Multisensory Teaching of Basic Language Skills

SECOND EDITION

Multisensory Teaching of Basic Language Skills

SECOND EDITION

edited by

Judith R. Birsh, Ed.D.

PAUL·H·
BROOKES
PUBLISHING CO.®

Baltimore • London • Sydney

Paul H. Brookes Publishing Co.
Post Office Box 10624
Baltimore, Maryland 21285-0624

www.brookespublishing.com

Typeset by Integrated Publishing Solutions, Grand Rapids, Michigan.
Manufactured in the United States of America by
The Maple Press Co., York, Pennsylvania.

The individuals and situations described in this book are based on the authors'
and volume editor's experiences. In all instances, names have been changed; in
some instances, identifying details have also been altered to further protect
confidentiality.

Readers may access free of charge from the Brookes Publishing Course Companion
Web Site for *Multisensory Teaching of Basic Language Skills, Second Edition,* various
resources that support instructors and students using the book. These materials are
available at http://textbooks.brookespublishing.com/birsh. Use of these materials
is granted for educational purposes only; the duplication and distribution of these
materials for a fee is prohibited.

A companion activity book, *Multisensory Teaching of Basic Language Skills Activity
Book* (ISBN 1-55766-723-3), by Suzanne Carreker and Judith R. Birsh, is also
available from Paul H. Brookes Publishing Co. (1-800-638-3775; 1-410-337-9580).
For more information on the *Multisensory Teaching of Basic Language Skills* materials,
go to www.brookespublishing.com

Excerpts from the *Open Court* reading program appearing on pages 102 and 103
are reprinted by permission of SRA/McGraw-Hill. From *Framework for Effective
Teaching, Grade 1: Thinking and Learning About Print,* by Adams, M.J., Bereiter, C.,
Hirschberg, J., Anderson, V., & Bernier, S.A. (pp. 304 and 84, respectively). Copyright © 1995 by Open Court.

Fourth printing, September 2008.

Library of Congress Cataloging-in-Publication Data
Multisensory teaching of basic language skills / edited by Judith R. Birsh.— 2nd ed.
    p.   cm.
  Includes bibliographical references and index.
  ISBN-13: 978-1-55766-676-5
  ISBN-10: 1-55766-676-8
  1. Dyslexic children—Education—United States. 2. Dyslexics—Education—
United States. 3. Language arts—United States. I. Birsh, Judith R.
  LC4708.85.M85 2005
  371.91′44—dc22
                                        2005003721

British Library Cataloguing in Publication data are available from the British Library.

Contents

The following chapters are available on-line at http://textbooks.brookespublishing.com/birsh

About the Editor

Judith R. Birsh, Ed.D., was founder and director of the Multisensory Teaching of Basic Language Skills program from 1985 until 2000 at Teachers College, Columbia University, in the Department of Curriculum and Teaching, Program in Learning Disabilities. Her primary interests are the teaching of literacy skills and the preparation of teachers who work with students with dyslexia. She is a consultant to public and private schools and is a Certified Academic Language Therapist.

Dr. Birsh was educational consultant on two videotape series for teachers and parents for Vineyard Video Productions, *Teaching the Learning Disabled: Study Skills and Learning Strategies* (1991) and *Learning Disabilities/Learning Abilities* (1997). She has served twice as president of the New York Branch of The International Dyslexia Association and was the 1995 recipient of the branch's award for achievement in the field of dyslexia education.

About the Contributors

Kay A. Allen, M.Ed., Director, Neuhaus Education Center, 4433 Bissonnet, Bellaire, TX 77401, has taught Orton-Gillingham–based teacher courses since 1982 and has worked for more than 20 years with adult students on improving their written language skills. She is an Academic Language Therapy Association Qualified Instructor, a Certified Academic Language Therapist, Secretary of the International Multisensory Structured Language Education Council, and co-author of *Multisensory Reading and Spelling* (Apple Core Press, 1993).

Marilyn C. Beckwith, B.A., Associate Director (Retired), Neuhaus Education Center, 4433 Bissonnet, Bellaire, TX 77401, has had a 40-year interest in the relationship of spoken language to written language, which resulted in her using multisensory structured techniques to teach basic language skills to both dyslexic and nondyslexic individuals. This interest also resulted in her following related research made possible by advancing technology, which confirms the principles taught to teachers at the Neuhaus Education Center.

Susan H. Blumenthal, Ed.D., Licensed Clinical Psychologist, Private Practice; Founder, The Learning Difficulties Program, Institute for Contemporary Psychotherapy, New York, NY, specializes in psychoeducational evaluations and cognitive remediation for adults and adolescents with learning difficulties and academic work output problems. She started an innovative program at the Institute for Contemporary Psychotherapy to train psychotherapists to work with adult patients with learning disabilities. In addition, she has trained teachers at Teachers College, Columbia University; Hunter College; and Manhattanville College.

Elsa Cárdenas-Hagan, M.A., CCC-SLP, CALT, Director, Valley Speech, Language and Learning Center, 856 West Price Road, Brownsville, TX 78520, is a bilingual speech-language pathologist and a Certified Academic Language Therapist. She is also co-principal investigator of a national longitudinal study on oracy and literacy development of Spanish-speaking children. In addition, she has worked extensively on the design of early literacy assessments in Spanish.

Joanne F. Carlisle, Ph.D., Professor of Education, University of Michigan, 610 East University Avenue, Ann Arbor, MI 48109, is Professor of Education at the University of Michigan. Her research interests focus on the acquisition of language and literacy, with a special focus on children for whom such acquisition is a challenge.

Suzanne Carreker, Director of Teacher Development, Neuhaus Education Center, 4433 Bissonnet, Bellaire, TX 77401, is a Certified Academic Language Therapist and Qualified Instructor. For 17 years, she has been involved with the preparation of teachers who provide instruction in basic literacy skills. She was a classroom teacher at and consultant to The Briarwood School in Houston for 13 years. She has served as President of the Houston Branch of The International Dyslexia Association and currently is Vice President of the Academic Language Therapy Association Centers Council.

Ellen Urquhart Engstrom, M.A., Associate Professor and Assistant Director of Educational Services, National Institute at Landmark College, 1 River Road South, Putney, VT 05346. Before joining the faculty of Landmark College, Ms. Engstrom taught at Groves Academy (an independent day school for students in grades K–12 with learning and attentional difficulties in Minneapolis, Minnesota), where she was the department head of the lower/middle school. Ms. Engstrom holds a B.A. from Wellesley College and a M.A. in educational psychology from the University of Minnesota. She has a long-standing interest in language and reading disorders, as well as the assistive technologies that support students with learning and attentional difficulties.

Mary L. Farrell, Ph.D., Professor, School of Education, Fairleigh Dickinson University, Bancroft Hall, Room 310, 1000 River Road, Teaneck, NJ 07666, is Director of Fairleigh Dickinson University's Learning Disabilities Program, which offers the Dyslexia Specialist Certificate Program that trains teachers in the Orton-Gillingham approach to teaching reading, spelling, and handwriting. Dr. Farrell also directs the Regional Center for College Students with Learning Disabilities, a comprehensive support program. She is a board member of the International Mutisensory Structured Language Education Council and the New Jersey Branch of The International Dyslexia Association and is a member of the Professional Advisory Board for the Masonic Children's Learning Centers.

Linda Hecker, M.Ed., Director of Educational Services, National Institute at Landmark College, 1 River Road South, Putney, VT, 05346, has taught at Landmark College since its founding in 1985. Appointed Director of Educational Services for the National Institute at Landmark College in 2001, she has overseen tutorial and teacher training programs; taught English, study skills, and music classes; and served as an academic advisor and academic dean. She frequently presents workshops and teacher training programs, has published several articles, including a study of the benefits of text-to-speech software, and has served as editor for Landmark College's *Assistive Technology Manual for Educators.*

Marcia K. Henry, Ph.D., Professor Emeritus and Former Director, Center for Educational Research, San Jose State University, Post Office Box 368, La Pointe, WI 54850, received her doctorate from Stanford University and was a Fulbright Lecturer/Research Scholar at the University of Trondheim, Norway, in 1991. Dr. Henry served as president of The International Dyslexia Association for 4 years. She now provides in-service training for schools and organizations across the country.

Holly Baker Hill, Ed.D., holds a doctorate in international and transcultural studies with a specialization in literacy and learning disabilities from Teachers College, Columbia University. She has worked for The International Dyslexia Association in establishing the Alliance for Accreditation and Certification of Structured Language Education. She has taught graduate and undergraduate reading and linguistics courses at the University of Texas at San Antonio and at St. Mary's University. Her primary research interests are international preservice teacher education in reading and multisensory structured language education. She currently resides in Melbourne, Australia, with her family.

Judith C. Hochman, Ed.D., holds a doctorate of education in curriculum and instruction from Teachers College, Columbia University. Dr. Hochman was the Head of Windward School, an independent school for students with learning disabilities, and was founder and is a senior faculty member of the Windward Teacher Training Institute. She was also Superintendent of Schools for the Greenburgh-Graham Union Free School District in Hastings, New York. She has been a teacher, administrator, and consultant in both general and special education

settings and has a particular interest in the teaching of expository writing. She is the author of *Basic Writing Skills* (GSL Publications, 1995), which is used extensively by educators throughout the country in all grades. In 1998, she received the New York Branch Award of The International Dyslexia Association for her years of leadership in advancing the needs of people with dyslexia.

Lauren A. Katz, Ph.D., CCC-SLP, Postdoctoral Fellow, University of Michigan, 610 East University Avenue, Ann Arbor, MI 48109, received her master's degree in communication sciences and disorders from the Massachusetts General Hospital Institute of Health Professions and her doctorate from the University of Michigan. Her research interests include morphological awareness, vocabulary development, and reading achievement in children with language and learning difficulties.

Betty S. Levinson, Ph.D., Licensed Clinical Psychologist, Private Practice; Founder and Former Co-director, National Institute of Dyslexia, Chevy Chase, MD, has wide clinical and teaching experience in the psychology of children and adults and in psychotherapy. Dr. Levinson has been a consultant on child abuse to local and state governments. Among other honors, she has been appointed to the Section Committee on Psychology of the American Association for the Advancement of Science, is on the Board of Directors of The International Dyslexia Association, and chairs the Committee of Children and Adolescents of the Board of Social Responsibility for the Maryland Psychological Association.

Eileen S. Marzola, Ed.D., Educational Consultant, Adjunct Professor of Education, Fordham University, New York, NY, is an independent educational consultant who received her doctorate in special education (with a focus on learning disabilities) from Teachers College, Columbia University. She has taught for more than 35 years at every level from kindergarten through graduate school and conducted numerous staff development trainings for those interested in improving instructional strategies for struggling learners. Dr. Marzola has been a keynote speaker and presented papers at many national and international conferences, and published articles in professional journals including *Journal of Reading Instruction, The Journal of Learning Disabilities,* and *Journal of Reading, Writing, and Learning Disabilities International.* Dr. Marzola was recently honored by the New York State Federation of the Council for Exceptional Children with the New York State Teacher of the Year Award. She is currently an adjunct professor of education at Fordham University in New York City and President of the New York Branch of The International Dyslexia Association.

Louisa C. Moats, Ed.D., Post Office Box 3941, Hailey, ID 83333, has worked as a teacher, neuropsychology technician, and specialist in learning disorders. She was a licensed psychologist in private practice for 15 years in Vermont. Specializing in reading development, reading disorders, spelling, and written language, she has written and lectured widely throughout the United States and abroad. Her publications include journal articles, book chapters, a classroom basal spelling program, *Spelling: Development, Disability, and Instruction* (York Press, 1995), *Speech to Print: Language Essentials for Teachers* (Paul H. Brookes Publishing Co., 2000), and *Speech to Print: Language Exercises for Teachers* (Paul H. Brookes Publishing Co., 2003). Most recently, she completed 5 years as Clinical Associate Professor of Pediatrics at the University of Texas–Houston, co-directing a research project on reading instruction in high-risk schools.

Graham F. Neuhaus, Ph.D., University of Houston–Downtown, 1 Main Street, Houston, TX 77002, received her doctorate in individual differences from the University of Houston in 2000. She is a Licensed Psychological Associate and a Licensed Specialist in School Psychology. She is a member of the faculty at the University of Houston–Downtown, where she

teaches psychology, including courses in educational psychology, child development, and memory and cognition. Dr. Neuhaus publishes in the areas of early reading processes, reading fluency, letter priming, and the role that processing speed plays in reading achievement. Although her formal training has taught her much about learning and cognition, she credits her four dyslexic children and her dyslexic husband with teaching her about courage, persistence, humility, and advocacy.

Claire Nissenbaum, M.A., Director, Atlantic Seaboard Dyslexia Education Center, Rockville, MD 20850, is a board member of the International Multisensory Structured Language Education Council, which accredits professional training programs in dyslexia. She is a member of the Academic Language Therapy Association, is a Fellow of the Academy of Orton-Gillingham Practitioners and Educators, and serves on the Information and Referral Committee of The International Dyslexia Association. She has been a dyslexia specialist for more than 30 years and co-founded the TRI-Services Center for Children and Adults with Learning Disabilities in Rockville, Maryland, and the National Institute of Dyslexia in Chevy Chase, Maryland, which received national recognition for its programs. She was awarded the John Dewey Award for Outstanding Service to Public Education from the American Federation of Teachers.

Jean-Fryer Schedler, Ph.D., Educational Consultant, Schedler Educational Consulting, Severna Park, MD, was a classroom teacher, reading specialist, and director of a reading program in a private school before going into private practice. She evaluates and designs individualized education programs, conducts academic evaluations, provides teacher training and mentoring, is a coach for the Sonday System, and is a Fellow of the Academy of Orton-Gillingham Practitioners and Educators. Her clinical and research interests are in implementing reading comprehension intervention programs in middle and high school settings.

Margaret Jo Shepherd, Ed.D., founded the Program in Learning Disabilities and the Special Education Child Study Center at Teachers College, Columbia University, with colleague Dr. Jeannette Fleischner in 1967. In 1996, Professors Shepherd and Fleischner included a required course in multisensory instruction in the Teachers College curriculum for people preparing to teach students with learning disabilities. Since retirement from the active faculty at Teachers College, Professor Shepherd has been involved in a variety of professional activities on behalf of students with learning disabilities. Presently she is using skills acquired through experience in special education as the Program Officer for the Teachers College, Columbia University, Afghanistan Education Project. In that capacity, she works with Afghan educators to write new textbooks for primary school students and to create a new preservice teacher education curriculum for primary school teachers in Afghanistan.

Jo Anne Simon, J.D., is an attorney in private practice in Brooklyn, New York, concentrating on disability rights litigation and consultation in higher education and high-stakes testing. A former disability services provider, teacher of the deaf, and sign language interpreter, she is an adjunct professor at Fordham University School of Law and acted as lead counsel to the plaintiff in *Bartlett v. New York State Board of Law Examiners* from the case's inception. She is currently a Vice President of the New York Branch of The International Dyslexia Association. She writes often about the Americans with Disabilities Act and higher education. In addition, she regularly advises faculty and administrators regarding issues pertaining to higher education and transition for students with disabilities from high school to postsecondary education.

Lydia H. Soifer, Ph.D., Language and Speech Pathologist, Director, The Soifer Center for Learning and Child Development, 333 Old Tarrytown Road, White Plains, NY 10603; Assis-

tant Clinical Professor of Pediatrics, Albert Einstein College of Medicine of Yeshiva University, Jack and Pearl Resnick Campus, 1300 Morris Park Avenue, Bronx, NY 10461, is also a faculty member of the Early Intervention Training Institute of the Rose F. Kennedy Center for Research in Mental Retardation and Human Development. As a parent educator, teacher trainer, and staff developer in both public and private schools, Dr. Soifer's focuses have been the developmental needs of children regarding their learning, behavior, and communication and the nature of language functioning in academic performance and success. She regularly offers courses in language as it relates to learning, oral language as it relates to literacy, vocabulary development, and language assessment procedures.

Margaret B. Stern, M.Ed., Consultant in Mathematics Education to the National Council of Teachers of Mathematics and The International Dyslexia Association, is co-author of the *Structural Arithmetic* materials and workbooks and teachers guides I–IV (Educators Publishing Service, 1988) and *Children Discover Arithmetic* (HarperCollins, 1971), which earned two grants from the Carnegie Foundation. She has received awards for achievement in education from the New York Branch of The International Dyslexia Association and the Bank Street College of Education. At present, she is a math education consultant and private tutor.

Joanna K. Uhry, Ed.D., Professor of Education, Graduate School of Education, Fordham University, 113 West 60th Street, New York, NY 10023, teaches literacy education to graduate students. Her research interests include dyslexia as well as the underlying cognitive processes used by young children who are learning to read and how these processes are supported by instruction.

Barbara A. Wilson, M.S.Ed., Director, Wilson Language Training, 124 High Street, Newburyport, MA 01950, is the director of Wilson Language Training and co-founder of the Wilson Learning Center for children and adults with language learning disabilities. She is author of the *Wilson Reading System* (Wilson Language Training, 1988). Her experience includes being a special education teacher and consultant, team chairperson for individual education programs meetings, and reading therapist at the Language Disorders Unit at Massachusetts General Hospital. Ms. Wilson is a founding fellow of the Academy of Orton-Gillingham Practitioners and Educators and was the first chair of the Teaching Standards Committee for the International Multisensory Structured Language Education Council. She served as chair of the nominating committee for The International Dyslexia Association. Ms. Wilson is co-investigator of an NIH-funded research study on adult literacy. She is also chairperson of the Advisory Council for the Language and Literacy graduate program at Simmons College in Boston.

Beverly J. Wolf, M.Ed., Dean of Faculty, Slingerland Institute for Literacy; Director Emeritus, Hamlin Robinson School for Dyslexics, has worked with children and adults with language disabilities for more than 30 years. As a teacher, program administrator, school head, and dean of faculty of the Slingerland Institute for Literacy, she has provided instruction both for students and their teachers. She is a member of the adjunct faculty of Seattle Pacific University and has served on both local and national boards of The International Dyslexia Association. She is also author of independent activity and language materials for classroom use.

Foreword

Multisensory Teaching of Basic Language Skills, Second Edition, edited by Judith R. Birsh, is a treat for anyone interested in teaching reading. It is a book so chock-full of good, reliable, and extremely helpful information that anyone who teaches reading or who cares about struggling readers will not want to put it down. Judith R. Birsh is a highly skilled, knowledgeable educator who cares deeply about teachers and the children and adults who are trying to learn to read. So, it is not surprising that reading this book is like having a wise and wonderful teacher right next to you, anticipating, explaining, and providing both the broad conceptual framework and the specific content and practical details necessary for you to understand why and to know what to do at each and every step of teaching reading.

This second edition of *Multisensory Teaching of Basic Language Skills* has been updated in important ways; most critically, it reflects the extraordinary progress in the science of reading and in its implications for reading instruction. The imprint of modern science and its integral role in guiding reading instruction is found throughout the informative pages of this book. Judith R. Birsh and her distinguished group of contributors have covered each of the important topics relevant to learning to read in the fullest and most scientifically honest manner possible and ensured that the information is presented clearly.

This book not only has facts, it has heart and concern for all aspects of the struggling reader's life. Accordingly, there are chapters focused on older students, bilingual instruction for Spanish-speaking students, working with high-functioning dyslexic adults, helping parents of children with dyslexia, assistive technology, and the increasingly important role of legal issues in protecting the rights of dyslexic readers. Teachers will be better for having read this book, and their students will be incomparably better for their teachers having read this book.

We are now in a new era of teaching reading, one that is driven by rigorous science and guided by evidence of effectiveness. It is essential that those responsible for teaching reading are brought into this modern era of education. I view Judith R. Birsh as a true comrade-in-arms, a member of that small and special band of colleagues who understand the new science of reading and who are passionate about disseminating this important knowledge to hungry educators. This is why I wrote *Overcoming Dyslexia: A New and Complete Science-Based Program for Reading Problems at Any Level* (Alfred A. Knopf, 2003). I wanted to bring the extraordinary progress of modern neuroscience and reading research, and its implications for identifying and remediating reading problems, within reach of parents, educators, and those who struggle to read. This is why Judith R. Birsh has produced this book. *Multisensory Teaching of Basic Language Skills, Second Edition,* is a valuable addition to the small and growing library of up-to-date scientifically based resources for those who want to understand what to do and to know why they are doing it in teaching children and adults to read. I have found it to be a wonderful resource in my own work, and I know scores of researchers and educators will be most grateful to have this book in their personal library.

Sally Shaywitz, M.D.
Co-Director, Yale Center for the
Study of Learning and Attention
Author, *Overcoming Dyslexia*

Preface

This preface explains the reason for this new edition of *Multisensory Teaching of Basic Language Skills* and the history behind the need for the book. It describes this edition and explains the new chapters and revisions of standing ones. Then a summary follows of what is in each chapter to guide readers in their search for information. Appendices A and B are outlined, along with directions on how to access the book's companion web site, which features two new chapters and other items.

The field of reading and reading disabilities has undergone a transformation since the first edition of this book was published in 1999. Reading is now a primary issue in the education reform movement. Data from brain research (Shaywitz, 2003); the findings of the National Reading Panel (National Institute of Child Health and Human Development [NICHD], 2000); and the passing of federal legislation, the No Child Left Behind Act of 2001 (PL 107-110), have prompted responses from educators, parents, and politicians that have put those responsible for students' reading achievement on notice. It is essential that teacher educators and teachers themselves have the knowledge and the tools to meet these demands. After considering the new challenges in reading education and reading reviews from readers, I devised a plan for the new edition of this book.

The goal of the second edition is to bring to its readers an updated and expanded version of the first volume that will continue to provide an explanation of multisensory structured language education (MSLE). With the addition of new scientific evidence about our understanding of language learning disabilities and its biological bases and responsiveness to remediation from the fields of educational psychology, neuroscience, and cognitive psychology, this new edition, like the earlier one, provides the foundation for teacher knowledge about the components of informed, language-based reading instruction and effective teaching strategies. An important new feature to go along with this edition is the *Multisensory Teaching of Basic Language Skills Activity Book*, created by Suzanne Carreker and me (available from Paul H. Brookes Publishing Co.). With many activities tied directly to the chapters in this book, teachers can learn how to put this knowledge into practice with confidence. Together, the textbook and the activity book are guides for helping teachers gain the skills they need with numerous models of recommended, evidence-based practices essential for preparation in the complicated task of literacy instruction and related content areas.

NEW EDITION

There is a growing consensus from science-based evidence on the critical elements of informed reading instruction. The first edition of this book addressed these elements with evidence known at the time. Since then, however, a new and robust body of scientific data from peer-reviewed studies has converged to support carefully sequenced curriculum objectives, explicit strategies and scaffolds to meet the complex demands of teaching the phonologic, alphabetic, semantic, and syntactic systems of written lan-

guage to beginning readers and those who are at risk for reading and spelling difficulties (Simmons & Kame'enui, 2003). New information, confirming how to move along from phonemic awareness and decoding to reading to learn, places critical emphasis on fluency, vocabulary, and comprehension instruction. A necessary consequence of these findings is the need for teachers and those who prepare them to have specific and explicit linguistic knowledge and to have help obtaining a deep understanding of effective, intensive, structured language interventions. Along with understanding the complexities involved in reading acquisition must come the skills and techniques to deliver informed reading instruction and remediation to a wide range of students. The second edition of this book is dedicated to these priorities.

Contributors from the first edition have updated their chapters to include new scientific evidence, new instructional strategies, new sources of information for teachers to refer to in each content area, and suggestions from readers. Seven new chapters have been added to address the following: reading research and learning disabilities; planning multisensory instruction and the classroom environment; biliteracy for at-risk beginning readers; remediation for older students; vocabulary instruction; assistive technology and dyslexia; and the rights of individuals with dyslexia under the law (the latter two chapters are available on-line only at http://textbooks.brookespublishing.com). The companion activity book has many practice activities for both teachers and their students, providing teachers many opportunities to hone their skills while learning new linguistic concepts.

HISTORY OF THE BOOK

The idea for the first edition evolved from a gathering of forces beginning in 1990. The Committee on Teacher Education Initiatives of The International Dyslexia Association (IDA), 60 teacher trainers representing a wide range of MSLE programs in the preparation of teachers and academic therapists, met yearly to create an accrediting body for organizations that prepare specialists in the education of individuals with dyslexia. Their aim was to set high professional standards for teachers, clinicians, and teacher education programs in the field of dyslexia in college and university programs, hospitals, and other organizations that have MSLE preparation as their function. By 1995 the group incorporated as the International Multisensory Structured Language Education Council (IMSLEC) and is presently accrediting programs to ensure that individuals who need effective intervention and their families are indeed receiving help from well-prepared specialists who have been held to exemplary standards of teaching.

Today, there are four accrediting and/or certifying organizations committed to improving the teaching of reading and related language skills for special and general education students. IMSLEC, the Academic Language Therapy Association (ALTA), and the Academic Language Therapy Association Centers Council (ALTA CC) compose the Alliance for Accreditation and Certification of Structured Language Education, which is sponsored by The International Dyslexia Association. The fourth accrediting and certifying organization is the Academy of Orton-Gillingham Practitioners and Educators. (See the section for Chapter 1 in Appendix B for contact information for these organizations.)

During those early collaborative forums of expert teacher trainers and therapists, it became clear that there was a great need for a comprehensive textbook for MSLE teacher preparation that would present research in reading and learning disabilities. The first edition of this book was designed to reflect the group members' long years of professional experience in the classroom and in one-to-one and small-group practice.

It brought together research and clinical experience of the second half of the 20th century to teach written language skills to children and adults with dyslexia, the most prevalent learning disability. Still tuned to the same rich background of experience, the second edition builds on those priorities with enrichment from current research.

SUMMARY OF CHAPTERS

Each chapter begins with a conceptual framework based on research in a specific area, followed by content knowledge and explicit how-to information from working model programs. The text as a whole contains the essence of informed reading instruction and is suitable for use as a core text in university education courses, as a handbook for teacher practitioners, as a source of parent information, and as a guide to the field of dyslexia studies. It is a highly useful resource for schools of education, professional development personnel, and teacher training organizations because it offers in-depth treatment of all aspects of written language instruction; references, illustrations, and examples of hands-on procedures; a glossary of key terms; and an extensive appendix of materials and sources. Terms defined in the glossary are set in boldface on first occurrence in the text. Throughout the book, phonic symbols (e.g., /b/, /ă/, /th/) are used to refer to sounds, except when International Phonetic Alphabet symbols (e.g., /æ/, /θ/) appear in a figure reprinted from another source. This was done because teachers and remedial specialists are more familiar with phonic symbols and use them with their students.

In Chapter 1, Research and Reading Disability, I review the research pertaining to prevention and remediation of reading difficulties that supports the specific approaches set forth in the following chapters. I explain the volume's main focus on scientifically based instruction in reading and related literacy skills. Four major concerns from research are explored so that teachers may have at hand ways to think about and apply relevant theory and substantiated practices: 1) What is scientifically based reading research, and why is it important? 2) What has scientifically based reading research explained about the components of reading? 3) How has scientifically based reading research advanced our understanding of dyslexia? and 4) How can teachers deliver evidence-based reading instruction with fidelity of implementation? This chapter provides readers with a working definition of dyslexia and its relationship to teachers' knowledge of language and evidence-based reading instruction. The implications for teacher preparation and professional development are discussed, with suggestions for major changes in how teachers need to be educated to work successfully with students struggling with reading and related literacy issues.

In Chapter 2, Multisensory Structured Language Education, Louisa C. Moats and Mary L. Farrell define what MSLE is and provide a description and rationale for the teaching approaches explained in this book. They discuss how it has been implemented in the past by researchers and educators from the late 19th century to the present. They identify the instructional practices that are consistently supported by research and the role of the multisensory component in effective instruction of language skills. They review the progress that has been made in gathering evidence from neuroscience for the efficacy of the multisensory component and offer suggestions on what additional research might be needed to validate the beliefs and accepted instructional practices of experienced clinicians who subscribe to these approaches.

Chapters 3, 4, and 5 cover the early prerequisites to learning to read, write, and spell. In Chapter 3, Development of Oral Language and Its Relationship to Literacy, Lydia H. Soifer observes that language is perceived and used by humans on many lev-

els and for many purposes, including reading. She helps teachers understand language and its relationship to literacy and learning from developmental and pedagogical points of view and compares the differences and the similarities between oral and written language. Soifer focuses on making teachers aware of the role that oral language plays as a child learns to decode words and comprehend the meaning of written text. For each of the oral language components—form (phonology, morphology, and syntax), content (semantics), and use (pragmatics)—the patterns of typical and disordered development and their parallel relationships to reading and writing are explained. The chapter also discusses the possible effects of middle-ear infections on overall language and academic development and offers suggestions for working with children with recurrent middle-ear infections.

In Chapter 4, Phonemic Awareness and Reading: Research, Activities, and Instructional Materials, Joanna K. Uhry emphasizes how phonemic awareness is a critical predictor in how easily children will acquire reading, how early instruction turns children into more successful readers, and how children with dyslexia have great difficulty with phonemic awareness and other phonological processing skills. Phonemic awareness often is a stumbling block for children with dyslexia, and unless they receive explicit, direct phonemic awareness instruction before and while they are learning to read, their attempts may be extremely frustrating. Uhry describes the link between phonemic awareness and reading and reviews research on the benefits and effectiveness of phonemic awareness instruction. In addition, several programs are described that may be useful with all children but that are critical to the reading success of children at risk for reading failure.

Kay A. Allen, with Graham F. Neuhaus and Marilyn C. Beckwith, adds specific new evidence on the significance of letter identification and naming to the reading process in Chapter 5, Alphabet Knowledge: Letter Recognition, Naming, and Sequencing. The first section of this chapter advocates multisensory, structured, sequential teaching of letter recognition and naming. The second section of this chapter describes the development of letter recognition and naming skills in students with and without dyslexia. The final section of the chapter presents a variety of multisensory lessons, activities, and games to help students with dyslexia to develop reliable and rapid letter–sound associations and to develop facility using the dictionary. Students with dyslexia especially need to have facility with the dictionary to check their work.

Gillingham and Stillman (1997), whose work is the foundation of MSLE, deemed it essential that both the teacher and the remedial student be aware of the history of the English language. Keeping with that tradition, in Chapter 6, The History and Structure of Written English, Marcia K. Henry proposes that instruction in phonics alone is not sufficient. Once students have learned the basics of the letter–sound correspondences, syllable types, and syllable division patterns, they will need to gain facility with words of Anglo-Saxon, Latin, and Greek origin. Addressing through MSLE the historical forces that influenced written English also provides a framework for teaching a decoding and spelling curriculum based on word origin and word structure. Teachers who understand the origins of words can enhance their presentation of reading instruction, improve their assessment skills, communicate clearly about the features of the language, and convey useful strategies to their students. Henry outlines events in the development of English and then describes the letter–sound correspondences, syllable patterns, and morpheme patterns unique to English words of Anglo-Saxon, Latin, and Greek origin. This chapter also presents sample lessons centered on words from these origin languages.

Chapter 7 has added a new author, Eileen S. Marzola, who has revised the work of the original author, Margaret Jo Shepherd. Assessment of Reading Difficulties describes the comprehensive and extensive information gathered during an educational assessment that includes but is not limited to testing. Assessment of students' progress leads to information of great value to teachers, parents, and students. Marzola and Shepherd explain the classification of tests into the categories of formal and informal, as well as norm referenced, criterion referenced, and curriculum referenced. The importance of early identification and prevention is emphasized, with a thorough discussion of a substantial number of tools for screening for the signs of reading difficulties early in kindergarten and reading assessment instruments that cover the growth and development of reading skills through third grade. In terms of assessment of progress or learning of specific skills, Marzola and Shepherd discuss options for collecting formative and summative data. The chapter concludes with an explanation of the critical components of making a clinical diagnosis of dyslexia, based on the definition of dyslexia in Chapter 1 and tailored to problems of individuals according to age and level of education.

Chapter 8, Planning Multisensory Structured Language Lessons and the Classroom Environment, by Jean-Fryer Schedler and me is a new chapter. Schedler and I integrate planning of multisensory structured lessons with creating a positive classroom environment for students. Students benefit when the environment is conducive to learning and when teachers are well prepared to implement instructional goals. This chapter discusses first the classroom environment, which includes the physical space for both the students and the teacher. Then, for teacher organization, the chapter enumerates ways to organize and maintain the materials for instruction and record keeping, in order to maximize the time students spend engaged in productive activity and minimize the time lost during transitions or disruptions. Next, the chapter focuses on student expectations and behavior, with a strong emphasis on building a positive learning environment. The final section describes in detail the steps in planning daily and weekly multisensory structured language lessons from beginning to advanced levels.

In Chapter 9, Teaching Reading: Accurate Decoding and Fluency, Suzanne Carreker asserts that for students, especially those with dyslexia, to become fully literate, the bedrock components of reading—decoding, comprehension, and fluency—and all other elements of literacy instruction must be explicitly, directly taught in an informed, comprehensive approach. Citing findings from the National Reading Panel (NICHD, 2000) and other scientifically based evidence, Carreker outlines a blueprint for such a program and discusses both the developmental stages of learning to read and a precise, step-by-step curriculum appropriate for a range of students. Chapter 9 first delineates the key elements of a multisensory structured presentation of instruction in decoding, phonemic awareness, and letter recognition. Next, this chapter explains how to introduce the concepts of vowel and consonant sounds and blending sounds. The chapter also lists syllable types in English and how to introduce them to students. Morphemes (e.g., prefixes, suffixes) and syllable division are given the same careful analysis. In addition, the chapter presents a specific procedure of teaching irregular words and contains a new section on the development of fluency in both oral and silent reading.

In Chapter 10, Teaching Spelling, Suzanne Carreker explains that learning to spell is not simply a by-product of learning to read and is not learned by rote; it plays an important role in reading instruction and enhances reading proficiency by heightening awareness of phonemes and orthographic patterns. Spelling, however, is a far more difficult skill to learn than reading. Carreker explains how spelling requires explicit in-

struction supported by the teacher's knowledge of how spelling develops, the structure of spoken and written language and how the orthography is represented in English, an alphabetic language. Carreker describes spelling development and explores the problems of poor spellers, such as difficulties with phonological processing and with memory for letter patterns. Instructional strategies to develop spelling and sample daily lesson plans assist the teacher in implementation. The chapter suggests an order of presentation in spelling instruction and offers examples of multisensory guided discovery teaching procedures.

Chapter 11, Biliteracy Instruction for Spanish-Speaking Students, by Elsa Cárdenas-Hagan, introduces a new topic to this book. This chapter describes a model for MSLE instruction in Spanish, based on research in a Texas–Mexico border community, for students whose first language is Spanish and then carefully, using the same MSLE teaching approach, introducing literacy instruction in English. Many of the linguistic elements of Spanish and English overlap, and these commonalities can be emphasized in this instructional model. Cárdenas-Hagan offers many examples of similarities in phonology, semantics, morphology. and syntax to ease the transition. The aim is to have students literate—reading, writing and spelling—in both languages by third grade.

The addition of Chapter 12, Instruction for Older Students Struggling with Reading, by Barbara A. Wilson brings a much-needed body of information on methods for direct instruction of the older students who are struggling with reading and other related difficulties. Wilson, an expert in the field of adolescent and adult literacy, focuses on the students beyond the third grade who may have decoding as well as comprehension deficits. Many of these older students are identified late as having difficulties and need MSLE that targets their difficulties in a direct but sensitive manner. Wilson also addresses the discomfort on the part of both teachers and students who need to overcome reluctance to work with basic skills. She provides a step-by-step guide for intensive instruction that includes how to teach accuracy and automaticity of single-word reading; application of skills and fluency with controlled and decodable text; and development of vocabulary, background knowledge, and comprehension. The idea behind this chapter is that it is never too late to improve the reading skills of an older student.

Word Learning and Vocabulary Instruction, Chapter 13, is another new addition to the book. Word learning and vocabulary development are critical for language growth and are essential elements in reading comprehension. Joanne F. Carlisle and Lauren A. Katz inform us of the wide range of opportunities beyond content-area courses for learning new words and developing a strong background in vocabulary. They examine the process by which students learn words and the factors that affect vocabulary acquisition, giving special attention to the difficulties faced by students with language learning impairments. With exacting attention to research, Carlisle and Katz present studies on methods of vocabulary instruction that have suggested practical implications for both teaching word meanings and strategies for deriving word meanings. They provide extensive guidelines for effective instruction in a variety of classroom settings.

Eileen S. Marzola is the new author of Chapter 14, Strategies to Improve Reading Comprehension in the Multisensory Classroom. Relying on a growing body of research on metacognitive strategies, along with the importance of accurate, fluent reading, a rich vocabulary foundation, and active prior knowledge, Marzola takes us through how comprehension instruction has changed since the 1960s. She presents a developmental framework for comprehension, along with detailed descriptions of research-supported strategies and other promising methods designed to improve comprehension within

an MSLE learning environment. Many examples of how to put these methods into practice, with accompanying illustrations and lesson prompts, will help teachers adapt these strategies for their classrooms.

Beverly J. Wolf assumed full authorship of Chapter 15, Teaching Handwriting, after Lynn Stempel-Mathey passed away. This chapter is an expanded version of the earlier chapter, with the addition of a discussion of keyboarding and assistive technology alternatives to standard handwriting instruction. This chapter highlights the importance of handwriting instruction in early education and in remediation. It provides a brief history of handwriting instruction and a discussion of some of the syndromes related to difficulties with handwriting. Wolf reports research evidence of the efficacy of direct teaching of handwriting to dyslexic students, with detailed and specific information on how to teach print and cursive handwriting using a multisensory framework that integrates handwriting instruction with reading and spelling instruction.

Chapter 16, Composition: Expressive Language and Writing, provides a program in composition instruction with clear guidelines and goals and addresses what to teach. Judith C. Hochman emphasizes that mastering the skills associated with good writing is a daunting task for students with learning and language problems and presents activities for writing sentences, paragraphs, and compositions especially developed for these students. She advocates using these writing activities concurrently with the beginning of instruction in reading, spelling, and handwriting. Sentence writing is geared toward enabling students to write compound and complex sentences and to improve their revision and editing skills. There are activities for paragraph writing using topic sentences and supporting details. For various kinds of longer expository compositions, three useful outline forms are described, with preliminary activities and directions on carrying out these sequenced steps in writing. The chapter suggests techniques for revising and editing and lists many questions that teachers can use to help students focus on ways to improve and correct their written compositions.

The difficulties students with dyslexia have with language concepts and associations, memory, and sustained attention also affect these students' grasp of mathematical concepts. In Chapter 17, Multisensory Mathematics Instruction, Margaret B. Stern explains an MSLE teaching approach that helps children discover mathematical concepts and relationships through student and teacher manipulation of multisensory materials such as blocks, numbered tiles, and trays of various sizes. First Stern describes students' exploration of the materials and the many things that the students can do with numbers. After developing a language of mathematics as students naturally express their thoughts about their discoveries, the next step is to record the ideas with math symbols. Then, students learn number patterns related to addition and subtraction facts. They also learn how to record math facts as equations. The chapter explains numerous games and activities so that students can gain confidence in such concepts as place value, zero, and the meaning and structure of two-digit numerals. Next, students learn the concept of regrouping for addition and subtraction. The chapter then suggests a sequence for teaching the multiplication tables. Division, including division with a remainder and word problems, is addressed in the final section of the chapter.

Chapter 18, Learning Strategies and Study Skills: The SkORE System, focuses on the techniques for training students in organization, time management, and specific learning strategies and study skills, to be adapted immediately and applied to content subjects. Claire Nissenbaum describes the typical difficulties of dyslexic adolescents and the effect of these difficulties on learning and academic success. Next, tips on working

with preadolescent and adolescent dyslexic students are described, followed by a explanation of the materials to be used and the specific ways in which to arrange them. Nissenbaum then delineates learning strategies and study skills techniques. The preliminary step of this study skills training consists of Quick Tricks and Advanced Quick tricks to help improve the student's relationship with his or her teachers. The first main phase of training focuses on preparing to read a passage of text. The second phase addresses how to clear up high-frequency spelling and mechanics errors and to give the student strategies for completing work and dealing with long texts in emergencies. The third phase of study skills training attends to critical thinking and developing higher order language skills, such as writing summaries and creating outlines.

Many high-functioning adults with dyslexia seek to move on in their academic work or their careers yet suffer from chronic feelings of inadequacy, stress, and low self-esteem regarding their ability to learn new information, read, or write. For these individuals, a history of difficulty in the early grades and uneven functioning throughout school are common experiences. In Chapter 19, Working with High-Functioning Dyslexic Adults, Susan H. Blumenthal outlines how remedial specialists can work with these individuals on a one-to-one basis, starting with an assessment that includes tests and a writing sample that recounts school memories. This written passage provides a rich source of diagnostic information and a way for a remedial specialist to get to know the individual. Along with case histories, one of which is new to this edition, this chapter presents excerpts from adults' writing samples that illustrate the painful experiences and feelings arising from early schooling that have had an impact to this day. Blumenthal explains the areas in which high-functioning dyslexic adults often need help and names goals of remediation: helping each individual perceive him- or herself as a person who can learn, teaching the individual to be aware of his or her thinking process, and reducing learning-related anxiety. The chapter gives pointers on how to achieve these goals.

In Chapter 20, Helping Parents of Children with Dyslexia, Betty S. Levinson emphasizes the importance of guidance and counseling for parents and caregivers of children with dyslexia to help them deal with the many social, emotional, and behavioral issues that arise at home and at school because of the nature and implications of dyslexia. She uses case studies to make her points. Levinson offers information on matters such as enhancing communication; working with parents who may also have dyslexia; helping families with organization, time management, and prioritization; and helping parents who feel overwhelmed. Also included in the chapter are a suggested training regimen for professionals, including the knowledge and experience needed to work effectively with parents and families, and a recommended library of key books and resources created to provide information and support.

On-Line Chapters and Course Companion Web Site

An important innovation of the second edition is a companion web site devoted to the book (http://textbooks.brookespublishing.com/birsh). To help teacher educators and teachers use this book, chapter objectives, lists of key terms, suggested readings, and a searchable glossary are available on the companion web site. In addition, two new chapters are available only on the web site: Chapter 21, Assistive Technology and Individuals with Dyslexia, by Linda Hecker and Ellen Urquhart Engstrom, and Chapter 22, The Rights of Individuals with Dyslexia Under the Law, by Jo Anne Simon. These two chapters were placed on-line instead of in the print edition because of the frequent advances

in technology and changes in legislation affecting individuals with dyslexia. The online chapters and other materials available on the web site will be updated from time to time as needed.

In Chapter 21, Hecker and Engstrom offer an overview of assistive technology (AT) that defines AT and describes the types of AT available for individuals with dyslexia. They review the research regarding how AT contributes to the academic success of students with dyslexia. They then address specific language areas in which AT is being used with students: reading comprehension and fluency, study skills such as note taking, organization, research, and writing. Hecker and Engstrom explore likely areas for future development and provide rich resources for readers to explore AT further.

In Chapter 22, Simon, an attorney concentrating on disability rights, explains how the law both hinders and helps individuals with dyslexia. Simon discusses the Individuals with Disabilities Education Act (IDEA) and its amendments, the federal law that protects basic educational rights for qualified individuals with disabilities from birth through age 21. This law established specific procedural safeguards and rights for these individuals throughout the nation. Simon explains the requirement that special educational services ensure a meaningful educational benefit. She adds to our knowledge about other civil rights laws that mandate services, too. Sometimes these laws overlap, which may cause confusion, so it is important that teachers have a basic understanding of them. A case study of a landmark court decision offers insights into how the law and the diagnosis of dyslexia intersect. Simon also provides an update on the latest reauthorization of IDEA by the U.S. Congress.

Appendices

Holly Baker Hill has added new information and organized both Appendix A, Glossary, and Appendix B, Materials and Sources, which appear at the end of the print edition. The glossary terms appear in boldface at first occurrence in the chapters. Appendix B offers readers extended and updated resources on

- Training programs, professional development sources, and professional organizations

- Reference articles and books

- Curricula, teaching guides, and activities

- Sources for teaching materials, including manipulatives, for use with students

- Publishing companies and distributors

- Professional journals

- Web sites

- Software

- Videotapes, audiotapes, and CDs

A searchable version of the glossary is available on the textbook companion web site (http://textbooks.brookespublishing.com/birsh). Appendix B is also available on the companion web site.

CLOSING THOUGHTS

My hope is that you find this second edition a worthwhile resource for extending your knowledge and supporting your everyday work with students with dyslexia and others who are struggling with reading, writing, and spelling.

REFERENCES

Gillingham, A., & Stillman, B.W. (1997). *Remedial training for children with specific disability in reading, spelling and penmanship* (8th ed.). Cambridge, MA: Educators Publishing Service.

National Institute of Child Health and Human Development (NICHD). (2000). *Report of the National Reading Panel. Teaching children to read: An evidence-based assessment of the scientific research literature on reading and its implications for reading instructions: Reports of the subgroups* (NIH Publication No. 00-4754). Washington, DC: U.S. Government Printing Office. Also available on-line: http://www.nichd.nih.gov/publicatons/nrp/report.htm

No Child Left Behind Act of 2001, PL 107-110, 115 Stat. 1425, 20 U.S.C. §§ 6301 *et seq.*

Shaywitz, S. (2003). *Overcoming dyslexia: A new and complete science-based program for reading problems at any level.* New York: Alfred A. Knopf.

Simmons, D.C., &, Kame'enui, E.J. (2003, March 1). *A consumer's guide to valuating a core reading program grades K-3: A critical elements analysis* (Rev. ed.). Eugene: University of Oregon, National Center to Improve the Tools of Educators (NCITE) and Institute for the Development of Educational Achievement (IDEA). Also available on-line: http://reading.uoregon.edu/curricula/con_guide.php

Acknowledgments

I deeply appreciate the patience and skill of all the contributors, who despite the demands of their own priorities, revised their chapters and created new ones. Their understanding of the need for in-depth knowledge of how children learn to read and write and their commitment to pushing ahead the field of evidence-based reading instruction gave them the impetus to write and rewrite so that the second edition will be a useful source of long-term professional education and information.

Thanks go to all of the readers whose suggestions and criticisms helped refine and refocus the content of this volume. Ideas came from many teacher educators and professional development personnel who used the first edition of the book with novice teachers and those in need of further expertise.

I am grateful to Holly Baker Hill, who tried various versions of the new text with her education students, all the while querying them about what they needed to have at their fingertips to help them teach real students.

I would like to acknowledge Senior Acquisitions Editor Jessica Allan, able editor at Paul H. Brookes Publishing Co., who helped guide the preparation of the second edition, encouraging the addition of new chapters and responding to the need for having certain chapters appear on a companion web site. Mika Sam Smith, Editorial Supervisor at Brookes Publishing, also deserves special praise for her uncompromising pursuit of accuracy and clarity to help readers understand the content and find the information they are seeking.

And, finally, a broad acknowledgment of all of the people across the country, too numerous to mention in person, who have devoted themselves to improving the outcome of reading instruction: teachers, teacher educators, principals, administrators, and parents; researchers, including psychologists, neurologists, pediatricians, and speech-language specialists; and law makers. The work of all these constituencies is reflected in this volume.

With love and gratitude to my children, Andrew, Philip, and Joanne Hope,
and to their children, Alexander, Abigail, Mark, Neena, Charlotte, and Nikolai

1

Research and Reading Disability

Judith R. Birsh

Reading is indeed nearly boundless in its promise.
It can effect changes for the greatest good.

—Mark Edmundson

Reading does not develop naturally and calls on specific areas in the brain for language processing. Reading is highly dependent on language development and quality instruction. Teachers with a wide range of experience and a strong foundation of knowledge enhanced by scientifically based reading research, from which to make judgments about what to teach, how to teach it, when to teach it, and to whom (*Overview of Reading and Literacy Initiatives*, 1998) ensure a successful outcome when working with all students but especially with students at risk of failing to learn to read or with those who have already fallen behind. When a child struggles with written language, none of the myriad layers of language processing can be taken for granted. Appropriate instruction is language based—intensive, systematic, direct, and comprehensive. Each individual is different and brings to the task unique cognitive and **linguistic** strengths and weaknesses. Therefore, teachers who work at prevention, intervention, or remediation require a foundation based on scientific evidence and need to be informed about the complex nature of instruction in reading and related skills. Fortunately, since the early 1980s, a broad range of individuals have made major contributions to research on the component processes of learning to read, reading disabilities, and models of effective instruction.

This keen interest in the newly acknowledged science of reading has involved general and special educators, psychologists, linguists, neuroscientists, geneticists, speech and language specialists, parents, and children with and without reading difficulties. What has changed in reading instruction is that it is no longer based on opinion but is being informed by science in an orderly progression of research data that shows what works. This volume's main focus is scientifically based instruction in reading and related literacy skills. In this chapter, four major concerns from research are explored so that teachers may have at hand ways to think about and apply relevant theory and substantiated practices.

1. What is scientifically based reading research and why is it important?

2. What has scientifically based reading research explained about the components of reading?

3. How has scientifically based reading research advanced our understanding of dyslexia?

4. How can teachers deliver evidence-based reading instruction with fidelity of implementation so that students learn to read with accuracy, fluency, and comprehension?

DEFINITION AND IMPORTANCE OF SCIENTIFICALLY BASED RESEARCH

Scientifically based research, also referred to as *evidence-based research,* gathers evidence to answer questions and to bring new knowledge to a field of study so that effective practices can be determined and implemented. Scientific research is a process:

> A scientist develops a theory and uses it to formulate hypotheses. To evaluate the hypotheses, a study is designed. The methods used in the study depend on the hypotheses, and these methods result in findings. The scientist then integrates what is found from this particular study into the body of knowledge that has accumulated around the research question. As such, scientific research is a cumulative process that builds on understandings derived from systematic evaluations of questions, models, and theories. (Fletcher & Francis, 2004, pp. 60–61, emphasis added)

Lyon and Chhabra (2004) underscored that good evidence is derived from a study that asks clear questions that can be answered empirically, that selects and implements valid research methods, and that accurately analyzes and interprets data.

A critical factor in establishing strong evidence for what works (causation) in experimental research is the use of **randomized controlled trials.** This means that subjects in an intervention study are randomly assigned to experimental and control groups. With randomized controlled trials, all variables are held constant (e.g., gender, age, demographics, skill levels) except the one variable that is hypothesized to cause a change. This allows the researcher to show a causal relationship between the intervention and the outcomes; in other words, the intervention caused a change thus establishing what does and does not work. **Quasi-experimental research** attempts to determine cause and effect without strict randomized controlled trials and is valid but is less reliable. The **meta-analysis** done by the National Reading Panel (NRP; National Institute of Child Health and Human Development [NICHD], 2000), reviewed both experimental and quasi-experimental studies of instructional practices, procedures, and techniques in real classrooms. The NRP's criteria closely followed accepted practices for evaluating research literature found in other scientific disciplines such as medicine and in behavioral and social research (Keller-Allen, 2004).

Two other factors, **peer review** and the **convergence of evidence,** should also be considered. Peer review stipulates that the results of an intervention study be scrutinized and evaluated by a group of independent researchers with expertise and credentials in that field of study before the results are publicly reported in a journal article. Another avenue of critical review is through presentations and papers that are scrutinized by fellow scientists to bring objectivity and reliability into the process of educational research (Fletcher & Francis, 2004). Convergence of evidence derives from the identi-

cal replication of a study in a similar population by other researchers because the outcomes from a single study are not sufficient to generalize across all populations. Other caveats for educational research are to be clear about the specific intervention, monitor it, and then use valid and reliable outcome measures (Reyna, 2004).

There are two kinds of educational research methodology, qualitative and quantitative. **Qualitative research** involves observing individuals and settings and relies on observation and description of events in the immediate context. An example of qualitative research is an **ethnographic observation,** in which researchers observe, listen, and ask questions to collect descriptive data in order to understand the content, context, and dynamics of an instructional setting. Qualitative research can be scientific if it follows the principles of scientific inquiry. It is difficult to say what works or does not work (causation) in qualitative research; however, this kind of research affords a picture of what is happening and a description of the context.

Quantitative research uses large numbers of individuals to generalize findings to similar settings using statistical analyses. Quantitative research must use experimental or quasi-experimental design methods to gather data. The debate over whether quantitative or qualitative research is better obscures the principle that it is not the method of observation (qualitative versus quantitative) that qualifies a study as providing rigorous evidence, it is the design that follows scientific inquiry that qualifies a study as rigorous. For example, it is essential to have enough subjects in well-matched groups in a study so that statistical significance between groups can be established. For a user-friendly resource that further explains evidence-based research and provides educational practitioners with tools to distinguish practices supported by rigorous evidence from those that are not, see U.S. Department of Education, Institute of Education Sciences, National Center for Education Evaluation and Regional Assistance (2003). To find out what works in education, see the What Works Clearinghouse (http://w-w-c.org).

The National Reading Panel

In 1997, the U.S. Congress asked the

> Director of the National Institute of Child Health and Human Development (NICHD), in consultation with the Secretary of Education, to convene a national panel to assess the status of research-based knowledge, including the effectiveness of various approaches for teaching children to read. (NICHD, 2000, p. 1-1)

Thus, unlike previous inquiries, the National Reading Panel (NRP) set about analyzing experimental and quasi-experimental research literature, using rigorous research standards, to determine specifically how "critical reading skills are most effectively taught and what instructional methods, materials, and approaches are most beneficial for students of varying abilities" (NICHD, 2000, p. 1-1). The NRP reviewed intensively the following topics:

National Institute of Child Health and Human Development.

- Phonemic awareness

- Phonics instruction

- Fluency

- Comprehension

- Teacher education and reading instruction

- Computer technology and reading instruction

The findings from the meta-analyses by the subgroups in the above list of topics reviewed by the 14 members of the NRP (NICHD, 2000), that is, longitudinal studies; cognitive and linguistic studies; and studies in neurobiology, revealed consensus with effective educators of long experience in what works in reading instruction. Research by itself cannot improve practice. However, the importance of converging scientific evidence in reading research and its relationship to practice has begun to gain new prominence in the thinking of not only teacher educators and teachers but among government officials on the federal, state, and local levels charged with educational reform, and business people as well as parents and caregivers of young children. The report of the most recent National Assessment of Educational Progress (NAEP) that indicates that 4th-, 8th-, and 12th-grade reading scores are still very low, particularly among disadvantaged students (National Center for Education Statistics, 2003). We must adopt more effective instructional practices and policies to solve the problem of pervasive, persistent reading failure. Through scientifically based reading research, both the causes of reading failure and practices that help children learn to read, including those most at risk, have been identified. Snow (2004) emphasized that knowing which practices work to produce specific results in the critical areas of reading instruction could help many teachers use methods and approaches in their daily work that are consonant with research-based evidence and could thus help significantly more children learn to read proficiently.

As part of the federal legislation No Child Left Behind Act of 2001 (PL 107-110), the Reading First state grant program was initiated that promotes the use of scientifically based research to provide high-quality reading instruction for grades K–3. Using proven instructional and **assessment** tools consistent with research, Reading First is mandated to provide assistance to state and local education agencies to ensure that all children learn to read by the end of third grade. Accountability is established with yearly assessments to directly measure each child's progress and to seek out children who are not progressing and meeting specific reading standards. Each application undergoes thorough review by expert panels that make funding recommendations and provide critiques and technical assistance to the states to see that the funds are used for scientifically based reading programs for children and evidence-based professional development for teachers. The U.S. Department of Education, then, is charged with implementing the legislation; drawing on resources from research, development, dissemination, technical assistance, professional development, and evaluation; and working to apply research-based applications to improve reading throughout the country.

SCIENTIFICALLY BASED READING RESEARCH EXPLAINS THE COMPONENTS OF READING

While researchers were studying learning disabilities such as dyslexia, they learned how reading develops in both impaired and nonimpaired readers. This led to a rich resource of data over time on more than 42,000 readers participating in studies sponsored by the NICHD of both poor and skilled readers. These findings have straightforward practical implications for teachers of normally developing readers and those students with dyslexia and other related co-occurring problems (Lyon, 2004).

Today there is a broad scientific consensus on what is needed to become a good reader. Two important sources for this agreement are the report of the National Research Council (Snow, Burns, & Griffin, 1998) followed by the report of the National Reading Panel (NICHD, 2000). This consensus on instructional approaches that pro-

vide the skills children must acquire as they learn to read is based on clear evidence. On the basis of the review of the literature, the panel arrived at some very strong conclusions (Pressley, 2002) and has identified the following critical components that are essential for teaching young children to read:

[handwritten annotations: "NRP", "Big 5" reading", "PPVFC Components"]

- Phonemic awareness

- Phonics

- Vocabulary development

- Reading fluency, including oral reading skills

- Reading comprehension strategies

How the five essential components of reading instruction are taught based on accumulated scientific evidence subsequently became the essential ingredients of Reading First grants as part of the No Child Left Behind Act of 2001 to improve reading instruction for kindergarten through third grade students throughout the United States. These are sometimes referred to as the building blocks for reading (The Partnership for Reading, 2003). Most educators agree that no one single reading component is sufficient in itself. Students need to acquire all of the combined essential components in a balanced, comprehensive reading program to become successful readers The chapters in this book give detailed analyses of the research and provide the reader with in-depth discussions of approaches for developing and implementing instruction in each of these component areas. Let us begin here by considering the conclusions of the NRP on essential reading skills instruction.

Phonemic Awareness

Phonemic awareness is "the ability to notice, think about and work with the individual sounds in words" (The Partnership for Reading, 2003, p. 2). The National Reading Panel meta-analysis confirmed that phonemic awareness, along with knowledge of the names and shapes of both lower- and uppercase letters, is a key component "that contributes significantly to the effectiveness of beginning reading and spelling instruction" (NICHD, 2000, p. 2-43). Phonemic awareness plays a vital role in learning to read because it helps children connect spoken language to written language. It helps to expose the underlying sounds in language that consequently relate to the alphabetic symbols on the printed page. Phonemic awareness has a causal relationship with literacy achievement and in kindergarten is the single best predictor of later reading and spelling achievement in first and second grade. In kindergarten, phonemic awareness predicts growth in word-reading ability (Torgesen, Wagner, & Rashotte, 1994). Children at risk because of early speech and language impairments and those with dyslexia perform more poorly on tests of phonemic awareness than those gaining reading skills typically. When children do not have good word-identification skills, they fall behind in reading and without appropriate intervention have only a one in eight chance of catching up to grade level (Juel, 1998). Without the ability to think about and manipulate the individual sounds in words, beginning and remedial readers risk falling behind or never catching up to their peers.

Isolating and manipulating sounds in words, through the use of oral segmenting and blending activities, help children learn the alphabetic principle as they are learning to read and spell. Learning letter names and shapes is an important adjunct to these

skills. Although phonemic awareness is a means to understanding and using letters and sounds for reading and writing, it is not an end in itself (for a discussion, see NICHD, 2000, p. 2-43). Taught in small groups and in moderate amounts, it stands as one of the major components of a comprehensive program of instruction. Children differ in their need for instruction, but phonemic awareness benefits everyone, especially those with little experience with detecting and manipulating speech sounds.

Phonics

Systematic and explicit instruction in phonics, the relationship between letters or letter combinations in written language (graphemes) and the approximately 44 sounds in English spoken language (phonemes), has proven effective for improving children's reading (Adams, 1990; NICHD, 2000; The Partnership for Reading, 2003). This leads to the accurate recognition of familiar words and to the decoding of unfamiliar new words. Eden and Moats pointed out the reciprocal relationship between phonemic awareness and reading in that "learning how letters represent sounds (phonology) and seeing words in print (orthography) helps novice readers to attend to speech sounds" (2002, p. 1082). Phonics, deemed valuable and essential, should be integrated with other types of reading instruction in a comprehensive program that includes all of the reading components listed earlier in this chapter. The NRP found solid support for using systematic phonics rather than an unsystematic approach or no phonics at all because systematic phonics provided a more significant contribution to children's growth in reading (see NICHD, 2000, p. 2-132). It has a great impact on children in kindergarten and first grade, with the greatest effects shown with beginning at-risk readers and for students of low socioeconomic status (Keller-Allen, 2004). However, **effect sizes** among low- and middle-income children for the outcomes of phonics instruction did not differ, leading Ehri et al. to conclude that "phonics instruction contributes to higher performance in reading in both low and middle class students" (2001, p. 418). It is clear that systematic phonics has its greatest impact in the early grades, that is, in kindergarten and first grade for all beginning readers, children at risk, and children diagnosed with reading disabilities.

Another important finding of the NRP meta-analysis of phonics studies was that positive results were produced whether through one-to-one tutoring, in small-group instruction, or in whole-class programs (Ehri et al., 2001, p. 420). Furthermore, systematic phonics can be taught variously through synthetic phonics, analytic phonics, phonics through spelling, analogy phonics, and embedded phonics (see Ehri, 2004, p. 168, for descriptions of these methods). Pressley (2002) also agreed that phonics instruction calls for more than a one-size-fits-all approach. Many variations are possible as long as the program is both extensive and systematic. One added benefit of systematic phonics instruction is its impact on beginning readers' comprehension. The impact of phonics is less clear with older students, which is an area in need of further intervention research.

Fluency

Beginning readers need to be fluent in naming letters, knowing their sounds, and in phonemic awareness activities. Fluency, however, is most often referred to as "the ability to read a text accurately and quickly. . . . recognize words. . . . [and] gain meaning from text" (The Partnership for Reading, 2003, p. 22). This is a key concept, with well-documented converging evidence supporting the connection between fluency and reading comprehension (Snow et al., 1998). Without the advantage of fluency, children

remain slow and laborious readers. Meaningful improvements in reading fluency are well documented with the use of a range of well-described instructional approaches. (See Chapter 9 for a discussion of fluency.) Major approaches to teaching fluency include guided oral reading procedures that include repeated oral reading, with modeling by the instructor, in which students receive feedback from peers, parents, or teachers. Guided oral reading and encouraging students to read are effective in improving fluency and overall reading achievement (see NICHD, 2000, p. 3-28). However, gaps in fluency remain in older students especially those with extremely low, word-level reading skills.

Vocabulary

A major contributor to students' ability to communicate and to comprehend text is their knowledge of word meanings. The NRP analyses confirmed that there is a strong relationship between vocabulary learning and comprehension gains (see NICHD, 2000, p. 4-20). Although the database of studies on vocabulary instruction and measurement that qualified for the NRP review was small, the panel did find some trends in the data that have implications for instruction (NICHD, 2000, p. 4-27):

1. Vocabulary should be taught both directly and indirectly.
2. Repetition and multiple exposures to vocabulary items are important.
3. Learning in rich contexts is valuable for vocabulary learning.
4. Vocabulary tasks should be restructured when necessary.
5. Vocabulary learning should entail active engagement in learning tasks.
6. Computer technology can be used to help teach vocabulary.
7. Vocabulary can be acquired through incidental learning.
8. How vocabulary is assessed and evaluated can have a differential effect on instruction.
9. Dependence on a single vocabulary instruction method will not result in optimal learning.

Comprehension

Comprehension is making sense of what we read and is dependent on good word recognition, fluency, vocabulary, world knowledge, and verbal reasoning. Good instruction calls for attention to comprehension when children listen to books read aloud and as soon as they begin reading text. Since the 1980s, research on comprehension instruction has supported the use of specific **cognitive strategies**, either individually or in concert, to help readers understand and remember what they read (see NICHD, 2000, pp. 4-46 to 4-47, for a discussion of this research). Direct instruction of these cognitive strategies in the classroom leads to active involvement of the readers and helps readers across the range of ability. Chapter 14 presents many such research-supported strategies as well as other promising methods designed to improve this essential reading skill within a multisensory learning environment.

Metacognition is thinking about thinking. Good readers think about what they are reading in complex ways. What the research suggests is that through modeling and metacognitive instruction by the teacher, students will improve in their ability to comprehend text. Effective strategies include question answering and generation, summarization, graphic and semantic organizers such as story maps, comprehension monitoring, and cooperative learning. Many opportunities for discussion and writing enhance comprehension. The evidence reviewed by the NRP led the panel to conclude that in-

K-W-L

struction that provides a "variety of reading comprehension strategies leads to in-creased learning of the strategies, to specific transfer of learning, to increased memory and understanding of new passages, and in some cases, general improvements in com-prehension" (NICHD, 2000, p. 4-52).

Other Factors Critical to Reading

The research cited in this chapter has focused mainly on reading development and read-ing instruction from kindergarten to third grade. It has prominently addressed phone-mic awareness, phonics, and reading decodable texts. More research needs to be done in the areas of fluency, vocabulary, and comprehension, especially as they relate to older age groups and other special populations (McCardle & Chhabra, 2004). Along with these five broad areas of skills that are needed to learn to read, scientifically based reading research has identified other critical factors needed for children to become good readers. These factors are delineated in Table 1.1.

SCIENTIFICALLY BASED READING RESEARCH HAS ADVANCED OUR UNDERSTANDING OF DYSLEXIA

One way to have a sophisticated understanding of the reading process is to have an understanding of dyslexia. Let us begin by examining the current definition of **dyslexia** adopted in 2003 by the International Dyslexia Association (IDA) in collaboration with the NICHD:

> Dyslexia is a specific learning disability that is neurobiological in origin. It is character-ized by difficulties with accurate and/or fluent word recognition and by poor spelling and decoding abilities. These difficulties typically result from a deficit in the phonologi-cal component of language that is often unexpected in relation to other cognitive abili-ties and the provision of effective classroom instruction. Secondary consequences may include problems in reading comprehension and reduced reading experience that can impede growth of vocabulary and background knowledge. (Lyon, Shaywitz, & Shaywitz, 2003, p. 2)

Dyslexia is a *specific learning disability* because it is associated with specific cogni-tive deficits in basic reading skills (Lyon et al., 2003). It affects 80% of those identified with learning disabilities and is one of the most common learning problems in children and adults (Lerner, 1989). Dyslexia is estimated to occur in approximately 5%–17% of the population in the United States (Shaywitz, 1998), with up to 40% of all fourth graders and almost 30% of all eighth graders scoring below the basic level in reading on the NAEP assessment (National Center for Education Statistics, 2003). Among these children not showing even partial mastery of grade-level skills in reading, there is a dis-proportionate representation of those who are poor, racial minorities, and nonnative speakers of English. However, large numbers of children from every social class, race, and ethnic group have significant difficulties with reading. Children most at risk for reading failure have limited exposure to the English language; have little understand-ing of phonemic awareness, letter knowledge, print awareness, and the purposes of read-ing; and lack oral language and vocabulary skills. Children raised in poverty, children with speech and hearing impairments, and children whose parents' or caregivers' read-ing levels are low are also at risk for reading failure.

"Children with reading disability differ from one another *and* from other readers along a continuum" (Lyon, 1996, p. 64) with reading disability representing the lower

Table 1.1. Consensus from scientifically based reading research on factors influencing becoming a good reader

---

Oral language

Long before children begin to read, they need language and literacy experiences at home and in preschool to develop a wide range of knowledge that will support them later in acquiring linguistic skills necessary for reading. These include language play such as saying rhymes, writing messages, listening to and examining books, developing oral vocabulary and verbal reasoning, and learning the purposes of reading. Exposure to reading aloud and oral language play fosters development of phonemic awareness.

Phonemic awareness

Reading development depends on the acquisition of phonemic awareness and other phonological processes. Phonemic awareness is the ability to understand the sound structure in spoken words. To learn to read, however, children must also be able to pay attention to the sequence of sounds or phonemes in words and to manipulate them. This is difficult because of the coarticulation of the separate sounds in spoken words. Children learn to do this by engaging in intensive oral play activities of sufficient duration, such as identifying and making rhymes, counting and working with syllables in words, segmenting initial and final phonemes, hearing and blending sounds, analyzing initial and final sounds of words, and segmenting words fully before learning to read and during beginning reading. This training facilitates and predicts later reading and spelling achievement.

Alphabet knowledge

It is essential that children learn the alphabet and be able to say the names of the letters, recognize the shapes, and write the letters. These skills are powerful predictors of reading success.

Phonics

Along with instruction on letter names, children need well-designed and focused phonics instruction to learn letter–sound correspondences. Fast and efficient decoding and word-reading skills rest on the alphabetic principle: how the written spellings of words systematically represent the phonemes in the spoken words. The beginning reader must begin to connect the 26 letters of the alphabet with the approximately 44 phonemes in English.

Practice with decodable texts

Children need to practice new sounds and letters using materials (i.e., controlled decodable texts) that directly reinforce the new information and that review what children already know for maximum gains in fluency and automaticity.

Exposure to sight words and irregular words

Sight word reading happens when children are able to read words from memory. Repeated exposures build the alphabetic features in memory so words can be read by sight.

It is also important for children to have a store of high-frequency irregularly spelled words so that they can read more than just controlled texts when they are ready.

Accurate and automatic word recognition

Fluency and comprehension depend on accurate and automatic word recognition. Slow decoders are poor at comprehension due to reduced attentional and memory resources. Systematic word recognition instruction on common, consistent letter–sound relationships and syllable patterns supports successful word recognition skills.

Spelling

When children are familiar with the spelling regularities of English, their reading and spelling are strengthened. Opportunities to apply the predictable and logical rules and spelling patterns that match the reading patterns being learned give children a double immersion in the information. Spelling is an essential and interconnected complement to reading instruction.

Comprehension

Comprehension depends on the activation of relevant background knowledge and is related strongly to oral language comprehension and vocabulary growth. Along with explicit vocabulary instruction, metacognitive strategies such as questioning, predicting, making inferences, clarifying misunderstandings, and summarizing while reading should be included in comprehension instruction.

Systematic, explicit instruction

Poor readers need highly systematic, structured, explicit, and intensive one-to-one or small-group instruction that recognizes their developmental level in phonemic awareness, word recognition, and comprehension processes. Implicit instruction has been found to be counterproductive with children with learning disabilities or children at risk for not learning to read and produces fewer gains in word recognition and decoding skills than does explicit, intensive instruction based on systematic phonics.

Well-trained teachers

Well-trained, accomplished teachers who can analyze instruction and monitor progress, set goals, and continue to learn about effective practices are the mainstay of children's success in learning to read.

Sources: Adams, 1990; Center for the Improvement of Early Reading Achievement, 1998; Lyon, 1999; Torgesen, 2004.

tail of a normal distribution of reading ability (Shaywitz, 2003). It is typical that a person with dyslexia will have some but not all of the problems that are described next because of individual differences and access to early remediation. Dyslexia is a language-based **learning disability** and is the most widespread form of learning disability. Some common signs of dyslexia are difficulties in learning to speak; problems organizing written and spoken language; difficulty learning the letter names and their sounds; inaccurate decoding; slow, laborious reading lacking fluency; conspicuous problems with spelling and writing; difficulty learning a foreign language; having a hard time memorizing number facts; and difficulty with math operations. Dyslexia varies in severity, and the prognosis depends on the severity of the disability, each individual's specific patterns of strengths and weaknesses, and the appropriateness and intensity of intervention. Dyslexia is not caused by a lack of motivation to learn to read, sensory impairment, inadequate instruction, a lack of environmental opportunities, or low intelligence.

The present working definition, based on empirical support, emphasizes that dyslexia is *neurobiological in origin* in that neural systems in the brain, in place for processing the sounds of language, critical to reading, are involved, as shown in Figure 1.1. Dyslexia is manifested by a disruption in these language systems, which leads to phonological weaknesses. The phonologic weakness occurs "at the lowest level of the language system," and in turn impairs decoding (Shaywitz, 2003). In fact, there are two neural systems for reading: one for word analysis in the parieto-temporal region and the other for automatic, rapid responses localized in the occipito-temporal area that is used by skilled readers for rapid word recognition. Low phonological processing skills are the result of left hemisphere posterior processing anomalies typical of children with dyslexia.

This means that individuals with dyslexia have difficulty accessing and manipulating the sound structure (phonemes) of spoken language. Such a deficit prevents easy and early access to **letter–sound correspondences** and decoding strategies that foster accurate and fluent word decoding and recognition. A vast majority of individuals with dyslexia have a phonological core deficit (Morris et al., 1998; Ramus et al., 2003). Phonological abilities include awareness of the sounds of words in sentences, awareness of syllables in words, and awareness of phonemes in words or syllables. (See Chap-

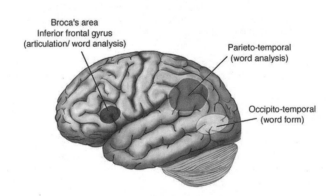

Figure 1.1.   Brain systems for reading. The left hemisphere has three important neural pathways: 1) an anterior system in the left inferior frontal region (Broca's area) for articulation and slower word analysis; 2) a parieto-temporal region for step-by-step analytic word reading; and 3) an occipito-temporal word-form area for skilled, rapid reading. (From OVERCOMING DYSLEXIA [p. 78] by Sally Shaywitz, M.D., copyright © 2003 by Sally Shaywitz, M.D. Used by permission of Alfred A. Knopf, a division of Random House, Inc.)

ter 4 for further discussion.) Approximately 17%–20% of school-age children are affected to some degree by deficits in phonemic awareness (Lyon, 1999). The result is that dyslexics have difficulty recognizing both real and **pseudowords.** This leads to over-reliance on context and guessing, which prevents the building of words in memory, instead of the use of the alphabetic principle to decode words. Readers with dyslexia may also have difficulties with processes underlying the rapid, precise retrieval of visually presented linguistic information. Measures of letter, digit, and color naming are predictors of later reading fluency (Wolf, Bowers, & Biddle, 2000).

Difficulties with accurate and/or fluent word recognition mean that poor readers lack the ability to read quickly, accurately, and with good understanding (The Partnership for Reading, 2003) and thus do not get to the meaning of the text, avoid reading, and fail to develop the necessary *vocabulary and background knowledge* for comprehension. *Poor spelling* assumes importance as a hallmark of dyslexia because of its intimate connection to reading. Educators can identify students with phoneme and word-recognition weaknesses early by administering screening tools for phonemic awareness and other prereading skills validated by research, and promptly applying appropriate intervention in kindergarten and first grade before failure sets in, creating a pattern later on of compromised text reading fluency, deficient vocabulary acquisition, and difficulties with reading comprehension (Eden & Moats, 2002).

Another aspect of the biological origin of dyslexia is that it runs in families. It is common for a child with dyslexia to have parents and siblings who also are dyslexic. Having a dyslexic parent means that between one quarter and one half of the children will have dyslexia, too (Shaywitz, 2003). According to Olson (2004), genetic influences on reading disability are just as important as shared environmental ones. Both are dependent on the quality of instruction available because improper instruction and lack of reading might affect brain processes. A number of different genes play a part in individual differences in phonemic awareness, word reading, and related skills. Deficits in phonemic awareness and reading of pseudowords are heritable. Evidence from research on identical and fraternal twins, funded by NICHD and conducted at the Colorado Learning Disabilities Research Center, has shown that these genetic constraints can be remediated so that children read normally after engaging in intensive practice with an early emphasis on phonological skills and more time in later grades spent reading for accuracy and fluency to promote continued growth. Olson (2004) suggested that there may be a genetic influence on learning rates for reading and related skills. Children with a family history of dyslexia should be monitored for early signs of oral language problems and attention given to prereading language play at home and the opportunity for effective beginning reading instruction at school.

Data from the Connecticut Longitudinal Study, funded by the NICHD, underscored that early identification along with intensive scientifically based instruction can bring poor readers up to grade level. Unless these readers receive intensive help early on, the gap between good and poor readers stays the same although both groups progress over time. What needs to be understood by all concerned with reading instruction is that children facing reading difficulties at the beginning of school remain poor readers as shown in Figure 1.2. As noted by Lyon, a reading disability "reflects a persistent deficit rather than a developmental lag" and "longitudinal studies show that of those children who have a [reading disability] in the third grade, approximately 74% continue to read significantly below grade level in the ninth grade" (1996, p. 64). Without informed teaching they are unlikely to catch up. Compounding that dire circumstance is the fact that students who receive help often receive it for a short period of time, in-

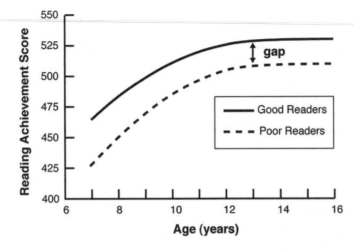

Figure 1.2. Trajectory of reading skills over time in readers with and without dyslexia. The y axis indicates Rasch scores (*W* scores) from the Reading subtest of the Woodcock–Johnson–Revised Tests of Achievement (Woodcock & Johnson, 1989). Both readers with and without dyslexia improve their reading scores as they get older, but the gap between the two groups remains. Thus, dyslexia is a deficit and not a developmental lag. (From OVERCOMING DYSLEXIA [p. 34] by Sally Shaywitz, M.D., copyright © 2003 by Sally Shaywitz, M.D. Used by permission of Alfred A. Knopf, a division of Random House, Inc.)

consistently, from untrained teachers using methods that lack a scientific base (see Shaywitz, 2003, pp. 34–35).

Dyslexia is recognized in the definition as difficulty in learning to read that is *unexpected in relation to other cognitive abilities and the provision of effective classroom instruction.* The discrepancy formula in which decoding and word-recognition deficits need to be lower than IQ in order to be considered dyslexic is no longer recognized. Rather, in its place is the need to compare reading age with chronological age or, in the case of adults, career attainment level. New to the definition is the idea that effective classroom instruction to meet the range of needs children bring to school must be factored in to recognizing dyslexia to tease out reading failure from inadequate instruction, poor preschool preparation, and lack of response to quality instruction.

Along with the specific reading disability just described there are *secondary consequences* such as weaknesses in vocabulary development and *reading comprehension* due to less developed accuracy and fluency and a smaller store of *background knowledge* to support comprehension. Much of this is due to *reduced reading experience.* Deficits in attention, problems in short verbal memory, and difficulty with word retrieval and mathematics have also been identified in students with dyslexia. These deficits can affect listening and reading comprehension. Students with dyslexia who spell poorly often have difficulty with the motor aspects of writing. Poor pencil grip and messy handwriting persist. Expression of ideas clearly in both written and oral form is slow to develop. According to Ramus et al. (2003), it is not clear why sensory and motor disorders are often associated with phonological deficits.

Parents and teachers, therefore, should be aware of the manifestations of dyslexia in early childhood, such as difficulty learning to talk and lack of correct pronunciation of words. Following directions, retrieving names of things such as letters of the alphabet, **sequencing**, and/or forming letters or numbers also can be areas of poor functioning. Characteristics that may accompany dyslexia include time management and organization problems, lack of social awareness, difficulty with attention (e.g., **attention-**

deficit/hyperactivity disorder), poor spatial sense, and difficulty with motor skills. Between 12% and 24% of those with dyslexia also have disorders of attention (Shaywitz, 2003). Reading disabilities and disorders of attention, however, are distinct (Lyon, 1996; Shaywitz, 2003). Although they are separate from learning disabilities, attention disorders and organization difficulties frequently co-occur with language-based reading disability. The severity of a reading disability may be compounded by attention disorders (Lyon, 1996). A good resource that explains these symptoms and offers timely and research-based information is the web site of the International Dyslexia Association (http://www.interdys.org). Hallmarks of good reading assessment are laid out in Chapter 7.

Perhaps what puzzles teachers and parents the most is that students who fail to learn how letters represent speech sounds and how sounds are represented by the letters in words often are good thinkers and are talented in other areas. Since dyslexia is domain specific, other cognitive abilities such as reasoning, comprehension, vocabulary, syntax, and general IQ typically are unaffected (Shaywitz & Shaywitz, 2004). People with dyslexia may excel in the arts, sports, computer technology, architecture, or science, for example. Data from the representative sample of children tested in the Connecticut Longitudinal Study showed that although boys are identified as having dyslexia four times more often than girls are, there are as many females as males with dyslexia. Boys are more often referred for special services due to behavior that signals problems, whereas girls in need of help are less likely to be identified (Shaywitz, 2003).

There are accurate and reliable screening and identification procedures available that are linked to prevention programs. Early identification and intervention are essential to successful treatment of children who are at risk for reading failure. See Chapters 4 and 7 for full discussions of these measures. In the identification of specific reading disability, there has been a shift in approach. According to Lyon, "Definitions that measure the discrepancy between IQ and achievement do not adequately identify learning disabilities, particularly in the area of beginning reading skills" (1996, p. 64). There is growing evidence in support of an alternative approach. Fletcher, Coulter, Reschly, and Vaughn (2004) stated, "Our most pressing challenge is conveying urgency about preventing disabilities through early screening and effective instruction, and for those who do not respond sufficiently, providing effective special education interventions that change achievement and social/behavioral outcomes." Using response to instruction as identification criteria can lead to targeted, timely intervention first and then to assessment; the use of formal progress monitoring with data on student response for accountability and planning; and building bridges between general and **special education** (Fletcher et al., 2004).

As mentioned previously, dyslexia persists across the lifespan and is not a developmental lag. This is most clearly seen in the manifestations of dyslexia among adults (Brozgold, 2002). As in children, it exists across a continuum, with varying indications depending on the individual. Adults with dyslexia vary greatly, with some individuals whose achievement is much lower than expected given their education and experience to gifted people in every field. Adults with dyslexia show decreased reading efficiency (i.e., slower reading rate and lower accuracy) relative to individuals without dyslexia despite good intelligence, education, and career attainment. Their phonetic decoding is impaired relative to their reading comprehension, which may be better due to reliance on context cues and knowledge of the subject about which they are reading. When tested, their decoding of pseudowords is impaired. Other language-based difficulties can be observed, such as mispronunciation of words and names and word-retrieval difficulty. Because writing calls on the integration of so many language skills, written

composition is problematic. Spelling is likely to be persistently weak. Unless the text is of particular interest, the individual may have ongoing difficulty retaining information that he or she reads. A diagnosis of dyslexia in adults can have significant therapeutic and practical value, as it confirms and validates the individual's strengths and weaknesses and leads to interventions that can improve academic skills, vocational functioning, and self-esteem (Brozgold, 2002).

TEACHERS CAN DELIVER EVIDENCE-BASED READING INSTRUCTION TO ALL STUDENTS

Effective Instruction Improves Reading and Changes the Brain

Although dyslexia affects individuals over the lifespan and cannot be cured, with the right early intervention and prevention programs, individuals with dyslexia and other poor readers can increase reading skills. Specifically, when children with reading disability were given intensive, systematic phonics-based reading interventions, they demonstrated increased activation in the left occipito-temporal brain region and also made significant gains in reading fluency and comprehension 1 year after the intervention had ended. Shaywitz et al. (2004) reported that this outcome provides evidence of plasticity of neural systems for reading and demonstrates that a scientifically based reading intervention brings about significant and durable changes in brain organization so that the brain facilitates the development of those fast-paced neural systems that underlie skilled reading.

Using a scientifically based reading intervention with reading disabled children who participated in a functional magnetic resonance imaging study, researchers showed that the intensive, phonologically based intervention made "significant and durable changes in brain organization so that brain activation patterns resemble those of typical readers" of the neural system for reading (Shaywitz et al., 2004, p. 931). The children's reading fluency improved. NICHD-supported research also has found that older individuals with dyslexia can improve with intervention that focuses on remediation of reading and writing skills and other areas of weakness. Sometimes, it is a matter of learning how to learn. (See Chapter 19, which discusses high-functioning adults with dyslexia.) As children get older, however, "the intensity and duration of reading interventions must increase exponentially" (Lyon, 1999) to achieve the same improvement possible with younger children. Effective programs involve intensive instruction using a systematic, structured language approach. It is crucial that the programs be consistent and of sufficient duration for individuals to make progress in improving reading and related skills (Shaywitz, 2003). Modifications and **accommodations**, while not a substitute for remediation, along with the use of technology to support learning, can pave the way for many poor readers to gain information, expand their world knowledge, and to be successful at school or work. They can improve their decoding and comprehension skills but often remain slow readers. Accommodations that build on the strengths of older students and adults with dyslexia can help them to lead successful lives. (Guides to instruction and resources for the older student are discussed in Chapters 12, 18, 19, and 21.)

The Content and Delivery of Reading Instruction Is Critical

It is clear from the consensus of scientifically based reading research that the nature of the educational intervention for individuals with reading disabilities and dyslexia is critical. Central to every aspect of intervention for individuals with language-based

learning disabilities is the characterization of reading and writing as language. For those who do assessments and interpret them, for those who are trained to deliver instruction, and for those who design and carry out programs at all levels, knowledge of language development and disabilities is essential (Dickman, Hennessy, Moats, Rooney, & Tomey, 2002, p. 23). As teachers learn about underlying concepts and instructional strategies in the components of reading accompanied by comprehensive instruction and practice, they begin to incorporate these ideas into their everyday work and student achievement improves (Moats & Foorman, 2003). There is evidence to show that student achievement and teacher preparation and specific domain knowledge are correlated (Darling-Hammond, 2000; Moats & Foorman, 2003; NICHD, 2000).

Too often, content knowledge and depth of training are lacking in the most basic areas of preparation for reading instruction. For example, Cheesman (2004) found that the beginning certified teachers she surveyed lacked the ability to differentiate between phonemic awareness and phonics and the ability to segment written words by phonemes. This raises questions about the quality of preservice teacher education and the availability of quality professional development and mentoring for beginning certified teachers.

To minimize reading failure, classroom reading approaches must include systematic, explicit instruction in phonemic awareness (orally identifying and manipulating syllables and speech sounds); particular attention to letter–sound knowledge (phonics); spelling integrated with reading; fluency (developing speed and automaticity in accurate letter, word, and text reading); vocabulary building; and text comprehension strategies. If such classroom programs prove to be not sufficient for students with dyslexia, the students will need to have a **multisensory structured language education (MSLE)** program, one that incorporates systematic, cumulative, explicit, and sequential approaches taught by teachers trained to teach language structure at the levels of sounds, syllables, meaningful parts of words, sentence structure, and paragraph and discourse

Table 1.2. Multisensory structured language education (MSLE) programs: Content of instruction (what is taught)

Phonology and phonological awareness: Phonology is the study of sounds and how they work within their environment. A phoneme is the smallest unit of sound in a given language that can be recognized as being distinct from other sounds. Phonological awareness is the understanding of the internal linguistic structure of words. An important aspect of phonological awareness is the ability to segment words into their component phonemes [phonemic awareness].

Sound–symbol association: This is the knowledge of the various sounds in the English language and their correspondence to the letter and combinations of letters that represent those sounds. Sound–symbol association must be taught (and mastered) in two directions: visual to auditory and auditory to visual. Additionally, students must master the blending of sounds and letters into words as well as the segmenting of whole words into the individual sounds.

Syllable instruction: A syllable is a unit of oral or written language with one vowel sound. Instruction must include the teaching of the six basic types of syllables in the English language: closed, open, vowel-consonant-*e*, *r*-controlled, and vowel pair [or vowel team]. Syllable division rules must be directly taught in relation to the word structure.

Morphology: Morphology is the study of how morphemes are combined to form words. A morpheme is the smallest unit of meaning in the language. The curriculum must include the study of base words, roots, and affixes.

Syntax: Syntax is the set of principles that dictate the sequence and function of words in a sentence in order to convey meaning. This includes grammar, sentence variation, and the mechanics of language.

Semantics: Semantics is that aspect of language concerned with meaning. The curriculum (from the beginning) must include instruction in the comprehension of written language.

From McIntyre, C.W., & Pickering, J.S. (1995). *Clinical studies of multisensory structured language education for students with dyslexia and related disorders* (p. xii). Poughkeepsie, NY: Hamco; reprinted by permission.

Table 1.3. Multisensory structured language education (MSLE) programs: Principles of instruction (how the programs are taught)

Simultaneous, multisensory (VAKT): Teaching is done using all learning pathways in the brain (visual, auditory, and kinesthetic-tactile) simultaneously in order to enhance memory and learning.

Systematic and cumulative: Multisensory language instruction requires that the organization of material follow the logical order of the language. The sequence must begin with the easiest and most basic elements and progress methodically to more difficult material. Each step must also be based on those [elements] already learned. Concepts taught must be systematically reviewed to strengthen memory.

Direct instruction: The inferential learning of any concept cannot be taken for granted. Multisensory language instruction requires the direct teaching of all concepts with [continual] student-teacher interaction.

Diagnostic teaching: The teacher must be adept at prescriptive or individualized teaching. The teaching plan is based on careful and [continual] assessment of the individual's needs. The content presented must be mastered to the degree of automaticity.

Synthetic and analytic instruction: Multisensory structured language programs include both synthetic and analytic instruction. Synthetic instruction presents the parts of the language and then teaches how the parts work together to form a whole. Analytic instruction presents the whole and teaches how this can be broken down into its component parts.

From McIntyre, C.W., & Pickering, J.S. (1995). *Clinical studies of multisensory structured language education for students with dyslexia and related disorders* (p. xii). Poughkeepsie, NY: Hamco; reprinted by permission.

organization (Eden & Moats, 2002; see also Tables 1.2 and 1.3). Some commercial programs that fit this description are *Alphabetic Phonics, Slingerland, Project Read, LANGUAGE!,* the *Sonday System, Orton-Gillingham, Wilson Language,* the *Spalding Method, Lindamood-Bell,* and others (see the sections for Chapters 9 and 10 in Appendix B for more information). In all of these programs instruction is multisensory, engages the learner in visual, auditory, and kinesthetic responses and feedback with deliberate and intensive practice in reading and spelling controlled for what has been taught. Teachers use structured lesson planning and ongoing monitoring of progress to organize instruction and chart the growth in skills.

From 25 years of prevention and intervention research targeting five major components of reading (phonemic awareness, phonics, fluency, vocabulary, and comprehension), Torgesen (2004) concluded that the key ingredient in teaching this knowledge and these skills to students who are struggling greatly with reading is explicitness and intensity of instruction. By that he meant, "Explicit instruction is instruction that does not leave anything to chance and does not make assumptions about skills and knowledge that children will acquire on their own" (p. 363).

In contrast to leaving things to chance or assuming that students are absorbing the necessary concepts to decode new word or comprehend text, explicit instruction calls on teachers to make clear connections between letters and sounds and their consistent, systematic relationships; to teach individual word meanings and word learning strategies; to provide modeling for fluent reading and have students engage in repeated oral reading; and to learn how to use explicit, carefully sequenced instruction in comprehension strategies. Research has shown that more favorable outcomes are associated with systematic phonics instruction than with an approach emphasizing implicit phonics (Lyon, 1996; NICHD, 2000). Furthermore, Torgesen (2004) reinforced the importance of explicit instruction for remediation and intervention by including the need for intensity, which is wholly different from regular classroom experiences. Through small-group instruction of 1:1 and 1:3 with intensity guided by students' rate of progress (Vaughn & Linan-Thompson, 2003), students with reading problems have a better chance of closing the grade gap with their peers in reading accuracy and reading com-

prehension than in larger group configurations. To make gains students need to engage in highly structured, sequential activities and be closely monitored in ways not possible in the general classroom, forming direct connections between the known and the new, with time for explicit practice of what is being learned to build automaticity and fluency. In addition, there should be a sequential order in the curriculum for instruction and practice. Teachers in the general classroom can also apply these practices with students struggling with reading by incorporating these teaching approaches and rethinking their grouping of students. Intervention research showing evidence of practices that work such as these will find a ready and willing audience among the readers of this volume. The instructional practices and curriculum content in the following chapters fit this model of intervention and remediation. It is encouraging to realize that the research evidence has arrived at a consensus on the critical element of instruction and how it is to be delivered.

Reading disability has far-reaching consequences, which is why we must be prepared to intervene early and intensively until the reader is on target for success. It is important for pre- and in-service teachers to be prepared to work directly with children with reading, writing, and spelling disabilities who also may have other co-occurring difficulties, such as difficulties with arithmetic calculation and mathematical reasoning. Without question, both general and special education teachers need the tools to identify students with language-based learning disabilities, to intervene with explicit instructional procedures, and to continue to sustain their students with intensive support for as long as they need it.

CONCLUSION: IMPACT OF RESEARCH ON PRACTICE

There have been more than 45,000 participants in the NICHD-funded research programs in reading development, reading disorders, and reading instruction, begun in 1965. Both children and adults have participated, including more than 22,500 good readers at the 50th percentile and above and about 22,500 struggling readers below the 25th percentile (Lyon, 2004). From these studies and others we have learned how children read, why some children have difficulties, how we can prevent difficulties from being ingrained, and how to provide intervention when readers continue to struggle.

The beginnings of reading emerge from substantial and significant oral language experiences from birth onwards. The importance of providing oral language and literacy experiences from birth onward, including reading to children, playing with language through rhyming and games, and encouraging writing activities is well documented. These activities encourage vocabulary development and enhance verbal reasoning, semantic, and syntactic abilities. The importance of early assessment and intervention for reading problems is borne out by the findings that show that reading problems identified in Grade 3 and beyond require considerable intervention because children do not just outgrow reading problems. In fact, 74% of children identified as having a reading disability in grade 3 still had a reading disability in the 9th grade according to a study by Francis, Shaywitz, Steubing, Shaywitz, and Fletcher (1996). Measures of intelligence do not predict reading or math achievement well and if used as identifying tools, they become a "wait to fail" model.

The risk factors for dyslexia can be seen in kindergarten and first grade: trouble with letter–sound knowledge, phonological awareness, and oral language development. The earliest clue to dyslexia is "a weakness in getting to the sounds of words" (Shaywitz, 2003, p. 93). Lyon noted that "the best predictor of reading ability from kinder-

garten and first-grade performance is phoneme segmentation ability" (1996, p. 64). It is best to assess all children and intervene first in the classroom, with explicit instruction in phonemic awareness, phonics, and comprehension with an emphasis on fluency in all these competencies. The instruction should be guided by a carefully constructed sequenced curriculum that is designed to be explicit about language structure and that leaves nothing to chance. The texts chosen for practice need to be controlled and later decodable so that children are taught to mastery. The development of phonemic awareness is necessary but not the sole component of learning to read. From the beginning, reading instruction must include attention to phonics principles for accurate and rapid decoding and active use of comprehension strategies.

"The ability to read and comprehend is dependent on rapid and automatic recognition and decoding of single words. Slow and inaccurate decoding are the best predictors of deficits in reading comprehension" (Lyon, 1996, p. 64). Additional factors impeding reading comprehension include vocabulary deficits, lack of background knowledge for understanding text information, deficient understanding of semantic and syntactic structures, insufficient knowledge of writing conventions for different purposes, lack of verbal reasoning, and inability to remember and/or retrieve verbal information. There are now proven strategies to maximize reading comprehension, to develop background knowledge and vocabulary through reciprocal teaching and monitoring feedback.

Educators can make changes by intervening early with instruction that changes the way the brain learns. Much has happened to disseminate the new science of reading. For example, neurobiologic investigations show that there are differences in the temporo-parietal and occipital-temporal brain regions among people with dyslexia from those without dyslexia. Although these differences affect the ability to read, neural systems for reading are malleable and highly responsive to effective reading instruction. In their research using functional magnetic resonance imaging to study the effects of a systematic phonics-based intervention with 6- to 9-year-old children, Shaywitz et al. (2004) found evidence of plasticity of neural systems for reading. The changes in the brain made these readers comparable to good readers. The children were still making gains in reading fluency and comprehension 1 year later after the intervention ended. The conclusion is that providing "evidence-based reading intervention at an early age improves reading fluency and facilitates the development of those neural systems that underlie skilled reading. . . . Teaching matters and can change the brain" (p. 931).

Many states are using research to guide their policy in reading education. The federal government has enacted legislation based on NICHD scientific criteria such as the No Child Left Behind Act of 2001 and the act's Reading First grants to the states. With high-level preservice preparation and professional development efforts that pay strict attention to this evidence, the impact of science should bring about changes at the school level. This book is dedicated to that goal and to teachers in the classroom.

There is still serious underpreparation among teachers regarding the theory and contents of language instruction. Teachers need to have multiple layers of expertise on how children acquire reading, the relationship between language development and reading development, the characteristics of disabilities, and the basic tenets of reading instruction methodologies. There needs to be serious reform in colleges of education and professional development programs.

The time has come to merge the evidence from the science of reading, the knowledge gained from research on what works in the classroom, with serious and sustained preservice training and ongoing professional development so that teachers can better carry out the complex demands of reading instruction. Efforts are going on in many

colleges and universities and private training organizations to rethink and explore new ways of delivering coursework, on-line and in the classroom, in conjunction with innovative ways of gaining practical, hands-on experience with validated practices (Moats, 2003). The way to proceed has been explicitly described by many guides who understand what expert teachers should know and be able to do (Brady & Moats, 1997; Clark & Uhry, 1995; Learning First Alliance, 2000; NICHD, 2000; Snow et al., 1998).

Teachers have to know how reading develops from prereading to reading for information and enjoyment. Detecting reading difficulties early and providing appropriate intervention in time to keep children from failing is critical. A thorough knowledge of the structure of language and how to teach it layer by layer helps teachers to monitor their students' progress and gives them the tools to pace lessons and move their students along based on consistent monitoring of progress (American Federation of Teachers, 1999; Moats & Brady, 1997). This ensures that special educators, who work with the students with the most serious problems, and general educators, who must reach a range of students with diverse needs on a daily basis, receive the best professional development based on what scientifically based reading research shows is effective. Good instruction can prevent a lifetime of difficulties: A good beginning has no end.

REFERENCES

Adams, M.J. (1990). *Beginning to read: Thinking and learning about print.* Cambridge, MA: MIT Press.

American Federation of Teachers. (1999, June). *Teaching reading is rocket science: What expert teachers of reading should know and be able to do* (Item No. 372 6/99). Washington, DC: Author. Also available on-line: http://www.aft.org/pubs-reports/downloads/teachers/rocketsci.pdf

Brady, S., & Moats, L.C. (1997). *Informed instruction for reading success: Foundations for teacher preparation.* Baltimore: The International Dyslexia Association.

Brozgold, A.Z. (2002, March 22). *The diagnosis of dyslexia in adults.* Paper presented at the 29th Annual Conference on Dyslexia and Related Learning Disabilities, New York Branch of The International Dyslexia Association.

Center for the Improvement of Early Reading Achievement. (1998). *Improving the reading achievement of America's children: 10 research-based principles.* Retrieved December 13, 2004, from http://www.ciera.org/library/instresrc/principles/

Cheesman, E.A. (2004). *Teacher education in phonemic awareness.* Unpublished doctoral dissertation, University of Connecticut.

Clark, D.B., & Uhry, J.K. (1995). *Dyslexia: Theory and practice of remedial instruction.* Timonium, MD: York Press.

Darling-Hammond, L. (2000). Teacher quality and student achievement: A review of state policy evidence. *Educational Policy Analysis Archives, 8*(1). Retrieved October 12, 2004, from http://epaa.asu.edu/epaa/v8n1/

Dickman, G.E., Hennessy, N.L., Moats, L.C.,

Rooney, K. J., & Tomey, H.A. (2002). *The nature of learning disabilities: Response to OSEP Summit on Learning Disabilities.* Baltimore: The International Dyslexia Association.

Eden, G.F., & Moats, L.C. (2002). The role of neuroscience in the remediation of students with dyslexia. *Nature Neuroscience, 5*(Suppl.), 1080–1084.

Edmundson, M. (2004, August 1). The risk of reading: Why books are meant to be dangerous. *The New York Times Magazine,* pp. 11–12.

Ehri, L.C. (2004). Teaching phonemic awareness and phonics: An explanation of the National Reading Panel meta-analyses. In P. McCardle & V. Chhabra (Eds.), *The voice of evidence in reading research* (pp. 153–186). Baltimore: Paul H. Brookes Publishing Co.

Ehri, L.C., Nunes, S.R., Stahl, S.A., & Willows, D.M. (2001). Systematic phonics instruction helps students learn to read: Evidence from the National Reading Panel's meta-analysis. *Review of Educational Research, 71*(3), 393–447.

Fletcher, J.M., Coulter, W.A., Reschly, D.J., & Vaughn, S. (2004). Alternative approaches to the definition and identification of learning disabilities: Some questions and answers. *Annals of Dyslexia, 54*(2), 304–331.

Fletcher, J.M., & Francis, D.J. (2004). Scientifically based educational research. In P. McCardle & V. Chhabra (Eds.), *The voice of evidence in reading research* (pp. 59–80). Baltimore: Paul H. Brookes Publishing Co.

Francis, D.J., Shaywitz, S.E., Stuebing, K.K., Shaywitz, B.A., & Fletcher, J.M. (1996). Developmental

lag versus deficit models of reading disability: A longitudinal, individual growth curve analysis. *Journal of Educational Psychology, 88*(1), 3–17.

Juel, C. (1988). Learning to read and write: A longitudinal study of 54 children from first through fourth grades. *Journal of Educational Psychology, 80,* 437–447.

Keller-Allen, C. (2004). *The National Reading Panel: The accuracy of concerns about the report.* Unpublished manuscript.

Learning First Alliance. (2000). *Every child reading: A professional development guide.* Washington, DC: Author.

Lerner, J. (1989). Educational interventions in learning disabilities. *Journal of the American Academy of Child and Adolescent Psychiatry, 28,* 326–331.

Lyon, G.R. (1996, Spring). Learning disabilities. *The Future of Children, 6*(4), 54–76.

Lyon, G.R. (1999). The NICHD research program in reading development, Reading disorders, and reading instruction: A summary of research findings. In *Keys to successful learning: A national summit on research in learning disabilities.* New York: National Center for Learning Disabilities.

Lyon, G.R. (2004). *The NICHD research program in reading development, reading disorders, and treading instruction initiated: 1965.* Paper presented at the 31st annual conference of the New York Branch of The International Dyslexia Association.

Lyon, G.R., & Chhabra, V. (2004). The science of reading research. *Educational Leadership, 61*(6), 13–17.

Lyon, G.R., Shaywitz, S.E., & Shaywitz, B.A. (2003). A definition of dyslexia. *Annals of Dyslexia, 53,* 1–14.

McCardle, P., & Chhabra, V. (Eds.). (2004). *The voice of evidence in reading research.* Baltimore: Paul H. Brookes Publishing Co.

McIntyre, C.W., & Pickering, J.S. (1995). *Clinical studies of multisensory structured language education for students with dyslexia and related disorders.* Salem, OR: International Mulitsensory Structured Language Education Council.

Moats, L.C. (2003). *Language essentials for teachers of reading and spelling (LETRS).* Longmont, CO: Sopris West.

Moats, L.C., & Brady, S. (1997). *Informed instruction for reading success: Foundations for teacher preparation.* Baltimore: The International Dyslexia Association.

Moats, L.C., & Foorman, B.R. (2003). Measuring teachers' content knowledge of language and reading. *Annals of Dyslexia, 53,* 23–45.

Morris, R.D., Stuebing, K.K., Fletcher, J.M., Shaywitz, S.E., Lyon, G. R., Shankweiler, D.P., et al. (1998). Subtypes of reading disability: Variability around a phonological core. *Journal of Educational Psychology, 90,* 347–373.

National Center for Education Statistics. (2003). *National assessment of educational progress: The nation's report card.* Washington, DC: U.S. Department of Education.

National Institute of Child Health and Human Development (NICHD). (2000). *Report of the National Reading Panel. Teaching children to read: An evidence-based assessment of the scientific research literature on reading and its implications for reading instruction: Reports of the subgroups* (NIH Publication No. 00-4754). Washington, DC: U.S. Government Printing Office. Also available on-line:http://www.nichd.nih.gov/publicatons/nrp/report.htm

No Child Left Behind Act of 2001, PL 107-110, 115 Stat. 1425, 20 U.S.C. §§ 6301 *et seq.*

Olson, R.K. (2004). SSSR, environment, and genes. *Scientific Studies of Reading, 8*(2), 111–124.

Overview of reading and literacy initiatives: Hearing before the Senate Committee on Labor and Human Resources, 105th Cong. (1998, April 28) (testimony of G. Reid Lyon). Also available on-line: http://www.nichd.nih.gov/publications/pubs/jeffords.htm

The Partnership for Reading. (2003, June). *Put reading first: The research building blocks for teaching children to read. Kindergarten through grade 3* (2nd ed.). Washington, DC: Author. (Available from ED Pubs, 800-228-8813, Post Office Box 1398, Jessup, MD 20794-1398, edpuborders@edpubs.org; also available on-line: http://www.nifl.gov/partnershipforreading/publications/PFRbookletBW.pdf)

Pressley, M. (2002). *Reading instruction that works* (2nd ed.). New York: The Guilford Press.

Ramus, F., Rosen, S., Dakin, S.C., Day, B.L., Castellote, J.M., White, S., et al. (2003). Theories of developmental dyslexia: Insights from a multiple case study of dyslexic adults. *Brain, 126,* 841–865.

Reyna, V.F. (2004). Why scientific research?: The importance of evidence in changing educational practice. In P. McCardle & V. Chhabra (Eds.), *The voice of evidence in reading research* (pp. 47–58). Baltimore: Paul H. Brookes Publishing Co.

Shaywitz, B.A., Shaywitz, S.E., Blachman, B.A., Pugh, K.R., Fulbright, R.K., Skudlarski, et al. (2004). Development of left occipitotemporal systems for skilled reading in children after a phonologically-based intervention. *Biological Psychiatry, 55*(9), 926–933.

Shaywitz, S.E. (1998). Current concepts: Dyslexia. *The New England Journal of Medicine, 338*(5), 307–312.

Shaywitz, S. (2003). *Overcoming dyslexia: A new and complete science-based program for reading problems at any level.* New York: Alfred A. Knopf.

Shaywitz, S.E., & Shaywitz, B.A. (2004). Neurobiologic basis for reading and reading disability.

In P. McCardle & V. Chhabra (Eds.), *The voice of evidence in reading research* (pp. 417–442). Baltimore: Paul H. Brookes Publishing Co.

Snow, C. (2004). Foreword. In P. McCardle & V. Chhabra (Eds.), *The voice of evidence in reading research* (pp. xix–xxv). Baltimore: Paul H. Brookes Publishing Co.

Snow, C.E., Burns, M.S., & Griffin, P. (Eds.). (1998). *Preventing reading difficulties in young children.* Washington, DC: National Academies Press.

Torgesen, J.K. (2004). Lesson learned from intervention research on interventions for students who have difficulty learning to read. In P. McCardle & V. Chhabra (Eds.), *The voice of evidence in reading research* (pp. 355–382). Baltimore: Paul H. Brookes Publishing Co.

Torgesen, J.K., Wagner, R.K., & Rashotte, C.A. (1994). Longitudinal studies of phonological processing and reading. *Journal of Learning Disabilities, 27,* 276–286.

U.S. Department of Education, Institute of Education Sciences, National Center for Education Evaluation and Regional Assistance. (2003). *Identifying and implementing educational practices supported by rigorous evidence: A user friendly guide.* Washington, DC: Coalition for Evidence Based Policy. Also available on-line: http://www.excelgov.org/usermedia/images/uploads/PDFs/User-Friendly_Guide_12.2.03.pdf

Vaughn, S., & Linan-Thompson, S. (2003). Group size and time allotted to intervention: Effects for students with reading difficulties. In B.R. Foorman (Ed.), *Preventing and remediating reading difficulties: Bringing science to scale* (pp. 299–324). Timonium, MD: York Press.

Wolf, M., Bowers, P., & Biddle, K. (2000). Naming-speed processes, timing, and reading: A conceptual review. *Journal of Learning Disabilities 33,* 322–324.

Woodcock, R.W., & Johnson, M.B. (1989). *Woodcock-Johnson Psycho-Educational Battery–Revised* (WJ-R). Allen, TX: Developmental Learning Materials.

2

Multisensory Structured Language Education

Louisa C. Moats and Mary L. Farrell

ultisensory structured language education (MSLE) is commonly endorsed and practiced by teachers of students with a wide range of learning difficulties. Although clinicians and teachers have embraced multisensory teaching techniques since the earliest teaching guides were written (e.g., Fernald, 1943; Gillingham & Stillman, 1960; Montessori, 1912; Strauss & Lehtinen, 1947), these techniques have seldom been well defined and clinical wisdom has been waiting for scientific research validation and explanation. With current consensus findings regarding the nature of reading development, the efficacy of certain reading instruction practices, and the relationship between brain function and learning, we are closer to understanding why expert teachers have, for generations, been committed to structured language approaches.

This chapter defines what MSLE is, discusses how it has been implemented in the past, identifies the instructional practices that are consistently supported by research, discusses the role of the **multisensory** component in effective instruction of language skills, reviews some recent findings from neuroscientific studies, and describes what additional research might be needed to validate the beliefs and practices of experienced clinicians who subscribe to these approaches.

DEFINITION AND HISTORY

Since the mid-1990s, a number of prominent instructional programs have become organized under the description *multisensory structural language education (MSLE)* (see Appendix B). These approaches are dedicated to the structured, systematic, direct teaching of the organization of language. They also share a belief in the importance of **multisensory strategies**, which include techniques for linking eye, ear, voice, and hand in symbolic learning. Although devoted practitioners emphasize the significance of the

multisensory component as pivotal for student success, it is perhaps this component that is least understood, so it is here that we should begin with both a description of multisensory strategies and a rationale for why they are used in the teaching approaches described in this book.

The term *multisensory* is used generically to refer to any learning activity that includes the use of two or more sensory modalities simultaneously to take in or express information. In this volume, the term does not mean *multimedia* as in playing videotapes or audiocassettes. The term *multisensory* in this volume pertains to techniques for novice or poor readers that involve visual, auditory, tactile-kinesthetic, and/or articulatory-motor components in the carefully sequenced teaching of language structure. For example, students learn alphabet letters by feeling, naming, and matching three-dimensional forms or tracing on rough surfaces; teachers and students model paragraph structure with **graphic organizers**; or students learn the identity of phonemes by feeling and seeing the position of the mouth, lips, and tongue (see Figure 2.1).

Farrell, Pickering, North, and Schavio (2004) investigated the use of multisensory strategies within MSLE programs. In the initial phase of the study, approximately 30 senior clinicians who were directors of MSLE teacher education programs were asked in a survey to specify multisensory strategies incorporated into each of the instructional objectives typical for MSLE lessons in their program (e.g., phonology, sound-symbol association, syllables, morphology, syntax, semantics). For each instructional objective, clinicians were asked to classify multisensory strategies into a description of the spe-

Teacher:	Today we're going to learn a new sound. Listen and say these words while you watch your mouth in the mirror. *Mop, mess, milk, mat, mud.* What sound is your mouth making when you get ready to say those words?
Student:	*Mop, mud, milk.* [Says /m/]
Teacher:	What part of your mouth moved when you started those words?
Student:	My lips!
Teacher:	Were your lips closed or open when you started those words?
Student:	Closed.
Teacher:	Is the sound blocked or unblocked?
Student:	Blocked.
Teacher:	Right. Where does the air come out?
Student:	I don't know.
Teacher:	Hold your nose, and try to say /m/. Where does the air need to come out?
Student:	[Holding nose, tries to say /m/] Through my nose.
Teacher:	Hold your throat. Is your throat buzzing? Are your vocal cords buzzing?
Student:	[Holding throat, says /m/] Yes.
Teacher:	What letter makes that sound, /m/?
Student:	*M.*
Teacher:	Vowels are open, and consonants are blocked. Is *M* a vowel or a consonant?
Student:	A consonant.
Teacher:	[Shows the *M* card; helps the student discover a key word; and asks student to trace the letter on a rough board, chalkboard, or salt tray while saying the name of the letter, the key word, and the sound it makes]

Figure 2.1. A multisensory sound-symbol activity.

cific involvement of each of the sensory systems. A survey item was written for each strategy identified by clinicians and items were organized and listed within instructional objectives. The table in the appendix to this chapter lists, by instructional objective, the multisensory strategies reported and incorporated in the survey.

A multisensory strategy, as mentioned previously, is one that combines the use of two or more senses simultaneously. Implicit in the table in the chapter appendix, for example, is the understanding that in a multisensory approach, a visual strategy is being used simultaneously with an auditory strategy and that for many learning tasks, **kinesthetic** and/or **tactile** strategies are also being used. For example, in working toward the sound–symbol objective (sound–symbol association), if the student's visual reinforcement is looking at a letter, the auditory reinforcement is to listen to and hear the sound and identify it with its symbol. The kinesthetic reinforcement stems from the child's feeling the articulatory muscle movement associated with saying the phonemes, as well as writing the letter on a roughened surface and feeling the associated sensations.

The directors, 19 of whom provided completed surveys, were asked to rate the frequency of use of each of the strategies represented in the survey items according to the following scale: 0 (*never*), 1 (*occasionally*), 2 (*as needed for certain students*), 3 (*systematically used for certain students*), 4 (*systematically used for all students*), and 5 (*other*). The table in the chapter appendix presents, for each survey item, the percentage of use of the strategies.

Multisensory instruction is one dimension of the practices and approaches useful with students who have problems with language learning, including reading and writing. Although some traditional multisensory approaches (e.g., Fernald, 1943) have not emphasized the structure of spoken and written language, most programs that follow **Orton-Gillingham** principles for teaching language-related academic skills (see Clark & Uhry, 1995) have emphasized that the core content for instruction is the carefully sequenced teaching of the structure and use of sounds, syllables, words, sentences, and written discourse. Orton-based approaches, such as *Alphabetic Phonics*, *Project Read*, *LANGUAGE!*, the *Sonday System*, *Wilson Language*, *Slingerland*, and the *Spalding Method* (see the sections for Chapters 9 and 10 in Appendix B) emphasize the necessity for explicit language teaching to be systematic, cumulative, direct, and sequential. It is the combination of these principles, according to clinical consensus (see the training guidelines of the members of the Alliance for Accreditation and Certification of Structured Language Education, 2003) that will facilitate students' ability to learn and recall information.

The idea that learning experienced through all senses is helpful in reinforcing memory has a very long history in pedagogy. Educational psychologists of the late 19th century promoted the theory that all senses, including the kinesthetic sense, are involved in learning. The second volume of James's (1890) *The Principles of Psychology* discussed Binet's theory that all perceptions, in particular those of sight and touch, involve movements of the eyes and limbs and that because such movement is essential in seeing an object, it must be equally essential in forming a visual image of the object. This theory was illustrated through descriptions of typical individuals who used tracing to bolster visual memory. Consistent with this theory were observations that the loss of acquired reading ability as a result of impaired visual memory in adults with brain injury could be bypassed through the use of a kinesthetic **modality** (tracing letters):

> Individuals thus mutilated succeed in reading by an ingenious roundabout way which they often discover themselves: It is enough that they should trace the letters with their finger to understand their sense. . . . The motor image gives the key to the problem. If the patient can read, so to speak, with his fingers, it is because in tracing the letters he

gives himself a certain number of muscular impressions which are those of writing. In one word, the patient reads by writing. (James, 1890, p. 62)

The late 19th-century medical literature also contained discussions about the use of "by-pass" strategies in individuals who had lost their ability to read because of cerebral dysfunction (Berlin, 1887; Dejerine, 1892; Morgan, 1896). Hinshelwood (1917) was the first physician to advocate a specific instructional approach for written language disorders in children identified as "word blind." On the supposition that reading failure was due to underdevelopment or injury of the brain, he recommended instruction using an alphabetic method in a manner that would appeal to as many cerebral centers as possible.

S.T. Orton, a neurologist, was the first person to report in the American medical literature on **word blindness** (1925, 1928). He proposed that there was a physiological failure of the brain to develop a clearly dominant language hemisphere to subsume reading, writing, and spelling (1937). The lack of dominance, he hypothesized, led to an unusual persistence of symbolic reversals in dyslexic individuals. Like Hinshelwood (1917), he advocated the use of all sensory pathways to reinforce weak memory patterns. Orton (1928) called for education methods based on simultaneous association of visual, auditory, and kinesthetic fields, for example, by having a person sound the visually presented word and establish consistent **directionality** by following the letters with the fingers during sound synthesis of syllables and words. He stressed the unity of the language system and its sensorimotor connections and stated that listening, speaking, reading, and writing were interrelated functions of language that must be taught in tandem.

It is clear that the medical and psychological literature reviewed previously had a long-term impact on educational practice. Hunt (1964) reported that in the early 20th century, motor response was considered extremely important in learning. Fernald (1943) described how the kinesthetic aspect of multisensory learning, primarily used for reinforcing word recognition through writing, was incorporated into the approaches of many leading practitioners of the time, including Dearborn (1929); Gates (1927); Hegge, Sears, and Kirk (1932); and Monroe (1932). The methods that have come to be most strongly associated with multisensory instruction today, however, are those developed by educators such as Montessori (1912), Fernald and Keller (1921), and Strauss and Lehtinen (1947), who were challenged by children with dyslexia, learning disabilities, and attention disorders.

The methods for the teaching of reading developed by Montessori, Fernald and Keller, and Strauss and Lehtinen are summarized in Table 2.1. A review of their methods reveals the multisensory nature of their instruction and, in particular, the strong role that the tactile-kinesthetic component plays in the learning process. These practitioners' rationales for tactile and kinesthetic teaching methods reflected their belief in the tenacity of muscle memory (Montessori, 1912) and the belief that children with nonspecific, developmental neurological impairments would profit from compensatory or bypass techniques used effectively with children with brain injury (Fernald, 1943; Strauss & Lehtinen, 1947). Fernald also asserted the need for tactile experience in word learning and reported the learning rate to be much more rapid when finger tracing was used than when a stylus or pencil was used. She quoted the work of Husband (1928) and Miles (1928) on maze learning to support her assertion.

The practitioners who are listed in Table 2.1 all reported very positive results in the educational growth of individual students and attributed their success to the use of

Table 2.1. Overview of early 20th-century multisensory programs

Montessori (1912)

Population: Children 3–7 years old from the tenements of Rome

Cause of disability: Economic and cultural deprivation

Method

1. Daily practice with pencil is given in nonwriting activities to develop muscles for holding and using pencil.
2. The child is prepared to write through daily use of light sandpaper. Vowels are taught, then consonants are begun.
    *   The teacher presents two vowel cards and says sounds. The child traces the letters repeatedly, eventually with eyes closed.
    *   The child is asked to give the teacher cards corresponding to two sounds the teacher pronounces. If the child does not recognize letters by looking, then he or she traces them.
    *   The teacher asks the child to give sounds for letters that the teacher presents.
    *   When the child knows some vowels and consonants, the teacher dictates familiar words that the child "spells" by selecting cardboard letters from a set containing only letters he or she knows.
3. After about 1 month (for 5-year-olds), the child spontaneously begins to write; that is, he or she uses a pencil for composing words.
4. When the child knows all of the sounds, he or she reads slips of paper with names of objects that are well known or present.

Length of training: Average time for learning to read and write, starting from moment at which the child writes, is about 2 weeks. The child begins reading phrases that permit teacher and child to communicate; they play games in which the child reads directions alone and then implements them.

Curriculum control: Although Montessori reported no control for difficulty of words, there is strict control of graphemes written and read through preparatory stages. The child then reads only familiar words only after learning all of the sounds.

Phonics: Within the writing program, presentation of graphemes is sequential and cumulative.

Kinesthetic component: "There develops, contemporaneously, three sensations when the teacher shows the letter to the child and has him trace it: the visual sensation, the tactile sensation, and the muscular sensation. In this way the image of the graphic sign is fixed in a much shorter space of time than when it was, according to ordinary methods, acquired only through the visual image. It will be found that the muscular memory is in the young child the most tenacious and, at the same time, the most ready. Indeed, he sometimes recognizes the letters by touching them, when he cannot do so by looking at them. These images are, besides all this, contemporaneously associated with the alphabetical sound." (p. 277)

Strauss and Lehtinen (1947)

Population: Children with brain injury, that is, with organic impairment resulting in neuromotor disturbances in perception, thinking, and/or emotional behavior

Cause of disability: Disturbances caused by accidental damage to the brain before, during, or after birth

Method

1. Readiness exercises "emphasize perception and integration of wholes; visual discrimination of forms, letters, and words; organization of space; [and] constructing a figure against a background" (p. 176) as well as "ear training" (p. 177).
2. The child learns to discriminate and reproduce sounds and to blend orally. Next, the child learns to associate visual symbols and writing with sounds. The child learns to articulate sound(s) while writing single letters and then pairs. The child attends to auditory components and visual words, makes words on cards or paper with a stamping set, copies them with crayons emphasizing significant features with color, writes them on the blackboard, and builds them with letter cards.
3. Before the child reads a story, he or she will have learned approximately 10 words in the story as single words, simple sentences, or phrases. The words are later presented in varying contexts or exercises to check comprehension. The child is not expected to conform to absolute standards of accuracy while reading words.
4. The child composes short story to be dictated to the teacher. These are then written or typed with a primer typewriter to be read again.

Length of training: Not specified

(continued)

Table 2.1   *(continued)*

Curriculum control: "The child's study of phonics is systematically enlarged. He prepares study materials for himself in the form of lists, cards, sliding devices, booklets, etc. using the phonograms [graphemes] which he encounters in his reading lesson. The work is extrinsic, i.e., the phonic study is supplemental to the reading lesson but closely correlated with it." (p. 180)

Phonics: No phonics training given

Kinesthetic component: "The reading instruction emphasizes accurate perception of words and very early attempts to make the relationship between visual and auditory perception a functioning one. In as many ways as possible, his attention should be drawn to the components of a word, both visual and auditory. He should build words from copy, making them on cards or paper with a stamping set; he should copy them with crayons, emphasizing significant features with color, write them on the blackboard, and build them with letter cards." (p. 179)

Fernald and Keller (1921)

Population: Nonreaders, that is, children of typical intelligence who failed to read after individual instruction by other recognized methods in Fernald's clinic

Cause of disability: "Certain variations" (Fernald, 1943, p. 164) in the integrated brain functioning of the same region in which lesions are found in acquired alexia

Method

1. A word that the child requests is written in large script. The child repeatedly traces the word with index and middle fingers, saying it over to him- or herself until he or she can write it from memory. The word is erased and the child writes it, saying the syllables to him- or herself while writing. If word is incorrect, the process is repeated until the word can be written without the script copy. After a few words are learned, the child is asked to read the word in manuscript print as well as in cursive and then in print only. If incorrect, the word is retaught as in the first presentation.

2. The child starts writing stories initially on subjects of interest to him or her and then, as the child's skill increases, on projects in the various school subjects. The child asks for any word he or she does not know how to write, and it is taught as described before he or she uses it. After the story is finished, the child files new words under the proper letters in his or her word file.

Length of training: Average tracing period is about 2 months, with range of 1–8 months. After period of tracing, the child develops ability to learn any new word by simply looking at a word in script, copying it, and saying each part of the word while writing it.

Curriculum control: Because the child usually is able to recognize words after having written them, this provides a reading vocabulary that usually makes it unnecessary to simplify the content of the first reading.

Phonics: The sound of each letter is never given separately, yet the child is instructed to segment the word into syllables while writing.

Kinesthetic component: "Individuals who have failed to learn to read by visual and auditory methods show a spurt of learning as soon as the kinesthetic method is used. . . . The end product is a skill equal to that of individuals who learn by ordinary methods" (Fernald, 1943, p. 168). Fernald and Keller (1921) reported that the learning rate is much more rapid when using tracing with finger contact than when using a stylus or a pencil.

kinesthetic methods. In each method, however, there was also an emphasis on language components and systematic, sequential, organized teaching. Fernald's (1943) technique differed from the others in that whole words or whole syllables were taught, not individual phoneme–grapheme relationships (apparently she was unable to perform phoneme segmentation tasks herself). In contrast, Montessori (1912) and Strauss and Lehtinen (1947) did emphasize direct teaching of phonics.

Given the multiple factors that may have accounted for these practitioners' successes with individuals, including the intensity of their small-group and individual interventions, their case study reports and anecdotal claims cannot be taken as proof of the efficacy of multisensory instruction. Even Strauss and Lehtinen (1947) acknowledged that the effect attributed to multisensory teaching could be a primary consequence of augmented attention rather than of kinesthetic learning per se.

Bryant (1979) continued to explore these questions, providing a history of the use of multisensory instruction up to 1979, a summary of the research examining the theoretical assumptions underlying multisensory approaches, and a review of empirical studies on the use of multisensory instruction in reading with individuals with reading disabilities. She reported that until the 1970s, special education teachers had firmly believed in the value of kinesthetic reinforcement, and she cited a number of well-known names in the fields of reading and learning disabilities who stressed the importance of multisensory approaches (Ayres, 1972; Cruickshank, Betzen, Ratzeburg, & Tannhauser, 1961; Dearborn, 1940; Frostig, 1965; Gates, 1935; Hegge, Kirk, & Kirk, 1940; Johnson, 1966; Kephart, 1960; Money, 1966; Monroe, 1932; Strauss & Lehtinen, 1947; Wepman, 1964). Bryant also found that textbooks training teachers on the treatment of learning disabilities typically recommended the use of multisensory techniques in word-recognition instruction and for other domains of symbolic and conceptual learning.

However, Bryant was unable to find any evidence to support the then-current theories (e.g., the theory of deficient **cross-modal integration**) for explaining why students with learning disabilities would need multisensory instruction to learn effectively.

In addition, Bryant noted that the popularity of both generic and reading-specific multisensory practices was attributable primarily to reports of success rather than to empirical evidence supporting either the theory or the practice of multisensory teaching. Bryant's review as well as subsequent reviews of the research literature in learning disabilities (e.g., Lyon & Moats, 1988; Moats & Lyon, 1993; Torgesen, 1991) failed to muster evidence in support of any explanations of learning or reading disorders that would provide a rationale for the power of multisensory strategies. In addition, the existing studies of multisensory teaching methods were either conflicting or inconclusive. Bryant herself compared visual-auditory-kinesthetic word-study techniques with visual-auditory word-study techniques and reported that young readers responded equally well to both. She concluded that other principles of good instruction, including enhancing student attention, providing feedback and modeling, avoiding overloading the student, giving sufficient practice, and providing effective reinforcement, accounted for student success.

Almost a decade after Bryant's (1979) review and intervention study, Clark (1988) also concluded that despite the widespread inclusion of multisensory techniques in remedial programs for students with dyslexia and the strong belief among practitioners using these techniques that they work, there was little empirical evidence to support the techniques' theoretical premises. Although many of the programs incorporating these strategies have been effective according to clinical reports, the specific contribution of the multisensory component to the overall success of those programs has not yet been thoroughly documented or explained through rigorous manipulation of instructional conditions and subsequent measurement of outcomes. Current reading research, however, does offer strong support for the *content* and overall approach of MSLE programs because they address language processing skills necessary for both decoding and comprehension.

CURRENT RESEARCH CONSENSUS ON TEACHING READING

The Content of Instruction: Why We Teach Phonics

Traditionally, methods for teaching reading in an **alphabetic language**, beginning with the methods used by teachers in ancient Greece, have included direct teaching of

the links between sounds and symbols (Matthews, 1966). Even before the work of the National Reading Panel (National Institute of Child Health and Human Development, 2000), several comprehensive reviews (Adams, 1990; Anderson, Hiebert, Scott, & Wilkinson, 1985; Chall, 1967, 1983), concluded that direct, systematic teaching of phonics for beginning and remedial readers, along with much practice in text reading and instruction in various comprehension skills, was a necessary component of effective instruction if all students were to be successful. The studies reviewed reflected a variety of research methodologies, including small, well-controlled laboratory experiments and large-scale, multiple-classroom research. None of the major, comprehensive evaluations of research in reading instructional methods ever concluded that phonics was unnecessary or unimportant in elementary instruction. It has always been the case that children who have received direct instruction in speech–print correspondences learn to read words, spell, and define vocabulary better than children who do not receive such instruction, especially if they are defined as at risk for failure, even though educators have eschewed those research findings with regularity (Moats, 2000; Snow, Burns, & Griffin, 1998).

Research has contributed an explanation of why phonics instruction is necessary and effective for children learning to read and spell an alphabetic orthography. Skilled reading requires accurate processing of the internal details of words—their phonological, morphological, and orthographic features (see Adams, Treiman, & Pressley, 1998; Rayner, Foorman, Perfetti, Pesetsky, & Seidenberg, 2001; Share & Stanovich, 1995; and Vellutino et al., 1996, for reviews). Beginning readers must be aware or must learn that words are made up of individual speech sounds (phonemes). They must be able to represent in their minds the linguistic structure of words they are learning to read, primarily at the phoneme level (Ehri et al., 2001) but at other levels of language structure as well, especially morphology or the meaningful parts of words (Henry, 2003). Although it appears that good readers guess at words or that they read whole words as units, good readers in fact process virtually every letter of the words they read and are able, on demand, to translate print to speech rapidly and efficiently. It is the fluency of this translation process that permits a good reader to attend to the meaning of what is read. Therefore, it is logical that effective instruction with poor readers would seek to increase their awareness of phonemes and other linguistic units and that the speech-to-print translation process would become a focus of teaching until the children read fluently enough to focus on comprehension.

Indeed, a wide range of studies has shown that poor readers are marked by weaknesses in **phoneme awareness**, slow and inefficient decoding skills, inaccurate spelling, and related language-processing difficulties. Poor readers' problems are linguistic in nature and are related both to inaccurate and to inefficient linguistic coding at very basic levels of word and subword processes. When readers cannot decode print accurately, comprehension is impaired; too much mental energy is being used to recode the message, and too little is available for making meaning. Effective instruction addresses these issues as directly and systematically as possible (Blachman, Schatschneider, Fletcher, & Clonan, 2003; Lyon, Fletcher, & Barnes, 2003; Torgesen et al., 2001; Vellutino et al., 1996).

Theoretical Support for the Use of Multisensory Strategies

The efficacy of structured, systematic, explicit teaching of all language-based skills is no longer questioned by leading researchers (Lyon, Fletcher, Fuchs, & Chhabra, 2005), but evidence is still needed to explain the popularity of multisensory activities in language

learning. Empirical support for the power of multisensory techniques remains illusive in recent studies of reading instruction. Nevertheless, theoretical support for the added benefit of multisensory techniques can be sought from the cognitive and neurological sciences. One logical explanation might be based on the design of memory itself.

The Nature of Memory

According to Wagner's (1996) overview of research on memory processes, **short-** and **long-term memory** are not separate functions that reside in different circuits or locations in the brain. Rather, short-term memory, or working memory, is most likely the temporary activation of selected and established long-term memory stores. During the conscious learning of any new information, a large number of organized patterns of neural networks are activated temporarily. This activation of selected circuitry lasts as long as attention is focused on a specific bit of information; otherwise, the activation pattern decays quickly as attentional shift occurs. Control processes such as **selective attention**, attentional shift, and employment of strategies for remembering such as **verbal rehearsal** or use of imagery are features of working memory as well.

Within working memory are specialized storage mechanisms including a **phonological loop** that can store small bits of speech information as they are being processed and a **visuospatial loop** that can store print or graphic information. The functional separation of these parts of working memory have long been evident in various experiments, including those that show that it is easier to integrate multiple sources of information during learning when the material is physically integrated, auditorily and visually, than when information is presented to each modality separately (Mousavi, Low, & Sweller, 1995).

Bits of speech information held in the phonological loop are interpreted in another workspace that subsumes comprehension or the construction of meaning. Previous knowledge of the domain of information being processed determines comprehension more than any limitation of working memory capacity. Therefore, the processes of initial word identification and subsequent interpretation of those words are served by different functions within working memory, and comprehension is very much a product of prior knowledge. Storage and retrieval of knowledge from long-term memory improve with practice and vary with subject-matter familiarity. Long-term memory content is created differently according to the different types and purposes of memories, including experiential, semantic, procedural, and automatic response memories.

The phonological loop is the special part of working memory that has been implicated in dyslexia or in reading and spelling disabilities. It is responsible for such feats as remembering a novel list of unrelated digits or words or a novel phonological string such as a **nonsense word** or an unfamiliar word from a foreign language. According to Torgesen's (1996) review, the phonological loop includes a phonological memory store to hold speech information for a brief period while speech is being interpreted and an articulatory control process that activates speech-motor programs. This articulatory control process is central, not peripheral, in its location and function: It is functionally dissociated from the parts of the brain that control speech musculature and the peripheral hearing mechanism. One can have a severe disorder of speech production and/or a hearing loss but have intact central articulatory control processes.

Items such as names of letters, individual speech sounds (phonemes), and words are represented in the phonological memory store as a set of distinctive features. For example, the /m/, /n/, and /ng/ phonemes all are nasal stop consonants that differ only

in place of articulation. When features are shared among phonemes, those units of sound are likely to be confused with one another. When a child says "aminal" for *animal,* or when the child spells *CON* for *comb,* the exact features of the nasal consonants in those words are not being processed accurately in the phonological memory store. To improve pronunciation, word recognition, or spelling, the child needs to establish memories for words with nasal consonants in which the features of sounds are fully specified and differentiated from one another. To reduce the possible confusion of speech sounds with shared features, the child can be enrolled in a speech-motor program that provides an internal image of the gestures involved in saying the phonemes. There is evidence that children with phonological disabilities improve in phoneme awareness, reading, and spelling when they are sensitized to both the articulatory features of the phonemes and phoneme sequences in words and when they learn the written symbols that represent them as linguistic units (Gillon, 2003).

Functional Neuroimaging

Neuroscience has advanced significantly our understanding of language learning disabilities, their biological bases, and their responsiveness to treatment (Eden & Moats, 2002; Lyon, Shaywitz, & Shaywitz, 2003; Shaywitz, 2003). **Functional neuroimaging**, in which images are constructed of the brain activity of subjects performing specific tasks while awake, can provide concrete evidence of how the brain is organized for reading. Multiple sites and multiple connections among those sites are activated during typical reading. The brain does not store information in localized compartments but rather establishes highly specialized and widely distributed networks that can be interrupted when damage occurs to specific areas. Messages from print are processed first in the visual (occipital) cortex, then in the left angular gyrus, which is linked to the left hemisphere's speech-processing centers. The **left angular gyrus** is the primary location for translating visual-orthographic information into phonological representations (linking symbol to sound). The nearby language association areas connect meaning to those phonological codes. Other connections also link the visual association cortex to speech-processing areas. (Figure 1.1 in Chapter 1 shows the areas of the brain that are involved in reading.) The neural connections for reading are so specialized that the type of word one is reading—for example, a noun or an adjective—affect the exact sites that are activated for processing. Processing proceeds simultaneously and interactively, even though specific modules or neural connections are highly specialized for processing jobs (Rumsey, 1996). During reading, when compared with children without reading disabilities, children with poor phonological processing show reduced cerebral blood flow in the left frontal and temporal cortices (where incoming language is coded and interpreted) and reduced activation of language areas normally involved in reading. Dyslexic readers also overrely on the right cerebral hemisphere (Shaywitz & Shaywitz, 2003). Underactivation of left hemisphere language areas and abnormal activation patterns continue to characterize dyslexic adults, even when they have learned to read reasonably well.

From this functional neurological model, one possibility is that dyslexic individuals with weak phonological processing must establish alternative circuits for word recognition to compensate for disruption of circuitry normally relied on for reading. It is possible, when sensorimotor pathways are activated through use of the fingertips, hand, arm, whole body, and/or vocal speech apparatus during symbolic learning, that circuits necessary for word recognition are more easily accessed and established. Sev-

eral recent studies of the impact of intensive, systematic, structured language instruction on children with reading disabilities have shown that functional brain patterns are normalized as a consequence of instruction (Berninger et al., 2003; Blachman et al., 2003; Shaywitz, 2003; Simos et al., 2002). Left hemisphere temporal-parietal and temporal-occipital regions can be activated in response to teaching and are able to subsume responsibility for automatic word recognition. The neurobiological mechanisms by which these changes are achieved are largely unknown.

Principles of Cognition

Even before so much was known about the nature of linguistic processing in reading disabilities, there was substantial evidence that successful instructional practices with students who had learning disabilities included deliberate provision of reinforcement and conscious employment of responsive, strategic learning (Lyon & Moats, 1988; Swanson, 1999; Wong, 1991). As cognitive psychologists have repeatedly demonstrated, learning is an active, constructive process in which new information is linked with established schemata (Wittrock, 1992). The brain transforms new information in accordance with stored information that it has activated during the learning process. **Active learning** is that which causes the learner to mentally search for connections between new and already-known information. That is, instruction that includes teaching of metacognition—the deliberate rearrangement, regrouping, or modal transfer of information, and the conscious choice of and evaluation of the strategies used to accomplish a task—is more effective than rote or passive memorization approaches in almost every domain of learning. For example, students who create their own **mnemonic strategies** tend to learn from those more readily than students who are provided with a mnemonic strategy. Students who think aloud while working remember more and make fewer errors. Students who respond motorically, who must do something as they learn, attend better to the details and meaning of a stimulus and are likely to remember more.

Adams and her colleagues (1998) completed an extensive review of the research literature on reading comprehension instruction. They concluded that the active (vocal) modeling and rehearsal of basic comprehension functions such as summarizing, questioning, and predicting during an interaction among a teacher and group of students was much more effective in improving comprehension than was structured seatwork or independent silent reading. The high rate of active response on the part of students, the combination of reading and verbalization of ideas, and the emphasis on deliberate employment of learning strategies characterized instructional conditions that resulted in retention and generalization of reading comprehension skills.

SUMMARY

Multisensory teaching links listening, speaking, reading, and writing. The simultaneous and alternative deployment of visual, auditory, kinesthetic, and tactile sensory modalities has traditionally been a staple of remedial and preventive intervention for students with learning disabilities and/or dyslexia. Multisensory methods support the connection of oral language with visual language symbols and can involve the use of touch and movement to facilitate conceptual learning in all academic areas. The appeal of multisensory instruction endures even though it has been poorly defined and is not well validated in existing intervention studies.

As noted in this chapter, MSLE techniques have been cited and recommended by experts in learning disorders before and throughout the 20th century. Although respected instructional programs incorporate similar instructional principles, research has contributed more to the definition and explication of the nature of dyslexia and learning disorders than it has contributed to supporting the use of MSLE. Science has substantially redefined the nature of dyslexia and learning disabilities. In other words, practitioners' beliefs about what works have remained quite stable even though conceptualizations of dyslexia and learning disabilities have changed substantially.

Prior to the conceptualization of dyslexia as a language-based disorder of phonological origin, many proponents of structured, multisensory, explicit language teaching endorsed the view that reading disability was primarily a visually based disorder. For many years, practitioners invoked various theories of modality preference, modality bypass, interhemispheric dominance, intersensory integration, and other ideas alluding to neurological organization to justify and explain the power of multisensory, structured teaching of language organization and other content. Most of those theories have been decidedly disproved or radically revised to accommodate the findings of cognitive, neuropsychological, neurological, and psycholinguistic research.

It is ironic that research-based conceptions of reading and language-based learning disabilities may provide a better theoretical rationale to explain why MSLE works than are provided by the theories of the methods' originators. It is known that poor and novice readers at risk for reading and spelling difficulties are usually lacking in phonological skill and often have related problems with short-term memory of verbal information and rapid retrieval of verbal information. In addition, at least one third of children with language-based learning disabilities also have coexisting attention disorders. Current research has demonstrated unequivocally that such learners benefit when the structure of spoken and written language, beginning with phonemes, is represented for them explicitly, sequentially, directly, and systematically, in the context of balanced and comprehensive reading instruction. Multisensory experiences with linguistic units such as single phonemes, letters, morphemes, words, and sentences may in fact activate more circuitry during language learning than unisensory experiences do.

Conceptions of memory organization, neural activation patterns in language processing, and the importance of metacognition are consistent with the efficacy of multisensory techniques. New neural networks, which in the human brain are highly specialized for certain processing functions, are established through repeated activation. When attention to linguistic detail is enhanced through multisensory involvement, a more complete and explicit registration of linguistic information (phonological and other) is likely to occur in the learner's working memory. Those transient associative memories are more likely to be stored in connection with existing information in the language processor if other movement or sensory events occur with them. Most likely, it is not simply the multimodal nature of such practice that explains its power but the mediating effect of various sensory and motor experiences on attention and recall.

Knowledgeable clinicians have been hoping for a scientific explanation for accepted instructional practices for many years, and much progress has been made. Eventually, cognitive psychology, educational psychology, and the neurosciences may provide even more definitive support for specific techniques of teaching and refinements of practice. Research is slowly but surely addressing the question of what to do, for what types of children, when, how much, for how long, and in what environments. While neuroscience, cognitive psychology, educational psychology, and educational intervention research pave the way toward an even better understanding of reading de-

velopment and reading remediation, the practices detailed in this book rest on both clinical experience and good science.

REFERENCES

Adams, M.J. (1990). *Beginning to read: Thinking and learning about print.* Cambridge: The MIT Press.

Adams, M.J., Treiman, R., & Pressley, M. (1998). Reading, writing, and literacy. In I. Sigel & A. Renninger (Eds.), *Handbook of child psychology: Vol. 4. Child psychology in practice* (5th ed., pp. 275–355). New York: John Wiley & Sons.

Alliance for Accreditation and Certification of Structured Language Education, Inc. (2003). *Alliance directory: A list of accredited training courses and certified individuals* [CD-ROM]. Baltimore: The International Dyslexia Association.

Anderson, R.C., Hiebert, E.H., Scott, J.A., & Wilkinson, I.A.G. (1985). *Becoming a nation of readers: The report of the Commission on Reading.* Washington, DC: U.S. Department of Education, The National Institute of Education.

Ayres, J. (1972). Improving academic scores through sensory integration. *Journal of Learning Disabilities, 5*(6), 338–343.

Berlin, R. (1887). *Eine besondere art der wortblindheit: Dyslexia* [A special kind of word blindness: Dyslexia]. Wiesbaden, Germany: J.F. Bergmann.

Berninger, V.W., Nagy, W.E., Carlisle, J., Thomson, J., Hoffer, D., Abbott, S., et al. (2003). Effective treatment for children with dyslexia in Grades 4–6: Behavioral and brain evidence. In B.R. Foorman (Ed.), *Preventing and remediating reading difficulties: Bringing science to scale* (pp. 381–417). Timonium, MD: York Press.

Blachman, B.A., Schatschneider, C., Fletcher, J.M., & Clonan, S.M. (2003). Early reading intervention: A classroom prevention study and a remediation study. In B.R. Foorman (Ed.), *Preventing and remediating reading difficulties: Bringing science to scale* (pp. 253–271). Timonium, MD: York Press.

Bryant, S. (1979). *Relative effectiveness of visual-auditory vs. visual-auditory-kinesthetic-tactile procedures for teaching sight words and letter sounds to young disabled readers.* Unpublished doctoral dissertation, Teachers College, Columbia University, New York.

Chall, J.S. (1967). *Learning to read: The great debate.* New York: McGraw-Hill.

Chall, J.S. (1983). *Stages of reading development.* New York: McGraw-Hill.

Clark, D.B. (1988). *Dyslexia: Theory and practice of remedial instruction.* Timonium, MD: York Press.

Clark, D.B., & Uhry, J. (1995). *Dyslexia: Theory and practice of remedial instruction* (2nd ed.). Timonium, MD: York Press.

Cruickshank, W.M., Betzen, F.A., Ratzeburg, F.H., & Tannhauser, M.T. (1961). *A teaching method for brain-injured and hyperactive children: A demonstration-pilot study.* Syracuse, NY: Syracuse University Press.

Dearborn, W.F. (1929). Unpublished paper presented at the Ninth International Congress of Psychology, Yale University, New Haven, CT.

Dearborn, W.F. (1940). On the possible relations of visual fatigue to reading disabilities. *School and Society, 52,* 532–536.

Dejerine, J. (1892, February 27). Contribution a l'étude anatomo-pathologigue et clinique des différentes variétés de cécité verbale [Contribution to the anatomo-pathological and clinical studies of different types of word blindness]. *Mémoriale Société Biologigue, 61.*

Eden, G.F., & Moats, L.C. (2002). The role of neuroscience in the remediation of students with dyslexia. *Nature Neuroscience, 5,* 1080–1084.

Ehri, L.C., Nunes, S.R., Willows, D.M., Schuster, B.V., Yaghoub-Zadeh, Z., & Shanahan, T. (2001). Phonemic awareness instruction helps children learn to read: Evidence from the National Reading Panel's meta-analysis. *Reading Research Quarterly, 36,* 250–287.

Farrell, M., Pickering, J., North, N., & Schavio, C. (2004, Fall). What is multisensory instruction? *The IMSLEC Record, 8*(3).

Fernald, G.M. (1943). *Remedial techniques in basic school subjects.* New York: McGraw-Hill.

Fernald, G.M., & Keller, H. (1921). The effect of kinesthetic factors in development of word recognition in the case of non-readers. *Journal of Educational Research, 4,* 355–377.

Frostig, M. (1965). Corrective reading in the classroom. *The Reading Teacher, 18,* 573–580.

Gates, A.I. (1927). Studies of phonetic training in beginning reading. *Journal of Educational Psychology, 18,* 217–226.

Gates, A. (1935). *The improvement of reading: A program of diagnostic and remedial methods.* New York: Macmillan.

Gillingham, A., & Stillman, B. (1960). *Remedial training for children with specific disability in reading, spelling, and penmanship* (6th ed.). Cambridge, MA: Educators Publishing Service.

Gillon, G.T., (2003). *Phonological awareness: From research to practice.* New York: Guilford Press.

Hegge, T.G., Kirk, S.A., & Kirk, W.D. (1940). *Remedial reading drills.* Ann Arbor, MI: George Wahr.

Hegge, T.G., Sears, R., & Kirk, S.A. (1932). Reading cases in an institution for mentally retarded problem children. In *Proceedings and Addresses of*

the *Fifty-Sixth Annual Session of the American As-sociation for the Study of the Feebleminded, 15,* 149–212.

Henry, M.K. (2003). *Unlocking literacy: Effective de-coding and spelling instruction.* Baltimore: Paul H. Brookes Publishing Co.

Hinshelwood, J. (1917). *Congenital word blindness.* London: H.K. Lewis.

Hunt, J.M. (1964). Introduction: Revisiting Mon-tessori. In M. Montessori, *The Montessori method* (A.E. George, Trans.). New York: Schocken Books.

Husband, R.W. (1928). Human learning on a four-section elevated finger maze. *Journal of General Psychology, 1,* 15–28.

James, W. (1890). *The principles of psychology* (Vol. 2). New York: Henry Holt & Co., Inc.

Johnson, M. (1966). Tracing and kinesthetic tech-niques. In J. Money (Ed.), *The disabled reader: Education of the dyslexic child* (pp. 147–160). Bal-timore: The Johns Hopkins University Press.

Kephart, N.C. (1960). *The slow learner in the class-room.* Columbus, OH: Charles E. Merrill.

Lyon, G.R., Fletcher, J.M., & Barnes, M.C. (2003). Learning disabilities. In E.J. Mash & R.A. Barkley (Eds.), *Child psychopathology* (2nd ed., pp. 520–586). New York: Guilford Press.

Lyon, G.R., Fletcher, J.M., Fuchs, L.S., & Chhabra, V. (2005). Learning disabilities. In E. Mash & R. Barkley (Eds.), *Treatment of childhood disorders* (2nd ed.). New York: The Guilford Press.

Lyon, G.R., & Moats, L.C. (1988). Critical issues in the instruction of the learning disabled. *Journal of Consulting and Clinical Psychology, 56,* 830–835.

Lyon, G.R., Shaywitz, S.E., & Shaywitz, B.A. (2003). A definition of dyslexia. *Annals of Dyslexia, 53,* 1–14.

Matthews, M.M. (1966). *Teaching to read: Historically considered.* Chicago: University of Chicago Press.

Miles, W. (1928). The high finger relief maze for hu-man learning. *Journal of General Psychology, 1,* 3–14.

Moats, L.C. (2000). *Whole language lives on: The il-lusion of "balance" in reading instruction.* Wash-ington, DC: Thomas B. Fordham Foundation.

Moats, L., & Lyon, G.R. (1993). Learning disabili-ties in the United States: Advocacy, science, and the future of the field. *Journal of Learning Dis-abilities, 26,* 282–294.

Money, J. (Ed.). (1966). *The disabled reader: Educa-tion of the dyslexic child.* Baltimore: The Johns Hopkins University Press.

Monroe, M. (1932). *Children who cannot read.* Chi-cago: University of Chicago Press.

Montessori, M. (1912). *The Montessori method.* New York: Frederick Stokes.

Morgan, W.P. (1896, November 7). Word blind-ness. *British Medical Journal, 2,* 1378.

Mousavi, S.Y., Low, R., & Sweller, J. (1995) Reduc-ing cognitive load by mixing auditory and visual presentation modes. *Journal of Educational Psy-chology, 87,* 319–334.

National Institute of Child Health and Human De-velopment. (2000). *Report of the National Reading Panel. Teaching children to read: An evidence based assessment of the scientific research literature on reading and its implications for reading instruction: Reports of the subgroups* (NIH Publication No. 00–4754): Washington, DC: Government Printing Office. Also available on-line:http://www.nichd .nih.gov/publications/nrp/report.htm

Orton, S.T. (1925). "Word-blindness" in school children. *Archives of Neurology and Psychiatry, 14,* 581–615.

Orton, S.T. (1928). Specific reading disability-strephosymbolia. *JAMA: Journal of the American Medical Association, 90,* 1095–1099.

Orton, S.T. (1937). *Reading, writing, and speech prob-lems in children.* New York: W.W. Norton.

Rayner, K., Foorman, B., Perfetti, C., Pesetsky, D., & Seidenberg, M.S. (2001). How psychological science informs the teaching of reading. *Psycho-logical Science in the Public Interest, 2*(2), 31–74.

Rumsey, J.M. (1996). Neuroimaging in develop-mental dyslexia: A review and conceptualization. In G.R. Lyon & J.M. Rumsey (Eds.), *Neuroimag-ing: A window to the neurological foundations of learning and behavior in children* (pp. 57–77). Bal-timore: Paul H. Brookes Publishing Co.

Share, D., & Stanovich, K.E. (1995). Cognitive processes in early reading development: Accom-modating individual differences into a mode of acquisition. *Issues in Education: Contributions from Educational Psychology, 1,* 1–57.

Shaywitz, S. (2003). *Overcoming dyslexia: A new and complete science-based program for reading prob-lems at any level.* New York: Alfred A. Knopf.

Shaywitz, S.E., & Shaywitz, B.A. (2003). Neurobio-logic basis for reading disability. In P. McCardle & V. Chhabra (Eds.), *The voice of evidence in read-ing research* (pp. 417–442). Baltimore: Paul H. Brookes Publishing Co.

Simos, P.G., Fletcher, J.M., Bergman, E., Breier, J.I., Foorman, B.R., Castillo, E.M., et al. (2002). Dyslexia-specific brain activation profile be-comes normal following successful remedial training. *Neurology, 58,* 1203–1213.

Snow, C.E., Burns, M.S., & Griffin, P. (Eds.). (1998). *Preventing reading difficulties in children.* Wash-ington, DC: National Academies Press.

Strauss, A., & Lehtinen, L.E. (1947). *Psychopathol-ogy and education of the brain-injured child.* New York: Grune & Stratton.

Swanson, H.L. (1999). Reading research for students with LD: A meta-analysis of intervention out-comes. *Journal of Learning Disabilities, 32,* 504–532.

Torgesen, J. (1991). Learning disabilities: Historical and conceptual issues. In B. Wong (Ed.), *Learning*

about learning disabilities (pp. 3–37). San Diego: Academic Press.

Torgesen, J.K. (1996). A model of memory from an information processing perspective: The special case of phonological memory. In G.R. Lyon & N.A. Krasnegor (Eds.), *Attention, memory, and executive function* (pp. 157–184). Baltimore: Paul H. Brookes Publishing Co.

Torgesen, J., Alexander, A.W., Wagner, R., Rashotte, C.A., Voeller, K., Conway, T., et al. (2001). Intensive remedial instruction for children with severe reading disabilities: Immediate and long-term outcomes from two instructional approaches. *Journal of Learning Disabilities, 34,* 33–58.

Vellutino, F.R., Scanlon, D.M., Sipay, E.R., Small, S.G., Pratt, A., Chen, R., et al. (1996). Cognitive profiles of difficult to remediate and readily remediated poor readers: Early intervention as a vehicle to distinguish between cognitive and experiential deficits as basic causes of specific reading disability. *Journal of Educational Psychology, 88,* 601–638.

Wagner, R. (1996). From simple structure to complex function: Major trends in the development of theories, models, and measurements of memory. In G.R. Lyon & N.A. Krasnegor (Eds.), *Attention, memory, and executive function* (pp. 139–156). Baltimore: Paul H. Brookes Publishing Co.

Wepman, J.M. (1964). The perceptual basis for learning. In H. Robinson (Ed.), *Meeting individual differences in reading.* Chicago: University of Chicago Press.

Wittrock, M.C. (1992). Generative learning processes of the brain. *Educational Psychologist, 27,* 531–541.

Wong, B.Y.L. (1991). Assessment of metacognitive research in learning disabilities: Theory, research, and practice. In H.L. Swanson (Ed.), *Handbook on the assessment of learning disabilities: Theory, research, and practice* (pp. 265–283). Austin, TX: PRO-ED.

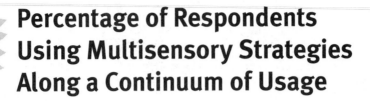

Percentage of Respondents Using Multisensory Strategies Along a Continuum of Usage

MODALITY	STRATEGY	% USAGE BY SCORES[a]					
		0	1	2	3	4	5
	Phonology						
Visual	Look at mouth of teacher to discriminate mouth positions (e.g., vowel versus consonant)	5.26	0	5.26	21.05	68.42	0
Visual	Look at mouth in mirror to discriminate mouth positions	15.79	0	15.79	21.05	47.37	0
Visual	Look at pictures or other graphic representations to discriminate mouth positions	36.84	5.26	21.05	5.26	31.58	0
Auditory	Listen (hear) to discriminate individual sounds	0	0	0	0	100	0
Auditory	Discriminate voiced and unvoiced sounds	0	5.26	5.26	5.26	84.21	0
Auditory	Discriminate number of sounds in spoken words	0	0	0	0	100	0
Auditory	Identify location of each sound in spoken word	0	5.26	0	5.26	89.47	0
Kinesthetic	Feel movement of articulatory muscles when phonemes are spoken	0	0	10.53	15.79	68.42	2.63
Kinesthetic	Tap out individual sounds in spoken words	0	5.26	10.53	15.79	63.16	2.63
Tactile	Feel placement of articulators and verbalize the placement when phonemes are spoken	0	5.26	15.79	26.32	52.63	0
Tactile	Feel presence or absence of voicing airflow	0	5.26	5.26	21.05	68.42	0
	Sound–symbol association						
Visual	Look at mouth of teacher to discriminate mouth positions	0	0	10.53	15.79	73.68	0
Visual	Look at letter or letter combinations	0	0	0	0	100	0
Visual	Discriminate letters	0	0	5.26	89.47	0	5.26
Visual	Look at a card with letter(s) and key word or picture	15.79	0	10.53	5.26	68.42	0
Auditory	Listen to (hear) the sound and identify its name with symbol	10.53	0	5.26	0	84.21	0
Auditory	Listen to (hear) the sound and identify it with its symbol	0	0	0	0	100	0
Auditory	Say key word and sound(s) or letter name identified with symbol	10.53	5.26	10.53	5.26	68.42	0
Auditory	Discriminate sounds	0	0	0	0	94.74	5.26

MODALITY	STRATEGY	% USAGE BY SCORES[a]					
		0	1	2	3	4	5
Kinesthetic	Feel articulatory muscle movement when phonemes are spoken	0	0	10.53	15.79	68.42	5.26
Kinesthetic	Use sky writing	5.26	5.26	10.53	15.79	63.16	0
Kinesthetic	Write letter on roughened surface with fingertip	5.26	5.26	15.79	15.79	57.9	0
	Syllables						
Visual	Look at mouth of teacher to discriminate syllable division	26.32	10.53	10.53	10.53	36.84	5.26
Visual	Look at printed words to identify vowel sounds and number of syllables	0	0	0	0	94.74	5.26
Visual	Look at syllable division markers (e.g., slashes, blank spaces) to determine number of syllables	5.26	0	0	5.26	84.21	5.26
Auditory	Listen for (hear) syllables in spoken words	0	0	5.26	0	89.47	5.26
Auditory	Discriminate number of syllables in spoken words	0	0	5.26	0	89.47	5.26
Auditory	Segment spoken words into syllables	0	0	0	0	94.74	5.26
Auditory	Blend syllables into a word	0	0	0	0	94.74	5.26
Kinesthetic	Feel movement of articulatory muscles when syllables are spoken	0	0	15.79	5.26	68.42	10.53
Kinesthetic	Pat or tap out syllables	0	5.26	5.26	0	84.21	5.26
Kinesthetic	Build syllables with letter cards	15.79	5.26	15.79	10.53	47.37	5.26
Kinesthetic	Build words with syllable cards	36.84	0	5.26	10.53	42.11	5.26
Kinesthetic	Segment words into syllables	0	0	0	0	94.74	5.26
Kinesthetic	Use syllable markers to break word into syllables	0	0	0	5.26	89.47	5.26
Tactile	Feel placement of articulators and verbalize the placement when syllables are spoken	15.79	5.26	26.32	10.53	31.58	10.53
Tactile	Pat or tap out syllables	0	5.26	5.26	0	78.95	10.53
Tactile	Build words with syllable cards	26.32	0	10.53	10.53	36.84	15.79
	Morphology						
Visual	Look at mouth of teacher to discriminate word parts	21.05	0	15.79	21.05	31.58	10.53
Visual	Look at bases and roots and affixes	0	0	0	10.53	89.47	0
Visual	Identify prefixes, base words, and suffixes in printed words	0	0	0	10.53	89.47	0
Auditory	Listen for (hear) bases and roots, affixes	0	0	10.53	5.26	84.21	0
Auditory	Identify prefixes, base words, and suffixes in spoken words	0	0	5.26	5.26	89.47	0
Kinesthetic	Feel movement of the articulatory muscles when morphemes are spoken	21.05	5.26	36.84	0	26.32	10.53
Kinesthetic	Segment words into prefixes, base words, and suffixes	0	0	0	10.53	89.47	0
Kinesthetic	Build words with base and/or root and affix cards	5.26	0	10.53	21.05	57.9	5.26
Tactile	Feel placement of articulators and verbalize the placement when morphemes are spoken	21.05	5.26	31.58	5.26	15.79	21.05

(continued)

MODALITY	STRATEGY	% USAGE BY SCORES[a]					
		0	**1**	**2**	**3**	**4**	**5**
Tactile	Segment words into prefixes, base words, and suffixes	0	0	0	10.53	84.21	5.26
Tactile	Build words with base and/or root and affix cards	5.26	0	10.53	21.05	52.63	10.53
	Syntax						
Visual	Look at mouth of teacher (e.g., to discriminate word parts)	31.58	5.26	21.05	0	26.32	15.79
Visual	Look at sentences to identify sentence parts (e.g., subject/verb, parts of speech)	0	0	10.53	5.26	84.21	0
Visual	Look at diagrammed sentences to label parts of speech	15.79	5.26	15.79	5.26	57.9	0
Visual	Look at graphic or symbol to identify part of speech	15.79	5.26	5.26	5.26	63.16	5.26
Auditory	Listen to sentences	0	0	0	0	94.74	5.26
Auditory	Say and read sentences	0	0	0	0	94.74	5.26
Auditory	Explain diagrammed sentences	15.79	5.26	10.53	15.79	52.63	0
Kinesthetic	Feel movement of the articulatory muscles	26.32	5.26	15.79	0	31.58	21.05
Kinesthetic	Diagram sentences	15.79	5.26	5.26	15.79	52.63	5.26
Kinesthetic	Build sentences with word cards	15.79	0	15.79	10.53	47.37	10.53
Kinesthetic	Use graphics or symbols to signify parts of speech	15.79	5.26	5.26	0	68.42	5.26
Kinesthetic	Manipulate cards to represent parts of speech	21.05	5.26	5.26	10.53	52.63	5.26
Kinesthetic	Write sentences	0	0	0	0	100	0
Kinesthetic	Write sentences from dictation	0	0	10.53	5.26	84.21	0
Tactile	Feel placement of articulators and verbalize the placement	26.32	5.26	21.05	0	26.32	21.05
Tactile	Diagram sentences	15.79	5.26	5.26	15.79	52.63	5.26
Tactile	Build sentences with word cards	15.79	0	15.79	10.53	47.37	10.53
Tactile	Use graphics or symbols to signify parts of speech in sentences	15.79	5.26	5.26	0	68.42	5.26
Tactile	Manipulate cards to represent parts of speech in sentences	15.79	5.26	15.79	5.26	52.63	5.26
Tactile	Write sentences	0	0	0	0	94.74	5.26
Tactile	Write sentences from dictation	0	0	10.53	5.26	78.95	5.26
	Semantics						
Visual	Look at mouth of teacher to discriminate easily confused words, (e.g., *from* and *form*)	15.79	0	31.58	15.79	36.84	0
Visual	Look at word	0	0	5.26	0	94.74	0
Visual	Look at graphic or symbol to represent meaning	10.53	5.26	15.79	5.26	57.9	5.26
Auditory	Say words and/or definitions	0	0	0	5.26	94.74	0
Auditory	Listen to sentences and explain meaning	5.26	0	0	5.26	89.47	0
Auditory	Use words in oral sentences that demonstrate meaning	0	0	0	5.26	94.74	0
Auditory	Read sentences and explain meaning	0	0	0	0	100	0
Auditory	Paraphrase sentences accurately	0	0	5.26	5.26	89.47	0
Auditory	Paraphrase paragraphs accurately	0	0	5.26	10.53	84.21	0

MODALITY	STRATEGY	% USAGE BY SCORES[a]					
		0	**1**	**2**	**3**	**4**	**5**
Kinesthetic	Feel movement of articulatory muscles	31.58	0	21.05	0	26.32	21.05
Kinesthetic	Draw graphics to represent meaning	0	21.05	21.05	15.79	36.84	5.26
Kinesthetic	Act out meaning (pantomime)	5.26	15.79	31.58	15.79	42.11	10.53
Tactile	Feel placement of articulators and verbalize the placement	31.58	0	0	0	31.58	15.79
Tactile	Draw graphics to represent meaning	0	26.32	26.32	10.53	26.32	10.53

From Farrell, M., Pickering, J., North, N., & Schavio, C. (2004, Fall). What is multisensory instruction? *The IMSLEC Record, 8*(3); adapted by permission.

[a]*Key:* 0, *never;* 1, *occasionally;* 2, *as needed for certain children;* 3, *systematically used for certain children;* 4, *systematically used for all children;* 5, *other.*

3

Development of Oral Language and Its Relationship to Literacy

Lydia H. Soifer

Imagine the elegant intricacies of Beethoven's "Ode to Joy" or Mozart's Serenade in G Major (*Eine Kleine Nachtmusik*) played captivatingly by an artist. It is as beguiling to the experienced listener as to the naïve ear. Now imagine pages of musical notation, an array of dots and lines splayed across a page, interrupted by assorted squiggles and swirls. If you can read music, then you may sense the beauty in your mind's ear, much the way Beethoven did. Can't read music? Then what remains is a morass of dots, lines, squiggles, and swirls. The same is true with language, an amazing latticework of interrelated complexities in which the oral (spoken) and aural (heard) in combination with memory, sensory, and motor function; environment; and culture form the basis from which literacy evolves. The challenge of teaching about language is that the language itself is the vehicle for learning. Thus, in large part the very thing that you are attempting to learn about consciously in this chapter is exactly what you are experiencing spontaneously as you comprehend or generate language. Learning about language is a **metalinguistic** task in which language is analyzed and considered as an entity and behavior. When a person speaks or listens, reads or writes, and effectively communicates or understands a particular purpose or intention, the language system has performed efficiently.

Mattingly suggested that there was something "devious" (1972, p. 133) about the relationship between the processes of speaking and listening and the process of reading. Listening and reading both are linguistic processes but are not really as parallel or analogous as many people assume. The differences are in the form of information being presented (complex auditory signals versus more static visual symbols), in the linguistic content (additional information available from the intonational and speech patterns that can be perceived in listening versus the many possible pieces of **phonological** information contained in one symbol), and in the relationship of the form to the content (enormous variation in what can be produced by voice versus alphabets with

limited information carried by any single symbol). Listening and speaking are automatic and natural ways of perceiving and using language, acquired as part of a developmental process. In contrast, the written form of a language must generally be taught, and not all individuals are able to learn it with ease. In addition, not all spoken languages have a written form.

There is agreement that reading is a language-based skill (Catts & Kamhi, 1986; Liberman, 1983; Perfetti & Lesgold, 1977; Snyder, 1980; Vellutino, 1979) and that the relationship between oral language and reading is reciprocal (Kamhi & Catts, 1989; Stanovich, 1986; Wallach & Miller, 1988), with each influencing the other at different points in development (Menyuk & Chesnick, 1997; Snyder & Downey, 1991, 1997). Oral and written language, although intimately and intricately related, are not the same. Teachers need to be aware of the similarities and differences (Moats, 1994; Moats & Lyon, 1996) so that they can facilitate students' language learning and academic success (Bashir & Scavuzzo, 1992). This chapter helps to foster in teachers an awareness of the inextricable role of language in learning to decode and comprehend. The processes of language learning (on which reading is based) begin long before children receive reading instruction. This chapter provides an insight into each component of the language system, including patterns of typical and disordered development and their analogous relationships to the higher-level language skills of reading and writing. In this chapter, oral and written language are viewed as a continuum, and the varying influences of oral language knowledge and use on the development of early decoding processes and subsequent comprehension processes are considered. Furthermore, to enhance teachers' ability to be informed observers and, as a result, to be more effective in planning instruction, this chapter offers a discussion of the oral–written language connection; the different levels of language processing; and the effects of chronic, intermittent, conductive hearing loss secondary to **otitis media** (middle-ear infections).

LANGUAGE: A DYNAMIC, RULE-GOVERNED PROCESS

Learning to talk appears easy but in fact is enormously complex. The marvel is that most children learn to talk so well and so quickly (Hart & Risley, 1999). The enormity of the task is confounded by the fact that most children are not taught to use language but rather discover the rules that govern language in the context of social interaction as they strive to understand and to convey meaning.

What is language? Bloom and Lahey offered a superb definition of language: "Language is a code whereby ideas about the world are represented through a conventional system of arbitrary signals for communication" (1978, p. 4). The key concepts to be considered are *communication, ideas, code, system,* and *conventional.* The purpose of language is *communication.* We use language for a variety of purposes in vastly different ways according to our needs, the needs of the listener, and the circumstances surrounding us. Language enables us to express an array of *ideas.* We have ideas about objects, events, and relationships. Our ability to express those ideas through language is different from the objects, events, or relationships themselves. Think about the page you are reading and the words you have available to represent your ideas about the page, what is on it, what you are doing with it, and your relationship to it. Each is different from the page itself, the writing on it, the act of reading, and how you are relating to the page by viewing it or touching it. In this way, language is a *code,* a means of representing one thing with another in a predictable and organized system. There are many different codes, from maps, to Morse code, to words spelled in a book. Sounds

may be combined into words, words into sentences, and sentences into conversation. The rule-governed predictability of the system enables us to understand it and learn how to use it.

Consider the following:

'Twas brillig, and the slithy toves
Did gyre and gimble in the wabe:
All mimsy were the borogoves,
And the mome raths outgrabe. (Carroll, 1865/1960, p. 134)

If asked, one could identify the parts of speech, such as noun (*toves, raths*), verb (*gyre, gimble*), adjective (*outgrabe*), or adverb (*brillig*); the subject, predicate, and object; have a reasonable idea of how to pronounce these novel words; and answer comprehension questions ("Were the borogoves mimsy?"). All of these tasks are possible because Carroll used the predictable, rule-governed nature of the sounds and grammar of English to create "Jabberwocky."

The code of language is also *conventional*. It consists of a socially based, tacitly agreed-on set of symbols and rules that govern their permissible combinations. The conventions of language allow users to share their ideas. Linguistic competence is a person's implicit knowledge about the rules of the language. Possessed of linguistic competence, a child or an adult has the knowledge to be a competent language user. In general, unless called on to do so specifically, a language user need not state the rules of language explicitly. The ability to generate an infinite number of sentences and understand varying forms of language across a plenitude of environments demonstrate knowledge of the rules.

THE ORAL–WRITTEN LANGUAGE CONNECTION

Literacy is much like a great pyramid. It is built on a broad foundation that is linguistic, sociological, cognitive, and pedagogic. Literacy evolves from well-developed oral language abilities; exposure to written language that gives rise to a child's notions of how print works and what it can do, called **emergent literacy** (Sulzby & Teale, 1991; Van Kleeck, 1990); a level of cognitive maturation that allows for metalinguistic awareness that permits a youngster to view language as an entity, something to be considered and analyzed; and a reasonable quality of instruction that can provide varying degrees of facilitation and support.

Language is the vehicle that drives curriculum. Although one may study aspects of the language in discrete ways (e.g., **phonics**, grammar, **vocabulary**), even then the very language being studied is the one that is employed to learn. In no instance does this resonate with greater truth than in the acquisition of literacy skills—reading and writing. "Learning to read and write is part of, not separate from, learning to speak and comprehend language" (Wallach & Butler, 1994, p. 11). Despite **whole language** arguments to the contrary, however, "learning to read is not the same as learning to speak" (Wallach, 1990, p. 64).

Indeed, Van Kleeck (1990) allowed that the foundations of literacy are created at birth and are interrelated with the evolution and fullness of a child's oral language because reading is a language-based skill dependent on a set of well-developed oral language abilities. Language learning and literacy learning are actually reciprocal. That is to say the relationship between the two is dynamic and changes over time with each influencing the other at different developmental stages (Kamhi & Catts, 1989; Sawyer,

1991). Nonetheless, there are very considerable differences between language learning and literacy learning (Scott, 1994) because reading is not just speech written down (Liberman, Shankweiler, Camp, Blachman, & Werfelman, 1990).

Understanding oral language requires a well-integrated knowledge of the form, content, and use of the language. Recognizing word patterns, word structure, and sentence forms; knowing the meaning of words, how words relate to one another, and how they are influenced by their position in the sentence; and interpreting the intent of the speaker with the context and in relationship to one's own knowledge base enable a listener to understand. Understanding written text requires the same linguistic knowledge that is necessary for understanding spoken language. The analogy of hearing spoken language to decoding print serves quite well: "I heard what you said, but I don't know what you mean" is similar to the phenomenon of asking a youngster to tell about what he or she has just read and being met with a look of noncomprehension that implies, "I know that I read [decoded] it, but I don't know what it means!" As described throughout this chapter, deficits in oral language, **syntax**, **morphology**, **semantics** (word meaning and relationships), **pragmatics**, and narrative structure have a negative impact on reading comprehension.

In addition to oral language skills, emergent literacy is a foundation for literacy development (see Van Kleeck, 1990, for an extended discussion of emergent literacy). Emergent literacy is an outgrowth of "literacy socialization" (Snow & Dickinson, 1991). When children are exposed to print by being read to, whether from books, signs or instructions, or birthday cards, they begin to develop a sense that the marks on the page, box, or card are related to the words being said (Linder, 1999). They also begin to develop an awareness of how books are manipulated, literally which way is up and in which direction the text flows and the pages turn. Children who have been exposed to print in early caregiver–child interactions also benefit from the positive emotional connection between reading and nurturing experiences. Provided with **literacy socialization** experiences and as a result the emergent literacy skills that precede learning to decode, children who have been read to as preschoolers unquestionably find the process of learning to read an easier experience (Dickinson & McCabe, 1991; Wolf & Dickinson, 1993).

Metalinguistic ability, as discussed later in this chapter, permits a child to focus on language from a distance; to view language as an object of consideration; and to reflect on its discrete, particular aspects and characteristics. It is metalinguistically that children recognize word boundaries; make letter–sound correspondences; consider which printed sequences of letters represent which words and meanings; and analyze, blend, and reconstruct words. Little, if anything, in the oral language experience prepares children to view words as discrete units (e.g., *sit*) to isolate the parts of each unit (e.g., *s-i-t*) in order to reformulate and orally produce them (e.g., "sit"). Certainly, phonological awareness activities are dependent on metalinguistic skills. Beyond the task of decoding, conscious use of linguistic knowledge strongly influences reading comprehension. Oral language development, however, does not require these metalinguistic abilities. The speech stream is continuous with boundaries that are not discrete, and the context is immediate and supported environmentally by the situation in which the talking is occurring. In oral language development, reflection on linguistic knowledge is not part of the process until a fair degree of cognitive maturity and linguistic sophistication has been attained.

Literacy is also built on good teaching. Moats and Lyon (1996) strongly urged changes in teacher education related to reading instruction to place a greater emphasis

on knowledge of language structure. They cited very disturbing findings in a survey of 103 teachers in which fewer than one third were proficient in basic knowledge of language structure, such as identification of an inflected ending (*-ed* in *instructed*) or the number of phonemes in words such as *ox, precious,* or *thank.* Teaching children to read requires teaching them language at a higher and conscious level. Successful teaching, particularly of those children who bring linguistic, experiential, cognitive, or environmental vulnerabilities to the task, requires a powerful, integrated knowledge of the language that is being taught.

ORAL–WRITTEN LANGUAGE DIFFERENCES

There is no doubt that reading is a language-based skill, yet there are numerous and obvious differences between oral and written language. These differences have been considered from a variety of different vantage points, either as parallels or continua (Horowitz & Samuels, 1987; Kamhi & Catts, 1989; Rubin, 1987; Scott, 1994; Wallach, 1990; Westby, 1985). In the course of human development, literacy is recent. Learning to read and write does not come naturally to everyone, and these skills are not a requirement in every society. Writing, as anyone who has ever struggled with a blank page or experienced writer's block well knows, requires a much greater effort than does producing oral language. Rubin highlighted his difficulty when he wrote that "no one is a native speaker of writing" (1987, p. 3). Human beings are socialized to communicate, and they have a biological predisposition to oral language that enables societal groups to have and pass on oral language systems. Reading and writing are acquired deliberately, rather than spontaneously and more naturally. The differences are in the aspects of production, influences of context, grammar, and vocabulary and in the degree of explicitness.

Oral language is transient and ephemeral. It exists only at the moment when it is spoken. It can be repeated or clarified, but that occurs at the request of the listener. Written language is permanent and more enduring than oral language, except when the latter is audiotaped or videotaped. Print allows the reader multiple opportunities for exposure and decision-making authority regarding the rate and depth of analysis with which the text is read. In oral language, the rate of presentation is at the discretion of the speaker. In oral language, temporal sequencing is most crucial, whereas in print, spatial sequencing is important. Print can be revisited more readily. A word, sentence, or paragraph can be reread or rewritten. It is rather a different experience to have someone attempt to repeat, exactly, the sentence just uttered.

Most oral language occurs face to face. Reciprocity exists between the speaker and listener. Interpersonal context and situational support exist in the form of vocal, facial, and physical gestures. When people are engaged in conversation or discussion, less needs to be explicitly stated and sentence structures can be more fragmentary. Vocabulary and syntax can be more familiar and less sophisticated. To appreciate the lack of explicitness, as well as the fragmentary, familiar, and contextually and physically supported nature of oral language, request a transcript of a television talk show that you have watched. While watching and listening to the discussion, you probably had little difficulty understanding the ebb and flow, intent, and effect of the exchanges among the participants. Reading the transcript of the same exchange will provide an immediate insight into the significant differences in the explicitness of a written text and the literate, grammatically dense nature of written language versus oral language that has

been written down. In oral language, cohesion between sentences and ideas can be established grammatically or paralinguistically through physical signals such as the shrug of a shoulder or a pregnant pause. In a written text, the cohesive devices and transitional markers that bind ideas or shift focus must be conveyed concretely and explicitly through a careful choice of words. The conventions of punctuating written language that are communicated orally through intonational gestures must be taught specifically; however, written text does provide other cues to organization and meaning through the structure of paragraphs and the use of boldface, italics, underlining, and other typography.

Although written language contains the intent to communicate with another or others or to interpret another person's message, the experience is generally more solitary and involves only the reader and the book, the page, or the computer screen. The interaction between writer and reader is limited and is decontextualized—separated by time and distance. In print it is necessary for the communicator to be more explicit and succinct.

Written language relies on the **lexicon** [vocabulary] to create the melody and meaning provided by the intonation, stress, pause, and juncture patterns of spoken language as well as the vocal characteristics of the speaker. An anxious tone, a sinister laugh, or a lascivious lilt can be heard, recognized, and interpreted without being explicitly stated by the speaker as such. What is said and meant can be potently influenced by how it is said, and thus the message and intent of the speaker and the response of the listener may vary. The most literate of writers attain a level of mastery that enables them to arrange, adapt, maneuver, integrate, and entwine words and sentences in ways that communicate so effectively that it seems as though these writers are talking to the reader. With that level of written language mastery, it is possible to write the same thing in so many different ways, ranging from the most informal to the most deliberately formal tone.

Following a consideration of the oral–written continuum, it is important to look at writing itself. Writing is the most sophisticated, complex, and formal aspect of language. Even the most well-read and literate individuals may not have equivalent skill in expressing thoughts on paper. Writing is a dynamic interaction among cognitive and linguistic factors, motor skills, and emotional considerations. The most sophisticated language act, writing, involves the simultaneous convergence of cognitive factors (abstracting, generating, and ordering ideas), linguistic factors (arriving at semantic [word meaning and choice] and syntactic [grammar] production appropriate to the nature of what is being written, such as a thank-you note versus an expository paragraph), narrative considerations (structuring information for varied purposes), graphomotor skills (recalling, planning, and executing complex motor acts), visual ability (recalling sequences of letters with **phonetic** rules for spelling), and temporal factors (writing legibly and appropriately under specific time constraints) while controlling for the emotional factors involved in risk, exposure, and evaluation of the final product. It is readily apparent why many children (and adults) might prefer to speak rather than to write! The teaching of writing can be an art form (see Chapter 16 for a discussion of teaching the writing process).

THE COMPONENTS OF LANGUAGE

Bloom and Lahey (1978) conceptualized three major, interactive components of language: form, content, and use (see Figure 3.1). Each component is governed by a complex set of rules that together compose language.

Language Form

Language form consists of the observable features of language. It includes the rules for the combination of sounds (*phonology*), the structure of words (*morphology*), and the order of words in sentences (*syntax*). These features and their development and the relationship of disorders in these elements of language form are described in the sections that follow.

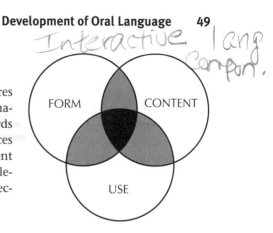

Figure 3.1. Venn diagram illustrating language form, content, and use. (From Bloom, L., & Lahey, M. [1978]. *Language development and language disorders* [p. 22]. Published by Allyn & Bacon, Boston, MA. Copyright © 1978 by Pearson Education. Reprinted by permission of the publisher.)

Phonology

Phonology is the sound system of a language. It comprises **suprasegmental** aspects (**intonation**, **stress**, loudness, pitch level, **juncture**, and speaking rate) and **segmental** aspects (phonemes: **vowels** and **consonants**).

The *suprasegmental*, or paralinguistic, aspects of phonology provide the melody of speech. They are related to speech because they are produced by the vocal tract but are concerned with larger units of production: **syllables**, words, phrases, and sentences. They are significant in our ability to communicate emotions and attitudes. These suprasegmental features help us to recognize different sentence types, declarative (*Joshua eats pizza.*), interrogative (*Does Russell like ice cream?*), or imperative (*Sit down now!*). Awareness of phrase structure helps us to understand where a comma might be placed in a sentence. These suprasegmental aspects also permit us to say the same sentence and communicate markedly different meanings. Varied aspects of **prosody** (the suprasegmental features of language) are used in talking to different people of different ages and status. Consider the number of ways to say "Don't be silly" to a baby, to a spouse, or to an employer. At a conversational level, the suprasegmental characteristics of language also may be used to convey sarcasm, to tease, and to mock.

The suprasegmental aspects of phonology are influential in reading. When reading aloud, fluent readers read with full intonation, communicating an understanding of the intent of the author. Early readers or those who struggle to decode may read each word individually, then, having derived meaning, reread with appropriate inflection. Inefficient readers may pause with a downward intonation at the end of a printed line of words rather than at the end of the sentence. Thus, the suprasegmental features of language play an essential role in comprehension.

Vowels and consonants compose the *segmental* features of language. Each language has a set of vowels and consonants, or phonemes, that may be combined to form words. A phoneme is the smallest linguistic unit of sound that can change meaning in a word. Consider the word family of *bat*. Changing any of the phonemes could produce a variety of new words (e.g., *sat, bit, ban*).

Standard English orthography has only 26 letters with which to represent the approximately 44 phonemes of English. More striking still, there are only 5 vowel letters available to represent the approximately 15 vowel sounds. Knowledge of phonemes and their role in language and reading is essential for teachers. Long before children are able to recognize, read, and write the letters that represent the sounds of English, they must begin to master the elaborate task of making those speech sounds correctly so that they

are able to clearly produce the sounds of the language. Children learn each of those 44 sounds and the possible variations on them by being exposed to them, by hearing others speak, and by storing information about the qualities that make up each sound. It is an unconscious and intricate task.

Speech production is the complex coordination of respiration (breathing), phonation (the vibration of the vocal folds), resonation (the quality of voice affected by the shape and density of the neck and cavities of the head), and **articulation** (the rapid, alternating movements of the jaw, tongue, lips, teeth, and soft palate). When we speak, the flow of speech is generally uninterrupted. Speech is produced in breath groups ("Whenneryagoin?") rather than in individual words ("When are you going?"). Yet early readers decode word by word and, at times, sound by sound. Liberman noted that "if speech were like spelling, learning to read would be trivially easy" (as cited in Brady & Shankweiler, 1991, p. xv). Awareness that the flow of coarticulated, overlapping phonemes can be segmented into sounds, syllables, and words is a precursor to cracking the code of language in print (see Chapter 4 for an extended discussion of phonological processes). Although speech and reading are clearly related, they are not equal. Oral language, of which speech is the observable form, is learned naturally. Reading is not (Liberman & Liberman, 1990). A bounty of literature, however, emphasizes the role of phonological awareness (the ability to attend to and recognize the sound structure of language) in the acquisition of early reading (Adams, 1990; Blachman, 1989, 1991; Blachman, Ball, Black, & Tangel, 2000; Stanovich, 1987; Wagner & Torgesen, 1987).

The speech-sound segments, vowels and consonants, may vary in their productions (**allophones**) and are guided by a set of rules for their production and placement in words. From the earliest moments of life, babies are acquiring information about the sounds of their language (Eimas, Siqueland, Jusczyk, & Vigorito, 1971). Through continuous exposure, babies acquire the set of acoustic features that define the sounds of their language. Over time the speakers of a given language come to recognize the possible variations in phoneme production while remaining able to recognize the specific phoneme. For example, the phoneme /p/ is a voiceless stop plosive (i.e., there is no vocal fold vibration, it is not produced in a long stream as /s/ is, and it produces a puff of air). Yet, the production of /p/ varies by the amount of **aspiration** (puff of air) produced according to where it appears in a word. Pronounce *pot* and *spot* aloud to feel the different amount of aspiration. Nonetheless, speakers of English recognize these variations as the phoneme /p/. Moreover, any of the plosive sounds (i.e., /p/, /b/, /t/, /d/, /k/, and /g/) when said in isolation or as a segmented phoneme must be produced with an accompanying vowel sound, the **schwa** (/ə/), typically produced as "uh." This is particularly relevant for teachers; as Liberman noted, "The word is 'bag,' not 'buh-a-guh'" (as cited in Brady & Shankweiler, 1991, p. xv) The distortion can be so great for some children that they are unable to recombine the sounds into the word *bag* that is readily recognizable to most. Combining /b/ and /ĕ/ in a smooth, connected production eliminates the /ə/. In addition, by not producing the /g/ with an overemphasis, the /ə/ is once again reduced, thus allowing the word being analyzed and synthesized to sound more like its real-world production. This enables the young reader to use language knowledge of the word to recognize it as a phonological/phonemic phenomenon.

Other phonetic distinctions may be made by limitations of the vocal tract. These distinctions may become important for spelling, particularly for children with vulnerabilities in phonological awareness. Plurals, possessives, and the third-person singular marking of the verb all are accomplished by the addition of -*s* (or -*es* for certain plurals) when being spelled. The sounds produced, however, may be /z/ or /s/. This is deter-

mined by the nature of the preceding phoneme. **Coarticulation** with a voiced consonant (one produced with the vocal folds closed) or a vowel will create /z/ or /ĭz/. Say *hugs, kisses,* and *hits* aloud to hear and feel the distinctions. A similar pattern emerges for the creation of the regular past tense, typically created in print as *-ed*. In speech, however, it may be produced as /d/, /t/, or /ĭd/, as in *hugged, kissed,* or *lifted*.

Vowels and consonants, which combine to form syllable structures, are separated into distinct classes by the nature of their production. A vowel is typically "formed as sound energy from the vibrating folds escapes through a relatively open vocal tract of a particular shape" (Bernthal & Bankson, 1998, p. 12). The tongue, jaw, and lips serve to create the shape of the vocal tract. Because the jaw and tongue work together, vowels are classified by identifying the position of the tongue during articulation (front, mid, or back; high or low) and the lips (rounded or unrounded). Vowels may also be tense or lax. **Tense vowels** (e.g., /ē/ in *bee*) are longer in duration; **lax vowels** (e.g., /ĭ/ in *bin*) are shorter in duration. Figure 3.2 demonstrates the position in the mouth of each vowel's production. Table 3.1 shows the spellings of different vowels. Moats's (2000) view of sound production in its relationship to spelling gives an accompanying image of the appearance of vowels (see Figure 3.3).

Consonants, unlike vowels, are created by either a complete or a partial constriction of the air stream along the vocal tract. The closure is affected by the position of the lips and the placement of the tongue in relation to the teeth and its position in the mouth. Consonants are classified as **stops** (e.g., /t/, /k/), **nasals** (/n/, /m/, /ng/), **fricatives** (e.g., /f/, /z/), **affricates** (/ch/, /j/), **glides** (e.g., /w/, /y/), or **liquids** (/l/, /r/).

Table 3.2 provides a clear view of where consonants are produced in the vocal tract. In addition, consonants may be described as **voiced** (caused by vibrations of the vocals folds when closed) or **voiceless** (open vocal folds). Several sets of phonemes, called **voiced–voiceless cognates**, are produced in the same place in the mouth, in the same manner, but vary only in the voicing characteristic. They are /p/ and /b/, /f/ and /v/, /t/ and /d/, /s/ and /z/, /k/ and /g/, /th/ (*think*) and /th/ (*this*), /sh/ and /zh/, and /ch/ and /j/. (The distinction between a voiceless and voiced phoneme can be felt as well as heard by placing the fingers gently against the throat. Start to say /s/, and without altering the position of the tongue and jaw, then say /z/.) In addition, the environ-

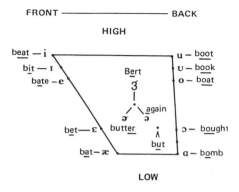

Figure 3.2. Vowel chart. (From Bernthal, J.E., & Bankson, N.W. [1998]. *Articulation and phonological disorders* [4th ed., p. 16]. Published by Allyn & Bacon; Boston, MA. Reprinted by permission fo the publisher.)

Table 3.1. American English vowels

Phonetic symbol	Phonic symbol	Spellings
/i/	ē	beet
/ɪ/	ĭ	bit
/e/	ā	bait
/ɛ/	ĕ	bet
/æ/	ă	bat
/ɑj/	ī	bite
/ɑ/	ŏ	bottle
/ɨ/	ŭ	butt
/ɔ/	aw, ô	bought
/o/	ō	boat
/ʊ/	o͝o	put
/u/	o͞o	boot
/ə/	ə	between
/ɑj/	oi, oy	boy
/æw/	ou, ow	bow

From Moats, L.C. (2000). *Speech to print: Language essentials for teachers* (p. 35). Baltimore: Paul H. Brookes Publishing Co.; reprinted by permission.

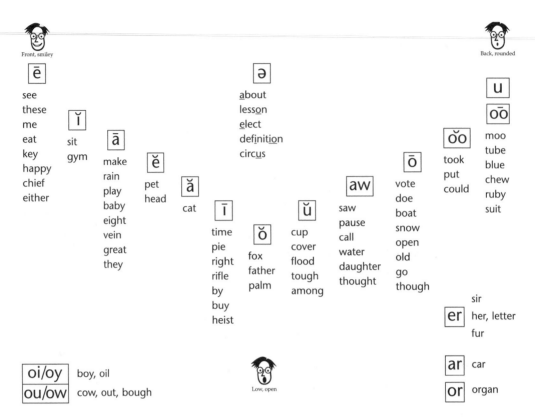

Figure 3.3. Vowels (phonic symbols) by mouth position. (Moats, L.C. [2000]. *Speech to print: Language essentials for teachers* [p. 94]. Baltimore: Paul H. Brookes Publishing Co.; adapted by permission.)

ment in which a consonant or vowel exists, that is, the other phonemes near it, may vary the production of that consonant or vowel. The relationship of vowel, consonant, and syllable production and **discrimination** and phonological awareness leading to more effective reading and spelling is significant.

In addition to rules for the production and perception of phonemes, there are rules that apply to how phonemes may be combined into meaningful words. These rules allow some sounds to appear in certain positions in a word but not in others. For example, in English, /ng/ may appear in the middle or at the end of a word but never at the beginning. Furthermore, certain combinations of sounds are restricted so that /ts/ may occur at the end of a word but not at the beginning. This set of **phonological rules** has implications for early reading and spelling as children learn to segment the flow of speech and recognize and represent it in print.

Phonological Development   Traditionally speech-sound development was thought to occur through unit-by-unit learning of each phoneme in a developmental sequence. In fact, phonological development is integrally related to the language system as a whole. Phonological development progresses with physical maturation, the mastery of sound features and phonological processes that reflect the linking of sounds to words and meaning, and the growth of syntactic and semantic rule knowledge and ability. Children employ phonological or natural processes to master adult-level speech productions.

Typically, children produce their first recognizable words by 12–18 months of age. The ability of toddlers to make themselves fully understood (without available **context**

Table 3.2. American English consonants (phonic symbols)

Class of consonant	Lips	Lips/ teeth	Tongue between teeth	Tongue behind teeth	Roof of mouth	Back of mouth	Throat
Stop							
voiceless	/p/			/t/		/k/	
voiced	/b/			/d/		/g/	
Nasal	/m/			/n/		/ng/	
Fricative							
voiceless		/f/	/th/	/s/	/sh/		
voiced		/v/	/th/	/z/	/zh/		
Affricate							
voiceless					/ch/		
voiced					/j/		
Glide							
voiceless						/wh/	/h/
voiced					/y/	/w/	
Liquid				/l/, /r/			

From Moats, L.C. (2000). *Speech to print: Language essentials for teachers* (p. 28). Baltimore: Paul H. Brookes Publishing Co.; reprinted by permission.

clues) is often limited by inadequate production of sounds. However, 3-year-olds are generally intelligible and by age 4 have suppressed or eliminated the remaining phonological processes that hinder their intelligibility (Hodson, 1994).

Typically developing children are able to produce speech sounds adequately by age 4 and require additional time (until age 7) for complete mastery, including the elimination of lisps and the production of **multisyllabic** words (see Table 3.3).

Relationship of Phonological Disorders to Literacy When preparing to teach early reading skills, teachers should be aware of two areas of consideration: intelligibility of speech production and its relationship to phonological awareness. Children who have problems with speech-sound production at the time they are being introduced to reading instruction or who have a history of such difficulties have been shown to be less adept at tasks of phonological awareness than their typically developing peers (Webster & Plante, 1992). Webster and Plante explained that "productive phonological impairment may hinder performance in phonological awareness because it precludes efficient phonological coding in working memory" (p. 176). In the same vein, Fowler (1991) suggested that articulation ability may be an important prerequisite for acquiring an awareness of phoneme structures.

Consider the dilemma of a child who does not have a stable speech production system. Certain speech production problems may be caused by neurological oral-motor dysfunction, including weaknesses of the musculature necessary for making the coordinated movements to produce speech (**dysarthria**). Other speech problems may be caused by sensorimotor disruptions in which the signals to the muscles necessary for speech production are not consistently or efficiently received (**dyspraxia**). When children encounter a new word, they must be able to store it in phonological short-term (working) memory as part of the process of creating a phonological representation for it. Children who have speech articulation difficulties, however, are at a disadvantage: What they are able to say may not match what they have heard. In the phonological awareness tasks of rhyme, segmentation, and blending and in spelling tasks, being able

to rehearse a word with proper production plays a contributing role in the successful completion of those tasks. Thus, for some children, speech disorders are a hidden contributor to the apparent phonological processing and spelling difficulties (Stackhouse & Wells, 1997).

Children with reading disabilities have been found to make more speech production errors than their typical peers (Catts, 1986; Snowling, 1981). This difficulty also has been found in college-age dyslexic students (Catts, 1989). The college-age dyslexic students had greater difficulty in repeating complex phrases rapidly and made significantly more errors than their typical peers. It is hypothesized that children and adults with reading difficulties have more difficulty in encoding phonological information and in planning (for articulation) of complex sequences of sounds (Catts, 1989).

Table 3.3. Phonemic acquisition—age at which 75% of children tested correctly articulated consonant sounds

Age	Sounds
2.0	/m/, /n/, /h/, /p/, /n/, /r/ (ring)
2.4	f, j, k, d
2.8	w, b, t
3.0	g, s
3.4	r, l
3.8	/sh/ (shy), /ch/ (chin)
4.0	/th/ (father), /zh/ (measure)
4.01	/j/ (jar), /th/ (thin), v, z

From Prather, E., Hedrick, D., & Kern, C. (1975). Articulation development in children aged two to four years. *Journal of Speech and Hearing Disorders, 40;* adapted by permission.

Phonological processing difficulties may manifest differently across the developmental continuum. They may stem from a variety of causes and vary in severity (Spear-Swerling & Sternberg, 1994). In the preschool years the development of oral language may be related to slower vocabulary growth (Catts, Hu, Larrivee, & Swank, 1994), and children may be less sensitive to rhyme, alliteration, and nonsense words (Fey, Catts, & Larrivee, 1995). During the elementary school years, children with phonological processing difficulties may be weaker in using segmentation strategies to analyze phonemic structure and slower in word recognition secondary to having reduced awareness of the relationship between phonemes and the alphabet (Catts, 1989; Ehri, 1989). If a child persists in having significant speech production difficulties, spelling ability may be affected (Clark-Klein & Hodson, 1995). Reduced rate of vocabulary acquisition and difficulty acquiring words with **multiple meanings** and **figurative language** as well as word-retrieval difficulties may become obvious (Catts et al., 1994; Milosky, 1994; Snyder & Godley, 1992). Comprehension problems may begin to emerge both orally and in print (Catts, 1996; Snyder & Downey, 1991).

In the 1990s, a great deal of attention was generated by the concept of temporal auditory processing deficits and their role in language and reading disabilities as well as their remediation by a specialized computer program commercially marketed as Fast ForWord (Scientific Learning Corporation) (Merzenich et al., 1996; Tallal et al., 1996). A temporal auditory processing deficit is said to occur when a child has difficulty rapidly processing the acoustic (sound energy) changes that occur between sounds in connected speech. While anecdotal evidence indicates positive changes in the language abilities of those children who participate in the highly intensive and restrictive computer training program that requires involvement with the computer program for 1 hour and 40 minutes daily for 6 weeks, only limited research has been published regarding the benefits of the treatment.

Tallal and Merzenich (1997) presented the results of a large field study of 500 children treated with the Fast ForWord program. Interpreting the results is problematic as the population of children studied varied in the degree of severity of their learning impairment, their diagnosis, and the amount of training they received in the Fast ForWord program. Furthermore, as suggested by Gillam (1999), caution must be applied

when pre- and posttest measures are the same, when there is no control group and the tasks being trained are similar to the format of the pre- and posttests. Results can be misinterpreted when performance may have been influenced by teaching to the test (Silliman & Wilkinson, 1994).

Hook, Macaruso, and Jones (2001) completed a longitudinal study of children treated for difficulties in phonemic awareness and word identification with either Fast ForWord or Orton-Gillingham training and compared them with a control group over the course of two academic years. Fast ForWord training did improve phonemic awareness immediately after the treatment program was completed; however, the gains were no greater than those achieved by those treated with the less intensive Orton-Gillingham methodology. Furthermore, the children receiving Orton-Gillingham instruction made greater improvement in word attack skills and sustained their gains. The authors question the efficacy of Fast ForWord given the intensity, time commitment, and cost of the program.

It is noteworthy that the concept of a temporal auditory processing deficit remains controversial. Of continued interest and concern is the ongoing debate about the very existence of a temporal auditory processing disorder (Mody, Studdert-Kennedy, & Brady, 1997; Studdert-Kennedy, 1998; Studdert-Kennedy et al., 1994–1995; Studdert-Kennedy & Mody, 1995). Studdert-Kennedy and Mody took the position that the problem with rapid temporal order processing for some poor readers has its genesis in "independent deficits in discrimination capacity of unknown origin" (1995, p. 513). The difficulty in discrimination they suggested is phonetic, resulting from similarity in production of phonemes not the speed and timing of an acoustic experience, that is, formant transitions (the shift in the resonance features of the vocal tract) from consonant to vowel. Still another intriguing approach to the problem of processing deficits in children with language impairments was offered by Montgomery (2002), who examined the nature of lexical processing in children with regard to both temporal processing and more generalized processing capacity deficits. He offered a compelling argument for the impact of the processing capacity limitations identified in language impaired children as an explanation for their performance difficulties in temporal processing tasks, in which resource allocation is a significant component. Further research and documentation are necessary before a full evaluation of this controversial conceptualization and approach can be made.

Phonological awareness abilities (see Chapter 4) have been identified as critical to the development of early reading. The evidence is so strong that commercial materials have begun to appear with increasing regularity to aid educators in identifying weaknesses in phonological awareness abilities (Robertson & Salter, 1997) and in developing these skills (Adams, Foorman, Lundberg, & Beeler, 1998; Catts & Vartiainen, 1997). The main point of the research is not only that phonological skills underlie early reading but also that they can be taught. Catts (1997) developed a checklist to aid in the early identification of language-based reading difficulties. The value of the checklist is twofold. The first benefit is its structure, which identifies six significant areas of observation for the teacher: speech-sound awareness, word retrieval, verbal memory, speech production and perception, comprehension, and expressive language. The second benefit is that when such a checklist is used in collaboration with a speech-language pathologist, it can be of enormous value in targeting students who may be vulnerable to reading difficulty and in pinpointing their particular areas of need (see Figure 3.4).

Phonology is too often simplified to its superficial relationship to speech or phonics instruction. In reality it has far-reaching significance for the rate of language acqui-

Early Identification of Language-Based Reading Disabilities: A Checklist

Child's name: _____   Birthday: _____

Date completed: _____   Age: _____

This checklist is designed to identify children who are at risk for language-based reading disabilities. It is intended for use with children at the end of kindergarten or beginning of first grade. Each of the descriptors listed below should be carefully considered and those that characterize the child's behavior/history should be checked. A child receiving a large number of checks should be referred for a more in-depth evaluation.

Speech sound awareness
_____ Doesn't understand and enjoy rhymes
_____ Doesn't easily recognize that words begin with the same sound
_____ Has difficulty counting the syllables in spoken words
_____ Has problem clapping hands or tapping feet in rhythm with songs and/or rhymes
_____ Demonstrates problems learning sound–letter correspondences

Word retrieval
_____ Has difficulty retrieving a specific word (e.g., calls a sheep a "goat" or says, "you know, a woolly animal")
_____ Shows poor memory for classmates' names
_____ Speech is hesitant, filled with pauses or vocalizations (e.g., "um," "you know")
_____ Frequently uses words lacking specificity (e.g., "stuff," "thing," "what you call it")
_____ Has a problem remembering/retrieving verbal sequences (e.g., days of the week, alphabet)

Verbal memory
_____ Has difficulty remembering instructions or directions
_____ Shows problems learning names of people or places
_____ Has difficulty remembering the words to songs or poems
_____ Has problems learning a second language

Speech production/perception
_____ Has problems saying common words with difficult sound patterns (e.g., *animal, cinnamon, specific*)
_____ Mishears and subsequently mispronounces words or names
_____ Confuses a similar sounding word with another word (e.g., saying, "The Entire State Building is in New York")
_____ Combines sound patterns of similar words (e.g., saying "escavator" for *escalator*)
_____ Shows frequent slips of the tongue (e.g., saying "brue blush" for *blue brush*)
_____ Has difficulty with tongue twisters (e.g., *she sells seashells*)

Comprehension
_____ Only responds to part of a multiple element request or instruction
_____ Requests multiple repetitions of instructions/directions with little improvement in comprehension
_____ Relies too much on context to understand what is said
_____ Has difficulty understanding questions
_____ Fails to understand age-appropriate stories
_____ Has difficulty making inferences, predicting outcomes, drawing conclusions
_____ Lacks understanding of spatial terms such as *left/right, front/back*

Expressive language
_____ Talks in short sentences
_____ Makes errors in grammar (e.g., "he goed to the store" or "me want that")
_____ Lacks variety in vocabulary (e.g., uses "good" to mean *happy, kind, polite*)
_____ Has difficulty giving directions or explanations (e.g., may show multiple revisions or dead ends)
_____ Relates stories or events in a disorganized or incomplete manner
_____ May have much to say, but provides little specific detail
_____ Has difficulty with the rules of conversation, such as turn taking, staying on topic, indicating when he/she does not understand

Figure 3.4. Checklist for early identification of language-based reading disabilities. (From Catts, H.W. [1997]. Appendix A: Early identification of language-based reading disabilities. A checklist. *Language, Speech, and Hearing Services in Schools, 28,* 88–89; reprinted by permission. Some descriptors have been taken from *Language for learning: A checklist for language difficulties,* Melbourne, Australia: OZ Student.)

Other important factors
_____ Has a prior history of problems in language comprehension and/or production
_____ Has a family history of spoken or written language problems
_____ Has limited exposure to literacy in the home
_____ Lacks interest in books and shared reading activities
_____ Does not engage readily in pretend play
Comments

_____

_____

_____

sition (Paul & Jennings, 1992), vocabulary size (Stoel-Gammon, 1991), working memory (Adams & Gathercole, 1995), word retrieval (Katz, 1986; McGregor, 1994), and phonological awareness skills (segmentation, **sound deletion**, blending, and counting) that are believed to underlie early literacy (Catts, 1993). Expressive phonological disorders have negative effects on early literacy (Bird & Bishop, 1992; Bird, Bishop, & Freeman, 1995) and spelling (Moats, 1995). The relationship between speech and print is anchored by an understanding of phonology and phonological processes. For children, making this connection is a vital step in the development of literacy. For teachers, understanding this connection brings power of knowledge to teaching.

Teachers are faced with a daunting challenge in our increasingly multicultural society as the expectations of the No Child Left Behind Act of 2001 (PL 107-110) mandate universal literacy. As researchers work to understand the impact on literacy acquisition of variations in the language and cultural literacy of African American (Craig, Connor, & Washington, 2003; Laing & Kamhi, 2003) and Hispanic children (Gottardo, 2002; Hammer, Miccio, & Wagstaff, 2003), teachers must support the learning needs of culturally and linguistically diverse populations. A particular challenge facing teachers is the impact of variation in vowel and consonant production in the oral language of populations of linguistically diverse speakers. The relationship between phonology and decoding is affected at a fundamental level by these variations. For teachers to be fully effective in meeting the needs of struggling readers of cultural and linguistic backgrounds different than their own, they must know the structure of the linguistic knowledge that the children bring to school (Labov, 2003). Indeed, the task is daunting but not insurmountable for creative, devoted educators. (See Chapter 11 on biliteracy.)

Morphology

Language form, one of three major components of language (Bloom & Lahey, 1978), also includes a set of rules for the formation of words. *Morphology* is the study of word formation, or how *morphemes* (the smallest units of meaning in language) combine to form words. Morphemes (unlike phonemes) are endowed with meaning. Words are made up of one or more morphemes. A morpheme that can stand alone, such as smile, book, or cute, is called an **unbound morpheme** (or **free morpheme**). Another group of morphemes, called bound morphemes, must be attached to other morphemes. **Bound morphemes** are typically the affixes of a language, such as *un-* and *-ing* for the

word *unsmiling,* *-s* in the plural *books,* and *-est* in the superlative *cutest.* Unbound morphemes have lexical (word) meaning of their own. They are the content words of the language: nouns, main verbs, adjectives, and adverbs. Other morphemes, called *function words* or *grammatical morphemes,* such as prepositions, articles, conjunctions, and auxiliary verbs, serve grammatical functions in a sentence by creating the connection between **lexical** morphemes. Bound morphemes may be either inflectional or derivational. **Inflectional morphemes** modify tense (*-ed* in *played*), possession (*-'s* in *Vicki's*), or number (*-s* in *dollars*). The acquisition of inflectional morphemes is a hallmark of early language development and reflects a child's increasing analysis of the structure and meaning of words. **Derivational morphemes** change one part of speech to another; for example, the verb *argue* plus *-ment* becomes the noun *argument,* and the adverb *happy* plus *-ness* becomes the noun *happiness.* The changes in spelling that result are another indication of the underlying complexity of the relationship between speech and print. Morphemic structure allows the language user to extend and modify meaning. Young language learners, making their way through the dense forest of sounds, words, and meanings, learn to mark the differences in tense, number, or possession by attending to the ends of words. Older children learn to recognize the relationships among words (e.g., *nation, national, nationality, nationalism, nationalistic*). Indeed, prefixes and suffixes, which are most commonly derived from Greek and Latin, permit a learner to extend lexical knowledge (White, Power, & White, 1989; see Chapter 6).

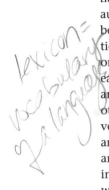

A further intrigue exists in the **morphophonemic relationship**: change in pronunciation caused by change in the **morphological** structure in a word, such as the changes that occur when the following words are said aloud: *sign, signature; medicine, medical.* Although phonemically such pronunciation changes may seem irregular, from a morphological view many of these changes are predictable.

Morphological Development   In the earliest stages of language development, morphological development is measured by the acquisition of the first 14 morphemes that emerge in children's language (Brown, 1973). As morphemes may either be words (unbound) or affixes (bound), the first 14 morphemes range from the present progressive marker *-ing,* to the use of the irregular third-person singular verb form *has,* to the contracted copula (*to be*) such as *-'m* in *I'm going.* These acquisitions generally occur between the ages of 2 or 2½ years and 4 years. Brown identified this initial phase of acquisition as occurring across five stages of development that span the period of approximately 1½–5½ years of age. During early language development, children acquire pronouns, articles, and adjective and noun suffixes. At a certain point in early development, morphological and syntactic development merge as indicated by the development of the negative forms *no* and *not* that become part of the evolution of negative sentence structures.

Later morphological development involves the acquisition of comparatives (*-er*) and superlatives (*-est*), irregular forms (*children*), and advanced prefixes and suffixes (*un-, dis-, -ness, -ment*), including those that mark noun (*-er* in *baker*) and adverb **derivation** (*-ly* in *slowly*). Spelling and pronunciation are affected by the structure of more advanced morphological development (e.g., *child/children, happy/happiness*). Wiig and Semel provided a sequence of acquisition of morphological or word formation rules:

> 1) Regular noun plurals, 2) noun–verb agreement for singular and plural forms of irregular nouns and verbs in the present tense, 3) regular noun possessives in the singular and plural form, 4) irregular noun plurals, 5) irregular noun possessives, 6) regular past tense

verbs, 7) irregular past tense verbs, 8) adjectival inflections for the comparative and super-lative forms, 9) noun and adverb derivation, 10) prefixing. (1980, p. 50)

Carlisle (1988), in her studies of fourth, sixth, and eighth graders, demonstrated that children know more about derivational morphology than they use in their spelling. Her recommendation was for direct instruction of words that undergo both phonologi-cal and orthographic changes (e.g., *deep/depth*) as opposed to those that undergo only phonological change (e.g., *equal/equality*).

Morphology plays an interesting role in language development and growth. From their earliest role in the emergence of grammar as a child passes beyond the single-word stage to the adolescent's urgent need to master Greek and Latin roots and affixes in preparation for the SAT, morphological knowledge and mastery contribute to vocabu-lary growth, spelling, comprehension, and the richness of a student's written language.

Relationship of Morphological Disorders to Literacy   Children with language learning disabilities often present with impairments in reading as their primary aca-demic problem. The rate of morphological acquisition is slower for these children than for their typically developing peers. Although morphological acquisition has not been widely studied, several investigations have pointed to the relationship between morpho-logical awareness and literacy. Mahoney and Mann (1992) found positive correlations between second graders' ability to appreciate phonologically and morphologically based puns and their reading ability. Ruben, Patterson, and Kantor (1991) reported a relationship between morphological knowledge and spelling ability in typically devel-oping second graders, children with learning disabilities, and adults with literacy prob-lems. Ruben and colleagues demonstrated that the morphemic errors made in writing reflected impairments in both the implicit and explicit levels of morphological knowl-edge. What was most striking, however, was their evidence that these impairments do not resolve simply by maturation and increased exposure to written language. Further-more, underlying phonological weakness may contribute to the difficulty poor readers have with certain morphological relationships. Fowler and Liberman (1995) found that poor readers have greater difficulty in producing morphological forms that involve a phonological change (e.g., *courage/courageous*) than they do when there is no phono-logical change (e.g., *danger/dangerous*).

Morphology is relevant to both reading and spelling for several reasons. Among those reasons concerning English morphology, Elbro and Arnbak (1996, p. 212) iden-tified the following:

- The role morphology plays in orthography;
- The value of morphemes as indicators of meaning;
- The economical nature of storing words in written lexicon as morphemes rather than as wholes (because of the relative unpredictability of sound to letter accuracy);
- Morpheme analysis and recognition as a reading strategy may provide a more direct route to the lexicon of the spoken word; certain reading and spelling errors are mor-phologically based, e.g., "proceedure"/"proceed."

Morphological awareness has been shown to be a strong indicator of reading compre-hension (Carlisle, 1995), and morphological awareness training has been shown to have a positive effect on comprehension (Elbro & Arnbak, 1996). Morphological aware-ness, however, is not seen as fully independent from phonological awareness (Fowler

& Liberman, 1995). Although researchers endeavor to determine the specific nature and interrelatedness of the systems of language that influence reading, teachers must remain conscious of the constant reciprocity among language components.

Syntax

Syntax is a third aspect of language form. Syntax is the system of rules that directs the comprehension and production of sentences. Syntax (sometimes referred to as *grammar*) specifies the order of words and the organization of words within a variety of sentence types. Syntactic rules allow the user to combine words into meaningful sentences and to alter the form of a sentence; for example, *The boy is walking* may be transposed into *Is the boy walking?* Despite a finite set of sentence types, an infinite number of sentences can be generated. In addition, syntactic knowledge allows a language user to decide whether sentences are grammatical.

Syntactic Development   Typically developing children acquire the rudiments of syntax early in the language acquisition process. As they progress beyond the basic form of noun phrase and verb phrase, children master the variety of sentence types common in preschool language: negative, interrogative, and imperative forms. Subsequently they begin to develop the earliest complex sentence structures of coordination, demonstrated by the use of *and* ("Joshua went to grandma's house *and* had a good time"); complementation, indicated by the use of a clause structure that modifies the verb ("Tell me *what he is eating*"); and relativization, in which a clause restricts or modifies the meaning of another portion of the sentence ("The boy *who ate the cake* has a tummyache"). Use of early complex sentence structures generally emerges at approximately 3 years of age and is mastered by age 5 or 6. Complex sentence development continues through the school years. Embedding of clauses, either parallel ("She gave him a toy *that he did not like*") or nonparallel ("He called the man *who walked away*"); the use of gerunds (verbs with *-ing* that function as nouns; e.g., "*Cooking* is fun"); and passive structures ("The cookie *was* eaten by the boy") continue to emerge across the school years with mastery of some forms as late as 11 years old. Other, more mature grammatical structures also evolve with the mastery of new forms such as more sophisticated conjunctions (e.g., *although, nonetheless*), mass nouns and their quantifiers ("*How much* water do you want?" rather than "*How many* water do you want?"), and the use of reflexive pronouns (e.g., *himself, herself*). The mature language user can use sentence complexity to convey numerous relationships among actions, ideas, and locations.

Sentence complexity continues to grow through the high school years, with increased maturation reflecting the development and influence of written language skills. Sentence length continues to increase slowly but steadily through the adolescent years at approximately one word per year as formally measured (Scott, 1988). Changes in the sophistication of noun and verb phrases and the development of nominal, adverbial, and relative clauses contribute to the growth in complexity of syntax. Chaney (1992) suggested the value of good syntactic knowledge in reading comprehension and reported that readers with better awareness of grammatical structure have better paragraph comprehension, possibly because they are able to use strong grammatical knowledge to monitor comprehension.

The ability to deconstruct sentences for comprehension or to construct them either orally or in writing to convey meaning is dependent on knowledge of syntactic rules. In addition, to some extent syntactic interpretation relies on the ability to main-

tain sentences in working memory (Adams & Gathercole, 1995) and to exploit phonological memory (Montgomery, 1996).

Whereas phonological knowledge and skills are relevant to early decoding, morphological and syntactic knowledge are significant to **fluency** and comprehension in later reading development. Beyond the initial stages of reading, most typically in second grade (Chall, 1983), increased fluency and comprehension become the focus of reading instruction. Knowledge of syntax enables readers to make predictions from among a set of possibilities about what type of word or words must be coming next. This can be easily demonstrated using the **cloze** technique (fill-in-the-blank technique) common to research designs in the study of syntax: *Sam gave Ida the* _____. Knowledge of syntactic structure helps an individual to predict the likelihood of either an adjective or a noun or both coming next. This predictive ability aids in automaticity.

Relationship of Syntactic Disorders to Literacy   For children who have difficulty with expressive or receptive syntax, the impact on reading may not become obvious until later in elementary school when the emphasis shifts from decoding to comprehension. Moreover, comprehension difficulties may not emerge until the density of text increases beyond the reader's syntactic knowledge limits. As with all aspects of language, there is a continuum that reflects both a developmental sequence and degree of complexity (from single words to complex sentences). A parallel continuum involves the degree of severity and pervasiveness (one particular aspect or all aspects) of the language difficulty.

Studies of early syntactic delay were predictive of subsequent reading disability (Scarborough, 1990), as were studies of children identified more globally as having language impairments in which disordered syntax was a characteristic (Aram & Hall, 1989). Other research has shown that children with reading difficulties have sentence comprehension problems as well. In particular, children and adolescents have difficulty interpreting later occurring complex structures such as those that contain **embedded** or **relative clauses** (Byrne, 1981; Morice & Slaghuis, 1985; Stein, Cairns, & Zurif, 1984). Reliance on semantic (meaning) strategies and limitations in working memory that would enable the child to retain the sentence for a sufficient period of time to analyze are possible contributing factors to difficulty in sentence comprehension.

Lahey and Bloom (1994) offered that sentence comprehension is far more complex than issues of working memory limitations would imply. As always, they considered a more encompassing view of sentence comprehension that includes working memory capacity, the ability to automatically retrieve the language knowledge needed to construct in mind what the sentence (and its parts) is representing, the nature of the material being processed (in or out of a context familiar to the child), and the availability and strength of any context cues. Sentence comprehension is not a simple process for anyone, but for a youngster with learning and language difficulties, it is an even greater task. What remains unclear is the nature of the relationship between syntactic comprehension problems and reading disability, although there is sufficient evidence to suggest that they coexist.

Comprehension of spoken syntax is supported by the discourse (conversational) structure of the interaction as well as by the paralinguistic and situational cues. Far fewer cues are available to the reader, and, as such, failure to accurately analyze sentence structure can result in deficient comprehension.

The elements of language form (phonology, morphology, and syntax) have clear relationships to one another as one aspect of the foundation on which literacy is built.

Early reading ability is strongly connected to phonological knowledge, as is the later development of spelling. Morphological knowledge adds to the skills required for spelling and comprehension. Later reading development, fluency, and comprehension have their roots in morphology and syntax while continuing to rely on efficient phonological processing.

Language Content

Language content, often referred to as *semantics*, is the meaning component of language. Language content reflects our world knowledge, what we know about objects, events, and relationships. The study of semantics is concerned with the meanings of words and the relationship between and among words as they are used to represent knowledge of the world. As explained by Lahey (1988), language content involves both the endless number of particular topics that can be discussed and the general categories of objects, actions, and relationships. Thus, all children of different cultures or experiences talk about content in terms of the objects, events, and relationships of their world, but the topics within each of these categories are different. Children raised in Mexico City or in Brooklyn will talk about food (object), eating (action), and possession (relationship) but are likely to ask for different foods.

Language content involves not only individual word meanings, as in the analysis of a child's vocabulary, but also the understanding of the meaning features that compose a word; how a word may (or may not) be used in a phrase, a sentence, or discourse; and the literal and figurative meanings of words. Words are composed of clusters of meaning features that allow us to define words and to differentiate among them. Most often our knowledge of these features is unconscious. Try, for example, to define the word *walk*. Although all of us know what it means, and most are able to demonstrate it, defining *walk* is quite difficult. Furthermore, when asked, "What does *draft* mean?" one could potentially supply six different responses ranging from conscription (being drafted into the military) to an alcoholic beverage (an ice-cold draft beer). Thus, determining whether a person knows a word extends beyond checking his or her ability to point to a picture of it or even to use it in a sentence. Moreover, knowledge of the world and the words used to represent that knowledge grows continuously across the life span. Over time, a person may come to associate varied meanings with each word because of increased exposure to assorted usage or varied personal experience. With exposure to print, a person may read about places, events, or people not directly experienced but may acquire new knowledge as well as the lexicon (vocabulary) that represents the experience.

In addition, there are rules that govern how words may be used in combination. Consider, for example, *The bachelor's wife is beautiful*. Although superficially the sentence is grammatically acceptable, the relationship between *bachelor* and *wife* raises a serious question as to the meaning of the sentence. Furthermore, the varying roles that words may play in a sentence can result in ambiguity that requires the language user to consider not only word meaning but also context. Consider the sentence *Visiting relatives can be a nuisance*. The meaning varies depending on the grammatical role ascribed to *visiting* as either a gerund or an adjective. These rules for the use of words in combination begin to develop quite early in a child's language acquisition process and form part of the basis for later semantic knowledge.

Word meaning may be literal or figurative. Part of the richness of language is in the imagery that it can create to express the more emotional and ethereal aspects of the

human experience. Whether one has *had a ball* (had a good time at a party or possessed a baseball at some time) or *opened a can of worms* (went fishing or unintentionally caused a problem), the semantic knowledge and use are reflected in the way in which meaning is colored.

Meaning in language is conveyed through the use of words and their combinations. Language content is the knowledge of the vast array of objects, events, and relationships and the way they are represented.

Semantic Development

People talk or write to communicate meaning just as they listen or read to determine meaning. The process of learning to assign meaning begins in infancy during the preverbal stages of development. Meaning can be represented in a word, in a sentence, or across sentences, as well as in nonlinguistic ways.

Each of us has a lexicon, a mental dictionary within our semantic memory. Individual word meanings as well as how words may be used are found in the lexicon. In early development children may ascribe a word to represent a variety of objects or events or relationships. Thus, in the single-word stage of language development, *cup* pronounced as "kuh" may mean a request for a drink or a request that a fallen cup be returned to the tray of the highchair. In early stages of language acquisition, word meaning may be overextended so that, for example, any four-legged furry animal is called "cat." Obviously, children and adults do not use words in the same way. Although a child may use a word such as *cat* taken from adult lexicon, the meaning may be different as reflected in the overextensions of meaning that children make. Fortunately, word meanings are consistently refined over time so that speakers of the same language share common definitions for words.

In the early single-word stages of language development, children have already begun to code meaning for the words they use. They will use a word to indicate a variety of semantic categories such as existence (indicated by looking at, naming, touching, or referring to an object that exists in their world), nonexistence or disappearance (an object expected to be seen does not appear; "bye-bye"), or recurrence (the reappearance of an object or the recurrence of an event; "more").

As children progress to the two-word stage of language development, new semantic relations emerge, both individually and in combination. Between 18 and 36 months of age, children steadily acquire an increasing number of meaning relations that they can represent, such as agent–action ("Russell kiss") or attribute–entity ("big book").

With continued development children begin to acquire vocabulary at a very rapid rate. From the toddler years through first grade, children acquire new words at a pace of approximately 9 words per day. The vocabulary of a 6-year-old may be as large as 14,000 words (Carey, 1978). It is a massive task and remarkable feat to acquire sufficient information from interacting with the world (with little direct instruction) to develop a lexicon of nouns, verbs, adjective, adverbs, and prepositions, as well as the words to represent a huge array of concepts such as time, space, and causality.

The learning of a word is a long-term developmental process. It includes determining that a set of sounds are a word; learning the word's meaning components, privileges, and restrictions on its use; and learning its syntactic properties (parts of speech, how it may be used in a sentence) and the conceptual foundations on which that word is based. Not only must children develop word meanings, but they also must learn contextual meaning. In the preschool years words and sentence meaning expand. Later,

children must learn to discern meaning from context (both linguistic and nonlinguistic) as well as to use later developing, more sophisticated cohesive devices to connect sentences into discourse.

Cohesive devices (Halliday & Hasan, 1976) include the use of pronouns or definite articles that refer to someone or something previously mentioned. This process is called **anaphora** (e.g., "Marsha was hungry. *She* went out to get lunch"). Another cohesive device, **ellipsis**, is the deletion of information available in a portion of the discourse immediately preceding (e.g., "Can you ice skate? I can"). Still another cohesive device, called **lexical cohesion**, involves the use of synonyms that refer to previously identified referents (e.g., "The *puppy* excitedly chased his tail. Our new *pet* was very entertaining").

In addition to relational meanings and contextual meaning, children must master the nonlinguistic aspects of meaning. **Deictic terms** are words that shift in meaning depending on how the nonlinguistic context changes. The meanings of words such as *I, you, here,* and *tomorrow* depend on who is speaking, where the participants are, and when the words are spoken.

Children acquire meaning of words and sentences and meaning across sentences in discourse. They must master a vast amount of information about the semantic and syntactic roles of words and about contextual and nonlinguistic aspects of meaning. It is amazing that much of this is accomplished in the preschool years. Later semantic development is concerned with continued refinement of previous content knowledge as well as with ongoing growth in vocabulary and in the mastery of **nonliteral language** such as metaphors, idioms, proverbs, and humor.

The power of word knowledge is seen most clearly in its impact on listening and reading comprehension, as well as writing. The strong connection between vocabulary knowledge, both breadth and depth of word meanings, and reading comprehension has a long history in research. The logic of the relationship between lexical knowledge and reading is intuitive; you will understand what you read if you know the meaning of the words! Vocabulary growth is a function of exposure, reading and problem solving ability, and good instruction. Effective vocabulary instruction involves the creation of word-rich classroom environments, independence in word learning, development of authentic instructional strategies, and the use of realistic assessments (Blachowicz & Fisher, 2002). As children become literate, the opportunities for growth in semantic knowledge grow considerably. After children learn to read, reading becomes a vehicle for learning. (See Chapter 13 on vocabulary.)

Relationship of Semantic Disorders to Literacy

There is more to reading than decoding (determining the pronunciation of words by noting the positions of vowels and consonants). The proof of a skilled, fluent reader may be the ability to read a professional manual filled with unfamiliar technical jargon. Being able to decode the words may very well be insufficient to provide the intended meaning or comprehension of the text. Once the reader has gained access to the word through decoding, the meaning of the words and sentences must be analyzed and synthesized for comprehension to occur. Comprehension in reading then is dependent on semantic, syntactic, and world knowledge. Consider *diadochokinesis,* a word unfamiliar to most. A strong decoder can syllabicate and decode the word syllable by syllable, a likely approach given the length of the word, but may not be able to guess the meaning (rapid alternating movements such as those associated with speech articulation).

Gough and Tunmer (1986) made reference to two sets of skills in reading: decoding and linguistic comprehension. Reading is not a unitary action, nor is the use of oral

language. Rather, both activities reflect a complex integration of skills. When looking at different groups identified as having reading disorders, dyslexia, language disorders, or specific language impairment, it is important to consider the criteria that are selected to define the group and which skills are under investigation before generalizing the implications of research findings.

During a consideration of semantic deficits in vocabulary and word knowledge, word retrieval, and the relationship to syntax and sentence comprehension, it is necessary to be concerned with the dynamic relationship of form, content, and use. Specifically, weak phonological coding may be related to the establishment of poorer networks of word meanings as well as poorer access to those words. Thus, facility or difficulty in one aspect of language as it relates to reading does not preclude the same ease or difficulty in the other aspects of reading. Some good decoders have poor comprehension, just as in the early stages of reading mastery, poorer decoders may have adequate comprehension. Swank (1997) demonstrated that in addition to phonological coding, meaning and grammar are important to the decoding abilities of kindergarten and first-grade readers. Similarly, Snowling and Nation (1997) wrote that syntactic and semantic information derived from sentences allowed children to alter their inaccurate pronunciation of decoded target words so that the words made sense in the context of the sentence. In older children with reading difficulties, semantic deficits may be the result of what Vellutino, Scanlon, and Spearing referred to as having "accrued" (1995, p. 76) as a consequence of prolonged decoding difficulty in which poor readers are denied access to semantic information about word meaning and use. Early in their school careers children learn to read and for the remainder of their academic years, read to learn (Chall, 1983). Nippold suggested a "symbiotic" (1988, p. 29) relationship between literacy and learning during the later school years.

By fourth grade, reading becomes the primary means of acquiring new vocabulary. When children have inherent language deficits, semantic functions may be restricted, thus influencing learning to read as well as later reading to learn. Semantic deficits may manifest at different times in the reading process, dependent in part on the kind of reading instruction a child receives. Emphasis on phonics in a highly structured sound–symbol system in which word identification is emphasized may allow comprehension difficulties based on semantic deficits to go unnoticed for longer periods of time. When text-based approaches to early reading are stressed, semantic deficits are more likely to be exposed earlier in the process of learning to read.

Semantic competence involves a high degree of organization among the concepts that are being accumulated in the semantic system. Semantic networks must be formed to provide the structure for the concepts that a child is learning. Children who are weaker at concept formation are likely to have less robust vocabulary and weaker semantic networks. Lack of exposure to concepts or difficulties in concept formation or in the organization of the concepts may result in less effective reading comprehension. So, children with ongoing oral language difficulties remain at higher risk for reading comprehension difficulties if their oral language deficits result in depressed semantic knowledge.

Children with reading deficits have been shown to have difficulties in vocabulary, word categorization, and word retrieval. Many children with reading impairments have more difficulty than same-age peers in providing accurate definitions for words. Hoskins (1983) reported that children with reading impairments were more likely to offer descriptions and examples of words they were asked to define rather than to provide more formal, specific definitions. This is a frequently observed clinical behavior. It reflects one level of general comprehension of word meaning and use (e.g., "I know

how to use it, but I can't really tell you what it means"). For teachers who are concerned about the reading comprehension abilities of their students, defining versus describing is a skill to watch for.

Categorization, or word association, abilities, another semantic skill reflecting a knowledge base, is also frequently deficient in children with reading difficulties. Children with reading and other learning disabilities often demonstrate restricted word meanings as well as weakly developed associations among words and classes of words. Limitations in reading comprehension may result from restricted word meanings that reduce the reader's ability to interpret sentences; reduced vocabulary knowledge so that less familiar, multisyllabic words are more difficult to decode; and poorly developed semantic networks between word meanings and categories.

Other than word meaning itself, it is necessary to consider several other important aspects of semantics. Understanding a word also requires knowledge of **synonyms**, **antonyms**, and multiple meanings of a word. At higher levels of abstraction, semantic knowledge includes the appreciation and use of humor, slang, idioms, **similes**, and **metaphors** (Roth & Spekman, 1989). World knowledge also plays a considerable role in how semantics functions in reading comprehension. Lack of world knowledge means that a decoding error is more likely to remain uncorrected when reading on an unfamiliar topic. Lack of an adequate knowledge base to judge the content that is being read may result in comprehension errors as well.

Another frequently observed semantic deficit that affects literacy is word retrieval problems. Word retrieval problems may be described as a person's difficulty in gaining access to a specific, intended word from his or her vocabulary. So, despite knowledge of the word, there is a disruption in recovering or retrieving the phonetic structure (sound pattern) of the word to express it in spontaneous production. Common behaviors of people with word retrieval difficulties are delay in retrieving the word; substitution of other, similar words; circumlocutions (descriptions of aspects of the word, as when a person says, "You know, the place where you swim," but means *pool*); the use of gestures or demonstration to represent the word; and the substitution of nonspecific words (e.g., *thing, stuff, the place*) for the specific word. Children with reading disabilities have been shown to have a slower rate of naming, more frequent naming errors, and longer delays before responding (Denckla & Rudel, 1976; German, 1982; Wiig, Semel, & Nystrom, 1982). (See Chapter 4 on phonological awareness.)

Children with word-retrieval difficulties may read less fluently, with many hesitations and rephrasings. A youngster may look at a word and offer a definition but may be unable to say the specific word. Given the frequent substitution of similar or related words, comprehension may not be seriously affected; however, the dilemma may be in demonstrating comprehension when specific words are not readily accessible.

Finally, as children become more adequate decoders, they, similar to mature readers, read for meaning across sentences and through extended text rather than from individual words. At this juncture semantic knowledge must become integrated with syntactic knowledge and the more pragmatic, or discourse-related, aspects of language that include a knowledge of narrative structure and the ability to determine the writer's intent.

Language Use

Language use is frequently referred to as *pragmatics*. Pragmatics involves a set of rules that dictate communicative behavior in three main areas: reasons for which we communicate, called *communicative functions* or *intentions;* different codes or styles of com-

munication necessary in a particular context; and conversation or discourse. Each person speaks for a variety of purposes with an assortment of intentions. These intentions refer to the speaker's goals in talking. For example, one may speak to greet, to inquire, to answer, to request a behavior or information, to negotiate, or to teach, among many other possibilities.

Success in communicating intentions depends on several factors. A speaker must choose the appropriate code or style from among the variety of ways in which something can be said. To make that decision, a speaker must consider the context and the listener's needs. The words and sentences that are chosen to formulate the thought depend on the ages, knowledge bases, and relative status of speaker and listener. Imagine using the greeting, "Hi sweetie!" uniformly when greeting your 3-year-old, your pharmacist, and your boss. Similarly, the words chosen depend on what is occurring or what is present at the time the words are spoken. Two people standing on a train platform at 7 A.M. on a weekday would find it appropriate to hear, "Here it comes." The same utterance while standing in line at the supermarket might be met with a quizzical, "What?"

Finally, pragmatics involves rules of conversation or discourse. To communicate effectively, a speaker must be able to start a conversation, enter a conversation in process, and appropriately remain in a conversation. Moreover, competent communicators must be able to take turns within a conversation, recognize the need for clarification and provide it, change the subject appropriately, listen and respond meaningfully, and tell a coherent and cohesive story (narrative). The minutiae of competent conversation and narrative are an extensive area of study because of their significance in the social and academic lives of children (Applebee, 1978; Brinton & Fujiki, 1989; Dore, 1978; Halliday, 1975; Prutting & Kirschner, 1987; Rees, 1978).

Mastering the social uses of language is an ongoing process for young language learners. In school, classroom discourse patterns and a literate level of talking and understanding represent a level of language use that is critical for academic success. The difference between everyday discourse and the language of the classroom and **expository writing** is dramatic. Although a youngster may have adequate linguistic ability for everyday conversational interactions, the same youngster may not have achieved a level of language use that is necessary to comprehend the language of instruction, which requires an understanding of more sophisticated vocabulary, words with multiple meanings, figurative usages, more varied and complex sentence structures, the distinction between what the sentence is saying and what it is intended to have the listener do, and the higher (less direct in interpretation) levels of understanding. Such vulnerability can be easily overlooked and is seriously deleterious to a child's learning ability.

Pragmatic Development

The earliest observations of communicative development can be made during the period between birth and approximately 10 months of age. This stage of preverbal communication is the first of three periods identified by Bates, Camaioni, and Volterra (1975). In this earliest period the child is not aware of the communicative impact of his or her behavior. Although a child might point or reach toward an object of interest, he or she does not do this to elicit an adult's attention or action. In the next stage of communicative development, the one-word stage, between 10 and 15 months old, a child more definitely intends to communicate with the adults around him or her. Although these attempted communications may not involve speech, they are clearly recognized

by both the baby and the adult as having intent. These attempts may be gestural and/or gestural and vocal (as differentiated from verbal attempts alone). Once a baby begins to use words to communicate, he or she is at the multiword stage, the third stage of this early period of communicative development. The baby's intentions previously were conveyed by gesture and vocalization. Now, more conventional word forms begin to serve similar purposes. As the use of words accomplishes goals for an infant or a toddler, the child begins to monitor and learn from the listener's reactions. The baby begins to see the effects of his or her utterances; as such, social interaction provides the context for learning about communication.

Roth and Spekman (1984) identified three sets of categories of intentional behavior for children in preverbal, one-word, and multiword stages that reflect a developmental process. The evolution of intentional behavior from preverbal attention seeking, requesting, greeting, protesting or rejecting, responding/acknowledging, and informing, to the more refined stage in which words are added and allow for the refinement of the original intentions and the addition of naming and commenting, to multiword utterance stages in which intention are more varied and refined and may now express rules and opinions, is foundational for the use of language in a more adultlike manner for regulating and controlling conversational interactions.

As these multiword toddlers become preschoolers, they begin to learn more complex ways of using language for social purposes. Their conversational skills grow as do their discourse skills, such as telling stories, describing with greater clarity, and recounting personal experiences. As children's language skills grow, language can be used for an increasing number of school-related skills, such as instructing or reasoning. As they progress toward the school years, children begin to use their pragmatic skills for an ever-growing number of purposes at a higher, more refined level. Now language used to plan and organize must help to construct narratives of greater density and longer sequences of events. An increasing number of communicative intentions, more sophisticated conversational skills, and improved narrative (storytelling skills) all mark the development of language use in preschoolers.

Conversational skills develop further during the school years. In the preschool years conversation between children and adults is often supported by the adult. If a preschooler has not effectively communicated his or her intent, and a clarification is requested, most typically the youngster will repeat what he has just said. By the early elementary school years, however, a youngster will not only repeat but also will elaborate in an attempt to be more clear for the listener. By the middle elementary school years, a child can not only elaborate but also explain, provide additional background information, and monitor the listener's comprehension in an ongoing way (Brinton, Fujiki, Loeb, & Winkler, 1986). Conversation among school-age children also involves the mastery of slang. In addition children speak to each other in sentence structures that are more complex, elaborate, and varied than they do when speaking to adults. This is consistent with parents' observations of the difference in the way children talk at home versus how they communicate among friends (Owens, 1996). Certainly, among teenagers the use of language for social purposes becomes more crucial. Also important is the ability to effectively shift from one conversational style (social) to another (academic) to meet the higher expectations of teachers for a fully literate style of language use (Larson & McKinley, 1995).

The school-age years bring with them another level of maturation and an increased demand on children's pragmatic abilities. During the school years several important changes take place in pragmatic development and use. The number of com-

municative functions must expand. Children have to use their language skills but must do so with increased levels of appropriateness and often more indirectly. The demands on narrative production increase steadily. Preschoolers' simple storytelling of one or two facts or events grows to become the requirements of show-and-tell as well as book reports and essays. Children who have heard stories read and told throughout their lives come to these school-based narrative tasks better equipped than peers with fewer literacy experiences (Linder, 1999). There is a structure and pattern to the ways stories are constructed (Stein & Glenn, 1979). When children have been exposed to this pattern frequently because they have been read to on a regular basis, they come to school with a tacit knowledge of the structure of stories that becomes more available to them as it is required in the school environment.

The language of the classroom is greatly different from the everyday language that is used for social interaction. In school there is a greater degree of formality. The choice of words is often more abstract and unfamiliar; sentence structures are more complex; the interactions are planned and controlled; the topics, which are also controlled, are often related to texts; the rate of speech is faster; and, above all, the language of the classroom is decontextualized (Nelson, 1986). When language is decontextualized there are few contextual clues that children can use to understand the language of the classroom. As communicators, people are supported by context in such cues as facial expressions, gestures, intonational patterns, and the presence of the object being discussed. Unlike conversation, instructional discourse provides less meaning and support from context. Understanding is more fully dependent on the words. The purposes of language in the classroom are more instructive, regulatory, and acknowledging and are far less individualized and supportive than in conversation. There is a communicative imbalance that is particular to the classroom. Teachers control topics and turns. They ask questions to which they already know the answers (and judge the responses) and create an environment with the language of authority. Britton has written that in a conversation the partners both are participants who have a generally equal role in the course and direction of the conversation. He described another style of conversation in which one partner is dominant and the other is more of a "spectator" (1979, p. 192). Spectators, he noted, "use language to digest experience" (p. 192). Indeed, when considering classroom discourse, students most frequently play the role of spectators.

The differences between social discourse and instructional discourse can be highlighted by comparing a request for information and its aftermath in a social context and in a classroom environment. A special form of instructional dialogue exists within classrooms (Cazden, 1988; Nelson, 1985), referred to as the initiation-response-evaluation interaction pattern that consists of teacher initiation, student response, and teacher evaluation. Thus, in a classroom one might hear the following:

Teacher:　[Initiating] What is the capital of California?

Student:　[Responding] Sacramento.

Teacher:　[Evaluating] That's right. Very good.

In a social environment a similar exchange would end somewhat differently:

Speaker 1:　What is the capital of California?

Speaker 2:　Sacramento.

Speaker 1:　Thanks.

Table 3.4. Oral/literate language differences

Oral language	Literate language
Function	
Talking to regulate social interaction—requesting, commanding, protesting, seeking interaction	Talking to reflect on the past and future—predicting, projecting into thoughts and feelings of others, reasoning, imagining
Questions generally asked by speakers to gain information they do not have	Pseudoquestions asked to get the listener to perform for the speaker who knows the answers
Used to share understanding of the concrete and practical	Used to learn and teach
Symmetrical communication—everyone has an equal right to participate in the conversation; participants collaborate on the discourse	Asymmetrical communication—one person has the floor and is responsible for organizing the entire discourse
Content	
Talk is about the here and now—the concrete	Talk is about the there and then—the past and future; the abstract
Topic-associative organization; chaining of ideas or anecdotes	Topic-centered organization; explicit, linear description of single event
Meaning is in the context (shared information or the environment)	Meaning is in the text
Structure	
Use of pronouns, slang, and jargon; expressions known only to the in-group	Use of explicit, specific vocabulary
Familiar words	Unfamiliar words
Repetitive syntax and ideas	Minimal or no repetition of syntax and ideas
Cohesion based on intonation	Cohesion based on formal linguistic markers (*because, therefore, and so forth*)

From Westby, C. (1995). Culture and literacy: Frameworks for understanding. *Topics in Language Disorders, 16*(1), 59; reprinted by permission.

In the classroom the question is a test, although it is phrased as a request for information. In an everyday interaction the request for information is a genuine request. (See Table 3.4 for a discussion of the differences between oral language and literate [classroom] language.)

Relationship of Pragmatic Disorders to Literacy

The emphasis on the relationship between language and reading has grown ever stronger (Catts, 1996; Catts & Kamhi, 1986; Greene, 1996). For certain children whose oral language skills are age appropriate when they enter school, early literacy acquisition and accommodation to school discourse may not be negatively affected. Yet as the demands of the curriculum escalate, these same children may not have developed enough linguistically to meet expectations. Skills that were adequate in early grades when the emphasis was on decoding and when instruction was more experiential in nature are now insufficient as reading to learn (Chall, 1983) becomes the expected mode. Moreover, as the curriculum expands, topics become less familiar; new vocabulary and more complex sentences, paragraphs, and texts must be analyzed and interpreted; more reading and writing are expected; and the cognitive demands become more abstract.

Reading comprehension is an enormously complex integration of high-level linguistic ability and problem-solving skills. Approaching reading with the intent to understand and gain information and with the expectation that the text will make sense are the behaviors of good readers. They recognize that the goal of reading is to comprehend, and to that end they monitor their own comprehension. Poor readers, by

metacognition

contrast, will often perceive the purpose of reading as sounding out and saying the words aloud. The expectation or intent to understand what has been decoded is sharply reduced or is not a concern of poorer readers (Bos & Filip, 1982; Brown, 1982; Myers & Paris, 1978; Owings, Peterson, Bransford, Morris, & Stein, 1980). (See Chapter 14 on reading comprehension.)

An essential higher-order linguistic ability in text comprehension is the aspect of language use called *discourse,* which includes both conversational and narrative ability. Numerous higher-order language and cognitive skills are necessary for text comprehension including the following (as identified by Roth & Spekman, 1989): understanding the relationship between words and word parts, grasping sentence cohesion (i.e., the relationship between two sentences or parts of a sentence as signaled by cohesive devices), identifying words based on context or familiarity, determining vocabulary meaning based on context (including multiple meaning words and figurative language), understanding at different levels from literal to inferential (identifying main ideas, summarizing, predicting, and determining character traits and emotions), determining the communicative intent of the author, identifying and retaining relevant information, and using knowledge of narrative structure.

Knowledge of narrative structure and determining the author's intent can play crucial roles in comprehension when other syntactic (sentence structure) and semantic (meaning aspects) are otherwise intact. Recognizing narrative structure and the intention of the writer is part of the active construction of comprehension that extends beyond the interpretations of the grammatical and meaning components of a piece of writing.

The ability to appreciate and use narrative structure in comprehension (and oral and/or written production) has been studied in children with reading problems. The use of story grammars that describe the internal structure (both the components of the story and the rules for the order and relationship among the story components) of a story has been the most common way of analyzing narratives (Mandler & Johnson, 1977; Stein & Glenn, 1979).

Stein and Glenn's (1979) story grammar consists of a setting category and a system for ordering episodes within the story. This system is easily recognizable to those with the tacit knowledge of narrative structure and familiarity with literature. They are as follows: setting statements (*Marsha looked out across the expanse of land that she knew could now be hers*), initiating events (*The matching numbers were so unexpected*), internal responses (*Marsha remained numbed by the news*), plans for obtaining a goal (*Marsha started a telephone list. There was little time to waste*), attempts at achieving the goal (*Call after call, Marsha reported the news*), direct consequences of the attempts to reach the goal (*Everyone had been reached. They would arrive within 2 days*), and reactions that describe the emotional response (*With a grin on her face, she dropped into her favorite chair, exhausted and exhilarated!*).

Children with language and reading disabilities have less appreciation for narrative structure as defined by story grammar. Poorer understanding of temporal and causal relationships, limited detail, mistaken information, shorter retellings, and difficulty with inferential questions were also observed in children with language disorders (Gerber, 1993; Roth, 1986). Westby (1989) reported that children with language disorders tell shorter stories with fewer complete episodes, use a more restricted vocabulary, and have less well-organized stories than their peers who use language more typically.

In addition to knowledge and use of narrative structure, another, very pragmatically based aspect of comprehension is an understanding of the intent of the writer (or speaker, in oral discourse). This involves appreciating information that is not presented

explicitly. This grasp of suggested or implied information, called presupposition, is necessary for the message being communicated to be understood (Bates, 1976; Rees, 1978). In order to be a successful communicator, it is necessary to have sufficient language flexibility to adjust what is being said according to the needs of the listener. That may mean altering word choice, sentence structure, gestures, and paralinguistic features such as intonation patterns based on a variety of characteristics including age, relative status (of speaker and listener), intellectual level, and awareness of the listener's prior knowledge of the topic. Sociolinguist Dell Hymes (1972) offered a definition of pragmatics as "knowing what to say to whom, how and under what circumstances." A listener must monitor his or her comprehension and request clarification if necessary.

The parallels of pragmatics of oral language or discourse to reading are strong. Written language can be used for a variety of purposes with different intentions. In writing, one can request, create, solicit, inform, educate, entertain, describe, and persuade, among a lengthy list of other purposes. For the reader the mandate is to discern the communicative intent of the author in nonfiction and of the author and characters in fiction. When children have vulnerabilities in determining a speaker's intent in oral discourse, they are clearly at risk for failing to make these determinations from print. So much emphasis is placed on the decoding process in the early school years that the functional and communicative intents of writing are often neglected (Creaghead, 1986). Children who are weaker in understanding implied meaning in conversation (e.g., the sarcasm in "Nice haircut" said with a sneer) may struggle later on when they are expected to interpret humor, sarcasm, figurative language (idioms), metaphors, and other less explicitly stated intended meanings. Moreover, in reading, the physical and environmental cues on which speakers and listeners depend, such as an arched eyebrow, a falsetto voice, or the gape of onlookers, are absent or may be reflected in more abstract ways (should the author choose to do so) as italics or punctuation (! ; ? " "). In conversation the speaker may recognize a furrowed brow as confusion and attempt to clarify before asked to do so. No such author-given support is available to the reader. I have lost track of the number of times I have needed to help students recognize the need to actively construct their comprehension because Edgar Allan Poe, O. Henry, or Guy de Maupassant is unavailable to explain himself! Conversely, children can be motivated to consider the needs of their reader (typically a teacher) when writing an assignment via a reminder that the teacher is unlikely to call them at home and ask, "Just what did you mean in the second paragraph on page 3?" It is crucial for teachers to recognize and remember that when children have vulnerabilities in discourse, they are at risk for comprehension difficulties with conversation and narrative despite having decoding skill. Active participation in the process of comprehending what is read involves a complex amalgam of skills among which language use or pragmatics is a subtle and often unrecognized vulnerability. When a youngster has adequate social language skills, the more hidden pragmatic weakness that can negatively affect comprehension may be overlooked easily. Direct instruction in narrative structure via story grammars and in identifying and interpreting the communicative intentions of the author can markedly improve a student's level of reading comprehension.

Metalinguistic Development

At the most developed level of language use, beyond the basic pragmatic skills required for conversation and narrative is another tier of language competence called *metalinguistic abilities* (Miller, 1990). Metalinguistic abilities permit a child to view language as

an entity, something to talk about and think about. Metalinguistic skills enable a child to use language to talk about language. In preschoolers, language is viewed primarily as a means of communication, not as an object of consideration. During the school-age years, however, children become increasingly able to reflect on language and make conscious decisions about their own language and how it works. This is different from having tacit, underlying knowledge that allows the generation of sentences with specific words that are appropriate to a situation. Metalinguistic skills are essential to successful school learning because they influence a number of school-based tasks and are particularly important to the development of early decoding ability. Bunce (1993) identified the diverse nature of the metalinguistic skills required for literacy acquisition, comprehension, and successful school learning. At a phonological level a child must be able to segment a word into its sounds and determine whether two words have the same sound. Another metalinguistic task is to determine whether two sentences have equal meaning or to identify a sentence by its syntactic form (e.g., declarative, interrogative). Recognizing multiple meanings, summarizing, and analyzing information are metalinguistic tasks as well.

Wallach and Miller (1988) established a sequence in the development of metalinguistic skills that evolves from 1½ to 10 years of age and older. In the earliest stages children learn to recognize some printed symbols, such as McDonald's signs or the first letter of their name. By the beginning of the later stages of metalinguistic awareness, between 5 and 8 years of age, children's metalinguistic knowledge becomes an essential part of learning to read. Among these skills are those associated with phonological awareness, such as rhyming, **segmentation**, and **phoneme deletion**. It is widely agreed that phonological awareness makes a major contribution to early decoding ability. Well-developed metalinguistic skills are as crucial to early reading ability as they ultimately are to classroom success in understanding the discourse patterns of the classroom and the ongoing need to analyze the language being used to teach the language that must be learned.

When children have weaker skills in language comprehension and use, they are at risk for academic difficulty at many levels. For some children the shift from contextualized, social, familiar, adult-supported language to the decontextualized, pedagogic, novel, adult-directed, evaluative, metalinguistic language of the classroom is overwhelming. Such language difficulties can be virtually invisible in a child whose speech is clear and whose demeanor is undemanding. A common misperception is that these children lack motivation or interest; rather, their skills are not on the same level as the language and communication demands of the classroom. Language is a part of every aspect of the school day, and what appears to be inattention or lack of motivation may in fact be a lack of comprehension of the level of language presented and the rules of classroom discourse.

OTITIS MEDIA AND SPEECH, LANGUAGE, AND LITERACY

While you quietly read this chapter, it is easy to take typical hearing and sound discrimination (the ability to determine the difference between two sounds so that whisper is not processed as whisker) abilities for granted. Classrooms are rarely as quiet as libraries or studies, so for a youngster with a conductive hearing loss secondary to ear infections or allergies, the background noise and acoustic lapses of a classroom, such as open doors, many windows, and uncarpeted floors (which allow for scraping and echoing) can be an obstacle to learning.

Otitis media is inflammation of the middle ear. This inflammation can be accompanied by fluid in the middle ear. If the fluid is not infected, the inflammation is called *otitis media with effusion (OME)*. When an infection exists in the middle ear, it is called *acute otitis media*. Many children shift back and forth between OME and acute otitis media. Fluid in the middle ear may persist for weeks or months after the onset of acute otitis media. When fluid persists for more than 3 months, the OME is said to be chronic. Although some children display signs and symptoms of the discomfort associated with fluid and/or infection in the middle ear, others are asymptomatic. Infected or not, symptomatic or not, when there is fluid in the middle ear, a child will generally have a mild to moderate conductive hearing loss as fluid blocks the normal transmission of sound through the middle ear. Put your fingers in your ears, or try listening to music while sitting in the bathtub with your ears below the surface of the water. The experience will provide a sense of how arduous listening and learning are to a child who is experiencing a conductive hearing loss. The conductive hearing loss associated with OME can fluctuate. This poses an additional dilemma for the young student. The teacher's voice may not be heard at a consistent level. Depending on the level of fluid, a child may have better or worse hearing on a given day. He or she cannot predict what he or she will be able to hear. Furthermore, because this type of hearing loss is often invisible, teachers may be unaware of a child's need for additional support and accommodation. Children may appear uninterested or inattentive when they cannot adequately hear what is being said.

There is controversy regarding the effects of early otitis media on later language and academic development. A large body of research has provided evidence that children with persistent OME during their early years perform more poorly on tests of speech production (Roberts, Burchinal, Koch, Footo, & Henderson, 1988), speech processing (Gravel & Wallace, 1992), expressive language (Friel-Patti & Finitzo, 1990), and academic achievement (Silva, Chalmers, & Stewart, 1986). Children who have a history of otitis media are more frequently described by teachers as having behavioral and attentional problems (Roberts et al., 1989; Silva, Kirkland, Simpson, Stewart, & Williams, 1982). Although many studies support the relationship between OME and subsequent difficulties in speech, language, and learning, other studies fail to show a significant link between OME and difficulties in the same cluster of skills and abilities, such as speech production and reception, receptive and expressive language, and academic achievement (Bishop & Edmundson, 1986; Lous, Fiellau-Nikolajsen, & Jeppeson, 1988; Roberts, Bailey & Nychka, 1991; Wallace, Gravel, McCarton, & Ruben, 1988).

The conflicting findings are in part a function of the ways in which the studies were conducted, either retrospectively or prospectively. It is important to consider the differences. Retrospective data collection relies on recall of events that may have occurred years before during episodes of OME as well as on review of medical records. The opportunity for error is great. Prospective data collection involves following the course of the child's experience from the time of the earliest incidence of OME through the development of language and academic experience. More prospective studies are needed to identify further the nature of the relationship between early OME and later learning. One study, Friel-Patti and Finitzo (1990), provided support for the logical assumption that the relationship between OME and language is bridged by hearing. Thus the relationship between OME and language is indirect but assumes the more direct relationship between OME and hearing and between hearing and language. Crucial to this point is the importance of repeated measures of OME, hearing, and language ability

Table 3.5. Suggestions for teachers and child care providers working with children with otitis media with effusion (OME)

1. Be aware of the signs of an ear infection (e.g., ear pain, pulling on ear, discharge from outer ear, hearing loss, congestion related to cold, decreased attentiveness), and let parents know when you observe that the child may have an ear infection.

2. Be aware that children experiencing OME may have a related fluctuating mild hearing loss and thus may exhibit difficulties hearing others talking or paying attention.

3. Recognize that children with a history of chronic OME may exhibit language and learning problems related to earlier OME, although they may not presently have frequent ear infections.

4. Provide an optimal language-learning environment by being responsive to the child.

5. When talking, face the child and talk at his or her eye level.

6. Speak clearly, repeating important words but using natural intonation.

7. Gain the child's attention before telling information to ensure that the child has the opportunity to hear what you are saying.

8. Optimize the listening situation for the child who has attention difficulties by providing reminders to pay attention.

9. Provide visual supports for verbal learning situations; for example, give the school-age child written instructions along with oral instructions.

10. To provide a more quiet listening environment, reduce background noise and room echo, for example, by using carpeting and draperies and closing the door.

11. Give the child preferential seating to provide the clearest auditory signal. Allow the child to sit close to the teacher but in a position where the child can see other students (e.g., at the side of the room).

12. Be sure that the child is close to the person speaking (not more than 5 feet away).

13. Provide opportunities for small-group and one-to-one interactions.

14. Refer a child experiencing OME or with a history of OME to a speech-language pathologist and other appropriate specialists (e.g., psychologist, special educator) when the child is having difficulty learning classroom material.

From Roberts, J., & Schuele, M. (1990). Otitis media and later academic performance: The linkage and implications for intervention. *Topics in Language Disorders, 11*(1), 58; adapted by permission.

taken both concurrently and prospectively, given the unquestioned relationship between hearing and language and oral language and reading.

Although treatment of OME is a medical responsibility, teachers can play an important role in facilitating learning for children who have OME. Ear infections and hearing loss, particularly the mild to moderate losses associated with OME, can be unobserved in a classroom environment. The inattentiveness of a child with a mild to moderate hearing loss can easily seem behavioral or emotional. Table 3.5 provides suggestions for teachers working with children with OME to help make the learning experience more positive and robust.

CLOSING THOUGHTS

Consider once more the marvelous melodies and harmonies of *Eine Kleine Nachtmusik*. There are but 8 notes in the Western musical scale, yet the combinations and permutations are endless. In a similar vein, a language system has a set of components that are conceptualized as form, content, and use. Within each of these components are an uncountable number of combinations and variations that function alongside rules and regularities, permitting the language user, young or old, to communicate. No child is like every other child. Genetics, personality, experience, emotion, developmental patterns, intellect, neurology, perception, memory, and **linguistics** intertwine so that in every case, the whole is greater than the sum of its parts. Still, there are certain regu-

larities in language development that teachers must know so as to enrich the understanding of how language influences a child's ability to learn. Simultaneously, the variability from one child to another must be kept in mind so that teachers focus on the child and not only on the task. At times, the child's knowledge and ability as well as the task itself influence performance and learning.

Throughout this chapter, four strands of research have been woven together: language and speech-language pathology, learning disabilities, reading, and education. In-depth knowledge of oral language development and language related to learning and reading comes from the discipline of speech-language pathology. An understanding of the many aspects of learning and flexibility in skill and strategy development emerges from the study of learning disabilities. Reading research and instruction provide an intense consideration of all aspects of the enormous task of "breaking the code" and then encoding to complete the reading process. Educational theory and practice offer a wide array of techniques for encouraging and facilitating learning. For teachers an awareness and integration of this information offers the opportunity for greater power in teaching.

Language is omnipresent in education. It is an immutable aspect of literacy, a treasured gift that many but not all of us share. By understanding and appreciating the role that language plays in learning and literacy and by thinking about the needs of one child at a time, teachers have a greater opportunity to share the gift.

REFERENCES

Adams, A., & Gathercole, S. (1995). Phonological working memory and speech production in preschool children. *Journal of Speech and Hearing Research, 38,* 403–414.

Adams, M. (1990). *Beginning to read: Thinking and learning about print.* Cambridge, MA: The MIT Press.

Adams, M.J., Foorman, B.R., Lundberg, I., & Beeler, T. (1998). *Phonemic awareness in young children: A classroom curriculum.* Baltimore: Paul H. Brookes Publishing Co.

Applebee, A. (1978). *The children's concept of story.* Chicago: University of Chicago Press.

Aram, D., & Hall, N. (1989). Longitudinal follow-up of children with preschool communication disorders. *School Psychology Review, 18,* 487–501.

Bashir, A., & Scavuzzo, A. (1992). Children with language disorders: Natural history and academic success. *Journal of Learning Disabilities, 25,* 53–65.

Bates, E. (1976). Pragmatics and sociolinguistics in child language. In D. Morehead & A. Morehead (Eds.), *Normal and deficient child language* (pp. 411–463). Baltimore: University Park Press.

Bates, E., Camaioni, L., & Volterra, V. (1975). The acquisition of performatives prior to speech. *Merrill-Palmer Quarterly, 21,* 205–226.

Bernthal, J.E., & Bankson, N.W. (1998). *Articulation and phonological disorders* (4th ed.). Boston: Allyn & Bacon.

Bird, J., & Bishop, D. (1992). Perception and awareness of phonemes in phonologically impaired children. *European Journal of Disorders of Communication, 27,* 289–311.

Bird, J., Bishop, D., & Freeman, N. (1995). Phonological awareness and literacy development in children with expressive phonological impairments. *Journal of Speech and Hearing Research, 38,* 446–462.

Bishop, D., & Edmundson, A. (1986). Is otitis media a major cause of specific developmental disorders? *British Journal of Disorders of Communication, 21,* 321–338.

Blachman, B. (1989). Phonological awareness and word recognition: Assessment and intervention. In A.G. Kamhi & H.W. Catts (Eds.), *Reading disabilities: A developmental language perspective* (pp. 138–158). Boston: Little, Brown.

Blachman, B. (1991). Early intervention for children's reading problems: Clinical applications of the research in phonological awareness. *Topics in Language Disorders, 12*(1), 51–65.

Blachman, B.A., Ball, E.W., Black, R., & Tangel, D.M. (2000). *Road to the code: A phonological awareness program for young children.* Baltimore: Paul H. Brookes Publishing Co.

Blachowicz, C., & Fisher, P.J. (2002). *Teaching vocabulary in all classrooms* (2nd ed.). Upper Saddle River, NJ: Pearson Education.

Bloom, L., & Lahey, M. (1978). *Language development and language disorders.* Boston: Allyn & Bacon.

Bos, C., & Filip, D. (1982). Comprehension monitoring skills in learning disabled and average

readers. *Topics in Learning and Learning Disabilities, 2,* 79–85.

Brady, S., & Shankweiler, D. (Eds.). (1991). *Phonological processes in literacy: A tribute to Isabelle Y. Liberman.* Mahwah, NJ: Lawrence Erlbaum Associates.

Brinton, B., & Fujiki, M. (1989). *Conversational management with language impaired children: Pragmatic assessment and intervention.* Rockville, MD: Aspen Publishers.

Brinton, B., Fujiki, M., Loeb, D., & Winkler, E. (1986). Development of conversational repair strategies in response to requests for clarification. *Journal of Speech and Hearing Research, 39,* 75–82.

Britton, J. (1979). Learning to use language in two modes. In N. Smith & M. Franklin (Eds.), *Symbolic functioning in childhood* (pp. 185–198). Mahwah, NJ: Lawrence Erlbaum Associates.

Brown, A. (1982). Learning how to learn from reading. In J. Langer & M. Smith-Burke (Eds.), *Reader meets author: Bridging the gap.* Newark, DE: International Reading Association.

Brown, R. (1973). *A first language: The early stages.* Cambridge, MA: Harvard University Press.

Bunce, B.H. (1993). Language of the classroom. In A. Gerber (Ed.), *Language related learning disabilities: Their nature and treatment* (pp. 135–159). Baltimore: Paul H. Brookes Publishing Co.

Byrne, B. (1981). Deficient syntactic control in poor readers: Is a weak phonetic memory code responsible? *Applied Psycholinguistics, 3,* 201–212.

Carey, A. (1978). The child as word learner. In M. Halle, J. Bresnan, & G. Miller (Eds.), *Linguistic theory and psychological reality* (pp. 264–293). Cambridge, MA: The MIT Press.

Carlisle, J. (1988). Knowledge of derivational morphology in spelling ability in fourth, sixth and eighth graders. *Applied Psycholinguistics, 9,* 247–266.

Carlisle, J. (1995). Morphological awareness and early reading achievement. In L.B. Feldman (Ed.), *Morphological aspects of language processing.* Mahwah, NJ: Lawrence Erlbaum Associates.

Carroll, L. (1960). *Alice's adventures in wonderland and through the looking glass. A Signet Classic.* New York: The New American Library. (Original work published 1865)

Catts, H. (1986). Speech production/phonological deficits in reading disordered children. *Journal of Learning Disabilities, 19,* 504–508.

Catts, H.W. (1989). Phonological processing deficits and reading disabilities. In A.G. Kamhi & H.W. Catts (Eds.), *Reading disabilities: A developmental language perspective* (pp. 101–132). Boston: Little, Brown.

Catts, H. (1993). The relationship between speech and language impairments and reading disabilities. *Journal of Speech and Hearing Research, 36*(5), 948–958.

Catts, H. (1996). Defining dyslexia as a developmental language disorder: An expanded view. *Topics in Language Disorders, 16*(2), 14–25.

Catts, H. (1997). The early identification of language-based reading disabilities. *Language, Speech, and Hearing Services in Schools, 28,* 86–89.

Catts, H.W., Hu, C.-F., Larrivee, L., & Swank, L. (1994). Early identification of reading disabilities in children with speech-language impairments. In S.F. Warren & J. Reichle (Series Eds.) & R.V. Watkins & M.L. Rice (Eds.), *Communication and language intervention series: Vol. 4. Specific language impairment in children* (pp. 145–160). Baltimore: Paul H. Brookes Publishing Co.

Catts, H.W., & Kamhi, A. (1986). The linguistic basis of reading disorders: Implications for the speech-language pathologist. *Language, Speech, and Hearing Services in Schools, 17,* 329–341.

Catts, H.W., & Vartiainen, T. (1997). *Sounds abound.* East Moline, IL: LinguiSystems.

Cazden, C. (1988). *Classroom discourse: The language of teaching and learning.* Portsmouth, NH: Heinemann.

Chall, J. (1983). *Stages of reading development.* New York: McGraw-Hill.

Chaney, C. (1992). Language development, metalinguistic skills, and print awareness in 3 year old children. *Applied Psycholinguistics, 13,* 485–514.

Clark-Klein, S., & Hodson, B. (1995). A phonologically based analysis of misspellings by third graders with disordered-phonology histories. *Journal of Speech and Hearing Research, 38,* 839–849.

Craig, H., Connor, C., & Washington, J. (2003). Early positive predictors of later reading comprehension for African-American students: A preliminary investigation. *Language, Speech, and Hearing Services in the Schools, 34,* 31–43.

Creaghead, N. (1986). Comprehension of meaning in written language. *Topics in Language Disorders, 6*(4), 73–82.

Denckla, M., & Rudel, R. (1976). Rapid "automatized" naming (RAN): Dyslexia differentiated from other learning disabilities. *Neuropsychologia, 14,* 471–479.

Dickinson, D., & McCabe, A. (1991). The acquisition and development of language: A social interactionist account of language and literacy development. In J. Kavanagh (Ed.), *The language continuum: From infancy to literacy.* Timonium, MD: York Press.

Dore, J. (1978). Requestive systems in nursery school conversations: Analysis of talk in its social context. In R. Campbell & P. Smith (Eds.), *Recent advances in the psychology of language: Language development and mother–child interaction* (pp. 271–292). New York: Plenum.

Ehri, L. (1989). Movement into word reading and spelling: How spelling contributes to reading. In J. Mason (Ed.), *Reading and writing connections* (pp. 65–81). Boston: Allyn & Bacon.

Eimas, P., Siqueland, E., Jusczyk, P., & Vigorito, J. (1971). Speech perception in infants. *Science, 171,* 303–306.

Elbro, C., & Arnbak, A. (1996). The role of morpheme recognition and morphological awareness in dyslexia. *Annals of Dyslexia, 46,* 209–240.

Fey, M.E., Catts, H.W., & Larrivee, L.S. (1995). Preparing preschoolers for the academic and social challenges of school. In S.F. Warren & J. Reichle (Series. Eds.) & M.E. Fey, J. Windsor, & S.F. Warren (Vol. Eds.), *Communication and language intervention series: Vol. 5. Language intervention: Preschool through elementary years* (pp. 3–37). Baltimore: Paul H. Brookes Publishing Co.

Fowler, A. (1991). How early phonological development might set the stage for phoneme awareness. In S. Brady & D. Shankweiler (Eds.), *Phonological processes in literacy: A tribute to Isabelle Y. Liberman* (pp. 97–117). Mahwah, NJ: Lawrence Erlbaum Associates.

Fowler, A., & Liberman, I. (1995). Morphological awareness as related to early reading and spelling ability. In L. Feldman (Ed.), *Morphological aspects of language processing* (pp. 157–188). Mahwah, NJ: Lawrence Erlbaum Associates.

Friel-Patti, D., & Finitzo, T. (1990). Language learning in a prospective study of otitis media with effusion in the first two years of age. *Journal of Speech and Hearing Research, 33,* 188–194.

Gerber, A. (1993). *Language-related learning disabilities: Their nature and treatment.* Baltimore: Paul H. Brookes Publishing Co.

German, D. (1982). Word-finding substitution in children with learning disabilities. *Language, Speech, and Hearing Services in Schools, 13,* 223–230.

Gillam, R. (1999). Computer-assisted language intervention using Fast ForWord: Theoretical and empirical considerations for clinical decision making. *Language, Speech, and Hearing Services in the School, 30,* 363–370.

Gottardo, A. (2002). The relationship between language and reading skills in bilingual Spanish-English speakers. *Topics in Language Disorders, 22*(5), 46–70.

Gough, P., & Tunmer, W. (1986). Decoding reading and reading disability. *Remedial and Special Education, 7,* 6–10.

Gravel, J., & Wallace, I. (1992). Listening and language at four years of age: Effects of early otitis media. *Journal of Speech and Hearing Research, 35,* 588–595.

Greene, J. (1996). Psycholinguistic assessment: The clinical base for identification of dyslexia. *Topics in Language Disorders, 16*(2), 45–72.

Halliday, M.A.K. (1975). *Learning how to mean: Explorations in the development of language.* London: Edward Arnold.

Halliday, M.A.K., & Hasan, R. (1976). *Cohesion in English.* London: Longman Group.

Hammer, C., Miccio, A., & Wagstaff, D. (2003). Home literacy experiences and their relationship to bilingual preschoolers' developing English literacy abilities: An initial investigation. *Language, Speech, and Hearing Services in the Schools, 34,* 20–30.

Hart, B., & Risley, T.R. (1999). *The social world of children learning to talk.* Baltimore: Paul H. Brookes Publishing Co.

Hodson, B. (1994). Helping individuals become intelligible, literate and articulate: The role of phonology. *Topics in Language Disorders, 14*(2), 1–16.

Hook, P., Macaruso, P., & Jones, S. (2001). Efficacy of Fast ForWord training on facilitating acquisition of reading skills by children with reading difficulties—A longitudinal study. *Annals of Dyslexia, 51,* 75–96.

Horowitz, R., & Samuels, J. (1987). Comprehending oral and written language: Critical contrasts for literacy and schooling. In R. Horowitz & J. Samuels (Eds.), *Comprehending oral and written language* (pp. 1–52). San Diego: Academic Press.

Hoskins, B. (1983). Semantics. In C. Wren (Ed.), *Language learning disabilities* (pp. 85–111). Rockville, MD: Aspen Publishers.

Hymes, D. (1972). On communicative competence. In J.B. Pride & J. Holmes (Eds.), *Sociolinguistics* (pp. 269–293). London: Penguin Books Ltd.

Kamhi, A.G., & Catts, H.W. (1989). Language and reading: Convergences, divergences and development. In A.G. Kamhi & H.W. Catts (Eds.), *Reading disabilities: A developmental language perspective* (pp. 1–34). Boston: Little, Brown.

Katz, R. (1986). Phonological deficiencies in children with reading disability: Evidence from an object-naming task. *Cognition, 22,* 225–257.

Labov, W. (2003). When ordinary children fail to read. *Reading Research Quarterly, 38,* 128–131.

Lahey, M. (1988). *Language disorders and language development.* New York: John Wiley & Sons.

Lahey, M., & Bloom, L. (1994). Variability and language learning disabilities. In G. Wallach & K. Butler (Eds.), *Language learning disabilities in school-age children and adolescents: Some principles and applications* (pp. 354–372). Boston: Allyn & Bacon.

Laing, S. & Kamhi, A. (2003). Alternative assessment of language and literacy in culturally and linguistically diverse populations. *Language, Speech, and Hearing Services in the Schools, 34,* 44–55.

Larson, V., & McKinley, N. (1995). *Language disorders in older students, preadolescents and adolescents.* Eau Claire, WI: Thinking Publications.

Liberman, I. (1983). A language-oriented view of

reading and its disabilities. In H. Myklebust (Ed.), *Progress in learning disabilities* (Vol. 5, pp. 81–102). New York: Grune & Stratton.

Liberman, I., & Liberman, A. (1990). Whole language vs. code emphasis: Underlying assumptions and their implications for reading instruction. *Annals of Dyslexia, 40,* 51–76.

Liberman, I., Shankweiler, D., Camp, L., Blachman, G., & Werfelman, M. (1990). Steps toward literacy. In P. Levinson & C. Sloan (Eds.), *Auditory processing and language: Clinical and research perspectives* (pp. 189–215). New York: Grune & Stratton.

Linder, T.W. (1999). *Read, play, and learn!: Storybook activities for young children. Teacher's guide.* Baltimore: Paul H. Brookes Publishing Co.

Lous, J., Fiellau-Nikolajsen, M., & Jeppeson, A. (1988). Secretory otitis media and verbal intelligence: A six year prospective case control study. In D. Lim, C. Bluestone, J. Klein, & J. Nelson (Eds.), *Recent advances in otitis media with effusion* (pp. 185–203). Philadelphia: Decker.

Mahoney, D., & Mann, V. (1992). Using children's humor to clarify the relationship between linguistic awareness and early reading ability. *Cognition, 45,* 163–186.

Mandler, J., & Johnson, N. (1977). Remembrance of things parsed: Story structure and recall. *Cognitive Psychology, 9,* 111–151.

Mattingly, I. (1972). Reading, the linguistic process and linguistic awareness. In J. Kavanagh & I. Mattingly (Eds.), *Language by ear and by eye: The relationship between speech and reading* (pp. 133–144). Cambridge, MA: The MIT Press.

McGregor, K. (1994). Use of phonological information in word finding treatment of children. *Journal of Speech and Hearing Research, 37,* 1381–1393.

Menyuk, P., & Chesnick, M. (1997). Metalinguistic skills, oral language knowledge and reading. *Topics in Language Disorders, 17*(3), 75–87.

Merzenich, M., Jenkins, W., Johnston, P., Schreiner, C., Miller, S., & Tallal, P. (1996). Temporal processing deficits of language-learning impaired children ameliorated by training. *Science, 271,* 77–80.

Miller, L. (1990). The roles of language and learning in the development of literacy. *Topics in Language Disorders, 10,* 1–24.

Milosky, L. (1994). Nonliteral language abilities: Seeing the forest for the trees. In G. Wallach & K. Butler (Eds.), *Language learning disabilities in school-aged children and adolescents: Some principles and applications* (pp. 275–303). Boston, MA: Allyn & Bacon.

Moats, L.C. (1994). Honing the concepts of listening and speaking: A prerequisite to the valid measurement of language behavior in children. In G.R. Lyon (Ed.), *Frames of reference for the as-sessment of learning disabilities: New views on measurement issues* (pp. 229–241). Baltimore: Paul H. Brookes Publishing Co.

Moats, L.C. (1995). *Spelling: Development, disability, and instruction.* Timonium, MD: York Press.

Moats, L.C. (2000). *Speech to print: Language essentials for teachers.* Baltimore: Paul H. Brookes Publishing Co.

Moats, L.C., & Lyon, G.R. (1996). Wanted: Teachers with a knowledge of language. *Topics in Language Disorders, 16*(2), 73–86.

Mody, M., Studdert-Kennedy, M., & Brady, A. (1997). Speech perception deficits in poor readers: Auditory processing or phonological coding? *Journal of Experimental Child Psychology, 64,* 199–231.

Montgomery, J. (1996). Sentence comprehension and working memory in children with specific language impairment. *Topics in Language Disorders, 17*(1), 19–32.

Montgomery, J. (2002). Examining the nature of lexical processing in children with specific language impairment: Temporal processing or processing capacity deficit? *Applied Psycholinguistics, 23,* 447–470.

Morice, R., & Slaghuis, W. (1985). Language performance and reading ability at 8 years of age. *Applied Psycholinguistics, 6,* 141–160.

Myers, M., & Paris, S. (1978). Children's metacognitive knowledge about reading. *Journal of Educational Psychology, 70,* 680–690.

Nelson, N.W. (1985). Teacher talk and child listening: Fostering a better match. In C. Simon (Ed.), *Communication skills and classroom success: Assessment of language-learning disabled students* (pp. 65–102). San Diego: College-Hill Press.

Nelson, N.W. (1986). Individualized processing in classroom settings. *Topics in Language Disorders, 6*(2), 13–27.

Nippold, M. (1988). The literate lexicon. In M. Nippold (Ed.), *Later language development: Ages nine through nineteen* (pp. 29–47). San Diego: College-Hill Press.

No Child Left Behind Act of 2001, PL 107-110, 115 Stat. 1425, 20 U.S.C. §§ 6301 *et seq.*

Owens, R. (1996). *Language development: An introduction* (3rd ed.). Columbus, OH: Merrill/Macmillan.

Owings, R., Peterson, G., Bransford, J., Morris, C., & Stein, B. (1980). Spontaneous monitoring and regulation of learning: A comparison of successful and less successful fifth graders. *Journal of Educational Psychology, 72,* 250–256.

Paul, R., & Jennings, P. (1992). Phonological behavior in toddlers with slow expressive language development. *Journal of Speech and Hearing Research, 35,* 99–107.

Perfetti, C., & Lesgold, A. (1977). Discourse comprehension and sources of individual differ-

ences. In M. Just & P. Carpenter (Eds.), *Cognitive processes in comprehension* (pp. 141–184). Mahwah, NJ: Lawrence Erlbaum Associates.

Prather, E., Hedrick, D., & Kern, C. (1975). Articulation development in children aged two to four years. *Journal of Speech and Hearing Disorders, 40,* 179–191.

Prutting, C., & Kirschner, D. (1987). A clinical appraisal of the pragmatic aspects of language. *Journal of Speech and Hearing Disorders, 52,* 105–119.

Rees, N. (1978). Pragmatics of language: Applications to normal and disordered language development. In R. Schiefelbusch (Ed.), *Bases of language intervention* (pp. 191–268). Baltimore: University Park Press.

Roberts, J., Bailey, D., & Nychka, H. (1991). Teachers' use of strategies to facilitate the communication of preschool children with disabilities. *Journal of Early Intervention, 15,* 369–376.

Roberts, J., Burchinal, M., Collier, A., Ramey, C., Koch, M., & Henderson, F. (1989). Otitis media in early childhood and cognitive academic and classroom performance of the school-aged child. *Pediatrics, 83,* 477–485.

Roberts, J., Burchinal, M., Koch, M., Footo, M., & Henderson, F. (1988). Otitis media in early childhood and its relationship to later phonological development. *Journal of Speech and Hearing Disorders, 53,* 416–424.

Roberts, J., & Schuele, M. (1990). Otitis media and later academic performance: The linkage and implications for intervention. *Topics in Language Disorders, 11*(1), 53–62.

Robertson, C., & Salter, W. (1997). *The phonological awareness test.* East Moline, IL: LinguiSystems.

Roth, F. (1986). Oral narratives of learning disabled students. *Topics in Language Disorders, 7*(1), 21–30.

Roth, F., & Spekman, N. (1984). Assessing the pragmatic abilities of children: Part I. Organizational framework and assessment parameters. *Journal of Speech and Hearing Disorders, 49,* 2–11.

Roth, F., & Spekman, N. (1989). Higher order language processes and reading disabilities. In A.G. Kamhi & H.W. Catts (Eds.), *Reading disabilities: A developmental language perspective* (pp. 159–198). Boston: Little, Brown.

Ruben, H., Patterson, P., & Kantor, M. (1991). Morphological development and writing ability in children and adults. *Language, Speech, and Hearing Services in Schools, 22,* 228–235.

Rubin, D. (1987). Divergence and convergence between oral and written communication. *Topics in Language Disorders, 7*(4), 1–18.

Sawyer, D. (1991). Whole language in context: Insights into the great debate. *Topics in Language Disorders, 11*(3), 1–13.

Scarborough, H. (1990). Very early language deficits in dyslexic children. *Child Development, 61,* 1728–1743.

Scott, C. (1988). Spoken and written syntax. In M. Nippold (Ed.), *Later language development: Ages nine through nineteen* (pp. 49–96). San Diego: College-Hill Press.

Scott, C. (1994). A discourse continuum for school-aged students: Impact of modality and genre. In G. Wallach & K. Butler (Eds.), *Language learning disabilities in school aged children and adolescents: Some principles and applications* (pp. 219–252). Boston: Allyn & Bacon.

Silliman, E., & Wilkinson, L. (1994). Observation is more than looking. In G. Wallach & K. Butler (Eds.), *Language learning disabilities in school aged children and adolescents: Some principles and applications* (pp. 145–173). Boston: Allyn & Bacon.

Silva, P., Chalmers, D., & Stewart, I. (1986). Some audiological, psychological, educational and behavioral characteristics of children with bilateral otitis media with effusion: A longitudinal study. *Journal of Learning Disabilities, 19,* 165–169.

Silva, P., Kirkland, C., Simpson, A., Stewart, I., & Williams, S. (1982). Some developmental and behavioral problems associated with bilateral otitis media with effusion. *Journal of Learning Disabilities, 15,* 417–421.

Snow, C., & Dickinson, D. (1991). Skills that aren't basic in a new conception of literacy. In A. Purves & E. Jennings (Eds.), *Literate systems and individual lives: Perspectives on literacy and schooling.* Albany: SUNY Press.

Snowling, M. (1981). Phonemic deficits in developmental dyslexia. *Psychological Research, 43,* 219–234.

Snowling, M., & Nation, K. (1997). Language phonology and learning to read. In M. Snowling & C. Hulme (Eds.), *Dyslexia: Biology, cognition and remediation* (pp. 153–166). San Diego: Singular Publishing Group.

Snyder, L. (1980). Have we prepared the language disordered child for school? *Topics in Language Disorders, 1*(1), 29–45.

Snyder, L., & Downey, D. (1991). The language of reading relationship in normal and reading disabled children. *Journal of Speech and Hearing Research, 34,* 129–140.

Snyder, L., & Downey, D. (1997). Developmental differences in the relationship between oral language deficits and reading. *Topics in Language Disorders, 17*(3), 27–40.

Snyder L., & Godley, D. (1992). Assessment of word finding in children and adolescents. *Topics in Language Disorders, 12*(1), 15–32.

Spear-Swerling, L., & Sternberg, R. (1994). The road not taken: An integrative theoretical model of reading disability. *Journal of Learning Disabilities, 27,* 91–103.

Stackhouse, J., & Wells, B. (1997). How do speech

and language problems affect literacy development? In M. Snowling & C. Hulme (Eds.), *Dyslexia: Biology, cognition and intervention* (pp. 182–211). San Diego: Singular Publishing Group.

Stanovich, K. (1986). Matthew effects in reading: Some consequences of individual differences in the acquisition of literacy. *Reading Research Quarterly, 21,* 360–407.

Stanovich, K. (Ed.). (1987). Introduction: Children's reading and the development of phonological awareness [Special issue]. *Merrill-Palmer Quarterly, 33*(3).

Stein, C., Cairns, H., & Zurif, E. (1984). Sentence comprehension limitation related to syntactic deficits in reading disabled children. *Applied Psychology, 5,* 305–322.

Stein, N., & Glenn, C. (1979). An analysis of story comprehension in elementary school children. In R. Freedle (Ed.), *New directions in discourse processing* (pp. 53–120). Greenwich, CT: Ablex Publishing Corp.

Stoel-Gammon, C. (1991). Normal and disordered phonology in two year olds. *Topics in Language Disorders, 11*(4), 21–32.

Studdert-Kennedy, M. (1998, Winter). Letter to the editor. *Asha,* 7.

Studdert-Kennedy, M., Liberman, A., Brady, S., Fowler, A., Mody, M., & Shankweiler, D. (1994–1995). Lengthened formant transitions are irrelevant to the improvement of speech and language impairments. *Haskins Laboratory Status Report on Speech Research, SR-119/120,* 35–38.

Studdert-Kennedy, M., & Mody, M. (1995). Auditory temporal perception deficits in the reading impaired: A critical review of the evidence. *Psychonomic Bulletin and Review, 2,* 508–514.

Sulzby, E., & Teale, W. (1991). Emergent literacy. In R. Barr, M. Kamil, P. Mosenthal, & P.D. Pearson (Eds.), *Handbook of reading research* (Vol. II, pp. 727–757). New York: Longman.

Swank, L. (1997). Linguistic influences in the emergence of written word decoding in first grade. *American Journal of Speech-Language Pathology, 6*(4), 62–66.

Tallal, P. & Merzenich, M. (1997, November). *Temporal training for language-impaired children: National clinical trial results.* Paper presented to the annual convention of the American Speech-Language-Hearing Association, Boston.

Tallal, P., Miller, S., Bedi, G., Byma, G., Wang, X., Nagarajan, S., et al. (1996). Language comprehension in language-learning impaired children improves with acoustically modified speech. *Science, 271,* 81–84.

Van Kleeck, A. (1990). Emergent literacy: Learning about print before learning to read. *Topics in Language Disorders, 10*(2), 25–45.

Vellutino, F. (1979). *Dyslexia: Theory and research.* Cambridge, MA: The MIT Press.

Vellutino, F., Scanlon, D., & Spearing, D. (1995). Semantic and phonological coding in poor and normal readers. *Journal of Experimental Child Psychology, 59,* 76–123.

Wagner, R., & Torgesen, J. (1987). The nature of phonological processing and its causal roles in the equation of reading skills. *Psychological Bulletin, 101,* 192–212.

Wallace, I., Gravel, J., McCarton, C., & Ruben, R. (1988). Otitis media and language development at 1 year of age. *Journal of Speech and Hearing Disorders, 53,* 245–251.

Wallach, G. (1990). Magic buries Celtics: Looking for broader interpretations of language learning in literacy. *Topics in Language Disorders, 10*(2), 63–80.

Wallach, G., & Butler, K. (1994). Creating communication, literacy and academic success. In G. Wallach & K. Butler (Eds.), *Language learning disabilities in school-age children and adolescents: Some principals and applications* (pp. 2–26). Boston: Allyn & Bacon.

Wallach, G., & Miller, L. (1988).*Language intervention and academic success.* Boston: Little, Brown.

Webster, P., & Plante, A. (1992). Effects of phonological impairment on word, syllable and phoneme segmentation and reading. *Language, Speech, and Hearing Services in Schools, 23,* 176–182.

Westby, C. (1985). Learning to talk—talking to learn: Oral literate language differences. In C. Simon (Ed.), *Communication skills and classroom success: Therapy methodologies for language learning disabled students* (pp. 181–213). San Diego: College-Hill Press.

Westby, C. (1989). Assessing and remediating text comprehension problems. In A.G. Kamhi & H.W. Catts (Eds.), *Reading disabilities: A developmental language perspective* (pp. 199–260). Boston: Little, Brown.

Westby, C. (1995). Culture and literacy: Frameworks for understanding. *Topics in Language Disorders, 16*(1), 50–66.

White, T., Power, M., & White, S. (1989). Morphological analysis: Implications for teaching and understanding of vocabulary growth. *Reading Research Quarterly, 24,* 283–304.

Wiig, E., & Semel, E. (1980). *Language assessment and intervention for the learning disabled.* Columbus, OH: Charles E. Merrill.

Wiig, E., Semel, E., & Nystrom, L. (1982). Comparison of rapid naming abilities in language learning disabled and academically achieving eight year olds. *Language, Speech, and Hearing Services in Schools, 12,* 11–23.

Wolf, M., & Dickinson, D. (1993). From oral to written language: Transitions in the school years. In J. Gleason (Ed.), *The development of language.* Columbus, OH: Charles E. Merrill.

4

Phonemic Awareness and Reading

Research, Activities, and Instructional Materials

Joanna K. Uhry

I n the definition of dyslexia used by The International Dyslexia Association (IDA) and the National Institute of Child Health and Human Development (NICHD), the reading and spelling difficulties of dyslexia are said to "typically result from a deficit in the phonological component of language" (Lyon, Shaywitz, & Shaywitz, 2003, p. 2). That is, deficits in **phonemic awareness** and in other forms of phonological processing are the characteristic early markers of dyslexia. Neurological research using functional magnetic resonance imaging (fMRI) confirms this model of dyslexia. Yale pediatric neurologist Sally Shaywitz stated, "The pattern of underactivation in the back of the brain provides a neural signature for the phonologic difficulties characterizing dyslexia" (2003, p. 82). These difficulties, apparent to trained early childhood classroom teachers through listening attentively to children's oral language, can now be viewed in particular locations in the brain. Studies by Shaywitz and others indicate that children with weak phonemic processing skills compensate by using a part of the brain that is not used by typically developing readers and that is not very efficient for reading (for a discussion, see Shaywitz & Shaywitz, 2004). Furthermore, reading instruction that focuses on phonemic awareness and phonics can actually change the way the brain functions as these children's reading improves.

Phonemic awareness is a crucial factor in predicting how easily young children will acquire reading. Furthermore, phonemic awareness can be taught. When children receive instruction in phonemic awareness around the time they learn to read, their reading tends to be more skillful than that of children without this instruction. Children with dyslexia tend to be very poor at phonemic awareness and other forms of phonological processing. Direct instruction in phonological processing strategies is particularly beneficial to them. This chapter describes a model for the link between phonemic awareness and reading, reviews research suggesting the benefits of phonemic awareness instruction, and then describes instructional models and programs that may be

useful to all children but that are critical to reading success for children who are at risk for reading failure.

PHONEMIC AWARENESS AS A FORM OF PHONOLOGICAL PROCESSING

The term **phonological processing** is a general term for several oral language processing abilities that are related to the sounds in words and are associated with the ability to read well. A diagram of the relationships among these terms is presented in Figure 4.1. One of the four subcategories of phonological processing, phonological awareness, is directly related to beginning reading and is described here in more detail. The other three processes (verbal short-term memory, **rapid serial naming**, and articulation speed) are discussed in a later section on other phonological processing deficits.

Phonological awareness is the ability to focus on units of sound in spoken language. It includes awareness of the sounds of words (rather than the meaning) in sentences, awareness of syllables in words, and awareness of **phonemes**—or individual sounds—in short words or syllables. During the early reading process, this last ability, phonemic awareness, is the most critical of all the phonological processing components. Because phonemic awareness is the most important of the phonological awareness abilities, I use the term *phonemic awareness* throughout, rather than the more inclusive term, *phonological awareness*. Keith E. Stanovich defined phonemic awareness as "conscious access to the phonemic level of the speech stream and some ability to cognitively manipulate representations at this level" (1986, p. 362). This complex and sophisticated ability involves deep understanding of the phoneme and is necessary for the acquisition of reading.

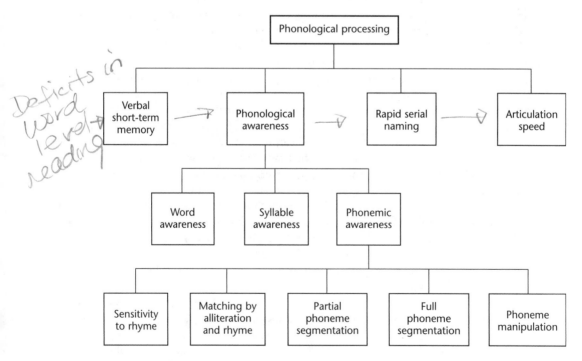

Figure 4.1. Relationships among phonological processing components.

Phonemes and Phonemic Awareness

A phoneme is the smallest unit of sound that can change the meaning of a word. Note that it is the initial phoneme that differentiates the spoken words "hug" and "bug." Toddlers can tell the difference between the spoken forms of "Give me a hug" and "Give me a bug." They can hear this fine distinction in sounds and can correctly interpret the meaning of either sentence. But by the time they are ready to read, they should be able to do more than hear differences that affect meaning. They should know that "hug" starts with the sound /h/ and "bug" starts with /b/. They should know that /h/ or /b/ comes at the beginning of the words and that the middle and end of both words are the same. These are crucial understandings for anyone engaged in learning how spoken words map onto print. In other words, children need to know more about oral language (i.e., phonemic awareness) in order to learn to read and write than they need to know in order to learn to talk and to listen (Liberman & Liberman, 1990). Keep in mind that Stanovich's definition of phonemic awareness uses the words "conscious access to the speech stream" (1986, p. 362). Strong beginning readers can segment, identify, locate, and sequence the phonemes that make the key difference in that access.

PHONEMIC AWARENESS AND BEGINNING READING

Phonemic awareness is only one of the skills necessary for beginning reading. English is an alphabetic language, meaning that **graphemes** (i.e., letters) represent phonemes. In addition, English is a complex language drawn from a number of other languages, with 26 letters, either alone or in combination, representing approximately 44 phonemes. Because there is more than one way to spell some of these phonemes and more than one way to pronounce some of these letters, there are roughly 98 different phoneme–grapheme associations that children need to learn in order to learn to read and spell in English (Cox, 1992). For example, in reading, the letter *o* has one sound at the beginning of the word *on* and another at the beginning of the word *onion*. And, in spelling, the words *bake* and *straight* provide two ways to spell the long /ā/ sound.

Phonics

The term *phonics* refers to knowledge of these combinations of graphemes and phonemes. For example, in phonics instruction, children learn that the letter *b* is sounded as the phoneme /b/ and the letters *ph* are sounded as the phoneme /f/. Some children acquire this knowledge intuitively, simply by noticing print while listening to stories read aloud or noticing ways in which words are alike and different while learning to read. Some children, however, do not acquire this knowledge on their own and need carefully sequenced, systematic direct instruction.

The Alphabetic Principle

The **alphabetic principle** is also critical to beginning reading. To be able to utilize phonemic awareness and phonics knowledge, children need additional understanding; they need to know how phonemes map onto letters in words. The term *alphabetic principle* refers to an understanding that letters represent sounds. It also implies an understanding that letters are ordered in a visual sequence in written words, that phonemes are ordered in a specific temporal sequence in speech, and that speech maps onto print.

Development of Phonemic Awareness

Knowledge of how to isolate, combine, and manipulate phonemes is critical to understanding the relationship between speech and print. That is, beginning readers need phonemic awareness, or awareness of phonemes in speech; they need phonics knowledge, or knowledge of the letters that are used to represent each of the 44 phonemes in English; and they need to know how sounds in speech relate to the letters on a printed page.

Phonemic awareness is a precursor to reading and begins to develop during the preschool years. Adams (1990) described phonemic awareness as progressing hierarchically through five levels of difficulty, outlined as follows.

An Ear for Rhymes

The first level in the development of phonemic awareness involves a sensitivity to rhyme. British researchers Maclean, Bryant, and Bradley (1987) followed preschoolers from age 3, when differences were found in children's ability to memorize nursery rhymes, through school age, when earlier ability with rhymes was found to be correlated with later reading ability. Children who can hear rhymes can intuitively recognize that part of the word, the initial phoneme, before the vowel, often called the **onset** by researchers, is exchanged for another phoneme in rhyming words. The word **rime** is a linguistic term for the spoken or written vowel and the final consonant(s) (if any) in a word. Even though 3-year-olds cannot consciously segment the initial phoneme, they are acquiring what Adams called "an ear" for this structure (1990, p. 80). This ability typically develops well before letters are taught. Teachers wishing to draw attention to letters at this stage need to be careful to use words that are look-alike rhymes (e.g., *mean* and *bean* but not *weigh* and *say*). Many rhyming picture books are not sensitive to this point. Keeping this in mind, the use of rhyming books is an ideal way to introduce phonemic awareness to classes or small groups of young children. Just listening to the rhymes can sensitize the ear, and more advanced children in a group can actually provide the rhyme if the teacher pauses as she or he comes to the end of the line.

Matching Words by Rhyme and Alliteration

The second level of phonemic awareness involves being able to match spoken words by either alliteration (i.e., similar onsets) or by rhyme. This can be assessed through use of a research task designed by Bradley and Bryant (1983) called the **oddity** or **odd-man-out task**. For example, with alliteration as the focus, a child is asked to listen to the words *ball, bat, tub,* and *bird* and to identify the odd man out (*tub*). Although adults process this task by looking at or conceptualizing letters, this is an auditory task for pre-readers. Again, teachers can use this task to introduce letters. The concept of the sound /b/ is developed through students listening and is then labeled with the letter *b*. Shoeboxes of objects sorted by initial phoneme and labeled with the initial letter can be used in classroom centers for play with sounds.

Partial Phoneme Segmentation

Adams (1990) described the third level of phonemic awareness tasks as syllable splitting. At this point, phonemes are not merely intuited but are consciously segmented from spoken words. The most common first attempts at segmenting involve the initial

phoneme or onset. Researchers have evidence that syllables break apart most easily at what is called the onset–rime division, with the initial phoneme being separated from the middle vowel and ending consonant(s) (if any) (Treiman, 1985). That is, it is easier to segment *map* into /m/-/ap/ than into /ma/-/p/. Kindergarten children are exhibiting this level of phonemic awareness when they segment initial phonemes and represent them with letters in **invented spellings**. For example, kindergarten children tend to spell *picking* as P and *dress* as J, the closest letter-name sounds to the onsets in these two words (Morris & Perney, 1984). Teaching children to listen to sounds for spelling can actually increase reading ability (Uhry 1993b; Uhry & Shepherd, 1993).

Segmenting is difficult because of a phenomenon known as coarticulation. Vowel sounds can exist on their own as short words or syllables (e.g., *oh, a, I*), but consonant sounds are always coarticulated with vowels. For example, when the sound of the letter *b* is said alone, it is hard to pronounce it without a following vowel (e.g., as "buh" or "bah"). What we conceptualize as the /b/ sound is really a series of /b/-like consonant sounds, each a little different depending on the vowel it accompanies. That is, the /b/ in *bake* is not quite the same as the /b/ in *bike*.

Perhaps because of the coarticulation phenomenon, the **medial** sounds in words are particularly hard for young children to segment. Medial vowels are coarticulated with both the initial and final consonants. For example, the short vowel sound in *mop* is coarticulated with initial /m/ and final /p/, making it hard to segment. Kindergarten children tend to segment this word as /m/-/p/ or as /m/-/ŏp/, leaving out the vowel or leaving it attached to the final consonant. Although medial vowels are especially difficult to segment in words with a **consonant-vowel-consonant** (CVC) structure, they are considerably easier to segment in short words beginning with vowels, such as *age* and *up* (Uhry & Ehri, 1999).

Adams (1990) included blending as a task at this level. Note that many children can blend spoken phonemes into words (e.g., blending /s/-/ă/-/m/ into "Sam") while still being unable to segment more than an initial phoneme.

Full Phoneme Segmentation

Not until around age 6, or the beginning of formal reading instruction, are children usually able to perform Adams's (1990) fourth level of phonemic awareness, in which all phonemes can be segmented (e.g., the spoken word *map* segmented as the sounds /m/-/a/-/p/). At this point a child is ready to understand and make use of the alphabetic principle to figure out how to read unfamiliar words on his or her own.

Manipulation of Phonemes

At the fifth and most complex of Adams's levels, children are able to delete or exchange phonemes; they can say the word *seat* without the /s/ sound as "eat," and they can reverse the sounds in *cat* to say "tack." Children who cannot carry out these phoneme manipulation activities as easily as age-peers are much more apt to have difficulty in reading and writing than those who can. This level is rarely reached in nonreaders.

Summary of Phonemic Awareness Development   At each of these levels of phonemic awareness, there is a wide range of differences in children's abilities. Although variation in performance is expected, children at the low end of the scale do not tend to catch up to peers if left on their own. They continue to have difficulty with both phonemic awareness and the alphabetic principle unless provided with direct instruction.

DYSLEXIA

Adams (1994) estimated that roughly 25% of beginning readers fail to grasp the alphabetic principle without direct instruction in phonics and phonological awareness. The percentage is even higher for poor children. Results of a longitudinal study that has now followed kindergarten children for over 20 years indicate that about 20% of all elementary-age children eventually develop symptoms of dyslexia, or word-level reading disability (Shaywitz, Fletcher, & Shaywitz, 1996). As stated earlier, dyslexia is associated with deficits in "the phonological component of language" (Lyon, Shaywitz, & Shaywitz, 2003, p. 1). The following four deficits in phonological processing are associated with deficits in word-level reading: 1) phonemic awareness, 2) rapid serial naming, 3) verbal short-term memory, and 4) speed of articulation.

Phonemic Awareness Deficits and Dyslexia

Children with dyslexia, or word-level reading disorder, typically memorize individual words but have difficulty generalizing from one word to another because of deficits in phonemic awareness. For example, knowing how to read the word *cat* does not generalize to knowing how to figure out sounds for *c* in *cup* or *a* in *map* or *t* in *nut*. See Chapter 1 or Clark and Uhry (1995) for a detailed description of readers with dyslexia. These children struggle with unfamiliar words, a characteristic that is often assessed through asking them to read phonetically regular nonwords. Children with dyslexia continue to be poorer at reading nonwords than real words relative to proficient readers (Rack, Snowling, & Olson, 1992). Research (DeFries et al., 1997) focused on reading disability and funded by the NICHD indicated that nonword reading disability is associated with a deficit in phonemic awareness. This deficit runs in families and is believed to be inherited through a specific gene. The deficit persists into adulthood for many people with dyslexia (Felton & Wood, 1989), even for those who have received remedial instruction.

Other Phonological Processing Deficits and Dyslexia

Phonological awareness, and more specifically, phonemic awareness, is only one of several forms of phonological processing related to reading and to dyslexia (see Figure 4.1). There are three other forms of phonological processing deficits, of which all relate to dyslexia. Wagner and Torgesen (1987) and Catts (1986) provided overviews of research on the relationship between reading and these other phonological processing deficits.

Rapid Serial Naming

Wagner and Torgesen's (1987) term for one of these processes, *phonological recoding in lexical access,* refers to the process of moving from one code to another, and in the case of reading, moving from letter symbols to a phonological code in terms of accessing or retrieving names for letters or words. This process can be measured in prereaders by asking them to name, as quickly as possible, a series of printed color swatches or pictured objects repeated over and over in random order in a matrix. Denckla and Rudel (1974) used colors, pictured objects, numbers, and letters in their Rapid Automatized Naming Test to demonstrate that children with dyslexia are much slower at continuous, serial naming than children with typically developing reading are. Children who are poor at naming on this test tend to be poor at word reading. Once they learn to read, they read slowly. See Wolf (1991) for a detailed description of this deficit and its effects. The com-

bination of phonemic awareness and rapid serial naming deficits is often called the **double deficit**. Uhry (1997) found that 9-year-old children with poor phonemic awareness made slower progress in reading after 2 years of phonemic awareness training if they were also slow at rapid serial naming in comparison with children who were poor at phonemic awareness alone. Wood and Felton (1994) found that adults with a childhood history of dyslexia often read accurately following remediation, but those who had had rapid serial naming difficulties as children continued to read quite slowly.

Verbal Short-Term Memory

Another phonological processing deficit, *phonetic recoding to maintain information in working memory* (Wagner & Torgesen, 1987), involves verbal short-term memory. The explanation of this reading disorder draws on information processing theory, a cognitive model in which there is a limited amount of storage space for holding on to verbal information long enough to carry out an operation using it. Storage involves use of phonological features. Young readers with this type of phonological processing difficulty can recode letters to sounds but have difficulty remembering the sounds long enough to blend them into words. Older readers can learn to decode words but have difficulty remembering them long enough to put them together in sentences and to extract meaning.

Articulation Speed

Catts (1986, 1989, 1993) described a fourth phonological processing deficit involving speech articulation. Some children with dyslexia scramble speech sounds (e.g., saying "aminal" for *animal*) and produce complex phonological sequences more slowly than children with typically developing reading. One task for measuring articulation speed involves repeating the nonsense syllables "pa-ta-ka" as quickly as possible (Wolff, Michel, & Ovrut, 1990). It may be that slow articulation rate interferes with ability to maintain phonological models in verbal short-term memory.

Summary of Phonological Processing Deficits

All four of the phonological processing deficits just discussed are associated with dyslexia, both in the research literature and in clinical findings with individual children. Phonemic awareness, however, is the only one for which there is a large body of research literature suggesting that treatment is effective. Because there is such strong evidence that symptoms of the phonemic awareness deficit can be remediated (discussed later in this chapter), it is critical to identify children with this deficit as early as possible.

Phonemic Awareness as a Predictor of Dyslexia

Researchers have demonstrated strong correlations between phonemic awareness tasks and later reading. Liberman, Shankweiler, Fischer, and Carter (1974) measured phonemic awareness with a phoneme tapping task in which a child was expected to tap once for each syllable (e.g., *elephant* has three taps) or for each phoneme in a word (e.g., *sat* has three taps). Bradley and Bryant (1983) used an initial phoneme oddity task, and Elkonin (1963, 1973) used tiles to represent phonemes. In these studies and in a number of others using phonemic awareness tasks with prereaders, children who were weak on the phonological tasks turned out to be weak readers later on and children who were

good at them turned out to be good readers. These researchers have demonstrated a strong association between phonemic awareness and reading. How important is phonemic awareness compared with other predictors of reading?

General Development

Since the 1950s researchers have investigated factors such as the age of a child relative to others in his or her class, general motor development as well as eye–hand coordination, and cognitive development as measured by IQ. Reading was considered to be related to a spectrum of developmental competencies. These competencies did predict how well a child would do in school in general but were not very good predictors of reading. Although children with overall slow development (i.e., mental retardation) are usually poor readers, not all poor readers are slow to develop in other ways. At the early stages of reading, in which word-level reading is so crucial, cognitive predictors can be particularly misleading. That is, some very bright children have inordinate difficulty with word reading.

Language Development

Current definitions of literacy focus on the relationships between oral language and written language, and it makes sense that aspects of oral language would be good predictors of written language. Children with language disorders often have difficulty learning to read. Not all children with reading difficulty, however, demonstrate early symptoms of language disorder. Just as children with dyslexia do not have overall slow development, they do not have grossly deficient skills in speaking and listening. Their language deficits are subtle and are often not evident until they have trouble with early reading. Catts (1989, 1993), a specialist in language disorders, refers to dyslexia as an oral language deficit, but one that is specific to phonemic awareness rather than to more global language skills.

Jansky and de Hirsch carried out seminal research in the 1960s in which the **reading precursor** field focused more and more on language. Their Screening Index (de Hirsch, Langford, & Jansky, 1966) was developed through a carefully researched narrowing-down process that started with 50 factors, including many of those general developmental characteristics mentioned previously. Their list of factors was narrowed to a screening with five assessment tasks, two of which are visual recognition or visual-motor tasks and three of which are language related: ability to retrieve names of 1) letters and 2) objects in response to visual stimuli and 3) ability to repeat back sentences from memory. Jansky and her colleagues reported that it was the balance between these five factors that accounted for reading difficulty; not all five factors needed to be areas of strength for a child so long as his or her total score was reasonably high. Together, these five tasks were quite accurate at predicting successful readers but not so accurate at predicting poor readers. Keep in mind that this screening did not include a measure of phonemic awareness.

Phonemic Awareness

Phonemic awareness turns out to be the single best predictor of risk for early reading failure. Researchers since the 1980s have found consistent and compelling experimental evidence of the importance of phonemic awareness in predicting reading. For example, Share, Jorm, Maclean, and Matthews (1984) tested 543 Australian children in

kindergarten and again in first grade using 39 measures (e.g., teacher predictions, letter copying, syntax comprehension, extent of parent–child reading, hours of television watched, IQ, preschool attendance). Measures of word reading, spelling, and reading comprehension were administered at the end of first grade, and a reading composite score was developed. The two factors with the highest correlations with this composite were phoneme segmentation ($r = .62$) and letter naming ($r = .58$). The statistical procedure **multiple regression analysis** was then used to see if these measures overlapped at all in their contribution or if they made unique contributions. That is, were the measures examining two manifestations of the same underlying factor or two different factors? Again, phoneme segmentation made the largest unique contribution, far surpassing all other predictors. Screening batteries using a variety of phonological and phonemic awareness tasks as well as letter identification tasks are consistently and strongly correlated with later reading. Screenings incorporating phonemic awareness tasks are quite accurate at identifying those children who are at greatest risk of struggling with first-grade reading.

Assessment of Phonological Processing Abilities

The following information on assessment of phonological processing is organized into three subsections, the first on tests that are formal, complex, and best administered by a specialist in assessment. The second subsection consists of short assessments that can be administered by classroom teachers or that can be assembled into a battery by a specialist. The third subsection outlines observations of phonological processing that can be made as children are engaged in authentic classroom activities. It is suggested that multiple sources of data be used in making decisions about both a child's phonological processing status and a possible intervention plan.

Formal Screening

One of the newest, most comprehensive, and best normed of the phonological processing tests is Wagner, Torgesen, and Rashotte's Comprehensive Test of Phonological Processing (CTOPP; 1999). It is based on phonological processing research, much of it carried out by the test authors and published in peer-reviewed journals, and it was normed on 1,656 individuals. It is widely used for both research and educational decision making. The subtests cover the elements of phonological processing described earlier in this chapter. The CTOPP is individually administered and has separate forms for different ages. The version for ages 5–6 has the following seven subtests: 1) Elision,[1] 2) Rapid Color Naming, 3) Blending Words, 4) Sound Matching, 5) Rapid Object Naming, 6) Memory for Digits, and 7) Nonword Repetition, as well as a supplemental subtest, Blending Nonwords. The version normed for ages 7–24 has six subtests: 1) Elision, 2) Blending Words, 3) Memory for Digits, 4) Rapid Digit Naming, 5) Nonword Repetition, and 6) Rapid Letter Naming. It also has norms for using certain subtests in the age 5–6 version with older individuals (i.e., Color and Object Naming, Blending Nonwords) as well as supplemental phonemic awareness subtests: Phoneme Reversal, Segmenting Words, and Segmenting Nonwords. It comes with a well-organized examiner's manual and with an audiotape for administering subtests in which phonemes need to

---

[1]The term *elision* means that a part is taken away. The word *deletion* is also used for this task. A word is said aloud by the examiner, the child repeats it, the examiner says to say it again but to leave out a part (e.g., say *picnic* without the *pic*; say *meat* without the /m/; say *clap* without the /k/).

be pronounced precisely. Standard scores are provided for each subtest and for three composite scores that combine sets of subtests: Phonological Awareness, Phonological Memory, and Rapid Naming. According to the manual, examiners should be highly trained (e.g., educational or psychological evaluators) and familiar with the statistical properties of tests.

The Lindamood-Bell Auditory Conceptualization Test–Third Edition (LAC-3; Lindamood & Lindamood, 2004) focuses on phonemic awareness. The examiner asks children to use small wooden cubes to represent sounds in a sequence. For example, the phoneme sequence /d/-/d/-/j/ could be represented by red-red-blue. Next, sounds are analyzed in nonwords (e.g., yellow-blue-red could represent the nonword *vop*). Performance criteria are provided for levels from kindergarten through adult readers. This latest revision includes more phonemes per syllable and more multisyllabic nonwords in comparison with earlier editions.

The Diagnostic Evaluation of Language Variation (DELV; Seymour, Roeper, & de Villiers, 2003a, 2003b) can be used with all 4- to 8-year-olds, but because it was designed to eliminate bias in testing, it is particularly appropriate for young African American children. It identifies both language dialect and language disorder so that speaking a dialect does not place children at risk for being misdiagnosed with a language disorder or for having a language disorder overlooked. The DELV–Criterion Referenced can be used for diagnosis, and a 15- to 20-minute screener (DELV–Screening Test; Seymour, Roeper, & de Villiers, 2003b) is available. The screener has two sections, Language Variation Status and Diagnostic Risk Status. In combination, these sections identify children who would benefit from the 45- to 50-minute criterion-referenced diagnostic assessment. Both the short and long versions include useful information on phonological processing as well as on other aspects of oral language.

The Early Reading Screening (ERS; Uhry, 1993a) includes a subtest with early literacy tasks such as **finger-point reading** and ability to read words found in the children's own kindergarten classrooms (e.g., job chart words, classmates' names) as well as a subtest with phonemic awareness tasks (e.g., matching by rhyme and alliteration, segmenting and blending phonemes). Correlations of the ERS in kindergarten with first-grade reading comprehension scores were .69 for middle SES children (Uhry, 1993a) and .75 for low SES children (Uhry, 1994). This test is individualized for particular classrooms or schools.

Classroom Assessments for Teachers

Rosner's Test of Auditory Analysis Skills (TAAS; 1975), which is called the Phonological Awareness Skills Program Test in its latest longer version (Rosner, 1999), is a set of deletion (i.e., elision), substitution, and analogy tasks. Tasks are progressively more difficult, moving from the deletion of syllables and initial consonants to deletion of interior consonants in initial clusters in such as *stale* and *smack* and substitution of the /ŭ/ sound for /ă/ in *crash* to make *crush*. The test ends with analogy items, such as "*Dim* is to *dip* as *rim* is to ____." It is short, fairly easy to administer, and provides age norms from age 5–10½. In my research I have used it in kindergarten and early first grade and have found it to correlate well with later word-level reading. The only difficult aspect of administering the test is making certain that one pronounces the phonemes correctly. The examiner should be careful not to add vowel sounds to consonants, some of which are very difficult to say in isolation. Say /m/ not /muh/. Unvoiced consonants such as /t/ are particularly difficult to say in isolation. Be sure the child is looking at your mouth as you say each phoneme.

The Roswell-Chall Auditory Blending Test (1963) involves saying parts of words aloud and asking the child to blend them into words. The test moves from the early first-grade level, in which the child blends two-phoneme words (e.g., *a-t, s-ay*), to blending onsets and rimes (e.g., *f-at, ch-ain*) and **blending** three sound segments (e.g., *c-a-t, t-oa-st*). The scoring system is easy to use but different from other tests in terms or interpretation. Whereas Rosner's test (1975, 1999) can show whether a child's phonemic awareness is similar to that of other first graders (i.e., typical of Grade 1 skills), the Roswell-Chall test shows whether a child's blending ability is strong enough to benefit from Grade 1 reading instruction. This 40-year old test still holds up well in terms of being both reliable and useful (Chall, Roswell, & Blumenthal, 1963; Roswell & Chall, 1963).

Morris's Developmental Spelling Test (Morris, 1999) provides a list of spelling words to dictate, as well as a developmental scoring system. Rather than use the usual spelling test scoring (either right or wrong), this system gives progressively higher scores for increments of spelling development as children move from using invented spellings using random strings of letters, to single initial letters to represent words, to unconventional vowel spellings, to orthographically conventional spellings. Morris's test works well as a quick screen for an entire kindergarten or early Grade 1 class. Invented spelling has been shown to be an excellent predictor of later reading skills (e.g., Morris & Perney, 1984). It is also a wonderful tool to use in planning instruction. For example, children spelling *back* as *BK* and *feet* as *FT* benefit from instruction focusing on the segmentation of medial vowels before instruction in vowel letter–sound associations.

The Dynamic Indicators of Basic Early Literacy Skills (DIBELS; Good & Kaminsky, 2002; Kaminski & Good, 1996) consists of a series of 1-minute measures of early reading fluency. Two of the subtests assess phonemic awareness. The Initial Sounds Fluency subtest asks children to point to the picture beginning with a designated sound or to tell the sound with which a designated picture begins. The Phoneme Segmentation Fluency subtest asks children to say phonemic segments in words such as *bad* and *beach*. Scores for both subtests are the number of items successfully completed in a minute. DIBELS is designed for multiple administrations during the kindergarten and Grade 1 school years, both to identify instructional needs and to track progress. It is short enough to be feasible as an ongoing classroom assessment.

Classroom Observations of Phonemic Awareness Indicators

Even before a classroom test or a more formal screening is administered, teachers often are able to spot weaknesses in phonemic awareness in preschool and kindergarten children if they are aware of possible indicators. Many of the research tasks mentioned previously can be observed in a natural classroom setting. Three-year-old children who have difficulty learning rhymes or rhyming songs may be at risk for reading difficulty. Four- and five-year-old children should be able to generate rhymes and to match classmates' names by initial sounds (e.g., Jim/Jasmine). During kindergarten children should be able to guess the word rhyming with the word containing the manipulated phoneme in playful songs such as "Willoughby Wallaby Wadeline, the elephant sat on . . . (Madeline)."

One of the best classroom-based indicators of at-risk status is inability to invent spellings for words during kindergarten or early first grade. This activity requires segmenting sounds but also requires matching the sound with a letter to represent it. Invented spelling is popular in whole language classrooms because it is advantageous to the creative writing process; children are encouraged to think about meaning as they write. However, there is a second advantage. Invented spellings to reflect a child's level

of phonemic awareness. Morris and Perney (1984) found significant correlations be-tween developmental invented spelling scores in September and reading scores in May of first grade. Invented spelling was found to be significantly correlated with word read-ing ($r = .68$) and with reading comprehension scores ($r = .61$) from the Metropolitan Achievement Tests. Although only about 9% of the spelling words were spelled con-ventionally in September, Morris and Perney used a developmental scoring system in which spellings were credited based on the degree to which they reflected the sound structure of the spoken word. For example, in the word *dress,* the spelling *J* received 1 point, *JS* 2 points, *JAS* 3 points, and *DRES* 4 points, although none provided the con-ventional spelling. Each of these scores represents a level in the development of spelling skills, ranging from *prephonetic* (i.e., not yet using all sounds) to *transitional* (i.e., near-ing conventional spelling). These spellings reflect the degree to which phonemic awareness is developed in a particular child.

Another classroom-based activity that is revealing in terms of phonemic awareness is a form of pretend reading called finger-point reading (Ehri & Sweet, 1991; Morris, 1983, 1993; Morris, Bloodgood, Lomax, & Perney, 2003; Uhry, 1999, 2002). Following shared readings by a teacher, children pretend to read by approximating familiar sto-ries or reciting memorized text. Those who are strong in phonemic segmentation can identify initial phonemes in the text they are reciting and match it with initial letters in printed words as they follow along, pointing from word to word. There is a strong research base for the role of phonemic awareness in success in matching voice with print. In a longitudinal study, Morris et al. (2003) found that partial phonemic aware-ness (ability to segment onsets) facilitated finger-point reading, which in turn facili-tated full phoneme segmentation and, later, word reading.

Classroom teachers can use invented spellings and finger-point reading to identify children who are at risk for later reading difficulties. Teachers can also use these indi-cators as diagnostic tools in establishing a starting point for providing more direct in-struction for children who appear weak in these areas. Systematic instruction in letter–sound associations and in segmenting provides effective boosts to both early spelling and early reading.

RESEARCH ON PHONEMIC AWARENESS INSTRUCTION

Important Early Studies

Three early sets of European studies (i.e., Bradley & Bryant, 1983, 1985; Elkonin, 1963, 1973; Lundberg, Frost, & Petersen, 1988) are often cited as seminal evidence of the ef-fectiveness of phonemic awareness training. In Denmark, Lundberg and his colleagues taught teachers to use games and songs with whole classrooms of preschoolers, 235 children in all, in order to increase their phonemic awareness before reading instruc-tion. An English-language version of this program (Adams, Foorman, Lundberg, & Beeler, 1998) is described in detail in the final section of this chapter. Bradley and Bryant used highly directed individual instruction in sorting words by rhyme and al-literation to teach phonemic awareness to at-risk British 4- and 5-year-olds, the lowest performing children in their longitudinal prediction study mentioned earlier. In both cases the children who had received training outperformed controls who had not in phonemic awareness at the end of the training period. They also outperformed them later on, in print-based tasks, long after the experimental training had been discontin-ued (Bradley & Bryant, 1985).

Lundberg et al.'s (1988) study is often used to make the point that phonemic awareness precedes and is causal to reading, as no experiences with print were offered during Lundberg's preschool training. However, Bradley and Bryant (1983) included two phonemic awareness training conditions, one with and the other without the use of letters. The training with letters had the most dramatic effect on later reading and spelling, indicating that whereas phonemic awareness may be a necessary precursor to reading, the use of letters increases the effectiveness of training and that the relationship between the two is reciprocal rather than unidirectional. Some researchers make the point that children may be overwhelmed by both sounds and letters and need to learn to listen selectively to phonemes before letters are used in this training. Hohn and Ehri (1983) found the opposite, that letters can actually help young children conceptualize the sound structure of words. The optimal time for introducing letters in phonemic awareness training continues to be a point of dispute in the reading field.

The third researcher, Elkonin (1963, 1973), described his Russian colleagues' and his own training studies with young children. The studies are important because the teaching method has been widely incorporated into training programs in the United States. Children were presented with a picture of an object, asked to say its name aloud, and then to represent its phonemes with small tiles that are moved into a square below the picture as each phoneme is pronounced. Providing, for example, three squares for three phonemes was believed to help children conceptualize the sound structure of words. Letters are used instead of blank tiles once phonemes are mastered.

Children with Dyslexia

Current research findings present a model of dyslexia as a reading disorder specific to word reading and associated, for many children, with familial difficulty in phonological processing (see Clark & Uhry, 1995; Shaywitz, 2003). Deficits in phonemic awareness are reported as causal to phonemic recoding deficits (Rack et al., 1992). That is, children with dyslexia are usually poor in code-based strategies, often measured through nonword reading. Remediation of this difficulty would allow a child to generalize phonics knowledge to new words, but until recently there has been little evidence that this could be done.

For many years, children with dyslexia have been provided with direct instruction in multisensory phonics as the remedial approach of choice (e.g., Black, Oakland, Stanford, Nussbaum, & Balise, 1994; Vickery, Reynolds, & Cochran, 1987). Phonics training alone (i.e., letter–sound associations) does not necessarily provide insight into phonemic awareness (i.e., the sound structure of words) or the alphabetic principle (i.e., how letters represent the sound structure of words in a particular order). Researchers have begun to combine phonological awareness training with code-based reading training in the remediation of children with dyslexia.

Alexander, Andersen, Heilman, Voeller, and Torgesen (1991) explored the effect of phonemic awareness training on nonword reading in 10-year-olds with dyslexia and effectively increased the ability of these children to read nonwords. This is an important study because it is the first documentation in the research literature of successful remediation of nonword reading. This training was carried out in a tutoring center with one-to-one instruction using a multisensory program developed by Lindamood and Lindamood (1975). The program begins with an emphasis on sensory feedback during the articulation of phonemes. For example, children are encouraged to notice in a mirror the various shapes of their mouth as different phonemes are uttered and to feel their

vocal cords to experience voiced and unvoiced consonants. The program also includes training in phoneme segmentation and phonics.

Uhry and Shepherd (1997) found equally dramatic gains in nonword reading with a group of 7-year-old children with dyslexia, also in a tutoring setting. Each session involved phonics (i.e., letter–sound training), and segmentation/spelling using letters to represent phonemes segmented from simple CVC words (see Uhry & Shepherd, 1993), and a chance to read words with these patterns in both phonics-controlled readers and narrative-controlled storybooks.

In both of these relatively small studies there was dramatic growth in nonword reading skills following phonemic awareness training. Whether increasing ability to use phonology to recode unfamiliar words is sufficient to increase children's reading comprehension is another issue currently being debated in the field. Phonemic awareness training may be necessary but not sufficient to ensure long-term progress in skilled reading of connected text and in comprehension. Two large-scale longitudinal studies with funding from the NICHD are exploring this issue (Foorman, Francis, Beeler, Winikates, & Fletcher, 1997; Torgesen, Wagner, Rashotte, Alexander, & Conway, 1997).

Early Intervention for Children at Risk

If phonemic awareness training can facilitate the growth of phonological recoding skills in older children with dyslexia, and the phonological processing deficit can be identified in young children, then the logical treatment for young at-risk children is early training in phonemic awareness. Bradley and Bryant's (1983) seminal study of at-risk 4- and 5-year-olds described previously is a model for studies that have followed.

Two large-scale, federally funded early intervention projects explored the longitudinal effects of early phonemic awareness training on various aspects of reading in young children at risk because of poor phonemic awareness. In a prevention study in Florida, Torgesen et al. (1997) provided 80 minutes per week of individual supplemental reading instruction to children with phonemic awareness deficits beginning at mid-kindergarten and continuing through fourth grade. Three instructional groups of about 35 children each were contrasted with typically achieving children and with classroom controls who had poor phonemic awareness. One group received instruction in the Lindamood (Lindamood & Lindamood, 1975) method of phonemic awareness and synthetic phonics (PASP) in which phonemic sound production is associated with articulatory gesture prior to training in sound analysis and synthesis of sounds from letters into words. A second group was trained in a method of **embedded phonics** in which phonemic awareness and phonics training were taught implicitly through the reading of real words in text. A third group received individual training in whatever method was being employed in the regular classroom reading program. By mid–second grade, all three groups receiving individual support could read words at a level close to that of typical readers, and the PASP group held a significant advantage in nonword reading over the other instructional groups.

The second of these NICHD-funded longitudinal studies (e.g., Foorman et al., 1997) was carried out in Texas. Foorman and her colleagues used an English-language adaptation of Lundberg's phonological awareness program (Adams et al., 1998) with seven kindergarten classes. Children were given 15 minutes per day of direct instruction in phonological awareness games, songs, and other activities. This program is described in detail later in this chapter in the section on *Phonemic Awareness in Young Children: A Classroom Curriculum*. The rate of growth in phonological tasks for these children was

significantly greater in comparison with that of controls in kindergartens using the school district's standard readiness program.

Children in Low Socioeconomic Status Schools

Phonemic awareness training has been used with children who are economically disadvantaged. Many of these children have poorly developed phonemic awareness. The same multisensory training programs that improve phonemic awareness in children with inherited reading disorders work effectively for these children as well. Benita Blachman and her colleagues (Blachman, Ball, Black, & Tangel, 1994; Tangel & Blachman, 1992) worked with at-risk preschoolers in upstate New York. Blachman trained kindergarten teachers to work with inner-city children from low socioeconomic status (SES) families for 11 weeks. Instruction for the kindergarten children included letter–sound associations; matching words by alliteration; and a segmenting activity called *Say-It-and-Move-It,* in which small disks are slid from a picture, one by one, as phonemes are segmented in order. Following this instruction, children were superior to untrained controls in phoneme segmentation, letter–sound knowledge, inventing spellings, and in reading word lists made up of phonetically regular real words and nonwords composed of target sounds from the training. These low-SES children were followed into first grade (Tangel & Blachman, 1995). First-grade training was similar but was embedded in a five-part reading program: 1) letter–sound correspondences; 2) phonemic awareness training; 3) **sight word** review, including **phonetically regular** words; 4) practice reading both phonetically regular text and trade books; and 5) writing. The authors reported that the experimental group had an advantage over controls in first grade in regard to ability to represent sounds on a developmentally scored test of invented spelling.

In another NICHD-funded study carried out by Foorman (Foorman, Francis, Fletcher, Schatschneider, & Mehta, 1998), first- and second-grade children eligible for Title I services received three forms of phonics and phonemic awareness instruction over the course of a school year: direct code instruction using a synthetic phonics basal series, less explicit phonics embedded in controlled text, and implicit code instruction through trade books. Children who were stronger in phonemic awareness on entry to the study tended to be stronger in reading by the end of the year regardless of group, but instructional group made a significant difference for those children who initially were weak in phonemic awareness. The growth rate and mean scores on word reading were significantly higher for the direct code group by the end of the year. In other words, direct instruction in phonics and phonemic awareness in the primary grades can help children recover from potentially detrimental effects of low levels of phonemic awareness. The direct code instruction, *Open Court,* is described in the section on programs later in this chapter.

Summaries of Research

Two important literature reviews published in the 1990s synthesized hundreds of research studies on phonemic awareness (Adams, 1990; Snow, Burns, & Griffin, 1998). Both reviews emphasized the importance of phonemic awareness as one component of a comprehensive reading program for young children. That is, the reviews placed high value on phonemic awareness instruction as a necessary component of early reading, together with early letter–sound instruction and a rich array of other activities such as

oral language development through conversation and listening to stories, writers' workshop, and other language-oriented, meaning-based experiences.

A third review was written in response to a charge by Congress to explore the state of scientifically researched reading instruction and the country's preparedness to use research findings in the classroom. This charge took place in the context of state and national initiatives centered on accountability for student learning outcomes around the turn of the century. This newest review, published in 2000 by the NICHD, is titled *Report of the National Reading Panel: Teaching Children to Read: An Evidence-Based Assessment of the Scientific Research Literature on Reading and its Implications for Reading Instruction: Report of the Subgroups* (see also Ehri et al., 2001). Whereas earlier reviews were collections of studies with summaries and recommendations for instruction, the National Reading Panel Report carried out what is called a meta-analysis. This statistical technique allows comparisons across studies, using effect size, the degree to which a form of instruction is more effective than another form. Prominent reading researcher Linnea Ehri headed a team that carried out the phonemic awareness portion of the report. She and her group looked at nearly 2,000 studies on phonemic awareness and selected those with a scientific design compatible with research criteria used by the panel (e.g., control groups, clear descriptions of participants and instruction). Some of the major findings and recommendations from the phonemic awareness report are as follows.

All young children benefit from phonemic awareness training. Overwhelmingly, the studies that Ehri's group looked at indicate that phonemic awareness is strongly correlated with later reading and that early instruction in phonemic awareness facilitates later reading skills. It was once a widely held belief that children with dyslexia and other learning disabilities needed different instruction than other children. What we know now is that all children benefit from this special teaching method. This instruction is effective for young readers as well as older readers who are still struggling with reading acquisition. It works for advantaged as well as disadvantaged children. Typically developing readers benefit in both reading and spelling. Although children with reading disabilities benefit in terms of reading, they have more difficulty learning to spell.

The most effective phonemic awareness instruction is direct and systematic. Instruction in phonemic awareness can take many forms. Some children can learn phonemic awareness from listening to rhyming text or stories with alliteration. Some teachers just present the material, whereas other teachers are careful to point out these rhymes. Some children "get it" from singing songs with rhyme or alliteration. There are games for teaching segmenting and blending. What the National Reading Panel (NICHD, 2000) found is that direct and systematic instruction works best. This is particularly true for children with dyslexia. Do not leave instruction to chance or hope that the teachable moment will arise. Make a plan for moving from easy to hard, aim instruction at the level of the learner, and teach directly. Do not try too many different forms of instruction. Choose a format and repeat it with increasingly more difficult linguistic combinations. Move from simple structures (words with two phonemes) to longer, more complex structures.

Using letters with phonemic awareness training is effective. A number of studies reviewed by the National Reading Panel (NICHD, 2000) support the use of letters in phonemic awareness training (Hohn & Ehri, 1983; Ehri & Wilce, 1987; Tangel & Blachman, 1992, 1995; Uhry & Shepherd, 1993). Using letters with phonemic awareness training provides a concrete way for children to hold onto and internalize what is, in essence, a very abstract concept. Invented spelling is really a form of phonemic awareness (segmenting sounds) coupled with letter–sound connections.

A little phonemic awareness instruction goes a long way. More is not necessarily better. One classic study of effective phonemic awareness instruction involved only 10 minutes twice per week (Bradley & Bryant, 1983). The National Reading Panel report (NICHD, 2000) raises the point that too much phonemic awareness training can actually take valuable time away from helping children apply this new learning to reading. If one plans instruction carefully and carries it out directly and systematically and uses letters, a short period of instruction on a regular basis can be highly effective.

Phonemic awareness instruction in small groups is effective. Of the studies reviewed, those with instruction in small groups were most effective. This may be due to the instruction itself rather than to group size, but the encouraging news is that effective instruction in phonemic awareness does not necessarily need to be carried out on an individual basis. Teachers can deliver short periods of effective phonemic awareness instruction to small groups of children several times a week right in the classroom. Small groups allow planning for instructional needs rather than trying to keep an entire class moving along at the same pace.

PHONEMIC AWARENESS INSTRUCTION

Classroom Instruction

Results of the studies just mentioned suggest an advantage for children receiving direct instruction in phonemic awareness. Older children diagnosed as dyslexic, younger children at risk because of poor phonemic awareness, and children just learning to read all benefit from this training. Phonemic awareness activities are often included in primary classrooms. In meaning-based classrooms, activities are usually contextualized within gamelike activities. Yopp described resources such as songs and games geared toward developing children's "curiosity about language and their experimentation with it" (1992, p. 702). Many kindergarten and first-grade teachers include phonemic awareness training during writing activities in which children are encouraged to sound out invented spellings rather than relying on conventional orthography. There is evidence that phonemic awareness plays a role in shared reading and finger-point reading activities in whole language classrooms (Ehri & Sweet, 1991; Morris, 1993, 2003; Uhry, 1999, 2002). Research suggests that ability to segment phonemes facilitates ability to coordinate memorized text with finger-point reading of printed words. To this end, Yopp (1995) describes read-aloud books with rhyme and alliteration that can be used to develop phonemic awareness.

These phonemic awareness activities enrich the beginning reading experiences of many young children. Without explicit instruction, however, children with dyslexia may not catch the alliteration or phoneme manipulation in songs and games. They may not learn to read from finger-point reading because often they are not able to segment phonemes. There is evidence in the research literature that children with dyslexia benefit from highly explicit instruction in phonemic awareness. In an often-cited study, Iverson and Tunmer (1993) added an explicit phonemic awareness and phonics instructional component to the *Reading Recovery* program for at-risk first graders. All *Reading Recovery* children in the study were provided with rich experiences reading text aloud under the one-to-one guidance of a highly trained tutor, but some children also received explicit phonemic awareness training and these children were ready sooner to rejoin peers for regular classroom reading instruction in comparison with control children trained in *Reading Recovery* alone.

Teachers and Phonemic Awareness

Although there is strong evidence supporting the benefits of phonemic awareness in-struction, many teachers are not adept at this sort of language analysis. Teachers are mature, capable readers, and most are not conscious of using the alphabetic principle themselves during reading for meaning and do not remember having learned about it in school. Moats (1994, 2000) pointed out that many teacher preparation programs neglect phonemic awareness as a topic for teacher education. Moats stressed the im-portance of teachers' having a firm grasp of the structure of spoken and written lan-guage in order to interpret children's **miscues** and in order to present solid examples through which patterns can be taught. For example, even though a teacher may not use terminology with 6-year-olds such as *consonant cluster* for the first two sounds in the word *clip* or *consonant digraph* for the first sound in *chin,* these labels will help the teacher conceptualize for him- or herself the idea of listening for two sounds in one case and just one in the other, respectively, as he or she works with a child trying to sound out and spell a word.

PHONEMIC AWARENESS PROGRAMS

There are currently a number of commercially available curriculum materials for use with emergent, beginning, and remedial readers. Most provide theoretical information as well as a systematic sequence and concrete ideas to use with children. Some, such as the Lindamood program (1975, 1998) have been available for a long time. Others, such as *Fundations* (Wilson, 2002) and the phonemic awareness component of the *Open Court* reading series (Adams, Bereiter, Hirshberg, Anderson, & Bernier, 1995), are rela-tively new. The explicit nature of instruction in these materials makes them appropri-ate for children with dyslexia, but these programs include activities that could be used in regular classrooms as well. These programs are all responsive to current research in that they tend to move through a common sequence of activities in which the focus moves toward smaller and smaller segments of sound in oral language and which the sound structure of words is established through oral activities prior to introducing let-ters. See Appendix B for a listing of the following and their sources.

Fundations

The *Wilson Reading System* (Wilson, 1996) is an Orton-Gillingham–based, systematic, multisensory remedial reading program that was originally designed for adolescents and adults. *Fundations* is Wilson's new program designed for beginning readers in kinder-garten and first grade (2002) and second grade (2004). *Fundations* is designed to be used for 30-minute classroom lessons that supplement meaning-based reading programs. It can also be used for small-group extension lessons in the classroom for children needing extra help or for pull-out programs for children with disabilities. It includes simplified versions of typical Orton-Gillingham lessons (e.g., letter–key-word–sound cards, link-ing handwriting with **sky writing** and with letter sounds and names). Two particu-larly nice materials are Wilson's magnetic letter cards for constructing words on small boards, with one board for each child, and an owl puppet named Echo used for re-peating oral material.

Wilson teaches phonemic awareness using letters right from the start. In this re-gard, *Fundations* is at one extreme in a continuum of programs ranging from full inte-gration of letters into phonemic awareness instruction to study of pure sound. At this

opposite extreme are programs such as *Lindamood Phoneme Sequencing Program for Reading, Spelling, and Speech* (Lindamood & Lindamood, 1998) and *Phonemic Awareness: A Classroom Curriculum* (Adams et al., 1998). These programs, which are discussed later, teach phonemic awareness without letters for a long time and only later begin to link phonemes with letters.

Ladders to Literacy

Ladders to Literacy (Notari-Syverson, O'Connor, & Vadasy, 1998; O'Connor, Notari-Syverson, & Vadasy, 1998b, 2005) was designed for young children with special needs but has also been found to be effective with their classmates without disabilities. The effectiveness of the program is well researched (O'Connor, Jenkins, & Slocum, 1995; O'Connor, Notari-Syverson, & Vadasy, 1996, 1998a, 2005), and several of O'Connor's studies using this instruction are included in the National Reading Panel report (NICHD, 2000). O'Connor was an early advocate of using phonemic awareness instruction with very young children at risk because of developmental disabilities, and the effects of her training seem to be particularly long lasting for these children. The program is based on two theoretical notions: the Vygotskian notion of providing a *scaffold* or support system to guide children in learning and the notion that cognitive processes such as phonemic awareness play a role in the development of reading. *Ladders to Literacy* includes activity books at both the preschool and kindergarten levels. The activity books differ from many other idea books in that these provide both a theoretical base and many examples of ways in which teachers can support children's learning through questioning and playful materials.

The version for preschool children is designed to be developmentally appropriate and to encourage emergent literacy in a print-rich environment. Activities involve direct instruction, can be used for groups or individuals, and are designed to be integrated into existing curricula. The curriculum begins with representational play and picture books and has sections on print and book awareness, metalinguistic skills (including phonological awareness), and oral language development. Preschool phonemic awareness activities include reciting nursery rhymes and changing the end rhymes, clapping syllables, drawing pictures of multisyllabic words and cutting the pictures apart to reassemble syllable by syllable (e.g., drawing a dinosaur and then cutting the picture into three parts), and listening for onsets in words with target sounds of the week. For each of these and many other activities, low, medium, and high levels of support are outlined as a guide for teachers to meet the needs of all individuals.

Ladders to Literacy: A Kindergarten Activity Book (O'Connor et al., 1998b, 2005) follows a similar format, with sections on **print awareness**, phonemic awareness, and oral language. Phonemic awareness activities overlap with those in the preschool book, but the end of the activity book includes sound matching, blending, and three-phoneme segmentation and incorporates the use of letters associated with sounds. As with the preschool book, teachers are guided through the possible difficulties of various task demands so that instruction can be made appropriate for each child.

Lindamood Phoneme Sequencing Program (LiPS)

Patricia and Charles H. Lindamood's program, *Auditory Discrimination in Depth* (*ADD*; 1975), is based on the Lindamoods' backgrounds in linguistics and speech-language pathology. The *ADD* program was revised by Patricia and Phyllis Lindamood, and its third edition was renamed the *Lindamood Phoneme Sequencing Program for Reading,*

Spelling, and Speech (LiPS; 1998). The distinguishing characteristic of the program continues to be its early focus on drawing a student's attention to the oral-motor processes used in articulating phonemes.

Special names describe the multisensory aspects of phoneme production. For example, the voiced and unvoiced **labiodental fricatives** /v/ and /f/ are called "Lip Coolers," with the former the "Noisy Brother" or voiced phoneme and the latter the "Quiet Brother" or unvoiced phoneme. Training involves helping students identify phoneme sounds by matching them with photographs of the lips, teeth, and tongue engaged in articulatory gestures. Changes in spoken words are analyzed or tracked as single-phoneme changes occur, first with the mouth pictures and later with colored blocks. For example, the teacher sets up a sequence of colored blocks (blue, red, green) and says, "That's *zab;* show me *zaf.*" The student exchanges the green block for a white one and responds, "The Lip Popper is gone and a Lip Cooler took its place" (Lindamood & Lindamood, 1998, p. 12). Note that this involves phoneme manipulation, Adams's (1990) highest level of phonemic awareness, and that at this point in instruction, letters are not yet associated with phonemes.

Once complex word structures such as CCVCC words (e.g., *stand*) can be segmented and manipulated, then lettered tiles are introduced for segmenting and spelling real words. Spelling instruction leads to reading instruction using lettered tiles and eventually to printed text, consistent with the Lindamoods' notion that speech should precede written work. Letter–sound associations are introduced in a carefully sequenced plan, and a set of readers is available for practicing reading. Word reading is done through a careful analysis of letter–sound correspondences, in the Orton-Gillingham tradition, with the focus initially on accuracy and later on fluency. Videotapes and a CD-ROM provide support for the teacher.

The Lindamood program (1975, 1998) was used by Torgesen et al. (1997) in an NICHD-funded longitudinal intervention study with at-risk first-grade children in Florida. Although long-term effects on reading comprehension are not yet known, there certainly is solid research evidence that the Lindamood program increases young children's ability in phonetic recoding.

Open Court

Open Court, a phonics-based basal-reading series, has been rewritten to include a phonemic awareness component in the early grades (Adams et al., 1995). Segmenting is taught in kindergarten and both blending and segmenting are taught in first grade. In both cases, instruction at the syllable level precedes instruction at the phoneme level. Activities are gamelike and playful and include clapping syllables for classmates' names, talking for a puppet who talks in segments rather than whole words, singing alliterative songs, and asking riddles (e.g., "What rhymes with *town* but begins with /br/?" [p. 304]).

In the *Open Court* program, phonemic awareness instruction precedes phonics instruction (i.e., instruction in letter–sound associations). Phonemic awareness activities are entirely oral and are described in red type in the teachers' manuals to differentiate these activities from reading instruction. Teachers are cautioned not to confuse phonemic awareness and phonics and to limit early phonics instruction to just those few patterns that have been explicitly taught. At the point in the first-grade curriculum where letter–sound correspondences are first introduced, phonemic awareness instruction has already covered many of the sounds.

Phonics lessons reinforce familiarity with phonemes previously taught. For instance, when the letter–sound association for the letter *t* is taught, the teacher uses the word *timer* as a **key word**, and leads the children in an activity in which they make the /t/ /t/ /t/ /t/ /t/ sound of a cooking timer. Repeating consonants rather than stretching them out (e.g., /tuuuuh/) avoids using the schwa vowel sound so that the sound of each consonant resembles the sound segmented in earlier oral activities. In addition to cards with letters and key-word pictures (e.g., *m* for *monkey*) there are short alliterative rhymes that are read aloud by the teacher while the children listen for the target sound at the beginnings of words. For example, the following is from Lesson 11 in the first-grade program: "For Muzzy the Monkey, bananas are yummy. She munches so many they fill up her tummy. When she eats, she says /m/ /m/ /m/ /m/ /m/" (Adams et al., 1995, p. 84).

Early reading activities repeat the structure of earlier phonemic awareness games. Whereas an earlier oral blending activity involves the riddle "What rhymes with *town* but begins with /br/?" (Adams et al., 1995, p. 304), beginning reading instruction involves blending activities such as teaching children to read the word *hamburger* on the chalkboard, erasing *h*, replacing it with *s,* and asking the children to blend and read the new word.

Phonemic Awareness in Young Children: A Classroom Curriculum

As mentioned previously, the Lundberg program (Lundberg et al., 1988) was used successfully in research with Danish kindergarten children. An English-language version was used in the Houston kindergartens where Foorman et al. (1997) carried out the early intervention portion of NICHD-funded research. Again, there is strong evidence that this program increases phonemic skills.

This phonemic awareness training program, which was subsequently published as *Phonemic Awareness in Young Children: A Classroom Curriculum* (Adams et al., 1998), is designed for kindergarten and first-grade classrooms and consists of a carefully sequenced hierarchy of games and activities. The sequence is arranged by chapters that focus on the following:

1. *Listening games:* Children are encouraged to listen selectively to environmental sounds, including the human voice, and to follow directions.

2. *Rhyming:* Children listen to and generate rhymes in order to become sensitive to the sound structure of words.

3. *Sentences and words:* This chapter includes activities for segmenting sentences into words.

4. *Syllables:* Children segment words into syllables and blend syllables into words.

5. *Initial and final sounds:* First initial and then final phonemes are segmented and blended in short, linguistically simple words.

6. *Phonemes:* At this level all phonemes in a word are segmented.

7. *Letters:* Phonemes are represented by letters to provide support for understanding the alphabetic principle.

Unlike many commercially available collections of ideas, there is sufficient theory throughout to enable a teacher to use the guide to plan his or her own program. A sample day-by-day schedule is included for both kindergarten and first grade in order to help

teachers select and repeat activities from the suggested sequence. The theoretical material is an exemplary feature of this program guide.

The activities are playful, child centered, and developmentally appropriate (e.g., clapping, dancing, whispering, tossing balls back and forth). Rhythmic dance and movement activities introduce a kinesthetic element to some of the early listening games. Later, children pull mystery objects from a box and then clap the syllables in the objects' names or guess classmates' names after listening to the teacher say the initial phoneme. Each activity is explained carefully not only in terms of procedures but also in terms of its linguistic features and possible pitfalls. The linguistic features of words have been carefully considered in the planning of the instructional sequences, and numerous word lists are included for playing the games at each level. Teachers are provided with clear guidelines for deciding when to move on to harder activities. Most of the games have variations so that children needing additional work at a particular level can be provided with extension activities.

Phonological Awareness Training for Reading

Torgesen and Bryant (1994) developed the *Phonological Awareness Training for Reading* program out of several research projects seeking to identify those components of phonological awareness that would most effectively increase reading-related skills in beginning readers. Torgesen and his colleagues at Florida State University carried out one training study using these materials in which they demonstrated that both **analytic** and **synthetic** phonological skills were advantageous in learning to read (Torgesen, Morgan, & Davis, 1992). In a second study (Torgesen & Davis, 1993), a revised program was used with minority children at risk for reading difficulty because of low phonemic awareness skills. These children outperformed controls on phonemic awareness tasks immediately after training in kindergarten and on a second testing early in first grade.

The program uses activities from a number of sources, including classroom teachers, and has been validated by research carried out by Torgesen and others in the field. It is designed for use with individuals or with small groups. It can be used during the second semester of kindergarten or for older at-risk children during first or second grade. The program is planned to last a semester when used in short sessions four times a week. There are four phases to the program:

1. *Warm-up activities: rhyming*—This short, introductory phase introduces the idea of listening to sounds through rhyming games and activities. The program includes sets of cards to match (e.g., pictures of an egg and a leg). The authors stress that the purpose of the activities should be made clear to the participants.

2. *Phonological training activities: blending*—Children begin by blending onsets and rimes (e.g., blending the phoneme /k/ with the rime unit /at/) and then later blend all three phonemes in short words (e.g., /k/-/a/-/t/ blended into /kat/). This leads into segmentation of the initial phoneme in a word.

3. *Phonological training activities: segmenting*—Phoneme segmentation activities use a sequence moving from initial to final to middle phonemes in words. Segmentation training also progresses from matching by phoneme to actually segmenting the phoneme in each of the three positions. There is a focus on awareness of the feeling the experienced in the mouth as various sounds are produced, and children are asked to listen for differences between voiced and unvoiced consonants.

4. *Phonological training activities: reading and spelling*—Letters are introduced to represent phonemes in the Level 4 activities for both reading and spelling. Letters are used to help children manipulate the sounds in words as in the following example from the manual in which the teacher uses letter cards to spell a word and then asks the children to change the letters to spell a second word: "This is the word *top*, /t/-/o/-/p/. What letter should we change to write the word *mop*?" (Torgesen & Bryant, 1994, p. 25).

Phonological Awareness Training for Reading (Torgesen & Bryant, 1994) includes a teacher's manual, game parts, and an audiotape. The game parts involve small pictures that can be used to play the games described in the manual. For example, a child says "cap" while looking at a picture of a cap, and then the teacher points to one of three blocks in a line and asks which sound it is (e.g., /k/ for the first block in *cap*). The audiotape provides sample pronunciations for words segmented into onsets and rimes and into all phonemic segments.

Reading Readiness

The Neuhaus Education Center in Houston, Texas, is an educational foundation that offers training to teachers in reading instruction. The Center uses *Alphabetic Phonics* (see Clark & Uhry, 1995, pp. 147–154) both as a remedial program and as the basis of beginning reading and spelling instruction in general education classes. In 1992 Benita Blachman presented a workshop at the center on the importance of phonemic awareness, and following this, center staff developed the *Reading Readiness* program for younger children (Carreker, 2002).

Reading Readiness (Carreker, 2002) involves many of the elements of *Alphabetic Phonics* lessons and introduces a new element involving phonemic awareness activities. The manual describes the program as being for use in the early grades. It begins with daily lessons in letter recognition and sequencing, phonemic awareness, and oral language skills. Once letter recognition and phonemic awareness are mastered, the lesson is extended from 20 to 30 minutes through the addition of handwriting and multisensory sound–symbol activities. Phonemic awareness activities such as the following examples from the program (Carreker, 2002) are presented in a sequence based on research.

1. Rhyming activities are presented at the initial level (e.g., "Do *go* and *top* rhyme? Find a rhyme for *cat*").

2. Awareness of words in sentences and syllables in compound and multisyllabic words is taught through clapping and counting activities.

3. Initial sound awareness is taught through attention to lip movements (e.g., "As I say *monkey*, what happens to my mouth? When I say the word *many*, what happens to my mouth? Are my lips together when I start to say each word?")

4. Phoneme segmentation is taught through a series of activities based on Ball and Blachman's (1991) *Say-It-and-Move-It* technique in which markers representing phonemes are moved from a picture down to a line below it in left-to-right order.

5. Segmenting and spelling are taught once students have learned **sound–symbol associations**. The phoneme segmentation activities are extended by segmenting and then using lettered markers to spell pictured words with simple consonant–

vowel–consonant constructions, such as *mop*. Note that this activity is similar to one first introduced by Elkonin (1963, 1973).

Road to the Code: A Phonological Awareness Program for Young Children

Road to the Code: A Phonological Awareness Program for Young Children was written by Blachman, Ball, Black, and Tangel (2000) as a teacher's guide for some of the activities used by the authors in their research with young readers. It is an 11-week sequence of 44 lessons for small groups or individuals in kindergarten and first grade. Although designed for children who need extra help in early literacy, the program would be beneficial in any classroom of emergent or beginning readers. Each lesson is constructed around three activities.

1. *Say-It-and-Move-It* is a phoneme segmentation game in which tiles representing phonemes are moved from a picture down onto an arrow pointing from left to right. The tiles are placed on the arrow in the order in which the children hear the teacher say them. Early in the program sounds are said in isolation (e.g., /t/-/t/ or /a/-/t/). Later words are said so that children need to segment them into phonemes and then represent the phonemes with sounds. Eventually lettered tiles are used so that segmenting becomes spelling.

2. *Letter Name and Sound Instruction* involves large cards with letters and pictures (e.g., a vampire playing a violin while lying across the top of a large *V*). The teacher teaches the sound directly, helps the children identify the pictures, and then encourages them to generate other words with the sound. Later lessons involve review through clapping games and chants.

3. *Phonological Awareness Practice* is carried out through a series of games, songs, and read-alouds designed to focus on sounds in words. For example, a set of sound categorization cards can be photocopied from the book and then used in a singing game to find the card whose sound does not match the others. The words *hat, cat,* and *bat* all rhyme, and *jug* does not. In another game pictures are "mailed" or sorted by initial sound into paper bags called "mailboxes."

Sounds Abound

Sounds Abound (Catts & Vartiainen, 1993) was developed by a university researcher and a speech-language pathologist. Catts, a professor who teaches courses in communication disorders and language-based learning disabilities at the University of Kansas, and Vartiainen, a speech-language pathologist in the public schools, have written a phonological awareness instructional program for children from ages 4–9. The program includes the following five components based on the research literature:

1. Rhyme awareness is encouraged through an extensive list of books of nursery rhymes, songs, poems, and sound play activities. Children listen to these read-alouds, join in once they know the rhymes, and ultimately create new verses.

2. Rhyme judgment and rhyme production are taught through activities, games, and songs. Sound sorting activities are similar to Bradley and Bryant's (1983) activities. Reproducible workbook pages provide pictures, and children are directed to mark the ones that rhyme.

3. Segmenting beginning and ending sounds is taught through workbook exercises followed by sound production activities. The authors include activities for songs in which alliteration is used (Yopp, 1992).

4. Full segmentation and blending are taught through oral activities such as the deletion of syllables from compound words (e.g., Say *railroad* without *rail*). There are workbook pages with Elkonin-type (1963, 1973) tasks using pictured objects and drawings of squares for sliding down a token for each phoneme in the word. There are also pictures to cut into three pieces to use in teaching blending.

5. Explicit instruction in mapping sounds onto letters is taught through the use of letters to represent phonemes in segmenting activities. Activities begin with word families (e.g., a rime such as *at* for producing the words *sat, fat,* and *mat*). Later students are taught to spell every segment of a word.

SUMMARY

Research demonstrates a strong link between children's early abilities in phonemic awareness and their later reading skills. Children with dyslexia are apt to have phonological processing deficits that are causal to their word-reading deficits. A number of phonemic awareness programs are commercially available, and most of these programs share the following principles derived from the research literature and mentioned in the recommendations of the National Reading Panel report (NICHD, 2000):

1. Teach phonemic awareness systematically and explicitly rather than implicitly and informally.

2. Teach phonemic awareness using a sequence similar to Adams's (1990) research-based hierarchy:

   a. Rhyming

   b. Matching by rhyme and alliteration

   c. Syllable splitting such as onset segmentation and partial segmentation and representation using invented spelling

   d. Full phoneme segmentation

   e. Manipulation of phonemes

3. Once children know letter names, teach letter–sound associations explicitly and then teach phonemic awareness using letters to represent sounds.

4. Link phonemic awareness activities to reading.

REFERENCES

Adams, M.J. (1990). *Beginning to read: Thinking and learning about print.* Cambridge, MA: The MIT Press.

Adams, M.J. (1994). Phonics and beginning reading instruction. In R. Lehr & J. Osborn (Eds.), *Reading, language, and literacy.* Mahwah, NJ: Lawrence Erlbaum Associates.

Adams, M.J., Bereiter, C., Hirshberg, J., Anderson, V., & Bernier, S.A. (1995). *Framework for effective teaching, Grade 1: Thinking and learning about print.* Chicago: Open Court.

Adams, M.J., Foorman, B.R., Lundberg, I., & Beeler, T. (1998). *Phonemic awareness in young children: A classroom curriculum.* Baltimore: Paul H. Brookes Publishing Co.

Alexander, A.W., Andersen, H.G., Heilman, P.C., Voeller, K.K.S., & Torgesen, J.K. (1991). Phonological awareness training and remediation of analytic decoding deficits in a group of severe dyslexics. *Annals of Dyslexia, 41,* 193–206.

Ball, E.W., & Blachman, B.A. (1991). Does phoneme segmentation training in kindergarten make a difference in early word recognition and developmental spelling? *Reading Research Quarterly, 26,* 49–66.

Blachman, B.A., Ball, E.W., Black, R.S., & Tangel, D.M. (1994). Kindergarten teachers develop phoneme awareness in low-income, inner-city classrooms: Does it make a difference? *Reading and Writing: An Interdisciplinary Journal, 6,* 1–18.

Blachman, B.A., Ball, E.W., Black, R., & Tangel, D.M. (2000). *Road to the code: A phonological awareness program for young children.* Baltimore: Paul H. Brookes Publishing Co.

Black, J.L., Oakland, T., Stanford, G., Nussbaum, N., & Balise, R.R. (1994). *An evaluation of the Texas Scottish Rite Hospital dyslexia program.* Unpublished report from the Texas Scottish Rite Hospital.

Bradley, L., & Bryant, P.E. (1983). Categorizing sounds and learning to read: A causal connection. *Nature, 301,* 419–421.

Bradley, L., & Bryant, P.E. (1985). *Rhyme and reason in reading and spelling.* Ann Arbor: University of Michigan Press.

Carreker. S. (2002). *Reading readiness.* Bellaire, TX: Neuhaus Education Center.

Catts, H. W. (1986). Speech production/phonological deficits in reading disordered children. *Journal of Learning Disabilities, 19,* 504–508.

Catts, H.W. (1989). Defining dyslexia as a developmental language disorder. *Annals of Dyslexia, 39,* 50–64.

Catts, H.W. (1993). The relationship between speech-language impairments and reading disabilities. *Journal of Speech and Hearing Research, 36,* 948–958.

Catts, H., & Vartiainen, T. (1993). *Sounds abound.* East Moline, IL: LinguiSystems.

Chall, J., Roswell, F.G., & Blumenthal, S.H. (1963). Auditory blending ability: A factor in success in beginning reading. *The Reading Teacher, 17,* 113–118.

Clark, D.B., & Uhry, J.K. (1995). *Dyslexia: Theory and practice of remedial instruction.* Timonium, MD: York Press.

Cox, A.R. (1992). *Foundations for literacy: Structures and techniques.* Cambridge, MA: Educators Publishing Service.

DeFries, J.C., Filipek, P.A., Fulker, D.W., Olson, R.K., Pennington, B.F., Smith, S.D., et al. (1997). Colorado learning disabilities center. *Learning Disabilities: A Multidisciplinary Journal, 8,* 7–19.

de Hirsch, K., Langford, W., & Jansky, J. (1966). *Predicting reading failure.* New York: HarperCollins.

Denckla, M.B., & Rudel, R.G. (1974). Rapid "automatized" naming of pictured objects, colors, letters, and numbers by normal children. *Cortex, 10,* 186–202.

Ehri, L.C., Nunes, S.R., Willows, D.M., Schuster, B.V., Yaghoub-Zadeh, Z., & Shanahan, T. (2001). Phonemic awareness instruction helps children learn to read: Evidence from the National Reading Panel's meta-analysis. *Reading Research Quarterly, 36,* 250–287.

Ehri, L.C., & Sweet, J. (1991). Fingerpoint-reading of memorized text: What enables beginners to process the print? *Reading Research Quarterly, 26,* 442–462.

Ehri, L.C., & Wilce, L.C. (1987). Does learning to spell help beginners learn to read words? *Reading Research Quarterly, 18,* 47–65.

Elkonin, D.B. (1963). The psychology of mastering the elements of reading. In B. Simon & J. Simon (Eds.), *Educational Psychology in the U.S.S.R.* (pp. 165–179). London: Routledge & Kegan Paul.

Elkonin, D.B. (1973). U.S.S.R. In J. Downing (Ed.), *Comparative reading* (pp. 551–579). New York: Macmillan.

Felton, R.H., & Wood, F.B. (1989). Cognitive deficits in reading disability and attention deficit disorder. *Journal of Learning Disabilities, 22,* 3–13

Foorman, B.R., Francis, D.J., Beeler, T., Winikates, D., & Fletcher, J.M. (1997). Early interventions for children with reading problems: Study designs and preliminary findings. *Learning Disabilities: A Multidisciplinary Journal, 8,* 63–71.

Foorman, B.R., Francis, D.J., Fletcher, J.M., Schatschneider, C., & Mehta, P. (1998). The role of instruction learning to read: Preventing reading failure in at-risk children. *Journal of Educational Psychology, 90,* 37–55.

Good, R.H., & Kaminski, R.A. (Eds.). (2002). *Dynamic Indicators of Basic Early Literacy Skills* (6th ed.). Eugene: OR; Institute for the Development of Educational Achievement. Also available online: http://dibels.uorgeon.edu

Hohn, W.E., & Ehri, L.C. (1983). Do alphabet letters help prereaders acquire phonemic segmentation skill? *Journal of Educational Psychology, 75,* 752–762.

Iverson, S., & Tunmer, W.E. (1993). Phonological processing skills and the Reading Recovery program. *Journal of Educational Psychology, 85,* 112–126.

Kaminski, R.A., & Good, R.H. (1996). Toward a technology for assessing basic early literacy skills. *School Psychology Review, 25,* 215–227.

Liberman, I.Y., & Liberman, A.M. (1990). Whole language vs. code emphasis: Underlying assump-

tions and their implications for reading instruction. *Annals of Dyslexia, 40,* 51–76.

Liberman, I.Y., Shankweiler, D., Fischer, F.W., & Carter, B. (1974). Explicit phoneme segmentation in the young child. *Journal of Experimental Child Psychology, 18,* 201–212.

Lindamood, C.H., & Lindamood, P.C. (1975). *The A.D.D. program, auditory discrimination in depth: Books 1 and 2.* Austin, TX: PRO-ED.

Lindamood, C.H., & Lindamood, P.C. (2004). *LAC-3: Lindamood-Bell Auditory Conceptualization Test–Third Edition.* Austin, TX: PRO-ED.

Lindamood, P., & Lindamood, P. (1998). *The Lindamood phoneme sequencing program for reading, spelling, and speech: Teacher's manual for the classroom and clinic.* Austin, TX: PRO-ED.

Lyon, G.R., Shaywitz, S.E., & Shaywitz, B.A. (2003). A definition of dyslexia. *Annals of Dyslexia, 53,* 1–14.

Lundberg, I., Frost, J., & Petersen, O.P. (1988). Effects of an extensive program for stimulating phonological awareness in preschool children. *Reading Research Quarterly, 23,* 263–284.

Maclean, M., Bryant, P.E., & Bradley, L. (1987). Rhymes, nursery rhymes, and reading in early childhood. *Merrill-Palmer Quarterly, 33,* 255–281.

Moats, L.C. (1994). The missing foundation in teacher education: Knowledge of the structure of spoken and written language. *Annals of Dyslexia, 44,* 81–102.

Moats, L.C. (2000). *Speech to print: Language essentials for teachers.* Baltimore: Paul H. Brookes Publishing Co.

Morris, D. (1983). Concept of word and phoneme awareness in the beginning reader. *Research in the Teaching of English, 17,* 359–373.

Morris, D. (1993). The relationship between children's concept of word in text and phoneme awareness in learning to read: A longitudinal study. *Research in the Teaching of English, 27,* 133–153.

Morris, D. (1999). *The Howard Street tutoring manual: Teaching at-risk readers in the primary grades.* New York: Guilford Press.

Morris, D., Bloodgood, J.W., Lomax, R.G., & Perney, J. (2003). Developmental steps in learning to read: A longitudinal study in kindergarten and first grade. *Reading Research Quarterly, 38,* 302–328.

Morris, D., & Perney, J. (1984). Developmental spelling as a predictor of first-grade reading achievement. *The Elementary School Journal, 84,* 441–457.

National Institute of Child Health and Human Development (NICHD). (2000). *Report of the National Reading Panel: Teaching children to read: An evidence-based assessment of the scientific research literature ion reading and its implications for reading instruction: Report of the subgroups* (NIH Publication No. 00-4754): Washington, DC: Government Printing Office. Also available on-line: http://www.nichd.nih.gov/publications/nrp/report.htm

Notari-Syverson, A., O'Connor, R.E., & Vadasy, P.F. (1998). *Ladders to literacy: A preschool activity book.* Baltimore: Paul H. Brookes Publishing Co.

O'Connor, R., Jenkins, J., & Slocum, T. (1995). Transfer among phonological tasks in kindergarten: Essential instructional content. *Journal of Educational Psychology, 87,* 202–217.

O'Connor, R., Notari-Syverson, A., & Vadasy, P. (1996). Ladders to literacy: The effects of teacher-led phonological activities for kindergarten children with and without disabilities. *Exceptional Children, 63,* 117–130.

O'Connor, R., Notari-Syverson, A., & Vadasy, P. (1998a). First-grade effects of teacher-led phonological activities in kindergarten for children with mild disabilities: A follow-up study. *Learning Disabilities Research and Practice, 13,* 43–52.

O'Connor, R.E., Notari-Syverson, A., & Vadasy, P.F. (1998b). *Ladders to literacy: A kindergarten activity book.* Baltimore: Paul H. Brookes Publishing Co.

O'Connor, R.E., Notari-Syverson, A., & Vadasy, P.F. (2005). *Ladders to literacy: A kindergarten activity book* (2nd ed.). Baltimore: Paul H. Brookes Publishing Co.

Rack, J.P., Snowling, M.J., & Olson, R.K. (1992). The nonword reading deficit in developmental dyslexia: A review. *Reading Research Quarterly, 27,* 28–53.

Rosner, J. (1975). *Helping children overcome learning difficulties.* New York: Walker & Co.

Rosner, J. (1999). *Phonological Awareness Skills Program.* Austin, TX: PRO-ED.

Roswell, F., & Chall, J. (1963). *Roswell-Chall Auditory Blending Test.* Cambridge, MA: Educators Publishing Service.

Seymour, H.N., Roeper, T., & de Villiers, J. (with de Villiers, P.). (2003a). *Diagnostic Evaluation of Language Variation (DELV–Criterion Referenced).* San Antonio, TX: Harcourt Assessment.

Seymour, H.N., Roeper, T., & de Villiers, J. (with de Villiers, P.). (2003b). *Diagnostic Evaluation of Language Variation–Screening Test (DELV–Screening Test).* San Antonio, TX: Harcourt Assessment.

Share, D., Jorm, A., Maclean, R., & Matthews, R. (1984). Sources of individual differences in reading acquisition. *Journal of Educational Psychology, 76,* 1309–1324.

Shaywitz, S. (2003). *Overcoming dyslexia: A new and complete science-based program for reading problems at any level.* New York: Alfred A. Knopf.

Shaywitz, S.E., Fletcher, J.M., & Shaywitz, B.A. (1996). A conceptual model and definition of

dyslexia: Findings emerging from the Connecticut Longitudinal Study. In J.H. Beitchman, N. Cohen, M.M. Konstantareas, & R. Tannock (Eds.), *Language, learning and behavior disorders* (pp. 199–223). New York: Cambridge University Press.

Shaywitz, S.E., & Shaywitz, B.A. (2004). Neurobiologic basis for reading and reading disability. In P. McCardle & V. Chhabra (Eds.), *The voice of evidence in reading research* (pp. 417–442). Baltimore: Paul H. Brookes Publishing Co.

Snow, C.E., Burns, M.S., & Griffin, P. (Eds.). (1998). *Preventing reading difficulties in young children.* Washington, DC: National Academies Press.

Stanovich, K.E. (1986). Matthew effects in reading: Some consequences of individual differences in the acquisition of literacy. *Reading Research Quarterly, 21,* 360–406.

Tangel, D. M., & Blachman, B. A. (1992). Effect of phoneme awareness on instruction on kindergarten children's invented spelling. *Journal of Reading Behavior, 24,* 233–261.

Tangel, D.M., & Blachman, B.A. (1995). Effect of phoneme awareness instruction on the invented spelling of first-grade children: A one-year follow-up. *Journal of Reading Behavior, 27,* 153–183.

Torgesen, J.K., & Bryant, B.R. (1994). *Phonological awareness training for reading.* Austin, TX: PRO-ED.

Torgesen, J.K., & Davis, C. (1993, April). Individual difference variables that predict response to training in phonological awareness. In R. Wagner (Chair), *Does phonological awareness training enhance children's acquisition of written language skills?* Symposium conducted at the annual meeting of the American Educational Research Association, Atlanta, GA.

Torgesen, J.K., Morgan, S., & Davis, C. (1992). The effects of two types of phonological awareness training on word learning in kindergarten children. *Journal of Educational Psychology, 84,* 364–370.

Torgesen, J.K., Wagner, R.K., Rashotte, C.A., Alexander, A.W., & Conway, T. (1997). Preventive and remedial interventions for children with severe reading disabilities. *Learning Disabilities: A Multidisciplinary Journal, 8,* 51–61.

Treiman, R. (1985). Onsets and rimes as units of spoken syllables: Evidence from children. *Journal of Experimental Child Psychiatry, 39,* 161–181.

Uhry, J.K. (1993a). Predicting low reading from phonological awareness and classroom print: An early reading screening. *Educational Assessment, 1,* 349–368.

Uhry, J.K. (1993b). The spelling/reading connection and dyslexia: Can spelling be used to teach the alphabetic strategy? In R.M. Joshi & C.K. Leong (Eds.), *Reading disabilities: Diagnosis and component processes* (pp. 253–266). Dordrecht, Netherlands: Kluwer Academic.

Uhry, J.K. (1994, April). *Early reading screening: Predicting reading outcomes in low SES urban kindergarten children.* Paper presented at the annual meeting of the American Education Research Association in New Orleans.

Uhry, J.K. (1997). Case studies of dyslexia: Young readers with rapid serial naming deficits. In R.M. Joshi & C.K. Leong (Eds.), *Cross-language studies of learning to read and spell: Phonological and orthographic processing* (pp. 71–88). Dordrecht, Netherlands: Kluwer Academic.

Uhry, J.K. (1999). Invented spelling in kindergarten: The relationship with finger-point reading. *Reading and Writing: An Interdisciplinary Journal, 11,* 441–464.

Uhry, J.K. (2002). Finger-point reading in kindergarten: The role of phonemic awareness, one-to-one correspondence, and rapid serial naming. *Scientific Studies of Reading, 6*(4), 319–342.

Uhry, J.K., & Ehri, L.C. (1999). Ease of segmenting two- and three-phoneme words in kindergarten: Rime cohesion or vowel salience? *Journal of Educational Psychology, 91,* 594–603.

Uhry, J.K., & Shepherd, M.J. (1993). Segmentation/spelling instruction as part of a first grade reading program: Effects on several measures of reading. *Reading Research Quarterly, 28,* 218–233.

Uhry, J.K., & Shepherd, M.J. (1997). Teaching phonological recoding to young children with dyslexia: The effect on sight vocabulary acquisition. *Learning Disabilities Quarterly, 20,* 104–125.

Vickery, K.S., Reynolds, V.A., & Cochran, S.W. (1987). Multisensory teaching for reading, spelling, and handwriting, Orton-Gillingham based, in a public school setting. *Annals of Dyslexia, 37,* 189–202.

Wagner, R.K., & Torgesen, J.K. (1987). The nature of phonological processing and its causal role in the acquisition of reading skills. *Psychological Bulletin, 101,* 192–212.

Wagner, R.K., Torgesen, J.K., & Rashotte, C. (1999). *Comprehensive Test of Phonological Processing (CTOPP).* Austin, TX: PRO-ED.

Wilson, B.A. (1988). *Wilson reading system program overview.* Millbury, MA: Wilson Language Training.

Wilson, B. (1996). *Wilson reading system instructor manual* (3rd ed.). Millbury, MA: Wilson Language Training.

Wilson, B.A. (2002). *Teacher's manual, Levels K-1* (Fundations). Millbury, MA: Wilson Language Training.

Wilson, B.A. (2004). *Teacher's manual, Level 2* (Fundations). Millbury, MA: Wilson Language Training.

Wolf, M. (1991). Naming speed and reading: The contribution of the cognitive neurosciences. *Reading Research Quarterly, 26,* 123–141.

Wolff, P.H., Michel, G.F., & Ovrut, M. (1990). The timing of syllable repetitions in developmental

dyslexia. *Journal of Speech and Hearing Research, 33,* 281–289.

Wood, F.B., & Felton, R.H. (1994). Separate linguistic and attentional factors in the development of reading. *Topics in Language Disorders, 14,* 42–57.

Yopp, H. (1992). Developing phonological awareness in young children. *The Reading Teacher, 45,* 696–703.

Yopp, H.K. (1995). Read-aloud books for developing phonemic awareness: An annotated bibliography. *The Reading Teacher, 48,* 538–542.

5

Alphabet Knowledge
Letter Recognition, Naming, and Sequencing

Kay A. Allen with
Graham F. Neuhaus
and Marilyn C. Beckwith

Awareness of the alphabetic principle, that letters represent the sounds of spoken language, is essential for learning to read an alphabetic language (Chall, 1996; Juel, 1988; Stanovich, 1986). When children can recognize and name the letters of the alphabet, they have a foundation for learning the alphabetic principle (Adams, 1990a; Ehri, 1983). After students learn the sequence of the alphabet, they have access to an organizational system ubiquitous in our culture from the telephone directory to the Internet. They can make efficient use of the dictionary to check spellings, pronunciations, definitions, and usage. This chapter offers a rationale and instruction for 1) the multisensory, structured, and sequential teaching of upper- and lowercase letter recognition and naming and 2) the use of alphabetical order as a sequencing tool, particularly for locating words in the dictionary easily and efficiently. This chapter describes principles of effective classroom teaching as well as the instruction, guided practice, and review that students with dyslexia require to fully develop their letter recognition and naming skills.

The first section of this chapter discusses the significance of letter identification and naming to the reading process. The second section discusses considerations in teaching these skills, especially to students with dyslexia. The third section offers activities for developing accuracy and **automaticity** in letter identification, letter naming, and alphabetizing and the application of these skills in using the dictionary and other reference materials.

THE ROLE OF LETTER RECOGNITION AND
NAMING WITHIN THE READING PROCESS

The compelling case for teaching letter recognition and naming includes several key points:

1. Letters are the written symbols that are cognitively processed to make reading possible (Adams, 1990b).

2. A beginning reader who readily recognizes individual letters can begin recognizing orthographic patterns (familiar letter sequences), an essential step in becoming a good reader (Ehri, 1980).

3. Knowing letter names provides a springboard for learning and remembering letter–sound relationships (Ehri, 1983; National Institute of Child Health and Human Development [NICHD], 2000; Treiman, Tincoff, Rodriguez, Mouzaki, & Francis, 1998).

4. The ease or difficulty with which a student acquires letter knowledge reliably predicts how easily and successfully the student will learn to read (Bond & Dykstra, 1967; Chall, 1996).

5. Letter names are the only stable property of letters (Cox, 1992), as shapes and sounds of letters vary.

6. The recognition of letters is a highly complex task that involves the transformation of graphemes into phonemes and is only slightly less complex than word reading (Neuhaus, 2002). Thus, single-letter knowledge is needed for a student to benefit from further reading instruction (Berninger et al., 2002; Vellutino, Scanlon, & Jaccard, 2003).

These points, as well as the relationship between letter recognition and dyslexia, are discussed in the sections that follow.

From Recognition of Individual Letters to Recognition of Letter Sequences

As unlikely as it may seem, "Skillful readers visually process virtually every individual letter of every word as they read, and this is true whether they are reading isolated words or meaningful, connected text" (Adams, 1990b, p. 18). Although this processing is not often perceived on a conscious level, studies show that misprints of even very familiar words are detected by readers. For example, when the letters *tqe* rather than the letters *the* are embedded in a sentence, the amount of eye fixation time increases (Adams, 1990b).

In a model of word recognition based on work by Seidenberg and McClelland (1989), Adams (1990a) defined the vital role of letter recognition and its relationship to the processing of speech sounds, meaning, and context. Print provides the data that the reader recognizes, recodes, and interprets in context (e.g., *rose* as flower or action). If a reader has fast, accurate recognition of individual letters, then he or she can identify rather than locate and learn familiar letter sequences. Through repeated reading of words, letter sequences are unitized. For fluent reading to develop, a student must learn to recognize frequently occurring orthographic (spelling) patterns in words. However, the student who struggles with recognition of individual letters will also struggle to identify familiar letter patterns. Adams described this paradox:

> Ultimately, readers come to look and feel like they recognize words holistically because they have acquired a deep, richly interconnected, and ready knowledge of their spell-

ings, sounds, and meanings. . . . Skillful readers automatically and quite thoroughly process the component letters of text because their visual knowledge of words is from memories of the sequences of letters of which the words are comprised. (1994, p. 9)

Ehri suggested that automatic word recognition, or sight word reading, involves recognizing the letters in the words, because ultimately letters are the "distinctive cues that make one word different from all the others" (1998, p. 13). Although necessary, letter recognition alone is not sufficient for good word reading because automatic word reading cannot occur without a complete understanding of the correspondences between the letters and their phonological realities (Ehri, 1998).

From Knowledge of Letter Names to Sound–Symbol Correspondences

In addition to recognizing letter sequences, children must learn how the phonemes of language map onto the letters that represent them. Phonemes are the smallest sound segments that make words distinguishable, such as /t/ and /d/ in *time* and *dime*. Learning the alphabetic code is an essential part of learning to read. In an alphabetic language such as English, the alphabet is the bridge from speech to literacy. To travel from the spoken language to the written code, children must acquire the conscious awareness "that all words are specified by an internal phonological structure, the shortest elements of which are the phonemes that the letters of the alphabet represent" (Liberman & Liberman, 1990, p. 60). It is now well understood that beginning readers must come to the same understanding that the inventors of the alphabet made: Words do not differ "holistically, one from another, but only in the particulars of their internal structure" (Liberman & Liberman, 1990, p. 61). Thus, a finite set of sounds arbitrarily rearranged over and over results in unique words that represent different concepts. This discovery led to the invention of the alphabet based on

> the idea that if each phonological element were represented by an identifiable, but wholly arbitrary, optical shape, then all could read and write, provided only that they knew the language and were consciously aware of the internal structure of its words. (Liberman & Liberman, 1990, p. 61)

An alphabet makes possible a highly efficient writing system that can represent all of the sounds in the language (Logan, 1986).

Alphabetic languages differ in how completely the alphabetic principle is realized (Hanna, Hanna, Hodges, & Rudorf, 1966). English has less-than-perfect sound–symbol correspondences and has been characterized as a river of words formed from the tributaries of many different languages (Gillingham & Stillman, 1960). Nevertheless, written English shares the advantages of all alphabetic languages: a relatively small number of symbols correspond to the phonemes that can be arranged and rearranged to represent a myriad of words. (See Chapter 6 for further discussion.)

Children who know letter names have an advantage for learning the alphabetic principle that children lacking that knowledge do not have. Vellutino et al. (2003) discovered that virtually all children who were later classified as poor readers entered kindergarten with poorly developed foundational reading skills such as letter knowledge and phonemic awareness. In an intervention study, Ehri and Wilce (1979) were successful in teaching letter sounds to kindergarten prereaders who already knew letter names; at the same time, Ehri and Wilce found that the children who did not know letter names experienced greater difficulty in learning letter sounds. Letter name knowledge not only helps students infer letter sounds but also helps students remember those sounds (Ehri & Wilce, 1979; Treiman et al., 1998).

A meta-analysis conducted by the National Reading Panel (NRP; National Institute of Child Health and Human Development [NICHD], 2000) also confirmed the importance of letter knowledge. Reading effects were significantly larger when children were taught to manipulate phonemes using letters than when they did not use letters. Similarly, spelling effects were found to be larger when children were taught to manipulate phonemes using letters.

Knowledge of letter names helps students read unknown words because phonemes represented by graphemes (letters or **letter clusters**) are often embedded in letters' names (Ehri, 1987). For example, the sound /m/ is found within the letter name "m." Similarly, vowels often have sounds that are identical to their names. The spellings of beginning readers (invented or transitional spellings) often reflect the use of this knowledge, such as in *PPL* for *people,* or *KAM* for *came,* in which letter names provide clues to letter sounds. Thus, letter names provide a foundation for learning the alphabetic principle: Letters represent sounds. When writing a word "the way it sounds," students begin to learn sound–symbol correspondences and an awareness of the sequencing of the sounds and letters in words. Both of these tasks are essential in the process of learning to read.

The Importance of Letter-Name Knowledge

Knowing letter names helps children recall letter–sound associations. Labeling an item helps store information about that item in long-term memory (Gibson, 1969, and Murray & Lee, 1977, both as cited in Walsh, Price, & Gillingham, 1988). Knowing the names of letters also facilitates communication about those letters. Teachers are more aware of students confusing letters if students use letter names, so letter names make instruction easier because there are common referents for letters (Walsh et al., 1988). Sulzby (1983) found that 5-year-olds used letter names in asking their parents questions about word boundaries. Knowing letter names makes it easier for children to ask for and receive information about the reading process.

There is an advantage to having a consistent common referent for letter shapes. The name of a letter is its only stable property (Cox, 1992). The shape may change (e.g., upper- and lowercase forms, cursive and printed forms, differing fonts), and the speech sounds represented by letters may change (e.g., long and short vowel sounds). However, the name of the letter remains the same, anchoring its other properties. According to Adams, "The provision of a distinctive and uniform label for a concept is especially important—perhaps critically so—for the attainment of concepts whose context and superficial expression varies across occurrences" (1990a, p. 352).

Knowing the different letter names allows children to uniquely label different letter shapes. Gibson, Gibson, Pick, and Osser (1962) described how children learn letter shapes: Children learn to distinguish one letter from another and to identify letters "by noting distinctive features such as whether lines are curved or slanted, open or closed" (as cited in Gunning, 1996, p. 55). Through many exposures children compare and contrast letters as they learn to identify and remember their distinctive features.

Some reading programs begin by teaching students to associate a letter shape with the sound it represents rather than with the letter's name. Because students will eventually need to associate symbols with sounds, some educators ask, "Why not go directly to sound–symbol association and bypass letter names?" According to Adams (1990a), there are some drawbacks to teaching only sound–symbol associations without teaching the names of the symbols:

- Several graphemes in English regularly represent more than one phoneme (e.g., *c* can be pronounced as /k/ as in *cat* or /s/ as in *city*). Learning to recognize letters may take longer if multiple sounds are associated with a letter.

- When trying to identify an unknown word, new readers are limited to the number of letter–sound correspondences that have been taught, whereas students with letter-name knowledge may be able to use this information to infer or retrieve the sound of the letter and thus identify the word.

Predictive Value of Letter-Name Knowledge

Since the late 1960s research consistently has shown that letter-naming accuracy predicts later reading achievement (Badian, 1994, 1995; Chall, 1996; Share, Jorm, Maclean, & Matthews, 1984). Bond and Dykstra (1967) found that the ability of prereaders to recognize and name upper- and lowercase letters was the single best predictor of end-of-year reading achievement. Badian (1995) reported results of a longitudinal study that followed 92 students from preschool through sixth grade to determine which of the students' prereading skills best predicted later reading ability. Preschool letter-naming accuracy (speed was not a factor in the letter-naming task) significantly predicted reading vocabulary, reading comprehension, and spelling achievement at each grade level, as well as phonemic awareness ability in the first and third grades.

The longitudinal prediction of word-reading ability from preschool letter-reading accuracy is based upon the similarity of letter- and word-reading tasks. Both letter- and word-reading require the ability to encode, store, and retrieve lexical labels for abstract symbols. Although letter naming has been assumed to be a prereading skill (Badian, 1995), it has recently been shown to be a simple form of reading (Neuhaus & Swank, 2002). Letter-reading success is dependent upon the same component skills that are necessary for accurate word reading. Single-letter reading is the simplest form of reading, and word-reading ability is the most robust predictor of reading comprehension (Perfetti, 1985). Importantly, letter-reading rather than naming ability is directly linked to reading comprehension skill through word-reading or decoding accuracy. Underdeveloped knowledge of single letters and letter clusters has been shown to "compromise early reading development for at-risk beginning readers in general, not just the slow responders, especially in application of alphabetic principal to unfamiliar words" (Berninger et al., 2002, p. 63). Moreover, inaccurate or inconsistent letter recognition prevents the developing reader from unitizing letters into whole words that he or she can recognize easily within 1 second (Ehri & Wilce, 1983).

Letter-Naming Errors and Dyslexia

Letter reversals and letter transpositions are commonly associated with beginning readers, and students with dyslexia often continue to reverse and transpose letters within words. Words containing *b, d,* or *p* may be read as though those letters were reversed or rotated, such as when *bad* is read as *dad* or *pad*. A transposition of letters results in *felt* being read as *flet* or *sacred* being read as *scared*.

Liberman, Shankweiler, Orlando, Harris, and Berti (1971) described several important findings about beginning readers' letter reversals and transpositions: 1) Letter reversals and letter transpositions of low-scoring second-grade readers are independent of each other. Together these two types of errors represented only 25% of misread letters; 2) less-skilled beginning readers make more errors when reading vowels than con-

sonants; and 3) letter reversals are rare when individual letters are presented at rapid exposures. Letter reversals occur at a much higher frequency within the context of a word. This suggests difficulty "with the rules governing the synthesis of syllables from combinations of letter segments, rather than with strategies for scanning connected text" (Liberman et al., 1971, p. 141).

Liberman and colleagues' (1971) research, supported by investigations by Shankweiler and Liberman (1972) and Vellutino (1979, 1980), is often credited with dispelling the belief that dyslexia results from deficiencies in the visual-perceptual system (i.e., that students with dyslexia perceive letters and words inaccurately). In a study by Vellutino, Smith, Steger, and Kaman (1975), readers with and without dyslexia who did not know Hebrew were given a brief exposure to unfamiliar Hebrew words and letters. Then the students were asked to copy the Hebrew symbols from memory. There was no difference in the two groups' ability to accomplish the task and no difference in orientation and sequencing errors. The readers with dyslexia actually made fewer orientation errors than did the readers without dyslexia. When linguistic processing was not included in the symbol memory task, that is, when sounds, verbal labels, and meanings were not required for the wordlike symbols, there was no difference in the ability to visually recall and reproduce the symbols. Individuals with dyslexia have difficulty when the task requires associating linguistic values with symbols such as letters. Some of these reading-related tasks include the following:

1. Associating a letter name with the letter form (the letter name "b" with the symbol *b*)

2. Mapping sounds onto symbols (the letter *b* represents the phoneme /b/)

3. Learning to associate orthographic patterns with the sounds they represent (*igh* = /ī/ as in *bright*)

4. Recognizing an orthographic pattern as a whole word (*bright* = /brīt/).

When students misidentify *b* as *d* or *p*, visual perception or visual memory are not the sources of the difficulty. The students may not have made a stable or fixed association between the letter name or sound and the spatial orientation of the letter (Vellutino, 1979). In other words, the student has not securely attached a verbal label to the letter. For many students, it is only through extensive practice that secure associations are formed between the visual form and its verbal label.

Stanovich and Siegel (1994) and Siegel, Share, and Geva (1995) have found that poor readers rely on an orthographic (visual) strategy to read words. Therefore, when students misread *flet* for *felt*, they most likely use a visual or orthographic reading strategy that includes very little phonological mediation or processing that provides an internal verbal affirmation of the appropriateness of the pronunciation (Siegel et al., 1995). Neuhaus (2000) documented that first-grade students who named letters with more inconsistent speed scored high on orthographic knowledge measures and low on phonological awareness measures, whereas first-grade students who named letters with a more consistent speed scored high on measures of phonological awareness. This significant interaction indicated that even letter reading requires well-developed orthographic and phonological knowledge. Overreliance on a visual reading strategy resulted in slow and inconsistent letter recognition, which was associated with inaccurate word recognition (Neuhaus, 2000). This again demonstrates the necessity for all readers to pair graphemes with their corresponding phonological labels.

Letter-Naming Speed and Dyslexia

It is thought that reading disability should be identified as early as possible so that children's reading difficulties can be remediated before they experience years of frustration and school failure. Vellutino et al. (2003) and Vellutino et al. (1996) suggested that the majority of middle- and upper middle-class students who are ultimately identified with reading difficulties have experiential or instructional deprivation rather than basic cognitive deficits. Therefore, deficient achievement levels of skills, known to predict later difficulty with word reading and reading comprehension, must be recognized early in a child's academic career so that effective instruction can target any skill deficits detected.

Denckla and Rudel (1974) developed the Rapid Automatized Naming (RAN) tests to predict whether young children were at risk for later reading failure. The RAN test measures how quickly individuals can name stimuli, and RAN tasks have consistently shown that the speed that young children name overlearned letters, numbers, objects and colors is a strong predictor of later word-recognition ability (Badian, 1994; Neuhaus, Foorman, Francis, & Carlson, 2001; Wolf, Bally, & Morris, 1986; Wolf & Bowers, 1999; Wolf & Obregón, 1992).

RAN tasks require students to name 50 items (five common letters, objects, numbers, or colors randomly arranged 10 times each) as rapidly as they can. RAN tasks have been used to show significant differences between the naming speed of readers with and without dyslexia (Ackerman & Dykman, 1993), readers whose poor reading skills are commensurate with their IQ scores (Wolf & Obregón, 1992), and students with attention deficit disorder (Felton, Wood, Brown, & Campbell, 1987). Significantly slower naming speed is present in kindergartners who are eventually classified as having severe reading impairments (Wolf et al., 1986), and slow naming persists in adults with dyslexia (Felton & Wood, 1989). Naming speed slowness in individuals with dyslexia does not appear to dissipate with age and has been found to predict reading ability independently of articulation speed (Neuhaus, Carlson, Jeng, Post, & Swank, 2001; Neuhaus, Foorman, et al., 2001; Obregón, 1994). It also predicts reading independently of phonological processing abilities (Neuhaus & Swank, 2002; Torgesen, Wagner, Rashotte, Burgess, & Hecht, 1997; Wolf, Bowers, & Biddle, 2000).

A naming speed deficit is hypothesized to represent a deficit that is distinct from a phonological processing deficit (Catts, Gillispie, Leonard, Kail, & Miller, 2002; Neuhaus & Swank, 2002; Wolf & Bowers, 1999). This has important implications for conceptualizing causes of dysfunctional reading and reading instructional strategies (Bowers & Wolf, 1993). Wolf (1997) distinguished four types of readers: 1) readers with no deficits; 2) readers with phonological processing deficits (difficulty encoding, storing, and/or retrieving phonological information); 3) readers with rapid-naming deficits; and 4) those with a double deficit, or difficulty with both phonological processing and rapid naming. The students with double deficits are most likely to be identified as having dyslexia and to have more severe reading problems (Wolf et al., 2003). Wolf suggested that if these students receive remedial instruction in the area of phonological processing alone, then they are receiving only a portion of what they need. Wolf and colleagues (2003) are studying the feasibility of increasing speed in naming, decoding, orthographic pattern recognition, and word retrieval through the RAVE-O intervention program (Wolf et al., 2003). The program is implemented only in conjunction with a program of systematic phonological analysis and blending and includes vocabulary development and the use of visual mnemonics (e.g., retrieving the meaning of *barometer* by previously having visualized a "tall Baron Meter") (Wolf & Segal, 1995, as cited in

Wolf, 1997). Importantly, the program always includes a daily practice of rapid recognition of common letter patterns (Wolf et al., 2003) and strives to build strong connections between letter patterns and their corresponding sounds.

An abundance of research points to the importance of fast and accurate letter recognition as a foundation for accurate word reading. Accurate word reading leads to good reading comprehension. Wolf and Obregón noted succinctly, "For children who are lagging behind in development for any environmental or physiological reason, or who are at risk for reading failure, the need to develop automatic letter and word recognition skills is critical" (1997, p. 200). Rapid letter reading is important to development of word-reading automaticity so that attention is freed for higher-level reading comprehension (LaBerge & Samuels, 1974). Letter and word recognition become automatic when letters and words are processed unconsciously. In other words, it is literally easier to recognize and read a letter or word than it is not to read it. The time and practice needed to reach an automatic level of letter reading, however, differs dramatically among students. Berninger (2000) found that students with dyslexia needed more than 20 times the amount of practice that students without dyslexia needed to learn letter sequences. Neuhaus, Carlson, et al. (2001) found that second-, third-, and fourth-grade students still have significant variation in their letter-naming speed. This suggests that letter knowledge is not necessarily fully developed by kindergarten or first grade for beginning readers and that secure letter knowledge requires more extensive practice for some students. Therefore, allowing each student sufficient time and practice to solidify knowledge of letter names, shapes, and sounds is imperative.

Letter-naming speed is influenced by a number of learned skills and cognitive abilities and has been found to be the single largest predictor of word-reading ability for first-grade students (Neuhaus & Swank, 2002). Neuhaus and Swank found that RAN letter naming is predicted by phonological awareness, orthographic recognition, general naming, and visual attention skills. When word-reading accuracy was modeled, general naming speed and letter-naming speed significantly predicted word reading over phonological awareness, orthographic recognition, and attention. This indicated that letter naming is only slightly less cognitively complex than word reading and that letter-naming tasks should more appropriately be termed single-letter word reading rather than letter naming. In other words, letter reading is a skill that requires the exacting coordination of multiple cognitive systems and is the most important predictor of identifying multiletter words.

The importance of good letter reading cannot be overstated. Fast and accurate letter reading must be developed in every student. However, fast and accurate letter reading is not the end goal; rather, it is the stepping-off point to accurate automatic word reading that leads to good reading comprehension. The teacher-led activities included later in this chapter have been successfully used to teach accurate and efficient letter recognition. These activities have been a part of a multisensory, structured, sequential reading instructional program that has been validated to increase reading skills for many students including general education elementary school students (Day, 1993); low socioeconomic status, minority students who changed schools frequently (Post, 1999); and high-achieving elementary school students (Frankiewicz, 1984b). These letter-learning activities were also included in a first- and second-grade multisensory reading intervention program (Carreker et al., 2003). The program was shown to significantly enhance the third-grade reading comprehension performance of both English-speaking and bilingual Hispanic elementary school students on a state-mandated achievement test over traditional instruction offered to the other students in the dis-

trict. In addition, the letter and alphabet activities presented in this chapter have been shown to significantly enhance the reading progress of learning disabled students in elementary, middle, and high school resource classrooms (Frankiewicz, 1984a; Reed, Selig, Young, & Day, 1995), and when implemented as one-to-one instruction (Frankiewicz, 1985; Stein, 1987). Together, the letter-naming activities and practices in this chapter can be effective for virtually any student beginning the journey toward literacy.

TEACHING LETTER IDENTIFICATION, NAMING, AND ALPHABETIZING SKILLS

This section provides information on how students, those with dyslexia in particular, can be helped to develop accurate and rapid associations of letter names and letter forms through a variety of instructional activities. The clinical experience of many practitioners has shown that use of these activities increases both accuracy and speed in letter identification and naming (Frankiewicz, 1985; Stein, 1987).

Development of Letter Recognition in Students without Dyslexia

It is helpful to view instruction in letter recognition for students with dyslexia in the context of how letter recognition develops in most students. Adams (1990a) outlined the process through which the majority of children develop this skill. Long before kindergarten, many children learn letter names before letter shapes through singing the alphabet. Some children can associate some letter names with letter shapes, particularly uppercase letters, before they enter school. They learn the associations through games, puzzles, television programs such as *Sesame Street,* and direct instruction from attentive adults.

Ideally, on entering kindergarten, children are given the chance to develop or consolidate letter identification with uppercase letters before lowercase letters are formally introduced. The same principle is seen in the recommendation that students know letter names well before instruction in sound–symbol association begins (Adams, 1990a; NICHD, 2000). Much confusion among kindergarten and first-grade students can be avoided if letter names are secure.

Writing plays a role in the beginning reader's ability to recognize letters. Practice in writing letters focuses students' attention on the particular features of the letter shape and thus helps reinforce letter recognition (Adams, 1990a).

Development of Letter Recognition in Students with Dyslexia

Often students with dyslexia are not identified until third or fourth grade or later. This means that students already have been exposed to both upper- and lowercase letters and probably to both print and cursive handwriting. In all likelihood, these students lack speed and accuracy in letter identification. In their own writing, they may mix together print and cursive and upper- and lowercase letters in the same sentence.

In several programs designed for students with dyslexia, letter identification is taught or improved through the use of uppercase block capitals because they contain fewer confusing letter shapes. The uppercase forms are more graphically distinct. Letter identification is reinforced through the use of three-dimensional (3-D) letters in alphabetizing activities as part of a comprehensive lesson plan. Alphabet sequencing activities reinforce left-to-right directionality as well, which is essential to the reading process.

Within the same lesson, a lowercase printed letter is taught through a multisensory letter introduction in which the letter's name, shape, and the sound it represents are linked (see Chapter 9 for more information on **linkages**). Students practice lowercase letter identification and naming with a letter deck. Handwriting practice within the same lesson provides kinesthetic reinforcement of letter name and shape. The cursive form of the letter is used for writing.

Principles of Effective Instruction

Principles of instruction that make letter identification instruction effective with students, including those with dyslexia, include the following.

1. *Multisensory teaching:* The purpose of multisensory teaching is to provide instruction that simultaneously engages multiple sensory receptors that encode the information concurrently in different forms. This provides an opportunity for knowledge to be retained in various domain specific memory stores, especially those associated with visual, verbal, kinesthetic, and tactile experiences. Recent studies have validated multisensory instruction as significantly more effective than traditional instruction for teaching phonological awareness, decoding skills, and reading comprehension (Carreker et al., 2003; Foorman, Francis, Shaywitz, Shaywitz, & Fletcher, 1997; Joshi, Dahlgren, Boulware-Gooden, 2002); however, it is not exactly clear how the multisensory procedures enhance achievement. Various explanations have been hypothesized.

   For example, Gardner (1985) has proposed that memory is composed of distinct modules that store different types of information. According to this theory, multisensory instruction would result in greater learning because information presented in two or more ways would be stored in different sensory-specific modular storage units. Multisensory reading instruction supplies the phonological and orthographic information associated with letters and words concurrently to these memory systems, so redundant information about each letter and letter pattern is stored in different modules. Therefore, a student who has a limitation in a storage system may be able to compensate by accessing the information available in other modules (Hallahan & Kauffman, 1976). This idea is consistent with connectionist models that suggest that reading ability is optimized when both phonological and orthographic representations are fully functional and are allowed to interact (Harm & Seidenberg, 2004; Plaut, McClelland, Seidenberg, & Patterson, 1996).

   Alternatively, it has been suggested that children's visual attention is focused by their manual tasks (Thorpe & Borden, 1985). Physical manipulation of a stimulus demands attention, and the enhanced attention to a manual task appears to increase the likelihood that the stimulus is remembered. Multisensory instruction may also improve memory of the linkages of specific sounds and symbols because teachers provide clear and concrete mnemonic strategies that young children may not initiate on their own. Finally, it is logical to assume that for a student to overtly demonstrate an ability to manipulate sounds, letters, and words correctly, he or she must understand the rules of the language activity. Oral responses and physical manipulation used in multisensory instruction allow the instructor to quickly and easily observe whether students understand the concepts underlying the activity. Consequently, the teacher can immediately reteach the information if students do not grasp the concept and can repeat activities to strengthen their knowledge.

Students with dyslexia often have difficulty with the storage and retrieval of lexical labels (including letter names) and need the opportunity to learn and practice especially through simultaneously engaging at least two or three learning modalities: visual, auditory, and tactile/kinesthetic (involving muscle memory). For example, students can say the names of letters as they see and touch 3-D plastic letters and place them in alphabetical order. This multisensory experience builds visual, verbal, and tactile/kinesthetic memories associated with letters and their order within the alphabet.

2. *Sequential presentation:* Information must be presented in a sequence that builds logically on previously taught material.

3. *Guided discovery:* The **Socratic method** leads learners to discover information through carefully guided questioning based on information they already possess. This method builds interest and aids memory. Also, when the teacher reviews by starting a sentence and then pauses for students to complete it, students are encouraged to participate rather than being placed on the defensive by a direct question, (e.g., *The initial letter of the alphabet is _____* , rather than *What is the initial letter of the alphabet?*).

4. *Brief instructional segments:* Frequent and brief instructional segments are more effective than less frequent segments lasting longer periods of time. Extensive guided practice is required for automaticity.

5. *Teaching to mastery:* After presenting the material through guided discovery, the teacher models and then provides practice activities; reviews the material on a regular basis; and, when students can be successful, assesses whether students have mastered the material. Students need many opportunities for practice with the material for long-term retention. The teacher should ensure success for all students by reviewing the procedure or concept before asking students to apply it. For example, a quick warm-up of touching and naming the letters on an alphabet strip is strongly recommended before students work on a sequencing, alphabetizing, or dictionary activity. In this way, students are set up for success.

   Students learn at different rates. As noted earlier in this chapter, Berninger (2000) found that students with learning disabilities needed more than 20 times the amount of practice that regular education students needed to reach equivalent levels of expertise in letter sequencing. The rate of letter mastery will differ among students and will vary according to a student's ability to consolidate the memories needed to recall the visual and verbal characteristics of each letter. Importantly, the teacher needs to individualize instructional practice time to allow varying amounts of time for students to acquire letter expertise.

6. *Teaching proofreading:* The teacher guides students through the process of proofreading by which they discover and correct their own errors instead of relying on an outside source (teacher or computer).

History of the Alphabet Promotes Interest in Learning Letter Names

The fascinating history of the alphabet can be used to encourage students' interest in developing letter recognition and alphabetizing skills. Students who have difficulty with the two-dimensional symbol system often enjoy learning about the 3-D objects

from which the letters of our alphabet are derived. Students can make helpful associations between a letter's history and the letter's name and shape.

The two letters from which we get the very word *alphabet* serve as examples. To the people of Phoenicia, who lived 4,000 years ago, the word for ox was *aleph*. When they wanted to send a message about an ox, they drew a simple line drawing of an ox head with two horns and a face in the middle. As time passed, the drawing was turned upside down and began to stand for the first sound of the word. Much later, the Greeks took the sign of the ox's head and called it *alpha,* which became the first letter of their alphabet. The letter we call *A* was the Greek alpha. The letter *B* comes down to us from the Phoenician word *beth,* meaning house, for which Phoenicians drew a triangle with a base. The Greeks borrowed the word and the sign, made two triangles, changed the orientation, and called it *beta.* Thus, we have our letter *B.* (See Chapter 6 for more on the history of the English language.)

The final section of this chapter contains questions for students to spark their interest in the history of writing and various alphabets. Student interest will be greatly increased if pictures and maps accompany this discussion.

ACTIVITIES

The following activities and recommended materials are drawn from the work and writings of Gillingham and Stillman (1960); Cox (1992) and the teaching staff of the Language Laboratory of the Scottish Rite Hospital in Dallas, Texas; Hogan and Smith (1987) of EDMAR Educational Associates in Forney, Texas; and the staff of the Neuhaus Education Center in Bellaire, Texas (1998). (See Appendix B at the end of the book for information on purchasing the materials for instruction.)

Materials for Instruction

Most materials used in the following activities are listed here; however, materials that are used only for a single activity or for variations on an activity are described later in the text.

- For each student, a small mirror, ideally a round one approximately 2″ in diameter with plastic encasing the edges. These are available from any company that produces marketing or promotional materials such as pencils, cups, and so forth.

- Classroom uppercase alphabet strip, a minimum of 3″ x 48″, with block letters, without pictures or graphics that can be visually distracting to students, mounted at students' eye level

- Set of 3-D plastic uppercase block letters for each student and for the teacher, stored in plastic bags or tubs

- Individual uppercase alphabet strip for each student, made of a laminated strip of cardstock, approximately 2″ x 17″, with block letters

- For each student, eight sets of 10 word cards approximately 1″ x 2″, with words printed in lowercase, to be used for alphabetization by 1) first letter; 2) second letter; 3) first and second letters; 4) third letters; 5) second and third letters; 6) fourth letter; 7) third and fourth letters; and 8) first, second, third, and fourth letters. The card sets should be identical across the class.

Use different colors of cards for the eight sets of cards. If eight colors are not available, card sets can be further differentiated by using a marker to draw a stripe along the top edge of certain card sets (e.g., sets of white, pink, yellow, and blue cards with and without a black stripe at the top). Word sets can be easily stored in small plastic sandwich bags. These card sets are described in further detail in the section on alphabetizing activities.

- For the teacher, eight sets of word cards approximately 5″ x 7″ with words printed in lowercase. The words used in the teacher's sets should not be identical to those in the students' sets. The teacher's cards are larger than the students' cards so that all students can see them.

- Container for each student in which to store the individual alphabet strip(s), plastic letters, and word cards to be alphabetized

- Guide-word practice dictionary for each student, purchased or teacher made

- Dictionary for each student, appropriate to the students' ability level

For younger students:

- Alphabet matching mat made of poster board or heavy laminated paper, approximately 24″ x 18″, with the outlines of uppercase block letter shapes arranged alphabetically in an arc (see Figure 5.1). Students can practice matching by placing plastic letters on the mat.

For students who do not need to start with a matching activity:

- Alphabet sequencing mat made of poster board or heavy laminated paper, approximately 24″ x 18″, with uppercase block letters in alphabetical order printed across

Figure 5.1. Alphabet matching mat.

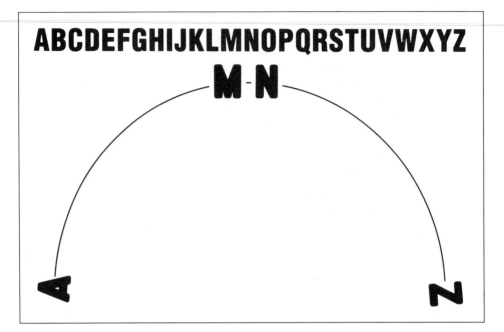

Figure 5.2. Alphabet sequencing mat. (A mat for learning the sequence of the Spanish alphabet appears in Figure 11.1 in Chapter 11.)

the top and the letters *A, M, N,* and *Z* forming an arc (or rainbow) beneath. *M* and *N* are printed at the top of the arc, *A* and *Z* are in the initial and final positions, and space is left for the missing letters to be placed within the arc (see Figure 5.2).

For students who have learned uppercase letters:

- Individual lowercase alphabet strip for each student, made of a 2″ x 17″ strip of laminated cardstock

- Classroom lowercase alphabet strip, minimum of 3″ x 48″, with block letters, without pictures or graphics, mounted at students' eye level

Activities for Developing Letter Identification, Naming, and Sequencing Skills

Schedule

Allot 5–7 minutes within a 50- to 60-minute lesson for letter identification, naming, and sequencing activities as outlined next. Continue using uppercase letters in these activities until students can rapidly and accurately identify all uppercase letters in sequence and at random.

Lowercase letters (and letter clusters) should be taught individually through a multisensory letter introduction procedure often referred to as *linking* (see Chapter 9) in which the letter's name, shape, and sounds it represents are concurrently linked in memory. Lowercase letter names should be reviewed daily through the use of a letter–sound deck or reading deck (see Chapter 9).

Younger students may need to reinforce speed and accuracy of lowercase letter recognition through the same activities discussed here for developing accurate and rapid recognition and sequencing of uppercase letters. Use 3-D lowercase letters and lowercase alphabet strips if needed.

The activities which follow can be rotated within a weekly lesson plan. Students should touch and name letters on an alphabet strip as a warm-up before each activity. The strip remains in place during the activity as a reference.

Matching and Naming

- 3-D uppercase letter sets

- Alphabet matching mats

Students who cannot match 3-D uppercase letters with the outlines of uppercase letters printed on paper should begin with this activity. The teacher has students turn the 3-D plastic letters right side up and facing the correct direction inside the arc on the alphabet matching mat. The teacher tells students that these are the letters found in the words we read and write. He or she points out the alphabet on the classroom alphabet strip and leads students to discover that an alphabet contains these same letters in a fixed order. The teacher asks students to name each letter before they place the plastic letter on top of the printed form on their individual alphabet matching mats. If all of the letters are not matched within 5 minutes, then the activity is repeated the next day, starting with the letters matched the day before and continuing with additional letters until students can place all of the letters on the mat. The teacher has students check their work each time by touching and naming the letters they have just placed (e.g., students say "A" and touch the plastic letter sitting on top of the printed letter).

The teacher leads students to discover the number of letters in the alphabet by pointing to each letter and counting. The teacher leads students in completing the sentence, "The number of letters in the alphabet is ____ [26]."

Students progress from 1) placing the plastic letters on top of the printed forms on the mat for matching, to 2) placing the letters beneath the printed letters on an alphabet strip, to 3) placing the letters in an arc on the mat for sequencing (see Figure 5.2). When students can accurately place plastic letters beneath the letters on an alphabet strip, they are ready for the following activity, Naming, Sequencing, and Discovery of Middle.

Naming, Sequencing, and Discovery of Middle

- Classroom uppercase alphabet strip

- Individual uppercase alphabet strips

Students who do not need to start with a matching activity will start here. If starting here, then the teacher leads students to discover the number of letters in the alphabet (see description in Matching and Naming).

The teacher asks students to join in naming each letter as he or she points to it in sequential order on the classroom uppercase alphabet strip. The teacher asks students to touch and name each letter on their individual uppercase alphabet strips as he or she leads them in naming the letters together.

The teacher asks younger students to discover the middle of the alphabet by putting one index finger on the first letter of the alphabet and one index finger on the last letter and moving in toward the middle. Students discover that the exact middle is between the letters *M* and *N*. The teacher leads students in completing the sentence, "The two middle letters of the alphabet are _____ [*M* and *N*]."

After students can accurately perform this touching and naming activity, any daily alphabet activity should begin with a warm-up in which students touch and name the letters of the alphabet on their strips. This warm-up activity provides the repetition that students with dyslexia require to develop automaticity.

Discovery of Vowel and Consonant Sounds

- Mirror for each student

Before students learn that there are two kinds of letters (consonants and vowels) in the alphabet, the teacher introduces the concept of two kinds of sounds. The teacher leads students to discover that we use only two kinds of sounds when we talk: the sounds we form when the mouth is open (vowels) and the sounds we form when the mouth is closed or partially closed (consonants). The teacher illustrates that when we say words, we open and close our mouths. The students try to talk by putting together only closed-mouth sounds, such as /m/, /l/, or /p/. The students try to talk using only open-mouth sounds, such as /ă/, /ĕ/, or /ŭ/. The teacher explains that to form words, we must both open and close our mouths. The teacher illustrates by slowly saying a word, such as *map,* and letting the students see the mouth closing for the consonant, opening for the vowel, and closing for the consonant.

The teacher asks students to look into a mirror as they say /ă/, /ĕ/, /ĭ/, /ŏ/, and /ŭ/ and leads them to discover that their mouths are open when they say these sounds. The shape of the mouth changes, but nothing blocks the air that comes out of the mouth to form these sounds. The teacher explains that vowel sounds open our mouths. Next, the teacher directs students to look in a mirror to see what happens when they say the sound /s/. The teacher explains that their teeth and tongue partially close their mouths. Then the teacher has the students say /l/ and notice that the tongue partially closes their mouths. Students then say /m/ and notice that their lips partially close their mouths. These are consonant sounds. The teacher says that consonant sounds close or partially close our mouths. The teeth, tongue, and/or lips block the air used in making these sounds. The teacher leads the students in saying, "Vowel sounds open our mouths, and consonant sounds close or partially close our mouths with our teeth, tongue, or lips." The teacher and students use gestures for open (hands open like a crocodile mouth) and closed (palms together) and point to their teeth, tongue, and lips.

The teacher provides practice for the students in differentiating between consonant and vowel sounds by having students look into their mirror, repeat sounds, and discover whether their mouth is open or closed (or partially closed) when they say the sound. The teacher starts with consonant sounds for which the mouth is very obviously closed or partially closed, such as /s/, /l/, /m/, or /n/, interspersed with both long and short vowel sounds. After students are aware of the difference between consonant and vowel sounds, they are ready to discover that the letters that represent these sounds are classified as consonant letters and vowel letters.

Discovery of Vowel and Consonant Letters

- Individual uppercase alphabet strips (for reference)

- Mirrors

The teacher tells the students that they are going to discover the two kinds of letters in the alphabet. The teacher explains that just as there are two kinds of sounds (vowels and consonants) in spoken words, there are two kinds of letters in our alphabet. The teacher and students review together, "Vowel sounds open our mouths, and consonant sounds close or partially close our mouths." The names of the letters give clues as to which letters will be called vowels and which will be called consonants. The teacher directs the students to look in a mirror to see what happens to their mouths when they say the names of the letters A, E, I, O, and U. Their mouths stay open when they say these letter names. The teacher tells students that these letters represent vowel sounds. Students use the mirror to discover that when they say the name of the letter S, the mouth is partially closed by the teeth and tongue. When they say the name of the letter L, the mouth is partially closed, with the tongue closing against the roof of the mouth. When they say the name of the letter M, the lips close the mouth.

After students are aware that the alphabet is made up of vowel and consonant letters that represent vowel and consonant sounds, the teacher varies the daily warm-up activity of touching and naming the letters by having students whisper or cheer for the vowel letters.

Discovery of Initial, Medial, and Final

- Classroom uppercase alphabet strip

- Individual uppercase alphabet strips

The alphabet can be used to teach students terminology that will be used in other aspects of written language training. For example, in phonemic awareness training, students will be asked whether they hear a specific sound in the **initial**, **medial**, or **final** position in a word. Students can be helped to understand the meaning of the abstract spatial terms *initial, medial,* and *final* by learning them first in relation to the alphabet strip. The terms *initial, medial,* and *final* can be introduced by teaching the initial, medial, and final letters of the alphabet.

The teacher writes the initials of his or her name on the board and leads students to discover that these letters are the first letters of his or her name. The teacher writes several students' initials on the board and helps students discover that initials are the first letters of names. The teacher explains that *initial* means first and that the alphabet also has an initial letter, A. The teacher points to the A on the classroom alphabet strip, asks students to touch the letter A on their alphabet strips, and leads them in saying, "A is the _____ [initial] letter of the alphabet."

The teacher touches Z on the classroom alphabet strip and asks students to touch Z on their strips. The teacher tells students that the last letter of the alphabet is Z and that another way of saying *last* is *final.* The teacher leads students in saying, "Z is the _____ [final] letter of the alphabet." The teacher tells students that all of the letters between A and Z are medial letters and that there is a difference between medial and middle. As students learned in Naming, Sequencing, and Discovery of Middle, the exact middle of the alphabet is found between the letters M and N. *Medial* means anything

between initial or final. A medial letter is any letter occurring between *A* and *Z*. The teacher asks students to name some of the medial alphabet letters (any letter that is not *A* or *Z*) and then to identify initial, medial, and final letters within other words written on the board, such as their own names or the teacher's name.

The teacher provides kinesthetic reinforcement for all of this information through gestures. The teacher stands with his or her back to the students, facing the classroom alphabet strip, and raises both arms, fingers pointing above his or her head. The teacher drops his or her left arm horizontally to the left (parallel to the floor) while saying, "Initial means first." The teacher drops his or her right arm horizontally to the right while saying, "Final means last." The teacher brings both arms back above his or her head and says, "Medial means anything between initial (dropping left arm to horizontal) and final (dropping right arm to horizontal)."

Sequencing with 3-D Letters

- Individual uppercase alphabet strips (for reference)

- 3-D uppercase letter sets

- Alphabet sequencing mats (most older students will place the letters on their desks rather than using mats)

The teacher writes *A, M, N,* and *Z* in an arc on the board with *M* and *N* at the top of the arc. The teacher directs students to name and place the initial letter of the alphabet on their alphabet sequencing mats (or desks). They name and place *A* and say, "*A* is the initial letter of the alphabet." Students name and place *Z* and say, "*Z* is the final letter of the alphabet." Students name and place *M* and *N* and say, "*M* and *N* are the two middle letters of the alphabet." The teacher directs students, "Name it, find it, place it," as they fill in the arc with missing letters in alphabetical order. Students say a letter, find it, and place it in the arc until the alphabet is complete. Students then proofread their work by touching and naming each letter from *A* to *Z*, using the index finger of their writing hand. Soon after beginning this activity, the teacher times students and compares the result with later timings. The initial goal is accurate naming and placement of all letters in less than 5 minutes, with an ultimate goal of 2 minutes or less. The reason that students place letters in an arc is that often there is not enough space on a desk or a tabletop to place all of the letters in a straight line.

Note for working with younger students: Some very young students may have difficulty crossing the mid-line (moving the right hand and arm into the space to the left of the mid-line of their body or vice versa for left-handed students). These students will want to place the first half of the alphabet letters with their left hand and the second half with their right hand rather than place all of the letters with their writing hand. This is a function of motor skill development; the teacher will encourage them to work toward the time when they can place all of the letters with their writing hand.

Note for working with older students: Older students may enjoy a variation of this activity. For sequencing, have students use plastic poker chips labeled with block capital letters. Older students particularly enjoy the challenge of being timed and having their progress charted. They can compete with themselves to improve their performance.

Other variations:
- Students proofread by returning letters to the storage container in sequence and naming each letter, rather than just touching and naming letters to check.

- After students are able to place the plastic letters in alphabetical order, students may place A, M, N, and Z as usual and then randomly select letters and place them one by one in the approximate place in the semicircle.

Discovery of Before and After

- Classroom uppercase alphabet strip

- Individual uppercase alphabet strips

Students with dyslexia often have difficulty with abstract spatial terms such as *before* and *after* and may be confused by directions such as "Look at the consonant after the vowel" or "Listen for the sound before the /k/ sound." To make the abstract terms *before* and *after* more concrete, the teacher directs students to place both hands below their alphabet strips and then models for students with the classroom alphabet strip. The teacher asks students to raise the hand that is closer to A and tells them that this is their *before* hand. The teacher asks students to raise the hand closer to Z, which is their *after* hand.

Next, the teacher names a letter, such as E, and places both index fingers under the letter on the classroom alphabet strip. The teacher moves the index finger of the *after* hand to the letter after E and says, "F is after E." Students then echo and place their index finger under the chosen letter (E) on their individual alphabet strips. With the index finger of their *after* hand, students touch and name the letter that comes after the named letter. Students say, "F is after E." The teacher names several other letters, and students respond appropriately.

The concept *after* is taught first because it reflects the left-to-right progression of the alphabet. The concept *after* should be practiced in several sessions until it is mastered. Then the teacher has students work with the concept *before*. The teacher names a letter, such as T, and asks students to tell which letter is before it. Students place both index fingers under T, point to S with the index finger of their *before* hand, and say, "S is before T." Finally, the teacher provides practice with both *before* and *after*: "Find W. Tell me what is before and after W."

Missing Letter Decks

- Individual uppercase alphabet strips (for reference)

- Missing letter decks (teacher-made uppercase decks and commercially available lowercase deck)

To make a missing letter deck with uppercase block letters, the teacher prints by hand or by computer the alphabet on cards, with two letters and a blank on each card. In the first set, the third letter is missing and is represented by a blank line (AB____, BC____, CD____). In the second set, the alphabet is printed in groups of three letters with the middle letter missing (A____C, B____D, C____E). In the third set, the first letter is missing (____BC, ____CD, ____DE). In the fourth set, the first and third letters are missing (____B____, ____C____, ____D____).

After students can place all 26 3-D letters of the alphabet in correct sequence within three minutes, the teacher introduces the uppercase missing letter deck. Only after students have been introduced to all lowercase letters should the commercially available Missing Letter Deck with lowercase block letters (Educators Publishing Service; see Appendix B) be used.

Students keep their alphabet strips in front of them to refer to if needed. The teacher makes sure the missing letter deck is in alphabetical order and holds up the first card in the first set of cards. Students name the two letters on each card and the missing letter: "AB____ [C], BC ____ [D]," and so forth. When students can rapidly and accurately name all three letters on each card with the cards in alphabetical sequence (after many practice sessions), the teacher shuffles the cards and presents them in random order. The students then progress to the second, third, and fourth teacher-made sets of the missing letter decks. As with the first set, these are practiced first in sequence, then shuffled. Students should be fluent at each level before progressing to the next level. Students do not have to have mastered all four levels before the teacher introduces the additional activities that follow. The teacher intersperses the Missing Letter Decks activity within a weekly lesson plan with more advanced activities for developing alphabetizing and dictionary skills.

Accent and Rhythm

- Mirrors

Students with dyslexia often have difficulty hearing the **accented** syllable in a word. This has consequences for written language skills, for spelling in particular. The following activity provides practice in hearing accented syllables, while also reinforcing alphabetic sequence. The teacher says the names of several students, overemphasizing the accented syllable in their names ("Ja mal', Sta' cy, Ta ke' sha, Ja' son, Jo sé'). The teacher asks students whether they hear a difference in the way one part of the name is said. The teacher models "robot talk" in which there is no accent. The students discover that we say some parts of spoken words louder than other parts. The teacher explains that when we accent one part of a word, the mouth opens wider, the voice is louder, and the tone is higher. The teacher reinforces each part of the definition with gestures: Mouth opens wider (hands open like a crocodile mouth), voice is louder (cupped hand behind ear), and tone is higher (flattened hand, palm to floor, is raised above head to designate higher).

Some students can learn to "see" accented syllables by using a mirror to notice when their mouths open wider. For students who find perceiving accent particularly difficult, the teacher models laying both hands along the jaw line so that students can feel the jaw opening wider on the accented syllable. Students may be better able to discern the change in pitch that occurs with accent if they place their hands over their ears and hum a word rather than say it.

The teacher recites the letters of the alphabet in pairs and accents the first letter of each pair: "A' B, C' D, E' F, G' H," and so forth. The teacher asks students whether the first or the second letter is being accented. The teacher encourages students to use a mirror to see their mouths opening wider and to cup their jaws in their hands to feel their mouth opening wider. Using block letters and accenting the first letter in each pair, the teacher writes the first eight letters of the alphabet on the board in pairs: A B, C D, E F, G H. Stressing the first letter in each pair, the teacher reads the list. With their alphabet strips in view, students say the alphabet and accent the first letter in each pair. Variations include having students clap on the accented letter.

After students are able to accent the first letter of each pair (after many practice sessions), the teacher writes on the board and leads students in accenting the second let-

ter: "*A B', C D', E F', G H',*" and so forth. Eventually, students practice accenting the first of a group of three letters ("*A' BC, D' EF . . .* "), then the second letter ("*A B' C, D E' F . . .* "), and finally, the third letter ("*AB C', DE F' . . .* "). Students will need to apply their knowledge of accenting patterns when reading unfamiliar longer words. In English, multisyllabic words are accented more often on the first syllable (e.g., bas' ket), next most often on the second syllable (pa rade', con ven' tion), and next most often on the third (guar an tee').

Random Naming of Uppercase Letters

- Classroom uppercase alphabet strip

To determine an individual student's accuracy and relative speed in naming uppercase letters, the teacher indicates letters in random order on the alphabet strip and the student names them. The teacher notes accuracy and relative speed with which responses are made.
   Variations:

- A student randomly selects and names alphabet letters from 26 plastic letters on his or her desktop.

- Students are presented with all 26 uppercase block letters of the alphabet printed in random order in a rapid naming letter chart. The grid has five rows of five letters each. The students name the letters. The teacher may time the students and chart progress for motivation.

Naming of Lowercase Letters

- Individual lowercase alphabet strips

   Chapter 9 describes the introduction of lowercase letters through multisensory letter introduction. If students need additional practice in naming the lowercase letters accurately and rapidly, many of the previous activities for uppercase letters may be adapted. The daily warm-up of touching and naming letters can be done with an alphabet strip of lowercase letters, as can activities such as Missing Letter Decks and Accent and Rhythm and the games Don't Say *Z* and Twenty Questions (described later).

Random Naming of Lowercase Letters

- Classroom lowercase alphabet strip

- 3-D lowercase letter set

The same activities to determine the accuracy and relative speed with which an individual student can name the uppercase letters can be used for the lowercase letters: 1) The student names letters designated in random order by the teacher on the lowercase alphabet strip, 2) the student randomly selects and names alphabet letters from 26 lowercase plastic letters on his or her desktop, or 3) the student names the 26 lowercase letters on a chart (five rows of five squares across, each with a letter in a square) in random order. The teacher may time the students and chart progress for motivation.

Games to Reinforce Letter Identification, Naming, and Sequencing Skills

Alphabet Battle

- Individual alphabet strip and 3-D letter set for each pair of students

Students are divided into pairs. Simultaneously, both players draw a letter from the set of 3-D letters without looking at the letters. Each player places his or her letter on the desk and says the name of the letter. The player whose letter is closer in alphabetical order to Z wins both letters. The student must say, for example, "U is after G. I win the letters." The winner is the player with the most letters at the end of the game.

Variation: The player whose letter is closer to A wins the letters (e.g., "J is before T. I win the letters").

Alphabet Bingo

- Individual alphabet strip (for reference) and 3-D letter set for each student

- 3-D letter set for the teacher

Each student selects any seven letters from his or her container of letters and places them on the desk in a vertical column on the *before* (left-hand) side. The other letters are put away.

The teacher selects one letter from another container, shows it to the students, and names it. Students repeat the name. If they have the letter on their desk, they move it to the after (right-hand) side of the desk to form a second vertical column. The first person to move all seven letters to the *after* side of the desk is the winner. The teacher checks for accuracy by having the winner name the seven letters. For a faster game, start with fewer than seven letters.

Alphabet Dominoes

SEQUENCING

- Individual alphabet strip (for reference) and 3-D letter set for each pair of students

Students should be proficient in *before* and *after* activities. Each pair of students places the letters M and N on the desk. Each student draws five letters without looking. The remaining letters become the "bone yard" and are placed inside the storage container on top of the desk. The teacher designates which student in each pair goes first. That student tries to play a letter immediately before M or after N. The student must have L or O to play initially. If not, then he or she draws a letter from the bone yard without looking. The letters are to be played in alphabetical order to the right of N and in reverse alphabetical order to the left of M. For example, if the letters JKLMNOPQ have been placed, then the next player may play I or R. If a player draws a letter from the bone yard that can be played, he or she must wait until the next turn to play it. Each player plays only one letter at a time. As each student places a letter, he or she says, "____ is before (or after) ____." The winner is the first student to play all of his or her letters (even if there are letters remaining in the bone yard).

Alphabet Relay

- Individual alphabet strip (for reference) and 3-D letter set for each team

Divide students into teams of two to four students. Each team receives an alphabet strip and container of letters and places them on a designated desk. At the teacher's signal,

the first person on each team goes to the team's desk, picks a letter at random, names it, and places it in its correct position in the alphabet. It may be necessary for students to place the letters in an arc if all 26 letters will not fit on the desk in a straight line. Each team member places a letter until all of the letters have been played by one team. The last person to play must check the sequence of the letters. If players see a letter out of sequence during play, then they may use a turn to correct one mistake. The first team to place the letters in correct sequence is the winning team.

Guess What?

- 3-D letter set for each pair of students

TACTILE

A student, with eyes closed, draws a letter from a container. The student tries to identify the letter by its shape. If successful, the student keeps the letter and his or her opponent takes a turn. If unsuccessful, the student returns the letter to the container and his or her opponent takes a turn. Play continues until all 26 letters have been named or time runs out. The student with the most letters at the end of play is the winner.

Don't Say Z

- Individual alphabet strip for each pair of students

Two players alternate saying letters of the alphabet in sequence. Each player may choose to say two or three letters in one turn. For example, if Player 1 says "*AB*" and Player 2 says "*CDE*," then Player 1 can say "*FG*" or "*FGH*," and so forth. The object is to avoid saying *Z*.

Variation: The game can be changed to Catch the *Z* in which the object is to be the player who says *Z*.

Twenty Questions

PH&P

The teacher prints the alphabet on the board (or on a sheet of paper, if working with one or two students). The teacher says, "I am thinking of a letter. I want you to try to guess the letter. You can ask me questions about the letter. I can only answer 'yes' or 'no.' See if you can guess the letter in fewer than 20 questions."

Students begin to ask questions about the letter. The teacher encourages students to ask questions that eliminate several letters at a time. Questions such as "Is it a vowel?" or "Is it made of only straight lines?" will eliminate several letters at a time. The teacher helps students to rephrase questions that require more than an answer of "yes" or "no."

As students eliminate letters, the teacher crosses the letters off the alphabet. The teacher records the number of questions required for students to guess the letter. The teacher can chart the number of questions. Students can compare the number of questions they ask each time the game is played.

Super Sleuth

Sequencing

- One individual alphabet strip (for reference) and 3-D letter set for each pair of students

- Pencil and paper

The students work together in pairs to arrange the 3-D letters in an arc. The first student closes his or her eyes while the second student removes one letter and closes the

gap left in the arc. The first student then must discover the missing letter. After the missing letter has been identified, it is replaced in the arc and the other student gets the chance to identify a missing letter. Students may keep track of correct guesses to determine the winner. The game continues until time runs out.

Activities for Developing Alphabetizing Skills

The alphabet provides a systematic approach to organizing, classifying, and codifying information in myriad fields, such as science, law, engineering, the social sciences, business, education, communication, and entertainment. The order of the alphabet in turn provides the order of words for every kind of information we seek, in libraries, books, and newspapers and on the Internet. The following activities help develop alphabetizing skills.

Schedule

Students are ready to learn to alphabetize words when they show competence with letter recognition, naming, and sequencing. They should be able to place the 3-D plastic letters in an arc within 2 minutes, be fluent with at least the first set of the uppercase missing letter deck (i.e., AB____, BC____, CD____), and be accurate with random naming of upper- and lowercase letters. Students begin alphabetizing word cards rather than lists of words. Mistakes can be easily corrected by rearranging a card rather than erasing a word in a list. Students move from alphabetizing word cards to alphabetizing lists of words, and then to locating words in the dictionary and other reference materials. The Missing Letter Decks activity should be interspersed among the following activities within the weekly schedule to provide review for letter sequencing.

Students touch and name letters on an alphabet strip as a warm-up before any sequencing-related activity. The strip remains in place as a reference.

Alphabetizing Word Cards by the First Letter

- Pocket chart

- For the teacher, a set of 10 cards, each of which bears a word beginning with a different lowercase letter

- For each student, a set of 10 cards, each of which bears a word beginning with a different lowercase letter

- Individual alphabet strips (for warm-up activity and reference)

The teacher places 10 cards in a vertical column on the *before* side of the pocket chart (or desk, if working with one or two students), ensuring that the words are not in alphabetical order. In keeping with the principle of having one focus, the words on these cards are for alphabetizing, not for reading. The teacher asks students whether the first letter of each word is the same as or different from the first letters of the other words. Students respond that they are different. The teacher asks the students which letter will guide them in putting these words into alphabetical order. The teacher explains that the letter used for alphabetizing is called the **guide letter**. The answer to the question is always an ordinal number (e.g., "The first letter is the guide letter").

The teacher points to the first letter of each word as the students recite the alphabet. For example, as students say, "*A*," the teacher points to the first letter of each word.

If the students see a word beginning with the letter *A* as they are saying, "*A*," then they say, "Stop!" The teacher forms a second column by placing the word card at the top of the pocket chart on the right side. The teacher points to the first word in the first column as the students say "*B*" and look at the first letter of each of the remaining words.

The students continue reciting the alphabet and saying, "Stop!" as the cards are aligned in alphabetical order. The students finish saying the alphabet even after all of the cards are placed. Students proofread by saying the alphabet again, and the teacher touches the first letter of each card when the students say that letter. The teacher taps the space to the left of the words when students say letters not found at the beginning of one of the words.

Students line up their set of word cards vertically on the *before* side of their desks. The teacher asks students which letter is their guide letter. The students reply, "The first letter is my guide letter." The students recite the alphabet while pointing to the first letter of each word. If students find a word beginning with *A*, they place it in a vertical column on the *after* side of the desk. They follow the same procedures for saying the entire alphabet and then proofread.

Have several different sets of word cards to be alphabetized by the first letter so that the students work with different sets over a period of time.

When students can perform this activity easily and efficiently, they are ready to progress to the next level, alphabetizing word cards by the second letter.

Alphabetizing Word Cards by the Second Letter

- Pocket chart

- For the teacher, a set of 10 cards with words that begin with the same first letter followed by a different letter, such as *set, sun, street, six, sled, sand, scout, show, sip,* and *snake*

- For each student, a set of 10 smaller cards with words that begin with the same first letter but are followed by different letter second letters

- Individual alphabet strips (for warm-up activity and reference)

The teacher places 10 cards in a vertical column on the *before* side of the pocket chart (or desk, if working with one or two students), ensuring that the words are not in alphabetical order. The students discover that the first letter of each of the words is the same. Students respond to the question "What is your guide letter?" by saying, "The second letter is my guide letter." The teacher points to the second letter of each of the words as students follow the procedures detailed in the previous activity for reciting the alphabet, forming a new column on the *after* side, and proofreading.

Students follow the same procedures as they practice with their word cards in columns on their desks.

Alphabetizing Word Cards by the First and Second Letters

- Pocket chart

- For the teacher, a set of 10 cards with words, some of which have the same first letter and some of which have a different first letter, such as *tent, can, brand, melt, trunk, slant, go, bake, free,* and *luck*

- For each student, a set of 10 cards with words, some of which have the same first letter and some of which have a different first letter

- Individual alphabet strips (for warm-up activity and reference)

The teacher places 10 cards in a vertical column on the *before* side of the pocket chart (or desk, if working with one or two students), ensuring that the words are not in alphabetical order. The students discover that some of the first letters are the same and some are different. Students respond to "What is your guide letter?" by saying, "For most of the words, the first letter is the guide letter; for some, the second letter is the guide letter." Students recite the alphabet, saying "Stop!" when they see a word beginning with the letter they are saying. For example, in a list of words that contains *tent* and *trunk*, when students say "*T*," they say, "Stop! Stop!" The teacher moves both *tent* and *trunk* to the column on the right and aligns them side by side, with a space beneath the two words. Students continue reciting the alphabet through *Z* as the teacher places the words in order in the column to the right. Students then come back to the two words beginning with *T* and say, "*Te* comes before *tr*." The teacher places *trunk* in the empty space below *tent*. Students recite the alphabet again to proofread their work as usual. After saying, "*T*," students say, "*Te* comes before *tr*, U, V, W, X, Y, Z." Students follow the same procedures as they practice with their word cards on their desks.

After students are proficient at this level, the teacher introduces and students practice alphabetizing by the third letter; by the second and third letters; by the fourth letter; by third and fourth letters; and finally by first, second, third, and fourth letters.

In typical classrooms, students can apply this procedure by alphabetizing their spelling or vocabulary words written on index cards.

After students can efficiently alphabetize a group of word cards with mixed guide letters, students are ready to alphabetize word lists.

Alphabetizing Words in Lists by the First Letter

- Individual alphabet strips (for warm-up activity and reference)

The teacher writes a list of words on the board to be alphabetized by the first letter. Students discover that the initial letter is their guide letter, and the teacher underlines each initial letter. Students recite the alphabet as the teacher points to the initial letter of each word. Students say, "Stop!" when they say a letter that matches the letter to which the teacher is pointing. The teacher numbers the words to the left of the word list to indicate alphabetical order. The teacher then gives students a list of words on paper to be alphabetized by first letter, and students follow the same procedure in numbering the words. As always, students check their work by reciting the alphabet again.

Alphabetizing a List of Words by the First and Second Letters

- Individual alphabet strips (for warm-up activity and reference)

The teacher writes on the board a list of words to be alphabetized by the first and second letters. Some words have the same first letters and some do not. The teacher draws a column of lines to the right of the list labeled *Letter* and a second column of lines labeled *Number*. An example follows.

Word	Letter	Number
track	————	————
den	————	————
tag	————	————
cube	————	————
bland	————	————
vote	————	————
same	————	————
gloss	————	————
camp	————	————
again	————	————

The students discover that the first and sometimes second letters are their guide letters. The teacher asks the students to name the initial letter of each word and writes the letter on the *Letter* line. If a letter is a duplicate, the students name and the teacher writes the second letter of the word beside the initial letter. An example follows:

Word	Letter	Number
track	_tr_____	————
den	_d_____	————
tag	_ta_____	————

Students then recite the alphabet as the teacher points to the letters in the *Letter* column. The teacher numbers the words when the students say the guide letter(s). When the second letter is the guide letter, as with *track* and *tag,* students say, "*Ta* comes before *tr.*" *Tag* is given the next number, and *track* the next.

The teacher gives students a list of words on paper with *Letter* and *Number* columns to the right of the list. Students follow the same procedures for numbering their list of words and checking their work.

Students progress to alphabetizing word lists by the third letter; by the second and third letters; by the fourth letter; by the third and fourth letters; and by the first, second, third, and fourth letters. Eventually students will number mixed word lists without the *Letter* column.

Activities for Developing Dictionary Skills

Schedule

After students can alphabetize word lists proficiently to the fourth letter, they are ready to develop skill in using the dictionary. The teacher includes the Missing Letter Decks and Alphabetizing Word Cards and Words in Lists activities within the weekly lesson plan as review activities. Students may not need to recite the alphabet as a warm-up activity at this point but the individual alphabet strips remain in place for reference.

Discovery of Quartiles

- Dictionary for each student

- Three 3″ × 5″ index cards for each student

- Individual alphabet strips (for reference)

The teacher leads students in dividing the dictionary into two parts and marking the location (in the words beginning with *m*) with a 3″ × 5″ index card. Dividing the first part into halves again, students place a card in the words beginning with *e*. Dividing the second part into halves, students place a card in the words beginning with *s*. The teacher explains that the four parts of a gallon are called *quarts* and that the four parts of a dollar are called *quarters*. The teacher then tells students that the four parts of a dictionary are called *quartiles*. The letters that begin the four quartiles are *a, e, m,* and *s.* Students create a sentence to aid memory, such as "All eagles must soar." If students ask why certain quartiles of the dictionary have fewer letters than others, the teacher can explain that certain letters in the dictionary have more entries (e.g., there are more words starting with *a* than with *x*). Placing the quartiles where they are (rather than having an equal number of letter groups in each quartile) divides the dictionary more evenly.

Quartile Practice with 3-D Letters

- 3-D letter set for each student

- Individual alphabet strips

- Paper clips

The teacher directs students to place the 3-D letters into the four quartiles:

ABCD
EFGHIJKL
MNOPQR
STUVWXYZ

The teacher names a letter, such as *q*. Students echo the letter name and say the letter's quartile ("Q. Q is in the third quartile"). Students practice designating quartiles. After students are proficient with this activity, students may mark the quartiles on their alphabet strips with paper clips and designate the quartile of target letters while looking at the strips.

Discovery of Guide Words and Cornering

- Dictionary for each student

- Individual alphabet strips (for reference)

After students have become proficient with designating quartiles, the teacher directs students to a designated page in their dictionaries. Students are told that the two words at the top of each page are called **guide words**. The teacher explains that the guide word on the left is the first **entry word** (in bold print) on the page. The guide word on the right is the last entry word on the page. Just as guide letters are useful when students

alphabetize words, guide words at the top of a dictionary page show the first and last entry words that will be on the page according to alphabetical order.

The teacher illustrates the cornering technique with the dictionary, an efficient way to focus only on the guide words. When the teacher looks forward in the dictionary (at the right-hand pages), the right hand turns only the corners of the pages while the left hand holds the turned pages. When the teacher looks backward in the dictionary (at the left-hand pages), the teacher's left hand "corners" the pages while the right hand holds those pages. Students practice cornering.

Locating a Letter Group within a Quartile by Cornering

- Dictionary for each student

- Individual alphabet strips (for reference)

The teacher directs students to find any guide word in the dictionary that begins with a designated letter, such as *r*. Students echo and say, "*R* is in the third quartile," and turn to the third quartile of their dictionaries. Students corner as they say, "*R* is after *o*. *R* is after *q*. Here is *r*." Students then name the letters of any guide word beginning with *r*. This activity is practiced several times until students can proficiently use the **cornering** technique.

Using Guide Words

- 3″ × 5″ index cards each bearing a **target word** in lowercase block letters

- Guide-word practice dictionary (contains only guide words and a **column word**)

- Individual alphabet strips (for reference)

The teacher writes two guide words with a target word between them on the board. The teacher explains that the word to be located in the dictionary is called the *target word*.

Example: beam   bet

bend

The teacher reviews the definition and purpose of guide words and target words. The guide word on the left is the first entry on the dictionary page; the guide word on the right is the last entry on the page. If the target word is on a particular page, the target word will come after the first guide word and before the second guide word alphabetically.

The teacher models by spelling the target word, *b e n d,* and comparing it with the guide word on the left, *b e a m.* (By naming the letters rather than the word, the teacher keeps the focus on the alphabetizing task rather than on reading.) The teacher asks, "What are your guide letters?" Students should respond, "The third letters are the guide letters because they are different." The teacher emphasizes the importance of starting with the letters of the target word and says, "*B e* ***n*** [emphasizing the guide letter] comes after *b e* ***a.*** I'll draw an arrow under *b e a m* that points to the *after* side. My target word may be on this page because it comes after the first guide word."

Example: beam   bet

⟶ bend

The teacher directs students to compare the target word with the guide word on the right and asks for the guide letters. The teacher leads the students in saying, "The third letters are the guide letters. *B e **n*** comes before *b e **t**.* I'll draw an arrow to the *before* side. The target word is on this page because it comes after the first guide word and before the second guide word. My arrows meet in the middle and show me that my target word is on this page."

Example: beam   bet
        ⟶ bend ⟵

The teacher gives each student a 3″ × 5″ index card on which a target word has been written.

> grant

The teacher directs students to a page in their guide-word practice dictionaries that contains only two guide words. A sample practice page follows:

glow | green

The teacher leads students in using guide words as detailed previously to discover whether the target word *grant* would be found on this page. (Students discover that the target word comes after the first guide word and before the second. The arrows meet in the middle, so the word is found on this page.) At first, all target words can be found on the page designated by the teacher. Sample guide words and target words for guide-word practice pages include

Guide words		*Target words*
bingo	bit	biology, biped, bird, bison
tumbling	turboprop	tumult, tuna, tune, turbine
sail	scout	saint, same, Saturday, scale

After students have had many practice sessions and are proficient at finding the target word when the teacher sends students to a designated page on which the target word is found, the teacher puts on the board two guide words and a target word that comes after the guide words.

Example: tumbling   turboprop
                          turtle

The teacher directs students to a matching page in their guide-word practice dictionaries. The teacher first models the procedure on the board and then directs students to do the activity in their guide-word dictionaries. Comparing the target word with the guide word on the left, the teacher asks which letters are the guide letters. The teacher leads the students in saying, "The third letters are the guide letters. *T u r* is after *t u m.* I'll draw an arrow to the *after* side. The target word may be on this page because it is after the first guide word. In the second guide word, the fourth letters are the guide letters. *T u r t* is after *t u r b.* I'll draw an arrow to the *after* side. The target word cannot be on this page because it is after the second guide word on this page. The arrow shows that I need to turn to the page after this one to see whether the target word is on that page." Students practice in their guide-word dictionaries with words found after the designated page occurs first because it reflects the left-to-right progression of the alphabet.

After students have had many practice sessions and are proficient at finding out that the target word is after the designated page, the teacher puts on the board two guide words and a target word that comes before the guide words. For example:

Example: glean   gluten
                       glad

The students discover that the target word given by the teacher comes before that page. Students practice in their guide-word dictionaries and progress to locating a written target word without the teacher's designating a page. Students verbalize as they compare the letters of their target word with those of the guide words at the top of the pages of their guide-word practice dictionaries (e.g., "*G e* is after *g a*")

Using Column Words

- Guide-word practice dictionary for each student

- Individual alphabet strips (for reference)

After students are proficient at locating the correct page in a guide-word dictionary with designated target words, they are ready to discover whether their target word falls within the first or second column of a dictionary page. The teacher writes two guide words and a target word on the board, for example, *tell* and *tent,* and target word *temper.* Students discover that their target word falls on this page. The teacher draws a line to indicate the two columns found on a dictionary page. At the top of the second column, the teacher writes a word representing the first entry in that column, such as *tend.* The teacher explains that this word is called the *column word* and it can be used to learn if the target word is in the first or second column. Students compare the target word (*temper*) with the column word (*tend*). The guide letter is the third letter. *M* comes before *n,* so the target word *temper* will be found in the first column.

Applying Skills Using a Regular Dictionary

- Dictionary for each student

- Individual alphabet strips (for reference)

After students are proficient at locating the correct page and column for written target words on pages in their guide-word practice dictionaries, the teacher leads them in applying the same skills using a regular dictionary. The dictionary should be appropriate for the level of the students with large print and no tabs. Students work with target words written by the teacher on 3" × 5" cards or on the board. Students locate the quartile, page, column, and word itself in the dictionary. Locating a word in 60 seconds or less is the goal.

Using Alphabetizing Skills with Other Reference Materials

- A variety of print and Internet reference materials

- Individual alphabet strips (for reference)

Students locate target words in a variety of other reference materials: computer listings, telephone directories, encyclopedias, and indexes in books.

Games to Reinforce Dictionary Skills

Dictionary Relay

- Dictionary Relay Page and dictionary for each team

- Individual alphabet strip for each team (for reference)

Students work in teams of four with one dictionary per team. Each team receives a Dictionary Relay Page of words to be found. A Dictionary Relay Page is a sheet of paper divided into four columns with the following headings: *Target word, Quartile, Page #,* and *Column #.* The first team member locates and records the quartile of the target word, the second team member finds and records the page number, and the third team member determines whether the word falls in the first column or second. The fourth team member locates and records the quartile of the second target word and passes the dictionary back to the first team member, who finds and records the page number, and so forth. The first team to correctly complete the Dictionary Relay Page is the winning team. If the teacher is working with an individual student, the student can work to improve his or her time completing the page.

Dictionary Scavenger Hunt

- Dictionary for each student

- Individual alphabet strips (for reference)

The teacher leads students in discovering **sound pictures** (phonetic respellings for pronunciation), word origins, parts of speech, and examples of usage in the dictionary. After students are familiar with these aspects of the dictionary, they may apply their knowledge in a Dictionary Scavenger Hunt for information.

Students work individually or in teams to complete a page. A sample Dictionary Scavenger Hunt follows.

1. Look up *telepathy.* What is the first entry word on that page?

    _____

2. What is the sound picture for *doubloon?* _____

    Copy a definition of *doubloon* from the dictionary. _____

3. Look up *run.* You may find more than one entry. This word can be used as how many different parts of speech? ____

    Write a sentence that illustrates *run* as a verb and another sentence that illustrates *run* as a noun. _____

4. Give the language of origin of these words or word parts:

    photo _____

    truck _____

    chiro _____

    tomato _____

    biped _____

    bio _____

Variation: Students can complete a Reference Scavenger Hunt using materials such as World Wide Web sites, encyclopedias, telephone books, and indexes in books.

Sample Questions to Spark Students' Interest in the History of Written Language and Alphabets

Student interest in the history of writing and various alphabets will be greatly increased by the presentation of pictures and maps to accompany the following questions.

History of Writing

- What are some of the ways people communicated before anyone could read or write?

- What are some hand signals and picture symbols that we use today that do not involve words?

- How long ago do you think human beings began to write?

- In what part of the world do you think the oldest writings have been found?

- What were the earliest writing instruments and on what did people write?

- Do you think that writing has always gone from left to right and top to bottom on the page?

History of Alphabets

- What are the differences between writing based on pictures and writing based on an alphabet?

- What group of people are credited with inventing the first alphabet?

- How did the English alphabet evolve from the Greek and Roman alphabets?

- From pictures of what objects did our two-dimensional letters evolve?

- What is the history of each of our letters?

CONCLUSION

Complete letter knowledge is essential for reading success. Knowledge of letters' shapes, names, and the phonemes they represent provides students with a solid foundation for using the alphabetic principle in learning to read. Moreover, this foundation needs to be strongly formed early in a child's academic career because word knowledge is built upon letter knowledge. Inaccurate, incomplete, or inconsistent letter knowledge jeopardizes a student's ability to unitize letter sequences that can be automatically recognized by sight.

The ability to learn letter knowledge is dependent upon multiple factors. First, some children are advantaged because they come to school with knowledge of letters' shapes, names, and sounds. Still other children begin school without any real letter knowledge and are already at an academic disadvantage when they begin formal schooling (Vellutino et al., 2003; Vellutino et al., 1996). Moreover, students learn about letters at inherently different rates. Regardless of each child's innate ability or preschool learning history, every child must know the shapes, names, and sounds of all the letters to be a good reader.

This presents a challenge to teachers because they must provide adequate letter learning experiences for each child regardless of his or her prior letter knowledge or inherent ability to remember letters. Consequently, instruction must be individualized to meet the specific needs of every child in the class. While some children may need only 10–20 exposures to a letter to recognize it automatically, other children may need 20 times that amount to overlearn the letters to the point of automaticity.

The NRP's meta-analysis (NICHD, 2000) stressed that letter knowledge enhances the effectiveness of both phonemic awareness and systematic phonics instruction for reading and spelling. In other words, students benefit more from instruction when the sound structure of words is linked to letters. Multisensory instruction directly and concretely links sounds and letter names to letter shapes to build a solid foundation of letter knowledge in the beginning reader. This type of instruction introduces letter knowledge and reinforces that knowledge by providing concrete mnemonic strategies and varied exercises designed to provide opportunities for letter mastery. Multisensory instruction is also paced so that prior knowledge is well-established before new knowledge is introduced.

Beginning readers must also learn to sequentially process the letters they see in words, as well as the phonemes the letters represent. Repeated exposure to letters in the alphabet and practice in sequencing the alphabet provide reinforcement of sequential processing of letters. Facility in using alphabetical order gives students efficient access to information available through reference materials such as dictionaries, encyclopedias, and the Internet.

In review, good word-reading ability starts with well-established letter reading. Letter reading may seem simple, but learning the alphabet is challenging for many young readers. Vellutino et al. (2003) and Vellutino et al. (1996) have found that dysfunctional

readers more often have experiential or instructional deprivation rather than an innate learning disability. Multisensory, structured, sequential instruction has been validated as instruction that enhances children's ability to develop well-established letter knowledge by directly and concretely linking the letter symbols with their names and sounds and by providing adequate practice of the linkages (Stein, 1987). Multisensory, structured, sequential instruction provides the strong foundation of letter knowledge that is required to support good word reading.

REFERENCES

Ackerman, P.T., & Dykman, R.A. (1993). Phonological processes, confrontation naming, and immediate memory in dyslexia. *Journal of Learning Disabilities, 26*(9), 597–609.

Adams, M.J. (1990a). *Beginning to read: Thinking and learning about print.* Cambridge, MA: The MIT Press.

Adams, M.J. (1990b). *Beginning to read: Thinking and learning about print* [A summary]. (Prepared by S.A. Stahl, J. Osborn, & F. Lehr). Cambridge, MA: The MIT Press.

Adams, M.J. (1994). Phonics and beginning reading instruction. In F. Lehr & J. Osborn (Eds.), *Reading, language, and literacy* (pp. 3–23). Mahwah, NJ: Lawrence Erlbaum Associates.

Badian, N.A. (1994). Preschool prediction: Orthographic and phonological skills, and reading. *Annals of Dyslexia, 44,* 3–25.

Badian, N.A. (1995). Predicting reading ability over the long term: The changing roles of letter naming, phonological awareness and orthographic processing. *Annals of Dyslexia, 45,* 79–96.

Berninger, V.B. (2000, November). *Language based reading and writing intervention: Findings of the University of Washington Multi-Disciplinary Disability Center.* Paper presented at the meeting of the International Dyslexia Association, Washington, DC.

Berninger, V.B., Abbott, R.D., Vermeulen, K., Ogier, S., Brooksher, L., Zook, D., et al. (2002). The comparison of faster and slower responders to early intervention in reading: Differentiating features of their language profiles. *Learning Disability Quarterly, 25*(1), 59–76.

Bond, G.L., & Dykstra, R. (1967). The cooperative research program in first-grade reading instruction. *Reading Research Quarterly, 2,* 5–142.

Bowers, P.G., & Wolf, M. (1993). Theoretical links among naming speed, precise timing mechanisms and orthographic skill in dyslexia. *Reading and Writing: An Interdisciplinary Journal, 5,* 69–85.

Carreker, S.H., Swank, P.R., Tillman-Dowdy, L., Neuhaus, G.F., Monfils, M.J., & Montemayor, M.L. (2003). *The effect of Language Enrichment teacher training delivered through interactive video conferencing on third grade reading achievement.* Manuscript submitted for publication.

Catts, H.W., Gillispie, M., Leonard, L.B., Kail, R.V., & Miller, C.A. (2002). The role of speed of processing, rapid naming, and phonological awareness in reading achievement. *Journal of Learning Disabilities, 35*(6), 509–525.

Chall, J.S. (1996). *Learning to read: The great debate* (3rd. ed.). Orlando, FL: Harcourt Brace & Co.

Cox, A.R. (1992). *Foundations for literacy: Structures and techniques for multisensory teaching of basic written English language skills.* Cambridge, MA: Educators Publishing Service.

Day, J.A. (1993). *Effectiveness of the Alphabetic Phonics teacher training course on student spelling ability for predictable and unpredictable words.* Unpublished manuscript, Neuhaus Education Center, Bellaire, TX.

Denckla, M., & Rudel, R. (1974). Rapid "automatized" naming of pictured objects, colors, letters, and numbers by normal children. *Cortex, 10,* 186–202.

Ehri, L.C. (1980). The development of orthographic images. In U. Frith (Ed.), *Cognitive processes in spelling* (pp. 311–338). San Diego: Academic Press.

Ehri, L.C. (1983). A critique of five studies related to letter-name knowledge and learning to read. In L.M. Gentile, M.L. Kamil, & J.S. Blanchard (Eds.), *Reading research revisited* (pp. 143–153). Columbus, OH: Charles E. Merrill.

Ehri, L.C. (1987). Learning to read and spell words. *Journal of Reading Behavior, 19,* 5–31.

Ehri, L.C. (1998). Grapheme-phoneme knowledge is essential for learning to read words in English. In J.L. Metsala & L.C. Ehri (Eds.), *Word recognition in beginning literacy* (pp. 3–40). Mahwah, NJ: Lawrence Erlbaum Associates.

Ehri, L.C., & Wilce, L.S. (1979). The mnemonic value of orthography among beginning readers. *Journal of Educational Psychology, 71,* 26–40.

Ehri, L.C., & Wilce, L.S. (1983). Development of word identification speed in skilled and less skilled beginning readers. *Journal of Educational Psychology, 75,* 3–18.

Felton, R.H., & Wood, F.B. (1989). Cognitive deficits in reading disability and attention deficit disorder. *Journal of Learning Disabilities, 22,* 3–13.

Felton, R.H., Wood, F.B., Brown, I.S., & Campbell,

S.K. (1987). Separate verbal memory and naming deficits in attention deficit disorder and reading disability. *Brain and Language, 31,* 171–184.

Foorman, B.R., Francis, D.J., Shaywitz, S.E., Shaywitz, B.A., & Fletcher, J.M. (1997). The case for early reading intervention. In B. Blachman (Ed.), *Foundations of reading acquisition and dyslexia* (pp. 243–264). Mahwah, NJ: Lawrence Erlbaum Associates.

Frankiewicz, R.G. (1984a). *An evaluation of the impact of the Alphabetic Phonics program in Cypress Fairbanks Independent School District from 1981 through 1984.* Unpublished manuscript, Neuhaus Education Center, Bellaire, TX.

Frankiewicz, R.G. (1984b). *An evaluation of the impact of the Alphabetic Phonics program in River Oaks Baptist School from 1983–1984.* Unpublished manuscript, Neuhaus Education Center, Bellaire, TX.

Frankiewicz, R.G. (1985). *An evaluation of the Alphabetic Phonics program offered in a one-to-one mode.* Unpublished manuscript, Neuhaus Education Center, Bellaire, TX.

Gardner, H. (1985). *Frames of mind: The theory of multiple intelligences.* New York: Basic Books.

Gibson, E.J., Gibson, J.J., Pick, A., & Osser, H. (1962). A developmental study of the discrimination of letter-like forms. *Journal of Comparative and Physiological Psychology, 55,* 897–906.

Gillingham, A., & Stillman, B.W. (1960). *Remedial training for children with specific disability in reading, spelling, and penmanship* (6th ed.). Cambridge, MA: Educators Publishing Service.

Grossman, R.P. (1981). In the field: Never too late. *Journal of Learning Disabilities, 14,* 554.

Gunning, T.G. (1996). *Creating reading instruction for all children* (2nd ed.). Boston: Allyn & Bacon.

Hallahan, D.P., & Kauffman, J.M. (1976). *Introduction to learning disabilities: A psychobehavioral approach.* Upper Saddle River, NJ: Prentice Hall.

Hanna, P.R., Hanna, J.S., Hodges, R.E., & Rudorf, E.H., Jr. (1966). *Phoneme–grapheme correspondences as cues to spelling improvement* (USOE Publication No. 32008). Washington, DC: U.S. Government Printing Office.

Harm, M.W. & Seidenberg, M.S. (2004). Computing the meanings of words in reading: Cooperative division of labor between visual and phonological processes. *Psychological Review, 111*(3), 662–720.

Hogan, E.A., & Smith, M.T. (1987). *Alphabet and dictionary skills guide.* Cambridge, MA: Educators Publishing Service.

Joshi, R.M., Dahlgren, M., & Boulware-Gooden, R. (2002). Teaching reading in an inner city school through a multisensory teaching approach. *Annals of Dyslexia, 52,* 229–242.

Juel, C. (1988). Learning to read and write: A longitudinal study of fifty-four children from first through fourth grade. *Journal of Educational Psychology, 80,* 437–447.

LaBerge, D., & Samuels, S.J. (1974). Toward a theory of automatic information processing in reading. *Cognitive Psychology, 6,* 293–323.

Liberman, I.Y., & Liberman, A.M. (1990). Whole language vs. code emphasis: Underlying assumptions and their implications for reading instruction. *Annals of Dyslexia, 40,* 51–76.

Liberman, I.Y., Shankweiler, D., Orlando, C., Harris, H.S., & Berti, F.B. (1971). Letter confusion and reversals of sequence in the beginning reader: Implications for Orton's theory of developmental dyslexia. *Cortex, 7,* 127–142.

Logan, R.K. (1986). *The alphabet effect.* New York: William Morrow.

National Institute of Child Health and Human Development (NICHD). (2000). *Report of the National Reading Panel. Teaching children to read: An evidence-based assessment of the scientific research literature on reading and its implications for reading instruction: Reports of the subgroups* (NIH Publication No. 00-4754). Washington, DC: U.S. Government Printing Office.

Neuhaus, G.F. (2000). An investigation of phonological awareness, orthographic recognition, and attention as predictors of Rapid Automatized Naming (RAN) and reading. *Dissertation Abstracts International,* 136–138. (UMI No. 9979233)

Neuhaus, G.F. (2002). What does it take to read a letter? *Perspectives, 28*(1), 6–8.

Neuhaus, G.F., Carlson, C., Jeng, M.W., Post, Y., & Swank, P.R. (2001) The reliability and validity of rapid automatized naming (RAN) scoring software for the determination of pause and articulation component durations. *Educational and Psychological Measurement, 61*(3), 490–504.

Neuhaus, G.F., Foorman, B.R., Francis, D.J., & Carlson, C. (2001). Measures of information processing in rapid automatized naming (RAN) and their relation to reading. *Journal of Experimental Child Psychology, 78*(4), 359–373.

Neuhaus, G.F., & Swank, P.R. (2002). Understanding the relations between RAN letters subtest components and word reading in first grade students. *Journal of Learning Disabilities, 35*(2), 158–174.

Neuhaus Education Center. (1998). *Basic language skills: Book 1.* Bellaire, TX: Author.

Obregón, M. (1994). *Exploring naming timing patterns by dyslexic and normal readers on the serial RAN task.* Unpublished master's thesis, Tufts University, Boston.

Perfetti, C.A. (1985). *Reading ability.* New York: Oxford University Press.

Plaut, D.C., McClelland, J.L., Seidenberg, M., & Patterson, K.E. (1996). Understanding normal

and impaired word reading: Computational principles in quasi-regular domains. *Psychological Review, 103,* 56–115.

Post, Y. (1999). *Building bridges: Literacy instruction links success to low-SES mobile minority population.* Unpublished manuscript, Neuhaus Education Center, Bellaire, TX, and Sam Houston State University, Huntsville, TX. Retrieved February 17, 2003, from http://www.neuhaus.org/Research/ BuildingBridges-070101.doc

Reed. L., Selig, H., Young, N., & Day, J.A. (1995). A working model for implementing multisensory teaching in the classroom. In C.W. McIntyre & J.S. Pickering (Eds.), *Clinical studies of multisensory language education for students with dyslexia and related disorders* (pp. 23–35). Dallas, TX: International Multisensory Structured Language Education Council.

Seidenberg, M.S., & McClelland, J.L. (1989). A distributed, developmental model of word recognition and naming. *Psychological Review, 96,* 523–568.

Shankweiler, D., & Liberman, I.Y. (1972). Misreading: A search for causes. In J.F. Kavanagh & I.G. Mattingly (Eds.), *Language by ear and by eye* (pp. 293–317). Cambridge, MA: The MIT Press.

Share, D.L., Jorm, A.F., Maclean, R., & Matthews, R. (1984). Sources of individual differences in reading acquisition. *Journal of Educational Psychology, 76,* 1309–1324.

Siegel, L.S., Share, D., & Geva, E. (1995). Evidence for superior orthographic skills in dyslexics, *Psychological Science, 6*(4), 250–254.

Stanovich, K.E. (1986). Matthew effects in reading: Some consequences of individual differences in the acquisition of literacy. *Reading Research Quarterly, 21,* 360–406.

Stanovich, K.E., & Siegel, L. (1994). Phenotypic performance profile of children with reading disabilities: A regression-based test of the phonological-core variable-difference model. *Journal of Educational Psychology, 86*(1), 24–53.

Stein, T. (1987). *An evaluation of the impact of the Alphabetic-Phonics program. One-to-one instruction from 1983 through 1986.* Unpublished manuscript, Neuhaus Education Center, Bellaire, TX.

Sulzby, E. (1983). A commentary on Ehri's critique of five studies related to letter-name knowledge and learning to read: Broadening the question. In L.M. Gentile, M.L. Kamil, & J.S. Blanchard (Eds.), *Reading research revisited* (pp. 155–161). Columbus, OH: Charles E. Merrill.

Thorpe, H.W., & Borden, K.S. (1985). The effect of multisensory instruction upon the on-task behaviors and word reading accuracy of learning disabled children. *Journal of Learning Disabilities, 18,* 279–286.

Torgesen, J.K., Wagner, R.K., Rashotte, C.A., Burgess, S., & Hecht, S. (1997). Contributions of phonological awareness and rapid automatic naming ability to the growth of word-reading skills in second-to-fifth grade children. *Scientific Studies of Reading, 1*(2), 161–185.

Treiman, R., Tincoff, R., Rodriguez, K., Mouzaki, A., & Francis, D.J. (1998). The foundations of literacy: Learning the sounds of letters. *Child Development, 69*(6), 1524–1540.

Vellutino, F.R. (1979). *Dyslexia: Theory and research.* Cambridge, MA: The MIT Press.

Vellutino, F.R. (1980). Dyslexia—perceptual deficiency or perceptual inefficiency? In J.F. Kavanagh & R.L. Venezky (Eds.), *Orthography, reading, and dyslexia* (pp. 251–270). Baltimore: University Park Press.

Vellutino, F.R., Scanlon, D.M., & Jaccard, J. (2003). Toward distinguishing between cognitive and experiential deficits as primary sources of difficulty in learning to read: A two year follow-up of difficult to remediate and readily remediated poor readers. In B.R. Foorman (Ed.), *Preventing and remediating reading difficulties: Bringing science to scale* (pp. 73–120). Timonium, MD: York Press.

Vellutino, F.R., Scanlon, D.M., Sipay, E.R., Small, S. G. Pratt, A., Chen, R., & Denckla, M.B. (1996). Cognitive profiles of difficult to remediate and readily remediated poor readers: Early intervention as a vehicle for distinguishing between cognitive and experiential deficits as basic causes of specific reading disability. *Journal of Educational Psychology, 88*(4), 601–638.

Vellutino, F.R., Smith, H., Steger, J.A., & Kaman, M. (1975). Reading disability: Age differences and the perceptual deficit hypothesis. *Child Development, 46,* 487–493.

Walsh, D.J., Price, G.G., & Gillingham, M.G. (1988). The critical but transitory importance of letter naming. *Reading Research Quarterly, 23,* 108–122.

Wolf, M. (1997). A provisional, integrative account of phonological and naming-speed deficits in dyslexia: Implications for diagnosis and intervention. In B. Blachman (Ed.), *Foundation of reading acquisition and dyslexia: Implications for early intervention* (pp. 67–92). Mahwah, NJ: Lawrence Erlbaum Associates.

Wolf, M., Bally, H., & Morris, R. (1986). Automaticity, retrieval processes, and reading: A longitudinal study in average and impaired readers. *Child Development, 57,* 988–1000.

Wolf, M., & Bowers, P.G. (1999). The double-deficit hypothesis for the developmental dyslexias. *Journal of Educational Psychology, 91,* 415–438.

Wolf, M., Bowers, P.G., & Biddle, K. (2000). Naming-speed processes, timing, and reading: A con-

ceptual review. *Journal of Learning Disabilities, 33,* 387–407.

Wolf, M., & Obregón, M. (1992). Early naming deficits, developmental dyslexia, and a specific deficit hypothesis. *Brain and Language, 42,* 219–247.

Wolf, M., & Obregón, M. (1997). The "double-deficit" hypothesis: Implications for diagnosis and practice in reading disabilities. In L. Putnam (Ed.), *Readings on language and literacy* (pp. 177–209). Cambridge, MA: Brookline Books.

Wolf, M., O'Brien, B., Adams, K.D., Joffe, T., Jeffrey, J., Lovett, M., et al. (2003). In B.R. Foorman (Ed.), *Preventing and remediating reading difficulties: Bringing science to scale* (pp. 355–380). Timonium, MD: York Press.

6

The History and Structure of Written English

Marcia K. Henry

This chapter presents a short history of written English and introduces the reader to the structure of English orthography, the English spelling system. English is a dynamic language, and numerous historical forces shaped the development of written English. The historical perspective is of primary importance to the study of word formation in English. As Nist (1966) and Venezky (1970) asserted, English orthography begins to make sense when understood from an historical perspective.

An understanding of the historical forces that influenced written English, along with a grasp of the structure of the English spelling system, provides teachers and their students with a logical basis for the study of English. Students who recognize letter–sound correspondences, syllable patterns, and morpheme patterns in words of Anglo-Saxon, Latin, and Greek origin have the strategies necessary to read and spell unfamiliar words. Students begin by learning phonics, basic orthographic patterns, and their related sounds and then learn **syllable types** and **syllable division patterns**. They move on to learn Latin **roots, prefixes**, and **suffixes** and Greek **combining forms**, which are the morpheme, or meaning, units in English. The importance of teaching more than basic phonics cannot be stressed enough. Brown (1947) found that 80% of English words borrowed from other languages came from Latin and Greek. Therefore, teaching relatively few Latin and Greek roots provides students with the key to unlocking hundreds of thousands of words!

HISTORY AND ENGLISH ORTHOGRAPHY

Among the important languages of the world, English is one of the youngest. The original inhabitants of the British Isles, the Celts, spoke a different language in the **Indo-European** family. They were conquered by Julius Caesar in 54 C.E. (Common Era). The

151

Table 6.1. Events related to periods in the development of the English language

Period	Year(s)	Event
Pre-English	54 B.C.E.	The ancient Britons (or Celts) defend their land from Julius Caesar and are defeated.
	50 C.E.	Roman Emperor Claudius I colonizes Britain; Celtic and Latin languages co-exist.
	450 C.E.	Romans leave Britain; the Teutonic tribes (the Jutes, Angles, and Saxons) invade.
	600	England divides into seven kingdoms; Northumbria emerges as the dominant Christian kingdom affiliated with the Roman Catholic Church.
Old English	800	The Danes (or Norsemen or Vikings) invade England and are defeated by King Alfred in 878.
	900	Old English reaches its literary peak under the West Saxon kings.
	1000	The Danes successfully invade Britain, yet the Anglo-Saxon language continues its dominant role.
	1066	William the Conqueror, Duke of Normandy, invades Britain; Norman French becomes the official language of state while English remains the language of the people.
Middle English	1350	Edward III takes control; English again becomes the official language of state.
	1400	Geoffrey Chaucer dies, leaving his classic *Canterbury Tales*.
	1420	Henry V becomes the first English king to write in Middle English.
	1475	The Renaissance reaches England. English borrows from Latin and Greek languages. William Caxton begins printing in English.
Modern English	1600	Queen Elizabeth I and William Shakespeare write in Modern English.
	1755	Samuel Johnson compiles the first comprehensive dictionary of English.
	1828	Noah Webster compiles a dictionary of American English.
	1857–1928	The Oxford English Dictionary is developed and published in parts; it is published in full in 1928.

From Henderson, Edmund, *Teaching Spelling, Second Edition.* Copyright © 1990 by Houghton Mifflin. Used with permission.

Britons continued to speak Celtic while the Romans spoke Latin. The Romans departed and returned almost a century later and stayed for nearly 400 years. Table 6.1 highlights important events contributing to the changes in written English over the centuries.

During the 5th century C.E., Germanic groups—the Jutes, Saxons, and Angles—began to settle in different parts of England. They did not speak the Celtic language and did not practice the Celtic religion (Balmuth, 1992). Rather, **Anglo-Saxon** became the dominant language, and the vocabulary stressed the people, objects, and events of daily life. The Roman alphabet, which the Romans had adapted from Greek via Etruscan, was reintroduced to the British Isles by Christian missionaries at this time.

Five major factors shaped the English language during the period of Old English between 450 and 1150 C.E.: Teutonic invasion and settlement; the Christianizing of Britain; the creation of a national English culture; Danish–English warfare, political adjustment, and cultural assimilation; and the decline of Old English as a result of the Norman Conquest (Nist, 1966). During this time Germanic, Celtic, Latin, Greek, Anglo-Saxon, Scandinavian, and French words entered Old English. At the end of the period, "that language was no longer the basically Teutonic and highly inflected Old English but the hybrid-becoming, Romance-importing, and inflection-dropping Middle English" (Nist, 1966, p. 107).

The period of Middle English (1150–1500) heralded great changes in the native tongue of Britain. Early Middle English (1150–1307) sounded much like present-day German. Claiborne estimated that after the Norman Conquest "more than ten thousand French words passed into the English vocabulary, of which 75 percent are still in use" (1983, p. 112). Anglo-French compounds (e.g., *gentlewomen, gentlemen; faithful, faithfulness*) appeared during this period.

A renewed Latin influence penetrated the language during the period of Mature Middle English (1307–1422) in the 14th and 15th centuries. Chaucer wrote *The Canterbury Tales* in the late 1300s. This was the time of the Renaissance, which brought a wave of cultural advancement. Hanna, Hodges, and Hanna observed,

> The Latin vocabulary was felt to be more stable and polished and more capable of conveying both abstract and humanistic ideas than was a fledgling language such as English. Further, Latin was something of a lingua franca that leaped across geographical and political boundaries. (1971, p. 47)

Many of the words used in English today are borrowed from the Latin of this period, including *index, library, medicine,* and *instant.* During the time of Mature Middle English, Latin **affixes** entered the language in great numbers. Prefixes (e.g., *ad-, pro-*) and suffixes (e.g., *-ent, -al, -ion*) were added to word roots to form words such as *adjacent, prosecution,* and *rational* (Claiborne, 1983).

During the period of Late Middle English (1422–1489), the written word grew in importance. English pressman William Caxton introduced the printing press to England and printed books using the English spoken in London by the well-to-do. Many spelling conventions were set into place at this time. Even more of English orthography was set during the period of Early Modern English (1500–1650).

During the periods of Late Middle English and Early Modern English, the sound patterns, especially the vowel sounds, of the language underwent changes. Nist commented that

> The changes in the pronunciation from the Mature Middle English of Chaucer to the Early Modern English of Shakespeare, insofar as these tense vowels were concerned, were so dramatic that Jespersen [1971] has named their phonemic displacement the Great Vowel Shift. (1966, p. 221)

The vowel shift resulted in certain vowel sounds' being articulated in new positions and ensured a sharp separation between phonology and spelling. For example, in Chaucer's time, the vowel sound in *bide* was pronounced as we pronounce /ē/ in *bee,* but in Shakespeare's time it shifted to /ā/ as in *bay.* This shift caused problems for spellers "because stabilized spellings now came to represent different sounds" (Hanna et al., 1971, p. 49). Changes continued through the periods of Authoritarian English (1650–1800) and Mature Modern English (1800–1920) to reach the pronunciation of today.

Also during the English Renaissance, words from Greek and Romance languages enriched English enormously. The Romance languages include the Latin-based languages (e.g., Portuguese, Spanish, French, Italian, Romanian). During the periods of Authoritarian English and Mature Modern English, vocabulary borrowed from these origins continued to expand, especially in the form of scientific terms that used Greek and Latin morphemes. English continues to develop. For example, words that were coined or that gained new usages in the 1980s and 1990s include *awesome, hunk, channeling, microwave, proactive, cybercafe,* and *decluttering.*

English, then, is a **polyglot**, and the Anglo-Saxon, Latin (Romance), and Greek languages all played a role in establishing the words as they are spoken and written today (Balmuth, 1992; Hanna et al., 1971; Nist, 1966). Claiborne noted,

> The truth is that if borrowing foreign words could destroy a language, English would be dead (borrowed from Old Norse), deceased (from French), defunct (from Latin) and kaput (from German). When it comes to borrowing, English excels (from Latin), surpasses (from French) and eclipses (from Greek) any other tongue, past or present. (1983, p. 4)

FRAMEWORK FOR CURRICULUM AND INSTRUCTION

One framework for teaching a decoding and spelling curriculum is based on word origin and word structure (Henry, 1988a, 1988b, 2003). The three origin languages most influential to English are Anglo-Saxon, Latin, and Greek. Teachers who understand the historical origins of words enhance their presentation of reading instruction. The major structural categories are letter–sound correspondences, syllables, and morphemes. By teaching all of the components of this framework, teachers can ensure that their students will learn the primary patterns found in English words. Teachers are encouraged to use a multisensory approach for teaching each component so that students will simultaneously link the visual symbol with its corresponding sound and form the pattern accurately. (See Chapter 2 for information on the basic principles of multisensory instruction.)

Teaching phonics offers a strategy for decoding and spelling that works when the letter–sound correspondence system carries all of the demands of word analysis. When students do not recognize syllabic and morphological patterns, however, they are constrained from using clues to identify long, unfamiliar words. Unfortunately, most decoding instruction largely neglects the instruction of syllable and morpheme patterns, perhaps because these techniques are only useful for the longer words found in literature and subject-matter text beyond second or third grade, at which point decoding instruction becomes virtually nonexistent in most schools.

Students in fourth grade and beyond are expected to read multisyllabic words. Those who know how to use rules for syllable division exhibit strategies for word analysis beyond the use of letter–sound correspondences. Students who recognize meaningful morpheme patterns incorporate still another word analysis strategy. Yet, many students in upper elementary school, secondary school, and adult literacy programs lack the strategies necessary to read and spell longer words. By learning basic syllable and morpheme patterns, these students will be able to analyze numerous multisyllabic words of Latin and Greek origin.

Figure 6.1 represents the categories in the word origin and word structure framework. Each entry in the matrix corresponds to words of Anglo-Saxon, Latin, or Greek origin that are related to letter–sound correspondences, syllables, or morphemes. In the following sections, the major components of the framework are discussed.

ANGLO-SAXON LAYER OF LANGUAGE

Words of Anglo-Saxon origin are characterized as the common, everyday, down-to-earth words that are used frequently in ordinary situations. Nist provided a clever example of Anglo-Saxon words:

> English remains preeminently Anglo-Saxon at its core: in the suprasegmentals of its stress, pitch, and juncture patterns and in its vocabulary. No matter whether a man is

	Letter–sound correspondences	Syllables	Morphemes
Anglo-Saxon	Consonants *bid, step, that* Vowels *mad/made, barn, boat*	Closed: *bat* Open: *baby* VCE: *made* Vowel digraph: *boat* Consonant-*le*: *tumble* *r*-controlled: *barn*	Compounds *hardware* *shipyard* Affixes *read, reread, rereading* *bid, forbid, forbidden*
Latin	Same as Anglo-Saxon but few vowel digraphs Use of schwa /ə/: *direction* *spatial* *excellent*	Closed: *spect* VCE: *scribe* *r*-controlled: *port, form*	Affixes *construction* *erupting* *conductor*
Greek	*ph* for /f/ *phonograph* *ch* for /k/ *chorus* *y* for /ĭ/ *sympathy*	Closed: *graph* Open: *photo* Unstable digraph: *cre-ate*	Compounds *microscope* *chloroplast* *physiology*

Figure 6.1. Word origin and word structure matrix. (*Source:* Henry, 1988b. Matrix from Henry, M.K. [2003]. *Unlocking literacy: Effective decoding and spelling instruction* [p. 30]. Baltimore: Paul H. Brookes Publishing Co; adapted by permission.)

> American, British, Canadian, Australian, New Zealander, or South African, he still *loves his mother, father, brother, sister, wife, son and daughter; lifts his hand to his head, his cup to his mouth, his eye to heaven and his heart to God; hates his foes, likes his friends, kisses his kin and buries his dead; draws his breath, eats his bread, drinks his water, stands his watch, wipes his sweat, feels his sorrow, weeps his tears and sheds his blood; and all these things he thinks about and calls both good and bad.* (1966, p. 9)

As the Nist passage shows, most words of Anglo-Saxon origin consist of one syllable and represent everyday objects, activities, and events. Although consonant letters are fairly regular (i.e., each letter corresponds to one sound), vowels are more problematic. Words that are learned early on in school are often irregular and may cause difficulty for students with specific reading disabilities. Students must memorize the spellings of these "weird" or "outlaw" words, such as *rough, does, only, eye, laugh, blood,* and *said,* because the vowels do not carry the normal short (lax) or long (tense) sound associated with these spellings.

Letter–Sound Correspondences

Letter–sound correspondences are the relationships between the consonant and vowel letters (graphemes) and their corresponding sounds (phonemes). Anglo-Saxon letter–sound correspondences are the first symbol–sound relationships taught to children learning to read and spell. Consonant letters (e.g., *b, c, d, f, m, p, t*) represent the speech sounds produced by a partial or complete obstruction of the air stream. The consonant

Table 6.2. English consonant spelling–sound correspondences with dictionary (phonic) and phonetic symbols

Consonant graphemes	Examples[a]	The American Heritage Dictionary, Fourth Edition (2000)[a]	International Phonetic Alphabet (IPA)
b	bib	b	b
d	deed	d	d
f, ph, gh	fife, phone, laugh	f	f
g	gag	g	g
h	hat	h	h
j, g, dge	jam, ginger, fudge	j	ʤ
k, -ck, c, ch, -que	kick, cat, chorus, unique	k	k
l, -le	lit, needle	l	l, ļ
m	mom	m	m
n	no, sudden	n	n, ņ
p	pop	p	p
r	roar	r	r
s, c, sc	sauce, science	s	s
t	tot	t	t
v	valve	v	v
w	with	w	w
y	yes	y	j
z, -s	zebra, dogs	z	z
-ng	thing	ng	ŋ
ch, -tch	church, pitch	ch	ʧ
sh	ship	sh	ʃ
th	thin	th	θ
th	that	*th*	ð
wh	when	hw	ʍ
si, su, -ge	vision, treasure, garage	zh	ʒ

[a]Copyright © 2000 by Houghton Mifflin Company. Adapted and reproduced by permission from *The American Heritage Dictionary of the English Language.*

pairs *gn-*, *kn-*, and *wr-* are Anglo-Saxon forms. Vowel letters (i.e., *a, e, i, o, u,* and sometimes *y* and *w*) represent the sounds that are created by the relatively free passage of breath through the larynx and oral cavity.

Liberman and her colleagues (Liberman, 1973; Liberman & Liberman, 1990; Liberman & Shankweiler, 1985, 1991; Liberman, Shankweiler, Fischer, & Carter, 1974) noted that children's phonological awareness, or understanding of the role that sounds play in the English language, is extremely important in learning to read. Before learning letter–sound correspondences, often called *phonics,* children benefit from training in phonological awareness. Phonological awareness is an awareness of all levels of the speech sound system, including rhymes, stress patterns, syllables, and phonemes. Students practice rhyming, segmentation, and blending (see Chapter 4) before learning letter names and letter formation (see Chapter 5). *Phonemic awareness,* which is only one component of phonological awareness, is the awareness that speech is made up of discrete sounds and the ability to manipulate sounds into words.

Balmuth (1992), as well as Adams (1990), Chall (1983), Chall and Popp (1996), and Richardson (1989), provided insights on the importance of phonics in education since the 19th century. When learning phonics, students must link the graphemes and phonemes of English. Tables 6.2 and 6.3 represent the primary graphemes that spell or correspond to each of the approximately 44 phonemes of English. Teachers generally

Table 6.3.   English vowel spelling–sound correspondences with dictionary (phonic) and phonetic symbols

Vowel graphemes	Examples[a]	The American Heritage Dictionary, Fourth Edition (2000)*	International Phonetic Alphabet (IPA)
a	pat	ă	æ
a, a-consonant-e, ai, ay, ei, eigh, ey	baby, made, pail, pay, veil, eight, they	ā	e
e	pet	ĕ	ɛ
e, e-consonant-e, ee, ea, ie, y, ey, ei	me, scheme, greet, seat, thief, lady, alley, ceiling	ē	i
i	bit	ĭ	ɪ
i, i-consonant-e, igh, ie, y	hi, kite, fight, pie, sky	ī	aj
o	hot	ŏ	ɑ
o, o-consonant-e, oa, ow, oe	go, vote, boat, grow, toe	ō	o
u	cut	ū	ɨ
a	father	ä	ɑ
(schwa)	alone, item, credible, gallop, circus	ə	ə
au, aw	fault, claw	ô	ɔ
ew, oo	chew, room	o͞o	u
oo	book	o͝o	ʊ
oi, oy	coin, toy	oi	ɔj
ou, ow	cloud, clown	ou	æw
ar	car	är	ɑːr**
are	care	âr	er**
er, ir, ur, or, ear (*stressed*)	fern, bird, burn, word, heard	ûr	ɜr**
er (*unstressed*)	butter	ər	ɚ
ier, eer	pier, deer	îr	ɪr, ir

*Copyright © 2000 by Houghton Mifflin Company. Adapted and reproduced by permission from *The American Heritage Dictionary of the English Language.*

**Phonetic notation for the *r*-controlled sounds varies.

use dictionary markings (phonic symbols) as guides to pronunciation. Linguists and specialists in speech-language disorders tend to use symbols from the International Phonetic Alphabet (IPA). Both ways of marking pronunciation are shown in Tables 6.2 and 6.3. (For further information on **phonetics**, the identification and description of speech sounds, and the articulation of specific sounds, see Chapter 1 of Moats, 1995, and Chapter 2 of Moats, 2000, as well as Chapter 3 in this book.)

Graphemes are organized either in consonant or in vowel patterns. Single-letter consonant spellings seldom vary; each letter stands for a specific sound. The letters *c* and *g*, however, have more than one possible pronunciation: a hard and soft sound. The letter *c* usually has the sound of /k/ as in *carrot* but becomes soft before *e, i,* and *y* as in *cell, city,* and *cypress.* Likewise, the *g* in *go* or *gas* is hard, whereas *g* before *e, i,* and *y* is soft as in *gem, ginger,* and *Gypsy.* The letter *s* is usually pronounced as /s/ as in *snake* but sometimes has the /z/ sound as in *dogs.* Note that *x* is omitted from Table 6.2; it represents two possible sounds. The letter *x* at the end of a word makes the sound of /ks/ as in *box* but makes the sound of /z/ at the beginning of some words, such as *Xerox.*

Consonant **blends** (sometimes called *consonant clusters*), made up of two or three adjacent consonants that retain their individual sounds in a syllable, are common (e.g., *bl* and *mp* in *blimp; spl* and *nt* in *splint*). In contrast to blends, consonant **digraphs**,

which evolved in Middle English times, are two or more adjacent letters that form only one speech sound. Often, one of the letters of a consonant digraph is *h* (e.g., *sh* in *ship*, *ch* in *chump*, *th* in *this*, *wh* in *when*).

Vowel graphemes tend to be more difficult to learn than consonant graphemes, as they can represent more than one sound and are often difficult to discriminate. Single vowels are generally either short or long. Words often contain clues, referred to as **markers**, that indicate whether the **short** or **long** sound should be used. A vowel with a consonant after it in the same syllable carries the short sound (e.g., *cat, let, fit, fox, fun*). In contrast, a vowel at the end of a syllable becomes long or "says its own name" (e.g., *go, baby, pilot*). A silent *e* at the end of a word, as in *shape* and *vote*, also signals that the word has a long vowel sound. A doubled consonant, as in *pinning* and *cutter*, marks that the preceding vowel has a short sound. The doubled consonant cancels the long-vowel signal that would otherwise be given by the *i* in *ing* and the *e* in *er*.

Students will also read words with a vowel plus *r* or *l*. The vowel sounds are often neither short nor long. These patterns are best taught as combinations, such as *ar* in *star, or* in *corn, er* in *fern, ir* in *bird, ur* in *church*, and *al* in *falter*. (See Appendix A at the end of this chapter for an example of a lesson contrasting *ar* and *or* patterns.)

Vowel digraphs consist of two adjacent vowel letters that represent one sound (e.g., *oa, ee, oi, ou, au*); these often occur in words of Anglo-Saxon origin. A vowel digraph usually occurs in the middle of a word. Vowel digraphs are often difficult for students to acquire because of their variability and because of interference from previously learned associations. They can be divided into two sets—those that are fairly consistently linked to a single sound (e.g., *ee, oa, oi, oy*) and those that may have either of two pronunciations (e.g., *ea* in *bead* or *bread, ow* in *show* or *cow*). (It should be noted that linguists differentiate between the terms *vowel digraph* and *diphthong*. Both contain two adjacent vowels letters in the same syllable. **Diphthongs** contain two vowels with a slide or a shift in the middle; they include *au/aw, oi/oy*, and *ou/ow*.) Balmuth provided the historical origins of vowel digraphs and diphthongs and noted that during Middle English times diphthongs were "especially varied in spelling because of the confusions that resulted from the separation of the written *i* and *y* and the introduction of the w and other French spelling conventions" (1992, p. 102).

By the end of the second grade, children should have mastered all of the common letter–sound correspondences and related spelling patterns (see Chapter 10 for further discussion of spelling patterns and rules). For example, children need to learn when to use *-ck* rather than *-k* at the end of a one-syllable word. The appendices at the end of this chapter provide examples of instruction on reading and writing words containing new target patterns.

Syllable Patterns

Syllables are units of spoken language consisting of a vowel sound or a vowel–consonant combination. Words of Anglo-Saxon origin have a variety of syllable patterns. Students first learn that each syllable must have a vowel. Children generally have less difficulty with hearing syllables in words than with identifying the syllables in written words (Balmuth, 1992; Groff, 1971). Therefore, teachers often begin by having children say their own names and count the number of syllables. Students also begin to listen for accent or stress in words of more than one syllable. Teachers can help students discover that words of Anglo-Saxon origin (e.g., *sleep, like, time*) tend to retain the accent when affixes are added (e.g., *asleep, likely, timeless*).

Groff (1971) emphasized that syllables are not units of writing, grammar, or structure. He noted that the boundaries of syllables rather than the number of syllables in a word cause difficulty in their analysis. He made the distinction between how linguists divide words based on morphemic boundaries and how dictionaries divide syllables based on sounds. For example, some linguists may prefer to divide the word *disruptive* as *dis|rupt|ive* (prefix, root, and suffix), whereas dictionaries usually divide the word as *dis|rup|tive*. Groff wondered whether teaching syllable division is an important part of teaching reading. Although this argument continues, it is useful for teachers to know the six major syllable types and the predominant syllable-division patterns because children will read multisyllabic words in the primary grades and will find syllable division useful in hyphenating words.

The major types of syllables are 1) closed, 2) vowel-consonant-*e,* 3) open, 4) vowel pair (or vowel team), 5) consonant-*le,* and 6) *r*-controlled (see Moats, 1995, 2000; Steere, Peck, & Kahn, 1971). Teachers introduce closed syllables first. In these syllables, the single vowel has a consonant after it and makes a short vowel sound (e.g., *map, sit, cub, stop, bed*). The final *e* in a vowel-consonant-*e* (VCE) syllable makes the vowel long (e.g., *made, time, cute, vote, Pete*). An open syllable contains a vowel at the end of the syllable, and the vowel usually has a long sound. Stanback (1992) found that closed syllables alone make up 43% of syllables in English words. Open syllables and closed syllables together account for almost 75% of English syllables. A vowel pair (or vowel team) syllable contains two adjacent vowel letters as in *rain, green, coil,* and *pause.* Children learn the long, short, or diphthong sound of each pattern. A syllable ending in -*le* is usually preceded by a consonant that is part of that syllable. For example, *bugle* has a long *u* because the *gle* stays together and makes *bu* a long syllable. *Tumble,* in contrast, contains *tum* and *ble;* with *tum* being a closed syllable. *Little* requires two *t*'s to keep the *i* in *lit* short. As discussed previously, vowel sounds in *r*-controlled syllables often lose their identity as long or short and are coarticulated with the /r/ (as in *star, corn, fern, church,* and *firm*).

Students also need to learn some common rules for syllable division so that multisyllabic words are easier to read and spell. By understanding and practicing identification of the various syllable types in one-syllable words first, readers will recognize these common syllable types as they learn to divide words into syllables. Understanding how to spell the vowel sounds in syllables gives readers an advantage and a more productive grasp of syllable-division rules. Readers may recognize syllable-division patterns such as vowel-consonant-consonant-vowel (VC|CV) and others (V|CV as in *hobo* and VC|CCV as in *hundred*). These are useful separations to know when analyzing unfamiliar words (see Chapter 9).

Morpheme Patterns

A morpheme is the smallest meaningful linguistic unit. Prefixes (beginnings), suffixes (endings), and roots are the morphemes that are helpful for students learning to read and write because they appear in literally hundreds of thousands of words (Brown, 1947; Henry, 1993). By knowing the common morphemes, students enhance not only their decoding and spelling skills but also their vocabulary skills.

Anglo-Saxon morphemes are found in both compound (e.g., *football, blackboard*) and affixed words (e.g., *lovely, timeless*). These words tend to be simple because they contain regular orthographic features. **Compound words** generally comprise two short words joined together to form new, **meaning-based words** (e.g., *blackboard* suggests a

black board, football refers to a *ball* for kicking with one's *foot*). Computer technology has been the impetus for many new compound words, such as *software* and *shareware*.

Words can also be expanded by affixing prefixes and suffixes to the **base word**. These base words, or free morphemes, can stand alone as words, such as *like* or *hope*. Morpheme affixes have two forms. Inflectional morphemes indicate grammatical features such as number, person, tense, or comparison (e.g., *dog, dogs; wait, waits; walk, walked; small, smaller*). Derivational morphemes, in contrast, change one part of speech to another, chiefly by adding affixes to root words (e.g., *hope, hopeless, hopelessly*). (See Chapter 3 for more on morphemes.)

Students begin learning morpheme patterns by adding suffixes to words requiring no change in the base form (e.g., *help, helpless; time, untimely*). Soon after that they must learn suffix addition rules that affect some base words, such as the rule about when to drop a final *e* or change *y* to *i* (see Chapter 10).

LATIN LAYER OF LANGUAGE

The Latin layer of the English language consists of words used in more formal settings. Latin-based words, including words from the Romance languages, are often found in the literature, social studies, and science texts in upper elementary school and later grades.

Letter–Sound Correspondences

Because Latin-based words are longer than Anglo-Saxon–based words, many students expect them to be more complex. Yet, in most cases the words follow simple letter–sound correspondences. Single consonants are identical to those found in Anglo-Saxon–based words, but words of Latin origin contain fewer vowel digraphs. Most Latin roots contain short vowels as in *dict, rupt, script, struct, tract, tens, pend,* and *duct*. The consonant combination *ct* is a signpost for words of Latin origin as in *contradict, construct,* and *viaduct*.

Latin-based digraphs generally appear in suffixes such as *-ion, -ian, -ient,* and *-ial*. When these vowel digraphs come after the letters *c, s,* and *t,* they combine with those letters as the /sh/ sound as in *nation, politician, partial, social,* and *admission* (*-sion* is also pronounced as /zhən/ in words such as *erosion* and *invasion*.)

The schwa (/ə/), or unstressed vowel sound, is often found in words of Latin origin in the unaccented prefixes and/or suffixes and is discussed next.

Syllable Patterns

The stress patterns in Latin-based words are fairly complex. The schwa (/ə/) is common in longer words of Latin origin such as *excellent* and *direction*. When one pronounces *excellent,* for example, stress occurs on the first syllable so the initial *e* receives the regular short sound. The following two *e*'s, appearing in unstressed syllables, have the schwa sound (/ə/). Listening for the unstressed vowels in open and closed syllables is an advanced skill that students with reading difficulties need to learn. Students who can discover the base word (e.g., *excel*) often will be able to spell the longer word.

Morpheme Patterns

Although Anglo-Saxon base words can make up compound words (e.g., *houseboat*) and can have affixes added to them (e.g., *hopelessly*) and become affixed, Latin roots may

only be affixed. Nist provided another key example: "So great, in fact, was the penetra*tion* of Latin *af*fixing during the *Renais*s*ance* that it quite *un*did the Anglo-Saxon habit of *com*pounding as the leading means of word form*ation* in English" (1966, p. 11). Words of Latin origin become affixed with the addition of a prefix and/or a suffix to a root, which rarely stands alone (e.g., *rupt, interrupt; mit, transmitting; vent, prevent*). For example, the prefix *in-* can be added to the bound morpheme *spect* to get *inspect,* and the suffix *-ion* can be added to get *inspection.* (*Note:* Some sources, such as Barnhart, 1988; Gillingham & Stillman, 1997; and Webster's New Universal Unabridged Dictionary, 1983, explain *-tion* and *-cian* as noun suffixes. Others teach only *-ion* and *-ian* as suffixes added to roots such as *invent* and *music,* respectively. Teachers and students need to know that *-ion* and *-ian,* are the suffixes but that these are often preceded by *t, s,* or *c.* These may be taught as specific patterns.)

The final consonant of a Latin prefix often changes based on the beginning letter of the root. For example, the prefix *in-* changes to *il-* before roots beginning with *l* (e.g., *illegal, illicit*), to *ir-* before roots beginning with *r* (e.g., *irregular*), and to *im-* before roots beginning with *m, b,* and *p* (e.g., *immobile, imbalance, important*). These **chameleon prefixes** are found in several forms (see Henry, 2003, and Henry & Redding, 1996).

Latin word roots form the basis of hundreds of thousands of words (Brown, 1947; Henry, 1993, 2003). These roots are useful not only for decoding and spelling words but also for enhancing vocabulary. Students can readily observe the prefixes, roots, and suffixes in such words as *prediction, incredible, extracting,* and *reconstructionist.*

Although most words of Latin origin follow regular letter–sound correspondences, some do not. Morphophonemic relations are the conditions in which certain morphemes keep their written spelling when affixes are added although their phonemic forms change. This concept provides students with a logical reason for many English spellings. For example, in *knowledge,* the morpheme *know* is pronounced differently than the base word know. The meaning of *knowledge,* however, is based on the base word *know.* Balmuth noted that

> It can be helpful to readers when the same spelling is kept for the same morpheme, despite variations in pronunciation. Such spellings supply clues to the meanings of words, clues that would be lost if the words were spelled phonemically, as, for example, if *know* and *knowledge* were spelled *noe* and *nollij* in a hypothetical phonemic system. (1992, p. 207)

GREEK LAYER OF LANGUAGE

Greek words, too, entered English by the thousands during the Renaissance to meet the needs of scholars and scientists. In addition, Bodmer noted that "the terminology of modern science, especially in aeronautics, biochemistry, chemotherapy, and genetics" (1944, p. 246), is formed from Greek. Greek roots are often called *combining forms* and compound to form words. Words of Greek origin appear largely in science textbooks (e.g., *microscope, hemisphere, physiology*). The following passage from a middle school science text (Cooper, Blackwood, Boeschen, Giddings, & Carin, 1985, p. 20) shows not only how short words of Anglo-Saxon origin mix with longer Romance words but also how the scientific terminology is couched in words of Greek origin:

> Suppose you could examine a green part of a plant under the *microscope.* What would you see? Here are some cells from the green part of a plant. The cells have small green bodies shaped like footballs. They give the plant its green color. They are called *chloroplasts.* A single green plant cell looks like this. *Chloroplasts* are very important to a plant.

As you know, plants make their own food. This food-making process is called *photo-synthesis.* It is in these *chloroplasts* that *photosynthesis* takes place.

Letter–Sound Correspondences

Greek letter–sound correspondences are similar to those of Anglo-Saxon, but words of Greek origin often use the sounds of /k/, /f/, and /ĭ/ represented by *ch, ph,* and *y,* respectively, such as in *chlorophyll.* These peculiar consonant combinations were introduced by Latin scribes and make words of Greek origin easily recognizable (Bodmer, 1944). Less common Greek letter–sound correspondences, found in only a handful of words, include *mn-* in *mnemonic, rh-* in *rhododendron, pt-* in *pterodactyl, pn-* in *pneumonia,* and the more well-known *ps-* in *psychology* and *psychiatry.*

Syllable Patterns

Syllable types most prevalent in Greek-based words are closed (CVC, as in *graph*) and open (CV, as in *photo*). In addition, a unique type of syllable can be found, that of adjacent vowels in separate syllables (CV|VC), as in *theater, create,* and *theory.* These vowels appear in distinct syllables and therefore have distinct sounds.

Syllable division in words of Greek origin generally follows the rules given for Anglo-Saxon words, especially the rules for open syllables (e.g., *phono, photo, meter, polis*). For example, the letter *y* sounds like short *i* in closed syllables (e.g., *symphony, gymnasium*), and these syllables are divided after the consonant. The letter *y* sounds like long *i* in open syllables (e.g., *cyclone, gyroscope, hyperbole*), and these syllables are divided immediately after the *y.* Combining forms such as *semi, hemi,* and *micro* do not follow traditional V|CV or VC|CV division. CVVC words such as *create* and *theory* divided between the vowels (*cre|ate, the|or|y*). Students rarely need to depend on strategies for syllable division because they learn the patterns as wholes.

Morpheme Patterns

If students recognize relatively few Greek roots (or combining forms), then they can read and spell many thousands of words. As students learn the common Greek roots that hold specific meaning, such as *micro, scope, bio, graph, helio, meter, phono, photo, auto,* and *tele,* they begin to read, spell, and understand the meaning of words such as *microscope, telescope, phonoreception, telephoto, telescopic, photoheliograph, heliometer, biography,* and *autobiography.* Many Greek roots are often called prefixes because they appear at the beginning of words (e.g., *auto* in *autograph, hyper* in *hyperbole,* and *hemi* in *hemisphere*). Numeral prefixes such as *mono-* (1), *di-* (2), *tri-* (3), *tetra-* (4), *penta-* (5), *hexa-* (6), *hepta-* (7), *octa-* (8), *nona-* (9), *deca-* (10), *centi-* (100), and *kilo-* (1,000) become useful in the study of mathematics and geometry.

Ehrlich (1972); Fifer and Flowers (1989); Fry, Polk, and Fountoukidis (1996); Henry (1990, 2003); and Henry and Redding (1996) provided numerous resources for words containing both Latin- and Greek-based words. Specific instructional activities can be found in the latter three sources. (See Appendixes B and C at the end of this chapter for examples of lessons for Latin and Greek morpheme patterns, respectively.)

CONCLUSION

Perfetti asserted that "only a reader with skilled decoding processes can be expected to have skilled comprehension processes" (1984, p. 43). When children are able to grasp

words important to the gist of a story or to the meaning of text, their understanding will be enhanced.

Teachers who comprehend the origins of the English language along with the primary structural patterns within words can improve their assessment skills, enhance their understanding of reading and spelling curricula, communicate clearly about language issues, and effectively teach useful language strategies to their students. Influences on English orthography stem from the introduction of letters and words from diverse origins. When teachers and their students understand the historical basis and structure of written English, they can better understand the regularities as well as the very few irregularities in English words.

Young students will use these language strategies to **decode** and spell short, **regular words** as well as Anglo-Saxon compound words and words using common prefixes and suffixes. Older students and adult learners receiving instruction in more advanced language structure will focus on Latin and Greek roots and affixes.

Finally, students of all ages often greatly enjoy learning about the structure and origins of English words. Students who are learning English as a second language find that English is quite regular after all and is not a language of exceptions. Children with or without specific language disabilities benefit as they learn effective and efficient strategies to read and spell numerous words.

REFERENCES

Adams, M.J. (1990). *Beginning to read: Thinking and learning about print.* Cambridge, MA: The MIT Press.

The American heritage dictionary (4th ed.). (2000). Boston: Houghton Mifflin.

Balmuth, M. (1992). *The roots of phonics.* Timonium, MD: York Press.

Barnhart, R.K. (1988). *The Barnhart dictionary of etymology.* New York: H.W. Wilson Co.

Bodmer, F. (1944). *The loom of language.* New York: W.W. Norton.

Brown, J.I. (1947). Reading and vocabulary: 14 master words. In M.J. Herzberg (Ed.), *Word study, 1–4.* Springfield, MA: Merriam-Webster.

Chall, J.S. (1983). *Learning to read: The great debate revisited.* New York: McGraw-Hill.

Chall, J.S., & Popp, H.M. (1996). *Teaching and assessing phonics.* Cambridge, MA: Educators Publishing Service.

Claiborne, R. (1983). *Our marvelous native tongue.* New York: Times Books.

Cooper, E.K., Blackwood, P.E., Boeschen, J.A., Giddings, M.G., & Carin, A.A. (1985). *HBJ science* (Purple ed.). Orlando, FL: Harcourt Brace & Co.

Ehrlich, I. (1972). *Instant vocabulary.* New York: Pocket Books.

Fifer, N., & Flowers, N. (1989). *Vocabulary from classical roots.* Cambridge, MA: Educators Publishing Service.

Fry, E.B., Polk, J.D., & Fountoukidis, D.L. (1996). *The reading teacher's new book of lists* (3rd ed.). Upper Saddle River, NJ: Prentice-Hall.

Gillingham, A., & Stillman, B.W. (1997). *Remedial training for children with specific disability in reading, spelling and penmanship* (8th ed.). Cambridge, MA: Educators Publishing Service.

Groff, P. (1971). *The syllable: Its nature and pedagogical usefulness.* Portland, OR: Northwest Regional Educational Laboratory.

Hanna, P.R., Hodges, R.E., & Hanna, J.S. (1971). *Spelling: Structure and strategies.* Boston: Houghton Mifflin.

Henderson, E.H. (1990). *Teaching spelling* (2nd ed.). Boston: Houghton Mifflin.

Henry, M.K. (1988a). Beyond phonics: Integrated decoding and spelling instruction based on word origin and structure. *Annals of Dyslexia, 38,* 259–275.

Henry, M.K. (1988b). Understanding English orthography: Assessment and instruction for decoding and spelling (Doctoral dissertation, Stanford University, 1988). *Dissertation Abstracts International, 48,* 2841–A.

Henry, M.K. (1990). *WORDS: Integrated decoding and spelling instruction based on word origin and word structure.* Austin, TX: PRO-ED.

Henry, M.K. (1993). Morphological structure: Latin and Greek roots and affixes as upper grade code strategies. *Reading and Writing, 5*(2), 227–241.

Henry, M.K. (2003). *Unlocking literacy: Effective decoding and spelling instruction.* Baltimore: Paul H. Brookes Publishing Co.

Henry, M.K., & Redding, N.C. (1996). *Patterns for success in reading and spelling.* Austin, TX: PRO-ED.

Jespersen, O. (1971). *Growth and structure of the English language.* New York: The Free Press.

Liberman, I.Y. (1973). Segmentation of the spoken word and reading acquisition. *Bulletin of the Orton Society, 23,* 65–77.

Liberman, I.Y., & Liberman, A.M. (1990). Whole language vs. code emphasis: Underlying assumptions and their implications for reading instruction. *Annals of Dyslexia, 40,* 51–78.

Liberman, I.Y., & Shankweiler, D. (1985). Phonology and the problems of learning to read and write. *Remedial and Special Education, 7,* 8–17.

Liberman, I.Y., & Shankweiler, D. (1991). Phonology and beginning reading: A tutorial. In L. Rieben & C.A. Perfetti (Eds.), *Learning to read: Basic research and its implications* (pp. 3–17). Mahwah, NJ: Lawrence Erlbaum Associates.

Liberman, I.Y., Shankweiler, D., Fischer, F.W., & Carter, B. (1974). Explicit syllable and phoneme segmentation in the young child. *Journal of Experimental Child Psychology, 18,* 201–212.

Moats, L.C. (1995). *Spelling: Development, disability, and instruction.* Timonium, MD: York Press.

Moats, L.C. (2000). *Speech to print: Language essentials for teachers.* Baltimore: Paul H. Brookes Publishing Co.

Nist, J. (1966). *A structural history of English.* New York: St. Martin's Press.

Perfetti, C. (1984). Reading acquisition and beyond: Decoding includes cognition. *American Journal of Education, 93,* 40–60.

Richardson, S.O. (1989). Specific developmental dyslexia: Retrospective and prospective views. *Annals of Dyslexia, 39,* 3–23.

Stanback, M.L. (1992). Syllable and rime patterns for teaching reading: Analysis of a frequency-based vocabulary of 17,602 words. *Annals of Dyslexia, 42,* 196–221.

Steere, A., Peck, C.Z., & Kahn, L. (1971). *Solving language difficulties.* Cambridge, MA: Educators Publishing Service.

Venezky, R.L. (1970). *The structure of English orthography.* The Hague, The Netherlands: Mouton.

Webster's new universal unabridged dictionary. (2nd ed.). (1983). New York: Simon & Schuster.

Chapter 6, Appendix A

Sample Lesson for Anglo-Saxon Letter–Sound Correspondences: *ar* and *or*

OPENING

State that students will review the pattern *ar* and learn a new pattern, *or*.

REVIEW

Have children write the pattern *ar* on their tablets and repeat the sound /är/. Remind them that the letter *r* with a vowel before it often changes the vowel sound from its typical short or long sound. Ask students whether they remember any words that use the pattern /är/ (as in *car*). As children generate words, write them on the chalkboard. Words could include the following:

car	dark	harm	starting	yard	target
par	stark	harming	started	arch	tarnish
jar	shark	harmed	charts	part	harmless
star	sharp	barn	mark	tarts	harmful
scar	march	farm	marking	partly	garden
park	starch	farmer	marked	discard	harvest
lark	harp	start	hard	market	alarm

After you write the words and add some of your own, have children read the words together. You may want to point out prefixes and suffixes if they have been included. Ask children to put their reading papers aside as you dictate a few of the words for spelling.

NEW

Write *or* on the board, and ask children whether they know what it says (/or/ as in *corn*). Have children write *or* on their tablets, first tracing, then copying, then writing while carefully monitoring the letter formation. As children write the pattern four or five

---

From Henry, M.K., & Redding, N.C. (1996). *Patterns for success in reading and spelling* (pp. 59–60, 81–82). Austin, TX: PRO-ED; adapted by permission.

times, they repeat the sounds. Have children generate words containing *or*. Words might include the following:

corn	pork	sport	morning	horse	record
for	stork	storm	thorn	order	report
fort	forth	north	shorn	forget	border
port	snort	scorch	short	hornet	
sort	form	morn	porch	sordid	

Again, add words of your own, and have the children read the words. Dictate a few of the words for spelling.

Now ask children to take a piece of paper and fold it in half, lengthwise. Have them write *ar* in the left-hand column and *or* in the right-hand column. Dictate a number of *ar* and *or* words. Children must listen carefully to the vowel sound and write words in the appropriate column.

Give students sentences containing *ar* and *or* words to read and spell. For example,

Please sort the cards.

They saw a shark jump in the storm.

He played many sports in the park.

The farmer planted corn on his farm.

She sat on the north side of the porch.

Her horse marched by the cars.

CLOSING

Review the two patterns emphasized in this lesson. Why are they important to learn?

Sample Lesson for Latin Roots

OPENING

After an introduction to common Latin prefixes and suffixes, students are now ready to learn many of the common Latin roots. Ask students whether they know what a root is (the main part of the word, to which prefixes and suffixes are added and which usually receives the accent or stress in Latin-based words). Tell students that roots are valuable not only as patterns for decoding and spelling but also as aids for learning new vocabulary to enhance reading, writing, listening, and speaking.

NEW

Begin by writing *rupt* on the chalkboard; students write *rupt* in their word booklets. Ask students to generate a number of words with *rupt* as the root. Write these words on the board. Words might include the following:

rupture	disrupt	corruptly	abruptly	interrupted
erupt	disrupting	bankrupt	interrupt	disruptive
eruption	corrupt	abrupt	interruption	irrupt

After students read all of the words that have been generated, see whether they can figure out the root's meaning (*to break*). Next, dictate some of the words for spelling.

Continue giving new Latin word roots in this manner. For each group of words, have students recognize the common roots. Have them note the placement of the root within the word (the beginning if there is no prefix, the end if there is no suffix, the middle if there are prefixes and suffixes). Show them how the root generally cannot stand alone—it is bound to the prefix and/or suffix.

Following are three Latin roots and only a few of the many words containing these roots. Additional suffixes may be added to most of the following words.

From Henry, M.K., & Redding, N.C. (1996). *Patterns for success in reading and spelling* (Part 3, Lesson 13, pp. 251–252). Austin, TX: PRO-ED; adapted by permission.

port (*to carry*)	form (*to shape*)	tract(*to pull*)
import	reform	tractor
export	deform	traction
portable	inform	attract
transport	transform	attraction
porter	transformer	attractive
transported	formula	contract
deport	informal	subtract
report	informative	retract
support	conform	protract
deportation	formal	distract
deportment	formality	distraction

Begin dictating sentences that contain the various roots that have been taught. For example,

> The contract supported the bankruptcy report.

> The exporter interrupted the attractive informant.

Continue teaching common roots such as *spect, scrib/script, stru/struct, dic/dict, flect/flex, mit/miss, cred, duce/duct, vert/vers, pend/pens, jac/jec/ject, tend/tens/tent,* and so forth.

FOLLOW-UP

Have students begin looking for Latin-based affixes and roots in their textbooks and in newspapers.

Chapter 6, Appendix C

Sample Lesson for Greek Roots (or Combining Forms)

OPENING

Tell students that many of the Latin roots just studied were actually borrowed from the Greeks. The Greek roots are often called combining forms because the two roots are of equal stress and importance and compound to form a word. Some of the forms appear only at the beginning of a word (and so may be considered prefixes), others come at the end (sometimes thought of as suffixes), and some forms can be used in either position. A few words contain three combining forms (e.g., *photoheliograph*).

Point out that although Greek-based words contain many of the same letter–sound correspondences found in Anglo-Saxon and Latin-based words, they also have unique letter–sound relationships (e.g., *ph* is pronounced as /f/ as in photograph; *ch* is pronounced as /k/ as in chemist; *y* is either a short or long *i* sound as in *physician* and *typhoon*).

NEW

As you introduce the combining forms, have students carefully write each form, along with its meaning.

>phon, phono (*sound*)
>
>auto (*self*)
>
>photo (*light*)
>
>tele (*distant*)
>
>graph, gram (*written/drawn*)
>
>ology (*study*, from logos/logue [*speech/word*])

Students generate words containing the combining forms. Students read long lists of words containing the previous forms, such as the following:

From Henry, M.K., & Redding, N.C. (1996). *Patterns for success in reading and spelling* (Part 3, Lesson 27, pp. 283–284). Austin, TX: PRO-ED; adapted by permission.

169

phone	graphite	photogram	automobile
phonics	graphics	telecast	photology
phonogram	autograph	telegram	telephotography
phonology	photograph	telephone	monologue
phonological	photography	telephoto	prologue
phoneme	photographer	telethon	dialogue
phonemic	photocopy	automation	epilogue
phonograph	photoflash	automatic	

Have students spell words from dictation. Have students read and spell sentences containing Latin- and Greek-based word parts. For example,

He collected several autographs from the conductors.

The TelePrompTer gave the television broadcaster visual messages.

Phonics instruction is useful in developing reading and writing skills.

Continue adding combining forms, including *micro, meter, therm, bio, scope, hydro, helio, biblio, crat/cracy, geo, metro, polis, dem, derm, hypo, chron, cycl, hyper, chrom,* and so forth.

FOLLOW-UP

Have students look for Greek-based words in science and mathematics textbooks.

7

Assessment of Reading Difficulties

Eileen S. Marzola and Margaret Jo Shepherd

In the minds of many people, assessment and testing are synonymous. People who believe this, however, miss an important point. Testing is a procedure for collecting data. In contrast, assessment is an ongoing process. Testing is subsumed within the process of assessment and is only one source of assessment data. Educators and psychologists who conduct educational assessments use several sources of data, including the following: family, developmental, medical, and educational histories; early screenings, school records, and examples of schoolwork, in particular, reading, spelling, and writing tasks; interviews; observations; both **formal** and **informal** tests; rating scales; and sample lessons. Depending on the purpose of the assessment and particularly in the case of identifying dyslexia, examinations will be requested from other people such as speech-language pathologists and physicians. Data collection for an educational assessment is comprehensive and extends far beyond the information provided by a test.

Three primary questions about assessment are addressed in this chapter:

1. Is this child's struggle with reading and spelling best described as dyslexia?

2. What remedial plan will facilitate learning to read and spell?

3. Is the remedial plan effective?

FACTORS TO CONSIDER WHEN BEGINNING ASSESSMENT

What Role Do Teachers Play in the Assessment Process?

Teachers commonly assess students' progress for two related reasons. First, teachers use data about students' progress to evaluate the effects of instruction. For example, a

teacher will decide that a particular lesson is too easy or too hard based on students' responses or that a particular student needs more practice based on that student's responses during a lesson. These decisions and others like them are made within a lesson or over a series of lessons. Assessment of students' progress, then, is a learning experience for the teacher. It provides information that the teacher uses to modify instruction. Second, a teacher assesses learning to give information to students and their parents. Information given to students is specific, meaningful, and immediate (i.e., provided during the lesson) and cumulative (e.g., collected in folders that are either kept by or easily accessible to the student). The same repositories of information that are available to students also provide information to parents. When parents need to know about their child's progress, the teacher can respond immediately. In addition to these two primary reasons for teachers' assessment of student progress, there is a peripheral benefit to this collection of data. Teachers' insights combined with the data they collect about their students' progress can provide valuable information to guide more comprehensive evaluations of students who continue to struggle in school despite good instruction (discussed later in the section called When Reading Difficulties Persist).

Types of Tests for Educational Assessment

Even though assessment does not depend exclusively on information obtained from tests, it is important to understand that different types of tests may be used during assessment. Tests can be classified as *formal* (standardized) or *informal*. **Standardized tests** must always be administered and scored following procedures that are prescribed in the manual accompanying the test. Unless people who give a standardized test follow the prescribed procedures exactly, the interpretation of test scores will be compromised. Such tests are standardized using a carefully selected sample of people who are representative of the larger group of people for whom the test was created. Informal tests, in contrast, are structured but not standardized. Typically, informal tests use the format of a standardized test, but the person giving the test can modify the presentation of test items and probe the student's responses in ways that are not permissible during the administration of standardized tests.

Tests can also be classified as **norm referenced**, **criterion referenced**, or **curriculum referenced**. Norm-referenced tests produce scores that permit comparisons among people. These tests allow a child's command of the knowledge measured by the test to be compared with that of other children of the same age or grade. Standards for judging the performance of the child taking a norm-referenced test have been determined by the performance of a group of children who took the test when it was standardized. The children whose performance created the norms, or standards, against which the test taker's performance is compared have been selected to be comparable to all children who might take the test with regard to characteristics that influence test performance (e.g., age, gender, race, ethnicity, socioeconomic status, geographic region of residence). Norm-referenced tests, then, give information about a child's development relative to the development of other children of the same age or grade. All norm-referenced tests are standardized.

The difference between criterion-referenced tests and norm-referenced tests is the standard used for judging performance. Norm-referenced tests produce an index (score) of one child's development relative to the development of other children, whereas criterion-referenced tests produce descriptions of one child's knowledge within the domain represented in the test. Criterion-referenced tests allow the test administrators to generate an item-by-item description of knowledge attained and knowledge yet to be

acquired. Curriculum-referenced tests are a variation on criterion-referenced tests. Questions included in a curriculum-referenced test are taken from the curriculum in use in the child's classroom. Curriculum-referenced tests avoid the error of testing a child on content that he or she has not had the opportunity to learn. Thus, curriculum-referenced tests allow for a good match between assessment and instruction. Children are only tested on material that they have been taught. Criterion- and curriculum-referenced tests can be standardized or informal. The important point about these two kinds of tests is that they allow comparisons to be made between a child's present performance and that child's immediate past performance. Thus, the child's previous performance (rather than other children's performance) is the standard for judging progress. Criterion- and curriculum-referenced tests were designed to guide teaching decisions.

Importance of Early Identification

In the not too distant past, parents of young children who struggled with beginning reading instruction were frequently advised by professionals in the schools to "sit and wait." It was assumed that these students would spontaneously catch up to their peers when they were "ready" to learn to read. Much more is known today about the dangers of waiting to intervene. As Torgesen advised, "The best solution to the problem of reading failure is to allocate resources for early identification and prevention" (1998, p. 1). The research is clear. The majority of young children entering kindergarten and elementary school at risk for reading failure have the potential to learn to read at average or above-average levels if they are identified early and given appropriate "systematic, intensive instruction in phonemic awareness, phonics, reading fluency, vocabulary, and reading comprehension strategies" (Lyon & Chhabra, 2004). Torgesen (2002) reported that the number of students who read below basic levels can be reduced to less than 6% if a combination of early identification and appropriate interventions are put in place. The consequences of delaying identification and intervention are ominous. The latest figures from the National Assessment of Educational Progress (U.S. Department of Education, National Center for Education Statistics, 2004) revealed that 37% of fourth graders tested in the United States scored below basic levels of reading in 2003. As Shaywitz (2003) reported, at least 70% of students who do not learn to read by age 9 will never catch up to their typically developing peers.

Even the youngest children who may be at risk for reading problems can be identified. For example, Adams (1990) cited rapid identification of upper- and lowercase letters of the alphabet as the single best predictor of early reading achievement. That, coupled with an assessment of phonemic awareness, which is shown to be directly related to the growth of early word-reading skills (Torgesen, 1998), can be very helpful in identifying young children at risk for reading failure.

Although common signs of reading difficulties may be apparent before a child even begins formal schooling, reviews of early identification research (Scarborough, 1998) have revealed substantial levels of false positives (an average of 45% of children identified during kindergarten as at risk for reading problems turn out not to be among the readers with the most serious problems by the end of first grade). Most of these identified at-risk children, however, are likely to be below-average readers (Torgesen & Burgess, 1998). The flip side is that about 22% of children who are later judged to have serious reading difficulties are not identified through kindergarten screenings. Torgesen (1998) recommended that screening begin in the second semester of kindergarten so that children may have some opportunity to learn the prereading skills that will later

be evaluated. To increase the efficiency of the screening procedure, Torgesen recommended that two tests be given: 1) a test of knowledge of letter names (most predictive for kindergarten children) and/or letter sounds (most predictive for first graders) and 2) a measure of phonemic awareness. Phonemic awareness is commonly measured through tasks grouped in three broad categories: sound comparison, phoneme segmentation, and phoneme blending. (See Chapter 4 for a discussion of phonemic awareness and Chapter 5 for a discussion of letter-name knowledge.)

Reading First and Assessment

The Reading First initiative, a component of the No Child Left Behind Act of 2001 (PL 107-110), passed by Congress and signed into law by President George W. Bush on January 8, 2002, lists assessment as one of its stated purposes. Specifically, one of the purposes of the legislation is "to provide assistance to state educational agencies and local educational agencies in selecting or administering screening, diagnostic, and classroom-based instructional reading assessments" (PL 107-110, § 1201[3]). In response to that call, the Reading First Assessment Committee, with Edward J. Kame'enui from the University of Oregon as its leader, sought to identify, review, and analyze screening, diagnostic, progress monitoring, and **outcomes** reading measures for students in kindergarten through Grade 3. The committee's final report defined these assessment measures in the following manner (Institute for the Development of Educational Achievement, 2002, p. 25):

- Screening measure: Brief assessment that focuses on critical reading skills strongly predictive of future reading growth and development, . . . conducted at the beginning of the school year with all children in grades K, 1, 2, and 3 to identify children likely to need extra or alternative forms of instruction.
- Diagnostic measure: Assessment conducted at any time during the school year when a more in-depth analysis of a student's strengths and weaknesses is needed to guide instruction.
- Progress monitoring measure: Assessment conducted a minimum of three times a year or on a routine basis (i.e., weekly, monthly, or quarterly) using comparable and multiple test forms to (a) estimate rates of reading improvement, (b) identify children who are not making adequate progress and therefore require additional or different forms of instruction, and/or (c) compare the effectiveness of different forms of instruction for struggling readers and thereby design more effective individualized instructional programs for those at-risk learners.
- Outcome measure: Assessment for the purpose of classifying students in terms of whether or not they achieved grade-level performance or improved.

The report focused on the five essential components of reading instruction as outlined in Reading First (PL 107-110, § 1208[3]):

(A) phonemic awareness;
(B) phonics;
(C) vocabulary development;
(D) reading fluency, including oral reading skills; and
(E) reading comprehension strategies.

Twenty-four of twenty-nine assessment measures reviewed by the committee were found to have sufficient evidence for use as screening, diagnosis, progress monitoring, and/or outcome instruments to assess one or more essential reading components at one or more grade levels K–3. Table 7.1 displays the type and use of each of the 24 measures.

Table 7.1. Assessment measures found to have sufficient evidence for use as screening, diagnosis, progress monitoring, and/or outcome instruments to assess essential reading components, grades K–3

Assessment measure	Author(s) and copyright year (if available)	Publisher
CBM Oral Reading Fluency	S. Deno (2002)	Unpublished assessment
Clinical Evaluation of Language Fundamentals–Third Edition (CELF-3)[a]	E. Semel, E.H. Wiig, & W.A. Secord (1995)	Harcourt Assessment San Antonio, TX 800-872-1726 www.psychcorp.com
Comprehensive Test of Phonological Processing (CTOPP)	R.K. Wagner, J.K. Torgesen, & C.A. Rashotte (1999)	PRO-ED Austin, TX 800-897-3202 www.proedinc.com
Degrees of Reading Power (DRP)	B. Koslin, S. Zeno, S. Koslin, & H. Wainer (2000)	Touchstone Applied Science Associates Brewster, NY 800-800-2598 www.tasaliteracy.com
Dynamic Indicators of Basic Early Literacy Skills–Fifth Edition (DIBELS)[a]	R. Good	University of Oregon Eugene, OR 541-346-3562 http://dibels.uoregon.edu
Early Reading Diagnostic Assessment (ERDA)[a]	D.R. Smith (2000)	Harcourt Assessment
Gray Oral Reading Test–Fourth Edition (GORT-4)	J.L. Wiederholt & B.R. Bryant (2001)	PRO-ED
Iowa Test of Basic Skills (ITBS)	H. Hoover, S. Dunbar, D. Frisbie, K. Oberley, V. Ordman, G. Naylor, et al. (2001)	Riverside Chicago, IL 800-323-9540 www.riverpub.com
Letter Sound Fluency	D. Fuchs & L. Fuchs	Vanderbilt University Nashville, TN
Lindamood Auditory Conceptualization Test (LAC Test)[a]	C. Lindamood & P. Lindamood (1979)	PRO-ED
Peabody Picture Vocabulary Test–Third Edition (PPVT-III)	L.M. Dunn & L.M. Dunn (1997)	American Guidance Service Circle Pines, MN 800-328-2560 www.agsnet.com
Phonological Awareness Test (PAT)	C. Robertson & W. Salter (1997)	LinguiSystems East Moline, IL 800-776-4332 www.linguisystems.com
Slosson Oral Reading Test–Revised (SORT-R)[a]	R.L. Slosson (revised by C.L. Nicholson) (1990)	Slosson Educational Publications East Aurora, NY 888-756-7766 www.slosson.com
Stanford Achievement Test–Ninth Edition[a]	(1997)	Harcourt Assessment
Terra Nova, The Second Edition (CAT/6)	(2001)	CTB/McGraw-Hill Monterey, CA 800-538-9567 www.ctb.com
Test of Language Development–Primary: 3 (TOLD-P:3)	P.L. Newcomer & D.D. Hammill (1997)	PRO-ED

(continued)

Table 7.1   *(continued)*

Assessment measure	Author(s) and copyright year (if available)	Publisher
Test of Phonological Awareness (TOPA)[a]	J.K. Torgesen & B. Bryant (1994)	PRO-ED
Test of Word Knowledge (TOWK)	E.H. Wiig & W. Secord (1992)	Harcourt Assessment
Test of Word Reading Efficiency (TOWRE)	J. Torgesen, R. Wagner, & C. Rashotte (1999)	PRO-ED
Texas Primary Reading Inventory (TPRI)[a]	University of Texas Health Science Center at Houston, Center for Academic and Reading Skills, & University of Houston (1999)	Texas Reading Instruments Austin, TX 800-758-4756 http://www.txreadinginstruments.com
Wechsler Individual Achievement Test–II (WIAT-II)	D.R. Smith (2001)	Harcourt Assessment
Woodcock Reading Mastery Test–Revised (WRMT-R)	R. Woodcock (1987)	American Guidance Service
Woodcock-Johnson III Tests of Achievement	R.W. Woodcock, K.S. McGrew, & N. Mather (2001)	Riverside www.woodcock-johnson.com
Yopp-Singer Test of Phoneme Segmentation	H.K. Yopp, & H. Singer (1995)	Published in *The Reading Teacher*, *49*(1), 20–29.

Source: Institute for the Development of Educational Achievement, 2002.

[a]Newer versions of the indicated assessments may be available.

Tools for Early Identification in Kindergarten

A substantial number of screening instruments (most of which have been reviewed in the Reading First Assessment Committee's final report, Institute for the Development of Educational Achievement, 2002) have become available in the past few years. These may be used to identify children in kindergarten or even prekindergarten who are at high risk for reading failure and who may require more intense, systematic reading instruction. Three short, direct, and relatively simple-to-administer screening tools hold particular promise: the Texas Primary Reading Inventory (TPRI; University of Texas Health Science Center at Houston, Center for Academic and Reading Skills, & University of Houston [UTH/UH], 2002); the Phonological Awareness Literacy Screening (PALS; Invernizzi, Juel, Swank, & Meier, 2003; Invernizzi, Meier, & Juel, 2002; Invernizzi, Sullivan, & Meier, 2001); and the Dynamic Indicators of Basic Early Literacy Skills (DIBELS; Good & Kaminski, 2002).

The TPRI (UTH/UH, 2002) is a one-to-one assessment tool designed to be used with students in kindergarten. Assessments for children in Grades 1, 2, and 3 are also available. The TPRI offers two levels of assessment. In January or February of the kindergarten year, students may take the brief Screening Section, which takes less than 10 minutes. Students who do not pass this initial screening may then take a more in-depth reading inventory that takes approximately 25–30 minutes to administer. In some schools, the entire Inventory Section is given to all students. This inventory can be used to help teachers identify student strengths and problem areas and also to monitor student progress.

The Screening Section of the TPRI (UTH/UH, 2002) focuses on three areas: **grapho-phonemic** knowledge in kindergarten and Grade 1 (recognition of letters of the alphabet and demonstrated understanding of sound–symbol relationships); phonemic awareness in kindergarten and Grade 1 (the ability to identify and manipulate sounds within spoken words); and word reading for kindergarten through Grade 3. The Inventory Section Assessment adds six new components: book and print awareness (general knowledge of the function of print as well as the characteristics of books and other print sources) to the kindergarten assessment; listening comprehension to the kindergarten and Grade 1 assessments; graphophonemic knowledge in the kindergarten through Grade 3 assessments (recognition of letters of the alphabet and demonstration of understanding of sound-symbol relations for kindergarten and Grade 1 students, word building activities for students in Grade 1 and spelling for students in Grades 2 and 3); and reading accuracy, reading fluency, and reading comprehension for Grades 1, 2, and 3. Each TPRI kit also includes an Intervention Activities Guide to guide instruction. A comparable assessment available from the same publisher measures student reading skills and comprehension development in Spanish for students in kindergarten through Grade 2: El Inventario de Lectura en Español de Tejas (Tejas LEE).

Another screening tool, the PALS (Invernizzi et al., 2003; Invernizzi et al., 2002; Invernizzi et al., 2001) is used twice a year beginning in prekindergarten and kindergarten. Assessments are also available for Grades 1–3. The first administration, in the fall of the school year, is used to guide instruction for students who do not meet early literacy standards. A second administration in the spring helps to evaluate progress after targeted interventions have been delivered.

The PALS-PreK (Invernizzi et al., 2001) measures skills such as name-writing ability, upper- and lowercase letter recognition, letter sounds and beginning sound production, print and word awareness, rhyme awareness, and nursery rhyme awareness.

The PALS-K (Invernizzi et al., 2003) focuses on five fundamental literacy skills. Skills assessed include phonological awareness (matching rhyming pictures plus beginning sound awareness demonstrated by matching words that begin with the same sound), alphabet recognition (26 lowercase letters), concept of word (touching words in a memorized rhyme, using context to identify individual words, and identifying words outside of the text), knowledge of letter sounds (producing sounds for 23 uppercase letters plus three digraphs), and spelling (five consonant–vowel–consonant words are targeted, and phonetically acceptable substitutions receive credit).

The PALS 1–3 (Invernizzi et al., 2002) for Grades 1–3 is a leveled instrument. Level A is used to identify students at risk of reading difficulties. Levels B and C provide teachers with information that can guide instruction by diagnosing specific skill deficits in students who do not meet the Level A criteria. Spelling, word recognition in isolation, oral reading in context (to assess oral reading accuracy, phrasing, intonation and expression), reading rate, comprehension, and fluency are all assessed. Students whose entry-level scores do not meet grade-level criteria are assessed with Level B tasks including alphabet recognition, letter sounds, and concept of word (the latter is explained in the previous PALS-K description). Finally, students who do not meet Level B benchmarks move to Level C for an even more in-depth evaluation of phonemic awareness skills, including blending and segmenting speech sounds.

A Teacher Checklist of Literacy Practices is included in the PALS-PreK kit. A video that includes demonstrations of instructional strategies for students can be found in both the PALS-K and the PALS 1–3 kits.

The third screening tool that is widely used in this country is the Dynamic Indicators of Basic Early Literacy Skills (DIBELS; Good & Kaminski, 2002), a free assessment

*DIBLES
download*

tool that was developed to identify children who are at risk for reading difficulties. It may be downloaded from the University of Oregon web site (http://dibels.uoregon.edu). These standardized, one-minute fluency measures can also be used to monitor progress in prereading and early reading skills. A Spanish version of DIBELS, Indicadores dínamicos del éxito en la lectura 6ta Edición (IDEL), is also available.

Student development of phonological awareness, understanding of the alphabetic principle, and automatic and fluent use of the reading code are assessed. For a small fee (currently $1.00 per student per year), DIBELS (Good & Kaminski, 2002) benchmark assessment scores may be tracked across years for grades currently covered by the assessments (kindergarten through Grade 3). Assessments may be administered three times per year (usually September, January, and May) if the students are progressing adequately. If not, however, DIBELS may be administered more frequently so that instructional interventions can be adjusted based on progress.

By the end of the school year, Kindergarten DIBELS (Good & Kaminski, 2002) will have assessed initial sound fluency, letter naming fluency, and phoneme segmentation fluency. Benchmarks are set for each skill. For example, the benchmark goal for the middle of kindergarten for initial sound fluency is 25–35 initial sounds correct. For phoneme segmentation fluency, the benchmark goal is 35–40 correct phonemes per minute in the spring of kindergarten and fall of first grade.

Skills are added to the DIBELS (Good & Kaminski, 2002) measures as students continue in school. For example, in Grade 1, nonsense word fluency and oral reading fluency are measured. In Grades 2 and 3, oral reading fluency continues to be measured. Word use and oral retell fluency measures are also available. Benchmark measures are set for nonsense word fluency, oral reading fluency, and oral retell fluency for first grade and above.

The DIBELS (Good & Kaminski, 2002) measures are standardized and designed to assess student development of phonological awareness, alphabetic understanding, and automaticity and fluency with the code. They are considered to be reliable, valid indicators of early literacy development. As with the TPRI (UTH/UH, 2002) and PALS (Invernizzi et al., 2003; Invernizzi et al., 2001), DIBELS can be used for early identification of students who are not progressing at expected levels and who need targeted intervention strategies. All three measures may also be used to provide grade-level feedback about whether interventions are effective for individual students.

PROGRESS MONITORING

Formative and Summative Data

In addition to classifying assessments as formal or informal, there is another way to classify data collection procedures that is particularly important when the assessment question is about progress or learning. Data collection can be *formative* or *summative*. **Formative data collection** applies to immediate or short-term instructional goals and yields information about a child's progress acquiring particular skills or knowledge. **Summative data collection** applies to long-term, comprehensive teaching goals and yields information about the accumulation and integration of knowledge. In the context of assessment of progress in literacy, formative procedures can be used to track the acquisition of word-recognition skills, whereas summative procedures can provide information about reading comprehension. Formative procedures include criterion- and curriculum-referenced tests (including tests constructed by teachers), checklists, anec-

dotal reports, examples of schoolwork, and records from trial teaching procedures. Formative procedures create an intimate record of progress. Summative procedures are typically norm-referenced tests. For example, a formative assessment might evaluate the students' knowledge of the *r*-controlled phonics rule using a list of *r*-controlled words in the assessment task, whereas a summative assessment might evaluate reading comprehension and, perhaps, reading fluency using a norm-referenced test.

Criterion- and curriculum-referenced tests can be used to collect summative data, but norm-referenced tests do not work well for formative data collection. Many norm-referenced tests are only available in one form and, therefore, cannot be given repeatedly to the same child because the child will learn the test and it will cease to be a reliable indicator of performance. A second limitation is the probability of a mismatch between the content of the test and the instruction the child has received, as is the case, for example, when the words on a norm-referenced test of word recognition are different from those words included in the lessons given to the child taking the test. Finally, norm-referenced test scores are, at best, gross indicators of progress. It is hard to recover from those scores detailed information about the knowledge a child has acquired since the last test was administered. Progress should be documented in smaller increments and in greater detail. Assessment of progress depends on both summative and formative procedures. The details of progress, however, are provided by formative procedures.

Information Needed for Assessment of Progress

This section discusses the specific information needed to assess students' progress. Some multisensory programs include information on how to make formative assessments of progress. For example, *Alphabetic Phonics* (Cox, 1992) uses curriculum-referenced tasks called Bench Mark Measures (Cox, 1986) and Progress Measurements (Rumsey, 1992), respectively, to assess progress in letter-knowledge acquisition and alphabetizing skills and to assess reading, spelling, and handwriting. Teachers who use the *Recipe for Reading* approach (Traub & Bloom, 1990) maintain an assessment folder for each student that includes a record of words the student has learned to read and spell. A list of books that the student has read is also included in the folder. Entries to the folder are dated and arranged chronologically to facilitate evaluation of progress. The *Wilson Reading System* (Wilson, 1996) and other multisensory structured language education programs include pre- and posttesting along with tests to evaluate **mastery** of knowledge taught in one curriculum unit before a student moves to the next curriculum unit. Assessment of progress in these programs does focus on students' mastery of word recognition and spelling skills.

To build on this tradition of assessing progress in multisensory programs, educators can identify the classes of data needed to assess progress and identify some methods of data collection. The following skills should be tracked: phoneme segmentation, letter identification, graphophonemic knowledge (letter–sound associations), word-recognition fluency, spelling, oral vocabulary, comprehension, and composition. Although it is useful to assess children's knowledge of letter–sound associations directly using checklists of phonics knowledge (e.g., Blachowicz, 1980), children's spellings also provide a window on their knowledge of letter–sound relationships. By examining children's spellings, teachers can gain insight into children's phonics knowledge (Treiman, 1998). Use of spelling to assess phonics knowledge requires a spelling curriculum that includes a systematic outline of English spelling, knowledge of the devel-

opmental sequence for acquiring English spellings, and a method for scoring spellings that evaluates spelling elements within words rather than simply marking words as correct or incorrect. Reading and spelling are usually taught as separate subjects; consequently, teachers might not think to use spelling to assess reading.

Although not intended for this purpose, the Spelling Performance Evaluation for Language and Literacy (SPELL) assessment tool, which includes a cross-platform CD-ROM and a manual (Masterson, Apel, & Wasowicz, 2003), is a criterion-referenced instrument that is organized to allow the simultaneous assessment of spelling and phonics knowledge. (For more information about spelling assessment, see Moats, 1995, and Mosely, 1997.) SPELL is composed of tests that assess knowledge of phonological awareness and alphabetic letter–sound relationships, letter patterns—vocabulary word parts, (prefixes, suffixes, base words), and mental images of words.

Informal reading inventories (see Leslie & Caldwell, 2001, and Woods & Moe, 2002) typically are used to obtain the data needed to plan remedial programs. The structure of these inventories could provide a model for teachers to use for ongoing assessment. Informal reading inventories are used to establish reading levels for individual students on the basis of accuracy in reading single words, words in text, and answering comprehension questions. These inventories include conventions for marking reading errors (insertions, hesitations, mispronunciations, omissions, regressions, substitutions, self-corrections, pauses, and repetitions) and, more important, provide classification systems for word-reading errors, which are commonly called miscues. Mispronounced words (words read incorrectly) are classified as graphically similar, semantically acceptable, or syntactically correct. This classification allows the teacher to make some inferences about the word-recognition strategies students are using. Given the view that word-recognition accuracy and fluency depend on the coordinated use of graphophonemic, semantic, and syntactic cues for word recognition (Ehri & McCormick, 1998), the analysis of miscues is important. Some informal reading inventories (e.g., Leslie & Caldwell, 2001) provide procedures for assessing reading rate for words and text and give standards for evaluating a student's fluency with word lists and text. In all informal reading inventories, comprehension is assessed by observing students thinking aloud as they read, retelling stories they have read, and answering questions about the text. Background knowledge is assessed by observing students making predictions about the text before they read based on the title and the first few sentences of the text. Vocabulary is assessed by observing students defining words encountered in the text.

Most inventories are organized to permit comparisons between a student's skills (i.e., fluency and comprehension) with narrative text and his or her skills with expository text. Comparisons can be made between a student's reading performance (i.e., accuracy and fluency) with word lists and his or her performance with text. Distinctions between reading and listening comprehension may also be drawn. Although the authors of informal reading inventories may not view the inventories from this perspective, these inventories are criterion-referenced tests. As indicated previously, data obtained from these inventories are used to construct remedial programs. The rules included in these inventories for marking reading errors, classifying miscues, and assessing reading rate can be used to create curriculum-referenced assessments based on the texts used for instruction. These structured observations of reading of texts that students use for reading instruction can also be used to assess comprehension, vocabulary, and use of background knowledge. It is easy to imagine an assessment folder that includes records of such observations made on a regular basis. These records would be

similar to the running assessment records recommended by Clay (1995). The text is from the students' reading lessons; the structure for assessing reading is borrowed from informal inventories.

WHEN READING DIFFICULTIES PERSIST

When a parent or teacher sees an intelligent child struggle to read and spell, three questions should come to mind: 1) Is this child's struggle with reading and spelling best described as dyslexia? 2) What remedial plan will facilitate learning to read and spell? and 3) Is the remedial plan effective? These questions are related to each other but have distinct answers. The first question seeks an explanation for the struggle with reading and spelling and requires information that compares the child's performance with the performance of other children of the same age. The second and third questions require detailed descriptions of the child's reading and spelling skills. The child's development is evaluated relative to knowledge attained and knowledge yet to be mastered. Direct comparisons with other children are less important. Assessment designed to answer the first two questions typically occurs during one, two, or three sessions. Assessment of the effectiveness of the remedial plan, or *assessment of progress,* is ongoing.

Which Skills Do We Assess?

When monitoring a student with persistent reading difficulties, it is essential to determine which skills to assess. Students' progress in mastering the skills with which they have difficulty should be documented. In other words, teachers should be particularly attentive to the effects of instruction on the persistent difficulties in reading and related skills. Assessment of progress, viewed from this perspective, emphasizes the following: phoneme segmentation, graphophonemic knowledge (letter–sound associations), word recognition, fluency and spelling, handwriting, comprehension, composition, oral language, and vocabulary. The assessment of such skills is consistent with the traditions of multisensory instruction, which emphasizes the acquisition of these skills. If teachers find evidence that students are not acquiring knowledge of the components of literacy, then they plan instruction accordingly. When reading difficulties persist in spite of informed instruction, a more comprehensive assessment is required and extends far beyond the information provided by tests. For example, this assessment may include input from a speech-language pathologist, diagnostician, and/or physician.

A physician can determine if there are vision or hearing difficulties that could interfere with reading development. The speech-language pathologist can assess speech production and oral language development. The diagnostician assesses key skills that might indicate an underlying cause of reading difficulties. (See Table 7.1 for a list of assessment measures.) These measures would include tests of phonological processing such as the Comprehensive Test of Phonological Processing (CTOPP; Wagner, Torgesen, & Rashotte, 1999), Lindamood Auditory Conceptualization Test–Third Edition (LAC-3; Lindamood & Lindamood, 2004), and or the Test of Phonological Awareness–Second Edition: PLUS (TOPA-2+; Torgesen & Bryant, 2004); and tests of single real word and pseudoword reading, such as the Test of Word Reading Efficiency (TOWRE; Torgesen, Wagner, & Rashotte, 1999), which can measure children as young as 6 years old, or the Letter-Word Identification subtest of the Woodcock-Johnson III Tests of Achievement (WJ-III; Woodcock, McGrew, & Mather, 2001). For oral reading, the Gray Oral Reading

Test (GORT-4; Wiederholt & Bryant, 2001) can be used. Measures of silent reading rate are also helpful, such as the Qualitative Reading Inventory–Third Edition (QRI3; Leslie & Caldwell, 2001) or the Nelson-Denny Reading Test (Brown, Bennett, & Hanna, 1985). The spelling subtest from the WJ-III or the Wechsler Individual Achievement Test-II (WIAT-II; Smith, 2001) may be used to examine spelling skills. Measures of fluency and listening comprehension are also needed. A writing sample will shed light on re-occurring errors in spelling and problems with sentence formation and organization of thoughts.

Are Persistent Reading Difficulties Dyslexia? Implications for Assessment from the Current Definition of Dyslexia

Let's revisit the International Dyslexia Association (IDA) definition of dyslexia that was discussed in Chapter 1 (Lyon, Shaywitz, & Shaywitz, 2003, p. 2).

> Dyslexia is a specific learning disability that is neurological in origin. It is characterized by difficulties with accurate and/or fluent word recognition and by poor spelling and de-coding abilities. These difficulties typically result from a deficit in the phonological component of language that is often unexpected in relation to other cognitive abilities and the provision of effective classroom instruction. Secondary consequences may include problems in reading comprehension and reduced reading experience that can impede growth of vocabulary and background knowledge.

There are significant implications for both assessment and intervention embedded in the new IDA definition of dyslexia. First, the description of dyslexia as neurobiological in origin, supported by what Lyon et al. proclaimed as "overwhelming and converging data from functional brain imaging investigations" (2003, p. 3), suggests that there is an observable difference in the way dyslexics' brains function. The differences have been observed in particular during phonological processing tasks including such activities as pseudoword rhyme detection. Shaywitz (2003) described how good readers show a consistent pattern of strong activation in the back of the brain with lesser activation in the front as they read. In contrast, the activation patterns of dyslexic children change with age. There is an underactivation of the neural pathways in the back of the brain that, when children are beginning to learn how to read, results in their having trouble analyzing words and transforming letters into sounds. As they get older, these children's reading remains slow and disfluent even if their accuracy improves. The frontal regions of the brain become overactive when adolescent dyslexics read. Shaywitz explained, "It is as if these struggling readers are using the systems in front of the brain to try to compensate for the disruption in the back of the brain" (p. 81). It is the pattern of underactivation in the back of the brain that provides the neural signature for the phonological difficulties apparent in dyslexics. This insight into the neurobiological source of dyslexia deepens our understanding of the challenges faced by dyslexic individuals. Today, however, few have the resources or the inclination to seek functional brain imaging as a practical tool to diagnose dyslexia. Fortunately, we do have other readily available instruments that can assess the specific manifestations of these neurobiological differences.

The inclusion of the characteristic of "accurate and/or fluent word recognition" in the definition of dyslexia suggests that fluency measures should be used in assessment. Oral reading rate measures for text of increasing length and complexity have long been included in tests such as the GORT-4 (Wiederholt & Bryant, 2001). Silent reading measures for reading rate are also available (e.g., QRI3, Leslie & Caldwell, 2001; Nelson-

Denny Reading Test, Brown et al., 1985). Newer tests, such as the TOWRE (Torgesen et al., 1999), can measure single real word and pseudoword reading fluency for children as young as 6 years of age.

Describing the reason for the difficulties in accuracy and fluency in word reading and spelling as "a deficit in the phonological component of language" certainly implies that tests measuring these phonological components should be included in any reading assessment. Tests such as the CTOPP (Wagner et al., 1999), the LAC-3 (Lindamood & Lindamood, 2004), and the TOPA-2+ (Torgesen & Bryant, 2004) evaluate these skills in kindergarten in children as young as 5 years of age.

The description of dyslexia as "often unexpected in relation to other cognitive abilities and the provision of effective classroom instruction" is significant for two reasons. First, it omits the requirement that basic decoding and word-recognition deficits must be significantly lower than IQ. As Shaywitz asserted, "There is an emerging consensus among researchers and clinicians that the dependence on a discrepancy between IQ and reading achievement for a diagnosis for dyslexia has outlived its usefulness" (2003, p. 137). Comparisons between reading and chronological age is only one suggested solution for preventing the delay in identification and subsequent intervention when relying on the IQ–achievement discrepancy formula (Shaywitz, 2003).

The second key point made in this portion of the dyslexia definition is that it stresses the importance of reviewing a student's instructional history before a diagnosis of dyslexia is made. The inclusion of information about a student's "lack of response to scientifically informed instruction is one factor that differentiates severe and intractable reading deficits from reading failure resulting from inadequate instruction" (Lyon et al., 2003, p. 9).

The final segment of the definition of dyslexia that connects to assessment issues is the description of "secondary consequences" of the disorder, i.e., "problems in reading comprehension and reduced reading experience that can impede growth of vocabulary and background knowledge" (Lyon et al., 2003, p. 2). As Lyon et al. noted, the addition of this sentence emphasizes how phonological deficits lead to other problems, including problems with accuracy and fluency, which can lead to still more problems in vocabulary and background knowledge. Professionals doing evaluations of poor readers need to know that they may have to look for phonological causal factors as the root of poor vocabulary and comprehension skills.

A Critical Assessment Principle

People who conduct educational assessments have at their disposal several procedures for collecting data. The overriding principle governing assessment is that the procedures that are selected from among these options depend on the assessment questions that have been chosen. The question "Is this child dyslexic?" obligates those conducting the assessment to look for word recognition, decoding, and spelling deficits. Such an assessment must also verify language competence alongside the reading deficits. If the child being assessed is 8 years old or younger, then the assessment must also verify the presence of a phonological processing deficit. These are all reasonably objective judgments. People making such an assessment would determine that a child has weak word-recognition skills by comparing his or her performance on a word-recognition test with the performance of other children of the same age, using norm-referenced tests. In contrast, when the assessment question is "What remedial plan will facilitate learning to read and spell?" criterion- and curriculum-referenced tests dominate the as-

sessment process. The people making the assessment can examine the knowledge and skill descriptions that these tests provide and determine goals for the remedial plan.

CONCLUSION

Assessment is defined as an information-gathering process that is guided by questions and that culminates in decisions that have an effect on an individual's life. We stand by that definition. Assessment of progress, however, is a special type of assessment and warrants a second definition. The English word *assess* derives from the Latin word *assidere* which means to *sit by one's side* (Wiggins, 1993). With this definition in mind, one can imagine a student and teacher sitting side by side and collecting evidence of learning to include in the student's assessment folder. First, critical questions must be investigated, including 1) Is this child's struggle with reading and spelling best described as dyslexia? 2) What remedial plan will facilitate learning to read and spell? and 3) Is the remedial plan effective? Once those questions have been answered, then one can imagine an assessment folder sitting beside the student so that it is easily accessible to anyone who is interested and has a right to gain access to the information. Assessment of progress is a learning experience for all involved. As a result of assessment of progress, a student's reading and spelling improves with the teacher's informed instruction and a greater understanding of the student's learning strengths and areas of need.

REFERENCES

Adams, M.J. (1990). *Beginning to read: Thinking and learning about print.* Cambridge, MA: MIT Press.

Blachowicz, C.L.Z. (1980). *Blachowicz Informal Phonics Survey.* Unpublished assessment device, National College of Education, Evanston, IL.

Brown, J.I., Bennett, J.M., & Hanna, G.S. (1985). *The Nelson-Denny Reading Test.* Chicago: Riverside.

Clay, M.M. (1995). *An observation survey of early literacy attainment* (Rev. ed.). Portsmouth, NH: Heinemann.

Cox, A.R. (1986). *Benchmark measures.* Cambridge, MA: Educators Publishing Service.

Cox, A.R. (1992). *Foundations for literacy: Structures and techniques for multisensory teaching of basic written English language skills.* Cambridge, MA: Educators Publishing Service.

Ehri, L.C., & McCormick, S. (1998). Phases of word learning: Implications for instruction with delayed and disabled readers. *Reading and Writing Quarterly, 14,* 135–163.

Good, R.H. & Kaminski, R.A. (Eds.). (2002). *Dynamic Indicators of Basic Literacy Skills* (6th ed.). Eugene, OR: Institute for Development of Educational Achievement.

Institute for the Development of Educational Achievement. (2002, May 15). *Final report: An analysis of reading assessment instruments.* Retrieved from http://idea.uoregon.edu/assessment/final_report.pdf

Invernizzi, M., Juel, C., Swank, L.,& Meier, C. (2003). *Phonological Awareness Literacy Screening:*
Kindergarten (PALS-K). Charlottesville: University of Virginia.

Invernizzi, M., Meier, J., & Juel, C. (2002). *Phonological Awareness Literacy Screening 1–3* (PALS 1–3). Charlottesville,: University of Virginia.

Invernizzi, M., Sullivan, A., & Meier, J. (2001). *Phonological Awareness Literacy Screening: Prekindergarten* (PALS-PreK). Charlottesville: University of Virginia.

Leslie, L., & Caldwell, J. (2001). *Qualitative reading inventory* (3rd ed.). Boston: Allyn & Bacon/Longman.

Lindamood, P.C., & Lindamood, P. (2004). *Lindamood Auditory Conceptualization Test–Third Edition* (LAC-3). Austin, TX: PRO-ED.

Lyon, G.R., & Chhabra, V. (2004). The science of reading research. *Educational Leadership, 61*(6), 12–17. Also available on-line: http://www.ascd.org/publications/ed_lead/200403/lyon.html

Lyon, G.R., Shaywitz, S.E., & Shaywitz, B.A. (2003). A definition of dyslexia. *Annals of Dyslexia, 53,* 1–14.

Masterson, J.J., Apel, K., & Wasowicz, J. (2003). *Spelling Performance Evaluation for Language and Literacy (SPELL)* [CD-ROM and manual]. Longmont, CO: Sopris West.

Moats, L.C. (1995). *Spelling: Development, disability, and instruction.* Timonium, MD: York Press.

Mosely, D.V. (1997). Assessment of spelling and related aspects of written expression. In J.R. Beech & C. Singleton (Eds.), *The psychological*

assessment of reading (pp. 204–223). London: Routledge.

No Child Left Behind Act of 2001, PL 107-110, 115 Stat. 1425, 20 U.S.C. §§ 6301 *et seq.*

Rumsey, M.B. (1992). *Dyslexia Training Program Progress Measurements* (Schedules I–III). Cambridge, MA: Educators Publishing Service.

Scarborough, H.S. (1998). Early identification of children at risk for reading disabilities: Phonological awareness and some other promising predictors. In B.K. Shapiro, P.J. Accardo, & A.J. Capute (Eds.), *Specific reading disability: A view of the spectrum* (pp. 75–120). Timonium, MD: York Press.

Shaywitz, S. (2003). *Overcoming dyslexia: A new and complete science-based program for reading problems at any level.* New York: Alfred A. Knopf.

Smith, D.R. (2001). *Wechsler Individual Achievement Test-II* (WIAT-II). San Antonio, TX: Harcourt Assessment.

Torgesen, J.K. (1998, Spring/Summer). Catch them before they fall: Identification and assessment to prevent reading failure in young children. *American Educator,* 1–8.

Torgesen, J.K. (2002). The prevention of reading difficulties. *Journal of School Psychology, 40*(1), 7–26.

Torgesen, J.K., & Burgess, S.R. (1998). Consistency of reading-related phonological processes throughout early childhood: Evidence from longitudinal-correlational and instructional studies. In J. Metsala & L. Ehri (Eds.), *Word recognition in beginning literacy* (pp. 161–188). Mahwah, NJ: Lawrence Erlbaum Associates.

Torgesen, J.K., & Bryant, B. (2004). *Test of Phonological Awareness–Second Edition: PLUS* (TOPA-2+). East Moline, IL: LinguiSystems.

Torgesen, J., Wagner, R., & Rashotte, C. (1999). *Test of Word Reading Efficiency* (TOWRE). Austin, TX: PRO-ED.

Traub, N., & Bloom, F. (1990). *Recipe for reading: New century edition.* Cambridge, MA: Educators Publishing Service.

Treiman, R. (1998). Why spelling? The benefits of incorporating spelling into beginning reading instruction. In J.L. Metsala & L.C. Ehri (Eds.), *Word recognition in beginning literacy* (pp. 289–313). Mahwah, NJ: Lawrence Erlbaum Associates.

University of Texas Health Science Center at Houston, Center for Academic and Reading Skills, & University of Houston (UTH/UH). (2002). *Texas Primary Reading Inventory (TPRI).* Austin: Texas Reading Instruments.

U.S. Department of Education, National Center for Education Statistics. (2004, March 8). *Percentage of students, by reading achievement level, grade 4: 1992–2003.* Retrieved from http://nces.ed.gov/nationsreportcard/reading/results2003/natachieve-g4.asp

Wagner, R.K., Torgesen, J.K., & Rashotte, C.A. (1999). *Comprehensive Test of Phonological Processing (CTOPP).* Austin, TX: PRO-ED.

Wiederholt, J.L., & Bryant, B.R. (2001). *Gray Oral Reading Test–Fourth Edition* (GORT-4). Austin, TX: PRO-ED.

Wiggins, G. (1993). *Assessing student performance: Exploring the purpose and limits of testing.* San Francisco: Jossey-Bass.

Wilson, B. (1996). *Wilson Reading System instructor manual* (3rd ed.). Millbury, MA: Wilson Language Training.

Woodcock, R.W., McGrew, K.S., & Mather, N. (2001). *Woodcock-Johnson III Tests of Achievement.*

Woods, M.L., & Moe, A. (2002). *Analytic reading inventory* (7th ed.). Upper Saddle River, NJ: Prentice-Hall.

8

Planning Multisensory Structured Language Lessons and the Classroom Environment

Judith R. Birsh and Jean-Fryer Schedler

L esson planning, designed for intervention and remediation, is at the heart of multisensory structured language education (MSLE). However, lesson plans cannot stand alone; the classroom environment is also important to consider. When a positive classroom environment is in place for effective teaching and learning for students struggling with academic subjects, explicit lesson planning assumes its powerful place. To meet these dual criteria, this chapter is divided into four main sections that discuss aspects of the classroom environment and lesson planning for MSLE that will help teachers implement scientifically based literacy instruction. The first part of the chapter considers the classroom environment, that is, the physical space for both the students and the teacher. The second part, on teacher organization, enumerates ways to organize and maintain materials for instruction and recordkeeping to maximize the time spent engaged in productive activity and minimize the time lost during transitions or disruptions. The third section focuses on student behavior, with a strong emphasis on how teachers can build a positive learning environment. The final section, on planning multisensory structured language lessons, describes in detail the steps in planning MSLE lessons for both small and large groups. Daily and weekly plans for MSLE lessons from beginning to advanced levels are discussed. Students benefit when the environment is conducive to learning and when teachers are well prepared to implement MSLE instructional goals.

The authors would like to acknowledge the assistance of Valerie G. Tucker, Director of LEAD/Literacy Education & Academic Development, Inc., Argyle, Texas, in planning and offering ideas for this new chapter. Her insights and understanding of MSLE lesson planning are reflected throughout.

CLASSROOM ENVIRONMENT

Effective teachers manage their classrooms;
ineffective teachers discipline their classrooms.
—Wong and Wong (1998, p. 83)

When considering the classroom environment, the first question teachers need to ask is, "Am I spending most of my time disciplining my students?" If your answer is yes, then this chapter is for you. It is designed to change your approach from one of responding to students' actions to an approach of reinforcing students' positive performance. In order to be effective and successful, you will need to step back and take a broad survey of the entire environment in which you and your students are interacting. It is important to structure every component of the learning environment for success.

The classroom is defined here as the space that you have been assigned to instruct your students. This space might be a room with four walls and a door, a space marked off by bookcases, an alcove in a hallway, or a space no bigger than a broom closet. However big or small or permanent or temporary the space may be, it is the space in which you are assigned to teach. The organization of that space must be carefully thought out and arranged. There is no *one* right plan or organization to any given space. Rather, the space must work for you as the teacher and for the specific students assigned to that space. Often, this means doing the best you can with few resources in terms of physical space, desks, and chalkboards.

The first space to plan is the main teaching space. Begin by standing in the space and mentally listing what you have for classroom furniture (e.g., desks, file cabinets, tables, chalkboards, bulletin boards, shelves, cubbies). Ask yourself these questions:

- Where will you stand (or sit, if it is a small-group tutorial setting) during the major portion of classroom instruction?

- Where are the chalkboards or magnetic whiteboards located in relation to the instructional position? Sometimes boards can be moved or added if need be.

- Where will the other teaching equipment (e.g., easels, overhead projectors) that are used during daily instruction be placed?

- How best can the student desks be arranged so that all students can see you during instruction? What works best for you and your students—desks in rows, desks touching, or desks in a four-square pattern?

- Are the desks the correct size for your students? Students should be able to sit comfortably with feet flat on the floor and knees not hitting the bottom of the desk. Take the time at the beginning of the year to adjust the desks to fit the size of each student. It may be necessary for you to trade desks with other teachers or to add wooden boxes to the bases of desks for your shorter students.

- Where will students keep their books and supplies? What works best for you and your students should be the deciding factor. Do you want them to keep their materials in their desks? If lockers are available, what will be kept in them and what will be kept in students' desks? Even if there is space in the desks for supplies, you may still want to have students keep supplies and books in an assigned tote located elsewhere in the classroom. This will enable students to have only the needed materi-

als at their desks during instruction. It may take several attempts to get the board(s), easels, overhead projector, and student desks to fit and work in the teaching space.

The next decision is where to locate the teacher's desk(s). Decide where to place and how to situate the teacher desk(s), filing cabinets, and bookcases that are to be used exclusively by you and/or classroom assistants. It is often a good idea to locate the teacher desk(s) and confidential materials away from the student traffic pattern. If you plan to have students sit with you at your desk for individualized instruction, you will need to plan how that area will work as well. Planning the teacher's space may require slight changes to the instructional space. Organization of the teacher's space is discussed more in the following section.

The third important space to plan is the small-group instructional area or study center. This could be a reading corner and/or a learning center based on a topic of study. Once the areas of use for a classroom have been identified and the furniture dragged to their respective places, you will need to check the traffic pattern that results from the current placement of furniture.

- Are the students able to enter and exit the classroom without bumping into desks, bookcases, and tables stacked with papers?

- Is the teacher's desk still situated so as to be undisturbed by students?

- Is there still a place to easily store and access confidential information, such as tests and progress reports, away from students?

- Where will papers be placed that are to be handed in for grading?

- Where will sets of workbooks, teacher's manuals, card decks, reading lists, dictation materials, and alphabet letters and other manipulatives be stored?

- Where are the pencil sharpener, other classroom supplies, and trash can located?

- Is there a space or desk set off as a quiet corner if needed?

- How will the bulletin boards and countertops (if any) be used?

Every need and movement of students from the time they enter until they exit the classroom must be arranged for what will be most efficient given the classroom size and furniture. The classroom set-up may not be perfect; however, it needs to be well thought through for what works best for your teaching style, the students assigned to your class, and the furniture and space available. After your classroom has been set up, take a critical look around the room with an eye toward limiting classroom distractions.

Finding what works best for you may take several attempts, extending over several years. But you will be fine tuning the physical surroundings of the instructional environment with a heightened awareness of your needs as the teacher and your students' needs for logical, systematic order in the classroom's physical environment.

TEACHER ORGANIZATION

Teacher organization encompasses the organization of 1) the space used exclusively by the teacher, 2) teaching materials, and 3) teacher transitions. There has been research consensus that the proportion of time in which students are actively and productively engaged in learning best predicts academic achievement and the overall quality of the

classroom (Mather & Goldstein, 2001). For a teacher to be successful in keeping students actively and productively engaged in learning, the teacher must be efficient in having available the materials necessary for a lesson.

The organization of a teacher's personal space is often overlooked yet is so critical for effective, efficient instruction. Begin by thinking of all of the requests made of you as a teacher. Requests come from students, administrators, colleagues, student teachers, and parents. There is the need to communicate with school personnel and supervisors requiring documentation. Students request materials such as paper, tape, scissors, passes, and forms. If these items are going to be stored on your desk, consider how to make them readily accessible without students accidentally having access to confidential materials. Next, take time to set up folders or files for confidential student information, information for parents, routine memos from the administration, and committee information. This organization is done prior to the arrival of students. The organization of your desk, drawer space, desktop supplies, as well as the set-up of any filing cabinets, bookcase, and storage closets need to be well thought out for accessibility and keeping daily clutter to a minimum. Make your personal space efficient so that you do not dread sitting down to a disheveled desk at the end of a productive day. By having everything organized, the items are readily accessible and do not become distractions or disruptions to the implementation of the lesson.

At the start of a school year, teaching materials are usually neatly stacked and ready for use. As the school year progresses, however, the stacks become untidy, materials get lost or damaged, and needed supplies get depleted. At the beginning of the year, set up labeled shelves or containers to accommodate materials that are critical to the success of your lessons. Each group or individual student should have the core daily lesson materials in a clearly marked bin. The bin could contain card decks for review and teaching new concepts, current reading lists, workbooks, manipulatives, extra pencils, and index cards. Nearby should be student notebooks used in the lesson. For older students, it is helpful to number handheld spell checkers and assign each student a specific spell checker. Provide a labeled storage box that can hold the entire set of spellcheckers at the end of the lesson. Store the spellcheckers in the same place on the shelf for the entire year. This thoughtful attention to detail will enable the lessons to move efficiently and smoothly.

Teachers, as well as their students, have transitions in their academic day. Teachers may make transitions from subject to subject or from instructional group to instructional group, including from one discrete instructional component to the next within a lesson. Teachers are usually thoughtful about making sure they have all the necessary materials needed for implementing a lesson. Time also needs to be spent planning what to do with teacher and student materials at the end of a specific lesson or component so that the next subject or instructional group can be initiated efficiently. Furthermore, keeping track of teaching and student materials during each component of the lesson leads to better planning and scaffolding of instruction for the next day. For example, enclosed plastic folders with multiple sections are ideal for students for holding letter tiles, writing boards, and student composition books.

An effective teacher organizes and maintains the classroom learning environment to maximize the time spent engaged in productive activity and minimizes the time lost during transitions or disruptions due to disciplinary action (Mather & Goldstein, 2001). Taking the time to get one's personal space organized; setting up a system for storage of instructional materials; and being able to efficiently access teaching materials before, during, and after instruction contributes to a productive classroom environment.

STUDENT BEHAVIOR

So far this chapter has considered structuring the physical space and organizing one-self for success, all prior to students' arrival in the classroom or tutorial space. The effect of the classroom environment on student behavior begins the second the students step through the doorway into the room. First of all, some students actively seek and draw attention to themselves more than others. Teachers should structure the environment so that attention directed to students is positive, while keeping negative attention to the absolute minimum. Often teachers are so focused on the curriculum to be taught that not enough time is allocated to developing positive student behavior.

One way to visualize the importance of positive student interactions is to think of each student as an individual drinking glass. The size of this glass varies according to the amount of attention that each student requires. A student will strive to keep his or her glass full of attention. It often does not matter to some students whether the attention is positive or negative, rather that attention is given. Your objective is to keep each glass filled to the brim with positive attention. False praise does not work. If students know the expectations for a classroom in terms of behavior, participation, or routine, there will be a lot of naturally occurring opportunities for giving praise. Use these opportunities to compliment students who require a lot of attention. It will take concerted and conscientious efforts on your part not to criticize an attention-seeking student for what he or she is doing wrong. Rather, you should keep an eagle eye out for ways to sincerely and appropriately compliment such a student for specific actions that merit praise. Beware of false praise, however, which is often more general and less tangible. For example, praising a student for better behavior after she or he has repeatedly been disruptive is false praise. A sincere praise is to compliment the student for the specific appropriate behavior of entering the classroom quietly. The goal is to drain the negative attention from the glass and fill the glass to the brim with positive attention.

The way to build a positive environment begins with thinking through expected student behavior and classroom procedures from the moment students enter the classroom. These expectations need to be explained to the students, clearly understood by the students, and reinforced by you in a positive manner. The next key piece is to maintain consistent rules and expectations from one day to the next. It is important to take the time (even if it reduces the amount of instruction) to reinforce the established rules and expectations. It is better to do this at the beginning of the year than to have the students repeatedly disrupt instruction throughout the rest of the year. When reinforcing classroom expectations, explain these in a patient, nonjudgmental tone. Use a tone that firmly repeats what the students may already know but have yet to internalize. Once classroom rules and expectations have been established, the key is to be consistent and *follow through* on those rules and expectations. Students are better able to be successful in environments in which they know what to expect. They need to be held accountable for classroom rules and expectations on the days when everything is going well, as well as on the days when nothing is going right.

For example, one middle school special education teacher successfully used one and only one rule in her classroom: "You are responsible" (E.-F. Bitler, personal communication, 2004). Her focus was to keep the rule simple and applicable to the real world. Whatever the difficulty (lost homework, broken pencil, inappropriate behavior) the student is held responsible for the action as well as determining an appropriate solution. Teachers may need to model how one determines or problem-solves an appropriate solution.

Along with using clear classroom expectations, there are many ways for teachers to reduce student anxiety starting in the first days of school. Wong and Wong (1998) identified questions students have as they begin the school year:

- *Am I in the right room?* Have your room number clearly visible.

- *Where am I supposed to sit?* Assign seats or have a sign indicating that students may select their own seats.

- *What are the rules in this classroom?* Have rules clearly visible, and take time to discuss the rules and reasons and to follow through on them.

- *What will I be doing this year?* Make available a syllabus or lesson plan chart.

- *How will I be graded?* Furnish a record keeper for grades.

- *Who is the teacher as a person?* Introduce yourself and tell something about your experience, hobbies, and interests.

- *Will the teacher treat me as a human being?* Your actions will speak louder than your words.

In the face of such uncertainties, teachers need to ensure that the classroom is a safe environment for students to be able to take academic risks, explore friendships, learn to negotiate a classroom setting, and learn appropriate expectations and behaviors that are transferable to the outside world. Students must know that the classroom is where unexpected negative things are not going to happen. It is okay to be incorrect; it is not okay to not try. There will be time and opportunity to develop social skills. Students will learn how to be students. They will be explicitly guided toward learning appropriate expectations and behaviors. A well-managed classroom is task-oriented and predictable. This kind of environment has

- A high level of student involvement with work

- Clear student expectations

- Relatively little wasted time, confusion, or disruption

- A relaxed and pleasant climate

Building the Student–Teacher Connection

It is important to bond and connect with all students, but especially with students who have experienced limited academic success. A key behavior is to establish eye contact during teaching and while conversing with a student. When you first meet, shake hands and look the student in the eye. It may feel corny, but this is a powerful first tool for establishing a unique, caring connection. Using students' names is critical especially when working with adolescents. Eye contact and addressing a student by name are powerful constructive tools in providing positive attention.

Once students begin to feel that you are an approachable teacher, it is critical that you practice active listening. Active listening involves maintaining attention to the students by simultaneously looking at the students while they are talking and keeping focused on what is being said. It is important not to interrupt the student. Acknowledge that you have listened by neutrally responding to what the student has said even

though you might disagree with what he or she has said. This will often require momentarily setting aside the agenda you have for a student so that you can hear and understand what information or request the student wishes to convey.

Another important way to gain students' confidence is to assure them that you will not ask them to do what you know they have not learned yet and what you have not already taught them. This helps to eliminate guessing and encourages them instead to practice the strategies you are instructing them to use to master the intricacies of the language. Being successful on a daily basis builds trust and confidence so much that students are quick to recognize your inadvertent use of something in a lesson they have not yet learned.

Another key strategy to improve student–teacher interactions is to use less teacher talk. By using active listening and structuring lessons to engage learners by using Socratic questioning, a skillful teacher is able to use what students already know to further their understanding and to help them integrate their knowledge of the components of reading. Concentrating on asking content- or process-related questions of students and then engaging in dialogue with students creates respect for what they are learning and helps them verbalize their understandings (Swanson, 1999). Very often it is possible to use only quick prompts such as verbal cues, gestures, and visual reminders to keep students on track.

There are many ways to build relationships with students, including those just described. Effective teachers know that it is important to acknowledge each student, to engage in meaningful feedback dialogues during teachable moments, and to recognize individual student successes. Other ways to engage students positively are to establish classroom traditions to celebrate successes and possibly even to disclose something meaningful about yourself. During student–teacher interactions, it is important to genuinely convey an attitude of respect, to make oneself available for individual questions, and to care enough to make a difference by doing what is needed to assist the student.

The appendix at the end of this chapter provides the Building Block Checklist for Effective Classroom Management (Schedler & Bitler, 2004). Teachers can use this checklist to review what they are already doing and to evaluate what further actions need to be taken to build a good classroom environment.

PLANNING MULTISENSORY STRUCTURED LANGUAGE LESSONS

Other chapters in this book describe the individual components of MSLE, such as phonological awareness (Chapter 4), alphabet and letter knowledge (Chapter 5), reading (Chapter 9), spelling (Chapter 10), vocabulary (Chapter 13), comprehension (Chapter 14), handwriting (Chapter 15), and composition (Chapter 16). Structured lesson planning supports and integrates these components, giving the teacher the framework to deliver the systematic sequence of the individualized curriculum the students need to master. Lesson planning brings together "the content to be taught, the most effective way to teach it . . . and the principles of learning and instruction" (Spalding, 2003, p. 193).

This section first discusses the history of lesson planning for MSLE and how it evolved from the original Orton-Gillingham approach (Gillingham & Stillman, 1956, 1997). Next, this section highlights the common features of various MSLE curricula. Then there is a discussion of the rationale for structured lesson planning, which derives from the experience of clinicians and program developers, and the growing research that supports these principles of instruction for students at risk for difficulty in learn-

ing to read. The following section enumerates the benefits of planning MSLE lessons for teachers and students. Lastly, implementing lesson planning through a variety of planning strategies and formats for the MSLE lesson is discussed. Through the sample lessons, teachers have the opportunity to examine varied levels of lesson planning for MSLE. Beginning teachers may find the sample lesson plans particularly useful.

The Orton-Gillingham Approach: History and Evolution

The Orton-Gillingham approach to remedial instruction began in the 1930s when Anna Gillingham and Bessie Stillman collaborated to develop remedial techniques based on Dr. Samuel T. Orton's neurological explanation for language learning disabilities. Dr. Orton's approach was derived from his neuropsychiatric background and his case studies of children whose individual learning differences and instructional needs did not match the sight word method reading curriculum then being used in the traditional classroom (Henry & Brickley, 1999).

In 1932, Dr. Orton appointed Anna Gillingham, an experienced psychologist at the Ethical Culture School in New York, as a research fellow in language disabilities at The Language Research Project of the New York Neurological Institute. Gillingham had recognized and worked with bright children with academic problems for many years. She and Bessie Stillman, a gifted teacher, researched ways to organize remedial techniques to meet the unique needs of these students who were struggling to read and spell. The understanding that "such children present a challenge which customary teacher-training does not enable the teacher to meet" (Gillingham & Stillman, 1956, p. 1) fueled their efforts. What emerged from their meticulous work with students and teachers was a system of teaching language-related skills incorporating letter sounds, syllables, words, sentences, and writing, contained within a daily lesson plan in which all aspects of the alphabetic phonetic approach to reading and spelling were detailed. The instruction was to be explicit, systematic, cumulative, direct, and sequential. In contrast to the sight word method, their technique was based on the close association of visual, auditory, and kinesthetic elements to teach the phonetic units step by step. Their basic multisensory teaching techniques to remediate reading problems, with many adaptations, are still used today (Gillingham & Stillman, 1997). What evolved over time is the essence of the MSLE lesson, which is now consistent with the effort to implement evidence-based instructional approaches to assist struggling readers.

Essence of an MSLE Lesson

The plan for an MSLE lesson includes a specific order of activities taught for a prearranged period of time so that all components of the structure of language are included each time the teacher meets with students. Conscious multisensory procedures using the student's eyes, ears, hands, and mouth help to link the sound, sight, and feel of the spoken language to the printed language on the page.

All MSLE programs rely on these important instructional design principles for diverse learners. Some examples of programs developed from the original Orton-Gillingham multisensory approach are: *Slingerland, Spalding, Alphabetic Phonics, Multisensory Teaching Approach, Sonday System, Wilson, LANGUAGE!* and *Project Read* (see the sections for Chapters 9 and 10 in Appendix B for information on how to obtain these curricula).

Discrete Components of Language

To build the associations necessary for successful reading, spelling, and writing, daily MSLE lessons typically include the following discrete components of language, which are modified for each student or group and for different levels of instruction. Not all components appear every day. They are rotated through the weekly lesson plans to help students establish mastery across the linguistic concepts. The list that follows is an amalgam of language lesson components derived from accredited teacher education programs. (See the section for Chapter 2 in Appendix B for accredited MSLE programs.)

- Alphabet sequence and letter naming

- Phonemic awareness activities

- Review of sound–symbol associations, learned in previous lessons using letter decks, and review of letter clusters, using cards and key words to aid memory

- Spelling these same sounds to integrate reading and spelling

- Introduction of new sounds and language concepts and/or review of previously introduced concepts

- Reading phonetically regular words in lists and sentences with letter patterns already taught and developing automatic recognition of high-frequency sight words to build automaticity.

- Vocabulary study

- Reading connected controlled and/or decodable text to develop fluency

- Spelling and writing words and sentences from dictation using words from reading practice

- Handwriting practice, with explicit instructions in letter formation

- Comprehension and listening strategies for use with connected text

- Oral language practice and written composition

It is necessary for these discrete components of language to be incorporated into lesson planning. During 10 years of research on 1,000 students with dyslexia, the Texas Scottish Rite Hospital in Dallas developed a way to integrate these elements in a lesson plan to facilitate learning. From the research, certain elements were shown to be essential to the successful teaching of the students (Cox, 1984). One element is a daily lesson plan that follows a set format. Cox suggested four types of structure that are essential in the remediation of language-related skills (1984, p. 35):

1. Ordered daily presentation of activities and materials
2. Precise steps in procedures
3. Rapid rotation of activities
4. Periodic measurement of progress.

The lesson activities are short and focused, with small steps taken in sequence, at first easy and then more difficult. The principles of instruction include multisensory presentation of each component of the lesson, using visual, auditory, and tactile/kinesthetic cues. The simultaneous presentation through these modalities, within the daily structure of the lesson plan ensures learning.

1. review
2. intro new material
3. scaffolded prac ε.in controlled environment

Structured lessons allow a systematic presentation of concepts, based on the order established by Gillingham and Stillman. Three major components are always present: review of what has been learned, introduction of new material, and scaffolded practice in a controlled environment.

Common Features Among Multisensory Structured Language Education Curricula

With the success of the original Orton-Gillingham approach, many teachers began to individualize their implementation of Orton-Gillingham programs to meet the needs of their school settings. The goal, to serve as many children as possible in many geographic locations, needed to be approached in a manner which was both acceptable and affordable to schools across the nation. Programs that are similar in structure and philosophy have been developing since the 1970s. They adhere to the principles learned from research studies and clinical experiences documented by Dr. Samuel T. Orton (1937), Anna Gillingham (Gillingham & Stillman, 1956), and many allied professionals from the fields of education, psychology, neuroscience, medicine, and speech-language pathology.

All of the programs accredited by the Alliance for Accreditation and Certification of Structured Language Education share the philosophy that effective MSLE includes instruction that is explicit, systematic, cumulative, direct, and sequential (Tucker, 2003). (See the section for Chapter 2 in Appendix B for more information on The Alliance.) Some MSLE programs are derived from the original Orton-Gillingham approach and bear the name of their authors, such as Slingerland, Sonday, Spalding, and Wilson. Many emphasize different content areas of the MSLE curriculum, depending upon the needs of the students they are designed to serve. This is reflected in the lesson plans of each program, which are variations on the same theme. Furthermore, all programs based on the Orton-Gillingham approach present the building blocks of written language in a comprehensive sequence that addresses phonemic awareness, sound–symbol relationships, phonics, syllable types, structural analysis, spelling, fluency, vocabulary, comprehension, composition, and handwriting.

Rationale and Research Support for Lesson Planning

The rationale for the MSLE lesson plan is based mainly on clinical experience. Since the 1980s, however, research in reading development and reading disabilities has influenced the creation and organization of the content of sequential language programs and materials needed for the variety of activities incorporated in MSLE lessons. For example, many programs include specific activities for developing phonemic awareness and building on the critical aspects of fluency needed for word identification and text reading.

Research in general education has shown that effective teachers are those who specify their objectives in detailed lesson plans. In working with students with learning difficulties, it is crucial that students have interventions that are carefully constructed based on known components that influence remediation outcomes. Structured lesson planning is the opposite of incidental learning. It plans for deliberate, conscious attention to all components of language, from phonemes to written text (Tucker, 2003). (See Chapter 2 for a discussion of MSLE and research on instructional practices.)

Swanson (1999) concluded in an extension of an earlier meta-analysis (Swanson & Hoskyn, 1998) that the most effective treatment outcomes for students with learning

Table 8.1. Effective instructional components for students with learning disabilities

---

Sequencing

Breaking down the task, fading of prompts or cues, sequencing short activities, and step-by-step prompts

Drill (repetition) and practice (review)

Daily testing of skills (e.g., statements in the lesson plan relating to master criteria, distributed review and practice, redundant materials or texts, repeated practice, sequenced review, daily feedback, and/or weekly review)

Segmentation

Breaking down the targeted skill into smaller, step-by-step sequences and then synthesizing the parts into a whole

Directed questioning and responses

The teacher verbally asking process- and/or content-related questions of students and engaging in dialogue with students

Controlled difficulty of processing demands of a task

Tasks sequenced from easy to difficult, with only necessary hints and probes provided; short activities with the level of difficulty controlled (the teacher provides the necessary assistance and a simplified model; teacher and students discuss task analysis)

Technology

Use of a computer, structured text, flowcharts, a structured curriculum, pictorial representations, specific or structured material, and/or media to facilitate presentation and feedback

Group instruction

Instruction that occurs in a small group, with students and/or the teacher interacting within the group

Supplement to teacher and peer involvement

Homework, parent involvement, or others supplements to assist instruction

Strategy cues

Reminders to use strategies or multiple steps (the teacher verbalizes problem solving with think-aloud models and presents benefits of using strategies or procedures)

From Swanson, H.L. (1999). Instructional components that predict treatment outcomes for students with learning disabilities: Support for a combined strategy and direct instruction model. *Learning Disabilities Research and Practice, 14*(3), 137; adapted by permission.

disabilities (including dyslexia) resulted from using nine key instructional components. These instructional components are summarized in Table 8.1. Structured lesson planning supports and deliberately integrates these components, thus giving the teacher a scaffold on which to build the sequence of the individualized curriculum for the students to master. Teachers and students both benefit from the explicit systematic approach, but for different reasons, which are discussed in the following sections.

Benefits of Lesson Planning: The Teacher's Point of View

All Components of Language

Structured lesson planning ensures that teachers include

All levels of language in the same instructional session: the sub word level (phonological awareness, letter formation and orthographic awareness); the word level (multiple strategies for connecting spoken and written words while spelling); and [the] text level (constructing sentences and discourse). (Berninger, 1999, p. 20)

An instructional model that contains these elements formed the basis of a classroom prevention study and a remediation study. In a 2-year prevention study of developing phonological awareness and word-recognition skills with low income inner-city kindergarten children, Blachman, Tangel, Ball, Black, and McGraw (1999) used a daily, five-step, 30-minute lesson using all components of language for explicit systematic instruction in the alphabetic code. The participating children showed a significant advantage in reading at the end of Grades 1 and 2. In the prevention study, the five-step core to develop accurate and fluent word recognition included group instruction in sound–symbol associations both previously learned and new; phoneme analysis and blending while manipulating letters to help synthesize sounds; practice in reading phonetically regular words and high-frequency words, as well as irregular words, to develop fluency; reading connected text both controlled and uncontrolled; and a short dictation activity. In the remediation study with children already experiencing reading difficulties in second and third grades, the same core was taught one to one, augmented by an emphasis on complex word structure, such as multisyllabic words in a wide array of reading materials with, again, a strong emphasis on fluency and daily spelling dictation (Blachman, Schatschneider, Fletcher, & Clonan, 2003). After a year of tutoring, the children in the remediation program showed significant differences in their word reading, spelling, paragraph reading, and reading rate on standardized measures. Furthermore, 1 year later, the children in the treatment group maintained their gains without the program as a result of the intensive, explicit instruction. The content of the lessons and the principles of instruction in the prevention and remediation studies were based on effective models used by other researchers (e.g., Foorman, Francis, Fletcher, Schatschneider, & Mehta, 1998, and Torgesen et al., 1999) and are practices supported by Snow, Burns, and Griffin (1998) and the National Reading Panel (National Institute of Child Health and Human Development, 2000).

A typical MSLE lesson starts out with a review of sounds and letters previously taught. Phonemic awareness activities at appropriate levels are incorporated. There is systematic review of words for oral reading, then these words are incorporated into separately read sentences and short paragraphs of connected text, based on what has been taught. Students then spell words from dictation that reflect the same letter patterns. New concepts are carefully introduced and linked to students' prior knowledge. Everything is taught cumulatively to build the concepts for reading and spelling one step at a time. Handwriting is integrated deliberately to help reinforce the memory for letter sounds and forms and to stress automaticity and legibility of writing. At the connected text level, teachers plan oral reading of narrative and expository texts using appropriate materials. Specific sections of the lesson have activities for comprehension strategies and composition, including direct instruction of vocabulary development. In this repetitive teaching format, fidelity of implementation is more likely to occur. In sum, a lesson plan for MSLE ensures a comprehensive presentation in which all components of language are practiced and reviewed systematically in the tightly focused, intensive lessons.

Opportunity for Multisensory Learning

Inherent in the planning of an MSLE lesson is the opportunity to incorporate many instances of multisensory instruction. (See Chapter 2 for a detailed analysis.) During the review sections, teachers use simultaneous visual, auditory, and kinesthetic/tactile activities to reinforce the concepts. This ensures that all pathways to learning are engaged

every lesson. For example, cards with individual letters and letter clusters printed on them are displayed to the students, who say and hear the letter names and sounds. The teacher dictates sounds, and the students say and write the letters, often naming a key word as well. Students trace and copy new letters that they are learning, using a variety of materials and surfaces, including writing in the air. During practice activities, students segment spoken words into phonemes for spelling and tap out syllables or divide written words into syllables with markers to aid reading. Students often use special **diacritical markings** for vowels, consonants, prefixes, and suffixes to highlight their importance. Because of the variety of modalities and media and the consistency of the approach, teachers experience enthusiastic interaction with their students. Lesson plans for MSLE help teachers establish a positive rapport with their students.

Diagnostic and Prescriptive Instruction

How do you know when to reteach a rule or model an application of a strategy? MSLE lessons are meant to be flexible and diagnostically attuned to students' needs and learning rate on a daily basis. The **diagnostic** part of the lessons occurs while the students are engaged in the discrete components of the lesson. The teacher is constantly observing and noting how students are handling the lesson components. When students are having difficulties, teachers can ask themselves if they have taught the **subskills** necessary for students to do the activity, if it is necessary to reintroduce the concept, or if the strategy for comprehending text is clear to the student. The **prescriptive** part of the lessons entails the changes the teacher makes to tailor the lessons for more practice, review, and/or multisensory activities. Lesson planning gives the teacher a concrete way to analyze where the students' learning gaps are and what needs to be included in instruction. The lesson plan is sensitive to the age of students, their level of skills, and the time and space allotted for instruction. When planning lessons for each student or group of students, the teacher keeps long-term goals in mind with regard to the scope and sequence of the curriculum. This roadmap for instruction tells the teacher where he or she is going with the students, but the teacher must decide how to get there and how fast to go (Tucker, 2003).

Two important sources of data influence the planning involved: data from informal curriculum-based probes given frequently to monitor progress and data from formal testing. (See Chapter 7 for more about informal and formal assessment.) Frequent informal assessment is needed to determine how much review to build into lessons, how often to review material taught in the past, when to introduce the next concepts, and what multisensory components of the lessons are most effective for the students. To aid planning, the daily lesson plan has a column for notes. At the end of each lesson the teacher writes down any significant needs for future lessons. When a teacher has a busy schedule, it is easy to forget that the 10:00 students need more practice on a certain activity or that he or she did not remember to make a certain point about a new concept that was introduced to the 2:00 group. When the teacher is making plans for the next week, the notes column of the lesson plan serves as a record of concepts that can be built into the lessons. It is helpful to document what was especially effective as well as to note details of presentations that did not have the planned impact.

Because the lessons are clearly demarcated into discrete language components, as discussed previously, the teacher can observe where students' strengths and weaknesses are and can monitor and adjust the instruction from day to day. He or she can allow for uneven development of knowledge and skills by offering different levels of practice

Socratic = questions that prompt thinking

activities for each component (Tucker, 2003). For example, it is not unusual for a student to master the ability to read closed syllables with short vowel sounds before mastering the ability to spell them. This is an opportunity to repeat material already presented in the spelling section until students master it. The lesson format also acts as a blueprint for task analysis so that student knowledge and skills can be monitored and built gradually and consistently toward automaticity.

There is another helpful adjunct to lesson planning. By keeping careful records—for example, by charting words and language concepts the student knows—the teacher has a ready reference to report current progress directly to the students themselves, as well as to parents and caregivers. This is a way for the teacher to be accountable and have evidence of gains and areas of weakness to address in ongoing future sessions.

Introduction of New Language Concepts

MSLE is based on teachers using a well-defined scope and sequence so that there is systematic introduction of new information in small steps for the precise teaching of skills. This feature of MSLE affords the opportunity for guided discovery through Socratic questioning to learn new language concepts based on what the student already knows. As Carreker notes in Chapter 9, "Guided discovery teaching uses the Socratic method of asking questions to lead students to discover new information. When students make a discovery, they understand and connect the new learning to prior knowledge." Many programs also have students organize this information in language notebooks, categorized into subsections, for ready reference and a record of their learning. In this way the learning strategies are made conspicuous as each concept is developed. Scaffolding and feedback continuously occur during the lessons. The choice of new material to introduce and the number and choice of words to spell can be tailored to what students can learn easily. Similarly, the teacher assigns an adequate amount of oral reading that is consistent with material that has been covered so that students read at a comfortable pace with 80%–90% accuracy. In this way, the lesson encourages integration of the lower level skills into the students' ability to handle multisyllable words and connected decodable text.

While working at the many complex layers of the language, teachers and students develop together a consistent language about language that is used along with multisensory techniques to help students attend to language concepts they need taught directly. For example, in the *Wilson Reading System* (Wilson, 2002), questioning techniques are used throughout the lesson after new material is introduced to ensure that the student has understood. Such terminology as *digraph, blend, syllable,* and *schwa sound* gives students and teachers a common vocabulary to discuss new concepts, review what they have learned, and to make corrections. Again, using leading questions about what the student already knows, teachers can prompt students to self-correct their errors "creating a positive, success-oriented lesson" (Wilson, 2002, p. 25).

Pacing of Learning

Structured lesson planning encourages appropriate pacing with specific objectives in each section of the lesson. Since the lesson ideally runs from 45 minutes to 1 hour, each section is limited to a short interval of intensive instruction. As teachers gain experience through observing lessons and through mentoring, they develop the skill of adjusting the pacing of parts of the lesson. Spalding (2003) pointed out the importance

of teaching students how to maintain and switch attention so that they can manage the transitions within the lesson easily. This promotes good pacing and helps students to work independently.

Benefits of Lesson Planning: The Student's Point of View

Structure

Structured lesson planning is essential for successful teaching of students with language learning disabilities and attention issues for a number of important reasons. From the students' point of view, MSLE lessons fit students' need for structure, limits, and an anxiety-free atmosphere in which to learn. Students do not like surprises or last-minute changes that can confuse them and affect their performance. They like to know what is coming next to prepare for it (Frank, 2002). MSLE lessons adhere to a daily structure to ensure that students feel secure in knowing that the lesson is stable and predictable and that it is designed for their success. The agenda of the lesson plan is often displayed using words and symbols for the activities listed. The students and teacher refer to this agenda as the lesson progresses. Often, students use a paperclip to mark each step on the daily lesson plan chart as they work through each task in order. They are frequently surprised at the fast pace and amount accomplished at the end of the session.

Less Anxiety

The daily presentation of activities in the same order removes students' anxiety over time. Students know what to expect and when. Because the activities rotate rapidly, none lasting more than 10 minutes, students' attention is better focused. In addition, students' active participation increases through verbalizing, generalizing, and comparing and contrasting language elements while building the structure of the language for themselves.

Use of Visual Reminders

Most MSLE systems have a structured lesson chart, as described previously, that is a visual reminder of the order of the lesson and, incidentally, how they are slowly mastering the components of written language (Smith, 1989). Spelling, handwriting, and composition lessons have procedure charts that prompt the students to use the strategies they are learning. These familiar structured procedures promote readiness for learning (see Chapters 9, 10, and 15 for specific examples of charts to use with students).

All Components of Language

Careful planning guarantees that all aspects of language are practiced and integrated systematically based on an organized curriculum. Students experience short, intensive, interactive activities that integrate reading, writing, and spelling. What they read they write; what they write they read; what they read they spell. Students are taught to use all pathways to learn in every lesson as they work on letter sounds, reading words, spelling, handwriting, vocabulary, comprehension, and composition. This seamless presentation ensures that the basic skills needed for students to become skilled readers are not presented in a disjointed, disconnected way. Grasping written language concepts presents difficulties for students, especially when attention is a problem. Therefore, ac-

tivities are short and focused with small steps taken in sequence, at first easy and then more difficult. With the rapid changing of learning modalities (visual, auditory, and tactile/kinesthetic) and media, the teacher keeps the lesson interesting. Students learn to accept and even anticipate variety within the structure (Tucker, 2003). Necessary repetition builds toward mastery while all taught concepts are maintained in the lessons (Wilson, 2002). New learning and practice with prior learning are well balanced. Review is automatically built in for purposes of fluency and automaticity of the essential components of reading and writing.

Better Organization

Clinicians and teachers have often observed that students barely notice the time passing during well-planned MSLE lessons. Teachers often report that when they inadvertently leave out a portion of the lesson, students quickly notice the omission. The emphasis on consistency and structure promotes student organization in a predictable and consistent environment. Students are aware of the forward motion of the daily schedule and depend on it for keeping organized and sequenced in time and space.

Students often feel less anxiety as they understand the expectations within the lesson structure and begin to experience success, often for the first time. The consistent daily review of learned information and guided practice of new concepts gradually leads to students' mastery and independent application of what has been learned. As students gain mastery of the subskills, teachers continue to introduce new content in the curriculum sequence. Some students take longer to reach mastery during remediation. However, the strong organization of well-planned MSLE lessons often help students improve their memory over time and thus have better retrieval of information.

Implementing Lesson Planning

Implementing planning for MSLE lessons requires the use of several different lesson plan formats: a daily lesson plan; a weekly lesson plan; and a summary worksheet or scope and sequence, which denotes progress. We suggest that teachers begin with formats provided by a certified trainer or coach. However, teachers should be encouraged to fine-tune their lessons to match their style of instruction as they become experienced in the implementation of the steps in the curriculum from basic to complex.

A lesson plan is built on a scope and sequence of an MSLE curriculum, as well as prior testing of the students. The teacher begins by identifying the individual components of the reading lesson in the suggested daily lesson plan and the sequence of these components. When the teacher begins planning for a new student or group of students, he or she can assume nothing about the students' previous mastery of material. If prior progress monitoring or report cards are available, the teacher can refer to these to identify the highest level of mastery attained for each component. If a student is new to a reading tutorial approach, a quick probe of all skills beginning with letter names and letter sounds is recommended. Each student must be evaluated to determine what material has been mastered and what knowledge is yet to be learned or needs to be reviewed. Once lessons have begun, succeeding steps will be driven by assessment data obtained from records of informal curriculum-based probes and later formal testing. It is important for students to know what they know and for the teacher to be aware of the gaps in students' skills. For students struggling with reading, it is a well-accepted axiom that remediation begins at the beginning and goes as slowly as necessary and as quickly as possible.

Daily Lesson Plan

A detailed daily lesson plan is needed to plan and organize skills, materials, and presentation. Lesson planning can be thought of as a concrete way to analyze the needs of each student. When teachers sit down to plan lessons, they need to keep long-term goals in mind according to the scope and sequence of the MSLE curriculum that delineate the discrete components of language and subskills to be mastered. When teachers are new to this kind of instruction, it often takes 2 or even 3 hours to plan and organize the materials for a 1-hour tutorial. After teaching through all of the elements of the curriculum, with several different groups of students, teachers find the planning process becomes easier.

The *first* daily lesson plan is generally a probe of or review of the student's known skills that are to be mastered in each component of the lesson. Every MSLE program has a beginning series of skills to be mastered. For example, the teacher should check new students for knowledge of the following: the alphabet, sequence, letter names, phonemic awareness of beginning sounds of words, writing upper- and lowercase print letters, some consonants sounds and short vowel sounds on cards, spelling individual sounds, and blending sounds into words (Sonday, 1997).

A variety of daily and weekly lesson plan formats are provided here for review. Figure 8.1 is an example of a beginning-level daily lesson plan after several consonants and two short vowels have been introduced. Figure 8.2 is an example of a more advanced daily lesson plan after the students have progressed to two-syllable words for reading and spelling. The students have worked with the dropping rule and spelling **derivatives**. The students have also been introduced to four syllable types: closed, vowel pair, vowel-*r*, and vowel-consonant-*e*. The daily lesson plan shown in Figure 8.2 introduces the open syllable.

For a description of the precise steps in a multisensory introduction of letter sounds and concepts, see Chapter 5, 9, and 10 for elementary students and Chapter 12 for older students. The times given for each lesson component are approximate. It is likely that teachers may or may not have the opportunity to include every component each day; with the use of the weekly lesson plan, however, all activities will be incorporated consistently over time. Figures 8.1 and 8.2 list chapters from this book that contain information and guidance on what can be included in each step of the daily lesson plan. Figures 8.1, 8.3, and 8.4 provide guidance for a beginning-level weekly lesson plan.

The explicit and systematic instruction used in MSLE lessons plays an important role in recent efforts to improve reading instruction and to link instruction to how children are identified with learning disabilities. Using the response-to-instruction criteria to assess and identify struggling readers calls for a three-tiered system of intervention. The first tier is screening for reading difficulties in preschool, kindergarten, and first grade and placement in early intervention programs in the general education classroom. The second tier is the provision of small-group intervention and progress monitoring to support students with similar needs for effective instruction in reading along with the general education program. For children who do not progress in reading at a reasonable rate, the poorest readers, the third tier would include special education services using scientifically based programs with progress regularly monitored (Fletcher, Coulter, Reschly, & Vaughn, 2004).

Regarding the three-tier system of intervention programs in U.S. public schools for students struggling with reading, Dickman, Hennessy, Moats, Rooney, and Tomey (2002)

Instructional component	Approximate time	Refer to . . .
ALPHABET KNOWLEDGE AND PHONEMIC AWARENESS *Alphabet Knowledge* Students touch and name the letters of the alphabet in sequence as warm-up. Students match plastic uppercase letters to grid of alphabet letters on a mat. *Phonemic Awareness* Ask students if these words rhyme: *pill/hill, tip/lip, yes/my, run/sun, mice/nice, now/nap.*	5 minutes	Chapters 4 and 5
READING DECKS Show letter cards for quick drill for students to name. Give key words and sounds: *i, t, p, n, s, a, l, d, f, h, g, o.* Use irregular word deck: *said, the, of, one.*	3 minutes	Chapter 9
SPELLING DECK Using a spelling deck (cards bearing letters and sounds introduced for reading), dictate sounds to students, who repeat the sounds, say the letter names, and write them on chalkboard: /ĭ/, /t/, /p/, /n/, /s/, /ă/, /l/, /d/, /f/, /h/, /g/, /ŏ/.	3 minutes	Chapter 10
MULTISENSORY INTRODUCTION OF LETTER OR CONCEPT Provide multisensory introduction of digraph *ng* using guided discovery of sound, letters, key words, and mouth position. Discovery words: *sing, sang, sting, ding* Reinforce with sky writing, handwriting, reading the sound, and spelling the sound.	5 minutes	Chapters 2 and 9
READING PRACTICE Students prepare and read orally closed-syllable words: *hint, stand, tint, slap, split, spat, spin, snap, nips, plant* *Dad lifts the sand in a tin pan.*	5–10 minutes	Chapter 9
SPELLING Give warm up, with review of sounds to be spelled: /ĭ/, /t/, /s/, /a/, /l/, /f/, /h/. Review Floss Rule and spell these words: *sniff, tiff, staff, till, hill, spill.*	5–10 minutes	Chapter 10
HANDWRITING Students practice writing *d* on folded newsprint paper. Students trace the letter three times while listening to guided stroke description: "Curve under, over, stop, back around, up, down, release." Students make three copies, saying the letter name each time.	3 minutes	Chapter 15
COMPREHENSION AND LISTENING STRATEGIES Read "The Tortoise and the Hare" to students. Have students retell the fable with a graphic organizer for stories (simple story map).	10 minutes	Chapter 13
ORAL LANGUAGE PRACTICE AND COMPOSITION Introduce vocabulary: *boasted, plodding, patient.* Have students find and discuss meanings for the descriptive words from the story, use words in sentences, and enter words in the vocabulary section of their language notebook.	10 minutes	Chapters 3, 13, and 14

Figure 8.1.   Beginning-level daily lesson plan. (*Source:* Cox, 1984.)

Instructional component	Approximate time	Refer to . . .
ALPHABET AND DICTIONARY, PHONOLOGICAL AWARENESS, AND MORPHOLOGY STUDY Students review guide words, target words, and first and last entry words on a dictionary page. Students do guide-word practice in the dictionary with alphabet strip as reference (e.g., if guide words are *lop* and *lot,* students determine whether the entry word *loss* would appear on that page).	5 minutes	Chapters 4 and 5
READING DECKS Students say the sounds represented by symbols in the letter card deck. Students also use a deck of word parts: suffixes, prefixes, and roots.	3 minutes	Chapters 9 and 12
MULTISENSORY INTRODUCTION OF LETTER OR CONCEPT Students learn vowels in open syllables through auditory/visual discovery. Discovery words: *able, ogle, idle, bugle* Explain to students, "All words end in final stable syllables; the first syllable is open and accented. A vowel in an open, accented syllable is long. Long vowels say their names." **sta**ꞌ|ble **ri**ꞌ|fle **no**ꞌ|ble	10 minutes	Chapters 2, 9, 10, and 12
READING PRACTICE Read words with vowels in open syllables: *table, cradle, trifle, stable, ruble, sable, title, maple, staple.* Read sentences: *The wooden cradle was carved from pinewood.* Read a review list of words and a short story in a controlled reader.	10 minutes	Chapters 9, 10, and 12
SPELLING Students spell on paper from dictation: *maple, stifle, table, noble, bugle, staple, stable.* Students categorize list of words for spelling as regular, irregular, or rule words: *tank, tail, swimming.* Students write sentences dictation: *The fish nibbles on the worm on the hook.*	10 minutes	Chapters 10 and 12
HANDWRITING *(does not occur every lesson)* Students practice writing capital letters *T, S,* and *I* in cursive.	5 minutes	Chapter 15
EXTENDED READING AND WRITING Goal is accuracy, fluency, and comprehension. Students read from connected decodable text with controlled vocabulary that is geared to the students' levels. Students write sentences using vocabulary they are reading and spelling.	10 minutes	Chapters 9, 12, 14, and 16
COMPREHENSION AND LISTENING STRATEGIES Read students stories or expository texts that match their age and interests. Include comprehension strategies (see Chapter 14).	5 minutes	Chapters 14 and 18
ORAL LANGUAGE PRACTICE AND COMPOSITION Begin expanding written sentences using *where* and *when.* Practice orally, starting with basic simple sentences: *The baseball player left his mitt (where?).* *Molly called her best friend Sara (when?).*	5 minutes	Chapters 3, 16, and 18

Figure 8.2. Intermediate-level lesson plan. (*Sources: Basic language skills: Concept manual, book two,* 2000; Cox, 1984.)

Instructional component	Day 2	Day 3
ALPHABET KNOWLEDGE AND PHONEMIC AWARENESS	**Alphabet knowledge** Students touch and name the alphabet on strip. Students practice accent and rhythm, naming the letters in pairs. Students accent the first letter of pairs. (**A'**B, **C'**D, **E'**F). **Phonemic awareness** Students add a sound to a word: Add /p/ to the beginning of these words: *each, in, age, ill, inch*	**Alphabet knowledge** Students touch and name the alphabet on strip. With model available, students put plastic letters in alphabetical order. **Phonemic awareness** Students identify the sound at the beginning of each word: *beach, ball, bark, boil, bus.* (Students use mirrors to check lips.)
READING DECKS	Show letter cards for quick drill for students to name and give key words and sounds: *i, t, p, n, s, a, l, d, f, h, g, o, a,* and (new card) *ng.* Use irregular word deck: *said, the, of, one.*	Repeat Day 2 activity.
SPELLING DECK	Dictate sounds to students, who repeat the sounds, says the letter names, and write them on rice tray: /ĭ/, /t/, /p/, /n/, /s/, /l/, /d/, /f/, /h/, /g/, /ŏ/, /ă/, /k/, and (new sound) /ng/.	Repeat Day 2 activity, on table top instead of using rice tray.
MULTISENSORY INTRODUCTION OR REVIEW OF LETTER OR CONCEPT	**Review of Day 1's new concept** Review /ng/ sound, letters, key word (*king*) and mouth position. Review digraph *ng* final: *sing, hang, long.* Discover /ng/ medial (*link, sank, honk*) where /ng/ is represented by letter *n* (key word: *sink*) Students draw *g*-curve on *n* to mark new sound: ŋ.	**Review of Day 1's new concept** Review /ng/ sound, letters, key words, and mouth positions. Reinforce with sky writing, hand-writing, reading sound, spelling sound (sometimes *n* = /ng/). Students puts /ng/ in student note-book, with spelling examples of digraph *ng* and *n* with key words.
READING PRACTICE	Students prepare and read orally words with *ng* and other short *a* words: *pat, tang, lap, sat, pang, sap, sang, dad, fang* Read sentences with *ng* words.	Students prepare and read orally words with short *i* words: *sit, hit, tip, dip, tin, pin, lid, did, pig, sis.* Read controlled sentences for fluency.
SPELLING	Give warm-up, with review of sounds to be spelled: /ĭ/, /p/, /n/, /s/, /ŏ/, /t/, /d/, /g/, /l/ Review suffix *s* rule (/z/ and /s/ = *s*): *pins, pots, tops, digs, dogs, logs, nips* Students write sentences from dictation: *Dan sits on the logs.*	Give warm-up, with review of sounds to be spelled: /h/, /ĭ/, /l/, /s/, /f/, /p/, /ŏ/ Review Floss Rule and suffix *s* rule, and have students spell words from dictation: *hills, pills, fills, dolls, sills.* (Also discuss word meanings.)
HANDWRITING	Review guided stroke description for letters *d, p,* and *a.* At the chalkboard, students practice *a, p,* and *d,* connecting them in random order: *adp, pda, dpa*	Review guided stroke description, and have students practice connecting bridge letter *o.* Students trace *op, od,* and *og* on folded newsprint. Students write copies after tracing.
COMPREHENSION AND LISTENING STRATEGIES	Reread fable ("The Tortoise and the Hare") to students. Using a simple story map as a prompt, have the students describe the actions of the hare.	Using a simple story map, have students describe the actions of the tortoise.
ORAL LANGUAGE PRACTICE AND COMPOSITION	**Vocabulary** List adjectives used in the fable to describe the hare.	**Vocabulary** List adjectives used in the fable to describe the tortoise.

Figure 8.3. Days 2 and 3 of a 5-day weekly lesson plan, beginning level.

Instructional component	Day 4	Day 5
ALPHABET KNOWLEDGE AND PHONEMIC AWARENESS	***Alphabet knowledge*** Students touch and name the alphabet on strip. Point to a letter on the alphabet strip. Students name what comes after and before the letter. ***Phonemic awareness*** Using letter tiles *p* and *b*, students point to the first sound in dictated words: *pill, bat, pet.*	***Alphabet knowledge*** Students touch and name the alphabet on strip. Students play Alphabet Bingo. ***Phonemic awareness*** Students add /d/ to the beginning of each syllable: *ear, esk, ock, og, ust, oll, ive, ime, itch.*
READING DECKS	Repeat Day 2 activity.	Repeat Day 2 activity.
SPELLING DECK	Repeat Day 2 activity on chalkboard.	Repeat Day 2 activity on lined paper.
MULTISENSORY INTRODUCTION OR REVIEW OF LETTER OR CONCEPT	***Introduction of new concept*** New letter *c* = /k/ before *a, o,* and *u* Visual discovery: *can, cop, cup* Students form linkages with key word *cup* and letter *c* pronounced as /k/. Reinforce with sky writing, handwriting, reading sound, and spelling sound. Students add *c* to the /k/ page in their notebooks.	***Review of digraph <u>ng</u> and <u>n</u> before /k/*** Present mixed review of *ng* and *nk* words presented during the week: *sing, sang, song, ding, dong, gong, tank, pink, honk, stink.* Students read sentences and underline *ng*: He sa<u>ng</u> a so<u>ng</u>. The bell went di<u>ng</u>-do<u>ng</u>.
READING PRACTICE	Students prepare and read orally nonsense words with *c read as /k/ before a* and *o*: *cass, coll, caff, scad, scop, scap.* Read sentences with review of new sight words *said, of, the,* and *one*: *One of the cops said, "Stop!"* *Pat spills one of the cans of pop.* Students draw boxes around words containing the suffix *-s*, which says /s/ or /z/.	Present mixed review of words read this week, through the use of a deck of word cards or words listed on the board or on chart paper: *tank, gang, tong, sing, king, sting, pink, honk, dank, sink, lank, stink, cast, cod, can, cop, cap.* Students read sentences listed on chart paper or on strips.
SPELLING	Students review suffix *s* rule, referring to their notebooks. Students write sentences from dictation: *Sis fills the gas can.* *Tad pats the cats.* *One of the kids hits the logs.*	Have students explain the Floss Rule and the suffix *-s* rule. Have students give two examples for each. Students write sentence from dictation: *The dog sniffs the pan and spills the fat.*
HANDWRITING	Students write five previously learned letters three times each (to stress size proportion). Each student places a star by one of each letter that he or she feels is best.	Students write five tall letters (*k, h, t, l, d*) three times each (to stress size proportion). Each student places a star by one of each letter that he or she feels is best.
COMPREHENSION AND LISTENING STRATEGIES	With aid of graphic organizer, students identify and explain the turning point of the fable "The Tortoise and the Hare."	Students identify which character they feel they are most like or give a situation when they were most like each character.
ORAL LANGUAGE PRACTICE AND COMPOSITION	***Vocabulary*** Students list adjectives used to describe the turning point of the fable.	Students lay graphic organizers on the table and generate one or two clear, concise sentences for each map.

Figure 8.4. Days 4 and 5 of a 5-day weekly lesson plan, beginning level.

noted that MSLE lessons ought to fit into the third-tier intervention in special education for the poorest readers. However, merely using direct instruction and strategy instruction are not sufficient. Students engaging in second- and third-tier intervention must have "structured teaching of language systems" (p. 24):

> Structured language interventions must be intensive to be effective. As students reach the third grade, up to two hours daily are necessary to remediate severe reading disabilities. Remediation programs with demonstrated effectiveness, staffed by teachers with appropriate training in language and remedial instruction, should be available to older poor readers in lieu of other academic requirements. *Accommodations and modifications are never a substitute for intensive remediation.* (2002, p. 25)

Weekly Lesson Plan

In addition to a daily lesson plan, a weekly lesson plan is also needed. A model is provided in Figures 8.1, 8.2, and 8.3. This can be in a separate plan book or more often is the same plan book if there is enough space. Some teachers use a teacher planner. If the planner contains a block for each class, each block is instead used for one component within a lesson. Sometimes a 9" × 12" sketch pad is used to accommodate daily and weekly plans on the same page. When a teacher first begins to organize MSLE lesson plans, each daily plan may require a full sheet of paper, as shown in Figure 8.1. As the teacher becomes more experienced with planning and implementing the lessons, five daily lessons (a week's worth) can be recorded on a single sheet of paper or in a teacher's plan book.

The weekly plan enables the instructor to always be looking ahead to focus the direction of the instruction. In that way, the teacher can ensure that the same components are practiced using different multisensory pathways and media. It is easy to fill a lesson with instructional activities. The real expertise is in continuing to move the lessons and the instruction forward. Pacing is the most difficult skill for inexperienced teachers to acquire because it only comes with experience. Working with both a daily and a weekly lesson plan format (under the guidance of a coach) enables a novice teacher to begin to see when instruction is moving too quickly or when it is moving too slowly. As mentioned previously, the idea is to move as quickly as possible but as slowly as necessary. By sketching out five lessons and then adjusting this plan on a daily basis, the teacher is able to begin to recognize and pace instruction based on the performance of his or her students. Figures 8.1, 8.3, and 8. 4 provide a model for a weekly lesson plan that shows the interplay of new information, review of concepts, and practice in controlled lists and texts for reinforcement and the variety of multisensory interactions between teacher and students. Unquestionably, as the week unfolds, the teacher adjusts the lesson plan to suit the needs of the students.

CONCLUSION

Change done to you is debilitating; change done by you is exhilarating.
—Anonymous

Be exhilarated by making needed changes to your classroom: your space, your interactions with your students, and your lesson planning. The aim of this chapter is to provide you with fresh ideas and a new perspective on your instruction of students with specific language learning disabilities. Use the Building Block Checklist for Effective Classroom Management in the appendix at the end of this chapter to reflect on what you are presently doing and what you want to do differently.

A lesson plan for MSLE instruction is the framework for interaction between the teacher and the student. It is designed to support teachers in their efforts to teach the linguistic content to be mastered, using the most effective ways to teach according to informed principles of learning and instruction. An MSLE lesson highlights the progression of time-intensive activities that include reviews of previously taught information, practice in all levels of language, and the introduction of new concepts based on a systematic curriculum. Careful planning of MSLE lessons builds the foundation for discovery learning and enables both the teacher and the students to work within a framework designed for explicit individualized instruction. Time spent ensuring that each part of the lesson includes multisensory components provides students with multiple opportunities to be active participants in the learning process.

As mentioned at the beginning of this chapter, although lesson planning is at the heart of MSLE, it cannot stand alone. It is important that teaching and learning take place in a positive environment. Multisensory structured language lesson planning assumes its powerful place when the teacher creates a positive classroom environment. A primary consideration is organizing the physical space for both the students and the teacher. The next priority is teacher organization and organization and maintenance of materials for instruction and recordkeeping, in order to maximize the time spent engaged in productive activity and minimize the time lost during transitions or disruptions. The third focus is student expectations and behavior, with a strong emphasis on building a positive learning environment. Once the learning environment has been addressed, the teacher can create and implement detailed daily and weekly MSLE lesson plans. Students benefit when the environment is conducive to learning and when teachers are well prepared to implement instructional goals.

REFERENCES

Basic language skills: Concept manual, book two. (2000). Bellaire, TX: Neuhaus Education Center.

Berninger, V. (1999). The "write stuff" for preventing and treating writing disabilities. *Perspectives, 25*(2), 20–22.

Blachman, B.A., Tangel, D.M., Ball, E.W., Black, R., & McGraw, C.K. (1999). Developing phonological awareness and word recognition skills: A two-year intervention with low-income, inner-city children. *Reading and Writing: An Interdisciplinary Journal, 11,* 239–273.

Blachman, B.A., Schatschneider, C., Fletcher, J.M., & Clonan, S.M. (2003). Early reading intervention: A classroom prevention study and a remediation study. In B.R. Foorman, (Ed.), *Preventing and remediating reading difficulties: Bringing science to scale* (pp. 253–271). Timonium, MD: York Press.

Cox, A.R. (1984). *Structures and techniques: Multisensory teaching of basic language skills.* Cambridge, MA: Educators Publishing Service.

Dickman, G.E., Hennessy, N.L., Moats, L.C., Rooney, K.J., & Tomey, H.A., III. (2002). *Response to OSEP Summit on Learning Disabilities.* Baltimore: The International Dyslexia Association.

Fletcher, J.M., Coulter, W.A., Reschly, D.J., & Vaughn, S. (2004). Alternative approaches to the definition and identification of learning disabilities: Some questions and answers. *Annals of Dyslexia, 54*(2), 304–331.

Foorman, B.R., Francis, D.J., Fletcher, J.M., Schatschneider, C., & Mehta, P. (1998). The role of instruction in learning to read: Preventing reading failure in at-risk children. *Journal of Educational Psychology, 90*(1), 37–55.

Frank, R. (with Livingston, K.E.). (2002). *The secret life of the dyslexic child: How she thinks, how he feels, how they can succeed.* Emmaus, PA: Rodale Press.

Gillingham, A., & Stillman, B.W. (1956). *Remedial training for children with specific disability in reading, spelling and penmanship* (5th ed.). Cambridge, MA: Educators Publishing Service.

Gillingham, A., & Stillman, B.W. (1997). *The Gillingham manual: Remedial training for children with specific disability in reading, spelling, and penmanship* (8th edition). Cambridge, MA: Educators Publishing Service.

Henry, M.K., & Brickley, S.G. (1999). *Dyslexia: Samuel T. Orton and his legacy.* Baltimore: The International Dyslexia Association.

Mather, N., & Goldstein, S. (2001). *Learning disabilities and challenging behaviors: A guide to intervention and classroom management.* Baltimore: Paul H. Brookes Publishing Co.

National Institute of Child Health and Human Development (NICHD). (2000). *Report of the National Reading Panel. Teaching children to read: An evidence-based assessment of the scientific research literature on reading and its implications for reading instruction: Reports of the subgroups.* (NIH Publication No. 00-4754). Washington, DC: U.S. Government Printing Office. Also available on-line: http://www.nichd.nih.gov/publications/nrp/report.htm

Orton, S.T. (1937). *Reading, writing and speech problems in children.* New York: W.W. Norton.

Schedler, J.-F., & Bitler, E.-F. (2004). *A classroom management secret: Keep the glasses full.* Workshop presented at the annual conference of the New York Branch of The International Dyslexia Association, New York.

Smith, M.T. (1989). *MTA classroom charts.* Cambridge, MA: Educators Publishing Service.

Smith, M.T. (1996). *Multisensory teaching system for reading.* Forney, TX: MTS Publications.

Snow, C.E., Burns, M.S., & Griffin, P. (Eds.). (1998). *Preventing reading difficulties in young children.* Washington, DC: National Academies Press.

Sonday, A. (1997). *The Sonday System: Learning to read.* St. Paul, MN: Winsor Corporation.

Spalding, R.B. (North, M.E., Ed.). (2003). *The writing road to reading: The Spalding method for teaching speech, spelling, writing, and reading* (5th rev. ed.). New York: HarperCollins.

Swanson, H.L. (1999). Instructional components that predict treatment outcomes for students with learning disabilities: Support for a combined strategy and direct instruction model. *Learning Disabilities Research and Practice, 14*(3), 129–140.

Swanson, H.L., & Hoskyn, M. (1998). A synthesis of experimental intervention literature for students with learning disabilities: a meta-analysis of treatment outcomes. *Review of Educational Research, 68,* 277–321.

Torgesen, J.K., Wagner, R.K., Rashotte, C.A., Rose, E., Lindamood, P., Conway, T., et al. (1999). Preventing reading failure in young children with phonological processing disabilities: Group and individual responses to instruction. *Journal of Educational Psychology, 91,* 579–593.

Tucker, V. (2003). *Planning multisensory structured language lessons.* Manuscript in preparation.

Wilson, B. (2002). *Wilson reading system instructor manual* (3rd ed.). Millbury, MA: Wilson Language Training.

Wong, H.K., & Wong, R.T. (1998). *The first days of school: How to be an effective teacher.* Mountain View, CA: Harry K. Wong Publications. Available from the publisher: http://www.firstdaysofschool.com/

Building Block Checklist for Effective Classroom Management

Things I *am* doing	Aspect of planning	Things I want to do differently
	Classroom environment	
	Bulletin boards	
	Furniture	
	Student desks	
	Traffic pattern(s)	
	Teacher organization	
	Teacher(s) desk(s)	
	Organization of teaching materials	
	Plan for instructional transitions	
	Student behavior	
	Establishment of classroom rules and expectations	
	Reduction of student anxiety	
	Bonding and connecting with all students	
	Connecting with individual students	
	Active listening to students	
	Self-evaluation of classroom needs	
	Is it a safe environment?	
	Can students take academic risks?	
	Are students exploring friendships?	
	Are students negotiating the classroom setting?	
	Are students learning appropriate expectations and behaviors?	
	Are students' behaviors transferable to the outside world?	

Directions:

1. Read through all items in the Building Block Checklist.

2. In the left column, place a check mark next to each item currently being addressed.

3. In the right column, place a check mark next to each item that needs to change to improve classroom management.

From Schedler, J.-F. & Bitler, E.-F. (2004). *A classroom management secret: Keep the glasses full.* Workshop presented at the annual conference of the New York Branch of The International Dyslexia Association, New York; adapted by permission.

9

Teaching Reading
Accurate Decoding and Fluency

Suzanne Carreker

The main goal of reading is comprehension. In order for a person to read, symbols on the printed page must be translated into spoken words (i.e., decoding), and meaning must be connected to those words. Reading is, according to the Simple View of Reading (Gough & Tunmer, 1986; Hoover & Gough, 1990), the product of decoding and language comprehension. These two components work together in a delicate, interdependent balance. Inefficiency in one of the components can lead to overall reading failure. The reader who has difficulty with decoding will not be able to derive meaning from the text; conversely, the reader who has difficulty with specific levels of spoken language will receive little reward for his or her decoding efforts. Joshi and Aaron (2000) expanded the Simple View of Reading to include fluency as a critical component of the reading competency formula. According to their model, the Componential Model of Reading, a person may have efficient decoding and language comprehension but may demonstrate difficulties in reading comprehension because of a slow processing rate, which results in dysfluent reading. Dysfluent reading diverts attention from the meaning of the text and adversely affects comprehension. For students to become fully literate, especially students with dyslexia, the components of reading—decoding, comprehension, and fluency—and all other elements of literacy instruction must be explicitly or directly taught in an informed, comprehensive approach (Adams, 1990; Brady & Moats, 1997; National Institute of Child Health and Human Development [NICHD], 2000). The focus of this chapter is the explicit, systematic, and sequential instruction of decoding and fluency, which leads to efficient comprehension and reading achievement.

THE ROLE OF DECODING

Decoding facilitates the reader's linkage of the printed word to the spoken word (Beck & Juel, 1995). A reader sees a page full of symbols. The reader's success in making sense of these symbols depends on how well he or she understands that the symbols represent spoken language. The extent to which the reader succeeds in establishing the relationship between the symbols and spoken language is dependent on his or her sensitivity to the internal sound structure of language (i.e., phonemic awareness; Adams, 1990). The reader must realize that spoken words have constituent sounds. In addition to recognizing that words have sounds, the reader must realize that printed words consist of letters that correspond to those speech sounds. These insights enable the reader to establish the alphabetic principle or code that is necessary for acquiring decoding skills. The importance of phonemic awareness (Adams, 1990; Bradley & Bryant, 1983; Goswami & Bryant, 1990; Liberman, Shankweiler, & Liberman, 1989; Stanovich, 1991) cannot be overemphasized as it provides the foundation for decoding, enabling the reader to unlock the printed word (see Chapter 4 for further discussion).

Decoding Strategies

Decoding requires knowledge of the phonemic, graphophonemic, syllabic, and morphemic structures of the language. A skilled reader uses a variety of strategies for translating the printed word into its spoken equivalent: sound–symbol correspondences, structural analysis, **instant word recognition**, and contextual clues. Although the primary focuses of this chapter are decoding and fluency, the crucial role of oral language in the reading process, as discussed in Chapter 3, must be stressed. Not only is oral language the foundation of comprehension, but it also greatly influences and assists the reader's efficient, effective use of the various decoding strategies.

A reader's appreciation of the relationship between sounds and letters develops through phonemic awareness and instant letter recognition (i.e., print awareness; Adams, 1990). This understanding, in turn, develops sound–symbol correspondences (i.e., graphophonemic patterns) that enable the reader to sound out unfamiliar words. Initially, the beginning reader recognizes words by associating a word with some visually distinguishing characteristics (e.g., *dog* has a circle in the middle and a tail at the end) (Gough & Hillinger, 1980). As the reader encounters more and more words, the visual characteristics that make words distinguishable diminish. The reader begins to cue recognition by selecting some of the letters in a word, usually the first and last letters (Ehri, 1991). He or she is now better able to distinguish words, but accuracy is limited as many words share the same initial and final letters. When the reader attends to all of the letters, he or she can sound out the correct pronunciation of an unfamiliar word (Gough & Hillinger, 1980).

Both phonological awareness and sound–symbol correspondences are critical co-requisites in reading acquisition (Share & Stanovich, 1995). The reader needs an introduction to a few sound–symbol patterns to begin sounding out words. As the reader sounds out words, he or she reinforces the sound–symbol correspondences that have been introduced and establishes new ones (Adams, 1990). New sound–symbol correspondences are acquired through a "self-teaching mechanism" (Share & Stanovich, 1995, p. 17). By using known sound–symbol correspondences and phonological sensitivity, the reader approximates the pronunciation of the unknown word. This approximate pronunciation combined with available contextual clues enables the reader to deter-

mine the correct pronunciation and thereby provides the reader an opportunity to acquire knowledge of the sound–symbol correspondences within the unknown word.
With repeated encounters, the reader builds an **orthographic memory** (i.e., memory
for patterns of written language) of words so that eventually he or she instantly recognizes the words without having to sound them out (Adams, 1990).

In addition to letters, printed words have syllables (i.e., speech units) and morphemes (i.e., meaning units). Structural analysis, the perception of orthographic syllables and morphemes, enables the reader to decode long, unfamiliar words and fosters
a decoding process that is less cumbersome and more efficient than sounding out each
letter. Once the reader can recognize different kinds of syllables, he or she can accurately predict the sound of the vowel in a syllable. With knowledge of morphemes, the
reader can focus on units of letters that recur in words (e.g., the reader sees *tract* in *tractor, attractive,* and *subtraction*). The reader does not have to sound out every letter in an
unknown word, only the letters that he or she does not recognize as part of a morpheme (Henry, 1988). Morphemes also give clues that allow the reader to infer the
meanings of words (Henry, 1988, 2003; Moats, 1994). Orthographic patterns established through graphophonemic, syllabic, and morphemic awareness greatly econo-
mize the learning of a reader's lexicon (i.e., spoken and written word knowledge). Every
word in the reader's lexicon, which may number 50,000 words by the time he or she
reaches college, does not have to be stored in memory as 50,000 separate items, and the
reader has a way of dealing with the words that he or she may use in speaking but has
never seen in print before (Gough & Hillinger, 1980).

The ease and automaticity with which a skilled reader is able to read individual
words is known as instant word recognition. Instant word recognition is achieved by
repeated encounters with words and by overlearning (i.e., learning to automaticity) the
orthographic and phonological patterns of the language. The ultimate goal of decoding instruction is the immediate, facile translation of a printed word into its spoken
equivalent. Automaticity with this translation has a significant impact on the reader's
attitude toward reading, comprehension, and overall reading success. Word recognition makes reading effortless, and reading becomes enjoyable. When reading is enjoyable, the reader will read more and, thereby, increase his or her word-recognition skills
(Beck & Juel, 1995; Juel, 1991). Inadequate word recognition has a negative effect on
fluency and comprehension. The reader who does not attain automaticity in word
recognition is said to be "glued" to the print (Chall, 1983, p. 17). The reader must focus
all of his or her attention on sounding out words and is diverted away from figuring
out the meaning (Adams, 1990; Liberman & Liberman, 1990). Evidence suggests that
word-recognition speed in first graders is predictive of later reading comprehension
success (Beck & Juel, 1995; Juel, 1991).

The skilled reader uses contextual clues to predict unfamiliar words, but evidence
suggests that context is not the primary strategy used for word recognition (Juel, 1991;
Share & Stanovich, 1995). First, the text may prove to be unreliable in yielding clues
for accurate prediction. In most cases, context enables the reader to predict accurately
only one of four words (Gough & Hillinger, 1980), and the content words that carry
meaning are predictable only 10% of the time (Gough, 1983). Therefore, context is not
useful when it is needed (Share & Stanovich, 1995). Second, eye-movement research
shows that the eyes fixate on a majority of words in a text and do not skip over long
words as a heavy reliance on context as a means for predicting words would suggest.
Only the short, predictable words are skipped. The duration of fixation depends on the
length, frequency, and predictability of the word as the reader processes its component

letters (Rayner & Pollatsek, 1986). The use of context facilitates the recognition of an unfamiliar word only when it is coupled with the reader's orthographic knowledge. When context clues are combined with knowledge of sound–symbol correspondences, the skilled reader should be able to identify words that are part of his or her listening vocabulary (Adams, 1990; Perfetti, 1985).

The skilled reader monitors his or her decoding using syntactic (i.e., sentence structure) and semantic (i.e., word meaning) cues (Tunmer, Herriman, & Nesdale, 1988). With the use of such cues and sound–symbol correspondences, the reader is able to detect and self-correct a misread word in a sentence. This combination of knowledge used in detecting and self-correcting errors also builds sound–symbol correspondences and word recognition as the reader deals with unfamiliar words. It is a particularly beneficial combination with the reader's discovery of more complex sound–symbol relationships.

The reader does not have to learn all of the possible sound–symbol correspondences before learning about and using structural analysis, and word recognition does not occur only after the reader has learned everything about the letter–sound and structural patterns of the language. The reader's use of a given strategy depends on his or her available knowledge about language patterns, the length and complexity of the words, the frequency of encounters with the words, and/or the availability of useful contextual clues. These decoding strategies provide the reader a means of translating the printed word into spoken language. Decoding is not an end in itself but is a necessary step in getting to the heart of reading: comprehending meaning.

Dyslexic Readers' Difficulty with Decoding

There is considerable agreement that at-risk and dyslexic readers are unable to decode and recognize words accurately and fluently (Adams & Bruck, 1993; Lyon, Shaywitz, & Shaywitz, 2003; Perfetti, 1985; Share & Stanovich, 1995; Stanovich, 1986). Dyslexia stems from a core deficit in phonological processing, not a deficit in visual processing (Adams, 1990; Goswami & Bryant, 1990; Stanovich, 1991; Vellutino, 1980). This difficulty with phonological processing is not a developmental delay. It is a deficit that interferes with reading and spelling development (Foorman, Francis, Shaywitz, Shaywitz, & Fletcher, 1997). Students who have difficulty learning to read have difficulty discovering that spoken words are made up of units of sounds (i.e., phonemic awareness) that relate to letters (Adams, 1990; Adams & Bruck, 1995; Brady & Moats, 1997; Brady & Shankweiler, 1991; Gough, Ehri, & Treiman, 1992; Rack, Hulme, Snowling, & Wightman, 1994). Without this realization, students fail to learn the alphabetic principle and how to decode words accurately. Subsequently, they fail to thrive in reading (Stanovich, 1986). Early intervention is essential.

Evidence suggests that in addition to deficits in phonological processing, students may also exhibit a deficit in naming speed, which can interfere with the development of automatic decoding and fluent text reading (Wolf, 1997; Wolf & Obregón, 1992; Wolf & Bowers, 1999, 2000; see also Chapters 4 and 5). This deficit and intervention strategies are discussed later in this chapter.

Teaching Decoding Skills

The English language, a language of approximately 44 speech sounds and 26 letters, operates on an alphabetic principle or code. The speech sounds are represented in print by letters. About 75% of the school population will deduce the alphabetic principle regardless of how they are taught (Liberman & Liberman, 1990). The other 25% of students, including dyslexic students, will not intuit this principle and will require ex-

plicit, systematic, and sequential instruction. Failure to receive such instruction can intensify these students' reading difficulties (Brady & Moats, 1997; Felton, 1993; Foorman, Francis, Beeler, Winikates, & Fletcher, 1997). The beneficial effects of explicit teaching of the alphabetic principle are not limited to students who have difficulty with reading. There is evidence that all students benefit from such instruction (Adams & Bruck, 1995; Beck & Juel, 1995; Brady & Moats, 1997; Chall, 1996; Joshi, Dahlgren, & Boulware-Gooden, 2002; Liberman & Liberman, 1990; NICHD, 2000).

Decoding requires knowledge of orthographic patterns of the language that is based on solid phonological processing. Key elements of decoding instruction include the following:

- Phonological awareness training, especially in phonemic awareness

- Instant letter-recognition training

- Introduction of sound–symbol correspondences

- Introduction of the six orthographic types of syllables

- Introduction of common syllable-division patterns

- Introduction of morphemes—prefixes, suffixes, roots, and combining forms

- Training in recognizing and understanding word origins (see Chapter 6)

- Teaching of a procedure for learning to read **irregular words**

- Instruction in the orthographic patterns for encoding (spelling)

- Practice for accuracy and fluency

The teaching of decoding is not an incidental part of reading instruction. It is not done through the use of worksheets or rote learning. Successful decoding instruction is a vital part of reading instruction that engages students in active, reflective, inductive learning. Students learn to be analytic and scientific in their approach to learning the structure of the language. The intensity of instruction will depend on the instructional needs of the students.

MULTISENSORY STRUCTURED INSTRUCTION

Decoding instruction requires a multisensory structured presentation within a language content. The characteristics of this instruction are outlined in Chapter 2 of this book. The introduction of decoding concepts and the discussion of instruction presented in this chapter exemplify these characteristics. The National Reading Panel (NRP; NICHD, 2000) emphasized that any decoding or phonics instruction should be incorporated with other reading instruction such as vocabulary and reading comprehension instruction to create a comprehensive reading program.

Students must apprehend phonemes and instantly recognize letters (see Chapters 4 and 5) before they are ready for careful instruction in sound–symbol correspondences and structural analysis. For the purpose of introducing the concepts necessary for successful decoding, this chapter presents concepts in concentrated form. It is important, however, to remember that these concepts must be introduced to students according to a systematic order of presentation. A systematic, sequential order of presentation ensures that all important concepts are taught and maximizes the learning of these concepts. To be successful with sound–symbol correspondences, students must understand

the concepts of vowels and consonants and the blending of consonant and vowel sounds. Success with structural analysis is dependent on students' knowledge of syllables, syllable-division patterns, prefixes, suffixes, and roots. Information about structural analysis can be introduced when students can read simple words with affixes.

The patterns and structure of the language are taught through a logically ordered presentation that begins with the most basic concepts and progresses to more difficult concepts, with the new learning building on prior knowledge. A systematic order of presentation begins with the establishment of phonemic segmentation and letter recognition. It proceeds to the introduction of the concepts of vowel and consonant sounds (i.e., vowel sounds are open; consonant sounds are blocked or partially blocked by the tongue, teeth, or lips). At first, three or four high-frequency consonants with predictable sounds (see Table 9.1) along with a short vowel (see Table 9.2) are taught. The concept of blending letter sounds together to form words is introduced, and students begin to read words. Students are taught that a vowel in a syllable that ends in at least one consonant (i.e., closed syllable) is short. After a few more consonants and short vowels are taught, one-syllable words in word lists and sentences are presented for students to read. Common suffixes such as -s or -ing are introduced. One-syllable words and derivatives are presented for practice. Once students understand closed syl-

Table 9.1. Consonants and consonant clusters

Consonants with one frequent, predictable sound			
b = /b/ (*bat*)	j = /j/ (*jam*)	**p** = /p/ (*pig*)	w = /w/ (*wagon*)
d = /d/ (*dog*)	k = /k/ (*kite*)	r = /r/ (*rabbit*)	z = /z/ (*zipper*)
f = /f/ (*fish*)	**l** = /l/ (*leaf*)	**t** = /t/ (*table*)	
h = /h/ (*house*)	**m** = /m/ (*mitten*)	v = /v/ (*valentine*)	

Consonants with more than one sound

c = /k/ (*kite*)—before *a, o, u,* or any consonant
/s/ (*city*)—before *e, i,* or *y*

g = /g/ (*goat*)—before *a, o, u,* or any consonant
/j/ (*gem*)—before *e, i,* or *y*

n = /n/ (*nest*)
/ng/ (*sink or finger*)—before any letter that says /k/ or /g/

s = /s/ (*sock*)
/z/ (*pansy*)

x = /z/ (*xylophone*)—in initial position*
/ks/ (*excite, box*)—in medial or final position*

Consonant digraphs with one frequent sound

ck = /k/ (*truck*)
ng = /ng/ (*king*)

sh = /sh/ (*ship*)
wh = /hw/** (*whistle*)

Consonant digraphs with more than one sound

ch = /ch/ (*chair*)
/k/ (*school*)—in words of Greek origin
/sh/ (*chef*)—in words of French origin

th = /th/ (*thimble*)
/th/ (*mother*)

Trigraphs with one sound

dge = /j/ (*badge*)

tch = /ch/ (*witch*)

Special situations

y = /y/ in initial or medial position*
as a consonant

qu = /kw/ (*queen*)—*q* is always followed by *u*

The boldface letters are frequently used consonants that are good to use when beginning to introduce sound–symbol correspondences. When these frequent consonants are combined with short *a, i,* and *o,* many simple words can be presented for reading.

*Initial refers to the first position of a syllable or word; *final* refers to the last position of a syllable or word; and *medial* refers to any position between the first and last positions of a syllable or word.

**This exaggerated pronunciation aids in establishing a strong orthographic memory of words that contain *wh.*

Table 9.2.   Vowels and vowel pairs

Short vowels in closed syllables

a = /ă/ (*apple*)	**i** = /ĭ/ (*it*)	u = /ŭ/ (*up*)
e = /ě/ (*echo*)	**o** = /ŏ/ (*octopus*)	

Long vowels in open, accented syllables

a = /ā/ (*apron*)	i = /ī/ (*iris*)	u = /ŭ/ (*unicorn*)
e = /ē/ (*equal*)	o = /ō/(*open*)	y = /ī/ (*fly*)

Vowels in open, unaccented syllables

a = /ŭ/ (*alike*)	i = /ĭ/ (*divide*)	y = /ē/ (*penny*)

Long vowels in vowel-consonant-e syllables

a-consonant-*e* = /ā/ (*cake*)	*i*-consonant-*e* = /ī/ (*five*)	*u*-consonant-*e* = /ū/ (*cube*)
e-consonant-*e* = /ē/ (*athlete*)	*o*-consonant-*e* = /ō/ (*rope*)	*y*-consonant-*e* = /ī/ (*type*)

Vowels in vowel-r syllables

ar = /âr/ (*star*)—accented	or = /ôr/ (*fork*)—accented
/er/ (*dollar*)—unaccented	/er/ (*world*)—after *w*
er = /êr/ (*fern*)	/er/ (*doctor*)—unaccented
ir = /êr/ (*bird*)	ur = /êr/ (*turtle*)

Vowel pairs with one frequent sound

ai = /ā/ (*sail*)	ei = /ē/ (*ceiling*)	oe = /ō/(*toe*)
au = /au/ (*August*)	eu = /ū/ (*Europe*)	oi = /oi/ (*boil*)
aw = /au/ (*saw*)	ew = /ū/ (*few*)	oy = /oi/ (*toy*)
ay = /ā/ (*play*)	ey = /ē/ (*monkey*)	ue = /ū/ (*rescue*)
ee = /ē/ (*feet*)	ie = /ē/ (*chief*)	

Vowel pairs with more than one frequent sound

ea = /ē/ (*eat*)	ou = /ou/ (*out*)	ow = /ou/ (*cow*)
/ě/ (*head*)	/o͞o/ (*soup*)	/ō/ (*snow*)
oo = /o͞o/ (*food*)		
/o͝o/ (*book*)		

Special situations

a = /ŏ/ (*watch*)—after *w*	eigh = /ā/ (*eight*)	o = /ŭ/ (*onion*)
a = /au/ (*ball*)—before *l*	igh = /ī/ (*light*)	

The boldface letters are good concepts and letters for beginning reading instruction.

lables, they are taught that two-syllable words with two medial consonants are divided between the consonants (e.g., VC|CV syllable-division pattern as in *mascot* or *napkin*), and, subsequently, one- and two-syllable words and derivatives are presented for practice. After letter clusters such as -*ck* and *sh* along with additional syllable types such as open, consonant-*le,* and vowel-consonant-*e* syllables are taught, many words of various lengths can be read. The introduction of concepts—more letters, letter clusters, syllable types, syllable-division patterns, suffixes, stems, and prefixes—continues, progressing systematically from simple to complex, with each concept building on those previously mastered. As each concept is introduced, it is practiced to mastery, first through **homogeneous practice** and then in **heterogeneous practice**. (See Appendix B at the end of this book for a listing of curricula with systematic orders of presentation.)

SOUND–SYMBOL CORRESPONDENCES

Generalizations about sound–symbol correspondences are introduced to provide students with a direct link between the printed word and the spoken word and to guide students' attention to the sound-spelling patterns of words. These generalizations are

not learned through rote memorization but rather through frequent practice both in and out of context. Once patterns are established, the generalizations are dispensable (Adams, 1990).

Solid Foundation for Sound–Symbol Correspondences

Awareness of the speech sounds of language and awareness of print provide the foundation for sound–symbol correspondences. Phonological awareness involves a sensitivity to the sound structure of language, such as rhyming, counting words in sentences, counting syllables in words, and identifying specific sounds in a word. The key component of phonological awareness is the ability to perceive the constituent sounds of a word (i.e., phonemic awareness) (Adams, 1990; Ball & Blachman, 1988; Liberman, 1987; Lundberg, Frost, & Petersen, 1988; Yopp, 1992). Print awareness involves sensitivity to the conventions of the printed page, such as top to bottom, left to right, punctuation, indentations, spaces between words, and the awareness that words consist of letters. The key component of print awareness is the ability to instantly recognize letters (Adams, 1990).

Instant Letter Recognition

A beginning reader's instant recognition of letters is a strong predictor of reading success. Knowledge of the names of the letters can facilitate the learning of the letter sounds as many sounds are embedded in the letter names (e.g., students can hear the /m/ sound in the name of the letter *m*) (Adams, 1990; Gough & Hillinger, 1980). All letters have four properties: name, sound, shape, and feel (i.e., the sensation of muscle movements while writing the letter or while producing the sound). The name is the only property that does not change. The name of the letter is an anchor to which the reader can attach the other properties of the letter. Automatic letter recognition allows the reader to see words as groups of letters instead of as individual letters that must be identified (Adams, 1990). Activities to reinforce letter recognition are easily incorporated into the classroom routine:

- The teacher writes a letter on the board. All students whose names begin with that letter line up.

- The teacher writes a letter on the board and calls on a student, who must name the letter before lining up.

- The teacher writes a letter on the board and calls on a student, who must name the target letter and the letter that comes after (or before) the target letter before lining up.

See Chapter 5 for other suggestions for activities that develop letter recognition.

Phonemic Awareness

A beginning reader's ability to segment a word into its phonemes (i.e., phoneme segmentation) is one of the best predictors of reading success. A phoneme is the smallest unit of speech that makes a difference in the utterance of a word. Thus, the reader's awareness of individual sounds in a word increases his or her understanding of the role of the individual letters in words and how the written letters can be mapped onto the sounds. Without these insights, the reader will not successfully learn the code of the language (Adams, 1990; Ball & Blachman, 1988; see also Chapter 3). Because of the impor-

tance of phonemic awareness, activities for reinforcing phonemic awareness should be ongoing. They are easily incorporated into the classroom routine:

- The teacher guesses what was for lunch. Students give the teacher rhyming clues so that the teacher can guess what students ate for lunch (e.g., "I had a mapple, a mandwich, and a mookie;" Rubin & Eberhardt, 1996).

- The teacher says a sound. All students whose names begin (or end) with the sound take their place in line (Rubin & Eberhardt, 1996).

- The teacher takes the class roll using blending. The teacher calls out the names slowly. Students guess the name, and the named student indicates his or her presence.

- The teacher says a word with three or four phonemes (e.g., *lap, sit, run, top, dog, jump, stop*). The teacher calls on a student to unblend the word (i.e., say the word slowly) before lining up.

- To hone their attention, students establish a word of the week. The teacher gains students' attention by saying the word. Students respond by unblending the word.

- After the teacher reads a book, students apply their phonological awareness skills to play with words from the book (Rubin & Eberhardt, 1996; Yopp, 1995). For example, after reading *The Wind Blew* (Hutchins, 1974), students discover that various items were blown into the air. Students can play with the names of the items. They say words that rhyme with *wig, hat,* and *flag*. They count the syllables in *balloon, letters, umbrella,* and *newspapers*. They segment the words *kite, shirt,* and *scarf* into their component sounds.

See Chapter 3 for more suggestions of activities to develop phonological awareness.

Orthographic Patterns

As students acquire basic sound–symbol correspondences, they build their knowledge of orthographic patterns in the language and create a scaffold for refining and expanding their knowledge of the spelling-sound system (Share & Stanovich, 1995). Some letters have one frequent sound or a one-to-one correspondence with a sound (e.g., letters such as *d, m, p,* and *v* have one sound). Two adjacent letters in a syllable that represent one speech sound are called digraphs. Digraphs that consist of two adjacent consonants are called consonant **digraphs** (e.g., *sh, ng, ck, th*); digraphs that consist of two adjacent vowels are called vowel digraphs (e.g., *ai, ea, ee, oa*). Some digraphs have one frequent sound (e.g., *sh* as in *ship, ng* as in *king, ck* as in *truck, oa* as in *boat*). Other digraphs have several sounds (e.g., *th* as in *thimble* and *mother; ea* as in *each, head,* and *steak*). Three adjacent letters in a syllable that represent one speech sound are called **trigraphs** (e.g., *tch, dge*). **Quadrigraphs** consist of four adjacent letters in a syllable that represent one speech sound (e.g., *eigh*). Two adjacent vowels whose sounds blend together are called diphthongs (e.g., *ou, ow, oi, oy*). Considerable attention to **orthography** is needed for readers to deal with letters that have more than one possible sound. The pronunciation of such a letter may depend on its occurrence with other letters (e.g., *c* is pronounced as /k/ before *a, o, u,* or any consonant but as /s/ before *e, i,* or *y*) and/or its position in a word (e.g., *y* is a consonant in initial position pronounced as /y/ but is a vowel in final position pronounced as /ī/ or /ē/). Knowing these patterns of language helps the reader choose the best pronunciation of a letter with more than one possible sound. In addition, there are constraints to the orthography of English. Some

letters and letter clusters may not occur in certain positions in a word (e.g., English base words do not end in *j* or *v*). Some letters may or may not occur adjacent to certain letters (e.g., *q* is almost always followed by *u; scr* occurs within a syllable, but *skr* does not). Finally, some letters never or rarely double (e.g., *h, j, k, v, w, x, y*) (Moats, 1995; Perfetti, 1985). Careful, reflective study of orthography for reading reinforces information readers need for spelling.

Multisensory Letter Introduction

Sound–symbol correspondences are established via thorough instruction of letters and letter clusters. The three major learning modalities or pathways—auditory, visual, and kinesthetic—are engaged in the introduction of a letter or letter cluster. Students link the look of a letter (visual) with its sound (auditory) and its feel (kinesthetic) to form the letter sound and written shape. The information received through more than one sensory pathway increases the certainty of learning and retrieval. The grouping of the modalities strengthens the weaker pathway(s) as the strongest pathway assumes the lead in learning. The following terms and procedures are helpful in understanding multisensory instruction.

Kinesthetic Awareness

Kinesthetic awareness involves sensitivity to muscle movement. Kinesthetic information heightens students' memory and ability to discriminate speech sounds. Students' awareness of the position of the mouth, tongue, teeth, or lips and the activity of the vocal cords during the production of a sound assists the definitive learning of speech sounds. Kinesthetic information also heightens students' visual memory and ability to discriminate letter shapes. Students' awareness of how a letter feels when written in the air (i.e., sky writing) or on paper connects kinesthetic and visual information so that the letter shapes can be thoroughly learned.

Sounds

The exact individual sounds of letters (i.e., phonemes) are difficult to isolate. Speech sounds do not occur as single units in running speech. In spoken language, sounds in a word are blended together into units with other sounds so that when the speaker says a word, it does not sound as though he or she is spelling the word out loud sound by sound (e.g., *bag* is not pronounced /b/-/ă/-/g/ but rather /bă/-/g/) (Liberman, 1987). The blending of speech sounds into units is termed coarticulation. For students to learn the sound–symbol correspondences, it is necessary for them to be able to isolate the sounds as close approximations of the actual sounds that, in running speech, will be coarticulated with other sounds. The following terminology helps build the teacher's understanding of sound–symbol relationships:

- A *voiced speech* sound is a sound in which the vocal cords vibrate during its production.

- An *unvoiced speech* sound is a sound in which the vocal cords do not vibrate during its production.

- A *vowel sound* is an open speech sound, produced by the easy passage of air through a relatively open vocal tract. It is unblocked by the tongue, teeth, or lips and is

voiced. (The sound /h/ opens the mouth, but because it is not voiced, it is a consonant sound.)

- A *consonant sound* is a sound that is blocked (e.g., /l/, /s/, /m/) or partially blocked (e.g., /p/, /b/) by the tongue, teeth, or lips and may be voiced (e.g., /m/, /l/, /r/) or unvoiced (e.g., /t/, /s/, /k/).

    Note: For decoding instruction, the terms *blocked* and *partially blocked* refer to the kinesthetic feel and visual display of the position of the tongue, teeth, or lips during the production of sounds in isolation. *Blocked* refers to the steady position of the tongue, teeth, or lips during the entire production of a sound (e.g., the lips stay together in a steady position as /m/ is pronounced). *Partially blocked* refers to a released position of the tongue or lips during production (e.g., the tongue is released from the ridge behind the teeth as /t/ is pronounced). These terms are used in decoding instruction because students can easily and clearly feel or see the characteristics that distinguish consonant sounds from vowel sounds.

Table 9.3. Voiced and unvoiced pairs

Unvoiced	Voiced
/p/	/b/
/t/	/d/
/k/	/g/
/f/	/v/
/s/	/z/
/th/	/th/
/ch/	/j/
/sh/	/zh/

- *Voiced and unvoiced pairs* (see Table 9.3) are sounds with the same visual display (i.e., the same position of the tongue, teeth, and lips) and kinesthetic feel, but the vocal cords vibrate during the production of one (voiced) and not the other (unvoiced).

- A *continuant speech sound* is prolonged in its production (e.g., /m/, /s/, /f/).

- A *stop consonant* is obstructed at its **place of articulation** and not prolonged in its production (e.g., /g/, /p/, /t/, /k/). These sounds must be clipped to prevent the addition of /ŭh/ at the end of the sound (e.g., /p/ not /pŭh/). *Note:* The terms *continuant* and *stop consonant* are linguistic terms. In decoding instruction, the term *continuant consonant* is synonymous with *blocked consonant*. The term *stop consonant* is synonymous with *partially blocked*.

- A *fricative* is produced by forcing air from the mouth through a narrow opening (e.g., /f/, /v/, /sh/, /s/, /z/).

- A nasal sound is produced by forcing air out through the nose (e.g., /n/, /m/, /ng/).

Use of Key Words

Key words serve as a memory device to unlock letter sounds and as a trigger for rapid elicitation of letter sounds. A key word illustrates the sound of a letter and provides a connection of that sound to a written symbol (Cox, 1992; Gillingham & Stillman, 1997). A letter–sound deck can be used to systematically review key words and sounds. When students are shown a letter card, they name the letter, say a key word and produce the sound (e.g., when shown a card with the letter *a*, students respond, "*a, apple,* /ă/"). Pictures of the key words may be added to the letter cards.

Coding

The use of diacritical markings for vowels and other code marks provides students with additional visual and kinesthetic information to reinforce the letter sounds. Short vowels are coded with a **breve** (˘). Long vowels are coded with a **macron** (¯). The obscure *a*, found in the word *along* and pronounced /ŭ /, is coded with a dot: *a·* . Vowel digraphs

(e.g., *ai, ea, ee, oa*), consonant digraphs (e.g., *ch, ng, sh*), and trigraphs (e.g., *tch, dge*) that represent one speech sound are underlined. Vowel diphthongs that represent two speech sounds that are blended together are coded with an arc:

$$ou \quad ow \quad oi \quad oy$$

Silent letters are crossed out:

$$a\cancel{i} \text{ or } \cancel{t}ch$$

Additional codes are introduced later in this chapter.

Sky Writing

Sky writing involves the engagement of the large "learning" muscles of the upper arm and shoulder. The movement of these muscles produces a strong neurological imprint of letter shapes (Waites & Cox, 1976). For sky writing, the arm of the writing hand is fully extended and tensed. Students use the whole writing arm, with fingers extended, to write large letters in the air, with a large model in front of them, to develop muscle memory. The nonwriting hand is placed on the upper arm or shoulder of the writing arm to create tension and help students feel the individual strokes more discernibly.

Guided Discovery Teaching

The instructional approach called **guided discovery teaching** is effective in ensuring that students learn sound–symbol correspondences and other patterns of language. The word *education* comes from the Latin word *educere,* which means *to lead out.* Guided discovery teaching uses the Socratic method of asking questions to lead students to discover new information. When students make a discovery, they understand and connect the new learning to prior knowledge.

Students, for example, are led to discover the difference between vowel and consonant sounds. The teacher asks students to repeat each of the following sounds one at a time while looking in a mirror: /ă/, /ĕ/, /ĭ/, /ŏ/, /ŭ/. The teacher asks, "What do you feel happening to your mouth as each sound is pronounced?" (The mouth is open.) The teacher asks students to say the sounds again while placing their fingers on the vocal cords. The teacher asks, "What do you feel?" (The vocal cords are activated, or the throat vibrates.) The teacher explains that these sounds are vowel sounds. Students verbalize what they have learned about vowel sounds through discovery: Vowel sounds are open and voiced (make the throat vibrate).

The teacher can also use guided discovery teaching to help students make discoveries about consonant sounds. When students are asked to repeat consonant sounds such as /l/, /s/, /m/, /b/, and /p/ while looking in a mirror, they discover that these sounds are blocked (/l/, /s/, /m/) or partially blocked (/b/, /p/) by the tongue, teeth, or lips. Consonant sounds can be voiced or unvoiced. Students verbalize what they have learned about consonant sounds through discovery: "Consonant sounds are blocked or partially blocked by the tongue, teeth, or lips. They may be voiced or unvoiced."

Multisensory Procedure for Introducing a Letter or Letter Cluster

Letter–sound relationships are introduced through discovery teaching and a multisensory structured procedure (Cox, 1992; Gillingham & Stillman, 1997):

1. The teacher reads five or six **discovery words** that contain the new letter sound.

2. Students repeat each word while looking in a mirror and listening for the sound that is the same in all of the words.

3. While looking in the mirror, students repeat the sound and discover the position of the mouth. Is it opened or is it blocked or partially blocked by the tongue, teeth, or lips?

4. While placing their fingers on their vocal cords, students repeat the sound to discover whether the sound is voiced (i.e., the vocal cords vibrate) or unvoiced (i.e., there is no vibration).

5. Students determine whether the new sound is a vowel or a consonant sound. Vowel sounds are open and voiced. Consonant sounds are blocked or partially blocked by the tongue, teeth, or lips. They may be voiced or unvoiced.

6. Students guess the key word for the new sound by listening to a riddle or by feeling an object obscured in a container. The key word holds the new sound in memory.

7. The teacher writes the discovery words on the board.

8. Students determine the letter that is the same in all of the words and that represents the new sound.

9. The teacher shows a card with the new letter on it.

10. Students name the letter, say the key word, and give the sound.

11. The teacher names the new letter just before writing a large model of the letter on the board.

12. The teacher names the letter and then demonstrates sky writing. The teacher describes the letter strokes while sky writing the letter.

13. Students stand and sky write, naming the letter before writing.

14. The teacher distributes papers with a large model of the new letter.

15. Students trace the model three times with the pointer finger of the writing hand and three times with a pencil. Students name the letter each time before writing.

16. Students turn the model over, and the teacher dictates the name of the letter.

17. Students repeat the letter name and write the letter.

18. The teacher shows the letter card again as students name the letter, say the key word, and produce the sound.

During the various steps in this procedure, the four properties of the letter—name, sound, shape, and feel—are being connected through the use of the auditory, visual, and kinesthetic modalities. This multisensory teaching reinforces the discovery information and builds associations in memory.

Blending

Once students have identified the letter–sound relationships of a word, they must meld the sounds to produce a word. The blending of the sounds in a word is a critical component of learning sound–symbol correspondences. Fluid blending of letter sounds aids students in producing recognizable words. Before students begin reading words,

they should have opportunities to blend sounds together orally with the use of manipulatives (e.g., blocks, buttons, math counters, pennies).

Because of the effects of coarticulation on sounds, letter-by-letter blending in reading does not always produce a recognizable word. Several different strategies, best presented one-to-one or in small groups, are used to promote the skill of blending when reading words. When introducing any of the blending activities for reading, it is desirable to begin blending words that have continuant initial sounds (e.g., /f/, /l/, /m/, /n/, /s/). Continuant sounds are easier to blend than the stop consonant sounds (e.g., /d/, /p/, /k/). The continuant sounds allow students to slide into the vowel sound. Blending with initial stop consonants is introduced after students have demonstrated facility with the blending of continuant initial sounds.

Say it Slowly

Using one set of letter cards or lettered tiles, the teacher sets out *m, e,* and *t.* The teacher demonstrates how to say the word *met* slowly by blending the sounds together in units—by saying /m/, then /mĕ/, then /mĕt/, not by saying /m/-/ĕ/-/t/ (Beck & Juel, 1995).

Say it Faster, Move it Closer

Using one set of letter cards or lettered tiles, the teacher sets out *s* and, separated by a wide space, *a.* The teacher points to the first letter. Students say /s/ and hold it until the teacher points to the second letter and students produce /ă/. The letters are moved closer together and the procedure is repeated, with students blending the sounds together faster. The letters are moved closer together and sounds are produced together faster until students can produce the two sounds as a single unit, /să/. A final consonant is added and blended with the unit to produce a word (e.g., *sat, sad, sap;* Blachman, 1987; Englemann, 1969).

Onsets and Rimes

Using letter cards or lettered tiles, the teacher sets out *a* and *t.* Students blend the letter sounds to produce /ăt/. This /ăt/ unit is the rime, the combination of the vowel and the consonant(s) that comes after it in a syllable. The teacher places the letter m before the rime. This letter is the onset, the consonant(s) of a syllable before the vowel. Students blend /m/ and /ă/ to produce/măt/. The teacher changes the onset to create new words that students blend and read (e.g., *sat, rat, fat, bat*). Other rimes for practice include the following: *in, it, an, am, op, ang, ing,* and *ink* (Adams, 1990; Goswami & Bryant, 1990).

Playing with Sounds

Using one set of letter cards or lettered tiles, the teacher sets out *a* and *t.* The student blends the letter sounds to produce /ăt/. The teacher asks the student to change /ăt/ to /săt/. The student adds the card or tile with *s* and reads /săt/. The teacher asks the student to read new words by changing or adding new letter sounds (e.g., change *sat* to *mat, mat* to *map, map* to *mop, mop* to *top, top* to *stop*) (Beck & Juel, 1995; Blachman, 1987; Blachman, Ball, Black, & Tangel, 2000; Slingerland, 1971).

Tapping Out

The teacher lays out or displays letter cards or lettered tiles to form a word such as *mat.* Using one hand, students quickly tap the pointer finger to the thumb and say the sound of the first letter, /m/. In quick succession, they tap the middle finger to the

thumb and say the sound of the second letter, /ă/. Finally, they tap the ring finger to the thumb and say the sound of the final letter, /t/. When all of the letter sounds have been tapped out, students say the word as they drag the thumb across their fingers, beginning with the index finger (Wilson, 1996).

Tapping and Sweeping

The teacher lays out letter cards or lettered tiles to form a word such as *mat*. Each student takes a turn. He or she makes a fist and taps under the *m* as he or she says the sound /m/. Next, he or she taps under the *a* and says /ă/. Finally, he or she taps under the *t* and says /t/. After the student has said each sound, he or she sweeps a fist under the letters and says the word (Greene & Enfield, 1985).

Strategies for Accuracy

Accurate reading of words is key to associating pronunciations with correct orthographic patterns as well as to facilitating comprehension. The teacher can use the following strategies to guide a student to the accurate decoding of a word or to correct a mistake when he or she is reading:

- *Misreading or skipping letters:* If a student misreads a letter in a word (e.g., *lid* for *lip*) or skips a letter in a word (e.g., *pat* for *past*), then the teacher directs the student to name the letters in the word. The naming of the letters focuses the student's attention on the letters and also strengthens the orthographic identity of the word.

- *Misreading a word:* If a student misreads a word (e.g., *pane* for *plant*), the teacher directs the student to use a backing-up procedure. The student identifies the syllable type, determines the vowel sound (short or long), and codes the vowel accordingly (i.e., marks it with a breve or a macron). The student produces the appropriate vowel sound and blends it with the consonant sound immediately after the vowel. He or she blends this unit with any remaining consonant sounds after the vowel, adding sounds one at a time. The reader then blends the vowel and all of the consonant sounds after the vowel with the consonant sound immediately before the vowel. Any remaining consonants that precede the vowel are blended on one at a time. The backing-up procedure with the word *plant* looks like this:

Step 1: The student codes *a* with a breve and says /ă/	plănt
Step 2: The student blends /ă/ with /n/.	plănt
Step 3: The student blends /ăn/ with /t/.	plănt
Step 4: The student blends /l/ with /ănt/.	plănt
Step 5: The student blends whole word.	plănt

STRUCTURAL ANALYSIS

Knowledge of sound–symbol correspondences enables a reader to successfully read one-syllable base words. Once the reader has established a few sound–symbol correspondences and can blend them together successfully to form words, information about structural analysis is taught concurrently with new sound–symbol correspondences. Structural analysis of the syllabic and morphemic segments of language facili-

tates the recognition of longer words. *Syllables* are speech units of language that contain one vowel sound and can be represented in written language as words (e.g., *cat, mop, sad*) or parts of words (e.g., *mu, hin, ter*) with a single vowel or pair of vowels denoting the vowel sound. When a syllable is part of a word, it does not necessarily carry meaning (e.g., *mu* in *museum* or *music*). Awareness of syllables helps the reader perceive the natural divisions of words to aid recognition. Six types of syllables are represented in written English (e.g., a closed syllable ends in at least one consonant; an open syllable ends in one vowel). (The types of syllables are discussed in detail later in this chapter.) Awareness of the syllable types gives the reader a way to determine how to pronounce the vowel sound in a syllable (e.g., the vowel in a closed syllable is short; the vowel in an open, accented syllable is long). Morphemes are meaning-carrying units of written language (Moats, 1994) such as base words (e.g., *cat, number, salamander*), prefixes (e.g., *un-, re-, mis-*), suffixes (e.g., *-ful, -ness, -ment*), combining forms (e.g., *bio, helio, polis*), and roots (e.g., *vis, struct, vert*). Awareness of morphemes aids recognition as well as word meaning.

Syllables

The teacher leads students to discover the concept of a syllable. Students are asked to repeat words of varying lengths (e.g., *mop, robot, fantastic*), one at time, while looking in a mirror and observing how many times their mouths open when each word is pronounced. They are asked to repeat each word again while cupping their jaws in their hands and feeling how many times their jaws drop or their mouths open. This visual information of seeing the mouth open and kinesthetic information of feeling the mouth open reinforces students' understanding of a syllable. The teacher explains that a syllable is a word or a part of a word made with one opening of the mouth.

Students are asked to think about which kind of letter sounds open the mouth. (Vowel sounds open the mouth.) The teacher explains that a syllable has one vowel sound. When students say a word, they determine the number of syllables by counting the number of times the mouth opens when pronouncing the word. This concept carries over when students look at a printed word; they determine the number of syllables in the word by counting the number of sounded vowels.

Auditory Awareness of Syllables

The following activities promote awareness of syllables in words:

- Syllable awareness begins early, with students identifying or generating short words (*farm, feet, fat, fork, food*) and long words (*February, firefighter, fisherman*). The chosen words might begin with a certain sound or pertain to a particular unit of study (*plants, animals, ocean, United States;* Rubin & Eberhardt, 1996).

- Students repeat words dictated by the teacher. They clap or tap out the number of syllables. The teacher starts with compound words (*playground, flashlight, cowboy*), then moves on to two-syllable words (*velvet, plastic, mascot*) and then on to words with three or more syllables (*fantastic, investment, invitation*).

- Students repeat words dictated by the teacher and move a counter (e.g., *block, button, penny*) for each syllable they hear. The use of the counters provides a visual and kinesthetic anchor for the sounds.

- Students repeat a word with two or more syllables dictated by the teacher. Students are asked to repeat the word again, omitting a designated syllable (Rosner, 1975), as illustrated in the following dialogue:

    Teacher: Say *transportation.*

    Students: Transportation

    Teacher: Say *transportation* without *trans.*

    Students: Portation

    Teacher: Say *transportation* without *tion.*

    Students: Transporta

This activity is effective in helping students with the correct pronunciations of words and becomes important reinforcement for reading and spelling words of more than one syllable.

Awareness of Accent

Correct placement of the accent or stress on a syllable supports students in the pronunciation and subsequent recognition of words. The mouth opens wider and the voice is louder and higher when the accented syllable is pronounced. The following activities promote awareness of accent:

- Students practice accent by saying the alphabet in pairs, accenting the first letter in the pair: "**A′** B, **C′** D, **E′** F, **G′** H, **I′** J."

- Students practice flexibility in accenting by saying the alphabet in pairs and shifting the accent to the second letter in the pair: "A **B′**, C **D′**, E **F′**, G **H′**, I **J′**." (See Chapter 5 for additional accenting activities.)

- Students practice accenting by saying two-syllable words, first placing an exaggerated accent on the first syllable and then placing it on the second. They then choose the correct accent placement (e.g., ***bas′***|*ket,* not *bas*|***ket′***; *can*|***teen′***, not ***can′***|*teen*). Some words have a noun form and a verb form, and the accent may fall on either syllable depending on the form of the word. The nouns are accented on the first syllable, and the verbs are accented on the second (e.g., ***con′***|*duct,* con|***duct′***; ***ob′***|*ject,* ob|***ject′***).

Six Types of Syllables

A complicating factor in learning the sound–symbol correspondences of written English is the instability of the vowels; they have more than one sound (e.g., short sound, long sound, unexpected sound when followed by *r* or in combination with another vowel). Knowledge of syllable types is an important organizing tool for decoding unknown words. Students can group letters into known syllable types that give clues about the sounds of the vowels. There are six orthographic types of syllables: **closed, open, vowel-consonant-*e*, vowel pair (vowel team), vowel-*r* (*r*-controlled),** and ***consonant-le*** (which is one kind of **final stable syllable**) (see Table 9.4; Steere, Peck, & Kahn, 1984). A high percentage of the more than 600,000 words of English can be categorized as one of these syllable types or as a composite of different syllable types.

Table 9.4. Six syllable types

Closed	Open	Vowel-consonant-*e*	Vowel pair (vowel team)	Vowel-*r*	Consonant-*le*[a]
it	hi	name	each	fern	-dle
bed	no	five	boil	burn	-fle
and	me	slope	sweet	thirst	-gle
lost	she	these	tray	star	-ple

[a]A consonant-*le* syllable is a kind of final stable syllable. Other final stable syllables include -*age,* -*sion,* -*tion,* and -*ture.*

Combining this knowledge of syllable types with known morphemes (e.g., suffixes, prefixes) simplifies the decoding of words with more than one syllable.

The closed syllable is the most frequent syllable type in English (Stanback, 1992). Students can be introduced to the closed syllable when they have learned the letter sounds that make up this pattern (i.e., three or four consonants and one short vowel). The remaining sound–symbol correspondences and syllable types are taught sequentially and cumulatively until all have been introduced, and then students practice them until all are mastered.

Guided discovery teaching techniques for the six syllable types are discussed in the sections that follow. The syllable types are introduced in the order that they might be presented to students. Students are led to discover the salient characteristics of each syllable type and the effect of the syllabic pattern on the vowel sound. The teacher pauses after the questions to solicit answers from students.

Closed Syllable

Teacher: [Writes discovery words on the board and directs students' attention to them] Look at these words: *hat, got, hip, mend.* How many vowels are in each word?

Students: There is only one vowel in each word.

Teacher: Look at the end of each word. How does each word end?

Students: Each word ends in at least one consonant.

Teacher: When the words are read, how are the vowels pronounced? [Reads the words]

Students: The vowels are pronounced with their short sounds.

Teacher: Each of these words ends in at least one consonant. What happens to the mouth when a consonant sound is made?

Students: The tongue, teeth, or lips close the sound.

Teacher: What would be a good name for a syllable that ends in a consonant?

Students: A good name is *closed syllable.*

Teacher: A closed syllable ends in at least one consonant. Therefore, these words are closed syllables. The vowel in a closed syllable is short; the vowel is coded with a breve that is written as (˘). [Writes a breve over the vowel in each word] The word *breve* comes from the Latin word *brevis,* which means *short.* What other words might come from the same Latin word?

Students: *Brief, brevity,* and *abbreviate* also come from the same Latin word.

Teacher: Let's review what you have discovered about closed syllables. A closed syllable ends in at least one consonant. The vowel is short; code it with a breve.

Note: When reviewing the concept of a closed syllable, or any kind of syllable, a cloze procedure can be used, with students filling in the most salient characteristics of the syllable type. Pausing for students' replies, the teacher says, "A closed syllable ends in at least one ——————— [consonant]. The vowel is ——————— [short]; code it with a ——————— [breve]."

Students must be sensitive to the fact that accent may affect the sound of a vowel in a syllable. Short vowel sounds in unaccented closed syllables, particularly before *m, n,* or *l,* may be distorted. The resultant vowel sound is schwa, which is denoted as /ə/ and is pronounced approximately as /ŭ/. This sound does not build a strong orthographic memory of the words because the schwa sound is not uniquely represented by one letter (Ehri, Wilce, & Taylor, 1987). Students should use an **exaggerated pronunciation**, or spelling-based pronunciation, when decoding these words (e.g., students pronounce *ribbon* as /rĭbŏn/). The teacher helps students match the printed word to a familiar word in running speech.

Short vowels before nasal sounds /m/, /n/, or /ng/ are nasalized and may seem distorted (e.g., *jam, ant, drank, thing*). Awareness of this possibility helps students better match the orthographic representation with a known word in their listening and speaking vocabularies. (See Ehri et al., 1987, for more discussion of short vowels.)

Open Syllable

Teacher: [Writes discovery words on the board and directs students' attention to them] Look at these words: *he, go, hi, me.* How many vowels are in each word?

Students: There is only one vowel in each word.

Teacher: Look at the end of each word. How does each word end?

Students: Each word ends in one vowel.

Teacher: Could these words be called closed syllables?

Students: No, closed syllables end in at least one consonant.

Teacher: When the words are read, how are the vowels pronounced? [Reads the words]

Students: The vowels are pronounced with their long sounds.

Teacher: Each of these words ends in one vowel. What position is the mouth in when a vowel sound is made?

Students: The mouth is open.

Teacher: What would be a good name for a syllable that ends in one vowel?

Students: A good name is *open syllable.*

Teacher: An open syllable ends in one vowel. The vowel in an open, accented syllable is long; the vowel is coded with a macron, which is written as (¯). [Writes

a macron on the board] The word *macron* comes from the Greek word *makros,* which means *long.* Let's review what you have discovered about an open syllable: An open syllable ends in one vowel. The vowel is long; code it with a macron.

Vowel-Consonant-e Syllable

Teacher: [Writes discovery words on the board] Look at these words: *cake, theme, five, rope, cube.* How many vowels are in each word?

Students: There are two vowels in each word.

Teacher: Look at the end of each word. How does each word end?

Students: They end with an *e.*

Teacher: What comes between the vowel and the final *e* in each word?

Students: One consonant.

Teacher: When the words are read, what happens to the final *e*? [Reads the words]

Students: The *e* in final position is silent.

Teacher: How are the vowels pronounced?

Students: They are pronounced with their long sounds.

Teacher: Each of these words ends in one vowel, one consonant, and a final *e.* What would be a good name for this kind of syllable?

Students: A good name is *vowel-consonant-e* syllable.

Teacher: The vowel in a vowel-consonant-*e* syllable is long. How is a long vowel coded?

Students: A macron shows a long vowel.

Teacher: The final *e* in this syllable is silent. How can the *e* be coded?

Students: The silent *e* can be crossed out: *e̸.*

Teacher: Let's review what you have discovered about the vowel-consonant-*e* syllable: A vowel-consonant-*e* syllable ends in one vowel, one consonant, and a final *e.* The *e* is silent; cross it out. The vowel is long; code it with a macron.

Vowel-Pair (Vowel-Team) Syllable

Teacher: [Writes discovery words on the board in two columns] Look at these words: *sea, feet, paint, boat, zoo, book, point, head.* How many vowels are in each word?

Students: There are two vowels in each word.

Teacher: Look at the end of each word. How does each word end?

Students: Some words end with at least one consonant.

Teacher: Are they closed syllables?

Students: No, a closed syllable has only one vowel.

Teacher: How about the other words?

Students: They end in a vowel.

Teacher: Are they open syllables?

Students: No, an open syllable has only one vowel.

Teacher: These words are called *vowel-pair syllables* or *vowel-team syllables* because
they have two vowels next to each other. Each vowel pair has a different letter combination and sound. Let's review what you have discovered about
the vowel-pair syllable: A vowel-pair (or vowel-team) syllable has two vowels next to each other.

Note: The generalization of "when two vowels go walking, the first one does the
talking" is only reliable about 45% of the time (Adams, 1990). The first four discovery
words (*see, feet, paint, boat*) in this activity follow this generalization; the last four discovery words (*zoo, book, point, head*) do not. For accuracy, each pair must be explicitly
taught.

Vowel-r (R-Controlled) Syllable   "Bossy R"

Teacher: [Writes discovery words on the board] Look at these words: *met, red, step,
hen, her.* How many vowels are in these words?

Students: There is one vowel in each word.

Teacher: Look at the end of each word. How does each word end?

Students: They end in at least one consonant.

Teacher: What kind of syllable ends in at least one consonant?

Students: A closed syllable ends in at least one consonant.

Teacher: Tell me about the vowel in a closed syllable.

Students: The vowel in a closed syllable is short; code it with a breve.

Teacher: Let's code and read these words. [Students direct the teacher to code each
word. Students read each word after it is coded. When students reach the
word *her,* they discover they cannot read the word with a short *e* sound.]
What happened when you tried to read the word *her*?

Students: The vowel is not short in the word *her.*

Teacher: Something unexpected happens to the vowel in this word. We expect the
vowel to be short because it is in a closed syllable. What letter do you see
after the vowel?

Students: The letter *r* is after the vowel.

Teacher: In the word *her,* the *r* comes after the vowel. What would be a good name
for this syllable?

Students: A good name would be *vowel-r syllable.*

Teacher: What happens to the vowel in a vowel-*r* syllable?

Students: The vowel makes an unexpected sound.

Teacher: When an *r* comes after a vowel, the vowel and the *r* are coded with an arc beneath them:

$$h\underset{\smile}{er}$$

The vowel-*r* combination in an accented syllable is also coded with a circumflex:

$$h\underset{\smile}{êr}$$

Let's review what you have discovered about a vowel-*r* syllable: A vowel-*r* syllable has an *r* after the vowel. The vowel makes an unexpected sound; in an accented syllable, code the vowel-*r* syllable with an arc and code the vowel with a circumflex.

Note: The vowel before an *r* in an accented syllable is coded with a **circumflex** (^). In an unaccented syllable, the vowel-*r* combination is coded with an arc and the vowel with a tilde (˜). The vowel-*r* combinations *er, ir,* and *ur* in an accented or unaccented syllable are pronounced /er/. The vowel-*r* combination *ar* in an accented syllable is pronounced /ar/ as in *star.* In an unaccented syllable, *ar* is pronounced /er/ as in *dollar.* The vowel-*r* combination *or* in an accented syllable is pronounced /or/ as in *fork.* In an unaccented syllable, *or* is pronounced /er/ as in *doctor.*

The terms *vowel-r syllable* and *r-controlled syllable* are used interchangeably. The term *vowel-r* focuses attention on the orthographic pattern, and the term *r-controlled* focuses attention on the influence of the *r* on the vowel.

Consonant-le (Final Stable) Syllable

Teacher: [Writes discovery words on the board] Look at these words: *ramble, uncle, candle, simple, table.* What looks the same in all of these words?

Students: They all have a consonant and *l* and *e* at the end.

Teacher: When these words are pronounced, how many syllables do you hear or feel? [Reads the words one at a time as students echo each word]

Students: There are two syllables.

Teacher: The second syllable in these words is spelled with a consonant, an *l,* and a final *e* and is called a consonant-*le* syllable. Tell me about the sound of the *e* in final position.

Students: It is silent.

Teacher: Because the final syllable in each of these words does not have a sounded vowel, these syllables are rule breakers. The final syllable is coded with a bracket: [. The accent falls on the syllable before the final syllable. Let's code the discovery words. [Students verbalize coding of the final syllable and the syllable before the consonant-*le* syllable. Students read words.] Let's review what you have discovered about a consonant-*le* syllable: A consonant-*le* syllable ends in a consonant, an *l,* and a final *e.* Code the syllable with a bracket, and accent the syllable before.

Note: The consonant-*le* syllable is one of several syllables that are referred to as *final stable syllables* (Cox, 1992). These syllables appear in the final position in words, and their pronunciations are fairly stable. Advanced final stable syllables, which include syllables such as *ture, age, sion,* and *tion,* are also coded with a bracket. Some of the advanced final stable syllables are also identified as suffixes. The advantage of treating these units as final stable syllables is twofold (Cox & Hutcheson, 1988): 1) They serve as an early, interim bridge to reading words of more than one syllable before the introduction of syllable division or advanced morphemes (e.g., **pic**′[*ture*, **man**′[*age*, **mo**′[*tion*); and 2) they provide predictable identification of the accent, which usually falls on the syllable before the final stable syllable (e.g., *va*|**ca**′[*tion, ex*|**plo**′[*sion*).

Morphology

Morphology comes from the Greek *morphe,* meaning *form,* and *ology,* meaning *study of.* Morphemes are the smallest forms or units of language—base words, prefixes, suffixes, roots, and combining forms—that carry meaning. A word may contain several syllables but may represent only one morpheme (e.g., *salamander;* Moats, 1994), or a word may contain several syllables and represent several morphemes (e.g., *instructor* contains three syllables and the morphemes *in-, struct,* and *-or*). Study of morphemes not only facilitates decoding but also provides a springboard for vocabulary development and spelling (Adams, 1990) and bridges the gap between alphabetic reading (i.e., word-level reading) and comprehension (Foorman & Schatschneider, 1997).

The following definitions are important to the study of morphemes.

- A *base word* is a plain word with nothing added to it.

- An *affix* is a suffix or a prefix that is added to a base word or a root.

- A root is an essential base of letters to which prefixes and suffixes are added (e.g., *audi, vis, struct*). Roots are primarily of Latin origin. A root that stands alone as a word is called a *free morpheme;* a root that requires the addition of an affix(es) to form a word is called a *bound morpheme* (Moats, 1995).

- A *suffix* is a letter or a group of letters added to the end of a base word or a root to change its meaning, form, or usage. A suffix that begins with a consonant is called a **consonant suffix** (e.g., *-ful, -less, -ness, -ment, -cian*). A suffix that begins with a vowel is called a **vowel suffix** (e.g., *-en, -ist, -ible*). *Derivational suffixes* are added to a base word or root and change the part of speech or the function of the base word or root (e.g., *-ful, -less, -cian, -or;* Moats, 1995, 2000). Some suffixes are grammatical endings called *inflections* or *inflectional endings* (e.g., *-s, -ed, -er, -est, -ing*), which, when added to base words, change their number, tense, voice, mood, or comparison (Moats, 1995, 2000).

  For the most part, the spelling of a suffix does not change. The spelling of the base word, however, may change when a vowel suffix is added. In the initial stages of introduction and practice, suffixes are added to base words. The suffix can be coded with a box. This coding visually separates the base word and the suffix, making it easier for students to attend to the base word:

  stand⟨*ing*⟩

- A *prefix* is a letter or a group of letters added to the beginning of a base word or a root to change its meaning (e.g., *mis-, un-, con-, re-*). A prefix that ends in a conso-

nant is called a **consonant prefix**. The spelling of a consonant prefix may change (e.g., *in-* may be spelled *il-, im-,* or *ir-*). A prefix that ends in a vowel is called a **vowel prefix**. The spelling of a vowel prefix does not change.

- A *derivative* is a base word or root plus an affix.

- *Combining forms* are similar to roots, but they are combined with equal importance in a word (e.g., *auto* and *graph,* which are neither affixes nor base words, combine to make *autograph;* see Henry, 1990, and Chapter 6 in this book). Words that are derived from combining forms can be affixed (e.g., *autobiography, autobiographic*). Combining forms are primarily of Greek origin.

Multisensory Introduction of Affixes

Quite often the means to reading multisyllabic words is identifying affixes (i.e., prefixes and suffixes) that are part of the word. Students may be able to recognize an unfamiliar word simply by identifying the affixes and then the remaining base word or root. Affixes can be introduced using a multisensory guided discovery teaching approach:

1. The teacher reads a list of five or six derivatives that have a common trait as students repeat each word (e.g., *joyful, careful, helpful, graceful, cheerful*).

2. Students discover what sounds the same in each word.

3. The teacher writes the derivatives on the board.

4. Students discover which letters are the same in each word and where the letters are found.

5. Students discover whether the same letters (the affix) are a suffix or a prefix, and they discover the meaning of the affix.

6. Students verbalize what they have discovered (e.g., *-ful* is a consonant suffix that means *full of*).

7. The teacher writes the new affix on an index card and adds it to an affix deck that is systematically reviewed. During review, students identify and spell the affix, give a key word, give the pronunciation, and give the meaning of the affix (e.g., when looking at the affix card for suffix *-ful*, students say, "Consonant suffix *f-u-l,* hopeful, /fŭl/, *full of*").

Syllable Division

Skilled readers are able to sense where to divide longer words because they have an awareness of syllables and have internalized the orthographic patterns of the language so well (Adams, 1990). The following activities heighten students' visual awareness of syllables and syllable division patterns.

Separated Syllables

Students identify syllable types of separated syllables, join them into words, and read the words aloud (Gillingham & Stillman, 1997):

cac|tus   *mas|cot*   *ban|dit*   *nut|meg*

mag|net   *gob|let*   *prob|lem*   *nap|kin*

Manipulation of Multisyllabic Words

Students identify syllables written on individual cards, arrange them into words, and read the words aloud (Gillingham & Stillman, 1997):

Scooping the Syllables

As students read multisyllabic words on a worksheet, they call attention to the syllables in the words by scooping the syllables. Using a pencil, students "scoop" (i.e., draw an arc underneath) the syllables from left to right, identify the syllable type, place a syllable code under each syllable (e.g., *o* for open, *r* for *r*-controlled) and code the vowel (Wilson, 1996):

Common Patterns for Dividing Words into Syllables

There are four major patterns in English (VCCV, VCV, VCCCV, and VV) that indicate that a word will be divided into syllables according to how it is pronounced. For each of these four patterns, there are different choices for division and accent placement. The best choices for dividing and accenting are listed here in order of frequency. Students must learn to be flexible when they make choices about dividing and accenting multisyllabic words. If the first choice of a pattern does not produce a recognizable word, then they need to try a second choice, which usually requires a change in accent placement. If necessary, they may need to try a third choice, which usually requires a change in the division of the word. Familiarity and flexibility with syllable-division patterns help students develop strategies for reading multisyllabic words; students do not have to guess or give up when they encounter unfamiliar long words.

VCCV—Two Consonants Between Two Vowels

- **VC′|CV**—When two consonants stand between two vowels, the word is usually divided between the two consonants. The accent usually falls on the first syllable. Examples include the following: ***nap′***|*kin,* ***vel′***|*vet,* ***can′***|*did,* ***cac′***|*tus,* ***cam′***|*pus,* ***mag′***|*net,* ***bas′***|*ket,* ***in′***|*sect,* ***op′***|*tic,* and ***mus′***|*lin.*
    Note: Consonant digraphs such as *ch, ck, sh, ph, th,* and *wh* are treated as single consonants because they represent single speech sounds (***ath′***|*lete,* ***dol′***|*phin*).

- VC|**CV′**—The word may be divided between the consonants, with the accent falling on the second syllable. Examples include the following: *un|**til′**, pas|**tel′**, dis|**cuss′**, can|**teen′**, in|**sist′**.*

- **V′|CCV**—The word may be divided before both consonants with the accent falling on the first syllable. Examples include the following: ***se′***|*cret,* ***fra′***|*grant,* and ***ma′***|*cron.*

Note: Consonant digraphs, two adjacent consonants that represent one sound (e.g., *sh, th, ck, ng*), are never divided. Some consonant clusters contain two adjacent consonants, commonly known as *consonant blends,* whose sounds flow together. It is not necessary for these clusters to be introduced as separate sound–symbol correspondences because each sound in a consonant cluster is accessible. Consonant blends may divide (e.g., *fab|ric*) or may not divide (e.g., *se|cret*).

VCV—One Consonant Between Two Vowels

- **V'|CV**—When one consonant stands between two vowels, the word is usually divided before the consonant. The accent usually falls on the first syllable. Examples include the following: *i'|ris, o'|pen, u'|nit, o'|ver, ro'|tate, a'|corn, mu'|sic, tu'|lip, va'|cate, si'|lent, su'|per,* and *e'|ven.*

- **V|CV'**—The word may be divided before the consonant, with the accent falling on the second syllable. Examples include the following: *re|quest', e|vent', o|mit', u|nite', pa|rade', a|like', a|lone', sa|lute',* and *di|vine'.*

  Note: The vowels in an open, unaccented syllable require careful attention during syllable division. If students are overly sensitive to sounds in their speech, they may not make the connection between orthography and speech (Ehri et al., 1987). For example, the *e* in the word *elect* sounds more like /ĭ/ in running speech. If students are too sensitive to the /ĭ/ sound, they will not build an orthographic memory of *elect* spelled with *e.* The *e* in an open, unaccented syllable should be perceived as having a pronunciation that is long (e.g., *e|vent'*) but is shorter than an *e* in an open, accented syllable (e.g., *ze'|ro*). In an open, unaccented syllable, *o* and *u* remain long, but their pronunciations are shortened (e.g., *o|mit', u|nite'*). The *e, o,* and *u* are coded with a macron. The *a* in an open, unaccented syllable is obscure and pronounced as /ŭ/ (e.g., *a|long'*). The *a* is coded with a dot. The *i* in an open, unaccented syllable is short (e.g., *di|vide'*). The *i* is coded with a breve.

- **VC'|V**—The word may be divided after the consonant, with the accent falling on the first syllable. Examples include the following: *rob'|in, riv'|er, cab'|in, trav'|el, mag'|ic, tim'|id, mod'|ern, plan'|et, sol'|id,* and *sev'|en.*

  Note: As mentioned previously, consonant digraphs (i.e., two adjacent consonants that represent one sound) are treated as one consonant. Words with consonant digraphs may be divided before the digraph (e.g., *go'|pher*) or after the digraph (e.g., *rath'|er*).

VCCCV—Three Consonants Between Two Vowels

- **VC'|CCV**—When three consonants stand between two vowels, the word is usually divided after the first consonant. The first syllable is usually accented. Examples include the following: *pil'|grim, chil'|dren, pan'|try, spec'|trum, mon'|ster, lob'|ster, hun'|dred, scoun'|drel, ham'|ster,* and *os'|trich.*

- **VC|CCV'**—The word may be divided after the first consonant, with the accent falling on the second syllable. Examples include the following: *im|ply', com|plete', sur|prise', in|trude', en|twine', em|blaze',* and *ex|treme'.*

- **VCC'|CV**—The word may be divided after the second consonant or after a final consonant cluster (e.g., *mp* and *nd* are consonant clusters that often occur in final position in one-syllable words); the accent falls on the first syllable. Examples include the following: *pump'|kin, sand'|wich, bank'|rupt, part'|ner, musk'|rat,* and *irk'|some.*

VV—Two Adjacent Vowels

- **V′|V**—A word with two adjacent vowels that typically form a vowel pair may be divided between the vowels, with the accent falling on the first syllable. Examples include the following: ***po′**|em*, ***qui′**|et*, ***sto′**|ic*, ***bo′**|a*.

  Note: Adjacent vowels that frequently form digraphs or diphthongs include *ai, ay, au, aw, ea, ee, ei, ey, eu, ew, ie, oa, oe, oi, oo, ou, ow,* and *oy*. Although consonant digraphs are not divided, adjacent vowels that can form digraphs and diphthongs may be divided. A reader first tries reading an unfamiliar word with two adjacent vowels using the pronunciation of the digraph or diphthong that the vowels represent (e.g., reading *poem* as /pōm/). If reading the words in this manner does not produce a recognizable or a correct word, he or she divides the words between the vowels and reads it.

- **V′|V**—A word with two adjacent vowels that *do not* form a vowel pair is divided between the vowels, with the accent falling on the first syllable. Examples include the following: ***di′**|al*, ***cha′**|os*, ***tru′**|ant*, ***tri′**|umph*, and ***li′**|on*.

  Note: Because the vowel pairs in these words (i.e., *ia, ao, ua, iu, io*) do not constitute digraphs or diphthongs, a reader knows immediately to divide the words between the two vowels.

- **V|V′**—The word may be divided between the vowels, with the accent falling on the second syllable. Examples include the following: *du|**et′***, *cre|**ate′***, and *co|**erce′***.

Procedure for Dividing Words

A structured procedure provides readers with a systematic approach for reading long, unfamiliar words and builds an orthographic memory for syllable-division patterns. Dyslexic students may need additional visual and kinesthetic information to build the memory of these patterns. Information helpful to dyslexic and at-risk students (Cox & Hutcheson, 1988) is given in parentheses.

1. *Count the vowels.* To determine the number of syllables in a word, students count the number of sounded vowels from left to right. Vowel pairs count as one sounded vowel. (The vowel pairs can be underlined to call attention to the fact that the two vowels make one sound.) All suffixes are boxed. By boxing suffixes, students may see a base word that requires no further division. Students place brackets before any final stable syllables. By bracketing a final stable syllable, students may see that no further division is needed.

2. *Touch the vowels.* Using the index fingers of both hands, students touch the sounded vowels or vowel pairs and identify them. (A line can be drawn over the word from sounded vowel to sounded vowel. The vowels can be labeled by writing a small *v* over each vowel.) Example:

   v   v
   mascot

   The word *mascot* has two syllables because it has two sounded vowels. The vowels are *a* and *o*.

3. *Count the consonants.* Students count the number of consonants between the two vowels or vowel pairs and identify the division pattern. (Consonant digraphs can be underlined to call attention to the fact that the two letters are treated as one con-

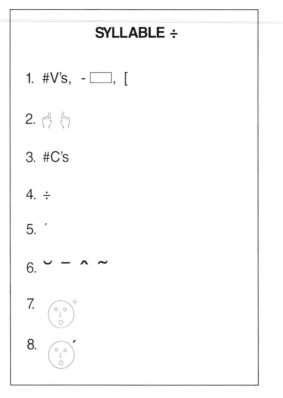

Figure 9.1. The syllable-division procedure provides ready access to multisyllabic words. Students 1) count the vowels, box suffixes, and add a bracket to mark a final stable syllable; 2) touch the vowels; 3) count the consonants; 4) draw a vertical line to divide the word; 5) mark the accent; 6) code the vowels; 7) read without accent; and 8) read with accent.

sonant sound. Each consonant or consonant digraph can be labeled with *c*. The labeling of the vowels and consonants expedites the orthographic memory of the syllable-division patterns.) Example:

$$\overset{\text{v c c v}}{\text{mascot}}$$

There are two consonants between the vowels in *mascot*. The syllable-division pattern is VCCV.

4. *Divide.* Students draw a vertical line to divide the word according to the most frequent division of this pattern. *Example:* Because the most common division choice for VCCV is to divide between the consonants, *mascot* is divided between *s* and *c*.

5. *Accent.* Students place an accent mark on the appropriate syllable according to the most frequent accent of the pattern. *Example:* With a VC|CV word, the accent is most frequently placed on the first syllable.

6. *Code.* Students identify each syllable type and code the vowels accordingly. *Example:* The first syllable of *mascot* is closed. The vowel is short; code it with a breve. The second syllable is closed. The vowel is short; code it with a breve.

7. *Read.* Students read each syllable without accenting either syllable.

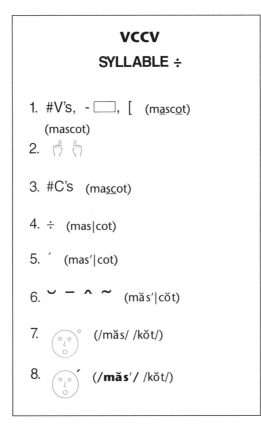

Figure 9.2. The word *mascot* is divided using the syllable-division procedures.

8. *Read again.* Students read the syllables together with the appropriate accent.

9. *Adjust.* Students adjust the accent or division if the word is not recognizable. Adjusting the accent or the division to produce a recognizable word teaches students to be flexible with language.

(See Figure 9.1, which is a pictorial representation of the previously delineated steps and is helpful for students with limited reading skills to use; Figure 9.2 shows the use of the steps when dividing the word *mascot*).

Reading Practice

Reading practice to reinforce a syllable-division pattern or any other decoding concepts must be focused. The teacher reviews all information that is pertinent to the reinforcement of the concept. For example, before reviewing a syllable-division pattern, the teacher might review the definition of a suffix, the syllable types that are germane to the pattern, the pattern itself, and the procedure for dividing words into syllables. After a review of relevant information, the teacher models the coding of a word while verbalizing the process and then reads the word. The teacher presents three or four additional words. Students verbalize the coding and/or division of these words and read them. The teacher then presents a list of words that contain the new concept for students to read, silently and then aloud. The teacher provides immediate feedback and

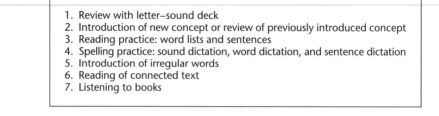

1. Review with letter–sound deck
2. Introduction of new concept or review of previously introduced concept
3. Reading practice: word lists and sentences
4. Spelling practice: sound dictation, word dictation, and sentence dictation
5. Introduction of irregular words
6. Reading of connected text
7. Listening to books

Figure 9.3.   Daily reading lesson plan.

leads students to self-correct errors so that students connect the correct orthographic patterns and pronunciations (Foorman, 1994). Students use words orally in complete sentences to ensure they understand the meanings of the words so that even at the word level, comprehension is attained (Foorman & Schatschneider, 1997). Students also read sentences. Spelling practice with the dictation of sounds, words, and sentences follows the reading practice. After the practice of skills, equal time is given to reading from connected text that mirrors what students have recently learned. Comprehension and fluency are addressed using this text. Irregular words that will be encountered in the text are reviewed before students read the text. Composition activities can also be incorporated at this time.

Well-matched reading text extends and reinforces the learning of orthographic patterns and gives relevance to what is being learned (Adams, 1990). When reading in connected text, the reader should be encouraged to pause and study unknown words instead of to skip or to guess an unfamiliar word. (Figure 9.3 shows how reading practice can be incorporated into an intensive, therapeutic reading lesson, with extended reading of text. See Chapter 8 for more on lesson planning.)

Dividing Words with Three or More Syllables

The same procedure is used for dividing words of three or more syllables. Students choose the most frequent division of a pattern (e.g., VCCV is usually divided between the consonants; VCV is usually divided before the consonant). Choosing accent requires the following considerations:

1.   Roots draw the accent; prefixes and suffixes are rarely accented (e.g., *in*|**vest***'*|*ment, re*|*con*|**struct***'*|*ing*).

2.   The syllable before a final stable syllable is usually accented (e.g., *im*|*mi*|**gra***'* [*tion*).

3.   A final syllable that ends in *-a* or *-ic* is not accented, and the accent usually falls on the syllable before the final syllable (e.g., *va*|**nil***'*|*la, At*|**lan***'*|*tic*).

4.   If there are no clues for accent, try accenting the first syllable (e.g., ***cu***'|*cum*|*ber*) or the second syllable (e.g., *es*|**tab***'*|*lish*).

   Careful attention to vowels in **polysyllabic** words is needed. The *a* in an open, unaccented syllable is obscure and is coded with a dot (e.g., *al*|**fal***'*|*fȧ*). The *i* in an open, unaccented syllable is short and coded with a breve (e.g., **ar***'*|*tĭ*|*chōke*). The *i* before a final stable syllable is short and is coded with a breve (e.g., *ig*|**nĭ***'* [*tion*). The *i* in an open, unaccented syllable before another vowel is pronounced as /ē/ (e.g., **sta***'*|*di*|*um*).

Advanced Morphemes

In addition to benefiting from learning about prefixes and suffixes, students benefit from learning about roots and combining forms. These morphemes are predominantly of Latin and Greek origins, respectively (see Chapter 6). The ability to instantly recognize roots and combining forms gives students a ready strategy for decoding longer words as well as insight into the meanings of the words.

Common Latin Roots

Words of Latin origin are common in literature and academic writing. Latin words generally are characterized as having a root with affixes. The root carries the base of the meaning:

- *audi* (to hear)—*auditory, audience, audit, auditorium, audible, inaudible, audition*

- *dict* (to say)—*dictate, predict, dictator, edict, contradict, dictation, indict, prediction*

- *ject* (to throw)—*reject, inject, projection, interjection, eject, objection, dejection*

- *port* (to carry)—*transport, transportation, import, export, porter, portable, report, support*

- *rupt* (to break)—*rupture, erupt, eruption, interrupt, interruption, disruption*

- *scrib, script* (to write)—*scribe, describe, manuscript, inscription, transcript, descriptive, prescription*

- *spect* (to watch)—*spectator, inspect, inspector, respect, spectacle, spectacular*

- *struct* (to build)—*structure, construct, construction, instruct, destruction, reconstructionist*

- *tract* (to pull)—*tractor, traction, attract, subtraction, extract, retract, attractive*

- *vis* (to see)—*vision, visual, visit, supervisor, invisible, vista, visualize, visionary*

Common Greek Combining Forms

Words of Greek origin are most often scientific, medical, and technical terms. They are characterized as having combining forms that carry equal importance in the meaning of the word:

- *auto* (self)—*automatic, autograph, autobiography, automobile, autocracy*

- *bio* (life)—*biology, biosphere, biography, biochemistry, biometrics, biophysics*

- *graph* (write, recording)—*graphite, geography, graphic, photograph, phonograph*

- *hydro* (water)—*anhydrous, dehydration, hydrogen, hydrant, hydrostatic, hydrophobia, hydrotherapy, hydroplane*

- *meter* (measure)—*speedometer, odometer, metronome, thermometer, chronometer, perimeter, hydrometer*

- *ology* (study of)—*geology, theology, zoology, meteorology, phonology*

- *photo* (light)—*photography, photocopy, photosynthesis, phototropism, Photostat, photogenic*

- *scope* (view)—*periscope, stethoscope, telescope, microscope, microscopic*

- *tele* (at a distance)—*telephone, telepathy, telegraph, television*

- *therm* (heat)—*Thermos, thermodynamics, thermostat, thermophysics*

Introduction of Roots and Combining Forms

The teacher writes a root or combining form on the board. Students generate derivatives of the word part. The teacher writes the derivatives on the board so that the new word part in each word is aligned. Students determine the meaning of the word part (Henry, 1990):

struct

structure

destruction

instructor

reconstructionist

The teacher writes the new root or combining form on an index card and adds it to a deck that is systematically reviewed. During a review, students read the word part on each card, give the meaning, and generate derivatives of the root (e.g., students say, "*struct; to build; construct, structure, instructor,* and *destruction*").

RECOGNITION OF IRREGULAR WORDS

Knowledge of the orthographic patterns of the language and practice with these patterns develop instant word recognition. But how do readers learn those words with irregular orthographic patterns? Despite claims to the contrary, English is a highly reliable language for reading (Gough & Hillinger, 1980). Approximately 87% of the English language is regular and can be predictably decoded using the orthographic patterns described in this chapter; this leaves only 13% of the language as irregular (Hanna, Hanna, Hodges, & Rudorf, 1966). The irregularities of written English are generally limited to the vowels and silent consonants. For most irregular words, the consonants offer sufficient support so that when the reader encounters an irregular word in everyday reading, he or she can determine the correct pronunciation of the word with partial decoding (Share & Stanovich, 1995).

Irregular words, particularly high-frequency irregular words (e.g., *the, said, have*), are learned through repeated encounters in text. An understanding of word origins further assists students' orthographic memory of irregular words by giving insight into the spellings of words that do not match their pronunciations. Analyzing irregular words to determine their irregularities reinforces reliable sound-letter relationships, helps students build an orthographic memory of the words, and establishes that the irregularities in English words are not arbitrary (Gough & Hillinger, 1980). Patterns, even if infrequent, can be found in irregular words (e.g., *gh* may be silent as in *taught*, pronounced /g/ in initial position as in *ghost*, or pronounced /f/ as in *laugh*). When students discover an irregularity in a word, a resounding "Good for you! You found a word that doesn't fit the pattern!" from the teacher confirms that the students are thinking about the language and acquiring a flexible understanding of the language.

Procedure for Teaching Irregular Words

A multisensory structured procedure helps students to achieve permanent memorization of irregular words (Cox, 1992; Gillingham & Stillman, 1997):

1. The teacher writes an irregular word on the board, such as *said.*

2. Students identify the syllable type and code the word according to the regular patterns of reading. Students read the word and discover it does not follow the reliable patterns of the language: /sād/.

3. The teacher erases the coded word and rewrites the word on the board: *said.* Beside the word, the teacher writes the pronunciation in parentheses: (sĕd).

4. Students compare the word and the pronunciation. They decide which part is irregular.

5. The teacher circles the irregular part:

    s (ai) d

6. The teacher writes the word on the front of a 4″ x 6″ index card. On the back of the card, the teacher writes the pronunciation. The teacher cuts off the upper left-hand corner of the front of the card. The irregular shape of the card cues students that the word printed on it is an irregular word.

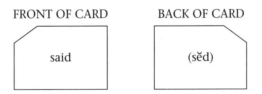

FRONT OF CARD   BACK OF CARD

said   (sĕd)

7. The teacher holds up the card so that students see the front of the card. Students read the word aloud.

8. The teacher turns the card around, and students read the pronunciation aloud.

9. The teacher slowly turns the card from front to back four or five times as students read the word and then read the pronunciation aloud.

10. The new card is added to a deck of irregular words that is reviewed daily.

Review of Irregular Words

Use of a rapid word-recognition chart (RWRC; see Figure 9.4) builds instant recognition of high-frequency irregular words. The chart contains five rows of six irregular words. Each row contains the same six words in a different order. The teacher makes an RWRC transparency. After placing the transparency on the overhead projector, the teacher points to 8–10 words at random as a warm-up. After the warm-up, students are timed for 1 minute. The teacher points to each square in order on the transparency, starting with the top row and working across each row. Students read aloud the word in each of the squares. In the 1-minute time frame, students may read through the chart more than

RAPID WORD RECOGNITION CHART

pretty	said	who	there	they	what
said	pretty	there	who	what	they
there	who	they	said	pretty	what
who	what	said	they	there	pretty
they	there	pretty	what	who	said

Figure 9.4. The rapid word recognition chart (RWRC) increases instant word recognition, particularly the recognition of words with phonetically irregular orthography.

once. At the end of 1 minute, students count and record the number of words they have successfully read. Progress can be graphed. The practice concludes with the teacher pointing at random to any troublesome words to provide further practice and secure the recognition of those words.

Word Origins

A brief overview of word origins helps students develop an understanding of why some words are pronounced in an unexpected way. This understanding allows students to forgive the language for being irregular and, more important, allows them to forgive themselves for having difficulty with the language (Cox, 1992; Gillingham & Stillman, 1997). Words may be pronounced irregularly for four reasons:

1. They are borrowed from another language such as French (*hors d'œuvre*), Dutch (*yacht*), or Greek (*ocean*).

2. They are **eponyms**, or words derived from proper names, such as the German botanist L. Fuchs (*fuchsia*) or the French statesman E. de Silhouette (*silhouette*).

3. They are words from the Anglo-Saxon language whose spellings did not keep pace with their changing pronunciations, such as *laugh, enough, said, through,* and *where.*

4. They are irregular with no easily identifiable reason or "just because," such as *curmudgeon.*

Investigation into the irregularities of words raises students' word consciousness. Becoming more sensitive to the irregular spellings of these words builds students' memory for instant recognition.

THE SPELLING CONNECTION TO READING

Noah Webster once wrote, "Spelling is the foundation of reading and the greatest ornament of writing" (as cited in Venezky, 1980, p. 12). Spelling, by its nature, is a multisensory skill, involving the translation of auditory sounds into visual symbols that are reinforced with the kinesthetic act of writing. A beginning reader's use of invented spelling (Read, 1971) provides the teacher with considerable insight as to how well the reader is learning and internalizing information about the language. The beginning reader applies his or her phonological awareness and acquired knowledge of sounds and patterns to the task of spelling an unfamiliar word. Students who have a sense of how the language works become risk takers. They attempt to sound out and spell words for which they may not have a strong visual image but that are, nevertheless, the best, most appropriate words for their writing (e.g., students attempt *tremendous* or *gigantic* instead of using *big*). In their trials of spelling these unfamiliar words, they reinforce and enhance their reading skills. The use of these more sophisticated words embellishes their writing and better reflects their oral vocabulary. Although it is important for students to become confident risk takers, it is also imperative for them to learn to spell words correctly because their spelling knowledge has a direct impact on their reading proficiency (Adams, 1990). (Chapter 10 provides suggestions for spelling instruction and the use of spelling practice to reinforce reading.)

FLUENCY

The NRP (NICHD, 2000) selected fluency in its study of effective reading instruction because of the concern that students are not achieving fluency in reading and dysfluent reading hinders comprehension and overall reading achievement. Fluency is the rapid, prosodic flow with which a skilled reader reads. When a fluent reader reads aloud, it sounds as though he or she is speaking. His or her reading is fluid and accurate, with adequate speed, appropriate phrasing, and correct intonation. This mirroring of spoken language supports comprehension, facilitates self-monitoring and self-correction, and makes reading enjoyable. Lack of fluency is marked by a slow, halting, spasmodic pace; mistakes; poor phrasing; and inadequate intonation (Samuels, 1979). A slow, labored rate of reading seriously impairs comprehension because it diverts attention away from the meaning of the text (LaBerge & Samuels, 1974) and overloads working memory at the word level so that this memory is not available for understanding the meaning of the text (Perfetti, 1985).

Instant, efficient word recognition, which is the result of familiarity with letter–sound correspondences and orthographic patterns (Adams & Bruck, 1995), greatly facilitates fluency. Explicit instruction in decoding improves word recognition. However, for some at-risk students, their difficulty in learning to read manifests itself in a lack of fluency even with improved word-recognition skills. These students are characterized as having a double deficit (Wolf & Bowers, 1999, 2000). In addition to a deficit in phonological processing that affects the development of accurate word recognition, they have a deficit in naming speed or rapid automatized naming (RAN; i.e., speed in

naming colors, numbers, letters, and objects; Denckla & Rudel, 1974) that interferes with the development of automatic word recognition and fluency (Blachman, 1984; Wolf, 1997; Wolf & Obregón, 1992; see also Chapter 5).

Fluency Practice

Fluency has been referred to as a neglected goal of reading (Allington, 1983). Most successful readers seem to move from word-level reading to the fluency of phrase reading easily. Their development of fluency is due, in part, to the fact that because successful beginning readers learn the alphabetic code early, they have more time to read (Adams & Bruck, 1995; Juel, 1988) and receive more encouragement to attend to fluency (Allington, 1983; Chall, 1983). It cannot be assumed, however, that the development of accurate decoding skills guarantees the application of those skills to fluency (Torgesen, 1997). Fluency development requires intentional, well-designed practice. Researchers are currently studying the brain and the time it takes the brain to process written language, and they are investigating sources for speed-related deficits that affect reading fluency. As more becomes known about the sources of speed-related deficits, the best designs for fluency interventions will be ascertained. To date, research suggests the most effective practices for the improvement of fluency are those that involve the repeated reading of letters, words, phrases, and text and are supported by increased knowledge of the systems of oral and written language (Wolf, 2001). Figure 9.3 delineates a daily reading lesson in which activities that improve fluency at the letter, word, and text levels are easily incorporated.

Rapid Letter Naming

Neuhaus and Swank (2002) proposed that letter naming is only slightly less complex than word reading and that automatic letter recognition is the key to automatic word recognition. Rapid letter recognition is dependent upon the familiarity of the orthographic and phonological properties of letters and directly predicts rapid recognition of words. Therefore, students benefit from overlearning the associations of letter shapes, names, and sounds. The use of a letter–sound deck in a daily reading lesson (see Figure 9.3) firmly secures these associations. Chapter 5 outlines many activities that can be used for the rapid naming of letters.

Rapid Word Reading

Evidence indicates that practice that involves the rapid reading of single words can result in improved speed and comprehension of text reading (Tan & Nicholson, 1997). The use of flash cards or an RWRC to preview words in a passage before reading keeps the words in memory for students to refer to as they read. In addition to using an RWRC for high-frequency, irregular words as shown in Figure 9.4, the chart can be used for repeated exposure to an orthographic pattern found in words in the planned passage (Fisher, 1999). For example, an RWRC could be filled with words that contain trigraph *tch* (e.g., *match, etch, itch, blotch, Dutch, catch*). Using the procedure described previously, students read these words and build a memory of a frequent, reliable orthographic pattern that is found in the planned passage as well as in other text.

Repeated Reading

The NRP (NICHD, 2000) concluded that guided oral reading, including repeated reading, is the most effective technique for improving word recognition, speed, accuracy, and fluency. Repeated reading involves the oral reading and rereading of the same passage of 50–200 words several times. The rereading of the same text provides the repeated exposures of words needed for the reader to form new or access previously formed orthographic images of letter patterns and words (Torgesen, Rashotte, & Alexander, 2001). Oral reading fluency is enhanced when repeated readings are proceeded by teacher modeling of fluent reading (Rose, 1984). The modeling provides a positive framework for students to strive for when they read. The teacher should provide guidance and feedback as students read and reread the passage (NICHD, 2000). Because the goal of fluency training is to aid comprehension and because comprehension of text aids fluency by allowing students to anticipate what is to come in the text (Wood, Flowers, & Grigorenko, 2001), background knowledge should be activated before the initial reading of the passage and comprehension should be assessed, even informally, after the initial reading of the passage. Repeated reading can be incorporated in the daily reading lesson plan during the reading of connected text (see Figure 9.3).

Decodable Text

Decodable text is text that matches the sound–symbol correspondences and irregular words that have been systematically introduced and is a logical choice for fluency practice. Decodable text provides practice of previously introduced sound–symbol correspondences and irregular words, which builds automatic word recognition. The repeated reading of decodable text further secures those concepts in memory. A second benefit of decodable text is that it develops independence in dealing with new words. Students learn that they can sound out most unfamiliar words while reading. When selecting text to read for fluency practice, students should be able to read the text with 95% accuracy. In other words, students misread only 1 of every 20 words of text (NICHD, 2000).

Measuring Oral Reading Rate

Measures of oral reading rate (i.e., the number of words read correctly in 1 minute) should be recorded regularly. These measures need to be assessed on a one-to-one teacher–student basis. There are two methods in which rate can be determined. In one method, a student orally reads a passage from the beginning or from another starting point within the text for one minute as the teacher times the student with a stop watch. While the student reads, the teacher records any errors (e.g., a misread word, a skipped word, a substituted word). At the end of the minute, the teacher stops the stop watch. He or she counts the total number of words read and subtracts the errors. This number represents the rate and is recorded in *number of words correct per minute (wcpm)*.

A second way to establish rate is to mark 100 words at the beginning of or within the passage. When the student begins to orally read the first of the 100 words, the teacher begins timing. Errors are recorded. When the student has finished reading the last of the 100 words, the stop watch is stopped. The teacher subtracts the errors from 100 and divides the number of words read correctly by the total time. It may be neces-

sary to convert the total time into a decimal. For example, if a student reads 96 of 100 words correctly in 1 minute and 20 seconds (80 seconds), the teacher converts the time into a decimal to represent the total time in minutes (80 seconds ÷ 60 seconds = 1.33 minutes). The teacher then divides 96 by 1.33. The resultant number is the rate (72) and is recorded as wcpm (72 wcpm). Although the calculations are more cumbersome in this method, it is easier to use this method if the rates of many students are being measured at one time. The teacher does not have to individually count the words each student reads. The difficulty of a text can be assessed quickly because more than 5 errors in 100 words means that the text is too difficult for fluency practice. Because all students read the same 100 words, the teacher can judge overall mastery of concepts and determine if the pace of instruction for the group of students is appropriate.

The NRP (NICHD; 2000) suggested that an appropriate oral reading rate by the end of first grade is 60 wcpm. By the end of second grade, students should read orally at a rate of 90–100 wcpm and approximately 114 wcpm by the end of third grade. A rate of 120–150 wcpm is desired by end of fifth grade and beyond (Meyer & Felton, 1999).

Additional Practice to Develop Prosody

Successful decoding requires the reader to translate printed words into their spoken equivalents, whereas successful fluency requires the reader to connect the flow of printed text to the flow of spoken language. Spoken language has intonation, phrasing, and stress, which are not present in written language. Early on children rely on all of these features to understand speech (see Chapter 3 for more information). When these features are present in oral reading, there is a rhythmic flow that makes it sound as if the reader is speaking. This rhythmic flow is known as *prosody*. Although fluency practice that includes attention to prosodic features does not produce stronger gains (Torgesen et al., 2001), it is prudent to practice such features because lack of prosody results in word-by-word reading and prevents some readers from learning to group words into meaningful units that support comprehension. Oral fluency, which leads to reading fluency, can be taught to readers who do not move from the word level to the phrase level of reading. Phrasing, intonation, and stress can be applied to written language with oral practice, the study of punctuation, and the study of grammar. This practice can take place during the daily reading lesson plan (see Figure 9.3) as a prelude to reading in connected text.

Oral Practice and the Study of Punctuation

Although phrasing and intonation are not conventions of written language, these features can be developed and practiced orally so that students will be able to incorporate them into their reading:

1. *Phrasing:* Phrasing can be taught by using the sequence of the alphabet. Students recite the alphabet in phrases of two or three letters as the teacher draws an arc under each letter grouping. Three possibilities follow:

AB CDE FG HIJ KL MNO PQ RST UV WXY Z

ABC DE FGH IJ KLM NO PQR ST UVW XY Z

ABC DEF GHI JKL MNO PQR STU VWX YZ

2. *Practice with phrases:* The teacher writes phrases of three, four, and five words (e.g., *a little dog, up the steep hill, sat on a green mat*) on the board, and students practice phrasing the words fluently.

3. *Segmented sentences:* The teacher writes five- or six-word sentences on the board in segments that represent the subject and the predicate. Students read the sentences in phrases as the teacher draws an arc under each phrase:

The mouse   ate the cheese.

A little dog   ran home.

When students become fluent in phrasing simple five- or six-word sentences, students can practice with segmented sentences that have prepositional phrases:

The big dog   chased the cat   up the street.

4. *Intonation and punctuation:* Students recite the alphabet as a conversation with appropriate inflection. The class can do this as a group or divided into two halves. The teacher writes the conversation on the board or on sentence strips. Two possibilities follow:

ABCD? EFG. HI? JKL. MN! OPQ. RST? UVWX. YZ!

ABC. DEFGHI? JKL! MN? OPQRS! TUV. WXY? Z.

5. *Intonation and punctuation with sentences:* The teacher writes a two-word sentence three times on the board and punctuates one with a period, one with a question mark, and one with an exclamation point (e.g., *Birds fly. Birds fly? Birds fly!*). The teacher discusses the effect of the different punctuation marks on intonation. Students read each sentence three times, changing their inflection to match the punctuation. The teacher can increase sentence length as students become secure with intonation.

6. *Intonation and stress:* The teacher writes a three-word sentence on the board three times. The teacher underlines the initial word in the first sentence, the second word in the second sentence, and the final word in third sentence (e.g., *I am hungry, I am hungry, I am hungry*). Students read the three sentences, stressing the underlined word. They discuss the subtle variations in the meaning of each sentence.

7. *Imitation of spoken language:* The teacher writes a five- or six-word sentence (e.g., *The game will begin at two*) on the board. Students read the sentence once for accuracy. They then read it as though they were talking to a friend. The teacher can add quotation marks to some sentences to reinforce the idea that these marks indicate conversation in written text.

The Study of Grammar

The study of grammar benefits students' use of phrasing and intonation. An understanding of the concepts of *subject* and *predicate* aids phrasing because many sentences can be segmented into these two syntactic units. Parts of speech such as *prepositions* and *subordinating conjunctions* also provide clues for phrasing and intonation. Skilled readers characteristically pause at the end of syntactic units, which aids the flow of their reading (Adams, 1990).

Subject and Predicate   The subject is the word or words that tell who or what a sentence is about. The predicate tells what the subject is doing or did. An understanding of subject and predicate is taught with simple, two-word sentences such as *Dogs bark* or *Children sing*. Students study a sentence and determine the word that tells who the sentence is about. The teacher explains that this word is the subject. Students then look for the word that tells what the subject is doing. The teacher explains that this word is the predicate. Students color code the parts of the sentence (e.g., subject is yellow, predicate is orange) (Carreker, 2002) or mark the subject and predicate with a special code (e.g., subject is underlined with a straight line, predicate is underlined with a jagged line) (Greene & Enfield, 1993). Knowledge of subject and predicate provides clues for phrasing. Once students have established the concepts of *subject* and *predicate* with two-word sentences, sentences with multiword subjects and predicates are presented. As students read these longer sentences, all of the words in the subject are spoken together as a phrase, and then all of the words in the predicate are spoken together.

Prepositions and Subordinating Conjunctions   Prepositions are the small words (e.g., *in, out, up, down, over, under*) that show the relationship of one noun, pronoun, or proper noun phrase to another element. Students code prepositions with a special color or mark. Because prepositions occur in phrases, students have a signal for reading the words in the prepositional phrase as a unit. When a prepositional phrase of four or more words occurs at the beginning of a sentence, students have a cue that a comma is coming, which will necessitate a pause as they read.

Subordinating conjunctions (e.g., *because, if, while, when*) signal a dependent clause (a group of words with a subject and a predicate that is not a complete sentence) that is spoken together as a unit (e.g., *before the game begins; while he was jogging*). Students code subordinating conjunctions with a special color or mark to flag the dependent clause. A subordinating conjunction at the beginning of a sentence cues students that a comma is coming and a pause will be needed as they read (e.g., *Before the game begins, the band will practice*).

SUMMARY

Reading is a complex process involving decoding, which enables a reader to translate printed symbols into words, and comprehension, which enables the reader to derive meaning from the printed page. With the insight that spoken words consist of sounds and that printed words consist of letters, the beginning reader is able to connect sounds to letters and to read words. Initially the reader is focused on sounding out words. With practice of graphophonemic, syllabic, and morphemic patterns through the use of word lists, sentences, and repeated readings of connected text, the reader's decoding skills become automatic, and he or she is able to give greater attention to the prosodic features of reading such as phrasing and intonation, which further aid fluency. The fluent translation of the flow of print to the flow of spoken language enables the reader to attend to the meaning rather than to the features of the printed text. Fluency is vital to comprehension, which is the main goal of reading.

REFERENCES

Adams, M.J. (1990). *Beginning to read: Thinking and learning about print*. Cambridge: The MIT Press.

Adams, M.J., & Bruck, M. (1993). Word recognition: The interface of educational policies and scientific research. *Reading and Writing: An Interdisciplinary Journal, 5*, 113–139.

Adams, M.J., & Bruck, M. (1995, Summer). Resolving the "great debate." *American Educator, 19,* 7–12.

Allington, R.L. (1983, February). Fluency: The neglected reading goal. *The Reading Teacher,* 556–561.

Ball, E.W., & Blachman, B.A. (1988). Phoneme segmentation training: Effect on reading readiness. *Annals of Dyslexia, 38,* 208–225.

Beck, I., & Juel, C. (1995, Summer). The role of decoding in learning to read. *American Educator, 19,* 8–12.

Blachman, B. (1984). Relationship of rapid naming ability and language analysis skills to kindergarten and first-grade reading achievement. *Journal of Educational Psychology, 76,* 610–622.

Blachman, B.A. (1987). An alternative classroom reading program for learning disabled and other low-achieving children. In R. Bowler (Ed.), *Intimacy with language: A forgotten basic in teacher education* (pp. 49–55). Baltimore: The International Dyslexia Association.

Blachman, B.A., Ball, E.W., Black, R., & Tangel, D.M. (2000). *Road to the code: A phonological awareness program for young children.* Baltimore: Paul H. Brookes Publishing Co.

Bradley, L., & Bryant, P.E. (1983). Categorizing sounds and learning to read: A causal connection. *Nature, 303,* 419–421.

Brady, S., & Moats, L.C. (Eds.). (1997). *Informed instruction for reading success: Foundations for teacher preparation.* Baltimore: The International Dyslexia Association.

Brady, S., & Shankweiler, D. (1991). *Phonological processes in literacy: A tribute to Isabelle Y. Liberman.* Mahwah, NJ: Lawrence Erlbaum Associates.

Carreker, S. (2002). *Multisensory grammar and written composition.* Bellaire, TX: Neuhaus Education Center.

Chall, J.S. (1983). *Stages of reading development.* New York: McGraw-Hill.

Chall, J.S. (1996). *Learning to read: The great debate revisited* (3rd ed.). Orlando, FL: Harcourt Brace & Co.

Cox, A.R. (1992). *Foundations for literacy: Structures and techniques for multisensory teaching of basic written English skills.* Cambridge, MA: Educators Publishing Service.

Cox, A.R., & Hutcheson, L.M. (1988). Syllable division: A prerequisite of dyslexics' literacy. *Annals of Dyslexia, 38,* 226–242.

Denckla, M.B., & Rudel, R. (1974). Rapid "automatized" naming of pictured objects, colors, and letters, and numbers by normal children. *Cortex, 10,* 186–202.

Ehri, L.C. (1991). Development of the ability to read words. In R. Barr, M.L. Kamil, P.B. Mosenthal, & P.D. Pearson (Eds.), *Handbook of reading research* (Vol. 2, pp. 383–417). Reading, MA: Addison Wesley Longman.

Ehri, L.C., Wilce, L.S., & Taylor, B.B. (1987). Children's categorization of short vowels in words and the influence of spelling. *Merrill-Palmer Quarterly, 33,* 393–421.

Englemann, S. (1969). *Preventing failure in the primary grades.* Chicago: Science Research Associates.

Felton, R. (1993). Effects of instruction on decoding skills of children with phonological processing problems. *Journal of Learning Disabilities, 26,* 583–589.

Fisher, P. (1999). Getting up to speed. *Perspectives, 25*(2), 12–13.

Foorman, B.R. (1994). The relevance of a connectionist model for reading for "The Great Debate." *Educational Psychology Review, 6,* 25–47.

Foorman, B.R., Francis, D.J., Beeler, T., Winikates, D., & Fletcher, J.M. (1997). Early intervention for children with reading problems: Study designs and preliminary findings. *Learning Disabilities: A Multidisciplinary Journal, 8,* 63–71.

Foorman, B.R., Francis, D.J., Shaywitz, S.E., Shaywitz, B.A., & Fletcher, J.M. (1997). The case for early reading intervention. In B. Blachman (Ed.), *Foundations of reading acquisition and dyslexia: Implications for early intervention* (pp. 243–264). Mahwah, NJ: Lawrence Erlbaum Associates.

Foorman, B.R., & Schatschneider, C. (1997). Beyond alphabetic reading: Comments on Torgesen's prevention and intervention studies. *Journal of Academic Language Therapy, 1,* 59–65.

Gillingham, A., & Stillman, B. (1997). *The Gillingham manual: Remedial training for children with specific disability in reading, writing, and penmanship* (8th ed.). Cambridge, MA: Educators Publishing Service.

Goswami, U., & Bryant, P. (1990). *Phonological skills and learning to read.* Mahwah, NJ: Lawrence Erlbaum Associates.

Gough, P.B. (1983). Context, form and interaction. In K. Rayner (Ed.), *Eye movements in reading: Conceptual and language processes* (pp. 203–211). San Diego: Academic Press.

Gough, P.B., Ehri, L., & Treiman, R. (Eds.). (1992). *Reading acquisition.* Mahwah, NJ: Lawrence Erlbaum Associates.

Gough, P.B., & Hillinger, M.L. (1980). Learning to read: An unnatural act. *Bulletin of The Orton Society, 30,* 179–196.

Gough, P.B., & Tunmer, W.E. (1986). Decoding, reading and reading disability. *Remedial and Special Education, 7,* 6–10.

Greene, V.E., & Enfield, M.L. (1985). *Project Read reading guide: Phase I.* Bloomington, MN: Bloomington Public Schools.

Greene, V.E., & Enfield, M.L. (1993). *Framing your thoughts.* Bloomington, MN: Language Circle Enterprise.

Hanna, P.R., Hanna, J.S., Hodges, R.E., & Rudorf, E.H. (1966). *Phoneme–grapheme correspondences*

as cues to spelling improvement. Washington, DC: U.S. Government Printing Office, U.S. Office of Education.

Henry, M.K. (1988). Beyond phonics: Integrating decoding and spelling instruction based on word origin and structure. *Annals of Dyslexia, 38,* 259–277.

Henry, M.K. (1990). *WORDS: Integrated decoding and spelling instruction based on word origin and word structure.* Austin, TX: PRO-ED.

Henry, M.K. (2003). *Unlocking literacy: Effective decoding and spelling instruction.* Baltimore: Paul H. Brookes Publishing Co.

Hoover, W.A., & Gough, P.B. (1990). The simple view of reading. *Reading and Writing: An Interdisciplinary Journal, 2,* 127–160.

Hutchins, P. (1974). *The wind blew.* New York: Scholastic.

Joshi, R.M., & Aaron, P.G. (2000). The component model of reading: Simple view of reading made a little more complex. *Reading Psychology, 21,* 85–97.

Joshi, R.M., Dahlgren, M., & Boulware-Gooden, R. (2002). Teaching reading in an inner city school through a multisensory teaching approach. *Annals of Dyslexia, 52,* 229–242.

Juel, C. (1988). Learning to read and write: A longitudinal study of 54 children from first to fourth grades. *Journal of Educational Psychology, 80,* 437–447.

Juel, C. (1991). Beginning reading. In R. Barr, M.L. Kamil, P.B. Mosenthal, & P.D. Pearson (Eds.), *Handbook of reading research* (Vol. 2, pp. 759–788). Reading, MA: Addison Wesley Longman.

LaBerge, D., & Samuels, S.J. (1974). Toward a theory of automatic information processing in reading. *Cognitive Psychology, 6,* 293–323

Liberman, I.Y. (1987). Language and literacy: The obligation of the schools of education. In R. Bowler (Ed.), *Intimacy with language: A forgotten basic in teacher education* (pp. 1–9). Baltimore: The International Dyslexia Association.

Liberman, I.Y., & Liberman, A.M. (1990). Whole language vs. code emphasis: Underlying assumptions and their implications for reading instruction. *Annals of Dyslexia, 40,* 51–76.

Liberman, I.Y., Shankweiler, D., & Liberman, A.M. (1989). The alphabetic principle and learning to read. In D. Shankweiler & I.Y. Liberman (Eds.), *Phonology and reading disabilities: Solving the reading puzzle* (pp. 1–33). Ann Arbor: University of Michigan Press.

Lundberg, I., Frost, J., & Petersen, O.P. (1988). Effects of an extensive program for stimulating phonological awareness in preschool children. *Reading Research Quarterly, 23,* 264–284.

Lyon, G.R., Shaywitz, S.E., & Shaywitz, B.A. (2003). A definition of dyslexia. *Annals of Dyslexia, 53,* 1–14.

Meyer, M.S., & Felton, R.H. (1999). Repeated reading to enhance fluency: Old approaches and new directions. *Annals of Dyslexia, 49,* 283–306.

Moats, L.C. (1994). The missing foundation in teacher education: Knowledge of the structure of spoken and written language. *Annals of Dyslexia, 44,* 81–102.

Moats, L.C. (1995). *Spelling: Development, disabilities and instruction.* Timonium, MD: York Press.

Moats, L.C. (2000). *Speech to print: Language essentials for teachers.* Baltimore: Paul H. Brookes Publishing Co.

National Institute of Child Health and Human Development (NICHD). (2000). *Report of the National Reading Panel. Teaching children to read: An evidence-based assessment of the scientific research literature on reading and its implications for reading instruction: Reports of the subgroups* (NIH Publication No. 00-4754). Washington, DC: U.S. Government Printing Office. Also available online:http://www.nichd.nih.gov/publicatons/nrp/report.htm

Neuhaus, G.F., & Swank, P.R. (2002). Understanding the relations between RAN letters subtest components and word reading in first grade students. *Journal of Learning Disabilities, 35*(2), 158–174.

Perfetti, C.A. (1985). *Reading ability.* New York: Oxford University Press.

Rack, J., Hulme, C., Snowling, M., & Wightman, J. (1994). The role of phonology in young children learning to read words: The direct-mapping hypothesis. *Journal of Experimental Child Psychology, 57,* 42–71.

Rayner, K., & Pollatsek, A. (1986). *The psychology of reading.* Upper Saddle River, NJ: Prentice Hall.

Read, C. (1971). Pre-school children's knowledge of English phonology. *Harvard Educational Review, 41,* 1–34.

Rose, T.L. (1984). The effects of two prepractice procedures on oral reading. *Journal of Learning Disabilities, 17,* 544–548.

Rosner, J. (1975). *Test of auditory analysis skills. Helping children overcome learning difficulties.* New York: Walker and Co.

Rubin, H., & Eberhardt, N.C. (1996). Facilitating invented spelling through language analysis instruction: An integrated model. *Reading and Writing: An Interdisciplinary Journal, 8,* 27–43.

Samuels, S.J. (1979, January). The method of repeated readings. *The Reading Teacher, 32,* 403–408.

Share, D.L., & Stanovich, K.E. (1995). Cognitive processes in early reading development: Accommodating individual differences into a model of acquisition. *Issues in Education, 1*(1), 1–57.

Slingerland, B.A. (1971). *A multi-sensory approach to language arts for specific language disability children: A guide for primary teachers.* Cambridge, MA: Educators Publishing Service.

Stanback, M.L. (1992). Analysis of frequency-based vocabulary of 17,602 words. *Annals of Dyslexia, 42,* 196–221.

Stanovich, K.E. (1986). Matthew effects in reading: Some consequences of individual differences in the acquisition of literacy. *Reading Research Quarterly, 21,* 360–407.

Stanovich, K.E. (1991). Cognitive science meets beginning reading. *Psychological Science, 2,* 70–81.

Steere, A., Peck, C.Z., & Kahn, L. (1984). *Solving language difficulties: Remedial routines.* Cambridge, MA: Educators Publishing Service.

Tan, A., & Nicholson, T. (1997). Flashcards revisited: Training poor readers to read words faster improves their comprehension of text. *Journal of Educational Psychology, 89*(2), 276–288.

Torgesen, J.K. (1997). The prevention and remediation of reading disabilities: Evaluating what we know from research. *Journal of Academic Language Therapy, 1,* 11–47.

Torgesen, J.K., Rashotte, C.A., & Alexander, A.W. (2001). Principles of fluency instruction in reading: Relationships with established empirical outcomes. In M. Wolf (Ed.), *Dyslexia, fluency, and the brain* (pp. 333–355). Timonium, MD: York Press.

Tunmer, W.E., Herriman, M.L., & Nesdale, A.R. (1988). Metalinguistic abilities and beginning reading. *Reading Research Quarterly, 23,* 134–158.

Vellutino, F.R. (1980). Perceptual deficiency or perceptual inefficiency. In J. Kavanagh & R. Venezky (Eds.), *Orthography, reading and dyslexia* (pp. 251–270). Baltimore: University Park Press.

Venezky, R.L. (1980). From Webster to rice to Roosevelt. In U. Frith (Ed.), *Cognitive processes in spelling* (pp. 9–30). London: Academic Press.

Waites, L., & Cox, A.R. (1976). *Remedial training programs for developmental language disabilities.* Cambridge, MA: Educators Publishing Service.

Wilson, B. (1996). *Wilson reading system instructor manual* (3rd ed.). Millbury, MA: Wilson Language Training.

Wolf, M. (1997). A provisional, integrative account of phonological and naming speed deficits in dyslexia: Implications for diagnosis and intervention. In B. Blachman (Ed.), *Foundations of reading acquisition and dyslexia: Implications for early intervention* (pp. 67–92). Mahwah, NJ: Lawrence Erlbaum Associates.

Wolf, M. (Ed.). (2001). *Dyslexia, fluency, and the brain.* Timonium, MD: York Press.

Wolf, M., & Bowers, P. (1999). The "double deficit hypothesis" for the developmental dyslexias. *Journal of Educational Psychology, 91*(3), 1–24.

Wolf, M., & Bowers, P. (2000). The question of naming-speed deficits in the developmental reading disabilities: An introduction of the double-deficit hypothesis. *Journal of Learning Disabilities, 33,* 322–324.

Wolf, M., & Obregón, M. (1992). Early naming deficits, developmental dyslexia, and a specific deficit hypothesis. *Brain and Language, 42,* 219–247.

Wood, F.B., Flowers, L., & Grigorenko, E. (2001). On the functional neuroanatomy of fluency or why walking is just as important to reading as talking is. In M. Wolf (Ed.), *Dyslexia, fluency, and the brain.* Timonium, MD: York Press.

Yopp, H.K. (1992). Developing phonemic awareness in young children. *The Reading Teacher, 45*(9), 696–703.

Yopp, H.K. (1995). Read-aloud books for developing phonemic awareness: An annotated bibliography. *The Reading Teacher, 48,* 538–542.

10

Teaching Spelling

Suzanne Carreker

In many classrooms spelling instruction is treated as an afterthought to or as a by-product of reading. The assumption is that if students learn to read, they learn to spell; therefore, spelling instruction is given little importance and minimal attention during the instructional day. Frequently, it is confined to irrelevant spelling exercises (Cronnell & Humes, 1980) or relegated to the memorization of word lists with little or no instruction (Peters, 1985; Treiman, 1998). The prevailing philosophy in some classrooms (Goodman, 1986) is that if students are immersed in print and given opportunities to write, then they will learn to spell without formal instruction. These views fail to recognize the integral role spelling instruction plays in learning to read. Spelling is the foundation of reading and, until the 20th century, was the primary method of teaching reading (Venezky, 1980). Spelling instruction enhances reading proficiency through the reinforcement of phonemes and letter patterns (Adams, 1990). Spelling is a complex process, a more difficult skill to learn than reading (Frith, 1980; Johnson & Myklebust, 1967). Learning to spell requires explicit instruction (Brady & Moats, 1997; Moats, 1995).

THE DISTINCTIVENESS OF SPELLING

In order to decode text, a reader must translate symbols on a printed page that represent spoken words (see Chapter 9 for more on decoding). To each letter in a printed word, the reader must attach a speech sound. In this manner the reader can sound out or pronounce the word that is represented by printed symbols. In order to spell, the speller must translate spoken words into printed symbols. To each speech sound in a spoken word, a speller must attach a written letter or letters. In this manner the speller can represent spoken words with printed symbols. It would appear from these simple descriptions that decoding and spelling are simply inverse operations that require knowl-

edge of sound–symbol correspondences and are performed in opposite order. Following this logic, it could be assumed that if a student can read a word, then he or she can also spell it. Although both decoding and spelling require phonological and orthographic knowledge, they are not simply inverse operations (Frith, 1980). First, sound-to-spelling translations are less dependable than spelling-to-sound translations (Adams, 1990). Second, decoding requires recognition of words, whereas spelling requires complete, accurate recall of letter patterns and words (Frith & Frith, 1980; Fulk & Stormont-Spurgin, 1995).

Orthography refers to how spoken words are represented in written language. When the reader has the decoding skills discussed in Chapter 9, English orthography is 87% reliable (regular) for reading (Hanna, Hanna, Hodges, & Rudorf, 1966). The reader needs to memorize or infer from the context only about 13% of the words he or she will encounter. The rest of the words that are not instantly recognized can be sounded out. To sound out an unfamiliar word, the reader assigns known sounds to known letters in the word. With the assistance of phonological awareness, approximate pronunciations, and contextual clues, the reader can accurately pronounce the unfamiliar word (Share & Stanovich, 1995). When a letter or group of letters has more than one possible pronunciation (e.g., *ea* can be pronounced /ĕ/, /ē/, or /ā/), the reader affirms his or her pronunciation choice by determining whether the chosen word makes sense in the sentence (e.g., one nods one's /hĕd/, not one's /hēd/ or /hād/). The more the reader knows about decoding, the easier it is for him or her to recognize words, but even with partial decoding, a reader can read unfamiliar words.

The 87% reliability of English orthography (Hanna et al., 1966) may make the task of spelling an unfamiliar word that one can read seem deceptively simple. The speller must rely on phonological awareness to segment the unfamiliar word into its constituent sounds and then determine how those sounds are best represented in print, however, because many speech sounds in English are represented by multiple spellings (e.g., initial or medial /ā/ in a one-syllable word can be spelled *a*-consonant-*e* as in *cake*, *ai* as in *rain*, *ei* as in *vein*, *eigh* as in *eight*, or *ea* as in *steak*), making the correct choice can be confusing to the speller. Contextual clues do not affirm the speller's choice of spelling (Fulk & Stormont-Spurgin, 1995). After all, the word that is pronounced /tām/ (*tame*), spelled incorrectly as *taim*, *teim*, *teighm*, or *team*, would share the same context. The speller's only confirmation of a correct spelling is to compare the spelled word with a word held in memory. If the word is not held in memory because the speller has not seen it before or because the speller has a poor memory for letters and words (i.e., poor orthographic memory), it is difficult for him or her to independently confirm that the spelling choice is correct. Spelling requires an awareness of and exact memory for letter patterns and words that reading does not require.

In addition to the need for exact recall and the ambiguities of sound-to-spelling translations, spelling is a complex linguistic skill that demands simultaneous integration of syntactic (see Bryant, Nunes, & Bindman, 1997, for a discussion), phonological, morphological, semantic, and orthographic knowledge (Frith, 1980; Moats, 1995; Smith, 1980). This integration can be illustrated as a speller attempts to spell /jŭmpt/. Phonological awareness enables the speller to hear all of the sounds and play with the idea that /jŭmpt/ without /t/ is /jŭmp/. Syntactic awareness alerts the speller that /jŭmp/ can be used as a verb and that verbs have tenses. Morphological awareness helps the speller realize that /jŭmpt/ consists of two meaningful units—base word /jŭmp/ and suffix /t/. Semantic awareness provides the speller with the understanding that /t/ represents the past tense. Finally, using orthographic knowledge, the speller apprehends that /t/ will

be spelled *ed* and not *t*. Spelling obligates the speller to attend to multiple layers of language concurrently.

Knowing how to read a word does not guarantee that a person can spell the word correctly. If this were true, then there would be no individuals who read quite well but are poor spellers, and spelling development would not lag behind reading development. Spelling instruction should be intimately integrated with the teaching of reading, but because spelling has its own distinctive characteristics and demands, it also must be distinct from reading and explicitly taught. Spellers must be taught in a manner that will increase their awareness and memory of letter patterns and words. Sequential, structured spelling instruction is essential.

SPELLING DEVELOPMENT

To understand the vital role spelling plays in learning to read and the spelling errors students make, it is important to understand how spelling develops. Evidence suggests that spelling is a unitary, interactive process that requires both phonological and orthographic knowledge (Lennox & Siegel, 1998). Beginning spellers take advantage of both phonological and visual strategies (Bryant & Bradley, 1980; Treiman, Cassar, & Zukowski, 1994).

A young child's first writing experience is usually in the form of drawing. As the child is exposed to print, he or she begins to differentiate writing from drawing and begins to imitate the print he or she has seen, using letterlike or numberlike forms (Cassar & Treiman, 1997). In this precommunicative or **prephonetic stage** (Moats, 1995), the child's writing shows a lack of understanding of the **concept of a word**, the alphabetic principle, or the conventions of print such as spaces between words and the left-to-right progression of writing. The organization of the child's writing may be described as "willy-nilly" (Bear, Invernizzi, Templeton, & Johnston, 1996, p. 16). At age 3 or 4, the child may think that the length of the word reflects the size of the object it names instead of the sounds of language (e.g., *cow* should have more letters than *chicken* because a cow is bigger than a chicken) (Treiman, 1997). To the 3- or 4-year-old child, meaning takes precedence over spelling. Only when the child becomes aware that print is related to speech does he or she come to understand that letters represent speech sounds.

A grasp of the **alphabetic principle** emerges with the child's realization that spoken words are made of sounds that can be represented in print. He or she will first attempt to connect speech to print at the level of the syllable instead of at the level of the phoneme and will write a symbol for each syllable, for example, *b* for *be* or *nf* for *enough* (Ferreiro & Teberosky, 1982). As the child becomes more aware that individual letters represent individual sounds, he or she enters this **semiphonetic stage** (Moats, 1995) and uses incomplete but reasonable phonetic representations of words. The child usually uses the initial or salient consonants of a word, such as *s*, *c*, or *sd* for *seed* (Rubin & Eberhardt, 1996), or the child may use letter names, such as *left* for *elephant* (Adams, 1990; Treiman, 1994). At this semiphonetic stage, the child demonstrates awareness of left-to-right progression, but he or she tends to run letters together with little or no sense of word boundaries (e.g., RUDF for *Are you deaf?*) (Moats, 1995).

Further experiences with print and writing move the child to a stage of complete phonetic representations, or the **phonetic stage** (Moats, 1995). Every sound in a word is represented, but the child does not demonstrate knowledge of conventional spelling patterns. The child may spell *same* as *sam*, thus neglecting the final silent *e* (Treiman,

Zukowski, & Richmond-Welty, 1995). The inflection -ed may be represented as t as in askt or d as in hugd (Read, 1971). At this phonetic stage, the child is aware of not only sounds but also the mouth positions used to make sounds. The child may seem to be "spelling by mouth" (Moats, 1995, p. 37). For example, the child may use y to spell /w/ because not only does the letter name contain /w/, but also the mouth position to say the letter name y is the same as to say /w/. Other odd but linguistically understandable spelling choices may be observed at this stage, such as spelling /t/ before /r/ as ch as in chrie for try or /d/ before /r/ as j as in jragin for dragon (Read, 1971). Phonetically, /t/ or /d/ would not be spelled with ch or j, but when /t/ or /d/ occur before /r/, the place of articulation (i.e., where the sound is obstructed in the mouth during production) matches the place of articulation for /ch/ and /j/, respectively (Treiman, 1998). Consistent spelling anomalies may occur, such as /r/ overwhelming the vowel as in hr for her or the omission of nasal (i.e., /m/, /n/, /ng/) and liquid sounds (i.e., /l/, /r/) as in drik for drink, jup for jump, and od for old (Treiman, 1998; Treiman et al., 1995).

In these early stages of spelling development, a child is literal in his or her spelling of words (e.g., /k/ is almost always spelled k). As the child begins to read more, he or she becomes more sensitive to the letter patterns in words. Without being taught, he or she may discover an orthographic pattern and sense its constraints. The child may discover that /k/ can be spelled ck and may sense that it does not occur in the initial position of a word. He or she is more likely to spell cake as kack than ckak (Treiman, 1997). In this transitional stage of spelling, as the child becomes more aware of letter patterns in words, his or her spelling may seem "off-base" (Moats, 1995, p. 40). From exact phonetic representations of every sound, the child's spelling may become a mixture of phonetic components and salient visual features in words. This change in spelling usually signals a heightened awareness of letter patterns.

Through their early spelling experiences, children build a foundation for reading as they begin to establish sound–symbol correspondences and develop a sensitivity to letter patterns. But just as beginning readers need explicit teaching to become good readers, beginning spellers need explicit teaching to become good spellers. Without this formal instruction, beginning spellers will not establish the awareness and memory of letter patterns that will make them good spellers.

GOOD AND POOR SPELLERS

Good spelling ability is contingent on a speller's sensitivity to letter patterns (Adams, 1990). Research has shown that good and poor spellers do not differ greatly in their visual memory abilities (Lennox & Siegel, 1996). What differs in good spellers is that they possess well-developed phonological processing skills that not only make them aware of the sounds in words but also support the learning of letter patterns in words (Lennox & Siegel, 1998; Moats, 1995). Good spellers possess an orthographic memory. This orthographic memory is a more specific memory than visual memory; it is specific to remembering letter patterns and words. The development of this memory is dependent on well-developed phonological processing skills. Good spellers know not only how sounds are represented in language but also how words should look (Adams, 1990). They are able to deal with the ambiguities of orthography (e.g., the multiple spellings of /ā/) by weighting the variable spellings by their frequency or exposure in reading (e.g., the good speller weights a-consonant-e as a more frequent or stronger connection to /ā/ than eigh because he or she sees it more frequently) (Adams, 1990; Foorman, 1994; Seidenberg & McClelland, 1989). In addition to possessing phonological and or-

thographic knowledge, good spellers are able to simultaneously draw support from their awareness of syntax, morphology, and semantics. Because good spellers possess the very skills that are needed for good decoding, good spellers are good readers (i.e., decoders). It is unusual to find a good speller who is a poor reader (decoder).

The definition of dyslexia endorsed by The International Dyslexia Association (Lyon, Shaywitz, & Shaywitz, 2003) includes reading disabilities as well as specific spelling disabilities. As noted in Chapters 4 and 9, dyslexic students have difficulty learning to decode because of a core deficit in phonological processing (Adams, 1990; Bradley & Bryant, 1983; Goswami & Bryant, 1990). It is rare for dyslexic students who have difficulty with reading not to have difficulty with spelling. It is possible, however, for students to be fairly good readers but poor spellers. Moats (1995) made these observations about poor spellers. Good readers who are poor spellers have problems with the exact recall of letter sequences and subtle difficulties with complex spelling patterns and aspects of language structure, but they do not have a deficit in phonological processing. Poor readers who are poor spellers have a deficit in phonological processing that interferes with their mastery of spelling. They also have a specific problem with memory of letter patterns, which is rooted in their poor phonological processing. In addition, poor spellers do not possess the ability to deal with several layers of language simultaneously. With proper instruction, poor spellers who are poor readers will improve their decoding skills, but they seldom master spelling (Moats, 1994; Oakland, Black, Stanford, Nussbaum, & Balise, 1998).

Roberts and Mather (1997) characterized poor spelling as the result of difficulties in both phonological and orthographic processing. Difficulties with phonological processing may include poor sequencing of sounds, omission or addition of sounds, confusion with similar-sounding phonemes (e.g., /f/ and /th/, /p/ and /b/), and limited knowledge of spelling rules. Orthographic processing difficulties are manifested as poor sequencing of nonphonetic patterns, confusion with graphemes that look similar (e.g., *b* and *d*, *n* and *u*), transposition of letters (e.g., *fro* instead of *for*), overgeneralization of rules, and overreliance on auditory features (e.g., *becuz* for *because*).

Poor spellers may be perceived as "free-spirit" spellers who spell words the way they sound without regard to conventional letter patterns. They may spell *does* as *duz*, *dress* as *dres*, or *girl* as *gerl*. They may spell the same word several different ways within the same paragraph, such as *thay, tha*, and *thai* for *they*. The true dyslexic spellers may be perceived as "bizarre" spellers. They struggle with the conventional letter patterns of words and use inappropriate letter sequences, such as *oridr* for *order*; transpositions, such as *gril* for *girl*; letter reversals, such as *dady* for *baby*; or incomplete letter patterns, such as *boht* for *bought*. Not only do dyslexic spellers lack the ability to use conventional letter patterns, but they also are unable to fully or correctly translate the sounds in words. They may have difficulty hearing the word correctly (e.g., hearing "fan" instead of "van"), hearing all of the sounds in a word (e.g., hearing "butful" for *beautiful*), or keeping the sounds in sequence (e.g., using *slpit* for *split*). They may have difficulty discriminating similar sounds as (e.g., hearing "baf" for *bath* or "wint" for *went*).

Problems with spelling persist in dyslexic adolescents and adults. Moats (1996) found that dyslexic adolescents showed lingering, subtle signs of phonological difficulty, primarily in segmenting words into their phonemic and morphemic units, as evidenced by their consistent omissions, substitutions, and misrepresentations of inflected morphemes (e.g., *-ed* spelled as *t* or *d*). Their errors in spelling **high-frequency words** suggested that their underdeveloped phonological and linguistic awareness compromised the development of orthographic memory. When comparing the writing

samples of dyslexic and nondyslexic adults, Sterling, Farmer, Riddick, Morgan, and Matthews (1998) found that the sentences of dyslexic adults were no shorter or longer than those of their peers but that there was a conspicuous use of **monosyllabic** words and misuse of **homophones**. Spelling errors suggested specific phonological impairment as well as problems with the complexities of English. Adolescents and adults who are poor spellers demonstrate the tenacious nature of the phonological processing deficit and its chronic effect on spelling development. Phonological awareness along with morphemic and orthographic awareness must be considered significant elements of spelling instruction.

It is important to note that spelling ability and IQ scores are not related. Poor spelling does not reflect a lack of intelligence (West, 1991). Take, for example, the spelling errors of neurosurgeon Harvey Cushing: *swoolen* for *swollen, neybour* for *neighbor,* and *quire* for *choir.* He was a brilliant man who was a *"mediocher"* speller.

KNOWLEDGE NECESSARY FOR SPELLING

Traditional spelling instruction that involves the repetitious copying of words or the memorization of word lists does not promote active, reflective thought about language. Informal spelling instruction that assumes that spelling will develop through writing experiences does not provide students with the necessary knowledge of language structure they need to become correct spellers. Students must be explicitly taught about language structure for spelling, and they must be actively engaged in thinking about language. The teacher must assume an active role in spelling instruction. It is imperative that the teacher have and be able to impart knowledge about the sounds of the language; the most frequent and reliable letter patterns; and rules of English orthography, morphology, and word origins (Brady & Moats, 1997; see Chapter 6 for a discussion of English word origins).

Phonetics, Phonology, and Phonics

Phonetics is the study of the characteristics of individual speech sounds (i.e., phonemes) that occur in all languages. There are approximately 44 speech sounds in English, with some variants of these sounds (i.e., allophones) that are not considered separate speech sounds (e.g., the /ă/ in the word *sank* is different from the /ă/ in *sack* but is not a separate speech sound). Phonetics involves the categorization or description of the articulation of each speech sound—where the sound is produced, the way in which air stream flows through the mouth and nose, and the activity of the vocal cords during production.

Spoken words are made up of the speech sounds. Every language has its own set of rules that governs the utterance of these sounds and the sound patterns that are allowed. This system of rules that determine how sounds are used in spoken language is called phonology (Moats, 1995). There are constraints about sound sequences in spoken language based on what humans are capable of producing easily (e.g., /np/ rarely occurs in spoken English, hence the pronunciation /ĭm|pôrt/ rather than /ĭn|pôrt/). Pronunciation variations may occur because of a phoneme's position in a word (e.g., /p/ in *pot* is different from the /p/ in *spot* or *top*) or because of surrounding sounds (e.g., the vowel in *sank* may be perceived as a long vowel instead of a short vowel because it is nasalized before nasal /ng/). These perfunctory pronunciation differences do not affect meaning (Treiman et al., 1994). Accent may vary pronunciations as well as the meanings of words (e.g., /**ŏb'**|jĕkt/ is a noun, and /ŏb|**jĕkt'**/ is a verb). It is not neces-

sary to teach the rules that govern the use of speech sounds when a child is learning to speak (Read, 1971); the rules are unconscious rules that automatically occur in spoken language.

Phonics is an instructional method that teaches the use of written symbols to represent speech sounds for reading and spelling. Phonics provides a visual representation of the phonology of spoken language (e.g., the /ă/ in *sank* is nasalized before *n,* which is nasalized; the *n* is pronounced /ng/ instead of /n/ before any letter pronounced /k/ or /g/). In order for students to be successful with phonics, they must be aware of the sounds in spoken words.

Brady and Moats (1997) contended that knowledge of phonetics and phonology assists the teacher in understanding the reading and spelling errors of students, increases his or her ability to provide **corrective feedback**, and enables him or her to plan instruction that is linguistically informed. Knowledge of phonetics heightens the teacher's awareness of speech sounds and how they are produced so that he or she can provide correct models for students. Knowledge of phonology also gives the teacher insight into why students might have difficulty segmenting or spelling words. For example, a nasalized vowel plus a nasal consonant sound is pronounced as a unit. Therefore, students may have difficulty hearing that /jŭmp/ consists of four separate sounds. They may segment it as three sounds: /j/, /ŭm/, and /p/. When spelling, students may hear /t/ before /r/ as /ch/ and spell it accordingly. As mentioned previously, /t/ before /r/ has a place of articulation in the mouth that is similar to /ch/, so the use of *ch* is not outrageous but instead is "reasonable and well motivated" (Treiman et al., 1994, p. 1336) and worthy of recognition (Read, 1971). The teacher need not be a linguist but rather should have phonemic awareness and a working knowledge of the sound structure of English.

Production of Speech Sounds

Correct pronunciation of speech sounds is encouraged through an understanding of the descriptions of the individual speech sounds (Moats, 1995). When students understand the kinesthetic feel and the visual display of the mouth as a sound is pronounced, they are better able to distinguish sounds.

In decoding instruction, students learn that vowel sounds are open and voiced. (See Figure 3.3 for the vowel sounds, arranged by mouth position.) The short vowels are most difficult to discriminate. Figure 10.1 (Cox, 1992) illustrates the mouth posi-

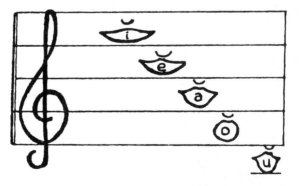

Figure 10.1. Mouth position for the short vowel sounds. (From Cox, A.R. [1992]. *Foundations for literacy: Structures and techniques for multisensory teaching of basic written English language skills* [p. 129]. Cambridge, MA: Educators Publishing Service; reprinted by permission.)

Table 10.1. Places of articulation of consonant sounds

Both lips	Teeth and lower lip	Between the teeth	Ridge behind teeth	Roof of mouth	Back of mouth	From the throat
/b/	/f/	/th/	/d/	/ch/	/g/	/h/
/m/	/v/	/th/	/l/	/j/	/k/	/hw/
/p/			/n/	/sh/	/ks/*	
			/r/	/y/	/kw/*	
			/s/	/zh/	/ng/	
			/t/		/w/	
			/z/			

*These combination sounds represent the most frequent sounds of *x* (/ks/) and *q* (/kw/), which is usually followed by *u*.

tions of the short vowel sounds. The teacher should study and share this figure with students. Visual awareness of the mouth positions for the production of vowel sounds heightens students' ability to discriminate the vowel sounds. Awareness of the distinctive, kinesthetic feel of sounds as they are produced also assists in discriminating easily confused vowel sounds (e.g., /ĭ/ makes you grin, /ĕ/ drops your chin).

To be able to provide correct models of consonant sounds, the teacher should study the production of consonant sounds according to three properties: the place of articulation, the flow of the air stream, and the activity of the vocal cords. Table 10.1 provides information about the place of articulation of the consonant sounds, using the phonic spellings that often are used in reading and spelling instruction. Table 10.2 provides information on the kinesthetic feel of the mouth and how the air stream flows from the mouth or nose during production of consonant sounds. Table 10.3 presents information about voiced and unvoiced consonant sounds. With awareness of each aspect of consonant sounds, the teacher will be better able to provide correct models for students.

Table 10.2. Flow of air during production of consonant sounds

Partially blocked and clipped	Blocked and continuous	Unblocked and aspirated	Through the nose, blocked, and continuous
/b/	/f/	/h/	/m/
/ch/	/hw/		/n/
/d/	/ks/		/ng/
/g/	/kw/		
/j/	/l/		
/k/	/r/		
/p/	/s/		
/t/	/sh/		
/y/	/th/		
	/th/		
	/v/		
	/w/		
	/z/		
	/zh/		

The terms *blocked, partially blocked,* and *unblocked* are used in spelling instruction to refer to the kinesthetic feel of the position of the tongue, teeth, or lips during the production of sounds in isolation. *Blocked* refers to the steady position of the tongue, teeth, or lips during the entire production of a sound. *Partially blocked* refers to a released position of the tongue or lips during the production of a sound. *Unblocked* refers to no obstruction of the sound by the tongue, teeth, or lips during the production of a sound. These terms are used to aid students in clearly feeling and distinguishing sounds for spelling.

Phonemic Awareness

The importance of phonemic awareness in learning to read and spell has been well documented (Adams, 1990; Bradley & Bryant, 1983; Goswami & Bryant, 1990; Liberman, Shankweiler, & Liberman, 1989). Spelling begins with the speller's awareness that spoken words are made up of sounds that are represented in print by letters. For the speller to represent those sounds in print accurately, he or she must be able to pronounce them correctly and discriminate them clearly.

Activities that promote phonological awareness, especially phonemic awareness, are outlined in Chapter 4 and must be included in beginning reading and spelling instruction. As students prepare to spell words, they need to engage in activities that promote the recognition or discrimination of specific sounds in words:

- *To heighten sensitivity to a particular sound in a word:* The teacher says a word and asks students to listen for a certain sound. Students repeat the word, listening for the sound. If they hear the sound, then they say the sound. If they do not hear the sound, then they say, "No."

- *To heighten sensitivity to the position of a particular sound in a word:* The teacher says a word and asks students to listen for the position of a particular sound in the word. Students repeat the word, listening for the position of the sound. Students indicate the position: initial, medial, or final (see Chapter 5 for activities that explore the concepts initial, medial, and final).

- *To promote spelling by analogy* (Goswami, 1988; Nation & Hulme, 1998): The teacher says a word, and students repeat it. The teacher tells students to change a sound (not a letter name) in the word and to pronounce the new word (e.g., change /s/ in *sat* to /m/ and pronounce the new word, change /t/ in *bat* to /g/ and pronounce the new word).

Table 10.3. Unvoiced and voiced consonant sounds

Unvoiced	Voiced
Pairs (read across)	
/p/	/b/
/t/	/d/
/k/	/g/
/f/	/v/
/s/	/z/
/th/	/th/
/ch/	/j/
/sh/	/zh/
Nonpairs (read down)	
/h/	/kw/
/hw/	/l/
/ks/	/m/
	/n/
	/ng/
	/r/
	/w/
	/y/

Orthography

Orthography refers to the rules that govern how words are represented in writing. Chapter 9 contains information that assists the student in managing English orthography for reading. With this information, the reader knows how to translate the orthography into its spoken equivalents. The speller's task is to determine how the phonemes of oral language are transcribed into the graphemes (i.e., letters or letter clusters) of written language. There are constraints in English orthography; for example, certain letters never double (e.g., *j, y, w*), certain letters do not occur in sequence (e.g., *skr* does not occur within a syllable), and words do not end in certain letters (e.g., *v, j*). Formal spelling instruction calls attention to these constraints and helps students manage English orthography for spelling by establishing a sense of the **frequency** and reliability of letter patterns (Brady & Moats, 1997).

Twenty-four speech sounds can be established as having a one-to-one correspondence with written letters (see Table 10.4). These sounds have only one spelling (e.g., /m/ is spelled *m*, /p/ is spelled *p*), or they have one spelling that is far more frequent

Table 10.4.   Sound-to-spelling translations of speech sounds, based on frequency

Vowel sounds with one frequent spelling	Consonant sounds with one frequent spelling	Vowel sounds with more than one frequent spelling	Consonant sounds with more than one frequent spelling
/ă/ = a (apple)	/b/ = b (bat)	/ŏ/ = o (octopus)	/ch/ = ch (cheek)
/ĕ/ = e (echo)	/f/ = f (fish)	a (watch)	ch (lunch, speech)
/ĭ/ = i (itch)	/g/ = g (goat)	/ŭ/ = u (cup)	tch (catch)
/ŏŏ/ = oo (book)	/h/ = h (house)	a (banana)	/d/ = d (dog)
/ōō/ = oo (moon)	/l/ = l (leaf)	/ā/= a-consonant-e (cake, vacate)	ed (smelled)
/âr/ = ar (star)	/m/ = m (mitten)	a (apron)	/j/ = j (jam)
/ôr/ = or (fork)	/n/ = n (nest)	ay (tray)	g (gentle, giant, biology)
	/p/ = p (pig)	/ē/= ee (feet)	dge (edge)
	/kw/ = qu (queen)	e-consonant-e (athlete)	ge (hinge)
	/r/ = r (rabbit)	e (equal)	/k/ = c (cat, cot, cut, clam, crab)
	/w/ = w (wish)	ee (three)	k (keep, kite, sky)
	/ks/ = x (box)	y (penny)	ck (pocket)
	/y/ = y (yarn)	/ī/ = i-consonant-e (five, invite)	ck (back)
	/th/ = th (rather)	i (iris)	k (book, milk)
	/th/ = th (thimble)	y (fly)	ke (make)
	/hw/ = wh (whistle)	/ō/ = o-consonant-e (rope, remote)	c (music)
	/sh/ = sh (ship)	o (open)	/ng/ = ng (king)
	/zh/ = si (erosion)	ow (snow)	n (sink, angle)
		/ū/ = u-consonant-e (cube, infuse)	/s/ = s (sock)
		u (unicorn)	c (grocery, icicle)
		ue (statue)	ss (kiss, discuss)
		/er/ = er (fern)	s (cactus)
		or (world)	ce (mice)
		/au/ = au (saucer)	se (horse, mouse)
		aw (saw)	/t/ = t (table)
		a (ball)	ed (jumped)
		/oi/ = oi (boil)	/v/ = v (valentine)
		oy (boy)	ve (have)
		/ou/ = ou (out)	/z/ = z (zipper)
		ow (cow)	s (pansy)
			s (has)
			se (cheese)

than any other spelling (e.g., /f/ is spelled *f* much more often than *ph* or *gh*, /ĕ/ is spelled *e* much more often than *ea*) (Hanna et al., 1966). This information will enable students to spell more than half of the phonemes of English.

The other speech sounds of English have a more precarious link to orthography (see Table 10.4). The transcription of each of these sounds depends not only on frequency but also on the position of the sound in a word, the length of the word, the accent, or the influence of surrounding sounds. To make sense of spelling choices, students must realize there is a difference between decoding and spelling. When decoding, students look at the printed symbols and translate those graphemes into phonemes. Students have no difficulty reading *gate* because they know that the vowel sound in an *a*-consonant-*e* syllable is pronounced as /ā/. They can read *bait* because they know that *ai* is pronounced /ā/. Knowing that *eigh* is pronounced /ā/ enables readers to pronounce the word *weight*. All of these words follow frequent, reliable patterns for reading.

Spelling a word starts with sounds, not letter sequences. For spelling, students hear /gāt/, /bāt/, and /wāt/. Except for the initial phonemes, these words sound similar. They all are one-syllable words with medial /ā/ that end in /t/. Students will have little trouble spelling the initial or final sounds, but spelling the medial sounds may be problematic. Without the memory of letter patterns, either because of lack of exposure to print or because of poor orthographic memory, spellers have difficulty knowing whether to use *a*-consonant-*e*, *ai*, or *eigh*. They must be taught that when they hear /ā/ before a final consonant sound, it is most frequently represented with *a*-consonant-*e* (e.g., *cake*, *insane*, *equivocate*). With this information, students will be able to spell correctly a high percentage of words with initial or medial /ā/ (Hanna et al., 1966). Not only does their spelling accuracy increase, but also the focus on one spelling establishes that pattern well and actually heightens awareness of other possible spellings of /ā/. If all of the possible spellings of /ā/ are taught at one time, however, beginning spellers and poor spellers in particular will be overwhelmed with choices. Words such as *bait* and *weight*, which contain less frequent spellings of /ā/, are best learned or memorized as whole words.

This problem exists with most published spelling series. The weekly spelling lists confuse students with multiple choices and seldom offer direction in terms of establishing frequency or reliability, as in the following example (Cook, Farnum, Gabrielson, & Temple, 1998, p. 28):

Words with /ū/ and /o͞o/

1. bloom	6. few	11. clue	16. dew
2. ruler	7. used	12. rescue	17. flute
3. broom	8. loose	13. movie	18. due
4. usual	9. whose	14. human	19. tune
5. roof	10. glue	15. avenue	20. beautiful

This list has two sounds, /ū/ as in *use* and /o͞o/ as in *moon*. These two sounds are auditorily similar with similar visual displays. The only noticeable difference is in the production of the two sounds. The tongue is tensed when pronouncing /ū/, so it sounds like /yo͞o/. But because /ū/ is often pronounced /o͞o/ in running speech, it will be difficult for students to clearly discriminate the two sounds. The other problem with this list is the number of spelling choices (seven) for these two sounds: *u*-consonant-*e*, *ue*, *u*, *oo*, *o*, *ew*, and *eau*. Some of the choices are extremely infrequent (see Table 10.5). Few words

Table 10.5.   Infrequent spellings of vowel sounds

/ă/ = pl*ai*d, l*augh*

/ā/ = r*ai*n, caf*é*, st*ea*k, matin*ee*, v*ei*n, *eigh*t, th*ere*, th*ey*, ball*et*

/au/ = c*augh*t, br*ough*t, br*oa*d

/ĕ/ = h*ea*d, s*ai*d, *a*ny

/ē/ = b*ea*ch, c*ei*ling, vall*ey*, sk*i*, pr*ie*st, pet*ite*

/er/ = doll*ar*, b*ir*d, anch*or*, b*ur*n, s*ear*ch, j*our*nal

/ĭ/ = capt*ai*n, clim*ate*, forf*ei*t, frag*ile*, g*y*m

/ī/ = *ai*sle, k*ay*ak, h*eigh*t, t*ie*, l*igh*t, n*y*lon, st*y*le, d*ye*, b*uy*

/ō/ = b*eau*, b*oa*t, t*oe*, d*ough*

/o͝o/ = p*u*sh

/o͞o/ = s*ou*p, d*o*, sh*oe*, thr*ough*, fr*ui*t

/ou/ = pl*ough*

/ŭ/ = s*o*n, bl*oo*d, t*ou*ch

/ū/ = b*eau*ty, *Eu*rope, n*ew*

have the /ū/ or /o͞o/ sound spelled with *o* as in *move,* *ew* as in *dew,* or *eau* as in *beautiful.* Helpful information for students includes the following: /ū/ is best spelled with *u*-consonant-*e* before a final consonant sound as in *cube* or *infuse;* /ū/ at the end of a syllable is spelled *u* as in *human* or, at the end of a word, *ue* as in *statue;* and the /o͞o/ sound in initial, medial, or final position is best spelled *oo* (Cox, 1977). It also may be helpful for students to overpronounce or to exaggerate the /ū/ sound in some words as /yo͞o/ to differentiate it from /o͞o/ and to clarify the best spelling choice (e.g., an overpronunciation of *tube* as /tyo͞ob/ rather than /to͞ob/ clarifies the spelling as *u*-consonant-*e* instead of *oo*).

Good spellers, who of course are good readers (decoders), begin to weight the frequency of these spellings as they read (Adams, 1990; Foorman, 1994; Seidenberg & Mc-Clelland, 1989) and are better able to deal with a list that has multiple spellings of one sound. Poor spellers who are poor readers do not receive sufficient exposure to these patterns to weight them. Poor spellers who are good readers do not have adequate sensitivity to letter patterns to determine frequency. The goal of effective spelling instruction is to make the reliability of English orthography obvious to all students by teaching the most frequent, reliable orthographic patterns of English (Post & Carreker, 2002; Post, Carreker, & Holland, 2001).

Morphology

Morphology is the study of *morphemes,* the smallest units of language that carry meaning (prefixes, suffixes, roots, and combining forms; see Chapters 6 and 9 for more information on morphemes). Morphemic knowledge advances students from the spelling of one-syllable base words to the spelling of one-syllable base words with suffixes and eventually to the spelling of other derivatives (i.e., a base word plus one or more affixes) and multisyllabic words. Knowledge of suffixes and inflectional morphemes signals to students that /pĭnz/ contains two morphemes or meaningful units: the base word /pĭn/ and the suffix /z/, which makes the word plural; therefore, /z/ is spelled *s* not *z*. Without the understanding of suffixes and inflectional morphemes, students remain literal in their spellings and write /jŭmpt/ as *jumpt* and /băngd/ as *bangd* because that is what they hear. The understanding that a suffix that begins with a consonant is a consonant suffix and a suffix that begins with a vowel is vowel suffix helps students when they add suffixes to base words to spell derivatives. The final letter of a base word may be doubled or dropped, but this is true only when adding a vowel suffix (e.g., *starring* but not *starrless, hoping* but not *hopful*).

Knowledge of prefixes and roots facilitates students' spelling of multisyllabic words (Adams, 1990; Brady & Moats, 1997; Henry, 1988). For example, the word *attraction* contains three morphemes. These morphemes serve not only as meaning-filled units but also as spelling units. The word attraction can be spelled in chunks instead of sound by sound. Knowing that some consonant prefixes change their spellings for **euphony** (i.e., to ease pronunciation; see Table 10.6), students know to spell a word such as *attraction* with two *t*'s because the *at-* in *attraction* represents a spelling deviation of the prefix *ad-*. The prefix changes the final letter to match the initial letter of the root *tract*. With knowledge of morphology, students can clarify spelling choices and contend with more complex levels of orthography.

Word Origins

Chapter 6 outlines the Anglo-Saxon, Latin, and Greek layers of language in English (see also Henry, 2003). These languages and others have shaped the orthography of En-

glish as evidenced in the spelling of /sh/. Fourteen different spellings have been noted in English (Bryson, 1990): *sh* as in *ship; ch* as in *chef; ti* as in *nation; si* as in *discussion; ci* as in *special; xi* as in *anxious; sci* as in *conscious; sch* as in *schnauzer; ce* as in *ocean; se* as in *nauseous; s* as in *sugar; ss* as in *tissue; psh* as in *pshaw;* and *chsi* as in *fuchsia.* These spellings represent different layers of language within English: *sh* from Anglo-Saxon; *ch* from French; *ti, ci, si, xi,* and *sci* from Latin; *sch* from German; *ce* from Greek, and *chsi* after German botanist Fuchs. The layers of other languages make English a rich tapestry of words, but they create a confusing orthography, thus compounding the difficulties poor spellers have with spelling. It would seem logical to change orthography to make it less confusing and to make words easier to spell.

Table 10.6. Prefixes that change spelling for euphony

Prefix	Prefix changed for euphony
ab-	*a-, abs-*
ad-	*a-, ac-, af-, ag-, al-, an-, ap-, ar-, as-, at-*
con-	*co-, col-, com-, cor-*
en-	*em-*
ex-	*e-, ec-, ef-*
in-	*il-, im-, ir-*
ob-	*oc-, of-, op-*
sub-	*suc-, suf-, sup-, sur-, sus-*

There have been attempts to reform English orthography but to no avail. Benjamin Franklin proposed a phonetic alphabet with a better one-to-one letter–sound correspondence, which in the end did not gain much favor. Noah Webster, who advocated educational reform and America's own form of spelling to complement its unique form of government, proposed changes such as *bred* for *bread, laf* for *laugh,* and *crum* for *crumb.* Although these changes were not accepted, Webster was successful in changing the spellings of words such as *honour* to *honor, centre* to *center,* and *publick* to *public.* An organization dedicated to spelling reform, the American Philological Association, made concerted efforts to change the orthography of English in the late 1800s and early 1900s but had little success. In the 1930s, *The Chicago Tribune,* in an effort to increase readership by making words easier to read, used these spellings in their newspaper: *thru, tho,* and *thoro* (Venezky, 1980). Although it seems reasonable to simplify and unify orthography, such attempts have failed. Perhaps this is because changing the orthography of English would mask its rich, interesting history and the interrelatedness of words (e.g., *muscle* is related to *muscular,* which accounts for the silent *c* in *muscle;* see Henry, 2003).

Rather than bemoan the inconsistencies of English, students can take advantage of information about word origins to refine their spelling knowledge. Initially, students are taught that the most frequent, though not the only, spelling of /f/ is *f.* This information serves them well for spelling most words. With the knowledge that long, scientific terms are usually of Greek origin and that Greek words containing /f/ are spelled with *ph,* students have information that will help them to spell words such as *chlorophyll* and *photosynthesis.* Students will also note that words of Greek origin containing /k/ are often spelled with *ch* and those containing /ĭ/ are often spelled with *y.* With knowledge of word origins, students come to understand why some words are spelled in unexpected ways, and, more important, students can determine the appropriate spellings for these words. (See Henry, 1988, 2003, for more on spellings according to word origin.)

FORMAL SPELLING INSTRUCTION

Spelling is a skill that must be formally taught. In preschool and kindergarten, the use of invented spelling should be encouraged and supported with phonological awareness

training (Blachman, Ball, Black, & Tangel, 1994, 2000; Castle, Riach, & Nicholson, 1994; Rubin & Eberhardt, 1996). (See Chapter 4 for activities that can be incorporated into the classroom routine; see also Adams, Foorman, Lundberg, & Beeler, 1998.) Through the use of invented spellings, students learn the essence of spelling: translating sounds to symbols. Good spelling, however, requires more than translating sounds to symbols; it also demands a sensitivity to letter patterns in words. Although invented spelling reinforces sound–symbol correspondences, it does not provide the correct models that students need to build orthographic knowledge. Students must be formally taught the patterns and rules of English orthography, beginning in the middle of first grade. Learning the patterns and rules cannot be left to chance. Correct spelling has a direct impact on students' reading proficiency (Adams, 1990). Formal spelling instruction should include the following:

- Phonological awareness training

- Opportunities for kindergarteners and beginning first graders to experiment with writing using invented spelling

- Multisensory guided discovery teaching introductions to the sounds, sound–symbol correspondences, patterns, rules, and morphemes of English, beginning in the middle of first grade and using a systematic, sequential, cumulative order of presentation

- Opportunities to analyze and sort words

- Practice using multisensory structured procedures

- A multisensory procedure for learning irregular words

- Opportunities to use the words in writing through dictation and personal writing

Invented Spelling

Students' use of invented spelling provides the teacher with information about how well students have learned and internalized information about language structure. When students use invented spelling, they are not reinventing the spelling of words. They are applying their acquired knowledge of sounds, symbols, and letter patterns to the task of spelling an unfamiliar word (Read, 1971). As students learn more about language structure, their knowledge is reflected in the spelling. The development of invented spelling should follow the definite stages of spelling development. These stages match students' acquisition of language knowledge (Rubin & Eberhardt, 1996): 1) Students spell words that represent partial phonetic patterns (e.g., *s, c,* or *sd* for *seed*), 2) students spell words that represent complete phonetic patterns (e.g., *sed, ced,* or *cd* for *seed*), and 3) students spell words that represent complete phonetic patterns and use conventional orthographic patterns (e.g., *sead, ceed, sede,* or *cede* for *seed*). Children who demonstrate progression through these stages in their invented spelling are gaining a solid foundation for spelling as well as reading. When children can use word structure to spell phonetically, they are better able to learn more complex spellings; they also make rapid progress in learning to read (Moats, 1995). The teacher must be alert to the children who are not moving through this sequence and give them guidance to ensure they will have the necessary foundation for reading and spelling.

Formal spelling instruction extends the spelling information students gain through invented spelling and teaches the structure of the language for spelling, thus enabling students to move from invented spelling to conventional spelling. Words can be cate-

gorized as regular, rule, and irregular (Carreker, 2002). It will be helpful to introduce information for spelling instruction in these same categories.

Regular Words

Regular words are spelled the way they sound. They follow the frequent, reliable sound-to-letter translations or patterns of the language (see Table 10.4). Some regular words are transparent in their spellings, such as *in*, *rag*, or *help*. There is only one spelling or only one predominant spelling of the sounds; hence there is no confusion about how to spell the sounds in these words. Not all regular words are as transparent in their spellings. Some regular words contain sounds with indefinite spellings, such as /k/, which can be spelled *k*, *c*, or *ck*. One spelling is not overwhelmingly apparent as the best choice. Students need to be taught generalizations about the use and frequency of letter patterns in English (Cox, 1977; Hanna et al., 1966; Post & Carreker, 2002; Post et al., 2001.).

Sounds with Multiple Spelling or Letter Patterns

When there is more than one frequent spelling or letter pattern for a sound, the best choice of the pattern is based on the frequency of the pattern and the situation of the sound in a word. The **situation** (i.e., the particular circumstances of how a sound occurs in a word) of the sound may be based on the position of the sound in a word, the placement of accent (see Chapters 5 and 9 for activities that promote awareness of accent), the length of the word, the influence of surrounding sounds, or a combination of these factors. Awareness of sounds and syllables in words is important in determining the best choice of letters or letter patterns (see Chapter 9 for activities that promote awareness of syllables). The terms that are introduced in decoding to express the positions of letters in words—*initial*, *medial*, and *final*—are also used to describe the positions of sounds in words. *Initial* refers to the first position in a syllable. *Final* refers to the last position in a syllable. *Medial* refers to any position between the first and last positions.

Students need not guess or give up when dealing with the sounds that have more than one frequent spelling or letter pattern. Instead, they consider the situation of the sound that may be represented by more than one spelling. The situation provides clues that will help students in their decision-making process. For example, in considering the spelling of /măch/, students think about possible, frequent spellings of /ch/ (*ch* or *tch*). To decide which spelling is the best choice, students determine the situation of the sound in the word. The sound is in the final position of a one-syllable word, and it comes after a short vowel. On the basis of this situation, students know that *tch* is the best choice for spelling /ch/ in the word *match*. The following examples of spelling patterns show the best choices for spelling sounds according to their situations. Each pattern should be introduced one at a time and practiced to mastery. A suggested order of introducing these patterns is mentioned later in this chapter.

Spelling Choices with Situations Based on Position

1. When is /oi/ spelled *oi*, and when is it spelled *oy*?

oil	*boy*
ointment	*toy*
boil	*joy*
coin	*enjoy*
joint	*employ*

In initial or medial position, /oi/ is spelled *oi*.	In final position, /oi/ is spelled *oy*. (A less frequent but reliable spelling choice for /oi/ at the end of a syllable is *oy* as in *royal* or *voyage*.)

2. When is /ou/ spelled *ou*, and when is it spelled *ow*?

out	*cow*
ouch	*how*
found	*plow*
shout	*meow*
ground	

In initial or medial position, /ou/ is spelled *ou*.	In final position, /ou/ is spelled *ow*.

(Less frequent but reliable spelling choices that could be introduced later as refinement include the following: /ou/ is spelled *ow* in a one-syllable word before final /l/ or /n/ *owl* or *down*, and /ou/ is spelled *ow* before /er/ as in *shower* or *flower*.)

Spelling Choices with Situations Based on Surrounding Sounds or Letters

1. When is /k/ spelled *k*, and when is it spelled *c*?

keep	*cat*
kit	*cost*
sky	*cup*
Before any sound represented by *e, i,* or *y*, /k/ is spelled *k*.	*clasp*
	cramp
	Before everything else, /k/ is spelled *c*.

2. When is /j/ spelled *g*, and when is it spelled *j*?

gem	*jam*
giant	*jot*
biology	*just*
Before any sound represented by *e, i,* or *y*, /j/ is spelled *g*.	Before everything else, /j/ is spelled *j*.

Spelling Choices with Situations Based on Position, Length, and Surrounding Sounds

1. When is final /ch/ spelled *tch*, and when is it spelled *ch*?

catch	*speech*
sketch	*porch*
pitch	*pouch*
blotch	*belch*
Dutch	*sandwich*
Final /ch/ in a one-syllable base word after a short vowel is spelled *tch*.	Final /ch/ after two vowels or a consonant or in a word of more than one syllable is spelled *ch*.

2. When is final /j/ spelled *dge*?

badge
edge
ridge
dodge
fudge
Final /j/ in a one-syllable base word after a short vowel is spelled *dge*.

3. When is final /k/ spelled *ck,* and when is it spelled *c?*

back	*picnic*
peck	*music*
sick	*lilac*
block	
stuck	

Final /k/ after a short vowel in a one-syllable word is spelled *ck.*

Final /k/ in a multisyllabic base word after a short vowel is spelled *c.*

Spelling Choices for Vowels

1. What are the best choices for spelling /ŏ/?

odd	*want*
hot	*wash*
top	*wand*
lost	*wasp*
spot	*wall*

The sound /ŏ/ is spelled *o,* except after /w/, when /ŏ/ is spelled *a.*

2. What are the best choices for spelling /ŭ/?

up	*alike*
us	*along*
cup	*parade*
rust	*tuba*
shut	*sofa*

The sound /ŭ/ is spelled *u,* except at the end of an unaccented syllable, when /ŭ/ is spelled *a.*

3. What are the best choices for spelling /ā/?

ate	*day*
ape	*say*
made	*play*
insane	*delay*
evaluate	*repay*

Initial or medial /ā/ before a final consonant sound is spelled *a*-consonant-*e.*

Final /ā/ is spelled *ay.*

table
baby
lady
basic
paper

At the end of a syllable, /ā/ is spelled *a.*

4. What are the best spelling choices for /ē/?

eel	*stampede*
feet	*complete*
green	*extreme*
need	*intervene*

Initial or medial /ē/ in a one-syllable word is spelled *ee.*

Before a final consonant sound in a word word of two or more syllables, /ē/ is spelled *e*-consonant-*e.*

meter	*bee*	*tardy*
fever	*see*	*sixty*
even	*free*	*ugly*
evil	*three*	*candy*

At the end of a syllable, /ē/ is spelled *e*.

In final position of a one-syllable word, /ē/ is spelled *ee*. In final position of a word with two or more syllables, /ē/ is spelled *y*.

5. What are the best choices for spelling /ī/?

ice	*fly*
five	*try*
recline	*deny*
excite	*reply*

Initial or medial /ī/ before a final consonant sound is spelled *i-consonant-e*.

At the end of a word, /ī/ is spelled *y*.

iris
fiber
tiger
lilac

At the end of a syllable, /ī/ is spelled *i*.

6. What are the best ways to spell /ō/?

rope	*show*
home	*slow*
explode	*window*
trombone	*yellow*

Initial or medial /ō/ before a final consonant sound is spelled *o-consonant-e*.

Final /ō/ is spelled *ow*.

open
over
robot
polite

At the end of a syllable, /ō/ is spelled *o*.

7. What is the best way to spell /ū/?

use	*sue*
cube	*cue*
infuse	*rescue*
constitute	*continue*

Initial or medial /ū/ before a final consonant sound is spelled *u-consonant-e*.

Final /ū/ is spelled *ue*.

unit
tunic
music
tuna

At the end of a syllable, /ū/is spelled *u*.

Note: When spelling words with /ū/, it may be necessary to overpronounce or to exaggerate the sound as /yoo/.

Summary of Sounds with Multiple Spelling or Letter Patterns   These spelling patterns offer students a way to manage English orthography for spelling. There will be exceptions to these patterns. It is exciting when students discover the exceptions. To find an exception, students must understand the pattern when it is introduced and remember it. They must compare that pattern with words they hold in memory and realize that there are words that share the same sound but have different spelling patterns. That is active reflection about language. An enthusiastic "Good for you! You found a word that doesn't fit the pattern!" from the teacher affirms that students are thinking about language.

The patterns are not to be memorized. They will be established in memory through multisensory guided discovery introductions, multisensory practice, and opportunities to write through spelling dictation and personal writing. The teacher should direct students' attention to spelling patterns as they occur in the reading. The teacher should refrain from describing the patterns as rules. The term *rule* should be reserved for situations in which a letter in a base word is doubled, dropped, or changed (**rule words** are discussed later in this chapter).

Order of Presentation of Spelling Patterns

When students are deciding the best spelling choice for a sound with multiple spellings, the situation of the sound and the frequency of possible letter patterns are important determiners. Students first learn the letter patterns that occur with greater frequency so that they can spell many words. Less frequent patterns are taught later. For dyslexic and beginning spellers, the introductions of the multiple spelling patterns of a sound should be separated to allow these students time and practice to master one possible pattern before another is introduced. In considering the sounds with multiple spelling patterns just delineated, which represent a sampling of patterns, the approximate order of introduction based on frequency might be as follows. It is important to note that other spelling patterns not delineated previously (e.g., /ĭ/ = i, /p/ = p, /ă/ = a) will be interspersed in the order of introduction.

1.	/ŏ/ = *o* as in *octopus*	14.	/ē/ = *y* as in *penny*
2.	/ŭ/ = *u* as in *up*	15.	/ā/ = *ay* as in *tray*
3.	/k/ = *k* as in *kit*	16.	/ā/ = *a* as in *apron*
4.	/k/ = *c* as in *cup*	17.	/ē/ = *e* as in *even*
5.	/k/ = *ck* as in *truck*	18.	/ī/ = *i* as in *iris*
6.	/j/ = *j* as in *just*	19.	/ō/ = *o* as in *open*
7.	/ē/ = *ee* as in feet and *three*	20.	/ū/ = *u* as in *unit*
8.	/ā/ = *a*-consonant-*e* as in *cake*	21.	/k/ = *c* as in *music*
9.	/ī/ = *i*-consonant-*e* as in *five*	22.	/oi/ = *oi* as in *oil*
10.	/ō/ = *o*-consonant-*e* as in *rope*	23.	/oi/ = *oy* as in *boy*
11.	/ū/ = *u*-consonant-*e* as in *cube*	24.	/ch/ = *ch* as in *chip*
12.	/ē/ = *e*-consonant-*e* as in *athlete*	25.	/ch/ = *tch* as in *witch*
13.	/ī/ = *y* as in *fly*	26.	/ou/ = *ou* as in *out*

27. /ou/ = *ow* as in *cow*   31. /j/ = *dge* as in *badge*

28. /ŭ/ = *a* as in *along* or *sofa*   32. /ū/ = *ue* as in *statue*

29. /ō/ = *ow* as in *snow*   33. /ŏ/ = *a* as in *watch*

30. /j/ = *g* as in *giant*

Introduction of Spelling Patterns with Guided Discovery Teaching

The patterns of spelling are introduced using a guided discovery teaching procedure, similar to that used in the introduction of reading concepts. The guided discovery teaching procedure uses a Socratic method in which the teacher asks questions to lead students to discover a new spelling pattern. This procedure heightens students' awareness of sounds in words; encourages students to think about how sounds are represented in words; and gives students the opportunity to notice letters in words, thereby heightening their sensitivity to letter patterns.

1. *Auditory discovery:* The teacher reads five to seven discovery words one by one, which contain the same sound and spelling pattern. Students repeat each word after the teacher. Students discover the sound that is the same in all of the discovery words and the position(s) of the sound. It is helpful for students to look in small mirrors as they repeat the words. The visual display on the mouth helps students discriminate the sound. Attention to the kinesthetic feel of the mouth also helps students discriminate the sound. **Auditory discovery** heightens students' awareness of a particular sound in words.

2. *Prediction:* After students have discovered the sound, they predict how the sound might be spelled. The sound students are discovering has been previously introduced for reading. This step encourages students to reflect on their language knowledge.

3. *Visual discovery:* After students have made their predictions, the teacher writes the discovery words on the board. Students carefully look at all of the words and decide which letter or letters are the same and where the letter or letters are located in the words. They also notice any other common features about the words, such as number of syllables, accent, or surrounding sounds. This step heightens awareness of letter patterns.

4. *Verbalization of the pattern:* With the discovery of the sound and its spelling, students verbalize the pattern (e.g., final /k/ after a short vowel in a one-syllable word is spelled *ck*) in their own words. Students then apply this information by spelling five to seven new words with the pattern.

Introducing a Spelling Pattern

Teacher: Listen as I read some words. I want you to repeat each word after me. Listen for the sound that is the same in all of the words. [The teacher reads the words *pick, sack, luck, clock,* and *peck* one at a time as students repeat.] What sound (not letter name) do you hear in all of the words?

Students: /k/

Teacher: Where do you hear the sound? In what position(s)?

Students: The sound is in the final position.

Teacher: Make a prediction about how this sound might be spelled. Think about what you know about the language. How might this sound be spelled? [Stu-

dents might predict *c, k,* or *ck.*] Watch carefully as I write the discovery words on the board. What letter or letters are the same?

Students: All of the words have the letters *ck*.

Teacher: In what position(s) do you see the letters?

Students: The letters *ck* are in final position.

Teacher: Is there anything else that is similar about these words?

Students: All of the words have short vowel sounds and have one syllable.

Teacher: What does the pattern seem to be?

Students: Final /k/ after a short vowel in a one-syllable word is spelled *ck*.

Teacher: I want you to apply what you have discovered. I will dictate some words for you to spell. [The teacher dictates five to seven words with the pattern one at a time as students write them on paper. The Simultaneous Oral Spelling (S.O.S.) procedure described later in this chapter is a helpful tool in word dictation.]

Multisensory Practice of Sounds and Patterns

Spelling sounds and patterns are practiced daily using multisensory structured procedures.

Sound Dictation   Daily review with a sound or spelling deck develops automaticity in translating sounds to spellings (Cox, 1992). Each introduced sound is written on a separate index card. The sounds are represented by letters with appropriate diacritical markings that are enclosed in parentheses or slash marks; for example, (ā) or /ā/. The possible spellings of the sound are written on each card. Key words that unlock the spellings of each sound are also written on the cards.

While looking at a card that is not shown to the students, the teacher dictates the sound written on the card. Students repeat the sound and name the letter or letters that spell the sound as they write them. If students hesitate about the spelling of a sound, the teacher cues students with the appropriate key word. (See Appendix B at the end of this book for multisensory structured reading programs with spelling components. Several of these programs have commercially produced spelling decks that provide daily review of sounds that have been taught through a multisensory procedure for reading.)

When students are spelling sounds with multiple spellings, they repeat the sound and name and write the frequent, reliable spelling choices. For example, if the teacher dictates /ā/, students repeat /ā/ and say, "*a*-consonant-*e, a;* final, *ay.*" In this abbreviated response, the best spelling choices for /ā/ are recognized. Students write this information in shorthand: *a-e, a // ay*. The double slash marks (//) define the spellings according to their positions in words. Everything to the left of the slash marks represents possible spellings of a sound in initial or medial position. Everything to the right represents possible spellings of a sound in final position.

The media that students use to write their responses can be varied daily to provide different kinesthetic reinforcement. Students may write responses on unlined paper, on the chalkboard, on their desktops, on carpet squares, or in salt trays.

Word Dictation   As each new spelling pattern is introduced, it is practiced to mastery first through the use of homogenous practice sessions in which every word contains the new pattern. When students demonstrate success in spelling the new pattern, het-

erogeneous practice sessions that contain the new pattern and previously introduced patterns are used. The words used for these practice sessions are not words that students have memorized or will need to memorize. At first, the words for heterogeneous practice should be one-syllable words that progress from two to three sounds to five to six sounds. When students are ready, they start with the spelling of one-syllable base words with suffixes, then move on to multisyllabic words, and finally, to multisyllabic derivatives. Word dictation practices provide review of sounds and patterns and instills a thinking process for spelling.

To establish this thinking process for spelling, a structured procedure is used for word dictation practice. S.O.S. was introduced by Gillingham and Stillman (1960) and adapted by Cox (1992; see Figure 10.2). At each step the teacher provides the necessary corrective feedback. The steps and rationale are as follows:

1. *Look and listen.* Students look at the teacher and focus on his or her mouth as he or she dictates the word. By focusing on the teacher's mouth, students use the visual display to clarify the sounds in the dictated word. For example, /f/ will be visually displayed with the upper teeth resting on the lower lip, whereas /th/ will be displayed with the tip of the tongue protruding between the teeth.

2. *Repeat and segment.* Students repeat the word while looking in a small mirror. The use of a mirror provides visual cues such as the position of the mouth or the placement of the tongue, teeth, or lips. The repetition of the word affirms that students heard the word correctly and gives them additional auditory input and kinesthetic feedback. The kinesthetic feedback clarifies the sounds in the dictated word. For example, with /f/, students feel the upper teeth resting on the lower lip, and with /th/, they feel the tip of the tongue protruding through the teeth.

   The segmenting part of this step depends on the kind of word students are spelling and the needs of students. Initially, students segment monosyllabic words

Figure 10.2. Simultaneous oral spelling (S.O.S.) procedure. 1) Look and listen, 2) repeat (echo) and segment, 3) name the letters, 4) name and write, and 5) read to check. (Used by permission of Neuhaus Education Center, Bellaire, TX. *Sources:* Cox, 1992; Gillingham & Stillman, 1960.)

with two to five sounds. Students segment each word into its constituent sounds. They may use their fingers to mark the sounds. They make a fist, and beginning with the thumb of their nonwriting hand (left palm up for right-handers; right palm down for left-handers) and moving in a left-to-right progression, students extend a finger for each sound that they hear as they segment the word. Instead of using their fingers, students may move counters such as blocks, buttons, or pennies for each sound they hear as they segment the word. Students continue spelling monosyllabic words until they can segment words into constituent sounds with ease.

When students can successfully spell monosyllabic words of five sounds, they are ready to advance to the spelling of derivatives and multisyllabic words. A derivative should be orally separated into morphemic units (e.g., /jŭmpt/ is base word /jŭmp/ plus suffix /t/). A multisyllabic word should be segmented into its component syllables. Students may use the fingers of their nonwriting hand, blocks, buttons, or pennies to segment the words into morphemic units or syllables.

3. *Name the letters.* Before writing the word on paper, students spell the word aloud. This is a rehearsal step for writing. The teacher can guide students to the correct spelling before they write. The naming of letters impresses letter sequences in memory (Gillingham & Stillman, 1997).

   If students have segmented the word using their fingers or counters, then they may want to touch each finger or counter as they spell, thereby reinforcing the sound–letter connection and sequence.

4. *Name and write.* Students write the word while naming the letters (Cox, 1992; Gillingham & Stillman, 1997). The rationale for this step is that naming letters builds the visual sequence of letters in the word through auditory and kinesthetic input. It is important for students to see the word they have spelled orally. If handwriting is not fluent, students can use plastic letters or letter cards to spell the words, or the teacher could serve as an **amanuensis** by writing for students on paper or on the board.

5. *Read to check.* After students have written the word, they read the word silently, using their decoding information. Knowledge of syllable types and syllable-division patterns will aid students' accurate reading of the word and confirmation of the spelling (see Chapter 9). This final step is intended to build independence in knowing that the word is spelled correctly and to teach proofreading skills. To monitor a large group in a class environment, the teacher may have students read the word aloud together and then touch and name the letters of this word. The teacher gives appropriate corrective feedback.

The S.O.S. procedure provides a structure for teaching students how to think about the process of spelling a word. Instead of impulsively writing a word on paper, students think about the sounds in the word and how those sounds can be spelled. They also impress the letter sequence in memory by naming the letters, monitor the spelling of the word by naming the letters while writing, and check the spelling by reading the word. In the initial stages of spelling instruction with dyslexic students, it may be necessary to build an understanding and memory of the five steps gradually by breaking the procedure down into smaller parts. Students may begin with Steps 1 and 2. The teacher says the word, and students repeat the word and segment it into its constituent

sounds. Students with recalcitrant spelling deficits may require practice with this abbreviated procedure for several days or weeks.

When students are secure with these two steps, Step 3 may be added, in which students spell the word aloud. When these three steps are secure, students can add Steps 4 and 5, with the teacher serving as the amanuensis. When the teacher writes the word, students can better attend to the letter sequence in the word and do not have to worry about the formation of the letters. Eventually, students will complete all five steps of the S.O.S. procedure independently.

Sentence Dictation   When students' handwriting is fluent and students have demonstrated success with word dictation, the dictation of phrases and sentences can begin. The dictation practice sessions are designed to review previously introduced spelling patterns and irregular words in context. Only three or four phrases or simple sentences are used for a dictation session. A structured procedure for dictation (Cox, 1992; Gillingham & Stillman, 1997; see Figure 10.3) aids this process. The steps and rationale of the procedure are as follows:

1. *Look and listen.* Students look at the teacher and listen as the teacher dictates a sentence. As with S.O.S., students look at the teacher's mouth to clarify the sounds in the words.

2. *Repeat.* Students repeat the sentence. Using a nonverbal cue, the teacher signals that students should repeat the sentence. Students continue to repeat the sentence until it is secure.

3. *Write.* When the teacher believes that the sentence is secure, he or she indicates that students should begin writing the sentence. The teacher again uses a nonverbal

Figure 10.3.   Dictation procedure. 1) Look and listen, 2) repeat (echo), 3) write, and 4) proofread. (Used by permission of Neuhaus Education Center, Bellaire, TX. *Sources:* Cox, 1992; Gillingham & Stillman, 1960.)

cue to indicate that students should begin to write. The use of nonverbal cues does not interrupt students' auditory memory of the sentence sequence.

4. *Proofread.* When students have finished writing the sentence, the teacher dictates it three times as students check for missing words, for capitalization and punctuation, and for spelling errors. As students check each feature, they place a checkmark at the end of the sentence. Three checkmarks after the sentence indicates that all three features have been checked. Students can extend this method of checking to their written composition. After writing a paragraph, they should check it three times for these same features. Three checkmarks in the top margin of a paper indicate that all three features have been checked.

It is suggested that students be given one more opportunity on another day to check the dictation paper for spelling errors. A freshly completed dictation paper is considered "hot" (Cox, 1992). It is difficult to see errors in a "hot" dictation paper. When students have the opportunity to review the dictation sentences at another time, they are better able to see errors. With knowledge of the frequent, reliable patterns in English, orthography is no longer a conundrum to students. They have a means of organizing and managing the language for spelling.

Rule Words

Rule words are spelled the way they sound, but certain information needs to be considered before the word is written. There are five major rules that indicate when a letter should be doubled, dropped, or changed. Two of these rules are used for doubling consonants within a base word. The other three major rules deal with spelling derivatives. They involve a change to the spelling of a base word (i.e., a letter is doubled, dropped, or changed) when adding a suffix. All of the rules are introduced through guided discovery teaching procedures.

Major Spelling Rules

The five major rules include the Rule for Doubling the Final Consonant (the Floss Rule), the Rule for Doubling a Medial Consonant (the Rabbit Rule), the Doubling Rule, the Dropping Rule, and the Changing Rule. Each rule has a set of **checkpoints**. These checkpoints signal students that a letter may be doubled, dropped, or changed. All of the salient checkpoints must be present for a letter to be doubled, dropped, or changed.

The Rule for Doubling the Final Consonant (the Floss Rule)

Discovery words:

tiff	*tell*	*toss*
puff	*doll*	*pass*
staff	*hill*	*mess*

In a one-syllable base word after a short vowel, final /f/, /l/, and /s/ are spelled *ff*, *ll*, and *ss*, respectively. When deciding whether to apply this rule, students must think about these checkpoints: 1) one syllable; 2) short vowel; and 3) final /f/, /l/, or /s/. If all three checkpoints are present, then the final consonant is doubled. If any one of the checkpoints is missing, then the final consonant will not be doubled.

Note: The term *floss* is a mnemonic device that reminds students that *f, l,* or *s* will double in a one-syllable base word after a short vowel.

The Rule for Doubling the Medial Consonant (the Rabbit Rule)

Discovery words:

sudden

tennis

mitten

pollen

muffin

In a two-syllable base word with one medial consonant sound after a short vowel, the medial consonant is doubled. The three checkpoints for this rule are 1) two syllables, 2) one medial consonant sound, and 3) a short vowel in the first syllable. If all of the checkpoints are present, then the medial consonant is doubled. If any checkpoint is missing, then the medial consonant will not be doubled. When a reader encounters these words in text, the doubled medial consonants indicate to the reader that the first vowel is short.

Note: The term *rabbit* is a mnemonic device that reminds students that a medial consonant doubles in a two-syllable base word after a short vowel.

The Doubling Rule

Discovery words:

hop + ed = hopped   *star + ing = starring*

red + ish = reddish   *begin + er = beginner*

When a word ends in one vowel and one consonant and the final syllable is accented (all one-syllable words are accented), and a vowel suffix is being added, the final consonant is doubled before the suffix is added. There are four checkpoints for consideration: 1) one vowel in the final syllable, 2) one consonant after that vowel, 3) final syllable accented, and 4) a vowel suffix that is being added. If all four checkpoints are present, then the final consonant is doubled. If one checkpoint is missing, then the suffix is just added on. A doubled final consonant before a vowel suffix indicates to the reader that the vowel before the final consonant is short (e.g., in *hopping* the final consonant is doubled before the vowel suffix and the vowel is short; in *hoping* the final consonant is not doubled before the vowel suffix and the vowel is long).

Seven letters in English orthography never or rarely double. Knowing these seven letters assists students in deciding whether to double a letter. These letters can be taught as a cheer:

h, k

y, j

v, w, x

Never or rarely double in English words.

With this bit of information, students will understand why the *x* in *faxing* or *relaxing* does not double or why the *v* in *river* or *seven* does not double.

The doubling rule is an extremely important rule for students to know for writing, as it is used often in spelling participles and the past tense of verbs. Figure 10.4 (Carreker, 2002) shows a visual aid that students can use to remember the four checkpoints of this rule. The four-leaf clover can be reproduced on green cardstock and cut apart for each student. As students search for the checkpoints in a word, they build the four-leaf clover. If all four leaves of the clover are used, students are lucky. The stem is added to the clover, and students know they must double the final consonant. If any leaf is missing, they will not double the final consonant.

The Dropping Rule

Discovery words:

bake + er = baker

solve + ed = solved

blue + ish = bluish

house + ing = housing

complete + ed = completed

When a base word ends in *e* and a vowel suffix is being added, the final *e* is dropped before the suffix is added. The two checkpoints are 1) final *e* and 2) a vowel suffix that is being added. If a consonant suffix is being added, then the final *e* is not dropped. As mentioned previously, a single final consonant before a vowel suffix indicates to a reader that the vowel before the final consonant is long.

The Changing Rule

Discovery words:

try + ed = tried

silly + est = silliest

penny + less = penniless

happy + ness = happiness

When a base word ends in a consonant before a final *y* and a suffix that does not begin with i is added, the final *y* changes to *i* before the suffix is added. The checkpoints for this rule are 1) a consonant before a final *y*, 2) final *y*, and 3) a suffix that does not begin with *i*. If the base word has a vowel before the final *y*, the *y* does not change to *i* (e.g., *boys, enjoying, stayed*). If a suffix that begins with *i* is added, the *y* does not change to *i* (e.g., *crying, babyish, lobbyist*). The teacher can explain to students that the *y* does not change when adding a suffix that begins with *i* because "two *i*'s are unwise." Of course, when students discover the word *skiing*, the teacher will say, "Good for you!"

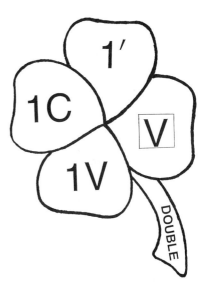

Figure 10.4. Manipulative four-leaf clover indicating checkpoints for the doubling rule: one vowel (1V), one consonant (1C), one accent (1´), and a vowel suffix (a boxed V). When a word has these checkpoints, students add the clover stem, indicating that the final consonant of the base word should be doubled. (From Carreker, S. [2002]. *Scientific spelling* [Rev. ed.; Section 3, p. 7]. Bellaire, TX: Neuhaus Education Center; reprinted by permission).

Introduction of the Spelling Rules

As mentioned previously, the introduction of the spelling patterns begins with an auditory guided discovery procedure to get students to focus on the sound. The goal of teaching the patterns is that when students hear a particular sound in a word, they will know the most frequent, reliable way to spell the sound. Spelling rules are introduced differently. Visual discovery is used to introduce the spelling rules because students must learn to recognize and remember not a sound but a distinguishing visual feature of the rule words.

Introducing the Rules with Doubled Consonants (the Floss Rule and the Rabbit Rule)

Teacher: Watch carefully as I write some words on the board. [When introducing the Rabbit Rule, for example, the teacher writes discovery words such as *rabbit, pollen, tennis, mitten,* and *sudden* on the board in a column as students watch.] What looks the same in all of these words? [Students notice doubled letters and the position of the doubled letters.] Do you notice anything else? [The teacher leads students to discover the other checkpoints of the rule.] Let's review the checkpoints and state the rule. [After students have reviewed the checkpoints and stated the rule, they spell five to seven new words that follow the rule.]

Introducing the Rules for Spelling Derivatives (the Doubling Rule, the Dropping Rule, and the Changing Rule)   The introduction of rules for spelling derivatives begins with the teacher writing a list of three to five discovery words on the board in a formula format: a base word + a suffix = the derivative. The teacher then leads students to discover similarities among all the base words, similarities among the suffixes, and similarities among the derivatives. The introduction of each of rule would be comparable to this introduction of the Doubling Rule.

Teacher: Watch carefully as I write some words on the board. [The teacher writes the discovery words in a formula format such as *run + er = runner, shop + ing = shopping,* and *stop + ed = stopped.*] The first column of words contains base words. The second column contains suffixes. The third column contains derivatives. Look at the column of base words. How are all the base words the same?

Students: They each have one vowel, one final consonant, and an accented final syllable.

Teacher: Look at the column of suffixes. How are all the suffixes the same?

Students: All of the suffixes are vowel suffixes.

Teacher: Look at the derivatives. How are all of the derivatives the same?

Students: The final consonant of each base word is doubled.

Teacher: Let's review the checkpoints and state the rule. [After students have reviewed the checkpoints and stated the rule, they spell five to seven new derivatives that follow the rule.]

Importance of Awareness of Language Domains

As mentioned previously, spelling requires attention to several domains of language (i.e., phonology, syntax, morphology, semantics, orthography) at once. If these different domains are taught as part of or concurrently with formal spelling instruction, the necessity of teaching many traditional spelling rules is eliminated. For example, the teacher could state the following spelling rule: "After the **sibilant** sounds /s/, /z/, /sh/, and /ch/, the plural form of a noun is spelled by adding *-es.*" This rule would help students spell the word *wishes,* but students might be able to spell the word correctly without knowing the rule. Students could do so with phonemic awareness (the word ends in /ĕz/) supported by awareness of syntax (a plural form is needed), morphology (the word has two meaningful units—/wĭsh/ and /ĕz/), semantics (/ĕz/ means more than one), and orthographic knowledge (suffix /ĕz/ is spelled *es*). Therefore, careful instruction with all language structures is important to support spelling. Learning too many rules is burdensome. Many rules are superfluous when instruction with all language structures is provided. Only the rules that aid in the memory of words by drawing attention to visual features (e.g., doubled letters) need to be introduced. These visual features cannot be accessed through awareness of any other language structure or system and must be taught through spelling rules.

Irregular Words

Irregular words have unexpected spellings. A word may be irregular for one of two reasons: 1) Its orthographic representation does not match its pronunciation (e.g., *should, enough, colonel*), or 2) it contains an infrequent orthographic representation of a speech sound (e.g., the spellings of the vowel sounds in *beach, train,* and *soap;* see Table 10.5). Words whose orthographic representations do not match their pronunciations are usually also irregular for reading. Words with infrequent orthographic representations are usually regular for reading, but because they contain less frequent representations of sounds, they are classified for spelling as irregular. Different procedures can be used to establish irregular words in memory. Various mnemonic strategies help students to learn words that contain less frequent patterns. A more structured and multisensory procedure (Cox, 1992; Fernald, 1943; Gillingham & Stillman, 1997) is needed to ensure the learning of some irregular words. The introduction of irregular words should be kept to a minimum when working with dyslexic students. They must establish a sense of the regular, reliable patterns of English before working extensively with irregular words.

Irregular Word Procedure

The following procedure uses visual, auditory, and kinesthetic input to assist in the permanent memorization of those words with truly atypical spellings. It is an involved but effective procedure that must be directed by the teacher. The efficacy of the procedure depends on students' naming the letters. This naming of letters as students trace or write is more effective than writing or copying words over and over because it focuses students' attention on the letter sequence in the word. The steps and rationale for each step follow:

1. *Circle the irregular part.* The teacher provides students with a large model of the irregular word on a sheet of paper. Students circle the part of the word that does not conform to the frequent, reliable patterns or rules. Analyzing the irregular part en-

gages students in active reflection of the language. Circling the irregular part draws their attention to the letter patterns in the word.

Because many irregular words are from Anglo-Saxon or are borrowed from other languages, a discussion of **etymology** can provide insight into the unexpected spelling of the word (see Chapter 6 for a discussion of words from Anglo-Saxon, Latin, and Greek). Over time students may begin to recognize patterns in irregular words (e.g., words from Anglo-Saxon are short, common, everyday words with the sound /f/ occasionally spelled as *gh* as in *enough* or *laugh*).

2. *Trace a model.* Students trace the model word three times, saying the word before they write and naming the letters as they write. Tracing the word while naming the letters provides the consummate multisensory experience. The students reinforce the letter sequence in the word through the visual, auditory, and kinesthetic modalities.

3. *Make copies.* Students make three copies of the word with the model in view, saying the word and naming the letters of the word as they write. This step extends the multisensory impressing of the letter sequence of the word in memory.

4. *Spell the word with eyes closed.* Students close their eyes and spell the word, imagining the word as they spell. They open their eyes and check the model. They close their eyes and spell the word two more times in this manner.

5. *Write from memory.* Students turn their papers over or fold them so that the model does not show. They write the word three times, saying the word before they write and naming the letters of the word as they write. Because students no longer have a model to rely on, they must call on their memory of the letter sequence of the word that was established through the multisensory input.

Other Procedures for Learning Irregular Words

Some irregular words do not require the intensity of the irregular word procedure just outlined. Instead, the use of exaggerated or spelling-based pronunciation builds a strong orthographic memory of these irregular words (Cox, 1992; Ehri, Wilce, & Taylor, 1987). Silent consonants often mark that a word will be irregular for spelling. When practicing irregular words, students may pronounce the silent *k* in words such as *knee, knife,* and *knock* or the silent *b* in words such as *comb, limb,* and *crumb* so that they will remember to write the silent *k* or *b* when they spell. They might exaggerate the pronunciation of *i* as /ī/ in *fragile* so that they will remember to spell the word with an *e* at the end. Schwa is not uniquely represented in English and therefore is difficult to spell. It is best managed with the use of the exaggerated or spelling-based pronunciation (e.g., students say /rĭbŏn/ instead of /rĭbŭn/) (Ehri et al., 1987).

To remember the spellings of certain irregular words, students could use a mnemonic association: "There is *a rat* in sep*arat*e," "The *capitol* has a d*o*me," or "The *principal* is your *pal*" (Moats, 1995). Students could group words in whimsical sentences as a mnemonic device to remember the infrequent spelling patterns that words share: "Whi*ch* ri*ch* people have so mu*ch* money and su*ch* big houses?" or "I am r*ea*dy to spr*ea*d the br*ea*d" (Cox, 1992).

Spelling Homophones

Homophones are words that share the same pronunciation but differ in their orthographic representations (e.g., *plane/plain, to/too/two, red/read*). Published spelling series

are notorious for presenting lists of homophones for students to learn. Students often find these words difficult to learn. The problem usually is not the spelling of homophones but rather their usage. Students are not sure when to use which spelling. To alleviate this confusion, homophones should not be introduced in pairs. Often one word in a pair of homophones is regular for spelling (e.g., *plane*) and the other word is not (e.g., *plain*). Students first should be introduced to the homophone with the regular spelling. When they are secure with the spelling of that word and are clear about its usage, the other homophone can be introduced. If both homophones are irregular for spelling (e.g., *there* and *their*), the word with the most frequent usage should be introduced first, followed by the other.

SPELLING LESSONS

This section discusses spelling lessons in therapeutic environments (one-to-one or small-group) with dyslexic students and spelling lessons in general classrooms. In any environment, it is important to remember that spelling is an interactive process that involves phonological and orthographic knowledge. Spelling instruction enhances this knowledge through synthetic and analytic teaching. Synthetic teaching (i.e., sounds to whole words) systematically builds awareness of sound–letter correspondences and provides a foundation for phonological knowledge and reinforcement of orthographic knowledge. Analytic teaching (i.e., whole words to sounds) builds awareness of letter patterns and provides the foundation for orthographic knowledge and reinforcement of phonological knowledge. Effective lesson planning employs both teaching strategies to provide opportunities for students to develop both phonological and orthographic knowledge. Appendix B at the end of this book lists programs for spelling and resources for planning spelling lessons.

Spelling Lessons for Dyslexic Students

Teaching dyslexic students to spell is a long, tedious process that requires careful lesson planning. The teacher must plan for success as success builds confidence and confidence builds independence. Dyslexic students need spelling instruction that is closely integrated with reading instruction. Because of the exacting demands of spelling on complete and accurate recall of letter patterns, dyslexic students need to spell words with sounds and patterns that have previously been introduced for reading and practiced. Reading words before spelling them heightens students' awareness of orthographic patterns. The number and choices of activities for a spelling lesson will depend on the readiness and needs of the student or students. The teacher will want to plan a rotation of activities that ensures that all areas of spelling are covered regularly. The teacher also will want to discuss the meanings and usages of spelling words to ensure that all of the different layers of language structure are covered in a lesson.

Because dyslexic students' primary deficit is in phonological processing, spelling instruction must be designed to address this deficit. Without phonemic awareness, dyslexic students will not be able to develop facility in reading or spelling. Initially, spelling instruction for dyslexic students should build phonemic awareness. Students should engage in activities that require the segmenting of words into sounds. As they prepare to spell words, they need to engage in activities that heighten the recognition or discrimination of specific sounds, such as listening for a specific sound in a word or listening for the position of a specific sound in a word. After letter–sound correspondences have been introduced for reading, they can be introduced for spelling. These

spelling associations are reviewed daily using a sound or spelling deck. Students spell words and derivatives with regular spellings using these sounds. Students should use the previously described S.O.S. procedure when spelling words. New spelling patterns or rules are introduced as needed. As described in previous sections, multisensory structured guided discovery teaching is used to introduce the new pattern or rule.

When students are ready, the lesson plan is extended. Students begin dictation practice, first with phrases and then with sentences. High-frequency irregular words can be introduced as needed, and students can use the irregular word procedure discussed previously. Analyzing and sorting activities focus students' attention on letter patterns in words, reinforce letter–sound correspondences, and help students generalize patterns and rules. Students can analyze and sort words written on individual index cards by sounds or letter patterns. As they gain greater knowledge of letter patterns, they may analyze and sort words as regular words, rule words, or irregular words. Students can compile a spelling notebook in which they record information about spelling. The notebooks could contain a section for spelling patterns, with one page for each speech sound (Figure 10.5). The reliable patterns for each sound are delineated on the pages. Student writes words that follow each pattern as well as exceptions to the patterns on each page as the sound and spelling(s) are taught. Students may also have a section for rule words, with one page for each rule, and a section for irregular words, with one page for each letter of the alphabet so that irregular words can be recorded on the pages by first letter. Once per week during a spelling lesson, students may record information in their spelling notebooks. On other days students may simply read information from the notebooks as a means of reviewing spelling information.

Initial Lesson Plan for Spelling

1. *Phonological awareness activities*

   The teacher chooses one or two of the following activities:

   - Students repeat words dictated by the teacher and listen for a specific sound.

   - Students repeat words dictated by the teacher and identify the position of a specific sound.

   - Students repeat and segment words dictated by the teacher.

   - Students repeat words dictated by the teacher and change a sound in a word as designated by the teacher to create a new word.

   - Students repeat words dictated by the teacher and say them again, leaving out a syllable designated by the teacher.

2. *Sound dictation*

   - The teacher dictates the sounds one at a time.

   - Students echo the sounds, then name and write the letter or letters that spell each sound. (A mirror is available for students who are unable to discriminate the sounds.)

   - The teacher cues students with a key word if they cannot remember the spelling.

   - The teacher varies the media for the response daily (e.g., unlined paper, chalkboard, desktop).

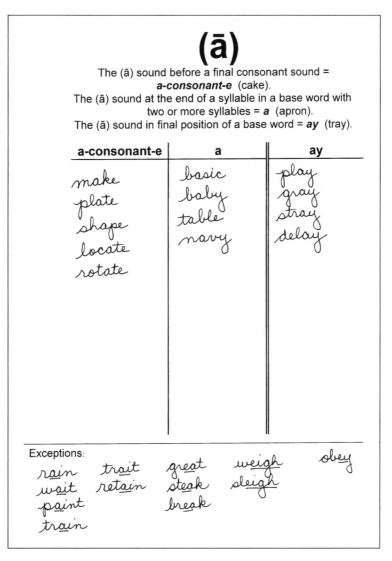

Figure 10.5. Spelling notebook page. This page reviews the most frequent spelling patterns of /ā/. The teacher dictates words that follow these patterns. Students write the words in the correct columns. Words with less frequent patterns that students find as they are reading are written at the bottom of the page. These words are not dictated. (From Carreker, S. [2002]. *Scientific spelling* (Rev. ed.; Student Notebook, p. 2). Bellaire, TX: Neuhaus Education Center; reprinted by permission.)

3. *Word dictation*

   • Before students spell words, the teacher reviews the patterns or rules that are germane to the practice session.

   • The teacher reviews the appropriate steps of S.O.S.

   • The teacher dictates the words (as few as 3–4 and no more than 10–12) as students spell using S.O.S. The words should be homogeneous when students are practicing a new spelling concept and then heterogeneous when students demonstrate mastery of the concept. The teacher should be careful to plan a lesson

rotation that includes the spelling of regular words on one day and the spelling of rule words on another day.

- The teacher provides immediate corrective feedback as needed.

4. *Introduction of new spelling concept (synthetic teaching)*

- The teacher introduces a new spelling pattern or rule following a sequential, cumulative order that allows time for concepts to be practiced to mastery.

- The teacher uses guided discovery teaching techniques.

- After the new pattern or rule has been introduced, students apply the concept by spelling three to five words with the pattern or rule.

Extended Lesson Plan for Spelling

This extended lesson plan for spelling includes the four activities of the initial lesson plan plus three additional activities. The word dictation activity is expanded to include the dictation of phrases and simple sentences. This new lesson plan can be used after students have been introduced to 10–12 spelling patterns and the Floss Rule and are spelling words with these concepts with relative ease and accuracy.

1. Phonological awareness activities

2. Sound dictation

3. Word dictation and/or sentence dictation

4. Introduction of a new spelling concept (synthetic teaching)

5. Introduction of a high-frequency irregular word

6. Analyzing or sorting spelling words (analytic teaching)

7. Use of spelling notebook

Technology Available to Spellers

Although complete mastery of spelling for dyslexic students is a rather elusive goal (Oakland et al., 1998), the teacher must be tenacious in pursuing this goal. The technology of computer and hand-held spell checkers greatly aids dyslexic students with the accuracy of their spelling when writing compositions and reports, but it is not a substitute for systematic instruction in spelling patterns and rules and procedures for dealing with irregular words. Knowledge of the structure of the language for spelling increases the effectiveness and efficiency of this technology. If students' spelling attempts do not match the probable patterns in English, then the spell checker may not be able to choose the correct word, or it may overwhelm students with too many choices. Such technology is not a replacement for explicit instruction for dyslexic students but instead serves as a complement to this instruction.

Spelling Lessons for the Classroom

Spelling instruction that requires the copying of words or the memorization of lists is dull and uninspiring. Spelling instruction that engages students in active, reflective thought about language is exciting. The goal of spelling instruction is to teach the re-

liable patterns and rules of English for spelling, thereby creating enthusiasm for language. Effective spelling instruction provides students with meaningful lists of words they will use in their academic work.

Order of Presentation

The order of presentation of spelling concepts should follow the order of presentation of reading concepts (see Chapter 9 for order of presentation of reading concepts). Because of the demands of spelling, the introduction of spelling concepts will lag behind the introduction of reading concepts.

Weekly Lesson Plan

The following weekly lesson plan systematically teaches the patterns and rules of English for spelling and provides opportunities for students to generalize and apply this information. The plan allows for modification to meet the needs of dyslexic students in the general classroom. These activities could also be incorporated into therapy lessons with dyslexic students.

Monday (15 minutes)   A new spelling pattern (e.g., initial or medial /ou/ is spelled *ou*) or rule is introduced through multisensory guided discovery teaching. Students spell five to seven words with the new pattern or rule, using S.O.S. This synthetic teaching ensures that students are systematically learning information about the structure of language for spelling. The words that students practice on Monday become the first words of the weekly spelling list.

Tuesday (15–20 minutes)   The rest of the words for the weekly spelling list come from the content area (e.g., words from a map skills unit in social studies). The number of words presented depends on the age or the needs of the students. Because the words are selected from the content area, students will need to know and use them. The need for and use of the words increases the likelihood that students will learn the words. Arbitrary lists of words from published spelling series seldom present words commensurate with students' classwork.

Students must analyze the words on the weekly spelling list and decide whether the words are regular words, rule words, or irregular words. To be successful with analyzing, students must disengage what they have learned about decoding. It is true that they will be able to read a word such as *east,* but for spelling purposes, it is considered irregular because *ea* is not the most frequent spelling of /ē/ in initial or medial position of a one-syllable base word. Words such as *eel* or *street* follow the frequent, reliable patterns of the language and would be analyzed as regular words.

The Tuesday lesson provides analytic teaching that ensures that students will look carefully at words to notice how they are spelled. It helps them generalize the patterns and rules they have learned. It engages students in active reflective thought about language. Students cannot decide the category of a word without thinking about all of the aspects of the word.

When students have finished analyzing and sorting the words, they have strategies for learning them. The regular words are spelled just the way they sound and can be sounded out. The rule words can be sounded out, but students must remember there is a letter that must be doubled, dropped, or changed before they write each word. Irregular words have unexpected spellings. They cannot be sounded out and must be memo-

rized (see Table 10.7). No more than three or four irregular words should be included in the Tuesday lesson.

The weekly spelling list is easily modified for dyslexic students in the classroom. Rather than require these students to learn all of the words in the list, the teacher may ask them to be responsible for only the discovery words from the Monday lesson (e.g., all of the words with /ou/ that are spelled *ou*), or if students are ready, the teacher may ask them to be responsible for all of the regular words in the weekly list. The addition of the daily use of a spelling deck and phonological awareness activities for these students creates a pattern of covering all areas of the spelling curriculum routinely and intensively.

Table 10.7. Weekly spelling list with five discovery words from the Monday lesson and 10 words from content areas

Regular	Rule	Irregular
found	mapping	ocean
mouth		country
ouch		east
count		
shout		
north		
south		
west		
globe		
river[a]		
continent		

[a]Note that the inclusion of *river* shows an example of how *v* usually is not doubled in English.

Wednesday (15 minutes)   Students practice the irregular words that were sorted in the Tuesday lesson. They decide the best way to learn them: using the irregular word procedure, a mnemonic device, or a spelling-based pronunciation. If time permits, they use the dictionary to determine why each word is irregular: 1) They are from Anglo-Saxon; 2) they are borrowed from another language; 3) they are slang or an abbreviated form of a word; 4) they are borrowed from a proper name; or 5) they are spelled that way "just because," with no apparent reason listed in the dictionary.

Thursday (15 minutes)   The teacher uses the spelling words in various phonological awareness activities segmenting words into sounds, counting syllables, omitting syllables, and changing sounds in words. Students also practice words through word or sentence dictation.

Friday (15 minutes)   Throughout the week students have had the opportunity to analyze, play with, read, and write the spelling words. On Friday, students are tested on the words through word and/or sentence dictation.

Effective Spelling Instruction

Effective spelling instruction does not teach students how to spell individual words. It teaches students how to think about spelling. An old adage says that if you give a man a fish, he eats for a day. If you teach a man how to fish, he eats for a lifetime. So it is with effective spelling instruction. Effective spelling instruction teaches students to think about language so that they know how to spell the words they need.

SUMMARY

Spelling serves as a foundation for reading; provides a means of communication; and, even if not rightly or fairly, is used by society to judge one's level of literacy and intelligence. Spelling is a valuable skill, yet it receives a modicum of attention and respect in schools. It has been reduced to mindless busywork or has been subjugated by the content in writing. Perhaps this has happened because of the misconception that En-

glish orthography is impossibly irregular and that there is no way to teach it or because of the perception that spelling is a rote, mechanical skill that does not promote cognition. The time has come to view spelling instruction in a different light.

The orthography of English is not hopeless. There are frequent, reliable patterns and rules that can be taught, which thus equip students with a system for managing the orthography of English for spelling. These patterns and rules are not taught through passive, rote memorization. Spelling instruction is deeply ensconced in a rich study of language structures and takes place in a manner that promotes active, reflective thought. Spelling instruction does not distract from the content of writing but rather enhances it by enabling students to choose the words that best express their thoughts instead of those words that are easy to spell. Effective spelling instruction is engaging, thought provoking, and exciting.

REFERENCES

Adams, M.J. (1990). *Beginning to read: Thinking and learning about print.* Cambridge: The MIT Press.

Adams, M.J., Foorman, B.R., Lundberg, I., & Beeler, T. (1998). *Phonemic awareness in young children: A classroom curriculum.* Baltimore: Paul H. Brookes Publishing Co.

Bear, D.R., Invernizzi, M., Templeton, S., & Johnston, F. (1996). *Words their way: Word study for phonics, vocabulary, and spelling instruction.* Upper Saddle River, NJ: Prentice Hall.

Blachman, B.A., Ball, E.W., Black, R., & Tangel, D.M. (1994). Kindergarten teachers develop phoneme awareness in low-income, inner-city classrooms: Does it make a difference? *Reading and Writing: An Interdisciplinary Journal, 6*(1), 1–18.

Blachman, B.A., Ball, E.W., Black, R., & Tangel, D.M. (2000). *Road to the code: A phonological awareness program for young children.* Baltimore: Paul H. Brookes Publishing Co.

Bradley, L., & Bryant, P.E. (1983). Categorizing sounds and learning to read: A causal connection. *Nature, 303,* 419–421.

Brady, S., & Moats, L.C. (1997). *Informed instruction for reading success: Foundations for teacher preparation.* Baltimore: The International Dyslexia Association.

Bryant, P.E., & Bradley, L. (1980). Why children sometimes write words which they do not read. In U. Frith (Ed.), *Cognitive processes in spelling* (pp. 355–370). London: Academic Press.

Bryant, P.E., Nunes, T., & Bindman, M. (1997). Children's understanding of the connection between grammar and spelling. In B. Blachman (Ed.), *Foundations of reading acquisition and dyslexia: Implications for early intervention* (pp. 219–240). Mahwah, NJ: Lawrence Erlbaum Associates.

Bryson, B. (1990). *The mother tongue and how it got that way.* New York: Avon Books.

Carreker, S. (2002). *Scientific spelling* (Rev. ed.). Bellaire, TX: Neuhaus Education Center.

Cassar, M., & Treiman, R. (1997). The beginnings of orthographic knowledge: Children's knowledge of double letters in words. *Journal of Educational Psychology, 89*(4), 631–644.

Castle, J.M., Riach, J., & Nicholson, T. (1994). Getting off to a better start in reading and spelling: The effects of phonemic awareness instruction within a whole language program. *Journal of Educational Psychology, 86*(3), 350–359.

Cook, G.E., Farnum, M., Gabrielson, T., & Temple, C. (1998). *McGraw-Hill spelling.* New York: McGraw-Hill School Division.

Cox, A.R. (1977). *Situation spelling: Formulas and equations for spelling the sounds of spoken English.* Cambridge, MA: Educators Publishing Service.

Cox, A.R. (1992). *Foundations for literacy: Structures and techniques for multisensory teaching of basic written English language skills.* Cambridge, MA: Educators Publishing Service.

Cronnell, B., & Humes, A. (1980). Elementary spelling: What's really taught? *Elementary School Journal, 81,* 59–64.

Ehri, L.C., Wilce, L.S., & Taylor, B.B. (1987). Children's categorization of short vowels in words and the influence of spelling. *Merrill-Palmer Quarterly, 33,* 393–421.

Fernald, G. (1943). *Remedial techniques in basic school subjects.* New York: McGraw-Hill.

Ferreiro, E., & Teberosky, A. (1982). *Literacy before schooling.* Portsmouth, NH: Heinemann.

Foorman, B.R. (1994). The relevance of a connectionist model for reading for "The Great Debate." *Educational Psychology Review, 6,* 25–47.

Frith, U. (1980). Unexpected spelling problems. In U. Frith (Ed.), *Cognitive processes in spelling* (pp. 495–515). London: Academic Press.

Frith, U., & Frith, C. (1980). Relationships between reading and spelling. In J.P. Kavanagh & R.L. Venezky (Eds.), *Orthography, reading, and dyslexia* (pp. 287–295). Baltimore: University Park Press.

Fulk, B.M., & Stormont-Spurgin, M. (1995). Spelling interventions for students with disabilities:

A review. *Journal of Special Education, 28*(4), 488–513.

Gillingham, A., & Stillman, B.W. (1960). *Remedial training for children with specific disability in reading, spelling, and penmanship* (6th ed.). Cambridge, MA: Educators Publishing Service.

Gillingham, A., & Stillman, B.W. (1997). *The Gillingham manual: Remedial training for children with specific disability in reading, writing, and penmanship* (8th ed.). Cambridge, MA: Educators Publishing Service.

Goodman, K. (1986). *What's whole in whole language: A parent–teacher guide.* Portsmouth, NH: Heinemann.

Goswami, U. (1988). Children's use of analogy in learning to spell. *British Journal of Developmental Psychology, 6,* 21–23.

Goswami, U., & Bryant, P. (1990). *Phonological skills and learning to read.* Mahwah, NJ: Lawrence Erlbaum Associates.

Hanna, P.R., Hanna, J.S., Hodges, R.E., & Rudorf, E.H. (1966). *Phoneme–grapheme correspondences as cues to spelling improvement.* Washington, DC: U.S. Government Printing Office, U.S. Office of Education.

Henry, M. (1988). Beyond phonics: Integrating decoding and spelling instruction based on word origin and structure. *Annals of Dyslexia, 38,* 259–277.

Henry, M.K. (2003). *Unlocking literacy: Effective decoding and spelling instruction.* Baltimore: Paul H. Brookes Publishing Co.

Johnson, D., & Myklebust, H.R. (1967). *Learning disabilities: Educational principles and practices.* New York: Grune & Stratton.

Lennox, C., & Siegel, L.S. (1996). The development of phonological rules and visual strategies in average and poor spellers. *Journal of Experimental Child Psychology, 62,* 60–83.

Lennox, C., & Siegel, L.S. (1998). Phonological and orthographic processes in good and poor spellers. In C. Hulme & R.M. Joshi (Eds.), *Reading and spelling development and disorders* (pp. 395–404). Mahwah, NJ: Lawrence Erlbaum Associates.

Liberman, I.Y., Shankweiler, D., & Liberman, A.M. (1989). The alphabetic principle and learning to read. In D. Shankweiler & I.Y. Liberman (Eds.), *Phonology and reading disabilities: Solving the reading puzzle* (pp. 1–33). Ann Arbor: University of Michigan Press.

Lyon, G.R., Shaywitz, S.E., & Shaywitz, B.A. (2003). A definition of dyslexia. *Annals of Dyslexia, 53,* 1–14.

Moats, L.C. (1994). Assessment of spelling in learning disabilities research. In G.R. Lyon (Ed.), *Frames of reference for the assessment of learning disabilities: New views on measurement issues* (pp. 333–349). Baltimore: Paul H. Brookes Publishing Co.

Moats, L.C. (1995). *Spelling: Development, disabilities, and instruction.* Timonium, MD: York Press.

Moats, L.C. (1996). Phonological spelling errors in the writing of dyslexic adolescents. *Reading and Writing, 8*(1), 105–119.

Nation, K., & Hulme, C. (1998). The role of analogy in early spelling development. In C. Hulme & R.M. Joshi (Eds.), *Reading and spelling development and disorders* (pp. 433–445). Mahwah, NJ: Lawrence Erlbaum Associates.

Oakland, T., Black, J.L., Stanford, G., Nussbaum, N., & Balise, R.R. (1998). An evaluation of the dyslexia training program: A multisensory method for promoting reading in students with reading disabilities. *Journal of Learning Disabilities, 31*(2), 140–147.

Peters, M.L. (1985). *Spelling, caught or taught?* London: Routledge & Kegan Paul.

Post, Y.V. & Carreker, S. (2002). Orthographic similarities and phonological transparency in spelling. *Reading and Writing: An Interdisciplinary Journal, 15,* 317–340.

Post, Y.V., Carreker, S., & Holland, G. (2001) The spelling of final letter patterns: A comparison of instruction at the level of the phoneme and the rime. *Annals of Dyslexia, 51,* 121–146.

Read, C. (1971). Pre-school children's knowledge of English phonology. *Harvard Educational Review, 41*(1), 1–34.

Roberts, R., & Mather, N. (1997). Orthographic dyslexia: The neglected subtype. *Learning Disabilities Research & Practice, 12*(4), 236–250.

Rubin, H., & Eberhardt, N.C. (1996). Facilitating invented spelling through language analysis instruction: An integrated model. *Reading and Writing: An Interdisciplinary Journal, 8,* 27–43.

Seidenberg, M., & McClelland, J. (1989). A distributed developmental model of word recognition and naming. *Psychological Review, 96,* 523–568.

Share, D.L., & Stanovich, K.E. (1995). Cognitive processes in early reading development: Accommodating individual differences into a model of acquisition. *Issues in Education, 1*(1), 1–57.

Smith, P.T. (1980). Linguistic information in spelling. In U. Frith (Ed.), *Cognitive processes in spelling* (pp. 33–49). London: Academic Press.

Sterling, C., Farmer, M., Riddick, B., Morgan, S., & Matthews, C. (1998). Adult dyslexic writing. *Dyslexia: An International Journal of Research and Practice, 4*(1), 1–15.

Treiman, R. (1994). Use of consonant letter names in beginning spelling. *Developmental Psychology, 30*(4), 567–580.

Treiman, R. (1997). Spelling in normal children and dyslexia. In B. Blachman (Ed.), *Foundations of reading acquisition and dyslexia: Implications for early intervention* (pp. 191–218). Mahwah, NJ: Lawrence Erlbaum Associates.

Treiman, R. (1998). Beginning to spell in English.

In C. Hulme & R.M. Joshi (Eds.), *Reading and spelling development and disorders*. Mahwah, NJ: Lawrence Erlbaum Associates.

Treiman, R., Cassar, M., & Zukowski, A. (1994). What types of linguistic information do children use in spelling? The case of flaps. *Child Development, 65,* 1318–1337.

Treiman, R., Zukowski, A., & Richmond-Welty, D.A. (1995). What happened to the "n" in sink? Children's spelling of final consonant clusters. *Cognition, 55,* 1–38.

Venezky, R.L. (1980). From Webster to rice to Roosevelt. In U. Frith (Ed.), *Cognitive processes in spelling* (pp. 9–30). London: Academic Press.

West, T.G. (1991). *In the mind's eye*. Buffalo, NY: Prometheus Books.

11

Biliteracy Instruction for Spanish-Speaking Students

Elsa Cárdenas-Hagan

Biliteracy is the ability to speak, read, and write in two languages. As the number of Hispanics living in the United States increases, the necessity for English–Spanish **biliteracy** has grown. In fact, Spanish speakers are the second-largest language group in the country. The first section of this chapter reviews the changing demographics in the United States and the need for educating the Hispanic population. For the purpose of extending the knowledge base of most teachers, the second section reviews briefly the structure of the Spanish language: its phonology, morphology, and syntax. The third section discusses multisensory techniques for literacy development in students' native language. The fourth section describes the transfer of language and literacy skills from the native language to the second language using a well-designed, evidence-based instructional approach.

DEMOGRAPHICS

According to the U.S. Census Bureau (2000), there are more than 39 million Hispanics living in the United States. This population now accounts for 20% of births in the United States. In addition, more than half of this population is less than 27 years old. It is estimated that there are 3 million children in the United States, ages 5–17, who speak Spanish and that 21% of Hispanic children are living at the poverty level (U.S. Census Bureau, 2000). In the United States the dropout rate for Hispanic youth is 21% and this group is more likely to drop out of school than any other group (Fry, 2003). The dropout rate of Hispanic immigrants is 46% (U.S. Census Bureau, 2000). In Texas 96% of second language learners speak Spanish in the home (Texas Education Agency, 2002). Literacy outcomes have been unsatisfactory (August & Hakuta, 1997). This booming population speaks Spanish and faces the necessity of learning English as a second language.

One of the main concerns in states such as Texas, California, Florida, and New York is the fact that many of the children in state-supported schools speak Spanish as their primary language. Many of these students enter school with limited world knowledge and limited exposure to reading and literature even in their first language. There is no doubt that educators need to concentrate on increasing the academic achievement of our nation's Hispanic students (Fry, 2003). However, how can an **English language learner** acquire a second language and become literate in that language when his or her first language is not fully established?

LANGUAGE COMPONENTS AND LEARNING A SECOND LANGUAGE

Research demonstrates that learning a second language is much easier for a child than an adolescent or adult (August & Hakuta, 1997). Therefore, timing is crucial if the student is to become bilingual and biliterate. Early training in kindergarten through third grade can make a difference.

It is also well known that cognitive skills transfer. Understanding the structure of one's native language is beneficial for learning a second language. Moreover, exploring the common ties between languages is extremely beneficial for biliteracy. This may be especially true for Spanish–English biliteracy. The Spanish language has many similarities to the English language. Both languages are based on the alphabetic principle. The two languages share common sounds. They also share common words and word parts that are derived from Latin. There are linguistic elements that can transfer from one language to the other. Focusing on the similarities of Spanish and English can promote biliteracy. The second language learner's understanding of concepts in the second language can be facilitated by explicit instruction in the commonalities between the two languages.

Spanish is considered a Romance language. Like English, it is based on an alphabetic system. Language has four distinct systems: phonology, morphology, syntax, and pragmatics. In addition, orthography is a convention of written language. It relies on phonology and morphology. *Phonology* includes the study of the sounds of a language. It incorporates the rules that determine how sounds can be combined. *Morphology* includes the study of word meanings and the structure of the language. Morphemes are the smallest units of meaning in a language. These include word parts such as roots, prefixes, and suffixes. *Syntax*, another characteristic of language, includes the rules for word usage and word order. One might describe *pragmatics* as the social rules of a language necessary for language usage (Bloom & Lahey, 1978). Rules of conversation, turn-taking, and initiating a topic appropriately are all considered pragmatic language skills. Bloom and Lahey defined language as the integration of content (semantics and morphology), form (syntax and phonology), and use (pragmatics). This model can be applied to all languages. A strong foundation in language is necessary for literacy development. Finally, *orthography* can be considered a system for written language. Orthography incorporates the rules for how sounds can be represented in print. The Spanish language is mostly regular in its orthographic patterns. Knowledge of sound–symbol relationships assists students with spelling development. In addition, there are spelling and morphological patterns in Spanish that transfer to English.

Language and Literacy Connections

Language is a natural system. Humans have the ability to understand and communicate. Reading is also a language-based process. However, reading is not a natural process since it is a skill that must be taught. Thus, in order to read, one's language system should be developed or developing. Language skills are necessary for successful reading skills. For

example, phonology is necessary for phonological awareness, phonics, and orthography development. Morphology is necessary for understanding the structure of text, thus contributing to understanding. Semantics is necessary for understanding the words that are read. Pragmatics is necessary for composing and creating written language that is comprehensible. Biliteracy therefore requires knowledge of phonology, morphology, syntax, and pragmatics in both Spanish and English. Working with students in small groups is helpful for engaging students in using their pragmatic language skills. These skills can be facilitated through role playing, giving a topic, and determining how students maintain the topic and take turns. Often there are differences across cultures and languages in the social use of language. See Chapter 3 for a fuller explanation of the components of oral language and their relationship to reading.

Spanish and English can serve mutually as resources for second language acquisition. Understanding the structure of one language facilitates the acquisition of the second language. Children who are provided with explicit instruction in all components of language and literacy are more likely to achieve biliteracy.

According to Bialystok (2002), when children learn literacy skills in a weak language at the same time as they learn to read in their strong language, the transfer of skills from the dominant language facilitates literacy attainment in the weaker language. Individual differences in reading ability account for variance in performance. Bialystok also reported that intact language proficiency skills increase the probability of literacy acquisition. Chiappe, Hasher, and Siegel (2002) determined that the acquisition of basic literacy skills for children with different backgrounds and cultures developed in a similar manner. Alphabetic knowledge and phonological processing were important contributors to children's early literacy performance. Phonological awareness is the ability to process, segment, and manipulate the sounds and syllables of a language. Phonological awareness includes skills such as rhyming, identifying sounds and syllables, and adding or deleting sounds and syllables within words. Phonemic awareness is the ability to process and manipulate the smallest unit of sound, known as a phoneme. Phonological awareness was correlated with literacy skills by the end of kindergarten. In Spanish, phonemic awareness tended to be highly related to literacy. Other researchers report similar results (Francis & Carlson, 2001).

The importance of early development of strong second language skills is indicated by the fact that Hispanic 16- to 19-year-olds who have poor English language skills have dropout rates as high as 60% (Fry, 2003). It is possible to prevent reading disabilities when individuals have the opportunity to learn in an explicit, systematic manner (National Institute for Child Health and Human Development [NICHD], 2000).

Spanish Phonology and Orthography

Phonology is the system of rules that determine how sounds exist and can be combined in a language. Processing and understanding sounds of a language is a necessary skill for reading English (Adams, 1990). Proficient Spanish readers also transfer phonological awareness skills to their reading (Quiroga, Lemons-Britton, Mostafapour, Abbott, & Berninger, 2000). Although Spanish is a syllabic language in that it has reliable syllable patterns, knowledge of sounds (phonemes) at the beginning of reading instruction can assist with the prediction of future reading ability (Francis & Carlson, 2001). There are 23 phonemes in the Spanish language (Barrutia & Schwegler, 1994): 5 vowel sounds and 18 consonant sounds. In addition, variations in Castilian Spanish include /th/, /zh/, and /v/.

The structure of the Spanish language consists of common syllable patterns. Some of the most common syllable patterns in Spanish are also common syllable patterns in

English. The Spanish consonant–vowel (CV) pattern, as in *ma, pa, la,* and *sa* is a basic syllable pattern and can be combined to form a CV|CV pattern, as in the words *mala, pala, sala, masa,* and *pasa.* Thousands of words can be formed from this common syllable pattern, which is regular in Spanish. The CV|CV pattern is divided after the first vowel. The vowel-consonant-vowel (VCV) syllable pattern is common in the Spanish language. It can be divided after the first vowel. Spanish words such as *uno, oso,* and *ala* represent this syllable pattern. The English language also has the vowel-consonant-vowel (VCV) syllable type. It can be divided after the first vowel as in the English words *pilot, token,* and *model.* It can also be divided after the consonant as in the words; *visit, exit,* and *valid.* Another common syllable pattern is the VC|CV pattern, as in the Spanish words *lista, isla, esta, hasta,* and *norte.* This syllable pattern is also common in the English language. In Spanish and English, the VC|CV pattern is divided between the two consonants. Reading teachers may utilize these common syllable patterns to practice reading multisyllabic words. In Spanish the CVC syllable pattern is present, but fewer words in Spanish than in English utilize this pattern. Words in Spanish with this pattern include *mes, dos, las, son, gis,* and *luz.* Words in English using this pattern include *pat, met, his, cot,* and *cut.* (For a discussion of English syllable division, see Chapter 9.)

Table 11.1 categorizes Spanish vowel sounds by tone and place of production. The vowel sounds produced in the back of the mouth are /o͞o/ and /ō/. When /o͞o/ and /ō/ are uttered, as in *uno* and *hola,* they produce high and middle tones, respectively. The vowel /ä/ is produced in the central position of the mouth and has a low tone as in the Spanish word *amigo.* The vowels /ē/ and /ĕ/ are produced toward the front of the mouth and have high and middle tones, as in the Spanish words *iguana* and *elefante.*

Spanish consonant sounds can be characterized by the placement of the tongue and the **manner** of production. Table 11.2 categorizes Spanish consonant sounds by the place and manner of production.

The sounds /b/ and /p/ are made with the two lips and are considered **bilabial** sounds. The manner in which they are produced is considered a stop since the air is abruptly stopped by the lips when the sound is produced. Some examples of Spanish words with bilabial sounds include *bate, beso, piano,* and *peso.* The consonant sound /f/, a labiodental sound, is produced with the upper teeth placed on the lower lip. It is a fricative sound since it is produced by the friction of the teeth upon the lower lip. The Spanish word *fiesta* begins with this sound. Speakers of Castilian Spanish produce the fricative sound /th/, which is produced like the English /th/ sound as in the English word *bath.* This sound may also be produced as a dialectal variant for the /s/ sound in Spanish. The ridge behind the front teeth is known as the **alveolar ridge.** Sounds such as /s/ and /n/, which are produced with the tongue touching this ridge, are categorized as **alveolar sounds.** The Spanish words *sol* and *noche* begin with alveolar sounds. Palatal sounds are produced by the tongue touching the palate in the medial position. The Spanish words *yoyo* and *llanta* begin with the **palatal** sound /y/. Speakers of Castil-

Table 11.1.   Spanish vowel sounds, by tone and mouth position

Tone	Mouth position		
	Front	Central	Back
Low	/ē/		/o͞o/
Middle		/ĕ/	/ō/
High		/ä/*	

*This is the obscure *a* sound as in the Spanish word *mañana.*

Table 11.2. Spanish consonant sounds, by manner and place of articulation

Manner of articulation	Place of articulation							
	Bilabial	Labiodental	Interdental	Dental	Alveolar	Palatal	Velar	Glottal
Stop	/p/, /b/*			/t/, /d/			/k/, /g/	
Nasal	/m/				/n/	/ñ/**		
Fricative		/f/, /v/*	/th/***		/s/	/zh/***	/h/****	/x/*****
Affricate						/ch/		
Liquid					/r/, /l/, /rr/	/y/		
Glide	/w/							

*Some dialects of Spanish do not use the /v/ sound and use the bilabial /b/ sound in its place. English language learners would benefit from learning these two sounds, as they correlate with the English sounds and thus facilitate the transfer to English.

**The /ñ/ sound in Spanish can be an alveolar-palatal nasal sound.

***The unvoiced /th/ sound and the /zh/ sound exist in Castilian Spanish.

****The /h/ sound exists in Spanish and is spelled with the letter *j* or the letter *g* before *e* or *i*.

*****The /x/ sound is a glottal fricative as in the words *Xavier* and *Oaxaca*.

ian Spanish produce this as the sound /zh/. Sounds such as /k/ and /g/ are produced close to the structure in the back of the mouth known as the **velum**. These two particular **velar** sounds are categorized as stops since the air is stopped abruptly by the tongue. Some Spanish words with these velar sounds include *kilo* and *gusano*.

By comparing the placement of the tongue and the manner of production of Spanish consonant sounds in Table 11.2 with those of English consonant sounds in Table 11.3, the well-informed teacher can understand the commonalities and possible sources of difficulty in learning the sounds in a second language. For example, the /ng/ sound can be difficult to produce for English language learners; however, it does exist in Spanish, as represented by the letter *n* before the /k/ sound as in *nunca*. In English the letter *n* before the /k/ sound is produced as /ng/ as in the word *sink*. The Spanish sound represented by the letter *ñ* is not represented in English. Although the letter *r* transfers from Spanish to English, the sound is mostly trilled in Spanish and is not as trilled in English. It is also important to understand that the medial *r* in Spanish when placed between two vowels is soft and not trilled; rather, it is pronounced as a **flap** sound. (A flap sound is produced when the tongue strikes against another articulator, such as the palate, and then returns to its rest position.) The flapping of medial Spanish *r* is similar to the flap sounds of medial *t* and *d* in English as in the words *battle* and *ladder*. Examples of Spanish words with a medial flap sound are *cara* and *pera*. Therefore, medial *r* between two vowels transfers to medial *t* and *d* in English.

There are a total of 44 phonemes in English. These sounds are represented by 26 alphabetic symbols. Many sounds in Spanish and English directly transfer from one language to the other. The place, manner, and production are directly related in English and

Table 11.3. English consonant sounds, by manner and place of articulation

Manner of articulation	Place of articulation					
	Bilabial	Labiodental	Interdental	Alveolar	Palatal	Velar
Stop	/p/, /b/			/t/, /d/		/k/, /g/
Nasal	/m/			/n/		
Fricative		/f/, /v/	/th/ (unvoiced), /th/ (voiced)	/s/, /z/	/sh/,/zh/	/h/
Affricate					/ch/, /j/	
Liquid				/l/, /r/		
Glide	/hw/, /w/				/y/	

Table 11.4.   Common consonant sounds of Spanish and English

Manner of articulation	Placement						
	Bilabial	Labiodental	Interdental	Alveolar	Palatal	Velar	Glottal
Stops	/p/, /b/			*		/k/, /g/	
Nasals	/m/			/n/			
Fricatives		/f/, /v/	/th/**	/s/	/zh/**		/h/
Affricates					/ch/		
Liquids				/l/, /r/***			
Glides	/w/				/y/		

*The /t/ and /d/ sounds in Spanish are dental as they are produced in a slightly more forward position of the mouth than the English /t/ and /d/ sounds.

**The unvoiced /th/ sound and the /zh/ sound exist in Castilian Spanish and in English.

***This symbol represents the flap sound, which occurs as a medial sound in the American English pronunciation of the words *ladder* and *bottle* and in the Spanish words *cara* and *pera*.

Spanish. As noted before, this facilitates the acquisition of phonology in the two languages. Table 11.4 illustrates the common consonant sounds between the two languages.

Although Spanish and English have some sounds in common, the orthographic representations of some of these sounds may differ. For example, /h/ is spelled with the letter *h* in English but with the letters *j* or *g* (before *e* or *i*) in Spanish. The /w/ exists in Spanish. In English the /w/ sound is spelled with the letter *w*. In Spanish, the /w/ sound can be heard in words such as *guante*, pronounced /gwäntĕh/. This sound is produced in Spanish when the letter *g* or *c* is followed by *u*.

Spelling patterns also transfer from one language to another. For example in Spanish as well as English, the letter *c* before *a, o, u,* and consonants is produced as /k/. The letter *c* before *e* or *i* changes to the /s/ sound as in words *mice* and *cinema* in English. In Spanish, words such as *centavo* and *cinco* are examples of this pattern. The spelling of the letter *g* before *a, o, u,* and consonants is produced as /g/ in English and Spanish. However when the letter *g* is immediately before *e* or *i*, the sound changes to /j/ in English (e.g., *gem, gin*) and /h/ in Spanish (e.g., *gente, gigante*).

Spanish Morphology

Morphology, the study of morphemes, assists students in decoding and also provides a foundation for vocabulary development and spelling in both Spanish and English. (See Chapters 6 and 9 for a fuller discussion of morpheme instruction.) For example, in Spanish, the word *xilófono* contains the morpheme *fono*, which means *sound*. Another example is the word *incompleto*, which contains the morpheme *in-*, meaning *not*. The Spanish word *adorable* includes the morpheme *-able*, which means *able to do*. Teachers can take advantage of the fact that Spanish consists of morphemes whose meanings are similar in English. These morphemes can take the form of base words, roots, prefixes, and suffixes that carry meaning (see Chapter 6 for further discussion of these word parts). The study of morphemes can assist children in developing reading as well as increase vocabulary skills. Approximately 60% of English is derived from Latin (Lindzey, 2003). Spanish cognates therefore are extremely useful for English language learners. One study showed that Spanish cognates and word knowledge facilitated English vocabulary and reading comprehension (Durgunoglu, Nagy, & Hacin-Bhatt, 1993). Studying word families as groups of words helps readers to infer meaning especially when encountering words in context (Anderson & Nagy, 1992). Corson (1998) reported marked improvement for children who have studied the etymology of words and word relationships. Morphology is helpful for learning words and word meanings in first and second languages.

Table 11.5.   Regular Spanish verb endings

	Verb ending		
Person	-ar	-er	-ir
yo	-o	-o	-o
tú	-as	-es	-es
él, ella, usted	-a	-e	-e
nosotros	-amos	-emos	-imos
vosotros	-amaís	-eis	-is
ellos, ellas, ustedes	-an	-en	-en

Spanish Syntax

Spanish has its unique grammatical rules. In Spanish as well as English, children learn the concept of nouns, which name a person, animal, place, or thing. Verbs are considered action words. Adjectives and adverbs have a primary job of describing. Adjectives describe nouns and adverbs describe verbs. The order of a grammatically correct sentence is what often causes the most difficulty when learning a language. In Spanish, for example, the adjective typically follows the noun. In order to describe pretty hair, one would say *pelo bonito,* with the noun placed before the adjective. In English, the adjective is typically placed before the noun.

Nouns in Spanish have either a masculine or feminine gender. To learn the grammatical rules, an English language learner may learn the rules in his or her native language and then apply or compare them with the rules of English syntax. For example, if a teacher is male, he is referred to in Spanish as *maestro.* Nouns denoting males or animals that are males end in the letter *o.* Nouns denoting females or animals that are generally feminine must end with the letter *a.* A female teacher therefore is referred to as *maestra.* Spanish speakers must not only learn nouns but must also learn how to apply the rules of gender. Therefore, English language learners should be able to understand the concept of nouns since unlike for Spanish they do not have to learn rules of gender for English.

The Spanish language has three regular classes of verbs, with infinitives ending in *-ar, -er,* and *-ir.* The regular tenses of verbs are formed by dropping the ending of the base and adding the endings shown in Table 11.5.

Spanish adjectives ending in *o* change the *o* to *a* in the feminine gender. Adjectives ending in a vowel other than *o* often have the same form for masculine or feminine. Adverbs related to manner are often formed in Spanish by adding the suffix *-mente* to the feminine form of the adjective:

Adjectives		
Masculine	Feminine	Adverbs
rápido	rápida	rápidamente
lento	lenta	lentamente
correcto	correcta	correctamente
triste	triste	tristemente
alegre	alegre	alegremente

COMMON TIES BETWEEN SPANISH AND ENGLISH

Alphabets

There are 29 letters and digraphs that are regarded as individual letters in the Spanish alphabet and 26 letters in the English alphabet:

Spanish: a b c ch d e f g h i j k l ll m n ñ o p q r s t u v w x y z

English: a b c d e f g h i j k l m n o p q r s t u v w x y z

Although there is a movement to remove *ch, ll, ñ,* and *rr* from the alphabet system, students at risk for reading difficulty benefit from one-to-one correspondence that is regular and stable. Each language has five letters to represent the vowels. Spanish vowels have consistent sounds and consistent spellings. They can also be combined to form diphthongs (two adjacent vowels in a syllable that blend together to make a new sound). English vowels can be short or long, can form diphthongs, or can have unaccented sounds. English vowel sounds can have more than one frequent spelling. The sequential order of the English and Spanish alphabet is similar. In some cases it is useful for teachers to remove the digraphs from the Spanish alphabet; however, doing so can cause a decrease in the one-to-one letter–sound correspondences within the alphabet. Struggling readers require regularity of the language and literacy system. It is therefore recommended that these digraphs remain within the Spanish alphabet during early reading instruction.

As noted previously, many sounds and symbols transfer from the Spanish language to English. There are 23 phonemes in Spanish compared with 44 phonemes in English. Some examples of phonemes that directly transfer from English to Spanish include /b/, /ch/, /d/, /ĕ/, /f/, /g/, /k/, /l/, /m/, /n/, /ō/, /p/, /s/, /t/, /w/, and /y/ (see Table 11.4 for Spanish–English consonant correlations). English and Spanish sound systems can be described by their articulatory manner of production. These concepts are useful for literacy in two languages.

Diphthongs

Table 11.6 depicts the Spanish–English consonant and diphthong correlations, respectively. Notice that Spanish vowels can combine to form diphthongs. Diphthong spellings such as *oy* and *au* directly transfer to the English language. If a Spanish vowel pair is accented, the two vowels are produced separately and are not combined. Examples include the Spanish words *oído* and *tía.*

Table 11.6. Spanish–English diphthong correlations

Spanish	English
ai (*bailarina*)	i (*light, like*)
au (*autobús*)	ou (*out*)
ey (*rey*)	ey (*they*)
ei (*peine*)	a (*pay*)
oi, oy (*oigan, voy*)	oi, oy (*oil, joy*)
ia (*media*)	ya (*yarn*)
ua (*cuando*)	wa (*wand*)
ie (*hielo*)	ye (*yet*)
ue (*cuete*)	we (*went*)
io (*radio*)	yo (*yoke*)
uo (*cuota*)	uo (*quote*)
iu (*ciudad*)	yu (*Yule*)
ui (*cuidar*)	wee (*week*)

MULTISENSORY INSTRUCTION OF LANGUAGE COMPONENTS IN SPANISH

Reading in two languages is possible when students' strengths and knowledge base are considered. The National Reading Panel (NICHD, 2000), reported important findings regarding the development of English reading skills. The results acknowledged the importance of direct, systematic instruction in phonological awareness, phonics, vocabulary, read-

ing fluency, and reading comprehension as skills important for successful reading development. Considering the challenge of biliteracy, learning to read in two languages can be facilitated by transferring these skills from one language to the other. The following exercises, which are similar to English reading instruction, were developed to facilitate teaching reading in Spanish. The first groups of activities presented are several levels of phonological awareness in a developmental progression of difficulty.

Phonological Awareness

Rhyme Identification

As children rhyme they are in fact manipulating an initial sound or cluster of sounds. This is sound manipulation and is necessary as a step toward achieving a higher level of phonological awareness, such as phoneme manipulation. Students and the teacher can utilize mirrors and observe that only the initial sound is substituted when rhyming words.

Teacher	*Students*	*Teacher*	*Students*	*Teacher*
(Digan = Say)		(¿Riman? = Do they rhyme?)		(Cambiamos . . . por . . . = We change . . . for . . .)
Digan *mía tía.*	mía tía	¿Riman?	Sí	Cambiamos /m/ por /t/.
Digan *sol gol.*	sol gol	¿Riman?	Sí	Cambiamos /s/ por /g/.
Digan *las mas.*	las mas	¿Riman?	Sí	Cambiamos /l/ por /m/.
Digan *sí no.*	sí no	¿Riman?	No	Cambiamos todos los sonidos. (We change all of the sounds.)
Digan *luna cuna.*	luna cuna	¿Riman?	Sí	Cambiamos /l/ por /k/.

Rhyme Generation

Rhyme generation is the ability to produce rhyming words. The teacher can scaffold this skill by using flash cards of the Spanish letters. The ultimate goal is for students to perform this skill by listening. Therefore the teacher dictates words that end in the same VCV pattern and asks the students to change the initial sound. One example is the ending *-asa.* Children can change the initial sound and generate rhyming words, such as *asa, casa, masa, pasa,* and *taza.* (In Spanish *s* and *z* are produced as /s/.) Examples of other endings include *-eso, -ano, -ala, -elo,* and *-una.*

Rhyming

Teacher: Digan *mía.* (Say *mía.*)

Students: Mía

Teacher: Digan una palabra que rime con *mía.* (Say a word that rhymes with *mía.*)

Students: Tía

The teacher continues the activity with the following Spanish words: *sol, las, mes, gato, casa, luna, pino, nido, mal, pala,* and *usa.*

Alliteration Repetition and Identification

Alliterations are called *trabalenguas* in Spanish. It is important to initially have students repeat the alliteration and identify the common initial sound. Later, students can sing and generate Spanish alliterations.

1. Mi mamá me mima.

2. ¿Cómo como? Como, como, como.

3. Tres tristes tigres tragan tres tragos.

4. Pepe Pecas pica papas con un pico pica papas Pepe Pecas.

Alliteration Generation

The teacher can scaffold the ability to produce alliterations by providing the first two words of the alliteration and asking the students to extend the alliteration with words that begin with the same initial sound. As students progress they can generate their own alliterations.

Teacher	*Students*
Manuel mira _____.	mangos, muebles, mariposas
Consuelo come _____.	carne, caldo, cacahuates
Triana toca _____.	tomates, tamales, timbres
Daniel debe _____.	dinero, donas, dulces

Syllable Blending

Children are asked to listen, repeat, and blend syllables to form words. They can use counters or their fingers to blend syllables and form words.

Teacher	*Students*	*Teacher*	*Students*
(Digan = Say)		(La palabra es = The word is)	
Digan /mä/ /sä/.	/mä/ /sä/	La palabra es	masa
Digan /lōō/ /nä/.	/lōō/ /nä/	La palabra es	luna
Digan /säl/ /gō/.	/säl/ /gō/	La palabra es	salgo
Digan /bä/ /tĕ/.	/bä/ /tĕ/	La palabra es	bate
Digan /mĕ/ /sä/.	/mĕ/ /sä/	La palabra es	mesa

Syllable Omission

Students can clap their hands, use counters, or their fingers to practice syllable omission activities. Deletion of an initial or a final syllable is easier than deletion of a medial syllable, so the teacher should first ask students to delete initial and final syllables before moving on to deletion of medial syllables.

Teacher	Students	Teacher	Students
(Digan = Say)		(Ahora digan . . . sin . . . = Now say . . . . .)	
Digan *mango.*	mango	Ahora digan *mango* sin *man.*	go
Digan *asiento.*	asiento	Ahora digan *asiento* sin *a.*	siento
Digan *silla.*	silla	Ahora digan *silla* sin *lla.*	si
Digan *rápido.*	rápido	Ahora digan *rápido* sin *rá.*	pido
Digan *abajo.*	abajo	Ahora digan *abajo* sin *ba.*	ajo

Phoneme Blending

Students can listen, repeat, and blend sounds to form words. They can use counters or their fingers to illustrate the concept of blending phonemes.

Teacher	Students	Teacher	Students
(Digan = Say)		(La palabra es = The word is)	
Digan /s/ /ä/ /l/.	/s/ / ä / /l/	La palabra es	sal
Digan /m/ /ĕ/ /s/.	/m/ /ĕ/ /s/	La palabra es	mes
Digan /g/ /ō/ /l/.	/g/ /ō/ /l/	La palabra es	gol
Digan /g/ /ä/ /t/ /ō/.	/g/ /ä/ /t/ /ō/	La palabra es	gato
Digan /b/ /ä/ /t/ /ĕ/.	/b/ /ä/ /t/ /ĕ/	La palabra es	bate

Phoneme Substitution

Students can use mirrors to view the position of the mouth as they substitute the initial sounds.

Teacher	Students	Teacher	Students
(Digan = Say)		(Cambia . . . por . . . = Substitute/change . . . for . . .)	
Digan *mesa.*	mesa	Cambia /m/ por /p/.	pesa
Digan *luna.*	luna	Cambia /l/ por /t/.	tuna
Digan *sal.*	sal	Cambia /s/ por /m/.	mal
Digan *gato.*	gato	Cambia /g/ por /p/.	pato
Digan *cena.*	cena	Cambia /s/ por /p/.	pena

Alphabet Knowledge

Alphabet knowledge can be taught using manipulatives. Activities such as singing the alphabet, placing letters in order, and identifying missing letters can be performed in Spanish as well as in English. The alphabet activities described in Chapter 5 can be incorporated into reading instruction in Spanish. One example is sequencing and ma-

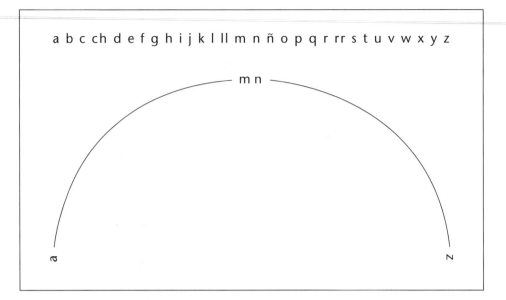

a b c ch d e f g h i j k l ll m n ñ o p q r rr s t u v w x y z

m n

a ... z

Figure 11.1.   Alphabet sequencing mat for the Spanish alphabet.

nipulating plastic letters into an arc and teaching the sequential order of the alphabet. An example of a Spanish arc is depicted in Figure 11.1 (an English version appears in Chapter 5). The same procedures incorporated for acquiring alphabet knowledge in English can be utilized in Spanish. In addition, games that focus on a missing letter (see Chapter 5) or a game of alphabet bingo can be used. As students begin to master phonological awareness and letter knowledge, they are prepared to learn letter–sound correspondences.

Letter–Sound Correspondences

To learn new sounds, children listen to words with common initial sounds, look at the letter that represents the sound, and feel their mouth and throat as they produce the sound. They discover the letter, a key word, and a sound to facilitate the letter and sound correlation. Using flash cards depicting each letter, key word, and sound is helpful as students learn the letter–sound correspondences.

Teacher: Digan *pala, pesa, punto.* (Say *pala, pesa, punto.*)

Students: pala, pesa, punto

Teacher: ¿Cuál sonido oyeron? (What sound did you hear?)

Students: /p/

Teacher: Miren su boca. ¿Está abierta o cerrada? (Look at you mouth. Is it open or closed?)

Students: Cerrada por los labios (Closed by the lips)

Teacher: ¿Es vocal o consonante? (Is it a vowel or consonant?)

Students: Es consonante. (It is a consonant.)

Teacher: La palabra clave es *piano*. (The key word is piano.)

Students: Piano

Teacher: Letra *p,* piano, /p/ (Letter *p,* piano, /p/)

Students: Letra *p,* piano, /p/ (Letter *p,* piano, /p/)

In order to learn to decode, it is important for Spanish speakers to learn the letter–sound correspondences. In one program, Spanish speakers are exposed to sounds, symbols, and words that directly transfer to the English language (Cárdenas-Hagan, 1998). For example, when learning the short *e* vowel sound, students learn the key word, *elefante* (elephant). This letter, sound, and word can directly transfer to English, therefore facilitating the knowledge of letter–sound correlations from one language to the next. Letters, sounds, and key words in Spanish and English are illustrated in Table 11.7; Figure 11.2 shows key word pictures and letters.

Morphemes

Word meaning and the structure of words are helpful for vocabulary, comprehension, and spelling instruction. Because 60% of the English language is derived from Latin word parts and 80% of Spanish is derived from Latin, Spanish word parts can be useful for learning to read, write, and understand English (Lindzey, 2003). Many morphemes are similar in Spanish and English. Studying base words, affixes (prefixes and suffixes), and roots helps decoding and builds vocabulary for reading and spelling. The ability to immediately recognize prefixes, suffixes, and roots in both Spanish and English gives students access to decoding longer words and insight into these words' meanings. Procedures for teaching these word parts are described in detail in the chapters on the history and structure of English (Chapter 6), reading (Chapter 9), and vocabulary (Chapter 13). Pages 310–311 contain multisensory discovery activities that deal with Spanish morphemes.

Table 11.7. Key words and sounds in Spanish and English

Letter	Sound(s)	Spanish key word	English key word
b	/b/	bate	bat
c	/k/	cámara	camera
d	/d/	doctor	doctor
e	/e/	elefante	elephant
f	/f/	fuego	fire
g	/g/	ganso	goose
i	/i/	iguana	iguana
k	/k/	kilo	kilo
l	/l/	limón	lemon
m	/m/	mamá	mother
n	/n/	nido	nest
p	/p/	piano	piano
r	/r/	rosa	rose
s	/s/	sol	sun
t	/t/	tomate	tomato
y	/y/	yoyo	yoyo
x	/ks/	saxofón	saxophone

From Cárdenas-Hagan, E. (2000). *Esperanza training manual* (p. 18). Brownsville, TX: Valley Speech, Language, and Learning Center; reprinted by permission.

Figure 11.2. Key word pictures and letters. (From Cárdenas-Hagan, E. [1998]. *Esperanza: A multisensory Spanish language program* [Reading deck cards]. Brownsville, TX: Valley Speech, Language, and Learning Center; adapted by permission.)

Auditory Discovery

Teacher: Estudiantes, saquen sus espejos y miren su boca mientras que repiten estas palabras que tienen la misma raíz: *teléfono, micrófono, xilófono.* (Students, take out your mirrors and look at your mouth as you repeat these words that have the same root: *telephone, microphone, xylophone.*)

Students: Teléfono, micrófono, xilófono

Visual Discovery

Teacher: Miren el pizarrón mientras que yo escribo las palabras *teléfono, micrófono* y *xilófono.* Cada palabra tiene la misma raíz. La raíz es_____. (Look at the board as I write the words *telephone, microphone,* and *xylophone.* Every word has the same root. The root is _____.)

Students: Fono (phone)

Tactile/Kinesthetic Discovery

Teacher: Miren y toquen mi teléfono. Yo uso el teléfono para oír los sonidos de la voz de otra persona. Miren y toquen mi xilófono. Ustedes pueden escuchar el sonido de este instrumento. Miren el micrófono. Ustedes pueden escuchar los sonidos de mi voz muy recio. Entonces el significado es _____. (Look at and touch my telephone. I use the telephone to listen to the sounds of another person's voice. Look and touch my xylophone. You can listen to the sounds of this instrument. Look at the microphone. You can hear the sounds of my voice. It is loud. Therefore, the meaning of *phone* is _____).

Students: Sonidos (sounds)

Teacher: Miren la tarjeta de la raíz *fono*. La palabra clave es *micrófono*. ¿Conocen otras palabras con la raíz *fono?* (Look at this card with the root *phone*. The key word is *microphone*. Do you know other words with this root?)

Students: Audífonos, fonología, megáfono (audiophones, phonology, megaphone)

Teacher: Muy bien. Ahora pueden usar estas palabras con la raíz *fono*. (Very good. Now you can use these words with the root *phone*.)

Ahora pueden crear oraciones con as palabras *audíofonos, fonologia y megafono*. (Now can you create sentences with the words *audiophones, phonology,* and *megaphone*.)

Tables 11.8–11.10 are helpful to teachers working with English language learners. These tables display the correlations between Spanish and English prefixes, suffixes, and roots and their meanings in both languages. Reaching beyond phonics and basic orthographic patterns, these comparisons can lead to a wider understanding of the similarities and differences in the meaning units of Spanish and English. Students can write the affixes and roots on index cards, with meanings and examples on the backs of the cards, to form a deck for review and practice during reading lessons. Teachers may use the graphic organizer shown in Table 11.11 as a tool for a multisensory introduction of base words and affixes.

Table 11.8.   Spanish prefixes and their English correlations

Spanish		English	
Prefix	Meaning	Prefix	Meaning
ante-	antes	ante-	before
anti-	contra	anti-	against
con-	unión	con-	with
contra-	contra	contra-	against
des-	negación	dis-	not
dis-	oposición	dis-	not
ex-	afuera de-	ex-	outside of
extra-	más	extra-	above
in-	no	in-	not
inter-	entre	inter-	between
intro-	dentro	intro-	within
multi-	mucho	multi-	many
pre-	antes	pre-	before
pro-	por	pro-	for
re-	repetir	re-	again
sin-	con	syn-	with
sub-	debajo	sub-	under
super-	sobre	super-	above
trans-	al otro lado	trans-	across
tri-	tres	tri-	three
uni-	uno	uni-	one

From Cárdenas-Hagan, E. (2000). *Esperanza training manual* (p. 19). Brownsville, TX: Valley Speech, Language, and Learning Center; reprinted by permission.

Table 11.9. Spanish suffixes and their English correlations

Spanish		English	
Suffix	Meaning	Suffix	Meaning
-able	capaz de	-able	able to
-ancia	forma de ser	-ance	state of being
-ano	nativo	-an	native of
-ante	alguien que	-ant	one who
-cial	en relación con	-cial	related to
-ción	estado de	-tion	state of being
-encia	estado de	-ence	state of being
-idad	calidad de	-ity	quality of
-ido	en relación con	-id	related to
-ista	alguien que	-ist	one who
-itis	inflamación	-itis	inflammation
-ito	diminutivo	-ite	related to
-ivo	causa de	-ive	causing
-lento	en relación con	-lent	relating to
-osis	enfermedad	-osis	disease
-oso	lleno de	-ous	full of
-sión	estado de	-sion	state of being
-tad	forma de ser	-ty	state of being
-undo	en relación con	-und	related to
-ura	estado de	-ness	state of being

From Cárdenas-Hagan, E. (2000). *Esperanza training manual* (p. 20). Brownsville, TX: Valley Speech, Language, and Learning Center; reprinted by permission.

Syntax

The Spanish language has the same parts of speech with the same functions as English: nouns, verbs, articles, adjectives, adverbs, conjunctions, and prepositions. Knowing the rules of one language and the similarities and differences with the second language is helpful for learning to read and write. Students can be taught the similarities between Spanish and English:

- Nouns name a person, place, or thing.

- Verbs are used for depicting action.

- Articles come before a noun.

- Adjectives describe nouns.

- Adverbs typically describe verbs but may also describe adjectives or other adverbs.

- Conjunctions connect thoughts.

- Prepositions are words that relate to other words.

Activities for Learning Syntax in Spanish

Teacher: Miren, yo hablo español. Miren, ahora yo camino. Miren, ahora yo brinco. (Look, I speak Spanish. Look, I walk. Look, I jump.)

Table 11.10. Spanish roots and their English correlations

Spanish		English	
Root	Meaning	Root	Meaning
audi	oír	audi	to hear
auto	solo	auto	by itself
cent	cien	cent	one hundred
ducto	guiar	duct	to lead
fam	fama	fam	famous
fin	final	fin	final
fono	sonido	phono	sound
graf	escribir	graph	written
gram	peso	gram	weight
kilo	mil	kilo	one thousand
liber	libre	liber	free
lingua	lengua	lingua	tongue
logía	estudio de	ology	study of
luna	lunar	luna	moon
metro	medida	meter	measure
novel	nuevo	novel	new
port	cargar	port	carry
semi	mitad	semi	half
tract	estirar	tract	to pull
trans	cruzar	trans	across
vis	ver	vis	to see
voc	voz	voc	voice

From Cárdenas-Hagan, E. (2000). *Esperanza training manual* (p. 21). Brownsville, TX: Valley Speech, Language, and Learning Center; reprinted by permission.

Digan *hablo, camino, brinco.* (Say *hablo, camino, brinco.*)

Estas palabras son verbos. Cada palabra termina en la letra *o.* El verbo es *hablar.* En el presente indicativo pongo la letra *o* al final de cada palabra. (These words are verbs. Each word ends in the letter *o.* The verb is *hablar.* In the present indicative I place the letter *o* at the end of each word. Now you can use the verb *apagar.*)

Students: Yo apag*o.*

Teacher: Muy bien usaron la letra *o* al final del verbo *apagar.* (Very good. You used the letter *o* at the end of the verb.)

Sigue con los verbos. (Continue with the following verbs.)

1. hallar
2. lavar
3. llamar
4. llevar
5. pintar
6. recomendar
7. sacar
8. tirar
9. trabajar
10. visitar

Table 11.11. Enseñanza de prefijos, sufijos o raices (in Spanish and English)

Descubrimiento auditivo	Nombra tres palabras con el prefijo, sufijo o raíz. Los estudiantes repitan la palabra. Los estudiantes nombren el prefijo, sufijo o raíz gue oyeron.
Visual	La maestra escribe tres palabras en el pizarrón. Los estudiantes pueden ver el prefijo, sufijo o raíz.
Significado kinestético	La maestra usa cada palabra en una oración. La maestra puede demostrar el significado de la palabra. La maestra usa las tarjetas de prefijos, sufijos o raíces. Los estudiantes escriben una oración para cada palabra. Los estudiantes usan y escriben los palabras en sus cuadernos de vocabulario.
Auditory discovery	Name three words with the prefix, suffix, or root. The students repeat the words. The students name the prefix, suffix, or root that they heard.
Visual discovery	The teacher writes three words on the board. The students can see the prefix, suffix, or root.
Kinesthetic discovery	The teacher uses each word in a sentence. The teacher can demonstrate the meaning of the word. The teacher uses prefix, suffix, or root cards. The students write a sentence for each word. The students use the words and write them in their vocabulary notebooks for further reference.

BILITERACY EDUCATION MODEL

In a small city along the Texas–Mexico border, a biliteracy education model was implemented. Indeed, the citizens shared the necessity to speak in two languages. The community also shared a vision with the local public school district that it was important to become bicultural and biliterate. A 5-year strategic action plan was developed by the school district that included intensive professional development for all kindergarten through third-grade teachers in two programs, *Esperanza* (Cárdenas-Hagan, 1998) for Spanish literacy and *Language Enrichment* (Carreker, 1992) for English literacy. Bilingual classrooms were provided on-site training with the *Esperanza* program. The school district considered these two programs as the core reading programs. Its strategic plan was approved by the local school board. This demonstrated a commitment to the reading reform effort from the classroom to the top administrators of the school district, to the school board and to the community.

During the 90-minute language arts block, the students in bilingual classrooms participated on a daily basis in the *Esperanza* program (Cárdenas-Hagan, 1998). The students were therefore exposed to phonological awareness, phonics, vocabulary, reading fluency, and reading comprehension practice in their native language, Spanish. In January of the first-grade year, students continued with their Spanish literacy instruction but were also introduced to the *Language Enrichment* (Carreker, 1992) program during their English as a second language period. Both of these programs are multisensory, systematic structured language approaches for language and literacy instruction. Parallel activities were conducted in the two languages. Each lesson incorporated systematic and structured reviews of previous lessons. Students were exposed to auditory, visual, tactile, and kinesthetic modalities in order to learn new reading, language, and writing concepts. As the students learned a new concept, they immediately applied it to reading, writing, and spelling.

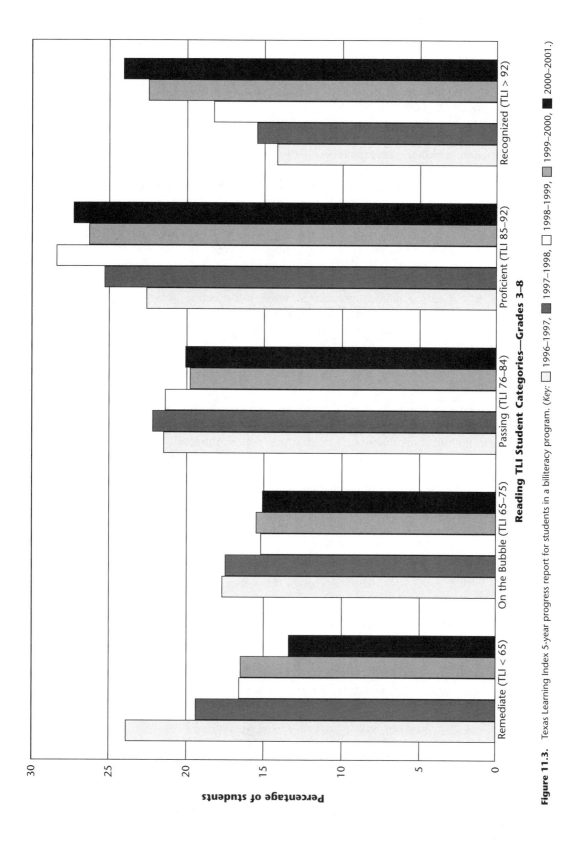

Figure 11.3. Texas Learning Index 5-year progress report for students in a biliteracy program. (*Key:* ☐ 1996–1997, ■ 1997–1998, ☐ 1998–1999, ▨ 1999–2000, ■ 2000–2001.)

From second grade to the end of third grade, the students in the bilingual classrooms continued with vocabulary and comprehension instruction in Spanish and focused on English reading using the *Language Enrichment* (Carreker, 1992) program until the end of third grade.

Teachers were provided with monthly updates and at least two *Esperanza* (Cárdenas-Hagan, 1998) coaching sessions during the school year. The program included instruction in phonological awareness, letter–sound correspondences, decoding, reading fluency, alphabet knowledge, writing, spelling, vocabulary, syntax, oral language, and comprehension. Once students demonstrated grade-level literacy in Spanish, the *Language Enrichment* (Carreker, 1992) program was implemented. This involved a 5-day training for teachers, with at least one mentoring session. Instructional facilitators were trained to provide staff support at the campus level. The school district reported an 84% reduction in referrals for special education services such as dyslexia by Year 3 of the project. Figure 11.3 shows that the percentage of students requiring intervention (the students in the Remediate group) in the school district dropped from 26% to 13%. The school district made progress in the delivery of effective literacy instruction for English language learners. Biliteracy for the border community is a necessity and can be achieved. This model can be replicated in other communities, and students can attain biliteracy.

CONCLUSION

Reading in two languages is possible when students' strengths and knowledge base are considered. The National Reading Panel (NICHD, 2000) reported important findings regarding the development of English reading skills. The results acknowledged the importance of phonemic awareness, phonics, vocabulary, reading fluency, and reading comprehension as skills important for successful reading development. Learning to read in two languages can be facilitated by incorporating similar skills from one language to the next in a multisensory, systematic, direct, and comprehensive instructional program that focuses on the structure of each language to facilitate learning.

REFERENCES

Adams, M.J. (1990). *Beginning to read: Thinking and learning about print.* Cambridge, MA: The MIT Press.

Anderson, R.C., & Nagy, W.I. (1992). The vocabulary conundrum. *American Educator, 16*(4), 14–18, 44–47.

August A., & Hakuta, K. (Eds.). (1997). *Improving school for language-minority children: A research agenda.* Washington, DC: National Academies Press.

Barrutia, R., & Schwegler, A. (1994). *Fonética y fonología españolas* (2nd ed.). New York: John Wiley & Sons.

Bialystok, E. (2002). Acquisition of literacy in bilingual children: A framework for research. *Language Learning, 52*(1), 159–199.

Bloom, L., & Lahey, M. (1978). *Language development and language disorders.* New York: John Wiley & Sons.

Cárdenas-Hagan, E. (1998). *Esperanza: A multisensory Spanish language program.* Brownsville, TX: Valley Speech Language and Learning Center.

Cárdenas-Hagan, E. (2000). *Esperanza training manual.* Brownsville, TX: Valley Speech Language and Learning Center.

Carreker, S. (1992). *Language enrichment: Reading concepts manual.* Houston, TX: Neuhaus Education Center.

Chiappe, P., Hasher, L., & Siegel, L.S. (2000). Reading-related skills of kindergartners from diverse linguistic backgrounds. *Applied Psycholinguistics, 23,* 95–116.

Corson, D. (1998). *Language policy in schools: A resource for teachers and administrators.* Mahwah, NJ: Lawrence Erlbaum Associates.

Durgunoglu, A.Y., Nagy, W.E., & Hacin-Bhatt, B.J. (1993). Cross-language transfer of phonological awareness. *Journal of Education Psychology, 85*(37), 453–465.

Francis, D., & Carlson, C. (2001). Presentation at

Tejas LEE Early Spanish Reading Symposium. Houston, TX.

Fry, R. (2003, June 12). *Hispanic youth dropping out of U.S. schools: Measuring the challenge.* Washington, DC: Pew Hispanic Center.

Lindzey, G. (2003). *Why study Latin?* [Brochure]. Retrieved December 23, 2004, from http://www.promotelatin.org/latin.htm

National Institute of Child Heath and Human Development (NICHD). (2000). *Report of the National Reading Panel. Teaching children to read: An evidence-based assessment of the scientific research literature on reading and its implications for reading instructions. Report of the subgroups* (NIH Publication No. 00-4754). Washington, DC: U.S. Government Printing Office. Also available on-line: http://www.nichd.nil.gov/publications/nrp/report.htm

Quiroga, T., Lemons-Britton, Z., Mostafapour, E., Abbott R.D., & Berninger, V.W. (2000). Phonological awareness and beginning reading in Spanish-speaking ESL first grade: Research into practice. *Journal of School Psychology, 40*(1), 85–111.

Texas Education Agency. (2002). *Snapshot 2001-02: School district profiles.* Retrieved from http://www.tea.state.tx.us/perfreport/snapshot/2002/index.html

U.S. Census Bureau. (2000). Washington, DC: U.S. Government Printing Office. Retrieved from http://www.census.gov/population

12

Instruction for Older Students Struggling with Reading

Barbara A. Wilson

INTRODUCTION

Jeanne S. Chall (1983) explained it well. First students learn to read, and then students read to learn. Students are expected to read to learn beginning in the upper elementary grades. If, however, students in grades 4–12 have not yet learned to read, this expectation places extraordinary demands upon them. Although the evidence for early intervention for struggling readers is clear (National Institute of Child Health and Human Development [NICHD], 2000; Torgesen, 1998; Vellutino et al., 1996), what happens to the students who do not get this intervention?

The statistics about reading failure in the United States are astounding. The 2002 National Assessment of Educational Progress (Grigg, Daane, Jin, & Campbell, 2003) reported that 36% of fourth-grade students, 25% of eighth-grade students, and 26% of the twelfth-grade students scored below the basic level in overall reading skill.

Clearly, this means that millions of students in middle and high schools across the nation struggle to read in school every day. Children in primary grades with reading difficulty usually have decoding deficits. Children beyond Grade 3 who have reading difficulty may have decoding deficits, comprehension deficits, or both (Leach, Scarborough, & Rescorla, 2003). This chapter focuses on instruction for those students beyond Grade 3 who have decoding deficits with or without an accompanying comprehension deficit. This accounts for 67% of students who have late-identified reading disabilities (Leach et al., 2003). These students need instruction that targets their deficits.

Intervention is not too late even if students are beyond Grade 3, as indicated by the analysis of pre- and posttest results for 319 students with significant decoding deficits in grades 4–8 (Wood, 2002; see Table 12.1). Table 12.1 shows reading growth after 60 hours of multisensory structured language teaching with the *Wilson Reading*

Table 12.1. Mean reading scores by grade, before and after multisensory structured language (MSL) teaching

Subtest	Grade 3 (*n* = 52)	Grade 4 (*n* = 106)	Grade 5 (*n* = 88)	Grade 6 (*n* = 54)	Grades 7/8 (*n* = 71)
Word Identification					
Pretest	90.51	88.55	84.74	81.22	75.83
Posttest	94.28	93.37	88.27	84.35	82.51
Word Attack					
Pretest	92.50	90.00	87.93	85.88	83.31
Posttest	101.82	100.94	99.19	95.67	95.49
Passage Comprehension					
Pretest	91.15	90.24	87.23	82.65	81.14
Posttest	97.12	96.71	92.64	87.15	88.81
Basic Skills Cluster					
Pretest	90.21	87.99	85.16	82.72	77.73
Posttest	96.44	96.10	92.11	88.08	87.05
Total Reading Cluster					
Pretest	89.81	88.37	85.00	81.17	76.72
Posttest	94.90	94.25	89.49	84.46	84.39

From Wood, F. (2002). Data analysis of the Wilson Reading System. In *Literacy solutions: Evidence of effectiveness*. Millbury, MA: Wilson Language Training.

System (Wilson, 1996). The scoring data were collected by school districts at multiple sites across the United States and analyzed across several variables. Comparison of pre- and posttest scores within each grade level revealed statistically significant improvements among all five measures of the Woodcock Reading Mastery Test–Revised (Woodcock, 1987) for each grade level (all $p < .001$) This indicates that older students benefit from structured language intervention just as much as do younger students.

Overcoming Discomfort

Although the majority of struggling readers lack basic language skills, most teachers are uncomfortable presenting older students with phonics. Teachers expect resistance and avoid this instruction. Teacher must overcome this discomfort in order to achieve success. Part of the discomfort is likely to be from their inexperience with teaching basic skills and their lack of preparation. Unfortunately, all too often teachers are not knowledgeable about how to teach word structure in depth. Furthermore, they lack core information about phonology, orthography, and morphology (American Federation of Teachers, 1999). This makes basic skills instruction challenging for a teacher working with elementary school students but it makes it even more difficult for a teacher working with older students. Older students will be hesitant to work on basic skills, so precise, experienced teaching is necessary. The teacher should be skilled and proficient with multisensory teaching methods. It is also important to present the multisensory structured language program with confidence and not in an apologetic manner whatsoever. In order to do this, the teacher must believe that this teaching is appropriate and necessary.

Another discomforting factor for teachers to overcome relates to a misconception. It is commonly believed that when teaching students basic word structure, one should not use grade-appropriate narrative and expository text. From the beginning, however, instruction should include work with such texts.

Student Expectations

Older students who are struggling with reading have likely met with much failure throughout the years. Regardless of their failure and varied reasons for it, students in middle school have a high interest in learning to read (McCray, 2001). It is hard to imagine the feelings these students have when facing undecodable words on a page. Most do not believe they can improve, so they do not want to show their interest. Expect this. They may protect their self-esteem by resisting instruction. It has failed them in the past; why should this be different? For this reason, teachers must not be thwarted when students initially say, "This is stupid." In the beginning, this is a very likely response. Students say it to protect their egos. If a teacher is understanding, he or she can respond sympathetically that it feels stupid but it is actually the beginning of a detailed study of the English language. It will soon get very sophisticated. If a student has a diagnosed language learning disability that interferes with ease of reading and spelling, the teacher can explain the abundant research that now indicates that many people share the difficulty of mastering the sound system and that systematic, sequential instruction has been proven to make mastery of it possible.

It is very important to explain to the students that they will be studying the structure of the English language in depth and that English is based upon a sound system. Explain to students that they will learn that just about 44 sounds are put together to make thousands and thousands of words. Show students that even with three-sound words, there are endless options. Use sound cards to demonstrate, changing just one letter at a time to make another word and stating, "Change just one letter and you have another word." Change from *hat* to *mat* to *mad* to *mud* to *bud* to *bid* to *bit* to demonstrate.

Most people think of English as a jumbled mix of words without rhyme or reason. However, a study conducted by Hanna, Hanna, Hodges, and Rudorf (1966) determined that the spellings of a majority of words in English follow a system. Explain that English is logical if one carefully studies sound–symbol correspondence as related to syllable patterns; orthographic (spelling) rules; and prefixes, roots, and suffixes. You can tell the students that they will learn more about English than most people know and that this will help them tremendously with both reading and spelling.

PLANNING FOR INSTRUCTION

Failing to prepare is preparing to fail.
—Anonymous

There are several key considerations when planning and implementing a multisensory structured language education (MSLE) program for older students (fourth grade and above):

1. Conducting an assessment of reading skills

2. Providing differentiated instruction

3. Scheduling a class with an appropriate group size for a sufficient amount of time in an appropriate setting

Conduct an Assessment of Reading Skills

Students beyond third grade vary in reading in more ways than younger students. For one thing, the range of overall reading levels in a given grade is much greater in the

later grades. An eighth-grade class, for example, might include some students who are nonreaders as well as some who read at a high school level. This, in itself, poses many challenges for instruction.

Students who are identified with a reading difficulty in the elementary grades usually have poor decoding (Shankweiler et al., 1999). For older students with reading difficulty there is an additional variable—the specific area of deficit. Unlike students in early elementary grades, students with late-identified reading disabilities may have word-level processing deficits or comprehension deficits or both (Leach et al., 2003).

Reading tests need to be comprehensive enough to determine subskills so that instruction can be properly planned and executed. (See Chapter 7 for further discussion of reading assessment.) Students who will benefit from the multisensory structured language instruction described in this chapter obtain low scores when tested on the following subskills, which indicates weak decoding:

- Phonological awareness

- Sound–symbol relationships

- Word attack (decoding)

- Rapid naming

- Word identification

- Fluency

- Spelling

These students most likely will have low comprehension scores due to their decoding and fluency deficiencies. Their energy and effort go to determining the words rather than understanding their meaning (Perfetti, 1985). Sufficient scores on listening comprehension tests indicate that poor comprehension scores are due to poor decoding, not to a lack of understanding. Some poor decoders, however, also have poor listening comprehension and thus, in addition to word-level deficits, they are likely to have vocabulary and comprehension deficits. Even when text is read to these students, they do not understand it, so listening comprehension measures yield a low score. These students will benefit from the MSLE instruction described here as well as more in-depth comprehension instruction.

Lastly, some older students decode fluently but have poor comprehension. These adolescents require specific methods of teaching comprehension skills and strategy instruction (Deshler et al., 2001; Moore, Bean, Birdyshaw, & Rycik, 1999). They have a very different profile on reading assessments. They usually score adequately on phonological awareness, word attack, and word identification subtests. They may also (though not always) score at grade level on spelling assessments. They may have weak vocabularies and lack background information. They score poorly on comprehension subtests (both reading and listening). These individuals are not candidates for the multisensory structured language instruction described in this chapter.

Provide Differentiated Instruction

Determining students' specific area(s) of deficit is a critical first step in addressing the reading difficulties of students beyond the elementary grades. Reading classes need to be well planned in order to succeed. Beyond elementary grades, this includes offering

classes that provide appropriate instruction. Therefore, students' scores on specific skill area subtests, rather than total reading scores, should determine instruction (Leach et al., 2003; Wilson, 1988). Reading assessments of subskills should be used to help design an appropriate program of instruction.

Poor decoders need very different instruction from students who lack adequate comprehension skills. Unfortunately, students are often treated the same beyond elementary grades regardless of their specific area(s) of deficit. Systematic instruction in decoding skills, if available at all, generally ends in the early elementary grades. Even when reading classes are available in middle and high schools, most do not include basic skills instruction. Students with poor word attack skills often find themselves in classes where they struggle to participate. Some students cannot even read basic text. Too often, even their reading intervention class instruction presents them with text that is too difficult for them to read. They frequently are placed in a reading class that focuses on comprehension regardless of their deficit, or they no longer get any direct reading instruction at all. These students require direct and systematic instruction of the sound system and word structure of the English language. Their instruction needs to focus on phonological awareness; phonics; reading accuracy, automaticity, and fluency; spelling; and vocabulary and comprehension. Students with both decoding and comprehension deficits can be grouped with the low-level decoders but they will likely require additional instructional time to sufficiently address both areas of need.

Conversely, students who read grade-level text fluently do not require any instruction in phonology; rather they require help with comprehension, including strategy instruction. They should not follow the same instructional course as students with primary decoding deficits. In fact, with older students, if these two groups are placed together for instruction, the teacher is unable to adequately address the needs of either group. If these students are misplaced with the poor decoders, they will be frustrated with instruction that includes sound–symbol relationships. They will likely say, "This is stupid," and for them, they are right on target. They might say it quietly at first but more loudly as time goes on. This will undermine the work that the teacher needs to accomplish with the students who do need phonology instruction.

Thus, students with primary decoding deficits should not be grouped for intervention with students who decode adequately but lack comprehension skills. If a more comprehensive reading evaluation is not available, then the teacher can place students in groups according to their percentile scores on *decoding* assessments. For example, students in Grade 8 who have scored below grade in reading might be placed in groups for differentiated instruction in the following manner:

Group 1: decoding and spelling below the 20th percentile*

Group 2: decoding and spelling between the 20th and 50th percentiles*

Group 3: decoding above the 50th percentile, with poor comprehension

*Students with weak comprehension in Groups 1 and 2 will also need additional work in comprehension.

Schedule Classes with Appropriate Group
Sizes and Sufficient Time in an Appropriate Setting

Older students with reading deficits are often placed in general education classes with accommodations and/or modifications. These students may not be getting enough di-

rect instruction in reading to progress. They may be getting support for their regular class content but not the intensive reading instruction they need (Deshler et al., 2001; McCray, 2001).

Although many older students with reading difficulties receive special education services in general education classrooms, some students are placed in pull-out programs. These, too, have yielded limited results. Unfortunately, for students with weak reading skills who are in pull-out classes, the instruction there has often produced very little reading growth. An analysis of a large data set reported that children in special education classes had only 0.04 standard deviations of growth in a year. (Hanushek, Kain, & Riuka, 1998). That is not closing the gap! These classes have not provided the structured, systematic teaching these students need. However, when pull-out programs do address students' specific deficits with sustained, systematic instruction, these students make significant gains (Deshler et al., 2001; O'Connor & Wilson, 1995; Wood, 2002).

When older students have not been successful, there is so much catching up to do. Reading instruction takes time. Students with a diagnosed reading disability need more intensive instruction than do other students (Lyon et al., 2001). It is not sufficient to squeeze this instruction into short periods of time.

Regardless of whether intensive instruction is provided in a general education reading class or in a pull-out setting, students with reading deficits require substantial time scheduled in a class that provides direct, systematic, and sustained instruction 5 days per week in the specific area(s) of deficit. For instruction to be adequate, it must be given at a regularly scheduled time, not fit in when possible. Students assigned to these classes should be grouped as previously discussed.

Classes for students with poor decoding that have a 90-minute block of time can then address the following three essential components of instruction on a daily basis:

1. *Accuracy and automaticity of single-word reading:* Focusing on accuracy and automaticity with single words includes a drill of sounds; a study of word structure; and practice with both decoding and encoding (spelling) single words, phrases, and sentences.

2. *Application of skills and fluency instruction:* This includes having students read **controlled text** to develop their independent reading skills as well as noncontrolled **decodable text**, as appropriate, to develop their application of skills and fluency.

3. *Development of vocabulary, background knowledge, and comprehension:* This work with vocabulary, background knowledge, and comprehension includes reading enriched text to students to develop critical skills with more challenging text. (Enriched text is sophisticated text with vocabulary and content written at a level higher than a student's decoding level.)

In addition to ensuring an appropriate group size and instructional setting, providing enough instruction time is important. Margaret B. Rawson (1988), a pioneer in the educational therapy for students with dyslexia, recognized that older students with significant reading deficits need sufficient time to achieve their potential:

> These children *can* succeed, if circumstances are even reasonably favorable and if they are given appropriate help over a long enough period. This must be at least a year, and preferably they should have two or three years, because there is much to learn about the language, and often much for the student to unlearn and to catch up on. No dyslexic child, I think we can say, *need fail because of his dyslexia.*

ACCURACY AND AUTOMATICITY OF SINGLE-WORD READING

The object of teaching a child is to enable
him to get along without his teacher.
—Elbert Hubbard

Get Underway with Sounds

Older students with decoding deficits lack phonological coding skills. They have not readily internalized the sound system of the language, and they do not understand the structure of words in English. As a result, they cannot accurately or fluently read text and they are poor spellers. It may seem awkward to present basic skills to older students, but if it is what they need and if the skills are taught in a multisensory, systematic way, students make substantial progress. This instruction needs to focus on developing the students' phonemic awareness, sound–symbol knowledge, understanding of word structure (syllable patterns and affixes), and high-frequency irregular words.

The National Reading Panel (NRP; NICHD, 2000) reported that phonemic awareness instruction is most effective when students are taught to manipulate phonemes by using the letters of the alphabet. Thus, phonemic awareness training is closely linked with the direct teaching of letter–sound (grapheme–phoneme) correspondences. The teacher begins instruction with the teaching of letter names and sounds for consonants, short vowels, and consonant digraphs. Accuracy with sounds is a crucial first step for students.

Many older students know most of the consonant sounds. However, they often add a vowel sound to each consonant, for example, saying /muh/ rather than /m/. It is more natural to say /muh/, and therefore /m/ must be carefully practiced. Teach students how to clip consonant sounds, explaining that it is important to clip sounds in order to blend them into words. Illustrate this using sound or phoneme cards. Make the word *mat.*

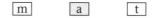

With the word *mat,* if the sounds are said /muh/ /ă/ /tuh/, the word will not blend to make the word *mat.* The sounds /m/ /ă/ /t/, on the other hand, do blend to say *mat.* It is helpful to explain that when pronouncing consonant sounds, one should minimize the dropping of the chin. Say /tuh/, then /t/. When the sound is clipped, the chin does not drop. Present each consonant with a phoneme card, and have the students practice saying the consonant sounds, carefully clipping them. Older students only need key words for consonant sounds that are either unknown or are not well established. An assessment such as the Word Identification and Spelling Test (WIST; Felton & Wilson, 2004) can help the teacher determine a baseline of sound knowledge.

Use key words (see Table 9.1 in Chapter 9) for any troublesome consonants. Key words aid memory and provide a reference to help students access the sound. The same key word should be consistently used to represent a sound. For example, many students say that the sound for *y* is /w/ because the name of the letter *y* starts with a /w/ sound. The key word *yellow* can help students remember that the sound for *y* is /y/, not /w/.

Typical consonants needing key words include *qu, w, x,* and *y.* Key words are also useful for the consonants *g* and *c* to emphasize the primary sound (*g, game,* /g/; *c, cat,* /k/) because students who have not mastered the sound system often say the secondary sound of each of these letters when trying to decode unfamiliar words, especially with the sound of the letter *g* (/j/ for *g*).

Short Vowels

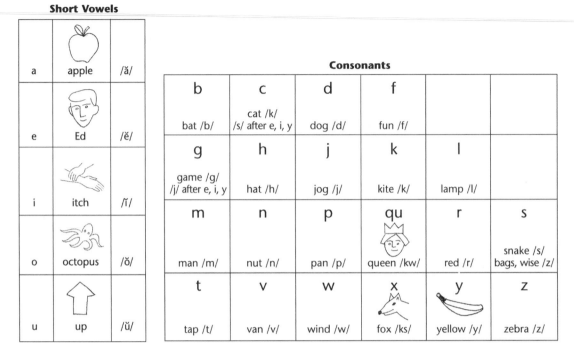

Figure 12.1. Pages from a student notebook for noting key words and pictures for short vowel and consonant sounds.

Regardless of baseline assessments, it is wise to use key words for all of the short vowels. (see Table 9.2 in Chapter 9). These sounds are critical and are easily confused. Help the students know exactly *how* to access the sound with the help of the key word by extending the vowel sound at the beginning of the key word. The key word *apple* is used for short *a*. Say "aaaaaaaapple" and have students repeat it. Ask students to say the sound until they run out of breath or to extend the sound at the beginning of the key word until you hold up your hand. Have them repeat each letter, key word, and sound after you: "Say *a, apple, /ă/.*"

Also, teach students the basic consonant digraphs: *sh, th, wh, ch,* and *ck.* Using a sound card with two letters on one card, show students that digraphs are two letters that have only one sound (*sh, ship, /sh/*).

Each student should begin a notebook divided into several sections to study the word structure of the English language. The first section of the notebook can be labeled *Sounds* and is used for reference. Have students enter the short vowel sounds on one page, the consonants on another page, and basic digraphs on a third page. See the student notebook sample in Figure 12.1 and note that the consonant page only has three key-word pictures drawn, indicating that for this particular student, those three consonant sounds were unknown or insecure. The rest of the notebook is devoted to recording word structure, spelling rules, vocabulary, and high-frequency nonphonetic irregular words (Wilson, 1988).

Initially, model the sounds and have students repeat after you until the students can accurately pronounce each sound independently. Begin each lesson with a quick 5-minute drill of these sounds so that students become automatic with them. During this kind of drill, initially the teacher presents a phoneme card and says the letter, key word, and sound and the students repeat these. Eventually, the teacher presents the card and the students respond, using their notebooks for reference as needed.

Not all of the sounds are taught at once. These are presented both incrementally and cumulatively. Carefully teach all sounds to mastery. As each sound is introduced, practice it in two directions, first for decoding and second for spelling:

1. Students look at the letter and name the sound,

2. Students hear the sound and identify the letter.

To practice the sounds for spelling, dictate a sound, such as /m/, and have students repeat it. Then have them name the letter (*m*) that makes that sound. Do this prior to the spelling instruction in each lesson.

Teach Blending and Segmenting

Mastery of sounds is critical; however, knowing the sounds of the English language does not ensure successful decoding or spelling. Students must know the sounds of English and be able to pronounce them quickly and efficiently. They must also be able to blend and segment these sounds.

Phoneme segmentation, the ability to pull apart the sounds in a given word, is a critical skill for reading and spelling success. Poor readers often need direct teaching of this skill. Students can learn how to blend and segment three sounds, then four, five, and six sounds, using one-syllable short-vowel words. This phoneme blending and segmentation training can be accomplished by using a combination of phoneme cards, blank cards (for segmenting), and a finger-tapping procedure.

First teach students how to segment and blend familiar three-sound words such as *map*. Put three phoneme cards (*m a p*) on a table surface or in a pocket chart. The card with the vowel should be represented by a different color.

Teach students how to say each sound as they tap a finger to their thumb: As they say /m/ they tap their index finger to their thumb, as they say /ă/, they tap their middle finger to their thumb, and as they say /p/ they tap their ring finger to their thumb.

Then have students say the sounds as they drag their thumb across their fingers, starting with their index finger for /m/. It does not matter whether or not this is done with the left or right hand. It does matter, however, to change fingers. This is an amazing way to get students to blend sounds (Wilson, 1988).

The tactile input to the fingertips appears to aid in the blending process. With a word such as *math*, the *th* digraph should be one card to represent one sound. The student also taps only three times because the digraph *th* stays together to make only one sound.

Some students prefer to tap on the table surface rather than the thumb. This still provides tactile feedback. To tap out the word *map* on the table, a student says /m/ while tapping the index finger on the table, /ă/ while tapping the middle finger and /p/ while tapping the ring finger. The student then taps all fingers to the table and says the word *map*.

With older students, it is important to immediately show them that they can decode a word that they have never seen before. They will usually read three-sound words

such as *map* without a problem, but there are many words that have three-sounds that are unfamiliar. Tell the students that the tapping-out method works with these unfamiliar words as well. Examples of three-sound words that are often unknown by sight are: *vat, shod, posh, thud, yen,* and *sod.* Form these words, one at a time, with cards. Be sure students say the sounds accurately with each tap, clipping the consonant sounds.

Model the blending as needed. When you make a three-sound word that the students do not know, help them decode it with tapping. You will create the opportunity to explain that this is exactly what they will be learning to do to figure out words that they may never have seen before. Tell the students that you will be showing them ways to determine hundreds of words without memorizing them. When they are successful with some of these words that they do not know by sight, they often feel encouraged. Be sure to take the time to talk about this with them and give them hope. They have tried to memorize so many words. Tell them, "See you don't need to memorize. I'm going to show you how to figure words out!" Students should not progress to words with four sounds until they can read and spell the three-sound words without tapping. For some students this might take several lessons.

When students know the basic sounds and can blend three sounds together in one-syllable words to read and segment them to spell, teach them how to identify closed syllables. Closed syllables are the most common of the six syllable types in English.

Students must learn to visually recognize if a syllable is closed. This tells them that the vowel in that syllable has a short sound. A very effective way to teach how to recognize a closed syllable is with the manipulation of sound cards. As mentioned previously, the vowel cards should be a different color from the consonant cards so that the students can see the vowel patterns. There are six kinds of syllables. All the words used as examples in this chapter so far have been closed syllables.

Form the word *bat.*

Tell the students that a closed syllable has one vowel only (point to *a*) and must be closed in (move the *t* closer to the *a* to show how it closes it in). A closed syllable gives the vowel the short sound: /ă/ is the short sound of *a.*

Now remove the *b* to leave the word *at.* Tell the student that there need not be a consonant in front of the vowel. The important point is that *one* vowel (point to *a* and stress **one**) is closed in (move *t*) by at least one consonant.

Make the word *bath.*

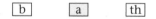

Tell the students that a closed syllable can have more than one consonant letter at the end (point to *th*).

Gradually build closed-syllable words with three sounds (e.g., *cap, cash*), then four (e.g., *step, stash*), then five (e.g., *stump, shrimp*), and at last six sounds (e.g., *script*). This teaching of sounds, phoneme segmentation, and blending sets the essential groundwork for successful and fluent decoding. Before progressing to multisyllabic work, students must easily blend and segment the sounds in a single syllable. In addition to the methods already described, be sure to give students much application practice with short-vowel words on flash cards, on word lists, and within connected text (Wilson, 1988).

To develop accurate reading of words, help students become metacognitive thinkers about word structure. They should know what they know and understand how it helps

them determine an unknown word. Use questioning techniques to facilitate this. For example, when a student reads the word *shop* instead of *chop,* ask, "What is the digraph in that word?" "What sound does the digraph make?" to lead to the correction. When the student determines the correct word, say, "That is the word! What did you do to figure it out?" Use the questioning to emphasize word structure and to correct errors, but do not overuse it. Reduce questioning as a student becomes more and more accurate so that you can then work on quick and automatic word recognition. When students become accurate, you can do timed drills to increase their automaticity. This is just the beginning for decoding and encoding, but it is a very crucial one.

Introduce Multisyllabic Words

Next, teach students how to combine closed syllables so that they succeed with multisyllabic words. The word *combat,* for example, combines two closed syllables. The word *Wisconsin* combines three closed syllables. With older students, it is important to give them this feeling of accomplishment with longer words. Combine closed syllables first rather than introducing another syllable type. When students master one type of syllable, teach them the next type, manipulating sound cards to teach the concept (see Table 9.4 in Chapter 9 for further discussion of syllable types).

With each new syllable type introduced, words combining different syllable types can be used (Wilson, 1988). For example, after students have learned closed and vowel-consonant-*e* syllables, present words such as *reptile, inflate,* and *compensate* to read and spell. The word *compensate,* for example, has two closed syllables (with short vowels) and a vowel-consonant-*e* syllable. With older students, you can present long words containing only one or two types of syllables. This allows students to read longer words and thus feel successful with decoding as soon as possible. Students should practice reading and spelling these words in isolation as well as within sentences and passages. The teaching of basic syllable patterns should be done gradually and cumulatively. As students learn these, they add the definition of each pattern, word examples, and corresponding rules of syllable division to their student notebooks. Teaching the students more detail about word structure helps them to apply the sounds in longer words accurately. Students need to learn the sounds of the language, but they must also go beyond the sounds to learn total word structure. Syllable patterns are a very important part of that instruction because the type of syllable regulates the vowel sound.

Teach Rules of Orthography

Students with a language learning disability actually can learn rules, although they might have difficulty with the language of the rules. Words get in their way. For students with a language learning difficulty, instruction must include demonstration and practice with manipulatives to clarify verbal explanations. The students add the language of the rule to their notebooks; however, they need to learn all about word structure in detail by means other than memorization of the wording of the rule. Manipulate word parts to help them see and feel the structure. For example, the silent *e* spelling rule can be taught with sound cards and suffix cards. Present suffixes to students on individual cards. First have the students categorize suffixes into two columns, putting the suffixes that begin with a vowel in one column and the suffixes that begin with a consonant in another column.

Vowel suffixes   Consonant suffixes

Vowel suffixes	Consonant suffixes
-ed	-ful
-ing	-less
-ive	-ness
-able	-ly
-er	-ty

Make the word *hope* with the sound cards:

h	o	p	e

Tell the students that words ending in silent *e* follow a rule when a vowel suffix is added. Put the -*ing* suffix cards beside the word *hope*. Tell the student that whenever a vowel suffix (point to the column of vowel suffixes) is added to a word with a silent *e*, the *e* must drop from the end. Pull down the silent *e* card and move the -*ing* suffix card over to form *hoping*. Put the *e* back and make *hope* again. Tell the student that whenever a consonant suffix is added to a silent *e* word (point to the column of consonant suffixes), the suffix is simply added and the *e* does not drop. Add the suffixes -*ful* and -*less* to demonstrate. Next, explain that this rule applies no matter when there is a silent *e*. Add suffixes to several words and explain the addition of the vowel versus consonant suffixes. Help students to understand the dropping of the *e* because the *e* is literally dropped whenever the vowel suffix is added. Some word examples include the following:

Word	*Reason for silent e*	*Addition of suffixes*
shape	Vowel-consonant-*e* syllable	shaped, shaping, shapeless
give	No English word ends in *v*	giving, giver, gives
settle	Consonant-*le* syllable	settling, settler, settlement
infringe	Letter *g* with a /j/ sound	infringing, infringement
nice	Two jobs: vowel-consonant-*e* and *c* with an /s/ sound	nicest, nicer, nicely

Demonstrate word structure for this and other rules of orthography with sound cards and suffix cards. This is usually necessary for students to process the information, understand it, and thus succeed in the learning and application. Teach and thoroughly practice each rule. Provide multiple opportunities to read words in isolation on flash cards and on word lists. Also, dictate the words for spelling. When students demonstrate mastery, introduce another rule, but continue to practice and review all rules previously taught. Students must overlearn the application of the rule as opposed to the wording of the rule. The wording is added to their notebooks for reference only.

Teach Morphology

A morpheme is the smallest unit of meaning. The word *predict,* for example, has two morphemes: *pre* and *dict.* When you teach students about syllables and suffix rules (as previously discussed), you are moving them to change their focus of attention from individual sounds to word parts. The direct teaching of morphology is another effective means to help older students understand and apply word structure for decoding and spelling. This instruction has the added benefit of teaching vocabulary as well. Use

flash cards to gradually teach the recognition, spelling, and meaning of prefixes, roots, and suffixes (Henry, 1993). You can introduce the Anglo-Saxon roots, then the Latin and Greek structures. (See Chapter 6 for suggestions.)

Move from Accuracy to Automaticity

Learning to read involves increasing automaticity in processing word units such as letter–sound correspondences, syllables, and affixes. As you present the structure of words, work with students to determine words accurately to break their habit of guessing. The older the student, the more established the guessing habit has probably become. It takes concerted effort to break this habit. The goal is to be able to say to the student, "Look. You didn't need to guess." Before progressing to the next concept, work on developing the students' automatic recognition of the words within the specific target pattern(s). The more automatic single-word reading becomes, the more a reader's cognitive attention can be focused on comprehension when reading connected words in a passage (LaBerge & Samuels, 1974; Perfetti, 1977, 1985).

APPLICATION OF SKILLS AND FLUENCY INSTRUCTION

If they don't read much, how they ever gonna get good?
—Richard Allington (1977)

The Need to Read

From the early grades, poor readers are exposed to much less text than students who read well. Although this is true in the primary grades, the gap increases dramatically as students progress into higher grades. A study of fifth-grade students conducted by Anderson, Wilson, and Fielding (1988) clearly shows an enormous gap in independent reading practices. Students at the 98th percentile of reading read approximately 4,358,000 words per year versus 8,000 words per year by students at the 10th percentile and 0 words by students at the 2nd percentile.

Reading develops reading skills (Cunningham & Stanovich, 1997). A 10-year longitudinal study conducted by Cunningham and Stanovich (1997) shows that the very act of reading can help children build their vocabulary, general knowledge, and cognitive structures. This is true even for children with poor comprehension skills. The amount or volume that a student reads makes a difference. However, the NRP (NICHD, 2000) suggested that sustained silent reading does not demonstrate benefits with students who have not yet developed the critical alphabetic and word-reading skills. Thus, most reading opportunities for these students must be with direct teacher instruction.

Reading builds comprehension. It also builds fluency. Students need to practice reading in order to become fluent (NICHD, 2000). The Partnership for Reading explained:

> Fluency develops as a result of many opportunities to practice reading with a high degree of success. Therefore, your students should practice orally rereading text that is reasonably easy for them—that is, text containing mostly words that they know or can decode easily. In other words, the texts should be at the students' independent reading level. . . . If the text is more difficult, students will focus so much on word recognition that they will not have an opportunity to develop fluency. (2003, p. 27)

Motivation to read is an important factor in getting students to practice. Students report that having the right materials motivates them to read (Ivey & Broaddus, 2001). If

Use of Differentiated Texts and Their Interrelationships for Students with Primary Decoding Deficits

FOCUS: ACCURACY & AUTOMATICITY OF SINGLE WORD READING	FOCUS: FLUENCY	FOCUS: VOCABULARY AND COMPREHENSION
Goals of instruction To develop the student's basic skills for both reading and spelling, including phonemic awareness, phonics, understanding of word structure (syllable patterns and affixes), and high-frequency irregular words	**Goals of instruction** To develop the student's fluent and rate-appropriate independent reading of connected text for meaning and to develop a student's oral reading with ease and expression	**Goals of instruction** To develop the student's vocabulary and understanding of both narrative and expository text and to increase a student's background knowledge and schema
CONTROLLED TEXT	**DECODABLE TEXT**	**ENRICHED TEXT**
Controlled text flash cards, pseudowords, word lists, phrases, and sentences Text is determined by the word structure that has been directly taught. It is 95%–100% controlled to have graphemes, pseudowords, syllables, and phonetically regular and irregular words with high potential for accuracy measured against curriculum.	**Controlled decodable text passages** Text is determined by the word structure that has been directly taught. It is 95%–100% controlled to have graphemes, pseudowords, syllables, and phonetically regular and irregular words with high potential for accuracy measured against curriculum. **Noncontrolled decodable text passages** Text is determined by a student's decoding response to a given passage. The student must read 95%–100% of the words independently. Important considerations are student interest and/or background schema.	**Enriched text passages** Narrative and expository text is determined by highest appropriate instructional listening comprehension level of student. Passage is read to the students so that they can develop comprehension skills at a higher level than their decoding ability.
Example of controlled text sh shop from from the shop Jack will get the subs from the shop. *Use to build skills for controlled decodable text reading.*	**Examples of decodable text** Subs in the Mud The men on the job got subs from the sub shop. They set the bag of subs on the top of Ben's van. Then Ben had to dash off. He had to pick up a set of hubcaps for his van . . . Monkey Face A study shows that a monkey knows what another monkey's face is saying. A Rhesus monkey has one look on its face when it makes a happy sound. When it makes a sound because it is afraid, its face looks different . . .	**Example of enriched text** Rhesus Monkeys Demonstrate Language Skill Research conducted at the Max Planck Institute for Biological Cybernetics in Germany suggests that human's capacity to read facial expressions may have evolved from monkeys. Asif Ghazanfar, who studied the monkeys, reports that rhesus monkeys can combine visual and auditory information to perceive vocal signals . . . *Use to build schema for noncontrolled decodable text reading.*

Focus on Phoneme–grapheme and grapheme–phoneme correspondences Blending and segmenting with letter manipulation Six syllable types in English Orthographic rules and affixes High-frequency irregular words Phrasing	**Focus on** Application and mastery of specific decoding skills Breaking an established guessing habit Helping students see the structure of words in English Reading for meaning Prosody	**Focus on** Application and generalization of decoding skills in a noncontrolled environment Use of context clues in conjunction with decoding strategies, as appropriate Reading for meaning Prosody	**Focus on** Vocabulary Comprehension of narrative text Comprehension of expository text Mental imagery and retelling
Instruction Cumulative building of skills Manipulation of word parts (letter cards, syllables, affixes) Concurrent teaching of decoding and spelling Repetition and practice Timed drills	**Instruction** Teacher-assisted silent and oral reading with retelling Teacher modeling of phrasing and expression Repeated reading Echo, choral, and shared reading Tape-assisted reading		**Instruction** Teacher modeling of fluent reading (passage is read by teacher—students do not track) Teacher modeling of thinking Pictorial representations of content Retelling Graphic organizers
Increase difficulty of text Difficulty increases in relation to taught patterns of word structure: *mash > script > contract > compensate > compensation > illustrious.*	**Increase difficulty of text** Difficulty increases in relation to size of font, length of passage, decoding level of text and complexity of content, and themes and ideas.		**Increase difficulty of text** Difficulty increases in relation to complexity of content, themes, and ideas.
	Difficulty also increases in relation to taught patterns of word structure: *mash > script > contract > compensate > compensation >illustrious.*	Difficulty also increases in relation to increase of a student's overall ability to apply decoding and context clues	

↓ ↓ ↓ ↓

Goal: The convergence of the skills that enable the student to independently read high-level text with ease, expression, and comprehension

Figure 12.2. Use of differentiated texts and their interrelationships for students with primary decoding deficits. (From Wilson, B.A. [2003]. *Uses of differentiated texts & their interrelationships for students with primary decoding deficits.* Retrieved from http://www.wilsonacademy.com; used by permission. Copyright © 2003 Wilson Language Training. All rights reserved.)

Subs in the Mud

The men on the job got subs from the sub shop. They set the bag of subs on the top of Ben's van. Then Ben had to dash off. He had to pick up a set of hubcaps for his van. But the subs sat on the top of the van. On his run to the shop, a big log fell in the path of his van. Ben hit the log with a thud, and the subs fell off in the mud. . . .

Figure 12.3. Sample of controlled decodable text for use after short vowels, consonants, and basic consonant digraphs in three-sound words have been introduced. (From Brown, J. [1998b]. Subs in the mud. In *Stories for older students [Books 1-2-3]*. Millbury, MA: Wilson Language Training. Copyright © 1998 Wilson Language Training; reprinted by permission.)

the material used with students is too difficult, it is discouraging and frustrating. If the material seems too babyish, it is demeaning. The students must practice, practice, practice to develop their skills. Thus, the challenge in your reading class is to find decodable text passages written on subjects that interest the students. As the students skill level for single-word decoding increases due to your instruction, then the level of text difficulty should gradually be increased as well. Throughout, you should be interactively working with the students as they read in order to help them integrate their decoding skills and to model both fluent reading and thinking. Figure 12.2 outlines the concurrent uses of controlled decodable text, noncontrolled decodable text, and enriched text instruction for students.

Application of Skills and Fluency Work: Controlled Decodable Text

Controlled decodable text is limited to text with words that contain only the sounds and structures that have been taught. If students have been introduced to the sounds of the short vowels, consonants, and basic consonant digraphs in three-sound words, a controlled text such as the one shown in Figure 12.3 could be used. The passage shown in Figure 12.4 is a sample of controlled text that can be presented when students have learned multisyllabic words combining closed syllables and vowel-consonant-*e* syllables.

Controlled text for older students should be written specifically for them to provide them with substantial practice within context. This kind of text is key for students with emerging decoding skills for the following reasons:

- To give students practice applying specific word attack skills, to develop accuracy, and to break the habit of guessing

---

Flipping Pancakes

Jim has a job at the Esquire Pancake Shop. His boss is Mr. Musgrave, but they call him "Bigtime." Bigtime has the shop as a franchise. On the front of the shop, in big print, is
HANDMADE PANCAKES
Jim, Helene, and a kid they call "Wishbone" run the shop. Jim and Wishbone make pancakes. Helene sets up the plates and flatware. They all help with the milkshakes. Jim gets up at sunrise and commutes to the shop on his bike. He has to compete with the traffic stampede, inhale its fumes. . . .

Figure 12.4. Sample controlled decodable text for use after multisyllabic words with closed syllables and vowel-consonant-*e* syllables have been introduced. (From Brown, J. [1998a]. Flipping pancakes. In *Stories for older students [Books 4-5-6]*. Millbury, MA: Wilson Language Training. Copyright © 1998 Wilson Language Training; reprinted by permission.)

- To give students repeated practice for mastery of skills

- To demonstrate word structure so that they "see" the system of the language

- To provide them with text to develop fluency

According to the NRP (NICHD, 2000), decodable text is necessary to develop fluency. Decodable text is text that is written at the independent reading level of a student. For the text to be decodable, the student should be able to read 95%–100% of the words independently, with no more than one error per 20 words. If a student is able to read a given passage with ease and accuracy, then it is decodable to that student. In other words, readability depends on the student, not the text. Thus to be decodable a text does not necessarily need to be controlled (limited to studied word structures). Initially, however, if a student is very dyslexic or has very limited word attack skills, then the text will likely need to be controlled to achieve 95% accuracy for independent reading.

Application of Skills and Fluency Work: Noncontrolled Decodable Text

Adequate progress in learning to read beyond the initial
level depends on . . . sufficient practice in reading to achieve
fluency with different kinds of texts written for different purposes.
—Snow, Burns, and Griffin (1998, p. 223)

Noncontrolled decodable text (containing patterns and sounds not already taught) should also be used with students as skills allow them to read the noncontrolled decodable text with 95% accuracy or better. Interest-driven text is beneficial because the subject is familiar and therefore the student will know the vocabulary. It will also be more motivating to students to read something that is of interest when decoding skills are just emerging (Fink, 1998).

The term **high interest–low level readers** has been used to describe text written at a basic decoding level with older students in mind. These are intended to provide older students with text written at the level at which they scored on reading assessments. The level of text difficulty might be reported by grade level.

A variety of methods have been used to determine the difficulty level of written text such as readability formulas, the lexile system, and text leveling (Hiebert, 2002). With each of these systems, there is an attempt to determine the difficulty of text using various factors. These may include print features (e.g., length of passage, layout, font), text structure (e.g., narrative, expository), vocabulary, predictability (e.g., repeated patterns, familiar concepts), syntactic difficulty (e.g., sentence length and structure), and semantic difficulty. Ways of measuring text difficulty are not consistent. To date, there is not one clear way to measure the real difficulty level of text, although it may be assigned a grade level or a lexile by a particular rating system. Student assessment scores will not necessarily match a text's assigned difficulty level. Although a student's reading assessment may indicate a reading grade-level score of 5.0, a text assigned a grade 5.0 level of difficulty may not be decodable text for that student. The student may struggle to read too many of the words in the passage despite the text's seeming appropriateness due to the correspondence between the score of the reading test and the assignment of text difficulty. Thus, text cannot truly be determined decodable for a student by lexiles, readability formulas, or grade-leveling systems. These can simply be used as guides. Text can be determined as decodable only by a student's response to the given passage. Again, in order for text to be decodable, a student must read 95%–100% of the words independently.

Because these students require substantial practice applying their developing skills with noncontrolled decodable text, you need a way to find suitable passages. Though imperfect, various measures of text difficulty can be useful as a guide when searching for appropriate reading material for emergent older readers. Use test scores and text difficulty guidelines to help select reading material. Also, use student interest and student background knowledge because the more a student knows about a topic, the more likely he or she will be able to successfully determine the words. Then have the student read the text orally so that you can determine if indeed it is truly decodable.

The primary aim of your instruction with decodable text is to increase students' independent ability to decode a passage and comprehend it at the same time. Once identified, this text should be used for guided reading instruction. Help the students with the application and generalization of decoding skills in the noncontrolled text environment. Encourage them to use context clues in conjunction with their decoding strategies, as appropriate. Work with your students, showing them how to apply the decoding skills (such as tapping) if they struggle with a word that contains elements that have been taught. Students are usually accustomed to teachers telling them the unknown words. Instead, use questioning techniques, described earlier, to guide students whenever words correspond to the structures you have taught. If students struggle with a word with untaught elements, first direct them to use the context and/or the word's structure if these will be helpful, and if not, tell them the word. Be sure that passages are read for meaning, helping the students to focus on comprehension as they successfully decode.

Decodable text should also be used to practice fluent reading. Older students with decoding deficits are disfluent, halting readers. This interferes with their comprehension. Findings from a synthesis of fluency research suggest that interventions that involve repeated reading for students with learning disabilities are associated with improvements in reading rate, accuracy, and comprehension (Chard, Vaughn, & Tyler, 2002).

For fluency practice, select a decodable passage and use shared reading to complete the passage. The term **shared reading** is sometimes used to mean reading to students. Here it is used to describe the taking of turns. You read a paragraph, and then a student reads a paragraph, with you assisting with words as needed. Scoop the passage into phrases to model phrasing and expression. You can draw scooped lines under the text to illustrate phrasing:

Next Monday, our class will visit the New England Aquarium.

Then you can read the text to the students and have them echo your phrasing and expression. Do this in a manner that emphasizes the meaning of the passage. Model this for a paragraph and then have the students read a paragraph silently to practice phrasing and expression before reading it aloud.

Be sure that students understand the text's meaning. Again, comprehension is the aim of reading and must always be presented as the foremost purpose. Research also suggests that fluency aids comprehension and comprehension aids fluency (Chard et al., 2002). If a student understands what he or she is reading, he or she will likely read more fluently. Repeated reading does improve fluency, but too much attention to it may detract from reading comprehension (Anderson, Wilkinson, & Mason, 1991).

After reading a passage one time for decoding with understanding, explain that the passage will be used again with a purpose to develop fluency. Students can then read the passage orally two or three more times with a focus on ease of reading and expression. You can also use echo and choral reading:

Echo reading: You read a paragraph and have students read it after you.

Choral reading: You and the students read the passage together.

The purpose of these methods is to provide a model for fluent reading. Read the same passage up to four times because it appears that most of the benefit from multiple readings are achieved by then (O'Shea, Sindelar, & O'Shea, 1985).

The text your students practice rereading orally should be relatively short—approximately 50–200 words—with many words repeated. As students are able to demonstrate sufficient success with more challenging text, gradually increase the level of text difficulty in relation to length of passages, size of font, complexity of content, and overall level of difficulty, being careful to present text that is decodable.

Students with emerging reading ability must *read, read, read*. In addition to the decodable nonfiction passages, use high-interest fiction at a decodable level to provide reading practice. Do not use fiction for repeated reading and fluency work. This will likely destroy the story and reduce the students' interest in reading it. In addition, vocabulary is not repeated as often in fiction and is less predictable (Hiebert, 2002). Thus, it is better to use relatively short nonfiction passages for the repeated reading and fluency work. There are limited sources for controlled text but many sources of potential decodable fiction and nonfiction text passages for older students (see Appendix B).

DEVELOPMENT OF VOCABULARY, BACKGROUND KNOWLEDGE, AND COMPREHENSION

The man who can make the hard things easy is the educator.
—Ralph Waldo Emerson

Reading develops general language skills, vocabulary, background knowledge, and familiarity with complex syntax structures (Cunningham & Stanovich, 1997). Good readers may read as many as 10 times as many words as poor readers (Nagy & Anderson, 1984). Students who do not learn to read fluently in elementary school are at a big disadvantage in regard to background knowledge and vocabulary development. Vocabulary is developed through print. It is dependent upon exposure to written text rather than oral language alone (Nagy & Anderson, 1984; Stanovich, 1986). Students who are unable to access print will have limited exposure to vocabulary. Students at the bottom percentiles of reading ability cannot read independently, so they do not. Over time, they exhibit what has become widely known as **Matthew effects** (Stanovich, 1986): Students who are behind get further and further behind.

Older students who are just entering an MSLE program have much catching up to do. True, they need to learn how to decode and read text fluently in a multisensory, sequential manner. However, this will not happen overnight. In the meantime, these students need as much exposure to enriched text as possible in order to develop their background knowledge, vocabulary, and comprehension.

Reading to Students

Too often, reading to students ends in the primary grades. Although older students are being taught with appropriate structured phonics to develop their decoding, enriched text should be read to them at a higher level than what they can independently decode. Controlled and noncontrolled decodable text is not usually enriched with vocabulary and content. Reading more sophisticated text to students who cannot do so inde-

---

Rhesus Monkeys Demonstrate Language Skill

Research conducted at the Max Planck Institute for Biological Cybernetics in Germany suggests that humans' capacity to read facial expressions may have evolved from monkeys. Asif Ghazanfar, who studied the monkeys, reports that rhesus monkeys can combine visual and auditory information to perceive vocal signals.

Both in captivity and in the wild, Rhesus moneys (*Macaca mulatta*) produce a variety of noises. Dr. Ghazanfar states that almost all noises have a unique facial expression. Rhesus monkeys were videotaped in a standard primate restraint chair in order to capture facial expressions associated with their two most common calls–a long, tonal coo which is a friendly call and a short, pulsed noisy threat call.

Monkey Face

A monkey knows what another monkey's face is saying. A study shows that the Rhesus monkey can tell if another monkey is happy by looking at its face. It can also tell if the other monkey is afraid. When the monkeys were tested, 65% could connect an expression with a sound of fear or a sound of gladness. Children and adults also use this skill. Did they learn it from monkeys? Maybe they did.

Figure 12.5.   Sample enriched text passages. Copyright © 2003 Wilson Language Training.

pendently will expose them to more advanced vocabulary, substantially more background knowledge, more complex syntax structure, and higher-level thinking. Include both narrative and expository selections in your choices. An important part of instruction, then, is to read to the students at a much higher level than they could comprehend on their own.

Students can track the words when you read decodable text to them because they are working on their application of decoding skills at that time. However, when reading enriched text to students, do not have them follow along while you read. They can simply listen and visualize or create a mental image of the text. Because you are reading text at a much higher level than students can independently decode, following the text does not contribute to their word-level understanding. When the text is too difficult to decode, students will likely lose their place if they try to follow along. You do not want to distract them from the meaning by having them try to stay on track and attempt to decipher the words. Help students focus on meaning through periodic discussion, modeling of thinking, and retelling of the story using mental imagery as a guide for words. Help them with challenging vocabulary, providing student-friendly explanations using everyday language. Draw simple picture representations of the concepts to aid students' understanding of the content. Literally pull apart the text with them to create understanding by using comprehension strategies such as retelling and making graphic organizers. (See Chapter 14 for specific comprehension strategies.) Identify vocabulary words to target for further study (see Chapter 13).

It can be helpful to match the content of the enriched text to a decodable text passage provided to students. First read the enriched text to the students while at the same time structuring their comprehension. Then present the same topic with similar information written at a decodable level. Because you have provided the **schema**, or background information, you will have the opportunity to teach the students how to use context clues in combination with their decoding strategies. The passages shown in Figure 12.5 are examples of enriched text for use with older students.

Exposure to Print Through Technology

Electronic text with screen reading software and books on audiotape can also provide students with the essential access to enriched text. Digital or electronic text can be extremely useful in assisting students who struggle with reading (Higgins, Boone, & Lovitt, 1996; Raskind, Goldberg, Higgins, & Herman, 1999). If the text is on a computer screen, it can be enlarged. The enlarged font size is very helpful to students who are just learning to read. More importantly, this digital text can be read aloud by screen-reading software with speech synthesizers. The NRP (NICHD, 2000) could not make specific instructional conclusions about computer technology and reading instruction due to the small sample of available experimental research studies. However, the report noted, "It is possible to use computer technology for reading instruction. All studies in the analysis report positive results" (NICHD, 2000, p. 6-2). Particularly of note, 6 of the 21 studies examined by the NRP found that adding speech synthesis to the print material presented on computers was an effective practice for reading instruction. **Speech synthesis software** (sometimes called *text-to-speech software*) may therefore be an effective component of instruction for older students.

Books on audiotape and screen reading software are very appropriate for students who have poor decoding with adequate listening comprehension. However, caution must be used with students who have poor decoding *and/or* poor comprehension. The tools might be helpful only if these students are closely monitored and given much assistance with comprehension.

Universal design provides access to digitized versions of curricular materials for use by students with print-based learning disabilities. Universal learning provides exciting potential for all students. This access to print should allow students to more fully participate in all classes. However, it is important that it does not supplant the creation of classes that provide the direct, systematic instruction that will yield independence.

OTHER CONSIDERATIONS

Provide Assistance in Content Classes

> *There is one thing worse than not communicating—*
> *it is thinking you have communicated when you have not.*
> —Edgar Dale

It is hard to imagine the daily challenges of older students who are unable to read grade-level text. Throughout the entire day, they must rely on others for information. These students should have access to the content in all classes, but they need a tremendous amount of support in order to succeed. The Joint Committee on Teacher Planning for Students with Disabilities (1995) defined *supported inclusion* as a set of instructional conditions in which teachers

- Are philosophically committed to meeting the needs of all students, including those with [learning disabilities], in the general education classroom
- Have sufficient time to think about and plan for the diverse needs of students in their class(es)
- Incorporate teaching practices that enable them to better meet the needs of all students in their class(es)
- Work collaboratively with special education teachers to assess, teach, and monitor student progress

- Have the option for their students to receive short-term, intensive instructional support from a special education teacher; and
- Have the option for their students [to leave the general education classroom] to receive sustained instruction in basic skills or learning strategies that could not be provided in the general education classroom

Provide Successful Classroom Practices

As discussed throughout this chapter, students in Grades 4 and beyond should have reading classes to develop their independent skills as indicated by testing. In addition, students should participate in content-area classes with the supported inclusion or differentiated instruction necessary to succeed.

Textbooks are often the sole source of reading material for subject-matter content. If a student's reading level is below the text level, the student cannot independently gain access to the information. He or she requires instruction that integrates reading with subject area content. All students can benefit from the integration of reading comprehension instruction specific to content. Anderson, Hiebert, Scott, and Wilkinson (1985) noted that "the idea that reading instruction should be integrated is an old one in education, but there is little indication that such integration occurs often in practice." Content-area teachers have resisted an integrated approach over the years (O'Brien, Dillon, Wellinski, Springs, & Stith, 1995; Ratekin et al., 1985). The following four-step process can assist teachers with a systematic approach to integrating reading and vocabulary instruction with content (Wilson, 1987). For students who cannot decode, the process assists them because the text is read to them. For students who can decode but lack comprehension, the process supports them through discussion and the modeling of the thinking processes used to understand text.

1. *Advance organization:* This first step requires some kind of discussion to direct the focus of the students' attention. The teacher might provide background information, or the class might discuss previously taught material that is related to the new information. The teacher might also state the reason for reading the text or the objective of the instruction. Advance organization was one of two instructional components found to consistently enhance outcomes with adolescents in a study looking at the challenges faced by adolescents with learning disabilities (Swanson, Hoskyn, & Lee, 1999).

2. *Picture concepts:* This step involves the teacher using an overhead projector to sketch the concepts as they are explained in his or her own words. The teacher dramatizes and draws out the information without getting bogged down by the specific vocabulary words, substituting easy words as necessary to develop understanding. The vocabulary labels are then attached to concepts by writing the words into the picture.

3. *Reading aloud and thinking aloud from text:* This step involves a teacher reading and periodically stopping to discuss the text and describe his or her own thinking process and to help the students create a visual image of the text in their minds. The teacher can relate back to the drawing and label it with more specific vocabulary as appropriate.

4. *Study cards and retelling:* In this last step, students develop study cards to help them learn the vocabulary and integrate the information. The teacher provides the list of vocabulary words, divided into syllables. Students write each word, divided into

Figure 12.6.   Writing and illustration created by a sixth-grader with dyslexia.

syllables, on one side of a card. On the other side, students draw a picture and/or write a user-friendly definition of the word. The cards are then spread out to display their relationships. This can be done with the picture sides up or with word sides up. Students then retell the information with the cards as a guide. This retelling can be done in pairs, in small groups, and/or with the whole class.

It is important to note that content-area vocabulary words present a significant challenge to students with poor decoding and spelling. When assessing their knowledge of content, it is best to avoid word-retrieval questions and instead ask students about the material. If they must come up with the labels, provide a word bank to select from.

Develop Students' Belief in Their Potential

Older students who have had a history of academic failure need help to program them for success. Several studies have demonstrated that students with learning disabilities who possess certain personal attitudes and behaviors have more successful life outcomes. Specifically, the attributes of self-awareness, perseverance, proactivity, emotional stability, and goal setting and the use of support systems are powerful predictors of success (Raskind et al., 1999; Reiff, Gerber, & Ginsberg, 1997; Wehmeyer, 1996; Werner & Smith, 1992). Help students become aware of their strengths as you work with them to overcome their difficulties. Many students with phonological weaknesses have strengths in areas other than phonological coding (Geschwind, 1982; Shaywitz, 2003; West, 1997).

The writing sample and drawing shown in Figure 12.6 illustrate the strengths of a sixth-grade student diagnosed with dyslexia. Clearly, he has difficulty with the basics of written language. However, his creativity shines through with his choice of words, such as "I scream and the echo fades into the dark void in my heart." The same student quickly copied the illustration by freehand within minutes.

The goal of your instruction should include an increased understanding of your students' strengths so that they can have a clearer direction for their future. Combined

with the skills that will develop with sufficient multisensory structured language instruction, students can begin to believe in themselves. Given appropriate instruction and time, you can help them set goals and develop support systems for success.

REFERENCES

Allington, R.L. (1977). If they don't read much, how they ever gonna get good? *Journal of Reading, 21,* 57–61.

American Federation of Teachers. (1999). *Teaching reading is rocket science: What expert teachers of reading should know and be able to do.* Washington, DC: Author.

Anderson, R.C., Hiebert, E.H., Scott, J.A., & Wilkinson, I.A.G. (1985). *Becoming a nation of readers: The report of the Commission on Reading.* Washington, DC: U.S. Department of Education, The National Institute of Education.

Anderson, R.C., Wilkinson, I.A.G., & Mason, J.M. (1991). A microanalysis of the small-group, guided reading lesson: Effects of an emphasis on global story meaning. *Reading Research Quarterly, 26,* 417–441.

Anderson, R.C., Wilson, P.T., & Fielding, L.G. (1988). Growth in reading and how children spend their time outside of school. *Reading Research Quarterly, 23,* 611–626.

Brown, J. (1998a). Flipping pancakes. In *Stories for older students (Books 4-5-6).* Millbury, MA: Wilson Language Training.

Brown, J. (1998b). Subs in the mud. In *Stories for older students (Books 1-2-3).* Millbury, MA: Wilson Language Training.

Chall, J.S. (1983). *Stages of reading development.* New York: McGraw-Hill.

Chard, D.J., Vaughn, S., & Tyler, B.J. (2002). A synthesis of research on effective interventions for building reading fluency with elementary students with learning disabilities. *Journal of Learning Disabilities, 35,* 386–406.

Cunningham, A.E., & Stanovich, K.E. (1997). Early reading acquisition and its relation to reading experience and ability 10 years later. *Developmental Psychology, 33,* 934–945.

Deshler, D.D., Schumaker, J.B., Lenz, B.K., Bulgren, J.A., Hock, M.F., Knight, J., et al. (2001). Ensuring content-area learning by secondary students with learning disabilities. *Learning Disabilities Research & Practice, 16*(2), 96–108.

Felton, R., & Wilson, B.A. (2004). *Word Identification and Spelling Test (WIST).* Austin, TX: PRO-ED.

Fink, R. (1998). Literacy development in successful men and women with dyslexia. *Annals of Dyslexia, 48,* 311–346.

Geschwind, N. (1982). Why Orton was right. *Annals of Dyslexia, 32,* 13–30.

Grigg, W.S., Daane, M.C., Jin, Y., & Campbell, J.R. (Eds.). (2003). *The nation's report card: Reading 2002* (NCES 2003–521). Washington, DC: U.S. Department of Education. Institute of Education Sciences. National Center for Education Statistics.

Hanna, P.R., Hanna, J.S., Hodges, R.E., & Rudorf, E.H., Jr. (1966). *Phoneme–grapheme correspondences as cues to spelling improvement* (USOE Publication No. 32008). Washington, DC: U.S. Government Printing Office.

Hanushek, E., Kain, J. & Riuka, S. (1998). *Does special education raise academic achievement for students with disabilities?* (NBER Working Paper No. 6469). Cambridge, MA: National Bureau of Economic Research.

Henry, M.K. (1993). Morphological structure: Latin and Greek roots and affixes as upper grade code strategies. *Reading and Writing: An Interdisciplinary Journal, 5*(2), 227–241.

Hiebert, E.H. (2002). Standards, assessment, and text difficulty. In A.E. Farstrup & S.J. Samuels (Eds.), *What research has to say about reading instruction* (3rd ed., pp. 337–369). Newark, DE: International Reading Association.

Higgins, K., Boone, R., & Lovitt, T. (1996). Hypertext support for remedial students and students with learning disabilities. *Journal of Learning Disabilities, 29*(4), 402–412.

Ivey, G., & Broaddus, K. (2001). Just plain reading: A survey of what makes students want to read in middle school classrooms. *Reading Research Quarterly, 36,* 350–377.

Joint Committee on Teacher Planning for Students with Disabilities. (1995). *Planning for academic diversity in America's classrooms: windows on reality, research, change and practice.* Washington, DC: U.S. Department of Education, Office of Special Education and Rehabilitative Services, Office of Special Programs.

LaBerge, D., & Samuels, S.J. (1974). Toward a theory of automatic information processing in reading. *Cognitive Psychology, 6,* 293–323.

Leach, J., Scarborough, H., & Rescorla, L. (2003). Late-emerging reading disabilities. *Journal of Educational Psychology, 95,* 211–224.

Lyon, G.R., Fletcher, J.M., Shaywitz, S.E., Shaywitz, B.A., Torgesen, J.K., Wood, F.B., et al. (2001). Rethinking learning disabilities. In C.E. Finn, Jr., A.J. Rotherham, & C.R. Hokanson, Jr. (Eds.), *Rethinking special education for a new century* (pp.

259–287). Washington, DC: Thomas B. Fordham Foundation and Progressive Policy Institute.

McCray, A.D. (2001, November). Middle school students with learning disabilities. *Reading Teacher, 55*(3), 298–310.

Moore, D.W., Bean, T.W., Birdyshaw, D., & Rycik, J.A. (1999). *Adolescent literacy: A position statement for the Commission on Adolescent Literacy of the International Reading Association.* Newark, DE: International Reading Association.

Nagy, W.E., & Anderson, R.C. (1984). How many words are there in printed school English? *Reading Research Quarterly, 19,* 304–330.

National Institute of Child Health and Human Development (NICHD). (2000). *Report of the National Reading Panel. Teaching children to read: An evidence-based assessment of the scientific research literature on reading and its implications for reading instruction: Reports of the subgroups* (National Institute of Health Pub. No. 00–4754). Washington, DC: U.S. Government Printing Office. Also available on-line: http://www.nichd.nih.gov/publicatons/nrp/report.htm

O'Brien, D.G., Dillon, D.R., Wellinski, S.A., Springs, R., & Stith, D. (1997). *Engaging "at-risk" high school students.* Athens, GA: National Reading Research Center.

O'Connor, J. & Wilson, B. (1995). Effectiveness of the Wilson Reading System used in public school training. In McIntyre and Pickering (Eds.), *Clinical studies of multisensory structured language education for students with dyslexia and related disorders.* Salem, OR: International Multisensory Structured Language Education Council.

O'Shea, L.J., Sindelar, P.T., & O'Shea, D.J. (1985). The effects of repeated readings and attentional cues on reading fluency and comprehension. *Journal of Reading Behavior, 17,* 129–142.

The Partnership for Reading. (2003, June). *Put reading first: The research building blocks for teaching children to read. Kindergarten through grade 3* (2nd ed.). Washington, DC: Author. (Available from ED Pubs, 800-228-8813, Post Office Box 1398, Jessup, MD 20794-1398, edpuborders@edpubs.org; also available on-line: http://www.nifl.gov/partnershipforreading/publications/PFRbookletBW.pdf)

Perfetti, C.A. (1977). Language comprehension and fast decoding: Some psycholinguistic prerequisites for skilled reading comprehension. In J.T. Guthrie (Ed.), *Cognition, curriculum, and comprehension* (pp. 20–41). Newark, DE: International Reading Association.

Perfetti, C.A. (1985). *Reading ability.* New York: Oxford University Press.

Raskind, M.H., Goldberg, R.J., Higgins, E.L. & Herman, K.L.(1999). Patterns of change and predictors of success in individuals with learning disabilities: Results from a twenty-year longitudinal study. *Learning Disabilities Research & Practice, 14*(1), 35–49.

Ratekin, N., Simpson, M., Alvermann, D., & Dishner, E. (1985). Why teachers resist content reading instruction. *Journal of Reading, 28,* 432–437.

Rawson, M.B. (1988). *The many faces of dyslexia.* Baltimore: The International Dyslexia Association.

Reiff, H.B., Gerber, P.J., & Ginsberg, R. (1997). *Exceeding expectations: Successful adults with learning disabilities.* Austin, TX: PRO-ED.

Shankweiler, D., Lundquist, E., Katz, L., Stuebing, K.K., Fletcher, J. M., Brady, S., et al. (1999). Comprehension and decoding: Patterns of association in children with reading difficulties. *Scientific Studies of Reading, 3,* 69–94.

Shaywitz, S. (2003). *Overcoming dyslexia: A new and complete science-based program for reading problems at any level.* New York: Alfred A. Knopf.

Snow, C.E., Burns, M.S., & Griffin, P. (Eds.). (1998). *Preventing reading difficulties in young children.* Washington, DC: National Academies Press.

Stanovich, K.E. (1986). Matthew effects in reading: Some consequences of individual differences in the acquisition of literacy. *Reading Research Quarterly, 21,* 369–407.

Swanson, H.L., Hoskyn, M., & Lee, C. (1999). *Interventions for students with learning disabilities: A meta-analysis of treatment outcomes.* New York: The Guilford Press.

Torgesen, J.K. (1998, Spring/Summer). Catch them before they fall: Identification and assessment to prevent reading failure in young children. *American Educator,* 1–8.

Vellutino, F.R., Scanlon, D.M., Sipay, E.R., Small, S.G., Pratt, A., Chen, R., et al. (1996). Cognitive profiles of difficult to remediate and readily remediated poor readers: Early intervention as a vehicle to distinguish between cognitive and experiential deficits as basic causes of specific reading disability. *Journal of Educational Psychology, 88,* 601–638.

Wehmeyer, M.L. (1996). Self-determination as an educational outcome: Why is it important to children, youth, and adults with disabilities? In D.J. Sands & M.L. Wehmeyer (Eds.), *Self-determination across the lifespan: Independence and choice for people with disabilities* (pp. 17–36). Baltimore: Paul H. Brookes Publishing Co.

Werner, E.E., & Smith, R.S. (1992). *Overcoming the odds: High risk children from birth to adulthood.* Ithaca, NY: Cornell University Press.

West, T. (1997). *In the mind's eye: Visual thinkers, gifted people with dyslexia and other learning difficulties, computer images and the ironies of creativity.* New York: Prometheus Books.

Wilson, B.A. (1987). *Wilson study and writing skills.* Millbury, MA: Wilson Language Training.

Wilson, B.A. (1988). *Wilson Reading System.* Millbury, MA: Wilson Language Training.

Wilson, B. (1996). *Wilson Reading System instructor manual* (3rd ed.). Millbury, MA: Wilson Language Training.

Wilson, B.A. (2003). *Uses of differentiated texts & their interrelationships for students with primary decoding deficits.* Retrieved from http://www .wilsonacademy.com

Wood, F. (2002). Data analysis of the Wilson Reading System. In *Literacy solutions: Evidence of effectiveness.* Millbury, MA: Wilson Language Training.

Woodcock, R.W. (1987). *Woodcock Reading Mastery Tests–Revised.* Circle Pines, MN: American Guidance Service.

13

Word Learning and Vocabulary Instruction

Joanne F. Carlisle and Lauren A. Katz

S tudies of instructional practices have shown that little attention is paid to vocabulary, except perhaps in content-area courses in which students must learn the meanings of the topical words that are needed to understand concepts in specific knowledge domains (e.g., in a unit on plant biology, words such as *osmosis*) (see Baumann & Kame'enui, 1991). Because vocabulary instruction has been so seriously neglected and yet is generally agreed to be a critical aspect of language development, this chapter helps teachers understand the process by which students learn words and factors that affect vocabulary acquisition. This foundation will aid teachers in making informed decisions about instructional methods and practices. Thus, the first section of this chapter focuses on the process of word learning and individual differences in vocabulary acquisition. The second section is devoted to discussion of methods of vocabulary instruction, and the third to guidelines for teachers.

LEARNING WORDS

Early Childhood

In the first stage of language learning, infants extract meaning from communicative intent and familiar expressions that are phonologically global but contextually linked, such as "Say bye-bye." These infants are not yet able to encode a fine-grained phonological representation of the word or words in a phrase (Fowler, 1991). They need to break into the speech stream so that they can begin to identify meaningful units of sound. In this way, the process by which children learn their first words is different from the process by which they will learn words for the rest of their lives. The closest experience adults have is trying to understand a foreign language that they are not fa-

miliar with. At first it seems impossible to distinguish words in the seemingly continuous flow of speech sounds, but with experience, patterns emerge that provide clues to sound units that have meaning and syntactic function. This process takes time, as children need to gather sufficient information from the language that they hear to distinguish meaningful units (words or morphemes, such as *teach* and *-er* in *teacher*) from units of language that are not meaningful (such as *-er* in *corner*) (Clark, 2003; MacWhinney, 1978).

Children's first words refer to things and actions in their daily environment. A child usually uses words in familiar contexts (saying "up" with arms uplifted when he or she wants to be picked up). Children's comprehension far outstrips their ability to pronounce words, in part because of the relatively slow development of their ability to articulate words. As children learn to use words, they tend to overgeneralize the meanings. Clark (2003) gave the example of a child using "ticktock" to refer to clocks, watches, a gas meter, and a scale with a round dial, among other things.

By 2 or 3 years of age, children's invented words show that they have mastered principles of word formation. Clark (1995) has given numerous examples of children's productive use of the agentive *-er*, for example, from a 2-year-old child, "You're the sworder and I'm the gunner," and from a 3-year-old child, "You be the storyer, Daddy." Children also coin verbs and adjectives; a good example comes from a 4-year-old child who, when talking about a box of cocoons, asked when they would be "flyable." These examples show that between 2 and 4 years children are able to analyze the internal structure of words and learn combinatory principles. The child who came up with "flyable," for example, has implicit awareness that "-able" is added to the end of a verb to make a descriptor. This child never heard "flyable" before but devised it to express a thought for which he or she did not have a readily available word. Vocabulary grows through productive uses of words and morphemes, not just through mimicry of expressions the child hears others use.

Acquiring understanding of words happens incrementally. The process of word learning begins with **fast mapping**. This involves picking up from context an initial impression of the meaning of a word. Working with preschoolers, Carey and Bartlett (as cited in Clark, 2003) found that preschoolers learned something about unfamiliar color words (e.g., *chromium*) from a single exposure. When contrasted with another color (e.g., "That's chromium, not red"), it seemed that a single exposure had a lasting impression on a child, contributing to the color terms in memory. However, for the child to acquire a more complete understanding of a word (e.g., to understand how *chromium* differs from *gray*), he or she must first encounter it in different linguistic contexts that provide further information about the semantic features of the word.

Exposure to a wide variety of unfamiliar words (that are, of course, within the conceptual grasp of a young child) is an important impetus to vocabulary development. Not surprisingly, therefore, the amount of language that parents or caregivers direct toward the child is reflected in the size of the preschooler's vocabulary (Hart & Risley, 1995). One study looked at the number of unusual or rare words (i.e., words not included in the 3,000 most common words of the Dale-Chall list; Dale & Chall, 1948) that 3- and 4-year-old children heard during dinnertime conversations. Results showed that the frequency of use of such words was significantly related to a child's receptive vocabulary at ages 5 and 7 (Beals, 1997). Furthermore, the extensiveness of a child's vocabulary is related to school learning. Studies have shown that the more extensive word knowledge a child has in kindergarten, the more likely he or she is to be a strong reader in second grade (Dickinson & Tabors, 2001; Hart & Risley, 1995).

To summarize, beginning in early childhood and continuing through the life span, word learning is characterized by certain basic principles and processes:

- Word learning takes place when a child encounters an unfamiliar word or words in a context that provides some basis for inferring meaning.

- The meaning of the word must be relevant in some way to the child.

- Development of a more complete understanding of the word's meaning depends on encountering that word in different contexts, and this is usually a slow process.

School Years

Acquiring depth of word knowledge is dependent on the development of a child's cognitive system. Through experience and exposure to language, the child develops conceptual and semantic relations, some of which involve understanding of categories and hierarchical structures within categories (Nelson, 1996). In her discussion of this process, Clark (1995) provided helpful examples. At about age 1, the child might understand the words *bird, duck, chicken,* and *goose.* By age 2 to 3, the child may know *stork, ostrich, robin, sparrow, dove,* and numerous other words for birds. Categories or taxonomies also become differentiated so that the child has a hierarchical structure, knowing, for example, that *robin* and *dove* are kinds of birds (Nelson, 1996). Elaboration of word meanings depends on seeing relations—spatial, temporal, and causal (among others).

The fundamental processes that influence children's development of categories is just one aspect of children's conceptual and semantic development. Again, combined cognitive and linguistic development plays a major role in the increasing breadth and depth of the word knowledge. Conceptual relations within domains of knowledge (e.g., how trees and bushes or flowers are different from one another) become a central factor affecting the depth of word knowledge (Nelson, 1996). Students' grasp of conceptual relations and knowledge structures influences the breadth and depth of their word knowledge, and this in turn affects the ease with which they learn the content of their courses in such areas as science and history. For example, understanding why some trees drop leaves and others do not provides a conceptual grasp of one aspect of the change of seasons.

Clearly, word learning in the school years is a dramatic if underappreciated process. Researchers' estimates of the vocabulary size of school-age children and the number of words they learn in a year vary markedly. Estimates might vary because researchers define knowing a word in different ways and use different methods to assess word knowledge. However, most researchers would agree that during the school-age years, students learn on average about 3,000 words a year, or about 7 new words a day (Beck & McKeown, 1991). As impressive as this figure is, it is extremely important to take into account individual differences in word learning. Beck and McKeown commented that "even if some students are learning as many as seven new words a day, many others may be learning only one or two" (p. 795). The relative rates of word learning are important because students' word knowledge, even in the preschool years, is a good predictor of reading skill years later (Snow, Burns, & Griffin, 1998).

Learning several new words in a day does not mean that all words are thoroughly understood. To provide a way of thinking about what it means to know a word, researchers (e.g., Beck & McKeown, 1991) have offered schemes for describing variations in the depth of word knowledge with three levels; these include full concept knowledge, partial concept knowledge, and verbal association knowledge. For example, a fourth

grader who knows that insulation is found in houses has associative knowledge. A peer who explains that insulation keeps a house warm in winter has partial conceptual knowledge. Another peer who explains that the insulation in his jacket keeps his body warm because heat cannot escape so easily through the jacket is on his way to having full conceptual knowledge. Through exposure to the use of a word in natural contexts (e.g., conversation, reading), students may pick up some information about its meaning, but as we noted earlier, the process of acquiring depth of word knowledge is incremental, depending in part on additional encounters with the word in different contexts.

Not only do the number of exposures to a word but also the nature of the discourse context in which a word appears affect word learning. This includes the richness of the oral or written discourse clues that are available for the student to infer word meaning. If a word is encountered in a rich context, the student has a better chance of inferring its meaning than if it is encountered in a lean context.

Students have the opportunity to learn numerous words from incidental exposure to words used in their classroom instruction and discussion. It is easier to learn words from oral contexts than from written language contexts, not only because oral contexts afford opportunities to ask clarifying questions but also because there are likely to be referents that provide visual, nonverbal support for word learning (Miller & Gildea, 1987). Students with good language-learning skills are likely to benefit from classroom discussions more than their peers with language-learning disabilities do. All students are likely to acquire some amount of word knowledge through oral discourse in content-area courses such as science, but the students with a better fund of word knowledge benefit more than those with smaller vocabularies (Carlisle, Fleming, & Gudbrandsen, 2000). Teachers can foster the acquisition of word knowledge by providing opportunities for diverse learning experiences in the classroom (Dickinson, Cote, & Smith, 1993).

Reading and Word Learning

Once students become readers of natural texts, they are exposed to a wealth of different words, and reading becomes a context for learning words as well as acquiring information and ideas. Much emphasis has been placed on acquiring words from written texts. There is evidence that the amount of reading children do is related to growth in their vocabulary and comprehension capabilities (Anderson, Wilson, & Fielding, 1988; Greaney, 1980). There are also studies that show that students acquire word knowledge from reading texts (e.g., Jenkins, Stein, & Wysocki, 1984; Nagy, Herman, & Anderson, 1985). Not surprisingly, these results have led experts in reading (e.g., Fielding, Wilson, & Anderson, 1984; Nagy et al., 1985) to suggest that the best way to learn words is to read and, ideally, to read a lot.

Teachers have taken this advice to heart and introduced programs such as sustained silent reading (SSR) or Drop Everything and Read (DEAR). There are also "book wars" in many schools, which provide an incentive for students to read a lot of books. Stahl and Kapinus (2001) described several such wide reading programs that can be implemented in schools, individual classrooms, and other settings. These methods can be motivating, and some students might find reading sufficiently pleasurable so that it becomes a lifelong habit.

The amount and kind of reading a student does is likely to affect his or her word learning if he or she is proficient in reading. Less skilled readers, who read fewer books and easier books, are less likely to benefit from reading than skilled readers (Stanovich,

1986). Because less skilled readers struggle with reading, they quickly come to dislike reading and lack the motivation to read as much as their peers do (Juel, 1988). When they do read, they may also engage less actively in constructing meaning from the text (Paris, Wasik, & Turner, 1991). There are very large differences in the amount of reading accomplished by able and less able readers in a year (Nagy & Anderson, 1984). In second or third grade, a less able reader might average 10 pages per day; for 100 days of the school year, 100,000 words of running text would be covered. In contrast, a more able reader might read 20 pages per day, doubling the number of words encountered in a year and the opportunity to encounter and infer the meaning of unfamiliar words.

Several factors influence word learning during reading. One factor is the number of times a word is repeated in the passage (Jenkins et al., 1984). Another is the nature of clues to the word's meaning in the surrounding text/discourse (Nagy et al., 1985). A third factor is the difficulty of the text. The degree of unfamiliarity of the word and of other words in the passage plays a role. Schatz and Baldwin (1986) found that unusual or uncommon words in natural texts may not be learned through incidental exposure to them. If students read books that are moderately challenging, they have a better opportunity to learn new words than if they were to read books that are easy for them (Carver, 1994). On the other hand, if the text contains too many unfamiliar words and concepts, word learning will be very difficult. This is in part because useful clues to a word's meaning will be hard to come by.

It is important to point out that students can learn words from books that are read aloud to them—they do not need to read them independently. Studies have shown that kindergartners and sixth graders learn words by listening to books read aloud (Eller, Pappas, & Brown, 1988; Stahl, Richek, & Vandevier, 1991). These results suggest ways to provide support for the vocabulary development of students with severe reading disabilities: Parents can read to them regularly and these students can listen to audio-recordings of the books.

Because vocabulary instruction is often structured by selecting words from students' textbooks, it is important to consider the relation of vocabulary knowledge and reading comprehension. Although these two aspects of comprehension (word and passage) are significantly related at all grade levels and in different languages and countries around the world (e.g., Anderson & Freebody, 1983), it is still important to consider the *nature* of this association. After all, it is possible to understand individual words in a sentence or passage *but not* fully understand the ideas or information conveyed by those words. In fact, in many studies of vocabulary instruction, students make progress on tests of the words they worked on, but it is uncommon to find improvement on general measures of reading comprehension. For example, in a recent study (Tomesen & Aarnoutse, 1998), fourth graders were given an instructional program for deriving word meanings from context and morphological analyses. The students showed improvement in the ability to derive word meaning, but there was no transfer of this ability to more general reading comprehension. The findings are more positive when students learn words from a chapter or unit of study and comprehension of that chapter or unit is assessed. Although it is likely that knowing words related to the topic of a text contributes to comprehension of that text, there is no guarantee that such instruction in the short term will affect the breadth of students' vocabulary knowledge, in general, or their achievement in reading comprehension.

Several characteristics of vocabulary instruction that are linked to reading textbooks might ensure the best possible impact on general vocabulary development and

comprehension skills. First, vocabulary instruction should stress not just memorization of words but also strategies for learning words, so that students have ways to tackle unfamiliar words in any passages they are reading. Second, vocabulary should be a regular part of the students' reading activities. Third, students should have regular opportunities to analyze and discuss the meanings of words in different contexts. And finally, efforts should be made to link vocabulary study with the development of conceptual frameworks and background knowledge about a given topic or domain of knowledge. Familiarity with the topic is likely to affect word learning—word knowledge and world knowledge go hand in hand. Students who know what an anchor is are likely to know such words as *yacht, wharf,* and *buoy.* Students with limited previous knowledge of a topic are likely to be overwhelmed by the many unfamiliar words that are used to discuss the topic (Carlisle et al., 2000).

Individual Differences in Word Learning

As Beck and McKeown (1991) have pointed out, there is enormous variation in the number of words children learn in a year. Although exposure to words influences students' word learning, their cognitive and linguistic capabilities also play an important role. Children with language disabilities often have significant delays, relative to their peers, in vocabulary knowledge. Not only do they learn fewer words than their peers when exposed to the same oral language experiences (e.g., a videotaped story), but also they recall fewer word meanings thereafter (see Oetting, Rice, & Swank, 1995). Similarly, poor readers learn fewer words from reading than good readers (Jenkins et al., 1984).

Many students with reading disabilities have lower levels of vocabulary development than their peers, but not always for the same reason. In some cases, students with reading disabilities have specific problems acquiring word-reading skills. Their reading comprehension is often an area of underachievement, but this is because their word reading is inaccurate and/or lacking in fluency (Mezynski, 1983). These students do not demonstrate significant weaknesses in listening comprehension, and some of them may show facility for acquiring vocabulary from oral language contexts. For example, Fawcett and Nicolson (1991), who studied vocabulary acquisition of dyslexic adolescents, reported that for some students oral vocabulary was a noticeable strength, whereas for others it was a significant weakness. In short, some students with reading disabilities have specific difficulties with word-reading accuracy and fluency, whereas others also have subtle or pronounced problems with language development, and vocabulary is an area of underachievement.

The nature of the language-learning difficulties of students with specific language impairments also varies, but most of these students appear to have underlying problems with phonological processing, including verbal working memory, and these problems impede word learning over time (Ellis Weismer & Thorardottir, 2002). Students with relatively poor verbal ability (evidenced by significantly lower vocabulary scores than their peers) make slower progress than their peers in learning words both from direct instruction and through the process of inferring meanings from context (Curtis, 1987; McKeown, 1985; Shefelbine, 1990). Their knowledge of word meaning is less thorough, and they seem to have less flexibility in interpreting a partially familiar word in a new context. They may recognize words as familiar but may not be able to explain the meaning clearly.

For students with language-learning disabilities, instructional programs need to be tailored to the nature and severity of the language-learning problems. Students are

likely to benefit from instructional programs that make explicit semantic and conceptual features of words and word relations.

METHODS OF INSTRUCTION

Even though many methods of vocabulary instruction have yielded significant improvements in research studies (National Institute of Child Health and Human Development, 2000), teachers are understandably uncertain about the best way or ways to go about fostering vocabulary development amongst their students, with a particular eye toward optimal long-term growth of their students' word knowledge. Teachers might be accustomed to asking students to learn words that are important to the topic under study but might be unsure what other methods are likely to lead to growth in students' vocabulary, particularly with the diverse learning abilities that are typically found in today's classrooms.

Approaches to vocabulary instruction can be classified into two main categories: teaching individual word meanings and teaching strategies for deriving word meanings. Within each of these categories, there are a variety of instructional methods that have been implemented both in classrooms and in clinical settings, with varying degrees of success. This section provides descriptions of various research-supported methods to vocabulary instruction. Following this section, we offer some guidelines for effective instruction.

Teaching Individual Word Meanings

Teaching individual word meanings is not uncommon in classroom settings. There might be predetermined sets of words to be taught (e.g., words in bold print in science passages), but how the teacher teaches them can vary in terms of his or her involvement and method. One teacher might give the students a list of words to look up in a dictionary and learn. Another might provide the students with the meanings or engage the class discussions about the word meanings as they relate to text. Students learn a relatively small number of words through this approach. Stahl and Fairbanks (1986) reported that direct instruction programs typically teach 10–12 words per week (approximately 400 words per year), only about 75% of which are actually learned (approximately 300 words). However, instructional methods used with this approach are not without value; many lead to significant increases in vocabulary knowledge (Stahl & Fairbanks, 1986). Two of these are the key-word method and computer-assisted (or computer-aided) instruction.

Key-Word Method

Rationale   The key-word method provides specific assistance in the recall of information and is considered especially appropriate for students with learning disabilities because they are likely to have difficulties committing information to memory (Scruggs & Mastropieri, 1990). Key-word methods or mnemonic strategies for teaching vocabulary are prevalent in the learning disabilities literature and have been shown to be effective in promoting word recall comprehension in students with learning disabilities (e.g., Condus, Marshall, & Miller, 1986; Mastropieri, Scruggs, & Fulk, 1990; Scruggs & Mastropieri, 1990; Veit, Scruggs, & Mastropieri, 1986) and in students with limited English proficiency (Zhang & Schumm, 2000).

Procedures   Vocabulary learning via the key-word method links an acoustic cue to a pictorial representation associated with the meaning of the word. The association need not make a lot of sense; in fact, the novelty of the link may be a central feature of its memorability. The key word is a word that is acoustically similar to the target word. For example, in one study, middle-school students with learning disabilities were trained in mnemonic learning that involved word parts (Veit et al., 1986). The word part to be learned was *ornith* (as in the word *ornithology,* the study of birds). To learn the word part *ornith,* the student was given a picture of a bird with an oar over its shoulder. The bird stood for *ornith,* and the oar was the key word. When a student is asked to define *ornith,* he or she would presumably recall the oar over the shoulder of the bird and in this way retrieve the first sound of the word and its associated meaning.

Comments   The key-word method has been effective in helping students with learning disabilities learn terms in science and social studies. Pfeiffer (1999) found that the key-word method works well if the students are given the word and asked to come up with the definition, but not if the students are given the definition and asked to recall the word. This may be because the definition does not trigger recall of the acoustically similar key word. Understandably, there are also concerns about the time-consuming process of developing the materials for use with mnemonic methods The teachers need to select the words to be learned, invent the key words, and so on. Although key-word and mnemonic methods have been used with middle-school and junior-high students in content-area courses with and without learning disabilities, they are likely to be less effective with younger students.

Computer-Assisted Instruction

Rationale   Computer programs have been developed primarily as a way to increase instructional time without placing greater demands on the time teachers need to spend working on vocabulary (Johnson, Gersten, & Carnine, 1987). Other advantages of computer-assisted instruction include the opportunity to individualize the content, to self-pace the lesson, to provide immediate feedback for the students, and to give a wealth of opportunities for repetition and practice.

Procedures   Drill-and-practice software programs appear to be the most widely used methods of computer-based vocabulary learning. In adopting such methods, teachers should consider the characteristics of instruction that leads to significant growth in word knowledge. For example, through selection menus, the teacher can control the particular words to be learned (and the number in a given set). In addition, the amount and type of practice may need to be monitored even though students work on their own. Providing extra review, for instance, has been found to lead to quicker recall and better transfer to passage comprehension (Johnson et al., 1987).

Johnson and colleagues (1987) utilized computer-assisted instruction for teaching high school students with learning disabilities sets of vocabulary words. In this method, a word is presented with its definition and then the word and its definition are each used in the same sentence (e.g., "Susie will ESTABLISH a new procedure for our meetings. Susie will SET UP a new procedure for our meetings," p. 208). Then, the students are presented with multiple-choice practice exercises that require them to select the best meaning for the target word used in a sentence.

Some computer-assisted instructional programs produce speech output. Students simultaneously read and hear a word, its definition, and a sentence containing the

word, and students control when they move to the next word by hitting the return key. Such programs have been found to be effective in promoting word learning for middle-school students with learning disabilities (Hebert & Murdock, 1994).

Comments In their computer-assisted instructional program, Hebert and Murdock (1994) found that students learned better when the computer-assisted instruction had speech output than when it did not have speech output. The speech component may have been effective because students could hear the words they were learning and thereby develop an understanding of the relationship of the pronunciation and the spelling. In addition, hearing the words may have made students aware that they had some knowledge of the words. That is, the words were in their oral recognition vocabulary, even if the words were not recognized in print. The speech-output mode is especially likely to make a difference for students with reading difficulties, as they are not required to rely on their reading for learning the words.

Proponents of computer-assisted instruction have argued that computers are motivating for students with learning disabilities. However, it is important to keep in mind that the ability to work independently over a period of time on abstract tasks may be an important prerequisite when selecting students who would benefit from computer-assisted instruction in vocabulary. Students who show difficulties working independently for extended periods of time might not benefit from this approach.

Teaching Word Learning in the Context of Reading

Unlike the two methods just described, in which vocabulary instruction is not provided in the context of broader reading activities, other effective methods for teaching individual words combine instruction in vocabulary with academic reading experiences (e.g., story books, literature selections, content-area chapters or units). There are benefits to learning words drawn from passages students are reading or words used to discuss a topic. Effective instructional methods make use of both definitional and contextual sources of information. When students study definitions for words and also study words in natural sentences or passages, they can see how the definition of the word sheds light on the meaning of the word in the context (Stahl & Fairbanks, 1986). Another advantage to vocabulary instruction given in conjunction with reading activities is that the recall and sharing of prior knowledge about a topic helps students to link topical words to their knowledge about the topic. For example, preteaching vocabulary from stories students were about to read was found to enhance fifth graders' comprehension of stories (Wixson, 1986).

School-age students are most effective in learning unfamiliar words when they are actively involved in meaning making. Interactive learning strategies help focus students' attention on the passage context and on the relations among concepts and words in the unit of study (Bos & Anders, 1990). Sharing ideas and activating prior knowledge are benefits of these elaborated methods of vocabulary instruction, which can also help to facilitate reading comprehension for students with learning disabilities.

Semantic Mapping

Rationale Semantic mapping is a highly interactive instructional activity for teaching vocabulary words as part of a reading activity. The belief is that knowledge is organized hierarchically and that by teaching a child to connect his or her background knowledge with new information (vocabulary and concepts) encountered in text, the child will learn and store the new concepts.

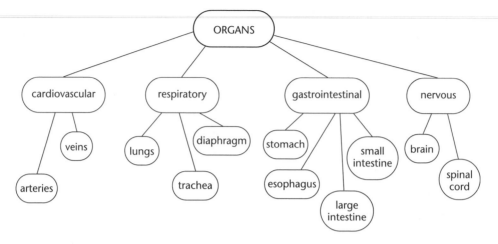

Figure 13.1. A semantic map.

Procedures   A semantic map is constructed prior to reading a specified passage, and it is verified during and following reading. The semantic map in Figure 13.1 is an example of what might be constructed prior to reading a biology chapter on organs of the body. Notice that the paths from word to word show both semantic and conceptual relations. Semantic relations are ways that words are related in meaning (e.g., synonym, part–whole). Conceptual relations are underlying abstract connections, indicating, for example, how two words convey principles in a domain of knowledge. Identifying such paths helps the students learn to reason about word relations. This too is an important indicator of effective word-learning processes.

In *Word Power: What Every Educator Needs to Know About Teaching Vocabulary*, Stahl and Kapinus (2001) stressed that active discussion is an important element of semantic mapping, especially for children with small vocabularies. They outlined three general procedures for engaging in semantic mapping:

1.   Brainstorm and discuss words that go with a topic.

2.   Develop a map with the topic printed in a circle in the middle, have the students come up with categories for the brainstormed words, add the words to the categories, connect the categories to the topic, and add a blank category circle to use after reading.

3.   Read the selection and follow-up with the map, adding additional terms and categories from the text when appropriate.

Comments   Semantic mapping has been found to be effective in promoting both word learning and reading comprehension. It has been useful for demonstrating relationships between language, subject-matter content, and students' own linguistic and cultural backgrounds. Furthermore, this method has been found to be effective for upper elementary bilingual students with learning disabilities as well as for secondary students with learning disabilities (Bos & Anders, 1990).

Semantic Feature Analysis

Rationale   Another interactive approach to teaching vocabulary and reading comprehension is semantic feature analysis. This method helps students learn the topi-

Bodies of water	Partially surrounded by land	Connects two larger bodies of water	Salt water	Shallow	Surrounded by land on all sides	Flowing	Located alongside a coast
bay	✓		✓				
channel		✓	?				
cove	✓		?				✓
gulf	✓		✓				
lagoon			?	✓			✓
lake					✓		
ocean			✓				?
pond				?	✓		
river				?		✓	
strait	✓		?				
stream				✓		✓	

Figure 13.2. A semantic feature analysis matrix.

cal vocabulary presented in a passage they are reading. More than semantic mapping, semantic feature analysis helps students to see relations among concepts, vocabulary words, and ideas or information in the text (Anders & Bos, 1986; Bos & Anders, 1990).

Procedures In semantic feature analysis the teacher and students predicted relations among concepts using a relationship matrix. Students can identify each relationship by placing a checkmark or a plus sign in the appropriate cell. Question marks can be placed when a student is not sure of the relationship, if the relationship is not explicitly mentioned in the text, or if the concept and the feature are sometimes related. It is also acceptable to mark nonrelationships; this can be done using a minus sign or an *X*.

In the example in Figure 13.2, the semantic feature analysis matrix provides a way to distinguish between some similar terms, based on their semantic features. For example, the students learn that a lagoon and a cove are located on the coastline, whereas a stream is not. This semantic feature analysis matrix, however, does not illustrate some relevant distinctions between similar terms, and the students might find themselves confused. For example, a bay and a gulf are both bodies of salt water that are partially surrounded by land; however, a bay is smaller than a gulf. Although this distinction is not made in the matrix, questions generated by the students can lead to useful and rich classroom discussion.

As with semantic mapping, active discussion is an important part of semantic feature analysis. First, students can work as a class to construct a matrix of vocabulary words and their associated concepts, examples, and/or characteristics. Then, students can work together in pairs to check off those words and concepts that are associated with one another. Finally, the class can come together to discuss the matrices and raise questions about specific words and concepts, including questions about words and concepts that do not seem to differ from each other at all.

Comments Stahl and Kapinus (2001) described this activity as being particularly effective in content-area classes. Furthermore, semantic feature analysis is an effective method for both junior high and high school students with learning and reading disabilities (Anders & Bos, 1986; Bos & Anders, 1990).

Define the new concept.
A reptile is a cold-blooded animal that has a backbone, is covered by scales or horny plates, breathes by means of lungs, and usually lays eggs.
Distinguish between new concept and similar concepts.
A reptile is different from a mammal because a mammal is warm-blooded.
Give examples of concept and explain.
Common reptiles are turtles, alligators, lizards, and snakes. These are reptiles because they have backbones, they are cold-blooded, they are covered with scales or horny plates. They also breathe air through lungs.
Give nonexamples and explain.
Fish are not reptiles because they breathe water through their gills; they cannot breathe air. Horses, birds, and whales are not reptiles because they are warm-blooded.
Distinguish between examples and nonexamples.
Which of the following are reptiles? bear, crocodile, cow, frog, newt, goldfish, dinosaur

Figure 13.3.   Learning new concepts and words.

Teaching Unfamiliar Words Through Discussion

Rationale   Discussion has been found to be an effective way to learn unfamiliar words. Researchers have found that when teachers present unfamiliar words in context and ask students to offer possible meanings, the ensuing discussion leads to significant improvement of their understanding of the words (Jenkins, Matlock, & Slocum, 1989). McKeown and Beck (1988) and Mezynski (1983) recommended the introduction of words for discussion before the group reads the passage.

In content-area courses, students may learn vocabulary effectively by participating in interactive discussions that focus on the important terms used in a given unit of study. It is typical for students to be faced with new words that represent new and unfamiliar concepts, and these words are not as easily learned as new words that represent known concepts. Graves (2000) suggested that teachers engage in more robust discussions with students when teaching words that express new and unfamiliar concepts. He cited the Frayer method as an effective method for teaching such words, as a prereading and postreading activity.

Procedures   Graves (2000) listed the steps teachers would take in teaching words with unfamiliar concepts, using the Frayer method. These steps are shown in Figure 13.3. First, the teacher provides the students with a good definition of the new concept. Then he or she distinguishes between the new concept and similar and different concepts. Next, examples and nonexamples of the concept with explanations should be provided. Finally, the students should take an active role in generating and distinguishing between examples and nonexamples and then presenting these to the class.

Comments   Graves (2000) explained that this method is highly effective for promoting word learning and comprehension in the middle grades. However, he acknowledged that the method can take a great deal of effort and time, even just to discuss one word. Although the effectiveness of this method for students with reading or learning disabilities has not been determined, the method holds promise for such students because, like semantic feature analysis, it helps students understand the conceptual basis of word meanings.

Discussion of Unfamiliar Words: Literature Discussion Groups

Rationale   Discussion of vocabulary can also be carried out in literature discussion groups. In literature discussion groups, students work cooperatively to understand and reflect on the meaning of texts that they are reading. Cooperative learning groups promote participation and students' investment in their reading. When vocabulary is built in as a planned activity in the daily discussion, students have a chance to select words they think are important to learn and to work together to come to an understanding of the meanings of unfamiliar words in context.

Procedures   In a study carried out by Fisher, Blachowicz, and Smith (1991), fourth-grade students in mixed-ability reading groups worked cooperatively in groups of four. Each group member had a role with specific responsibilities for each day; these roles were discussion director, vocabulary researcher, literary luminary, and secretary-checker. The four roles rotated each day. The vocabulary researcher selected five or six words from the chapter of the book the group was reading to teach the group members. Along with identifying appropriate meanings for the words, the vocabulary researcher led a discussion about the words and asked students to derive meanings from context. The vocabulary researcher confirmed group members' predictions or gave a better meaning.

Comments   The fourth graders' performance on a vocabulary test showed that they had made noticeable gains in their understanding of the words they discussed in their groups. A method such as this one may help students take an interest in words and understand the value of studying unfamiliar words in texts they read. To our knowledge, however, there have been no studies of vocabulary acquisition of students with reading or language-learning disabilities who participated in such literature discussion groups.

Discussion of Unfamiliar Words: Possible Sentences

Rationale   Stahl and Kapinus (1991) explored another discussion method, the "possible sentences" technique, which appears to help students access prior knowledge and share knowledge and experiences with each other. Furthermore, it might foster students' ability to consider the meanings of words as they are used in content-area textbooks.

Procedures   In this study, fifth graders were given about six difficult words from the passage they were about to read (e.g., *barometer, humidity*). Six familiar words from the text (e.g., *rain, predict*) were also written on the board. The teacher or students provided a short definition of each word. Students were then asked to think of possible sentences containing the words that might be in the passage they were about to read. These were written on the board. After contributing possible sentences, students read the chapter or passage. The class then discussed the possible sentences, determining whether they were true or not. Untrue sentences were modified on the basis of information in the text. Generating sentences before reading and discussion of the sentences after reading fostered vocabulary knowledge and text comprehension.

Comments   This method holds promise for students who struggle with reading and with language learning. Moreover, Stahl and Kapinus (1991) suggested that this approach is easy to implement as well as effective for preparing children to read content-area and narrative texts. There is no need for teachers to prepare worksheets or other

materials. The approach simply requires familiarity with the text (including selection of vocabulary words) and class time for discussion. Although these researchers argued in favor of the possible sentences approach, they emphasized that it should not be used in place of other methods (e.g., semantic mapping); rather, it should be used in conjunction with other methods.

Discussion of Unfamiliar Words: Text Talk

Rationale   Discussion methods can also be carried out when reading books aloud to young students. Beck and McKeown described *Text Talk,* an approach designed to promote comprehension and language development in kindergartners and first graders through "in-depth and extensive experiences in listening to and talking about stories read to them" (2001, p. 10). Although the program is geared toward overall language development, specific and explicit attention is given to the acquisition of vocabulary.

Procedures   Using a trade book, the teacher selects words that are likely to be unfamiliar to the children but still represent identifiable concepts that could be used in normal conversations (e.g., reluctant). The teacher calls the children's attention to each target word as it appears in the context of the story and then defines it in a child-friendly way (e.g., "In the story, Lisa was *reluctant* to leave the Laundromat without Corduroy. *Reluctant* means you are not sure you want to do something"). The children are asked to repeat the word so that they encode the phonological representation. The teacher gives examples of how the word could be used (e.g., "Someone might be *reluctant* to eat food they had never had before") and then asks the children to come up with their own examples, starting their phrases with "I might be reluctant to _____" (Beck & McKeown, 2001, p. 19). After each child's example, another child is asked to explain what the example means.

Comments   Beck and McKeown (2001) emphasized that although reading aloud to children is not a difficult task for literate adults, taking full advantage of a reading-aloud experience can be challenging. They offered the following guidelines for ensuring effective book-reading experiences:

- Be aware of the difference between constructing meaning of ideas and simply retrieving information from the text.

- Understand that children have difficulty gaining meaning from words presented out of context.

- Use questions to help children talk about and connect ideas in the text, and develop follow-up questions that build on those ideas.

- Help students meaningfully incorporate their background knowledge.

- Be aware that pictures can draw attention away from processing the linguistic information in the text—attend to the timing of the use of pictures.

- Take advantage of sophisticated words in texts.

Resources for Deriving Word Meaning

Comprehension of texts is dependent to a large extent on the reader's understanding of the words in the text. Sometimes it is difficult for students to infer the meanings of unfamiliar words from passage contexts. They need to know about resources they might

use to learn about word meanings (e.g., dictionary, thesaurus). Students also need to learn how to use information from such sources to figure out the meanings of unfamiliar words.

Dictionary Methods

Rationale   Although it may not seem obvious, being able to use a dictionary when one encounters an unfamiliar word can be a useful strategy for deriving meaning from unfamiliar words. Of course, for the strategy to be effective, students need to be comfortable using a dictionary. Schatz and Baldwin (1986) argued in favor of teaching students how to use dictionaries and glossaries to determine the meanings of unfamiliar words that are encountered in texts.

Procedures   Definitions can be a source of independent learning, but for this to happen, students need to know how to find the definition of a word in the dictionary and how to regard the definition as an "initiating event," not a final step in the process (McKeown, 1991). For students to become independent consumers of resources such as the dictionary and thesaurus, they must first become familiar with techniques for finding words. They need to learn how to use headings and how to read entries (including common abbreviations). They also benefit from activities in which definitions from the dictionary are used to interpret a word in context. (See Chapter 5 for dictionary activities.)

Beck, McKeown, and Kucan (2002) suggested that students be introduced to the variability that exists from one type of dictionary to another. These authors explained that through this, teachers can help students to understand the "openness and flexibility of language—particularly that there is nothing absolute about a dictionary definition" (p. 123). In terms of recommendations for specific dictionaries to use, Beck et al. suggested learners' dictionaries, such as the *Collins COBUILD English Language Dictionary* (1987), which contain much more comprehensible definitions than traditional dictionaries.

Comments   Although using dictionaries or glossaries does have its benefits (e.g., a practical and useful skill that can be utilized independently), it has many potential limitations. First, for students with reading difficulties, remembering a word's spelling in order to search for it might be a difficult task. Second, these resources often do not yield helpful information to students because of the complexity of the wording of definitions (McKeown, 1991; Miller & Gildea, 1987; Scott & Nagy, 1997). Dictionary entries tend to be most useful to people who already have a good sense of the meaning of the word they are looking up! Moreover, as many words are defined by multiple definitions in the dictionary, students must be able to detect and make sense of the most relevant definition for a given word in a given context, and this can be especially difficult for students with language and learning difficulties.

Using Computer-Mediated Texts

Rationale   The problem with using a dictionary the old-fashioned way is that students are often not exposed to the word they are seeking to learn in a comprehensible context. Reinking and Rickman (1990) addressed this problem in a study in which word meanings were supplied by the computer program as students read a passage. They found that sixth graders learned significantly more vocabulary words and demonstrated greater passage comprehension with computer-mediated texts than with a tra-

ditional printed passage and access to a dictionary or glossary. The computer-mediated texts provided the students with the appropriate meanings for the difficult words they encountered while reading a passage on the screen, thus saving the students from having to stop to look up words and then struggle to find and understand the appropriate definitions in a dictionary or glossary.

Procedures   Reinking and Rickman (1990) described two equally effective options for using computer-mediated texts. One option allows a student to simply click on any word for which he or she wants a definition. The definition for that word, in that context, is then presented to the student on the computer. The other option did not allow the student the same level of control. This option was designed so that the student was given definitions for all of the difficult words; he or she had no choice in the matter.

Comments   The researchers suggested that learning of difficult words during independent reading of texts might be enhanced with the aid of a computer. Computer-mediated texts can expand or control students' options for deriving meaning from texts, and they are particularly attractive for students who have difficulties with language learning and/or reading. However, because computer-mediated texts are not likely to be readily available outside of the classroom, this method may not be a practical long-term strategy for students with language-learning and reading difficulties. Still, this approach is likely to promote word learning, and it might possibly help to shape effective reading behaviors (e.g., monitoring comprehension, stopping to make sense of unfamiliar words in text).

Teaching Word- and Context-Analysis Strategies

Students need a variety of strategies to infer the meanings of unfamiliar words during reading. Two useful strategies are **context analysis**, which refers to using clues from the passage to infer the meaning of unfamiliar words, and **structural analysis** (or word analysis), which refers to using word parts (i.e., prefixes, suffixes, bases, and roots) to infer the meanings of words (Baumann & Kame'enui, 1991). These two strategies often complement one another.

Context Analysis

Rationale   Because incidental word learning during reading exerts an influence on students' vocabulary growth, it is important to improve students' ability to infer word meanings from context. By itself, increasing the volume of reading that students do may not lead to significant increases in word knowledge for students with language-learning disabilities; in contrast, increasing their awareness of unfamiliar words and the value of context as a way to understand unfamiliar words may lead to better comprehension of words and texts.

Procedures   Students can be taught a step-wise process to analyze a word in context; sometimes, they are also taught to look for different types of context clues (Buikema & Graves, 1993; Herman & Dole, 1988; Jenkins et al., 1989; White, Sowell, & Yanagihara, 1989). Once the process is introduced, the teacher should give guided practice using the process in short passages with specific words that students can work on. An important step in the process is identifying context clues that are relevant. The steps in the process vary in different studies, but they often include the following:

- Write the unknown word.

- Look for passage clues.

- Write the passage clues below the word.

- Think about what the word might mean, based on the clues.

- Try this meaning in the passage to see if it makes sense.

- If it does, move on to see if there are helpful clues later in the passage. If it does not make sense, revise your guess about the meaning of the word.

Teaching types of context clues that can help students understand unfamiliar words is recommended by some experts. Sternberg, Powell, and Kaye (1983) advocated teaching a number of different types of clues (e.g., temporal, spatial). However, examples of what these clues look like and steps involved in teaching these and other kinds of clues have not been well described in the research literature. One study in which context clues descriptions were provided was carried out by Carnine, Kame'enui, and Coyle (1984). They studied fourth, fifth, and sixth graders' use of three different types of context clues for deriving meaning from unfamiliar words. They used the following types of context clues in their instruction (p. 190):

1) *Synonym*s (e.g., The starfish has a most *idiosyncratic* way of eating. It certainly is *strange.*)
2) Contrast in which an antonym of the unfamiliar word is preceded by the adverb not (e.g., The starfish has a most *idiosyncratic* way of eating. It certainly is *not normal.*)
3) *Inference relationships* in which a chain of words allows the formation of a deduction (e.g., The starfish has a most *idiosyncratic* way of eating. *Most animals do not eat this way.*)

For students with learning disabilities, the most useful type of clue was synonyms.

Comments   Researchers who have reviewed studies designed to teach students to infer meanings from context have found that this method is modestly effective (Fukkink & de Glopper, 1998; Kuhn & Stahl, 1998). Studies have often been short term. They have not provided structured activities designed to help students practice the process of deriving word meaning from context over an extended period of time. Students need to practice this strategy until they find that they are using it habitually. For this method to be a useful means of word learning, students need to monitor their own comprehension and learn to deploy some repair strategies when they find they are not understanding words or sentences. If they do not do so, they are unlikely to notice the words that are unfamiliar and that affect their ability to understand a text. A second problem is that the types of context clues students should be taught are a matter of debate.

Structural Analysis and Word Analysis

Rationale   Along with analysis of the passage context to infer word meanings, students can be taught to infer meanings from analysis of meaning-bearing parts of words. These include prefixes, base words or roots, and suffixes. Learning to analyze word parts may be very important as students move into the middle school years. Nagy, Anderson, Schommer, Scott, and Stallman (1989) estimated that about 60% of the unfamiliar words that middle school students encounter in books are morphologically complex words with relatively transparent structure and meaning, such as *replacement* or *undamaged*. Awareness of the structure of complex words is likely to pay off in terms

of both vocabulary development and reading comprehension (e.g., White, Power, & White, 1989).

Procedures   Henry (1988, 2003) described a program of instruction that includes a focus on structural analysis and word etymology. The first part of this program involved teaching words of Anglo-Saxon origin, because the base word is usually a free-standing word form that students may recognize (e.g., *help*). Next, Latinate prefixes, suffixes, and roots are taught; roots are usually not free-standing words (e.g., *duc* means to lead and is found in such words as *induce* and *reduce*). Finally, students learn Greek roots and compounds (e.g., *microphone*). The primary emphasis of this program is on decoding and spelling, but understanding the meanings of word parts are a definite part of the process of becoming aware of the structure of the word. Other instructional programs link reading and spelling and the meaning of words and word parts but without a specific focus on the origins of words (e.g., Bear, Invernizzi, & Templeton, 1996; Templeton, 1989).

Comments   Henry's (1988, 2003) research has indicated that students with and without learning disabilities make significant improvements in word learning, as well as in word-reading and spelling skill. Analysis of words with prefixes and suffixes might be particularly helpful for older students with reading disabilities (Elbro & Arnbak, 1996). However, there have been few well-designed studies of the effectiveness of word-analysis strategies (and context-analysis strategies, too) as used by struggling readers and students with language-learning disabilities during reading.

Combined Strategies   Some studies have shown that deriving word meanings from morphological analysis is only partially successful in getting students close to knowing the meaning of a word (Wysocki & Jenkins, 1987). Students (particularly those who are younger or less able readers) may focus particularly on the base word, neglecting analysis of the syntactic and semantic aspects of some suffixes. For example, students may indicate that they understand the word *talkativeness*, but their sense of knowing this word may derive entirely from their familiarity with the word *talk*. Their neglect of the two suffixes that follow the base word becomes apparent when they are asked to use the word in a sentence and produce such sentences as "My cousin was talkativeness, and she spent all her time on the telephone." White et al. examined the extent to which "misleading analysis" (1989, p. 287) might occur (e.g., the word *unassuming* means *modest*, not *not assuming*). Their findings suggested that students who are able to think of only the most familiar meaning of a base word have a 40% chance of defining its derived forms incorrectly. They noted, however, that this figure did not account for the contribution that context makes in deriving meaning from unfamiliar words.

White et al. (1989) suggested that context cues might activate less familiar definitions, which would improve readers' chances for successful analysis. Nagy and Herman (1987) have emphasized the value of combining analysis of word structure and context to determine the meanings of unfamiliar words during reading. A student who devotes some attention to analyzing word parts in relation to the whole might be able to come to an understanding of the possible meaning of the word. Then, examination of context clues can often provide a way to check the estimated meaning of the word. For example, consider the sentence *Realignment of the car's wheels made for a much smoother ride.* Analysis of the parts of *realignment* would yield the probable meaning of *state of lining up again,* and clues in the sentence (e.g., *much smoother*) provide some confirmation that the structural analysis process was helpful in understanding the word.

Bauman and his colleagues (2002) compared fifth-grade students' learning of morphological analysis, context analysis, and combined morphological and context analysis. Morphological analysis focused on groups of prefixes that had a common meaning (e.g., *not,* exemplified by *unbroken, impassive,* and so forth). Context analysis involved the use of social studies texts. Twelve lessons were given, and performance on both trained and transfer words was assessed. The results showed that after morphological or context analysis training, students improved in their understanding of words from their lessons both immediately and at a later date; students also improved in their understanding of words similar to the trained words. The students who received the combined training performed like the groups who received only one form of strategy instruction. There was no impact on reading comprehension as a result of any type of training, but this may be because the students received only 12 lessons overall. Perhaps only long-term experience with word analysis and context analysis strategies will affect general performance on measures of reading comprehension.

GUIDELINES FOR EFFECTIVE INSTRUCTION

In order to provide effective instruction in vocabulary, teachers need to consider not only the words, texts, and methods but also the broader instructional context. Among the important areas are the students (e.g., their ages and learning capabilities) and the goals of instruction and the instructional setting. Teachers also need to think about how to align assessment with the goals of instruction, how to select words for instruction, how to structure learning activities in order to provide sufficient practice and reinforcement. Vocabulary instruction can and should occur in all content areas. All of these aspects of instruction influence the effectiveness of vocabulary instruction.

Consider the Students

Students of Different Ages

Students of all ages benefit from vocabulary instruction; however, not all methods are well suited for every age group. Instruction that incorporates silent or independent reading would not be appropriate for young children who are not yet reading on their own, and as mentioned earlier, the key-word method is thought to be less effective for younger children than for older children. However, many instructional methods (e.g., semantic mapping, semantic feature analysis, context analysis, word analysis) can be modified for use with very young children. For example, the teacher can always read a piece of text aloud and then work with young students to create a pictorial or iconic semantic map, and teachers may be able to help young children start to think about how to derive meaning from words using context and word structure. Remember also that everyone (even prereaders) can learn words through listening to books read aloud; discussing words and concepts during or after the teacher's reading is a good way to promote word learning for students of all ages.

As far as using word analysis strategies, there is evidence that children as young as 4 years old are able to think about language and show an awareness and understanding of word structure (Berko, 1958; Carlisle & Fleming, 2003; Rubin, 1988). Although, at this time, this morphological knowledge is immature, there is significant growth in the ability to analyze words in Grades 3 and 5, so this kind of instruction would be appropriate throughout the elementary years.

Students with Language-Learning or Reading Disabilities

Students with language-learning or reading disabilities generally lag behind their peers in the development of their reading skills, and this affects their ability to learn vocabulary from reading. They are therefore more dependent on explicit methods of instruction than their peers. Most methods discussed earlier can be effective for students with language-learning disabilities; these include the key-word method, computer-assisted instruction, semantic mapping, semantic feature analysis, and word analysis strategies. The characteristics of instruction, however, need to be tailored to these students' learning needs. Teachers should be careful not to give these students too many words to work on at the same time. In addition, these students need more review of principles and strategies, and more practice and support in applying word-learning strategies than their peers need.

Students with language-learning disabilities lag behind their peers in the development of their word knowledge because of difficulties with semantic and conceptual aspects of word learning (Kamhi & Catts, 1986). For this reason, some approaches may not be as ideal or may require special considerations. Students with language-learning or reading disabilities are likely to have trouble using a dictionary as a regular strategy for learning words. They have trouble with densely worded definitions and with multiple definitions provided for a given word. It is hard for them to tell which definition is appropriate for a word in a given context. These students should be helped to learn techniques for using a dictionary or glossary as a strategy for figuring out the meaning of a word in a specific context.

These students are also likely to have trouble using context clues for deriving word meanings. They may lack the semantic and conceptual knowledge needed to infer meanings of words from context (whether oral or written language is involved). The usefulness of any context clue is likely to depend on a reader's typical and linguistic knowledge. Not surprisingly, therefore, students with limited language or cognitive capabilities will have difficulty learning new words by this method.

In general, teaching such students the meanings of individual words is likely to be most effective when there is active involvement on the part of the student and when conceptual and semantic features of words are made clear through the instructional activities. These conditions can be met with a number of approaches, such as semantic mapping and semantic feature analysis. The presence of limitations in cognitive or linguistic development does not necessarily mean that teachers should avoid instruction in using context clues to learn new words; rather, the plan for instruction should be carefully thought out. The amount of guided practice that is provided, as well as the number and types of clues the students are given to work with, should be adjusted so that the student benefits from the use of inferential methods.

For students with specific reading disabilities, the primary weakness is poor decoding or word-reading skill, which hinders the learning of new words as well as the acquisition of ideas and information from written texts (Mezynski, 1983). As long as the oral vocabulary is strong, improvements in students' basic reading skills should over time lead to improvements in their ability to learn words through reading as well as access to ideas and information from written text. Strategies such as context analysis and word analysis may be very helpful ways for these students to monitor their comprehension of words and sentences during reading. General education and special education teachers should work together to make sure that students develop the decoding strategies needed to identify unfamiliar words in texts. If the students are unable to

read the words, they are also unlikely to process them for meaning or, in fact, derive meaning from reading the text.

It is important to remember that some students who appear to struggle with reading may have more general difficulties with language learning, as noted previously. Teachers should not assume that a poor reader has trouble with reading only. Instead, they should determine whether the student's vocabulary development is age appropriate and whether other language-learning skills support learning words from oral and written discourse. With a profile of each poor reader's strengths and weaknesses, a teacher is in a good position to select appropriate methods for vocabulary learning (Carlisle, 1993).

Students with specific reading disabilities are likely to learn vocabulary effectively through listening but not through reading. This is not likely to be the case for students with language-learning disabilities. However, in general, students with language-learning or reading disabilities need support in order to benefit from independent reading. They might benefit from reading books aloud with a peer or an adult, listening to audio-recordings of books, or using computer-mediated texts, but it is best if some discussion of the text is part of the reading activity.

Students Who Are English Language Learners

Students who are learning English as a second language often need particular assistance learning vocabulary, and this is especially true of those thought to have language-learning disabilities (Gersten & Baker, 2003). Although exposure to oral language will gradually build students' comprehension of English, many scholars have pointed out that vocabulary is specific to the areas of learning the students are engaged in, and deep learning does not take place through passive listening. Explicit instruction should be balanced by opportunities for interactions with others who speak English well (Fillmore & Snow, 2002).

Although some aspects of language learning are quite readily transferred from the native language to the second language, vocabulary is not one of these. A student can have a concept that is not language specific (e.g., understanding the concept of *jump*), but the exact word or words available in the language to convey that idea need to be learned; they are not transferred from native to second language. Experts suggest that because memory for large numbers of unfamiliar words is often a challenge, teachers need to take steps to assist their students in any way possible (Blachowicz & Fisher, 2000). This might include encouraging a variety of memory strategies, such as imagery; verbal associations or elaboration; repetition and practice; and of course, use of words that are being learned in natural contexts. Interactive discussions about words in texts (e.g., inferring word meanings from context) are helpful, particularly when they emphasize the relation of language and culture to subject matter content (Bos, Allen, & Scanlon, 1989). Speaking and writing serve to build the language learners' sensitivity to meaning and the grammatical roles of words as they are used in English.

Gersten and Baker (2003) provided the following recommendations concerning the characteristics of vocabulary instruction for English language learners: 1) the number of vocabulary terms introduced at one time should be limited, 2) high-utility words and words that express key concepts should be selected for study, 3) visual aids (e.g., semantic maps, concept and story maps, word banks) effectively support word learning, and 4) teachers should consider varying the cognitive and linguistic demands. Regarding this last suggestion, Gersten and Baker explained that in some cases it might be appropriate to lower the linguistic demands (e.g., accepting one-word answers to

questions when content is the focus), whereas in other cases, expecting more complete explanations from students would provide a way for students to try out aspects of expressive language (including vocabulary) that they are learning.

Consider the Goals of Instruction and the Instructional Setting

Goals of Instruction

One issue that teachers must be concerned with as it relates to instruction (and assessment, which is discussed later) is what it means to *know* a word. A teacher may feel that certain words need only to be understood at a general or shallow level—enough so that the student can make sense of the text. For example, it may not be necessary to deeply understand the meaning of *furbelow* (a ruffle or flounce on a garment) in the context of reading an adventure book; it would be enough to understand that the word refers to something having to do with a garment. However, there are other words and concepts that students should deeply learn so that the words can be understood and used intelligently. Stahl and Kapinus referred to such words as "sophisticated words," which they described as "frequently encountered and employed by mature, informed language users, such as 'consistent,' 'representative,' and 'fluency'" (2001, p. 13). The extent to which the teacher believes a given word should be understood should be taken into consideration when choosing and implementing an instructional approach, and teachers should be aware that it might take more robust discussions about words and more exposures to the words for some students to gain deep knowledge about words.

Settings for Instruction and Classroom Organization

One of the biggest challenges of teaching in classrooms is managing the diversity of students in the room. This is particularly the case in inclusive settings in which there are students with language-learning or reading disabilities and students with limited English proficiency. Using mixed-ability groups with methods such as semantic feature analysis and literature discussion groups has been found to be effective for working with heterogeneous classrooms. When children of mixed learning abilities are paired or grouped together to engage in structured and meaningful discussions in a cooperative manner, language learning can occur for all students. In addition, employing computer-assisted methods can help teachers individualize instruction for each student.

There are certainly benefits to working with students in a one-to-one setting or even in small groups; it is easier to individualize instruction when working with small groups or individual students. Although an individualized instructional setting does not allow for peer interactions utilizing such methods as semantic feature analysis and literature group discussions, most of the methods discussed in this chapter can be used or easily modified for use with individuals or small groups. Modifications might include the number and type of words students work on, the extent of teacher support (explicit explanation, modeling of strategies), and the amount of practice provided over time.

When working with students in a resource room or clinical setting, teachers might make use of the vocabulary and texts that the students are already using for their schoolwork. There is no need to present students with additional words and reading assignments. Because students with special needs are typically struggling to keep up with their typically achieving peers, they appreciate assistance with content-area texts. Furthermore, many are motivated when they see some value in the task (e.g., it will help them earn a better grade) (Duffy, Roehler, & Rackliffe, 1986).

Finally, fostering students' interests in self-regulated word learning is an important goal in individual and small-group settings as well as in the classroom. Students reap long-term benefits when they acquire an interest in word learning and an interest in taking responsibility for their own word learning. Graves offered a number of ways for helping students become consciously aware of words and their importance (2000, pp. 128–131). Some of his points are summarized here:

- teachers should deliberately use and explain words that students might not know;
- teachers should point out interesting words that authors use in texts;
- teachers should recognize and encourage students' adroit word choices in their speaking and writing;
- teachers should promote word play, such as clichés and puns; and
- teachers should promote engagement with word-play books.

Align Assessment with Goals of Instruction

Consider Levels of Word Knowledge

Teachers must be concerned with what it means to know a word as it relates to assessment. A student may be able to demonstrate shallow knowledge of a word when asked to recognize its meaning in a multiple-choice format, but correct identification of a word's meaning does not necessarily imply that the student truly understands and can use the word. Therefore, when assessing students' vocabulary knowledge and progress, teachers might consider the instructional goals. For example, if it is important for students to have a good grasp of the conceptual foundations of word meanings (e.g., *condensation* in a science lesson), a multiple-choice test would be a less useful measure than a test that asked students to define or use the terms in context.

Carry Out Pre- and Postreading Assessments

When assessing word knowledge before or after instruction, teachers can consider giving several different tasks (i.e., both recognition and recall) in order to accommodate the expressive language difficulties of students with language-learning disabilities. Such students are able to recognize the meanings of words that they have trouble defining (Curtis, 1987; Simmons & Kame'enui, 1990). (This difference is true for all students but is more pronounced for students with language-learning disabilities.) A test that includes both multiple-choice items and writing definitions or using words in context might provide insights into the depth and breadth of students' word knowledge.

Assessing progress regularly provides a way to make sure that students are benefiting from the vocabulary instruction they are receiving. With frequent measures of students' word learning, the teacher can make adjustments in instruction as necessary. Long-term retention should be assessed as well. Teachers should not assume that word learning has taken place merely because performance on a weekly quiz is adequate. Ideally, students will learn words so that they will understand and use them well beyond the period of instruction. In short, assessment (as well as instruction) should be ongoing and cumulative.

Assessing Strategy Usage

Teachers may make the mistake of assuming that lessons on strategies for word learning will be sufficient. In fact, it is necessary that a teacher determine whether the students have internalized the strategy and are using it as appropriate during reading. This

is a difficult phase to assess. To evaluate student progress in using strategies for deriving word meanings, a teacher might observe and record students' use of strategic behaviors during oral reading. For example, do students stop reading when they encounter unfamiliar words? Do they attempt to use context- and/or word-analysis clues to derive meaning from unfamiliar words? Do they demonstrate success in using these strategies? Another method, recommended by Pressley and Afflerbach (1995), is using talk-aloud protocols as a way to assess students' efforts to make texts meaningful. With this method, at regular intervals a student is asked to stop reading and to explain his or her thinking (e.g., predictions, confusions about words). Although time consuming, this method holds promise for assessing strategy usage.

A related issue is how to assess the depth of the students' word knowledge. Beck et al. (2002) offered several suggestions for ways to assess students' deep knowledge of word meanings:

- Ask students what words mean.

- Have students respond to questions such as "Describe what a person who is *stingy* is like," and "Tell about a time when you behaved *impulsively.*"

- Have students distinguish between appropriate and inappropriate uses of a word.

- Have students describe how pairs of words are alike and/or different (e.g., delicious and tasty, sour and sweet).

- Have students place word phrases on a continuum and then explain their placements (e.g., on a continuum from least sad to most sad, the phrase *their **despondent** faces* would go at one end and *the **ebullient** crowd* would go at the other, with other phrases in between).

- Have students answer questions about sentences containing target words (e.g., "When Sam received his grade on the math test, he was *elated.* How do you think Sam did on the test?").

Make the Most of Instruction

Selecting Words to Teach

When students are learning the meanings of individual words, several factors should influence a teacher's selection of words. It is important to teach words that students do not already know (or have an incomplete understanding of). It can be useful to assess students' knowledge of a set of words prior to teaching the words. This can be accomplished by presenting the students with an ungraded quiz, or more informally, by presenting students with a list of words and asking them to mark the words they do or do not know.

It is also important to select words that might be practical or essential to know. For example, if the students are reading *Twelve Angry Men*, it would be practical for them to know not only words that appear repeatedly in the play but also words and concepts that relate to trials (e.g., *plaintiff, defendant, sustained, sequestered, jury of your peers*). In content-area courses, such as science, social studies, and math, there are always new words and concepts that occur and that are critical for understanding the unit being studied. Beck et al. (2002) have provided a thoughtful discussion for teachers about how to select words for instruction in *Bringing Words to Life: Robust Vocabulary Instruc-*

tion. Their general criteria include 1) importance and utility (words that appear frequently across domains), 2) instructional potential (words that can be worked with in a variety of ways and can be connected to other words and concepts valuable to the students, and 3) conceptual understanding (words for which students understand the general concept but are likely to deepen their understanding of concepts).

Graves and Slater offered four questions to help teachers select the most important words to teach (1996, p. 274): 1) "Is understanding the word important for understanding the selection in which it appears?" 2) "Are students likely to be able to assign the word a meaning using their context or structural analysis skills?" 3) "Can this word be used to further students' context, structural analysis, or dictionary skills?" and 4) "How useful is this word outside of the selection being currently taught?"

The authors suggested that selecting words that students can understand using word analysis is useful in promoting students' word learning as well as use of context- and structural-analysis strategies. In addition, a word's frequency in a text has a lot to do with how useful it is. If the word is a high-frequency word, it is likely to be encountered numerous times and is likely an important word to know.

Providing Explicit Instruction with Modeling

In an examination of the nature of instruction that led to effective learning by students with learning disabilities, Swanson (1999) found that explicit instruction and interactive learning opportunities mutually support one another. In terms of vocabulary instruction, then, we recommend that teachers provide explicit instruction in the specific strategies that students are learning. Such instruction can be accompanied by modeling of the use of the strategy so that students can see how the strategy is carried out.

Explicit instruction incorporates a number of different components. First, effective teachers present information within a meaningful framework (Duffy, Roehler, & Rackliffe, 1986). Students have trouble understanding information that is presented out of context, particularly if it is not relevant to their own lives. Thus, instead of simply telling students to look up unfamiliar words in the dictionary, a teacher might emphasize the value of the skill to her students. He or she might say, "This is a skill you can use any place you read . . . the newspaper . . . your social studies book, or your library book . . . the cereal package in the morning" (Duffy, Roehler, & Rackliffe, 1986, p. 8).

When teachers explain the purpose behind learning particular information, their students benefit. Students are more likely to perceive the value in learning a task when they understand its potential relevance. Duffy, Roehler, Meloth, and Vavrus (1986) provide a thoughtful explanation. After placing the instruction in a meaningful framework, effective teachers explain precisely so that students become aware of the lesson content. Students learn better when teachers introduce each lesson with explicit statements about its structure, goals, and purpose. Procedural information must also be provided explicitly and precisely, especially when the procedures are unfamiliar and require students to reason in new ways (e.g., using context clues to help derive meaning from unfamiliar words). Effective teachers use task analysis to identify and then explain their own reasoning skills in explicit and precise ways to students who are learning to employ new procedures. Effective teachers are also conceptually accurate in their explanations. Students are better able to explain what they have learned from teachers who correctly communicate the intended curricular outcomes.

A teacher can use modeling to show students how to do something that they do not know how to do. Modeling allows for explicit presentation of word-learning strate-

gies (e.g., context analysis). Thus, it reduces the likelihood that students will misinterpret the teacher's intentions. One effective approach that teachers can use to model mental processes used in analysis of unfamiliar words is the think-aloud approach. Just as it sounds, a teacher thinks aloud, stating his or her own reasoning as he or she analyzes an unfamiliar word so that the students can "see" the invisible process (Davey, 1983; Duffy, Roehler, Meloth, & Vavrus, 1986). For example, a teacher might note that she does not understand a particular word and that she will need to look for clues in the surrounding context as well; she would follow the steps in the process of using context clues described previously, talking about her thinking as she does so. For example, she might name possible context clues, suggest a possible meaning for the word, and speculate on whether she has come to a reasonable understanding of the word's meaning in that context.

In addition to thinking aloud, a teacher should elicit students' responses. This provides a way to assess students' understanding of the process. The students' responses influence the teacher's subsequent interactions and vice versa, so the process becomes cyclical in nature. Eventually, through this process, the students move closer toward understanding the strategy and how it might be useful to them, and, as a consequence, they are in a position to take on more of the responsibility for their word learning.

Practice and Reinforcement

There is no question that words are best learned through repeated encounters or multiple exposures (Nagy, 1988; Stahl & Fairbanks, 1986). Repetition is key if words are to be deeply learned. Nagy suggested that this is best accomplished by providing students with encounters with words that require meaningful use (i.e., uses that parallel normal speaking, reading, and writing). For example, if a word is taught on one occasion by way of presenting a definition and an example in context, it can later be revisited by asking students to use the meaning of the word to make an inference (e.g., if students learn that a *furbelow* is a ruffle or flounce on a garment, they could then infer that it is more likely to be seen on a dress than on a pair of men's socks). The word could come up again in an activity originally described as "frequent contact" by Jantzen (1985; as cited in Nagy, 1988). In this activity, students can discuss inferences about clusters of related words. For instance, students could be asked to draw three columns on a sheet of paper with category headings listed at the top of each column (e.g., *Designers, Soldiers,* and *Archeologists*). Then, the teacher would give the students a list of 20 or so words and instruct them to place the words in each of the columns based on whether a designer, soldier, or archeologist would be most likely to have the frequent contact with each item. Students would be encouraged to use a dictionary when needed, and they would be allowed to place a word in more than one column if it had several meanings (e.g., the word *arms* could fit into the categories of designers and soldiers). There are countless other possibilities for creating meaningful encounters with vocabulary words (e.g., sentence completion activities, writing activities).

In their program *Text Talk,* Beck and McKeown (2001) also stressed the importance of maintaining words after the initial instruction, as words that children are exposed to are not likely to be deeply learned if they are not revisited. Therefore, in conjunction with *Text Talk,* the researchers created charts for the teachers and the students to keep track of words that the children saw, heard, and/or used following their initial introduction. The children responded very well to this tool for practice and reinforcement. For example, for the words *nuisance* and *commotion,* the children pointed out their

classmates who were nuisances in the classroom, and they brought commotions in the hallway to the attention of their teachers. When reading new stories, the children were also observed to comment on words they had already learned from earlier stories. It seemed that keeping a tally of the number of encounters with each word was motivating for both the teachers and the students and encouraged practice and promoted learning. In short, both the type and number of exposures to unfamiliar words play a role in building deep and lasting understanding.

Include Vocabulary Instruction in the Content Areas

It should be obvious from much of the discussion in this chapter that vocabulary instruction should not be limited to the language-arts or English classroom. In content areas such as science and social studies, specific meanings of words and concepts are central to learning the ideas and information in units of study.

Awareness of strategy knowledge and use is important for older students in content-area courses. Carr (1985) has identified three main strategic processes that students engage in while learning words in content areas: 1) Students need to develop independent selection of strategies for identifying important words to be learned, 2) they need to understand words central to the unit of study but also need to be able to use them in speaking and writing, and 3) they need to retain the vocabulary and use it as part of their learning of the information and idea in that unit of study. A key to fostering this degree of independent word learning is having students learn multiple strategies with sufficient support and practice so that students have ownership of them.

Teachers in different content areas can work together to coordinate instruction in several ways. For example, teachers of different subjects might consider teaching and using context analysis strategies at the same time. In this way, students will have multiple opportunities for practice and they will hopefully recognize the value of the strategy, in that it can be used successfully for more than one class. Teachers might also help support one another's instructional goals. For example, if the language arts teacher intends to work on dictionary skills, other content-area teachers can have students use these skills to reinforce and improve their word learning in different domains. Teachers might use team meetings of grade-level curriculum committees to coordinate the goals and methods of vocabulary instruction within a school.

An important issue to consider when teaching vocabulary across the curriculum is overload, particularly for students with language and learning disabilities. Requiring students to learn too many words in different courses, particularly if the words are unrelated to one another, may be counterproductive, as it may overload students' capacities for comprehension and recall. It is sometimes best to teach fewer words at a time, as this will allow the students to learn the words' meanings deeply. One possible way to achieve this is for each teacher to limit the number of words that he or she teaches per week. Alternatively, teachers might share some of the same words so that students are given plenty of opportunities for practice and reinforcement.

CONCLUSIONS

In summarizing insights about vocabulary instruction culled from research studies since the 1980s, Blachowicz and Fisher (2000) found that the following principles are generally recommended as guides to instruction: 1) Students need to be active in developing their understanding of words and ways to learn them, 2) students benefit

from personalizing word learning, 3) students should be immersed in words, and 4) students build knowledge of words through exposure to multiple sources of information and repeated exposures.

Researchers have provided analyses of effective vocabulary instruction that is aligned with these principles (Johnson & Pearson, 1984; McKeown & Beck, 1988; Nagy, 1988; Stahl, 1986). These characteristics of effective vocabulary instruction pertain to all students, including those with reading and language-learning problems (Carlisle, 1993). Effective vocabulary instruction

- Provides exposure to different meanings of words

- Provides illustrations of word usage in natural contexts

- Builds conceptual and semantic foundations for word knowledge

- Builds understanding of links among members of word families

- Assists students' efforts to derive meanings from context

- Provides ways to remember word meanings

- Integrates new information with prior knowledge

- Facilitates opportunities for meaningful use

- Seeks to engage the students in inquiry about words

REFERENCES

Anders, P.L., & Bos, C.S. (1986). Semantic feature analysis: An interactive strategy for vocabulary development and text comprehension. *Journal of Reading, 29*(7), 610–616.

Anderson, R.C., & Freebody, P. (1983). Vocabulary knowledge. In H. Singer & R.B. Ruddell (Eds.), *Theoretical models and processes of reading* (3rd ed., pp. 343–371). Newark, DE: International Reading Association.

Anderson, R.C., Wilson, P.T., & Fielding, L.G. (1988). Growth in reading and how children spend their time outside of school. *Reading Research Quarterly, 23,* 285–303.

Baumann, J.F., Edwards, E.C., Font, G., Tereshinski, C.A., Kame'enui, E.J., & Olejnik, S.F. (2002). Teaching morphemic and contextual analysis to fifth-grade students. *Reading Research Quarterly, 37,* 150–176.

Baumann, J.F., & Kame'enui, E.J. (1991). Research on vocabulary instruction: Ode to Voltaire. In J. Flood, J.M. Jensen, D. Lapp, & J.R. Squire (Eds.), *Handbook of research on teaching the English language arts* (pp. 604–632). New York: Macmillan.

Beals, D.E. (1997). Sources of support for learning words in conversation: Evidence from mealtimes. *Journal of Child Language, 24,* 673–694.

Bear, D., Invernizzi, M., & Templeton, S. (1996). *Words their way: Word study for phonics, vocabu-lary, and spelling instruction.* Upper Saddle River, NJ: Prentice Hall.

Beck, I.L., & McKeown, M.G. (1991). Conditions of vocabulary acquisition. In R. Barr, M.L. Kamil, P. Mosenthal, & P.D. Pearson (Eds.), *Handbook of reading research* (Vol. II, pp. 789–814). New York: Longman.

Beck, I.L., & McKeown, M.G. (2001). Text talk: Capturing the benefits of reading aloud experiences for young children. *The Reading Teacher, 55,* 10–20.

Beck, I.L., McKeown, M.G., & Kucan, L. (2002). *Bringing words to life: Robust vocabulary instruction.* New York: Guilford Press.

Berko, J. (1958). The child's learning of English morphology. *Word, 14,* 150–177.

Blachowicz, C.L.Z., & Fisher, P. (2000). Vocabulary instruction. In M.L. Kamil, P. Mosenthal, P.D. Pearson, & R. Barr (Eds.), *Handbook of reading research* (Vol. III, pp. 503–523). Mahwah, NJ: Lawrence Erlbaum Associates.

Bos, C.S., Allen, A.A., & Scanlon, D.J. (1989). Vocabulary instruction and reading comprehension with bilingual learning disabled students. *National Reading Conference Yearbook, 38,* 173–179.

Bos, C.S., & Anders, P.L. (1990). Effects of interactive vocabulary instruction on the vocabulary learning and reading comprehension of junior-

high learning disabled students. *Learning Disability Quarterly, 13,* 31–42.

Buikema, J.L., & Graves, M.L. (1993). Teaching students to use context clues to infer word meanings. *Journal of Reading, 36,* 450–457.

Carlisle, J. F. (1993). Selecting approaches to vocabulary instruction for the reading disabled. *Learning Disabilities Research and Practice, 8,* 97–105.

Carlisle, J.F., & Fleming, J. (2003). Lexical processing of morphologically complex words in the elementary years. *Scientific Studies of Reading, 7,* 239–253.

Carlisle, J.F., Fleming, J.E., & Gudbrandsen, B. (2000). Incidental word learning in science classes. *Contemporary Educational Psychology, 25,* 184–211.

Carnine, D., Kame'enui, E.J., & Coyle, G. (1984). Utilization of contextual information determining the meaning of unfamiliar words. *Reading Research Quarterly, 19,* 188–204.

Carr, E.M. (1985). The vocabulary overview guide: A metacognitive strategy to improve vocabulary comprehension and retention. *Journal of Reading, 28,* 684–689.

Carver, R. (1994). Percentage of unknown vocabulary words in text as a function of the relative difficulty of the texts: Implications for instruction. *Journal of Reading Behavior, 26,* 413–438.

Clark, E.V. (1995). Later lexical development and word formation. In P. Fletcher & B. MacWhinney (Eds.), *The handbook of child language* (pp. 393–412). Oxford, UK: Blackwell Publishers.

Clark, E.V. (2003). *First language acquisition.* Cambridge, UK: Cambridge University Press.

Collins COBUILD English language dictionary. (1987). London: Collins.

Condus, M.M., Marshall, K.J., & Miller, S.R. (1986). Effects of the keyword mnemonic strategy on vocabulary acquisition and maintenance by learning disabled children. *Journal of Learning Disabilities, 19,* 609–613.

Curtis, M.E. (1987). Vocabulary testing and instruction. In M.G. McKeown & M.E. Curtis (Eds.), *The nature of vocabulary acquisition* (pp. 37–51). Mahwah, NJ: Lawrence Erlbaum Associates.

Dale, E., & Chall, J. (1948). A formula for predicting readability. *Educational Research Bulletin, Ohio State University, 27,* 11–20, 28, 37–54.

Davey, B. (1983). Think-aloud modeling the cognitive processes of reading comprehension. *Journal of Reading, 27,* 44–47.

Dickinson, D.K., Cote, L., & Smith, M.W. (1993). Learning vocabulary in preschool: Social and discourse contexts affecting vocabulary growth. In C. Daiute (Ed.), *The development of literacy through social interaction* (pp. 67–78). San Francisco: Jossey-Bass.

Dickinson, D.K., & Tabors, P.O. (Eds.). (2001). *Be-ginning literacy with language: Young children learning at home and school.* Baltimore: Paul H. Brookes Publishing Co.

Duffy, G.G., Roehler, L.R., Meloth, M.S., & Vavrus, L.G. (1986). Conceptualizing instructional explanation. *Teaching and Teacher Education, 2,* 197–214.

Duffy, G.G., Roehler, L.R., & Rackliffe, G. (1986). How teachers' instructional talk influences students' understanding of lesson content. *The Elementary School Journal, 87,* 3–16.

Elbro, C., & Arnbak, E. (1996). The role of morpheme recognition and morphological awareness in dyslexia. *Annals of Dyslexia, 46,* 209–240

Eller, R.G., Pappas, C.C., & Brown, E. (1988). The lexical development of kindergartners: Learning from written context. *Journal of Reading Behavior, 20,* 5–24.

Ellis Weismer, S., & Thorardottir, E.T. (2002). Cognition and language. In P.J. Accardo, B.Y. Rogers, & A.J. Capute (Eds.), *Disorders of language development* (pp. 21–37). Timonium, MD: York Press.

Fawcett, A.J., & Nicolson, R.I. (1991). Vocabulary training for children with dyslexia. *Journal of Learning Disabilities, 24,* 379–383.

Fielding, L.G., Wilson, P.T., & Anderson, R.C. (1984). A new focus on free reading: The role of trade books in reading instruction. In T.E. Raphael & R.E. Reynolds (Eds.), *The contexts of school-based literacy* (pp. 149–162). New York: Random House.

Fillmore, L.W., & Snow, C.E. (2002). What teachers need to know about language. In C.T. Adger, C.E. Snow, & D. Christian (Eds.), *What teachers need to know about language* (pp. 7–53). McHenry, IL: Delta Systems.

Fisher, P.J.K., Blachowicz, C.L.Z., & Smith, J.C. (1991). Vocabulary learning in literature discussion groups. In J. Zutell, S. McCormick, L.L.A. Caton, & P. O'Keefe (Eds.), *Learner factors/teacher factors: Issues in literacy research and instruction* (pp. 201–209). Chicago: National Reading Conference.

Fowler, A.E. (1991). How early phonological development might set the stage for phoneme awareness. In S.A. Brady & D.P. Shankweiler (Eds.), *Phonological processes in literacy: A tribute to Isabelle Y. Liberman* (pp. 97–117). Mahwah, NJ: Lawrence Erlbaum Associates.

Fukkink, R.G., & de Glopper, K. (1998). Effects of instruction in deriving word meaning from context: A meta-analysis. *Review of Educational Research, 68,* 450–469.

Gersten, R., & Baker, S. (2003). English-language learners with learning disabilities. In H.L. Swanson, K.R. Harris, & S. Graham (Eds.), *Handbook of learning disabilities* (pp. 94–109). New York: Guilford Press.

Graves, M.F. (2000). A vocabulary program to com-

plement and bolster a middle-grade comprehension program. In B.M. Taylor, M.F. Graves, & P. van den Broek (Eds.), *Reading for meaning: Fostering comprehension in the middle grades* (pp. 116–135). Newark, DE: International Reading Association.

Graves, M.F., & Slater, W.H. (1996). Vocabulary instruction in the content areas. In D. Lapp, J. Flood, & N. Farnan (Eds.), *Content area reading and learning instructional strategies* (2nd ed., pp. 261–275). Boston: Allyn & Bacon.

Greaney, V. (1980). Factors related to amount and type of leisure time reading. *Reading Research Quarterly, 15,* 337–357.

Hart, B., & Risley, T.R. (1995). *Meaningful differences in the everyday experiences of young American children.* Baltimore: Paul H. Brookes Publishing Co.

Hebert, B.M., & Murdock, J. (1994). Comparing three computer-aided instruction output modes to teach vocabulary to students with learning disabilities. *Learning Disabilities Research and Practice, 9,* 136–141.

Henry, M.K. (1988). Beyond phonics: Integrated decoding and spelling instruction based on word origin and structure. *Annals of Dyslexia, 38,* 258–275.

Henry, M.K. (2003). *Unlocking literacy: Effective decoding and spelling instruction.* Baltimore: Paul H. Brookes Publishing Co.

Herman, P.A., & Dole, J.A. (1988). Theory and practice in vocabulary learning and instruction. *Elementary School Journal, 89,* 43–54.

Jenkins, J. R., Matlock, B., & Slocum, T. A. (1989). Two approaches to vocabulary instruction: The teaching of individual word meanings and practice deriving word meaning from context. *Reading Research Quarterly, 24,* 215–235.

Jenkins, J.R., Stein, M.L., & Wysocki, K. (1984). Learning vocabulary through reading. *American Educational Research Journal, 21,* 767–787.

Johnson, D., & Pearson, P.D. (1984). *Learning vocabulary through reading* (2nd ed.). New York: Holt, Rinehart & Winston.

Johnson, G., Gersten, R., & Carnine, D. (1987). Effects of instructional design variables on vocabulary acquisition of LD students: A study of computer-assisted instruction. *Journal of Learning Disabilities, 20,* 206–213.

Juel, C. (1988). Learning to read and write: A longitudinal study of 54 children from first though fourth grades. *Journal of Educational Psychology, 80,* 437–447.

Kamhi, A.G., & Catts, H.W. (1986). Toward an understanding of developmental language and reading disorders. *Journal of Speech and Hearing Disorders, 51,* 337–347.

Kuhn, M.R., & Stahl, S.A. (1998). Teaching children to learn word meanings from context: A synthesis and some questions. *Journal of Literacy Research, 30,* 119–138.

MacWhinney, B. (1978). The acquisition of morphophonology. *Monographs of the Society for Research in Child Development, 43*(Whole No. 1).

Mastropieri, M.A., Scruggs, T.E., & Fulk, B.M. (1990). Teaching abstract vocabulary with the keyword methods: Effects on recall and comprehension. *Journal of Learning Disabilities, 23,* 92–96, 107.

McKeown, M.G. (1985). The acquisition of word meaning from context by children of high and low ability. *Reading Research Quarterly, 20,* 482–496.

McKeown, M.G. (1991). Learning word meanings from definitions: Problems and potential. In P.J. Schwanenflugel (Ed.), *The psychology of word meaning* (pp. 137–156). Mahwah, NJ: Lawrence Erlbaum Associates.

McKeown, M.G., & Beck, I.L. (1988). Learning vocabulary: Different ways for different goals. *Remedial and Special Education, 9,* 42–52.

Mezynski, K. (1983). Issues concerning the acquisition of knowledge: Effects of vocabulary training on reading comprehension. *Review of Educational Research, 53,* 253–279.

Miller, G.A., & Gildea, P.M. (1987, September). How children learn words. *Scientific American, 257,* 94–99.

Nagy, W.E. (1988). *Teaching vocabulary to improve reading comprehension.* Newark, DE: International Reading Association.

Nagy, W.E., & Anderson, R. (1984). How many words are there in printed school English? *Reading Research Quarterly, 19,* 304–330.

Nagy, W.E., Anderson, R., Schommer, M., Scott, J.A., & Stallman, A.C. (1989). Morphological families and word recognition. *Reading Research Quarterly, 24,* 262–282.

Nagy, W.E., & Herman, P.A. (1987). Breadth and depth of vocabulary knowledge: Implications for acquisition and instruction. In M.G. McKeown & M.E. Curtis (Ed.), *The nature of vocabulary acquisition* (pp. 19–45). Mahwah, NJ: Lawrence Erlbaum Associates.

Nagy, W.E., Herman, P.A., & Anderson, R. (1985). Learning words from context. *Reading Research Quarterly, 20,* 233–253.

National Institute of Child Health and Human Development (NICHD). (2000). *Report of the National Reading Panel. Teaching children to read: An evidence-based assessment of the scientific research literature on reading and its implications for reading instruction: Reports of the subgroups* (NIH Publication No. 00-4754). Washington, DC: U. S. Government Printing Office. Also available on-line: http://www.nichd.nih.gov/publications/nrp/report.htm

Nelson, K. (1996). *Language in cognitive development.* Cambridge: Cambridge University Press.

Oetting, J.B., Rice, M.L., & Swank, L.K. (1995). Quick incidental learning (QUIL) of words by school-age children with and without SLI. *Journal of Speech and Hearing Research, 38,* 434–445.

Paris, S.G., Wasik, B.A., & Turner, J.C. (1991). The development of strategic readers. In R. Barr, M.L. Kamil, P. Mosenthal, & P.D. Pearson (Eds.), *Handbook of reading research* (Vol. II, pp. 609–640). New York: Longman.

Pfeiffer, J. (1999). *Long-term retention of novel information learned via the keyword mnemonic method.* Unpublished doctoral dissertation, Northwestern University, Evanston, IL.

Pressley, M., & Afflerbach, P. (1995). *Verbal protocols of reading.* Mahwah, NJ: Lawrence Erlbaum Associates.

Reinking, D., & Rickman, S.S. (1990). The effects of computer-mediated texts on the vocabulary learning and comprehension of intermediate-grade readers. *Journal of Reading Behavior, 22,* 395–411.

Rubin, H. (1988). Morphological knowledge and early writing ability. *Language and Speech, 31,* 337–355.

Schatz, E.K., & Baldwin, R.S. (1986). Context clues are unreliable predictors of word meanings. *Reading Research Quarterly, 21,* 439–453.

Scott, J.A., & Nagy, W.E. (1997). Understanding the definitions of unfamiliar verbs. *Reading Research Quarterly, 32,* 184–200.

Scruggs, T.E., & Mastropieri, M.A. (1990). Mnemonic instruction for students with learning disabilities: What it is and what it does. *Learning Disability Quarterly, 13,* 271–280.

Shefelbine, J.L. (1990). Student factors related to variability in learning word meanings from context. *Journal of Reading Behavior, 22,* 71–97.

Simmons, D.C., & Kame'enui, E.J. (1990). The effect of task alternatives on vocabulary knowledge: A comparison of students with and without learning disabilities. *Journal of Learning Disabilities, 23,* 291–297, 316.

Snow, C.E., Burns, M.S., & Griffin, P. (Eds.) (1998). *Preventing reading difficulties in young children.* Washington, DC: National Academies Press.

Stahl, S.A. (1986). Three principles of effective vocabulary instruction. *Journal of Reading, 29,* 662–668.

Stahl, S.A., & Fairbanks, M.M. (1986). The effects of vocabulary instruction: A model-based meta-analysis. *Review of Educational Research, 56,* 72–110.

Stahl, S.A., & Kapinus, B.A. (1991). Possible sentences: Predicting word meanings to teach content-area vocabulary. *The Reading Teacher, 45,* 36–43.

Stahl, S., & Kapinus, B. (2001). *Word power: What every educator needs to know about teaching vocabulary.* Washington, DC: National Education Association.

Stahl, S.A., Richek, M.A., & Vandevier, R.J. (1991). Learning meaning vocabulary through listening: A sixth-grade replication. *National Reading Conference Yearbook, 40,* 185–192.

Stanovich, K.E. (1986). Matthew effects in reading: Some consequences of individual differences in the acquisition of literacy. *Reading Research Quarterly, 21,* 360–406.

Sternberg, R.J., Powell, J.S., & Kaye, D.B. (1983). Teaching vocabulary-building skills: A contextual approach. In A.C. Wilkinson (Ed.), *Classroom computers and cognitive science* (pp. 121–143). San Diego: Academic Press.

Swanson, H. L. (1999). Reading research for students with LD: A meta-analysis of intervention outcomes. *Journal of Learning Disabilities, 32,* 504–532.

Templeton, S. (1989). Tacit and explicit knowledge of derivational morphology: Foundations for a unified approach to spelling and vocabulary development in the intermediate grades and beyond. *Reading Psychology, 10,* 233–253.

Tomesen, M., & Aarnoutse, C. (1998). Effects of an instructional programme for deriving word meanings. *Educational Studies, 24,* 107–128.

Veit, D.T., Scruggs, T.E., & Mastropieri, M.A. (1986). Extended mnemonic instruction with learning disabled students. *Journal of Educational Psychology, 78,* 300–308.

White, T.G., Power, M.A., & White, S. (1989). Morphological analysis: Implications for teaching and understanding vocabulary growth. *Reading Research Quarterly, 24,* 283–304.

White, T.G., Sowell, J., & Yanagihara, A. (January 1989). Teaching elementary students to use word-part clues. *The Reading Teacher,* 302–308.

Wixson, K.K. (1986). Vocabulary instruction and children's comprehension of basal stories. *Reading Research Quarterly, 21,* 317–329.

Wysocki, K., & Jenkins, J. (1987). Deriving word meanings through morphological generalization. *Reading Research Quarterly, 22,* 66–81.

Zhang, Z., & Schumm, J.S. (2000). Exploring effects of the keyword method of limited English proficient students' vocabulary recall and comprehension. *Reading Research and Instruction, 39*(3), 202–221.

14

Strategies to Improve Reading Comprehension in the Multisensory Classroom

Eileen S. Marzola

For many years educators believed that when individuals had at least average intelligence and could decode accurately and fluently, good reading comprehension would naturally follow (Allington, 2001; McNeil, 1987). Although few would deny the critical importance of accurate, fluent decoding as a requirement for strong comprehension (Adams, 1990; Ehri, 1998; see Chapter 9 for more on this topic), there has been a growing awareness of other factors that promote successful development of this skill. For example, expanding as well as activating prior knowledge, maintaining a rich vocabulary foundation (see Chapter 13), and employing **metacognitive strategies** are also fundamental components of the reading process. Fortunately, a growing body of research has demonstrated that students can be taught the strategies that good readers use spontaneously and that when students are taught those strategies, both their recall and their comprehension of text improve (Pressley, 2002; Stahl, 2004). After a brief history of how comprehension instruction has changed over the last 50 years, this chapter presents a developmental framework for comprehension followed by a review of research-supported strategies as well as other promising methods designed to improve this essential reading skill within a multisensory learning environment.

HISTORICAL PERSPECTIVE OF COMPREHENSION

Although reading comprehension is viewed as the "essence of reading" (Durkin, 1993) and the "ultimate goal of reading education" (Adams, Treiman, & Pressley, 1998), much of the reading research since the 1980s has focused more on understanding the development of word reading as well as improving instruction for children who struggle with reading at the word level. During the scant occasions when instructional strategies for comprehension were proposed, moreover, they were rarely validated by con-

trolled studies to see if their adoption really did improve student performance (for reviews, see Adams et al., 1998). More recently, however, an explosion of research about teaching comprehension has begun to come to light, offering tantalizing guides to improving reading instruction.

Comprehension instruction was largely absent from classrooms throughout the 1960s and 1970s (Durkin, 1979; Williams, 1987). Durkin's (1979) observational studies of reading instruction in fourth-grade classrooms revealed that of more than 4,000 minutes of reading, only 20 minutes of comprehension instruction were observed. Instead of the focus being on teaching comprehension, the focus was on testing it. More than 25 years later, little has changed (Pressley, 2000; Taylor, Pearson, Clark, & Walpole, 1999). For many years, students were required to answer questions included at the end of packaged reading selections as a way of testing comprehension and sometimes stimulating discussion and/or reflection. This was done even though little thought had been given to the steps readers go through to process and understand what they read. Most often teachers spent no time instructing students about the strategies required to answer those questions (Maria, 1990). At best, if difficulties were noted in responding to questions after reading a text, a quick dip into a specific skill exercise (e.g., finding the main idea, drawing inferences, determining sequence) was a common (and frequently the only) prescription recommended. There was little, if any, transfer to real-text reading. Allington (2001) labeled this approach "assign and assess" because no instruction was provided with the materials used. This method rarely met students' needs. Activities were usually completed silently, with no direct instruction. Students were expected to acquire useful comprehension strategies through self-discovery, but many students were not able to discover effective reading strategies without teacher modeling.

Much reading comprehension instruction today is constructivist in nature. It focuses on the distinctive knowledge base each reader brings to the text and results in a unique interpretation of the text for each reader (Williams, 2002). The role of the teacher in this model is one of facilitator. Instruction is organized around discussion, with each student contributing his or her own individual interpretation that can then be expanded and refined as discussion evolves. Although this constructivist model has been noted to be effective for many students (Allington, Guice, Michelson, Baker, & Li, 1996), Williams argued, "This constructivist approach would not fully meet the needs of students with learning disabilities, who have been shown to respond well to structured, direct instruction" (2002, p. 129). Weak readers can be taught to improve their thinking and reasoning skills and can be taught interactive reading strategies to bolster their comprehension of text (Simmons, Fuchs, Fuchs, Mathes, & Hodge, 1995).

With the Reading First program, a component of the No Child Left Behind Act of 2001 (PL 107-110), major financial awards have been made available to states that demonstrate that they are using scientifically based reading programs in their schools. The result has been a flood of interest in scientifically validated strategies to improve instruction. A foundation of research has been building that tells us what cognitive processes are involved in text comprehension and which comprehension strategies are most effective for improving the skills of students who struggle to understand what they read.

STRATEGIES USED BY GOOD READERS

Much of the research done in the past about reading comprehension has focused on strategies used by good readers. Table 14.1 outlines the differences between behaviors

Table 14.1. Behaviors of good and poor readers before, during, and after reading

GOOD READERS	POOR READERS
Before reading . . .	
Activate prior knowledge	Begin to read without preparation
Understand what they need to do and set a purpose for reading	Are unaware of their purpose for reading
Are self-motivated to read	Tend to read only because they have to
Make positive self-statements about their progress	Make negative self-statements about their progress
Choose strategies that are appropriate for the task	Begin to read without any specific plan or strategy in mind
During reading . . .	
Are focused	Are distracted easily
Monitor their understanding as it is occurring	Are often unaware of their lack of understanding
Anticipate and predict what is likely to happen next	Read just to get it over with
Are able to use fix-up strategies if their comprehension gets off track	Do not know what to do to help themselves if they begin to lose understanding
Can use context to understand the meaning	Do not recognize which of new vocabulary is important
Recognize and use text structure to support their comprehension	Do not recognize any organization within the text
Organize and integrate new information	Tend to add on rather than integrate new information with what they already know
After reading . . .	
Think about what was read	Stop both reading and thinking
Summarize main ideas in some manner	
Seek more information from other sources	
Affirm that their success is a result of their effort	Believe that any success they experience is a result of luck

From Deshler, D.D., Ellis, E.S., & Lenz, B.K. (1996). *Teaching adolescents with learning disabilities: Strategies and methods* (2nd ed., p. 68). Denver, CO: Love Publishing. Originally adapted by Deshler et al. (1996) from Grover, H., Cook, D., Benson, J., & Chandler, A. (1991). *Strategic learning in the content areas.* Madison: Wisconsin Department of Public Instruction.

of good and poor readers before, during, and after reading. Good readers have many strengths that prevent them from encountering the pitfalls experienced by less skilled readers. For example, good readers understand the complexities of the reading process. They can identify key ideas from the text they are reading, and they are aware of text structures that can assist their comprehension (e.g., headings, subheadings). Good readers rarely allow themselves to get too lost in the text they are reading. They monitor their comprehension and know how to employ fix-up strategies to get back on track before they have gone too far astray. Good readers tend to have a stronger background knowledge and vocabulary foundation than poor readers have. They have knowledge of and use a variety of reading strategies effectively. They are flexible in adjusting their understanding of the topic to fit in new information.

In contrast to the powerful behaviors of good readers, poor readers have a weak understanding of the variables that are part of the reading process. They struggle to separate important from unimportant information in text. They are often unaware of text structures that could aid their understanding. Even if they do not understand what they are reading, they still continue reading until the end. Completing the task, rather than understanding the text, becomes the primary goal. Finally, poor readers do not

make adjustments in their background knowledge to accommodate the new information they are taking in. Instead, they make adjustments in the information they are absorbing so that it fits with their previous understanding (Deshler, Ellis, & Lenz, 1996).

SOURCES OF COMPREHENSION DIFFICULTIES

Individuals who are strong comprehenders bring rich experience with literacy; strong oral language ability; breadth of background knowledge (including understanding of both high-utility and content-specific vocabulary); accurate, fluent decoding skills; and efficient, active comprehension strategies to their interactions with text (Gambrell, Block, & Pressley, 2002; Shaywitz, 2003). The two essential tools required for good reading comprehension are strong general language comprehension skills and accurate, fluent word-reading skills (Gough, 1996; Torgesen, 1998). Comprehension cannot occur without them.

Dyslexia is a language-based disorder, and some individuals with dyslexia may have more pronounced deficits in language beyond difficulty with written language comprehension. Individual deficits in oral language, syntax, morphology, semantics, pragmatics, and understanding narrative structure will negatively affect reading comprehension for those individuals with more global language impairments (see Chapter 3 for more on the relationship of oral language to literacy).

Many times, however, a dyslexic's difficulty with language is much more apparent at the word-reading level. Individuals may appear to be poor comprehenders when, in reality, their difficulties lie in decoding accuracy and reading fluency (see Chapter 9 for more on this). If an individual has strong listening comprehension skills but stumbles when asked to demonstrate understanding of something read independently, it is often because higher-order thinking and reasoning skills cannot be accessed until the words on the page can be read accurately and fluently. Individuals who are dyslexic must allocate their effort to sound out words strategically at the expense of using that same effort to monitor comprehension strategically (Rose & Dalton, 2002). Pressley stated it succinctly: "If the word-level processes are not mastered (i.e., recognition of most words is not automatic), it will be impossible to carry out the higher order processes that are summarized as reading comprehension strategies" (2000, p. 551).

Another group of individuals is not able to maintain the balance between reading fluency and reading comprehension. They focus too much on the word level and fail to derive meaning from what has been read. When asked what is the most important part of reading, getting all of the words right or understanding what has been read, they answer without hesitation, "Getting all of the words right." They miss the point of reading; they are not always aware of when they become lost in the text; and, if they are aware, they lack the active comprehension strategies needed to get themselves back on track and away from the detour they have taken.

A CONTINUUM OF COMPREHENSION DEVELOPMENT WITHIN A MULTISENSORY TEACHING ENVIRONMENT

There is a continuum of comprehension development beginning at the word level and progressing through increasingly complex units of text. The more students are actively involved in their learning, the more the retention and application of strategies are apparent. Dyslexic students benefit from multisensory learning that captures their attention. Involving at least two or more modalities in teaching simultaneously helps stu-

dents to solidify their grasp of the strategies they are being taught. (See Chapter 2 for further discussion of multisensory teaching.)

When Adams and her colleagues (1998) reviewed research on reading comprehension instruction, they concluded that silent reading and independent seatwork were not nearly as effective as active verbal modeling by the teacher coupled with active, vocal student practice of basic comprehension techniques including summarizing, questioning, and predicting. This model of active involvement by both student and teacher may begin at the earliest levels of instruction.

Aural activities coupled with opportunities for students to articulate the strategies they are using to comprehend text are good ways to begin comprehension instruction. Creating and using visual representations of the organization as well as the content of the text through graphic organizers add yet another modality. As students gain in skill, they can demonstrate their understanding through drawing or writing. Examples of specific strategies to involve students actively as they create meaning from text are woven throughout the rest of this chapter.

BEGINNING COMPREHENSION INSTRUCTION

Planning for instruction must begin with a good assessment (see Chapter 7 for more about evaluation and assessment of reading difficulties). Is a student having difficulty reading the words with accuracy and fluency? How extensive is the student's prior knowledge? Vocabulary? Does the size of the text affect the student's comprehension? Can the student make sense of what he or she reads when only a sentence or a short paragraph is presented? What happens when the individual is asked to retell what he or she has read? Is the student able to make connections between what is known and what is new? Can the individual answer questions whose answers are explicitly stated in the text? Is there evidence of higher level thinking, or is the student bound to the concrete level of understanding? Is there evidence of self-monitoring of comprehension, or is the student merely "word-calling"? Is there any evidence of active repair strategies if something read obviously does not make sense? Is there a difference between the student's silent and oral reading comprehension? What about listening comprehension?

Developing Listening Comprehension Skills

Students who are dyslexic and others who have not yet mastered decoding skills need not wait until they become fluent readers to begin addressing comprehension skills. Instruction can be started early by bypassing reading altogether and focusing instead on an aural level (Williams, 2002).

Kindergarten and even preschool-age children can improve their comprehension performance through experiences that support both oral language and reading skills. If students have adequate listening skills, stories can be read to them and oral discussion can be the mode of instruction. Students can be encouraged to "read" picture books to hone their comprehension skills. Describing the characters and actions in pictures begins the process of comprehension. Students can listen to stories read by older students, parents, teachers, and other adults. At this age, students can participate in analytic conversations in which they practice connecting events in stories with their own experiences. They can learn about predictable story structure and use graphic organizers such as story maps to aid their recall and retelling of stories. They can be engaged in drawing inferences, making predictions, analyzing characters, and following sequences of events. They can be exposed to rich vocabulary within meaningful contexts. Teachers can begin modeling their own thinking at this early level.

Visual presentations (e.g., short films or stories on CD-ROMs coupled with conventional text stories) may entice young children's attention and draw the children more deeply into stories they hear. A word of caution is necessary here, however. Williams warned,

> If our ultimate goal is reading comprehension, we do not want to overemphasize nontext presentation. That would reduce the amount of textual language the children hear, and familiarity with the linguistic features of written language fosters the acquisition of reading comprehension. (2002, p. 136)

Developing Reading Comprehension at the Sentence Level

There are times when decoding and fluency are in place, yet an individual still struggles to gain meaning from the page. Once students have adequate decoding skills to begin to read independently, the unit size of the presentation must be considered. Some students may need to begin at the word level as they develop their understanding of the meanings of single words (see Chapter 13), whereas the sentence level may be the most appropriate starting point for other students.

Carnine, Silbert, and Kame'enui (1990) described a sequence of sentence comprehension activities designed to teach students how to identify what has happened in a sentence, who was involved, when the event occurred, where the event took place, and why the event happened. Use of this strategy can serve as a foundation for comprehension activities using larger chunks of text later.

The question words *who, what, when, where, why,* and *how* are used during this exercise. A prerequisite skill for engaging in this activity is the ability to repeat five- to seven-word statements (e.g., *The girl skipped up the street; The boy jumped over the fence*). If individuals cannot retain the information in a sentence long enough to repeat it, they are unlikely to be able to recall the information needed from those sentences to answer simple questions.

Instruction begins with the introduction of *who* and *what* questions and is followed by extensive practice until the students can answer questions independently:

Teacher	*Students*
1. The teacher models:	
a. "Betty went to school."	
Who went to school? Betty."	
b. "What did Betty do? She went to school."	
2. The teacher provides practice and tests:	
"Listen. The dog ate his food. Say that."	"The dog ate his food."
"Who ate his food?"	"The dog"
"What did the dog do?"	"Ate his food"
3. The teacher repeats Step 2 with more sentences and questions.	

A similar procedure follows for *when* and *where* words:

Teacher	***Students***

1. Teacher models:

   a. "I'll say phrases that tell *when. To-morrow morning* tells *when. Last Friday* tells *when. Before the sun rises* tells when. After breakfast tells *when.*"

   b. "Now I'll say phrases that tell *where. In the backyard* tells *where. At the pool* tells *where. On the sofa* tells *where. Under the bed* tells *where.*"

2. The teacher tests. "I'll say a phrase. You say if it tells *when* or *where.*"

a. "In the backyard"	"Where"
b. "After breakfast"	"When"
c. "Tomorrow morning"	"When"
d. "On the sofa"	"Where"
e. "At the pool"	"Where"
f. "Last Friday"	"When"

Once students can discriminate between *where* and *when* phrases, they are introduced to *where* and *when* questions.

Teacher	***Students***
1. The teacher says, "'Jane played in the backyard yesterday afternoon.' Say the sentence."	"Jane played in the backyard yesterday afternoon."
"Where did Jane play?"	"In the backyard."
"When did Jane play?	"Yesterday afternoon."

A similar procedure is used for modeling answers to *why* and *how* questions. The teacher gives examples using these question words and then provides discrimination practice. Carnine et al. (1990) cautioned against using only predictable words such as *because* in sentences requiring a response to a *why* question because students may fall into the trap of learning a misrule that *because* is the only word that tells *why*. In order to prevent this, teachers are advised to use examples with words such as *to* (He ran *to* catch the bus); *since* (She couldn't buy the toy *since* she lost her money); and, finally, *and* (They stumbled *and* fell).

Once students demonstrate understanding of the application of these important question words at the simple sentence level, students may be asked to respond to multiple sentences, paragraphs, and eventually longer texts.

"GOOD READER" STRATEGIES FOR COMPREHENSION OF LONGER TEXTS

A major goal for teachers of reading is to teach poor readers to use strategies that good readers use spontaneously. Can this be done? Fortunately, the explicit teaching of reading comprehension strategies has been highly effective (Deshler et al., 1996; National Institute of Child Health and Human Development [NICHD], 2000; Sweet & Snow, 2002). It is one thing, however, to be able to demonstrate that a student has mastered the steps to a reading comprehension strategy but quite another to have evidence that use of the strategy has been generalized to daily reading experiences. Students need to know not only how to operationalize the strategies but also why they are learning them and under what conditions they should apply them. Mason and Au (1986) outlined six steps to ensure that comprehension strategies will not only be learned, but also applied.

1. Set the stage by discussing how reading activity changes depending on the purpose for reading and the nature of the text.

2. Explain and model the steps in the strategy. Begin with clear, simple examples.

3. Present more than one situation or one kind of text in which the strategy would be useful.

4. Provide many opportunities for practice, starting with easy examples.

5. Encourage students to think out loud when they use the strategy so that they can correct misunderstandings or mistakes.

6. Have students suggest times and conditions when they would use the strategy on their own. When these occasions arise, remind students to use the strategy.

Choosing Research-Validated Strategies for Comprehension Instruction

Once we have a good picture of what exactly is working and what is not effective when a student reads, the next question is how shall we choose which strategies to teach? How do we know which strategies are truly effective? In 1997 an important step was taken in gathering and disseminating information about the effectiveness of different approaches used to teach children to read. At that time, Congress approached the Director of NICHD at the National Institutes of Health, in consultation with the Secretary of Education, to form a national panel to review research-based knowledge on reading instruction. The result of this collaboration was the *Report of the National Reading Panel* (NRP; NICHD, 2000). One of the research areas the panel chose to evaluate was reading comprehension.

After identifying almost 500 studies on comprehension published since 1970, the NRP (NICHD, 2000) applied a very strict selection process, choosing only those studies that were relevant to instruction of reading or comprehension among typical readers; were published in a scientific journal; had an experiment involving at least one treatment and an appropriate control group; and, if possible, had random assignment of subjects to treatment and control groups. Application of these criteria whittled the number of studies down to about 200. Before conclusions could be drawn about the effectiveness of the strategies selected, the next step for the panel was to select only those studies that had an experimental effect that was "reliable, robust, replicable, and general" (p. 4-42).

The NRP (NICHD, 2000) identified 16 categories of comprehension instruction, 7 of which appear to have a strong scientific basis for concluding that they improve comprehension in typical readers:

- Comprehension monitoring, in which readers learn how to be aware of their level of understanding as they read

- Cooperative learning, in which students work together in pairs or small groups as they learn reading strategies

- Graphic and semantic organizers (including story maps) that help students make graphic representations of the material they are reading in order to bolster comprehension

- Question answering, in which teachers ask questions and students receive immediate feedback about their responses

- Question generation, in which students ask themselves questions to clarify understanding

- Story structure, in which students learn how to use the structure of the text to help them recall content to answer questions about what they have read

- Summarization, to encapsulate and remember important ideas from the text

Many of these strategies have also been included in an eighth category, multiple strategies. In general, the research suggests that teaching a combination of techniques to bolster comprehension works the best (NICHD, 2000). When these seven strategies are used appropriately, they improve recall, question answering, question generation, summarization of text, and, ultimately result in improved performance on standardized comprehension tests.

Although not identified as one of the "super seven" strategy categories, the other eight categories (integrating strategies into the normal curriculum, listening actively, mental imagery, mnemonics [including pictorial aids and key words], building prior knowledge, psycholinguistic strategies relating to learning relevant knowledge about language, teacher preparation to learn effective transactional strategies, and the vocabulary–comprehension relationship) should not be dismissed out of hand. Many were eliminated because there were simply too few studies in a category to make a determination of the scientific merit of the treatment.

Comprehension Monitoring

Comprehension monitoring may be defined as "the active awareness of whether one is understanding or remembering text being processed" (Pressley, Brown, El-Dinary, & Afflerbach, 1995, p. 218). Comprehension monitoring can also be seen as one of the two components of self-regulation as they apply to reading: 1) monitoring and evaluating comprehension and 2) implementing strategies when comprehension breaks down (Klingner, Vaughn, Dimino, Schumm, & Bryant, 2001). The second component may also be looked at as "strategic effort" (RRSG, 2002). The temptation to go on automatic pilot and just read on is very common for nonstrategic, weak readers. They are much less likely to be tuned in to the need for comprehension monitoring than their more able peers (Oakhill & Yuill, 1996).

The goals of comprehension monitoring are to help readers to become aware of whether they are understanding a text as they read and, equally important, to help them identify where their understanding has been blocked. Children as young as first graders can be taught to ask themselves questions as they read and monitor their understanding:

- Does this make sense?

- Do I understand what I am reading?

- What does this have to do with what I already know?

- What will happen next?

If they do encounter blocks to their understanding, readers need to be aware of what cognitive processes are involved in their own reading as they employ fix-up strategies to correct their comprehension difficulties. Teacher modeling of the process readers go through when they struggle to understand words, phrases, clauses, sentences, or longer chunks of text is critical to learning this strategy. Students need to know that even good readers encounter obstacles to their understanding as they read; that it is perfectly acceptable to stop when that occurs; and, most important, that there are effective strategies students can use to bypass those blocks.

Steps readers can take when their comprehension monitoring reveals a roadblock to their understanding include:

- Identifying the difficulty

- Using think-aloud procedures that highlight where and when the difficulty began

- Restating what was read

- Looking back through the text (rereading)

- Looking forward in the text to find information that might help (reading ahead)

When comprehension-monitoring strategies were taught to students in Grades 2–6 in the studies reviewed by the NRP (NICHD, 2000), improved detection of text inconsistencies and memory of the text were noted as compared with the performance of control groups. In addition, students also made gains on standardized reading comprehension tests. Transfer and generalization of this strategy were critical outcomes of instruction.

Cooperative Learning

Diversity in classrooms has been increasing dramatically since the 1990s. In addition to rising numbers of children who come from homes where English is not the first language (Hodgkinson, 1991), more and more children are coming from families below the poverty level (Pallas, Natriello, & McDill, 1989). Also, growing populations of children with handicapping conditions are appearing in general education classrooms. The typical range of academic performance in urban classrooms is 5.4 years (Jenkins, Jewell, Leceister, & Troutner, 1990). Classroom teachers' instructional skills are being challenged as never before as they try to meet the wide range of students' needs. Cooperative or **collaborative learning** is a promising alternative for teaching students with mixed abilities in the same class.

Students involved in clearly defined activities in which students work together to achieve their individual goals are engaged in cooperative learning. A related ap-

proach, collaborative learning, is "learning by working together in small groups, so as to understand new information or to create a common product" (Harris & Hodges, 1995, p. 35). Research has demonstrated growth in elementary school–age children in reading competence when they work collaboratively on structured activities (Greenwood, Delquadri, & Hall, 1989; Rosenshine & Meister, 1994). The benefits of cooperative learning are clear. The creators of the *Collaborative Strategic Reading (CSR)* program noted,

> Cooperative learning fosters the development of higher-level reasoning and problem solving skills. Cooperative learning is effective in diverse classrooms that include a wide range of achievement levels, and has been recommended by experts in the fields of multicultural education, English as a second language (ESL), special education and general education. (Klingner et al., 2001, p. 6)

In addition, the NRP's summary evaluation of cooperative learning stated, "Having peers instruct or interact over the use of reading strategies leads to an increase in the learning of the strategies, promotes intellectual discussion and increases reading comprehension" (NICHD, 2000, p. 4-45). The panel also cited the social benefits of this approach in addition to students' increased control over their own learning.

Collaborative Strategic Reading

The program *From Clunk to Click* is a *CSR* program drawn from original research conducted by Klingner, Vaughn, Hughes, Schumm, and Elbaum (1998). It was designed primarily for students in Grades 3–8 who are in mixed-level classrooms and are reading expository or content-area text drawn from textbooks. Although the program was designed with middle school students in mind, adaptations for high school students are also included in the instructional materials (Klingner & Vaughn, 2000).

Students work together to reach five main goals as they read these content-area selections:

1. Discuss the material.

2. Help each other understand it.

3. Encourage each other to do their best.

4. Learn collaborative skills while mastering content.

5. Learn comprehension strategies that are likely to improve reading comprehension.

Each student must participate with a partner or as part of a small group in a cooperative or collaborative learning environment. Students assume specific, meaningful roles within the group as they work on clearly outlined tasks. In some programs, students may exchange roles as part of their activity. All students contribute to the overall success of the group. In this *CSR* program, at least three roles are essential: Leader, "Clunk" Expert, and "Gist" Expert. Other roles are included in the program, but they may be shared because they require fewer discrete skills: Encourager, Announcer, and Timekeeper. Roles and responsibilities of each member of the group are clearly outlined on cue cards or sheets that can be referred to as needed:

> Leader: Helps the group stay on track and guides them in the use of the four strategies:
>
> - Preview
>
> - Click and clunk

- Get the gist
- Wrap up

Announcer: Makes sure that each member of the group participates by sharing his or her good ideas

Clunk Expert: Helps the group members figure out words they do not understand and helps the group members clarify any misunderstandings they may have

Gist Expert: Works with the group to decide on the best gist (main idea to write in their learning logs for each section of the reading assignment)

Encourager: Watches the group and lets group members know when they are doing something well

Timekeeper: Helps the group complete the reading assignment in a timely manner

Each member of the group has a cue sheet. These sheets have scripted dialogue to help students know what to say as they assume their roles. Descriptions of extensive practice activities including question stems, question types (see the description of the *Question-Answer Relationships* strategy later in this chapter), time allotment sheets, learning logs, and graphic organizers are included in the manual for the program.

This *CSR* program's plan for strategic reading includes three phases of activity: before reading, during reading, and after reading. Before reading, students preview by brainstorming what they already know about the topic and predicting what they will learn about the topic when they read the passage.

During reading, students identify and repair "clunks" (parts of text that were hard to understand, including challenging vocabulary). See Figure 14.1 for a sample cue sheet for the Clunk Expert that includes examples of fix-up strategies. Students also work at getting the gist of the text during reading. They identify the most important person, place, or thing in the section they are reading and then identify the most important idea about that person, place, or thing.

After reading, students wrap up. They identify what questions will check their understanding of the most important information in the passage and then determine if they can answer those questions. Finally, they review what they have learned.

Research evaluating the effectiveness of *CSR*, most of which was conducted after the NRP (NICHD, 2000) review, has been very promising. For example, when middle school students in Grades 4 and 6 engaged in *CSR* activities were compared with others in a control group, *CSR* students outperformed the controls on standardized comprehension tests. Even more encouraging was the finding that low-achieving students showed the greatest gains (Klingner et al., 2001). Another study showed gains in vocabulary knowledge based on text read by English language learners engaged in *CSR* (Klingner & Vaughn, 2000).

Peer-Assisted Learning Strategies

Another popular cooperative learning strategy with a strong research base behind it is *Peer Assisted Learning Strategies (PALS)*. Although it was originally designed to work in classrooms for Grades 2–6, a kindergarten and high school version of the strategy have been added (Fuchs et al., 2001).

In the original model, teachers implement three 35-minute *PALS* sessions each week. Students are paired by the teacher so that a higher- and a lower-performing student work together. The teacher splits the class in half and pairs the highest performer

---

Clunk Expert's Cue Sheet

1. What is your clunk?

2. Does anyone know the meaning of the clunk?

   YES
   - Announcer, please call on someone with their hand raised.
   - Ask them to explain how they figured out the clunk.
   - Everyone, write the meaning in your Learning Log.

   NO
   - If NO, follow these steps until you know the meaning of the clunk and are ready to write it in your Learning Log.

     STEP 1: Read the sentence with the clunk and look for key ideas to help you figure out the word. Think about what makes sense.

     Raise your hand if you can explain the meaning of the clunk.
     (If NO, go to STEP 2)

     STEP 2: Reread the sentence with the clunk and the sentences before and after the clunk looking for clues.

     Raise your hand if you can explain the meaning of the clunk.
     (If NO, go to STEP 3)

     STEP 3: Look for a prefix or suffix in the word that might help.

     Raise your hand if you can explain the meaning of the clunk.
     (If NO, go to STEP 4)

     STEP 4: Break the word apart and look for smaller words that you know.

     Raise your hand if you can explain the meaning of the clunk.
     (If NO, go to STEP 5.)

     STEP 5: Ask the teacher for help.

Figure 14.1. Clunk Expert's cue sheet. (From Klingner, J.K., Vaughn, S., Dimino, J., Schumm, J.S., & Bryant, D. [2001]. *From clunk to click: Collaborative strategic reading* [p. 91]. Longmont, CO: Sopris West; reprinted by permission of Sopris West Educational Services; *Collaborative Strategic Reading*, copyright 2001.)

in the top half of the class with the highest performer in the bottom of the class and so forth. *PALS* sessions are quite structured and include frequent verbal interaction and feedback between tutor and tutee.

An exchange of roles within the pairs is built in so that each student has the opportunity to assume the role of both tutor and tutee during each session. It is important to note, however, that the higher-performing student in each pair reads first for each activity, serving as a model for the lower-performing reader. Material chosen for reading is literature that is appropriate for the lower-performing reader. Each 35-minute session is divided into three 10-minute segments for Partner Reading, Paragraph Shrinking, and Prediction Relay, plus an additional 2 minutes are used for a retelling activity that follows partner reading. The remaining time is used for setting up and putting away materials during transitions.

The goal of Partner Reading is to improve reading accuracy and fluency (Simmons, Fuchs, Fuchs, Hodge, & Mathes, 1994). In Paragraph Shrinking, students develop comprehension through summarization and main idea identification (Doctorow, Wittrock, & Marks, 1978; Palincsar & Brown, 1984). In Prediction Relay, students practice formulating expectations about what is likely to follow in their reading. Students who practice making predictions have been shown to improve in reading comprehension (Palincsar & Brown, 1984).

Pairs of students are assigned to one of two teams. They earn points from the teacher for being engaged in their reading activities and helping their partners in a constructive and collaborative manner. Each student acting as the tutor also awards points as activities are completed successfully. Point cards represent joint effort, progress, and achievement. At the end of each week, the points are tallied for each team and the winning team is announced and cheered for. Students are assigned to new pairs and new teams every 4 weeks.

Careful training is required to make *PALS* work in classrooms. Teachers are expected to model key procedures and allow students to role-play them. It usually takes about seven 45-minute sessions for teachers to train their students. The first session is a general orientation in which students learn how set up materials, be a helpful partner, use a scorecard, and report points. After this first orientation session, each of the three reading activities takes about two 45-minute sessions to teach. Teachers are encouraged to teach one *PALS* activity at a time, taking at least a week to practice an activity before introducing a new one.

PALS has been approved by the U.S. Department of Education's Program Effectiveness Panel for inclusion in the National Diffusion Network of effective educational practices. Research conducted in second- through sixth-grade classes where *PALS* has been implemented has shown an enhancement of reading development in low- and typically achieving students as well as students with learning disabilities (Fuchs, Fuchs, Mathes, & Simmons, 1997; Simmons et al., 1994).

Cue cards that may be used by reading partners are found in Figure 14.2. The content of *PALS* reading activities proceed as follows.

Partner Reading The Partner Reading activity is designed to increase students' reading fluency. Beginning with the stronger reader, each student reads connected text

---

Prompt Card 1: Retell

1. What did you learn first?
2. What did you learn next?

Prompt Card 2: Paragraph Shrinking

1. Name the who or what.
2. Tell the most important thing about the who or what.
3. Say the main idea in 10 words or less.

Prompt Card 3: Prediction Relay

Predict _____ What do you predict will happen next?
Read _____ Read half a page.
Check _____ Did the prediction come true?

Figure 14.2. Partner reading question cards from *Peer Assisted Learning Strategy (PALS).* (From Fuchs, D., Mathes, P.G., & Fuchs, L.S. [2001]. *Peer-assisted learning strategies: Reading methods for Grades 2-6* [teacher manual, pp. A26–A27]. Nashville: Vanderbilt University; adapted by permission.)

aloud for 5 minutes, for a total of 10 minutes. Students are given guidance about how to identify and correct word-recognition errors as they occur.

Retelling After partner reading by both students, the lower-performing reader retells in sequence what has been read. Prompts from the student tutor (the higher-performing reader) during this 2-minute retelling include questions such as, "What did you learn first?" and "What did you learn next?" If the weaker reader has difficulty remembering the next piece of information or struggles with sequence, the tutor can provide help and retelling continues.

Paragraph Shrinking The Paragraph Shrinking activity is designed to develop comprehension through identification and summarization of the main idea. Unlike partner reading, both readers read new text during this activity. Beginning with the stronger reader, the partners alternate reading one paragraph at a time for five minutes, stopping after each paragraph to identify the main idea in 10 words or fewer. The tutor must make a judgment about whether the main idea is correct as stated. Errors trigger a supportive response by the tutor ("That's not quite right. Skim the paragraph and try again") If the reader is still incorrect, the tutor supplies the answer.

Prediction Relay The Prediction Relay activity requires students to think ahead because it extends paragraph shrinking to larger chunks of connected text. There are five steps in this activity. In each step the reader has a specific job:

1. Predict what will be learned on a half-page of text.

2. Read the half-page out loud.

3. Confirm or refute the prediction.

4. Summarize the half-page in 10 words or fewer.

5. Make a new prediction about the next half-page.

Graphic and Semantic Organizers

A graphic or semantic organizer is a visual representation of knowledge. Essentially it is a diagram or picture that structures information to demonstrate relationships. It has been used effectively for a wide range of purposes, including the following:

- Generating lists of character traits with supporting evidence within narrative text (see Figure 14.3 for an example of a character map)

- Deepening understanding of unfamiliar vocabulary (see Figure 14.4 for an example and also Chapter 13 for more on vocabulary word study)

- Depicting relationships in expository texts in social studies or science (see Figure 14.5 for an example of an animal map)

- Activating background knowledge and setting a purpose for reading (see Figure 14.6)

- Helping students to see the text structure of stories, which can enhance students' ability to retell stories they have heard or read themselves (see Figure 14.9 on p. 402)

The NRP, in its review of research on graphic or semantic organizers, cited three important uses for these visual cues: "(1) help students focus on text structure while reading, (2) provide tools to examine and visually represent textual relationships, and (3) assist in writing well-organized summaries" (NICHD, 2000, p. 4-73).

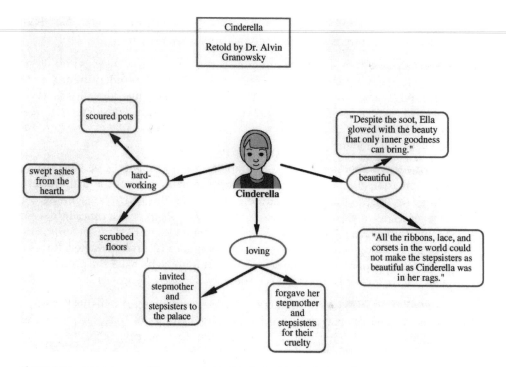

Figure 14.3. Character map. (Diagram created in Kidspiration® by Inspiration Software®, Inc.) (Text of story from *That awful Cinderella,* © 1993, Steck-Vaughn. All Rights Reserved. Used with permission of Harcourt Achieve.)

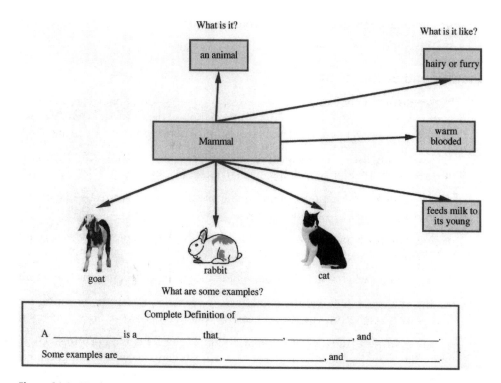

Figure 14.4. Word structure map. (Diagram created in Kidspiration® by Inspiration Software®, Inc.)

The most robust finding of the studies reviewed by the NRP (NICHD, 2000) was that the use of graphic organizers can facilitate memory of the content of what has been read for many students. This may be the result of having a means to retrieve information in a more organized manner because clear relationships between concepts or events are displayed visually. This may also generalize to better comprehension and achievement, particularly in content-area instruction.

Pearson and Johnson talked about comprehension as the process of "building bridges between the new and the known" (1978, p. 24). If a reader has some accurate and appropriate knowledge of the topic, that building can be accomplished more easily. One comprehension strategy using a structured graphic organizer, *K-W-L*, has facilitated that process for many struggling readers.

K-W-L (Ogle, 1986) and *K-W-L Plus* (Carr & Ogle, 1987) are procedures that have been used to help both elementary and secondary students to become more active readers of expository text. The two strategies are essentially the same except that in *K-W-L Plus*, semantic mapping and written summaries have been added to the three basic *K-W-L* steps.

K-W-L stands for three basic cognitive steps that are often particularly challenging to students with learning disabilities but that are essential to reading comprehension:

K   Accessing what I already **K**now about the topic (activating prior knowledge)

W   Deciding what I **W**ant to learn (setting a purpose for reading, including deciding what categories of information or ideas are likely to be discovered)

L   Recalling what I **L**earned as a result of my reading (including integrating that new information with what I already know)

The teacher plays a critical role in students' mastering this strategy by acting as both a guide and model for the think-aloud strategies that are essential for *K-W-L*'s implementation.

Step K—What I Know   There are two parts to this step. First, the teacher selects a central idea or concept of the text the students are about to read. Next, the students list as many words or phrases as they can associate with the concept. Either the teacher or individual students may record the results of this brainstorming. In order to deepen the thinking of the students, the teacher may ask, "Where did you learn that?" or "How do you know that?" Students may share information they have learned through personal experience, books they have read or listened to, television, films, videotapes, computer software, or other sources. It is important for students to be aware that they can turn to many places to broaden their background knowledge.

For the second part of the first step, the teacher cognitively models or thinks aloud the process of classifying pieces of information and then labeling the resulting categories. Figure 14.6 shows an example of a Brainstorming Map about pandas that was created with Kidspiration software (Inspiration Software, Inc.). The information collected has been categorized by creating a question for each set of grouped facts. For example, *bamboo and sometimes meat, flowers* follow the question, "What do they eat?"

Step W—What I Want to Learn   During this step, students set their purpose for reading. They generate questions they want to have answered by reading the text. Sometimes these questions grow out of the brainstorming. Sometimes they arise because of conflicting information supplied by the students that needs to be sorted out or clarified. Questions can also be added as the students begin to read.

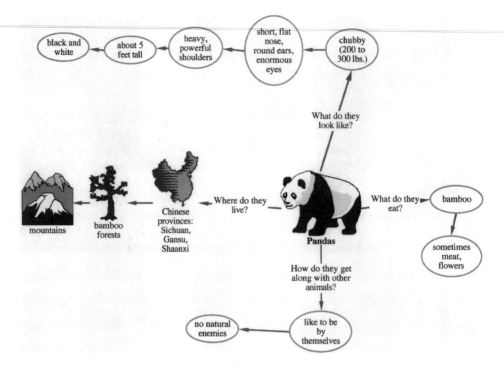

Figure 14.5. Brainstorming map. (Diagram created in Kidspiration® by Inspiration Software®, Inc.)

Step L—What I Learned   As students read, they record new information in this last step. They and the teacher review the questions generated in Step W to see if they have been answered by their reading. Questions that have not been answered may be highlighted for further study. If there was any disagreement at the beginning over conflicting information supplied by students, there should be discussion to see if those conflicts have been resolved by reading. If questions have not been answered, and if conflicts have not been resolved, teachers and students together should discuss other resources that could be consulted.

The "Categories of information we expect to use" section of the *K-W-L* Strategy Sheet (Ogle, 1986; see Figure 14.3) is particularly useful for creating written summaries or expanded writing about the topic at hand. For example, when reading a text about an animal, some of the expected categories might be *appearance, habitat, food,* and *behavior.* If the topic is a person, categories might include information about *birth, childhood, family influences, education, pivotal life events, important contributions,* and *death.* Each category of information can represent a new paragraph.

Generating these categories very early in the *K-W-L* procedure helps students to select and organize information for their writing. Ogle suggests discussing with students how the results of their brainstorming could help them to generate categories. For example, in the brainstorming graphic organizer about pandas (see Figure 14.6) student attention could be brought to the fact that many of the terms relate to the way pandas look. The name of a category they can expect to use, therefore, might be *appearance.* That category would then be written on the bottom of the *K-W-L* Strategy Sheet (Ogle, 1986; see Figure 14.3).

KWL Strategy Sheet

1. K—What we know	W—What we want to find out	L—What we learned and still need to learn

2. Categories of information we expect to use
    A.
    B.
    C.
    D.
	E.
	F.
	G.	

Figure 14.6.   K-W-L Strategy Sheet. (From Ogle, D.M. [1986, February]. K-W-L: A teaching model that develops active reading of expository text. *The Reading Teacher, 39,* 565; reprinted by permission.)

The results of research on *K-W-L* and *K-W-L Plus* conducted by Carr and Dewitz (1988) indicate that these strategies are effective in helping students learn new social studies content, develop both literal and inferential comprehension, and improve their summary-writing skills.

The NRP's (NICHD, 2000) summary evaluation of graphic and semantic organizer instruction noted students' improvements in remembering what they read after they used this strategy. The panel also suggested that "this may transfer, in general, to better comprehension and achievement in Social Studies and Science content areas" (p. 4-45).

Question Answering

Good readers ask themselves questions before, during, and after reading. Yet, many students do not self-question spontaneously. They need to have good models of questioning during all three periods of the reading process to have impact on their comprehension. Results of the NRP's (NICHD, 2000) review of research on questioning confirmed that teaching question-answering strategies can improve student performance in this area. Teaching these strategies before, during, and after reading can have a positive effect on students' comprehension of text.

Before Reading

Teacher questions before reading can help teachers to evaluate (and if necessary supplement and/or modify) students' prior knowledge about a topic. The *K* segment of the *K-W-L* strategy outlined previously, for example, functions well in this role. Activating prior knowledge and then organizing it into schema can integrate learning more readily into an already existing framework. Asking predictive questions before reading also helps to set readers' purposes for reading and can improve motivation to read. Forming hypotheses about what will happen next has been shown to aid comprehension (Hammond, 1983).

During Reading

Teachers asking questions during reading can help their students to direct their attention to important sections of the text, monitor their comprehension and serve as a catalyst to get them to activate fix-up strategies when comprehension is blocked (see the previous discussions of comprehension monitoring and the *CSR* program for more on this).

After Reading

Questions asked after reading can encourage students to reprocess what they have read, thereby creating new associations as they review information.

If students are to learn to be good self-questioners, they need to see their teachers as strong models. Although teachers may ask a question or two before reading to motivate students' interest, questioning by the teacher often functions primarily as an evaluative activity following reading (Durkin, 1979). Questions can have a more far-reaching effect, however, if they are used to teach more than to test. Quality of questions asked, feedback given to student responses, and instruction in how to answer challenging questions are critical to the success of this process.

Obviously, attention must be paid to the quality of questions teachers ask. Yet, when researchers have looked at this area, the findings have been dismal. For example, Guszak (1967) observed that about 70% of the questions teachers asked were literal and required only recognition (locating information in the text) or recall (answering from memory) of factual information. Worse yet, the majority of the questions asked neglected literal understanding of essential information presented in stories (e.g., characters, plot, sequence of critical events) in favor of "trivial factual makeup of stories" (p. 233).

Although the need to ask students text-related questions that tap both literal and inferential comprehension is important, questions that extend the discussion beyond the text should also be posed. Unfortunately, however, many struggling readers are unsure of what to do if answers to questions are not immediately obvious. Raphael (1982) found that students did not employ effective strategies when reading and answering questions. Instead of applying specific strategies to meet the demands of different kinds of questions, she found that many readers' approaches to question-answering fell into two broad categories: 1) They overrelied on the content of the text and neglected their own background knowledge, or 2) they ignored the text and answered questions only from their prior experiences. It is obvious that applying either of these approaches exclusively negatively affects question-answering skill.

Categorizing Questions to Aid Comprehension

Learning how to categorize questions into those that can be answered by referring back to the text and those that require higher level thinking based on personal knowledge can be an effective strategy to improve question-answering performance. Pearson and Johnson (1978) created a model to describe three different types of questions that teachers can ask to help their students to develop both text-related (literal and inferential comprehension) and beyond-text (critical analysis, interpretation, generalization, and extension of ideas from the text) comprehension skills:

1. *Text explicit:* The answer to this type of question can be cleanly lifted verbatim from the text.

2. *Text implicit:* Rather than being explicitly stated, the answers to these questions are suggested in the text. It may be necessary to gather information from several sentences or integrate information from larger sections of text in order to answer this type of question.

3. *Script implicit:* The reader's background knowledge, rather than information from the text, is required to answer this kind of question.

There is a relationship between children's recall of passages they have read and the types of questions they have been asked. If they are asked text-explicit questions, they recall parts of the text verbatim. If they are asked text-implicit questions, they tend to draw more inferences from text. If they are asked script-implicit questions they make more interpretive and evaluative connections between their own prior knowledge and new information from their readings (Wixson, 1983). If we want children to be able to respond to a variety of question levels, we must give them opportunities to observe good models and practice extensively.

Question-Answer Relationships

Raphael and her colleagues (Raphael, 1982, 1984, 1986) designed an instructional program, *Question-Answer Relationships (QAR),* that is based on Pearson and Johnson's (1978) taxonomy. The program was designed to help students to label the type of questions being asked and then, as they considered both the text and their prior knowledge before they answered a question, use this information to assist them in formulating answers.

Two major categories of relationships are taught: *In the Book* and *In My Head.* Readers must refer back to the text to answer *In the Book* questions, but in order to respond to *In My Head* questions correctly, looking back at the text will not give students the answers they seek. At least some reference to prior knowledge is required in order to answer this type of question adequately.

Each of these two primary *QAR* categories is then divided into two subcategories. Within the *In the Book* group, two kinds of questions may be found: *Right There* and *Think and Search* (also called *Putting It Together*). There is one primary difference between *Right There* and *Think and Search* questions. Although the answers for both categories of questions may be found in the text, the answers for *Right There* questions are found in one sentence. In addition, many of the same words used in the question are also in the answer. For example, in a passage about Harriet Tubman, these sentences might be found:

> Harriet Tubman was a nurse and a spy for the Union Army during the Civil War. When the War ended she continued to help people. Harriet worked to raise money for schools for black children. She also worked for funds to establish a home for old black people. Five years before she died, she established the Harriet Tubman home in Auburn, New York for poor, elderly black people.

A *Right There* question about this passage might be "What kind of work did Harriet Tubman do during the Civil War?" The answer, "Harriet Tubman was a nurse and a spy for the Union Army during the Civil War," can be lifted from one sentence and uses many of the same words as the question.

In contrast, a *Think and Search* question might be "How did Harriet Tubman help black people before and after the Civil War?" The answer might be, "Harriet Tubman helped black people before the Civil War by being a nurse and a spy for the Union Army. After the war she continued to help by raising money for schools for black chil-

dren and a home for old black people." The answer, although clearly in the book, requires a bit more work. The reader needs to put together information found in several sentences in order to answer.

Turning to the *In My Head* broad category, there are also two subcategories: *Author and You* and *On My Own*. The main difference between these two is whether the reader must read the text for the questions to make sense (Raphael, 1986). If it is necessary for the reader to connect his or her background knowledge with the information in the text in order to answer the question, then the question fits into the *Author and You* category. For example, the question "Why was Harriet Tubman a spy for the Union Army even though she was born a Southerner?" requires that readers know at least two things:

1. The fact that Harriet was a black woman who was born a slave in the South (drawn from the text)

2. The conditions black slaves lived under in the South during the Civil War period (drawn from the reader's background knowledge)

Neither piece of information is sufficient alone to answer the question. The reader needs to integrate those two facts in order to formulate a reasonable answer to the question. As a result, this must be categorized as an *Author and You* question.

Referring once again to the text about Harriet Tubman, two examples of *On Your Own* questions might be:

Why was the Civil War fought?

How were black children educated before the Civil War?

In both cases, the author has not given the information needed in order to answer the question. The reader needs to either have the prior knowledge necessary to answer it or has to look to another source to find it.

The general sequence of procedures for teaching the *QAR* strategy are as follows:

*   The teacher introduces the concept of the *QAR* strategy with the two broad categories (*In the Book* and *In My Head*).

*   The teacher demonstrates the *QAR* strategy with several short passages by modeling the thinking behind each label.

*   The teacher gives students the text, questions, answers, and *QAR* label for each question. The students now supply the reason for the label.

*   The teacher gives the text, questions, and answers, and the students provide both the *QAR* label and the reason for the label.

*   The teacher gives students the text and questions, and the students supply the answers, the *QAR* labels, and the reasons for the labels.

At the beginning, the teacher needs to provide much modeling and immediate feedback as students begin to assume responsibility for labeling the relationships. Students progress from shorter to longer texts and build independence by moving from group to independent activities. After the two broad *QAR* categories have been mastered, the teacher repeats the teaching sequence with the two subcategories under each: *Right There* and *Think and Search* for *In the Book* questions, and *Author and You* and *On My Own* for *In My Head* questions. (See Figure 14.7 for an illustration of the cue card used to explain the *QAR* strategy to students.)

In the Book QARs

Right There
The answer is in the text, usually easy to find. The words used to make up the question and words used to answer the question are **Right There** in the same sentence.

In My Head QARs

Author and You
The answer is *not* in the story. You need to think about what you already know, what the author tells you in the text, and how it fits together.

Think and Search
(Putting It Together)
The answer is in the story, but you need to put together different story parts to find it. Words for the question and words for the answer are not found in the same sentence. They come from different parts of the text.

On My Own
The answer is not in the story. You can even answer the question without reading the story. You need to use your own experience.

Figure 14.7. Illustrations to explain Question-Answer Relationships (QARs) to students. (From Raphael, T.E. [1986]. Teaching question answer relationships, revisited. *The Reading Teacher, 39*(6), 519; copyright © 1986 by International Reading Association; reprinted by permission.)

The most important things about the *QAR* strategy are not only that students learn to identify different categories of questions but that also they use this information as a signal to try different strategies to answer those questions. Students become active learners who come to value both their own prior knowledge about a topic and the information the author of the text has presented to them.

After reviewing 17 studies on question-answering instruction, the NRP (NICHD, 2000) noted student improvement both in answering questions after reading passages and in strategies of finding answers.

Question Generation

The NRP's review of the research found "the strongest scientific evidence . . . for the effectiveness of asking readers to generate questions during reading" (NICHD, 2000, p. 4-45). It has the strongest evidence for a single reading comprehension strategy among the seven listed. An eighth, that combines several strategies, including self-questioning, is also promising for struggling readers. Self-questioning has been demonstrated to distinguish effective readers and learners from those who have more difficulty with reading (Bransford et al., 1982; Cote & Goldman, 1999).

Strickland, Ganske, and Monroe stated, "Readers who don't think while they read do not generate questions. . . . The most direct and effective way for teachers to help stu-

dents do this is by demonstrating self-questioning through think-alouds" (2002, p. 162). Opening a window for students onto the kind of self-questioning good readers do as they read can in fact be a powerful strategy, but there are other more systematic, explicit methods (e.g., the *ReQuest* strategy) that can also be used to promote students to begin to interrogate the text.

As early as 1969, Manzo demonstrated that students could be taught to create their own questions. His technique, *ReQuest,* was designed to "improve the student's reading comprehension by providing an active learning situation for the development of questioning behaviors" (p. 123). *ReQuest* can be used with either narrative or expository text and is effective in jump-starting students on the road to active comprehension. It makes heavy use of modeling, an important feature of cognitive behavior modification. *ReQuest* has been shown to be particularly effective in helping students to focus their attention on the text and pay attention to detail.

ReQuest follows a simple sequence:

1. *Silent reading:* The students and the teacher silently read a common segment of text (1–2 sentences to 1–2 paragraphs).

2. *Student questioning:* The teacher closes the book, and students ask him or her as many questions as possible. The teacher models appropriate answers and also provides substantial feedback to students about the questions they generate. Students are asked to "try to ask the kinds of questions a teacher might ask in the way a teacher might ask them" (Manzo, 1969, p. 124).

3. *Teacher questioning:* The students close their books, and the teacher asks the questions. The teacher helps students to sharpen their questions by modeling good questioning behavior that includes a range of question types (see the previous discussion of QAR for ideas).

4. *Repetition of sequence:* When questions are exhausted, the students and the teacher read the next segment of text and repeat the procedure. New sections of the text should be integrated with old sections. Questions may relate to new and old sections.

5. *Predictions:* When enough text has been processed for the students to make predictions about the remainder of the text, the exchange of questions stops. The teacher asks predictive questions ("What do you think the rest of the story will be about? Why do you think so?")

6. *Reading:* The teacher and the students read to the end of the passage, verifying and discussing predictions made.

ReQuest was first tested under clinical conditions with students receiving one-to-one remedial instruction, but both Manzo (1969; Manzo & Manzo, 1993) and others (Mason & Au, 1986) have supported its effectiveness when it is used with larger groups. In order to encourage students to generalize questioning to other situations, Bos and Vaughn (1998) advise cuing students to remember to stop while reading and ask themselves questions as they did during *ReQuest.*

In its summary evaluation of question generation, the NRP (NICHD, 2000) cited significant scientific evidence that instruction on question generation during reading improves reading comprehension in terms of memory and answering questions based on text as well as integrating and identifying main ideas through summarizing. The panel recommended this strategy as part of a multiple-strategy instruction program. (The use of multiple strategies is discussed later in this chapter.)

Story Structure

The bulk of texts used in elementary school reading are stories. Story structure pertains to how stories and their plots are organized into a predictable format that includes characters, setting, problem, goal, action, and outcome (or resolution of the problem). When students are taught about story structure, they have an easier time retelling stories within a logical framework. They also show improvements in asking and answering *who, what, when, where, why,* and *how* questions about the story (NICHD, 2000).

Lorna Idol (1987) developed a simple story map with a visual representation of story components and their relationship to one another (see Figure 14.9 on p. 402). She offered one straightforward approach for presenting story mapping in a classroom:

1. *Model:* After introducing the purpose of the strategy, the teacher presents the story elements that are on the story map. The teacher reads a story out loud and stops periodically when story elements are presented in the text. If certain story elements are not presented explicitly, the teacher needs to model the thinking required to generate the inferences. Students label the parts and write them in the appropriate places on the story map.

2. *Lead:* Students read the story and complete their story maps independently. The teacher gives students feedback about their maps and encourages them to add details they may have omitted.

3. *Test:* Students read a story, generate a story map, and then answer questions that relate to the story elements on the map (e.g., *Who are the characters in the story? Where did the story take place? What was the main problem in the story?*).

Four optional supports to the story mapping strategy may be helpful for some students. These additions to classic story structure instruction may facilitate recall of story elements for students and spur more active reading of text.

In the first modification, students who have difficulty remembering story elements may use a "five finger retelling" (Stahl, 2004). In this strategy, each finger is used as a reminder or prompt for an element in story structure: characters, setting, problem, plot, and resolution/solution. A chart may serve as an additional reminder of these elements.

For a second modification using the elements from the story map, Bos (1987) proposed a mnemonic, STORE, to help students to retell the story. See Figure 14.8 for a cue card for this story retelling strategy.

Story-Retelling Strategy

Setting:	Who, What, When, Where
Trouble:	What is the trouble/problem to be solved?
Order of Action:	What happened to solve the problem? (correct/logical order)
Resolution:	What was the outcome (resolution) for each action?
End:	What happened in the end?

Figure 14.8. Story-retelling strategy. (From Bos, C.S. [1987]. *Promoting story comprehension using a story retelling strategy.* Paper presented at the Teachers Applying Whole Language Conference, Tucson, AZ.)

Simple Story Map

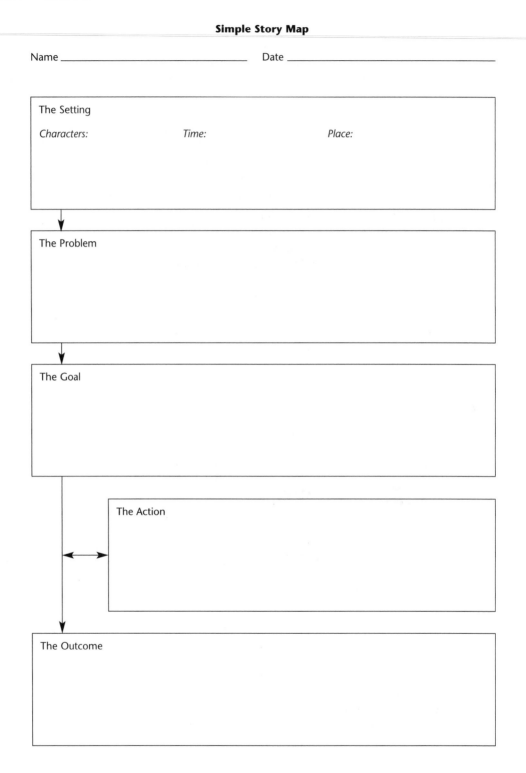

Name _____   Date _____

The Setting

Characters: *Time:*   *Place:*

The Problem

The Goal

The Action

The Outcome

Figure 14.9.   Simple story map. (From Idol, L. [1987]. Group story mapping: A comprehension strategy for both skilled and unskilled readers. *Journal of Learning Disabilities, 20,* 199; copyright © 1987 by PRO-ED, Inc.; reprinted by permission.)

For a third option, the Language Circle (see Appendix B) created a set of story elements on Post-it notes. Students can use the Post-it notes to flag the elements of the story as they read.

According to the NRP (NICHD, 2000) report, instruction in story structure improves students' ability to understand stories, answer questions about them, and remember what was read. The weakest readers benefit the most from this strategy, although even strong readers improve their performance after instruction.

Summarization

In order to summarize, students must orchestrate three important tasks (NICHD, 2000, p. 4-92):

1. Decide what are "the most central and important ideas in the text"

2. "Generalize from examples or from things that are repeated"

3. "Ignore irrelevant details"

Researchers who have studied the behaviors of students with learning difficulties have long been aware that these tasks are particularly challenging for these students (Brown & Palincsar, 1982; Graves, 1986; McCormick, 1992; Wong, 1979).

The University of Kansas Center for Research on Learning (Schumaker, Denton, & Deshler, 1984) developed the RAP Paraphrasing Strategy,[1] which helps students to bypass these difficulties and improve their ability to recall the main ideas and important facts from text they have read. The RAP Paraphrasing Strategy has three specific steps (1984, p. 66):

1. **R**ead a paragraph.
2. **A**sk yourself, "What were the main idea and details in this paragraph?"
3. **P**ut the main idea and details into your own words.

The teacher begins by describing the rationale for learning RAP. If students learn to put information into their own words, they will more likely think about what they have read and understand and remember it. Next, the general conditions under which the strategy may be used are noted. Students will be able to use the strategy any time they are reading something in paragraph form that they want to understand and remember. Finally, the teacher shares the positive results that students can expect after learning and applying the strategy.

Next, the teacher describes the three steps of the strategy. As students do Step 1, "Read a paragraph," the teacher reminds them to think about what the words they are reading mean. As students do Step 2, "Ask yourself, 'What were the main idea and details in this paragraph?,'" they are guided to look back over the paragraph quickly to

---

[1]The steps of the remembering system for the Paraphrasing Strategy listed on this page are part of an instructional program developed and researched at the University of Kansas Center for Research on Learning (Schumaker, Denton, & Deshler, 1984). This remembering system is used to cue strategic thinking. Each step involves a variety of strategic questions and prompts that are described in step-by-step detail in written materials that can only be obtained as part of guided professional development experiences that are offered throughout the nation and are designed to ensure high-quality implementation with students. This program is one of several research-based programs designed for teachers to use as they teach learning strategies to students. For information, go to http://www.kucrl.org.

find the main idea and details. The teacher reminds them that the first or last sentence, key vocabulary, and repetitions of the same word or words in the whole paragraph often give hints about the main idea. Important details are related to that main idea. The teacher then describes how to locate the main idea.

Throughout the description of the strategy, students are reminded of certain requirements of each paraphrased statement (Schumaker et al., 1984).

- It must contain a complete thought, with a subject and a verb.

- It must be totally accurate.

- It must have new information and must not be a repetition of something that was already said.

- It must make sense.

- It must contain useful information.

- It must be in the students' own words.

- Only one general statement per paragraph is permitted.

As students continue to learn the strategy, modeling by the teacher (and by students); verbal practice; controlled practice with short, simple passages; advanced practice; and generalization become integral parts of the instruction.

The NRP's (NICHD, 2000) final evaluation of summarization as a targeted strategy was quite positive. The panel noted that this is a sound method for connecting ideas and making generalizations from text. Other benefits were also listed for summarization, including improving memory of what is read, both for free recall and for answering questions. This strategy has been incorporated successfully into other multiple-strategy interventions, most notably reciprocal teaching (discussed next). In addition, *PALS* and *CSR*, both described previously, include a summarization step in their approaches.

Multiple Strategies

Although research on individual reading strategies has yielded many positive results, these strategies may even be more powerful when they are combined into a multiple strategy instructional program. "This method finds considerable scientific support for its effectiveness, and it is the most promising for use in classroom instruction where teachers and readers interact over texts" (NICHD, 2000, p. 4-46).

Probably the most well-known method for teaching multiple comprehension strategies is reciprocal teaching (Palincsar & Brown, 1984). This approach combines several of the most effective comprehension strategies reviewed by the NRP (NICHD, 2000): prediction, questioning, seeking clarification when comprehension monitoring reveals confusion, and summarization.

As a reciprocal teaching lesson begins, the teacher explains the purpose of the work the students and teacher will do together and describes the four strategies they will be using in the lesson. The teacher models the activity, and the students try to emulate the process. Throughout the lesson, the teacher provides corrective feedback so that students have ample opportunity to be supported in their steps to independence. Students silently read passages that are appropriate to their age and ability. Very young children (or very weak readers) may have passages read aloud to them. After a passage has been read, children are asked to state the topic and summarize the important information they have read.

The teacher always models the reciprocal teaching procedure first, but eventually a student is chosen to act as the teacher and asks an important question about the passage that was just read. Next, he or she will summarize, making a prediction and, if necessary, asking for clarification of confusing terms or concepts. The teacher provides support during this process by prompting students to guide them in the right direction, instructing (reminding them about the important steps to the procedure if they have forgotten), modifying the activity for students who appear to be stuck, or asking for other students to step in and help.

Carlisle and Rice (2002) caution practitioners to make sure that sufficient time is devoted to the instructional process in reciprocal teaching, that they allow adequate chances for students to practice the strategies, and that they provide continued guidance and support for students to reach independent application of the embedded strategies. Rosenshine and Meister's (1994) review of the research on reciprocal teaching concluded that more time should be spent teaching the individual strategies directly before beginning the more interactive segment of the technique.

Project WebSIGHT, a joint project of the Miami-Dade County Public Schools, the University of Miami, and the Florida Department of Education, has designed a teacher education course incorporating the Internet to bring recommended teaching practices to Florida schools. The project provides support materials for reciprocal teaching lessons on its web site (http://www.miamisci.org/tec). Lesson plans and instructional materials, including student cue cards and bookmarks, may be found on the site.

Reciprocal teaching is similar to *CSR*, a cooperative learning strategy discussed previously. Klingner et al. (2001) acknowledged that *CSR* is an outgrowth of reciprocal teaching and, in fact, used reciprocal teaching in their earlier work (Klingner & Vaughn, 1996). After adopting many changes to reciprocal teaching over time, they felt that they had created a substantially different approach that deserved its own name (Klingner et al., 2001). An outline of the differences the authors cited between *CSR* and reciprocal teaching may be found in Table 14.2.

Other Promising Strategies

Experimental research examining various approaches to instruction is relatively new. As a result, there are other reading comprehension strategies that have not yet been confirmed by pretest–posttest control-group studies even though initial, limited research has been promising and reports from practicing teachers suggest that they have merit.

Visualization or Mental Imagery

One strategy with tantalizing potential is visualization or mental imagery. **Imagery training** has been found to improve students' memory of what they read (Pressley, 1976) as well as improve inferential reasoning about written text (Borduin, Borduin, & Manley, 1994). Depending on the program used, individuals are guided to create visual images to represent a picture or a text as they read it.

Researchers and practitioners in reading have offered several models of visualization strategies. For example, *Visualizing and Verbalizing for Language Comprehension and Thinking,* developed by Nanci Bell (1991) for Lindamood-Bell products, is widely used. This program may be particularly helpful for individuals with weak language skills. The program begins with the picture level, so even individuals who are poor decoders can start to address comprehension.

Beginning at the picture level and gradually moving through word imaging, single sentences, and multiple sentences (in which higher-order thinking skills, or HOTS, are

Table 14.2.   How reciprocal teaching and *Collaborative Strategic Reading (CSR)* differ

Reciprocal teaching	Collaborative Strategic Reading
Designed primarily for use with narrative text	Designed primarily for use with expository text
No **brainstorming** before reading	Students **brainstorm** to activate prior knowledge as part of preview (before reading).
Students predict what they think will happen next before reading each paragraph or segment of text.	Students only **predict** as part of the Preview strategy (before reading), making informed guesses about what they think they will learn.
Students **clarify** words or chunks of text they don't understand by rereading the sentences before and after the sentence they don't understand and/or asking a peer for assistance.	Students use fix-up strategies to clarify **clunks** (words they don't understand). • Reread the sentence. • Reread the sentences before and after. • Break apart the word and look for smaller words they know. • Look for a prefix or suffix they know. • Look at the picture for clues. • Ask for help.
Students **summarize** the paragraph or segment of text they have just read.	Students **get the gist** of the paragraph or segment of text they have just read, identifying "the most important who or what" and the most important thing about the who or what. They then say the gist in ten words or less.
Students **generate questions** after each paragraph or segment of text they have just read.	Students only **generate questions** as part of a **wrap up** after they have read the entire day's selection. Students answer each other's questions.
No **review** after reading	Students **review** what they have learned after reading the day's selection.
8–12 students in the group; the teacher in the group	An entire class is divided into **cooperative groups** of 2–5; the teacher circulates rather than staying with a group.
No learning logs	Students record their previews, clunks, questions, and what they've learned in individual **CSR Learning Logs.**
The leader (a student) facilitates the discussion about a paragraph or section of text; this role rotates after each paragraph.	Every student in the group has a meaningful role; one of these roles is to be the leader. Roles are assigned for an entire lesson (only rotating biweekly in some classes).
No cue cards	Students use **Cue Cards** to help them implement their roles and the comprehension strategies.

From Klingner, J.K., Vaughn, S., Dimino, J., Schumm, J.S. & Bryant, D. (2001). *From clunk to click: Collaborative strategic reading* (p. 7). Longmont, CO: Sopris West; reprinted by permission of Sopris West Educational Services; *Collaborative Strategic Reading,* copyright 2001.

introduced), single and multiple paragraphs, and eventually whole pages, *Visualizing and Verbalizing* uses a very structured format of modeling, questioning, and helping students to expand descriptions of visual images to improve understanding. Using structure words (e.g., *what, size, color, number, shape*) written on cards, students build their mental images in increasing complexity and depth. Clinical studies conducted at the Lindamood-Bell Learning Processes Center showed highly significant gains in oral and silent reading comprehension measures after individuals received intensive therapy in the *Visualization and Verbalizing* strategy (Bell, 1991).

The *Visual Imagery Strategy*[2] (Schumaker, Deshler, Zemitzch, & Warner, 1993), developed at the University of Kansas Center for Research on Learning, requires students to make pictures in their minds as they read each sentence in a passage. This strategy is designed for students who are reading at the second-grade level or above, are decoding words with fluency, have adequate background knowledge to connect words with pictures, and are able to describe a picture in words. To use this strategy independently, however, students need to be reading at or above the fourth-grade level. There are five steps to this strategy (1993, p. 94):

1. **S**earch for picture words.
2. **C**reate or change the scene.
3. **E**nter a lot of details.
4. **N**ame the parts.
5. **E**valuate the picture.

In the first step, students search for picture words that will give them ideas for the movie they will create in their mind as they read. These are words that can be turned into pictures, primarily nouns and verbs. In Step 2, students create a backdrop for the movie in their minds by deciding which picture words are related to the scene they will be describing. In the third step, students enter details about the people or animals or whatever is creating the action in the scene in their minds. In Step 4, students describe the scene and the action to themselves in their own words. In the final step, students self-check their progress, evaluating their pictures to see whether they have included everything in their mental pictures that they need. They do this by looking back at the sentences that they have read to check whether they have something in their mental pictures that represents the picture words provided by the author.

University of Kansas research (Clark, Deshler, Schumaker, Alley, & Warner, 1984) has demonstrated that after students have mastered the *Visual Imagery Strategy*, the quality and quantity of the visual images they make while reading a passage increase and, more important, that their comprehension and retention scores also grow. Several reasons are offered for these phenomena. Many of the components of effective reading comprehension are embedded within this strategy. First, the *Visual Imagery Strategy* requires students to interact actively with the text rather than just passively read it. Second, attention to task is increased when the reading passage is divided into small units with alternating reading and visualizing activities. Third, students must connect new information from a reading passage to their prior knowledge as they make new pictures of the new information using images already stored in their memories. Finally, students are required to translate the new information they have learned into their own words.

Both Lindamood-Bell and the University of Kansas offer extensive training to help teachers to implement their strategy instruction appropriately to achieve maximum effectiveness. In fact, to ensure that their strategies are used correctly, the University of Kansas does not even sell its materials to professionals until they have completed training in their strategies.

---

[2]The steps of the remembering system for the *Visual Imagery Strategy* listed on this page are part of an instructional program developed and researched at the University of Kansas Center for Research on Learning (Schumaker, Deshler, Zemitzch, & Warner, 1993). This remembering system is used to cue strategic thinking. Each step involves a variety of strategic questions and prompts that are described in step-by-step detail in written materials that can only be obtained as part of guided professional development experiences that are offered throughout the nation and are designed to ensure high-quality implementation with students. This program is one of several research-based programs designed for teachers to use as they teach learning strategies to students. For information, go to http://www.kucrl.org.

Although a promising technique, more research is needed to measure the effectiveness of programs that use visualization strategies. Existing research tends to be limited to experimenter tests tapping recall and ability to answer questions that have short answers. Studies using control groups as well as those identifying transfer of comprehension improvement to standardized test performance would be a welcome addition to research.

Computer Technology

Since 1984, the Center for Applied Special Technology (CAST), a research and development group, has been addressing the application of computer technology to individualize reading instruction and improve effective practice of reading strategies in schools today. To combat the lack of time and resources available to provide adequate opportunities for supported practice that struggling readers need, CAST has been involved in research for the Engaging the Text Project (Dalton, Pisha, Eagleton, Coyne, & Deyster, 2001).

CAST is working with middle school teachers in this project to see whether their use of computer-supported strategy instruction can be helpful in improving the comprehension of struggling readers' in both resource room and inclusive settings. Most of the students in this project have been identified as having learning disabilities and are reading three to four grade levels below their grade placement. Using Palincsar and Brown's (1984) reciprocal teaching method (outlined earlier in this chapter), students employ strategies such as summarizing, question generating, clarifying, and predicting to increase comprehension using digitized versions of novels that are embedded with reading strategy supports. The built-in instructional supports include decoding help, embedded assessments, and graphic organizers as well as interactive reading strategies.

For more information about technological supports for individuals with dyslexia, see Chapter 22, Assistive Technology and Individuals with Dyslexia, available on-line at http://textbooks.brookespublishing.com/birsh.

NEXT STEPS

We cannot afford to wait to address the needs of students who struggle to gain meaning from text. As Stanovich (1986) noted, students who do not read well read less and when they read less, they learn less; Stanovich dubbed this "Matthew effects." As a result, students' comprehension difficulties complicate their learning in all academic areas (Chall, 1996). And although Michael Pressley's observations conflict with common philosophy and practice in many schools today, Pressley noted,

> Despite the improvements in fluency and knowledge permitted by extensive reading, the "read, read, read" approach does not lead to as active meaning construction during reading as occurs when students are taught explicitly to use and articulate comprehension strategies when they read. (2000, p. 554)

There are many powerful, research-supported strategies that hold promise for struggling readers who may be able to decode but who still struggle to understand what they read. Although a good amount is known about effective (and ineffective) reading comprehension strategies, there are still many unanswered questions. Concerns about understanding the multiple sources of variance in the reading comprehension process and outcomes, continuing national demand for high literacy skills but stagnant read-

ing test performance, weak teacher preparation, minimal or ineffective reading comprehension instruction in the schools, and a persistent achievement gap between children of different demographic groups continue to trouble us.

In 2000, the RAND Reading Study Group (RRSG) of the RAND Foundation was formed when the U.S. Department of Education's now-defunct Office of Educational Research and Improvement (OERI) asked RAND to look at how OERI could improve the quality and relevance of research that the agency funded (RRSG, 2002). The RRSG called for an ambitious federally funded research effort on reading comprehension to address proposed questions such as the following:

- What instructional conditions should accompany strategy instruction to encourage students to generalize strategic approaches to learning across texts, tasks, contexts, and different age levels?

- How should teachers of poor comprehenders who are in general education classes prioritize time and instructional emphasis among the many competing calls for their attention to everything from building fluency, to teaching vocabulary, to using computer technology, to improve reading skills?

- What variations in instructional time and practice optimize opportunities for students who are English language learners to improve their comprehension skills?

The RRSG's research agenda for reading comprehension promises to "build new knowledge that will be helpful to all concerned with reading education—practitioners, teacher educators, policymakers, and parents" (Sweet & Snow, 2002, p. 47). All of us have been given an opportunity to have a huge impact on the lives of children now and on their futures as productive, literate adults.

REFERENCES

Adams, M.J. (1990). *Beginning to read: Thinking and learning about print.* Cambridge: The MIT Press.

Adams, M.J., Treiman, R., & Pressley, M. (1998). Reading, writing and literacy. In W. Damon (Series Ed.), & I.E. Sigel & K.A. Renninger (Vol. Eds.), *Handbook of child psychology: Vol. 4. Child psychology in practice* (pp. 275–355). New York: John Wiley & Sons.

Allington, R.L. (2001). *What really matters for struggling readers: Designing research-based programs.* New York: Longman.

Allington, R., Guice, S., Michelson, N., Baker, R., & Li, S. (1996). Literature-based curricula in high poverty schools. In M.F. Graves, P. van den Broek, & B.M. Taylor (Eds.), *The first R: Every child's right to read* (pp. 73–96). New York: Teachers College Press.

Bell, N. (1991). *Visualizing and verbalizing for language comprehension and thinking.* Paso Robles, CA: Academy of Reading Publications.

Borduin, B.J., Borduin, C.M., & Manley, C.M. (1994). The use of imagery training to improve reading comprehension of second graders. *Journal of Genetic Psychology, 155*(1), 115–118.

Bos, C.S. (1987). *Promoting story comprehension using a story retelling strategy.* Paper presented at the Teachers Applying Whole Language Conference, Tucson, Arizona.

Bos, C.S., & Vaughn, S. (1998). *Strategies for teaching students with learning and behavior problems* (4th ed.). Boston: Allyn & Bacon.

Bransford, J., Stein, B., Vye, N., Franks, J., Auble, P., Mezynski, K., et al. (1982). Differences in approaches to learning: An overview. *Journal of Experimental Psychology, 111,* 390–398.

Brown, A.L., & Palincsar, A.S. (1982). Including strategic learning from texts by means of informed, self-control training. *Topics in Learning and Learning Disabilities, 2*(1), 1–17.

Carlisle, J.F., & Rice, M.S. (2002). *Improving reading comprehension.* Timonium, MD: York Press.

Carnine, D., Silbert, J., & Kame'enui, E.J. (1990). *Direct instruction reading* (2nd ed.). Columbus, OH: Charles E. Merrill.

Carr, E., & Dewitz, P. (1988). *Teaching comprehension as a student-directed process.* Paper presented at the meeting of the International Reading Association, Toronto.

Carr, E., & Ogle, D. (1987). K-W-L Plus: A strategy for comprehension and summarization. *Journal of Reading, 30,* 626–631.

Clark, F.L., Deshler, D.D., Schumaker, J.B., Alley, G.R., & Warner, M.M. (1984). Visual imagery and self-questioning: Strategies to improve comprehension of written material. *Journal of Learning Disabilities, 17,* 145–149.

Chall, J. (1996). *Stages of reading development* (2nd ed.). Orlando, FL: Harcourt.

Cote, N., & Goldman, S. (1999). Building representations of informational text: Evidence from children's think-aloud protocols. In H. Van Oostendorp & S. Goldman (Eds.), *The construction of mental representations during reading* (pp. 169–193). Mahwah, NJ: Lawrence Erlbaum Associates.

Dalton, B., Pisha, B., Eagleton, M., Coyne, M., & Deyster, S. (2001). *Engaging the text: Computer-supported reciprocal teaching and strategy instruction. Final report to the U.S. Office of Special Education Programs.* Peabody, MA: CAST.

Deshler, D.D., Ellis, E.S., & Lenz, B.K. (1996). *Teaching adolescents with learning disabilities: Strategies and methods* (2nd ed.). Denver, CO: Love Publishing.

Doctorow, M., Wittrock, M., & Marks, C. (1978). Generative processes in reading comprehension. *Journal of Educational Psychology, 70,* 109–118.

Durkin, D. (1979). What classroom observations reveal about reading comprehension. *Reading Research Quarterly, 14,* 518–544.

Durkin, D. (1993). Teaching them to read (6th ed.). Boston: Allyn & Bacon.

Ehri, L. (1998). Word reading by sight and by analogy in beginning readers. In C. Hulme & R.M. Joshi (Eds.), *Reading and spelling development and disorders* (pp. 87–111). Mahwah, NJ: Lawrence Erlbaum Associates.

Fuchs, D., Fuchs, L.S., Mathes, P.G., & Simmons, D.C. (1997). Peer assisted learning strategies: Making classrooms more responsive to diversity. *American Educational Research Journal, 34,* 174–206.

Fuchs, D., Fuchs, L.S., Thompson, A., Svenson, E., Yen, L., Al Otaiba, S., et al. (2001). Peer-assisted learning strategies in reading: Extensions for kindergarten, first grade, and high school. *Remedial and Special Education, 22,* 15–21.

Fuchs, D., Mathes, P.G., & Fuchs, L.S. (2001). *Peer-assisted learning strategies: Reading methods for Grades 2-6* [teacher manual] (pp. A26–A27). Nashville: Vanderbilt University.

Gambrell, L.B., Block, C.C., & Pressley, M. (2002). Introduction: Improving comprehension instruction: An urgent priority. In C.C. Block, L.B. Gambrell, & M. Pressley, (Eds.), *Improving comprehension instruction* (pp. 3–16). San Francisco: Jossey-Bass.

Gough, P.B. (1996). How children learn to read and why they fail. *Annals of Dyslexia, 46,* 3–20.

Granowsky, A. (n.d.). *Point of view stories series: Cinderella.* Orlando, FL: Harcourt Achieve.

Graves, A.W. (1986). Effects of direct instruction and metacomprehension training on finding main ideas. *Learning Disabilities Research, 1*(2), 90–100.

Greenwood, C.R., Delquadri, J.C., & Hall, R.V. (1989). Longitudinal effects of classwide peer tutoring. *Journal of Educational Psychology, 81,* 371–383.

Guszak, F.J. (1967). Teacher questioning and reading. *The Reading Teacher, 21,* 227–234.

Hammond, D. (1983). How your students can predict their way to reading comprehension. *Learning, 12,* 62–64.

Harris, T.L., & Hodges, R.E. (Eds.). (1995). *The literacy dictionary: The vocabulary of reading and writing.* Newark, DE: International Reading Association.

Hodgkinson, H. (1991). Reform versus reality. *Phi Delta Kappan, 73,* 9–16.

Idol, L. (1987). Group story mapping: A comprehension strategy for both skilled and unskilled readers. *Journal of Learning Disabilities, 20,* 196–205.

Jenkins, J.R., Jewell, M., Leicester, N., & Troutner, N.M. (1990). *Development of a school building model for educating handicapped and at-risk students in general education classrooms.* Paper presented at the annual meeting of the American Educational Research Association, Boston.

Klingner, J.K., & Vaughn, S. (1996). Reciprocal teaching of reading comprehension strategies for students with learning disabilities who use English as a second language. *Elementary School Journal, 96,* 275–293.

Klingner, J.K., & Vaughn, S. (2000). The helping behaviors of fifth-graders while using collaborative strategic reading (CSR) during ESL content classes. *TESOL Quarterly, 34,* 69–98.

Klingner, J.K., Vaughn, S., Dimino, J., Schumm, J.S., & Bryant, D. (2001). *From clunk to click: Collaborative strategic reading.* Longmont, CO: Sopris West.

Klingner, J.K., Vaughn, S., Hughes, M.T., Schumm, J.S., & Elbaum, B. (1998). Academic outcomes for students with and without learning disabilities in inclusive classrooms. *Learning Disabilities Research & Practice, 13,* 153–160.

Manzo, A. (1969). The ReQuest procedure. *Journal of Reading, 13,* 123–126.

Manzo, A.V., & Manzo, U.C. (1993). *Literacy disorders: Holistic diagnosis and remediation.* Orlando, FL: Harcourt.

Maria, K. (1990). *Reading comprehension instruction: Issues and strategies.* Timonium, MD: York Press.

Mason, J.M., & Au, K.H. (1986). *Reading instruction for today.* Glenview, IL: Scott Foresman.

McCormick, S. (1992). Disabled readers' erroneous responses to inferential comprehension questions: Description and analysis. *Reading Research Quarterly, 27,* 54–77.

McNeil, J.D. (1987). *Reading comprehension.* Glenview, IL: Scott Foresman.

National Institute of Child Health and Human Development (NICHD). *(2000). Report of the National Reading Panel. Teaching children to read: An evidence-based assessment of the scientific research literature on reading and its implications for reading instruction: Reports of the subgroups* (NIH Publication No. 00-4754). Washington, DC: U.S. Government Printing Office. Also available on-line: http://www.nichd.nih.gov/publicatons/nrp/report.htm

No Child Left Behind Act of 2001, PL 107-110, 115 Stat. 1425, 20 U.S.C. §§ 6301 *et seq.*

Oakhill, J., & Yuill, N. (1996). Higher order factors in comprehension disability: Processes and remediation. In C. Cornoldi & J. Oakhill (Eds.), *Reading comprehension difficulties: Processes and intervention* (pp. 69–92). Mahwah, NJ: Lawrence Erlbaum Associates.

Ogle, D.M. (1986). K-W-L: A teaching model that develops active reading of expository text. *The Reading Teacher, 39,* 564–570.

Palincsar, A.S., & Brown, A. (1984). Reciprocal teaching of comprehension-fostering and comprehension-monitoring activities. *Cognition and Instruction, 1,* 117–175.

Pallas, A.M., Natriello, G., & McDill, L. (1989). The changing nature of the disadvantaged population: Current dimensions and future trends. *Educational Researcher, 18,* 16–22.

Pearson, P.D.& Johnson, D.D. (1978). *Teaching reading comprehension.* Austin, TX: Holt, Rinehart & Winston.

Pressley, G.M. (1976). Mental imagery helps eight-year-olds remember what they read. *Journal of Educational Psychology, 68,* 355–359.

Pressley, M. (2000). What should comprehension instruction be the instruction of? In M. Kamil, P. Mosenthal, P.D. Pearson, & R. Barr (Eds.), *Handbook of reading research* (Vol. III, pp. 545–562). Mahwah, NJ: Lawrence Erlbaum Associates.

Pressley, M. (2002). Comprehension strategies instruction: A turn-of-the-century report. In C.C. Block & M. Pressley (Eds.), *Comprehension instruction: Research-based best practices* (pp. 11–27). New York: The Guilford Press.

Pressley, M., Brown, R., El-Dinary, P., & Afflerbach, P. (1995). The comprehension instruction that students need: Instruction fostering constructively responsive reading. *Learning Disabilities Research and Practice, 10,* 215–224.

RAND Reading Study Group (RRSG). (2002). *Reading for understanding: Toward an R&D program in reading comprehension.* Retrieved January 25, 2005, from http://www.rand.org/publications/MR/MR1465/MR1465.pdf

Raphael, T.E. (1982). Teaching children question-answering strategies. *Reading Teacher, 36,* 186–191.

Raphael, T.E. (1984). Teaching learners about sources of information for answering comprehension questions. *Journal of Reading, 28,* 303–311.

Raphael, T.E. (1986). Teaching question-answer relationships, revisited. *Reading Teacher, 39,* 516–522.

Rose, D., & Dalton, B. (2002). Using technology to individualize reading instruction. In C.C. Block, L.B. Gambrell, & M. Pressley (Eds.), *Improving comprehension instruction* (pp. 257–274). San Francisco: Jossey-Bass.

Rosenshine, B., & Meister, C. (1994). Reciprocal teaching: A review of the research. *Review of Educational Research, 64*(4), 479–530.

Schumaker, J.B., Denton, P.H., & Deshler, D.D. (1984). *The paraphrasing strategy (learning strategies curriculum).* Lawrence: University of Kansas.

Schumaker, J.B., Deshler, D.D., Zemitzch, A., & Warner, M.M. (1993). *The visual imagery strategy.* Lawrence: The University of Kansas Center for Research on Learning.

Shaywitz, S. (2003). *Overcoming dyslexia: A new and complete science-based program for reading problems at any level.* New York: Alfred A. Knopf.

Simmons, D.C., Fuchs, D., Fuchs, L.S., Hodge, J.P., & Mathes, P.G. (1994). Importance of instructional complexity and role reciprocity to classwide peer tutoring. *Learning Disabilities Research and Practice, 9*(4), 203–212.

Simmons, D.C., Fuchs, L.S, Fuchs, D., Mathes, P.G., & Hodge, J.P. (1995). Effects of explicit teaching and peer tutoring on the reading achievement of learning-disabled and low-performing students in regular classrooms. *Elementary School Journal, 95,* 387–408.

Stahl, K.A.D. (2004). Proof, practice, and promise: Comprehension strategy instruction in the primary grades. *The Reading Teacher, 57*(1), 598–609.

Stanovich, K.E. (1986). Matthew effects in reading: Some consequences of individual differences in the acquisition of literacy. *Reading Research Quarterly, 21,* 360–406.

Strickland, D.S., Ganske, K., & Monroe, J.K. (2002). *Supporting struggling readers and writers.* Portland, ME: Stenhouse Publishers.

Sweet, A.P., & Snow, C. (2002). Reconceptualizing reading comprehension. In C.C. Block, L.B. Gambrell, & M. Pressley (Eds.), *Improving comprehension instruction* (pp. 17–53). San Francisco: Jossey-Bass.

Taylor, B.M., Pearson, P.D., Clark, K.F., & Walpole, S. (1999). Effective schools/accomplished teachers. *The Reading Teacher, 53*(2),156–159.

Torgesen, J.K. (1998, Spring–Summer). Catch them before they fail. *American Educator,* 1–8.

Williams, J. (1987). Educational treatments for dyslexia at the elementary and secondary levels. In R. Bowler (Ed.), *Intimacy with language: A forgotten basic in teacher education* (pp. 24–32). Baltimore: The International Dyslexia Association.

Williams, J. (2002). Using the theme scheme. In C.C. Block & M. Pressley (Eds.), *Comprehension instruction: Research-based best practices* (pp. 126–139). New York: The Guilford Press.

Wixson, K. (1983). Questions about a text: What you ask about is what children learn. *The Reading Teacher, 37,* 287–293.

Wong, B.Y.L. (1979). Increasing retention of main ideas through questioning strategies. *Learning Disability Quarterly, 2*(2), 42–47.

15

Teaching Handwriting

Beverly J. Wolf

In many textbooks on teaching reading, handwriting is classified as one of the mechanics along with spelling, punctuation, and grammar. Rarely is handwriting given the importance it deserves in the overall language arts program for typical students or even in intervention programs for students with learning disabilities, although writing disabilities are often more persistent than reading disabilities. This chapter gives the rationale for including handwriting as a vital component of multisensory instruction of literacy skills and a component skill for developing a functional writing system (Berninger, 1999).

This chapter 1) highlights the importance of handwriting instruction in early education and in remediation, 2) provides a brief history of handwriting instruction, 3) discusses some of the syndromes related to difficulties with handwriting, 4) reports research evidence of the efficacy of direct teaching of handwriting to dyslexic students, 5) presents general principles and specific information on how to teach print and cursive handwriting using a multisensory framework that integrates handwriting instruction with reading and spelling instruction, and 6) offers a brief discussion of keyboarding and **assistive technology** alternatives.

THE IMPORTANCE OF HANDWRITING
INSTRUCTION IN EARLY EDUCATION AND REMEDIATION

Writing has added a timeless dimension to oral communication, expanding communicative capabilities the way mathematics did to counting on fingers and toes, and has made possible our modern world (vos Savant, 1988). Henry (2003) provided a review of the establishment of early writing systems and the historical milestones of written English.

Current research emphasizes the importance of handwriting in developing the orthographic skills needed for reading. Adams suggested that the activities of letter tracing and copying "may contribute valuably toward the development of those fine motor skills that determine the willingness as well as the ability to write" and help in "developing necessary skills for reading as well as writing" (1990, p. 357). Instruction in writing and spelling often comes before instruction in reading during efforts to promote phonemic awareness through the teaching of letter names and sounds and phonemic segmentation while children are in kindergarten (Rubin & Eberhardt, 1996). At this point it is important for children to know the names of the letters and to distinguish between upper- and lowercase letters (see Chapter 5).

Children begin the writing process with motivating and meaningful experiences in preschool and kindergarten. They have opportunities to trace and copy letters using markers, pencils, and crayons. Models of letters on alphabet strips or letter cards showing upper- and lowercase letters are available for the children to observe. They progress from drawing and scribbling, to creating strings of letter-like forms, to generating invented spellings (Snow, Burns, & Griffin, 1998). Although Snow et al.'s recommendations for practice do not suggest that teachers, even professional reading specialists, should be prepared to teach handwriting, Snow et al. clearly outlined the handwriting demands for kindergarten and first-grade reading accomplishments (pp. 80–81):

Kindergarten

- Writes own name (first and last) and the first names of some friends or classmates
- Can write most letters and some words when they are dictated

First grade

- Composes fairly readable first drafts using appropriate parts of the writing process (. . . planning, drafting, rereading for meaning, and some self correction)
- Produces a variety of types of compositions (e.g., stories, descriptions, journal entries) showing appropriate relationships between printed text, illustrations, and other graphics.

To meet the demands of these accomplishments, children need direct, explicit instruction in letter formation and much guided practice to become proficient in the task of handwriting.

Berninger emphasized that handwriting is not merely a motor act: "It is a written language act that taps the processes of creating letter representations in memory and then retrieving them" (1998, p. 47). She explained that difficulty with "the ability to code an identified language symbol (letter) in memory" (1998, p. 47) accounts for handwriting problems more than trouble with **fine motor skills** do. Although motor skills contribute to handwriting (Graham & Weintraub, 1996), orthographic coding has a more direct relationship to handwriting than do fine motor skills (Abbott & Berninger, 1993). When children do not remember the sequence of movement required in speech or letter formation, voluntary motor function cannot be triggered. That lack of kinesthetic recall for speech and/or for letter formation may hinder fluent speech and penmanship (Slingerland, 1976).

Even though the computer is a tool for writers that facilitates the act of writing and increases the volume of written material, it is not always as readily available as the pencil and pen, which are easily carried in the pocket. Nor is the computer a substitute for kinesthetic reinforcement provided by manual writing when learning to read. Furthermore, with the advent of high-stakes testing, the quality and utility of accessible and

legible handwriting skills have become more essential. Students with writing difficulties are much more likely to stand out.

Many teachers encourage their students to write journal entries to practice letter formation but do not give students an appropriate model and accept either print or cursive as long as it is legible. These teachers appear to be bypassing the use of formal instructional material (Tabor, 1996).

There are many advantages to formal handwriting instruction. McMenamin and Martin (1980) explained that time spent on handwriting practice to improve legibility and develop fluency is a time saver for both the teacher, who spends less effort deciphering the writing, and the pupils, who complete written assignments in less time. Strickling (1974) observed that spelling improves when legibility increases. A writer can discover errors more easily with fewer ambiguously formed letters, which interfere with proofreading, and a greater amount of reinforcement of correct word patterns becomes available. College students have difficulty with lecture comprehension when their note taking is too slow (Blalock, 1985). An additional bonus is the pride the students have in a product that is neat, legible, and attractive (Phelps & Stempel, 1987). Automaticity and fluency in handwriting are also important because they give individuals the freedom to concentrate on accurate spelling, higher level thought processes, and written expression. Berninger (1999) suggested that the more fluent and automatic handwriting is, the more working memory is available for higher level composing processes. Automaticity is also a strong predictor of the quality of composition in typically developing writers and writers with disabilities (Berninger, 1999).

Individuals need to be able to write for others to have something to read. People of any age suffer embarrassment when they feel that their writing is inadequate. In most school districts formal training in handwriting appears to be limited to the first three or four grades. Some poor handwriting may be caused by students not having enough training to form letters automatically when rapid writing is needed as a tool to perform assigned writing tasks (Hamstra-Bletz & Blöte, 1990). For most students, motor skills used in handwriting can be improved with guided practice once correct models are demonstrated, and many models are made available. Self-help workbooks for students and adults have been developed.

Kinesthetic memory, the earliest, strongest, and most reliable form of memory, may aid spellers in remembering orthographic patterns. As a final point, students need to be aware that teachers often judge students' abilities and grade them based on the appearance of their written work.

A BRIEF HISTORY OF HANDWRITING INSTRUCTION

The history of teaching handwriting begins in ancient times. Richardson (1995) noted that Plato (428 B.C.–348 B.C.), Horace (65 B.C.–9 B.C.), and Seneca (4 B.C.–A.D. 65) were specific in their instructions to those who taught handwriting. Plato instructed the master to draw lines (letters) for the student to copy, Horace incorporated the idea of using pastry formed in the shape of letters, and Seneca had the teacher guide the student's hand as the letters were traced. Quintilian (A.D. 35–A.D. 100) suggested using a board with letters cut into it so that the child could keep the pen within the letters to make the letter forms accurately. Quintilian also recommended that the student learn the sound and shape of a letter simultaneously.

Cursive letters have evolved over time from the highly ornamental and calligraphic forms used by medieval monasteries. Each monastery developed and used its

own alphabet until a common alphabet was established during the 9th century. Today the more simplified styles of Palmer, Zaner-Bloser, and the D'Nealian method are taught in the United States (Phelps & Stempel, 1987).

In a comprehensive review of research in reading, writing, and math disorders for the U.S. Interagency Committee on Learning Disabilities, Johnson (1988) described a shift in the teaching of penmanship. In the late 1800s and early 1900s, penmanship was taught as a separate subject, with copying drills that focused on the form of the letter itself and appropriate posture. After the 1940s curricular changes led to a broader emphasis on language arts that resulted in less time being devoted to handwriting instruction in schools. This reordering of priorities led to a debate about whether teachers should provide direct instruction in skills and processes or allow children to engage in extensive reading, writing, and speaking experiences without explicit input on component language subskills such as handwriting. Recently, as personal computers have become more common, school systems have placed even less importance on teaching handwriting.

SYNDROMES RELATED TO DIFFICULTIES WITH HANDWRITING

A 5-year longitudinal study at the University of Washington funded by the National Institute of Child Health and Human Development began in 1999 and will be reported on in a special issue of *Developmental Neuropsychology* (principal investigator, V. Berninger; see Berninger et al., in press). The study has found that printing manuscript letters, writing cursive letters, and finding letters on a keyboard have different early developmental paths. Printing letters in manuscript form and finding the manuscript letters on a keyboard have a low moderate, but statistically significant, correlation in typically developing first graders. Likewise, printing manuscript letters, writing cursive letters, and finding manuscript letters on a keyboard have low moderate, but statistically significant, correlations in typically developing third graders. However, different neurodevelopmental processes uniquely predict *automaticity* of handwriting or keyboarding, the ability to produce or find letters accurately, quickly, and effortlessly. For printing letters, the unique predictor is storing letter forms in short-term memory while the letter forms are analyzed in working memory. For finding the letters on the keyboard, the same letter-coding and -analyzing skill and rapid automatic naming of letters are the unique predictors. For writing cursive letters, the unique predictor is inhibition—an executive function that directs attention to the relevant linguistic information and suppresses the irrelevant linguistic information. Difficulty with inhibition is a nonlinguistic marker of dyslexia (Berninger et al., in press). Training in cursive writing may help dyslexics because it improves their inhibition. Additional information about the role of handwriting in beginning reading and treating dyslexia is forthcoming (Berninger et al., in press).

Moats (1995) pointed out that there is little research on the relationship between handwriting and spelling even though children and adults who have difficulty with handwriting often have impaired spelling abilities as well. In addition, it is possible to know how to spell words correctly but not be able to write them by hand. This condition, in which letter shapes, letter sequences, and motor patterns are impaired, is called **specific agraphia** (Goodman & Caramazza, 1986). In Samuel T. Orton's research on reading problems (as cited in J.L. Orton, 1966), he considered poor handwriting as both an interrelated and a separate language function. According to Orton, poor handwriting could result in poor visual reinforcement of word patterns and thus a weakened circuit between visual memory for printed words for writing, reading, and spelling and poor

auditory memory for words in speech, spelling, and writing. He recognized, too, that slow, messy handwriting could constitute a specific language disability itself.

Some students who have difficulty producing legible writing are diagnosed with **dysgraphia** (difficulty with handwriting). According to Levine (1994), many children have fine motor problems that affect only writing. These children's writing is slow and laborious as well as sometimes illegible. There are three common forms of this **grapho-motor** dysfunction. The first is motor memory dysfunction, in which there is trouble integrating motor output with memory input. Children with this condition have difficulty in recalling the sequence of motor engrams (muscle movements) that are needed to form a specific letter. The second is **graphomotor production deficit**, in which the larger muscles of the wrist and forearm are used during letter formation because they are under better control than the small muscles of the fingers. This results in laborious and slow but legible writing. The third is a motor feedback problem, sometimes referred to as **finger agnosia**, in which an individual has to visually monitor the location of the pencil point because the fingers do not report their location to the brain (Levine, 1994). A child with agnosia may use an awkward, fist-like pencil grip in which he or she places the thumb over the other fingers, preventing the fingers from moving the pencil efficiently. Handwriting for such a child is exhausting and painfully slow, to such an extent that it interferes with fluency.

Improvement can be achieved through formal handwriting programs that provide practice with appropriate models. School occupational therapists are often involved in providing the instruction (Reisman, 1991). The bypass strategy of learning keyboarding and using a computer is usually recommended for older students. When they write by hand, they are encouraged to utilize either print or cursive, whichever is their preference (Black, 1996). (See Appendix B for recommended keyboarding and handwriting programs.) Berninger and Amtmann (2003) cautioned, "It is important to remember that these technological tools bypass handwriting difficulties but create new tasks with processing requirements that may or may not be a challenge for an individual student." Early handwriting instruction and continued practice may reduce the number of students needing bypass strategies.

EVIDENCE FOR EFFICACY OF THE DIRECT TEACHING OF HANDWRITING TO DYSLEXIC STUDENTS

Initial Teaching of Manuscript Print versus Cursive Handwriting

Young children usually become aware of the concept of groups of letters as symbols with meaning (i.e., the alphabetic principle) through their most personal possession, their names. Caregivers or teachers who show children how their names are written with printed letters commonly introduce this concept. Whether a child's name is written in upper- or lowercase letters, it becomes a symbol of self. Manuscript print is customarily taught to first and second graders in most public schools, and cursive is introduced at the end of second grade or the beginning of third grade. Most public school districts use manuscript print when introducing handwriting to young children, perhaps because it is most consistent with preschool learning and because it is the writing style encountered in reading texts.

- Print writing introduces children to the letter forms they will need to recognize as they begin to learn to read.

- The typeface used in the basic readers is more like print writing than cursive in appearance.

- The use of print by the teacher allows primary-grade children to see the same symbol forms used for reading, writing, and spelling, thereby lessening confusion.

Proponents of the initial teaching of cursive writing, such as Cox (1992), have cited a number of advantages of cursive handwriting, especially for students with dyslexia (Phelps & Stempel, 1987) (Texas Scottish Rite Hospital for Children, Child Development Division [TSRHC], 1996). Cursive handwriting does the following:

- Eliminates a student's need to decide where each letter should begin because all cursive letter shapes begin on the baseline

- Provides directional movement from left to right

- Provides unique letter shapes that are not mirror images of other letters

- Reduces reversals by eliminating the need to raise the pencil while writing a single letter or a series of letters in a word

- Eliminates the need to learn two different writing skills, allowing the student to avoid confusion

Some school districts have devised their own handwriting curriculum by analyzing letters and developing directions for making them easily and legibly (Wessel, 1984). The goal is to provide a legible, automatic means of written expression.

Developmental Stages of Learning Handwriting

Levine (1987) suggested that the acquisition of the skills needed for writing occurs in six stages, with variation in the rate of progress of even typically achieving children.

1. *Imitation—preschool to first grade:* Children pretend to write by mimicking actual writing while acquiring skill in letter and number formation but lack precise graphomotor skill. Early warning signs of potential problems may be observed in children who have fine motor weaknesses and become frustrated and self-conscious as they notice their peers' proficiency. Hand preference is shown although not fully established in all children.

2. *Graphic presentation—first and second grades:* Children become more aware of spatial planning as they learn to form both lower- and uppercase letters and recognize the need for more space between words than between letters. Letter reversals are common, sometimes because of confusion over **directionality** and **laterality** and at other times because the need to concentrate and remember the configuration of the letter causes a child to overlook directionality. Fine motor control becomes better developed, and the child relies increasingly on **proprioception** and kinesthetic feedback (an inner sense of where the fingers are on the page). Letters become smaller to fit the lines on the paper.

3. *Progressive incorporation—late second to fourth grades:* Children produce print letters with less conscious effort, are less preoccupied with spatial and aesthetic appearance of their writing, and are ready to accept cursive writing as a more efficient system. Rules of capitalization, punctuation, syntax, and grammar are incorporated.

4. *Automatization—fourth through seventh grades:* Writing rate and efficiency become significant as children are expected to communicate in writing using correct grammar, spelling, punctuation, capitalization, and vocabulary while automatically recalling and producing legible letter forms.

5. *Elaboration—seventh through ninth grades:* Writing is used to establish and express a viewpoint. In proficient writers, written language exceeds everyday speech in complexity.

6. *Personalization-diversification—ninth grade and beyond:* Individual style and talent for writing, if any, develops. Students who find writing too difficult may never reach this stage.

Luria (1973) described the process of learning to write as initially depending on memorization of the graphic forms of every letter. It takes place through a chain of isolated motor impulses, each of which is responsible for the performance of only one element of the graphic structure. With practice this structure of the process is radically altered, and writing is converted into a single kinetic melody.

The child with learning disabilities apparently experiences a breakdown in the developmental continuum described by Luria (1973). Handwriting, according to Hagin (1983), should be taught at a level appropriate to the child's motor mastery and as a task that involves visual, motor, kinesthetic, temporal, and spatial skills. Getman (1984) cited research that showed that arm and hand movements that produced the least physiological and cognitive stress came from the shoulder with the full arm involved in the movements required for the formation of letters. The completion of the motor patterns eventually allows handwriting to become such a habitual skill that the mind is free to think while the arm and hand automatically produce the words chosen by the mind. A student experiencing a problem with the motor act of handwriting often resists writing anything at all because it is tiring or at best writes as little as possible (Cicci, 1995).

Rationale for Multisensory Teaching

Although it is not a handwriting program per se, the Fernald (1943) method is a special remedial approach to teaching reading and spelling that involves handwriting directly (see Table 2.1 for more on the **Fernald method**). The tracing of words to be learned involves all four sensory pathways: visual, auditory, kinesthetic, and tactile. For reading, the student traces the word the teacher has written (a process involving the visual, kinesthetic, and tactile senses) while saying the word (a process using the auditory sense). (See Appendix B at the end of this book for a listing of other programs utilizing multisensory approaches for teaching handwriting.)

Cox (1980, 1985, 1992) and Slingerland (1971, 1976, 1981), who adapted systems of teaching for children with dyslexia from the Orton (1937) and Gillingham approach (Gillingham & Stillman, 1960), stressed the multisensory aspects of teaching handwriting. Cox insisted on the use of cursive, suggesting that "a strong kinesthetic memory may reinforce the visual memory of letter shapes for reading" (1992, p. 19). Naming the letters aloud while tracing or copying them is not just a remedial technique. Adams pointed out that children often say the name or the sound naturally as they write, which helps to "bind the visual, motor, and phonological images of the letter together at once" (1990, p. 355). In the Slingerland approach,

> The process of learning to write is not part of phenomenal development and should be taught as a basic skill. As the form of each letter is introduced, review time should be

planned for strengthening the Visual-Auditory-Kinesthetic (VAK) associations of *sight-sound* (grapheme-phoneme)-*feel* (hand and mouth) of each letter as it is named. (Slingerland, 1981, p. 21)

Some students who have better kinesthetic memory than visual memory learn to write more easily than they learn to read; thus, writing training may take the lead in multisensory language training as these students' strongest pathway to learning (Cox, 1992). Difficulty with retrieval of letter symbols from visual memory, typically weak in dyslexics, is a major deterrent to rapid, automatic production of alphabet letters, which is a lower-order writing skill that is most important in the beginning stages of writing (Berninger, Mizokawa, & Bragg, 1991).

Kinesthetic performance with the use of visual symbols and their letter names forms a multisensory association that helps strengthen recall for both reading and writing (Cox, 1992; Slingerland, 1971). One activity that accomplishes this is forming a large letter shape made in the air with a straight arm while naming the letter, key word, and sound. The addition of this multisensory component is especially valuable for children with confusions between commonly reversed letters such as *b, d, g, p, q,* and *s.* Students with weaknesses in one modality area can use their strengths to achieve success in another.

GENERAL PRINCIPLES IN THE MULTISENSORY TEACHING OF HANDWRITING

Ready Reference

Alphabet wall cards provide easy reference for children. They may be made by the teacher or purchased. Some teachers prefer to use cards with key-word pictures that also serve to help children recall the sounds of the letters. Prepared materials used in the *Alphabetic Phonics* (Cox, 1992), Gillingham (Gillingham & Stillman, 1997), and Slingerland (Slingerland, 1976; Slingerland & Aho, 1985), and *Fundations* (Wilson Language Training, 2002) approaches are available (see Appendix B at the end of the book). The cards should be visible so that children can refer to them easily at any time. Most classroom teachers display them in alphabetical order above the chalkboard so that children have a ready reference to the different letter shapes.

Good Posture

Poor body position can significantly interfere with ease of coordinating the hand movements in writing (Kurtz, 1994). The student should use a chair with a flat back and a seat that allows the feet to rest flat on the floor, with the hips, knees, and ankles all at 90° angles. The desk should be 2 inches higher than the child's bent elbows (Benbow, 1988, as cited in Kurtz, 1994). A desk that is too high will cause the student to elevate the shoulders, which is tiring and restricts freedom of movement, whereas a desk that is too low could cause the student to slouch. The nonwriting hand and arm should be on the desk to hold the paper in place.

Proper Pencil Grasp

The child should use a normal tripod pencil grip (see Figure 15.1 for correct and incorrect writing grips). The pencil rests on the first joint of the middle finger with the thumb and index fingers holding the pencil in place and the pencil held at a 45° angle

Recognized Correct
and Incorrect Writing Grips

Correct

1. The pencil rests on the first joint of the middle finger with the thumb and index fingers holding the pencil in place.

2. Same as figure 1 except the fingers are closer to the pencil point.

3. Same as figure 1 except the pencil is held perpendicular to table.

Incorrect

4. Thumb and index finger holding pencil, with the index finger overlapping the thumb.

5. Pencil held by tips of fingers. Thumb on one side, middle and index finger on the other.

6. Thumb wraps around pencil with the index and middle fingers pressing pencil to ring finger.

7. Index, middle and ring finger tips hold one side of pencil, the thumb holds the other.

8. Pencil is held between the index and middle fingers, pressing pencil to the thumb.

9. Thumb on one side, index and middle fingers on the other, all pressing the pencil to ring finger.

10. Index finger holds pencil to middle finger, with the thumb overlapping the index finger.

11. The thumb holds the pencil along the first joints of the rest of the fingers.

12. The pencil is grasped in the fist, and held up against the thumb.

Thē Pencil Grip

P.O. Box 67096 Los Angeles, CA 90067   310-315-3545   Fax: 310-315-0607

Figure 15.1.   Recognized correct and incorrect writing grips. (Reprinted by permission of Thē Pencil Grip.)

to the page. An awkward pencil grip can indicate finger agnosia. The use of an auxiliary plastic pencil grip or a metal writing frame can aid in changing the fatiguing grip to a normal, less tiring one (Phelps & Stempel, 1985; TSRHC, 1990). Children may need to experiment with pencil grips or a writing frame to determine which one works best for them. Many become frustrated with these implements once the novelty has worn off. The pencil should point toward the shoulder of the writing arm for both left- and right-handed students.

An alert, diligent teacher can help a student change pencil position, but this requires consistency and patience. At any time that the teacher notes incorrect position, he or she can instruct the class as follows:

Teacher: Stop.

Students place their pencils on the desk with the point toward them.

Teacher: Pinch.

With the index finger and thumb in a "pinch" position, students lightly grasp their pencils where the paint begins (approximately 1 inch from the point).

Teacher: Lift.

As the children lift the pencil, it will fall back to correct writing position and rest on the first joint of the middle finger.

After a few practice sessions, this teacher interruption of the writing process is brief; students only need to hear, "Stop, pinch, lift," to adjust their pencil positions. Teacher perseverance will help students become accustomed to the feel of the new position and use it consistently. After a time, only the one or two children who have continued difficulty will need reminders. The older the child, the more difficulty he or she will have with changing the pencil position.

Writing Implement

"The complex motor action of writing is overwhelmingly dependent upon accurate, ongoing kinesthetic [reafferent] feedback" (Levine, 1987, p. 226). While the child is writing, he or she is receiving feedback in the form of pressure and the pull of the pencil against the paper. A No. 2 or softer pencil should be used. Pencils with soft lead require less pressure from the child, thereby reducing fatigue. Children with impaired kinesthetic feedback will benefit from the use of softer leads, which will not break as the children press firmly in an attempt to receive that feedback when writing (Levine, 1987). It is preferable to use pencils without erasers. Instead, the teacher can instruct children to bracket mistakes: *I [wahsed] washed my dog.* This reduces time spent erasing and allows teachers to see the errors children have made and incorporate reteaching into lesson planning.

Paper

Handwriting instruction begins with activities that involve gross motor movement so that children may feel the movement in the shoulder and arm and improve their kinesthetic memory. Tracing at the chalkboard is the first step. Paper patterns also should be large and gradually become smaller as children become proficient with letter forms. Children of any age should be introduced to folded newsprint or lined paper with the

widest spaces available. The space between lines should be reduced as children's formation of letters becomes automatic.

Initially, letter forms should be taught using a chalkboard or dry erase board, then using unlined paper, then wide-lined paper (1" between rows), next primary-grade lined paper (¾" ½" ⅜"), and finally regular lined notebook paper. The size of the spaces between lines is adjusted downward as the child masters the letter forms. The teacher should watch carefully to see that correct posture, full arm movement, and correct form are maintained. Additional practice utilizing other media such as carpet squares; Jell-O; salt or rice trays; sand; tabletops; and varying styles of columned paper such as newspaper want ads, telephone books, or computer paper will ensure large full, arm movement and can make handwriting practice game like.

Paper Position

To achieve the consistent slant that is needed in cursive writing, the edge of the paper should be parallel to the writing arm (at about a 45° angle to the edge of the desk) and anchored at the top by the nonwriting hand. After the child's writing is small enough to permit him or her to use regular notebook paper, a slant guide (a piece of paper with slanted lines that is positioned beneath the writing paper) can be helpful after the child forms all lowercase letters automatically, Some instructors prefer that a left-handed student write with a backward slant, placing the paper parallel to the left arm; others teach a forward slant to both left- and right-handed students (see Figure 15.2 for sample slant guides). It has been suggested that left-handers who write with a hook (the "curled wrist" method) were taught by teachers who insisted all students place their papers in the right-handed position. To avoid smudging the paper and to see what they have written, these left-handers curl their wrists while writing. Athènes and Guiard (1991) asked, "Is the inverted handwriting posture really so bad for left handers?" By compar-

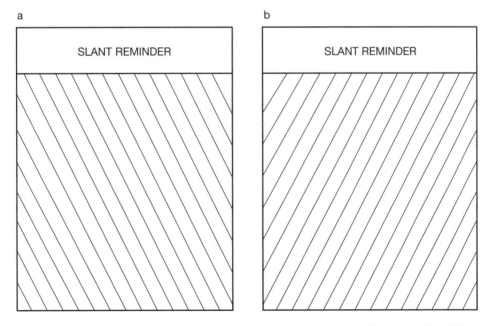

Figure 15.2.   Slant reminders for a) left-handers and b) right-handers. (From Texas Scottish Rite Hospital for Children, Child Development Division. [1996]. *Teaching cursive writing* [Brochure]. Dallas: Author; reprinted by permission.)

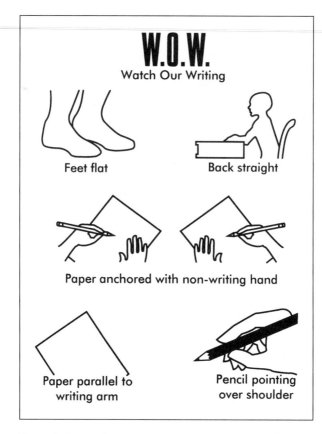

Figure 15.3. Watch Our Writing (W.O.W.) chart. (From Phelps, J., & Stempel, L. [1985]. *CHES's handwriting improvement program* [CHIP]. Dallas: Children's Handwriting Evaluation Scale; reprinted by permission.)

ing rate of writing of non-inverters with that of inverters in left-handed adults and children, they concluded that "the handwriting performance of inverters was just as good as that of non-inverters" (p. 149). Bertin and Perlman, authors of *Preventing Academic Failure* (1991), a multisensory curriculum for teaching phonics, spelling, and reading, have developed a handwriting program for teaching cursive to left-handers that is available commercially. See the **Watch Our Writing (W.O.W.)** chart developed by Phelps and Stempel (Figure 15.3) for illustrations of proper posture, pencil grasp, and paper position for both left- and right-handed students.

Slingerland recommended that the paper always be slanted with the upper left corner higher for left-handed students and the upper right corner higher for right-handed students when using cursive. She further recommended that right-handed students keep their papers parallel to the bottom of the desk when using manuscript print. This helped them keep their manuscript letters straight.

Importance of Motivation

Students will be motivated to improve their handwriting if they take part in deciding which areas need help. The teacher can help students analyze the quality of their writing, using generally accepted criteria: correct letter forms, rhythm (fluency), consistent slant, good use of space within and between words and lines, and general appearance

Lowercase Manuscript Letter Forms

All lowercase maunscript letters are made with a
continuous line, except for *f, i, j, k, t,* and *x.*

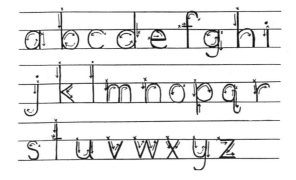

Uppercase Manuscript Letter Forms

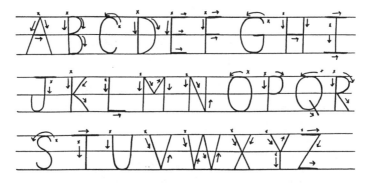

Figure 15.4.   Print letters, using a continuous stroke (when possible). (Developed by
the Renton School District, Renton, WA; reprinted by permission; versions taught in
other school districts may vary slightly.)

(copy is free of excessive strikeovers or erasures). The teacher should set daily goals for
the student or group. Writing is an acquired skill that requires good training in order
to write legibly and rapidly. Although not all individuals have superior handwriting,
many can achieve legibility with effort and practice (TSRHC, 1996).

Uppercase letters are introduced only after students write all lowercase letters automatically and legibly because uppercase letters are used in only about 2% of writing.
Some teachers prefer to introduce the capitals needed for student names on an individual basis. See Figures 15.4 and 15.5 for a version of simplified uppercase letters in
both manuscript and cursive.

TEACHING LETTER FORMS USING A MULTISENSORY FRAMEWORK

Handwriting instruction and practice are the same for both manuscript and cursive
writing and are appropriate for one-to-one therapy, small groups, or general education
classrooms at any age. It is neither necessary nor desirable to keep the alphabet in sequence while teaching handwriting. It is preferable to teach the reading, spelling, and
writing of sounds and letters that reflect ease of learning and frequency in English and

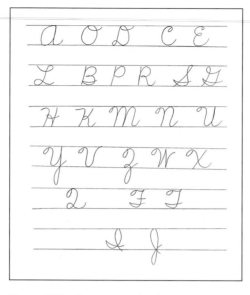

Figure 15.5. Uppercase cursive letters. (From Texas Scottish Rite Hospital for Children, Child Development Division. [1996]. *Teaching cursive writing* [Brochure]. Dallas: Author; reprinted by permission.)

similarities of strokes in writing. When planning the presentation of print letters, the following should be considered:

- Ease of production of the letter

- Continuity of stroke

- Similarity of strokes to those letters previously taught

- Ease of perception and production of the sound associated with the letter

Although sounds are not taught during handwriting class, their associations with letter forms are part of the multisensory experience. For example, the manuscript letter *l* is the simplest to write, but its sound is more difficult for young children, so it is

a	Around, down.	t	Down, cross.
n	Down, hump.	h	Down, hump.
b	Down, up, around.	u	Down, curve up, down.
o	Around, close.	i	Down, dot.
c	Around, stop.	v	Slant down, up.
p	Down, up, around.	j	Down, hook, dot.
d	Around, up, down.	w	Slant down, up, down, up.
q	Around, down, flag.	k	Down, slant in, out.
e	Across, around, stop.	x	Slant right. Slant left.
r	Down, up, over.	l	Down.
f	Curve, down, cross.	y	Slant right. Slant left.
s	Curve, slant, curve.	m	Down, hump, hump.
g	Around, down, hook.	z	Across, slant, across.

Figure 15.6. Continuous stroke descriptions of print letters. (Used by permission of Neuhaus Education Center, Bellaire, TX.)

a poor choice as the first letter to be introduced. It may be taught more easily after a few letters and their sounds have been presented.

Students appear to recall the sequence of movements of a given letter better if the instructor verbalizes consistent, precise directions for writing each letter shape (see Figures 15.6–15.10). The descriptive phrases should be repeated each time the letter is traced or written to reinforce motor memory until the letter shape is automatic (Slingerland, 1971; TSRHC, 1996). Each time students start to write a letter, it is important for him or her to name it while writing. This is an adaptation of Gillingham and Stillman's (1960) Simultaneous Oral Spelling, which provides kinesthetic reinforcement in which movements of the speech organs help the memory for letter names, sounds, and shapes.

Manuscript Print Handwriting

Print handwriting introduces primary-grade children to the symbol forms used in printed text. Through multisensory association of sight, sound, and feel, children integrate each letter name with its visual form and the feel of how the letter is written, strengthening intersensory associations. The procedure for instruction for print is the same as that for cursive writing, described later in this chapter, but pace will be slower for younger children. As much as 1 week or more may be spent on each letter when working with kindergarten or first-grade students.

There are many forms of print writing, but the one most often recommended for dyslexic children is one that utilizes a continuous stroke whenever possible (Beery, 1982; Slingerland, 1971). A continuous stroke letter is most similar to cursive writing in that lines are retraced whenever possible and the pencil is lifted only when necessary, for example, to cross a *t* or to dot an *i*. This helps prepare the child for a natural transition to cursive writing. Continuous stroke letters also reduce the opportunities for reversals that may occur each time that the child lifts the pencil. (Figure 15.4 shows lower- and uppercase print alphabets that use continuous strokes when possible; Figure 15.6 shows descriptions for writing print letters using continuous strokes.)

When a letter such as *h* is taught first, it introduces children to the idea of using a continuous stroke to form a letter because the child starts at the top of the letter, pulls down to the baseline, slides up almost to the midline, curves out and down without lifting the pencil. When a letter such as *t* is taught first, students must lift the pencil to cross the downstroke line; thus, children have more difficulty adjusting to moving their arms without lifting the pencil from the paper when *h* is presented later.

Grouping Printed Letters by Similar Strokes

The h Group

The sound of the letter *h* is easy to hear and reproduce. The print letter form introduces the idea of continuous stroke. Its basic arm movement is also used in such letters as *b, m, n, r,* and *p*. Be prepared to spend considerable time on the letter *b* because of the confusions between *b* and *d*. Slingerland (1971) recommended preparing students for the introduction of the letter *b* with an auditory-motor activity in which students stand and hold their writing arms in front of their bodies. The teacher then separates right- and left-handed students and helps them understand that to move in the direction that handwriting should go, right-handed students move their arms away from their bodies, whereas left-handed students move their arms across their bodies. Then, when patterns are introduced at the chalkboard, the teacher verbalizes, "Tall stem down and away from my body (if right-handed)," and, "Tall stem down and across my body (if

left-handed)," to help both right- and left-handed students understand and remember the direction of the letter. The students are expected to subvocalize whispering the same language as they practice the letter *b*.

The *a* Group

The *a* group consists of letters that start with the same movement as the letter *a*. It includes *a, c, d, g, o, q*, and *s*. These letters begin at the 2 o'clock position just below the mid-line. As children begin to form these letters, they should move their pencils at approximately a 45° angle toward the mid-line, curving around toward the baseline. The exaggerated slant typical of beginning writers' letters will become more rounded as children's writing becomes automatic. The angle of the pencil will eliminate a nearly vertical upward stroke and produce a rounded letter.

Other Groups

The letters *i, j, k, l*, and *t* begin with straight downstrokes, whereas the letters *v, w*, and *x* start with slight slants. If the angle of the first slant is exaggerated, the resulting letter will be sprawled across the page. The letters *e, u, y*, and *z* do not belong to a particular group.

Cursive Handwriting

Lowercase letters are also taught first in cursive handwriting. A new letter is introduced each day, and previously learned letters are reviewed and practiced following the introduction of the new one. It is beneficial to follow the order and grouping of cursive letters by the four basic approach strokes (see Figures 15.7–15.10). Students learn the four approach strokes as they learn new letters. Each approach stroke always begins on the baseline and moves from left to right. An arrow is provided to establish a baseline when students practice on the chalkboard or on unlined paper. The drop stroke follows the approach stroke and ties the letter to the baseline. The remaining shape is added to form the letter, which is then finished by a release stroke. The release stroke is an important part of every letter because it allows for uniform spacing between letters and promotes rhythmic writing.

The Writing Lesson

Classroom teachers should plan to spend 20–30 minutes per day teaching handwriting. When all letter forms are taught, a 5- to 10-minute daily review of difficult letter forms or those that confuse students will maintain standards and automatic performance. The teacher should organize writing instruction with attention to posture, pencil grip, position of the writing surface, and emphasis on naming the letters before writing them. This daily attention to handwriting using a multisensory process helps students learn the letter shapes, increases their automaticity for writing, and facilitates the connection between the letters and the sounds they represent for reading and spelling. Children should be instructed to write, then trace over each letter rather than writing the same letter over and over, as the letters tend to deteriorate.

Berninger (1998) recommended a daily 5-minute handwriting warm-up before starting spelling or written language tasks. In the *Alphabetic Phonics* approach (see Appendix B for information on this program), during the handwriting part of the daily lesson, students can practice at different levels. Each practice session should establish a single focus. The focus can be practicing a selected approach stroke; exercising rhythm and control when writing by naming letters before writing; copying cursive letters directly on top of print to reinforce a letter shape; regulating letter proportion, especially

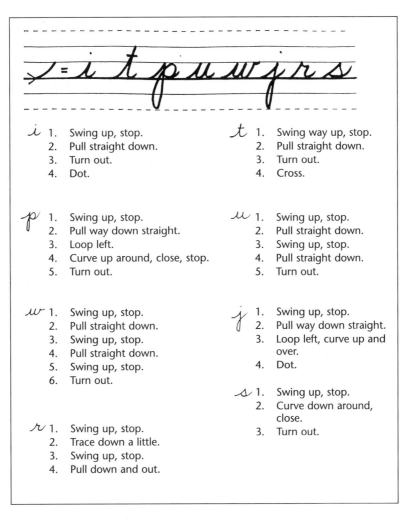

i 1. Swing up, stop.
2. Pull straight down.
3. Turn out.
4. Dot.

t 1. Swing way up, stop.
2. Pull straight down.
3. Turn out.
4. Cross.

p 1. Swing up, stop.
2. Pull way down straight.
3. Loop left.
4. Curve up around, close, stop.
5. Turn out.

u 1. Swing up, stop.
2. Pull straight down.
3. Swing up, stop.
4. Pull straight down.
5. Turn out.

w 1. Swing up, stop.
2. Pull straight down.
3. Swing up, stop.
4. Pull straight down.
5. Swing up, stop.
6. Turn out.

j 1. Swing up, stop.
2. Pull way down straight.
3. Loop left, curve up and over.
4. Dot.

s 1. Swing up, stop.
2. Curve down around, close.
3. Turn out.

r 1. Swing up, stop.
2. Trace down a little.
3. Swing up, stop.
4. Pull down and out.

Figure 15.7. Approach stroke: "Swing up, stop." (From Texas Scottish Rite Hospital for Children, Child Development Division. [1996]. *Teaching cursive writing* [Brochure]. Dallas: Author; reprinted by permission.)

of tall letters; or repeating individual strokes such as "pull down straight" strokes, circles, release strokes, and lower loops. The Slingerland format for instruction includes daily practice in moving from one letter to the next smoothly to develop a rhythmic tempo; students form one dictated letter, then trace until the next letter is named. "This automatic recall and rhythmic movement from one letter to the next should precede functional use of letters for writing words. . . . Controlled guidance and practice are essential" (Slingerland, 1981, p. 39).

After all lowercase letters are learned and can be written legibly, students should practice writing the alphabet in sequence in connected cursive, giving extra attention to the bridge strokes used to connect *b, o, v,* and *w* with the next letter. Extra practice should be provided for frequent combinations such as *br, oa, vi,* and *wh* (see Figure 15.11 for examples). Henry (2003) pointed out that third graders often need practice in these linkages when they are using cursive writing for spelling more complex words. Explicit practice should take place, with students tracing and copying these bridge stroke transitions when difficulties arise.

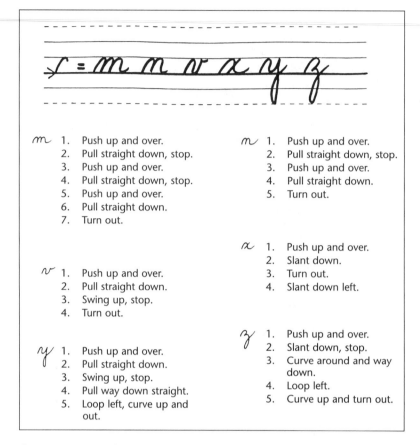

Figure 15.8. Approach stroke: "Push up and over." (From Texas Scottish Rite Hospital for Children, Child Development Division. [1996]. *Teaching cursive writing* [Brochure]. Dallas: Author; reprinted by permission.)

If a student is unable to write a letter satisfactorily, then he or she should return to the tracing step at the board or on a large paper pattern. This procedure should be followed meticulously with each letter until all have been learned and written legibly and automatically. For each activity, the teacher follows a hierarchy of modeling for the students; giving them specific wording to help them monitor their visual-motor responses; and having the students air write, trace, copy, and write on their own. In the Slingerland approach, handwriting practice and review are integrated into the written language lesson to provide success with spelling and written language tasks. For example, if students will be expected to write the word *book*, they first practice the letter forms and connections necessary to successfully write the word: *bo, ok, oo*.

Handwriting lessons should consist of teaching new letters, practicing letters already learned, and reviewing and practicing with letter connections in cursive writing. The following lesson is an excerpt adapted from the Teacher Procedure Cards of the Slingerland Institute for Literacy (2001).

Sample Lesson—Introducing a New Letter and Review

Learning New Letters

1.   Teacher: *Shows Wall Card or Class Alphabet Card. Places hand under the lowercase letter. Names the letter.*

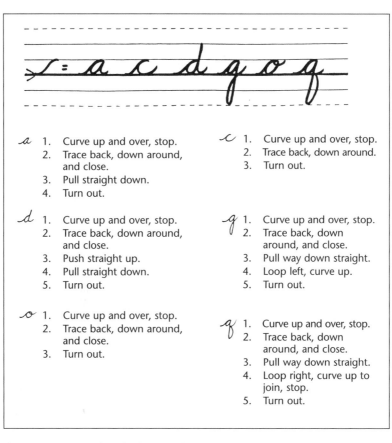

Figure 15.9. Approach stroke: "Curve under, over, stop." (From Texas Scottish Rite Hospital for Children, Child Development Division. [1996]. *Teaching cursive writing [Brochure]. Dallas: Author; reprinted by permission.)*

Children:	*Each individual child names the letter.*
2.	Teacher:	*Forms a large letter on the board, naming it as it is formed, stressing difficult parts*
	Children:	*Individual children—one at a time—trace and name the letter.*
3.	Teacher:	*Makes several patterns on the board*
	Children:	*Several children trace and name at one time.*
	Class:	*Children at seats who have traced (for input), form letter with arm swing, naming as it is formed. (The letter is formed with a full arm swing, 1–2 feet high.)*
4.	Teacher:	*Gives each child a prepared permanent pattern*
	Class:	*Children trace and name, using two fingers.*
5.	Class:	*On the same permanent pattern, children **trace** and name using the unsharpened end of the pencil.*
6.	Teacher:	*Provides a three-space expendable pattern for tracing and copying*
	Class:	*Traces the pattern, first with two fingers, then with the unsharpened end of the pencil.*
	Teacher:	*Monitors for full arm swing and correct formation*

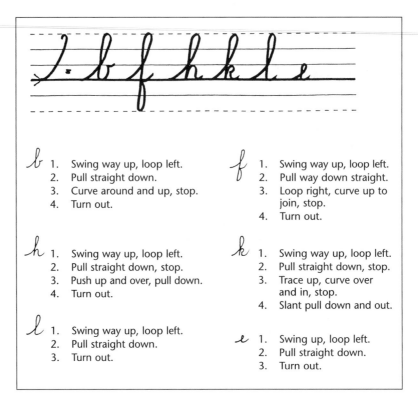

Figure 15.10. Approach stroke: "Curve way up, loop left." (From Texas Scottish Rite Hospital for Children, Child Development Division. [1996]. *Teaching cursive writing [Brochure].* Dallas: Author; reprinted by permission.)

Class: *Children **copy**, then trace the teacher's pattern until the teacher corrects them as needed.*

Teacher: *Moves about the classroom and corrects students as needed*

Class: *Children trace and name the pattern. Then they fold the paper so that only a blank space is visible and they write from memory in the last box of the three-space pattern. When the letter is complete, each child opens the paper to check for correct form and traces the pattern until teacher has checked for correct formation of the letter written from memory.*

Teacher: *Corrects students as needed*

Steps 2, 3, and 6 are also used for teaching difficult cursive letter connections.

Reviewing Letters

This is a time for practicing the spacing between letters, rhythm, and fluency.

Teacher: *Names a letter*

Class: *Children form the letter in the air, with arm swing, while naming it. They name the letter while writing on paper.*

Teacher: *Corrects students as needed*

Class: *Children name and trace the letter.*

Figure 15.11. Lowercase cursive bridge strokes between common letter combinations. (From Texas Scottish Rite Hospital for Children, Child Development Division. [1996]. *Teaching cursive writing* [Brochure]. Dallas: Author; reprinted by permission.)

When children are more automatic and need less structure, they may move to the next review step.

Teacher: *Names letter or letters to develop rhythm and fluency*

Class: *Children write, naming and tracing until the next letter is given (about three times). Each time the children write a letter, they should name the letter and, if necessary, remind themselves verbally of the correct formation.*

Teacher: *Corrects very little*

BYPASS TECHNOLOGY

Resources Available

Keyboarding, voice recognition software, and word prediction programs are among the resources currently available for bypassing handwriting problems. A teacher should use

caution and carefully consider the individual strengths and weaknesses of each student before substituting any of these alternatives. Each has distinct advantages and challenges for the dyslexic student. Continued research is needed to identify the students who will most benefit from using each of these resources as bypass tools.

Keyboarding

Keyboarding should be considered a complement rather than an alternative to handwriting skills. The motor process involved in selecting a key rather than writing a letter may be simpler, but it may require a greater degree of fine motor development. Thought should also be given to the amount of time required to develop fluency on the keyboard. Even students with sufficient dexterity may have difficulty developing automatic use of the keyboard, perhaps because of the difficulties in superimposing the keyboard alphabet (*asdf . . .*) upon the known alphabet (*abcd . . .*). King developed a multisensory approach to touch-typing that teaches the position of the keys in alphabetic order (see Appendix B). Students learn the position of the keys in as little as 30 minutes, followed by practice based on the Orton-Gillingham sequence of instruction. The ability to produce a document on the keyboard provides the psychological bonus of having an attractive document (Levine, 2003).

Effective word processing requires the integration of multiple operations such as selecting, saving, deleting, cutting, pasting, and formulating (Levine, 2003). When keyboarding and word processing skills become automatic for the dyslexic student, computers provide excellent support by facilitating written composition, simplifying the editing process, and providing a check for spelling. Berninger (1998) noted that a spell checker is most effective when children have achieved a fifth-grade spelling level so that their spellings can be recognized by the computer. Students must also have adequate reading ability and a sufficient grasp of vocabulary to discriminate between homographs (words that have the same spelling but that sound different and have different meanings) and homonyms (words that sound the same and that often have the same spelling but have different meanings). Grammar checks can also be excellent support for emerging writers.

Voice Recognition Software

Some students find that they are able to produce longer and more complex compositions when the chore of handwriting or keyboarding is eliminated by voice recognition software. They are required only to enter simple commands and monitor the text as it is produced on the screen. They are freed of the mechanics of writing and able to focus on content. This tool, however, may not be effective for children with limited working memory because of the demands of simultaneous tasks. Many children with expressive language difficulties are unable to use voice recognition software effectively because of the complexity of monitoring text and the amount of editing required to transfer their thoughts into readable form. Very often it is more frustrating rather than less. A computer-savvy dyslexic now employed in the computer industry said, "I'll just learn to write better; this is too much trouble." Levine recommended that "every effort should be made to enable such individuals to practice their graphomotor function as well" and noted that these individuals "are likely to need manual writing in the future" (2003, p. 189).

In the classroom, voice recognition technology may be a distraction to the other students, or may be less effective because of background noise. Each student and learn-

ing situation must be individually evaluated to monitor the effectiveness of this or any other adaptive tool.

Word Prediction Software

Word prediction software allows the child to complete a word, a phrase, or a sentence with only a few keystrokes. The program is based on the letters typed in the word. It generates words beginning in that particular way. As the writer progresses, the program examines syntax and continues to predict the structure of the sentence. As with voice recognition software, the student is expected to keep a number of tasks in working memory. Editing may be helped by programs that read aloud what the child has written. Headphones may be needed in a classroom environment.

Tablet PC Software

Innovative tablet PC software allows computer users to write directly on the computer screen with a stylus, then manipulate the handwritten text. It offers some of the advantages of keyboarding; ability to manipulate text, spell checking, and editing. However, it will not be as effective for a student with graphomotor or orthographic weaknesses.

As this and other new bypass technologies are developed and existing ones are refined, their effectiveness for individual students will be determined by the students' own individual strengths, weaknesses, and needs. (See Chapter 21 of this book, available on-line at http://textbooks.brookespublishing.com/birsh, for further discussion of assistive technology.)

CONCLUSION

This chapter has presented specific techniques for teaching handwriting utilizing a multisensory framework and integrating the teaching of print and cursive handwriting with reading and spelling. The importance of handwriting instruction in early education and in remediation, a brief history of the teaching of handwriting, techniques used to teach it in schools now, some syndromes related to difficulties with handwriting, research evidence of the efficacy of direct teaching of handwriting to dyslexic students, and the use of assistive technologies have been discussed.

Emphasis is placed on a hierarchy of skills—utilizing large-muscle movements at first, providing a model of cursive over print to tie how the letter is written to how it appears in printed reading material, practicing individual strokes within letters, and connecting letters. Spacing; proportion of single letter shapes, both individually and in relation to other letters; rhythm; and fluency are emphasized, leading to instant writing and writing from memory. All is done in a structured way in correct position, with models to refer to, with students naming the letters before writing to utilize the visual, auditory, kinesthetic, and tactile senses. The teacher does not hurry students to reduce the size of the letter shapes prematurely but demands automaticity at each level of **air writing**, tracing, copying, and writing from memory large letters before allowing smaller letters to be practiced.

A number of programs have been specifically developed to emphasize the proper formation of letters, treating handwriting as a basic skill to be taught systematically. All of the programs direct the writer's attention to the distinctive features of each letter. Letters are grouped by beginning strokes; by the number of spaces above and below the

lines; and by stopping points, vertical lines, loops, and curves. The main feature of these programs is consistent motor patterns supported by explicit verbalization of the proper order and direction of making the strokes as the letters are learned and practiced. Verbal descriptions have been developed for all 26 lowercase cursive and print letters. Uppercase cursive letters are usually taught later. (See Appendix B at the end of this book for a list of published multisensory structured language programs that deal directly and explicitly with handwriting as a remedial adjunct to reading and spelling.)

Research has shown that students who are unable to take notes and write papers at an efficient level fall behind not only in notation but also in comprehension (Phelps, Stempel, & Browne, 1989). Because the basic skill areas appear closely linked, handwriting should be integrated into curricula designed to help students who have academic difficulties. Very often the focus in language arts education is on spelling and reading to the exclusion of the technique of handwriting. This vital omission can lower overall achievement and affect a child's attitude toward all school learning (Askov & Peck, 1982).

Assistive or bypass technologies are available, but before adoption careful consideration of a child's strengths and weaknesses is required to determine the degree of assistance that the technologies might provide. Once keyboarding skills are automatic, the keyboard and word processor are useful tools. Students' needs and the limitations of other technologies will influence the effectiveness of these alternatives.

REFERENCES

Abbott, R., & Berninger, V. (1993). Structural equation modeling of relationships among developmental skills and writing skills in primary and intermediate grade writers. *Journal of Educational Psychology, 85,* 478–508.

Adams, M.J. (1990). *Beginning to read: Thinking and learning about print.* Cambridge, MA: The MIT Press.

Askov, E., & Peck, M. (1982). Handwriting. In *Encyclopedia of educational research* (5th ed., Vol. 2, pp. 764–766). New York: Free Press.

Athènes, S., & Guiard, Y. (1991). The development of handwriting posture: A comparison between left-handers and right-handers. In J. Wann, A.M. Wing, & N. Sovik (Eds.), *Development of graphic skills* (pp. 137–149). London: Academic Press.

Beery, K. (1982). *Administration, scoring, and teaching manual for the Developmental Test of Visual–Motor Integration* (Rev. ed.). Cleveland, OH: Modern Curriculum Press.

Berninger, V. (1998). *Guides for intervention.* San Antonio, TX: Harcourt Assessment.

Berninger, V. (1999). The "write stuff" for preventing and treating writing disabilities. *Perspectives, 25*(2), 20–22.

Berninger, V., Abbott, R., Jones, J., Wolf, B., Gould, L., Anderson-Youngstrom, M., et al. (in press.). Early development of language by hand: Composing, reading, listening, and speaking connections, three letter-writing modes and fast mapping in spelling. *Developmental Neuropsychology.*

Berninger, V., & Amtmann, D. (2003). Preventing written expression disabilities through early and continuing assessment and intervention for handwriting and/or spelling problems: Research into practice. In H.L. Swanson, K.R. Harris, & S. Graham (Eds.), *Handbook of research on learning disabilities* (pp. 345–363). New York: The Guilford Press.

Berninger, V., Mizokawa, D.T., & Bragg, R. (1991). Theory-based diagnosis and remediation of writing disabilities. *Journal of School Psychology, 29,* 57–79.

Berninger, V., Raskind, W., McCutchen, D., Richards, T., Cunningham, A., Nolen, S., et al. (1997). Educational and biological links to learning disabilities. *Perspectives, 23*(4), 10–13.

Bertin, P., & Perlman, E. (1991). *Preventing academic failure.* Cambridge, MA: Educators Publishing Service.

Black, J. (1996). *The clumsy child.* Unpublished manuscript, Texas Scottish Rite Hospital for Children, Dallas.

Blalock, J.W. (1985, November 13). *Oral language problems of learning-disabled adolescents and adults.* Paper presented at the 36th annual conference of The Orton Dyslexia Society, Chicago.

Cicci, R. (1995). *What's wrong with me? Learning disabilities at home and in school.* Timonium, MD: York Press.

Cox, A. (1980). *Structures and techniques: Multisensory teaching of basic language skills.* Cambridge, MA: Educators Publishing Service.

Cox, A. (1985). Alphabet phonics: An organization and expansion of Orton-Gillingham. *Annals of Dyslexia, 35,* 187–198.

Cox, A.R. (1992). *Foundations for oral literacy: Structures and techniques for multisensory teaching of basic written English language skills.* Cambridge, MA: Educators Publishing Service.

Fernald, G. (1943). *Remedial techniques in basic school subjects.* New York: McGraw-Hill.

Getman, G.N. (1984). About handwriting. *Academic Therapy, 19,* 139–140.

Gillingham, A., & Stillman, B.W. (1960). *Remedial training for children with specific disability in reading, spelling, and penmanship* (6th ed.). Cambridge, MA: Educators Publishing Service.

Gillingham, A., & Stillman, B.W. (1997). *The Gillingham manual: Remedial training for children with specific disability in reading, writing, and penmanship* (8th ed.). Cambridge, MA: Educators Publishing Service.

Goodman, R., & Caramazza, A. (1986). Dissociation of spelling errors in written and oral spelling: The role of allographic conversion in writing. *Cognitive Neuropsychology, 3,* 179–206.

Graham, S., & Weintraub, N. (1996). A review of handwriting research: Progress and prospects from 1980 to 1994. *Educational Psychology Review, 8,* 7–87.

Hagin, R.A. (1983). Write right or left—a practical approach to handwriting. *Journal of Learning Disabilities, 16,* 266–271.

Hamstra-Bletz, L., & Blöte, A. (1990). Development of handwriting in primary school: A longitudinal study. *Perceptual and Motor Skills, 70,* 759–770.

Henry, M.K. (2003). *Unlocking literacy: Effective decoding and spelling instruction.* Baltimore: Paul H. Brookes Publishing Co.

Johnson, D.J. (1988). Review of research on specific reading, writing, and mathematics disorders. In J.F. Kavanagh & T.J. Truss (Eds.), *Learning disabilities: Proceedings of the national conference.* Timonium, MD: York Press.

Kurtz, L. (1994, Fall). Helpful handwriting hints. *Teaching Exceptional Children,* 58–59.

Levine, M. (1987). *Developmental variations and learning disorders.* Cambridge, MA: Educators Publishing Service.

Levine, M. (1994). *Educational care: A system for understanding and helping children with learning problems at home and in school.* Cambridge, MA: Educators Publishing Service.

Levine, M. (2003). *The myth of laziness.* New York: Simon & Schuster.

Luria, A.R. (1973). *The working brain.* London: Penguin Books.

McMenamin, B., & Martin, M. (1980). *Right writing.* Spring Valley, CA: Cursive Writing Associates.

Moats, L.C. (1995). *Spelling: Development, disability, and instruction.* Timonium, MD: York Press.

Orton, J.L. (1966). The Orton-Gillingham approach. In J. Money (Ed.), *The disabled reader: Education of the dyslexic child.* Baltimore: The Johns Hopkins University Press.

Orton, S.T. (1937). *Reading, writing, and speech problems in children.* New York: W.W. Norton.

Phelps, J., & Stempel, L. (1985). *CHES's handwriting improvement program (CHIP).* Dallas: CHES. (Available from the publisher, Post Office Box 25254, Dallas, TX 75225)

Phelps, J., & Stempel, L. (1987). Handwriting: Evolution and evaluation. *Annals of Dyslexia, 37,* 228–239.

Phelps, J., Stempel, L., & Browne, R. (1989). *Children's handwriting and school achievement.* Unpublished manuscript, Texas Scottish Rite Hospital for Children, Dallas.

Reisman, J. (1991, September). Poor handwriting: Who is referred? *American Journal of Occupational Therapy, 45*(9), 849–852.

Richardson, S. (1995). Specific developmental dyslexia: Retrospective and prospective views. In C.W. McIntyre & J.S. Pickering (Eds.), *Clinical studies of multisensory structured language education* (pp. 1–15). Salem, OR: IMSLEC.

Rubin, H., & Eberhardt, N. (1996). Facilitating invented spelling through language analysis instruction: An integrated model. *Reading and Writing: An Interdisciplinary Journal, 8,* 27–43.

Slingerland, B.H. (1971). *A multisensory approach to language arts: Book I.* Cambridge, MA: Educators Publishing Service.

Slingerland, B. (1976). *Basics in scope and sequence of a multisensory approach to language arts: Book II.* Cambridge, MA: Educators Publishing Service.

Slingerland, B. (1981). *A multi-sensory approach to language arts for specific language disability children: Book 3. A guide for elementary teachers.* Cambridge, MA: Educators Publishing Service.

Slingerland, B., & Aho, M. (1985). *Manual for learning to use manuscript handwriting.* Cambridge, MA: Educators Publishing Service.

Slingerland Institute for Literacy. (2001). Teacher procedure cards. In *Slingerland Institute directors' manual.* Bellevue, WA: Author.

Snow, C.E., Burns, M.S., & Griffin, P. (Eds.). (1998). *Preventing reading difficulties in young children.* Washington, DC: National Academies Press.

Strickling, C.A. (1974). The effect of handwriting and related skills upon the spelling scores above average and below average readers in the fifth grade. *Dissertation Abstracts International, 34*(07), 3717A.

Tabor, M. (1996, May 8). Penmanship: Fine art to lost art. *The New York Times,* pp. B1, B12.

Texas Scottish Rite Hospital for Children, Child

Development Division (TSRHC). (1990). *Dyslexia training program developed in the Dyslexia Laboratory, Texas Scottish Rite Hospital* [Videotape]. Cambridge, MA: Educators Publishing Service.

Texas Scottish Rite Hospital for Children, Child Development Division (TSRHC). (1996). *Teaching cursive writing* [Brochure]. Dallas: Author.

vos Savant, M. (1988, June 5). Ask Marilyn. *Parade,* 8.

Wessel, D. (1984, June 27). Pupils are minding their P's and Q's and other letters. *The Wall Street Journal,* p. 1.

Wilson Language Training. (2002). *Fundations.* Millbury, MA: Author.

16

Composition
Expressive Language and Writing

Judith C. Hochman

Written language is considered by many to be the most challenging skill to teach and to learn. Some proponents of multisensory instruction believe that the teaching of written language skills should be delayed until students have achieved proficiency in decoding, spelling, and handwriting (Clark & Uhry, 1995). It is feared that dyslexic children will be overwhelmed if they are exposed to additional language training before they reach middle school. There is reason to believe, however, that there are large numbers of oral and written activities that teachers should use in the primary grades concurrently with the beginning of instruction in reading, spelling, and handwriting.

Many individuals with excellent reading and speaking skills have problems generating written language. Even for typical learners, mastering the skills associated with good writing is a daunting task, but those individuals with learning and language problems face especially formidable obstacles. Students with learning and language disabilities have difficulties with decoding, spelling, word retrieval, and syntax that are often exacerbated by a limited vocabulary. As a result, understanding what others say and expressing oneself with clarity and accuracy are significantly compromised. In addition, weak organizational skills often accompany learning and language problems. The inability to distinguish essential from nonessential information and to set forth facts or ideas in logical order can impede students as they try to formulate outlines or generate well-organized paragraphs and compositions.

Writing problems remain a persistent learning disability, personally, vocationally, and academically for many adults who were not taught specific strategies as young students (Scott, 1989, 1999). Because reading disabilities receive far more attention in school than do writing problems, many students receive little, if any, explicit instruction in written language (Scott, 1989, 1999). Too often it is assumed that mastery of the conventions of written language will naturally follow fluent decoding and good reading comprehension.

Competent writers are able to focus on the topic, meaning, purpose, and audience as they plan and organize information. These tasks require simultaneous processing at higher cognitive levels than are required in other areas of skills acquisition. Moreover, older students are often required to demonstrate in writing assignments their understanding of subject matter by paraphrasing or summarizing texts that are linguistically complex or densely loaded with factual information.

The development of **narrative** skills and sound expository writing abilities, that is, the discussion of ideas or explanation of processes, should be the primary aims of a written language curriculum. Given the limited time teachers have to provide instruction in writing, the goal should be to help students develop a solid foundation in those writing skills that are required most often in academic tasks and assignments. Writing and thinking are inextricably linked. Therefore, the most important instructional goals should be to enhance clarity and precision in both process and product. Although mechanics such as spelling and handwriting (see Chapters 10 and 15, respectively) are important and should not be ignored, they should be addressed separately from composition whenever possible so that students can focus on developing the higher level skills required for written language.

Creative writing activities, which center on self-expression rather than on communication with the reader, are frequently the major focus of elementary school writing programs. Imaginative stories, poems, journal writing, and descriptions involving personal perceptions are assigned in many classes, often with little or no guidance from the teacher. These activities are not the same as those used during direct instruction in how to write. Students with and without learning and language disabilities should be given opportunities to experiment with a variety of forms and styles only after they learn how to write sentences and paragraphs competently.

Although writing lessons should take place daily, tasks involving paper and pencil are not always necessary. For example, many sentence and paragraph activities can and should be done orally. This is particularly important in the primary grades. Activities for longer compositions should include carefully orchestrated discussions dealing with the identification of the audience, selection of a topic, and description of the purpose of the assignment. The teacher must provide explicit demonstrations of what is expected. Independent writing should not take place until a great deal of time has been spent on teacher modeling and group activities.

Because many students have difficulty applying the writing principles learned in one class to the subject matter of another, reinforcement is important. For the best results, writing instruction should be integrated into every content area and at all grade levels through secondary school. Students with a wide range of abilities will then have a chance of becoming better writers in all academic areas.

This chapter describes activities for writing sentences, paragraphs, and compositions. Most of them should take place concurrently. Sentence activities are the foundation for revising and editing skills, which are crucial in developing competency in writing. Activities for paragraphs and compositions are necessary to develop the thinking and study skills that students need.

SENTENCES

Sentence activities have two primary purposes. The first goal is to enable students to write compound and complex sentences rather than only simple, active, declarative forms. This will enhance reading comprehension (Maria, 1990). The second goal is to

improve revision and editing skills, which benefit critical thinking skills. Students' awareness of grammar and the functions of the parts of speech is enhanced by emphasizing sentence structure and sentence activities (Scott, 1989, 1999). The importance of allocating a great deal of time working with sentences cannot be emphasized enough.

Teachers may use many sentence activities, most of which can be performed both orally and in writing. They should provide as many opportunities as possible to practice developing sentence skills. These activities can be adapted to be made more challenging or easier, depending on the age and ability levels of the students.

Sentences and Fragments

Teacher: A sentence is a complete thought. Tell me whether the groups of words you hear (or read) are sentences or not: Jane gave me her book.

Student: *Sentence*

Teacher: Into the forest

Student: *Not a sentence*

Teacher: A fragment is a piece of a sentence. Change this fragment into a sentence: At night.

Student: *The deer ran at night.*

Note: Students often use **fragments** (incomplete sentences) in spoken language, and they do the same when they write. The teacher must explain that far more precision is necessary in writing than in speaking. Students should be able to locate fragments in a given selection or one that is read aloud before attempting to correct them in their own work.

Scrambled Sentences

Teacher: Rearrange the words into sentences, and add the correct punctuation and capitalization: live did where tim

Student: *Where did Tim live?*

Rearranging sequences of words into sentences and adding the correct punctuation and capitalization provide practice working with word order in sentences. Younger or less able students may need to be given the first word of the sentence with the first letter capitalized.

Sentence Types: Statements, Commands, Questions, and Exclamations

Teacher: Add the correct punctuation and capitalization to these sentences. Write this as a statement: john stayed at home

Student: *John stayed at home.*

Teacher: Write this as a command: give that to me immediately

Student: *Give that to me immediately!*

Teacher: Write this as a question: where are you going

Student: *Where are you going?*

Teacher:	Write this as an exclamation: my father hates cauliflower
Student:	*My father hates cauliflower!*
Teacher:	[Asks students to write on worksheets or on the chalkboard an example of each of the four sentence types, using a particular spelling or vocabulary word] Write a statement, a command, a question, and exclamation using the word *retract*.
Student:	*The teacher retracted what she said.* *Retract that statement.* *Will he retract that remark?* *I want you to retract that statement!*
Teacher:	[Asks students to change statements to questions (and vice versa)] He is the governor.
Student:	*Is he the governor?*
Teacher:	[Asks students to generate a question from an answer; students can do this orally or in writing] Albany
Student:	*What is the capital of New York?*
Teacher:	[Asks students to help develop essay questions for social studies, science, or literature tests]
Student:	*Discuss the events leading up to the War of 1812.* *Describe the process of photosynthesis.* *Explain the great and continuing public interest in* The Diary of Anne Frank.

It is as important to have students generate questions as it is for students to respond to them. For example, the teacher can show primary students a picture and ask them what question(s) the picture suggests. Older students should be asked to anticipate essay questions on upcoming tests or produce questions after reading comprehension exercises.

Sentence Expansion

The teacher should display the question words *who, what, when, where, why,* and *how* and then give students sentence kernels (simple sentences without modifiers), such as *Jane ran* or *Candidates debate*. The teacher should ask the class to expand the kernels by using one, two, three, or more of the question words. When introducing this strategy, it is best for the teacher to begin with *when, where,* or *why* because these are easier than *who, what,* and *how*. (Figure 16.1 shows an example of a sentence expansion worksheet.) Reading comprehension or knowledge in any content area can be assessed using sentence kernels and question words, such as *Colonists fled. Where? Why?* Students often assume that the reader has more prior knowledge than is actually the case; sentence expansion enables them to provide information with greater precision.

Conjunctions

Conjunctions are uninflected words that join words, phrases, or clauses. Their purpose is to link or relate parts of a sentence. Table 16.1 lists conjunctions that the teacher may use as a reference and insert in students' notebooks to aid them in independent writ-

Name:__________ Date:__________

SENTENCE EXPANSION

Expand the following kernels using three of the following question words: where, **when, why, how.**

Kernel: The boys ran.
when Tuesday
how quickly
where in the park
Expanded Sentence: Last Tuesday the boys ran quickly in the park.

Kernel: Rose entered.
when yesterday
how cautiously
why scared
Expanded Sentence: Yesterday, Rose entered cautiously because she was scared.

Figure 16.1. Sentence expansion worksheet. (From Hochman, J.C. [2001]. *Basic writing skills: A manual for teachers* [p. 66]. New York: GSL Publications; reprinted by permission.)

ing. Students should write sentences starting with conjunctions to construct linguistically complex sentences. The teacher can consider having students embed spelling or vocabulary words in their sentences or write about their experiences.

Teacher: Use the three following conjunctions, and write one sentence about the ice skating trip for each: whenever, since, after

Student: *Whenever we go ice skating, we have a great time.*
Since we are going ice skating, I am going to get my skates sharpened.
After we go ice skating, we will write about it in school.

Teacher: [Asks students to combine short, active, declarative sentences using conjunctions and explains that repetition can be avoided by using pronouns] Combine these sentences using a conjunction: John was at the bus stop. John's car was being repaired.

Student: *John was at the bus stop because his car was being repaired.*

Table 16.1.   Conjunctions for use in independent writing

after	but	if . . . then	since	until
although	either . . . or	in order to	so	when
and	even if	neither . . . nor	so that	whenever
as if	even though	nevertheless	than	where
as soon as	for (meaning *because*)	nonetheless	that	wherever
as though	how	or	then	while
because	however	rather than	though	yet
before	if	regardless of	unless	

Teacher: [Asks students to use conjunctions to create complete sentences] Mother was happy because . . .

Student: *Mother was happy because we cleaned our room.*

Teacher: Mother was happy, but . . .

Student: *Mother was happy, but she saw clothes on the floor.*

Teacher: Mother was happy, so . . .

Student: *Mother was happy, so she let us go to the movies.*

This activity is useful in assessing students' understanding of literature, social studies, or current events, as shown in the following examples:

Teacher: Andrew Jackson was a popular president, but . . .

Student: *Andrew Jackson was a popular president, but there were many critics of his Kitchen Cabinet and the spoils system.*

Teacher: Andrew Jackson was a popular president because . . .

Student: *Andrew Jackson was a popular president because he was a champion of the common people.*

Teacher: Andrew Jackson was a popular president, so . . .

Student: *Andrew Jackson was a popular president, so he won the election of 1828 easily.*

Teacher: Anne Frank and her family were hidden in the attic; however . . .

Student: *Anne Frank and her family were hidden in the attic; however, they were discovered by the Nazis.*

Grammar

The parts of speech and their usage should be taught within the writing program. Teaching grammar during sentence activities helps students gain an understanding of how parts of speech are used in context, which proves especially useful when students are expected to revise and edit their own work or assigned passages.

Teacher: [Asks students to change nouns to pronouns] Mary danced.

Student: *She danced.*

Teacher: [Asks the class to change tenses from present to past (or from present to future or vice versa)] The car races.

Student: *The car raced.*
The car will race.

Teacher: [Asks students to insert an adjective, an adverb, and a prepositional phrase]
The runner won.

Student: *The amazing runner won easily in spite of keen competition.*

Teacher: [Asks students to use an appositive after a proper noun (an appositive is a
second noun, placed beside the first noun to explain it more fully; it usually
has modifiers)] George Washington was a brilliant general.

Student: *George Washington, our first president, was a brilliant general.*

Topic Sentences

The teacher should show students how to generate topic sentences for given topics. "He
or she explains to the students that the topic sentence is the leading or controlling sentence of the paragraph" (Morgan, 2001, p. 152). Students brainstorm sentences about
a given topic. For example, if the topic is hiking, a range of topic sentences can emerge:
*Hiking can be dangerous. My favorite weekend activity is hiking. Hiking is a great way to enjoy
nature. Try hiking this summer!* The teacher should encourage students to experiment
using different sentence types and remind students that topic sentences do not necessarily have to begin with the topic word.

Teacher: Topic: New York City

Student: *I love New York City.*
Do you have a favorite place to visit in New York City?
Visit New York City!
New York City is a study in contrasts.

The teacher should make sure that students can distinguish between topic sentences and supporting details. *Visiting the Metropolitan Museum of Art is a wonderful experience* supports but does not convey the main idea, New York City. Selecting the topic
sentence from a group of sentences is a beneficial activity.

Teacher: I'm going to read you several sentences. One is a topic sentence. The others
are supporting details. Listen for the topic sentence, and tell me which one
you think it is. Remember, the topic sentence might not be the first one I
read to you.

The western frontier closed.
European nations were competing for resources and markets.
There were several causes for the United States' expansion overseas.
Businesses were seeking raw materials and new markets.

Student: *The topic sentence was the third one: There were several causes for the United States'
expansion overseas.*

PARAGRAPHS AND COMPOSITIONS

Very little has been written on the developmental stages of writing for children with
language disabilities (Clark & Uhry, 1995). Narratives setting forth a sequence of events

are the form of composition taught most frequently to younger or less skilled writers (Deshler, Ellis, & Lenz, 1996). Narrative writing relates events in chronological order, and sentences can be sequenced using **transition words**, such as *first, next, then,* and *finally* (see Table 16.2). Written in the first person (narrator as a participant) or third person (narrator as an observer), this type of composition is most beneficial when it is based on a personal or a class experience.

In contrast with narratives, expository writing explains or informs. Typically, students are asked to define, discuss, criticize, list, compare, contrast, explain, and/or summarize. Expository writing is also used to provide an example or describe a process. The topic sentence of a paragraph or thesis statement of a composition should clearly state the writer's objective, and the product should contain sufficient support for the writer's position. Because this type of assignment is the kind of writing most frequently required in school in fourth grade and beyond, teachers should spend the most time on it (Deshler et al., 1996). Several common types of expository writing are described next.

Persuasive writing presents a point of view to a specific audience, such as parents, fellow students, teachers, or the editor of a newspaper. Facts are gathered in order to convince the reader of the validity of the writer's position. The conclusion usually proposes the action that the writer would like the reader to take. Persuasive writing is usually considered the most difficult type of expository writing.

Descriptive writing taps the five senses in order to effectively transmit experiences about people, places, things, and thoughts. Varied and vivid vocabulary is especially important when developing a descriptive passage. Brainstorming and generating lists of adjectives and adverbs or more precise nouns and verbs are appropriate activities to use in conjunction with descriptive writing lessons.

The *compare-and-contrast composition* highlights the similarities (comparisons) and differences (contrasts) among two or more people, places, things, ideas, or experiences. A conclusion must be developed from the facts presented. When presenting this type of writing assignment, teachers should be aware that organizing compare-and-contrast essays can be particularly challenging for the less skillful writer. Teachers should explain that it is easier to compare and contrast two subjects in a composition with several paragraphs than in one paragraph.

A great deal of time must be spent teaching students how to develop a single good paragraph before moving on to longer compositions. Many teachers are eager to encourage their students to write at length about a topic, thus confusing quantity with quality. The chances are that if students write too much too soon, they may not stick to the topic and may not proofread and improve their writing effectively.

The following four steps are involved in most writing assignments. A lesson can end after any one of them, except that it is not a good idea to have students end an assignment with an uncorrected draft.

1. Planning and outlining

2. Drafting

3. Revising and editing

4. Writing a final copy

The first step, planning and outlining, and the third step, revising and editing, are the most important to master. Therefore, they should be given far more instructional time than drafting or producing final copies, which can be done independently by some students.

Planning and Outlining

Planning requires a great deal of instructional time. This is the point at which students begin to organize their assignments and thoughts systematically and sequentially. Class discussions that establish the topic, type, purpose, and audience of the paragraph or composition are extremely important. During the planning phase, information is gathered and shared. Students are guided to distinguish between relevant and nonessential material. Ideas and supporting details are categorized and sequenced in outline form. Topic sentences and, for older students, thesis statements can be developed at this time. Initially, all of these activities can be done as a class with teacher demonstrations and guidance. When students become more proficient, they can begin to work independently.

Initial lessons in how to develop outlines are done with the teacher guiding the development of a model for the class. By providing an overall view of the finished product, the outline serves as a map that allows students to visualize the project as a cohesive whole that has a beginning, middle, and end. Outlines help students to distinguish essential from nonessential material and to sequence information. As students become more proficient through practice and group work, they can develop their outlines independently.

Three useful outline forms are as follows (Hochman, 2001):

- The *Quick Outline* is used for developing a single paragraph and is intended to help the students discern the basic structure of the paragraph: topic sentence, supporting details, and concluding sentence.

- The *Transitional Outline* is useful when students are beginning to write compositions of two or three paragraphs.

- The *Multiple Paragraph Outline (MPO)* is for developing compositions of three or more paragraphs.

After students have mastered a particular outlining format, they should be encouraged to proceed to writing drafts. When teaching outlining, teachers should use topics that require no special prior knowledge unless something that has just been taught or experienced by the class is being reviewed or reinforced. The emphasis should be on the skills required to outline, not on the material to be learned or reviewed.

Quick Outline

Students must master several preliminary skills before they can develop a Quick Outline (see Figure 16.2) independently (Hochman, 2001). Several activities for developing and improving outlines are helpful in providing practice for students. First, the student must be able to produce a topic sentence for a given topic (e.g., if the topic is the Industrial Revolution, a topic sentence might be *There were several major causes and effects of the Industrial Revolution*). Second, the student has to learn to supply supporting details using key words or phrases (e.g., *Eli Whitney/cotton gin/interchangeable parts*). This skill is an important one and is a precursor to note taking. A great deal of practice is needed for students to convert sentences into phrases. Complete sentences should not be used on the outline except for the topic and concluding sentences. Third, the students have to understand that the concluding sentence is either a restatement of the topic sentence or a summary of the paragraph's main point (e.g., *The Industrial Revolution was a time of great change*). Topics can be easier or more challenging depending on

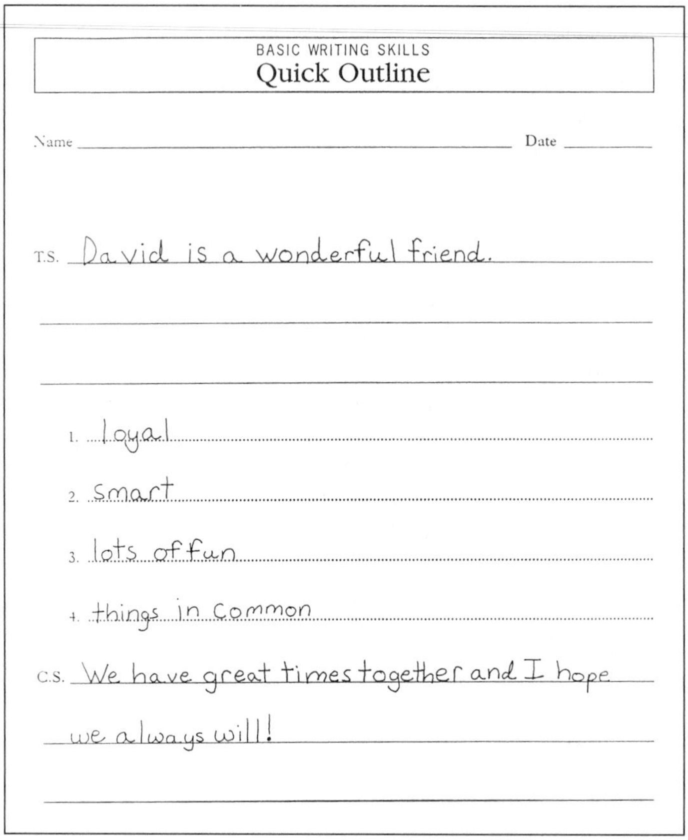

BASIC WRITING SKILLS
Quick Outline

Name ____________ Date ______

T.S. David is a wonderful friend.

1. loyal
2. smart
3. lots of fun
4. things in common

C.S. We have great times together and I hope we always will!

Figure 16.2. Quick Outline. (From Hochman, J.C. [2001 *Basic writing skills: A manual for teachers* [p. 75]. New York: GSL Publications; reprinted by permission.)

the age and abilities of the students. Teaching the skills used in the creation of Quick Outlines requires a great deal of teacher demonstration and group work.

Many activities focus on just one segment of the Quick Outline. These activities can be done before or concurrently with completing a full Quick Outline. An overhead projector is useful when working as a class. The students should have a copy of the overhead text so they can work along with the teacher.

Teacher: Provide the details for this topic sentence: Thanksgiving is a wonderful traditional holiday.

Student: *Pilgrims, Native Americans*
preparation, fun
family reunion
wonderful food

Teacher: Generate a topic sentence from the following phrases:

Pilgrims and Native Americans
family gets together
turkey, trimmings, desserts
football

Student: *Thanksgiving is my favorite holiday.*

Teacher: Identify the topic sentence and sequence the others.

> I ate too much candy.
> My sister and I selected our costumes.
> Sheila was a princess and I was a witch.
> Last Halloween was great!
> The next day we were exhausted.

Student: *The topic sentence is* Last Halloween was great! *The others should be in this order:*

> *My sister and I selected our costumes.*
> *Sheila was a princess and I was a witch.*
> *I ate too much candy.*
> *The next day we were exhausted.*

Teacher: Identify the topic sentence, and write the others in phrases and key words.

> Texas was perfect for raising cattle and growing cotton.
> There was fertile land in Oregon.
> Americans believed in Manifest Destiny.
> There were many causes of the westward expansion in the United States.
> Mormons wanted a safe haven.
> Gold was discovered in California.

Student: *The topic sentence is* There were many causes of the westward expansion in the United States. *Key words are:*

> *perfect/cattle/cotton*
> *Oregon/fertile*
> *belief in Manifest Destiny*
> *Mormons/safe haven*
> *California/gold*

Teacher: Here is a topic sentence: Autumn is my favorite season. Eliminate irrelevant phrases and those that do not relate directly to the topic sentence.

> go for drive/changing colors
> buy cider/doughnuts/pumpkin
> watch video
> carve jack-o'-lantern

> Concluding sentence: Some of my best memories take place in autumn.

Student: Watch video *is the irrelevant phrase.*

Teacher: Convert the following paragraph into a Quick Outline:

> Autumn is my favorite season. I love to drive through the country and look at the changing colors of the leaves. It's fun to stop for cider and doughnuts and to buy a pumpkin. Later, at home, we carve the jack-o'-lantern. Some of my best memories are of autumn.

Student: *Topic sentence: Autumn is my favorite season.*
> *go for drive/changing colors*
> *buy cider/doughnuts/pumpkin*
> *carve jack-o'-lantern*
> *Concluding sentence: Some of my best memories are of autumn.*

To develop a complete Quick Outline with the class, the following sequence is suggested:

1. Introduce and discuss a topic.

2. Identify audience and discuss purpose.

3. Present a topic sentence to the students, or have them generate one as a group. (Eventually students should do this independently.)

4. Elicit as many supporting details as possible from the class, and write them on the chalkboard or on a flipchart. If the details are stated as complete sentences, convert them into phrases or key words.

5. Depending on the topic and number of details, either select three or four of the most important ones or, whenever possible, group the details in categories for the outline.

Distribute a blank Quick Outline to each student.

1. Ask the students to write their preferred topic sentence (if more than one was generated) and to select details for the outline.

2. Generate a concluding sentence as a class. If students are able, they can do this independently.

Transitional Outline

The Transitional Outline (see Figure 16.3) is used after the students have had experience writing paragraphs and are ready to attempt to produce longer compositions. Students should be comfortable with the format of the Quick Outline before moving on to the Transitional Outline, and this generally does not occur before fourth or fifth grade. The Transitional Outline provides an overview of the whole composition, including topic sentences and details for every paragraph. A concluding sentence is not necessary for any paragraph other than the last one.

Multiple Paragraph Outline

The MPO (see Figure 16.4) is designed for students who are ready to develop unified, coherent compositions of three or more paragraphs. This type of outline poses a number of challenges for students with learning disabilities. These students must be careful not to select topics that are either too broad or too narrow. A specific purpose for writing as well as the audience must be identified. The thesis statement should be clear and succinct.

In order to develop an MPO, students must be able to construct a good paragraph. Unlike the Quick Outline, in an MPO the main idea of each paragraph is not written as a topic sentence but as a category on the left side of the outline (e.g., *pro, con; cause, effect; similarities, differences; 1st reason, 2nd reason*). Supporting details should be written as brief, clear phrases or key words. The MPO helps students learn to construct an introduction; a body, which can consist of several paragraphs; and a conclusion. This kind of outline guides students to stay with a consistent topic, purpose, and point of view by providing a clear visual diagram of the entire work. As with the other outlines, students will need group work and teacher modeling before they can develop an MPO independently.

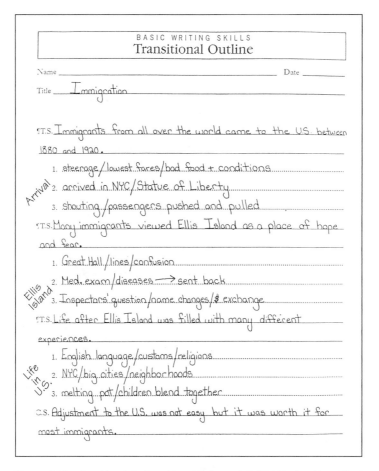

BASIC WRITING SKILLS
Transitional Outline

Name _____   Date _____

Title ___Immigration_____

¶T.S. Immigrants from all over the world came to the US between
1880 and 1920.

   1. steerage / lowest fares / bad food + conditions.........................

Arrival   2. arrived in NYC / Statue of Liberty..........................

   3. shouting / passengers pushed and pulled.............,........

¶T.S. Many immigrants viewed Ellis Island as a place of hope
and fear.

   1. Great Hall / lines / confusion..........................

   2. Med. exam / diseases → sent back..........................

Ellis Island   3. Inspectors' question / name changes / $ exchange..................

¶T.S. Life after Ellis Island was filled with many different
experiences.

   1. English language / customs / religions..........................

Life in U.S.   2. NYC / big cities / neighborhoods..........................

   3. melting pot / children blend together..........................

C.S. Adjustment to the U.S. was not easy but it was worth it for
most immigrants.

Figure 16.3. Transitional Outline. (From Hochman, J.C. [2001 *Basic writing skills: A manual for teachers* [p. 76]. New York: GSL Publications; reprinted by permission.)

The teacher does not need to move in sequence from three- to four- to five-paragraph compositions, because the number of paragraphs usually depends on the topic. For example, a book report may require three paragraphs, with categories such as introduction, plot summary, and opinion. A topic such as pollution might have four categories: introduction, causes, effects, and possible solutions. A biographical essay about Andrew Jackson may require five categories, such as introduction, early life, military career, presidency, and conclusion.

Depending on the topic, most MPOs require a thesis statement, which can be presented as one of the following:

- A personal judgment on a topic

- Advice or directions

- Consequences

- An argument for or against an issue

- An interpretation (usually when writing about fiction or poetry)

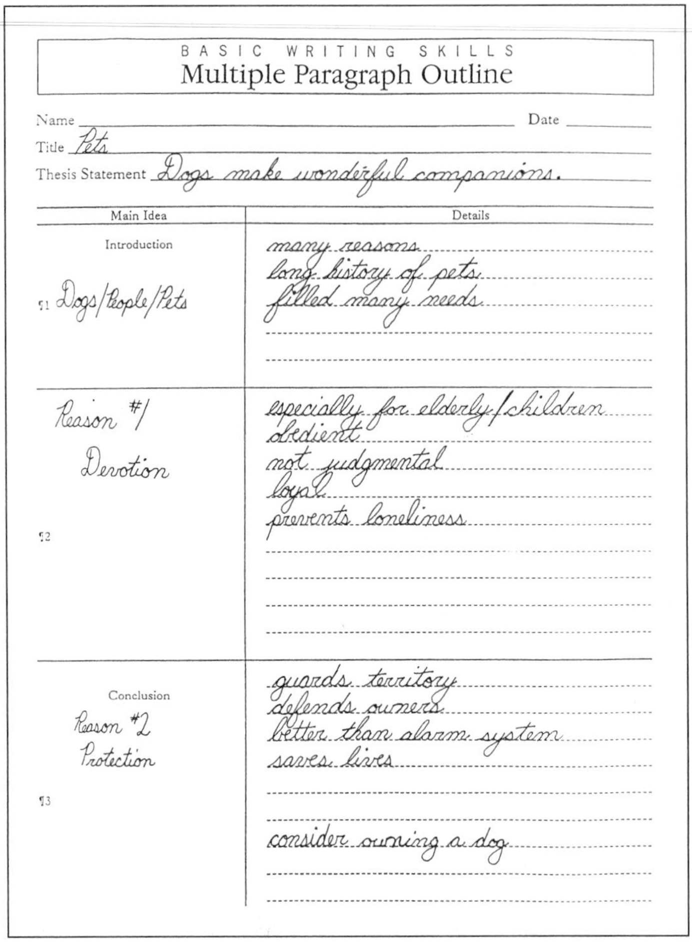

BASIC WRITING SKILLS
Multiple Paragraph Outline

Name ______ Date ______
Title Pets
Thesis Statement Dogs make wonderful companions.

Main Idea	Details
Introduction ¶1 Dogs/People/Pets	many reasons long history of pets filled many needs
Reason #1 Devotion ¶2	especially for elderly/children obedient not judgmental loyal prevents loneliness
Conclusion Reason #2 Protection ¶3	guards territory defends owners better than alarm system saves lives consider owning a dog

Figure 16.4. Multiple Paragraph Outline. (From Hochman, J.C. [2001]. *Basic writing skills: A manual for teachers* [p. 81]. New York: GSL Publications; reprinted by permission.)

At this point, older or more advanced students can be taught that it is not necessary for the topic sentence to be the first one in a paragraph. The teacher should explain that the last few words in a paragraph or composition have the most impact on the reader, and therefore the points the writer wishes to emphasize should be at the end. The last sentence of a selection is as important as the first one.

To develop a complete MPO, the following sequence is suggested:

1. Select the topic that will be the basis for the title when writing the draft.
2. Discuss purpose and audience.
3. Develop the thesis statement.
4. Write the main idea as a phrase or a category for each paragraph in the left-hand column. This prevents repetition and enables the students to plan the entire composition more effectively. Each paragraph must relate to the overall theme.
5. After determining the main idea for each paragraph, write the supporting details in the right-hand column and tell the students that it is acceptable to include more

items than they may eventually include in their draft. Remind students that each supporting detail should relate directly to the main idea of its paragraph.

Writing the introduction and the conclusion requires the ability to summarize information. Students should be given plenty of oral practice summarizing news stories, chapters, or plots in one or two sentences. The sentence expansion strategy (*who, what, when, where, why*) and conjunctions (especially *but, because,* and *so*) are helpful aids when summarizing. Because many writers have difficulty with summarizing, it is a good idea to provide lessons that focus exclusively on introductions and conclusions of given topics.

Drafting

Drafting begins with writing paragraphs or compositions based on Quick Outlines, Transitional Outlines, or MPOs. Inexperienced or less competent writers should limit their writing to one paragraph of five or six sentences because longer papers tend to discourage attempts to revise and edit. The teacher should tell students that a draft can never be left uncorrected or unimproved. Revisions and editing will always be expected. In order to provide room for improving their work, students must skip lines when writing drafts or leave sufficient space when working on a computer. A teacher may decide to end an activity with a corrected draft instead of moving on to a final copy if the objectives of the lesson have been met.

Even after a final copy is produced, drafts should not be discarded because they can be helpful in assessing how much the students have improved and the areas in which students need further work. Drafts also provide students with graphic examples of their progress.

Revising and Editing

It is important to stress revising and editing when teaching writing skills to students. Revision is the clarification or alteration of the meaning or structure of a draft. This is in contrast to editing, which involves proofreading and correcting errors in grammar, punctuation, syntax, and spelling. Highly competent writers spend the most time on revision, and consequently, it is the area in which the largest amount of instructional time should be invested. The sentence activities presented previously provide the foundation for developing the skills to improve written work. In order to teach students to refine their own or others' writing, the teacher can remind students that there are several ways to improve the quality of written language. The five fundamental techniques for revising and editing are as follows:

1. Adding words

2. Deleting words

3. Substituting words, phrases, or clauses

4. Rearranging words, phrases, clauses, and sentences

5. Proofreading for errors

All too frequently, students are given credit for the quantity of their written work rather than for the quality. They should be reminded regularly that clarity and accuracy, not length, are their goals. Assignments should be kept brief.

The teacher should provide students with checklists for revising and editing. Typical items include the following, with variations for age and ability:

- Does your draft follow your outline?

- Is your topic sentence clearly stated?

- Are your supporting details clear and in order?

- Do the details support the topic sentence?

- Did you use different types of sentences?

- Do your sentences vary in length?

- Are there sentences that should be combined or expanded?

- Did you use transition words or phrases?

- Are your word choices repetitive? vivid? accurate?

- Have you checked for **run-on sentences**? fragments? spelling, punctuation, or capitalization errors?

- Have you checked tense and number agreement?

Initially, only a few items should be selected from the checklist to provide a focus for the students as they improve and correct their work. As students become more adept, more checklist items can be added. Students will need reminders to revise style first, then edit the mechanics.

In addition to listing specific items on the checklist, it is often helpful for the teacher to give younger or less advanced students explicit instructions that will add flair to their compositions, such as "Add two adjectives," "Insert more transition words," or "Use **sentence starters**." At first, the teacher will have to show students exactly where to place the words and phrases. In time, students will be able to see where to insert them independently. Much attention should also be given to the selection of strong and varied nouns and verbs as well as modifiers. Time and sequence transitions should be taught first, followed by conclusions, and then illustration transitions. The remaining two groups can be taught in any order. (See Table 16.2 for examples of transition words and phrases.) The teacher should encourage students to use transitions even at the beginning stages of paragraph development. Together with the use of sentence starters and conjunctions, the application of these skills will raise the level of linguistic complexity and quality of the students' written work. The teacher should stress that a draft can be reworked at least two or three times and that the more often the draft is rewritten, the better the writer.

Students require a great deal of direct instruction, demonstrations, and group participation as they correct and improve their work. They have to understand that their goals should be compositions that flow smoothly, are properly organized, and maintain the reader's interest. Sentences should vary in length and style. Although short, simple, active, declarative sentences are useful for emphasis, too often they are the only forms used by less skillful writers. Teachers' comments and feedback should be explicit and plentiful during drafting and during revising and editing.

Students should routinely read their work aloud as an important component of any writing program. This can take place during sentence activities and the drafting or revising and editing stages. Students can read to a partner, to a small group, or to the

Table 16.2. Transition words and phrases

Group 1 *Time and sequence*	Group 2 *Conclusion*	Group 3 *Illustration*
first	in conclusion	for example
second	consequently	for instance
then	in closing	specifically
next	in summary	as an illustration
also	to conclude	
after	therefore	
later on	as a result	
in addition	thus	
before		
last of all		
finally		

Group 4 *Change of direction*	Group 5 *Emphasis*	
but	keep in mind	furthermore
however	remember that	undoubtedly
yet	a major concern	certainly
in contrast	the best thing	above all
otherwise	the biggest advantage	most important
still	it is valuable to note	primarily
on the other hand	obviously	
on the contrary		

entire class. One purpose of oral reading is to sharpen proofreading capabilities. Many students are able to correct their errors more accurately and effectively when they read their written work aloud. Another goal is to enhance critical listening skills. The reader's classmates can contribute suggestions based on the checklist for revision and editing explained previously, which will improve proficiency in these skills.

Writing a Final Copy

It is not advisable for students to spend a great deal of time recopying written work for final copies. Certainly, this type of activity should not be done during instructional time. Therefore, teachers must be selective as to which activities should be developed to this stage. If final copies are produced, every effort should be made to display them. Students should be given opportunities to see their written work on bulletin boards or published in a class journal, school or local newspaper, or parent bulletin. Writing letters that will accomplish a purpose or elicit a reply can also be rewarding.

CONCLUSION

Explicit instruction of narrative and expository writing skills is given very little time in most schools, although students are routinely given independent writing assignments. Because writing is the most difficult skill to teach and learn, teachers may need to use a writing program with clear guidelines and goals that will enable students to succeed. The key to helping all students, but especially those with learning and language disabilities, to develop proficiency in written language is to provide the students with the structure and strategies for building acceptable sentences, paragraphs, and composi-

tions. Goals should be established carefully but should not be overly ambitious. Teaching primary or elementary grade students strategies for sentence expansion and the use of sentence starters as well as activities for developing Quick Outlines in the course of a year can be considered a great accomplishment. If students move more quickly than anticipated, then the activities can easily be made more challenging. Composition skills do not develop automatically. Students need carefully sequenced direct instruction, teacher demonstrations, and a great deal of practice in order to succeed.

REFERENCES

Clark, D.B., & Uhry, J.K. (1995). *Dyslexia: Theory and practice of remedial instruction* (2nd ed.). Timonium, MD: York Press.

Deshler, D.D., Ellis, E.S., & Lenz, B.K. (1996). *Teaching adolescents with learning disabilities: Strategies and methods* (2nd ed.). Denver, CO: Love Publishing.

Hochman, J.C. (2001). *Basic writing skills: A manual for teachers*. New York: GSL Publications.

Maria, K. (1990). *Reading comprehension instruction: Issues and strategies*. Timonium, MD: York Press.

Morgan, C.G. (2001). *When they can't write*. Timonium, MD: York Press.

Scott, C.M. (1989). Learning to write: Context, form and process. In A.G. Kamhi & H.W. Catts (Eds.), *Reading disabilities: A developmental language perspective* (pp. 261–302). Boston: Little, Brown.

Scott, C.M. (1999). Learning to write. In H.W. Catts & A.G. Kamhi (Eds.), *Language and reading disabilities* (pp. 261–302). Boston: Allyn & Bacon.

17

Multisensory Mathematics Instruction

Margaret B. Stern

This chapter is devoted to the description of the Structural Arithmetic (Stern & Stern, 1971) method of teaching mathematical concepts, in which multisensory materials are used. In this method, children achieve mastery of arithmetic without being forced to learn only by memorization and parroting. The materials are designed to enable children to learn on their own; after giving such materials to her students, one first-grade teacher cried, "They teach themselves!"

A structured, multisensory teaching approach is of special importance to children with learning disabilities. These children have difficulty with language concepts and associations and memory. They are usually struggling with a combination of these deficits and may also have difficulties with attention. To understand concepts, students with learning disabilities must learn to receive and integrate information from as many different senses as possible. These students often have difficulty in "getting things" from books; however, they begin to trust their ability to learn when they have real experiences with multisensory materials. Because Structural Arithmetic is a multisensory approach, it enables children to develop concepts through experimenting with materials on their own.

The materials described in this chapter convey concepts through structures that are true to the mathematical relationships being taught. To understand these relationships, children pick up the materials and measure and compare them. A concept or a quantity is presented in context rather than in isolation so that children can explore and discover the many different mathematical relationships that are possible. Good multisensory materials not only stimulate such activities but also should present concepts so vividly and clearly that children can visualize them later. More than 100 sequenced activities and games have been gathered together in the teacher's guides titled *Experimenting with Numbers: A Guide for Preschool, Kindergarten, and First Grade Teachers*

(Stern, 1988) and *Structural Arithmetic Workbooks 1–3 and Teachers' Guides* (Stern & Gould, 1988–1992). They are the result of the further development of the original work published in *Children Discover Arithmetic: An Introduction to Structural Arithmetic* (Stern & Stern, 1971). These materials have been used successfully in classrooms for more than 45 years. Teachers also have expressed their appreciation for the illustrated directions that make teaching with multisensory structured materials much easier. (For more information on the Structural Arithmetic approach, go to http://www.SternMath.com.)

What is involved in the formation of concepts? Children seem to reason with mental pictures. Therefore, when teaching children to think, we must develop their ability to form images. Multisensory materials will have fulfilled their purpose when the children can visualize the concepts presented. It is not sufficient, however, for the children to visualize a quantity in isolation; they must be able to visualize it in relation to other numbers and turn it around in their minds, and they must understand the actions that can be performed on it. For example, a teacher turned face down a pattern board with blanks for eight cubes and asked Sean to build the cube pattern he thinks will fit into it. When Sean built the 8-pattern correctly, he explained, "I imagined it in my brain, then I built it, then I turned the board over, and the cubes all fit!"

In addition to mental pictures, language plays a crucial role in the formation of concepts. The best way to teach children the meaning of spoken language is to give them the opportunity to see and touch what the words describe and, thus, work out for themselves what the words mean. In many of the math games in this chapter, children are asked to follow spoken directions. This develops both their receptive language and their auditory memory. It is especially important for children with language deficits to develop these abilities.

In mathematics, as in any other subject, language is a vehicle for thought; therefore, students need many opportunities to put newly discovered concepts into their own words. Parroting the words of the teacher is not a sign of true learning. Instead, the teacher should often encourage students to talk about concepts by asking them, "How did you figure out your answer?"

In the Structural Arithmetic approach, the children progress from activities and games with concrete materials that help them form basic concepts to the final steps of recording addition and subtraction facts with number symbols, or numerals. Here are the steps of Structural Arithmetic, stated as goals and objectives, to be followed in the first years of mathematics instruction:

- *Level I:* To discover size relationships between amounts from 1 to 10, to know where each comes in the sequence from 1 to 10, to recognize odd and even numbers built as cube patterns, and to form number combinations with sums ranging from 1 to 10 using number blocks

- *Level II:* To learn number names and how to count from 1 to 10, to understand terms such as *bigger than* and *smaller than,* and to recite the addition facts with sums of 10 or less that have been discovered with the materials

- *Level III:* To identify and write the numerals 1–10 and 0, to understand the amount each numeral stands for, to understand the meaning of addition or subtraction equations, to write the answers to addition facts with sums of 10 or less and the answers to their related subtraction facts, and to demonstrate with materials the solution of a word problem and then record the addition or subtraction equation used to solve it.

At Levels I and II the amounts from 1 to 10 are introduced in two different ways: with groups of cubes to be counted and with number blocks. For example, the amount of 4 is introduced both with four single cubes and by a number block called a 4-block, which looks like four cubes glued together in a straight line. Number symbols or numerals are introduced later on. Children realize that they can name a small number block of 2 or 3 units at a glance but that they need to verify the name of a longer number block of 8 or 9 units by counting its units. They soon realize that each number block is easily recognized by its relative size, its position in the sequence from 1 to 10, and its color (a peripheral characteristic that is not mathematical). For example, children learn that the 10-block is the biggest number block, stands last in the sequence from 1 to 10, and is blue. The 9-block thus is recognized as the next-to-biggest number block, comes just before the last number block, and is black. These characteristics enable children to identify each number and study its changing role in different situations.

FIRST EXPERIMENTS: THE COUNTING BOARD

Children begin their explorations of number concepts by fitting cubes or number blocks into grooves of the counting board (see Figure 17.1). Using the board, the children carry out many experiments on their own. Concrete materials alone, however, do not lead to the development of mathematical thinking. The number blocks or cubes must be looked at, picked up, compared, and fit into activities that have been fashioned so as to make clear the structure of our base-10 number system. The teacher as well as children must put discoveries and relationships into words. Once the students understand these concepts, the teacher introduces the symbols that stand for them (see the section called Number Symbols and Signs: Level III).

Number Concepts and Language: Levels I and II

By experimenting with materials, children discover the many things they can do with numbers. Soon they are impatient to tell each other about their discoveries. Once they have learned the number names of the blocks, they begin to express their thoughts in language that comes to them naturally. (For example, Sumi might point to a 5-block

Figure 17.1. The counting board: Matching number markers to numerals on the number guide.

and a 3-block and say, "I am 5, but my brother is only 3.") When children express ideas about numbers in their own words, they will have a more secure understanding of the language of mathematics when they hear it later. Teachers who listen to their students' words are often alerted to difficulties in comprehension and are able to give help before the problems cause even more trouble. In more formal environments, teachers give children orders to carry out. In doing so, children show whether they understand new vocabulary. For instance, a teacher might say, "Add 3 and 2, and tell me what 3 plus 2 equals." Students respond by adding together a 3-block and a 2-block and placing them alongside a 5-block. The students see that 3 and 2 are "the same size as 5," which they learn is expressed by the words "equals 5." The relationship among the blocks enables the children to gain this insight. In contrast, the piecemeal act of counting single cubes often camouflages the meaning of the word *equal*.

Number Symbols and Signs: Level III

The teacher should introduce number symbols (numerals) after number concepts have been explored. The teacher fits the number guide into the slot at the top of the counting board (see Figure 17.1). When attached, the number guide shows where each numeral comes in the sequence from 1 to 10. Each numeral appears above the groove that holds the number of cubes or the number block for which it stands (e.g., the 10 on the number guide appears above the groove that can hold 10 cubes or a 10-block). Between the number guide and the grooves are empty spaces for number markers or tiles bearing the numerals 1–10. On each number marker a line beneath the numeral indicates the correct orientation of that numeral (e.g., 6 indicates the marker is for 6, not 9). Having children match the numerals on the markers to the numerals on the number guide is an excellent check of the children's ability to perceive symbols and to position them correctly. This step prevents errors that might arise when the children try to read or write numerals.

The teacher then lets the numerals "call back" the number blocks, which is an activity that the children enjoy. The teacher says, "Pick a number. Where does it go?" A child selects a number marker such as 3, matches it to the 3 on the number guide, then finds the 3-block and fits it into the 3-groove.

Building Basic Concepts

Children who do not know math facts (e.g., 4 + 4 = 8) will have had difficulty learning them by rote and will resort to counting them out over and over again because they have become rigidly attached to the "counting song." Such children profit from remedial work with basic math concepts. When they realize they can learn basic concepts by playing exciting games with the counting board, they respond with improved concentration, which helps them retain the new knowledge better. One such game follows.

The Snake Game

The object of the Snake Game is to build the longest snake of number blocks. The teacher fills a counting board with number blocks and divides students into two teams of six to eight players. The teams take turns selecting a number marker from the face-down number markers that are scattered on the table. Each number marker indicates which number block the team may add to their snake of blocks. Children give up counting individual units on the number blocks when they realize it is quicker to name and se-

lect the number block below the number on the guide that matches the marker drawn. The winning team is the one that has the longer snake of blocks after the counting board has been emptied.

The Snake Game prepares students to see and remember number combinations that they will discover when they later fill a number box with blocks (discussed later in this chapter). It is more impressive to note that working with counting board materials will enable children to move easily from addition to subtraction. But first they must be able to name the numbers and understand the concepts for which the number symbols stand.

DEVELOPING A NUMBER SENSE: PATTERN BOARDS

Each pattern board provides between 1 and 10 empty blanks in a set pattern into which cubes may be inserted (see Figure 17.2). Children show that they recognize a number pattern by building it with cubes. They then check the pattern they have built by placing the cubes into the blanks of the correct pattern board. To learn the name of each number pattern, they count the cubes.

Even and Odd Numbers

The characteristics of evenness and oddness cannot be taught with number blocks, but they can be taught with cubes and pattern boards. Even numbers are formed by pairs of cube partners so that the pattern ends evenly. They are named 2, 4, 6, and 8. Children see that even numbers are made with 1 + 1, 2 + 2, 3 + 3, 4 + 4, and 5 + 5 (math facts that are taught later). When one cube is added to an even number pattern, it becomes odd. Children learn that "one cube all alone" distinguishes an odd number and that odd numbers are named 1, 3, 5, 7, and 9. A stick or a pencil can be used to split an odd number pattern down the center to yield the two consecutive numbers that form it. These odd number patterns are 1 + 0, 2 + 1, 3 + 2, 4 + 3, and 5 + 4. When building the sequence from 1 to 10, the odd number patterns are positioned between the even patterns. These facts are studied later under the name Doubles and Neighbors (discussed later in this chapter). The structure of these patterns makes the relationships visible and easy to recall later as addition facts.

Figure 17.2. Pattern boards: matching cube patterns.

Introduction to Word Problems

Acting out word problems with multisensory materials will prepare children to analyze complex word problems later. It is important for children to learn how to demonstrate word problems of their own creation. Pattern boards and cubes are excellent materials with which to begin. Each child in the group selects a different pattern board. For example, Laura selected the pattern board for the number 6, filled it with cubes, and then acted out her problem, saying, "My dog had 6 puppies. I gave 4 away. How many are left?" Even though she had subtracted 4 cubes, the children could still see the original number she started with because she chose a pattern board with 6 blanks. The pattern board allowed Laura's classmates to see at the same time the 4 subtracted cubes, the remaining 2 cubes, and their relationship to the original total of 6 cubes. Teachers know that some children, when taking 4 loose cubes away from 6 loose cubes, cannot visualize the original amount and wonder just how much they began with. These children lose any sense of the relationship of 4 to 6 and of the remaining 2 to the 6 they began with. Well-planned lessons in which children act out word problems with multisensory materials such as pattern boards will help build strong foundations for later learning.

ADDITION AND SUBTRACTION WITH THE 10-BOX

Discovering Combinations that Make 10

The 10-box, a square measuring 10 units by 10 units, has a frame around the edge that tells children when the total units of the block-partners is 10 (see Figure 17.3). In the beginning, children fill the 10-box with pairs of number blocks in any sequence, as though they were working on a puzzle. Kindergartners often know which blocks go together in the 10-box before they can name them or designate them with number symbols. Each time these children put a number block in the 10-box, they measure with their eyes to judge the size of the block that will fit with it. Thus they systematically study the relationship between each separate number block and the total, which is 10 units long. When they make a mistake, they can see and feel how the block does not fit. The teacher does not need to say, "Wrong!" The emphasis is on experimenting.

Figure 17.3.   Filling the 10-box with number blocks.

When the children find pairs of blocks that fit, they feel a satisfaction that is unforgettable. This success with filling the 10-box helps them remember the block combinations that total 10 units. Once the children have learned the names of the blocks, they will find it easy to name the block partners that make 10 (see Figure 17.3).

When the combinations making 10 are placed in sequence, the combination in the middle is a double, a 5-block and a 5-block. A double, children will discover, can be found in the center of every even number. In addition, students will understand the zero fact even before it is recorded; they can put the 10-block in the 10-box and say, "10 needs no other block to make 10." The children can show that they understand the concept of equality when they place two number blocks next to the 10-block and say, for example, "8 and 2 are just as big as 10." This concept will be recorded later with the equal sign.

Building the Stair from 1 to 10 in the 10-Box

The teacher scatters number blocks 1–10 next to the 10-box and begins to build the stair in the lower left corner with the 1-, 2-, and 3-blocks. The teacher asks the children to complete the stair. When the children put in a block that is too long (e.g., placing the 5-block after the 3-block), they realize that the structure is wrong and they look for the correct block (e.g., the 4-block). The choices they make are guided by how the stair looks. The teacher can also challenge the children by removing one step of the completed stair while they are not looking and asking them to name the missing step.

Recording the Story of 10: Writing Equations

The goal is for students to record from memory the "Story of 10," the pairs of numbers that equal 10, but first students must learn how to record an equation after they fill a column in the 10-box. The teacher places the empty 10-box and two sets of number blocks before the children and sets to one side the number markers 1–10 and the plus and equal signs. The children put two number blocks (**addends**) into the 10-box and name them, for example, "6 and 4." The teacher records this by arranging the symbols 6 + 4 next to the 10-box. The students continue by saying, "equal 10," and the teacher records this by putting the appropriate symbols last, yielding 6 + 4 = 10. When the children later write equations, they understand the process from having recorded the combinations of blocks as they placed them in the box. Using the 10-box while recording equations also enables students to understand an equation when they read it.

For many children, the **missing addend** form of an equation (e.g., 6 + _____ = 10) is difficult to deal with as they do not understand what it means. When the children put a 10-block in the box and place a 6-block next to it, however, they find it natural to ask, "6 needs what to make 10?" They then record what they have just said with the number markers and symbols: 6 + _____ = 10. Students discover that the missing symbol is the numeral that stands for the missing block, which they know is the 4-block. Teachers often find that using the 10-box is the first time they have had an easy way of teaching equations with missing addends.

Subtraction and Its Relation to Addition

An addition example contains two or more addends, and students are asked for the sum or total; subtraction can easily be shown to have the opposite character. The children place a 6-block and a 4-block into the first column of the 10-box and note that they measure 10. The teacher states the addition fact 6 + 4 = 10. The teacher's next

step is to explain how this addition fact will yield two subtraction facts. To demonstrate the first fact, the children realize that they begin with the total, 10, from which they subtract the 4-block; the 6-block remains. This demonstration gives meaning to the words, "10 take away 4 leaves 6," which students record as $10 - 4 = 6$. The teacher then asks someone to demonstrate the other subtraction fact, $10 - 6 = 4$, and to record it below the first. The structure of the materials makes it obvious that the smaller number is always subtracted from the larger number.

Combinations that Make 10

Playing the Hiding Game (described next) gives children more than practice in remembering the combinations that make 10. To discover which combination has been hidden, the children must first figure out how the block combinations have been organized; they then find a strategy for identifying the missing combination. Afterward, it is interesting to ask students, "How did you do that?"

The Hiding Game

The teacher displays the 10-box filled with number block combinations in sequence from $1 + 9$, $2 + 8$, $3 + 7$, and so forth up to $10 + 0$. When the children's eyes are closed, the teacher removes one combination, such as $4 + 6$, and says, "Open your eyes. What did I hide?" A child answers, "$4 + 6$," and says while pointing to the blocks in the lower stair, "I counted each step, 1, 2, 3, and found 4 was missing, so I knew 4 and 6 were missing."

ADDITION AND SUBTRACTION: OTHER NUMBER BOXES

Children are delighted to find there are more number boxes smaller than the 10-box and enjoy fitting them inside one another to form a pyramid. On finding that the peak of the pyramid would be the 1-box, a precocious kindergartner called out, "I have the pièce de résistance!"

When asking the children to fill one of the smaller boxes, such as the 8-box, the teacher presents two sets of blocks as well as the box to be filled. Students respond by rejecting the blocks that are too big (the 9- and 10-blocks) and finding the block combinations that exactly fit the 8-box. They realize that this task has the same features as filling the 10-box and adjust their performance accordingly. This adjustment comes about as a result of learning through insight, not by rote. Students enjoy playing the same addition and subtraction games with each box as they played with the 10-box. They later write the number story for each box and give each a title, such as the "Story of 8."

Different Roles a Number Can Play

Students will be excited when they become aware that a number plays a different role in each number box. Each number block's distinctive size and color enables children to observe how a number changes its role as it comprises the total of each different box. For example, consider the changes in the role of the 5-block. When filling the 5-box, a kindergarten child said, "5 is the control of this box!" When discovering the combinations while filling the 6-box, another child ran to his teacher and said, "Look! 5 is the 9 of this box." He had noticed that the 5-block plays the same role in the 6-box as the 9-block does in the 10-box: Both are the next-to-biggest block and thus join with a 1-block to fill a column in the box.

In addition, when putting together the combinations to make 9, an odd number, children find that there are two sets of consecutive numbers that make 9; they see that a 5-block joins a 4-block to make 9 and that next to these blocks, a 4-block joins a 5-block to make 9. Finally, they discover that doubles are found only in the even-number boxes. Thus, when filling the 8-box, they find a pair of 4-blocks in the center.

SOLVING WORD PROBLEMS

It is easy for children to understand when to solve a word problem by addition: There are two or more addends, and the total is being asked for. Children have greater difficulty identifying problems that are to be solved by subtraction. When a total is stated and a smaller amount is lost, it is relatively easy for children to decide to solve the problem by subtraction. Children, however, are more confused when trying to solve problems that say nothing about an amount being lost or taken away. In this type of problem a total and one amount are given, and children must figure out the other amount (e.g., "The book costs $10. Tobias has $3. How much does he need to earn?"). The children have to learn that the way to solve this type of word problem, a missing addend problem, is to subtract. Teachers usually start with problems in which the numbers are small, as in the previous example. Unfortunately, the use of small numbers makes it difficult for children to understand why they must subtract because they can so easily solve this kind of problem in their heads: "3 needs what to make 10? 7." This type of problem is especially difficult for children to solve later when the problems deal with big numbers (e.g., "The television set costs $225. Tobias has $37. How much does he need to earn?") Children cannot solve 37 + _____ = 225 in their heads. The teacher must show the children how to think about this type of problem by setting up a model so that when the numbers are big, it will make sense to subtract. For example, the teacher can put 10 cubes in a number track (a grooved track with numerals on one side that holds cubes or number blocks in sections of 10 units, or decades; see Figure 17.4) and say, "The book costs $10. Tobias doesn't need to earn all $10; he already has $3." The teacher covers 3 cubes with a scarf and says, "I covered 3 cubes to show that Tobias doesn't need to earn those $3; he already has them. I've taken 3 away from 10." The teacher writes 10 − 3 = _____ and says, "Tobias needs to earn the rest." The children conclude in a full sentence, "Tobias needs to earn $7." The children now have a model of how to solve missing addend problems. Later, they will be able to substitute big numbers in this model. For example, "Ted wants $225. He has $37. He doesn't need to earn it all, so I'll take $37 away! He needs to earn the rest!" The students will understand that missing addend problems are solved by subtraction and will set them up correctly.

TEEN NUMBERS

It is important for the teacher to show mathematical concepts such as teen numbers in more than one way. The teen numbers are the numbers above 10 through 19, composed of a 10-block and a number of ones (the rest of the number). They will be shown first in the 20-tray (a square tray, similar to a 10-box, that measures 20 units by 20

Figure 17.4. Building 14 in the number track.

units), then in the number track (see Figure 17.4), and also in the dual board (see Figure 17.5 in the section on regrouping in subtraction).

Building the Stair from 1 to 20

In the 20-tray, children begin by building the familiar stair from 1 to 10. On reaching 10, they discover they must piece together the next numbers using a 10-block and another number block (e.g., 1 ten and a 1-block to make 11, 1 ten and a 2-block to make 12, 1 ten and a 3-block to make 13). Students will be surprised when they see that the stair from 1 to 10 repeats itself in the teen numbers on a base of 10-blocks. They name each number in the 20-tray by naming the steps from 1 to 20. To make certain that the students understand the structure of teen numbers, the teacher says, "Close your eyes," and hides the blocks composing a teen number such as 14. When the children look at the stair of teen numbers, they see which step is missing and cry, "14!" As the teacher replaces the number blocks in the missing step, the students name them: "10 and 4." After this activity they will think of the number 14 as the teacher has built it, with 1 ten and 4 ones (a 4-block). Visualizing the structure and naming the blocks enables students from the start to write the digits in the correct order as 14, not as the number is pronounced, "four-teen."

Measuring Teen Numbers in a Number Track

The numerals on the side of the number track record the total created by the number blocks that are placed in the track. Children need to be familiar with the structure of a teen number in the number track. Operating from this base, they will easily understand the next step, that of adding to 9, in which they first add a number block, such as a 3-block, to a 10-block and then to a 9-block. They can see that the 10-block and the 3-block reach 13 but that the 9-block and the 3-block only reach 12.

Building Teen Numbers in the Dual Board

The dual board has two compartments, a large tens compartment the same size as a 10-box, and a small ones compartment that holds a column of ten 1-blocks or several unit blocks from 1 to 9. Before using the dual board for purposes such as subtracting from 2-place numbers (see Figure 17.5 in the section on regrouping in subtraction), it is important for children to construct the teen numbers in the dual board.

When children first look at a written number such as 12, they see two numerals that seem to stand for numbers of about the same size. By building a number in the dual board, the children gain insight into the important role that the place, or the position, of each numeral plays. The teacher builds a number, such as 12, in the dual board by placing 1 ten in the tens compartment and a 2-block in the ones compartment. To record this number, the number marker 1 is put below the tens compartment and the number marker 2 is put below the ones compartment. This shows the meaning of each symbol in the written number 12. To make the term *place value* clear, the teacher can change the places of the number markers 2 and 1 and have children show the new value of each symbol, that is, 2 tens and a 1-block.

ADDITION FACTS WITH ANSWERS IN THE TEENS

There are 36 addition facts with answers in the teens (e.g., 9 + 2 = 11 to 9 + 9 = 18). These facts can be categorized into different groups of structurally related facts: Adding

9, Adding to 9, Combinations that Make 11 and 12, and Doubles and Neighbors. Children master them by understanding the general rules for each group.

Adding 9

There are eight facts in the Adding 9 group (2 + 9, 3 + 9, 4 + 9, 5 + 9, 6 + 9, 7 + 9, 8 + 9, 9 + 9). Children can master these eight facts at once by learning only one general rule. First they add a 10-block to any block, such as the 3-block, in the number track and realize that the digit in the ones place of the total, 13, is the same as the unit block that was added to the 10-block (e.g., 3 + 10 = 13). Students then add a 9-block to the 3-block and discover that they only reach 12, a number that is 1 less than if they had added a 10-block to the unit block they started with (e.g., 3 + 10 = 13, but 3 + 9 = 12). Students demonstrate that they understand these facts by adding a 9-block to each number block from 2 to 9.

Adding to 9

Eight addition facts result from adding a number to 9 (9 + 2, 9 + 3, 9 + 4, 9 + 5, 9 + 6, 9 + 7, 9 + 8, 9 + 9). To learn these Adding to 9 facts, which are the reverse of the Adding 9 facts, children add blocks to a 9-block. This time, the teacher places a 9-block in the number track, holds a 3-block above the track, and asks, "What do you think 9 + 3 equals?" The children have time to answer before the teacher places the 3-block after the 9-block in the number track. When the blocks are joined end to end, the children can see that the 3-block had to move down one unit to fill the gap between 9 and 10; thus, adding 3 to 9 reaches the number 12 (i.e., 10 + 3 = 13, but 9 + 3 = 12). They figure out all of the Adding to 9 facts adding the numbers 2 through 8 to 9.

Combinations that Make 11 and 12

The children begin working with the facts for Combinations that Make 11 and 12 by building a stair from 1 to 10 in the 10-box. They then fill the 10-box by adding the reverse stair of blocks (9, 8, 7, 6, 5, 4, 3, 2, 1) to this stair. Thus, each column in the 10-box is filled. Now the children move the whole top stair up and over one step. This move results in the combinations that make 11, by adding 1 to 10, 2, to 9, 3 to 8, and so forth. The children know the combinations that make 10, so when making combinations that total 11, they realize that one of the component parts will be 1 unit bigger. For example, 5 + 5 = 10, but 5 needs 6 to make 11; 7 + 3 = 10, but 7 needs 4 to make 11.

To build combinations that make 12, students again move the blocks of the top stair up one step. This time 2 units must be added to one of the component parts that totaled 10; for example, 5 + 5 = 10, but 5 needs 7 to make 12. The teacher can now use the clock on the wall as an unforgettable way to show the combinations making 12. The numbers that stand across from each other on the clock face add up to 12. For example, 9 is across from 3, and 9 + 3 = 12; 8 is across from 4, and 8 + 4 = 12; and 7 is across from 5, and 7 + 5 = 12. Once the children have learned Adding 9, Adding to 9, and Combinations that Make 11 and 12, they have studied two thirds of the addition facts with sums that are teen numbers.

Doubles and Neighbors in the Teens

The next group of structurally related addition facts is called Doubles and Neighbors in the Teens and consists of six new facts. Children usually find the doubles (6 + 6 = 12;

7 + 7 = 14; 8 + 8 = 16; 9 + 9 = 18; 10 + 10 = 20) easy to learn. To illustrate the doubles, the teacher places pairs of like blocks side by side and explains that the sum of each pair is an even number. For practice in learning doubles, children should play a game such as Stop and Go (described later in this chapter). To illustrate the facts that are neighbors of the doubles (5 + 6 = 11, 6 + 7 = 13, 7 + 8 = 15, 8 + 9 = 17, 9 + 10 = 19), the teacher places the pair of 6-blocks (12) next to the pair of 7-blocks (14) and leaves a space between the pairs. The teacher points to this empty space. To make the neighbor between 12 and 14, a child takes a 6-block from the pair that totals 12 and a 7-block from the pair that totals 14. This produces the number 13, built from the consecutive numbers 6 and 7. The teacher demonstrates how each odd teen number can be formed from two consecutive numbers. Once students have mastered Doubles and Neighbors in the Teens, there are only four final addition facts with answers in the teens to be learned: 8 + 5 and 8 + 6 and the reverse facts, 5 + 8 and 6 + 8.

Addition and Subtraction Facts in the Teens

Teachers often must work with children who find math especially difficult to comprehend. A teacher must first discover which concepts these students do not understand. Looking at students' final answers to math problems does not indicate students' level of understanding. For example, if the teacher sees that a student wrote 15 − 9 = 6, then the teacher still does not know how the student figured out the answer. If the teacher, however, sees that the student made 15 dashes, crossed off 9 of them, and counted the remaining dashes, then the teacher has gained valuable information. Students who have difficulty with math concepts need to work with materials structured so as to give them the foundation they never had to understand computation with answers that are teen numbers.

First, students must build the stair of teen numbers in the 20-tray using 10-blocks and unit blocks to construct the numbers 11–20. Second, they must build a teen number such as 15 in the number track using a 10-block and a 5-block. Then by substituting the 9-block and the 1-block for the 10-block, they should conclude that the result of taking 9 from a teen number such as 15 is easy to figure out. When the 9-block is removed, the 1-block remains in the number track with the 5-block to yield the answer, 6. Children find it easy to demonstrate similar examples with the same structure: 17 − 9 = 8 or 16 − 9 = 7. This kind of insight gives children confidence in their ability to answer difficult math problems without the endless counting of dots or dashes. In particular, children with learning disabilities profit most from such experiences. They need to realize that they can think and that they can do arithmetic.

Games with Teen Numbers

It is important for all children to learn the concepts about teen numbers and to practice them by playing games that they find challenging.

The Hard Snake Game

The Hard Snake Game may be played by two teams or two children. On each of 10 cards, the teacher writes a teen number and turns it face down. One member of Team A then selects a card and announces the number written on it. The player must form this total by adding two blocks, one of which must be a 9-block. Thus, if the card says 15, then the player must build 15 using a 9-block and a 6-block. If the player forms the

correct total, the blocks are then added to Team A's snake of blocks. The winner is the team with the longest snake of blocks. This game reinforces the students' learning of these difficult teen number facts.

The Probe Game

To prepare for the Probe Game, the teacher displays the number track from 1 to 20 and covers the numbers 1–10 with a cardboard box. The teacher has the children close their eyes and then hides a number block, perhaps the 5-block, under the cardboard box. The teacher lets the students open their eyes and asks a child to discover the size of the hidden block by using the 9-block as a probe. As he or she pushes the 9-block down the track and under the box, the children wait expectantly until it stops and shows that the sum is 14. The child must reason, "If this were the 10-block, then the hidden block would be the 4-block, but it is only the 9-block, so the hidden block has to be one bigger than 4: it must be the 5-block." At this point the teacher verifies the answer by lifting the cardboard box to reveal that the hidden block is indeed the 5-block.

PLACE VALUE OR POSITIONAL NOTATION

Giving up dealing with ones and grouping them into tens as a new unit of measure is one of the most ingenious ideas of humankind. Here is an experiment that will show the children how the use of place value, or positional notation, helps us deal with big numbers. The teacher throws only a few cubes on the table and explains that it is easy to say how many are in a small group of cubes. Next, the teacher throws more than 50 cubes onto the table and writes down a few of the children's estimates of the amount. To determine the exact number, the teacher arranges the cubes in rows of 10 in the tens compartment of the dual board and places any leftover cubes in the ones compartment. Students can see at a glance that the amount of cubes is 5 tens plus the 4 leftover cubes in the ones compartment (i.e., 54). The teacher can explain that grouping objects in tens and ones is one advantage of the structure of our number system.

Recording Teen Numbers and Understanding the Numeral 0

When students built the teen numbers, they discovered that the composition of each number corresponded exactly with its numerals: 1 ten and 1 one were recorded as 11, 1 ten and 2 as 12, and so forth, up to 1 ten and 9 as 19. The teacher asks the children to put two 10-blocks in the dual board and record it by placing the number marker for 2 below the tens compartment. The teacher then places the number marker for 0 below the empty ones compartment and explains why 0 is called a place holder: "If we write the numeral 2 and let it stand alone, it would mean 2 ones. So we write 0 in the ones place to tell us that this time the digit 2 stands for 2 tens and that there isn't anything in the ones place. Moreover, in 20, the 0 is also holding a place for another numeral. If we replace 0 with 1, we must also put 1 cube in the ones compartment." The teacher explains that the numeral is now 21, records the amount in the dual board, and says, "2 tens, 1 one."

Building 2-Place Numbers in the Dual Board and the Number Track

Children are now ready to discover the meaning behind the structure of the 2-place, or 2-digit, numerals between 10 and 100. The children first build a number such as 25

with 2 tens and 5 ones, then they reverse the digits and build 52, using 5 tens and 2 ones. They are now ready to play an interesting game.

Build Your Guess

The game Build Your Guess gives children practice building 2-place numbers in the dual board and then measuring them in the long number track to note where they come in the sequence of 1 to 100. To begin, the teacher writes a 2-place number on a piece of paper and hides it. The student who comes closest to guessing the teacher's number is the winner. Each child should guess a different number and must then build his or her guess in the dual board. For example, Erin decides to guess 39, so she puts 3 tens in the tens compartment and a 9-block in the ones compartment and records it with number markers for 3 and 9. She then measures her blocks in the number track; they reach 39. She places her number markers, 39, next to the track to show her guess. Then the teacher shows the hidden number, 36. Erin finds that her guess, 39, is 3 units bigger than 36, whereas Toshi's guess, 32, is 4 units smaller than 36. The others were even further away. Erin concludes she is the winner.

In this game and the other Structural Arithmetic activities, the children express their ideas by building numbers with blocks and recording them with numerals. This solid foundation in understanding 2-digit numbers will make regrouping in addition and subtraction (i.e., carrying and borrowing) easier to understand.

REGROUPING IN ADDITION

The procedure called **regrouping** is known to previous generations as *carrying and borrowing*. The teacher explains that in our system of positional notation, when the amount in one column exceeds 9, it can only be expressed by a 2-digit numeral that has a tens digit and a ones digit; therefore, the amount must be regrouped. For example, when dealing with an amount in the ones column such as 12 ones, 10 ones must be exchanged for or regrouped as 1 ten and carried to the tens column. That leaves 2 in the ones place. The numeral that records 1 ten and 2 ones is 12. When children work with the blocks in the dual board, these procedures will have meaning from the very start.

Students learn addition with regrouping step by step using the dual board. The first step in adding two numbers, such as 39 and 1, is to build the 2-place number in the dual board. The children place 3 tens in the tens compartment and 9 ones in the ones compartment and say the name of the number: "thirty-nine." The teacher adds 1 cube to the 9 cubes that are already in the ones compartment and explains, "We cannot record the 10 cubes in the ones compartment with a single numeral; we must regroup!" Students exchange the 10 cubes for 1 ten, carry it to the tens compartment, and add it to the 3 tens already there, resulting in a total of 4 tens.

Once the children have understood regrouping, they record each step on paper; writing on paper lined in half-inch squares is a great help. The children write 39, then they write + 1 below the 9 in the ones column, draw a horizontal line beneath it, and say, "9 plus 1 equals 10. I must regroup." They reenact the carrying of 1 ten to the tens compartment and record this move by writing a small figure 1 above the 3 in the tens column of their example. They write 0 in the ones place below the horizontal line (because there are no ones left). Next they add the digits in the tens column and say, "3 plus 1 equals 4." They write 4 in the tens place in their answer. The sum is written as 40 and named "forty," which accurately records the 4 tens in the dual board.

Next, the students add a bigger number, perhaps 3, to 39. When they add three cubes to the 9 that are already in the ones compartment, they see that they have twelve cubes and must regroup. They exchange ten cubes for 1 ten and carry it to the tens compartment to join the 3 tens. That move leaves 2 cubes in the ones compartment. The students record each step on paper and get the answer, 42, which they see accurately records the 4 tens and 2 ones in the dual board.

Money and Regrouping

To make clear the value of different coins, the teacher tapes a dime to each of several 10-blocks, a nickel to each of several 5-blocks, and a penny to each of about 20 cubes. Children are now able to see the relationship among the values of the different coins. The nickels are taped to blocks that are half the size of the blocks to which the dimes are taped. Students can see that nickels, which are larger in size than dimes, are worth less than dimes and that it takes 10 pennies (also larger in size than dimes) to equal a dime, or 10 cents. The children will enjoy using the money on blocks in a store game. They can also use the money on blocks in other games.

Score 1 if You Carry

This game is played with the dual board, money on blocks, and a die. The teams take turns tossing the die and placing pennies in the ones compartment of the dual board. For example, Team A tosses the die, gets 3, and places 3 pennies in the ones compartment. Team B tosses a 4 and adds 4 pennies, bringing the total to 7. Team A tosses the die and gets 5, which, when added to 7, yields 12 pennies. Team A must regroup; it exchanges 10 pennies for 1 dime and carries it to the tens compartment. The team puts the 2 remaining cents in the ones column. Team A "scores 1" because it got the chance to regroup, or "carry 1." The game continues. The game could end when one team's score is 5.

REGROUPING IN SUBTRACTION

The process of regrouping in subtraction has also been known as *borrowing*. The children again work in the dual board. They write 30 on their papers and build it with 3 tens. The teacher dictates, "Subtract 6." The children write − 6 below the 0 in 30 and draw a horizontal line below the subtraction example. The teacher explains that the students cannot take 6 cubes away from the ones compartment of the dual board because there are no cubes there and that they must regroup. They carry back 1 ten from the tens compartment and exchange it for 10 ones. On their papers they cross out the 3 and write a small 2 above it to indicate that there are only 2 tens left. The students write a small figure 1 above and to the left of the 0 in the ones place to indicate they now have 10 cubes in the ones column (see Figure 17.5). Now they can subtract 6 cubes, which leaves 4 cubes. The final amount is 2 tens and 4 ones, which matches the written answer, 24.

Regrouping with the Dual Board

After working with the blocks in the dual board, the children need to practice regrouping in a more exciting situation, such as a game.

Figure 17.5. A dual board. The example 30 − 6 is worked out by carrying back 1 ten to the ones compartment, exchanging it for 10 ones, and subtracting 6.

Your Answer Is Your Score

During each turn in the game Your Answer Is Your Score, one player selects two face-down number markers and uses them to build a two-digit number with number blocks in the dual board. He or she must then subtract from this number an amount that is large enough to require regrouping. The player's score is the number that remains after this subtraction operation; the player with the highest score wins. For example, Robert, who has selected the markers 6 and 3, understands that the goal is to get a big score, so he explains, "I don't want to build 36; I'll build 63, of course!" The teacher asks, "How much will you subtract from 63 so that you must regroup?" Robert reasons, "I have only 3 cubes in the ones compartment, so I think I'll subtract 4 from 63." He exchanges 1 ten for 10 ones and puts them into the ones compartment; he now has a total of 13 single cubes. He subtracts 4 cubes from the 13, and this leaves 9 cubes. Robert sees that there are now 5 tens and 9 ones in the dual board and exclaims, "My score is 59!" He writes 59 on the chalkboard. The rest of the players will try to beat his score.

MULTIPLICATION

To most people, multiplication still means the memorization of 100 facts, such as 7 × 6 = 42, which are repeated again and again until they have been learned by heart. Actually, multiplication and division are fascinating operations that, when studied with the Structural Arithmetic materials, allow children to discover new relationships among numbers. The children come to realize that they are viewing the same facts from opposite sides when they discover that the relationship between multiplication and division is one of doing and undoing, just as it is between addition and subtraction. Students will not only grasp this relationship but also understand, through their experiments with the materials, just how division is the opposite of multiplication.

The operation of multiplication can, of course, be taught by the addition of equal addends. For example, the answer to 5 × 2 can be figured out by addition: 2 + 2 = 4,

4 + 2 = 6, 6 + 2 = 8, and 8 + 2 = 10. In Structural Arithmetic, however, children produce an amount a given number of times, and by measuring it in the number track, they discover how this total is expressed in our base-10 system, that is, with tens and ones.

Discovery of What a Multiplication Table Is

The children will discover that multiplication is a new way of expressing number relationships. The essence of multiplication is that an amount is taken not once but several times. Therefore, to find the answer to 5×2, the children take a 2-block five times. The number 5 is not represented by a block but is the operator and plays a different role from the 2; it indicates how many times 2 is to be produced.

Multiplication tables are often recited by saying, for example, "5 times 1 equals 5, 5 times 2 equals 10, 5 times 3 equals 15," and so forth. To represent these facts with materials would mean changing the size of the number blocks used each time: five 1-blocks, then five 2-blocks, then five 3-blocks, and so forth. It makes more sense to demonstrate the multiplication table using the same size number block each time: one 5-block, then two 5-blocks, then three 5-blocks, and so forth (see Figure 17.6). By following this procedure children will be able to discover the products of any multiplication table by themselves. They can take a block a certain number of times and measure the total in the number track. They can find, for example, the way that three 5s are expressed in our base-10 number system: 1 ten and 5 ones, or 15 (see Figure 17.6). Students discover not only the interrelationship among the facts within one multiplication table (e.g., 1×5, 2×5, 3×5, and so forth up to 10×5) but also the interrelationship among the facts of different tables, such as the multiples that two or three tables have in common.

One approach used to teach children to represent a multiplication fact is to have them draw circles and stars. To demonstrate 3×4, they make three circles and put four stars in each circle. This arrangement shows the role of the **operator**, or **multiplier**, 3, and the size, 4, but does not show how the total is expressed in the denominations of our number system, tens and ones. There is no visible connection between the fact 3×4 and the product 12, which can only be found by counting. The same is true when children create arrays, such as 4 rows of 5 dots each.

Figure 17.6.   Discovering what 3 times 5 equals.

Sequence of Teaching the Multiplication Tables

Children begin by studying the 10-table because our number system is built on base 10. When the multiplicand is 10, each product can be expressed immediately. The product of 3×10, 30, does not have to be calculated but can be shown by writing 3 in the tens place of the numeral and adding a 0 as a placeholder; the multiple is already expressed in tens and ones. The need for multiplication tables arises because for any multiplicand other than 10, the products must be expressed in tens and ones.

The multiplication facts in the 1-table can be shown by producing the 1-block a certain number of times (5×1) or each number block one time (e.g., to show 1×5, a student produces a 5-block); the answer is the quantity the number block itself represents. The 2-table is studied next because its characteristic feature is that a given number of 2s is the same as the double of that given number (e.g., $6 \times 2 = 12$ and the double of 6 is 12). Because the children know the doubles, they easily master the 2-table. The 5-table is studied next because of the special relationship of 5 to 10 (5 is half of 10), followed by the 9-table because of the closeness of 9 to 10 (9 is 1 less than 10).

To teach the 9-table, the teacher puts one 10-block in the number track and writes $1 \times 10 = 10$. The 10-block is then replaced by a 9-block and a 1-block. The teacher then subtracts the 1-block and writes $1 \times 9 = 10 - 1$; beneath that he or she writes, $1 \times 9 = 9$. To show the second multiple of 9, the teacher places two 10-blocks in the track and writes $2 \times 10 = 20$. Next, the teacher replaces the 10-blocks with two sets of 9-blocks and 1-blocks. Both 1-blocks are subtracted, and the two 9-blocks are shoved together; they reach 18. The teacher writes $2 \times 9 = 20 - 2$. Below that he or she writes $2 \times 9 = $ _____ ; the children copy the fact and write 18 in the blank. By following this procedure the teacher and the children continue to demonstrate and record the 9-table and finish with $10 \times 9 = 100 - 10$; $10 \times 9 = 90$.

Multiplication Games

Stop and Go

Stop and Go is one of several exciting games that children can play to reinforce their understanding of a multiplication table. To play Stop and Go with the 5-table, the teacher fills the number track with 10 of the 5-blocks. He or she assigns a red cube to the Red Team and a blue cube to the Blue Team and places them at the beginning of the track. The stop-and-go cube has two red "Stop" sides and four green "Go" sides. The Red Team drops the stop-and-go cube and gets Go. The Red Team places its cube on the end of the first 5-block above the number 5 on the track, and one of the Red Team's players says, "1 times 5 equals 5." The Blue Team also gets Go, so it places its blue cube piggyback on top of the red cube. Here are the two possible moves for the Red Team: If Red gets Go, it must carry the Blue Team's cube, move both cubes up to the end of the number 10 on the number track, and say, "2 times 5 equals 10." If the Red Team gets Stop, however, both teams' cubes remain on 5. If the Blue Team gets Go at the next turn, it will move off of the red cube. In this way, they race each other up the track landing on each multiple of 5 until one team reaches the 10th multiple, 50.

When studying the multiples of the 5-table in the number track, as with Stop and Go, the children will discover that each decade in the number track holds 2 fives. Therefore, when the multiplier is even, the product ends in 0 because it equals a number of 10s; when the multiplier is an odd number, the product has 5 in the ones place

because an odd number of 5s reaches the middle of a decade: $1 \times 5 = 5$, $3 \times 5 = 15$, $5 \times 5 = 25$, $7 \times 5 = 35$, $9 \times 5 = 45$.

Capture Peaks

Capture Peaks is another favorite game. First, the children choose a multiplication table and place 10 of the appropriate blocks in the number track. For example, the children decide on the 4-table and place ten 4-blocks successively in the number track. Then they dictate each fact for the teacher to write on the chalkboard. On each of 10 dominoes a fact is printed in this form: $1 \times 4 = $ ____. The Red and Blue Teams each get 10 cubes of their respective color, which thus limits each team to 10 turns. A member of the Red Team turns up one of the face-down dominoes and reads it aloud: "3 times 4 equals 12." Then the team places its red cube on 12 in the number track. The domino is then returned to the pool so that each multiple in the number track can have more than one cube on it. After several more turns a member of the Blue Team might get $3 \times 4 = $ ____ and say, "3 times 4 equals 12! I'm on top of the Red Team!" At the end of the game, the color cube on top of each peak or multiple determines which team claims the entire tower of cubes beneath it. The team with the most cubes wins.

The Screen Game

The Screen Game, which focuses on the use of words in math, builds a foundation that will enable students to understand similar wording when they encounter it later in algebra problems. Children who have had difficulty understanding the meaning of words sometimes mistake the words *3 times as big as* to mean *3 times bigger than* and thus produce an amount *3 times as big as* the original and then add this tripled amount to the original amount. The result is an amount that is 4 times as big as the original. For children who make similar mistakes, the Screen Game is an important activity.

To begin, the teacher suggests that the children watch the Screen Game carefully so that they can invent similar problems of their own. Then the teacher writes a few math expressions on the chalkboard, such as *times as big as, times as long as, times as much as, times as heavy as,* and *times as old as.* The children then invent their own problems in which they use one of the expressions.

The teacher gives the children a pile of number blocks and stands a screen on a table. He or she places a 6-block in front of the screen and says, "This represents a stick 6 feet long—perhaps 6 doll-feet! In back of the screen is a stick 3 times as long. Show me with the blocks how long the hidden stick is." If the children have understood the words "3 times as long," they will build a stick with 3 of the 6-blocks. The hidden stick is then revealed for comparison. The children write their equations on paper ($3 \times 6 = 18$) and say, "The stick is 18 feet long." The teacher then asks several children to demonstrate a problem of their own.

For example, Chan invented this problem: "My dog weighs 20 pounds. I weigh 3 times as much. How much do I weigh?" The teacher had to help another student, Jim, to come up with the wording of his problem: "My father is 4 times as old as I am. I am 10 years old. How old is my father?"

After having students come up with their own problems, such as in the Screen Game, teachers often reflect that they have been too interested in leading every activity themselves. They realize that they must learn to stand back and encourage the children to develop and use their own powers of creation.

THE RELATIONSHIP BETWEEN MULTIPLICATION AND DIVISION

Students who have learned multiplication with the Structural Arithmetic materials have experienced for themselves how different the role is that each number in an equation plays. For instance, in a multiplication example, such as $3 \times 5 =$ _____ , the multiplier, 3, and the **multiplicand**, 5, are given; the product is to be found. In one of the related division examples, the total, called the **dividend**, is given and has to be divided into a given number of parts. The question is "What is the size of each part?" ($15 \div 3 =$ _____). This is the partition aspect of division. In contrast, when the total and the size of the part are given, the question is "How many times is the size, or part [5], contained in the dividend?"

$$5 \overline{)15}$$

The answer, 3, is called the **quotient**. This is the containing aspect of division.

Students can take the idea that three 5s make 15, turn it around to answer the new question, "How many 5s are in 15?" and immediately answer, "3." By contrast, children who learn the 100 multiplication facts by rote acquire a habit of absent-minded mechanical activity that does not allow them to see the relationship between multiplication and division.

The Partition Aspect of Division

Most children experience the partition aspect of division at home whenever food or toys are divided among a few children. For example, a total, such as 15 cookies, is divided among 3 children; the answer to the question "How many cookies will each child receive?" (5) is the answer to the division problem $15 \div 3$. The children can carry out many such problems and record them (e.g., $15 \div 3 = 5$).

The Containing Aspect of Division

When considering the partition aspect of division, the total and the number of shares are stated, and the question is to find the size of the share. In contrast, when considering the containing aspect of division, the total and the size of the part are given. The question is to find the number of shares (e.g., "How many times is the part contained in the total?"). For example, the previous problem changed to demonstrate the containing aspect of division would be stated like this: "Mother has 15 cookies. She wants to give 5 cookies to each child. How many children can she give cookies to?"

The containing aspect of division is taught first because it makes the structure of the division algorithm so clear. Children find they can solve a division example as soon as they understand multiplication.

The **division radical** looks like this: $\overline{)}$ and can be presented so as to make sense to students. The teacher places a small paper division radical on the number track over a multiple, such as 15. By doing this the teacher shows how the number 15 changes roles from being the product in a multiplication example to being the dividend in a division example. When the children see a division example, such as

$$5 \overline{)15}$$

the teacher explains that this asks, "How many 5s are in 15?" To answer this question, students lay their pencils across 15 on the number track and find it takes 3 of the 5-blocks to reach 15, thus 3 tells them "how many times" the **divisor** (5) is contained

in the dividend (15) (see Figure 17.6). The children then place the number marker for 3 on top of the number track above the number 15. This placement reminds them to write the quotient above the division radical when they record the answer to a division example (see Figure 17.7). By working with examples such as this one, the children begin to understand the relationship between multiplication and division.

Under the Box

The game called Under the Box helps children remember which number in a division example is written "under the box" (under the division radical). When children hear words such as "24 divided by 4," they often write the numbers in the order in which they hear them, like this:

$$24 \overline{)4}$$

The teacher hides several number blocks of the same size under a box, such as four 5-blocks, writes the total on a card, and says, "The blocks under the box make 20." The children write 20 under the box on their papers, like this:

$$\overline{)20}$$

The teacher continues, "The blocks under the box are 5-blocks. How many 5s are there?" The students ask themselves, "How many 5s are in 20?" and write

$$5 \overline{)20}$$

They answer "4" and lift the box, which reveals the four 5-blocks. They write 4 above the division radical:

$$5 \overline{)20}^{4}$$

Division with Remainder

When long division is presented with the Structural Arithmetic materials, children can see that each step of the process makes sense. The teacher dictates a division example that will have an answer with a remainder, such as "How many 5s are in 14?" (see Fig-

Figure 17.7. Division with remainder.

ure 17.7). The children place two 5-blocks in the number track plus 4 cubes to reach 14, and write

$$5 \overline{)14}$$

on their papers. The children see that there are 2 fives in 14, so they write 2 above the division radical, but they know that 2×5 is only 10. The teacher explains that now the students should find the number of cubes left, so he or she takes the 2 fives out of the track. The children say, "Subtract 10 from 14," and they write $- 10$ below 14 in their examples:

$$\begin{array}{r} 2 \\ 5 \overline{)14} \\ -10 \end{array}$$

Because 10 has been subtracted from 14, 4 cubes remain in the number track. Thus, the expression "remainder of 4" makes sense to the students. They complete their work by writing the remainder in their answers:

$$\begin{array}{r} 2R4 \\ 5 \overline{)14} \\ -10 \\ \hline 4 \end{array}$$

Division Word Problems

Division (Containing Aspect)

15 children want to go on boat rides (total). One boat holds 5 children (size of part). Question: How many boats will the children need? We want to find how many 5s are contained in 15, so we write

$$5 \overline{)15}$$

They will need 3 boats. We can check this: $3 \times 5 = 15$.

Division (Partition Aspect)

15 children want to go on boat rides (total). There are only 3 boats. Question: If there are an equal number of children in each boat, how many children are in each boat? We want to know the size of the part or the number of children in each boat. [To show that the students are finding the size of the part this time, the teacher can use a different way of writing the example, such as $15 \div 3 = 5$.] There will be 5 children in each boat. They can state that 3 boats containing 5 children in each will carry 15 children.

CONCLUSION

This chapter shows how the multisensory Structural Arithmetic materials enable children to discover mathematical concepts and relationships that they could not have discovered through counting procedures and memorization alone. Children often respond appreciatively when a demonstration gives them insight into a new concept by exclaiming, "How neat!" Such enthusiasm is quickly responded to by the other children and gives the teacher special pleasure in working with these materials.

Today educators and parents are concerned about the use of computers by children. What effect will their use have on the ability of children to develop intellectual competence and to learn effectively? Jane Healy has made extensive studies of children working with computers at different ages. In her book *Failure to Connect,* she wrote,

> It is no accident that formal schooling in most countries begins at the time when the brain is sufficiently organized to grasp abstract symbols. Prior to that time, young children are "concrete learners": They need to "mess around," experiment, and create meaning with their own symbol systems. Preschoolers don't learn language and concepts from two-dimensional flash cards, but from multidimensional experience. (1999, p. 221)

Premature reliance on abstractions, on visual images and mouse movements and clicks without sufficient exposure to 3-dimensional experience is likely to diminish the density of meaning children associate with symbols. To the extent that computers may deprive young children of such experience, or cut dramatically into the time they spend interacting with the concrete world, the symbols may come to hold less tangible associations.

Piaget (1952) explained that children develop an understanding of mathematical concepts as a result of the actions they perform with objects, not as a result of the objects themselves. This makes clear why pictures in workbooks do not teach children. The Structural Arithmetic blocks invite children to handle them and perform actions at every step. By the time students reach the level of writing in workbooks, they are free to focus on how to write numbers and equations; they have already worked out the concepts with the multisensory materials and are ready to record them.

By using these structured materials, children, especially children with learning disabilities, learn to trust their intelligence; they come to feel pleased with themselves and proud of their ability to think. This feeling of self-confidence increases their self-esteem and often spreads to their work in other fields. Furthermore, they have developed a reliable understanding of number concepts from the very beginning. They will not have to discard these early formulations as deceptively simple but can carry them forward as the building blocks of algebra.

When we teach mathematical truths and facts by rote, we take away from children not only the joy of using their minds but also their sense of independence. They feel manipulated, and the result is unimaginative mechanical work. In some cases, this causes students to be bored; in other cases, this leads students to turn off their minds, to withdraw, or to fail. What children crave is freedom to carry out their own experiments and draw their own conclusions. When they are permitted to do this to the degree that they can, their work will be fulfilling.

REFERENCES

Healy, J. (1999). *Failure to connect.* New York: Simon & Schuster.

Piaget, J. (1952). *The child's concept of number.* London: Routledge & Kegan Paul.

Stern, C., & Stern, M. (1971). *Children discover arithmetic: An introduction to Structural Arithmetic.* New York: HarperCollins.

Stern, M. (1988). *Experimenting with numbers: A guide for preschool, kindergarten, and first grade teachers.* Cambridge, MA: Educators Publishing Service.

Stern, M., & Gould, T. (1988–1992). *Structural Arithmetic workbooks 1–3 and teachers' guides.* Cambridge, MA: Educators Publishing Service.

18

Learning Strategies and Study Skills

The SkORE System

Claire Nissenbaum

I t is not necessarily the smartest student but the student who knows how to study who gets the highest marks. The most intellectually able students may be among the lowest-performing students in the class. Too often, these students are struggling with unrecognized language-based learning difficulties (dyslexia[1]), which affect performance in every area of the curriculum, especially if the students have not had effective training in learning strategies and study skills (Deshler, Ellis, & Lenz, 1996; Strichart & Mangrum, 1993; Wiig & Semel, 1990). Instructors who undertake to work on learning strategies and study skills with students with specific language-based learning difficulties should be fully trained in addressing the language-processing problems typical of these students. Training is available from programs across the country (see the section for Chapter 2 in Appendix B).

In this chapter, the terms *strategy* and *study skills* are used as follows:

> An individual's approach to a task is called a strategy. Strategies include how a person thinks and acts when planning, executing and evaluating performance on a task and its subsequent outcomes. (Deshler et al., 1996, p. 12)

> Study skills are those competencies associated with acquiring, recording, organizing, synthesizing, remembering and using information and ideas found in school . . . the ones more or less indispensable for success. (Devine, 1981, p. 4)

Systematic instruction in learning strategies and study skills may or may not be offered in middle or secondary school. Even if it is available, the instructor may not have

---

[1]The term *dyslexia* is used here to refer to language-based specific learning difficulties in receptive and expressive language skills, including conceptualization, decoding comprehension, grammar, memory (storage and retrieval), time-management, and organization, and—even in students who are talented in math—difficulties with math concepts and operations. Students with dyslexia may also have difficulties in social skills (Deshler et al., 1996; Wiig & Semel, 1990). At least 80% of students with learning disabilities have verifiable reading disorders (Lerner, 1989).

had adequate training to teach the course (Tonjes & Zintz, 1981). The time allotted may have been insufficient for students to develop mastery of the strategies and skills (Deshler et al., 1996). Practice in transferring the skills successfully to the classroom may have received little or no attention.

The lack of efficient, effective training in strategies and skills handicaps *all* students but is extremely handicapping to students with dyslexia, especially if they are included in general education classes. They are left to a demeaning and unrewarding struggle to survive academically, to narrowly limited college and vocational choices, and to the likelihood of physical and mental health problems (Kamhi & Catts, 1989). A few individuals develop self-destructive or antisocial behaviors (Levine, 1987).

Training in learning strategies and study skills must be as efficacious as possible and must be accomplished in the shortest possible time without sacrificing mastery. The strategies should be applicable in all subject classes with minimal teacher involvement. Well done, training in such skills facilitates change in the student, from passive involvement to proactive and productive participation in learning (Deshler et al., 1996).

OVERVIEW

This chapter discusses *unconventional* techniques that improve the performance of all students, but that make the critical difference between passing and failing for students with dyslexia. The techniques are useful for college and graduate school and later for work. After sections on the academic achievement of students with dyslexia and organization, time management, and self-management, this chapter describes the SkORE system, which is designed to help students achieve the goals of self-knowledge, self-management, and self-advocacy. In addition, strategies for improving memory and comprehension and for taking tests are discussed.

The Skills for Organizing and Reading Efficiently (SkORE) system begins by teaching students fast-working "Quick Tricks" that

- Engage the students' attention and cooperation

- Reduce high-frequency errors and common teacher irritants in written work

- Begin systematic memory training

- Provide strategies for handling long reading assignments on an emergency basis

Simultaneously, students are coached in organization and time-management skills. This introductory step usually has positive effects on students' motivation.

After this introductory step, the first phase of SkORE presents strategies for preparing to read a passage of text. The second phase presents strategies and techniques for mastering subject content and includes rapid improvement in vocabulary (including **nonliteral language**), comprehension, conceptual and critical thinking, writing skills, and self-confidence. There is strong emphasis on concept formation and explication of abstract terms. Written language skills are taught incrementally, beginning with the mechanics of English, accurate spelling, sentence and paragraph structure, and, in the third phase of SkORE, moving to summarizing, writing précis, outlining, and note taking. More extensive training in writing skills is not possible in a study skills course, due to time limitations (see Chapter 16 for more information on composition). Bringing students to mastery in the strategies and skills is crucial. To attempt to do both is to do an inadequate job of both (Deshler et al., 1996).

ACADEMIC ACHIEVEMENT OF STUDENTS
WITH DYSLEXIA: CONVENTION, PERCEPTION, AND REALITY

The problem with conventional courses in study skills is that there is too much *study* and not enough *skills*. This may be because teachers cannot teach what they themselves have not been taught (Askov & Kamm, 1982). College and university education courses for teacher preparation do not include methods in teaching study skills (Deshler et al., 1996). Notwithstanding, many elementary and secondary teachers are required to teach them. Teachers often lecture, provide worksheets in discrete skills (e.g., finding the main idea), and test students' knowledge. Students are expected to pay attention, listen, understand, take notes, remember, and apply the skills to content subjects. These are precisely the areas of greatest deficit for most students with dyslexia.

Many adults believe that academic achievement is a prerequisite to success in adult life. This belief is supported neither by research nor common experience. Parents typically believe that academic achievement is directly related to the time and effort spent on homework. Teachers may view parents of low achievers as unable or unwilling to make the students work harder. Both parents and teachers tend to view low-achieving students as unmotivated, lazy, and not invested in their work.

The reality is that students with learning disorders do poorly because of deficits in cognitive processing resulting from underlying differences in brain anatomy and physiology (Cruickshank, 1967; Gaddes & Edgell, 1994). These deficits may include one or more of the following:

- ***Concrete thinking*** results in difficulty with abstractions, multiple word meanings, nonliteral language such as idioms and metaphors (Cruickshank, 1967; Wiig & Semel, 1990).

- ***Rigidity,*** or inability to shift the frame of reference, can be manifest as difficulty with transitions or changing a routine or as perseveration (Cruickshank, 1967; Wiig & Semel, 1990).

- ***Difficulties with spatial and temporal sequence*** are evidenced in poor orientation in space, poor sense of direction, problems with telling time, sensing duration, estimating time, habitual tardiness, vocabulary of time and space (day after tomorrow, second from the last). These difficulties may affect interpersonal relationships.

- ***Unstable figure–ground perception*** results in difficulty with recognizing whole–part relationships (e.g., forest and trees) and the ability to analyze and synthesize. This affects handwriting, reading, subtraction and division, outlining and summarizing, and comprehension of complex subject matter (Cruickshank, 1967; Tomatis, 1969) because, as Johnson and Myklebust noted, "A perceptual disorder by reciprocation *disturbs all levels of experience that fall above it*" (1967, p. 33, italics added).

- ***Difficulty with focusing and sustaining attention*** affects all aspects of intellectual and social functioning.

- ***Poor and variable memory*** affects a person's ability to understand, store, retrieve, and use information (Neisser, 1976).

- ***Difficulty with symbolization*** can lead to problems understanding, learning, and using verbal symbols and symbol systems (Orton, 1937; Wiig & Semel, 1990). This difficulty affects speaking, reading, and writing skills.

- ***Deficits in receptive and expressive language*** affect vocabulary, grammar, all communication, and interpersonal relationships (Tomatis, 1969).

- ***Deficits in simultaneous integration of verbal symbolic data with motor output*** affect attention, memory, spelling, writing, and note taking.

- ***Difficulty processing rapidly spoken information*** (e.g., a lecture) can include problems with discrimination of discrete verbal sound units in words and sentences. This affects listening skills, vocabulary, following directions, note taking, and memory.

- ***Anxiety*** may appear as general anxiousness and can be compounded by stress, such as during classroom recitations, oral reading, tests, social introductions. Anxiety affects all areas of thought and learning, especially memory.

- ***Problems with abstraction*** include difficulties with classifying, categorizing, generalizing, and making analogies. These problems affect concept development, abstract thought (Lakoff & Johnson, 1980), comprehension, and understanding of logical relations (Wiig & Semel, 1990). Tomatis observed, "Categorization is the main way we make sense of experience" (1969, p. 32).

- ***Risk aversion*** can affect class participation, selection of courses, schools, jobs, and friendships.

WORKING WITH STUDENTS WITH DYSLEXIA

The need to prevent early failure is the strongest argument for aggressive intervention in the early school years. Students who have experienced continual failure inevitably have low self-esteem. Once eroded, self-esteem is difficult to restore. Adult achievement appears not to compensate for early traumas. Professor Seymour Martin Lipset, a fellow of the Hoover Institution at Stanford University and a member of the American Academy of Arts and Sciences, described himself as "the man whose wife had to write his thank-you notes for him" (personal communication, 1986). Katrina de Hirsch (1984) stated that the teacher of a student with language deficits must be the student's ego until he or she begins to experience success. Cruickshank held that a student with a learning disability "needs every stable external support possible to assist him in developing a strong ego" (1967, p. 9).

To provide this support, the study skills instructor functions as mentor, coach, and cheerleader, with unflagging faith in the student's ability to overcome or compensate for the difficulties. The instructor must make learning a process of communication, hope, and trust for the student (Tonjes & Zintz, 1981). All this requires good organization and thorough preparation, with the instructor working as "a manager, and instructional leader, and a mediator of learning who demonstrates how to think about a task, apply strategies, and problem-solve in novel situations" (Deshler et al., 1996, pp. 463–464).

What are the odds of getting the student to use learning strategies and study skills consistently and accurately in other classes? The obstacles are the persistent skills deficits, such as in memory, decoding, handwriting, spelling, and comprehension; lack

of sufficient time for practice in the transfer and application to content subjects; and lack of coordination with other teachers. Therefore, the instructor must be willing and able to work cooperatively with subject teachers. Teachers and students need to know that it takes much time to establish effective study skills. "The full benefits of effective programming are realized only . . . over a period of years" (Deshler et al., 1996, p. iii).

The study skills instructor is not a homework aide. Aspects of assignments in subject classes can serve as a vehicle for applying and practicing the techniques, but helping with class work and test preparation is not part of the coaching process. In the best case, subject teachers work closely with the study skills instructor to reinforce the skills by requiring, cuing, and monitoring the student's use of the strategies and techniques in the subject classroom. These include full use of the binder (described later), vocabulary work, consistent attention to spelling, note taking, use of mnemonics and cue cards, and use of procedures for homework assignments.

Students need to know that study skills training is a cooperative effort with the instructor, in which the instructor has the expertise to give the student the skills and to train him or her in the discipline needed for success. Giving the student the right to set his or her own priorities and goals is essential; it is not necessary for the student to get an A in every subject.

Catch Them Early

Dr. Helen Hall, an expert in working with failing adolescents, noted that "if you are going to catch them, you have six weeks to do it" (personal communication, 1977). A student with dyslexia must experience change for the better very quickly. He or she needs to know that it is indeed possible to improve performance and get better grades fairly soon after beginning the study skills course. This is the rationale for the Quick Tricks, described later in this chapter, the introductory step in SkORE.

ORGANIZATION, TIME MANAGEMENT, AND SELF-MANAGEMENT

The importance of structure and organization when working with students with dyslexia cannot be overemphasized. Strichart and Mangrum (1993) noted that students with learning disabilities typically experience disorganization. It is often overwhelming to a student, even threatening, to have to function in an unstructured environment (Cruickshank, 1967). A study skills instructor must impose and require maximum structure in every aspect of a student's work. The SkORE process accomplishes this by using structured procedures, an orderly sequence of steps in a process for acquiring and applying specific strategies and skills. Deshler et al. noted, "Structured teaching . . . unites the teacher and student in a learning partnership by providing informed, explicit, and interactive instruction" (1996, p. 459).

The Binder as a Central Organizing System

At the first session, the student receives basic equipment for the study skills course, a set of two sturdy three-inch three-ring binders, one for study skills and the other for *all other classes*. The study skills binder remains with the instructor for the duration of training. Use of a single binder for all other subjects requires the agreement of the subject teachers. (If a teacher requires a spiral notebook, it should be bound into the school binder in the appropriate class section.) The use of a single binder eliminates many of the organization and maintenance problems otherwise sure to occur. The study skills binder serves as a model for the all-subjects school binder.

Furnishings for Each Binder

Each binder should be outfitted with the following:

- *Large* plastic zipper case, preferably 7″ × 11″, containing
    - Two pens and two pencils
    - Set of colored felt-tipped pens
    - Gum eraser
    - Wedge-shaped metal pencil sharpener (flat and very small, such as the one made by Staedtler)
    - Paper clips
    - Rubber bands
    - Index cards: four sets of eight cards, each set a different color
    - Several double-fold industrial-quality paper towels
    - Banker's size manila envelopes (2½″ × 3½″)
    - Hole punch that can be clipped into the binder
    - Two sturdy double pocket dividers
    - Dividers for each subject
    - Two or more sheet protectors

The plastic pouch, with its contents, is inserted at the front of the binder. The hole punch is inserted in the middle of the binder (to prevent breakage). The pocket dividers are inserted at the front and the back of the binder. The pocket dividers are labeled as follows:

- Front side of first divider: *Handouts/Homework Sheets/Assignments*
- Back side: *Work in Progress*
- Front side of back divider: *For Consultation and Reworking*
- Back side: *Completed Assignments to Hand In*

After the pocket divider that is placed near the front of the binder, a copy of the school calendar, the student's class schedule, exam schedules, and a table of contents are inserted into sheet protectors. The contents of the binder may be arranged alphabetically or chronologically, according to the daily schedule.

All other papers from the day's work should be filed into the pocket on the inside back cover of the binder, to be filed as soon as possible in the appropriate section. The instructor checks the binder weekly to see that all papers are filed by the end of the week.

Organizing Space

The instructor has to work with the student to organize two different areas, the locker and the backpack. The locker is reorganized with specific arrangements for books, clothing, gym bag, and other items. Extraneous items should be eliminated. The locker

is inspected weekly and cleaned out once a month. The backpack must be even more organized, with specific places for the binder, textbooks, and reference books. No loose papers should be permitted in the backpack.

The home study area, although usually impossible for the instructor to monitor, also needs to be very organized, furnished with all books and supplies the student will need. These include the following:

- A good collegiate dictionary (hardback), such as the most recent edition of *Merriam Webster's Collegiate Dictionary*

- *Roget's Thesaurus* (original version)

- An etymological dictionary, such as *The Oxford Dictionary of English Etymology* (1996)

- Handbook of essential idioms, such as *A Dictionary of American Idioms* (Makkai, Boatner, & Gates, 1995)

- Dictionaries of literary and historical allusions, such as *Brewer's Dictionary of Phrase and Fable* (Evans, 1981)

- Reference book of English composition and grammar, such as *English Composition and Grammar: Complete Course* (Warriner, 1988)

- A handbook on English usage, such as *A Dictionary of Modern English Usage, Second Edition* (Fowler, 1983), or *Minimum Essentials of English, Second Edition* (Obrecht, 1999)

- General reference books, such as *The New York Public Library Desk Reference, Second Edition* (Gold, 1993)

- Optional items, such as an atlas and books of historical time lines

Time Management

Many people with dyslexia have difficulty with aspects of time, such as learning the language of time, learning to tell time, estimating the passage of time, projecting time budgets, planning and carrying out projects in time, and being punctual. No other aspect of study skills training is more critical to success than time management because these individuals must be more organized and efficient than other students to achieve mastery. Being organized alleviates the characteristic free-floating anxiety in students with dyslexia that impairs memory and impedes progress. The study skills instructor has the responsibility to help a student understand that he or she must spend more time on assignments than other students to achieve good grades. The initial training focuses on planning and scheduling.

The first section of the binder contains a set of coordinated calendars, schedules, and time sheets that the student fills out and uses daily, weekly, and monthly:

- Monthly calendar (for secondary students, 60-day calendar)

- Weekly calendar

- Daily time log

- Long-range assignments calendar and/or time logs

- Daily assignment sheet (optional)

- Exam schedule(s)

Monthly Calendar

On a blank calendar form, the instructor guides the student to note holidays, half-days, special events, and vacations. Next, standing commitments are filled in, such as daily classes, practices, regular meetings and appointments, volunteer work, and family commitments. Nonroutine commitments are then added, such as medical appointments and sports matches. Finally, deadlines for long-range assignments are added.

Each entry is made as a *block* of time, posted according to the time of day. Recording entries in this way provides a visual representation of the duration of each event. For example, an afternoon commitment is blocked in below the middle of the square. Initially, the instructor guides the student. Later, when the student can do this independently, the instructor should monitor updates to the calendar weekly.

Long-range assignments require special attention. The student should be trained to build in extra time in case of unexpected events, such as illness or greater than usual difficulty with an assignment. Ideally, the subject teacher is consulted to approve the schedule. The study skills instructor has a special responsibility to see that the student keeps to the schedule and that his or her work is appropriate and meets the teacher's standards. Some students work best with a separate planning worksheet for each long-range project on which the separate components can be checked off as completed.

Weekly Calendar

With the monthly calendar as reference, the student blocks out (colors in) the time for each commitment during the week on a blank weekly calendar. If Saturday morning is committed to soccer practice, for example, the time for the practice, as well as the time for travel, should be blocked out. Deadlines for short- and long-range assignments are noted, as are quizzes and tests. ***The white space remaining on the weekly calendar graphically displays the time available to study and to complete assignments.*** It is important that the student see clearly *when* time is available and *how much* time is available in each instance.

To complete the weekly calendar, the student estimates and schedules in the times needed for studying, completing homework, and working on long-range assignments. The student may lack adequate time sense to plan and schedule realistically, or he or she may have only a vague notion of the actual time needed. Students invariably underestimate the time needed for completing an assignment. The instructor must work with the student to break down every task incrementally and to make a realistic time budget.

Daily Schedule

On Friday, the student fills out the weekly and daily schedules for the next week. If homework is due on a certain day, the student can place an asterisk in red after the name of the class on that day on the daily schedule. A double asterisk can be used to indicate a quiz or test. Figure 18.1 shows a sample daily schedule. In addition, on Friday, the instructor and the student should review and assess the student's ability to schedule appropriately by comparing the estimated and actual time spent on assignments (using the past week's weekly schedule).

Self-Management

Many students with dyslexia actually do not perceive the connection between their academic behavior and their grades. For this reason, it is also useful to create a form to compare the time spent studying weekly on each subject with the grades received in

Wednesday, September 28	RETURN LIBRARY BOOKS

7:00	Review notes for math test.
7:15	Leave. Take LIBRARY BOOKS.
7:30	Spanish
8:40	*Social Studies
9:30	Math
10:20	Free. RETURN LIBRARY BOOKS. Work on math.
11:30	Lunch—Sit with Guy; discuss science project.
12:00	*Science
12:50	Phys. Ed. SEE MR. HASKINS ABOUT EQUIPMENT ROOM.
1:45	**English—Make appointment with Mrs. G to go over book report draft.
2:45	Meet Reshad to get math book.
3:00	Soccer practice
5:30	Nap
6:00	Dinner
6:45	Science project—Work with Guy, my house.
8:15	Read novel for book report, due 10/5, Chaps 6, 7 (30 pages; 67 to go).
9:00	Spanish assignment
9:20	Math assignment
9:45	Pack backpack; check off assignments.

Figure 18.1.   Sample daily schedule sheet. An asterisk indicates that homework is due; double asterisks indicate a quiz.

that class. The form should also note the number of assignments completed and handed in and the number not completed and/or not handed in or handed in late. *This recordkeeping is an important step in training the youngster to develop a more objective view of him- or herself as a student.*

QUICK TRICKS: STRATEGIES FOR CHANGING ATTITUDES AND REVIVING HOPE

At the first or second study skills session, the student is coached to use learning strategies known as Quick Tricks, the introductory step of SkORE. These are presented as strategies that can change teachers' attitudes and grading practices to the student's advantage. (Students will need to be cautioned against discussing this with other teachers.) Seemingly simplistic, Quick Tricks almost always result in perceptible changes that students themselves report with obvious satisfaction. Quick Tricks are designed to help the student begin using a more intentional, proactive, and responsible mode of behavior and especially to foster better relationships with teachers, thereby gradually reducing whatever tensions may exist. The instructor and student should role-play each set of Quick Tricks before the student implements them in his or her classes.

With the right sell by the instructor—enthusiasm mixed with confident assurances, the Quick Tricks produce results in a short time. After a few weeks students generally report more positive responses from teachers ("My teacher smiled at me today!"). These changes increase students' motivation to use the Quick Tricks more consistently. Because teachers see a student using Quick Tricks as making greater effort and having a better attitude, they may even give slightly better grades to encourage the student. A student using Quick Tricks often assumes that the teacher has changed; it is the student, of course, who is changing, but at this point, the student does not make this connection.

Level One (no extra time required, minimal effort required)

1. Look directly at the teacher when he or she is speaking. Look at his or her forehead, ears, or nose if you are uncomfortable with making eye contact.

2. Greet the teacher by name when speaking to him or her at least every other day.

3. In every class, speak at least once. Ask a question, make a comment, or ask to have something repeated.

4. Arrive on time; better yet, be a minute or two early.

5. Avoid watching the clock or glancing at your wristwatch. Do not begin to move out of your desk until the bell rings.

6. Leave only after the bell has finished ringing. Pack up only if the teacher has finished speaking. Never slam a book shut, slam it on the desk, or slam the seat up.

7. Say "thank you" at least once a week as you leave. (This can be combined with #2.)

   (After the student is comfortable using the Level One Quick Tricks, he or she learns the Level Two Quick Tricks.)

Level Two (no extra time required, slightly more effort required, bigger payoff)

1. Hand assignments in *on time,* no matter what you think of your work or whether the assignments have been completed. Ask for the opportunity to complete unfinished assignments, *even if they have already been graded.* Return them to the teacher for a better grade.

2. Always use the heading format the teacher requires. Be sure every paper is dated.

3. Draw only *one* line through an error. Never erase (unless instructed by the teacher) or cross out by scribbling.

4. Ask the teacher to explain anything you do not understand using different words and examples than he or she used the first time.

5. Type or have someone type your papers.

6. Proofread your work for capitalization and end punctuation.

Level Three (some time and effort required at first, but you save on both in the long run)

1. Make an appointment with the teacher to go over anything you are having trouble with.

2. Trade with a classmate who is good in a subject you need help in. Help him or her with computer skills, show him or her how to repair a bike, or coach the classmate in basketball in exchange for assistance in a subject you need help in.

3. Don't give up. Find someone who is able to help you.

Advanced Quick Tricks

Thus far, the work on organizing the binder and presenting the Quick Tricks may have taken two or three sessions, and this time is well invested. The novelty and pristine condition of the binders are attractive to the student. The greater attraction is in its clear order and structure, an attraction, in my experience, so strong as to be irresistible even to adults. This is the rationale for presenting the binder fully indexed, organized, and equipped.

With this beginning, the instructor has gained the student's attention and dawning respect. To capitalize on these gains, the instructor must move the student beyond the first three levels of the Quick Tricks to the next phase, which can be presented as advanced Quick Tricks. New gains must be more tangible and must come quickly. Otherwise, earlier gains will be lost, the student will revert to old ways, and it will be difficult to regain his or her attention. Although still preliminary to actual study skills training, training in and use of these advanced Quick Tricks will result in better grades. Askov and Kamm noted that "early success can have a very positive effect on students' attitudes about learning" (1982, p. 3).

The advanced Quick Tricks involve training in the following:

- Structured procedures for completing assignments

- Emergency techniques for handling assignments

- Structured procedures to reduce spelling errors

- Structured procedures to reduce errors in mechanics

- Spelling by "geometric progression"

Structured Procedures for Completing Homework Assignments

Students who do well in class and on tests may nevertheless receive poor grades because of missing homework assignments. Homework represents one of the most frustrating, contentious, and divisive issues for teachers and for students with dyslexia and their parents. The impact on family life can be extreme. As part of the Quick Tricks, students have been trained to hand assignments in on time, even if the assignments are unfinished, and to complete them later. As quickly as possible, the study skills instructor must train the student to complete assignments *before* handing them in. This is done through structured procedures for time management, for managing papers, and for self-monitoring and **tracking.**

Techniques for handling assignments are part of the structured procedures for using the binder. It is critical that the student observe these procedures faithfully. The procedure is the same for every class.

1. All handouts relevant to assignments are filed in the front side of the pocket divider inside the front cover of the general subject binder. This ensures that the student can locate them quickly and easily. This pocket was labeled *Handouts/Homework Sheets/Assignments* when the binder was set up.

2. All assignments that have been started but not completed are filed in the reverse side of the same pocket folder. This pocket is the one that was labeled *Work in Progress*.

3. Completed assignments are filed in the reverse side of the pocket divider in the back of the binder. This pocket is the one labeled *Completed Assignments to Hand In.*

4. Homework that has been graded and returned to the student is filed in the front side of the same divider for further processing. This pocket is the one that was labeled *For Consultation and Reworking.* At the first available opportunity, the student takes assignments returned with errors to the subject teacher to discuss the errors and to ask for the chance to correct them for a better grade. ***This practice is extremely important to ensure continual improvement in grades.*** Discussing assignments with the teacher further improves relationships with the teacher and parents. It prompts the subject teacher to go the extra mile to give the student extra assistance. Most important, it is another step in developing the student's ability to assess his or her own learning style, characteristic errors, strengths, and deficits. Asking for the chance to discuss and correct errors continues the process of self-monitoring; self-evaluation; and, ultimately, self-advocacy.

5. Papers free of errors are clipped to the inside front cover of the binder with a large spring clip, to be filed in the appropriate subject section as soon as possible, preferably the same day.

For a middle or secondary school student, the study skills instructor should work out a consistent system for recording assignments with subject teachers. If this is a problem, then the student should not leave class before the subject teacher has checked to see that the assignments have been recorded correctly and that the student has the books or materials he or she will need to complete the assignment. Assignments can be recorded on a specially designed form filed in the front side of the first pocket divider atop the day's worksheets or filed at the beginning of each subject section in the binder. Younger students should have a single form for listing all daily assignments. (Small assignment pads are easily misplaced or lost. If used, they should be kept in the zipper case.)

Students with dyslexia typically have difficulty remembering to take home what they need to do their homework. They also have difficulty remembering to bring books and homework back to school. Where this is a problem, the study skills instructor, subject teacher, student, and parents need to work out a structured routine whereby the student's book bag is checked by an adult before leaving home and school. A careful record should be kept of the student's ability to come to school and go home fully prepared. It is best that student and parent organize the backpack together the night before, using a checklist to make sure that nothing is forgotten. A few students may need to have two sets of textbooks, one for home and one for school.

Emergency Techniques for Last-Minute Reading Assignments

A long reading assignment, such as a social studies chapter, can be quite daunting for students with dyslexia. Students typically put off this kind of assignment until the last minute, when they have too little time and too little energy to do the job well. This procrastination becomes habitual. The anxiety and stress generated by the delay compound the problem. While coaching a student in scheduling, the study skills instructor can present techniques to compensate for reading at the last minute.

First, the student should get "psyched up" to be as focused and attentive as possible and form the intention to hold as much in memory as possible. Then, he or she should complete these steps:

1. Read the introduction, the advance organizer, or the first three paragraphs and the summary and questions, if any, at the end of the selection.

2. Read the text headings (boldface type) and subheadings *in order* from first to last.

3. Read all uppercase, boldface, and italic type embedded in the text.

4. Return to the beginning and read the first and last sentence of every paragraph.

5. Read the captions under all graphics, charts, or tables.

6. Copy onto 3″ × 5″ cards all definitions set apart in the text.

7. If time permits, read through the text rapidly without attempting to remember it, or scan it rapidly without stopping.

8. Discuss the highlights of the selection with a friend before class. This strategy lays the groundwork for later structured procedures for mastering course content. When it works, it has the advantage of increasing the student's trust in the study skills instructor, bolstering self-confidence, and strengthening motivation.

Structured Procedures to Reduce Spelling Errors: Multisensory Solutions

Misspellings account for the most frequent errors made by college freshmen (Deshler et al., 1996). When students with dyslexia have poor memories for auditory or visual sequential patterns, spelling is "the last skill acquired" (Tomkins, 1963, p. 127). In the initial stages, memory training is facilitated by the work on organizing, scheduling, and managing time; by the organization of the binder; and by the introduction of certain structured procedures, such as proofreading (described later).

Systematic memory training begins with the structured procedures for improving spelling. Success with these techniques fosters confidence and a new awareness in the student that success in academics does not depend on the ability to *memorize* information. At this stage, training to correct spelling weaknesses is *physical* and *mechanical*, relying principally on **overlearning** by frequent repetition and kinesthetic (muscle) memory—the most permanent sense memory. This does not involve memorizing or learning rules. Structured procedures for *internalizing* orthographic (spelling) patterns are employed, involving simultaneously *seeing, saying, hearing,* and *tracing* or *writing*. (See Chapter 10 for spelling patterns and rules and for more on spelling instruction.) Except where printing is specified, students should use cursive handwriting (see Chapter 15 for more on handwriting instruction). The several techniques for internalizing spelling patterns can be used simultaneously or rotated. When used daily, they result in rapid and significant improvement in spelling and can, in the best case, eliminate up to 50% of a student's habitual errors.

Copying   On wide-ruled paper, the instructor writes a model in cursive for the student to copy. The student copies *below* the model, keeping the letters aligned under those above. The instructor must check constantly to be sure that the student has not made an error. The student finger proofs *each* copy, saying the name of the letter aloud while touching the index finger of each hand to the same letter in the model and the copy (one above, one below). Experimenting will determine how many times the student must copy in order to retain the word. Making about 7–10 copies at a time is usually effective. If not, the **cloze technique** described next may be more effective.

Cloze Technique

t a u g h t	The complete word
_ a u g h t	Easiest letter/sound to remember omitted
_ a u g h _	Next easiest to remember omitted
_ a u _ _ _	Digraph *gh* omitted
_ _ _ _ _ _	Digraph *au* omitted.

After the word is prepared as just shown, the student begins to fill in the missing letters, at each step covering the word above and the word below, and *naming the letters* as he or she *prints* them. Finally, the student fills in all of the blanks. Then, the student covers all of the words and writes the word from memory. At each step, the student checks the newly filled-in line with the line above for accuracy by finger proofing, before moving to the next line.

It is important for the student to maintain vigilant attention while practicing this technique. To achieve the best results, he or she should actively *intend* to attend closely to spelling aloud, printing the letters neatly, and checking for accuracy. Being on automatic pilot will not do the trick. Occasionally, a student will display great agitation and resistance while doing the cloze procedure. In this case it should be dropped for the time being.

Tracing   All students with dyslexia should use tracing to learn irregularly spelled words, such as *their, llama, unique,* and *rough.* Materials needed are a medium felt-tip pen and double-fold industrial-strength paper towels, the scratchiest possible. Work can be done starting with three words per session, working up to five. No more than five should be attempted in a single session. With the paper towel folded and open at the top, the tracing procedure is as follows:

1. The student or the instructor writes the model in large, evenly spaced cursive letters, with the word centered on the upper front panel.

2. Using the fleshy ends of the index and middle fingers of the writing hand, the student traces the word **three times,** naming each letter or saying each sound as the fingers trace over it, naming the full word after each tracing.

3. If the student does the second step correctly, the top panel is dropped behind, and the bottom panel is lifted, exposing the center panel. The word is written again, on the center panel and compared to the model. If the student has written the word correctly, the bottom panel is folded up over the center panel, the top panel is dropped behind, and the word is written again and compared again to the original model on the top panel.

4. If correct, the procedure is repeated for 3 days, then once a week for 3 weeks, finally once a month for 3 months.

If the student is in error at any point, Step 1 is repeated. Each time, three tracings are made. Only two retries of the same target word may be made on the same day. If after 3 days, the student has not mastered the word, it should be an indication that the word is too difficult for him or her at this time.

Syllable Spelling   A student with fairly good skills in phonics, at least with closed (e.g., *cat*) and open syllables (e.g., *he, go*), should use the Simultaneous Oral Spelling (S.O.S.) procedure (Gillingham & Stillman, 1997): Listen to the dictated word, echo the word, tap out each sound while saying it (/k/ /à/ /t/), then write it in cursive letters.

Words of two, three, and four syllables combining the closed and open syllable patterns can be spelled this way (e.g., *open, event, remit, intended, discontented*). (See Chapters 9 and 10 for further discussion of syllable patterns and S.O.S. respectively.)

Structured Procedures to Reduce Errors in Mechanics

The habit of proofreading written work must become automatic. Teachers view errors in the mechanics of English—capitalization, punctuation, spelling, as carelessness and evidence of indifference, at best, or low ability, at worst. Spotting errors is problematic for students with dyslexia because of their difficulties with attention, memory, and systematic scanning, among others. It is important to prevent the student from surveying or her work for all possible errors at one time (Askov & Kamm, 1982). Instead, beginning with the first sentence and moving sentence by sentence, the student searches systematically for possible errors, *one at a time:*

1. Capitalization of the first word in a sentence

2. Punctuation mark at the end of the sentence

3. Capitalization of proper nouns

4. Apostrophes in contractions

Spelling by Geometric Progression

Students with dyslexia are at a disadvantage when required to make inferences; these students often do not see what is obvious to others. They do not perceive or translate patterns from one situation to another, unless these are highlighted, explicated, dramatized, or clearly delineated, with color coding, for example. This is true even for the spelling of inflected (e.g., *cat/cats*) and derived (e.g., *happy/happiness*) forms of a base word.

To bring orthographic patterns into sharp focus, the student should be given practice first in working with extending and then in creating arrays such as the one in Figure 18.2. Students should not be asked to memorize the spellings. The point is to get students to recognize—to see—the related patterns of roots and affixes. Arrayed in columns, one entry under another, each column of prefixes, roots, and suffixes is coded with a different color. This practice aids decoding as well as spelling. (Further gains in spelling as well as gains in reading speed, fluency, and comprehension can be realized through the

Anglo-Saxon			Latin
stand	**sew**	**friend**	**human**
stand s	**sew** s	**friend** s	**human** ness
stand ing	**sew** ed	**friend** ly	in **human** ness
un der **stand** ing	**sew** ing	**friend** ship	in **human** ity
un der **stand** ing s	**sew** er	be **friend**	**human** ize
mis un der **stand** ing	**sew** n	be **friend** ed	**human** iz ed
up **stand** ing	un **sew** n		**human** iz ing
out **stand** ing			

Figure 18.2. Spelling by geometric progression.

mastery of the meanings of roots and affixes, beginning with J.I. Brown's [1976] Fourteen Master Words: *detain, nonextended, indisposed, oversufficient, intermittent, offer, precept, uncomplicated, aspect, reproduction, mistranscribe, monograph, insist,* and *epilogue*.) For further discussion of spelling instruction, see Chapter 10.

MEMORY TRAINING

The student is now ready to begin to learn the specific techniques for mastering content subject material. The emphasis is on expanded memory training. In general, students with dyslexia have problems with memory. They may have unreliable, variable memory or, in the most serious cases, little or no memory for linguistic material (Deshler et al., 1996). Research has identified many contributing factors: lack of focus and attention, absence of intention, inability to sustain attention, lack of attention to detail, absence of neural mechanisms for filtering or screening irrelevant stimuli, problems with **figure–ground perception,** inability to organize and categorize, inadequate prior knowledge, inability to visualize, anxiety, situational stress, and expectation of failure.

Teachers need to be mindful of a dyslexic student's neuropsychological deficits and the resultant problems with association, classification, organization, storage, and recall of verbal information. Memory is inseparable from learning and is related to productivity, and "severe problems in memory equate to severe problems in school" (A.L. Brown, 1979). Consequently, students with dyslexia need techniques that enable them to internalize and remember information without memorizing; that is, these students need *mnemonics* (from *mnemon,* Greek for *mindful*). In the process of developing mnemonic devices, the student must work at forming associations that do not exist naturally in the content, a necessary condition for remembering (Trudeau, 1995). The use of mnemonics helps students to transform, store, and retrieve information in long-term memory by creating connections in otherwise unconnected data.

Mnemonic Devices

Most students are aware of simple mnemonic devices such as *acronyms,* words made up of the initial letters in a series of words (HOMES, for remembering the Great Lakes), and *acrostics,* groups of words that start with the specific letters or words to be recalled (**E**very **G**ood **B**oy **D**oes **F**ine, for the lines of the music staff). Other devices include the following:

- *The key word strategy:* Using a similar familiar word to cue the meaning of an unfamiliar word (*aberrant:* Abner is odd).

- *Chaining:* Linking the words to be recalled in a sentence or story (for a shopping list of bread, milk, party food, and fabric softener sheets: *Brad milked the company dry*).

- *Chunking:* Separating the information into manageable sets, to be worked on one at a time (the 50 states, by region; e.g., *New England*).

- *Creating rhymes:* Using rhyming lines to remember factual information (*Columbus sailed the ocean blue in 14 hundred and 92*).

- *Visualizing:* Calling up or forming a mental image (e.g., of the White House, of the numeral 8).

STRUCTURED PROCEDURES FOR MASTERING CONTENT SUBJECTS: SkORE

Students with dyslexia are at a particular disadvantage when the text (or the teacher) is not organized or well structured. This is especially true when the students come to the subject with inadequate background knowledge, which is often the case because they have read less than other students who are good readers or because they are unable to remember what they have read. Organization, however "plays an important role in memory and concentration" (Devine, 1981, p. 287).

Unless students process the information to be learned at a deep cognitive level, it is not stored in working or long-term (permanent) memory. Students with dyslexia, however, are rarely taught strategies and techniques for deep processing (Deshler et al., 1996; Levine, 1987; Maria, 1990; McNeil, 1992). They typically resort to rereading every word, from the beginning, a very ineffective way to learn content.

The study skills instructor can offer students with dyslexia faster, more reliable, and more effective alternatives. Storage in long-term memory can be secured by the use of Skills for Organizing and Reading Efficiently (SkORE)[2] procedures for organizing material, elaborating, deep processing, mind mapping, summarizing, writing précis, and note taking. Throughout, a high level of repetition and kinesthetic reinforcement is key to success. SkORE can also be referred to as a CRAP system because it is **c**ognitive, **r**epetitive, **a**ctive, and **p**hysical. The strategies and techniques comprise an integrated system of multisensory structured procedures that facilitate memory, comprehension, reasoning, and written expression. Closely articulated and cumulative skills are built systematically through explicit, direct instruction (especially for extracting meaning); modeling; demonstration; rehearsal; guided practice; transfer; and application to content subjects. The SkORE approach is one example of a *teaching device,* a construct that Deshler et al. noted helps

> Make abstract information more concrete, connect new knowledge with familiar knowledge, enable students who cannot spell well to take useful notes, highlight relationships and organizational structures within the information to be presented, and draw unmotivated learners' attention to the information. (1996, p. 445)

SkORE is designed to produce significant improvement in academic performance over the course of 1 school year. Students need at least 1 year to fully master the strategies and techniques and to transfer and apply them. The first two phases of the process, preparation and organization of the material, are critical to the student's mastery of the material to be learned.

The rationale for these two first phases is the characteristics of poor readers with memory problems, who

> Start reading without preparation . . . read without considering how to approach the task . . . are easily distracted . . . do not know they do not understand . . . do not know what to do when they lack understanding . . . do not recognize important vocabulary . . . do not see any organization . . . [and] add on rather than integrate information. (Deshler et al., 1996, p. 68)

---

[2]SkORE is a study skills approach developed in the late 1970s at the TRI-Services Center for Children and Adults with Learning Disabilities, Rockville, Maryland. The author gratefully acknowledges the writings of S.T. Orton (1925, 1937), Gillingham and Stillman (1956), Cruikshank (1967), and Alley and Deshler (1979) and the modeling and direct training of TRI-Services founder and former director Betty S. Levinson, Ph.D., and Alice A. Koontz, M.A., Jemicy School, Owings Mills, Maryland, as influential in the development of SkORE.

The first two phases of SkORE help students to understand what and how they need to study. Ellis and Colvert (as cited in Deshler et al., 1996) criticized instruction in which the student with learning disabilities is left alone to make discoveries because such teaching is not usually effective. Conversely, research has shown the effectiveness of explicit, direct teaching strategies with techniques continually demonstrated and modeled for the student.

SkORE strategies and techniques help a student compensate for difficulties with attention, scanning, memory, vocabulary, reading comprehension, abstract and nonliteral language, association and categorization, outlining, summarizing, paraphrasing, and critical thinking. The strategies require the following involvement of the student:

- Frequent consultation with subject teachers

- Continual self-generated questions

- Habitual use of reference books, especially the dictionary and *Roget's Thesaurus* (original version)

- Systematic extension of vocabulary

- Systematic explication of abstract and nonliteral language

- Systematic use of mnemonic devices

- Routine conversion of text to graphic displays

- Ongoing self-evaluation

There is little similarity between SkORE and SQ3R (Survey, Question, Read, Recite, Review; Robinson, 1946). SQ3R relies primarily on reading, mental rehearsal, and rote memory—which are weak areas for most students with dyslexia. With SkORE the student is trained to deal with text in five progressive sequences:

1. Preparing the text and setting up a skeleton web

2. Selecting and organizing salient information

3. Generating graphic displays

4. Extending vocabulary and understanding of concepts

5. Summarizing, composing précis, making conventional outlines, and taking notes

Materials Needed

The following materials should be on hand before beginning: binders with all furnishings (as described previously in this chapter), colored index cards, a banker's size manila envelope ($2\frac{1}{2}'' \times 3\frac{1}{2}''$), $11'' \times 17''$ unlined paper, wide-ruled loose-leaf paper, dictionary, and a thesaurus.

The Instructor's Role

The study skills instructor demonstrates the SkORE procedures for the student, beginning with short samples of text and proceeding to longer, more complex text. When the student has understood the structured procedures, the instructor and student together work through several rehearsals, as many as necessary, until the student reaches a comfort level with the process. Then under supervision and with guidance, the stu-

dent practices on new material. Concurrently, systematic instruction in the use of the dictionary (see Chapter 5) and the thesaurus is provided, along with techniques for abstracting, taking notes, creating cue cards and mnemonics, mind mapping (webbing), and writing précis.

Phase One: Preparing the Text

The first phase of SkORE training is designed to train the student to familiarize him- or herself in advance with the information, the vocabulary, and the important concepts of the text to be read and to begin the process of organizing and structuring the material. Specific tasks involve 1) surveying and scanning the text; 2) setting up the basic framework of the mind map; and 3) preparing rehearsal or cue cards for learning and reviewing vocabulary, definitions, major concepts, and spelling.

Surveying and Scanning

Beginning with the title and subtitle, if any, the student goes through the text and reads only what sticks up, stands out, or in some other way is different from the body of the text. This survey includes boldface and italic type, headings, marginal glosses (printed commentary in the margins), boxed text, diagrams, photographs, drawings, charts, and other graphics with captions. (Footnotes should be omitted.) Some students will gain from reading aloud or subvocalizing, but others may lose comprehension; a student should try both at first to determine what works best. Before going on, the student should formulate in one to three sentences what he or she believes is the important information or theme of the text.

Then, the student does a cursory reading of the text (scanning), beginning with the introductory questions, concepts, and/or summary (or the first three paragraphs); the first sentence of each subsequent paragraph; and the concluding summary and questions, if any.

Setting Up the Mind Map

After this cursory reading, the student sets up a mind map, using one to three words printed in block capital letters to designate the topic. A word or a brief phrase to correspond with the headings in the text serve as the main branches of the map. (To build skill in mapping, the student can start with brainstorming familiar topics.)

Preparing Cue Cards

Next, the student reads through the entire text rapidly but at a comfortable rate, making no effort to memorize or remember as he or she goes. During the reading, the student uses code symbols to mark unfamiliar vocabulary; definitions; important concepts; and, separately, vocabulary words that he or she does not know how to spell. The code symbols are arbitrary.

- Underline unfamiliar words.

- Circle unknown or difficult words for spelling practice.

- Place a single asterisk in the margin next to definitions.

- Place double asterisks in the margin for important concepts and abstract terms.

After the student has marked the text, he or she writes vocabulary words on cue cards using the following procedure (the colors of the cards are arbitrary):

- On white index cards, print each vocabulary word in the upper left-hand corner.

- On yellow index cards, using a medium-point black felt-tip pen, write the spelling words in cursive, centered on the cards. Write as large as possible in the space. Double-check accuracy by finger proofing, or have someone check the spelling for accuracy. (Tracing the spelling words is useful for acquiring cursive handwriting skill if the model is a good model of cursive writing.)

- On gold cards, copy the definitions exactly as they appear in the text. Start with the term being defined, and print it in block capital letters. Print the definitions in upper- and lowercase letters, as appropriate.

- On orange cards, write the concept words or phrases on one side. (It may be necessary to use 4″ × 6″ cards for concepts. Fold these cards to place them in the manila envelope.)

Next, the student adds definitions to the cue cards:

- From the most recent edition of *Webster's New World Dictionary,* copy onto the reverse side of the white vocabulary cards the first two definitions given, and number the definitions. Younger students should begin with just one definition. On the side of the cards containing the definitions, write a sentence that makes the meaning of the word very clear. If the target word is *planet,* the sentence *Earth is a planet* will not do.

- On the front of each white vocabulary card, right next to the word, copy from the dictionary the part of speech (e.g., n., adj.). In the upper right-hand corner, place an abbreviation for the language of origin—Anglo-Saxon (A.S.), Latin (L.), or Greek (G.). Later, the student can add inflected forms and extensions of the word on this side of the card—*planet-s, planet-ary, planet-ari-um, planet-oid*—that show the base word and affixes separately.

- The student should trace each spelling word daily by using the fleshy ends of the index and middle fingers, naming aloud each letter as the fingers trace over it, and finally saying the whole word. Each word should be traced three or more times at each rehearsal.

- On the reverse side of the orange concept cards, print the detailed aspects of the concept according to the related features semantic map (described later in this chapter) or in a similar manner (see Chapter 9 in Deshler et al., 1996, and Chapter 5 in Maria, 1990).

After the cards are prepared, they are banded together by color and kept in the manila envelope in the plastic zipper case at the front of the student's general subject notebook. Students are encouraged to review the cards daily at odd moments, such as in class, during lunch, while on the bus, while waiting for class to begin, and so forth.

Phase Two: Selecting and Organizing the Information

As an adjunct to the SkORE process, separate but concurrent systematic training in related subskills, such as cursive handwriting, abstracting, mind mapping, and **précis** writing, is necessary for the student to gain facility in these component techniques. To

self-monitor attention and concentration—or the extent of his or her distractibility—the student can be asked to complete a brief reading or exercise and to check a form or ring a bell each time his or her attention wanders. Exercises in abstracting should be given, beginning with underlining the most salient information in simple sentences and paragraphs and working up to doing this with a selection of several paragraphs and brief chapters (see Lehmann, 1960a, 1960b). The student should create a mind map or web first by filling in major details under the topic lines, then by creating topic words and phrases for subsections with details filled in (see Buzan, 1983, and Wycoff, 1991). (For students with more severe dyslexia who have difficulty with abstracting, note taking, and mind mapping, the instructor is referred to the *Reading and Thinking in English* series edited by Moore & Widdowson, 1981, especially the first volume, *Concepts in Use,* written by Moore & Munévar. This resource should be used in conjunction with the SkORE process.) The dyslexic student needs practice in categorizing and classifying, as well as practice in detecting and verbalizing relationships between and among concepts and terms.

The instructor should encourage the student to verbalize his or her thinking as he or she works. This gives the instructor the opportunity to help the student to clarify his or her thinking and the chance to model spoken English by repeating what the student says, in complete, grammatically correct, coherent sentences. More important, the student's verbalizations give the instructor a window on the student's thought processes.

In Phase Two of SkORE, the student must make the conscious decision to maintain attention and concentration to the best of his or her ability throughout each step. The tasks involve 1) abstracting the text, 2) taking notes on the mind map, 3) consulting with the instructor to correct and complete the mind map, 4) completing and enhancing the mind map by color coding and creating graphics, and 5) creating mnemonics.

Abstracting the Text

The process of abstracting (condensing) text forces the student to determine the essential information in the text. The abstract extracts the most important information from the paragraph or text. The goal is to reduce the text at least by half, and later by as much as two thirds. To do this, the student must ask him- or herself questions. The technique of questioning should be taught concurrently, with the teacher using both Socratic questioning (to get the correct answer) (see Murdoch, 1987; this book is out of print but is still available in many libraries and may also be found through on-line booksellers) and open-ended questioning (to provoke the student to think) (see Maria, 1990). For lengthy text, such as a chapter in a social studies, history, or science textbook, structured group discussion is a useful tool; in this type of discussion, the questions originate from the students (see Chapter 6 of Christensen, Garvin, & Sweet, 1991). An example of a text marked (underlined) for abstracting follows:

> <u>The student returns to the beginning</u> of the text <u>and,</u> reading paragraph by paragraph, <u>abstracts the text</u> by underlining only the salient parts. (Because dyslexic students have significant difficulty determining saliency (relative importance, from L. *salio,* leap, i.e., to be "over" others), <u>this will be</u> quite <u>difficult.)</u> <u>The finished abstract should be in</u> complete, <u>grammatically correct sentences, keeping the author's own words. Paraphrasing is not permitted. Minor changes are permitted</u> for smooth transitions and correct syntax; including transitional words and changes in tense or number. <u>The instructor must approve the final product.</u>

The previous paragraph (92 words) has been abstracted (42 words) to read as follows:

> The student returns to the beginning and abstracts the text. This will be difficult. The finished abstract should be in grammatically correct sentences [in] the author's words. Paraphrasing is not permitted; minor changes are permitted. The instructor must approve the final product.

For the dyslexic student, who has difficulty processing large volumes of language, it is vital that the text be reduced in this manner (Deshler et al., 1996). The advantages of abstracting are as follows: The student is not so overwhelmed by the reading task, his or her storage capacity is less taxed by the task (dyslexic students often think it is necessary to memorize everything), comprehension is improved because the essential information is laid bare, and the student can see the focus of the lesson more clearly. Maria (1990) stated that in "many texts . . . the real point of the lesson is often obscured." Once the abstract is approved by the instructor, the original text is put aside and is never referred to again.

Taking Notes on the Mind Map

Working from the abstract only, not from the original text, the student next fills in the details on the mind map, beginning at 12 o'clock and working clockwise. It is best to use unlined 11″ × 17″ paper. Single words or brief phrases should be printed in block capital letters (Buzan, 1983) to serve as cues for retrieving information. The student must not be permitted to print long phrases, clauses, or sentences or to write in cursive. Unless the headings of the text provide a clear structure for the web, the student usually must reorganize the map by grouping related details in narrower categories. With the instructor's guidance, the student should reexamine each cluster to determine whether details belong under that subtopic label, whether the heading should be reworded, and whether one cluster should be merged with another or, conversely, be made into two clusters.

It is expected that full mastery of the mapping technique will take time and much practice. Both instructor and student should regard the time invested as normal and productive in the learning curve. For a full treatment of mind mapping, see Buzan (1983) and Wycoff (1991). (*Note:* Buzan's system of note taking is not recommended for dyslexic students.)

Reexamining the details of the web, the student should next try to identify concepts and details that are grouped separately but somehow related. Connections can be shown by dotted lines ending in arrows. The relationships—the basis of the associations—should be verbalized by the student.

Consulting with the Instructor

When the student has finished the mind map, he or she should ask the study skills instructor to review the map with him or her to determine whether important information has been omitted and whether unimportant information has been included. (Later, the student will ask the subject teacher to review the map.) Appropriate corrections are made. This is an important step in facilitating the student's ability to assess his or her own work and monitor the outcomes.

Color-Coding and Creating Graphics

After consulting with the instructor, the student color-codes the web by lightly shading each module with a different pale pastel color, or by circling the modules in differ-

ent colors, or by underlining the branches and subbranches of separate modules with different colors. (Students must not be permitted to print the words in each block using different colors; this is time consuming, and the visual result is disorganized.) Color differentiation further structures the material by establishing boundaries, and enhances the graphic display by helping the student to focus on modules of information. Also, it adds to the sensorially pleasing quality of the mind map, which should not be underestimated as an additional reinforcer. In addition, the student creates cartoons, graphs, sketches, diagrams, maps, and other visual aids to illustrate the material to be learned. Students often produce maps that are beautiful and creative enough to display as graphic art.

Creating Mnemonics

After details have been filled in on the mind map, the student devises mnemonics as aids to remember specific data on the map, such as lists. These mnemonics are added to the map. All material is written on the same (front) side of the paper. (*Note:* Dyslexic students do better with mnemonics that are provided by the instructor, rather than ones they make up themselves, according to Deshler et al., 1996.)

Working with the Mind Map

Students often are amazed and shocked when, after completing the map, they are asked to recreate it without referring to the original. Invariably, they find that they already know 60%–80% of the material without having memorized it. This outcome has a dramatic effect because students typically protest throughout the mind-mapping process that they do not have time to "do all this" because they need the time to memorize the material. After recreating the mind map without referring to it, however, they know what they know and what they do not know. Instead of having to memorize the whole map, they only have to review the portion that has not already gone into working memory.

The colored mind map and cue cards should be reviewed and redrawn daily during the first week until the student can complete the entire map accurately without referring to the original. Thereafter, the mind map should be reviewed weekly, then monthly, to maintain it in long-term memory. The mind map should be reviewed together with the summary and précis of the material, which are described in the next section.

Phase Three: Summarizing, Writing Précis, Outlining, and Note Taking

In the final phase of the SkORE process, the student uses the mind map to write a summary of the information on the map; write a précis of the abstract; and if necessary, create an outline. The student also learns to taken notes from various sources.

Summarizing

After having converted the text into a visual display, the student now converts the visual display back to discursive English. This transformation is at first a mechanical process. Beginning at 12 o'clock on the map and moving clockwise, the student labels each main branch with a Roman numeral—I, II, III, and so forth—to set up the order of the paragraphs in the summary.

The first branch should be introductory. The details noted on subbranches under each main branch can be assigned letters—A, B, C, and so forth. If the subbranches are

further modified by subbranches, then the details are numbered with Arabic numerals—1, 2, 3, and so forth.

When the student has labeled all of the branches and subbranches of the mind map, he or she returns to the branch labeled with the Roman numeral I and begins to create the summary using the notation on the main branch as the topic sentence of the first paragraph. The word or phrase that appears at the center of the mind map, which states the general topic to be discussed, should be included in the topic sentence of the first paragraph. The student then makes the details on the subbranches into full sentences; these are the supporting detail sentences. The student follows this procedure for each main branch around the clock. Then the student creates a closing paragraph either by stressing the main point or by reemphasizing the import of the author's point(s). The précis (described later) can be used as a final paragraph. Finally, the student proofreads the summary for errors. The habit of proofreading has been established as an automatic practice long before this, beginning at Level 2 of the Quick Tricks, and has been reinforced during the abstracting procedure.

Writing Skills   To prepare for writing the summary, the study skills instructor should inform students that teachers require at least three sentences in a paragraph and at least three paragraphs in a theme or composition. If students follow this recipe, then their work will be accepted. This formulaic approach to devising summaries gives students an initial approach to expository writing that appears to reduce their characteristic resistance to writing by eliminating what they perceive as the vagueness of the process. To go beyond the mechanical, formulaic method of summarizing, students should receive instruction in sentence patterns (see Helson, 1971). They should be given practice in elaborating sentences, first with adjectives and adjective phrases, next with adverbs and adverb phrases, and then with clauses. Subjunctive clauses present a particular difficulty for dyslexic students.

Automaticity in handwriting skills is an absolute prerequisite for facility in written English. Students will be far less apt to want to write if they have not mastered automatic letter formation and connected writing; if their inappropriate grip causes unnecessary fatigue; or if they write with an uncorrected, obstructive hooking of the writing hand. (For an excellent handwriting program, see King, 1985. See Chapter 15 in this book for more on multisensory handwriting instruction.)

There is no good substitute for reading widely and deeply; it is the best way to learn to write. The study skills instructor can entice students in two ways into reading for information as well as for pleasure. After determining a student's interest or ambition (e.g., soccer, gymnastics, inventing, computers, space travel, dance), the instructor can get good, well-illustrated trade books, including biographies, in large, clear type from the public library. The first group of books should be written many years below the student's reading ability. For example, when working with a seventh grader, books written for fourth graders can be very useful for this stage. As the student gains facility in reading because of study skills training, more difficult texts can be used. The books should never be used for instruction; they are sources of information and pleasure. The instructor should also take a few minutes of every period to read aloud from works of fiction, biographies, essays, and poems of literary worth. These can be tied to classwork in English, science, history, mathematics, and even physical education.

Some dyslexic students have a talent for writing and intend to be journalists or authors despite their difficulties with written language. Notable authors who have experienced such difficulties include Agatha Christie, Winston Churchill, W. Somerset

Maugham, Beatrix Potter, and John Updike. These people, along with media men Fred Friendly (former *CBS News* president), Richard Cohen of *The Washington Post,* and Robert Scheer of *The Los Angeles Times* and others have demonstrated that dyslexics can be very successful writers. Students who desire to be writers should be encouraged.

Writing Précis

Unlike the abstract, which must keep to the author's words, the précis is a condensation of the text in the student's own words. The goal is to state the author's essential message, the main thrust of the selection, and the author's underlying thesis or a combination of these in a highly condensed form. A précis of a chapter or even a book might consist of just a few sentences or paragraphs. As an example, the moral that follows one of Aesop's fables can be considered a précis (e.g., *Slow and steady wins the race*); a proverb also can serve as a précis (e.g., *Pride goeth before a fall*). The practice of précis writing is an invaluable aid to comprehension. The précis should be no more than one third to one fourth as long as the abstract and may be much shorter. The best technique for formulating a good précis is a group discussion of the essence of the abstract. (See Christensen et al., 1991, for excellent discussion techniques focused on problem solving. For the subskills prerequisite to précis writing, see Lehmann, 1960a.)

Outlining

Ideally, subject teachers will agree to accept the mind map in lieu of traditional, linear outlines from students with dyslexia. Nevertheless, some teachers will not. In this case, it is a simple matter to convert the mind map to outline form. Using the numbers assigned for developing the summary, the student simply copies the Roman numerals, letters, and Arabic numerals onto a template provided by the study skills instructor. The words and phrases on the main branches and subbranches can be copied next to the appropriate number or letter. The outline should be checked by both the study skills instructor and the subject teacher before being put into final form. The study skills instructor should exert every effort, however, to have the mind map accepted by classroom teachers because there is nothing to be gained from the redundant activity of creating an outline from the mind map, and—more important to the student—doing so uses valuable time.

Note Taking from Works of Fiction

To retain information about works of fiction, the student should take notes on 3″ × 5″ index cards, using the following structured procedure. Information is entered onto the cards according to a preset pattern. When completed, the cards are arranged in vertical columns of one, two, or three cards, with each column representing one paragraph. The student may need 20 or more cards when taking notes on one work of fiction. The information is written on the front side of the cards only.

Data relevant to one topic, such as characters, may require more than one card. The information should be added to the cards in the order shown, and the cards should be numbered. When writing paragraphs, the student should keep the three-sentence rule in mind.

1.   Title, author, illustrator (if any), publisher, date of publication

2.   Setting: time (or times), place

3a.   Major characters

3b.   Major characters' traits

4.   Story type (e.g., action story, romance, historical account, fable)

5a.   Content: theme or main idea

5b.   The point at which the theme is expressed most clearly*

How often the theme is expressed*

Through which characters it is most clearly expressed*

5c.   Conflict(s)

6.   Author's purpose

7.   Actions that take place

8a.   Technique: how the text is organized*

8b.   Kinds of characters, incidents, or images used

Why these were used instead of others*

8c.   Style of writing used (e.g., realistic, formal, informal)

(Items marked by an asterisk are for use with older students.)

Note Taking from Lectures

Taking notes from lectures is very difficult for the dyslexic student because it requires competency in attention and concentration, processing and remembering rapid speech, rapid and accurate handwriting, vocabulary, determining saliency, prioritization, and proficiency in written English, among other skills. Instruction in note taking must be the most direct, explicit, supported, and sustained of all of the study skills to be learned. This training should not be attempted until the student has gained proficiency in handwriting (see Chapter 15) and note taking from text. These skills are prerequisites to taking notes from lectures because, as Deshler and colleagues explained,

> Notetaking skills and subskills must be applied at the same time and at a rapid rate if the lecture is fast. The student must attend to a lecture idea, process the meaning of the idea by associating or integrating it with prior learning, extract the important information from the lecture idea, retain the meaning in memory, use a framework for recording notes, and write the idea using sufficient speed and abbreviations while simultaneously listening to additional lecture information. (1996, p. 271)

These are formidable obstacles for the dyslexic student. He or she, however, will have addressed many of these areas during the previous phases of SkORE training.

The study skills instructor should begin by arranging for the student to receive lecture notes or a study guide from the subject teacher or from a fellow student by means of carbonless reproduction paper. According to federal, state, and local regulations (e.g., regulations governing the implementation of the Individuals with Disabilities Education Improvement Act of 2004, PL 108-446), students with language and learning disabilities have a legal right to this accommodation. The subject teacher(s) working cooperatively with the study skills instructor can be kept informed of the student's progress in the subskills for note taking, such as processing, memory, and use of short-

hand symbols and abbreviations. It is important for subject teacher(s) to know that the accommodation is temporary but may extend throughout the school year.

To assess processing and memory, the study skills instructor can read aloud very brief passages of three or four sentences; then the instructor should ask the student to repeat orally as much of the information as possible in his or her own words. If the student performs reasonably well, then the instructor can use other passages and ask the student to record on a simple web only a word or a phrase to cue memory of important information. This cuing system of simple webbing should be used without concern for classification or organization. The branches should simply be spokes radiating from the topic word or phrase in the center. It is critical to work at this level until the student has mastered the cuing system—recording a word or a phrase to call up the data—with about 80% accuracy. The length of the passage can be increased gradually as the student gains mastery.

The instructor can also offer direct, systematic instruction in simple shorthand symbols for common words:

> ⌐ for *the*
> • for *a*
> ⌡ for *if*

Other symbols can be taught: & for *and,* w/ for *with,* % for *percent,* and @ for *at.* Some students will do better with vowel-less writing: *Sm stdnts wll do bttr w/vwllss wrtng;* the instructor must check carefully, however, to determine whether the student can re-translate the notes accurately.

When the student is ready, the study skills instructor and the classroom teacher can monitor the notes that the student takes in class. As with notes taken during training, notes should be merely single words or phrases on spokes radiating from a wheel, recorded without regard to organization or classification. The student should be monitored for accuracy, completeness, and the ability to read back and translate the notes.

Once the radial web has been approved by the study skills instructor (later, by the classroom teacher), the student proceeds in the same fashion as with taking notes from the mind map by reordering and reorganizing the web according to classification, categorization, and associated ideas. Cue cards, semantic and concept maps (explained later in this chapter), mnemonics, and graphics are included as when working with text. Two advantages of taking notes from lectures this way is that lecture and reading notes can be merged into a single web later, and webs that are made on large enough paper can be amended and extended.

Key Words   The cue words on the simple webs developed by the student while taking notes from lectures are like the key words that are used in more conventional two- or three-column note-taking systems. Therefore, once the student has mastered the note-taking process just described, he or she will be able to use conventional systems well with a little guided practice. (See Chapter 6 of Deshler et al., 1996, for more on note taking and dyslexic students.)

COMPREHENSION

Good groundwork for improved comprehension has been laid by the training in the mechanics, such as the work on spelling and vocabulary development that occurs through the Quick Tricks, and by training in the SkORE processes for mastering con-

tent course information, especially the techniques for abstracting and mind mapping. Some of the benefits of this instruction in terms of comprehension are as follows:

- The improvement in spelling results in improved decoding and therefore greater speed and accuracy in reading, which facilitates comprehension.

- The practice of having the student identify and define unfamiliar words and explicate concepts and abstractions before reading the text improves comprehension.

- The process of abstracting forces the student to weigh and consider ideas by asking questions about the relevance and relative importance of every part of the text. Abstracting also clarifies the structure and development of the information, thereby greatly increasing comprehension.

- The process of mind mapping—which involves note taking, categorizing, identifying related concepts and details, and creating graphics and mnemonics—requires the deep processing and manipulation that is requisite to deriving meaning and storing information in long-term memory.

As this list demonstrates, students can significantly improve comprehension just by using SkORE strategies and techniques. To improve comprehension for all students, however, additional techniques are required, such as semantic mapping; concept mapping; creating lexicons by geometric progression; and systematically studying nonliteral language, especially idioms and metaphors. For dyslexic students, these collateral activities are critical to improvement in comprehension, writing, and higher-order thinking skills. (See Chapter 14 for a discussion of comprehension techniques for the multisensory classroom.)

For an excellent discussion of the specific comprehension problems of dyslexic learners, the reader is referred to Wiig and Semel (1990), who noted that students with learning disabilities have problems with syntax, semantics, and memory that may cause difficulty with comprehending complex texts. Kamhi and Catts (1989) commented that such problems with reading means reduced exposure to new vocabulary words, and Maria stated that "the reader's level of vocabulary is the best predictor of his or her ability to understand the text" (1990, p. 111). Therefore, as stated previously, the best tool to improve the reading comprehension of dyslexic students rapidly is discussion.

Semantic Mapping

In addition to vocabulary limitations that result from a combination of language problems, the dyslexic student typically has poor decoding ability (and thus tends to skip unknown words), has very limited reading experience (and may hate to read), and has a general distaste for multisyllabic words and specific terms (and may use words such as *stuff* or *things;* other contentless nouns; and, when all else fails, *y'know*).

To aid in comprehension, three kinds of semantic maps are recommended: synonym–antonym maps, related features maps, and multiple meanings maps. These maps are best developed through group discussion, with Socratic-type questioning from the teacher as the stimulus. By this process, the teacher asks questions designed to elicit the desired answers, such as "What is the missing word in 'Jack fell down and broke his _____?'"

Creating synonym–antonym maps (see Figure 18.3) benefits students' oral and written language ability by expanding vocabulary, offering the opportunity to discuss nuances of meaning (see Hayakawa, 1968), and facilitating the mastery of classification of parts of speech. Resources to use include synonym–antonym dictionaries, *Roget's*

```
┌─────────────────────────────────────────────────────┐
│                    JOY, L. n.                        │
│                                                      │
│   Synonyms              Antonyms                     │
│   (name for same)       (name for what is opposite)  │
│                                                      │
│   delight               sorrow                       │
│   gladness              sadness                      │
│   elation               depression                   │
│   lightheartedness      downheartedness              │
│   ecstasy               despair                      │
│   happiness             joylessness                  │
│                                                      │
└─────────────────────────────────────────────────────┘
```

Figure 18.3.   Synonym–antonym map. (*Key:* L., Latin; n., noun.)

Thesaurus (original version), and *The Oxford Dictionary and Thesaurus* (1996). In order to understand the words on the map, students must have extensive practice in using the words in sentences, both orally and in writing.

The related features map (see Figure 18.4) is a simple version of the concept map (explained in the next section); it is a good place to start with younger students, by brainstorming. The related features map can be organized to show different categories as the main entry, such as *weather, animals,* or *plants.*

Multiple meanings, many different meanings for the same word, is a characteristic of English that makes it very difficult for nonnative speakers to learn the language. Similarly, the concept of multiple meanings causes great problems for dyslexic learners in both oral and reading comprehension. This is all the more true of words that have metaphorical meanings, such as *foot, head, place, arm,* and *bloom,* and words that are part of an idiomatic expression (e.g., *I'm burning up*). It is important for the student to have practice with the different meanings of such words from the very beginning of study skills training. This practice begins when more than one definition is written on a vocabulary cue card that is made in preparation for mind mapping. That step is a good introduction, but it is an inadequate way to teach the numerous English words that have multiple meanings. Creation of multiple meanings maps similar to the one shown in Figure 18.5 is a good second stage. For further development, see the later section called Creating Lexicons by Geometric Progression.

These semantic maps are not to be memorized; students achieve better command by discussing the words on the maps and debating the nuances of meaning (e.g., "What is the same about seeing to a guest, seeing the waiter, and seeing someone home?") and by illustrating the meanings. (For more on semantic mapping, see Chapter 7 of McNeil, 1992.)

```
┌─────────────────────────────────────────────────────┐
│                   DESERT, L. n.                      │
│                                                      │
│      sand                  lizards                   │
│      dry                   tents                     │
│      oasis                 no rain                   │
│      camel                 palm trees                │
│      cactus                mirages                   │
│      sun                   sandstorms                │
│                                                      │
└─────────────────────────────────────────────────────┘
```

Figure 18.4.   Related features map. (*Key:* L., Latin; n., noun.)

SEE, A.S., Anglo-Saxon, v., verb

look at
See the boat?

view
We went to see the Alps.

understand[+]
I don't see your point.

learn, find out[+]
Go see what's happening.

think, consider[+]
I'll see if I can do it.

take care of[++]
I'll see to it.

finish[++]
Can you see the project through?

attend to[++]
See to the guests.

feel[++]
Mom sees red when I track in mud.

make sure[++]
See that it happens.

escort[++]
See her home.

encounter[++]
I'll see him tomorrow.

call on, consult[++]
Go see him about it.

receive[++]
The doctor will see you.

perceive, intuit[+]
She sees right through me.

help[++]
See me through my illness.

tip[++]
Did you see the waiter?

SEE, L., Latin (from *sedes,* seated), n., noun

bishopric[+]
The bishop's see is the jurisdiction of a seated bishop.

[+]metaphoric   [++]idiomatic

Figure 18.5.   Multiple meanings map. (*Source: The Oxford Dictionary and Thesaurus,* 1996.)

Concept Mapping

Dyslexic students may have significant difficulty understanding abstract terms; this difficulty can be a great barrier to comprehension for secondary and postsecondary students. Noting that their understanding of words is too concrete and literal, Levine (1987) pointed out that bright dyslexic students are able to get by with a very partial understanding (a corner) of an abstract concept (e.g., *democracy, latitude, empathy*). This literal understanding of the language, however, results in an imperfect, perhaps distorted, grasp of meanings and implications. Levine stressed that

> The ability to derive concepts is crucial. Several steps are involved: recognizing the salient properties of objects, actions, or events; categorizing those objects, actions, or events by identifying their common properties; forming a superordinate concept to other instances or settings. *The entire process can be viewed as a system of testing hypotheses by making careful decisions to accept or reject formulated hypotheses about problems.* (1987, p. 177, italics added)

The study skills instructor must train the student to understand concepts and abstract terms through the systematic creation of concept maps similar to the one in Figure 18.6 to accompany the cue cards for vocabulary. (For more detailed concept maps, see Deshler et al., 1996; Maria, 1990; and McNeil, 1992.)

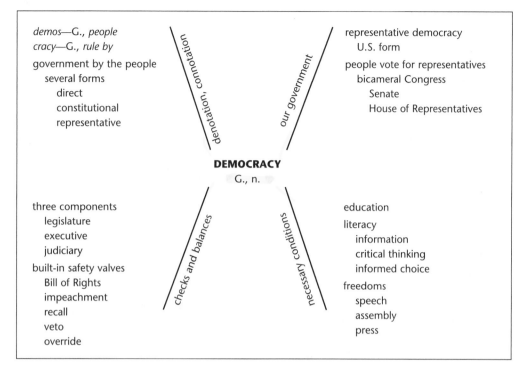

Figure 18.6.   Concept map. (*Key:* G., Greek; n., noun.)

Creating Lexicons by Geometric Progression

Because they come to the task of comprehension with a smaller personal lexicon than other students, dyslexic students must be enabled to enlarge their vocabulary very quickly and efficiently without memorization. Also, because of difficulties with pattern recognition, making associations, seeing relationships, and memorizing, dyslexic students need very explicit instruction, in which patterns are highlighted, extensions (e.g., affixes) are easy, and meaning is revealed in a logical and dramatic fashion. This training is best done using graphic arrays, or lexicons by geometric progression, that convey the morphological structure (the shape or form of units of meaning) of the language, such as roots and affixes. Bywaters (1998) and Murray and Munro (1989) are good resources for lexicons by geometric progression. Partridge (1966; out of print but in libraries) is the best reference for study skills instructors.

The lexicon work should begin with short, easy exercises, such as the one shown in Figure 18.7. It is very important to observe the spacing as indicated, to highlight the root in color (shown as gray shading in Figure 18.7), to include idioms, and to ask the student to generate short paragraphs using both literal and nonliteral words from the array.

Studying Nonliteral Language: Idioms, Metaphors, Proverbs, Puns, and Jargon

Dyslexic people commonly have difficulty with nonliteral language (Kamhi & Catts, 1989; Maria, 1990; Wiig & Semel, 1990), which uses words in an atypical way to convey meaning that is different from the standard usage, such as *a raging torrent, out of the mouths of babes, he got the axe, she's a peach, his crimes caught up with him, get off my back,*

Root	*dict* (from Latin, *dicere, dictus—to show, point out, tell, say, proclaim*)	
dic tate	**dic** tion ar y	pre **dict**
dic tate s	**dic** tion ar ies	pre **dic** tive
dic ta ted		pre **dic** tion
dic ta tion		contra **dict**
dic ta tor		contra **dic** tory
dic ta tor s		contra **dic** tion
dic ta tor ship		
dit to (from Italian, *the same as [was said] before*)		
	Idiomatic: He can't dictate what I do. Metaphor: He's a little dictator.	

Figure 18.7.   A lexicon by geometric progression.

and *an ounce of prevention is worth a pound of cure*. It is important for the study skills instructor to appreciate the vast amount of figurative language, especially idioms and metaphors, used in reading materials for even the youngest children. Moreover, metaphor appears every day in conversations and print media (Lakoff & Johnson, 1980). Although dyslexic children may not voice their difficulties, these students are often confused by figurative language.

A dyslexic student does not comprehend nonliteral language incidentally. He or she needs direct, systematic presentation and explication of the language. A good resource to begin with is Makkai and colleagues (1995), but the instructor must simultaneously search out, list, and teach all nonliteral language in the student's required reading. Students enjoy acting out some of the expressions (e.g., *His eyes are bigger than his stomach*) and creating stories and scenarios to illustrate meaning (e.g., *He did that to save face*). These exercises can take just a few minutes and can provide pleasant relief in the midst of hard work. All lexical arrays should include figurative uses of some of the words developed (see Figure 18.7).

TAKING TESTS

The goal of teaching study strategies and skills is for students to solve problems. Although study skills instruction focuses on learning how to learn—not on learning how to cram for tests—tests cannot be avoided in the academic setting. Study skills instruction should address test-taking issues in the following ways:

- Training in organizing and scheduling time, given at the outset of training, deals with the issue of time in preparing for tests and final exams.

- Training in semantics should include the distinctions in the vocabulary of testing: *define, discuss, detail, compare, contrast, list, explain, justify,* and *so forth*.

- The abstracts, mind maps, and summaries developed by the student in the SkORE process are the materials used for study; the student should refer back to these rather than to the original text.

- The periodic reviews are what constitute studying for tests and exams. This ongoing process is designed to retain and strengthen the information in the student's long-

term memory. In this way, the student comes to know the material; he or she does not need to struggle to remember and recall it. Thus, the stress and anxiety typically accompanying cramming and test taking are much abated, and the negative impact of stress on retrieval (memory) is avoided. In short, the student has a far better chance of doing his or her best on the test.

- Training in self-monitoring for attention should enable the student to sustain concentration during tests better than he or she could before the start of study skills training.

At this point in training, what remains is for the instructor to give the student test-taking savvy by coaching him or her on how to apportion time for each section; to read directions carefully and highlight critical words or phrases; to avoid guessing unless only correct answers are scored (i.e., points are not deducted for wrong answers); to eliminate answers in multiple-choice tests; and to proofread carefully at the conclusion, not only to catch the usual errors in writing but also to ensure that no question was overlooked.

Dyslexic students need to learn specific strategies for tracking during tests (following along with the text of the test). For example, when doing matching exercises, students may need to number the items on the left, letter those on the right, and cross out the words they have already matched as they work. Other specific strategies for test taking can be found in Deshler and colleagues (1996), Millman and Pauk (1969), and Strichart and Mangrum (1993).

CONCLUSION: STUDY SKILLS TRAINING AND METACOGNITION

Metacognition has been described as the individual's conscious awareness of his or her functioning and the ability to verbalize that awareness. Wiig and Semel (1990) and others have called metacognition the ability to use language as a tool. Deshler and colleagues wrote that the term "convey[s] the idea that the learner uses . . . processes to provide [him- or herself] with feedback on learning" (1996, p. 13). *Meta*, from Greek, means *beyond, above,* or *higher.* For the dyslexic student, the objective of study skills training is to develop higher-level thinking, objective judgment, and serious reflection, all of which the student can use to assess him- or herself as a learner.

The strategies and techniques discussed in this chapter build from the beginning techniques for self-monitoring and self-evaluation to the methods for taking notes from texts and lectures and call for frequent interaction with supportive adults who offer feedback and guidance. During study skills training, the student emerges from randomness and confusion to deliberate and focused behavior and develops the capacity to relate his or her habits and actions to achievements. All of the study skills activities contribute to metacognition. They demand more from the student, not less. The procedures take time, discipline, and the will to win. The study skills instructor is the mentor and supporter of the student while he or she acquires the necessary skills. Instructor and student have a formidable task, which was well articulated by Dr. Baruj Benacerraf, recipient of the 1980 Nobel Prize in Physiology or Medicine and former president of Harvard's Dana-Farber Cancer Research Center:

> Dyslexia is a challenge to overcome, rather than a deficiency to be sorry about. To achieve excellence, I found that I needed to always examine my own work with a merciless, critical eye. It is far better to be more severe and demanding of oneself than others can be. (personal communication, 1988)

Teachers, however, should also keep Torgesen's Law in mind: "Know your stuff. Know who you are stuffing. Stuff them as explicitly, as systematically, and as supportively as you possibly can" (Joseph K. Torgesen, personal communication, June 19, 1998).

REFERENCES

Alley, G.R., & Deshler, D.D. (1979). *Teaching the learning disabled adolescent: Strategies and methods.* Denver, CO: Love Publishing.

Askov, E.N., & Kamm, K. (1982). *Study skills in the content areas.* Boston: Allyn & Bacon.

Brown, A.L. (1979). The development of memory. In H.W. Reese (Ed.), *Advances in child development and behavior.* San Diego: Academic Press.

Brown, J.I. (1976). *Efficient reading: Revised form.* Boston: Houghton Mifflin.

Buzan, T. (1983). *Use both sides of your brain.* New York: Dutton/Plume. [*Note:* Buzan's note-taking system is not recommended for dyslexic students; this source is recommended for mind map design and enhancement only.]

Bywaters, D. (1998). *Affix and root cards.* Cambridge, MA: Educators Publishing Service.

Christensen, C.R., Garvin, D.A., & Sweet, A. (1991). *Education for judgment: The artistry of discussion leadership.* Boston: Harvard Business School Press.

Cruickshank, W.M. (1967). *The brain-injured child in home, school, and community.* Syracuse, NY: Syracuse University Press.

de Hirsch, K. (1984). Language and the developing child. *The Orton Society Monographs, 4.* Timonium, MD: York Press.

Deshler, D.D., Ellis, E., & Lenz, B.K. (1996). *Teaching adolescents with learning disabilities: Strategies and methods* (2nd ed.). Denver, CO: Love Publishing.

Devine, T.G. (1981). *Teaching study skills: A guide for teachers.* Boston: Allyn & Bacon.

Evans, H. (Ed.). (1981). *Brewer's dictionary of phrase and fable* (Centenary rev. ed.). New York: HarperCollins.

Fowler, H. (1983). *A dictionary of modern English usage* (2nd ed.). New York: Oxford University Press.

Gaddes, W.H., & Edgell, D. (1994). *Learning disabilities and brain function: A neuropsychological approach* (3rd ed.). New York: Springer-Verlag.

Gillingham, A., & Stillman, B.W. (1956). *Remedial training for students with specific disability in reading, spelling and penmanship* (5th ed.). Cambridge, MA: Educators Publishing Service.

Gillingham, A., & Stillman, B.W. (1997). *Remedial training for children with specific disability in reading, spelling and penmanship* (8th ed.). Cambridge, MA: Educators Publishing Service.

Gold, S. (Ed.). (1993). *The New York Public Library desk reference* (2nd ed.). Upper Saddle River, NJ: Prentice-Hall.

Hayakawa, S.I. (1968). *Choose the right word: A modern guide to synonyms.* New York: HarperCollins.

Helson, L.G. (1971). *Basic English sentence patterns.* Cambridge, MA: Educators Publishing Service.

Individuals with Disabilities Education Improvement Act of 2004, PL 108-446, 20 U.S.C. §§ 1400 *et seq.*

Johnson, D.J., & Myklebust, H.R. (1967). *Learning disabilities: Educational principles and practices.* New York: Grune & Stratton.

Kamhi, A.G., & Catts, H.W. (1989). *Reading disabilities: A developmental perspective.* Boston: Little, Brown.

King, D.H. (1985). *Writing skills for the adolescent.* Cambridge, MA: Educators Publishing Service.

Lakoff, G., & Johnson, M. (1980). *Metaphors we live by.* Chicago: University of Chicago Press.

Lehmann, P.W. (1960a). *The junior précis practice pad.* Cambridge, MA: Educators Publishing Service.

Lehmann, P.W. (1960b). *The senior précis practice pad.* Cambridge, MA: Educators Publishing Service.

Lerner, J. (1989). Educational interventions in learning disabilities. *Journal of the American Academy of Child and Adolescent Psychiatry, 28,* 326–331.

Levine, M. (1987). *Developmental variation and learning disorders* (2nd ed.). Cambridge, MA: Educators Publishing Service.

Makkai, A., Boatner, M.T., & Gates, J.E. (1995). *A dictionary of American idioms.* Hauppauge, NY: Barron's Educational Series.

Maria, K. (1990). *Reading comprehension instruction, issues, and strategies.* Timonium, MD: York Press.

McNeil, J.D. (1992). *Reading comprehension: New directions for classroom practice.* New York: HarperCollins.

Millman, J., & Pauk, W. (1969). *How to take tests.* New York: McGraw-Hill.

Moore, J., & Munévar, T. (1981). *Reading and thinking in English series: Vol. 1. Concepts in use.* New York: Oxford University Press.

Moore, J., & Widdowson, H. (Series Eds.). (1981). *Reading and thinking in English series.* New York: Oxford University Press.

Murdoch, I. (1987). *Acastos.* New York: Viking Penguin.

Murray, C., & Munro, J. (1989). *30 roots to grow on.* Cambridge, MA: Educators Publishing Service.

Neisser, U. (1976). *Cognition and reality: Principles and implications of cognitive psychology.* San Francisco: W.H. Freeman.

Obrecht, F. (1999). *Minimum essentials of English* (2nd ed.). Hauppauge, NY: Barron's Educational Series.

Orton, S.T. (1925). "Word-blindness" in school children. *Archives of Neurology and Psychiatry, 14,* 581–615.

Orton, S.T. (1937). *Reading, writing and speech problems in children.* New York: W.W. Norton.

The Oxford dictionary and thesaurus (American ed.). (1996). New York: Oxford University Press.

The Oxford dictionary of English etymology. (1983). New York: Oxford University Press.

Partridge, E. (1966). *Origins: A short etymological dictionary of modern English.* New York: Greenwich House.

Robinson, F.P. (1946). *Effective study.* New York: HarperCollins.

Roget's thesaurus (5th ed.). (1992). New York: HarperCollins. [*Note:* Only editions of the original *Roget's Thesaurus,* such as this version, are recommended.]

Strichart, S.S., & Mangrum, C.T., II. (1993). *Teaching study strategies to students with learning disabilities.* Boston: Allyn & Bacon.

Tomatis, A. (1969). *Dyslexia.* Ottawa, Ontario, Canada: University of Ottawa Press.

Tomkins, C. (1963, September 14). The last skill acquired. *The New Yorker,* 127–133.

Tonjes, M.J., & Zintz, M.V. (1981). *Teaching reading, thinking, study skills in content classrooms.* Dubuque, IA: William C. Brown.

Trudeau, K. (1995). *Megamemory.* New York: William Morrow & Co.

Warriner, J.E. (1988). *English composition and grammar: Complete course.* Orlando, FL: Harcourt Brace & Co.

Wiig, E.H., & Semel, E. (1990). *Language assessment and intervention for the learning disabled.* Columbus, OH: Charles E. Merrill.

Wycoff, J. (1991). *Mindmapping: Your personal guide to exploring creativity and problem-solving.* New York: Berkley Books.

19

Working with High-Functioning Dyslexic Adults

Susan H. Blumenthal

The population of high-functioning dyslexic adults is a specific but quite diverse group of individuals. They are studying and working in a variety of fields and include college students, graduate students, physicians, lawyers, and members of the clergy. Some adults, especially those in graduate school, are required to do tremendous amounts of reading each week. Other graduate students conduct experiments in science research, which may require less reading than is necessary in liberal arts programs. In science settings, however, graduate students need to perform sequential, multistep experiments with relative independence over a period of several days. Frequent shifting from abstract conceptualization to sequenced detail and back again requires a high degree of organization, which can be troublesome for some dyslexics.

Not all high-functioning dyslexics are in a school environment. Some dyslexic adults have already completed school and are working in a business setting. Whether a person runs his or her own business or is in a corporate setting, he or she usually has to do background reading in trade or professional journals to keep abreast of developments in the field. In addition, individuals in professional positions often have to write memos and reports on a regular basis as part of their job.

Virtually all high-functioning dyslexic adults are ambitious and highly motivated, but they also suffer from chronic feelings of inadequacy, stress, and low self-esteem regarding their ability to learn. Almost all of them had a difficult beginning in the early grades of elementary school and continued to function quite unevenly during their school years.

EMOTIONAL REPERCUSSIONS

Despite being above average or quite superior in general ability, nearly all of the high-functioning dyslexic adults who seek help with reading and writing skills experience anxiety about some aspects of their work and learning. They often do not know why they have so much difficulty with written language. Through the years, they have tried to both compensate for and hide the problem. They may have never read a book all of the way through but will rarely miss class so that they can pick up the necessary information from discussion. They may have to write multiple drafts of a term paper but often will ask and be allowed to give an oral presentation or work in tandem with another student. So many of these students have been told to "try harder" throughout their school careers. Nearly every dyslexic adult who goes for a psychoeducational consultation or evaluation thinks that he or she is "lazy," that everyone else is smarter, or that there is something wrong with his or her brain. It does not matter whether these individuals graduated from a state school or an Ivy League school, nor does it matter whether they were inducted into Phi Beta Kappa. They almost always are plagued by varying degrees of self-doubt.

There are important differences between children and adults who have learning difficulties that can have an impact on intervention. First, their basic attitudes generally are different. When children are referred for language intervention, they often are resistant at first. They have been identified as not doing well in school, and both the children and the parents may be upset with the children's school performance and/or with the school staff. In contrast, adults usually are highly motivated to improve their language skills. Many are self-referred or are referred by other professionals, such as psychotherapists or college teachers. Consequently, adults with learning difficulties often have definite goals. In addition, they often are relieved when they realize that they can get help.

A second difference between children and adults with learning difficulties is awareness. Children's awareness of their learning needs and difficulties usually is unformulated. In some way, the children sense that there is something wrong. They say, "Reading is not hard for me—I just don't like it." Adults are much more aware of how learning difficulties, especially reading difficulties, have affected their lives. They may feel self-conscious in a social group—not because they lack social skills but because they do not make the same kind of contributions as others. They may not make the same mental associations because they lack the underlying foundation of knowledge, which is often derived from reading. For example, a 35-year-old physician with a persistent reading problem who came for help had this comment: "I feel I am shallow, compared to all my friends. They read all of the time."

Another difference between children and adults with learning disabilities is how they cope. Children are part of an established support system; they are evaluated, tested, promoted to or held back from the next grade, and are often the focus of parent–teacher conferences. The responsibility of learning or not learning is shared. Adults with learning disabilities invariably seem to have a secret life. They do not have the same support system as children do. Adults have to work in an increasingly independent manner, and they worry about being "found out." Many adults with learning disabilities have learned to hide their problems and compensate as much as possible. Often, they focus on avoidance in order to escape potential humiliation.

Finally, the beginning of the referral process is also different for adults and children. Children are usually referred or evaluated because they are failing or not doing

well in school. Adults are referred for a variety of reasons. Some adults experience a change in their work requirements or in their educational setting, and they find that they cannot meet the expected level of the new requirements. For example, a member of the Coast Guard with severe dyslexia was promoted to petty officer. Instead of working on machines, at which he was an expert, he now had to do considerable paperwork and report writing. His performance ratings, which were formerly consistently high, fell below average. In another instance, an ambitious 31-year-old account executive who had a history of dyslexia was quite successful on her job. She had excellent verbal skills and was effective at meetings. Her new boss, however, insisted that there be more memos and outlines of marketing goals and fewer face-to-face meetings. The account executive knew that if she wanted to be promoted, then she would have to get her ideas down in writing.

Some adults who return to school for a higher degree refer themselves for a psychoeducational evaluation. For example, a successful 47-year-old businesswoman with a bachelor of arts degree decided to apply for a master of business administration program. She referred herself for evaluation because she suspected that she had a previously undiagnosed learning problem. When her son was diagnosed with dyslexia, she recognized similar patterns in her own academic life.

More adults are being referred by mental health workers, personnel in the workplace, and college and university faculty to explore whether there is an undetected learning problem. As awareness increases about the different forms that learning problems can take, psychotherapists, job supervisors, and professors have begun to notice areas of discrepancy in people who otherwise are functioning well. For example, an administrator at a university was referred for a psychoeducational evaluation after his boss wrote, "The communication area is of great concern and an obstacle to Mr. K's career development. He exceeds expectations in personal skills and in commitment to all aspects of his job. I recommend that he get help for problems in writing and other communications skills."

EVALUATION AND ASSESSMENT

The first component of a comprehensive assessment for an adult involves the gathering of information about the individual's early developmental, educational, and medical histories, and, if appropriate, employment history. The individual's own perception of the problem is particularly helpful. The latter information can be obtained from a writing sample called Educational Memories (Blumenthal, 1981), which is described later in this section.

The purpose of the assessment is to try to understand and evaluate the client's presenting problems in order to develop a treatment plan. The assessor tries to determine why the person is having difficulty functioning in an academic or a work setting and explores the client's capabilities and learning patterns to see what interferes with learning. Current information is as important as the individual's history. If the individual is in school, then it is important to read several recent term papers as well as look over class notes from lectures. Individuals with jobs can bring in reports, memos, or letters that are representative of work demands.

There is no specific test battery for diagnosing learning disabilities. Psychologists who specialize in working with people who have dyslexia or other types of learning disabilities use many of the same tests in their evaluation as are used in traditional psychological evaluations, but they view the results in a particular way (see Chapter 7 for

more on types of assessment tests). That is, during assessment of learning disabilities, qualitative information is always an important supplement to the quantitative results. The evaluator wants to know exactly what the client said and how he or she responded to each task. A trained diagnostician always administers tests in a standardized manner according to the test manual, but views each test as a vehicle for deriving other important, perhaps subtle currents of information. By listening carefully and recording precisely what the client says, an evaluator can pick up clues about receptive and expressive language problems, confusion in the use of prepositions, word substitutions, and so forth. Although this ancillary information may not directly affect the overall test results, it is important because it helps show vulnerabilities in the client's learning and performance and often illuminates why his or her performance in school or on the job has been uneven.

A typical test battery to identify learning disabilities in adults includes the Wechsler Adult Intelligence Scale–Third Edition (Wechsler, 1991); a silent reading test such as the Nelson-Denny Reading Test (Brown, Bennett, & Hanna, 1981) or the Gates-MacGinitie Reading Tests–Third Edition (MacGinitie & MacGinitie, 1989); the Wide-Range Achievement Test–Third Edition (Wilkinson, 1993), which has Word Recognition, Spelling, and Math Computation subtests; a test of oral reading such as the Gray Oral Reading Test–Third Edition (Wiederholt & Bryant, 1992) or the Diagnostic Assessments of Reading with Trial Teaching Strategies (Roswell & Chall, 1992); a design copying test such as the Bender Visual Motor Gestalt Test (Bender, 1938); and several writing samples (usually one written during the session and two written at home between testing sessions), including Educational Memories (Blumenthal, 1981). Depending on the client's presenting problems, other tests may be included, such as House-Tree-Person Drawing (Buck, 1978), selected cards form the Thematic Apperception Test (Murray & Bellak, 1973), and a sentence completion test such as the Rotter Incomplete Sentences Blank–Second Edition (Rotter, Lah, & Rafferty, 1992). Sometimes a client has had a prior psychological examination but has not undergone reading tests or a writing evaluation. Although it is not necessary to redo what has been done already, a reading and writing assessment should be done before the specialist begins to work with the client.

After the testing is completed, the evaluator interprets the findings and explains them to the client. It is important for the evaluator as well as the remedial specialist (if the specialist is different from the evaluator) to present the results in as constructive a manner as possible. When the evaluator uses trial teaching techniques and judiciously chosen teaching materials, the client can begin to sense how he or she can make progress. After test findings were explained to one young physician and he had begun working on his problems, he wrote the following:

> My diagnosis as dyslexic, i.e., reading more slowly in order to understand, was both difficult and refreshing. At first I had attached a stigma to it, yet it was also refreshing, since it validated my life experience. I now feel in control. Adequate time to read translates into adequate time to process and understand.

Educational Memories

The Educational Memories writing sample measure provides information that cannot be obtained through typical diagnostic tests. Between the initial telephone call and the time of the first testing appointment, clients receive a writing assignment that focuses on their school memories. Clients are asked to relate their own version of their educational experience, including both positive and negative memories. They are to write a first draft only, by hand, on 8½″ × 11″ paper. They are to avoid talking to family mem-

bers or using a dictionary or any other reference source. Educational Memories allows evaluators to get to know more about a client and at the same time obtain a writing sample for close examination. Most individuals write 7–9 handwritten pages.

Educational Memories serves as a valuable part of the diagnostic examination for a number of reasons. First, it is possible to find out what insights the client has about his or her own difficulties. Second, the writing sample reveals information about the individual's tendency to blame him- or herself or others for any difficulties faced. Third, the sample gives a sense of the emotional impact of years of struggling with school and/or work. Finally, the writing sample offers an initial view of the person's ability to organize information. This sample also allows an examination of handwriting, grammar, syntax, vocabulary, and spelling. The Educational Memories sample also is a useful part of the diagnostic process because it helps diagnosticians differentiate between people who have learning difficulties and people who do not. People with learning problems rarely report positive memories about school. Their negative memories always center around problems of mastery. In contrast, people with no learning difficulties have many more positive memories of school, and their negative memories relate not to mastery but instead to specific social problems (e.g., *I was never popular. I didn't get invited to parties*) or to the harshness of particular teachers.

Following are excerpts from the Educational Memories samples of four individuals, which illustrate how painful the introduction to school can be, particularly in the beginning years when children are especially vulnerable.

Bobbie

Bobbie, a 45-year-old woman with learning and memory problems, admitted during her first session that she has never read a book all of the way through. She is now in a graduate program with approximately 1,000 pages per week of assigned reading, such as Freud, D.W. Winnicott, and Melanie Klein. Bobbie wrote,

> I always have difficulty remembering what I read, and also I have trouble with facts and names. The memory of my education goes back to my very first day at school. I sat there and they debated whether or not I was retarded, because I did not know my name. I had been called Bobbie all my life, and had no idea my given name was Roberta.

Lana

A 30-year-old woman studying for her bachelor of science degree in physical therapy, Lana, wrote the following:

> From the time I was around 8 years old, I have had this underlying feeling of inadequacy and inferiority, which is very tied into my feelings about school. The two are almost synonymous. My driving force to get my B.S. is to rid myself of this burden.

Derek

A 27-year-old law student recalled the following in his write-up:

> I attended private school from nursery through third grade, and it was there where I encountered the most academic difficulty. The school told my parents that I was "unteachable." This attitude is reflected in a progress report from the third grade in which it was stated they no longer measured my advancement on a scale with other students: "His grades reflect individual progress rather than third-grade expectations." These are particularly painful years to remember as my self-esteem was significantly diminished.

Mark

A 22-year-old dental student wrote the following:

> My earliest academic memories are filled with anxiety—feeling the inability to master all of the spelling words for the Monday morning quiz. As I grew older, reading quickly and accurately became more important. I always had to work longer and concentrate more intently than my peers. Finally, my compensatory mechanisms of using extra time were inadequate, since I was confronted with timed exams, and no matter how much I prepared I was faced with my nemesis, only a limited amount of time to read. This forced me to skim over material rather than master it, and I therefore could not answer questions on topics I was familiar with.

THE MOST COMMON NEEDS OF HIGH-FUNCTIONING DYSLEXICS

Individuals with learning difficulties or dyslexia usually need help in one or more of the following areas: silent reading comprehension skills, vocabulary development, expressive language (writing) skills, spelling, study skills, and managing or allocating time in a constructive manner. Each person may have a greater or lesser degree of difficulty with any one of these areas and may not have difficulty with all of them. It is particularly important to remember that each person presents a unique combination of strengths as well as weaknesses. The remediation plan has to be tailored to that person's specific needs. Often the client manifests competence in unexpected areas as well as surprising gaps in background knowledge. Information gathered from the individual's history, diagnostic study, and examination of current work as well as trial teaching will help to pinpoint areas that need attention.

There are several important goals in treatment. The first goal is to change the individual's perception of him- or herself from someone who *cannot* learn to one who *can* learn. This is best accomplished by helping the person to become an active learner. Many dyslexic readers are too passive in relation to the material they read. As a result, their retention, understanding, and even appreciation are affected. Being an active learner means thinking about and evaluating the material being read. Active learning involves bringing prior information to the discussion of the subject at hand. The active reader tries to discern the author's point of view. Encouraging the transition from a passive to a more active approach to reading requires guidance from the remedial specialist. The remedial specialist needs to know when to pose evocative questions, how to elicit information, and when to prepare the client to develop insights about the material.

For example, Evelyn, an ambitious college graduate, was running a successful business and wanted to go to graduate school for her master of business administration degree. The evaluation showed that she had a slow reading rate and had difficulty retaining what she read. Evelyn thought that she often missed main ideas, which undermined her confidence in general. An intelligent woman, she was quite interested in world affairs. To improve her reading comprehension and retention of information, she was encouraged to read the editorial columns in the daily newspaper. Instead of skimming articles and retaining a minimal amount, as she had done formerly, Evelyn was asked to approach the reading material differently, in a four-step approach.

1. First, she should read the headline and subhead and before reading further, ask herself, "What do I think this article is about?" By posing this question, she immediately became more active and focused on the article's topic.

2. Next, she should read the article and then ask herself, "What did the author say?"

3. Then she should ask, "What did I learn that was new?"

4. Finally, she should ask, "What is my opinion about this subject? Do I agree or disagree?"

After using this approach with one newspaper article, Evelyn wrote a 1-page essay about the article, which she brought to the next session. The entire assignment took her about 1 hour at home. This active approach stimulated her ability to concentrate and fostered her retention. It also improved her writing skills. After approximately 2 months of remediation, Evelyn commented, "At first it seemed like I was taking baby steps, but the way I read is really changing. When we went out to dinner with friends, it was amazing, I found I had facts and opinions and held my own in the discussion." Evelyn also worked with a variety of other standardized reading comprehension materials, such as Six-Way Paragraphs (Advanced) by Pauk (1983), and in doing so improved her concentration, reading comprehension, and writing skills. At the end of the year, she took the Graduate Management Admissions Test with extended time and was accepted into business school, where she did well.

When the therapeutic alliance is optimal and the demands of the remedial work are challenging but not overwhelming, progress can be made. The client often will report a sense of excitement about his or her own potential being realized. For example, one graduate student declared, "I looked at this assignment and said, 'I know you, you sucker! I can do it.'" Another client said, "I know that what is coming next will be hard, but now I think there is nothing I can't handle."

The second goal of remediation is to help the individual to develop an awareness of his or her own thinking process. As individuals become aware of their own thinking, positive changes occur, and thinking, reading, and writing become more efficient. It is possible to stimulate and activate cognitive processes such as reasoning, organizing, generalizing, and planning so that these cognitive processes are enhanced across a broad range of content areas. One way to encourage this kind of awareness of how one thinks is through the use of Process Notes (Blumenthal, 1981).

When the clients are disturbed about their reactions to their pattern of work habits or ability to sustain attention, they can be taught to be more aware of how they think, or of what interrupts their reasoning, and what helps them to continue their work. When a client faces obstacles in doing his or her work, the remedial specialist can encourage the client to write Process Notes, that is, to evaluate in writing his or her own reactions to the assignment. This often helps the client to develop organizing principles, which facilitates his or her work.

For example, Process Notes were eventually used by Ted, a dyslexic doctoral student who referred himself for evaluation after he failed his written comprehensive exams. The members of the examining committee had harsh comments and remarked on how "poorly written" and how "disorganized" Ted's written effort was. They raised questions about Ted's suitability in a doctoral program, perhaps forgetting that he had completed all of the coursework up to that point with excellent grades. None of the committee members thought about the discrepancy between Ted's record and his performance on the comprehensives, yet unevenness in performance is the hallmark of almost all learning disabilities.

One of the first steps in helping Ted was for the remedial specialist to read Ted's comprehensive exam. Although the exam was more than 35 handwritten pages long,

it was necessary to read it carefully to understand how Ted performed under pressure, to evaluate exactly where he needed help, and to develop a treatment plan. Although Ted experienced both anger and mild depression in reaction to his failure, his drive to improve his writing was prodigious. He responded well to the varied writing assignments that the remedial specialist gave him, most of which he completed in the library between sessions. During sessions, all completed work was read aloud, sentence by sentence, and discussed in relation to clarity, organization, and effectiveness. Although the remedial specialist made no marks on Ted's paper, every unclear sentence was discussed. In essence, the remedial specialist *modeled an active approach* for Ted by questioning unclear areas rather than by writing correct answers. After the 20th session, the specialist encouraged Ted to write Process Notes. Ted wrote the following passage after the 21st session of work:

> I began writing this time before I began typing—I began to frame this essay in my mind ahead of time. I asked a main question, and then made myself ask "What does another person reading this have to know in order to understand both the question and the answer?" I asked myself, "Does the piece follow a logical and easily understood order?" and "Does each paragraph contain a logical order too? Do all the paragraphs fit together?" Although there were a good many spelling lapses, the general ordering of the ideas seem OK to me—and this is encouraging to me. I would have to say a guarded yes to my questions.

The working relationship between the remedial specialist and the client is never a static one. It draws its strength from the balance between necessary support and the increasing autonomy of the student as he or she becomes more able to compensate for his or her difficulties. In this particular case, we see that Ted has developed an awareness of the specific elements of effective and communicative writing. The revelation that one's writing always needs to be understood by others continued to transform Ted's efforts, and Ted eventually integrated this principle into most of his writing. By the end of the year, he retook the comprehensive exams and passed with high commendations.

Finally, the third goal of treatment is to reduce anxiety related to learning. A client can decrease anxiety while working on the area of his or her greatest vulnerability if a positive therapeutic alliance has been established, if materials appropriate to the client's intellectual level are used, and if each defined goal or task is broken down into manageable parts. Achievement of all three goals of treatment—helping the individual to change his or her self-perception, to develop an awareness of his or her thought processes, and to reduce anxiety—can help the individual to achieve a degree of mastery. The following three case examples illustrate these points.

Janet

The emotional repercussions of learning disabilities can interfere with a sense of positive self-worth and cause a person to feel intense shame. Janet, a friendly 30-year-old who works for a large corporation, graduated from a small liberal arts college with a degree in marketing.

Early History

Janet had difficulty learning to read in the early grades. During reading instruction, she was placed in a corrective reading group that met five times per week for 1 hour each time. Janet recalls that reading was always difficult for her. In high school, her parents helped her with assignments. They helped her review before tests and made editorial and spell-

ing changes on her papers. She graduated from high school with a C average. Janet's anxiety heightened in college, and she often stayed up all night before an exam. She made it a point to find a study group. Her friends read her papers and made corrections before she handed them in. She did well enough so that no professor ever identified her as someone who needed to be referred for psychoeducational evaluation. After passing all of her courses, she graduated in 4 years.

Work History

After college, Janet worked in sales. Her organizational ability was praised, but she decided to change jobs because she wanted a position that included some travel. She took a job with the large corporation for whom she currently works. Her new job required interpersonal and organizational skills and also involved some travel. After 1 year, she had her first job review. She was rated outstanding in interpersonal skills and in working as a member of a team. In fact, she was rated well above average in every category except writing and communication skills. The job review noted, *Written work is dramatically inadequate for her level of responsibility.* Janet was told that the quality of her written work would keep her from being promoted. Janet's boss told her that she thought that Janet had some kind of learning disability and strongly urged her to get help if she wanted to advance on the job.

Testing and Remediation

Janet was extremely anxious when she first consulted the psychoeducational diagnostician and wept helplessly when she talked about her learning problems. Confronting her problems with learning was so traumatic that a month passed after the first interview before she called to begin work. Her parents were supportive both emotionally and financially. Janet asked her parents not to tell anyone else in her family that she was getting help for her learning problems. She told her boss but did not tell any of her close friends. She felt stigmatized and very ashamed.

An intelligence test showed that Janet had average ability, but the unevenness of her subtest scores showed that she had higher potential ability. For example, her general knowledge clearly had been inhibited by lack of background reading. She also experienced considerable anxiety when asked to answer questions and do specific tasks; this anxiety had a definite negative impact on the intelligence test results.

On the Word Recognition subtest of the Wide Range Achievement Test–Third Edition (Wilkinson, 1993), Janet scored at the sixth percentile, which is equivalent to approximately an eighth-grade skill level. Her oral and silent reading were approximately at the 10th-grade level. When answering questions about the silent reading passages, Janet read the passages and had to look back at them to find every answer.

She was asked to write several short summaries. Although it was evident that she could express herself verbally, she was very uncertain about how to put what she wanted to say in writing. Her fear about making spelling errors made her choose a simple vocabulary that made her writing seem less mature.

The evaluation was stressful. The findings were interpreted and explained to her in as positive a manner as possible, but Janet felt despair about making progress. It seemed likely that Janet had had severe reading problems when she was a youngster. There was no indication in her history or in the current evaluation, however, that suggested that she would be unable to make progress during remediation, and the evaluator conveyed this positive outlook to her.

The Work

The first goal of treatment was to change Janet's perception of herself from *someone who could not learn to someone who could learn* by having Janet work on appropriate materials within the context of a supportive relationship. It was also necessary to reduce Janet's anxiety and despair related to learning.

Because of Janet's intense anxiety in relation to reading, writing, and words in general, it was particularly important for the remedial specialist to be supportive and non-pressuring and at the same time choose materials that were mature in format and content and appropriate to Janet's reading level. Janet and the remedial specialist met once per week, before Janet was due at work. Remediation focused on oral reading, vocabulary development, silent reading comprehension, and expressive language skills, including letter and memo writing, spelling, and word analysis. Janet reviewed expressive writing and vocabulary activities during the week at home.

Janet's first writing assignments were to write about members of her family. These assignments required no advance reading. Writing impressions about family and friends usually tends to be less stressful than a more formal assignment. The remedial specialist made no corrections on these first few writing assignments. After a few weeks the specialist asked Janet to summarize an article of her choice from a newspaper. Janet was able to find articles she could read in *USA Today*. Because she rarely had looked at a newspaper, she and the specialist looked at one together to see how to locate news articles, the weather section, and human interest stories. The specialist asked her to choose a newspaper article that appealed to her, read the article at home, and then summarize it in writing. Janet underlined any words in the article that she did not know or words that she thought she would have trouble defining. Each week at her remedial session, she read the summary aloud. Again, the specialist made no corrections at the time of the reading. Instead, the specialist chose one aspect of the writing—usually grammar, spelling, or general usage—for teaching during the next session. In this way, Janet felt less threatened because she was not corrected during her presentation and because skills were taught separately from the presentation. She began incorporating the grammar and usage lessons into her writing. After approximately 8 months, Janet started reading *The New York Times* instead of *USA Today*. This change boosted her self-esteem, because her family and friends also read *The New York Times*. She generally found at least one article of interest to write about.

The newspaper reading was important to remediation because Janet avoided reading in general and never read the newspaper at all. After she had been attending remediation sessions for a while, Janet started to read the newspaper once per week and consequently had more to contribute when she socialized with her co-workers. Each week she added new words to her vocabulary by underlining new words at home. During remediation sessions, she and the specialist discussed and defined each word with the aid of a dictionary. By herself, Janet felt intimidated by the dictionary, but she did use it during sessions. She wrote each new word on a 3″ × 5″ index card with the definition on the reverse side. She also added a sentence using the word to help her to retain the word. The specialist also encouraged Janet to keep and bring to her sessions a list of any unknown words that she might hear at work. In this way all of the new words studied were ones that Janet herself had selected rather than words from a list in a vocabulary book.

During each session Janet read silently a short selection and answered accompanying comprehension questions. She and the remedial specialist discussed any incor-

rect responses. The questions that posed the most problems for Janet were questions that required inferential thinking, a skill that is essential for advanced reading comprehension. Inferential thinking involves making accurate judgments and drawing conclusions about what is read. It was necessary for Janet to approach the text in a more interactive manner than she was accustomed to. She also tended to make literal interpretations that limited her understanding of subtleties. The remedial specialist helped her to make more accurate inferences in the following way. Through guided discussion, Janet was encouraged to identify relationships between events in a passage, as she and the specialist returned to the text for additional analysis of the content. The specialist helped Janet to recognize that she often could use some prior knowledge to figure out an answer. Increased self-monitoring of her own thought processes was also encouraged. In this way, Janet began to derive more meaning from what she read.

So that Janet could improve her spelling skills, misspelled words were identified both in her weekly writing assignments and in the memos or reports that she wrote for her job. When the words were common and likely to be used frequently, she copied them in a small, alphabetized notebook that she could carry in her pocketbook. The remedial specialist reviewed the words with Janet during the weekly sessions and added to the list each week so that Janet became familiar with the words. When she needed to use a word in her writing, she referred to her personal dictionary. As time went on, she memorized many of the words, and they were dropped from the list. New words were added as Janet began to expand her vocabulary. In this way, her spelling skills improved steadily and so did her confidence in including a more varied vocabulary in her writing.

Although Janet was reading at the high school level, she was not confident about applying word analysis skills or syllabication skills to figure out new multisyllabic words. Because review of basic word analysis skills was a painful reminder of early school failures, word analysis was taught in conjunction with the words from newspaper articles that Janet mispronounced. For example, when she was not able to pronounce *mirth,* an opportunity arose for the remedial specialist to introduce the pronunciation of the special letter combinations *ir, ur,* and *er* and to select different words for teaching and practice at the following session. Teaching was thus tied to *use* and did not take on the qualities of *drills.* Eventually, all of the necessary word analysis skills were reviewed.

Although Janet was motivated and conscientiously completed her writing and vocabulary review at home, she continued to hide her efforts from her friends and close family members. After approximately 8 months of remediation, Janet received a promotion and a pay bonus. Her boss no longer criticized her writing and communication skills. Janet was more confident and handled pressure and stress on her job with greater equanimity. She still tended to procrastinate when she had to write memos and letters, but brought them to the remedial sessions more readily to work on them with her remedial specialist. Janet still found reading to be a struggle, but she was more willing to try to get information from books and began to read some self-help books related to career advancement.

After 1½ years of remedial sessions, Janet had less anxiety and had increased confidence about reading and writing. As a result, she was able to learn and retain information more easily. At work she became more willing to write memos and letters and did not automatically think that whatever she wrote was of poor quality. Her vocabulary expanded, and she realized that she was aware of words in a way that she had not been before. She made an effort to retain what she knew by reviewing and by trying to use the words in conversation.

Roy

Many individuals with learning disabilities or symptoms of mild dyslexia who have struggled for years in school tend to become discouraged and take an increasingly passive approach to academic work. This was the case with Roy, an articulate 24-year-old college graduate who was distressed about his future. He wanted to decide on a career but did not think he could do anything well.

Early History

Roy's earliest memory of school was of feeling frightened. In the first and second grade, he did not make sufficient progress in reading and was assigned to remedial reading classes. In addition, he went to tutors periodically throughout elementary school. He never read for pleasure and read only what was assigned. Roy described elementary school as frustrating. Roy chose to attend an alternative high school that offered smaller classes and more individual attention to each student. He became a student government leader but never excelled in his studies. In college, he graduated with a B-minus average and felt he had not learned as much as he would have liked. Roy stated that he never put his full effort into schoolwork. He told himself that if he did not do well, then he could also comfort himself with the fact that he had not tried very hard.

Testing and Remediation

After college, Roy was evaluated by a neuropsychologist who administered a comprehensive testing battery. Roy had done mediocre academic work throughout college, and the testing showed Roy to have uneven abilities. He had above-average ability in verbal and math areas, but read very slowly and had a relatively limited vocabulary. He had extensive word retrieval problems. He also had difficulty interpreting visual or pictorial material. The neuropsychologist discouraged Roy from attempting graduate school. No silent reading test was administered at the evaluation. Instead of choosing a career, Roy, with the encouragement of his family, decided to seek remediation for his learning difficulties.

Roy was interested in learning more about his problem and wanted to improve his reading skills, but he was ambivalent about working on anything academic. The remedial specialist needed a baseline measure because there was no current information about how well Roy could read textbook-like material. The Nelson-Denny Reading Test (Brown et al., 1981) was administered. The specialist made a mark on Roy's answer sheet when the standard time had passed but then allowed Roy to complete the test to find out his accuracy if he had sufficient time to finish the test. The results (relative to the results of typical college seniors) were as follows:

Area tested	Standard time percentile	Extended time percentile
Vocabulary	12	82
Reading comprehension	31	85

The results indicated that although Roy had a slow rate of reading, he definitely could understand difficult material when he had sufficient time. At this point, Roy was

quite discouraged and did not see himself as capable of doing well in school because he had never done so.

Many students who read slowly and struggle constantly to keep up with their work also never learn how to study effectively or how to sustain effort in order to master material for a difficult course of study. Roy had shown very uneven ability on the intelligence test, but he had average ability, and the pattern of scores suggested that he had higher potential ability. The silent reading test helped confirm his good basic ability. When devising a plan of treatment, the remedial specialist took into account Roy's statement that he had never put in full effort. The specialist interpreted and explained the results of the reading test to Roy in as positive a manner as possible; that is, she told him that the results showed that he had good basic ability and that although he had a slow rate of reading, he definitely could improve. She also told him that he expressed his ideas well in writing.

It is possible to help an individual change from being a passive reader to being an active one if appropriate materials are chosen and if assignments are presented both supportively and incrementally. It was important that Roy not be overwhelmed. The plan was to help him gradually to perceive himself as a learner, as someone who could sustain effort even with difficult material. That Roy enjoyed expressing his ideas in writing was incorporated into the plan.

Roy came to weekly 1-hour remedial sessions and spent approximately 2 hours per week working at home. Each week he was assigned a short story by a writer such as Raymond Carver, Ernest Hemingway, George Orwell, Eudora Welty, or Italo Calvino. Roy was always able to complete each assignment because the stories were short. He felt positive about being able to do the assignments and, at the same time, learned about many new authors. After reading the week's story at home, he wrote a 1- or 2-page summary that included a discussion about the story's main theme. After a few weeks, he was also assigned to read an editorial essay in *The New York Times* by a regular editorial writer. Roy read and summarized these point-of-view articles at home. He was encouraged to agree or disagree with the columnist at the end of his summary. Roy was slowly but systematically beginning to acquire information both from literature and from current events. Roy liked to write, and the act of writing required him to become more interactive with the text. He began to discuss the new information with his family and his friends and engage more actively in discussion about politics.

Each week, Roy brought in a list of new words from the reading selection. Roy had an excellent speaking vocabulary but had a much more limited reading vocabulary because of his limited reading experience. He therefore had many new words to discuss each week. He and the remedial specialist chose 10 words per week to write on 3″ × 5″ cards and wrote the definitions on the reverse sides along with sentences from the article or book that included the new words. Roy and the remedial specialist discussed the meanings in the sessions, and Roy reviewed the words at home. Roy's vocabulary gradually improved. Other topical articles were introduced, for example, essays by Elisabeth Kübler-Ross and Betty Friedan, to broaden both his interests and his knowledge base. Finally, the remedial specialist asked Roy to get a book by a professional photographer. Every other week he wrote an essay about a photograph of his choice. He had to discern the story the photographer appeared to convey. The book contained no explanatory text, so Roy's entire essay had to be rooted in what he saw in the photograph. He got practice in interpreting visual and pictorial material, which had been identified as a problem area in his neuropsychological testing. His observations became more

acute, and with practice he began producing integrated essays that incorporated most of the visual details as well as the underlying drama in the photographs.

Roy's anxiety about learning and reading gradually lessened. All of Roy's written assignments were read aloud and discussed at the remedial sessions. He received general positive feedback as well as specific suggestions for improving his essays. At the end of 3 months, Roy began to think of himself as both well-informed and well-read. He saw that he had learned a great deal and had developed his own opinions about world events. He felt so energized by all of the information that he was absorbing and learning that he declared, "This has been the most exciting 3 months of my life!"

At this point, Roy began to have hope for his future. He decided that he might like to go to medical school. First, he had to prove to himself that he could put forth the effort in a sustained way. He and his remedial specialist found an undergraduate science course that he could take on a noncredit basis. He attended each week, did the reading and assignments, took the exams, and saw that he could master the material.

Next, as part of this new long-range plan, Roy had to apply for a program where he could take all of his pre-med requirements because he had not been a science major in college. He took these background science courses over a 2-year period so that he and his remedial specialist could concentrate on effective study skills. It was necessary for him not only to become an active learner but also to begin to work in an increasingly independent manner. The remedial specialist encouraged him to sit near the front of the lecture room, prepare for class *before* going to the lecture, take complete notes, and review the notes after the lecture, underlining important points in red pencil. He learned to apply these study skills as the first term progressed. Before the midterm exams, the specialist encouraged Roy to go to his professors during office hours to ask questions about anything that was not clear. He first wrote out a list of the questions and left space for the answers. Roy was surprised to find that he was the only student who visited during office hours, so each professor spent the entire hour with him. In addition, Roy and the remedial specialist looked over the questions together to see whether his questions were based on insufficient information, misreading the text, or topics that were not covered in lectures. He could then zero in on any vulnerable area when he studied.

During his first term, Roy definitely became a more active learner. He was introduced to the **SQ3R** method of study (Robinson, 1946), which helped him to be less overwhelmed by the science texts. These texts were difficult, but it was particularly helpful for Roy to find out that most of the information in each paragraph is represented in the first sentence of the paragraph and that the remaining sentences in the paragraph support the first sentence with details.

Roy remained motivated throughout the 2 years, even though the pre-med courses were difficult and demanding. At the end of the 2 years, he had earned seven As and one B. He took the Medical College Admissions Test (MCAT) with extended time because he had a diagnosis of dyslexia. His score on the MCAT was above average, and Roy was accepted to medical school. Although Roy's reading rate had improved, it still was slower than that of the average student. Consequently, he requested and was granted extended time on examinations in medical school. Roy continued to do well in medical school.

Evan

A student's reading comprehension, expressive writing, and mathematical skills can be above average, and still the student may not do well in college. Puzzled parents and

teachers often call these students "underachievers." However, when these students are helped to become more attentive to their own thinking processes, positive changes can occur. These cognitive processes are usually related to organizational, attentional, and strategy issues. *Executive function,* a concept from clinical neuropsychology, has been useful in understanding and working with these students. Often included under the rubric *executive function* are activities such as planning, prioritizing, sequencing, organizing, being able to shift focus, and following a project through to completion (Denckla, 1996). These students may not have actual deficits, but they seem unaware of what they need to do in order to be successful students. First, they tend to be passive learners and are overly dependent on their teachers or professors to provide them with information. They do not seem conscious of the fact that it is up to them to initiate ideas, to create outlines, and to organize their time so that all of the work can get done. They have trouble prioritizing the steps of a task, and they are not flexible in shifting their focus when the task demands it. These issues become increasingly important as the students advance through school. Evan is an example of a student with a mild learning disability combined with problems in executive functioning.

Early History

Evan, a well-spoken 20-year-old, reported that he always had difficulty concentrating in school and was easily distracted. He did not enjoy reading and tended to read only what was assigned for a class. In elementary school, he had been diagnosed as mildly dyslexic, but he did not receive any specialized help, probably because his grades were consistently above average. He did not excel in high school, but graduated with a B minus average and high SAT scores (Verbal, 680; Math, 710). When Evan was accepted at a competitive liberal arts college, he did not anticipate any difficulty with coursework. Not particularly self-reflective, Evan did not give much thought as to how to plan his time or how to study effectively when he began college. To his dismay, he did not do well in his academic subjects. The required reading was much more complex and dense than in high school, and the amount of new information to be absorbed and integrated was considerably higher. He found he could not sustain his concentration long enough to study and retain material at a satisfactory level. He was not used to organizing his time, and often he did not leave sufficient time to complete long assignments, much less do a first draft and revisions. He had trouble working independently, something that is increasingly necessary as a student advances through college. Note-taking was not easy for him. If his attention wavered in class, he often could not get back on track again for that class period. Sensing he might be in academic trouble, he began to put extra time into studying in the library and in doing his schoolwork, but much to his disappointment, the results were not commensurate with his effort. He began to experience anxiety about his ability to do well in college, and his confidence plummeted. By the end of his sophomore year, Evan had achieved a C plus average. He decided to take an official leave of absence and be evaluated for learning disabilities.

Testing and Remediation

The results of the neuropsychological evaluation showed Evan to be a cooperative and motivated student who was above average in general intelligence. He expressed a wish to do well in school, and he did not understand why his efforts did not result in better grades. He scored higher than the 85th percentile on a reading comprehension test and seemed to have good overall ability in reading. He could solve mental arithmetic prob-

lems quickly and accurately, was higher than average in abstract thinking, and had an excellent vocabulary. However, he was found to have mild organizational weaknesses. When a lot of unfamiliar information was presented, he seemed rattled and had difficulty deciding where to begin the task. Also it was noted that when encountering any degree of challenge in a task, Evan tended to give up easily, rather than plan an approach and then generate strategies to solve the problem. Finally, although Evan did well on reading the relatively short reading comprehension passages, he was slow to apply phonic principles to multisyllabic, unfamiliar words that he had to read. This suggested that there was a lack of *automaticity* in his reading ability that might account, in part, for some of his problems with assignments. In college, reading material is usually much more difficult than in high school and requires the reading of original sources as well as the ability to sustain attention over time.

According to the evaluation, Evan was both puzzled and demoralized by his college performance. He pictured himself as a good student, but at this point his confidence was quite low. He had put in effort but the results did not bear him out. He had tried studying by himself and with a small group of fellow students. Neither method led to success. A recurring comment by professors was that his papers were superficial and did not go deep enough.

After the results of the evaluation were interpreted to Evan, it was recommended that he begin work with a remedial specialist. Evan first found a part-time job, and then he began remediation. He had a wry, self-deprecating sense of humor, and from the start it was clear that he was eager to collaborate in finding ways to be a more effective student. The remedial specialist's first goal was to help Evan see himself as someone who could learn and succeed in an academic setting. As part of the remediation plan, Evan was asked to summarize and comment on one chapter per week from *Into Thin Air* by Jon Krakauer, a true adventure account of climbing Mt. Everest. He also was given a newspaper essay on a stimulating topic, which he was asked to summarize and critique. In the past, he had tended to procrastinate, and now he was urged to complete his assignments *during the week*, not at the last minute, so that he could improve and revise his writing if he wanted to. Evan and the remedial specialist particularly discussed the consequences of the themes included in both the essay and in the book. By starting his work in advance and looking for the ramifications and consequences in the essays, Evan began to spend more time on his own interpretations. As the weeks went on, he became more committed to the work.

During the session, Evan and the remedial specialist worked on improving inferential reading skills, expanding vocabulary, and focusing on writing as a way to communicate ideas. Evan began to care more about the words he chose to express himself and to reread to decide if he had communicated effectively.

After 15 sessions, Evan had to decide whether to reenroll at his college or transfer to a nearby university. Instead of making an impulsive decision, Evan was persuaded to write two essays: one to support reenrollment at his college and the other about whether to transfer to the nearby university. He wrote two detailed essays for and against reenrollment. Evan and the remedial specialist talked about the pros and cons, and he discussed the options with his family. In the end, he decided to enroll as a nonmatriculated student at a nearby university, with the understanding that if he did well he would apply as a matriculated student.

Evan registered for three courses, which he chose himself. All of the courses required a term paper, plus a good deal of reading. To Evan's surprise, he found the lectures, the reading, and the assignments much more stimulating and compelling than

he had ever experienced before. Together he and the remedial specialist worked on planning a study schedule that he agreed he could adhere to. They discussed the topics for the assigned papers, and he chose his topic early in the term. He was encouraged to keep up with the required reading, to participate in class discussions, and begin the research for his assigned papers early in the semester. The therapeutic alliance was positive, and he liked talking over the ideas from his courses. He was receptive to suggestions regarding to how to study effectively. He began to function increasingly as an organized student. Procrastination ceased to be a major problem, and he started to set priorities among the demands of his schedule. After two semesters as a nonmatriculated student, Evan had maintained a GPA of 3.5 and was able to matriculate as a regular student.

Evan was feeling much more confident in general, and he began to look to the future and consider law as a career. In preparation, he decided on political science as a major area of study. By this time, Evan's approach toward mastering his coursework was much more organized. He set aside blocks of time for writing papers. Occasionally he would procrastinate, but that became much less of a problem. He found his courses interesting, and his attitude toward schoolwork continued to be positive. His written assignments and term papers were no longer criticized for being superficial. Instead his professors tended to write "Good point" and "You write well." After two years, Evan graduated with a GPA of 3.5. Instead of going immediately to graduate school, Evan decided to work for 2 years as a paralegal. He found legal work interesting and was given increased responsibility and an opportunity to do legal research. At the end of 2 years he began law school. Law school demands a student's full attention because of the sheer quantity of reading material and the special requirements of detailed written briefs and notes. Evan experienced the academic work as challenging but manageable. He was conscious of allocating his time so that he could complete his work in a timely manner. He was particularly satisfied with the praise he received for his analytic reasoning ability and for the clarity of his writing.

SUMMARY

Although the three individuals described in these case studies are quite different, they made a lot of progress and developed a greater sense of self-confidence. Although learning differences in high-functioning dyslexics vary greatly, all individuals have the potential to make progress. It is important for each client to have a thorough and competent evaluation (which is interpreted to the client in the most positive manner possible), from which an effective treatment plan can be developed. When a treatment plan is successfully implemented, the clients take an active role in their own learning. Often when clients understand their strengths and weaknesses, they can advocate for the necessary accommodations in school or on the job. When these accommodations are made, clients can show the extent of their knowledge better. They perform better, receive recognition for their improved performance, can sustain hope about the future, and often achieve their goals.

REFERENCES

Bender, L. (1938). *Bender Visual Motor Gestalt Test*. San Antonio, TX: The Psychological Corporation.

Blumenthal, S. (1981). *Educational Memories*. Unpublished manuscript.

Brown, J.I., Bennett, J.M., & Hanna, G.S. (1981). *The Nelson-Denny Reading Test*. Chicago: Riverside.

Buck, J.N. (1978). *The House-Tree-Person Technique* (Rev. manual). Los Angeles: Western Psychological Services.

Denckla, M.B. (1996). A theory and model of executive function: A neuropsychological perspective. In G.R. Lyon & N.A. Krasnegor (Eds.), *Attention, memory, and executive function* (pp. 263–278). Baltimore: Paul H. Brookes Publishing Co.

MacGinitie, W.H., & MacGinitie, R.H. (1989). *Gates-MacGinitie Reading Tests* (3rd ed.). Chicago: Riverside.

Murray, H.A., & Bellak, L. (1973). *Thematic Apperception Test (TAT)*. San Antonio, TX: The Psychological Corporation.

Pauk, W. (1983). *Six-way paragraphs (Advanced)*. Providence, RI: Jamestown Publishers.

Robinson, F.P. (1946). *Effective study*. New York: HarperCollins.

Roswell, F.G., & Chall, J.S. (1992). *Diagnostic Assessments of Reading with Trial Teaching Strategies (DARTTS)*. Chicago: Riverside.

Rotter, J.B., Lah, M.I., & Rafferty, J.E. (1992). *Rotter Incomplete Sentences Blank* (2nd ed.). San Antonio, TX: The Psychological Corporation.

Wechsler, D. (1991). *Wechsler Adult Intelligence Scale–III*. San Antonio, TX: Harcourt Assessment.

Wiederholt, J.L., & Bryant, B.R. (1992). *Gray Oral Reading Test* (GORT-3) (3rd ed.). Austin, TX: PRO-ED.

Wilkinson, G.S. (1993). *Wide Range Achievement Test–Third Edition: Manual*. Wilmington, DE: Jastak Associates.

20

Helping Parents of Children with Dyslexia

Betty S. Levinson

I n the first edition of this book, published in 1999, this chapter stated the importance of helping the dyslexic child and the family to understand the nature and implications of dyslexia. Although there have since been some advancements in diagnostic and instructional procedures for dyslexics, there has not been a parallel gain in counseling families who have progressed beyond the diagnostic phase.

As this chapter was being prepared for this second edition, a literature search failed to find any significant improvement in the above-referenced areas. Although more has been written about what parents of dyslexics should know, there has been no emphasis on what is needed from helping professionals (HPs) to guide these parents in implementing the suggestions given to them. HPs who are typically engaged in helping parents include psychologists, psychiatrists, educational therapists, social workers, teachers, and counselors.

This chapter deals with issues relating to parenting a dyslexic youngster, including the similarities to and differences from raising a nondyslexic child. In addition, this chapter stresses the desperate need that parents of dyslexics have for sound, realistic guidance and the possible resulting despair and loss of human potential when appropriate advice is absent.

This chapter also addresses the language problems that often accompany dyslexia. Parents typically seek help from well-trained, knowledgeable HPs after witnessing the negative impact that these language problems have on the child both in school and at home. Finally, this chapter provides guidelines for assessing the training and qualifications of HPs who counsel parents of dyslexics. Intervention practices are compared with research findings and the clinical experience of HPs who have worked with dyslexics and their families over the years.

THE UNIQUENESS OF DYSLEXIA

When discussing child-rearing issues with the parents of dyslexic youngsters, it becomes apparent that these children are different from young people with other types of disabilities. Children who have a physical disability or severe cognitive impairments are observably different to both laypeople and HPs. A child with a specific language-based learning disability such as dyslexia, however, is said to have an invisible condition, which often goes undetected. Dyslexia's early signs vary greatly and are frequently mistaken for a developmental lag (Bernstein & Tiegerman, 1997). Consequently, by the time parents and teachers become convinced that a child needs help, the mystery surrounding the disability has deepened, and confusion has taken over.

Dyslexia is a language-based communication problem. Its remediation requires that several key concepts about communication be kept in mind. First, most communication problems are related to the language, not to the person's thoughts. Second, language is anything that transmits a message and, depending on the situation, can include the following:

- Words and other vocal sounds

- Silence

- Pitch, tone, and rhythm of voice

- Gestures

- Facial expressions

- Postures

- Body language

- Signs

- Clothing worn or objects carried

- Distance from other people or objects

Dyslexia is a disorder that interferes with communication—the acquisition, processing, and transmission of language—and consists of the symptoms illustrated in Figure 20.1.

It is crucial to consider genetic factors when dealing with dyslexia. There is an increased incidence of specific language disability among the parents of dyslexics. The parents' own language processing and general communication difficulties can thus complicate the assessment and intervention process. Unless this possibility is considered (and appropriate training is introduced), the ability of parents to assist their children may be reduced significantly. In other words, often the parents along with the child should receive help for specific language disability.

Dyslexia rates among parents of dyslexics are also high (ranging from 27% to 49%) and are consistent across studies. A dyslexic child is eight times as likely to have a parent with dyslexia as the general population (whose risk is only 5%)—a higher level than that found in many familial behavior disorders. In addition, in four family studies that addressed rates of recurrence and possible mechanisms of transmission of dyslexia, Pennington, Gilger, Olson, and DeFries (1992) showed that there is a high and consistent occurrence of dyslexia among siblings of dyslexics—ranging across studies from

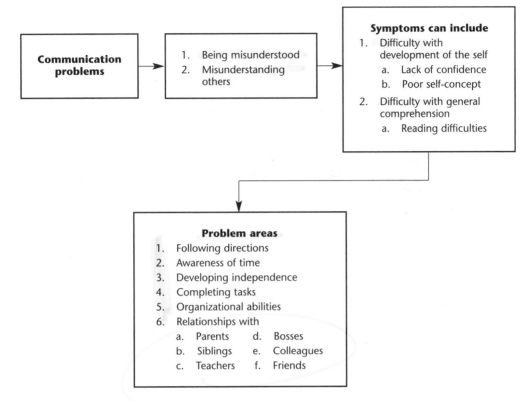

Figure 20.1. Symptoms of and problems resulting from communication problems such as dyslexia.

38.5% to 43%. These extensive longitudinal studies report strong evidence that dyslexia is both familial and heritable.

Arnold (1978) reminded HPs about the need to identify the parents' situation, to empathize with their feelings, and to enter into a cooperative alliance. A survey of parents of dyslexics would likely show that parents' experiences with HPs have been in direct contrast to Arnold's prescription. This discrepancy stems not from the helpers' unwillingness to assist but from a lack of knowledge about how to help.

Until the 1980s, many how-to books written for parents and the general public about dyslexia failed to take into account both the probable genetic factors (within parents) and many teachers' lack of training concerning typical language development in children. Consequently, advice that intended to help missed the target. Even now, parents who have dyslexia cannot implement suggestions that they are unable to assimilate, and most teachers cannot intervene in the manner prescribed by the how-to books because they lack appropriate training and necessary background information.

For instance, a parent with dyslexia might complain that weekends are a disaster. With several children in the family, all of whom have activities, homework, and chores, the child with dyslexia may seem to be the only one who cannot remember his or her responsibilities, cannot follow a task through to completion, and complains about everything. Often this occurs to the point that either the parent does things for the child or asks another child to do it.

One can readily see what the result of this approach will be. The parent becomes angry, despairing, and overwhelmed with a feeling of inadequacy. The child enlisted to help feels angry and burdened. This child with dyslexia gets the message that people are angry with him or her, which is true; that the parent does not love him or her, which is not true; and that he or she does not have to do what he or she does not want to do, which is certainly not true.

Rather, the parents should have a session with the learning disabilities specialist during which they go over everyone's weekend expectations and then reconsider the findings in the dyslexic child's diagnostic reports. Characteristics such as memory problems, organization, timing, retrieval, and insecurity difficulties, all would suggest why the child with dyslexia may have trouble carrying out an oral list of instructions.

The learning disabilities specialist can then explain to the parents new ways to approach weekends and can try role-playing strategies to help the child succeed. It is suggested that the entire family be included in the weekend plans to avoid singling out the child with dyslexia. One option is for the family to get together on Friday evening to list all of the chores and activities that need to be accomplished that weekend. Each individual should have his or her own list containing specific times to start and (if possible to determine) to stop. The overall family schedule should contain breaks, fun time, telephone time, and so forth. There is also a box to check off each task when it is finished.

This arrangement provides the parents with a way to monitor their child with dyslexia over the weekend from beginning to end. Any interruption during the process can be handled so that the list of tasks is completed without conflict or repeated failures.

This scheduling method is a didactic approach. It involves heightening awareness, teaching, monitoring, and following up. The HP never presumes that parents readily understand or can implement the necessary changes without rehearsing the script. The HP accepts that parents may lack the necessary repertoire of constructive behaviors and may require explicit instruction.

BACKGROUND KNOWLEDGE FOR HELPING PROFESSIONALS

Knowledge of typical language development must be a large part of HP training. One cannot recognize what is different unless he or she knows what is typical. Information from standard texts on child development cover the physical, emotional, psychological, and social arenas, which must be part of the knowledge base of individuals who work with the dyslexics. HPs also need a thorough understanding of dyslexia's neurobiological underpinnings, particularly the development of language and information processing (see Chapters 3 and 4). Understanding the neurobiological systems that are involved in communication (see, e.g., Chase, Rosen, & Sherman, 1996) increases the HPs' comprehension of the causation of language difficulties and aids in conveying this information to parents.

Communication with Parents

The HP who lacks the communication skills to translate complex information into understandable language may leave parents in the same state as when they initially arrived at the office—unable to understand the reasons behind their child's difficulties and lacking the knowledge about how to help their youngster. Unless parents

understand this information, the HP may be contributing unwittingly to an increase in parental depression, feelings of hopelessness, and anger. In addition, the child is not being helped.

To enhance communication with parents, the HP must be aware of the major difficulty that dyslexics often have with nonliteral language, such as idioms, proverbs, metaphors, similes, and slang and of these individuals' tendency often to become overloaded auditorially. Other symptoms, such as problems with time management and the inability to organize a response rapidly, can interfere with communication if a parent also has dyslexia. Consequently, HPs must be vigilant about the language they use. It should be simple but not demeaning. To ensure that parents have understood, it is imperative for the HP to ask for frequent feedback, for example, "Just so that I can be sure that my explanation was clear, tell me in your own words what we just talked about."

To address some of these communication difficulties, HPs and parents are advised to gain the listener's attention, speak concisely (using short sentences), eliminate figures of speech, and provide concrete examples from the family's daily experiences with the child. Doing so helps the parent make an immediate connection and illustrates (for the parent) useful behaviors that, in turn, bring more immediate positive changes.

Factors that Interfere with Communication

An example of the confusion that can happen (and what helps clear up the misunderstanding) when highly figurative language is used came up during a counseling session with a Mrs. C., a British-born mother married to an American. All three of her children were born in America; two are dyslexic. Everyone in the family is very intelligent. The mother continually reported, however, that the only child in the family with whom she did not have communication problems was her youngest boy, the one who was not dyslexic.

One day Mrs. C came to her counseling session quite distressed. She told the following story. Her oldest child, a 14-year-old girl, came home, dropped her books on the floor in the living room, threw her jacket on a chair, took a snack out of the refrigerator (leaving the refrigerator door open), and left her dirty glass and plate on the table. She then went into her parents' bedroom, sprawled across the freshly made bed while she used her parents' telephone to call a friend, and continued to munch on some crackers.

Mrs. C walked in the bedroom and screamed, "I'm speechless! Can you throw any light on this situation? Do you know how often you drive me around the bend? Do you have bats in your belfry? Oh, God! I think I'm losing it!"

At that point, the daughter (who was still on the telephone) turned to her mother and said, "What did you lose?"

Obviously, the mother became more upset and thought that her daughter was giving a smart-mouthed reply. It was even more obvious that the daughter had misunderstood her mother's tirade and only grasped the fact that her mother seemed upset. The girl later said that she was genuinely concerned about her mother's loss, which was totally "lost" on the mother who stomped out—crying in frustration—and called her HP for an extra session that week.

In part, the mother's session proceeded as follows:

Therapist: Try to tell me exactly what happened. I want to hear it all because I know how frustrating this was for you. [This gave the mother a chance to be heard in an environment in which she feels listened to and understood.]

Mrs. C: I'm not sure I can remember much, except how inadequate these blowups make me feel, but I'll try. [She went on to relate the story in a disorganized way, interrupting herself many times. The therapist recorded the session with Mrs. C's permission while helping her to organize her thoughts and also wrote down all of Mrs. C's nonliteral language and behaviors that might have interfered with communication.]

Therapist: Oh, my! I certainly can feel that you're upset, given how often you experience these situations that seem unforgivable, given that your daughter is so bright and already 14 years old. By now you had a right to expect more appropriate behavior. That is, if she were not dyslexic.

Mrs. C: Thank you for listening and understanding. But tell me what to do. It's upsetting the whole family.

Therapist: All right, I'll try. I know when we met to discuss the findings from the tests that I gave you a lot of information all at once. It was too much for any parent to remember to use in situations at home. So let me use your difficult time to go over some issues and to suggest ways to handle them in the future.

First, as you entered the house and followed the trail your daughter left, your agitation mounted as you climbed the steps that led to your bedroom. By the time you saw her, you were angry and certainly could not be expected to reflect on the traits that often coexist with dyslexia, such as difficulties with nonliteral language, problems when too many words are used, problems responding to questions, lack of ability to focus, and defensiveness (primarily because these youngsters feel as though they are constantly displeasing someone). Instead of yelling at the child, it's necessary, initially, to gain the child's attention.

I can go through your story and suggest a different approach to help you develop some effective ways to bring about change. Now, the next time you see the items your daughter leaves strewn about, you might begin an inner dialogue: Yes, she has a problem. Which symptom does this resemble— lack of focus? disorganization? Next, you need to take some deep breaths. Try to assess the situation quickly. Then in some way other than screaming, "I'm speechless," get your daughter's attention, and make eye contact.

Next, ask your daughter to please come to see you as soon as she is off the telephone. Or, hand her a note that says *Please end your conversation, now, and come see me in the kitchen.* Once your daughter gets to the kitchen, try to smile at her, as difficult as this may be for you. Ask how her day was. Keep looking at her. Then say what you want her to hear: "I came into the house and I saw your book bag on the floor, your jacket on the chair, your dirty dishes on the table, and then found you on my bed eating crackers and getting crumbs all over." You need to say this neutrally.

At this point, become an actress. Begin to laugh, and say, "You were expecting me to yell and punish, right? Well, to tell you the truth, I felt like it. But that's what I've done many times. Obviously, it doesn't work. So let's try to work this out together. Here's my thought on the subject. Number one, I love you. Second, I don't think you do this kind of thing on purpose. Third, I think when you come home you do things without thinking too

much about them. So let's you and I look at what happened today. Let's see if together we can plan some ways to prevent this kind of thing from happening."

Next, the therapist gave Mrs. C a list of suggestions and role-played with her to develop a plan for monitoring her daughter's progress. Mrs. C laughed as she and the therapist went over these things. She said that she saw the situation more clearly now. She went over her language and saw how it might seem incomprehensible to her daughter. She and the therapist both laughed.

Years later, Mrs. C reminded her therapist of this incident. She told her therapist how she brought it up with her daughter (now married, with three children of her own, all of whom are dyslexics). During their conversation, her daughter said, "I still don't have any idea what a belfry is. And Dad used to say, 'Hold your horses.' Pretty confusing, since I didn't have any. And you used to say, 'Don't count your chickens before they hatch.' I didn't have any of those either."

The daughter then listed a few other sayings her parents used, such as "Kill two birds with one stone," and "Don't cut off your nose to spite your face." The daughter said that her parents spoke like that so much that she often failed to understand. Yet they would invariably end up asking, "Do you understand?" She said it made her feel dumb and angry.

Unfortunately, her parents did not realize the impact of their daughter's language problems and how it led to her rebellious behavior. Because her language difficulties were discovered so late, they led to continual conflicts among family members.

Although the role playing and counseling were effective to some degree with Mrs. C, the truly beneficial outcome was that the daughter, now a mother of three children, had become more knowledgeable about dyslexia—its symptoms and what must be done. She identified it in her own children before their teachers recognized it. The daughter asked an advocate to help her at school meetings. Although the daughter had learned a great deal, she wanted an advocate to ensure that communication between her and school personnel would be effective for her children. In addition, this young mother is continuing to role-play with a therapist to acquire better communication skills.

Mrs. C stated that gaining a sense of humor is essential for parents. She learned to laugh at what used to make her cry. She said it also helped her when other parents of dyslexics shared their frustrating language experiences. Mrs. C remembered a friend who came to her and said, "You won't believe this. My son came to me yesterday and asked when his piano lesson was. I said, 'Tomorrow.' Then today he asked again when was his piano lesson going to be. I said, 'Today.' Then he said, 'But you told me tomorrow.'" In complete frustration, Mrs. C's friend had smacked her forehead, only to have her sweet little boy ask her whether she had a headache.

Mrs. C and her friend laughed, and one funny story after another followed. Mrs. C ended by telling her friend that when she was a little girl in England during World War II, she heard two adults speaking about two children who had been blown up. For days afterward she remembers looking up in the sky for the children. She was only 5 years old at the time, when such a concrete interpretation would have been considered normal and funny. For dyslexics, however, this concreteness goes on long beyond the time when it is considered developmentally appropriate. Therefore, dyslexics must be taught the whole range of language skills, including the use of nonliteral language; these skills are essential for their socialization. In addition, it is important for the HP

to explain to parents the difficulties that dyslexics have with nonliteral and abstract language.

One more brief vignette, involving Mrs. C, her dyslexic daughter, and Mrs. C's granddaughter, exemplifies dyslexia's genetic factor. One afternoon Mrs. C's daughter called to say, "I think dyslexia has struck again." When queried, her daughter reported that Mrs. C's granddaughter (age 9, IQ above 129), overheard that her mother's friend would not be going to the park with them because "he was all tied up." The granddaughter volunteered to help, saying, "Don't worry. I'll come right over and untie you, and then we can all go to the park."

For those who are not dyslexic, stories such as Mrs. C's bring laughter and amusement. For those who have difficulties with language, these stories may conjure up memories of embarrassment, withdrawal from social situations, and instances of limited comprehension in academic reading and conversation.

A Helpful Recordkeeping System

The HP can ask a child's parents to keep a journal of how each day went (including tasks finished/unfinished) so that adjustments can be made when needed. Keeping a record that includes successes is important. Parents often remember their failures but not their successes. Keeping records or journals is one of the most difficult tasks for parents to accomplish. Therefore, the HP should assist parents in devising a simple record-keeping system. For instance, a checklist of chores could be set up as a seven-column chart (one column for each day of the week). Each chore (one row for each chore) that the child finishes would be checked off using the child's favorite color. No crosses or Xs should be used to indicate unfinished chores; empty boxes seem to bring about more positive results.

Even when all of the boxes for the day are checked, no special award should be offered. I have found over the years that most children find it a challenge to fill all of the boxes—first for a day, then for a week. After the 7-day checklist has been used for a while, the parent can explain to the child that when all (or almost all) of the boxes are filled for 4 weeks, perhaps the chart will not be needed anymore.

This kind of chart brought about positive changes for John, a 9-year-old whose mother kept insisting that he never does what is asked of him, although John maintained that he does his chores most of the time. The goal was to see whether the boy could have all of the boxes filled in for a day. At the end of each day, mother and son would count the checks for that day. They enjoyed the fact that the checks showed that he was really trying and that he had accomplished some of what was expected. After the check marks were counted, the mother was to smile, give him a hug, and say, "Nice try! We'll see how tomorrow's chart looks. Before you go to bed, let's just see if you can say what happened that made you leave some of today's boxes empty. Maybe we can figure out something together so that all of the boxes will have checks soon."

The next week, John and his parents decided to stop using the chart, there was a real setback. His mother reported that John had stopped doing some of his chores. The HP advised her to say to her son, who had a real interest in becoming a scientist, "You know, John, some scientists need a checklist most of the time to be sure they remember all of the necessary steps when they do an experiment. Maybe you will need to do this for a while longer. Let's try it for a few more weeks."

After another week, the mother and son had a session with the therapist about what had happened and to discuss the empty boxes (see Figure 20.2).

CHORE	M	T	W	T	F	S	S
1. Brush teeth	✓	✓		✓	✓	✓	✓
2. Feed dog	✓	✓	✓	✓	✓	✓	✓
3. Walk dog			✓	✓	✓	✓	✓
4. Start homework w/o nagging				✓	✓	✓	✓
5. Take bath w/o arguing	✓			✓	✓		✓
6. Clear room floor before bedtime			✓		✓	✓	
7. Lay out clothes for next morning		✓	✓		✓	✓	✓

Figure 20.2. Chore chart for John, a 9-year-old with dyslexia.

Monday   John said, "I forgot to walk the dog because I was late for school." His mother suggested that she could wake him a little earlier. They addressed homework next. John did not agree that his mother had to nag him to do his homework. His mother followed one of the therapist's prior suggestions (when you are not sure about how to handle a situation, give yourself time to think before you attempt to deal with it) and let John's statement stand. Next, John said his mother didn't remind him to clear his bedroom floor and lay the next day's clothes out before going to bed; she said that she would remind him to look at the chart before he went to bed the next night.

Tuesday   When asked about the empty box for #4, "Start homework w/o nagging," John stated, "I hate homework." His mother said she understood but that maybe the next night he could just begin his homework by telling her how much he hates it and then ask for help. (This seemed to help; for the next 4 nights, John's mother did not have to nag him to start his homework.) When asked what happened on Sunday, John laughed and said that he didn't have any homework. Then they both laughed, and his mother said, "He should have given himself a check. Then he will reach his goal sooner."

Wednesday   When asked why he didn't put a check in the box for #6, "Clear room floor before bed," John laughed again and said, "There was nothing to pick up."

Thursday   The same thing happened for #6 as on Wednesday, and John added, "I'm a little more careful now about leaving things on the floor, because I hate picking up."

Friday   John's excuse for arguing about taking a bath was "I guess I'm a regular boy."

Saturday   Mother and son explained that they had celebrated on Saturday because all of the day's boxes had checkmarks. Mom had spontaneously offered him the opportunity to watch an especially long television show that would end past his bedtime.

Sunday   When discussing Sunday's empty boxes, John laughed as he explained why he hadn't cleared his floor before going to bed that day: His dad had said that he would do it for him because John had been trying so hard all week. His mom was so pleased with his honesty that she said he deserved a check in that box anyway.

The following weeks had some ups and downs, but the one wonderful result was the lessening of conflict and the family's working together more positively. When John was asked how everything was going, he said, "You know, they smile at me now!" His mom cried when he said this and told the therapist later that she never realized how angry and sullen she looked most of the time.

INCREASING PARENTS' UNDERSTANDING OF DYSLEXIA

When parents learn that their child is dyslexic, they frequently experience a mixed sense of relief (Houston, 1987) and comfort in finally knowing what is causing their child's problems. Some parents feel apprehension that they, too, may have the same problem with language. These parents may feel this apprehension when the diagnosticians describe the child's difficulties and give details concerning its negative impact on functioning at home and in the classroom. Hearing this information often triggers memories about their own past (or present) functioning.

As intervention progresses, the parents' memories of their own childhood experiences at home and at school may enhance their understanding and increase their level of empathy. This increased understanding may provide an opportunity for the parents to receive help and make changes that they never thought possible. Although the parents' discovery of their own problems can be difficult, gradually the process results in positive attitudinal changes that lead to better relationships with their dyslexic child and with others.

If a parent discovers that he or she is a dyslexic, then he or she may feel other emotions, such as denial, anger, fear, guilt, shame, loss, and panic. Some psychologists suggest that parents go through stages similar to those experienced when grieving after the loss of a loved one. The important point is that most parents, when given appropriate HP support and understanding, work through this spectrum of normal feelings. Through education and increased knowledge that the outlook for their youngster can be positive, parents can become strong advocates for their children. Many enter the field of language disorders or become advocates for other children.

Parents' initial negative feelings change as they observe progress such as obtaining an appropriate school placement, the implementation of the correct approach to teaching language skills. The child's improvement and successes change everyone's negative feelings. Given the right information and support, the parents regain confidence in themselves. When taught properly, the child also gradually gains confidence in him- or herself as a learner, and this leads to greater self-esteem and a more typical childhood.

Helping Parents Help Children

Teaching children who are dyslexic properly means addressing such stress areas for dyslexics as inability to follow directions, not having a sense of time, lack of organization, failure to complete assignments on time, leaving chores until the last minute, forgetting tasks such as homework, and being resistant when help is offered. Each of these

requires a teaching approach that includes a multisensory plan—one that encompasses structure, organization, integration, and feedback.

HPs need to become familiar with material that deals with organizational skills and time management. Then they can teach parents how this information can be applied to every facet of a child's functioning such as the child's morning routines, daytime activities, playtime, homework, and bedtime routines. The use of lists, calendars, and organizers of all types should be a focus in such learning (see Chapter 18).

Organization and time management must be a family affair. Every child and adult living under the same roof participates in and benefits from strategies that improve organization and time management. The advantage of such approaches is that they increase everyone's efficiency without placing a constant focus on one child and his or her problems. The plan, however, must be designed to fit the individual needs of the family. A plan that is effective for one family may not be suitable for another—only the general guidelines remain the same.

In addition, time, money, and progress all need to be discussed with the parents when intervention is being formulated. If the child attends a general education classroom in the local school, then the more individual sessions with direct explicit instruction, the better. Ideally, 1 hour per day, five times per week, provides the level of intensity from which most children benefit. This frequency of sessions, however, is rarely affordable; therefore, it is recommended that the child have individual sessions with the HP no less than three times per week. Anything less than this ignores the dyslexic's difficulty with memory and the need for frequent and intensive reinforcement.

Less experienced or uncertified tutors may recommend one session per week. Such an approach is both unproductive and harmful. Under such a regimen the dyslexic child will not acquire the necessary skills, and both child and parent will become discouraged and believe that they are at fault rather than blame the once-a-week schedule. The child will feel an additional reason to believe that he or she is "dumb"—and may feel that even with help (which, of course, is not of an appropriate intensity), he or she cannot learn. Moreover, when more appropriate, more intense help is found, the child who has failed recently will be less likely to want to try again—he or she may reason, "Why risk another failure?"

Helping Parents Who Feel Overwhelmed

Sometimes when parents learn more about the recommended intervention plan, they feel overwhelmed. They lament about how much time it will take. This is when HP support is most necessary. It often helps to remind parents of the enormous amount of time they now expend in coaxing, nagging, arguing, and battling resistance—most of which ends in failure for both the child and the parents. The HP can make this amount of time concrete by examining a situation the parents have related to the HP.

Help for parents can vary from several sessions per week with telephone feedback to one session per week with a therapist—until the parents and therapist agree that enough new parenting strategies have been learned. Parents should feel confident to move ahead on their own, with only an occasional session for monitoring.

Parents may sometimes consciously or unconsciously be resistant to making changes. Their resistance to change is no different from their child's opposition to change. In part such resistance may stem from prior, built-in thinking patterns coupled with a fear of failure. Resistance may also result from past successes that could not be sustained. When the HP communicates his or her understanding of these fears to the parents,

along with reassurances that the HP will be there to help, the parents' courage to try once again can be rebuilt. Much effort and many attempts are necessary before success is achieved, but it will happen.

Addressing Co-occuring Attention-Deficit/Hyperactivity Disorder

Language processing difficulties in a dyslexic child are frequently misidentified as **attention-deficit/hyperactivity disorder** (ADHD). This, in turn, often leads to the suggestion of a trial on medication. Regardless of whether the child is later determined to have ADHD, it is good for the HP to remember, as Healy stated, that showing the parents of children with ADHD some techniques to control behavior is at least as effective as, if not superior to, the use of medication alone:

> Whether we want to admit it or not, the way the parents and/or caregivers interact with children is critically important to teaching them how to pay attention. These interactions also communicate subtle messages about what is appropriate to pay attention to, the thing most children diagnosed with these difficulties don't seem to understand. (1990, p. 178)

Judging the Competence of Helping Professionals

Parents of children with learning disabilities may have questions concerning the competence of the HPs working with their child. Most often, more than one HP is involved in the intervention process. When team members disagree concerning a diagnosis or a course of action, the situation becomes highly problematic. Nothing is as destructive to a child and his or her family and can shake the confidence of parents more than observing conflicts among several HPs on whose knowledge they depend. The likelihood of such a traumatic situation is reduced when each person serving the family has been well trained in parent–HP relationships and can work with the others as a team to help the child and the family.

When the parents first become involved with their child's intervention, their focus is usually on why their child cannot read or succeed in school. To them academic achievement is the issue. As they become more knowledgeable, parents gain a greater awareness of the wide, negative effects that untreated dyslexia can have on children—diminished self-esteem, restricted socialization, delayed emotional development, and lifelong effects from depression. More often than not, there is no overall structure to the oral and/or written suggestions or reports given by HPs to parents. At its crux, this material deals only with how to bring help to the child through others. This material often omits the crucial contribution that parents can make to assist in their child's remediation process. As a consequence, coexisting problems in social, emotional, and behavioral areas frequently remain unresolved, and family difficulties persist.

During the initial stage of seeking information, parents often feel overwhelmed. They may have difficulty sorting out relevant information and understanding their role, and they may perceive that the HPs dealing with them (e.g., diagnosticians, physicians, teachers, special educators) do not agree on a definition of dyslexia (see Chapter 14), what constitutes a specific language-based learning disability, and what interventions have had demonstrated success.

Planning, timing, organization, and memory difficulties all may affect the parents' ability to understand and follow through with suggestions made by HPs. These capabilities constitute an individual's executive functioning ability. They are often poorly developed in dyslexics, including parents who have dyslexia. It is not unusual to hear

a psychologist, a psychotherapist, or a speech-language pathologist tell another HP (with great exasperation) how a child's parents failed to carry out a series of remedial suggestions. Such exclamations reflect the HP's inability to recognize in one or both parents symptoms that are similar to those in the child. Moreover, such HPs need to appreciate how their own lack of knowledge about effective interventions can produce such negative outcomes with parents. Mental health HPs who have obtained additional training in this area report increased successes in working effectively with the parents of dyslexic children.

If parents are to play their critical role in helping their dyslexic child, then the HP must develop and model a structured multisensory program for them. Parents of a youngster with learning disabilities continue to have more responsibility for their child over a significantly longer period of time than the parents of a nondyslexic (Fine, 1980). To help their child with organizing the basic routines of daily life, parents must become involved in showing their youngster how to do the following: ask the right questions; talk through problems; plan ahead; and, in general, insert language between impulse and behavior. HPs often urge parents to talk with their children; certainly, this is a reasonable suggestion. This advice ignores the fact, however, that many of these parents may not know how to talk to their children; they themselves need to be taught that skill.

An emphasis among the helping professions is teaching HPs in training to empower those whom they are assisting. When this principle is misunderstood, it can become not only less than helpful but also dangerous. Parents who feel inadequate and who have little knowledge about learning problems and few skills in this area initially cannot be empowered. To attempt to do so would be similar to telling a 6-year-old who has never been off a farm that he or she is empowered to cross a major street in a large metropolitan city. No one would do such a thing before instructing, practicing, and making certain that the child has the "tools" to cross the street without getting injured.

DIAGNOSIS AND BEYOND

It is difficult for parents to project themselves (and their child) into the future. Telling parents about all of the past and present famous/successful dyslexics is hardly reassuring. Once they hear the word *dyslexia,* emotional and intellectual turmoil often sets in. Parents frequently pass through several stages: denial, anger, guilt, shame, blame, overprotection, and (finally) emotional adaptation (Fine, 1980). They may have little idea about the competencies needed by the HPs who will work with their child and/or provide support. The HP needs to be prepared to deal directly with three questions the parents will bring up immediately:

1. "Will my child get better?" The HP must assure the parents that dyslexia is not new, that there are approaches for treating this condition that have proven successful, and that dyslexia is not a disease.

2. "How long will it take?" The HP's experience will help parents understand that they cannot expect overnight cures. Dyslexia's neurological factors preclude cures, but remediation can be attained with appropriate intervention. The process takes time, yet progress will be seen by the child and his or her parents and teachers.

3. "How much will it cost?" Not only is the diagnostic and intervention process both bewildering and overwhelming to the child's parents, often it also is financially

burdensome. Many parents may be unable to follow through with an elaborate evaluation or afford multiple sessions. Has help become unattainable? No!

The HP must indicate to the parents the difference between the ideal situation and reality. The emphasis should be on describing a step-by-step process. Explanation should focus on how much can be accomplished with some good information and on the need to begin intervention immediately. The HP should reassure parents that he or she will monitor the situation and seek further evaluations and/or intervention only when needed and in a way that will be affordable.

At this time, outreach is crucial; the list of community resources that the HP has built becomes essential. Knowing which HPs or agencies offer help and use sliding-scale fees is very helpful. It is necessary for parents to be aware that the public school system is bound by law to provide help to qualified students (e.g., under the auspices of the Individuals with Disabilities Education Improvement Act of 2004, PL 108-446). The more the HP demonstrates an unwillingness to give up seeking affordable help from HPs and legally required supports from schools, the less likely the parents will be to give up. Parents model the HP's actions and gain confidence in doing so.

The parents' next set of questions may include "Why didn't the school pick this up sooner?" or "Why can't the teacher help?" The parents' anguish about every aspect of their child's life will most likely be directed at the teachers and at the person who has just delivered the diagnosis of dyslexia. This situation requires that the HP be able to display a high degree of empathy and patience and have the ability to cope with a great deal of anger without taking it personally or withdrawing from it.

Parents are often furious at the school system. They may blame the school not only for failing to detect their child's condition earlier or even denying its existence but also for causing it. The HP must be careful not to appear to support this view by agreeing with the parents. Although the parents' frustration and anger with the school may be somewhat justified, seeing only the negatives will not help. Parents need to be guided in a more beneficial direction.

At this stage of the helping process, the HP's ability to accept the parents as they are and convey genuine respect for them and their situation is crucial. Establishing this type of atmosphere allows the parents to feel safe enough to hear what they must do. It enables them to become constructive members on the intervention team that will help their child.

INTERVENTION STRATEGIES

Houston (1992) asked the following: What good does it do to diagnose dyslexia, pinpoint the specific difficulties of the client, and then send the individual to someone for remediation if that person does not know what to do about alleviating the various problems? The way to avoid this dilemma lies in the HP's being well informed about research on effective intervention approaches, knowing how to gain access to appropriate community resources, and having a list of well-trained academic therapists to whom parents can be referred.

Most books on dyslexia for parents (and those written for HPs) indicate that dyslexia can affect every aspect of a child's life. They tend to reassure both parents and educators that all is treatable, that with proper intervention at home and at school, the child will succeed or can fulfill his or her potential. As a result, false hopes of quick remediation may be raised.

Parents of dyslexics may have read books or taken their child to participate in study groups for typical children, only to find such experiences of little or no help with their child. Parents may need to integrate a whole new body of knowledge with what they already know.

When interventions are designed and implemented for the dyslexic child, consideration must be given to the difficulties that parents may experience—often as a result of dyslexia—in following through on an intervention plan. Giving a list of suggestions to parents is often as ineffective as presenting the dyslexic child with a similar set of instructions. Scheduled activities may be forgotten, the list may be lost, or the date and/or time of appointments may be confused. HPs who are attempting to help the child may become frustrated with the parents. Consequently, attention needs to be given both to the parents' training program and to the child's intervention plan.

Parent Intervention

Parents need help not only with their own emotions but also with the school system and teachers as well as their friends, neighbors, and extended family. Grandparents can be a real source of help to both the parents and the dyslexic child. Or, they may be a great impediment by further undermining the confidence of the dyslexic child's parents at a time when they are feeling most inadequate and are questioning their ability to parent their child. It is often helpful to suggest that the grandparents visit the HP for their own session during which the diagnosis is interpreted and a plan is developed containing specific ways in which the grandparents can assist.

The dyslexic child's siblings are another group about which the parents will need guidance. If the parents do not bring up the subject, then the HP must not let it remain ignored. The well-trained HP will explain the issues directly to the brothers and sisters of the dyslexic child. When this is not possible, the information is conveyed by the parents. The HP, however, must assist the parents concerning how the message is to be delivered. The tone must be one that mutes difficulties and highlights strengths. The dyslexic child is not "a problem"; rather he or she is someone who has some difficulties with language and who has some skills in other areas, just as the siblings may be good at some activities but not others. For example, some dyslexics are quite talented musically. One such youngster might be the one chosen to sing a solo in the school chorus. This child's sibling, who is doing well in school, might be extremely embarrassed if asked to sing alone before a group of peers. The sibling with a "musical disability" can hide this lack of skill better. He or she is never considered as a child with a disability but merely as one who cannot carry a tune. The HP should have a repertoire of stories similar to this example. The intent of telling such stories is to make clear that the dyslexic child has a disability only in certain environments.

After hearing some of these examples, one 14-year-old brother of a child with dyslexia said, "Oh, I get it. It was like me in algebra. I just couldn't understand the teacher. A few other kids couldn't either, but my best friend could. That made me feel dumb. I was getting Ds and Fs. After Christmas, when we got back to school, we had a new teacher. The other one had gone skiing and got badly hurt. With the new teacher I began to get Bs and even As, sometimes. My parents asked me if I was working harder. I said, 'No. In fact I had to work harder with the other teacher because I couldn't understand his accent.' My parents never thought of that as being my problem and neither did I, until I realized how clearly my new teacher spoke." Then he laughed and said, "Maybe I have an auditory processing problem like my brother. I sure hope he gets teachers who speak the way he understands."

Even when the parents have been fortunate enough to secure a thorough, competent evaluation, their initial understanding of its implications may be hazy. Consequently, assisting parents becomes a process of providing information over a period of time. In addition, the HP will need to provide support to the parents as they cope with the many emotional issues that appear during the course of intervention. Consequently, the HP's assistance cannot be hurried, unsystematic, or brief. It must be thorough, comprehensible, and sufficiently flexible so that as changes occur over time, the type of support provided is appropriately modified.

Language learning disabilities change over time as the child develops and use of language becomes more complex. In a parallel fashion, the parents' problems also change as the dyslexic child develops. Although this also can be said about most children without dyslexia, the parents of a dyslexic youngster are confronted by a different timetable. In addition, the parents continually battle with the problem of how to help without adding to their child's negative self-esteem. For example, during adolescence, when most youngsters are beginning to separate from their parents and need less help from their parents, the dyslexic child still needs assistance. The child's wish to be more like his or her peers may lead the child to deny his or her learning needs and causes conflicts at home when refusing the help offered by his or her parents.

In this situation, the HP, the parents, and the adolescent dyslexic need a session together. During their interaction, the following should be outlined: where the adolescent was when he or she began the intervention, the progress that has been made, the areas of difficulty that remain, and new problems that may occur and that can result in a setback in school performance. The consequences of a refusal to participate in intervention and how this will limit the individual's choices in the future must also be discussed.

At the end of the session, the HP must give a clearly written document (in bullet style) to the adolescent. The HP should explain that the adolescent can use this document to monitor his or her situation and to know when to ask for or to reinstate help.

Consequently, the document must include clear descriptions of early warning signs, such as slipping grades; increased time to complete homework; a number of assignment deadlines missed; increasingly frequent conflicts with teachers and parents; the dyslexic's own disappointment regarding progress; and secretly felt anxiety, stress, and/or depression.

Both the joint session and the resulting document need to have a positive thrust. They should not be viewed as a warning or a prediction of doom and gloom but as a way to check for times when the student may need extra support or help with learning strategies. The session ends with positive statements by the HP that commend the adolescent on the progress made and that indicate that the dyslexic may be making the right decision for the moment but also mention the hope that the individual's good judgment will allow him or her to seek help when needed. The individual should not be made to feel that this refusal of help is a step backward but rather an opportunity to grow and gain control over the situation.

The parents will need support at this time. They also will benefit from suggestions and guidelines as to what to say and do as time passes and the adolescent makes no request for help. Parents need to know which clues signal that it is time to step in and when it is okay to allow the consequences of failure to provide the child with an impetus to seek help again.

The HP needs to make certain that the dyslexic child's parents understand how important it is that they encourage and support their youngster; unconditional love needs

to be not just the order of the day but also the order of a lifetime. Parents need to hear that they—with guidance from the HP—must become their child's advocate. Primarily, it will be the parents who will have to deal with the school system and find ways to elicit cooperation and understanding from their child's teachers. Finally, the overarching directive for parents is patience, patience, patience.

Child Intervention

The HP working with the parents and the child must be knowledgeable about the child's needs. The process of designing intervention for the dyslexic youngster begins with the development of an organizing structure. Both the parents and the HP must help the child become organized. For example, a written activity schedule needs to be generated—one that describes what is to happen and when it is to occur; a regular routine needs to be established and followed; an uncluttered, quiet workplace must be established for the child; and the parents should provide help with their youngster's school assignments. Getting organized is a monumental task, especially when the parents have their own problems in this area. Hence, the HP needs to teach such skills and help parents monitor the home front. (See Chapter 18 for tips on arranging the home environment for better organization and study.)

Once an intervention strategy for a dyslexic child has been implemented, close monitoring becomes a high priority. This will allow modifications to be made promptly when progress is not occurring as anticipated.

Often, when an intervention is implemented but the child's academic progress is not evident and coexisting emotional problems increase, the original learning disability diagnosis is questioned. Both parents and HPs may begin to believe that the child's emotional and psychological difficulties are the "real" cause. These issues, rather than the lack of a well-integrated intervention strategy, become the focus of attention. Rarely does the focus shift to more intensive help for the family. At this critical juncture, mental health services are often suggested. Such a recommendation fosters a greater loss of self-esteem and increased feelings of inadequacy in both the child and the parents.

Many HPs believe that prior to a shift away from school- and home-based intervention, the first attempts at adjusting a chosen intervention approach should include the following: effecting environmental changes at home and at school, securing an adequate academic program, offering more parental support, systematic monitoring, and making frequent reevaluations. A trial on medication should be the last resort.

THE ROLES OF MOTHERS AND FATHERS

The parenting roles of both the mother and the father have frequently been stressed as fathers have received more encouragement to participate actively in the home and in child rearing. This reflects changes in society as well as an increase in knowledge of men's and women's emotions and ways of interacting. Although many HPs recognize that the heavier burden of parenting still rests with the mother (even when both parents hold jobs outside the home), there is a noticeable trend toward the father's greater involvement. See the section for this chapter in Appendix B for more information on fathers' roles. To make generalizations in this area, however, would be a mistake, except that it is wise—although not always necessary—to encourage both parents to participate. Sometimes, in fact, this encouragement may have a negative effect. It is always prudent to also consider the cultural background and preferences of the family when making recommendations for what parents' roles should be in treatment.

The HP needs to assess the personalities and strengths and weaknesses of the child's parents. If one parent is more articulate with adults, then he or she may need to take the lead in school conferences. The more nurturing parent—not always the mother—needs to be encouraged to interact more directly with the child. What comes naturally to each parent will allow each to help his or her child more authentically and successfully. In addition, this approach helps each individual to feel more adequate with regard to his or her parenting skills.

Thus, the HP plays a very positive role for the parents by aiding them in discovering how each can best help and by showing each how to help the child. This directs their attention to how their spouse's strengths are an asset, thereby reducing the adversarial, conflictual environment that often develops. Parents should be trained in how to establish a co-equal relationship to help their dyslexic child. According to Shaywitz (2003), significant adults play a crucial role in their children's future outlook. Children with dyslexia need adults who are knowledgeable, patient, and persevering and who actively create change to support the children's efforts to succeed.

In cases in which only one parent is the child's primary caregiver or only one parent is participating in intervention, a support network needs to be established. The HP should see to it that no single parent or guardian is left alone to deal with the complexities brought on by dyslexia.

HELPING PARENTS PRIORITIZE

Because many professionals are involved in treatment for individuals with dyslexia, the HP must help parents set priorities and should recognize the critical nature of timing. All forms of intervention need to be considered in light of what will keep the situation for both child and parents as normal as possible. Often, parents express a desire to deal with all of the issues simultaneously, assuming that such an approach will hasten success. Not only is this far from the truth, but attacking all of the issues at once also can have the opposite effect—that of leading the child to feel like a "basket case." For example, some evaluations end with a statement recommending speech and language help, academic therapy, occupational therapy, computer keyboard training, and psychotherapy (individual and family). Needless to say, no child or family could tolerate all of this help at once emotionally, financially, or practically (in terms of time). It is possible, however, to prioritize and address a few issues at a time.

Depending on the age of the child, usually it is most urgent to secure academic therapy and to counsel the parents briefly. Other interventions should be postponed, if at all possible. If it seems urgent to implement many therapies at first, then placement in a special school may be warranted—one in which help is part of everyday school activity and in which the child will not be seen as being different from the other students.

Decisions about priorities should be made by a team consisting of all of the HPs that assessed the child and the child's parents. Each team member should be able to justify his or her list to the satisfaction of all team members. This should be done at a meeting designed specifically for that purpose.

THE HELPING PROFESSIONAL AS ADVOCATE

In addition to helping the child at home, the parents will have to communicate with the school. Therefore, the HP must ensure that the dyslexic child's parents are knowl-

edgeable about **due process** requirements, PL 108-446, the Family Educational Rights and Privacy Act of 1974 (PL 93-380), and the difference between advocacy and direct intervention.

Although the dyslexic child's parents must play the major role in being advocates for their youngster, particularly with the school system, they will need the guidance of the HP. This, in turn, means that the HP must develop considerable expertise in this arena.

TRAINING REGIMEN FOR THE HELPING PROFESSIONAL (HP)

As of 2005, there were no national standards for HPs who lead parent groups. If HPs are to be adequately trained to help parents assist their dyslexic child or to serve as direct agents of change, then minimum training requirements need to be put in place; these include the following:

- *Knowledge concerning typical child development:* HPs must understand the stages of development in order to help parents of a dyslexic child appreciate the complex nature of the physical, psychological, social, and language forces that influence children's behavior during each age period. Expectations for dyslexics, who develop differently in certain areas, must be explained in terms of what constitutes typical development (Berk, 1996).

- *Knowledge about neurobiology:* HPs should have an understanding of neurobiology to answer parents' "why" questions about dyslexia, which is a neurobiologically based syndrome. HPs need to learn some basic neurology and neuroanatomy and should have a working knowledge of **neuropsychology**. "Models [of human behavior] which leave out man's physical organism are bound to be inadequate for the task of making behavior intelligible" (Guthrie, 1950).

- *Knowledge about language development:* At a minimum, HPs should be familiar with the descriptive view of language development, which holds that a language disorder is "any disruption in the learning or use of the conventional system of arbitrary signals used by persons in the environment as a code for representing ideas about the world" (Bloom & Lahey, 1978).

- *Knowledge of assessment procedures:* HPs must understand assessment procedures; however, it must be stressed that the child is not a number, does not always fit into a discrepancy formula, and must never be dismissed as having "no problem" based on measurements alone. As Einstein stated, "Not everything that counts can be counted and not everything that can be counted, counts" (as quoted in *Albert Einstein: A Man for All Seasons,* 1995).

- *Up-to-date information concerning direct intervention techniques:* HPs must stay current about direct intervention techniques in use, particularly in regard to the teaching of language (reading, writing, spelling). The research literature (e.g., Brady & Moats, n.d.) supports code-based techniques for such teaching and strategies that include a simultaneous, multisensory, language-based approach.

- *An awareness that dyslexia's symptoms change:* HPs must recognize that the symptoms of dyslexia change as the individual's language becomes more complex and as the individual moves from oral to written expression and reading.

- *An ability to deal with the complexities and controversies concerning ADHD:* HPs should have an understanding of issues pertaining to ADHD, which can co-occur with dyslexia.

- *Supervised experience and training in intervention techniques:* HPs should learn how to implement intervention procedures that are structured and organized. Such intervention should include a monitored program for the parents of the dyslexic child, which can be intertwined with the intervention provided for the child.

- *Role playing and practicum experiences:* The student HP learns by doing; supervision during training must be part of the curriculum.

The well-trained HP who is helping the parents of a dyslexic child needs to be knowledgeable about the use of multiple therapies—often including the use of medication. (The use of medication is a highly charged topic for parents, teachers, and HPs.) If interventions are to be beneficial, then parents must have confidence in the competence of the HP making the suggestions. This, in turn, requires that the HP be knowledgeable and experienced and, most important, have a track record of successful past work with dyslexic children. HPs should take a stand on issues (e.g., the use of medication) by drawing support from a knowledge base that justifies the actions they take. Consequently, the student HP needs to read widely—across disciplines—to serve both children and their parents effectively. It is most important that practitioners be knowledgeable about these two issues:

1. *Differing definitions of dyslexia, learning disabilities, and specific language disability—and the confusions that still persist in the field:* For example, The International Dyslexia Association published its latest definition of dyslexia in 2003 (Lyon, Shaywitz, & Shaywitz, 2003; see Chapter 1 for the definition and a discussion), and this definition does not deal with often-found coexisting conditions such as difficulties with organization, timing, memory, and integration. It is when conditions such as these are addressed that the parents usually need to become involved.

2. *The major controversies in regard to diagnosis and intervention:* What constitutes a comprehensive evaluation for children suspected of having dyslexia is not agreed on. Recommendations often vary, depending on what is available and how costly it will be. (For further discussion of assessment see Chapter 7.) There also is no general agreement as to what the intervention for dyslexia should be. Its complexity precludes a quick and simple prescription.

Similar to the Hula-Hoop and other fads, the quick, unsubstantiated cures for learning disabilities come and go—vision training, tinted lenses, certain drugs, megavitamins, special diets, and neurological training. Vulnerable parents—those with children whose problems are not being remedied rapidly—are often ready to accept well-publicized claims about "successful" new approaches. What complicates matters is that frequently there is a HP in the community who supports one of these therapies or a handful of parents who swear by such a therapy because of how their children have been helped. HPs must exercise extreme caution when they are working with parents who reveal they have already started using one of these controversial therapies with their youngster. Criticizing the parents' action can lead to the premature termination of the HP's own intervention process. The HP can say, "I do not wish to undermine your previous choice, but I wonder if you would read some material that I have that raises questions about the effectiveness of the approach you have tried." The HP should then present

material from reputable sources that contain information on evidence-based interventions that target the needs of the child.

Research stresses the need for properly trained HPs in the learning disabilities and dyslexia field. The need is becoming increasingly apparent and is being addressed by an ever greater emphasis on preservice and in-service training for HPs. No longer is it appropriate for physicians, psychologists, psychiatrists, social workers, educators, speech-language pathologists, audiologists, occupational therapists, and members of any other discipline involved in helping dyslexics and their families to be knowledgeable only in their own field of expertise. Dyslexia is a complex condition that requires a multidimensional intervention approach.

Along with understanding the child's condition, it is necessary for the HP to attend equally intensively to the parents' needs on a continuing basis. To help the parents help their child, the HP should give them information about child development. Parents of dyslexics should understand differences in the learning patterns of children. HPs working with dyslexia must be knowledgeable and able to communicate accurate information on these topics. An HP can overcome a lack of training by working in a multidisciplinary setting.

HPs who help dyslexics usually have not been exposed to a special curriculum to teach them how to support their clients' parents. At best, training in how to assist these parents is generic. Most often it involves addressing only the anxieties, fears, denial, depression, and confusion that parents experience at the outset of an intervention with their dyslexic child. HPs must also learn what information parents need and must know how to convey this material so that parents will not only understand what is to be done but also will carry out the necessary actions.

To the student HP, all of this may seem overwhelming and may give rise to such questions as the following:

1. If my way of communicating is difficult for these parents to understand, then does that mean I cannot help them?

2. What is my way of communicating, and what can I do about it?

The answer to the first question is that the student HP can help the parents provided that he or she becomes knowledgeable about dyslexia and the other areas listed previously. Then the student HP follows specific guidelines for effective communication (outlined previously in this chapter).

With regard to the second question, the key is for the student HP to consult with an already trained HP who can assess both the student HP's knowledge about dyslexia and his or her style of communication. As stated previously, it is also necessary for the student to learn by doing, in a practicum situation that includes systematic supervision.

HPs must be trained so that they can help parents understand and accept the following: 1) the most current, widely accepted definition of dyslexia; 2) the fact that a thorough multidisciplinary evaluation has shown that their child is dyslexic; and 3) that specific interventions, based on research findings, will benefit their child.

It is of utmost importance that HPs avoid defining dyslexic children only in terms of their problem. A dyslexic child is a child with a specific problem and he or she is not the problem. Similarly, a child with blond hair is still a child first and foremost and would not be referred to as only a blond, which would ignore all of his or her other attributes. Children with dyslexia are multidimensional. Along with the loving and nurturing given by parents and teachers must also come positive ways to view the

child and to build up self-esteem and ways the child can stand out or excel. In other words, "Let his strengths and not his weaknesses define him as a person" (Shaywitz, 2003, p. 313).

Often when others hear the term *dyslexia,* it elicits a stream of negative verbalizations. Rarely do people respond, "Oh, he must be very bright," or, "Oh, she must be very talented." It is disheartening for the HP to hear this negativity about dyslexia. Often when parents or teachers of dyslexics are asked to name one positive trait, they cannot. Consequently, from the very outset, HPs dealing with dyslexia must emphasize the individual's strengths.

THE HELPING PROFESSIONAL'S LIBRARY

The well-trained HP needs to have a complete library of books, videotapes, and audiotapes that can be lent to and read by the parents of a dyslexic child. Providing books to the parents will be useful only when the HP offers additional, concrete help regarding how to use such information. No book should be given to the parents unless the HP has read it. This will ensure that the book is relevant to the child's situation. The HP could devote part of each session to planning with the parent how information in the book can be used with the child.

There are many well-written books on dyslexia for parents and teachers, such as the following, listed in from most to least recently published:

Ten in Every Hundred: The What, Who, How and Where of Dyslexia (Porch & Gilroy, 2003)

Overcoming Dyslexia: A New and Complete Science-Based Program for Reading Problems at Any Level (Shaywitz, 2003)

Parenting the Child with Learning Disabilities (Adelizzi & Goss, 2001)

Straight Talk About Reading (Hall & Moats, 1999)

What's Wrong with Me?: Learning Disabilities at Home and School (Cicci, 1995)

The Dyslexic Scholar (Nosek, 1995)

Understanding Dyslexia (Houston, 1992)

Understanding Learning Disabilities: A Parent Guide and Workbook (National Center on Learning Disabilities/Learning Disabilities Council, 1991)

Overcoming Dyslexia (Hornsby, 1984)

In addition, excellent videotapes are available, such as *How Difficult Can This Be?: F.A.T. City* (Eagle Hill School & Rosen, 1989), *Keeping Ahead in School* (Levine, 1990), and a series on learning disabilities—*LD/LA: Learning Disabilities/Learning Abilities* (Birsh, 1997)—that clarifies dyslexia as being distinct from other learning disabilities and explains that ADHD is different from a learning disability. Among some excellent reference books are *No Easy Answers: The Learning Disabled Child at Home and at School* (Smith, 1979), *Succeeding Against the Odds* (Smith, 1991), and *The Misunderstood Child* (Silver, 1988). These three books focus learning disabilities; dyslexia as a specific learning disability is not always addressed in these texts as it is in books on dyslexia.

Much new material is being published (books, audiotapes, videotapes, CD-ROMs; see Appendix B); the best advice to parents may be to check with their local dyslexia organization and HP. Special-needs librarians in public libraries can also be quite helpful.

Reading may be a problem for some parents because they have no time or have reading difficulties of their own. In such situations the HP might suggest that the parents obtain an audiotape of the book in question so that they could listen to it on their way to work or appointments. Those times may be some parents' only opportunity to listen to the audiotapes.

It is important that the HP keep current with the resources available for parents and teachers. Many parents will hear something on the radio, see something on television, or read an article in the newspaper or on the Internet about dyslexia, learning disabilities, or ADHD. Frequently, this will precipitate a call or visit from the parents because they want to discuss what they have just learned. Parents want HPs to have opinions on such matters. Not only do parents want to know what the HP thinks, but they also want those opinions to be supported by up-to-date research information.

QUALITIES NECESSARY IN HELPING PROFESSIONALS

If HPs are to help the parents of dyslexics be advocates for their children, then HPs must know what constitutes a comprehensive evaluation, who are the well-trained people in the community, and how to build a link between evaluation and help from these individuals. To do so effectively, HPs in a helping role must have the following qualities:

1. HPs must have a high level of empathy and a great deal of patience.

2. HPs must have the ability to listen with a "third ear"—to really hear what is being said while remembering that the parents may also be struggling with language.

3. HPs must be able to deal with the frustration and anger of others without taking it personally.

4. HPs must be able to offer emotional support while also teaching parents in concrete ways; suggestions that are only given orally and that are given without any follow-up often are useless.

5. HPs must be willing to secure additional knowledge (beyond coursework requirements) by reading, obtaining more academic training, and attending workshops and discussion groups in which experienced people in the field participate.

6. Early on, HPs must meet with other family members (even briefly) so that advice given later in the helping process will be more practical and relevant to the family.

7. HPs must be nonjudgmental and flexible when relating to others.

8. HPs must be able to empathize with the parents and communicate that empathy to the parents. This is crucial for building a trusting relationship in which the parents feel safe enough to try the HP's suggestions. For the parents, who already may feel inadequate, to risk trying is to risk failure. Unless they feel safe, they will often give up trying to help their child.

9. If the HP has children with dyslexia, then he or she must avoid frequent use of his or her children as an example. Not all children with learning disabilities are the same in terms of learning needs. Moreover, the child's parents may conclude that their youngster's situation is even more unfortunate because they lack the knowledge to help that the HP has. When such examples are used sparingly and appro-

priately, however, they can build the parents' confidence because they convey that the HP really does understand the family's situation.

10. The HP should recognize, as Carl Rogers once said, that being trustworthy does not mean being rigidly consistent but being dependably real. In other words, the HP should be consistent because the information is based on valid data and, therefore, is to be trusted.

Many other desirable qualities in HPs could be enumerated, but the list grows daunting. If a student HP thinks that he or she does not have some of the listed qualities, then these can be developed. Many of these attributes can be acquired through experience and direct teaching. Openness and a willingness to learn, coupled with meaningful interactions with experienced HPs, will help the student HP become an effective agent of change for the parents of dyslexic children. It will also mean that the HP will become a never-to-be-forgotten friend to both the child and the family.

The last but undoubtedly the most important quality the HP must have is a genuine sense of humor. It has been written that

> Joy and laughter are indispensable to emotional well being. To make others laugh is a talent but to be able to laugh at ourselves is as necessary to living as air is to breathing. Humor, when properly used, is a means of lessening personal hostility and dispelling self-hatred. Moreover, laughter is often effective in expressing the truth. We can often say in jest the things we would not dare to express directly. In situations of emotional tension, humor frequently helps those involved to gain the perspective they need to look at the situation realistically. (*Jewish Spirituality and Peace of Mind: Daily Meditations*, n.d., p. 5)

Dyslexic children and their parents must see others smile at them. Expressions of tension, discouragement, and frustration will appear on the faces of the HPs involved in helping dyslexics. Unlike normal youngsters, who see a lot of smiles, dyslexics are often robbed of this aspect of childhood. No child's world should be populated chiefly by serious faces.

The kind of humor that HPs should have is more than a knack for telling or laughing at jokes. It involves not taking oneself too seriously, appreciating the occasional absurdity of the human condition, and being able to smile and shake one's head at the kind of situations we all get ourselves into.

CONCLUSION

Those who diagnose and treat children with dyslexia need to be alert to the role that genetic factors play in this syndrome. Consequently, the well-trained HP will do more than merely recommend that parents of a dyslexic child complete a series of events. Knowledgeable HPs will monitor subsequent interventions and guide parents step by step through the process. Only in this way will the child with dyslexia be able to realize his or her true potential. Only in this way will everyone—child, parent, and society—benefit from the intellectual talent that lies within a child, for example, who says while riding in the car with his or her mother that she would see better if she turned on the "shinwield wiper."

As Adelizzi and Goss stated,

> Life is full of learning opportunities and your home is the most important class room your child will ever enter. Make it a place full of gentle words, warm conversation, and

careful listening. Make it a safe place where what your child says will be respected and what he doesn't say will be heard by the heart.

What a beautiful thought for HPs to help parents of dyslexic children live by.

REFERENCES

Adelizzi, J.U., & Goss, D.B. (2001). *Parenting children with learning disabilities.* Westport, CT: Bergin & Garvey.

Albert Einstein: A man for all seasons. (1995). Petaluma, CA: Pomegranate Calendars and Books.

Arnold, E.L. (1978). *Helping parents help their children.* New York: Brunner/Mazel.

Berk, L.E. (1996). *Infants, children, and adolescents* (2nd ed.). Boston: Allyn & Bacon.

Bernstein, D.K., & Tiegerman, E. (1997). *Language and communication disorders in children* (4th ed.). Boston: Allyn & Bacon.

Birsh, J.R. (1997). *LD/LA: Learning disabilities/learning abilities* [Videotape series]. West Tisbury, MA: Vineyard Video Productions.

Bloom, L., & Lahey, M. (1978). *Language development and language disorders.* Boston: Allyn & Bacon.

Brady, S., & Moats, L. (n.d.). *Informed instruction for reading success: Foundations for teacher preparation* [Position paper]. Baltimore: The International Dyslexia Association.

Chase, C.H., Rosen, G.D., & Sherman, G.F. (Eds.). (1996). *Developmental dyslexia: Neural, cognitive, and genetic mechanisms.* Timonium, MD: York Press.

Cicci, R. (1995). *What's wrong with me?: Learning disabilities at home and school.* Timonium, MD: York Press.

Eagle Hill School & Rosen, P. (Producers). (1989). *How difficult can this be?: F.A.T. city* [Videotape]. Alexandria, VA: PBS Video.

Family Educational Rights and Privacy Act of 1974, PL 93-380, 20 U.S.C. §§ 1221 *et seq.*

Fine, M.J. (1980). *Handbook on parent education.* San Diego: Academic Press.

Guthrie, E.R. (1950). The status of systematic psychology. *The American Psychologist, 5*(4), 97–101.

Hall, S.L., & Moats, L.C. (1999). *Straight talk about reading.* Chicago: Contemporary Books.

Healy, J.M. (1990). *Endangered minds: Why children don't think—and what we can do about it.* New York: Simon & Schuster/Touchstone.

Hornsby, B. (1984). *Overcoming dyslexia.* London: Martin Dunitz.

Houston, A.M. (1987). *Common sense about dyslexia.* Lanham, MD: University Press of America.

Houston, A.M. (1992). *Understanding dyslexia.* Lanham, MD: University Press of America.

Individuals with Disabilities Education Improvement Act of 2004, PL 108-446, 20 U.S.C. §§ 1400 *et seq.*

Jewish spirituality and peace of mind: Daily meditations. (n.d.). Hoboken, NJ: Ktav Publishing.

Levine, M. (1990). *Keeping ahead in school* [Audiotapes and book]. Cambridge, MA: Educators Publishing Service.

Lyon, G.R., Shaywitz, S.E., & Shaywitz, B.A. (2003). A definition of dyslexia. *Annals of Dyslexia, 53,* 1–14.

NCLD/Learning Disabilities. (1991). *Understanding learning disabilities: A parent guide and workbook.* Richmond, VA: Author.

Nosek, K. (1995). *The dyslexic scholar.* Dallas, TX: Taylor Publishing.

Pennington, B.F., Gilger, J.W., Olson, R.K., & DeFries, J.C. (1992). The external validity of age versus IQ-discrepancy definitions of reading disability: Lessons from a twin study. *Journal of Learning Disabilities, 29,* 562–573.

Porch, M., & Gilroy, M. (2003). *Ten in every hundred: The what, who, how and where of dyslexia* [Booklet]. Albuquerque, NM: Southwest Branch of The International Dyslexia Association. (Available from the publisher, 505-255-8234)

Shaywitz, S. (2003). *Overcoming dyslexia: A new and complete science-based program for reading problems at any level.* New York: Alfred A. Knopf.

Silver, L.B. (1988). *The misunderstood child.* New York: McGraw-Hill.

Smith, S.L. (1979). *No easy answers: The learning disabled child at home and at school.* New York: Bantam Doubleday Dell.

Smith, S.L. (1991). *Succeeding against the odds.* New York: Penguin Putnam.

Wechsler, D. (1991). *Wechsler Intelligence Scale for Children* (3rd ed.). San Antonio, TX: Harcourt Assessment.

Appendix A

Glossary

Holly Baker Hill

accent   Stress or emphasis on one syllable in a word or on one or more words in a phrase or sentence. The accented part is spoken louder, longer, and/or in a higher tone. The speaker's mouth opens wider while saying an accented syllable. *See also* suprasegmental.

accommodations   Changes within the general classroom to enable students to keep up with the education program, such as intensive instruction; reduced assignments; adapted test procedures; and use of computers, calculators, and tape recorders. The term *accommodations* is not used in the Individuals with Disabilities Education Improvement Act (IDEA) of 2004 (PL 108-446). That law, however, generally refers to supplemental services that are, for the most part, what Section 504 of the Rehabilitation Act Amendments of 1998 and the Americans with Disabilities Act of 1990 (PL 101-336) call *reasonable accommodations*.

active learning   Learning in which the learner mentally searches for connections between new and already known information.

active reading process   A reading method that offers the reader an effective system for processing the meaning of text in progressively deeper stages (e.g., preread, read, make margin notes, chunk, summarize).

addend   A number to be added to another. The numbers 1 and 2 are addends in $1 + 2 = 3$.

ADHD   *See* attention-deficit/hyperactivity disorder.

affix   A letter or a group of letters attached to the beginning or ending of a base word or root that creates a derivative with a meaning or grammatical form that is different than the base word or root. *See also* prefix, suffix.

affricate   A consonant speech sound that is articulated with the tongue touching the roof of the mouth (e.g., /ch/ in *chair*, /j/ in *judge*) (Henry, 2003; Moats, 2000).

agraphia   *See* specific agraphia.

air writing   *See* sky writing.

alexia   *See* word blindness.

allophones   Slight variations in production of vowels or consonants that are predictable variants of a phoneme (e.g., /p/ in *pot* and *spot*, /ă/ in *fast* and *tank*).

alphabet   A series of letters or signs arranged in a fixed sequence, each of which represents a spoken sound of that language. Knowledge of the 26 letters of the English alphabet is essential to the language skills—phonics, reading, writing, and spelling.

alphabetic language   A language, such as English, in which letters are used systematically to represent speech sounds, or phonemes.

alphabetic principle   The concept, understood by readers, that the letters on the page represent or map onto the sounds in spoken words.

alveolar   Pertaining to sounds produced with the tongue placed against the alveolar ridge behind the upper front teeth (e.g., /n/, /s/).

alveolar ridge   The gum ridge behind the upper front teeth.

amanuensis A person, such as a teacher, who writes while another person, such as a student, dictates words, sentences, or stories.

analytic Pertaining to instruction or a process that separates the whole into its constituent parts to reveal the relationships of the parts. Analytic phonics separates the whole word into its constituent parts so that students can deduce the phonic relationships of the separate orthographic patterns. *See also* synthetic.

anaphora Use of a pronoun or a definite article to refer to something already mentioned (e.g., The turtle moved slowly. *It* crept along the road).

Anglo-Saxon The language of the Germanic peoples (Angles, Saxons, and Jutes) who settled in Britain in the 5th and 6th centuries A.D. Anglo-Saxon was the dominant language in Britain until the Norman Conquest in 1066 and is a major contributor to the English language.

antonyms Words of opposite meaning.

appositive A noun or noun phrase that is placed after a noun to explain it more fully; it usually contains modifiers (e.g., Susan B. Anthony, *an influential suffragist,* appears on the silver dollar).

arbitrary learning New learning that has no logical connection to already acquired knowledge or practical relationships (in contrast to learning through guided discovery). *See also* guided discovery teaching, mnemonic strategies.

articulation The vocal production of speech, in which the mouth, tongue, lips, teeth, and other parts of the vocal tract are used in specific ways.

aspiration The push of air that accompanies the production of some stop consonants (e.g., /t/ in *top*) (Moats, 2000).

assessment Collection of information to make decisions about learning and instruction.

assistive technology Any item, piece of equipment, or product that is used to increase, maintain, or improve the functional capabilities of individuals with disabilities.

attention deficit disorder (ADD); attention disorder *See* attention-deficit/hyperactivity disorder.

attention-deficit/hyperactivity disorder (ADHD) Disorder characterized by difficulty with attending to and completing tasks, impulsivity, and/or hyperactivity that frequently co-occurs with but is not a learning disability. *Also called* attention deficit disorder (ADD), attention disorder. *See also* learning disability.

auditory discovery Listening and responding to guided questions to discover new information, such as when students echo words dictated by the teacher to discover a new common sound.

auditory discrimination *See* discrimination.

automaticity Ability to respond or react without attention or conscious effort. Automaticity in word recognition permits full energy to be focused on comprehension.

base word A word to which affixes are added (e.g., *whole* in *unwholesome*). A base word can stand alone. *See also* free morpheme.

bilabial Pertaining to consonant sounds produced with the two lips contacting each other.

biliteracy The ability to speak, read, and write in two languages.

blend Two or more adjacent consonants (a consonant blend) or two or more adjacent vowels (a vowel blend) whose sounds flow smoothly together. *See also* blending.

blending Fusing individual sounds, syllables, or words to produce meaningful units or to sound out (e.g., saying /m/ /ă/ /p/ as "map"; saying "tooth" and "brush" as "toothbrush").

blocked *See* continuant.

borrowing *See* regrouping.

bottom-up process *See* text-driven process.

bound morpheme A morpheme that must be attached to other morphemes (e.g., *-ed* in *spotted, -s* in *boys*, *pre-* in *preview*). *See also* free morpheme.

breve The curved diacritical mark (˘) above a vowel in a sound picture or phonic/dictionary symbol notation that indicates a short sound in a closed syllable, in which at least one consonant comes after the vowel in the same syllable (e.g., ĭt, căt, blĕnd; exception: dĭvide).

carrying *See* borrowing.

chameleon prefix A prefix whose final consonant changes based on the initial letter of the base word or root (e.g., *in-* changes to *ir-* before base words and roots beginning with *r*, such as *responsible*). *See also* euphony.

checkpoint *See* marker.

choral reading Reading in which the instructor and the student(s) read the passage aloud together. *See also* echo reading, shared reading.

circumflex A diacritical mark (^) placed over certain vowels when coding or when writing a sound picture to indicate an unexpected pronunciation. The circumflex is used in the *Alphabetic Phonics* (Cox, 1992) code to indicate when a vowel-*r* combination is accented (e.g., âr, êr, îr, ôr, ûr). The circumflex is also used over the circled *a* to indicate the /aw/ pronunciation before /l/ in a monosyllabic word (e.g., b â ll).

closed syllable A syllable ending with one or more consonants (e.g., *mat, hand*). The vowel is usually short. *See also* open syllable.

cloze technique Any of several ways of measuring a student's ability to restore omitted portions of an oral or written message from its remaining context. *Also called* fill-in-the-blank technique.

clue *See* context clue; *see also* marker.

coarticulation The phenomenon of word pronunciation in which adjacent sounds often are spoken in such a way that one phoneme seems to overlap, is changed by, and/or modifies another.

cognates *See* voiced–voiceless cognates.

cognitive strategies Self-regulating mechanisms, including planning, testing, checking, revising, and evaluating during an attempt to learn or to problem-solve. Use of cognitive strategies is a higher order cognitive skill that influences and directs the use of lower order skills.

collaborative learning Learning by working together in small groups, so as to understand new information or to create a common product.

column word The first word in the second column of a dictionary page. This word assists in determination of whether a target word will be found in the first or second column of the page.

combination *See* letter cluster.

combining form A morpheme to which other roots and/or affixes may be combined to form compound words or derivatives (e.g., *auto, hemi, bio*). Combining forms are usually of Greek origin and are sometimes referred to as roots instead of combining forms.

compound word A word composed of two or more smaller words (e.g., *doghouse*). A compound word may or may not be hyphenated depending on its part of speech and conventions of usage (e.g., in modern usage, *football* is not hyphenated). *See also* meaning-based word.

comprehension Making sense of what we read. Comprehension is dependent on good word recognition, fluency, vocabulary, worldly knowledge, and language ability.

comprehension monitoring The active awareness of whether one is understanding or remembering text being processed.

concept of a word Understanding that sentences are made up of strings of words; the ability to count words in oral sentences and to match spoken words to printed words as demonstrated by pointing to the words of a text while reading. *See also* finger-point reading.

conjunction A part of speech that serves to connect words, phrases, clauses, or sentences (e.g., *and, but, as, because*). *Also called* connectives.

consonant One of a class of speech sounds in which sound moving through the vocal tract is constricted or obstructed by the lips, tongue, or teeth during articulation.

consonant blend *See* blend.

consonant digraph *See* digraph.

consonant prefix A prefix with a consonant as the final letter. The spelling of a consonant prefix may change for euphony (e.g., *ad-* becomes *at-* in *attraction, in-* becomes *ir-* in *irresponsible*). *See also* euphony.

consonant suffix A suffix beginning with a consonant (e.g., *-ful, -ness*).

consonant-*le* syllable A syllable in final position of a word that ends in a consonant, an *l*, and final silent *e* (e.g., *mid*d*le, rif*le). *See also* final stable syllable.

consonant-vowel-consonant (CVC) Pertaining to a word or syllable composed of letters with a consonant-vowel-consonant pattern. Short words or syllables with this pattern are a common starting point for reading phonetically regular words.

context analysis Use of clues in a passage to infer the meaning of an unfamiliar word.

context clue Information from the immediate setting in which a word occurs, such as surrounding words, phrases, sentences, illustrations, syntax, or typography, that might be used to help determine the meaning and/or pronunciation of the word. *Also called* contextual clue, visual hint.

continuant Pertaining to speech sounds that are sustained in their production (e.g., /f/, /m/, /s/)

controlled text Text that is written using only sound–symbol relationships already taught to provide practice with specific decoding skills; used to apply phonics in reading of text.

convergence of evidence Evidence from the identical replication of a study in a similar population by other researchers. Convergence of evidence is important in drawing conclusion from research because the outcomes from single study are not sufficient to generalize across all populations.

cooperative learning Instructional approach in which students work together rather than compete to solve a problem or to complete a task.

cornering Use of thumb, index finger, and middle finger to expose only the guide words in the corners of dictionary pages in rapid succession to find the page on which the targeted entry word is defined.

corrective feedback Teacher responses during and following performance of a skill that is sensitive to the student's level and that guides him or her closer to mastery.

criterion-referenced test Test in which performance is assessed in terms of the kind of behavior expected of a person with a given score. A criterion-referenced test permits descriptions of a child's domain of knowledge represented in the test, allows an item-by-item description of knowledge attained and knowledge yet to be acquired, and may be standardized or informal. *See also* informal test, standardized test.

cross-modal integration Combination of information received as visual, auditory, kinesthetic, and tactile input.

curriculum-referenced test Test in which items are taken from the curriculum used in the child's classroom so that he or she is not tested on material that has not been taught. A curriculum-referenced test provides a good match between assessment and instruction and may be standardized or informal. *See also* informal test, standardized test.

cursive handwriting Handwriting with the slanted strokes of successive characters joined and the angles rounded.

CVC *See* consonant-vowel-consonant.

decodable text Text that is written at the independent reading level of a student; for the text to be decodable the student should be able to read 95%–100% of the words independently, with no more than one error per 20 words.

decode 1) To break the phonic code (to recognize a word). 2) To determine the pronunciation of a word by noting the position of the vowels and consonants.

deictic term A word whose use and meaning changes based on context (e.g., *I, you, tomorrow, here, there*).

deletion *See* elision; *see also* sound deletion.

derivation The process of building a new word from another word by adding affixes. For example, *deconstructing* is a derivative of *deconstruct,* which in turn is derived from *construct. See also* etymology.

derivational morpheme Morpheme added to a base word that creates a new word that is a different part of speech from that of the base word (e.g., *-ness* changes adjective *careless* into noun *carelessness*).

derivative A word made from a base word by the addition of one or more affixes.

detached syllable *See* nonsense word.

diacritical marking A distinguishing mark used in dictionaries and phonics programs to indicate the pronunciation of a letter or combination of letters. *See also* breve, circumflex, macron.

diagnostic Pertaining to instruction in which the teacher is constantly taking notice of how students are handling the lesson concepts. Diagnostic instruction is sometimes be used in conjunction with prescriptive instruction. *See also* prescriptive instruction.

diagnostic and prescriptive instruction Instruction in which students are engaged in components of the lesson while the teacher observes how students are handling the discrete components (diagnostic instruction) so that the teacher may plan instruction. The prescriptive part of the lesson may involve changes to permit additional practice, review, and/or multisensory activities.

digital texts *See* electronic texts.

digraph Two adjacent consonants (a consonant digraph) or two adjacent vowels (a vowel digraph) in the same syllable representing a single speech sound (e.g., *sh* in *wish, ee* in *feet*). *See also* diphthong, quadrigraph, trigraph.

diphthong Two adjacent vowels in the same syllable whose sounds blend together with a slide or shift during the production of the syllable (e.g., *oy* in *toy, ow* in *cow*). *See also* digraph.

directionality The direction used in a language for reading and writing. English is governed by left-to-right directionality.

discovery learning *See* Socratic method.

discovery words Group of related words used during guided discovery teaching to help students perceive a principle, pattern, or feature of the language. *See also* guided discovery teaching.

discrimination The process of noting differences between stimuli. Auditory discrimination involves listening for the position of a particular sound in a word.

dividend In division, the total amount that is to be divided into a given number of parts (divisor) (e.g., 15 is the dividend in $15 \div 3 = 5$). *See also* divisor.

division radical Mathematical symbol () used when writing long division facts.

divisor In division, the number that the total (dividend) is divided by (e.g., 3 is the divisor in $15 \div 3 = 5$).

double deficit Deficit in phonological awareness and rapid serial naming.

due process A requirement that basic procedural protections be provided before a school system can separate children with disabilities from those in general education; includes the

parents' right to receive notice of changes in their child's educational plan and a hearing if they disagree with the changes.

dysarthria   Neurological oral-motor dysfunction including weaknesses of the musculature necessary for making the coordinated movements of speech production.

dysgraphia   Extremely poor handwriting or the inability to perform the motor movements required for handwriting. The condition is associated with neurological dysfunction.

dyslexia   "Dyslexia is a specific learning disability that is neurobiological in origin. It is characterized by difficulties with accurate and/or fluent word recognition and by poor spelling and decoding abilities. These difficulties typically result from a deficit in the phonological component of language that is often unexpected in relation to other cognitive abilities and the provision of effective classroom instruction. Secondary consequences may include problems in reading comprehension and reduced reading experience that can impede growth of vocabulary and background knowledge" (Lyon, Shaywitz, & Shaywitz, 2003).

dyspraxia   Sensorimotor disruption in which the motor signals to the muscles, such as those necessary for speech production, are not consistently or efficiently received.

echo reading   Reading in which the instructor reads a paragraph aloud and has the student(s) read it aloud after the instructor has finished reading. *See also* choral reading, shared reading.

effect size   The degree to which a form of instruction is found through research to be more effective than another form.

electronic text   Text material that has been converted to a digital format on a computer. *Also called* e-text.

elision   A language task in which a part is taken away. *Also called* deletion.

ellipsis   Deletion of information from a portion of the discourse immediately preceding (e.g., "Do you like tortillas? I do").

embedded clause   A clause enclosed within a sentence (e.g., The hummingbird, *whose wings beat very rapidly,* has brilliant plumage).

embedded phonics   Phonological awareness and phonics taught implicitly through the reading of real words in text.

emergent literacy   A level of cognitive maturation characterized by well-developed oral language ability, exposure to written language, and metalinguistic awareness.

English language learner   A student who is learning English, who comes from a language background other than English, and whose English proficiency is not fully developed.

entry word   Word that is defined in a dictionary or glossary; may be divided into syllables.

eponym   A word for a place, an object, or an action that is named after an individual (e.g., *sandwich, Fahrenheit, diesel*).

e-text   *See* electronic text.

ethnographic observation   A type of qualitative research in which researchers observe, listen, and ask questions to collect descriptive data in order to understand the content, context, and dynamics of an environment. *See also* qualitative research.

etymology   The study of the origins and historical development of words.

euphony   Beautiful or pleasing sound (from Greek). A desire for euphony may explain why, in the development of the English language, the last letters of certain prefixes have changed to match the first letter of the base words or stems. The result is easier to say and often results in a double consonant (e.g., *irregular,* not *inregular*). Knowledge of this phenomenon is an aid to spelling.

evidence-based research   *See* scientifically based research.

exaggerated pronunciation   Overpronunciation of a word as an aid to spelling. Dyslexic students are encouraged to develop and practice exaggerated pronunciation at first as

needed to strengthen auditory memory. Thus, vowel sounds in unaccented syllables are not reduced to the indistinguishable schwa sound but are pronounced phonetically (e.g., the closed syllable in *vital* is exaggerated as /tal/ to emphasize the *a*). *Also called* spelling pronunciation, spelling-based pronunciation, or spelling voice.

executive function difficulties Difficulties with certain cognitive skills such as poor planning, disorganization of time and materials, difficulty narrowing a topic in writing, and procrastination.

experimental design Experimental educational research raises a question based on a theory, which determines the experimental design for directly investigating the question using scientific methods of collecting data using rigorously applied methods of instruction, with detailed descriptions of the participants and measures used. In this kind of experimental research, the data are interpreted to yield results of the impact of the manipulation and control of the conditions of observation. Studies thus designed can be analyzed for knowledge gained and can be replicated.

expository writing Writing that explains or informs, including persuasive or descriptive writing and compare-and-contrast compositions.

fast mapping Picking up from context an initial impression of the meaning of a word.

Fernald method Technique for learning words that involves the visual, auditory, kinesthetic, and tactile (VAKT) modalities. The student looks at a word while saying and tracing it.

figurative language *See* nonliteral language.

figure–ground perception The ability to attend to one aspect of a visual field while perceiving it in relation to the rest of the field; ability to identify and focus on salient information.

fill-in-the-blank technique *See* cloze technique.

final Pertaining to or occurring at the exact end; pertaining to the very last letter or sound in a word or syllable. *Z* is the final letter of the alphabet.

final stable syllable A syllable with nonphonetic spelling and relatively stable pronunciation that occurs frequently in final position in English words (e.g., *-tle, -sion, -cial*).

fine motor skills The strategic control of small sets of voluntary muscles such as in writing, grasping small objects, controlling eye movements, or producing speech.

finger agnosia A kinesthetic feedback disorder in which the fingers do not report their location to the brain.

finger-point reading A form of pretend reading in which prereaders point their fingers at the words on a page as they recite the story from memory and synchronize spoken words with words in print. Finger-point reading is facilitated by the ability to segment phonemes and match them with written letters. *See also* concept of a word.

flap The reduction of /t/ and /d/, such as in the American English pronunciations of *ladder* and *latter*, formed by the tongue flapping on the alveolar ridge.

fluency In reading, the ability to translate print to speech with rapidity and automaticity that allows the reader to focus on meaning.

formal test *See* standardized test.

formative data collection Procedure to gather information about a child's progress in acquiring particular skills or knowledge to be applied to short-term instructional goals; usually collected using criterion- and curriculum-referenced tests. *See also* criterion-referenced test, curriculum-referenced test, summative data.

fragment A phrase or subordinate clause that is not a sentence (e.g., *The girl who was standing*).

free morpheme A morpheme that can stand alone as a whole word (e.g., *box, plant, tame*). *Also called* unbound morpheme. *See also* bound morpheme.

frequency   The number of times an event occurs in a given category (e.g., frequency in English of multiple spellings of the long /ū/ sound as in *cube, human,* and *statue*) that guides the order of introduction for reading and spelling.

fricative   A consonant produced by a partial obstruction of the airflow, which creates friction and slight hissing noise (e.g., /s/, /f/).

functional neuroimaging   Pictures of brain activity of awake subjects performing specific tasks that allow researchers to investigate which brain areas are used during certain tasks. *See also* neuroimaging.

gerund   An English word ending in *-ing* when used as a noun (e.g., She loves *dancing* and *singing*).

glide   A vowel-like consonant (i.e., /w/ and /y/) produced with little or no obstruction of the air stream in the mouth. *Also called* semivowel.

glottal sound   A sound produced by use of the most posterior part of the mouth, known as the glottis. The sound is produced by complete or partial constriction of the glottis.

grapheme   A written letter or letter cluster representing a single speech sound (e.g., *i, igh*). *See also* digraph, quadrigraph, trigraph.

graphic organizers   Visual displays of information to help a student compose written material or study for tests (e.g., outlines, semantic maps, story grammars/diagrams).

graphomotor   Pertaining to the skillful coordination of the muscle groups involved in handwriting.

graphomotor production deficit   Difficulty writing in which the larger muscles of the wrist and forearm are used during letter formation because they are under better control than the small muscles of the fingers.

graphophonemic   Pertaining to letter-sound patterns.

guide letter   The letter in a word that guides the reader in alphabetizing a word or finding it in the dictionary (e.g., when determining if *plow* appears on a dictionary page with the guide words *please* and *prison,* the second letter is the guide word).

guide words   The two words usually found in the upper corner of each dictionary page indicating the first and last words on the page.

guided discovery teaching   Manner of presenting new material or concepts so that they can be deduced or discovered by the students. Only material that relates logically to their previous learning or that evolves through reason or sequence will lend itself to the students' discovery. Students will remember more readily that which they have been allowed to discover. Successful discovery teaching requires careful preparation. *See also* Socratic method.

heterogeneous practice   A spelling or reading practice session with more than one focus used only after the student has mastered each of the concepts contained in the practice.

high interest–low level readers   Used to describe text written at a basic decoding level with the subject interests of older students in mind. *Also called* high-interest text.

high-frequency word   A word that is encountered numerous times in text and is important to know.

high-interest text   *See* high interest–low level readers.

Hispanic   Relating to people descended from Spanish or Latin American people or their culture.

homogeneous practice   A spelling or reading practice in which every word contains the same pattern or rule that is the single focus of the practice.

homophones   Words that sound like another but have different spellings and meaning (e.g., *bare* and *bear; fourth* and *forth*).

IDEA   *See* Individuals with Disabilities Education Act of 2004 (PL 108-446).

IEP *See* individualized education program.

imagery training Training in the use of language to create sensory impressions and in the formation of imaginative mental images while reading or listening.

inclusion 1) The opportunity for all students with disabilities to have access to and participate in all activities of the neighborhood school environment. 2) An educational placement in which a qualified student with disabilities receives special education and related services in the least restrictive environment, which may involve (to the extent possible) placement in the general education classroom.

independent level That level of academic engagement in which an individual works independently without need for instructional support. Independent-level behaviors demonstrate a high degree of accuracy, speed, ease, fluency, and mastery. When used in the context of reading instruction, this is most often referred to as *independent reading level*. In reading, an independent level is usually defined as reading 95%–100% of the words in a given passage correctly, with no more than one error per 20 words.

Individuals with Disabilities Education Improvement Act (IDEA) of 2004 (PL 108-446) Special education legislation, originally passed in 1975 (PL 94-142) and amended in 1990 (PL 101-476) and 1997 (PL 105-17), that serves as a mechanism to help fund special education. This legislation mandates that states receiving federal monies must provide special educational and other services to qualified children (from birth through age 21) with disabilities or risk the loss of these dollars. IDEA protects a child's right to a free appropriate public education (FAPE) in the least restrictive environment (LRE).

individualized education program (IEP) A document that sets out the child's placement in special education as well as the specific goals, short-term objectives, and benchmarks for measuring progress each year. Creation and implementation of the IEP must include the opportunity for meaningful participation by the parents.

Indo-European A family of languages consisting of most of the languages of Europe, as well as those of Iran, the Indian subcontinent, and other parts of Asia. Most English words are ultimately of Indo-European origin.

inflectional morpheme A morpheme added to the end of a word that shows tense, number, or person of a verb; plural or possessive of a noun; or comparative or superlative form of an adjective (e.g., *-ed* in *floated*, *-s* in *tales*, *-er* in *thinner*).

informal test A test that is structured but not standardized; it typically follows the format of a standardized test, but presentation can be modified to probe the students' responses in ways that are not permissible with standardized tests. *See also* standardized test.

initial The first or beginning sound or letter in a word or syllable. *A* is the initial letter of the alphabet.

instant word recognition The ease and automaticity with which a skilled reader is able to read individual words.

intonation The pattern or melody of pitch changes revealed in connected speech.

invented spelling Spelling that is not the same as conventional orthography and that may be encouraged from preschool to first grade to help students develop phonemic awareness and apply their knowledge of sounds, symbols, and letter patterns. The use of invented spelling is temporary until regular orthography is learned.

irregular word A word that has an unexpected spelling either because its orthographic representation does not match its pronunciation (e.g., *colonel, Wednesday*) or because it contains an infrequent orthographic representation of a sound (e.g., *soap*).

juncture The transition or mode of transition from one sound to another in speech; a pause that contributes to meaning of words (e.g., to make *a name* distinguishable from *an aim*) or rising intonation, as in a question.

key word   A word emphasizing a particular letter-sound association that serves as the key to unlock the student's memory for that association (e.g., *apple* for /ă/, *itch* for /ĭ/).

kinesthetic   Pertaining to the sensory experience stimulated by bodily movements and tensions; often pertaining to the student's feeling of letter shapes while moving parts of the body through space.

kinesthetic memory   A voluntary motor sequence that is recalled by the student after repeated practice and training, such as daily writing of cursive letter shapes while associating them with the name and sounds represented by each.

labiodental fricative   A sound in which the lower lip and the upper teeth touch and partially obstruct the air flow (e.g., /f/, /v/).

language content   The knowledge of the vast array of objects, events, and relationships and the way they are represented.

laterality   The tendency to use either the left or the right side of the body; handedness.

lax vowel   *See* short vowel.

learning disability   "A generic term that refers to a heterogeneous group of disorders manifested by significant difficulties in the acquisition and use of listening, speaking, reading, writing, reasoning, and mathematics abilities, or of social skills. These disorders are intrinsic to the individual and presumed to be due to central nervous system dysfunction. Even though a learning disability may occur with other handicapping conditions (e.g., sensory impairment, mental retardation, social and emotional disturbance), with socioenvironmental influences (e.g., cultural factors), and especially with attention deficit disorder, all of which may cause learning problems, a learning disability is not the direct result of those conditions or influences." (The Interagency Committee, 1985, as cited in Kavanagh & Truss, 1988, pp. 550–551)

learning strategies model   *See* cognitive strategies.

left angular gyrus   Part of the left hemisphere of brain that is the primary location for translating visual-orthographic information into phonological representations (linking symbol to sound).

letter cluster   Group of two or more letters that regularly appear adjacent in a single syllable (e.g., *oo, ng, th, sh, oi, igh*). In spelling instruction, a pattern of letters in a single syllable that occurs frequently together. The pronunciation of at least one of the component parts may be unexpected, or the letters may stand in an unexpected sequence (e.g., *ar, er, ir, or, qu, wh*). A cluster may be a blend (two or more letters that represent more than one sound) or a digraph (two letters that represent one sound). *Also called* combination. *See also* blend, digraph, diphthong, quadrigraph, trigraph.

letter–sound correspondences   *See* phonics.

lexical   Relating to words or the vocabulary of a language or the meaning of the base word in inflected and derived forms.

lexical cohesion   The planning and organization of the content of a message before it is communicated.

lexicon   A body of word knowledge, either spoken or written.

linguadental   A sound produced with the tongue contacting the teeth.

linguistic   Denoting language processing and language structure.

linguistics   Study of the production, properties, structure, meaning, and/or use of language.

linkages   1) The associations developed in language training between students' visual, auditory, kinesthetic, and tactile perceptions by seeing the letter, naming it, saying its sound, and writing it in the air and on paper. 2) Connections between cursive letters. Students may need extra practice with the more difficult linkages such as the bridge stroke after the letters *b, o, v,* and *w*.

liquid A class of consonant sounds that contains /l/ and /r/ of American English.

literacy socialization As a result of being read to, the development of the sense that marks on a page relate to the words being said, that there is a correct way to manipulate books, and that there is a positive connection between reading and nurturing experiences (Snow & Dickinson, 1991).

long vowel A vowel sound that is produced by a slightly higher tongue position than the short vowels. The long sounds represented by the written vowels (i.e., *a, e, i, o,* and *u*) are usually the same as their names. When coding or when writing a sound picture, any long vowel is marked by a macron. *Also called* tense vowel.

long-term memory Permanent storage of information by means of primarily semantic links, associations, and general organizational plans; includes experiential, semantic, procedural, and automatic habit memories.

macron The flat diacritical mark (¯) above a vowel in a sound picture or phonic/dictionary notation that indicates a long sound (e.g., /fāvor/).

manner In phonology, the articulation and perceptual character of speech sounds.

manuscript handwriting *See* print handwriting.

marker A distinguishing feature of a word that signals the need to apply a spelling rule or a coding for reading. The student may literally place a mark at each crucial point as a reminder. *Also called* checkpoint, clue.

mastery Proficiency in specific subskills of a new task. Based on the bottom-up notion of gaining automatic recall of basic information or learning to automaticity. *Also called* overlearning.

Matthew effects A term coined by Stanovich (1986) to describe a phenomenon observed in findings of cumulative advantage for children who read well and have good vocabularies and cumulative disadvantage for those who have inadequate vocabularies and read less and thus have lower rates of achievement. The term is named after a passage from the New Testament: "For unto everyone that hath shall be given, and he shall have abundance: but for him that hath not shall be taken away even that which he hath" (Matthew XXV:29).

meaning-based word As a result of compounding, a word whose meaning may not always be inferred from the meaning of its components (e.g., *greenhouse, flyleaf*). *See also* compound word.

medial The letters or sounds that occur in the interior of a word or syllable. All of the letters in the sequential alphabet are medial except *A* and *Z*. *Medial* is not a synonym for *middle*. *See also* middle.

meta-analysis A statistical technique that allows comparisons of results across many studies.

metacognition The deliberate rearrangement, regrouping, or transfer of information; the conscious choice of the strategies used to accomplish a task and processes to provide feedback on learning and performance.

metacognitive strategies Strategies that students may use to think about what they are reading and the factors that influence their thinking.

metalinguistic Pertaining to an awareness of language as an entity that can be contemplated; crucial to early reading ability, to understanding discourse patterns in the classroom, and to analyzing the language being used to teach the language that must be learned. Metalinguistics is one kind of metacognition.

metaphor A word or phrase that means one thing and that is used, through implication, to mean something else (e.g., "His remark created a blizzard of controversy"). *See also* simile.

middle Equidistant from two extremes. *Middle* and *medial* are not synonymous. The middle letters of the alphabet are *M* and *N*. *See also* medial.

miscue   Used by reading specialists to refer to inaccurate reading responses to written text during oral reading.

missing addend equation   Addition equation in which only one addend and the sum are given (e.g., 5 + ___ = 10); the student must provide the missing addend.

mnemonic strategies   Formal schemes designed to improve memory, including using key words, chunking, rhyming, and visualizing. Arbitrary learning is more difficult for the dyslexic student than learning that is related and logical, so devices such as mnemonic strategies for grouping needed facts are essential. *See also* arbitrary learning.

modality   A specific sensory pathway. Multisensory instruction engages simultaneously the student's visual, auditory, and kinesthetic/tactile senses.

model   A standard or example provided by the teacher for imitation or comparison (e.g., a model of syllable division procedure before a reading practice); a structure or design to show how something is formed (e.g., teacher skywrites a cursive letter).

modifications   In the Individuals with Disabilities Education Improvement Act of 2004 (PL 108-446), a term used to refer to changes in how an alternate assessment is administered.

monosyllabic   Pertaining to a word of one syllable containing one vowel sound.

morpheme   The smallest meaningful linguistic unit. A morpheme may be a whole word (e.g., *child*), a base word (e.g., *child* in *childhood*), a suffix (e.g., *-hood* in *childhood*), or a prefix (e.g., *un-* in *untie*). *See also* derivational morpheme, inflectional morpheme.

morphological   In linguistic terms, pertaining to the meaningful units of speech; a suffix, for example, is a morphological ending.

morphology   1) The internal structure of the meaningful units within words and the relationships among words in a language. 2) The study of word formation patterns.

morphophonemic relations   The conditions in which certain morphemes keep their written spelling when affixes are added although their phonemic forms change.

motor feedback problem   *See* finger agnosia.

motor memory dysfunction   A disorder affecting handwriting in which a person has difficulty recalling the movements needed to form specific letters.

multiple meanings   Different meanings for the same word; characteristic of English language. Students with learning disabilities often have difficulty with multiple meanings of words.

multiple regression analysis   A statistical method that relates a dependent (or criterion) variable (*y*) to a set of independent (or predictor) variables (*x*) by a linear equation for the purposes of prediction, controlling confounding variables, evaluating sets of variables, accounting for multivariate interrelationships, and analyzing variance and covariance on levels of independent variables (Fruchter, as cited in Corsini & Auerbach, 1996).

multiple spellings   The various ways in which a sound may be spelled (e.g., long /ā/ may be spelled *a, ay, ei, eigh, ey,* or *ai*).

multiplicand   The number in a multiplication equation that states the size or amount that is to be multiplied (e.g., 5 is the multiplicand in 3 × 5 = 15).

multiplier   The number in a multiplication equation that states how many times a certain size is to be produced (e.g., 3 is the multiplier in 3 × 5 = 15). *Also called* operator.

multisensory   Referring to any learning activity that includes the use of two or more sensory modalities simultaneously for the taking in or expression of information.

multisensory strategy   A procedure, used most often for novice or poor readers, that involves an auditory, visual, tactile-kinesthetic, and/or an articulatory-motor component in the carefully sequenced teaching of language structure.

multisensory structured language education (MSLE) Instructional approach that incorporates the simultaneous use of visual, auditory, kinesthetic, and tactile sensory modalities to link listening, speaking, reading, and writing together.

multisyllabic Pertaining to a word of more than one syllable (e.g., *fantastic*). *Also called* polysyllabic.

narrative Composition containing a sequence of events, usually in chronological order.

nasal A sound produced in which air is blocked in the oral cavity but escapes through the nose. The consonants in *mom* and *no* are nasal sounds.

neuroimaging Diagnostic and research method of viewing brain structures and activity through the use of advanced medical technology, such as magnetic resonance imaging, in which the patient's body is placed in a magnetic field and resulting images are processed by computer to produce an image of contrasting adjacent tissues. *See also* functional neuroimaging.

neuropsychology The study of areas of the brain and their connecting networks involved in learning and behavior.

nonliteral language Language that avoids use of the exact meanings of words and uses exaggeration, metaphors, and embellishments. *Also called* figurative language.

nonsense word A word having no meaning by itself, the spelling of which is usually phonetic (e.g., *vop*). Reading and spelling nonsense words are phonic reinforcement for students who have already memorized a large number of words. Nonsense words can be used for teaching older students to apply phonetic decoding. *Also called* detached syllable, nonsense syllable, nonword, pseudoword.

norm-referenced test Assessment of performance in relation to that of the norm group (cohort) used in the standardization of the test. Norm-referenced tests produce scores that permit comparisons between a student and other children of the same age. All norm-referenced tests are standardized. *See also* standardized test.

oddity task Task or question in which student is presented with several items and must select the one that does not fit with the rest (e.g., "*Ball, call, tall, hop*. Which of these words doesn't belong?"). *Also called* odd-one-out task, odd-man-out task.

onset The initial written or spoken single consonant or consonant cluster before the first vowel in a syllable (e.g., /s/ in *sit*, /str/ in *strip*). Some syllables do not have an onset (e.g., *on, ask*). *See also* rime.

open syllable A syllable ending with a long vowel sound (e.g., the first syllables in *labor* and *freedom*). *See also* closed syllable.

operator *See* multiplier.

orthographic memory Memory of letter patterns and word spellings.

orthography 1) The writing system of a language. 2) Correct or standardized spelling according to established usage.

Orton-Gillingham approach Multisensory method of teaching language-related academic skills that focuses on the structure and use of sounds, syllables, words, sentences, and written discourse. Instruction is explicit, systematic, cumulative, direct, and sequential.

otitis media Inflammation of the middle ear that can lead to temporary conductive hearing loss or, sometimes, permanent hearing loss. A young child who experiences hearing loss from otitis media may have resulting speech or language difficulties.

outcomes In assessment, the measured results of an educational program.

overlearning *See* mastery.

palatal Pertaining to sounds produced by the tongue touching the hard palate.

paralinguistic *See* suprasegmental.

partially blocked   *See* stop.

pause   A break, stop, or rest in spoken language; one of the suprasegmental aspects of language. *See also* juncture, suprasegmental.

peer review   Scrutiny and evaluation of the results of a research study by a group of independent researchers with expertise and credentials in that field of study before the research findings are publicly reported.

phoneme   An individual sound unit in spoken words; the smallest unit of speech that makes one word distinguishable from another in a phonetic language such as English (e.g., /f/ makes *fat* distinguishable from *vat;* /j/ makes *jump* distinguishable from *chump*).

phoneme awareness   *See* phonemic awareness.

phoneme deletion   *See* sound deletion.

phonemic awareness   Awareness of the smallest units of sound in the speech stream and the ability to isolate or manipulate the individual sounds in words. Phonemic awareness is one aspect of the larger category of phonological awareness. *Also called* phoneme awareness. *See also* phonological awareness.

phonetic   Pertaining to speech sounds and their relation to graphic or written symbols.

phonetic stage   Stage in spelling development in which every sound is represented, but the complete knowledge of conventional orthography is not. *See also* prephonetic stage, semiphonetic stage.

phonetically regular word   *See* regular word.

phonetics   The system of speech sounds in any specific language.

phonics   Paired association between letters and letter sounds; an approach to teaching of reading and spelling that emphasizes sound-symbol relationships, especially in early instruction.

phonological   Pertaining to a speaker's knowledge about sound patterns in a language.

phonological awareness   Both the knowledge of and sensitivity to the phonological structure of words in a language. Phonological awareness involves a sophisticated ability to notice, think about, or manipulate sound segments in words. It can progress from rhyming; to syllable counting; to detecting first, last, and middle sounds; to segmenting, adding, deleting, and substituting sounds in words. Phonemic awareness is one component of phonological awareness. *See also* phonemic awareness.

phonological loop   Part of short-term memory that can store small bits of speech information as they are being processed.

phonological processing   An umbrella term for a large category of oral language processing abilities that are related to the sounds in words and are associated with the ability to read well.

phonological rules   Implicit rules governing speech sound production and the sequence in which sounds can be produced in a language.

phonology   The science of speech sounds, including the study of the development of speech sounds in one language or the comparison of speech sound development across different languages.

PL 108-446   *See* Individuals with Disabilities Education Improvement Act (IDEA) of 2004.

place of articulation   The place in the oral cavity where the stream of air is obstructed or changed during the production of a sound.

place value   The position of a digit in a numeral or series (e.g., the ones place, the tens place, the hundreds place).

polyglot   A language that is made up of words from several languages; English is a polyglot.

polysyllabic   *See* multisyllabic.

pragmatics   The set of rules that dictates behavior for communicative intentions in a particular context and the rules of conversation or discourse.

précis Condensation in the student's own words of an author's essential message, thesis, moral, or purpose.

prefix An affix attached to the beginning of a word that changes the meaning of that word (e.g., *tri-* in *tricycle*). *See also* consonant prefix, vowel prefix.

prephonetic stage Stage in spelling development in which not all of the sounds of the word are represented by letters (e.g., *JS* for *dress*). *See also* phonetic stage, semiphonetic stage.

prescriptive When used in the context of instruction, entailing the changes made to a lesson to tailor it for more practice, review, and/or multisensory activities.

print awareness Children's appreciation and understanding of the purposes and functions of written language.

print handwriting Unconnected letters formed using arcs and straight lines. *Also called* manuscript handwriting.

prosody Features of spoken language, such as intonation and stress, that fluent readers use for appropriate phrasing of text into meaningful units.

proprioception An individual's subconscious perception of movement and spatial orientation coming from stimuli within the body.

pseudoword *See* nonsense word.

quadrigraph Four adjacent letters in a syllable that represent one speech sound (e.g., *eigh*). *See also* digraph, trigraph.

qualitative research Research that involves observing individuals and settings and relies on observation and description of events in the immediate context.

quantitative research Research using experimental or quasi-experimental design methods to gather data. *See also* quasi-experimental research.

quasi-experimental research Research that determines cause and effect without strict randomized controlled trials and is valid but less reliable than randomized controlled trials.

quotient In division, the number of shares contained in a total (dividend) (e.g., 5 is the quotient in $15 \div 3 = 5$).

randomized controlled trial An intervention study in which subjects are randomly assigned to experimental and control groups; all variables are held constant except the one variable that is hypothesized to cause a change.

rapid automatic naming A speed naming task, most often administered to prereaders, in which the individual is asked to name quickly a series of printed letters, number, or blocks of color repeated over and over in random order. *Also called* rapid automatized naming, rapid serial naming.

***r*-controlled** Pertaining to the phenomenon in English in which the letter *r* affects the way a preceding vowel is pronounced. For example, the *a* in *bar* is influenced by the *r* and sounds different from the *a* in *bad*.

***r*-controlled syllable** A syllable containing the combination of a vowel followed by *r*. The sound of the vowel often is not short but instead may represent an unexpected sound (e.g., *dollar, star, her*). This kind of syllable is also called a *vowel-r syllable,* a term which focuses on the orthographic pattern (whereas the term *r-controlled syllable* focuses on the sound pattern).

reading disability *See* dyslexia.

reading fluency *See* fluency.

recognition The act of identifying a stimulus as the same as something previously experienced (e.g., auditory recognition is involved in listening for a particular sound).

regrouping New mathematical term for carrying (in addition) and borrowing (in subtraction); necessary in our base-10 positional notation system.

regular word A word that is spelled the way it sounds. *Also called* phonetically regular word.

relative clause A dependent clause introduced by a relative pronoun such as *who, that,*

which, or *whom* (e.g., We bought ice cream from the man *who was standing on the corner*). A relative clause is not a complete sentence on its own.

review   Look over again; bring back to awareness. Used twice in a multisensory lesson to increase automatic reaction to symbols for reading and spelling and to make a brief reference to the day's new material.

rime   The written or spoken vowel and the final consonant(s) in a syllable (e.g., *at* in *cat, itch* in *switch*). *See also* onset.

root   A content word (noun, verb, adjective, adverb) or word part to which affixes can be added (e.g., *hat, group, green, fast*). Some roots, usually of Greek or Latin origin, are morphemes that generally cannot stand alone as a word in English (e.g., *cred, dict, struct, tele*). *See also* base word, bound morpheme, free morpheme.

rule word   A word that carries information indicating when a letter should be dropped, doubled, or changed (e.g., *shiny, rabbit, bountiful*).

run-on sentence   Two main clauses incorrectly run together without any punctuation or conjunction separating them (e.g., *It began raining they parked the car*).

schema   A student's prior knowledge and experience relevant to a new topic insofar as it contributes to a frame of reference, factual or attitudinal, for the new information, thus creating links or structures through which the new information can be assimilated. *Also called* schemata.

schwa   An unaccented vowel whose pronunciation approximates the short /u/ sounds, such as the sound that corresponds to the first and last *a* in *America* or the second *a* in *sandal*.

scientifically based research   A process that gathers evidence to answer questions and to bring new knowledge to a field so that effective practices can be determined and implemented. *Also called* evidence-based research.

segmental   Pertaining to a feature of language that can be divided or organized into a class (e.g., place of articulation, voicing).

segmentation   1) Separating a word into units, such as syllables, onsets and rimes, or individual phonemes, for the purpose of reading or spelling. *Also called* unblending. 2) Breaking down a targeted skill into smaller step-by-step sequenced units and then synthesizing the parts into a whole.

selective attention   The ability to attend to certain stimuli while ignoring other stimuli; in working memory, putting ideas on hold while working on other ideas.

semantics   The meaning of words and the relationships among words as they are used to represent knowledge of the world.

semiphonetic stage   Stage in spelling development in which a child usually strings consonants together to represent speech sounds in words and syllables (e.g., *NTR for enter*). *See also* phonetic stage, prephonetic stage.

semivowel   *See* glide.

sentence expansion   Addition of details explaining who, what, where, when, and/or how to a sentence kernel (e.g., *Yesterday when I was at the store, I saw the woman with the brown dog* is an expansion of *I saw the woman*).

sentence kernel   A simple sentence without modifiers.

sentence starter   Words used specifically to begin a sentence or complete thought (e.g., *whenever, since, after*).

sequencing   In multisensory structured language education, the orderly presentation of linguistic concepts based on frequency and ease of learning in a continuous series of connected lessons.

shared reading   Reading in which the instructor reads a paragraph aloud and then the student reads a paragraph aloud, with the instructor assisting with words as needed. *See also* choral reading, echo reading.

short vowel   A vowel that is pronounced with a short sound, which is unrelated to the name of the letter. A short vowel usually occurs in a closed syllable and is marked with a breve. *Also called* lax vowel.

short-term memory   Memory that lasts only briefly, has rapid input and output, is limited in capacity, and depends directly on stimulation for its form. Short-term memory enables the reader to keep parts of the reading material in mind until enough material has been processed for it to make sense. *Also called* working memory. *See also* phonological loop, visuospatial loop.

sibilant   A speech sound that is uttered with or accompanied by a hissing sound (i.e., /s/, /z/, /ch/, /j/, /sh/, and /zh/).

sight word   A word that is immediately recognized as a whole and does not require decoding to identify. A sight word may or may not be phonetically regular (e.g., *can, would, the*).

simile   An explicit comparison of two unlike things, usually with the word *like* or *as* (e.g., *Her tousled hair was like an explosion in a spaghetti factory*). *See also* metaphor.

Simultaneous Oral Spelling (S.O.S.)   A structured sequence of procedures to teach the student how to think about the process of spelling. The student looks and listens to the word, unblends it, spells it aloud, writes it while naming each letter, codes it, and reads it aloud for proofreading (Cox, 1992).

situation   In reading and spelling instruction, a feature in a word that provides clues about how to spell or read a word. The situation refers to the position of letters or sounds, placement of accent, and the influence of surrounding sounds or letters.

sky writing   Technique of "writing" a letter or word in the air using arm and writing hand. Use of upper arm muscles during sky writing helps the student retain kinesthetic memory of the shape of letters. *Also called* air writing.

Socratic method   A teaching method that leads learners to discover information through carefully guided questioning based on information they already possess. *Also called* discovery learning; Socratic questioning. *See also* guided discovery teaching.

sound deletion   Early literacy task in which the student is presented with a word and is asked to say all of the sounds in the word except one (e.g., "Say *bat* without /b/"). Ability to delete sounds is an important component of phonemic awareness. *Also called* phoneme deletion.

sound dictation   Procedure in which the teacher dictates individual phonemes, words, or sentences, and the student repeats and responds by writing them down. Sound dictation may involve oral and/or written review with a sound or spelling deck to develop automaticity in translating sounds to spellings.

sound picture   Letter or word written with diacritical markings indicating pronunciation. Sound pictures are often enclosed in slashes or parentheses (e.g., /kup/ for *cup*).

sound–symbol associations; sound–symbol correspondences   *See* phonics.

special education   A federally defined type of education for a qualified child with a disability that is

> specially designed instruction, at no cost to the parents, to meet the unique needs of the child with a disability, including—
>
> (A)   instruction conducted in the classroom, in the home, in hospitals and institutions, and in other settings; and
> (B)   instruction in physical education. (PL 108-446, 20 U.S.C. § 1401 [29][a–b])

specific agraphia   Acquired disorder in which ability to form letter shapes, letter sequences, and motor patterns is impaired.

specific learning disability   *See* learning disability.

speech synthesis software   Software in which synthetic speech is added to the printed material presented on computers or other electronic devices. *See also* text-to-speech software.

spelling pronunciation, spelling voice   *See* exaggerated pronunciation.

SQ3R   *See* Survey, Question, Read, Recite, Review.

standardized test   A test that is standardized using a carefully selected sample of people representative of the larger group of people for whom the test was created; such a test must be administered and scored following procedures prescribed in the manual accompanying the test. *See also* informal test.

stop   In terms of speech sounds, a consonant that is produced with a complete obstruction of air (e.g., /p/, /t/, /k/).

strategy   An individual's approach to a task, including how the person thinks and acts when planning, executing, and evaluating performance on a task and its subsequent outcomes.

strategy cues   Reminders to use strategies or multiple steps. The teacher verbalizes problem solving. Instruction using strategy cues may include think-aloud models or charts with steps in a procedure.

stress   *See* accent.

structural analysis   The perception and examination of syllables and morphemes. Structural analysis enables the reader to recognize different kinds of syllables and decode long, unfamiliar words.

study skills   Those competencies associated with acquiring, recording, organizing, synthesizing, remembering, and using information and ideas learned in school or other instructional arenas.

subskill   A skill that is part of a more complex skill or group of skills. Subskills of reading include phonological awareness and knowledge of letter–sound correspondences.

suffix   A morpheme attached to the end of a word that creates a word with a different form or use (e.g., *-s* in *cats*, *-ing* in *lettering*). Suffixes include inflected forms indicating tense, number, person, and comparatives. *See also* consonant suffix, vowel suffix.

summative data collection   Procedure to gather information about the accumulation and integration of knowledge to be applied to long-term comprehensive teaching goals; typically collected using norm-referenced measures but sometimes collected with curriculum- and criterion-referenced tests. *See also* criterion-referenced test, curriculum-referenced test, formative data, norm-referenced test.

suprasegmental   Pertaining to the singular musical qualities of language, including intonation, expression, accent, pitch, juncture, and rhythm, which are significant in our ability to communicate and comprehend emotions and attitudes. *Also called* paralinguistic.

Survey, Question, Read, Recite, Review (SQ3R)   Study method in which student *s*urveys the assignment, poses a *q*uestion, *r*eads to answer the question, *r*ecites the answer to the question, and *r*eviews the material read (Robinson, 1946).

syllable   A spoken or written unit that must have a vowel sound and that may include consonants that precede or follow that vowel. Syllables are units of sound made by one impulse of the voice.

syllable division   The process of breaking down multisyllabic words into separate syllables for greater ease in learning, pronunciation, or spelling.

syllable division patterns   Patterns for dividing words into syllables. There are four major syllable division patterns in English: VCCV, VCV, VCCCV, and VV.

syllable types   Orthographic classifications for syllables. There are six syllable types in English: closed, open, vowel-consonant-*e*, vowel pair (vowel team), vowel-*r* (*r*-controlled), and consonant-*le*. *See also specific syllable types*.

synonyms   Words having similar meaning.

syntax The system by which words may be ordered in phrases and sentences; sentence structure; grammar.

synthetic Pertaining to instruction or a process that begins with the parts and builds to the whole. Synthetic phonics starts with individual letter sounds that are blended together to form a word. *See also* analytic.

tactile Relating to the sense of touch.

target word 1) A word that is being looked for in a dictionary or other reference source. 2) A word that is the focus of reading, spelling, vocabulary, handwriting, or other instruction.

template A blank pattern that can be used as a guide to be filled in by the student.

tense vowel *See* long vowel.

text-to-speech software Software that can convert computer-based text into spoken words.

top-down process *See* concept-driven process.

tracking The ability to finger point while reading a text, demonstrating the concept of a word. *See also* concept of a word, finger-point reading.

transition words Words that aid in changing a thought within a sentence or paragraph (e.g., *first, next, then, finally*).

trigraph Three adjacent letters in a syllable that represent one speech sound (e.g., *tch, dge*). *See also* digraph, quadrigraph.

unblending *See* segmentation.

unbound morpheme *See* free morpheme.

unvoiced *See* voiceless.

VAKT (visual, auditory, kinesthetic, tactile) *See* Fernald method; *see also* multi-sensory structured language education (MSLE).

VCE *See* vowel-consonant-*e* syllable.

velar Pertaining to sounds produced when the tongue and roof of the mouth contact near the soft palate.

velum The soft palate.

verbal rehearsal A strategy that can be used to help hold information in short-term memory.

verbalization The saying aloud of a pattern or rule for reading or spelling or strokes of a letter shape after that pattern or rule or letter shape has been discovered or learned.

visual, auditory, kinesthetic, tactile (VAKT) *See* Fernald method; *see also* multi-sensory structured language education (MSLE).

visual discovery 1) Information gained by sight. 2) Guided discovery of a reading or spelling rule through looking at written examples of the language concept.

visual hint *See* context clue.

visual mapping software Software that allows for visual representation of ideas and reduces the need for writing because concepts can be expressed in brief phrases while the visual array does the cognitively and linguistically taxing work of representing relationships among concepts. This software offers enhanced opportunities for brainstorming and organizing on the computer.

visuospatial loop Part of short-term memory that can store print or graphic information.

vocabulary A large store of words that a person recognizes and/or uses in his or her oral and written language for communication and comprehension.

voice recognition software Computer software recognizes the user's voice and provides an alternative to handwriting or keyboarding while drafting text.

voiced Pertaining to a consonant articulated with vocal vibration (e.g., /z/).

voiced–voiceless cognates Phonemes produced in the same place of the mouth and in the same manner, but that vary in the voicing characteristic (e.g., /k/ and /g/).

voiceless Pertaining to a consonant articulated with no vocal vibration (e.g., /s/). *Also called* unvoiced.

vowel A class of open speech sounds produced by the easy passage of air through a relatively open vocal tract. English vowels include *a, e, i, o, u,* and sometimes *y. See also* semivowel.

vowel blend *See* blend.

vowel digraph *See* digraph.

vowel pair syllable A syllable containing two adjacent vowels that have a long, short, or diphthong sound (e.g., *meet, head, loud*). *Also called* vowel team syllable.

vowel prefix A prefix with a vowel as the final letter. The spelling of a vowel prefix does not change when it is added to a base word, a root, or a combining form.

vowel suffix A suffix beginning with a vowel, such as *-ing* and *-ed.*

vowel team syllable *See* vowel pair syllable.

vowel-consonant-*e* syllable (VCE) A one-syllable word or a final syllable of a longer word in which a final silent e signals that the vowel before the consonant is long (e.g., *cake, rope, cube, five, athlete*).

vowel-*r* syllable *See* r-controlled syllable.

Watch Our Writing (W.O.W.) A checklist designed to help students write accurately, comfortably, and legibly: Place feet flat on the floor, sit up straight, slant the paper at a 45° angle, rest arms on the desk, and hold the pencil lightly while pointing its upper end toward the shoulder of writing arm (Phelps & Stempel, 1985).

whole language approach A perspective on teaching literacy based on beliefs about teaching and learning that include the following: Reading can be learned as naturally as speaking; reading is focused on constructing meaning from text using children's books rather than basal or controlled readers; reading is best learned in the context of the group; phonics is taught indirectly during integration of reading, writing, listening, and speaking; teaching is child centered and emphasizes motivation and interest; and instruction is offered on the basis of need.

word blindness Term used in the late 19th and early 20th centuries for dyslexia. Word blindness now refers to acquired alexia, "the loss or diminution of ability of reading ability resulting from of brain trauma, a tumor, or a stroke" (Shaywitz, 2003, p. 140).

word prediction software Software that uses spelling knowledge, grammar rules, and context clues to predict what word a student wants to type as he or she enters the first few letters into the computer.

working memory *See* short-term memory.

zero-reject principle The principle infused in special education legislation that no child's disabilities are too severe for him or her to learn or to be provided with educational services.

REFERENCES

This glossary was compiled using the following as resources: Fromkin, Rodman, and Hyams (2003), Harris and Hodges (1995), Lerner (1997), Moats (1995), and *Stedman's Medical Dictionary* (2000).

Americans with Disabilities Act (ADA) of 1990, PL 101-336, 42 U.S.C. §§ 12101 *et seq.*

Corsini, R.J., & Auerbach, A.J. (Eds.). (1996). *Concise encyclopedia of psychology* (2nd ed.). New York: John Wiley & Sons.

Cox, A.R. (1992). *Foundations for literacy: Structures and techniques for multisensory teaching of basic written English language skills.* Cambridge, MA: Educators Publishing Service.

Education for All Handicapped Children Act of 1975, PL 94-142, 20 U.S.C. §§ 1400 *et seq.*

Fromkin, V., Rodman, R., & Hyams, N. (2003). *An introduction to language* (7th ed.). Boston: Thomson/Heinle.

Harris, T.L., & Hodges, R.E. (Eds.). (1995). *The literacy dictionary: The vocabulary of reading and writing.* Newark, DE: International Reading Association.

Henry, M.K. (2003). *Unlocking literacy: Effective de-*

coding and spelling instruction. Baltimore: Paul H. Brookes Publishing Co.

Individuals with Disabilities Education Act Amendments of 1997, PL 105-17, 20 U.S.C. §§ 1400 *et seq*.

Individuals with Disabilities Education Act (IDEA) of 1990, PL 101-476, 20 U.S.C. §§ 1400 *et seq*.

Individuals with Disabilities Education Improvement Act of 2004, PL 108-446, 20 U.S.C. §§ 1400 *et seq*.

Kavanagh, J.F., & Truss, T.J. (Eds.). (1988). *Learning disabilities: Proceedings of the national conference*. Timonium, MD: York Press.

Lerner, J.W. (1997). *Learning disabilities: Theories, diagnosis, and teaching strategies* (7th ed.). Boston: Houghton Mifflin.

Lyon, G.R., Shaywitz, S.E., & Shaywitz, B.A. (2003). A definition of dyslexia. *Annals of Dyslexia, 53*, 1–14.

Moats, L.C. (1995). *Spelling: Development, disabilities, and instruction*. Timonium, MD: York Press.

Moats, L.C. (2000). *Speech to print: Language essentials for teachers*. Baltimore: Paul H. Brookes Publishing Co.

Phelps, J., & Stempel, L. (1985). *CHES's handwriting improvement program* (CHIP). Dallas: Children's Handwriting Evaluation Scale.

Rehabilitation Act Amendments of 1998, PL 105-220, 29 U.S.C. §§ 701 *et seq*.

Robinson, F.P. (1946). *Effective study*. New York: HarperCollins.

Shaywitz, S. (2003). *Overcoming dyslexia: A new and complete science-based program for reading problems at any level*. New York: Alfred A. Knopf.

Snow, C., & Dickinson, D. (1991). Skills that aren't basic in a new conception of literacy. In A. Purves & E. Jennings (Eds.), *Literate systems and individual lives: Perspectives on literacy and schooling*. Albany, New York: SUNY Press.

Stanovich, K.E. (1986). Matthew effects in reading: Some consequences of individual differences in the acquisition of literacy. *Reading Research Quarterly, 21*, 360–407.

Stedman's medical dictionary (27th ed.). (2000). Philadelphia: Lippincott, Williams & Wilkins.

Materials and Sources

Holly Baker Hill

CHAPTER 1—RESEARCH AND READING DISABILITY

Organizations for Information on Dyslexia, Learning Disabilities, and Attention Disorders

All Kinds of Minds
Post Office Box 3580
Chapel Hill, NC 27514
http://www.allkindsofminds.org

The Alliance for Technology Access (ATA)
2175 East Francisco Boulevard
Suite L
San Rafael, CA 94901
415-455-4575

Attention Deficit Disorder Association
Post Office Box 543
Pottstown, PA 19464
484-945-2101
http://www.add.org

Center for Accessible Technology
2547 Eighth Street 12A
Berkeley, CA 94710
510-841-3224
http://www.cforat.org

Center of Minority Researchers in Special
  Education (COMRISE)
Curry School of Education
University of Virginia
405 Emmet Street
Charlottesville, VA 22903
804-924-1022

Children and Adults with Attention Deficit
  Disorders (CHADD)
499 Northwest 70th Avenue
Suite 308
Plantation, FL 33317
305-587-3700
http://www.chadd.org

Division for Learning Disabilities (DLD)
The Council for Exceptional Children (CEC)
1110 North Glebe Road
Suite 300
Arlington, VA 22201
888-CEC-SPED
E-mail: cec@cec.sped.org
http://www.teachingld.org

Florida Center for Reading Research
277 North Bronough Street
Suite 7250
Tallahassee, FL 32301
850-655-9352
http://www.fcrr.org

HEATH Resource Center
American Council on Education
1 Dupont Circle NW
Suite 800
Washington, DC 20036
800-544-3284

The International Dyslexia Association (IDA)
8600 LaSalle Road
Chester Building
Suite 382
Baltimore, MD 21286
800-222-3123
E-mail: info@interdys.org
http://www.interdys.org

Learning Disabilities Association of America (LDA)
4156 Library Road
Pittsburgh, PA 15234
412-341-1515
http://www.ldanatl.org

National Association for the Education of
African American Children with Learning
Disabilities (NAEAACLD)
Post Office Box 09521
Columbus, OH 42309
614-237-6021
http://www.aacld.org

National Center for Learning Disabilities
(NCLD)
381 Park Avenue South
Suite 1401
New York, NY 10016
888-575-7373
http://www.ncld.org

National Dissemination Center for Children
with Disabilities (NICHCY)
Post Office Box 1492
Washington, DC 20013
800-695-0285
E-mail: nichcy@aed.org
http://www.nichcy.org

Schwab Learning
Charles and Helen Schwab Foundation
1650 South Amphlett Boulevard
Suite 200
San Mateo, CA 94402
650-655-2410
http://www.schwablearning.org

Trace Research and Development Center
University of Wisconsin–Madison
S-151 Waisman Center
1500 Highland Avenue
Madison, WI 53705
608-263-5776; 608-263-5910
http://trace.wisc.edu

Publishers of Information, Curricula, and Products on Dyslexia and Learning Disabilities

Academic Communication Associates
Publication Center, Department 698
4149 Avenida de la Plata
Post Office Box 586249
Oceanside, CA 92058
888-758-9558
E-mail: acom@acadcom.com
http://www.acadcom.com

Academic Therapy Publications
20 Commercial Boulevard
Novato, CA 94949
800-422-7249
http://www.academictherapy.com

Brookline Books
Post Office Box 1047
Cambridge, MA 02238
800-666-BOOK

C TECH
Post Office Box 30
2 North William Street
Pearl River, NY 10965
800-228-7798

CEC Publications
The Council for Exceptional Children
(CEC)
1110 North Glebe Road
Suite 300
Arlington, VA 22201-5704
888-CEC-SPED
http://www.cec.sped.org/bk/catalog2/
index.html

Center for Applied Research in Education
Book Distribution Center
Route 59 at Brook Hill Drive
West Nyack, NY 10995

Continental Press
520 East Bainbridge Street
Elizabethtown, PA 17022
800-233-0759
http://www.continentalpress.com

Corwin Press
2455 Teller Road
Thousand Oaks, CA 91320
805-499-9774
http://www.corwinpress.com

Educators Publishing Service
Post Office Box 9031
Cambridge, MA 02139-9031
800-435-7728
http://www.epsbooks.com

Franklin Electronic Publishers
1 Franklin Plaza
Burlington, NJ 08016
800-266-5626
http://www.franklin.com

Flyleaf Publishing
Post Office Box 185
Lyme, NH 03768
603-795-2875
http://www.flyleafpublishing.com/home.html

Gander Publishing
416 Higuera Street
San Luis Obispo, CA 93401
800-541-3836
http://www.ganderpublishing.com

Harcourt Assessment
19500 Bulverde Road
San Antonio, TX 78259
800-221-8378
http://www.harcourtassessment.com

High Noon Books
20 Commercial Boulevard
Novato, CA 94949
800-422-7249
http://www.academictherapy.com/support/
    hnb_intro/index2.tpl

Jamestown Publishers
A Glencoe/McGraw Hill Company
800-USA-READ
http://www.glencoe.com/gln/jamestown

Kurzweil Educational Systems
411 Waverley Oaks Road
Waltham, MA 02154
800-894-5374
http://www.kurzweiledu.com

Lawrence Erlbaum Associates
10 Industrial Avenue
Mahwah, NJ 07430
800-926-6579
http://www.erlbaum.com

Lindamood-Bell Learning Processes
416 Higuera Street
San Luis Obispo, CA 93401
800-233-1819
http://www.lblp.com

LinguiSystems
3100 4th Avenue
East Moline, IL 61244
800-776-4332
E-mail: service@linguisystems.com
http://www.linguisystems.com

Modern Learning Press
Post Office Box 167
Department 390
Rosemont, NJ 08556
800-627-5867
http://www.modlearn.com

MTS Publications
Post Office Box 2
Forney, TX 75126
972-564-5005
http://www.mtsedmar.com

Paul H. Brookes Publishing Co.
Post Office Box 10624
Baltimore, MD 21285-0624
800-638-3775; 410-337-9580
E-mail: custserv@brookespublishing.com
http://www.brookespublishing.com

Precious Memory Educational Resources
18403 Northeast 111th Avenue
Battleground, WA 98604
360-687-2082

PRO-ED
8700 Shoal Creek Boulevard
Austin, TX 78757
800-897-3202
http://www.proedinc.com

Recorded Books
270 Skipjack Road
Prince Frederick, MD 20678
800-638-1304
http://www.recordedbooks.com

Recording for the Blind & Dyslexic (RFB&D)
20 Roszel Road
Princeton, NJ 08540
800-221-4792
http://www.rfbd.org

Region XIII TAAS/Education Service Center
5701 Springdale Road
Austin, TX 78723
512-926-5593

Research Press
Post Office Box 9177
Champaign, Il 61826
800-519-2702
http://www.researchpress.com

Riverside Publishing
8420 Bryn Mawr Avenue
Chicago, IL 60631
800-767-8378
http://www.riverpub.com

Saxon Publishers
1320 West Lindsey Street
Norman, OK 73069
800-284-7019
http://www.saxonpublishers.com

S.I.S. Publishing Company
6344 Buenos Aires, NW
Albuquerque, NM 87120
505-881-0026

Slosson Educational Publications
Post Office Box 280
East Aurora, NY 14052
888-756-7766
http://www.slosson.com/index2.ivnu

Smart Stuff & Good Ideas
56 Ludlow Street
New York, NY 10002
800-20-SMART

Social Work, Psychology, and Disabilities
   Video Collection
Fanlight Productions
47 Halifax Street
Boston, MA 02130
800-937-4113

Sopris West
4093 Specialty Place
Longmont, CO 80504-5400
800-547-6747
http://www.sopriswest.com

Vineyard Video Productions
Post Office Box 370
West Tisbury, MA 02575
800-664-6119
E-mail: mpotts@vineyardvideo.org
http://www.vineyardvideo.org

Walker & Co.
435 Hudson Street
New York, NY 10014
800-AT-WALKER
http://www.walkerbooks.com

Winsor Learning
1620 Seventh Street West
Saint Paul, MN 55102
800-321-7585
http://www.sondaysystem.com

York Press
Books available through PRO-ED
800-897-3202

Zaner-Bloser Educational Publisher
2200 West Fifth Avenue
Post Office Box 16764
Columbus, OH 43216
800-421-3018
http://www.zaner-bloser.com

Teacher References

Blachman, B. (Ed.). (1997). *Foundations of reading acquisition and dyslexia: Implications for early intervention*. Mahwah, NJ: Lawrence Erlbaum Associates.

Cox, A.R. (1984). *Structures and techniques: Multisensory teaching of basic language skills*. Cambridge, MA: Educators Publishing Service.

Diamond, L., & Martin, J. (2004). *What reading leaders should know about successful reading instruction*. Emeryville, CA: Consortium on Reading Excellence. (Available from the publisher, http://www.corelearn.com)

Foorman, B.R. (Ed.). (2003). *Preventing and remediating reading difficulties: Bringing science to scale*. Timonium, MD: York Press. (Available from PRO-ED, 800-897-3202)

Gillingham, A., & Stillman, B.W. (1997). *The Gillingham manual: Remedial training for children with specific disability in reading, spelling, and penmanship* (8th ed.). Cambridge, MA: Educators Publishing Service.

Henry, M.K. (2003). *Unlocking literacy: Effective decoding and spelling instruction.* Baltimore: Paul H. Brookes Publishing Co.

Joshi, R.M., Dahlgren M., & Boulware-Gooden, R. (2002). Teaching reading in an inner city school through a multisensory teaching approach. *Annals of Dyslexia, 52,* 229–242.

Learning Disabilities Roundtable. (2002, July 25). *Specific learning disabilities: Finding common ground.* Washington, DC: U.S. Department of Education, Office of Special Education and Rehabilitative Services, Office of Special Education Programs, Division of Research to Practice.

Learning First Alliance. (2000). *Every child reading: A professional development guide.* Washington, DC: Learning First Alliance. (Available from the publisher, http://www.learningfirst.org/publications/reading)

Liberman, I.Y., & Liberman, A.M. (1990). Whole language vs. code emphasis: Underlying assumptions and their implications for reading instruction. *Annals of Dyslexia, 40,* 51–76.

McCardle, P., & Chhabra, V. (Eds.). (2004). *The voice of evidence in reading research.* Baltimore: Paul H. Brookes Publishing Co.

Moats, L.C. (2000). *Speech to print: Language essentials for teachers.* Baltimore: Paul H. Brookes Publishing Co.

Moats, L.C. (2000). *Whole language lives on: The illusion of "balance" in reading instruction.* Washington, DC: Thomas B. Fordham Foundation.

Neuman, S.B., & Dickinson, D.K. (Eds.). (2001). *Handbook of early literacy research.* New York: The Guilford Press.

The Partnership for Reading. (2003, June). *Put reading first: The research building blocks for teaching children to read: Kindergarten through grade 3.* Washington, DC: Author. (Available from ED Pubs, 800-228-8813, Post Office Box 1398, Jessup, MD 20794-1398, e-mail: edpuborders@edpubs.org; also available on-line: http://www.nifl.gov/partnershipforreading/publications/PFRbookletBW.pdf)

Rayner, K., Foorman, B.R., Perfetti, C.A., Pesetsky, D., & Seidenberg, M.S. (2001). How psychological science informs the teaching of reading. *Psychological Science, 2*(2), 31–74.

Scarborough, H.S., & Brady, S.A. (2002). Toward a common terminology for talking about speech and reading: A glossary of the "phon" words and some related terms. *Journal of Literacy Research, 34*(3), 299–336.

Simmons, D.C., &, Kame'enui, E.J. (2003, March 1). *A consumer's guide to valuating a core reading program grades K-3: A critical elements analysis* (Rev. ed.). Eugene: University of Oregon, National Center to Improve the Tools of Educators (NCITE) and Institute for the Development of Educational Achievement (IDEA). Also available on-line: http://reading.uoregon.edu/curricula/con_guide.php

Stanovich, K.E. (2000). *Progress in understanding reading: Scientific foundations and new frontiers.* New York: The Guilford Press.

Wolf, M. (Ed.). (2001). *Dyslexia, fluency and the brain.* Timonium, MD: York Press. (Available from PRO-ED, 800-897-3202)

Recommended Curriculum Guides for Early Reading Success

California Department of Education. (1997). *English-Language Arts content: Standards for California Public Schools, Kindergarten through Grade 12.* Sacramento: Author.

Connecticut State Department of Education. (2000). *Connecticut's Blueprint for Reading Achievement: The Report of the Early Reading Success Panel.* Hartford: Author. Also available on-line: http://www.state.ct.us/sde/dtl/curriculum/currcbra.htm

National Center of Education and the Economy (NCEE) and the University of Pittsburgh. (1999). *Reading and writing grade-by-grade: Primary literacy standards for kindergarten through third grade.* (Available on the NCEE web site: http://www.ncee.org/store/products/detail.jsp?setProtocol=true&id=7)

Professional Journals

American Educator
Annals of Dyslexia

Annals of Neurology
Brain
Brain and Language
Child Development
· *Cognition and Instruction*
Developmental Psychology
Dyslexia: An International Journal of Research and Practice
Educational Psychologist
Exceptional Children
JAMA: The Journal of the American Medical Association
Journal of Child Neurology
Journal of Child Psychology and Psychiatry and Allied Disciplines
Journal of Consulting and Clinical Psychology
Journal of Educational Psychology
Journal of Educational Research
Journal of Experimental Child Psychology
Journal of Experimental Psychology: Learning, Memory, and Cognition
Journal of General Psychology
Journal of Learning Disabilities
Journal of Literacy Research
Journal of Psycholinguistic Research
Journal of Psychology
Journal of Reading Behavior
Journal of Special Education
Journal of Speech and Hearing Disorders
Learning Disabilities Quarterly
Learning Disabilities: A Multidisciplinary Journal
Learning Disabilities: Research and Practice
Nature
Neurology
New England Journal of Medicine
Perspectives
Reading and Writing: An Interdisciplinary Journal
Reading Research Quarterly
The Reading Teacher
Remedial and Special Education
Science
Scientific Studies of Reading
Teaching Exceptional Children
Topics in Language Disorders
Trends in Neurosciences

Videotapes on Dyslexia, Learning Disabilities, and Attention Disorders

(*Source:* The International Dyslexia Association. [2004]. *Videos about dyslexia and other learning disabilities.* Retrieved March 28, 2005, from http://www.interdys.org/fact%20sheets/Video%20List%202004%20B.pdf)

ADD: From A to Z
by Edward Hallowell, M.D. (Available from Hallowell Center, http://www.drhallowell.com/store/add_az.html)

Come Inside Our World
(Available from Texas Scottish Rite Hospital for Children, 222 Wellborn Street, Dallas, TX 75219; 214-559-7525)

Dyslexics Talk About Attaining Success
(Available from Joan Kelly, 326 North Cove Road, Hudson, WI 54016; 715-386-2762)

Einstein and Me: Talking About Learning Disabilities
(Available from The British Dyslexia Association, 98 London Road, Reading, Berkshire RG1 5AU, UNITED KINGDOM; e-mail: admin@bda-dyslexiahelp-bda.demon.co.uk)

Ennis' Gift
(Available from the Hello Friend/Ennis William Cosby Foundation, Post Office Box 4061, Santa Monica, CA 90411; 800-343-5540; http://www.hellofriend.org)

Finding the Answers
(Available from The International Dyslexia Association [IDA], 8600 LaSalle Road, Chester Building, Suite 382, Baltimore, MD 21286; 800-ABC-D123; e-mail: info@interdys.org; http://www.interdys.org)

Fundamentals of Reading Success: An Introduction to the Orton-Gillingham Approach to Teaching Reading (video series, work booklet, and language kit)
(Available from Educators Publishing Service, 31 Smith Place, Cambridge, MA 02138-1000; 800-225-5750; http://www.epsbooks.com/dynamic/catalog/series.asp?seriesonly=7250M)

Gifts of Greatness
Written and directed by Joyce Bulifant. (Available from the National Dyslexia Research Foundation, Post Office Box 393, Boca Grande, FL 33921; 941-964-0999)

Homework and Learning Disabilities: A Common Sense Approach
(Available from Altschul Group Corporation Educational Media, 1560 Sherman Avenue, Suite 100, Evanston, IL 60201; 800-421-2363; e-mail: agcmedia@starnetinc.com)

How Difficult Can This Be? The F.A.T. City Workshop
(Available from LD Online, http://ldonline.learningstore.org/products/LD1001.html)

Last One Picked, First One Picked On
(Available from LD Online, http://ldonline.learningstore.org/products/LD1002.html)

Learning Disabilities: A Family Crisis
(Available for rent or purchase from Altschul Group Corporation Educational Media, 1560 Sherman Avenue, Suite 100, Evanston, IL 60201; 800-421-2363; e-mail: agcmedia@starnetinc.com)

Learning for Life: Kids and Learning Differences
(Available from Disney Educational Productions, 800-295-5010; http://www.Edustation.Disney.com)

LD/LA: Learning Disabilities/Learning Abilities (video series)
(Available from Paul H. Brookes Publishing Co., Post Office Box 10624, Baltimore, MD 21285-0624; 800-638-3775; 410-337-9580; http://www.brookespublishing.com)

Learning Disabilities: The Orton-Gillingham Approach
(Available from San Jose State University, 1 Washington Square, San Jose, CA 95192; contact: Paula Galvin; 408-924-3676)

Look What You've Done!
(Available from LD Online, http://ldonline.learningstore.org/products/LD1005.html)

Slingerland Institute Information Video
(Available from the Slingerland Institute for Literacy, 411 108th Avenue, N.E., Bellevue, WA 98004; 425-453-1190; e-mail: mail@slingerland.org; http://www.slingerland.org)

Unlocking the Written Word—Reading Assist
(Available from Reading ASSIST Institute, 100 West 10th Street, #910, Wilmington, DE 19801; 888-311-1156)

We Can Learn: Understanding and Helping Children with Learning Disabilities
(Available from National Center for Learning Disabilities [NCLD], 381 Park Avenue South, Suite 1420, New York, NY 10016; 888-575-7373; http://www.ncld.org)

When the Chips Are Down: Strategies for Improving Children's Behavior
(Available from LD Online, http://ldonline.learningstore.org/products/LD1004.html)

Wilson Language Training-Group Lesson: Step 6
(Available from Wilson Language Training, http://www.wilsonlanguage.com)

Web Sites

ERIC Clearinghouse on Disabilities and Gifted Education
http://ericec.org

Florida Center for Reading Research's web page on the science of reading
http://www.fcrr.org/science/science.htm

National Clearinghouse for Professions in Special Education (NCPSE)
http://www.specialedcareers.org

No Child Left Behind: A Toolkit for Teachers
http://www.ed.gov/teachers/nclbguide/index2.html

What Works Clearinghouse
http://w-w-c.org

Wrightslaw
http://www.wrightslaw.com/nclb/4defs.reading.htm

CHAPTER 2—MULTISENSORY STRUCTURED LANGUAGE EDUCATION

MSLE Teacher Training Programs and Accrediting Organizations

Accrediting Organizations

The Alliance for Accreditation and Certification of Structured Language Education
(sponsored by The International Dyslexia Association [IDA])
8600 LaSalle Road
Chester Building
Suite 382
Baltimore, MD 21286
800-ABC-D123
E-mail: alliance@interdys.org
The Alliance is composed of three organizations involved in the accrediting (of programs) and/or certifying (of individuals). These organizations are the Academic Language Therapy Association (ALTA), the Academic Language Therapy Association Centers Council (ALTA CC), and the International Multisensory Structured Language Education Council (IMSLEC). The International Dyslexia Association (IDA) sponsors the combined efforts of these organizations.

Accrediting and Certifying Organizations

Academic Language Therapy Association (ALTA) [*Certification*]
13140 Coit Road
Suite 320, LB 120
Dallas, TX 75240
972-233-9107 x204
E-mail: ALTAadmin@ALTAread.org
http://www.ALTAread.org

Academic Language Therapy Association Centers Council (ALTA CC) [*Accreditation*]
Nancy Coffman
c/o Shelton School
15720 Hillcrest Road
Dallas, TX 75248
972-774-1772
E-mail: ncoffman@shelton.org

International Multisensory Structured Language Education Council (IMSLEC) [*Accreditation*]
Joyce Pickering
c/o Shelton School
15720 Hillcrest Road
Dallas, TX 75248
972-774-1772
E-mail: jpickering@shelton.org

Academy of Orton-Gillingham Practitioners and Educators [*Accreditation/Certification*]
East Main Street
Post Office Box 234
Amenia, NY 12501
845-373-8919
E-mail: oga@mohawk.net

ALTA CC Accredited Centers

Centers for Youth and Families
Post Office Box 251970
Little Rock, AR 72225-1970
Director: Stacey Mahurin
501-666-8686

Katheryne Payne Education Center
3240 West Britton Road
Suite 104
Oklahoma City, OK 73120
Director: Janet Riggan
405-755-4205
E-mail: info@payneeducationcenter.org

Literacy Education & Academic Development
  (LEAD)
Post Office Box 262
Argyle, TX 76226
Director: Valerie G. Tucker
940-464-3752
E-mail: lead1234@gte.net

Multisensory Language Training Institute of
  New Mexico
6344 Buenos Aires NW
Albuquerque, NM 87120
Director: Sandra Dillon
505-898-7500
E-mail: sandradillon@msn.com

Neuhaus Education Center
4433 Bissonnet
Bellaire, TX 77401-3233
Director: Kay A. Allen
713-664-7676
E-mail: kayallen@neuhaus.org

The Scottish Rite Learning Center of Austin
508 West 14th Street
Austin, TX 78701
Director: Pat Sekel
512-472-1231
E-mail: psekel@austin.rr.com

The Scottish Rite Learning Center of West
  Texas
602 Avenue Q
Post Office Box 10135
Lubbock, TX 79408
Director: Doris Haney
806-765-9150
E-mail: lubsrite@door.net

Southern Methodist University Learning
  Therapy Program
Southern Methodist University
5236 Tennyson Parkway
Building 4
Suite 108
Plano, TX 75024
Director: Kay Vickery
214-768-7323
E-mail: learning.therapy@smu.edu

Southwest Multisensory Training Center
600 South Jupiter
Allen, TX 75002-4065
Director: Beverly Dooley
972-359-6646
E-mail: bevdool@aol.com

Stratford Friends School Multisensory Teacher
  Training Program
5 Llandillo Road
Havertown, PA 19083
Director: Sandra Howze
610-446-3144

Teachers College, Columbia University
Multisensory Teaching of Basic Language Skills
Post Office Box 31
New York, NY 10027
Director: Mary Hercus-Rowe
212-678-3080
E-mail: mcr30@columbia.edu

Texas Scottish Rite Hospital for Children
Lucius Waites Child Development Center
2222 Wellborn Street
Dallas, TX 75219
Director: Karen Avrit
214-559-7885
E-mail: kavrit@tsrh.org

IMSLEC Accredited Centers

The Association Method
University of Southern Mississippi
DuBard School for Language Disorders
USM Box 10035
Hattiesburg, MS 39406-0035
601-266-5223
E-mail: maureen.martin@usm.edu
Director: Maureen K. Martin, Ph.D.

Atlantic Seaboard Dyslexia Education Center
Expert Training Systems
1123 Nelson Street
Rockville, MD 20850
Director: Claire Nissenbaum
301-762-2414
E-mail: cnissen@aol.com

Basic Language Skills
Scottish Rite Learning Center of Austin
207 West 18th Street
Austin, TX 78701
Director: Pat Sekel
512-472-1231
E-mail: psekel@austin.rr.com

Dyslexia Therapist Training Course
Texas Scottish Rite Hospital for Children
Luke Waites Child Development Center
2222 Wellborn Street
Dallas, TX 75219
Director: Karen Avrit
214-559-7885
E-mail: kavrit@tsrh.org

Greenhills School
Box 15392 Ardmore Station
Winston-Salem, NC 27113
Director: Marjory Roth
336-924-4908
E-mail: greenhills@alltel.net

Greenwood Institute Training Program
The Greenwood Institute for Learning
  Disabilities
14 Greenwood Lane
Putney, VT 05346
Director: Mike Minsky
802-387-4545

The Hill Center Professional Education
   Programs
The Hill Center
3200 Pickett Road
Durham, NC 27705-6008
Director: Jean Neville
919-489-7464
E-mail: smaskel@da.org

Language Training Course—Orton Gillingham
Massachusetts General Hospital
Language Disorders Unit
WANG ACC Building
#737
Boston, MA 02114
Director: Phyllis Meisel
617-726-2764
E-mail: meiselp@aol.com

Literacy Education & Academic Development
   (LEAD)
Post Office Box 262
Argyle, TX 76226
Director: Valerie G. Tucker
940-464-3752
E-mail: lead1234@gte.net

Multisensory Integrated Reading &
   Composition
Southwest Academy
600 South Jupiter Road
Allen, TX 75002-4065
Director: Beverly Dooley
972-359-6646
E-mail: BevDool@aol.com

Multisensory Language Training of New
   Mexico
Multisensory Language Training
6344 Buenos Aires N.W.
Albuquerque, NM 87120
Director: Sandra Dillon
505-898-7500
E-mail: SandraDillon@msn.com

Neuhaus Education Center Dyslexia Specialist
   Program
Neuhaus Education Center
4433 Bissonnet
Bellaire, TX 77401-3233
Director: Kay A. Allen
713-664-7676
E-mail: kallen@neuhaus.org

Orton-Gillingham Dyslexia Specialist Training
   Course
Fairleigh Dickinson University
1000 River Road, T-RH5-02
Teaneck, NJ 07666
Director: Mary L. Farrell
201-692-2816
E-mail: farrell@fdu.edu

Orton Multisensory Structured Language
   Teacher Training Program
Greenhills School
Box 15392, Ardmore Station
Winston-Salem, NC 27113
Director: Marjory J. Roth
336-924-4908
E-mail: troth@nr.infi.net

Payne Education Center Therapist Training
   Course
Kathryne Payne Education Center
3240 West Britton Road
Suite 104
Oklahoma City, OK 73120
Director: Janet Riggan
405-755-4205
E-mail: mary@payneeducationcenter.org

Phonics First
Reading & Language Arts Center
36700 Woodward Avenue
#20
Bloomfield, MI 48340
248-645-9690

Reading ASSIST MSL Professional Course
Reading ASSIST Institute
100 West 10th Street
Suite 910
Wilmington, DE 19801
Director: Rebecca Combs
302-425-4080
E-mail: readinfo@readingassist.org

Shedd MSL Training Course
Shedd Academy
401 South 7th Street
Post Office Box 493
Mayfield, KY 42066
Director: Paul Thompson
207-247-8007
E-mail: thompsonp55@hotmail.com

Shelton MSL Training Course
Shelton School and Evaluation Center
15720 Hillcrest Road
Dallas, TX 75248
Director: Joyce S. Pickering
972-774-1772
E-mail: jpickering@shelton.org

Simultaneous Multisensory Institute of
    Language Arts
Binghampton Fellowship Foundation
2679 Kingham Drive
Memphis, TN 38119
Director: Rosemary Williams
901-754-1441
E-mail: rwilliams@bodineschool.org

SLANT System for Structured Language
    Training
Geller Educational Resources
2772 Whispering Oaks Drive
Buffalo Grove, IL 60089
Director: Marsha A. Geller
847-821-9609
E-mail: gellereducational@yahoo.com

Slingerland Multisensory Approach for
    Language Arts
Slingerland Institute for Literacy
411 108th Avenue, N.E.
Bellevue, WA 98004
Director: Susan Heinz, Ph.D.
425-453-1190
E-mail: mail@slingerland.org
http://www.slingerland.org

Southern Methodist University Learning
    Therapy Program
Southern Methodist University
5236 Tennyson Parkway
Building 4
Suite 108
Plano, TX 75024
Director: Kay Vickery
214-768-7323
E-mail: learning.therapy@smu.edu

Southwest Multisensory Training Center
600 South Jupiter
Allen, TX 75002-4065
Director: Beverly Dooley
972-359-6646
E-mail: bevdool@aol.com

The Spalding Method
Spalding Education International
2814 West Bell Road
Suite 1405
Phoenix, AZ 85053
Director: Carol Wile
602-866-7801
E-mail: mnorth@spalding.org

SSMALD Training Course, The Hardman
    Technique
Hardman & Associates
5746 Centerville Road
Tallahassee, FL 32309
Director: Patricia Hardman, Ph.D.
850-893-2216
E-mail: dri@talstar.com

Starting Over
317 West 89th Street
#9E
New York, NY 10024
Director: Joan Knight
212-769-2760
E-mail: kni.educ@att.net

Stratford Friends School Multisensory Reading
    Instruction
Stratford Friends School
5 Llandillo Road
Havertown, PA 19082
Director: Sandra Howze
610-446-3144
E-mail: showze@stratfordfriends.org

Structured Language Arts Teacher Education
    Program
Dyslexia Association of Greater Baton
    Rouge/Brighton Academy
3488 Partridge Lane
Baton Rouge, LA 70809
Director: Sophie C. Gibson
225-926-2844
E-mail: sgibson@brighton-academy.org

32 Masonic Orton Gillingham Training
    Program
32 Masonic Learning Centers for Children
33 Marrett Road
Lexington, MA 02421
781-862-8515
E-mail: info@childrenslearningcenters.org

Academy of Orton-Gillingham Practitioners and Educators Accredited Training Sites

ASSETS School
One Ohana Nui Way
Honolulu, HI 96818
Contact: Ronald Yoshimoto
808-423-1356

Camperdown Academy
501 Howell Road
Greenville, SC 29615
Contact: Pat Porter
864-244-8899
E-mail: camperdn@bellsouth.net

Commonwealth Learning Center
123 Highland Avenue
Needham, MA 02484-3005
Contact: Mary Briggs
781-444-5193
E-mail: lisambrooks@commlearn.com

The Garside Institute for Teacher Training at the
    Carroll School
Baker Bridge Road
Lincoln, MA 01773
Contact: Louise Freese
781-259-8342

Kildonan School
425 Morse Hill Road
Amenia, NY 12501
Contacts: Diana Hanbury King and William
    Van Cleave
845-373-8111
E-mail: DKING1066@optonline.net

Pine Ridge School
1075 Williston Road
Williston, VT 05495
Contacts: Jean Foss and Wendy Sweeney
802-434-2161
E-mail: jfoss@pineridgeschool.com

The Reading Center
847 5th Street, N.W.
Rochester, MN 55901
Contact: Jean Osman
507-288-5271

Riverside School
2110 McRae Road
Richmond, VA 23235
Contact: Ruth Harris
804-320-3465

Sandhills School
1500 Hallbrook Drive
Columbia, SC 29209
Contact: Anne Vickers
803-695-1400

Schenck School
282 Mount Paran Road, NW
Atlanta, GA 30327
Contacts: Eugenia Calloway and Rosalie Davis
404-252-2591

Other MSLE Training Programs

The Stern Center
135 Allen Brook Lane
Williston, VT 05495-9209
800-544-4863
E-mail: educator@sterncenter.org
http://www.sterncenter.org

Wilson Language Training
175 West Main Street
Millbury, MA 01527
800-899-8454 (ordering materials)
800-899-5699 (training information)
http://www.wilsonlanguge.com

Web Site

The DANA Foundation
http://www.dana.org

CHAPTER 3—DEVELOPMENT OF ORAL LANGUAGE AND ITS RELATIONSHIP TO LITERACY

Teacher References

Agin, M.C., Geng, L.F., & Nicholl, M.J. (2003). *The late talker: What to do if your child isn't talking yet.* New York: St. Martin's Press.

Allen, J. (1999). *Words, words, words: Teaching vocabulary in Grades 4-12.* Portland, ME: Stenhouse Publishers.

Apel, K., & Masterson, J. (2001). *Beyond baby talk: From sounds to sentences.* Roseville, CA: Prima Publishing.

Baron, N. (1992). *Growing up with language.* Reading, MA: Addison Wesley Longman.

Bielmiller, A. (1999). *Language and reading success.* Cambridge, MA: Brookline Books.

Butler, K.G., & Silliman, E.R. (2002). *Speaking, reading, and writing in children with language learning disabilities.* Mahwah, NJ: Lawrence Erlbaum Associates

Catts, H.W., & Kamhi, A.G. (Eds.). (2005). *Language and reading disabilities* (2nd ed.). Boston: Allyn & Bacon.

Hamaguchi, P. (1995). *Childhood speech, language and listening problems.* New York: John Wiley & Sons.

Hulit, L., & Howard, M. (1993). *Born to talk: An introduction to speech and language development.* New York: Macmillan.

Meltzer, L. (Ed.). (1993). *Strategy assessment and instruction for students with learning disabilities.* Austin, TX: PRO-ED.

Menyuk, P. (1999). *Reading and linguistic development.* Cambridge, MA: Brookline Books.

Merritt, D., & Culatta, B. (1998). *Language intervention in the classroom.* San Diego: Singular Publishing Group.

Owens, R. (1996). *Language development: An introduction* (3rd ed.). Columbus, OH: Charles E. Merrill.

Roberts, J.E., & Burchinal, M.R. (2001). The complex interplay between biology and environment: Otitis media and mediating effects on early literacy development. In S.B. Neuman & D.K. Dickinson (Eds.), *Handbook of early literacy research* (pp. 232–244). New York: The Guilford Press.

Stahl, S. (1999). *Vocabulary development.* Cambridge, MA: Brookline Books.

Wallach, G., & Butler, K. (1994). *Language learning disabilities in school-age children and adolescents.* Boston: Allyn & Bacon.

Instructional Materials

Dandy Lion Publications
3563 Sueldo Street
Suite L
San Luis Obispo, CA 93401
800-776-8032
E-mail: dandy@dandylionbooks.com
http://www.dandylionbooks.com

Janelle Publications
Post Office Box 811
DeKalb, IL 60115
800-888-8834
E-mail: info@janellepublications.com
http://www.janellepublications.com

Remedia Publications
15887 North 76th Street
#120
Scottsdale, AZ
800-826-4740
http://www.REMPUB.com

The Speech Bin
1965 25th Avenue
Vero Beach, FL 32960
800-4-SPEECH

Super Duper Publications
Department SD 2004
Post Office Box 24997
Greenville, NC 29616
800-277-8737
http://www.superduperinc.com

Thinking Publications
424 Galloway
Eau Claire, WI 54703
800-225-4769
http://www.ThinkingPublications.com

Professional Journals

American Journal of Speech-Language Pathology
Journal of Speech and Hearing Disorders
Language, Speech, and Hearing Services in the Schools
Topics in Language Disorders

Web Site

American Speech-Language-Hearing Association
http://www.asha.org

CHAPTER 4 — PHONEMIC AWARENESS AND READING: RESEARCH, ACTIVITIES, AND INSTRUCTIONAL MATERIALS

Teacher References

Adams, M.J., Bereiter, C., Hirshberg, J., Anderson, V., & Case, R. (1995). *Framework for effective teaching: Sounds and letters* (Teacher's guide). New York: McGraw-Hill.

Adams, M.J., Foorman, B.R., Lundberg, I., & Beeler, T. (1998). *Phonemic awareness in young children: A classroom curriculum.* Baltimore: Paul H. Brookes Publishing Co.

Blachman, B.A., Ball, E.W., Black, R., & Tangel, D.M. (1994). Kindergarten teachers develop phoneme awareness in low income inner-city classrooms: Does it make a difference? *Reading and Writing: An Interdisciplinary Journal, 6,* 1–18.

Byrne, B., & Fielding-Barnsley, R. (1991). *Sound foundations.* Artamon, New South Wales, Australia: Leyden Educational Publishers. (Available from the publisher, 36 Whiting Street, Artamon, New South Wales 2064, AUSTRALIA)

Carreker, S. (1992). *Reading readiness.* Bellaire, TX: Neuhaus Education Center.

Catts, H.W., & Vartiainen, T. (1993). *Sounds abound: Listening, rhyming, and reading.* East Moline, IL: LinguiSystems.

Clark, D.B., & Uhry, J.K. (1995). *Dyslexia: Theory and practice of remedial instruction* (2nd ed.). Timonium, MD: York Press. (Available from PRO-ED, 800-897-3202)

Conocimiento fonémico [Trans. and adapted by Sánchez Hart Consultants from *Phoneme awareness* by M.T. Smith, 1997]. Forney, TX: MTS Publications.

Cunningham, A.E. (1990). Explicit instruction in phonemic awareness. *Journal of Experimental Child Psychology, 50,* 429–444.

Griffith, P.L., & Olson, M.W. (1992). Phonemic awareness helps beginning readers break the code. *The Reading Teacher, 45,* 516–523.

Stanovich, K.E., Cunningham, A.E., & Cramer, B. (1984). Assessing phonological awareness in kindergarten children: Issues of task comparability. *Journal of Experimental Child Psychology, 38,* 175–190.

Torgesen, J.K. (1995). *Orton Emeritus series: Phonological awareness. A critical factor in dyslexia.* Baltimore: The International Dyslexia Association.

Uhry, J.K. (1993). Predicting reading from phonological awareness and classroom print: An early reading screening. *Educational Assessment, 1,* 349–368.

Yopp, H.K. (1995). A test for assessing phonemic awareness in young children. *The Reading Teacher, 49,* 20–29.

Curricula, Guides, and Activities

Bear, D.R., Invernizzi, M., Templeton, S., & Johnston, F. (1996). *Words their way: Word study for phonics, vocabulary, and spelling instruction.* Upper Saddle River, NJ: Prentice Hall.

Blachman, B.A., Ball, E.W., Black, R., & Tangel, D.M. (2000). *Road to the code: A phonological awareness program for young children.* Baltimore: Paul H. Brookes Publishing Co.

Gentry, J.R. (1982). An analysis of developmental spelling in GYNS AT WRK. *The Reading Teacher, 36,* 192–200.

Goldsworthy, C.L. (1998). *Sourcebook of phonological awareness activities: Children's classic literature.* San Diego: Singular Publishing Group.

Notari-Syverson, A., O'Connor, R.E., & Vadasy, P.F. (1998). *Ladders to literacy: A preschool activity book.* Baltimore: Paul H. Brookes Publishing Co.

O'Connor, R.E., Notari-Syverson, A., & Vadasy, P.F. (2005). *Ladders to literacy: A kindergarten activity book* (2nd ed.). Baltimore: Paul H. Brookes Publishing Co.

Opitz, M.F. (1998). Children's books to develop phonemic awareness—for you and parents too! *The Reading Teacher, 51,* 526–528.

Smith, M.T. (1999). *Phoneme awareness: Assessment, instruction, practice.* Forney, TX: MTS Publications.

Wilson, B.A. (2002). *Teacher's manual, Levels K-1 (Fundations).* Millbury, MA: Wilson Language Training.

Wilson, B.A. (2004). *Teacher's manual, Level 2 (Fundations).* Millbury, MA: Wilson Language Training. (Both *Fundations* manuals are available from the publisher, http://www.wilsonlanguage.com)

Yopp, H.K. (1992). Developing phonological awareness in young children. *The Reading Teacher, 45,* 696–703.

Yopp, H.K. (1995). Read-aloud books for developing phonemic awareness: An annotated bibliography. *The Reading Teacher, 48,* 538–542.

Instructional Materials

Lindamood Auditory Conceptualization complete kit. (1971). Austin, TX: PRO-ED.

Lindamood, P., & Lindamood, P. (1998). *Lindamood phoneme sequencing program for reading, spelling, and speech (LiPS): Teacher's manual for the classroom and clinic* (3rd ed.). Austin, TX: PRO-ED.

Torgesen, J.K., & Bryant, B. (1993). *Phonological awareness training for reading* [Kit]. Austin, TX: PRO-ED.

Torgesen, J.K., & Bryant, B. (2004). *Test of Phonological Awareness, 2nd Edition: PLUS (TOPA-2+)* [Complete kit]. Austin, TX: PRO-ED.

Assessment Tools

Denckla, M.B., & Rudel, R.G. (1976). *Rapid Automatized Naming Test.* Baltimore: Kennedy Krieger Institute.

Lindamood, C.H., & Lindamood, P.C. (1971). *The LAC Test: Lindamood Auditory Conceptualization Test.* Austin, TX: PRO-ED.

Robertson, C., & Salter, W. (1997). *The Phonological Awareness Test.* East Moline, IL: LinguiSystems.

Sawyer, D.J. (1987). *Test of Awareness of Language Segments.* Austin, TX: PRO-ED.

Seymour, H.N., Roeper, T.W., & de Villiers, J. (with de Villiers, P.A.). (2003). *Diagnostic Evaluation of Language Variance (DELV–Criterion Referenced).* San Antonio, TX: Harcourt Assessment.

Seymour, H.N., Roeper, T.W., & de Villiers, J. (with de Villiers, P.A.). (2003). *Diagnostic Evaluation of Language Variance–Screening Test (DELV–Screening Test).* San Antonio, TX: Harcourt Assessment.

Smith, M.T. (1999). *Phoneme awareness: Assessment, instruction, practice.* Forney, TX: MTS Publications.

Torgesen, J.K., & Bryant, B.R. (1994). *Test of Phonological Awareness (TOPA).* Austin, TX: PRO-ED.

Wagner, R., Torgesen, J.K., & Rashotte, C. (1999). *Comprehensive Test of Phonological Processing.* Austin, TX: PRO-ED.

Wolf, M., & Denckla, M.B. (2005). *Rapid Automatized Naming and Rapid Alternating Stimulus Tests.* Austin, TX: PRO-ED.

Yopp, H.K. (1995). A test for assessing phonemic awareness in young children. *The Reading Teacher, 49,* 20–29.

Videotapes

Birsh, J.R. (Consulting Ed.), & Potts, M., & Potts, R. (Producers). (1997). *LD/LA: Learning disabilities/learning abilities (Videotapes I–IV).* West Tisbury, MA: Vineyard Video Productions. (Available from Paul H. Brookes Publishing Co., Post Office Box 10624, Baltimore, MD 21285-0624; 800-638-3775; 410-337-9580; http://www.brookespublishing.com)

Software

Erickson, G.C., Foster, K.C., Forster, D.F., Torgesen, J.K., & Packer, S. (1992). *Daisyquest*. Scotts Valley, CA: Great Wave Software.

Erickson, G.C., Foster, K.C., Forster, D.F., Torgesen, J.K., & Packer, S. (1993). *Daisy's castle*. Scotts Valley, CA: Great Wave Software.

Parent Resources

With the exception of Adams, Foorman, Lundberg, and Beeler (1997), these parent resources are adapted from Yopp, H.K. (1995). Read-aloud books for developing phonemic awareness: An annotated bibliography. *The Reading Teacher, 48*(6), 538–542. Copyright © International Reading Association; adapted by permission.

Adams, M.J., Foorman, B.R., Lundberg, I., & Beeler, T. (1997). Annotated bibliography of rhyming stories. In *Phonemic awareness in young children: A classroom curriculum* (Appendix F, pp. 159–169). Baltimore: Paul H. Brookes Publishing Co.

Adams, M.J., Foorman, B.R., Lundberg, I., & Beeler, T. (1997). Poems, fingerplays, jingles, and chants. In *Phonemic awareness in young children: A classroom curriculum* (Appendix G, pp. 171–175). Baltimore: Paul H. Brookes Publishing Co.

Brown, M.W. (1983). *Four fur feet*. New York: Bantam Doubleday Dell.

Buller, J., & Schade, S. (1989). *I love you, good night*. New York: Simon & Schuster.

Carter, D. (1990). *More bugs in boxes*. New York: Simon & Schuster.

de Regniers, B., Moore, E., White, M., & Carr, J. (1988). *Sing a song of popcorn*. New York: Scholastic.

Deming, A.G. (1994). *Who is tapping at my window?* New York: Penguin USA.

Ehlert, L. (1989). *Eating the alphabet: Fruits and vegetables from A to Z*. Orlando, FL: Harcourt Brace & Co.

Emberley, B. (1992). *One wide river to cross*. Boston: Little, Brown.

Geraghty, P. (1992). *Stop that noise!* New York: Crown.

Gordon, J. (1991). *Six sleepy sheep*. New York: Puffin Books.

Hague, K. (1984). *Alphabears*. New York: Henry Holt.

Krauss, R. (1985). *I can fly*. New York: Young Scott Books.

Kuskin, K. (1990). *Roar and more*. New York: HarperCollins.

Lewison, W. (1992). *Buzz said the bee*. New York: Scholastic.

Martin, B. (1989). *Chicka chicka boom boom*. New York: Simon & Schuster.

Marzollo, J. (1989). *The teddy bear book*. New York: Dial.

Obligado, L. (1983). *Faint frogs feeling feverish and other terrifically tantalizing tongue twisters*. New York: Viking.

Ochs, C.P. (1991). *Moose on the loose*. Minneapolis, MN: Carolrhoda Books.

Otto, C. (1991). *Dinosaur chase*. New York: HarperCollins.

Parry, C. (1991). *Zoomerang-a-boomerang: Poems to make your belly laugh*. New York: Puffin Books.

Patz, N. (1983). *Moses supposes his toeses are roses*. Orlando, FL: Harcourt Brace & Co.

Pomerantz, C. (1993). *If I had a paka*. New York: Mulberry.

Prelutsky, J. (1982). *The baby Uggs are hatching*. New York: Mulberry.

Prelutsky, J. (1989). *Poems of A. Nonny Mouse*. New York: Alfred A. Knopf.

Raffi, D. (1989). *Down by the bay: Raffi songs to read*. New York: Crown.

Sendak, M. (1990). *Alligators all around: An alphabet*. New York: HarperCollins.

Seuss, Dr. (1963). *Dr. Seuss's ABC*. New York: Random House.

Seuss, Dr. (1965). *Fox in socks*. New York: Random House.

Seuss, Dr. (1974). *There's a wocket in my pocket*. New York: Random House.

Shaw, N. (1989). *Sheep on a ship*. Boston: Houghton Mifflin.

Showers, P. (1991). *The listening walk*. New York: HarperCollins.

Silverstein, S. (1964). *A giraffe and a half*. New York: HarperCollins.

Staines, B. (1989). *All God's critters got a place in the choir*. New York: Penguin.

Van Allsburg, C. (1987). *The Alphabet Theatre proudly presents the Z Was Zapped: A Play in Twenty-Six Acts.* Boston: Houghton Mifflin.

Winthrop, E. (1986). *Shoes.* New York: HarperCollins.

Web Sites

Get Ready to Read!
http://www.getreadytoread.org

Phonemic Awareness Activities for 4-5-6 Year Olds
http://www.iusd.k12.ca.us/parent_resources/phonemicawareness456.htm

CHAPTER 5—ALPHABET KNOWLEDGE: LETTER RECOGNITION, NAMING, AND SEQUENCING

Teacher References

Balmuth, M. (1982). *The roots of phonics.* New York: Teachers College Press.

Dowdell, D. (1965). *Secrets of the ABC's.* Fayetteville, GA: Oddo Publishing.

Logan, R.K. (1986). *The alphabetic effect.* New York: William Morrow and Company, Inc.

Museum of the Alphabet. (1990). *The alphabet makers.* Huntington Beach, CA: Summer Institute of Linguistics.

Ogg, O. (1971). *The 26 letters.* New York: Thomas Y. Crowell. (Out of print but still available in libraries.)

Patton, S.J. (1989). *Alphabetic: A history of our alphabet.* Tucson, AZ: Zephyr Press.

Curricula, Guides, and Activities

Cox, A.R. (1992). *Foundations for literacy: Structures and techniques for multisensory teaching of basic written English language skills.* Cambridge, MA: Educators Publishing Service.

Fisher, L.E. (1978). *Alphabet art: Thirteen ABC's from around the world.* New York: Macmillan.

Gillingham, A., & Stillman, B.W. (1997). *The Gillingham manual: Remedial training for children with specific disability in reading, spelling, and penmanship* (8th ed.). Cambridge, MA: Educators Publishing Service.

Hogan, E.A., & Smith, M.T. (1987). *Alphabet and dictionary skills guide.* Cambridge, MA: Educators Publishing Service.

Instructional Materials

Abecedarian
8025 Cobblestone
Austin, TX 78735-7901
Phone/fax: 800-342-1165
E-mail: info@alphabetletter.com
http://alphabetletter.com
Set of 26 plastic uppercase block letters (1¼", nonmagnetic, blue)
Set of 28 plastic lowercase letters (1¼", nonmagnetic, red with two styles of *g*)
Set of 29 plastic uppercase letters for Spanish (1¼", nonmagnetic, green)
Set of 30 plastic lowercase letters for Spanish (1¼", nonmagnetic, orange)
Plastic classroom-size uppercase alphabet strip (3" × 48")
Desk-size alphabet strip approximately (2" × 17½")

Dominie Press
1949 Kellogg Avenue
Carlsbad, CA 92008
800-232-4570
E-mail: info@dominie.com
http://www.dominie.com
EUC 3896—Set of 38 plastic uppercase magnetic letters (1¼", English)
ELC 9098—Set of plastic lowercase magnetic letters (1¼", 90- or 45-piece set)
SUC 4296—Spanish edition of uppercase letters (42-piece set)
SLC 6396—Spanish edition of lowercase letters (62-piece set)

Educators Publishing Service
Post Office Box 9031
Cambridge, MA 02139-9031
800-435-7728
E-mail: epsbooks@epsbooks.com
http://www.epsbooks.com
The following items are not on the web site and must be ordered by telephone.
5047—Set of plastic uppercase block letters (magnetic)
5107—Laminated individual alphabet strip (2½" × 22½")
409—Advanced Reading Deck (graphemes on cards)
413—Initial Reading Deck (pictures and graphemes on cards)
408—Missing Letter Deck (uppercase block letters on cards)
202—Phonics Drill Cards (no pictures on cards)
6202—Phonics Drill Cards (with pictures on cards)
1459—Skeleton Dictionary (guide-word practice dictionary)
1662—Teacher's Hand Pack for Classroom Use (letters of the alphabet, phonograms, digraphs, and letter combinations)

Software

Bailey's Book House (Edmark; available from Riverdeep; 800-825-4420; http://www.riverdeep.net)
Letter Machine (Edmark; available as a free download from Riverdeep; 800-825-4420; http://www .riverdeep.net)
Lexia Phonics Based Reading (Lexia Learning Systems, 2 Lewis Street, Post Office Box 466, Lincoln, MA, 01773; 800-435-3942; http://www.lexialearning.com)

CHAPTER 6—THE HISTORY AND STRUCTURE OF WRITTEN ENGLISH

General Teacher Resources

Ayto, J. (1999). *Twentieth century words.* New York: Oxford University Press.
Balmuth, M. (1982). *The roots of English.* Timonium, MD: York Press. (Available from PRO-ED, 800-897-3202)
Barnett, L. (1964). *The treasure of our tongue.* New York: Alfred A. Knopf.
Bryson, B. (1990). *The mother tongue: English and how it got that way.* New York: William Morrow.
Claiborne, R. (1983). *Our marvelous native tongue. The life and times of the English language.* New York: Times Books.
Lederer, R. (1991). *The miracle of language.* New York: Pocket Books.
Logan, R.K. (1986). *The alphabet effect.* New York: St. Martins Press.
Manguel, A. (1996). *A history of reading.* New York: Viking.
Martin, H.-J. (1994). *The history and power of writing.* Chicago: University of Chicago Press.

McCrum, R., Cran, S., & MacNeil, R. (1986). *The story of English.* New York: Viking.

Nist, J. (1966). *A structural history of English.* New York: St. Martins Press.

Pei, M. (1965). *The story of language.* New York: J.B. Lippincott. (Original work published 1949)

Pinker, S. (1994). *The language instinct.* New York: William Morrow.

Soukhanov, A.H. (1995). *Word watch.* New York: Henry Holt.

Curricula, Guides, and Activities

Bebko, A.R., Alexander, J., & Doucet, R. (2001). *LANGUAGE! Roots* (2nd ed.). Longmont, CO: Sopris West.

Blanchard, C. *Word roots series* (Level A, Grades 4–12+; Level B, Grade 7–12+). Pacific Grove, CA: Critical Thinking Books and Software.

Ehrlich, I. (1972). *Instant vocabulary.* New York: Pocket Books.

Fifer, N., & Flowers, N. (1990). *Vocabulary from classical roots.* Cambridge, MA: Educators Publishing Service.

Henry, M.K. (1990). *WORDS: Integrated decoding and spelling instruction based on word origin and word structure.* Austin, TX: PRO-ED.

Henry, M.K. (2003). *Unlocking literacy: Effective decoding and spelling instruction.* Baltimore: Paul H. Brookes Publishing Co.

Henry, M.K., & Redding, N.C. (1996). *Patterns for success in reading and spelling.* Austin, TX: PRO-ED.

Johnson, K., & Bayrd, P. (1998). *Megawords series.* (1998). Cambridge, MA: Educators Publishing Service.

Kleiber, M.H. (1990–2004). *Specific language training: An Orton-Gillingham curriculum for adolescents.* Yonkers, NY: Decatur Enterprises. (Available from the publisher, 26 Birch Road, Yonkers, NY 10705)

Marcellaro, E.G., & Ostrovsky, G.R. (1988). *Verbal vibes series.* Sacramento, CA: Lumen Publications.

Moats, L.C. (2000). *Speech to print: Language essentials for teachers.* Baltimore: Paul H. Brookes Publishing Co.

Morgan, K. (2002). *Dynamic roots.* Albuquerque: Morgan Dynamic Phonics.

Pinnell, G.S., & Fountas, I.C. (1998). *Word matters.* Portsmouth, NH: Heinemann.

Rome, P.D., & Osman, J.S. (1993). *Language tool kit.* Cambridge, MA: Educators Publishing Service.

Rome, P.D., & Osman, J.S. (2000). *Advanced language tool kit.* Cambridge, MA: Educators Publishing Service.

Steere, A., Peck, C.Z., & Kahn, L. (1971). *Solving language difficulties.* Cambridge, MA: Educators Publishing Service.

Wimer, D.B. (1994). *Word studies: A classical perspective, Prefixes + roots + suffixes* (Vol. 1). Richmond, VA: Author. (Available from the author, Post Office Box 5362, Richmond, VA 23220)

Instructional Materials

Student Dictionaries and Thesauri

Agnes, M.E. (Ed.). (1999). *Webster's new world children's dictionary* (2nd ed.) [For ages 7–12]. New York: John Wiley & Sons.

American Heritage student dictionary [For Grades 6–9]. (1998). Boston: Houghton Mifflin.

American Heritage student thesaurus [For Grades 7–10]. (1999). Boston: Houghton Mifflin.

Barnhart, R.K. (Ed.). (1988). *The Barnhart dictionary of etymology.* New York: The H.W. Wilson Co.

Bollard, J.K. (1988). *Scholastic children's thesaurus.* New York: Scholastic.

Crutchfield, R.S. (1997). *English vocabulary quick reference: A comprehensive dictionary arranged by word roots.* Leesburg, VA: LexaDyne Publishing.

Halsey, W.D. (Ed.). (2001). *MacMillan dictionary for children.* New York: Simon & Schuster.

Latimer, J.P., & Nolting, K.S. (2001). *Simon and Schuster thesaurus for children* [For ages 9–12]. New York: Simon & Schuster.

Levey, J.S. (Ed.). (1990). *Macmillan first dictionary* [For ages 4–8]. New York: Simon & Schuster.

Levey, J.S. (Ed.). (2002). *Scholastic children's dictionary* [For ages 8–12]. New York: Scholastic Reference.

Games

Johnson, P.F. (1999). *Word Scramble 2.* East Moline, IL: LinquiSystems.

UpWords. (1999). East Longmeadow, MA: Milton Bradley (a division of Hasbro).

Word Lists

Anderson, C.W. (1980). *Workbooks of resource words for phonetic reading* (Books 1–3). Lincoln, NE: Educational Tutorial Consortium. (Available from the publisher, http://www.etc-ne.com/rw100.lasso)

Bloom, F., & Coates, D.B. (2000). *Recipe for reading.* Austin, TX: PRO-ED.

Fry, E.B., Kress, J.E., & Fountoukidis, D. (2000). *The reading teacher's book of lists* (4th ed.). Upper Saddle River: Prentice Hall.

Henry, M.K. (2003). *Unlocking literacy: Effective decoding and spelling instruction* (Appendices B–G, pp. 167–283). Baltimore: Paul H. Brookes Publishing Co.

Jones, T.B. (1997). *Decoding and encoding English words.* Timonium, MD: York Press. (Available from PRO-ED, 800-897-3202)

Slingerland, B.H. (1982). *Phonetic word lists for children's use.* Cambridge, MA: Educators Publishing Service.

Software

Inspiration Software
http://www.inspiration.com

KidPix Deluxe 4 for Schools
http://www.kidpix.com

Student Resources

Brook, D., & Zallinger, J.D. (Illustrator). (1998). *The journey of English.* New York: Clarion Books.

Klausner, J. (1990). *Talk about English: How words travel and change.* New York: Thomas Y. Crowell.

Krensky, S. (1996). *Breaking into print: Before and after the invention of the printing press.* Toronto: Little, Brown.

Samoyault, T. (1996). *Alphabetical Order: How the alphabet began.* New York: Penguin.

Parent Resources

Beal, G. (1992). *Book of words: A–Z guide to quotations, proverbs, origins, usage, and idioms.* New York: Kingfisher Books.

Brook, D. (1998). *The journey of English.* New York: Clarion Books.

Web Sites for Teachers and Parents

American Speech-Language-Hearing Association
http://www.asha.org

Critical Thinking Books and Software
http://www.criticalthinking.com

Explore English Words Derived from Latin-Greek Origins
http://www.wordexplorations.com

The International Dyslexia Association (IDA)
http://www.interdys.org

Morgan Dynamic Phonics
http://www.dynamicphonics.com

Reading Rockets
http://www.readingrockets.org

Vocabulary University
http://www.vocabulary.com

A Word A Day
http://wordsmith.org/awad

CHAPTER 7—ASSESSMENT OF READING DIFFICULTIES

Teacher References

General Assessment

Chall, J.S. (1994). Testing linked to teaching. In N.C. Jordan & J. Goldsmith-Phillips (Eds.), *Learning disabilities: New directions for assessment and intervention* (pp. 163–176). Boston: Allyn & Bacon.

Choate, J.S., Enright, B.E., Miller, L.J., Poteet, J.A., & Rakes, T.A. (1995). *Curriculum-based assessment and programming*. Boston: Allyn & Bacon.

Cohen, L., & Spenciner, L. (1998). *Assessment of children and youth*. Reading, MA: Addison Wesley Longman.

Darling-Hammond, L., Ancess, J., & Falk, B. (1995). *Authentic assessment in action*. New York: Teachers College Press.

Idol, L.A., Nevin, A., & Paolucci-Whitcomb, P. (1996). *Models of curriculum-based assessment*. Austin, TX: PRO-ED.

Kubiszyn, T., & Borich, G. (1993). *Educational testing and measurement: Classroom application and practice* (5th ed.). Boston: Houghton Mifflin.

Nitkop, A.J. (1996). *Educational assessment of students*. Upper Saddle River, NJ: Prentice Hall.

Salvia, J., & Ysseldyke, J.E. (2004). *Assessment* (9th ed.). Boston: Houghton Mifflin.

Spenciner, L.J. (2002). *Assessment of children and youth with special needs*. Upper Saddle River, NJ: Pearson Education.

Wiggins, G. (1993). *Assessing student performance: Exploring the purpose and limits of testing*. San Francisco: Jossey-Bass.

Reading and Writing Development and Disorders

Coles, G. (1998). *Reading lessons: The debate over literacy*. New York: Hill & Wang.

Felton, R.H. (1998). The development of reading skills in poor readers: Educational implications. In C. Hulme & R.M. Joshi (Eds.), *Reading and spelling: Development and disorders* (pp. 219–233). Mahwah, NJ: Lawrence Erlbaum Associates.

Fink, R.P. (1996). Successful dyslexics: A constructivist study of passionate interest in reading. *Journal of Adolescent and Adult Literacy, 39*, 268–280.

Lyon, G.R., Shaywitz, S.E., & Shaywitz, B.A. (2003). A definition of dyslexia. *Annals of Dyslexia, 53*, 1–14.

Lyon, G.R., Fletcher, J.M., Shaywitz, S.E., Shaywitz, B.A., Torgesen, J.K., Wood, F.B., et al. (2001). Rethinking learning disabilities. In C.E. Finn, R.A.J. Rotherham, & C.R. Hokanson (Eds.), *Rethinking special education for a new century* (pp. 259–287). Washington, DC: Thomas B. Fordham Foundation & Progressive Policy Institute.

Olson, R.K., Wise, B., Ring, J., & Johnson, M. (1997). Computer-based remedial reading training in phoneme awareness and phonological decoding: Effects on the post-training development of word recognition. *Scientific Studies of Reading, 1*, 235–253.

Pennington, B.F., Gilger, J.W., Olson, R.K., & DeFries, J.C. (1992). The external validity of age-versus IQ-discrepancy definitions of reading disability: Lessons from a twin study. *Journal of Learning Disabilities, 25*, 562–573.

Rhodes, L.K., & Shanklin, N.L. (1993). *Windows into literacy*. Portsmouth, NH: Heinemann.

Shaywitz, S.E. (1996). Dyslexia. *Scientific American, 275*, 98–104.

Shaywitz, S.E. (1998). Dyslexia. *New England Journal of Medicine, 338*, 207–312.

Shepherd, M.J., Charnow, D.A., & Silver, L.B. (1989). Development of reading disorder. In H. Kaplan & B. Sadow (Eds.), *Comprehensive textbook of psychiatry* (5th ed., Vol. 2, pp. 1790–1800). Philadelphia: Lippincott, Williams & Wilkins.

Shepherd, M.J., & Uhry, J.K. (1993). Reading disorder. *Child and Adolescent Clinics of North America, 2*, 193–208.

Snowling, M., & Hulme, C. (1989). A longitudinal case study of developmental phonological dyslexia. *Cognitive Neuropsychology, 6*, 379–401.

Torgesen, J.K. (2000). Individual differences in response to early interventions in reading: The lingering problem of treatment resisters. *Learning Disabilities Research and Practice, 15,* 55–64.

Torgesen, J.K., Alexander, A.W., Wagner, R.K., Rashotte, C.A., Voeller, K., Conway, T., et al. (2001). Intensive remedial instruction for children with severe reading disabilities: Immediate and long-term outcomes from two instructional approaches. *Journal of Learning Disabilities, 34,* 33–58.

U.S. Department of Education, Office of Special Education and Rehabilitative Services. (2002). *A new era: Revitalizing special education for children and their families.* Washington, DC: U.S. Government Printing Office.

Reading and Writing Assessment

Anthony, R., Johnson, T., Midelson, N., & Preece, A. (1991). *Evaluating literacy: A perspective for change.* Portsmouth, NH: Heinemann.

Barr, R., Kaufman, B., Katz, C., Blachowicz, C.L., & Blachowicz, C. (2001). *Reading diagnosis for teachers: An instructional approach* (4th ed.). Upper Saddle River, NJ: Pearson Education.

Clay, M.M. (1995). *An observation of early literacy attainment.* Portsmouth, NH: Heinemann.

Glazer, S.M., & Brown, C.S. (1993). *Portfolios and beyond: Collaborative assessment in reading and writing.* Norwood, MA: Christopher Gordon.

Hewett, G. (1995). *A portfolio primer: Teaching, collecting, and assessing student writing.* Portsmouth, NH: Heinemann.

Kibby, M.W. (1995). *Practical steps for informing literacy instruction: A diagnostic decision-making model.* Newark, DE: International Reading Association.

Miller, W.H. (1995). *Alternative assessment techniques for reading and writing.* West Nyack, NY: Center for Applied Research in Education.

Rhodes, L.K., & Shanklin, N.L. (1993). *Windows into literacy.* Portsmouth, NH: Heinemann.

Roskos, K., & Walter, B.J. (1994). *Interactive handbook for understanding reading diagnosis.* Upper Saddle River, NJ: Prentice Hall.

Texas Scottish Rite Hospital for Children. (1992). *Dyslexia training program (Schedules I–III progress measurements: Teacher's guide and student's books).* Cambridge, MA: Educators Publishing Service.

Valencia, S.W., Hiebert, E.H., & Afflerbach, P.P. (Eds.). (1994). *Authentic reading assessment: Practice and possibilities.* Newark, DE: International Reading Association.

Torgesen, J.K., & Mathes, P. (2000). *A basic guide to understanding, assessing, and teaching phonological awareness.* Austin, TX: PRO-ED.

Walker, B.J. (1996). *Diagnostic teaching of reading: Techniques for instruction and assessment* (3rd ed.). Upper Saddle River, NJ: Prentice Hall.

Videotapes

Birsh, J.R. (Consulting Ed.), & Potts, M., & Potts, R. (Producers). (1997). *LD/LA: Learning disabilities/learning abilities: Videotape I. Introduction: Understanding learning disabilities through demonstration and description.* West Tisbury, MA: Vineyard Video Productions. (Available from Paul H. Brookes Publishing Co., Post Office Box 10624, Baltimore, MD 21285-0624; 800-638-3775; 410-337-9580; http://www.brookespublishing.com)

Birsh, J.R. (Consulting Ed.), & Potts, M., & Potts, R. (Producers). (1997). *LD/LA: Learning disabilities/learning abilities: Videotape IV. Children & parents & schools & strengths.* West Tisbury, MA: Vineyard Video Productions. (Available from Paul H. Brookes Publishing Co., Post Office Box 10624, Baltimore, MD 21285-10624; 800-638-3775; 410-337-9580; http://www.brookespublishing.com)

Parent Resources

Greene, J.F., & Moats, L.C. (2001). *The "T" book. Testing: Critical components in the clinical identification of dyslexia* (3rd ed.). Baltimore: The International Dyslexia Association. (Available from the publisher, http://www.interdys.org/servlet/bookstore?section=OrtonEmeritusSeries)

Hurford, D.M. (1998). *To read or not to read: Answers to all your questions about dyslexia.* New York: Scribner.

Smith, C., & Strick, L. (1997). *Learning disabilities: A to Z.* New York: The Free Press.

CHAPTER 8—PLANNING MULTISENSORY
LESSONS AND THE CLASSROOM ENVIRONMENT

Teacher References

Lesson Planning

American Federation of Teachers. (1999, June). *Teaching reading is rocket science: What expert teachers of reading should know and be able to do* (Item No. 372 6/99). Washington, DC: Author.

Clark, D.B., & Uhry, J.K. (1995). *Dyslexia: Theory and practice of remedial instruction* (2nd ed.). Timonium, MD: York Press. (Available from PRO-ED, 800-897-3202)

Foorman, B.R., Francis, D.J., Fletcher, J.M., Schatschneider, C., & Mehta, P. (1998). The role of instruction in learning to read: Preventing reading failure in at-risk children. *Journal of Educational Psychology, 90,* 1–15.

Henry, M.K. (2003). *Unlocking literacy: Effective decoding and spelling instruction.* Baltimore: Paul H. Brookes Publishing Co.

Joshi, M.R., Dahlgren, M., & Boulware-Gooden, R. (2002). Teaching reading in an inner city school through a multisensory teaching approach. *Annals of Dyslexia, 52,* 229–242.

McCardle, P., & Chhabra, V. (Eds.). (2004). *The voice of evidence in reading research.* Baltimore: Paul H. Brookes Publishing Co.

McIntyre, C.W., & Pickering, J.S. (1995). *Clinical studies of multisensory structured language education for students with dyslexia and related disorders.* Salem, OR: IMSLEC.

Moats, L.C. (1998, Spring/Summer). Teaching decoding. *American Educator, 42*–49, 95–96.

Moats, L.C. (2000). *Speech to print: Language essentials for teachers.* Baltimore: Paul H. Brookes Publishing Co.

Pressley, M. (2002). *Reading instruction that works: The case for balanced teaching* (2nd ed.). New York: The Guilford Press.

Shaywitz, S. (2003). *Overcoming dyslexia: A new and complete science-based program for reading problems at any level.* New York: Alfred A. Knopf.

Snow, C.E., Burns, M.S., & Griffin, P. (Eds.). (1998). *Preventing reading difficulties in young children.* Washington, DC: National Academies Press.

Torgesen, J.K., Alexander, A.W., Wagner, R.K., Rashotte, C.A., Voeller, K., Conway, T., et al. (2001). Intensive remedial instruction for children with severe reading disabilities: Immediate and long-term outcomes from two instructional approaches. *Journal of Learning Disabilities, 34,* 33–58.

Classroom Environment

Marzano, R.J., Marzano, J.S., & Pickering, D.J. (2003). *Classroom management that works: Research-based strategies for every teacher.* Alexandria, VA: Association for Supervision and Curriculum Development.

Mather, N., & Goldstein, S. (2001). *Learning disabilities and challenging behaviors: A guide to intervention and classroom management.* Baltimore: Paul H. Brookes Publishing Co.

McLeod, J., Fisher, J., & Hoover, G. (2003). *The key elements of classroom management: Managing time and space, student behavior, and instructional strategies.* Alexandria, VA: Association for Supervision and Curriculum Development.

Paine, S.C., Radicchi, J., Roselini, L.C., Deutchman, L., & Darch, C.B. (1983). *Structuring your classroom for academic success.* Champaign, IL: Research Press.

Pierangelo, R., & Guilani, G.A. (2002). *Creating confident children: Using positive restructuring in your classroom.* Champaign, IL: Research Press.

Pierangelo, R., & Giulani, G.A. (2001). *What every teacher should know about students with special needs.* Champaign, IL: Research Press.

Vail, P.L. (1993). *Emotion: The on/off switch to learning.* Rosemont, NJ: Modern Learning Press.

Curricula, Guides, and Activities

A more detailed listing of multisensory structured language education curricula appears in the Chapter 9 entries in this appendix.

Mamchak, P.S., & Mamchak, S.R. (1993). *Teacher's time management survival kit: Ready-to-use techniques and materials.* Upper Saddle River, NJ: Prentice Hall.

Murray, C. (2002). *Scope and sequence for literacy instruction* (2nd ed.). Los Altos, CA: Lexia Institute. (Available from PRO-ED, 800-897-3202; see also *LessonPlanner,* described later in the Software section.)

Royal, N.S. (2003). *Preparing children for success in reading; A multisensory guide for teachers and parents.* Timonium, MD: York Press. (Available from PRO-ED, 800-897-3202)

Smith, M.T. (1996). *Multisensory teaching system for reading.* Forney, TX: MTS Publications.

Instructional Materials

Minsky, M. (2003). *Greenwood word lists: One syllable words.* Longmont, CO: Sopris West.

Smith, M.T. *MTA lesson planner and record keeping CD.* Forney, TX: MTS Publications.

Web Sites

Lesson Planning

Big Ideas in Beginning Reading
http://reading.uoregon.edu

Dade-Monroe Teacher Education Center
http://www.miamisci.org/tec

Division for Learning Disabilities (DLD) and the Division for Research of The Council for Exceptional Children (CEC)
Current Practice Alerts
http://www.teachingld.org/ld_resources/alerts/default.htm

Reading ASSIST Institute: Free Downloads
http://www.readingassist.org/downloads.htm

Reading Rainbow
http://www.pbskids.org/readingrainbow

Reading Rockets
http://www.readingrockets.org

Resource Room
http://www.resourceroom.net/index.asp

Vaughn Gross Center for Reading and Language Arts
http://www.texasreading.org/utcrla/default.asp

Vocabulary University
http://www.vocabulary.com

Wilson Academy
http://www.wilsonacademy.com

Classroom Environment

http://www.BehaviorAdvisor.com

Videotapes

Beckham, P.B., & Biddle, M.L. (1988). *Dyslexia training program videotapes*. Dallas: Texas Scottish Rite Hospital, Child Development Division.

Birsh, J.R. (Consulting Ed.), & Potts, M., & Potts, R. (Producers). (1997). *LD/LA: Learning disabilities/learning abilities: Videotape II. The teaching: What students need.* West Tisbury, MA: Vineyard Video Productions. (Available from Paul H. Brookes Publishing Co., Post Office Box 10624, Baltimore, MD 21285-0624; 800-638-3775; 410-337-9580; http://www.brookespublishing.com)

Birsh, J.R. (Consulting Ed.), & Potts, M., & Potts, R. (Producers). (1997). *LD/LA: Learning disabilities/learning abilities: Videotape III. Reading is not a natural skill: Teaching children the code to unlock language.* West Tisbury, MA: Vineyard Video Productions. (Available from Paul H. Brookes Publishing Co., Post Office Box 10624, Baltimore, MD 21285-0624; 800-638-3775; 410-337-9580; http://www.brookespublishing.com)

Keagy, J., & Sanders, A. (1991). *Literacy program videotapes*. Dallas: Texas Scottish Rite Hospital, Child Development Division.

Lavoie, R. (1997). *When the chips are down: Strategies for improving children's behavior.* Washington, DC: WETA, The Learning Disabilities Project. (Available from LD Online, http://ldonline.learningstore.org/products/LD1004.html)

Software

LessonPlanner (This software compliments *Scope and Sequence for Literacy Instruction,* Murray, 2002, and is available from Lexia Institute, 766 Raymundo Avenue, Los Altos, CA; 650-964-3666; http://lexia.mgh.harvard.edu)

CHAPTER 9—TEACHING READING: ACCURATE DECODING AND FLUENCY

Teacher References

Adams, M.J. (1990). *Beginning to read: Thinking and learning about print.* Cambridge, MA: The MIT Press.

Adams, M.J. (1994). Phonics and beginning reading instruction. In F. Lehr & S. Osborn (Eds.), *Reading, language, and literacy* (pp. 3–23). Mahwah, NJ: Lawrence Erlbaum Associates.

Adams, M.J. (1995, Summer). Resolving the "great debate." *American Educator,* 7–20.

Bear, D.R., Invernizzi, M., Templeton, S., & Johnston, F. (1996). *Words their way: Word study for phonics, vocabulary, and spelling instruction.* Upper Saddle River, NJ: Prentice Hall.

Beck, I.L., & Juel, C. (1995, Summer). The role of decoding in learning to read. *American Educator,* 8–42.

Blachman, B.A. (1991). Getting ready to read: Learning how to print maps to speech. In J.F. Kavanagh (Ed.), *The language continuum: From infancy to literacy* (pp. 41–62). Timonium, MD: York Press. (Available from PRO-ED, 800-897-3202)

Bowers, P.G., Sunseth, K., & Golden, J. (1999). The route between rapid naming and reading progress. *Scientific Studies in Reading, 3*(1), 31–53.

Butler, K.G., & Silliman, E.R. (2002). Speaking, reading and writing in children with learning disabilities. Mahwah, NJ: Lawrence Erlbaum Associates.

Calfee, R. (1998). Phonics and phonemes: Learning to decode and spell in a literature-based program. In J.L. Metsala & L.C. Ehri (Eds.), *Word recognition in beginning literacy.* Mahwah, NJ: Lawrence Erlbaum Associates.

Calfee, R.C., & Patrick, C.P. (1995). *The portable Stanford book series: Teach our children well.* Stanford, CA: Stanford Alumni Association.

Chall, J.S. (1983). *Stages of reading development.* New York: McGraw-Hill.

Chall, J.S. (1992). The new reading debates: Evidence from science, art, and ideology. *Teachers College Record, 94,* 315–328.

Chall, J.S., & Popp, H.M. (1996). *Teaching and assessing phonics.* Cambridge, MA: Educators Publishing Service.

Cox, A.R. (1992). *Foundations for literacy: Structures and techniques for multisensory teaching of basic written English language skills.* Cambridge, MA: Educators Publishing Service.

Dickinson, D.K., & Tabors, P.O. (Eds.). (2001). *Beginning literacy with language: Young children learning at home and school.* Baltimore: Paul H. Brookes Publishing Co.

Ehri, L. (1998). Research on learning to read and spell: A personal-historical perspective. *Scientific Studies in Reading, 2*(2), 97–114.

Ehri, L. (1996). Development of the ability to read words. In R. Barr, M. Kamil, P. Mosenthal, & P.D. Pearson (Eds.), *Handbook of reading research* (Vol. II, pp. 383–417). New York: Longman.

Felton, R.H. (1993). Effects of instruction on the decoding skills of children with phonological-processing problems. *Journal of Learning Disabilities, 26*(9), 583–589.

Fry, E.B., Polk, J.K., & Fountoukidis, D.L. (1996). *The reading teacher's new book of lists* (3rd ed.). Upper Saddle River, NJ: Prentice Hall.

Henry, M.K. (1989). Children's word structure knowledge: Implications for decoding and spelling instruction. *Reading and Writing: An Interdisciplinary Journal, 2,* 135–152.

Honig, B. (1996). *Teaching our children to read: The role of skills in a comprehensive reading program.* Thousand Oaks, CA: Corwin Press.

Honig, B., Diamond, L., & Nathan, R. (1998). *Reading research anthology.* Novato, CA: Academic Therapy Publications.

Honig, B., Diamond, L., & Nathan, R. (1998). *Teaching reading sourcebook.* Novato, CA: Academic Therapy Publications.

Liberman, I.Y., & Liberman, A.M. (1990). Whole language vs. code emphasis: Underlying assumptions and their implications for reading instruction. *Annals of Dyslexia, 40,* 51–76.

Liberman, I.Y., Rubin, H., Duques, S.L., & Carlisle, J. (1985). Linguistic skills and spelling proficiency in kindergartners and adult poor spellers. In D.B. Gray & J. Kavanagh (Eds.), *Biobehavioral measures of dyslexia* (pp. 163–176). Timonium, MD: York Press. (Available from PRO-ED, 800-897-3202)

Mather, N. (1992). Whole language reading instruction for students with learning disabilities: Caught in the crossfire. *Learning Disabilities Research and Practice, 7,* 87–95.

Moats, L.C. (2000). *Speech to print: Language essentials for teachers.* Baltimore: Paul H. Brookes Publishing Co.

National Institute of Child Health and Human Development (NICHD). (2000). *Report of the National Reading Panel. Teaching children to read: An evidence-based assessment of the scientific research literature on reading and its implications for reading instruction: Reports of the subgroups* (NIH Publication No. 00-4754). Washington, DC: U.S. Government Printing Office. Also available on-line: http://www.nichd.nih.gov/publicatons/nrp/report.htm

Pressley, M. (2002). *Reading instruction that works: The case for balanced teaching* (2nd ed.). New York: The Guilford Press.

Richardson, S. (1991). The alphabetic principle: Roots of literacy. In W. Ellis (Ed.), *All language and the creation of literacy* (pp. 57–62). Baltimore: The International Dyslexia Association.

Snow, C.E., Burns, M.S., & Griffin, P. (Eds.). (1998). *Preventing reading difficulties in young children.* Washington, DC: National Academies Press.

Vail, P.L. (1991). *Common ground: Whole language and phonics working together.* Rosemont, NJ: Modern Learning Press.

Williams, J. (1991). The meaning of a phonics base for reading instruction. In W. Ellis (Ed.), *All language and the creation of literacy* (pp. 9–19). Baltimore: The International Dyslexia Association.

Wolf, M., & Katzer-Cohen, T. (2001). Reading fluency and its intervention. *Scientific Studies in Reading, 5*(3), 211–239.

Multisensory Structured Curricula

Bebko, A.R., Alexander, J., & Doucet, R. (2001). *LANGUAGE! Roots* (2nd ed.). Longmont, CO: Sopris West.

Bertin, P., & Perlman, E. (1980). *Preventing academic failure.* Cambridge, MA: Educators Publishing Service.

Bloom, F., & Traub, N. (2002). *Recipe for reading* (New century ed.). Cambridge, MA: Educators Publishing Service.

Carreker, S. (1992). *Language enrichment*. Bellaire, TX: Neuhaus Education Center.

Carreker, S. (1998). *Basic language skills* (Book 1–3). Bellaire, TX: Neuhaus Education Center.

Clark-Edmunds, S. (2000). *S.P.I.R.E.* Cambridge, MA: Educators Publishing Service.

Cox, A.R. (1992). *Foundations for literacy: Structures and techniques for multisensory teaching of basic written English language skills*. Cambridge, MA: Educators Publishing Service.

Dillon, S. (1987). *Sounds in syllables*. Albuquerque, NM: S.I.S. Publishing Co.

duBard, N.E., & Martin, M.K. (1994). *Teaching language deficient children: Theory and application of the Association Method for multisensory teaching* (Rev. ed.). Cambridge, MA: Educators Publishing Service.

Enfield, M.L., & Greene, V. *Project read*. Bloomington, MN: Language Circle Enterprise.

Gillingham, A., & Stillman, B.W. (1997). *The Gillingham manual: Remedial training for students with specific disability in reading, spelling, and penmanship* (8th ed.). Cambridge, MA: Educators Publishing Service.

Greene, J.F. (1995). *LANGUAGE! A reading, writing, and spelling curriculum for at-risk and ESL students* (Grades 4–12). Longmont, CO: Sopris West.

Henry, M.K., & Redding, N.C. (1996). *Patterns for success in reading and spelling: A multisensory approach to teaching phonics and word analysis*. Austin, TX: PRO-ED.

Herman, R.D. (1993). *The Herman Method for reversing reading failure*. Sherman Oaks, CA: The Herman Method Institute.

Jolly phonics. Chigwell, Essex, United Kingdom: Jolly Learning. (Available from the publisher, 50 Winter Sport Lane, Williston, VT 05495-0020; 800-488-2665; e-mail: jolly.orders@aidcvt.com)

Knight, J.R. (1986). *Starting over: A combined teaching manual and student textbook for reading, writing, spelling, vocabulary, and handwriting*. Cambridge, MA: Educators Publishing Service.

LEAD Educational Resources. *LEAD program: Logical encoding and decoding*. Bridgewater, CT: Author. (Available from the author, 144 Main Street North, Bridgewater, CT 06752; 860-355-1516)

Lindamood, P., & Lindamood, P. (1998). *Lindamood phoneme sequencing program for reading, spelling, and speech (LiPS): Teacher's manual for the classroom and clinic* (3rd ed.). Austin, TX: PRO-ED.

Pickering, J.S. *Sequential English education (SEE)*. Dallas, TX: The June Shelton School.

Reading mastery. Blacklick, OH: SRA/McGraw-Hill. (Available from the publisher, http://www.sraonline.com)

Redding, N.C., & Henry, M.K. (2004). *Patterns for success in reading and spelling activity book*. Austin, TX: PRO-ED.

Rome, P.D., & Osman, J.S. (1993). *Language tool kit*. Cambridge, MA: Educators Publishing Service.

Rome, P.D., & Osman, J.S. (2000). *Advanced language tool kit*. Cambridge, MA: Educators Publishing Service.

Simmons, L. (1997). *Saxon phonics*. Norman, OK: Saxon Publishers.

Slingerland, B.H., & Aho, M. (1994–1996). *A multi-sensory approach to language arts for specific language disability children* (Rev. ed., Vols. 1–3). Cambridge, MA: Educators Publishing Service.

Smith, M.T. (1996). *MTA reading and spelling program* (Kits 1–7). Cambridge, MA: Educators Publishing Service.

Smith, M.T. (1996). *Multisensory teaching system for reading (MTS)*. Forney, TX: MTS Publications.

Sonday, A. (1997). *The Sonday system: Learning to read* [Learning plan and word books]. Cambridge, MA: Educators Publishing Service.

Spalding, R.B. (with Spalding, W.T.). (1990). *The writing road to reading: The Spalding Method of phonics for teaching speech, writing, and reading* (4th rev. ed.). New York: Quill.

Wickerham, C.W., & Allen, K.A. (1993). *Multisensory reading and spelling* (Books 1–4). Bellaire, TX: Neuhaus Education Center.

Wilson, B.A. (1988). *Wilson reading system: Teacher's guide and student material*. Millbury, MA: Wilson Language Training. (Available from the publisher, http://www.wilsonlanguage.com)

Other Curricula, Guides, and Activities

Biddle, M.L., & Raines, B.J. (1980). *Situation learning: Teacher guides and student workbooks* (Vols. 1–3). Cambridge, MA: Educators Publishing Service.

Chall, J.S., & Popp, H.M. (1996). *Teaching and assessing phonics*. Cambridge, MA: Educators Publishing Service.

Hall, N., & Price, R. (1993). *Explode the code.* Cambridge, MA: Educators Publishing Service.

Henry, M.K. (1990). *WORDS: Integrated decoding and spelling instruction based on word origin and structure.* Austin, TX: PRO-ED.

Henry, M.K. (2003). *Unlocking literacy: Effective decoding and spelling instruction.* Baltimore: Paul H. Brookes Publishing Co.

Henry, M.K., & Redding, N.C. (1996). *Patterns for success in reading and spelling: A multisensory approach to teaching phonics and word analysis.* Austin, TX: PRO-ED.

Johnson, K., & Bayrd, P. (1988). *Megawords: Multisyllabic words for reading, spelling and vocabulary.* Cambridge, MA: Educators Publishing Service.

Smith, M.T. (1996). *Multisensory teaching system for reading.* Forney, TX: MTS Publications.

Steere, A., Peck, C.Z., & Kahn, L. (1971). *Solving language difficulties.* Cambridge, MA: Educators Publishing Service.

Wilson, R.Q., & Rudolf, M.K. (1986). *Merrill linguistic reading program* (4th ed.). New York: Merrill.

Wimer, D.B. (1994). *Word studies: A classical perspective. Prefixes + roots + suffixes* (Vol. 1). Richmond, VA: Author. (Available from the author, Post Office Box 5362, Richmond, VA 23220)

Instructional Materials

Carreker, S. (1999). *Practices for developing accuracy and fluency.* Bellaire, TX: Neuhaus Education Center.

Erwin, P. (1992). *Winston grammar cards.* San Diego: Farnsworth Books.

Gillingham, A., & Stillman, B.W. (1959). *Phonetic word cards: Remedial training for children with specific disability in reading, spelling, and penmanship.* Cambridge, MA: Educators Publishing Service.

Greene, J.F., & Woods, J.F. (1992). *J & J language readers for reading/language delayed and ESL/EFL students* (Levels I–III). Longmont, CO: Sopris West.

McCracken pocket charts. Seattle, WA: School Art Materials. (Available from the publisher, Post Office Box 94082, Seattle, WA 98124; 800-752-4359)

Montgomery, D.B. (1975). *Angling for words: The teacher's line.* Novato, CA: Academic Therapy Publications.

Neuhaus Education Center. *Procedure charts: LLP, WOW, SOS, Dict, Demo, Copy.* Bellaire, TX: Author.

Sands, E.M. *SANDS reading cards* [Picture sound cards, letter sound cards, audiocassette]. New York: Davick House. (Available from the publisher, Post Office Box 150136, Kew Gardens, NY 11415)

Smith, M.T. *MTA reading and spelling program* (Kits 1–7). Cambridge, MA: Educators Publishing Service.

Smith, M.T. (1987–1993). MTA reader series. Cambridge, MA: Educators Publishing Service:

Brubaker, S., & Jackson, N. (1988). *Tracks.*

Brubaker, S., & Jackson, N. (1988). *Wishes.*

Brubaker, S., Crouch, J., & Jackson, N. (1989). *Hurdles.*

Jackson, N. (1987). *Pals.*

Sokoloski, B. (1993). *Kids and critters.*

The following bookstore also carries instructional materials: BurnsBooks, 50 Joe's Hill Road, Danbury, CT, 08811; 203-744-0232.

Videotapes

Beckham, P.B., & Biddle, M.L. (1988). *Dyslexia training program videotapes.* Dallas: Texas Scottish Rite Hospital, Child Development Division.

Birsh, J.R. (Consulting Ed.), & Potts, M., & Potts, R. (Producers). (1997). *LD/LA: Learning disabilities/learning abilities: Videotape II. The teaching: What students need.* West Tisbury, MA: Vineyard Video Productions.

Birsh, J.R. (Consulting Ed.), & Potts, M., & Potts, R. (Producers). (1997). *LD/LA: Learning disabilities/learning abilities: Videotape III. Reading is not a natural skill: Teaching children the code to unlock language.* West Tisbury, MA: Vineyard Video Productions. (Available from Paul H. Brookes Publishing Co., Post Office Box 10624, Baltimore, MD 21285-0624; 800-638-3775; 410-337-9580; http://www.brookespublishing.com)

Keagy, J., & Sanders, A. (1991). *Literacy program videotapes.* Dallas: Texas Scottish Rite Hospital, Child Development Division.

Software

Texthelp Systems Ltd.
Enkalon Business Centre
25 Randalstown Road
Antrim, NORTHERN IRELAND BT41 4LJ
+44 (0)28 94 428105
http://www.texthelp.com

Dyslexia training program supplement. Richardson, TX: SofDesign International. (Available from the publisher, http://www.sofdesign.com/dyslexia/dtps/default.html)

Kurzweil 3000 [Provides visual and auditory feedback with printed material]. Waltham, MA: Kurzweil Educational Systems. (Available from the publisher, 411 Waverley Oaks Road, Waltham, MA 02452; 800-894-5374)

Lexia Reading SOS (Strategies for Older Students). Lincoln, MA: Lexia Learning Systems. (Available from the publisher, 2 Lewis Street, Post Office Box 466, Lincoln, MA, 01773; 800-435-3942; http://www.lexialearning.com)

Lexia Primary Phonics. Lincoln, MA: Lexia Learning Systems. (Available from the publisher, 2 Lewis Street, Post Office Box 466, Lincoln, MA, 01773; 800-435-3942; http://www.lexialearning.com)

ULTimate reader [Speaks back electronic printed matter]. Wauconda, IL: Don Johnston (Available from the publisher, Post Office Box 639, Wauconda, IL 60084; 800-999-4660; e-mail: info@donjohnston.com; http://www.donjohnston.com)

Web Sites

Center for the Improvement of Early Reading Achievement
http://www.ciera.org

Junior Great Books
http://www.greatbooks.org/typ/index.php?id=junior

U.S. Department of Education
http://www.ed.gov

Resources and Organizations for Parents and Teachers

Hall, S.L., & Moats, L.C. (1999). *Straight talk about reading: How parents can make a difference during the early years.* Chicago: Contemporary Books.

The International Dyslexia Association (IDA)
8600 LaSalle Road
Chester Building
Suite 382
Baltimore, MD 21286
800-ABC-D123
E-mail: info@interdys.org
http://www.interdys.org

International Reading Association (IRA)
Public Information Office
800 Barksdale Road
Post Office Box 8139
Newark, DE 19714
302-731-1600
http://www.reading.org

CHAPTER 10—TEACHING SPELLING

Teacher References

Cox, A.R. (1992). *Foundations for literacy: Structures and techniques for multisensory teaching of basic written English language skills.* Cambridge, MA: Educators Publishing Service.

Moats, L.C. (1995). *Spelling: Development, disability, and instruction.* Timonium, MD: York Press. (Available from PRO-ED, 800-897-3202)

Curricula, Guides, and Activities

Bear, D.R., Invernizzi, M., Templeton, S., & Johnston, F. (1996). *Words their way: Word study for phonics, vocabulary, and spelling instruction.* Upper Saddle River, NJ: Prentice Hall.

Bell, N. (1997). *Seeing stars: Symbol imagery for phonemic awareness, sight words, and spelling.* San Luis Obispo, CA: Gander Publishing.

Carreker, S. (1998). *Basic language skills* (Books 1–3). Bellaire, TX: Neuhaus Education Center.

Carreker, S. (2002). *Scientific spelling* (Rev. ed.; Grades 1–8). Bellaire, TX: Neuhaus Education Center.

Cox, A.R. (1992). *Alphabetic phonics.* Cambridge, MA: Educators Publishing Service.

Enfield, M.L., & Greene, V. *Project Read.* Bloomington, MN: Language Circle Enterprise.

Gillingham, A., & Stillman, B.W. (1997). *The Gillingham manual: Remedial training for children with specific disability in reading, spelling, and penmanship* (8th ed.). Cambridge, MA: Educators Publishing Service.

Hall, N.M. *Spellwell.* Cambridge, MA: Educators Publishing Service.

Henry, M.K. (1990). *WORDS: Integrated decoding and spelling instruction based on word origin and structure.* Austin, TX: PRO-ED.

Moats, L.C., & Rostow, B. (2003). *Spellography: Teacher's resource guide.* Longmont, CO: Sopris West.

Rak, E.T. *The spell of the word* (Grade 7–Adult). Cambridge, MA: Educators Publishing Service.

Rome, P.D., & Osman, J.S. (1993). *Language tool kit.* Cambridge, MA: Educators Publishing Service.

Rudginsky, L.T., & Haskell, E.C. (1985). *How to spell* (Grades 1–12). Cambridge, MA: Educators Publishing Service.

Simmons, L. (1997). *Saxon phonics.* Norman, OK: Saxon Publishers.

Slingerland, B.H., & Aho, M. (1994–1996). *A multi-sensory approach to language arts for specific language disability children* (Rev. ed., Vols. 1–3). Cambridge, MA: Educators Publishing Service.

Smith, M.T. (1996). *MTA reading and spelling program* (Kits 1–7). Cambridge, MA: Educators Publishing Service.

Texas Scottish Rite Hospital for Children. (1992). *Dyslexia training program: Teacher's guides and student's books* (Vols. 1–4). Cambridge, MA: Educators Publishing Service.

Wickerham, C.W., & Allen, K.A. (1993). *Multisensory reading and spelling* (Books 1–4). Bellaire, TX: Neuhaus Education Center.

Wilson, B.A. (1988). *Wilson reading system: Teacher's guide and student material.* Millbury, MA: Wilson Language Training. (Available from the publisher, http://www.wilsonlanguage.com)

Instructional Materials

Carreker, S., & Birsh, J.R. (2005). Four-leaf clover. In *Multisensory teaching of basic language skills activity book.* Baltimore: Paul H. Brookes Publishing Co.

Electronic spellers. Burlington, NJ: Franklin Electronic Publishers.

Manipulative four-leaf clover [For teaching the Doubling Rule]. Austin, TX: Region XIII Education Service Center. (Available from the publisher, 5701 Springdale Road, Austin, TX 78723; 512-926-5593)

McCracken pocket charts. Seattle, WA: School Art Materials. (Available from the publisher, Post Office Box 94082, Seattle, WA 98124; 800-752-4359)

Videotapes

Birsh, J.R. (Consulting Ed.), & Potts, M., & Potts, R. (Producers). (1997). *LD/LA: Learning disabilities/learning abilities: Videotape II. The teaching: What students need.* West Tisbury, MA: Vineyard Video Productions. (Available from Paul H. Brookes Publishing Co., Post Office Box 10624, Baltimore, MD 21285-0624; 800-638-3775; 410-337-9580; http://www.brookespublishing.com)

Birsh, J.R. (Consulting Ed.), & Potts, M., & Potts, R. (Producers). (1997). *LD/LA: Learning disabilities/learning abilities: Videotape III. Reading is not a natural skill: Teaching children the code to unlock language.* West Tisbury, MA: Vineyard Video Productions. (Available from Paul H. Brookes Publishing Co., Post Office Box 10624, Baltimore, MD 21285; 800-638-3775)

CHAPTER 11—BILITERACY INSTRUCTION FOR SPANISH-SPEAKING STUDENTS

Organizations

National Association for Bilingual Education (NABE)
1030 15th Street NW
Suite 470
Washington, DC 20005
202-898-1829
E-mail: nabe@nabe.org
http://www.nabe.org

National Clearinghouse for English Language Acquisition
   and Language Instructional Educational Programs
2121 K Street NW
Suite 260
Washington, DC 20037
800-321-6223
http://www.ncela.gwu.edu

Teacher References

Fitzgerald, J. (1995). English as a second language reading instruction in the United States: A research review. *Journal of Reading Behavior, 27*(2), 115–152.

Harrison-Harris, O.L. (2002, November 5) AAC, literacy, and bilingualism. *The ASHA Leader Online.* Retrieved March 8, 2005, http://www.asha.org/about/publications/leader-online/archives/2002/q4/fo21105.htm

International Dyslexia Association. (2000). *Sólo los hechos . . . Información de La Asociación Internacional de Dislexia.* Retrieved March 8, 2005, from http://www.interdys.org/pdf/spanish-what-is-dyslexia.pdf

Learning two languages [Brochure]. Rockville, MD: American Speech-Language-Hearing Association (ASHA). (Available from ASHA product sales, 888-498-6699, Product #0112544 [(English], Product #0112545 [Spanish])

Slavin, R.E., & Cheung, A. (2004). How do English language learners learn to read? *Educational Leadership, 61*(6), 52–57.

Stone, C.A., & Carlisle, J.F. (2005). Learning disabilities in English language learners: Research issues and future directions [Special issue]. *Learning Disabilities Research and Practice, 20*(1).

Tabors, P.O., & Snow, C.E. (2001). Young bilingual children and early literacy development. In S.B. Neuman & D.K. Dickinson (Eds.). *Handbook of early literacy research* (pp. 159–178). New York: The Guilford Press.

Teacher Resources

Devney, D.M. (1992). *Guide to Spanish suffixes*. Lincolnwood, IL: Passport Books.

Kendris, C. (1982). *501 Spanish verbs* (2nd ed.). New York: Barron's Educational Series.

Moore, B., & Moore, M. (1997). *NTC's dictionary of Latin and Greek origin*. Lincolnwood, IL: NTC Publishing Group.

Pierson, R.H. (1996). *A practical guide to 2,500 commonly used Spanish idioms: Guide to Spanish idioms/ Gaia de monism's Español es*. Lincolnwood, IL: Passport Books.

Prado, M. (1993). *NTC's dictionary of Spanish false cognates*. Lincolnwood, IL: NTC Publishing Group.

Assessment Tools

Muñoz-Sandoval, A.F., & Woodcock, R.W. (1996). *Batería Woodcock-Muñoz: Pruebas de aprovechamiento-revisada*. Itasca, IL: Riverside Publishing.

Office of Bilingual Education, University of Texas, & the Texas Center for Reading and Language Arts. (2003). *El Inventario de Lectura en Español de Tejas: Tejas LEE. A Spanish early reading assessment*. Austin, TX: CSI.

Riccio, C.A., Imhoff, B., Hasbrouck, J.E., & Davis, G.N. (2004). *Test of Phonological Awareness in Spanish (TPAS)*. Austin, TX: PRO-ED.

Semel, E., Wiig, E.H., & Secord, W.A. (1995). *Clinical Evaluation of Language Fundamentals* (3rd. ed., Spanish ed.). San Antonio, TX: Harcourt Assessment.

Zimmerman, I.L., Steiner, V.G., & Pond, R.E. (2002). *Preschool Language Scale* (4th ed.). San Antonio, TX: Harcourt Assessment.

Instructional Materials

Esperanza: A Multisensory Structured Spanish Language Program
856 West Price Road
Brownsville, TX 78520
956-504-2200
Email: valleyspeech@worldnet.att.net

Language Enrichment: A Multisensory Structured English Language Program
Neuhaus Education Center
4433 Bissonnet
Bellaire, TX 77401-3233
713-664-7676

TrabaLenguas: Educational Materials for Spanish Speech Language Therapy
Post Office Box 286
LaGrange, IL 60525
708-352-3502
http://www.spanishspeech.com

Web Sites

Schwab Learning
http://www.schwablearning.org

The White House Initiative on Educational Excellence for Hispanic Americans
http://www.yesican.gov

CHAPTER 12—INSTRUCTION FOR
OLDER STUDENTS STRUGGLING WITH READING

Teacher References

Adams, M.J. (1990). *Beginning to read: Thinking and learning about print.* Cambridge, MA: The MIT Press.

Alvermann, D.E., & Moore, D.W. (1996). Secondary school reading. In R. Barr, M.L. Kamil, P. Mosenthal, & P.D. Pearson (Eds.), *Handbook of reading research* (Vol. II, pp. 951–983). New York: Longman.

Barry, A.L. (1997). High school reading programs revisited. *Journal of Adolescent and Adult Literacy, 40*(7), 524–531.

Carr, S.C., & Thompson, B. (1996). The effects of prior knowledge and schema activation strategies on the inferential reading comprehension of children with and without learning disabilities. *Learning Disabilities Quarterly, 19*(1), 48–61.

Cornoldi, C., Logie, R., Brandimonte, M., Kaufmann, G., & Reisberg, D. (1996). *Stretching the imagination.* New York: Oxford University Press.

Cramer, E.E., & Castle, M. (Eds.). (1994). *Fostering the love of reading: The affective domain in reading education.* Newark, DE: International Reading Association.

Ehri, L.C., & Wilce, L.S. (1983). Development of word identification speed in skilled and less skilled beginning readers. *Journal of Educational Psychology, 75,* 3–18.

Finn, C.E., Rotherham, A.J., & Hokanson, C.R., Jr. (2001). *Rethinking special education for a new century.* Washington, DC: Thomas B. Fordham Foundation and the Progressive Policy Institute.

Gaultney, J.F. (1995). The effect of prior knowledge and metacognition on the acquisition of a reading comprehension strategy. *Journal of Experimental Child Psychology, 59*(1), 142–163.

Henry, M.K., & Brickley, S.G. (Eds.). (1999). *Dyslexia . . . Samuel T. Orton and his legacy.* Baltimore: The International Dyslexia Association.

Juel, C. (1996). Beginning reading. In R. Barr, M.L. Kamil, P. Mosenthal, & P.D. Pearson (Eds.), *Handbook of reading research* (Vol. II, pp. 749–788). New York: Longman.

Kos, R. (1991). Persistence of reading disabilities: The voices of four middle school students. *American Educational Research Journal, 28*(4), 875–895.

Maria, K. (1990). *Reading comprehension instruction issues and strategies.* Timonium, MD: York Press. (Available from PRO-ED, 800-897-3202)

Meyer, M.S., & Felton, R.H. (1999). Repeated reading to enhance fluency: Old approaches and new direction. *Annals of Dyslexia, 49,* 283–306.

Noble, A.J., Hackett, G., & Chen, E.G. (1992, April). *Relations of career and academic self-efficacy to the career aspirations and academic achievement of ninth and tenth grade at risk students.* Paper presented at the annual meeting of the American Educational Research Association, San Francisco.

Orton, J.L. (1964). *A guide to teaching phonics.* Winston-Salem, NC: Orton Reading Center and Salem College Book Store.

Orton, J. (1966). *The Orton Gillingham approach in the disabled reader.* Baltimore: The John Hopkins University Press.

Panagos, R., & DuBois, D. (1999). Career self-efficacy development and students with learning disabilities. *Learning Disabilities Research & Practice, 14*(1), 25–34.

Samuels, S.J. (2002). Reading fluency: Its development and assessment. In A.E. Farstrup & S.J. Samuels (Eds.), *What research has to say about reading instruction* (3rd ed., pp. 166–183). Newark, DE: International Reading Association.

Samuels, S.J., Miller, N., & Eisenberg, P. (1979). Practice effects on the unit of word recognition. *Journal of Educational Psychology, 71,* 514–520.

Sanacore, J. (1997). Promoting lifetime literacy through authentic self-expression and intrinsic motivation. *Journal of Adolescent and Adult Literacy, 40*(7), 568–571.

Scarborough, H.S. (1998). Predicting the future achievement of second graders with reading disabilities: Contributions of phonemic awareness, verbal memory, rapid naming, and IQ. *Annals of Dyslexia, 68,* 115–136.

Schupack, H., & Wilson, B.A. (1997). *Reading, writing and spelling: The multisensory structured language approach.* Baltimore: The International Dyslexia Association.

Shaywitz, B.A., Fletcher, J.M., Holahan, J.M., & Shaywitz, S.E. (1992). Discrepancy compared to low achievement definitions of reading disability: Result from the Connecticut longitudinal study. *Journal of Learning Disabilities, 25*(10), 639–648.

Stanovich, K.E., & Cunningham, A.E. (1993). Where does knowledge come from? Specific associations between print exposure and information acquisition. *Journal of Educational Psychology, 85*(2), 211–229.

Wagoner, S.A. (1983). Comprehension monitoring: What it is and what we know about it. *Reading Research Quarterly, 18*(3), 328–346.

Worthy, J. (1996). A matter of interest: Literature that hooks reluctant readers and keeps them reading. *The Reading Teacher, 50*(2), 2–10.

Curricula for Students Beyond Elementary Grades

Greene, J.F. (1995). *LANGUAGE! A reading, writing, and spelling curriculum for at-risk and ESL students* (Grades 4–12). Longmont, CO: Sopris West.

Kleiber, M.H. (1990–2004). *Specific language training: An Orton-Gillingham curriculum for adolescents.* Yonkers, NY: Decatur Enterprises. (Available from the publisher, 26 Birch Road, Yonkers, NY 10705)

Knight, J.R. (1986). *Starting over: A combined teaching manual and student textbook for reading, writing, spelling, vocabulary, and handwriting.* Cambridge, MA: Educators Publishing Service.

Tuley, A.C. (1998). *Never too late to read: Language skills for the adolescent dyslexic* (based on the work of Alice Ansara). Timonium, MD: York Press. (Available from PRO-ED, 800-897-3202)

Wilson, B.A. (1988). *Wilson reading system: Teacher's guide and student material.* Millbury, MA: Wilson Language Training. (Available from the publisher, http://www.wilsonlanguage.com)

Instructional Materials for Controlled Text

The following companies are sources of controlled text for older students. These contain passages with 95%–100% of the words following a specified word structuring.

Academic Therapy Publications
20 Commercial Boulevard
Novato, CA 94949
800-422-7249
http://www.academictherapy.com
 High Noon: Sound Out Series

Educators Publishing Service
Post Office Box 9031
Cambridge, MA 02139-9031
800-435-7728
http://www.epsbooks.com
 MTA Readers

Sopris West
Post Office Box 1809
Longmont, CO 80502
800-547-6747
http://www.sopriswest.com
 J & J Language Readers

Wilson Language Training
175 West Main Street
Millbury, MA 01527
800-899-8454 (ordering materials)
800-899-5699 (training information)
http://www.wilsonlanguage.com
 Student Readers: Steps 1-12 (by B. Wilson)
 Stories for Older Students (by J. Brown)
 Travels with Ted (by J. Brown)

Instructional Materials for Noncontrolled Decodable Text

The following sections list companies who offer text with passages written at easier levels, which may provide decodable text for students (depends upon individual students).

Fiction

The fiction stories listed here are written at varied levels and in varied subjects of interest.

Don Johnston
26799 West Commerce Drive
Volo, IL 60073
800-999-4660
http://www.donjohnston.com
> *Start to Finish Series* (classic stories available at two levels and in three formats—book, audiotape, and CD-ROM with text-to-speech features)

4Mation Educational Resources
Castle Park Road
Barnstaple, Devon
EX32 8PA UNITED KINGDOM
+44 (0)1271 325353
http://www.4mation.co.uk/contact.html
> *Spinout Stories* (CD-ROMs designed to promote literacy for older students with reading difficulties. Each story has three levels—the hardest has optional text links.)

Jamestown Education Press
A McGraw-Hill Company
800-USA-READ
http://www.glencoe.com/gln/jamestown
> *American Portraits* (historical novels with reading levels 5–8)
> *Best Series* (diverse nonfiction including poetry, plays, short stories, and selections from novels)
> *Five-Star Stories* (high-interest anthologies with short stories from around the world)

Wieser Educational
30281 Esperanza Rancho
Santa Margarita, CA 92688-2130
800-880-4433
http://www.wiesereducational.com
> *Cover to Cover Novels* (written at Grades 2–4 reading levels with stories of interest for students in Grade 4 to adult)
> *Passages Reading Program* (high-interest reading books written at Grades 3–6 reading levels with stories of interest for students from Grade 5 to adult)

Nonfiction

These nonfiction passages can be used for comprehension and fluency.

Jamestown Education Press
A McGraw-Hill Company
800-USA-READ
http://www.glencoe.com/gln/jamestown
> *Contemporary Reader* (diverse, nonfiction selections written at Grades 2–5 levels)
> *Six-Way Paragraphs* (a leveled series of high-interest nonfiction passages)

Phoenix Learning Resources
2349 Chaffee Drive
St. Louis, MO 63146
800-221-1274
http://www.phoenixlearninggroup.com/home.htm
> *New Practice Readers* (Reading levels 2–6, interest 2 to adult)

Reading for Concepts (Reading levels 1–6, interest 2 to adult)
Reading About Science (Reading levels 2–6, interest 2 to adult)
Building Reading Skills (Reading levels 2–7, interest 4 to adult. Six new vocabulary words are repeated several times in different contexts in each real-life story.)

Recording for the Blind & Dyslexic (RFB&D)
http://www.rfbd.org
A variety of titles are available from RFB&D.

Wilson Language Training
175 West Main Street
Millbury, MA 01527
800-899-8454 (ordering materials)
800-899-5699 (training information)
http://www.wilsonlanguage.com
http://www.wilsonacademy.com (Resources on this subscription-based web site provide nonfiction passages with text for teachers to read to students at a higher level, matched with same content text written at an easier, more decodable level.)

Achieve passages (Print version of passages from Wilson Academy.com written at two levels—one to be read to students, the other to be read by students)

Spellcheckers

Franklin Electronic Publishers
http://franklin.com
Handheld electronic spellcheckers that speak (from Franklin Electronic Publishers and other companies) can be used to help students read words that they cannot decode. They also assist students with spelling if they understand basic sound–symbol correspondence and word structure.

Text-to-Speech Supported Reading Software

EzDaisy and Scholar, Digital Talking Book Players
http://www.telex.com/86256BB50053ED61/0/2EC53A4BF998A9AA86256E4C0049F1EF
    ?Open&Highlight=0,digital,talking,book
and
http://www.telex.com/duplication/products.nsf/allpages/0313DC795FA04C8E86256BC2006F1EA6

Kurzweil 3000
http://www.kurzweiledu.com/products_k3000win.asp
and
http://www.kurzweiledu.com/products_k3000mac.asp

Literacy Productivity Package
http://www.premier-programming.com/LPP_packs.htm

Read & Write Gold
http://www.texthelp.com/rwg.asp?q1=products&q2=rwg

WYNN
http://www.freedomscientific.com/LSG/products/wynn.asp

E-text Sources

Bookshare.org
http://www.bookshare.org

Technology Resources

Audiobooks are available from a variety of stores and libraries, as well as from Recording for the Blind and Dyslexic (RFB&D), http://www.rfbd.org.

Web Sites

Adolescent Literacy
http://www.reading.org/resources/issues/focus_adolescent.html

Alliance for Excellent Education
http://www.all4ed.org/publications/ReadingNext

Literacy Education and Reading Programs in the Secondary School
http://www.nassp.org/news/bltnliteracyed0902.html

National Institute on the Education of At-Risk Students
http://www.ed.gov/offices/OERI/At-Risk

Strategic Instruction Model
http://www.ku-crl.org/iei/sim/index.html

Success of a Direct Instruction Model at a Secondary Level School with High-Risk Students
http://www.uoregon.edu/~bgrossen/page5.html
(Click on "ask for a copy.")

Wilson Academy
http://www.wilsonacademy.com

CHAPTER 13—WORD LEARNING AND VOCABULARY INSTRUCTION

Teacher References

Baumann, J.F., & Kame'enui, E.J. (2004). *Vocabulary instruction: Research to practice.* New York: The Guilford Press.

Fry, E.B., Kress, J.E., & Fountoukidis, D. (2000). *The reading teacher's book of lists* (4th ed.). Upper Saddle River, NJ: Prentice Hall.

Greenwood, S.C. (2004). *Words count: Effective vocabulary instruction in action.* Portsmouth, NH: Heinemann.

Henry, M.K. (2003). *Unlocking literacy: Effective decoding and spelling instruction.* Baltimore: Paul H. Brookes Publishing Co.

Henry, M.K., & Redding, N.C. (1996). *Patterns for success in reading and spelling: A multisensory approach to teaching phonics and word analysis.* Austin, TX: PRO-ED.

Rasinski, T.V., Padak, N.D., Church, B.W., Fawcett, G., Hendershot, J., Henry J.M., et al. (2000). *Teaching word recognition, spelling, and vocabulary: Strategies from* The Reading Teacher. Newark, DE: International Reading Association.

Stahl, S., & Kapinus, B. (2001). *Word power: What every educator needs to know about teaching vocabulary.* Washington, DC: National Education Association.

Web Site

Vocabulary University
http://www.vocabulary.com

CHAPTER 14—STRATEGIES TO IMPROVE READING COMPREHENSION IN THE MULTISENSORY CLASSROOM

Teacher References

Bell, N. (1992). *Visualizing and verbalizing for language comprehension and thinking* (Rev. ed.). San Luis Obispo, CA: Gander Publishing.

Carlisle, J.F., & Rice, M.S. (2002). *Improving reading comprehension.* Timonium, MD: York Press (Available from PRO-ED, 800-897-3202)

Carreker, S. (1993). *Multisensory grammar and written composition.* Houston, TX: S.S. Systems. (Available from the publisher, 5434 Darnell Street, Houston, TX 77096)

Deshler, D.D., Ellis, E.S., & Lenz, B.K. (1996). *Teaching adolescents with learning disabilities: Strategies and methods* (2nd ed.). Denver, CO: Love Publishing.

Harvey, S., & Goudvis, A. (2000). *Strategies that work: Teaching comprehension to enhance understanding.* York, Maine: Stenhouse Publications.

IRA Literacy Study Groups (2003). *Reading comprehension module.* Newark, DE: International Reading Association.

Maria, K. (1990). *Reading comprehension instruction: Issues and strategies.* Timonium, MD: York Press. (Available from PRO-ED, 800-897-3202)

McLaughlin, M. (2003). *Guided comprehension in the primary grades.* Newark, DE: International Reading Association.

National Institute of Child Health and Human Development (NICHD). (2000). *Report of the National Reading Panel. Teaching children to read: An evidence-based assessment of the scientific research literature on reading and its implications for reading instruction: Reports of the subgroups* (NIH Publication No. 00-4754). Washington, DC: U.S. Government Printing Office. Also available on-line: http://www.nichd.nih.gov/ publicatons/nrp/report.htm

RAND Reading Study Group (2002). *Reading for understanding: Toward an R & D program in reading comprehension.* Washington, DC: U.S. Office of Educational Research and Improvement.

Rasinski, T.V., Padak, N.D., Church, B.W., Fawcet, G. Hendersbot, J., et al. (2000). *Teaching comprehension and exploring multiple literacies: Strategies from* The Reading Teacher. Newark, DE: International Reading Association.

Smith, M.T., & Hogan, E.A. (1991). *MTA: Teaching a process for comprehension and composition.* Forney, TX: MTS Publications.

Strickland, D.S., Ganske, K., & Monroe, J.K. (2002). *Supporting struggling readers and writers: Strategies for classroom intervention 3-6.* Portland, ME: Stenhouse Publishers.

Curricula, Guides, and Activities

Carreker, S. (1992). *Language enrichment.* Bellaire, TX: Neuhaus Education Center.

Greene, J.F. (1995). *LANGUAGE! A reading, writing, and spelling curriculum for at-risk and ESL students (Grades 4–12).* Longmont, CO: Sopris West.

Greene, V., & Enfield, M.L. (1999). *Report form kit* (Contains materials for classroom display and for teacher and students). Bloomington, MN: Language Circle Enterprises.

Greene, V., & Enfield, M.L. (1999). *Story form comprehension kit* (Contains materials for classroom display and for teacher and students, including story element Post-it notes). Bloomington, MN: Language Circle Enterprises.

Greene, V., & Enfield, M.L. (1999). *Story form literature kit* (Contains materials for classroom display and for teacher and students, including story element Post-it notes). Bloomington, MN: Language Circle Enterprises.

Klingner, J.K., Vaughn, S., Dimino, J., Schumm, J.S., & Bryant, D. (2001). *From clunk to click: Collaborative Strategic Reading.* Longmont, CO: Sopris West.

Neuhaus Education Center. (2003). *Developing metacognitive skills: Vocabulary and reading comprehension with reusable magnetic webs*. Bellaire, TX: Neuhaus Education Center.

Neuhaus Education Center. *Colors and shapes of language*. Bellaire, TX: Neuhaus Education Center.

Smith, M.T. (1987). *MTA: Teaching a process for comprehension and composition*. Forney, TX: MTS Publications.

Instructional Materials

Auslin, M.S. (2003). *The idioms workbook* (2nd ed.). Austin, TX: PRO-ED.

Bell, N., & Lindamood, P. *See time fly: Visualizing and verbalizing history stories* (Vol. 1). San Luis Obispo, CA: Gander Publishing.

Bell, N., & Lindamood, P. *See time fly: Visualizing and verbalizing history stories workbook* (Vol. 1). San Luis Obispo, CA: Gander Publishing.

Bell, N., & Lindamood, P. (1993). *Vanilla vocabulary: A visualized/verbalized vocabulary program* (Level I). San Luis Obispo, CA: Gander Publishing.

Bell, N., & Lindamood, P. (1998). *Vanilla vocabulary: A visualized/verbalized vocabulary program* (Level II). San Luis Obispo, CA: Gander Publishing.

Bell, N., & Lindamood, P. *Visualizing and verbalizing CD-ROM: Adventures with Ivan* (Grades K–6). San Luis Obispo, CA: Gander Publishing.

Bell, N., & Lindamood, P. *Visualizing and verbalizing CD-ROMs* (Grades 3–6). San Luis Obispo, CA: Gander Publishing.

Bell, N., & Lindamood, P. *Visualizing and verbalizing kit* (includes manual and Stories Book 1). San Luis Obispo, CA: Gander Publishing.

Bell, N., & Lindamood, P. *Visualizing and verbalizing stories* (Book 1). San Luis Obispo, CA: Gander Publishing.

Bell, N., & Lindamood, P. *Visualizing and verbalizing stories* (Book 2). San Luis Obispo, CA: Gander Publishing.

Bell, N., & Lindamood, P. *Visualizing and verbalizing stories* (Book 3). San Luis Obispo, CA: Gander Publishing.

Bell, N., & Lindamood, P. *Visualizing and verbalizing video*. San Luis Obispo, CA: Gander Publishing.

Bell, N., & Lindamood, P. *Visualizing and verbalizing workbooks* (Grades 3 and 4). San Luis Obispo, CA: Gander Publishing.

Carlisle, J. *Beginning reasoning and reading* (Grades 3 and 4). Cambridge: Educators Publishing Service.

Carlisle, J. (1982–1983). *Reasoning and reading* (Levels 1 and 2 for Grades 5–8). Cambridge, MA: Educators Publishing Service.

Carlisle, J. (1987). *Beginning paragraph meaning: Beginning reasoning and reading*. Cambridge, MA: Educators Publishing Service.

Curriculum Associates (2000). *Strategies to achieve reading success*. North Billerica, MA: Curriculum Associates.

Einstein, C. (2002). *Einstein's who, what, and where* (Grades 4–7). Cambridge, MA: Educators Publishing Service.

Einstein, C. *Claims to fame* (Grades 2–5). Cambridge, MA: Educators Publishing Service.

Einstein, C. *Reading for content* (Grades 3–6). Cambridge, MA: Educators Publishing Service.

Ervin, J. (1993). *Early reading comprehension in varied subject area and reading comprehension in varied subject matter* (Books A & B for Grades 2–4). Cambridge, MA: Educators Publishing Service.

Ervin, J. *More reading comprehension in varied subject matter* (Middle school and up). Cambridge, MA: Educators Publishing Service.

Ervin, J. *Reading comprehension in varied subject matter* (Grades 3–8). Cambridge, MA: Educators Publishing Service.

Evans, A.J. (1979). *Reading and thinking: Exercises for developing reading comprehension and critical thinking skills* (Books I & II). New York: Teachers College Press.

Fry, E.B., Kress, J.E., & Fountoukidis, D.L. (2000). *The reading teacher's book of lists* (4th ed.). Upper Saddle River, NJ: Jossey-Bass.

Gwynne, F. (1987). *A chocolate moose for dinner.* Upper Saddle River, NJ: Prentice Hall.

Gwynne, F. (1987). *The king who rained.* Upper Saddle River, NJ: Prentice Hall.

Gwynne, F. (1987). *The sixteen hand horse.* Upper Saddle River, NJ: Prentice Hall.

Hall, K.L. (1996). *Reading stories for comprehension success: 45 high-interest lessons that make kids think* (Grades 1–3 & Grades 4–6). West Nyack, NY: Center for Applied Research in Education.

Kratoville, B.L. (1990). *Listen my children and you shall hear* (3rd ed.). Austin, TX: PRO-ED.

LinguiSystems staff (2002). *Strategic learning: Reading comprehension.* East Moline, IL: LinguiSystems.

Raphael, T.E., & Au, K.H. (2002). *Super QAR for test-wise students.* Bothell, WA: Wright Group.

Schumaker, J.B., Denton, P.H., & Deshler, D.D. (1984). *The paraphrasing strategy* (Learning Strategies Curriculum). Lawrence: University of Kansas.

Schumaker, J.B., Denton, P.H., & Deshler, D.D. *The self-questioning strategy* (Learning Strategies Curriculum). Lawrence: University of Kansas. (See http://www.ku-crl.org/iei/sim/strategies/selfquest.html for more information.)

Schumaker, J.B., Denton, P.H., & Deshler, D.D. *The visual imagery strategy* (Learning Strategies Curriculum). Lawrence: University of Kansas. (See http://www.ku-crl.org/iei/sim/strategies/vimagery.html for more information.)

Smith, M.T., & Hogan, E.A. (1991). *MTA: Teaching a process for comprehension and composition.* Forney, TX: EDMAR Educational Associates.

Staman, A.L. *Starting comprehension: Stories to advance reading & thinking.* Cambridge: Educators Publishing Service.

Weber, S.G. *Idioms fun deck.* Greenville, SC: SuperDuper Publications.

Web Sites

Award-Winning Children's Literature
http://www.ala.org/Template.cfm?Section=bookmediaawards
(The award descriptions on this page describe the awards that pertain to children's literature. Then click Award Recipients on the left of the screen, and scroll to and click the applicable award to find a listing of recipients of that award.)

Big Ideas in Beginning Reading
http://reading.uoregon.edu

Book Adventure
http://www.bookadventure.com

Center for the Improvement of Early Reading Achievement
http://www.ciera.org

Center on Accelerating Student Learning
http://www.vanderbilt.edu/casl

Computer-Based Study Strategies
http://cbss.uoregon.edu

Content Literacy Information Consortium
http://curry.edschool.virginia.edu/centers/clic/home.html

Dade-Monroe Teacher Education Center
http://www.miamisci.org/tec

Division for Learning Disabilities (DLD)
http://www.teachingld.org

Early Reading Success
http://www.haskins.yale.edu/haskins/ers/index.html

Florida Center for Reading Research
http://www.fcrr.org

Inspiration Software
http://www.inspiration.com

International Reading Association (IRA)
http://www.reading.org

International Reading Association Article Archive
http://pqasb.pqarchiver.com/reading
Articles from the International Reading Association journals *The Reading Teacher, Journal of Adolescent & Adult Literacy,* and *Reading Today* from January 1988 to the present are available from this archive. Articles from another International Reading Association journal, *Reading Research Quarterly,* are available at http://www.reading.org/publications/journals/rrq/archives.html.

LD Online
http://ldonline.org

Learning Strategies Database, Muskingum College Center for Advancement of Learning
http://www.muskingum.edu/~cal/database

Learning Toolbox
http://coe.jmu.edu/LearningToolbox

National Reading Panel
http://www.nationalreadingpanel.org

Peer-Assisted Learning Strategies (PALS)
http://kc.vanderbilt.edu/kennedy/pals

Read Across America
http://www.nea.org/readacross

Reading ASSIST Institute: Free Downloads
http://www.readingassist.org/downloads.htm

Reading Comprehension
http://www.literacy.uconn.edu/compre.htm

Reading Online
http://www.readingonline.org

Reading Rockets
http://www.readingrockets.org

ReadingQuest
http://curry.edschool.virginia.edu/go/readquest/strat

Resource Room
http://www.resourceroom.net/index.asp

SparkNotes
http://www.sparknotes.com

University of Texas at Austin, Vaughn Gross Center for Reading and Language Arts
http://www.texasreading.org

CHAPTER 15—TEACHING HANDWRITING

Teacher References

Cox, A.R. (1992). *Foundations for literacy: Structures and techniques for multisensory teaching of basic written English language skills.* Cambridge, MA: Educators Publishing Service.

Gillingham, A., & Stillman, B.W. (1997). *The Gillingham manual: Remedial training for children with specific disability in reading, spelling and penmanship* (8th ed.). Cambridge, MA: Educators Publishing Service.

Curricula, Guides, and Activities

Bertin, P., & Perlman, E. (1980). *Preventing academic failure.* Cambridge, MA: Educators Publishing Service.

Cox, A.R. (1992). *Alphabetic phonics.* Cambridge, MA: Educators Publishing Service.

duBard, N.E., & Martin, M.K. (1994). *Teaching language-deficient children: Theory and application of the Association Method for multisensory teaching* (Rev. ed.). Cambridge, MA: Educators Publishing Service.

Enfield, M.L., & Greene, V. *Project read.* Bloomington, MN: Language Circle Enterprise.

Gillingham, A., & Stillman, B.W. (1997). *The Gillingham manual: Remedial training for children with specific disability in reading, spelling, and penmanship* (8th ed.). Cambridge, MA: Educators Publishing Service.

Herman, R.D. (1993). *The Herman Method for reversing reading failure: Teacher's guide, set A.* Sherman Oaks, CA: The Herman Method Institute.

Knight, J.R. (1986). *Starting over: A combined teaching manual and student textbook for reading, writing, spelling, vocabulary, and handwriting.* Cambridge, MA: Educators Publishing Service.

Slingerland, B.H., & Aho, M. (1994–1996). *A multi-sensory approach to language arts for specific language disability children* (Rev. ed., Vols. 1–3). Cambridge, MA: Educators Publishing Service.

Smith, M.T. (1996). *MTA reading and spelling program* (Kits 1–7). Cambridge, MA: Educators Publishing Service.

Sonday, A.W. (1992). *Fundamentals of reading success: An introduction to the Orton-Gillingham approach to teaching reading and spelling.* Cambridge, MA: Educators Publishing Service.

Spalding, R.B. (with Spalding, W.T.) (1990). *The writing road to reading: The Spalding Method of phonics for teaching speech, writing, and reading* (4th rev. ed.). New York: Quill.

Texas Scottish Rite Hospital for Children. (1992). *Dyslexia training program: Teacher's guides and student's books* (Vols. 1–4). Cambridge, MA: Educators Publishing Service.

Wilson, B.A. (1988). *Wilson reading system: Teacher's guide and student material.* Millbury, MA: Wilson Language Training.

Wilson, B.A. (2002). *Teacher's manual, Levels K-1 (Fundations).* Millbury, MA: Wilson Language Training.

Wilson, B.A. (2004). *Teacher's manual, Level 2 (Fundations).* Millbury, MA: Wilson Language Training. (The *Wilson Reading System* materials and both *Fundations* manuals are available from the publisher, http://www.wilsonlanguage.com)

Handwriting and Keyboarding Curricula

Bertin, P., & Perlman, E. (1980). *Preventing academic failure handwriting program.* Cambridge, MA: Educators Publishing Service.

Cavey, D.W. (1993). *Dysgraphia: Why Johnny can't write. A guide for teachers and parents* (2nd ed.). Austin, TX: PRO-ED.

Duffy, J. (1974). *Type it.* Cambridge, MA: Educators Publishing Service.

Olsen, J.Z. (1998). *Handwriting without tears.* Cabin John, MD: Author. (Available from the author, 8001 MacArthur Boulevard, Cabin John, MD 20818; 301-263-2700; http://www.hwtears.com)

Johnson, W.T., & Johnson, M.R. (1975). *Let's write and spell.* Cambridge, MA: Educators Publishing Service.

Johnson, W.T., & Johnson, M.R. (1977). *Beginning connected, cursive handwriting.* Cambridge, MA: Educators Publishing Service.

King, D.H. (1986). *Keyboarding skills.* Cambridge, MA: Educators Publishing Service.

King, D.H. (1987). *Cursive writing skills.* Cambridge, MA: Educators Publishing Service.

Phelps, J., & Stempel, L. (1985). *CHES's handwriting improvement program (CHIP).* Dallas: CHES. (Available from the publisher, Post Office Box 25254, Dallas, TX 75225)

Slingerland, B.H., & Aho, M.S. (1971). *Manual for learning to use cursive handwriting.* Cambridge, MA: Educators Publishing Service.

Slingerland, B.H., & Aho, M.S. (1971). *Manual for learning to use manuscript handwriting.* Cambridge, MA: Educators Publishing Service.

Smith, M.T. *Handwriting masters guide.* Cambridge, MA: Educators Publishing Service.

Smith, M.T. *Handwriting practice guide.* Cambridge, MA: Educators Publishing Service.

Smith, M.T. *MTS handwriting program.* Forney, TX: MTS Publications.

Instructional Materials

Olsen, J.Z. (1998). *Handwriting without tears.* Cabin John, MD: Author. (Available from the author, 8001 MacArthur Boulevard, Cabin John, MD 20818; 301-263-2700; http://www.hwtears.com)

All the write news [Fits over pencil to assist grip]. Los Angeles: Thē Pencil Grip. (Available from the publisher, Post Office Box 67096, Los Angeles, CA 90062; 888-PEN-GRIP)

Pencil grips. Dallas, TX: CHES. (Available from the publisher, Post Office Box 25254, Dallas, TX 75225)

Writing frame (#C1590011) [Metal frame to help writer's grip and shaping of letters]. Columbus, OH: Zaner-Bloser.

Videotapes

Allen, K. (Director). *Help your child with handwriting.* Bellaire, TX: Neuhaus Education Center.

Multisensory typing program. Dallas: Texas Scottish Rite Hospital for Children, Child Development Division.

Software

Mavis Beacon teaches typing for kids. Novato, CA: Mindscape (Available from the publisher, 88 Rowland Way, Novato, CA 94945; 415-897-9900)

Texas Scottish Rite Hospital for Children. *Keyboarding for written expression.* Dallas, TX: Author. (Available from SofDesign International 1303 Columbia Drive, Suite 209 Richardson, TX 75081; 800-755-7344)

CHAPTER 16—COMPOSITION: EXPRESSIVE LANGUAGE AND WRITING

Teacher References

Bereiter, C., & Scardamalia, M. (1987). *The psychology of written composition.* Mahwah, NJ: Lawrence Erlbaum Associates.

Handbook of grammar and usage. (1972). New York: William Morrow & Co.

Kamhi, A.G., & Catts, H.W. (1999). *Language and reading: Convergence and divergence.* In H.W. Catts & A.G. Kamhi (Eds.), *Language and reading disabilities* (pp. 1–24). Boston: Allyn & Bacon.

King, D.H. (1985). *Writing skills for the adolescent.* Cambridge, MA: Educators Publishing Service.

Scott, C.M. (1999). Learning to write. In H.W. Catts & A.G. Kamhi (Eds.), *Language and reading disabilities* (pp. 224–258). Boston: Allyn & Bacon.

Scott, C.M. (2002). Sentence comprehension instruction. In J.F. Carlisle & M.S. Rice, *Improving reading comprehension: Research-based principles and practices* (pp. 115–138). Timonium, MD: York Press. (Available from PRO-ED, 800-897-3202)

Strunk, W., & White, E.B. (1979). *The elements of style* (3rd ed.). New York: Macmillan Publishing Co.

Westby, C.E., & Clauser, P.S. (1999). The right stuff for writing: Assessing and facilitating written language. In H.W. Catts & A.G. Kamhi (Eds.), *Language and reading disabilities* (pp. 259–324). Boston: Allyn & Bacon.

Curricula, Guides, and Activities

Carlisle, J.F. (1998). *Models for writing*. Novato, CA: Academic Therapy Publications.

Catts, H.W., & Kamhi, A.G. (Eds.). (1999). *Language and reading disabilities*. Boston: Allyn & Bacon.

Cheney, T.A.R. (1983). *Getting the words right: How to rewrite, edit, and revise*. Cincinnati, OH: Writer's Digest Books.

Clark, D.B., & Uhry, J.K. (1995). *Dyslexia: Theory and practice of remedial instruction* (2nd ed.). Timonium, MD: York Press. (Available from PRO-ED, 800-897-3202)

Collins, K.M., & Collins, J.L. (1996, October). Strategic instruction for struggling writers. *English Journal, 5*(6), 54–61.

Deshler, D.D., Ellis, E., & Lenz, B.K. (1996). *Teaching adolescents with learning disabilities: Strategies and methods* (2nd ed.). Denver, CO: Love Publishing.

Gunning, T.G. (1996). *Creating reading instruction for all children* (2nd ed.). Boston: Allyn & Bacon.

Johnson, D.J., & Grant, J.O. (1989). Written narratives of normal and learning disabled children. *Annals of Dyslexia, 39*, 140–158.

King, D.H. (1989). *Writing skills levels 1 and 2* (Grades 4–6 and 7–9). Cambridge, MA: Educators Publishing Service.

Levy, N.R. (1996, November). Teaching analytical writing: Help for general education middle school teachers. *Intervention, 32*(2), 95–96.

Maria, K. (1990). *Reading comprehension: Instruction, issues, and strategies*. Timonium, MD: York Press. (Available from PRO-ED, 800-897-3202)

Muschla, G.R. (1991). *The writing teacher's book of lists*. Upper Saddle River, NJ: Prentice Hall.

State University of New York & New York State Education Department. (1987). *The arts and learning: The write way on*. Albany: Authors.

State University of New York & New York State Education Department. (1988). *English language arts syllabus K–12 (1988)*. Albany: Authors.

State University of New York & New York State Education Department. (1988). *Helping student writers*. Albany: Authors.

Instructional Materials

Biddle, M.L. (1998). *Written basic English for dyslexic students*. Cambridge, MA: Educators Publishing Service.

Composition in the English language arts curriculum K–12. (1986). Boston: McDougal, Littell.

Region XIII TAAS/Education Service Center. *Reading activities supporting the Texas reading initiative* [Manipulative paragraph writing outlines]. Austin, TX: Author.

CHAPTER 17—MULTISENSORY MATHEMATICS INSTRUCTION

Teacher References

Burns, M. (1987). *50 problem solving lessons*. White Plains, NY: Cuisinaire Dale Seymour Publications. (Available from the publisher, Post Office Box 502, White Plains, NY 10602)

Burns, M. (1992). *About teaching mathematics: A K–8 resource*. Sausalito, CA: Math Solutions Publications.

Fennema, E., Carpenter, T.P., & Lamon, S. (Eds.). (1991). *Integrating research and teaching and learning mathematics*. Albany: SUNY Press.

Gardener, H. (1991). *The unschooled mind: How children think and how schools should teach*. New York: Basic Books.

Grouws, D.A. (1992). *Handbook of research on mathematics teaching and learning*. New York: Macmillan.

Healy, J. (1999). *Failure to connect*. New York: Simon & Schuster.

Jordon, N.C., & Montani, T.O. (1996). Mathematics difficulties in young children: Cognitive and developmental perspectives. *Advances in Learning and Behavioral Disabilities, 10A*, 101–134.

Kamii, C. (1985). *Young children reinvent arithmetic: Implications of Piaget's theory.* New York: Teachers College Press.

MacNeal, E. (1994). *Mathematics: Making numbers talk sense.* New York: Viking Penguin.

Montessori, M. (1964). *The Montessori method.* Cambridge, MA: Robert Bentley.

National Council of Teachers of Mathematics. (1991). *Professional standards for teaching mathematics.* Reston, VA: Author.

Piaget, J. (1952). *The child's concept of number.* London: Routledge & Kegan Paul.

Pimm, D. (1990). *Speaking mathematically: Communication in mathematics classrooms.* New York: Routledge.

Sawyer, W.W. (1964). *Introducing mathematics: Vision in elementary mathematics.* London: Penguin Books Ltd.

Steen, L.A. (1997). *Why numbers count: Quantitative literacy for tomorrow's America.* Reston, VA: National Council of Teachers of Mathematics.

Stern, M. *Experimenting with numbers: Developing number skills with Structural Arithmetic. A multi-sensory approach to the first years of mathematics instruction* (Book 1, 3–6 years). Warminster, United Kingdom: Maths Extra.

Stern, M., & Gould, T. (1988–1992). *Structural Arithmetic workbooks and teacher's guides 1–3.* Cambridge, MA: Educators Publishing Service.

Thiessen, D., Matthias, M., & Smith, J. (1998). *The wonderful world of mathematics: A critically annotated list of children's books in mathematics.* Reston, VA: National Council of Teachers of Mathematics.

Trafton, P.R. (Ed.). (1989). *New directions for elementary school mathematics.* Reston, VA: National Council of Teachers of Mathematics.

Tuley, K., & Bell, N. (1998). *On cloud nine: Visualizing and verbalizing for math* [Includes kit and graded workbooks]. San Luis Obispo, CA: Gander Publishing.

Instructional Materials (Manipulatives)

Base ten blocks [Plastic blocks with units marked, used to demonstrate place value: tens, hundreds, and thousands]. White Plains, NY: Cuisinaire Dale Seymour Publications.

Cuisinaire rods [Colored plastic rods with sizes in centimeters, units not marked]. White Plains, NY: Cuisinaire Dale Seymour Publications.

Structural Arithmetic materials [Includes wooden number blocks 1–10 with units marked, numerals, and devices into which the blocks fit; counting board; pattern boards; number track; and dual board for place value]. Cambridge, MA: Educators Publishing Service.

Unifix cubes [Set of colored interlocking plastic cubes and devices into which they fit]. White Plains, NY: Cuisinaire Dale Seymour Publications.

Assessment Tools

Ginsburg, H. (1987). *Assessing the arithmetic abilities and instructional needs of students.* Austin, TX: PRO-ED.

National Council of Teachers of Mathematics. (1995). *Assessment standards for school mathematics.* Reston, VA: Author.

Videotapes

Birsh, J.R. (Consulting Ed.), & Potts, M., & Potts, R. (Producers). (1997). *LD/LA: Learning disabilities/learning abilities: Videotape VI. Teaching math: A systematic approach for children with learning disabilities.* West Tisbury, MA: Vineyard Video Productions. (Available from Paul H. Brookes Publishing Co., Post Office Box 10624, Baltimore, MD 21285-0624; 800-638-3775; 410-337-9580; http://www.brookespublishing.com)

Birsh, J.R. (Consulting Ed.), & Potts, M., & Potts, R. (Producers). (1991). *Teaching the learning disabled: Study skills and learning strategies.* West Tisbury, MA: Vineyard Video Productions.

Web Sites

Centre for Innovation in Mathematics Teaching, University of Exeter, United Kingdom
http://www.ex.ac.uk/cimt

Math Parent Handbook: A Guide to Helping Your Child Understand Mathematics
http://www.eduplace.com/math/res/parentbk

Mathematics Learning Forum, Bank Street College
http://www.bnkst.edu/mlf

Stern Structural Arithmetic
http://www.sternmath.com

Sunburst Communications
http://www.sunburst.com

Organization

National Council of Teachers of Mathematics
1906 Association Drive
Reston, VA 20191
800-235-7566
http://www.nctm.org

CHAPTER 18—LEARNING STRATEGIES AND STUDY SKILLS: THE SkORE SYSTEM

Teacher References

Aaron, P.G., & Baker, C. (1991). *Reading disabilities in college and high school: Diagnosis and management.* Timonium, MD: York Press. (Available from PRO-ED, 800-897-3202)

Calfee, R.E. (1983). The mind of the dyslexic. *Annals of Dyslexia, 33,* 28.

Carlisle, J.F., & Rice, M.S. (2002). *Improving reading comprehension.* Timonium, MD: York Press.

Catts, H.W., & Kamhi, A.G. (Eds.). (2005). *Language and reading disabilities* (2nd ed.). Boston: Allyn & Bacon.

Christensen, C.R., Garvin, D.A., & Sweet, A. (1991). *Education for judgment: The artistry of discussion leadership.* Boston: Harvard Business School Press.

Foorman, B.R. (Ed.). (2003). *Preventing and remediating reading difficulties: Bringing science to scale.* Timonium, MD: York Press. (Available from PRO-ED, 800-897-3202)

Gaddes, W.H., & Edgell, D. (1994). *Learning disabilities and brain function: A neuropsychological approach* (3rd ed.). New York: Springer-Verlag.

Galaburda, A. (Ed.). (1993). *Dyslexia and development: Neurobiological aspects of extraordinary brains.* Cambridge, MA: Harvard University Press.

Levine, M. (1987). *Developmental variation and learning disorders* (2nd ed.). Cambridge, MA: Educators Publishing Service.

McCardle, P., & Chhabra, V. (Eds.). (2004). *The voice of evidence in reading research.* Baltimore: Paul H. Brookes Publishing Co.

Shaywitz, S.E. (1998). Current concepts in dyslexia. *New England Journal of Medicine, 338,* 307–312.

Steeves, K.J. (1983). Memory as a factor in the computational efficiency of dyslexic children with high abstract reasoning ability. *Annals of Dyslexia, 33,* 141–152.

Tuley, A.C. (1998). *Never too late to read: Language skills for the adolescent dyslexic* (based on the work of Alice Ansara). Timonium, MD: York Press. (Available from PRO-ED, 800-897-3202)

Wiig, E.H., & Semel, E. (1990). *Language assessment and intervention for the learning disabled.* Columbus, OH: Charles E. Merrill.

Curricula, Guides, and Activities

Abbamont, G.W., & Brescher, A. (1997). *Test smart: Ready-to-use test-taking strategies and activities for grades 5–12.* West Nyack, NY: Center for Applied Research in Education.

Askov, E.N., & Kamm, K. (1982). *Study skills in the content areas.* Boston: Allyn & Bacon.

Bragstad, B.J., & Stumpf, S.M. (1987). *Study skills and motivation: A guidebook for teaching.* Boston: Allyn & Bacon.

Coffman, N.W. (2002). *Shelton School study skills curriculum.* Dallas, TX: June Shelton School & Evaluation Center.

Coffman, N. (2002). *Shelton School study skills student resource binder.* Dallas, TX: June Shelton School & Evaluation Center.

D'Angelo Bromley, K. (1996). *Webbing with literature: Creating story maps with children's books.* Boston: Allyn & Bacon.

Deshler, D.D., Ellis, E., & Lenz, B.K. (1996). *Teaching adolescents with learning disabilities: Strategies and methods* (2nd ed.). Denver, CO: Love Publishing.

Devine, T.G. (1987). *Teaching study skills: A guide for teachers* (2nd ed.). Boston: Allyn & Bacon.

Ellis, E.S. (1984). An instructional model for integrating content-area instruction with cognitive strategy instruction. *Reading and Writing Quarterly, 1,* 63–90.

Foss, J. (1986). The tutor–student instructional interaction. *Annals of Dyslexia, 36,* 15–27.

Langan, J. (1979). *Sentence skills: A workbook for writers.* New York: McGraw-Hill.

McNeil, J.D. (1992). *Reading comprehension: New directions for classroom practice.* New York: HarperCollins.

Roman, N.V. *Get set for reading: Test preparation for reading assessment.* Elizabethtown, PA: Continental Press.

Strichart, S.S., & Mangrum, C.T., II. (1993). *Teaching study strategies to students with learning disabilities.* Boston: Allyn & Bacon.

Tonjes, M.J., & Zintz, M.V. (1992). *Teaching reading, thinking, study skills in content classrooms* (3rd ed.). Dubuque, IA: William C. Brown.

Vurnakes, C. (1995). *The organized student: Teaching time management.* Torrance, CA: Frank Schaffer Publications.

Instructional Materials

Ayto, J. (1990). *Dictionary of word origins.* New York: Arcade.

Benne, B. (1988). *WASPLEG and other mnemonics: Easy ways to remember hard things.* Dallas, TX: Taylor Publishing Co.

Budworth, J. (1991). *Instant recall: Tapping your hidden memory power.* Holbrook, MA: Bob Adams.

Buzan, T. (1991). *Use both sides of your brain* (3rd ed.). New York: E.P. Dutton. [*Note:* Buzan's note-taking system is not recommended for dyslexic students; this source is recommended for mind map design and enhancement only.]

Bywaters, D. (1998). *Affix and root cards.* Cambridge, MA: Educators Publishing Service.

Cherry, R.L. (1989). *Words under construction.* Tucson: University of Arizona Press.

Danner, H.G., & Noël, R. (1996). *Discover it!: A better vocabulary the better way.* Occoquan, VA: Imprimus Books.

Dillon, S. (2000). *Structure of the English language for reading and spelling.* Albuquerque, NM: S.I.S. Publishing Co.

Erwin, P. (1992). *The Winston grammar program.* Battleground, WA: Precious Memories Educational Resources. (Available from the publisher, 18403 Northeast 111th Avenue, Battleground, WA 98604, 360-687-2082)

Gilbert, S. (1990). *Go for it: Get organized. The perfect time-management system for busy teens.* New York: Morrow Junior Books.

Henry, M.K. (2003). *Unlocking literacy: Effective decoding and spelling instruction.* Baltimore: Paul H. Brookes Publishing Co.

Kesselman-Turkel, J., & Peterson, F. (1982). *Note-taking made easy.* Chicago: Contemporary Books.

Lakoff, G., & Johnson, M. (1980). *Metaphors we live by.* Chicago: University of Chicago Press.

Makkai, A., Boatner, M.T., & Gates, J.E. (1995). *A dictionary of American idioms.* Hauppauge, NY: Barron's Educational Series.

Merriam Webster's collegiate dictionary (10th ed.). (1993). Springfield, MA: Merriam-Webster.

Moore, B., & Moore, M. (1997). *NTC's dictionary of Latin and Greek origins.* Lincolnwood, IL: NTC Publishing Group.

Morwood, J., & Warman, M. (1990). *Our Greek and Latin roots.* London: Cambridge University Press.

Murray, C., & Munro, J. (1989). *30 roots to grow on.* Cambridge, MA: Educators Publishing Service.

The Oxford dictionary and thesaurus (American ed.). (1996). New York: Oxford University Press.

Partridge, E. (1966). *Origins: A short etymological dictionary of modern English.* New York: Greenwich House.

Roget's thesaurus (5th ed.). (1992). New York: HarperCollins. [*Note:* Only editions of the original *Roget's Thesaurus,* such as this version, are recommended.]

Trudeau, K. (1995). *Megamemory.* New York: William Morrow & Co.

Wycoff, J. (1991). *Mindmapping: Your personal guide to exploring creativity and problem-solving.* New York: Berkley Books.

Web Sites

Computer-Based Study Strategies
http://cbss.uoregon.edu

Learning Strategies Database, Muskingum College Center for Advancement of Learning
http://www.muskingum.edu/~cal/database
A collection of general learning strategies and content-specific strategies.

Learning Toolbox
http://coe.jmu.edu/LearningToolbox

ProQuest K–12
http://www.researchpaper.com

Videotapes

Birsh, J.R. (Consulting Ed.), & Potts, M., & Potts, R. (Producers). (1991). *Teaching the learning disabled: Study skills and learning strategies: Videotape III. Organizing time, materials, and information.* West Tisbury, MA: Vineyard Video Productions.

The University of Kansas Center for Research on Learning, Institute for Effective Instruction, has a variety of videotapes that can be ordered from its web site: http://www.ku-crl.org/iei/products/support.html

Software

Anderson, L. *Inspiration* [Outlining and graphic organizer software]. Portland: University of Oregon.

CHAPTER 19—WORKING WITH HIGH-FUNCTIONING DYSLEXIC ADULTS

Teacher References

Blumenthal, S.H. (1981). *Educational Memories as a diagnostic measure.* Unpublished manuscript. (Available from the author, shb280@aol.com)

Blumenthal, S.H. (1981). *Process Notes as a cognitive mediator.* Unpublished manuscript. (Available from the author, shb280@aol.com)

Fink, R.P. (1998). Literacy development in successful men and women with dyslexia. *Annals of Dyslexia, 48,* 311–346.

Gerber, P.J., Ginsberg, R., & Reiff, H.B. (1992). Identifying alterable patterns in employment success for highly successful adults with learning disabilities. *Journal of Learning Disabilities, 25*(8), 475–487.

Gerber, P.J., Ginsberg, R., & Reiff, H.B. (1996). Reframing the learning disabilities experience. *Journal of Learning Disabilities, 29*(1), 98–101.

Levine, M.D. (2002). *A mind at a time.* New York: Simon & Schuster.

Morris, B. (2002, May 13). Overcoming dyslexia. *Fortune,* 54–70.

Reiff, H.B., Gerber, P.J., & Ginsberg, R. (1994). Instructional strategies for long term success. *Annals of Dyslexia, 44,* 270–288.

Reiff, H.B., Gerber, P.J., & Ginsberg, R. (1997). *Exceeding expectations: Successful adults with learning disabilities.* Austin, TX: PRO-ED.

Roswell, F., & Chall, J. (1994). *Creating successful readers.* Chicago: Riverside.

Shaywitz, S.E. (1996). Dyslexia. *Scientific American, 275*(5), 98–104.

Instructional Materials

Cooley, T. (1993). *The Norton sampler: Short essays for composition* (4th ed). New York: W.W. Norton.

Milan, D. (1991). *Developing reading skills* (3rd ed.). New York: McGraw-Hill.

Milan, D. (1992). *Improving reading skills* (2nd ed.). New York: McGraw-Hill.

Pauk, W. (1983). *Six-way paragraphs: Advanced level* (Rev. ed.). Providence, RI: Jamestown Publishing.

Pauk, W. (1983). *Six-way paragraphs: Middle level* (Rev. ed.). Providence, RI: Jamestown Publishing.

Recording for the Blind & Dyslexic (RFB&D)
20 Roszel Road
Princeton, NJ 08540
800-803-7201
http://www.rfbd.org

Books by Adults with Learning Difficulties

Hampshire, S. (1982). *Susan's story.* New York: St. Martin's Press.

Simpson, E.M. (1998). *Reversals: A personal account of victory over dyslexia* (Reissue ed.). New York: Noonday Press.

West, T.G. (1991). *In the mind's eye.* Buffalo, NY: Prometheus Books.

Organizations

The International Dyslexia Association (IDA)
8600 LaSalle Road
Chester Building
Suite 382
Baltimore, MD 21286
800-222-3123
E-mail: info@interdys.org
http://www.interdys.org

Learning Disabilities Association of America
   (LDA)
4156 Library Road
Pittsburgh, PA 15234
412-341-1515
http://www.ldanatl.org

National Center for Learning Disabilities
   (NCLD)
381 Park Avenue South
Suite 1401
New York, NY 10016
888-575-7373
http://www.ncld.org

Web Sites

All Kinds of Minds
http://allkindsofminds.org

Cyberwink
http://cyberwink.com

Literacy & Learning Disabilities Special Collection: Success for Adults with Learning Disabilities
http://ldlink.coe.utk.edu/

Schwab Learning
http://schwablearning.org

CHAPTER 20—HELPING PARENTS OF CHILDREN WITH DYSLEXIA

The author of this chapter, who has more than 35 years of clinical experience with dyslexic children and their families, strongly recommends that the most recent definition of dyslexia be read (see Chapter 1) before consulting the following references. It is also important to consider the perspective of Shaywitz and Shaywitz (2004):

> Dyslexia, a developmental disorder, is characterized by an unexpected difficulty in reading in children and adults who otherwise possess the intelligence, motivation, and education considered necessary for developing accurate and fluent reading (Lyon, 1995). Dyslexia (or specific reading disability) represents one of the most common problems affecting children and adults; in the United States the prevalence of dyslexia is estimated to range from 5% to 17%, with up to 40% of school-age children reading below grade level (S.E. Shaywitz, 1998). Dyslexia is the most common and most carefully studied of the learning disabilities (LDs), affecting 80% of all individuals identified as having LD (Interagency Committee on Learning Disabilities, 1987; Lerner, 1989, S.E. Shaywitz, 1998).

Although individuals with dyslexia often have co-existing conditions, such as attention issues, not all individuals with dyslexia necessarily have attention-deficit/hyperactivity disorder (ADHD) or attention deficit disorder (ADD). Consequently, although medication may be one option for mediating attention issues, it is important to stress the need for a differential diagnosis prior to such an intervention. Psychotropic drugs will not improve reading and language disorders and, in fact, may preclude the implementation of the most successful education intervention.

Thomas Armstrong, M.D. (1995), wrote: "ADD has appeal because it implies a specific neurological condition for which no one can be held particularly responsible." Debra DeLee, a spokesperson for the National Education Association (the largest teacher organization in the United States), noted, "Establishing a new category [ADD] based on behavioral characteristics alone, such as over-activity, impulsiveness, and inattentiveness, increases the likelihood of inappropriate labeling for racial, ethnic, and linguistic minority students." This is particularly the case for dyslexic individuals, whose brains are wired differently for processing language and who need a very specific instructional approach based on scientific research.

The resources listed here for Chapter 20 include works related to ADHD, ADD, and LD to provide responsible information for parents regarding what is being said in the media and in the schools; along with this warning: ***Only a small percentage of dyslexics have ADHD or ADD.*** A comprehensive, responsible evaluation should lead to a primary choice of treatment, that is, a multisensory, systematic, structured language approach. Adjunctive therapies (e.g., counseling, medication, family help) should be secondary considerations.

The proliferation of ADHD and ADD literature, along with the increased use of drugs as the answer, is dangerous and can lead to inappropriate treatment. According to John S. Werry, M.D., "If ever any country badly needed a sobering does of science about ADHD to temper overenthusiastic diagnosis and treatment, it is the United States."

Teacher and Parent References

Armstrong, T. (1995). *The myth of the A.D.D. child.* New York: Dutton.
Barkley, R.A. (1995). *Taking charge of ADHD: The complete, authoritative guide for parents.* New York: The Guilford Press.
Betancourt, J. (1993). *My name is ~~Brain~~ Brian.* New York: Scholastic.

Cicci, R. (1995). *What's wrong with me?: Learning disabilities at home and in school*. Timonium, MD: York Press. (Available from PRO-ED, 800-897-3202)

Clark, D.B., & Uhry, J.K. (1995). *Dyslexia: Theory and practice of remedial instruction* (2nd ed.). Timonium, MD: York Press. (Available from PRO-ED, 800-897-3202)

Corcoran, J. (1994). *The teacher who couldn't read*. Colorado Springs: Focus on the Family Publishing.

Diller, L.H. (1998). *Running on Ritalin*. New York: Bantam Books.

Frank, R. (2002). *The secret life of the dyslexic child*. Emaus, PA: Rodale Press.

Griffith, J. (1998). *How dyslexic Benny became a star*. Dallas, TX: Yorktown Press.

Hall, S.L., & Moats, L.C. (1999). *Straight talk about reading: How parents can make a difference during the early years*. Chicago: Contemporary Books.

Hall, S.L, & Moats, L.C. (2002). *Parenting a struggling reader: A guide to diagnosing and finding help for your child's reading difficulties*. New York: Random House.

Hallowell, D.M., & Ratey, J.J. (1994). *Answers to distraction*. New York: Bantam Doubleday Dell.

Hallowell, D.M., & Ratey, J.J. (1994). *Driven to distraction*. New York: Pantheon Books.

Hampshire, S. (1982). *Susan's story*. New York: St. Martin's Press.

Honig, B. (1996). *Teaching our children to read: The role of skills in a comprehensive reading program*. Thousand Oaks, CA: Corwin Press.

Hurford, D.M. (1998). *To read or not to read: Answers to all your questions about dyslexia*. New York: Scribner.

Huston, A.M. (1992). *Understanding dyslexia: A practical approach for parents and teachers*. Lanham, MD: Madison Books.

Interagency Committee on Learning Disabilities. (1987). *Learning disabilities: A report to the U.S. Congress*. Washington, DC: U.S. Government Printing Office.

Janover, C. (1988). *Josh: A boy with dyslexia*. Burlington, VT: Waterfront Books.

Kurnoff, S. (2001). *The human side of dyslexia: 142 interviews with real people telling real stories about their coping strategies with dyslexia—kindergarten to college*. London: Universal.

Landau, E. (1991). *Dyslexia*. New York: Franklin Watts.

Lauren, J. (1997). *Succeeding with LD: 20 true stories about real people with LD*. Minneapolis, MN: Free Spirit.

Lerner, J. (1989). Educational interventions in learning disabilities. *Journal of the American Academy of Child and Adolescent Psychiatry, 28*, 326–331.

Levine, M. (1990). *Keeping ahead in school* [Audiotapes and book]. Cambridge, MA: Educators Publishing Service.

Levine, M. (1993). *All kinds of minds*. Cambridge, MA: Educators Publishing Service.

Levinson, B. (1987). *Fathers: Critical determinants of a child's success*. Chevy Chase, MD: National Institute of Dyslexia.

Lyon, G.R., Shaywitz, S.E., & Shaywitz, B.A. (2003). A definition of dyslexia. *Annals of Dyslexia, 53*, 1–14.

Marek, M. (1985). *Different, not dumb*. New York: Franklin Watts.

McCardle, P., & Chhabra, V. (Eds.). (2004). *The voice of evidence in reading research*. Baltimore: Paul H. Brookes Publishing Co.

National Association for the Education of African American Children with Learning Disabilities. (2003). *One child at a time: A parent handbook and resource directory for African American families with children who learn differently*. Columbus, OH: Author. (Available from the author, http://www.aacld.org)

National Center for Learning Disabilities. (1997–1998). *Their world*. New York: Author.

National Council on Learning Disabilities. (1991). *Understanding learning disabilities: A parent guide and workbook*. New York: Author.

Osman, B.B. (1995). *No one to play with: Social problems of LD and ADD children*. Novato, CA: Academic Therapy Publications.

Osman, B.B. (1998). *LD and ADHD: A family guide*. New York: John Wiley & Sons.

Parents Educational Resource Center. (1995). *Bridges to reading*. San Mateo, CA: Author.

Rawson, M.B. (1988). The many faces of dyslexia. *Monographs of the Orton Dyslexia Society, 5*.

Sedita, J. (1993). Landmark study skills guide. Prides Crossing, MA: Landmark Outreach Program. (Available from the publisher, Box 79, Prides Crossing, MA 01965)

Shaywitz, S. (1998). Current concepts: Dyslexia. *The New England Journal of Medicine, 338*(5), 307–312.

Shaywitz, S. (2003). *Overcoming dyslexia: A new and complete science-based program for reading problems at any level.* New York: Alfred A. Knopf.

Silver, L.B. (1998). *The misunderstood child: A guide for parents of learning disabled children* (3rd ed.). New York: Random House.

Simpson, E.M. (1998). *Reversals: A personal account of victory over dyslexia* (Reissue ed.). New York: Noonday Press.

Smith, S.L. (1987). *No easy answers: The learning disabled child at home and at school.* New York: Bantam Doubleday Dell.

Vail, P.L. (1987). *Smart kids with school problems: Things to know and ways to help.* New York: E.P. Dutton.

Vail, P.L. (1991). *About dyslexia: Unraveling the myth.* Rosemont, NJ: Modern Learning Press.

Vail, P.L. (1994). *Emotion: The on-off switch for learning.* Rosemont, NJ: Modern Learning Press.

Weinstein, L. (2003). *Reading David: A mother and son's journey through the labyrinth of dyslexia.* New York: Perigee Books.

West, T.G. (1991). *In the mind's eye.* Buffalo, NY: Prometheus Books.

Instructional Materials

Schmidt, J.J. (1997). *Making and keeping friends: Ready-to-use lessons, stories, activities for building relationships* (Grades 4–8). West Nyack, NY: Center for Applied Research in Education.

Organizations

Children and Adults with Attention Deficit
    Disorders (CHADD)
499 Northwest 70th Avenue
Suite 308
Plantation, FL 33317
305-587-3700
http://www.chadd.org

Division for Learning Disabilities (DLD)
The Council for Exceptional Children (CEC)
1110 North Glebe Road
Suite 300
Arlington, VA 22201
888-CEC-SPED
E-mail: cec@cec.sped.org
http://www.teachingld.org

Independent Educational Consultants Association
4085 Chain Bridge Road
Suite 401
Fairfax, VA 22030
703-591-4850
E-mail: iecaassoc@aol.com
http://www.educationalconsulting.org.

Institute of Education Sciences
U.S. Department of Education
555 New Jersey Avenue NW
Washington, DC 20208-5500
800-USA-LEARN
http://www.ed.gov/about/offices/list/ies/index
    .html

The International Dyslexia Association (IDA)
8600 LaSalle Road
Chester Building
Suite 382
Baltimore, MD 21286
800-ABC-D123
E-mail: info@interdys.org
http://www.interdys.org

Learning Disabilities Association of America
    (LDA)
4156 Library Road
Pittsburgh, PA 15234
412-341-1515
http://www.ldanatl.org

National Center for Learning Disabilities
    (NCLD)
381 Park Avenue South
Suite 1401
New York, NY 10016
888-575-7373
http://www.ncld.org

National Dissemination Center for Children
    with Disabilities (NICHCY)
Post Office Box 1492
Washington, DC 20013
800-695-0285
E-mail: nichcy@aed.org
http://www.nichcy.org

National Institute of Child Health and Human
  Development (NICHD)
National Institutes of Health
Post Office Box 3006
Rockville, MD 20847
800-370-2943
http://www.nichd.nih.gov

National Library Service for the Blind and the
  Physically Handicapped (Talking Books)
The Library of Congress
1291 Taylor Street NW
Washington, DC 20542
800-424-8567

Office of Special Education and Rehabilitative
  Services (OSERS)
U.S. Department of Education
400 Maryland Avenue SW
Washington, DC 20202-7100
202-245-7468
http://www.ed.gov/about/offices/list/osers/
  index.html?src=oc

Parents Educational Resource Center (PERC)
Charles and Helen Schwab Foundation
1650 South Amphlett Boulevard
Suite 200
San Mateo, CA 94402
800-230-0988
E-mail: infodesk@schwablearning.org
http://www.perc-scwhabfdn.org

Recording for the Blind & Dyslexic (RFB&D)
20 Roszel Road
Princeton, NJ 08540
800-803-7201
http://www.rfbd.org

Technical Assistance for Parent Programs (TAPP)
Federation for Children with Special Needs
95 Berkeley Street
Suite 104
Boston, MA 02116

Professional Journal

Parent Journal: A Quarterly Publication for Parents of Children with Learning Differences
published by Parents Educational Resource Center (PERC)
Charles and Helen Schwab Foundation
1650 South Amphlett Boulevard
Suite 200
San Mateo, CA 94402
650-655-2410

Videotapes

Birsh, J.R. (Consulting Ed.), & Potts, M., & Potts, R. (Producers). (1991). *Teaching the learning disabled: Study skills and learning strategies.* West Tisbury, MA: Vineyard Video Productions. (Available from Paul H. Brookes Publishing Co., Post Office Box 10624, Baltimore, MD 21285-0624; 800-638-3775; 410-337-9580; http://www.brookespublishing.com)

Birsh, J.R. (Consulting Ed.), & Potts, M., & Potts, R. (Producers). (1997). *LD/LA: Learning disabilities/learning abilities: Videotape IV. Children & parents & schools & strengths.* West Tisbury, MA: Vineyard Video Productions. (Available from Paul H. Brookes Publishing Co., Post Office Box 10624, Baltimore, MD 21285-0624; 800-638-3775; 410-337-9580; http://www.brookespublishing.com)

Birsh, J.R. (Consulting Ed.), & Potts, M., & Potts, R. (Producers). (1997). *LD/LA: Learning disabilities/learning abilities: Videotape V. ADD/ADHD/LD: Understanding the connection.* West Tisbury, MA: Vineyard Video Productions. (Available from Paul H. Brookes Publishing Co., Post Office Box 10624, Baltimore, MD 21285-0624; 800-638-3775; 410-337-9580; http://www.brookespublishing.com)

Eagle Hill School & Rosen, P. (Producers). (1989). *How difficult can this be? F.A.T. City.* Alexandria, VA: PBS Video. (Available from the publisher, 1320 Braddock Place, Alexandria, VA 22314; 703-739-5000)

Guilford Publications (Producer) & Barkley, R.A. (Director). (1992). *ADHD in the classroom: Strategies for teachers.* New York: Guilford Publications.

Guilford Publications (Producer) & Barkley, R.A. (Director). (1992). *ADHD—What do we know?* New York: Guilford Publications.

WETA-TV (Producer) & Lavoie, R. (Director). (1994). *Learning disabilities and social skills with Richard Lavoie: Last one picked . . . first one picked on.* Alexandria, VA: PBS Video. (Available from the publisher, 1320 Braddock Place, Alexandria, VA 22314; 703-739-5000)

Audiotapes

Dr. Alan Wachtel and Dr. Betty Levinson each have created audiotapes on the role of fathers, which might be useful both for HPs and for parents. These audiotapes are available from The International Dyslexia Association (IDA), 8600 LaSalle Road, Chester Building, Suite 382, Baltimore, Maryland 21286 (800-222-3123; http://www.interdys.org).

Web Sites

ERIC Clearinghouse on Disabilities and Gifted Education
http://ericec.org

LD Online
http://ldonline.org

Matrix Parent Network
http://marin.org/edu/matrix/index.html

Parents Helping Parents
http://www.php.com

SparkTop.org
http://www.sparktop.org

CHAPTER 21—ASSISTIVE TECHNOLOGY AND INDIVIDUALS WITH DYSLEXIA

Chapter 21 appears on-line at http://textbooks.brookespublishing.com/birsh

Web Sites

ABLEDATA
http://www.abledata.com

Adaptive Technology Center, Indiana University
http://www.indiana.edu/~iuadapts

The Alliance for Technology Access (ATA)
http://www.ATAccess.org

Assistive Technology for the Classroom, Landmark College
http://www.landmark.edu/institute/assistive_technology/index.html

Center for Applied Special Technology (CAST)
http://www.cast.org

Center for Assistive Technology & Environmental Access (CATEA)
http://www.catea.org

Closing The Gap
http://www.closingthegap.com

Community Technology Centers' Network
http://www.ctcnet.org

eduScapes
http://www.eduscapes.com

The Family Center on Technology and Disability
http://www.fctd.info

Johns Hopkins University Center for Technology in Education
http://www.cte.jhu.edu

LD Online's Technology section
http://ldonline.org/ld_indepth/technology/technology.html

LD Resources
http://www.ldresources.com

Learning Aids, Washington Assistive Technology Alliance
http://www.wata.org/resource/learning

National Center to Improve Practice in Special Education through Technology, Media and Materials
http://www2.edc.org/NCIP

Schwab Learning
http://www.schwablearning.org

Speaking to Write
http://www.edc.org/spk2wrt

University of Toronto, Adaptive Technology Resource Centre
http://www.utoronto.ca/atrc/index_E.html

Listservs and Discussion Boards

Closing The Gap Forums
http://www.closingthegap.com/cgi-bin/ultimatebb.cgi

Kurzweil
http://www.kurzweiledu.com/support_listserv.asp

Speak to Write
http://www.edc.org/spk2wrt/spk2wrt.html

Software and Hardware

This list of software and hardware resources is not exhaustive, but surveys the field and offers some leading products in each category. Listing here does not imply endorsement of a particular product. (*Source:* Pisha, B., Hitchcock, C., & Stahl, S. [2003, Fall]. Assistive technologies resource list. *Perspectives, 29*[4], 14–18.)

Text-to-Speech Software

Although some text-to-speech software, which reads digitized text aloud, is available as a free download or as shareware, the features vary greatly among products, and not all digital text can be read by all products.

Freeware
Freeware can be downloaded from the Internet without charge.

HearIt! (http://allmacintosh.xs4all.nl/preview/205274.htm)
HELP Read (http://www.pixi.com/~reader1/allbrowser)
Microsoft Reader (http://www.microsoft.com/reader)
Text Talkster v1.0 (http://yippee.i4free.co.nz/html/win/desktopenhancements/title10699.htm)

Shareware

Shareware can be downloaded from the Internet and used without cost for a trial period. After the trial ends, users should pay a shareware fee, which is usually relatively inexpensive.

TextAloudMP3 (http://www.nextup.com/TextAloud/download.html)

Commercial Software

Following are more expensive choices that offer integrated scanning, improved voices, and maintain original page layout.

CAST eReader
CAST
http://www.cast.org/products/ereader/index.html

Kurzweil 3000
http://www.kurzweiledu.com/products_k3000win.asp
and
http://www.kurzweiledu.com/products_k3000mac.asp

Read & Write Gold and Screenreader v4
Texthelp Systems Ltd.
http://www.texthelp.com/rwg.asp?q1=products&q2=rwg

Reading Assistant
Soliloquy Learning
http://www.soliloquylearning.com

WordQ Writing Aid Software
http://www.wordq.com

WYNN
Freedom Scientific
http://www.freedomscientific.com/LSG/products/wynn.asp

Voice Recognition Software

Dragon NaturallySpeaking
ScanSoft
http://www.scansoft.com/naturallyspeaking

MacSpeech iListen (Macintosh only)
http://www.macspeech.com/products/ilisten

ViaVoice
http://www-3.ibm.com/software/speech
(ViaVoice products are available through ScanSoft, http://www.scansoft.com/viavoice)

Graphic Organizer Software

Inspiration and Kidspiration
http://www.inspiration.com

Inexpensive Portable Word Processors

AlphaSmart 3000
AlphaSmart
973 University Avenue
Los Gatos, CA 95032
408-355-1000

LaserPC6 (with text-to-speech option)
http://www.perfectsolutions.com/pc6f.asp

Other Technology Tools

Draft:Builder, Write:OutLoud, Co:Writer 4000, and Co:Writer SmartApplet
Don Johnston
http://www.donjohnston.com

Reading Pen
WizCom Technologies
257 Great Road
Acton, MA 01720, USA
888-777-0552

Sources for Digital Text

General

(*Source of general digital text listing:* Center for Applied Special Technology. *Web resources: Digital media.* Retrieved from http://dev.cast.org/castweb/udl/index.cfm?i=206&s=y&searchby=level1&level1_ID=1#1)

Abacci Books
http://abacci.com/books

Accessible Book Collection
http://accessiblebookcollection.com

Alex: A Catalog of Electronic Texts
http://sunsite.berkely.edu/alex

Audible
http://www.audible.com

Bookshare.org
http://www.bookshare.org

CAST eText Spider
http://www.cast.org/udl/index.cfm?1=1300

EBooks
http://www.eBooks.com
A digital bookstore

Elibrary
http://www.elibrary.com

The eText Archive
http://www.etext.org

Internet Public Library
http://www.ilp.org

Literature Online from Chadwyck
http://lion.chadwyck.com

The Online Books Page
http://www.ul.cs.cmu.edu/

Project Gutenberg
http://www.promo.net/pg/

Search eBooks
http://www.searcheBooks.com

SearchGov.com
http://www.SearchGov.com

The Texas Text Exchange
http://www.tte.tamu.edu

Elementary Level

Accessible Book Collection
http://www.accessiblebookcollection.org/default.htm

African Stories
http://artsedge.kennedy-center.org/aoi/literary/storytelling/trove.html

Best Children's Lit (On The Net)
http://www.geocities.com/Paris/Jardin/1630/

The Children's Literature Web Guide
http://www.acs.ucalgary.ca/~dkbrown

Cinderella Stories
http://www.ucalgary.ca/~dkbrown/cinderella.html

Fairrisa Cyber Library
http://www.fairrosa.info/

KidSpace @ The Internet Public Library
http://www.ipl.org/youth

The Princess and the Pea by Hans Christian Andersen
http://hca.gilead.org.il/princess.html

Stories, Folklore, and Fairy Tales Theme Page
http://www.cln.org/themes/fairytales.html

Academic Texts, Secondary Level and Above

American Literary Classics
http://www.americanliterature.com

Bartleby.com
http://www.bartleby.com/

Bookshare
http//www.bookshare.org

Camera Obscura
http://www.hicom.net/~oedipus/etext.html

Carnegie Mellon's Universal Library
http://www.ulib.org/html/index.html

CCBC Publications
http://www.education.wisc.edu/ccbc/public2.htm

Electronic Text Center, The University of Virginia
http://etext.lib.virginia.edu/eng-oth.html

English Language Resources, The University of Virginia
http://etext.lib.virginia.edu/english.html

Hypertexts: Electronic Texts for the Study of American Culture
http://xroads.virginia.edu/~HYPER/hypertex.html

Internet Archive of Texts and Documents, Hanover College History Department
http://history.hanover.edu/texts.html

Literature Project Sites
http://www.literatureproject.com/site-map.htm

University of Toronto English Library, Authors Database
http://www.library.utoronto.ca/utel/indexauthors.html

CHAPTER 22—THE RIGHTS OF INDIVIDUALS WITH DYSLEXIA AND OTHER DISABILITIES UNDER THE LAW

Chapter 22 appears on-line at http://textbooks.brookespublishing.com/birsh

Organizations

Council of Parent Advocates and Attorneys
1321 Pennsylvania Avenue SE
Washington, DC 20003-3027
202-544-2210
http://www.copaa.org

Division for Learning Disabilities (DLD)
The Council for Exceptional Children (CEC)
1110 North Glebe Road
Suite 300
Arlington, VA 22201-5704
888-CEC-SPED
E-mail: cec@cec.sped.org
http://www.teachingld.org

The International Dyslexia Association (IDA)
8600 LaSalle Road
Chester Building
Suite 382
Baltimore, MD 21286
800-222-3123
E-mail: info@interdys.org
http://www.interdys.org

Learning Disabilities Association of America (LDA)
4156 Library Road
Pittsburgh, PA 15234
412-341-1515
http://www.ldanatl.org

National Dissemination Center for Children with Disabilities (NICHCY)
Post Office Box 1492
Washington, DC 20013
800-695-0285
E-mail: nichcy@aed.org
http://www.nichcy.org

Web Sites

LD Online
http://ldonline.org

U.S. Department of Justice, ADA home page
http://www.usdoj.gov/crt/ada

Wrightslaw
http://www.wrightslaw.com

Index

Page numbers followed by *f, t,* and *n* indicate figures, tables, and footnotes, respectively.

Companion workbook—
ideal for sharpening language and teaching skills!

Multisensory Teaching of Basic Language Skills Activity Book

Suzanne Carreker & Judith R. Birsh

US$24.95 · 2005
208 pages · 8 ½ x 11
layflat paperback
Stock number: 67236
ISBN 978-1-55766-723-6

Multisensory Teaching of Basic Language Skills Activity Book

By Suzanne Carreker & Judith R. Birsh, Ed.D.

With this companion workbook to Multisensory Teaching of Basic Language Skills, Second Edition, current and future educators can advance their knowledge of multisensory teaching and hone their language skills. Ideal for preservice teacher education courses and in-service professional development, the workbook includes 101 activities that cover all the areas in the text.

Teachers will learn how to use multisensory instruction to help students with dyslexia and other learning disabilities improve their phonological awareness, letter recognition, syllable division, spelling, decoding, fluency, comprehension, and more. They'll also find forms to help them with lesson planning and practical activities and handouts they can use with their own students. With this easy-to-use activity book, educators will get the practice they need to put multisensory teaching to work in their classrooms.

Convenient ways to order:

CALL toll-free
1-800-638-3775
M-F, 9 a.m. to 5 p.m. ET.

FAX
410-337-8539

MAIL order form to:
Brookes Publishing Co.
P.O. Box 10624
Baltimore, MD 21285-0624

ON-LINE
www.brookespublishing.com

❑ **Yes!** Please send me:

Quantity_____   Stock # BA-67236

Title: *Multisensory Teaching of Basic Language Skills Activity Book*   Price: *US$24.95*

❑ Check enclosed (payable to Brookes Publishing Co.)

❑ Purchase Order attached (bill my institution) *Add 2% to product total for P.O. handling fee

❑ Please charge my credit card: ❑ American Express ❑ MasterCard ❑ Visa

Credit Card #_____ Exp. Date: _____

Signature (required with credit card use):_____

Name:_____ Daytime Phone: _____

Street Address: _____ ❑ residential ❑ commercial

Complete street address required.

City/State/Zip:_____ Country: _____

E-mail Address:_____

❑ Yes! I want to receive special web site discount offers! My e-mail will not shared with any other party.

ABOUT YOU

Write in your title and check area of specialty: _____

❑ Birth to Five   ❑ K–12   ❑ 4-year College/Graduate   ❑ Community College/Vocational
❑ Clinical/Medical   ❑ Community Services   ❑ Association/Foundation

Shipping & Handling

Continental USA, AK, HI, PR, and USA territories & protectorates

For subtotal of	Add*
US$55.00 and under	$6.49
US$55.01 and over	12%

Canada

For subtotal of	Add*
US$67.00 and under	$9.99
US$67.01 and over	15%

*calculate percentage on product total

Orders within continental USA ship via Ground Delivery. Orders for AK, HI, PR, USA territories & protectorates ship via USPS. For other shipping options and rates, call 1-800-638-3775 (in the USA and CAN) and 1-410-337-9580 (worldwide).

Subtotal $ _____
6% sales tax, Maryland only $ _____
5% business tax (GST), CAN only $ _____
2% P.O. handling fee $ _____
Shipping (see chart) $ _____
Total (in U.S. dollars) $ _____

Your savings code is **BA**